Raoul Wren

HANDBOOK OF EMOTIONS

HANDBOOK
OF
EMOTIONS

Edited by
MICHAEL LEWIS
Robert Wood Johnson Medical School
University of Medicine and Dentistry of New Jersey

JEANNETTE M. HAVILAND
Rutgers—The State University of New Jersey

THE GUILFORD PRESS
New York   London

© 1993 The Guilford Press
A Division of Guilford Publications, Inc.
72 Spring Street, New York, NY 10012

Printed in the United States of America

This book is printed on acid-free paper.

Last digit is print number: 9 8 7 6 5 4 3 2 1

Library of Congress Cataloging-in-Publication Data

Handbook of emotions / edited by Michael Lewis and Jeannette M.
  Haviland
    p. cm.
  Includes bibliographical references and index.
  ISBN 0-89862-988-8
  1. Emotions. 2. Emotions—Sociological aspects. I. Lewis,
Michael, 1937 Jan. 10–   II. Haviland, Jeannette M.
  [DNLM: 1. Emotions—handbooks. BF 531 H236]
BF561.H35 1993
152.4—dc20
DNLM/DLC
for Library of Congress   92-48999
                                           CIP

Contributors

JAMES R. AVERILL, PhD, Department of Psychology, University of Massachusetts at Amherst, Amherst, Massachusetts

GARY G. BERNTSON, PhD, Department of Psychology, The Ohio State University, Columbus, Ohio

STEVEN J. BRECKLER, PhD, Department of Psychology, Johns Hopkins University, Baltimore, Maryland

LESLIE R. BRODY, PhD, Psychology Department, Boston University, Boston, Massachusetts

JOHN T. CACIOPPO, PhD, Department of Psychology, The Ohio State University, Columbus, Ohio

SUSAN D. CALKINS, PhD, Institute for Child Study/Department of Human Development, University of Maryland, College Park, Maryland

LINDA A. CAMRAS, PhD, Department of Psychology, DePaul University, Chicago, Illinois

RICHARD J. DAVIDSON, PhD, Department of Psychology, University of Wisconsin, Madison, Wisconsin

ED DIENER, PhD, Department of Psychology, University of Illinois, Champaign, Illinois

KENNETH A. DODGE, PhD, Department of Psychology and Human Development, Vanderbilt University, Nashville, Tennessee

SEYMOUR EPSTEIN, PhD, Department of Psychology, University of Massachusetts at Amherst, Amherst, Massachusetts

NATHAN A. FOX, PhD, Institute for Child Study/Department of Human Development, University of Maryland, College Park, Maryland

NICO H. FRIJDA, PhD, Department of Psychology, University of Amsterdam, Amsterdam, The Netherlands

H. H. GOLDSMITH, PhD, Department of Psychology, University of Wisconsin, Madison, Wisconsin

JOHN MORDECHAI GOTTMAN, PhD, Department of Psychology, University of Washington, Seattle, Washington

LESLIE S. GREENBERG, PhD, Department of Psychology, York University, North York, Ontario, Canada

JONATHAN HAIDT, PhD, Department of Psychology, University of Pennsylvania, Philadelphia, Pennsylvania

JUDITH A. HALL, PhD, Department of Psychology, Northeastern University, Boston, Massachusetts

PAUL L. HARRIS, DPhil, Department of Experimental Psychology, University of Oxford, Oxford, England, United Kingdom

ELAINE HATFIELD, PhD, Department of Psychology, University of Hawaii, Honolulu, Hawaii

JEANNETTE M. HAVILAND, PhD, Department of Psychology, Rutgers—The State University of New Jersey, New Brunswick, New Jersey

DAVID R. HEISE, PhD, Department of Sociology, Indiana University, Bloomington, Indiana

ELIZABETH A. HOLLAND, MA, Department of Psychology, DePaul University, Chicago, Illinois

JILL HUNZIKER, MA, Department of Psychology, Long Island University, Brooklyn, New York

ALICE M. ISEN, PhD, Johnson Graduate School of Management, Cornell University, Ithaca, New York

CARROLL E. IZARD, PhD, Department of Psychology, University of Delaware, Newark, Delaware

PATRICIA KAHLBAUGH, PhD, Neuro-psychiatric Institute, University of California, Los Angeles, California

THEODORE D. KEMPER, PhD, Department of Sociology, St. John's University, Jamaica, New York

DAVID J. KLEIN, BA, Department of Psychology, The Ohio State University, Columbus, Ohio

RANDY J. LARSEN, PhD, Department of Psychology, University of Michigan, Ann Arbor, Michigan

JOSEPH E. LeDOUX, PhD, Center for Neural Science, New York University, New York, New York

ELIZABETH A. LEMERISE, PhD, Department of Psychology, Western Kentucky University, Bowling Green, Kentucky

HOWARD LEVENTHAL, PhD, Institute for Health, Health Care Policy and Aging Research, Rutgers University, New Brunswick, New Jersey

MICHAEL LEWIS, PhD, Institute for the Study of Child Development, University of Medicine and Dentistry of New Jersey, Robert Wood Johnson Medical School, New Brunswick, New Jersey

MARIA LIWAG, MA, Department of Psychology, University of Chicago, Chicago, Illinois

PAUL D. MacLEAN, MD, Laboratory of Neurophysiology, National Institute of Mental Health, Bethesda, Maryland

CAROL MAGAI, PhD, Department of Psychology, Long Island University, Brooklyn, New York

CLARK R. McCAULEY, PhD, Department of Psychology, Bryn Mawr College, Bryn Mawr, Pennsylvania

TERRY R. McGUIRE, PhD, Department of Biological Science and Bureau of Biological Research, Nelson Biological Laboratories, Rutgers University, Piscataway, New Jersey

DANIEL N. McINTOSH, MA, Department of Psychology, University of Michigan, Ann Arbor, Michigan

THOMAS A. MORE, PhD, Northeastern Forest Experiment Station, Burlington, Vermont

SHEILA T. MURPHY, PhD, Annenberg School for Communication, University of Southern California, Los Angeles, California

KEITH OATLEY, PhD, Centre for Applied Cognitive Science, Ontario Institute for Studies in Education, Toronto, Ontario, Canada

JOHN O'BRIEN, PhD, Department of Sociology, Indiana University, Bloomington, Indiana

ARNE ÖHMAN, PhD, Department of Clinical Neuroscience and Psychiatry, Karolinska Hospital, Stockholm, Sweden

JAAK PANKSEPP, PhD, Department of Psychology, Bowling Green State University, Bowling Green, Ohio

LINDA PATRICK-MILLER, MA, Institute for Health, Health Care Policy and Aging Research, Rutgers University, New Brunswick, New Jersey

MARY JILL PATTERSON, MA, Department of Psychology, DePaul University, Chicago, Illinois

LAWRENCE A. PERVIN, PhD, Department of Psychology, Rutgers University, New Brunswick, New Jersey

JEFFERY PITTAM, PhD, Department of English, University of Queensland, Brisbane, Queensland, Australia

ROBERT PLUTCHIK, PhD, Department of Psychiatry, Albert Einstein College of Medicine, Bronx, New York

RICHARD RAPSON, PhD, Department of History, University of Hawaii, Honolulu, Hawaii

PAUL ROZIN, PhD, Department of Psychology, University of Pennsylvania, Philadelphia, Pennsylvania

WILLIBALD RUCH, PhD, Department of Physiological Psychology, University of Düsseldorf, Düsseldorf, Germany

CAROLYN SAARNI, PhD, Department of Counseling, Sonoma State University, Rohnert Park, California

KLAUS R. SCHERER, PhD, Department of Psychology, University of Geneva, Geneva, Switzerland

RICHARD A. SHWEDER, PhD, Committee on Human Development, University of Chicago, Chicago, Illinois

ROBERT C. SOLOMON, PhD, Department of Philosophy, University of Texas, Austin, Texas

CAROL ZISOWITZ STEARNS, MD, PhD, Department of Psychiatry, University of Pittsburgh School of Medicine, Pittsburgh, Pennsylvania; Pittsburgh Psychoanalytic Institute, Pittsburgh, Pennsylvania

PETER N. STEARNS, PhD, Department of History, Carnegie Mellon University, Pittsburgh, Pennsylvania

NANCY L. STEIN, PhD, Department of Psychology, University of Chicago, Chicago, Illinois

TOM TRABASSO, PhD, Department of Psychology, University of Chicago, Chicago, Illinois

GEOFFREY M. WHITE, PhD, Program on Cultural Studies, East–West Center, Honolulu, Hawaii

R. B. ZAJONC, PhD, Department of Psychology, University of Michigan, Ann Arbor, Michigan

Preface

No one would deny the proposition that in order to understand human behavior, one must understand feelings. The interest in emotions has been enduring; however, within the discipline of psychology at least, the study of feelings and emotions has been somewhat less than respectable. Learning, cognition, and perception have dominated what have been considered the legitimate domains of inquiry. Yet interest in and discussion about emotions have never ceased. How are we to understand this distorted historical commitment to the study of some aspects of human behavior but not others?

The answer lies in the particularly Western idea of the duality between mind and body. In this idea of the dual nature of human life, the mind is elevated to a place of honor, whereas the body is relegated to necessity and baseness. Emotions are held to belong to the realm of the body. Thus debased, emotions have been considered in need of control by the beauty and grace of mind. Freud's century-old tripartite division of the psyche into ego, superego, and id reflects this Western view of the nature of emotion. In this division of psychic life, emotion is relegated to the id, and although the id contains the life force, Freud viewed the task of the ego and superego as one of checking the id's coarse and base impulses. But this view of the emotions existed long before Freud, and even before Descartes wrote of emotions as the "sweat" of the activity of mind. Emotions have been relegated not only to secondary citizenship in the study of human behavior, but also to an epiphenomenological position.

The ancient distinction between mind and body has permeated our view of emotion and had a corresponding impact on our research and understanding. When the romanticists claim that emotion is all spiritual transcendency, or when the classicists claim that emotion is all mundane physical physiology, there can be no dialogue or growth in our understanding of either emotional or mental operations. However, as new paradigms arise and new ways of viewing behavior emerge, the mind–body distinction necessarily gives way to more complex models. With the emergence of new paradigms in science—of interactive feedback models, dynamic systems, top-down and bottom-up networks, information-processing systems, and so forth—we have seen a growing increase of interest in the study of emotion. No longer the outcast that it was, the study of emotion has been legitimized by the development of new measurement techniques, as well as by new ways to conceptualize behavior and feeling.

The blossoming of research in emotion that has occurred in the last decade gives rise to the need for an up-to-date *Handbook of Emotions* that can serve many functions. We see this handbook, first, as providing a basic research source for what is known about emotion; it can serve as a starting point for investigating the field. Second, it can provide an informed researcher in one domain with background information on other aspects of emotion. Third, it can be a source of interdisciplinary dialogue, presenting some of the newest ways of conceptualizing issues. Fourth, for those not yet involved in the study of emotion, it can signal that there is a growing and important body of work to take into account in attempts to explain human and animal behavior. Finally, and perhaps not least, it can provide a body of work that can say to people who have been working in the field, as well as to those for whom it is a new field, "Emotion has come of age as a legitimate domain of study."

This new interest in the study of emotion has been building and is reflected in new publications, in new journals, and in new scientific societies. The accumulation of several decades of scholarly work is represented in this handbook. Although there is a history to the study of emotion, this history is limited; almost everything that is presented here is new. The pioneers in scholarship on emotion, many of whom are represented in this handbook, have often had to make leaps of intellectual genius. Along with such insights have come the hard work and commitment to detailed research and conceptual systems that now mark the study of emotion.

The study of emotions transcends many of the traditional lines of inquiry. By its dynamic nature, it has become an interdisciplinary effort involving psychophysiology, cognition, cultural studies, linguistics, and many other fields. This interdisciplinary activity is reflected in this handbook. Because of the newness of our studies, traditional lines of inquiry demarcating the study of human behavior have been less rigidly attended to than in older domains of science. At least at this juncture, the study of emotion transcends the limited boundaries of the older disciplines. Nevertheless, we have no doubt that as the field matures, more differentiation will occur. Even today, we see the beginnings of this: The research on basic physiological processes of emotion has become highly technical, as have studies of developmental processes and of select problems in facial measurement. This handbook therefore includes not only chapters that bridge domains, but chapters that express the diversity of approaches to the study of emotion. We present a sample of the technologies and theories that have resulted both from research within selected domains and from cross-domain research. Models and research from sociology, history, anthropology, philosophy, biology, neurophysiology, behavior genetics, and developmental, clinical, and social psychology are represented. It is our hope that the presentation of diverse sets of perspectives will allow the general reader to appreciate the broad scope of effort in the study of emotion, and at the same time will allow the more technical and specific reader to focus on aspects not heretofore considered.

The *Handbook of Emotions* is organized into five sections. We begin with a broad overview, an interdisciplinary foundation. In this section the reader can grasp the vast territory that is affected by scholarship in the field. Section II concerns biological and neurophysiological approaches to emotion. Section III presents the basic psychological processes; here we see the examination of the relation between emotion and other aspects of human behavior. Section IV deals with social processes related to emotion. Whereas the previous sections have looked at chapters dealing principally with emotions within the individual, this section looks directly at group and family processes as they relate to emotion. Here, too, one can find the relation of affect to clinical issues being addressed. The fifth section focuses on some of the more widely studied select emotions, such as happiness, exhilaration, disgust, fear, anxiety, and shame.

The creation of the *Handbook of Emotions* was no easy task. Some topics that could have been included in this first major study of the field have not been, and some that are included may seem from some perspectives tangential. The collection procedure and the content of this handbook were made possible by the generous support and help of our editorial committee. We should like to thank Paul Ekman, Alice M. Isen, Anthony Manstead, Robert Plutchik, and Klaus R. Scherer for their efforts; at the same time, we emphasize that any error of omission or inclusion rests firmly with us, the editors. We hope that this handbook will be the first in a long line of volumes aimed at presenting the newest and most exciting work in the field of emotional study. We hope that clinicians, scholars, and students from a variety of disciplines and interests will find our effort useful.

MICHAEL LEWIS
JEANNETTE M. HAVILAND

Contents

SECTION IV. SOCIAL PROCESSES RELATED TO EMOTION

SECTION V. SELECT EMOTIONS

HANDBOOK OF EMOTIONS

I
INTERDISCIPLINARY FOUNDATIONS

1

The Philosophy of Emotions

ROBERT C. SOLOMON

"What is an emotion?" That question was asked in precisely that form by William James, as the title of an essay he wrote for *Mind* over 100 years ago (James, 1884). But philosophers have been concerned and often worried about the nature of emotion since Socrates and the "pre-Socratics" who preceded him, and although the discipline has grown up (largely because of Socrates and his student Plato) as the pursuit of reason, the emotions have always lurked in the background—as a threat to reason, as a danger to philosophy and philosophers, as just plain unreasonable. Perhaps that is why one of the most enduring metaphors of reason and emotion has been the metaphor of master and slave, with the wisdom of reason firmly in control and the dangerous impulses of emotion safely suppressed, channeled, or (ideally) in harmony with reason. But the question "What is an emotion?" has proved to be as difficult to resolve as the emotions have been to master. Just when it seems an adequate definition is in place, some new theory rears its unwelcome head and challenges our understanding.

The master–slave metaphor displays two features that still determine much of the philosophical view of emotion today. First and foremost, there is the inferior role of emotion—the idea that emotion is as such more primitive, less intelligent, more bestial, less dependable, and more dangerous than reason, and thus needs to be controlled by reason (all argument that Aristotle and other enlightened Athenians used to justify the political institution of slavery as well). Second, and more profoundly, there is the reason–emotion distinction itself—

as if we were dealing with two different natural kinds, two conflicting and antagonistic aspects of the soul. Even those philosophers who sought to integrate them and reduce one to the other (typically reducing emotion to an inferior genus of reason, a "confused perception" or "distorted judgment") maintained the distinction and continued to insist on the superiority of reason. It was thus a mark of his considerable iconoclasm that the Scottish skeptic David Hume (1739/1888), in the 18th century, famously declared that "reason is, and ought to be, the slave of the passions." But even Hume, despite an ingenious analysis of the structure of emotions, ultimately fell back on the old models and metaphors.

Whatever else it may be, philosophy is a historical discipline, and the theories and debates of today cannot be understood or appreciated without some understanding of philosophy's rich and convoluted past. Even when a philosopher pretends to understand the phenomenon of emotion "in itself" or analyze the language of emotion without reference to history or to any earlier attempts to do so, both the wisdom and the folly of generations of accumulated reflection and argument are already embedded in the subject matter. And although one might impatiently demand from the outset that one "define the terms" before the current discussion commences, the truth is that a definition will emerge only at the end of a long discussion, and even then it will be merely tentative and appropriate only within a limited context and a certain model of culture and personal character.

In what follows, I have tried to sketch a somewhat selective history of philosophical

attempts to understand emotion, followed by
a brief summary of questions still central to
philosophical debate. Given the nature of philosophy and its emphasis on reason, however,
we would expect that the focus of most philosophical analysis has been and remains the
more cognitive aspects of emotion, with the
physiological and to a certain extent the social
and behavioral dimensions of emotion diminished or in many cases even denied. That will
be, I should admit from the outset, the bias
of this account as well. But the dialectic of
philosophy tends to go back and forth in
its emphasis and rediscovery of these often
neglected dimensions. Sometimes emotions
are dismissed as mere feelings and physiology,
utterly unintelligent, even inhuman. In reaction, emotions are ascribed the virtues of true
wisdom; they are seen as the proper masters
of reason and the very foundation of our
being-in-the-world. Most philosophers, however, try to find some more moderate, multidimensional position.

One might object that philosophical theories
of emotion tend to be "armchair" speculation,
devoid of the empirical support supplied by
social scientists. However, this objection ignores the fact that philosophers, contrary to
their own self-styled reputations as men and
women of pure reason, have emotions themselves, and in most (but not all) cases a sufficiently rich repertoire of emotions to fund and
support a dozen theories of emotion. As
Descartes (1649/1989) said, in his introduction
to the subject, "everyone has experience of the
passions within himself, and there is no necessity to borrow one's observations from elsewhere in order to discover their nature." Ultimately, there is no need for the perennial (in
fact century-old) feud between philosophy and
psychology, and the phenomenon of emotion
lies equally open to both of them.

THE HISTORY OF THE
PHILOSOPHY OF EMOTION

Although the history of philosophy has often
been described as the history of the development of reason—for example, by the great
19th-century German philosopher G. W. F.
Hegel—philosophers have never entirely
neglected emotion, even if they have almost
always denied it center stage. It would be a
mistake, however, to put too much emphasis

on the term "emotion," for its range and meaning have altered significantly over the years, in
part because of changes in theories about emotion. So, too, the word "passion" has a long and
varied history, and we should beware of the
misleading assumption that there is a single,
orderly, natural class of phenomena that is
simply designated by different labels in different languages at different times. The language
of "passion" and "emotion" has a history into
which various feelings, desires, sentiments,
moods, attitudes, and more explosive responses enter and from which they exit,
depending not on arbitrary philosophical stipu-
lation but on an extensive network of social,
moral, cultural, and psychological factors. Thus
we will often find that the focus is not emotion as such, but rather some particular class
of emotions or particular emotion and its role
in the manners or morals of the time.

The emotions as such, accordingly, do not
form one of the three aspects of Plato's
(c. 428–347 B.C.) tripartite soul as defined in
The Republic (1974). These aspects are reason,
spirit, and appetite; not only does what we call
"emotion" seem divided between spirit and
appetite, but, considering Plato's discussion of
eros as the love of the Good in his dialogue
The Symposium (1989), there are emotions
involved in reason as well. Aristotle (384–322
B.C.), by contrast, did seem to have a view of
emotion as such; but although he had a mania for taxonomies, he spent relatively little
time listing or analyzing the emotions, as he
did, for example, the virtues and the various
kinds of birds. In his *Rhetoric* (1941), however,
he defined emotion "as that which leads one's
condition to become so transformed that his
judgment is affected, and which is accompanied by pleasure and pain. Examples of emotion include anger, fear, pity, and the like, as
well as the opposites of these."[1] (He did not
specify what these "opposites" might be.)
Aristotle discussed certain emotions at length,
notably anger, which he described in remarkably modern terms. In the *Rhetoric* he defined
anger as "a distressed desire for conspicuous
vengeance in return for a conspicuous and
unjustifiable contempt of one's person or
friends." He added that "anger is always
directed towards someone in particular, e.g.

[1]This and other quotations from Aristotle in this chapter have been newly translated by Jon Solomon.

Cleon, and not towards all of humanity," and mentioned (if only in passing) the physical distress that virtually always accompanies such emotion. The key to his analysis, however, is the notion of a "slight" as the cause of anger, and may be an instance of "scorn, spite, or insolence." Aristotle made allowances for only imagined slights (in other words, unwarranted anger is nevertheless anger), and he gave a central place to the desire for revenge, thus introducing a behavioral component at the heart of the emotion. We might note that Aristotle, who was so precocious in so many disciplines, seems to have anticipated most of the main contemporary theories. His analysis of anger includes a distinctive cognitive component, a specified social context, a behavioral tendency, and a recognition of physical arousal. He even noted that physical or psychological discomfort—sickness, poverty, love, war, breached expectations, or ingratitude—yields a predisposition for anger. It is worth noting that Aristotle had little to say of "feeling," presumably not because the Greeks were anesthetic, but rather because what we (inconsistently) call "affect" and inner sensation generally held little interest for them and played no significant role in their language or their psychology.

Perhaps the most important single point to make about Aristotle's view of emotion is the fact that his analyses make sense only in the context of a broader *ethical* concern. Anger was of interest to him because it is a natural reaction to offense and a moral force, which can be cultivated and provoked by reason and rhetoric. (Thus its inclusion in a book on that topic.) Anger (and several other emotions, notably pride) are also prominent in Aristotle's classical list of virtues in his *Nicomachean Ethics* (1941), where he discussed in some detail those circumstances in which it is appropriate to get angry, those in which it is not, and what amount or intensity of anger is justified. He suggested that forgiveness may be a virtue, but only sometimes. He also insisted that only fools don't get angry, and that although overly angry people may be "unbearable," the absence of anger (aimed at the right offenses) is a vice rather than a virtue. In this, as in all else, Aristotle defended moderation, the "mean between the extremes." So too, he discussed fear at length in the *Ethics* with regard to courage, which is not fearlessness or "overcoming" fear so much as it is having just the right

amount of fear—not to be foolhardy or a coward either. The emotions, in other words, are central and essential to the good life, and the analysis of their nature is part and parcel of an ethical analysis.

So, too, in Roman times, we find the conjunction of ethics and emotion in the philosophy of the Stoics (see Rist, 1969). But whereas Aristotle took emotion to be essential to the good life, the Stoics analyzed emotions as conceptual errors, conducive to misery. In modern terms, the Stoics Seneca and Chryssipus developed a full-blooded cognitive theory of the emotions, two millenia ago. Emotions, in a word, are judgments—judgments about the world and one's place in it. But the world of Roman society was not a happy or a particularly rational place. (Seneca served under the Emperor Nero, and ultimately committed suicide at his behest.) And as the Stoics saw the world they lived in as out of control and beyond any reasonable expectations, they saw the emotions, which impose such expectations on the world, as misguided judgments about life and our place in the world. The emotions, consequently, make us miserable and frustrated. Accordingly, the Stoics made a careful study of the component judgments that compose the emotions—the presumptuousness of moral judgment in anger, the vulnerability of love, the self-absorption of security in fear. The alternative was seen as "psychic indifference," or *apatheia* (apathy). The Stoics did believe, we might add, in a "higher" reason, one transcending the vanities of the social world. But they felt that the best life in that world could be achieved only by getting straight about the pointlessness of emotional attachments and involvement.

Throughout the Middle Ages, the study of emotion was again typically attached to ethics, and it was central to Christian psychology and the theories of human nature in terms of which the medievals understood themselves (see Hyman & Walsh, 1973). There were elaborate, quasi-medical studies of the effects of the various "humours" (gall, spleen, choler, and blood itself) on emotional temperament, but there were (as there were among the Stoics) especially rich studies of the cognitive and "conative" aspects of the emotions. Emotions were essentially linked with desires, particularly self-interested, self-absorbed desires. And so the Christian preoccupation with sin led to elaborate analyses of those emotions, passions, and desires designated as sins (notably greed, lust, anger, envy, and pride). The tight linkage between the study of emotion and ethics is particularly evident in the curious fact that the highest virtues, such as love, hope, and faith, were not classified as emotions as such, but were rather elevated to a higher status and often (e.g., by Thomas Aquinas) equated with reason. The old master–slave metaphor remained alive and well, and as some emotions were seen as sins, the highest virtues could hardly be counted among the mere emotions.

Reviewing the ancient and medieval literature on emotion, René Descartes (1596–1650) was provoked to write that what they taught was "so slight, and for the most part so far from credible, that I am unable to entertain any hope of approximating the truth excepting by shunning the paths they followed" (1649/1989). Descartes is typically recognized as the "father" of modern philosophy, and, in a more scholarly vein, as the bridge between the scholastic world of the Middle Ages and our own. But Descartes was fundamentally a scientist and a mathematician, awed by "the natural light of reason"; accordingly, he disdained the bodily and the bestial, insisting that the mind is a separate "substance" from the body (and that beasts do not have minds). The separation of mind and body proved to be a famously difficult problem for Descartes and his successors, however, and nowhere was that problem more evident than in his attempt to deal with the emotions. Thoughts about mathematics may be clearly "in" the mind, as stomach contractions are in the body, but an emotion seems to require the interaction of mind and body in an undeniable way. Accordingly, Descartes defended a theory in his treatise *On the Passions of the Soul* (1649/1989), in which the mind and body "meet" in a small gland at the base of the brain (now known as the pineal gland), and the latter effects the former by means of the agitation of "animal spirits" (minute particles of blood), which bring about the emotions and their physical effects in various parts of the body. But the emotions involve not only sensations caused by this physical agitation, but perceptions, desires, and beliefs as well. Thus over and above the physical agitation and familiar sensations, the emotion hatred, Descartes declared, ultimately arises from the perception of an object's potential harmfulness and involves a desire to avoid it. Accordingly, it is not as if an emotion is merely

a perception of the body; it is rather, as Descartes put it, a perception of the soul, and some perceptions (as in dreams) may in fact be of things that do not exist at all.

An emotion is one type of "passion," and Descartes defined the passions in general as "the perceptions, feelings or emotions of the soul which we relate specifically to it, and which are caused, maintained, and fortified by some movement of the [animal] spirits." The passions in general are distinguished from "clear cognition," and render judgment "confused and obscure." Emotions are particularly disturbing passions. And yet emotions can be influenced by reason. For example, writing of courage, Descartes stated:

> To excite courage in oneself and remove fear, it is not sufficient to have the will to do so, but we must also apply ourselves to consider the reasons, the objects or examples which persuade us that the peril is not great; that there is always more security in defense than in flight, that we should have the glory and joy of having vanquished, while we should expect nothing but regret and shame for having fled, and so on.

And so the physiological account gives way to a cognitive account, and the emotions move from the merely bodily to an essential ingredient in wisdom: "The utility of the passions consist alone in their fortifying and perpetuating in the soul thoughts which it is good that it should preserve, and which without that might easily be effaced from it." How then can there be "bad" emotions? "The harm is that they fortify these thoughts more than necessary, or they conserve others on which it is not good to dwell." So, bewildered by the physiology (though he was at the head of his class in the latest scientific knowledge), Descartes too tended to a value-oriented, wisdom-minded analysis of emotion. His six "primitive passions—wonder, love, hatred, desire, joy, and sadness—are not meaningless agitations of the animal spirits, but ingredients in the good life.

Baruch (Benedict) Spinoza (1632–1677) might well be considered to be a latter-day Stoic, like Chrysippus and Seneca in ancient Rome. Just as the Stoics saw the emotions as misguided judgments about life and our place in the world, Spinoza too saw the emotions as a form of "thought" that, for the most part, misunderstand the world, and consequently make us miserable and frustrated. But unlike the Stoics, Spinoza did not aspire to that "psychic indifference" known as *apatheia* (apathy); rather, in his *Ethics* (1677/1982), he urged the attainment of a certain sort of "bliss," which can be achieved only once we get straight our thinking about the world. In particular, we have to give up the idea that we are or can be in control of our own lives, and adopt instead the all-embracing idea of ourselves and our minds as part of God. Most of the emotions, which are passive reactions to our unwarranted expectations of the world, will leave us hurt, frustrated, and enervated. The active emotions, by contrast, emanate from our own true natures and heighten our sense of activity and awareness. Spinoza, like the Stoics, developed an early version of the cognitive theory of emotion. But Spinoza also defended a grand and complex metaphysics, in which all substance is one and mind and body are but dual "aspects" of one and the same being. Accordingly, he did not face Descartes's formidable "mind–body" problem"; although he himself could not have attempted to work this out, he anticipated the subtle emotion–brain research that is being carried out today by some philosophers as well as by neuropsychologists.

David Hume (1711–1776) was one of the most outspoken defenders of the Enlightenment, that very vocal and often rebellious intellectual movement that challenged old orthodoxies, elevated science and put religion on the defensive, attacked superstition and irrationality in all quarters, practiced and encouraged vigorous debate and discussion, and put a premium on the virtues of reason. But Hume, in carrying out the directives of reason to challenge, debate, and question, came to question the role and capacities of reason itself, and in particular the power of reason to motivate even the most basic minimum of moral behavior. "It is not against reason," he declared in one of his most outrageous proclamations, "to prefer the destruction of half the world to the scratching of my finger" (1739/1888). What motivates us to right (and wrong) behavior, Hume insisted, are our passions, and rather than being relegated to the margins of ethics and philosophy, the passions deserve central respect and consideration. Accordingly, he gave the passions large middle portion of his great first book, *A Treatise of Human Nature* (1739/1888). Not surprisingly, however, most philosophers then and since have preferred to

read the first and third parts, on knowledge and ethics, and to ignore the central position of the passions.

Hume's theory is especially important not only because he challenged the inferior place of passion in philosophy and questioned the role of reason. He also advanced a theory of the passions that, although limited and encumbered by his general theory of mind, displayed dazzling insight and a precocious attempt to grapple with problems that would only be formulated generations later. Hume, like many of his contemporaries and predecessors, defined an emotion as a certain kind of sensation, or what he called an "impression," which (as in Descartes) is physically stimulated by the movement of the "animal spirits" in the blood. Such impressions are either pleasant or unpleasant, but the differentiation of the many emotions is not to be found in the nature of these impressions as such. Rather, the impressions that constitute our emotions are always to be located within a causal network of other impressions and, importantly, ideas. Ideas cause our emotional impressions, and ideas are caused in turn by them. The pleasant impression of pride, for example, is caused by the idea that one has achieved or accomplished something significant, and the impression in turn causes another idea, which Hume described as an idea of the self, *simpliciter*. The emotion, in other words, cannot he identified with the impression or sensation alone, but can only be identified by the whole complex of impressions and ideas. What Hume again acknowledged with his emphasis on the essential place of ideas in emotion is what we now call the cognitive dimension of emotion, in addition to the physiological ("animal spirits") and merely sensational ("impression") aspects of emotion. Moreover, his inclusion of the second idea of the self in this example indicates his grappling with the notion of intentionality (the "aboutness" of emotions)—an effort that is further reinforced by his somewhat obscure insistence that the connection between an emotion (the impression) and this consequent idea is "original" or "natural," or something more than the merely causal associations that form the usual bonds between ideas and impressions.

The emotions, for Hume, form an essential part of ethics. There are good emotions and bad emotions. Pride, he declared, is a good emotion; humility, its opposite (an unpleasant feeling brought about by the idea that we have accomplished something), is a bad emotion, a "monkish" emotion. Here we can see again the extent to which, as so often, a theory of emotion serves to grind some larger philosophical ax—in this case, Hume's Enlightenment attack on religion. In this regard too, we might mention another aspect of Hume's moral philosophy, followed in kind by his illustrious Edinburgh friend and colleague Adam Smith (1723–1790, also the author of *The Wealth of Nations* [1776/1976], the bible of modern capitalism). Hume and Smith both defended the importance of what they called "the moral sentiments" (see Smith, 1759/1976), the foremost of which is sympathy, our ability to "feel with" other people and appreciate (if not suffer with) their misfortunes. Sympathy, they argued, is a universal feature of human nature (countering and mitigating the self-interest that Smith in particular famously championed in *The Wealth of Nations*), and it is the bedrock foundation of society and morality. Emotion, in other words, is not an embarrassment or part of the refuse of the human psyche, but rather the very essence of human social existence and morality. It is not to be unfavorably contrasted and opposed to reason, but, on the contrary, is to be celebrated and defended along with it.

Immanuel Kant (1724–1804) was also a champion of the Enlightenment, but he too questioned the capacities and limits of reason. He was uncompromising in its defense, however, against Hume's skepticism, against any attempt to replace reason by irrational faith, and against any attempt to ground ethics on fleeting human feeling instead of the universal and necessary dictates of reason. Thus Kant reinforced the crucial distinction between reason and what he called "the inclinations" (emotions, moods, and desires), and dismissed the latter (including the moral sentiments) as inessential to morals at best and intrusive and disruptive or worse. And yet, although Kant felt no need to develop a theory of emotion to accompany his elaborate and brilliant "critiques" of reason, his position on the "inclinations" is more ambiguous than is usually supposed, and his "respect for feeling" more significant. It was Kant, a quarter-century before Hegel (who is credited with it), who insisted that "nothing great is ever done without passion," and it was Kant, in his *Critique of Judgment* (1793/1951; concerned in part

with art and aesthetics), who celebrated the importance of shared ("intersubjective") feeling in the appreciation of beauty and the awe with which we try to comprehend the wonder of God's creation. Indeed, even Kant's central notions of respect and human dignity, the very heart of his rationalist ethics, are sometimes suggested to be matters of feeling as well as reason, thus calling into question the harshness of his ruthlessly divided self. When his successor Hegel (1770–1831) took over the reins of German philosophy in the early 19th century, the overstated distinction between reason and passion was again called into question, and Hegel's own odyssey of reason (in an epochal book called *The Phenomenology of Mind,* 1807/1977) has rightly been called a "logic of passion" as well.

Friedrich Nietzsche (1844–1900) was a philosopher for whom passion was the watchword and reason a source of suspicion. He was the culmination of a long line of "Romantics," beginning with the *Sturm und Drang* poets of the 18th century and continuing through the philosophy of Nietzsche's own favorite influence, the neo-Kantian pessimist Arthur Schopenhauer. Nietzsche anticipated the global skepticism and conceptual chaos of the 20th century; like Freud, who admired him, he described (and celebrated) the darker, more instinctual, and less rational motives of the human mind. Accordingly, in his *On the Genealogy of Morals* (1887/1967), he praised the passions and, in an ironic twist, described the passions as themselves having more reason than Reason. But this was not to say that all passions are wise; some, he declared, "drag us down with their stupidity," and others, notably the "slave morality" emotion of resentment, are devious and clever but to a disastrous end, the "leveling" of the virtuous passions and the defense of mediocrity. Nietzsche never developed a "theory" of emotions, but his distinctions were remarkable in their insight and subtlety. His celebration of passion scared the wits out of a great many philosophers in Europe, however, who saw more than enough passion and irrationality in the Great War and then the rise of National Socialism in Germany. Accordingly, the ancient celebration of reason would once more rule philosophy, and emotion was again relegated to the sidelines.

In the 20th century, one can trace the fate of emotion in Western philosophy through two very different tracks. In North America and in England, the emotions were given particularly short *schrift,* in large part because of the newly exaggerated emphasis on logic and science. The great British philosopher Bertrand Russell gave elaborate praise to love and passion in the opening pages of his autobiography (1967), but in his philosophy he said virtually nothing about them. Of course, the nature of emotion was a major concern of William James and the young John Dewey in the early years of the century, but with James's emphasis on the physiological nature of emotion (he argued [1884] that an emotion is a sensation or set of sensations caused by a physiological disturbance, which in turn is prompted by some "perception" or other), coupled with the subsequent and quite unfortunate split between philosophy and psychology as academic discipline, questions about emotion were relegated to the realm of psychology (where they were also treated with less than the full respect due them). Indeed, the first major attention to emotion in Anglo-American philosophy came in midcentury, when an ethical theory named "emotivism" came to dominate both the English and the North American scene. But emotivism, which was part and parcel of an across-the-board philosophical purgative known as "logical positivism," was essentially a dismissal of ethical (and many other) questions in philosophy as "meaningless" (i.e., unscientific and without verifiable solutions). Emotion came back onto the stage of philosophy, but only as the butt of the argument: Ethical statements were meaningless because they were *nothing but* expressions of emotion.

During the same period in Europe, however, the emotions enjoyed more attention. Franz Brentano (1874/1971) succeeded the British "moral sentiment" theorists in attempting to found an ethics on a foundation of emotions. (Sigmund Freud was one of his students.) Following the "phenomenology" of Edmund Husserl (1938/1960) (another Brentano student and a mathematician who showed little or no interest in emotion), Max Scheler (1916/1970), Martin Heidegger (1927/1962), and more recently Paul Ricouer (1950/1966) developed ambitious philosophies in which emotions were given central place in human existence and accorded considerable respect. In the shadow of World War II, Jean-Paul Sartre offered the slim but important *The Emotions: Sketch of a Theory* (1939/1948), fol-

lowed by his monstrous tome *Being and Nothingness* (1943/1956), which includes embedded within its many pages a number of detailed "phenomenological" analyses of emotion. Sartre's conception of emotions as "magical transformations of the world"—willful stratagems for coping with a difficult world—added a new "existential" dimension to the investigation of emotion. But, predictably, philosophy in both France and Germany turned again to other interests, though the study of emotion continued despite the perennial shift in fashions.

In Anglo-American philosophy, however, the fortunes of emotion were also to change. In an article simply entitled "Emotion" (indicating how rarely the topic had even been broached), Errol Bedford (1956/1964) addressed the Aristotelean Society in London on the nature of emotion and the errors of thinking of emotions as "feelings." The essay might have sat on the shelves gathering dust except for the fact that the then dean of Oxford philosophers, J. L. Austin (1956–1957), took it upon himself to remark on one of Bedford's claims. (Austin's own essay was not about emotions at all.) Austin's attention kept the article alive and occasionally anthologized until the 1960s, when the subject seemed to come to life again.

Today, one finds a rich variety of arguments about emotions on both sides of the Atlantic Ocean and the English Channel. Given the nature of philosophy and its current concern with epistemological matters, it is again not surprising that the focus is on the conceptual structures of emotion, rather than the sensory, social, or physiological aspects of emotion. But there has been a reaction even within philosophy to the "hypercognizing" of emotion; consequently, there has been a serious effort to join forces with psychologists, neurologists, anthropologists, and moral philosophers to obtain a more holistic theory of emotion.

SOME PHILOSOPHICAL QUESTIONS ABOUT EMOTION

What is an emotion? Because philosophy is a discipline concerned with the essential nature and the "definition" of things, the basic question facing theories of emotion in philosophy is still the question posed by James and answered in a fashion by Aristotle. It is, on the face of it, a quest for a definition, a conceptual analysis. But it is also a much larger quest for an orientation: How should we think about emotion—as intrusive, as essential to our rationality, as constitutive of meaning, as dangerous, as dispensable, as an excuse for irresponsibility, or as a mode of responsibility? Which of the evident aspects of emotion—that is, the various sensory, physiological, behavioral, cognitive, and social phenomena that typically correspond with an emotion—should we take to be essential?

Many philosophers hold onto the old "Cartesian" view that an emotion cannot lack its "subjective" or "introspective" aspect, although what this means (and how accessible or articulate an emotion must be on inspection) is itself a subject of considerable dispute (Lyons, 1980; Sartre, 1943/1956; Freud, 1915/1935). Many philosophers have become skeptical about such subjective essentialism, however; like their associates in the social sciences, they have pushed the analysis of emotion toward more public, observable criteria (formulating their own versions of behaviorism, physiologism, and social construction theory, for example). But the seemingly self-evident Cartesian demand that first-person experience is seemingly ineliminable is evident in even the most radical of them, although its place and significance are greatly diminished. Can one have an emotion without feeling? What is a "feeling"? The virtue of the Jamesian theory is that it ties down the nature of emotional sensation to quite particular and therefore verifiable visceral responses. Unfortunately, the Jamesian theory is wrong, at least in its details. How specifically are emotional feelings tied to physiological processes? To be sure, whatever goes on in the mind must now be supposed to have some correlate and cause in the brain, but can we not and should we not describe the "phenomenology" of those feelings quite apart from their brain correlations and causes?

Some theorists have tried to save feeling theory by employing the vague, general (and technical) notion of "affect" and its cognates ("affective tone"). But do such terms do anything more than cover up the problem with another word, whose meaning can only be explained by "the kind of feeling you get when you have emotion X"? It is a mistake, moreover, to suppose that such feelings are indescribable or "ineffable," whether out of excessive romanticism (as if understanding always undermines passion) or dismissive scientism (why talk about feelings if we can't experimentally test them?). Most feelings have at least an "as if" recognizability ("It feels as if I'd known him for years" or "It felt as if he had shot me through the heart, it was so sudden and so traumatizing"). Many feelings have a distinctive structure, which (not surprisingly) emerges in the thoughts (and then in the verbal expression) of the emotion. In general, one must ask how much cognition and learning is presupposed in the feelings that we identify as emotions. One does not need an elaborate Schachter and Singer (1962) scenario to do the *Gedanken* experiment, which shows that certain feelings typical of, say, fear and anger do not actually constitute fear and anger if there are no appropriate beliefs accompanying them. A person may well feel flushed, uncomfortable, and "as if" he or she wanted to flee or start a fight with someone, but if there is no fearful object (more precisely, if the person has no sense of a fearful object) or if there is nothing objectionable, frustrating, or offensive (to the person), then those feelings do not count as fear and anger (or even as "feeling afraid" or "feeling angry"). Whatever else we may say about the place of feeling in emotion, feeling alone is not sufficient. Of course, this same term "feeling" can be expanded to include all sorts of thoughts, cognitions, and attitudes about the immediate situation, and not only tendencies to behave but even the behavior itself (as subjective experience rather than observable action). But this only shows that the seemingly innocuous notion of "feeling" also needs careful analysis, and the commonsense notion that an emotion is basically a feeling (perhaps a feeling in a certain context or brought about by a certain kind of cause) is accordingly still a prominent focus in philosophy. (For example, see Kraut, 1987; Stocker, 1990.)

Recent advances in neurology disclose structural and functional patterns in the central nervous system that are correlated with, and that under experimental conditions bring about, certain emotional reactions. Do these patterns dictate the structure of an adequate theory of emotion, or are those findings simply one more set of (contingent) considerations for inclusion in an all-embracing theory? Whatever the case, it is now clear that philosophers cannot ignore or neglect the rich neurophysiological literature on emotions. Indeed, there is now a new (inter)discipline in philosophy called "neurophilosophy," which makes the new neurology central to any adequate analysis of emotion and "the mind" (Churchland, 1986). Philosophers may continue to argue that Aristotle knew all about emotions even though he did not know beans about the brain, but they do so at their peril—and in the face of the obvious fact that among the factors that have altered the history of philosophy and its concepts most radically have been new advances in previously unknown or undeveloped sciences.

Virtually all emotions get expressed (however minimally) in behavior. Should behavioral tendencies or sequences of actions or certain basic gestures be taken as essential? A great deal of detailed work in psychology has shown the enormous subtlety and the seemingly "hard-wired" nature of basic patterns of facial expression. Philosophers remain skeptical (Neu, 1989). The data are not in question, but the implied shift in conception from the emotion to the symptom of emotion is. What is it that causes the twitch or a gesture? The emotion would seem to be the perception, the awareness, the realization that is expressed, not the expression itself. On the other hand, many philosophers of a somewhat behaviorist bent (following Wittgenstein's later *Philosophical Investigations* [1953] and Gilbert Ryle's *The Concept of Mind* [1951]) have suggested that an emotion is nothing but its behavioral expression, though certainly not a single gesture but an openended sequence of actions. An emotion is not a "ghostly inner event," Ryle tells us, but a "multitrack disposition" to behave in any number of recognizable ways. So, too, philosophers have tried to understand emotion not as an inner feeling but as a value-laden description of a social situation. Thus Errol Bedford (1956/1964), in his pioneering article in the 1950s, suggested that the difference between shame and embarrassment, for example, is not some shade of difference between internal *qualia,* but the differences between descriptions of an awkward situation in terms of responsibility or innocence.

What remains at the core of all such theories, however, is an awareness that all emotions presuppose or have as their preconditions certain sorts of cognitions—an awareness of danger in fear, recognition of an offense in anger, appreciation of someone or something lovable in love. Even the most hard-headed neurological or behavioral theory must take account of the fact that no matter what the neurology or the behavior, if a person is demonstrably ignorant of a certain state of affairs or facts, he or she cannot have certain emotions. If neurologically induced rage does not include some object of anger, that rage (whatever else it may be) cannot be anger. So, too, Freud's "free-floating anxiety" would count as an emotion only insofar as it does indeed (as Freud [1915/1935] argued) have an object, albeit "unconscious." Philosophers (following Aristotle and the scholastics of the Middle Ages) have come to call this the "formal object" of emotion, and one might well think of this as the minimum essential set of "beliefs" defining an emotion and an emotional experience. The formal object of fear, to take an obvious case, is a fearful object, and the beliefs that constitute the awareness of the presence or threat of such an object. Other emotions are more complicated and, accordingly, more the topics of debate and disagreement. Anger would seem to require a formal object involving an offense, but some authors would allow frustration alone to count as anger (Gordon, 1987). Jealousy is more difficult still, for its object seems to involve not only a threatened loss but a perpetrator as well (perhaps the threatened object as a perpetrator too), and possibly the larger social situation in which jealousy involves not only loss but humiliation as well (Neu, 1980). But though the exact natures of the formal objects and requisite beliefs of various emotions is a matter of lively debate (and there is some doubt and debate over the very possibility of a generalized formal object for all emotions or emotions *sui generis*), the presumption is that every emotion must have a cognitive basis and an object. (There is some corollary debate concerning the status of moods and mood-like emotions [e.g., joy], which do not have a determinate object).

There is also considerable debate over the nature of cognition itself. I have used the word "belief" above, but that seems to me to be unsatisfactory for a variety of reasons Beliefs are too much like established states rather than the spontaneous acts or events that characterize many emotions. Beliefs seem to be too fully articulate and already verbalized for the unreflective reactions that characterize most emotions. For that reason, I prefer to use the concept of "judgment" in this regard (like the ancient Stoics), whereas others (Neu, 1977) prefer the term "thought" (like Spinoza, for example). Some have simply stuck with the notion of evaluation (Pitcher, 1965), while others have preferred the less cognitively commital notion of a way of seeing ("seeing as")—sometimes as a rejection of the cognitive view, but more appropriately, I believe, as a refinement of it (Calhoun, 1984). The nature of an emotional cognition, and whether it must be fully conscious or capable of articulation, remain matters of considerable debate. Indeed, if certain holistic suggestions can be worked out, it may be that the very distinctions that philosophers have so long presupposed among cognition, behavior, physiology, and feeling are themselves inadequate and ought to be integrated.

One way of putting the point that emotions must have a cognitive component—that they cannot be simply feelings or physiological processes, or even "mindless" bits of behavior—is to insist that they have *intentionality*. "Intentionality" is a technical notion, but its common-sense meaning can be captured by the idea that emotions are always "about" something or other. One is always angry about something; one is always in love with someone or something (even if one is also "in love with love"); one is always afraid of something (even if one doesn't know what it is) Thus we can understand the "formal object" of an emotion as its essential intentionality—the kind of object (event, person, slate of affairs) to which it must be directed if it is to be that emotion. But intentionality has also been the object of philosophical consternation for over a century now, because despite its appeal as a way of understanding the nature of perception and other mental "acts" (which gets us away from the image of images or representations "in" the mind), intentionality has its own peculiar complications (Kenny, 1963; Searle, 1983). Most troubling for philosophers is the obvious fact that an emotion may be "about" some non-existant, merely imagined object. The object of fear may be nowhere around. The imagined threat in jealousy may not exist. The person one still loves may be dead. (Indeed, the problem seems to remain whether the lover knows of the death or not. In either case, the emotion is directed at a person who is in no position to receive it.) Moreover, the object of an emotion would seem to be one and the same object, whether or not it exists or not. (It is one and the same devil that is the object of a child's fear, whether the devil exists or not.) Thus the ontological status of the intentional object of emotion causes considerable commotion. In recent decades, many Anglo-American language-oriented or "analytic" philosophers have reduced the seemingly mysterious notion of intentionality to the supposedly more manageable notion of "intensionality," a precisely defined feature of certain sorts of sentences (Dennett, 1978, 1987). But whether intensionality does in fact capture the necessary features of intentionality is itself a topic of considerable debate, and at least seems to confuse the language with which we ascribe emotions with the nature of the emotions themselves (Searle, 1983).

Philosophers have also become concerned with the "why?" of emotions—their function and their explanation. Most of the work here has been done on the explanation of particular instances of emotion, although a few investigators have recently tackled the much larger question of the evolution and function of emotions as such (de Sousa, 1987; Gibbard, 1990). Particular instances of emotion seem to be subject to two different sorts of explanations. On the one hand, because they are intentional and essentially involve beliefs (also desires, needs, attitudes, and values), emotions seem to require an explanation that invokes a person's beliefs and attitudes toward the world. A person is angry because he believes that so-and-so wronged him, or someone is saddened because she has found out that she has just lost a loved one, and so on. But this cannot be a complete account of emotional explanation. We also explain emotions by citing the fact that a person has been sleepless all week, or is ill, or has been given some medication. In other words, explanation of emotion may cite an underlying cause that may or may not make mention of the object of emotion. The cause may be physiological—for example, an underlying state of irritability, an ingested drug, or a direct surgical stimulation of the brain. The cause may be some state of affairs or incident that "triggered" the person's emotion, but this may not be the object of the person's emotion, nor need he or she have any memory or awareness of it. ("Subliminal" messages presumably work this way.)

But how this causal explanation can be reconciled with an explanation in terms of beliefs and attitudes is not always obvious, and many philosophers tend to emphasize the importance of one over the other or to reduce all explanations to causal explanations or belief-and-desire explanations. On the one hand, one provides a fuller account of the intentionality of an emotion by describing not only its formal object ("He's angry because he's been offended"), but the specific details of the situation, as well as the person's beliefs and various attitudes. On the other hand, one provides an explanation in terms of an underlying cause that may or may not make mention of the object of emotion. Very often, however, the citation of a cause of emotion (its initiating stimulus or "trigger") and the account of the object of the emotion will be nominally the same ("He got mad because she stepped on his toe"). The problem that has been addressed by many philosophers (and has been the subject of several weighty studies) is the relation between these two and the various problems in understanding them together (Rorty, 1980).

The cognitive basis of emotions also raises another question, one that was often a matter of deep concern for earlier philosophers: the question of the *rationality* of emotions. Many thinkers have written as if the emotions were not only irrational but also nonrational—not even candidates for intelligence. Accounts of emotions as mere feelings or physiological processes would make them no more than nonrational (one cannot have a "stupid" headache, except by way of a roundabout complaint about its inconvenience). Aristotle, on the other hand, simply assumed that an emotion can be appropriate or inappropriate, foolish or prudent, not just on the basis of whether or not it is acceptable in the circumstance in question (though that social dimension is certainly essential), but on the basis of the perceptions, beliefs, and desires of the individual. The fact that emotions consist at least in part of cognitions means that they can be evaluated in terms of the same epistemic and ethical criteria that we use to evaluate beliefs and intentions: Are they appropriate to the context? Do they consider the facts of the matter? Are their perceptions fair and their evaluations reasonable? Indeed, the argument is now prevalent and persuasive that we cannot understand emotions without grasping their reasons, and these reasons in turn give us a basis for evaluation (de Sousa, 1987; Greenspan, 1988). The current debate, however, concerns how these reasons are to be understood,

and whether the rationality of emotions can indeed be fairly compared to the evaluation of more fully deliberative, articulate activities.

The rationality of emotions also moves to center stage the question of emotions and ethics that we have been following through the history of philosophy. How does emotion enter into ethical understanding, and how do our ethics affect our emotions? One thing is clear: The commingling of emotions and ethics is not grounds for dismissing either ethics or emotion, as the old emotivists suggested. It is worth noting that a new conception of the emotional foundations of ethics has taken root in the Anglo-American tradition and, an appropriate irony, has taken the name "emotivism" (Gibbard, 1990). Of course, one of the questions that remains, left over from the old rationalist charges that emotions are "merely subjective," is that emotions vary too much from culture to culture to provide firm basis for ethics; in other words, they are "relative." But though philosophers cannot (and should not try to) answer the empirical question of the universality or relativity of emotions, they can and should clear away the dogmatic assumptions and mistaken conceptions that have often occupied philosophy in the past. There is nothing in the nature of emotion (including the human brain, which changes significantly with experience and varies considerably from person to person) that assures universality, but neither is it so obvious that emotions differ so much from place to place either. (This is indicated not only by studies of facial expression, but by the logic of the "human condition" and its more general features.) This also raises the question of emotions and choice—the supposed passivity of emotions. Sartre (1939/1948, 1943/1956) suggested that the emotions are willful, but many philosophers who do not share Sartre's extreme voluntarism would agree that emotions are indeed ways of coping, whether inherited through natural selection or cultivated in the less articulate practices of a society. But are we at the mercy of our emotions? Do we simply "have" them, or do we perhaps, to some extent, cultivate and "do" them ourselves? Obviously, a good deal of ethics and our attitudes toward ourselves depend on this. The study of emotion in philosophy is, accordingly, not a detached and marginal discipline, but the very core of our inquiry into ourselves and our own natures. It was Socrates, the great champion of reason, who took as his mottos the slogan at Delphi ("Know thyself") and the rather extreme injunction that "The unexamined life is not worth living." But part of that knowledge is surely our understanding and appreciation of our emotions, which are, after all, much of what makes life worth living.

REFERENCES AND FURTHER READING

Aristotle. (1941). *The basic works of Aristotle* (R. McKeon, Ed.; J. I. Beare, Trans.). New York: Random House. See also W. Fortenbaugh (1975), *Aristotle on emotion*. London: Duckworth.

Austin, J. L. (1956–1957). Pretending. *Proceedings of the Aristotelean Society*, 57.

Bedford, E. (1964). Emotion. In D. Gustafson (Ed.), *Essays in philosophical psychology*. Garden City, NY: Doubleday/Anchor. (Original work published 1956)

Brentano, F. (1971). *Psychology from the empirical standpoint*. London: Routledge & Kegan Paul. (Original work published 1874)

Calhoun, C. (1984). Cognitive emotions? In C. Calhoun & R. C. Solomon (Eds.), *What is an emotion?* New York: Oxford University Press.

Churchland, P. S. (1986). *Neurophilosophy—toward a unified science of the mind–brain*. Cambridge, MA: MIT Press.

Dennett, D. (1978). *Brainstorms*. Montgomery, VT: Bradford Books.

Dennett, D. (1987). *The intentional stance*. Cambridge, MA: MIT Press.

Descartes, R. (1989). *On the passions of the soul* (S. Voss, Trans.). Indianapolis: Hackett. (Original work published 1649)

de Sousa, R. (1987). *The rationality of emotion*. Cambridge, MA: MIT Press.

Freud, S. (1935). The unconscious (C. M. Baines, Trans.). In *Essays in metapsychology*. London: Liveright. (Original work published 1915)

Gibbard, A. (1990). *Ethics and emotion*. New York: Oxford University Press.

Gordon, R. M. (1987). *The structure of emotion*. Cambridge, England: Cambridge University Press.

Greenspan, P. (1988). *Emotions and reasons*. New York: St. Martin's Press.

Hamlyn, D. W. (1978). The phenomenon of love and hate. *Philosophy*, 53. (Includes a discussion of Brentano's theory.)

Heidegger, M. (1962). *Being and time*. New York: Harper & Row. (Original work published 1927) See also the following explications of Heidegger: C. Guignon (1984), Moods in Heidegger's *Being and time*. In C. Calhoun & R. C. Solomon (Eds.), *What is an emotion?* New York: Oxford University Press; H. Dreyfus (1991), *Being-in-the world: A commentary on Heidegger's Being and time*. Cambridge, MA: MIT Press.

Hegel, G. W. F. (1977). *The phenomenology of mind* (A. N. Miller, Trans.). Oxford: Oxford University Press. (Original work published 1807)

Hume, D. (1888). *A treatise of human nature* (L. A. Selby-Bigge, Ed.). Oxford: Oxford University Press. (Original work published 1739) See also A. Baier (1991), *A*

progress of sentiments. Cambridge, MA: Harvard University Press.

Husserl, E. (1960). *Cartesian meditations* (D. Cairns, Trans.). The Hague: Nijhoff. (Original work published 1938)

Hyman, A., & Walsh, J. (1973). *Philosophy in the Middle Ages*. Indianapolis: Hackett.

James, W. (1884). What is an emotion? *Mind*, 9, 188–205.

Kant, I. (1951). *Critique of judgment* (J. H. Bernard, Trans.). New York: Hafner. (Original work published 1793)

Kenny, A. (1963) *Action, emotion and will*. London: Routledge & Kegan Paul.

Kraut, R. (1987). Feelings and contexts. *Journal of Philosophy*, 80. See R. C. Solomon (1990), Emotions, feelings and contexts: A reply to Robert Kraut. *Dialogue*, 29.

Lyons, D. (1980). *Emotion*. Cambridge, England: Cambridge University Press. For an unusual but entertaining philosophical use of Lyons's theory, see N. Carroll (1991), *The philosophy of horror*. London: Routledge & Kegan Paul.

Neu, J. (1977). *Emotion, thought and therapy*. Berkeley: University of California Press.

Neu, J. (1980). Jealous thoughts. In A. Rorty (Ed.), *Explaining emotions*. Berkeley: University of California Press.

Neu, J. (1989). *A tear is an intellectual thing*. Unpublished manuscript.

Nietzsche, F. (1967). *On the genealogy of morals* (W. Kaufmann, Trans.). New York: Random House. (Original work published 1887)

Pitcher, G. (1965). Emotion. *Mind*, 74.

Plato. (1974). *The republic*. Indianapolis: Hackett.

Plato. (1989). *The symposium* (A. Nehamas & P. Woodruff, Trans.). Indianapolis: Hackett.

Ricouer, P. (1966). *The voluntary and the involuntary* (E. Kohak, Trans.). Evanston, IL: Northwestern University Press. (Original work published 1950)

Rist, J. M. (1969). *Stoic philosophy*. Cambridge, England: Cambridge University Press.

Rorty, A. (1980). Explaining emotions. In A. Rorty (Ed.), *Explaining emotions*. Berkeley: University of California Press.

Russell, B. (1967). *The autobiography of Bertrand Russell* (Vol. 1). Boston: Little, Brown.

Ryle, G. (1951). *The concept of mind*. New York: Barnes & Noble.

Sartre, J.-P. (1948). *The emotions: Sketch of a theory* (B. Frechtman, Trans.). New York: Philosophical Library. (Original work published 1939) See the commentary in R. C. Solomon (1988), *From Hegel to existentialism*. Oxford: Oxford University Press.

Sartre, J.-P. (1956). *Being and nothingness* (H. Barnes, Trans.). New York: Washington Square Press. (Original work published 1943) See also J. Fell (1965), *Sartre's theory of the passions*. New York: Columbia University Press.

Schachter, S., & Singer, J. (1962). Cognitive, social and physiological determinants of emotional state. *Psychological Review*, 69(5), 379–399. For a good philosophical rejoinder, see R. M. Gordon (above), Chapter 5.

Scheler, M. (1970). *The nature of sympathy*. New York: Archon. (Original work published 1916)

Searle, J. (1983). *Intentionality*. Cambridge, England: Cambridge University Press.

Smith, A. (1976). *Theory of the moral sentiments*. Oxford: Oxford University Press. (Original work published 1759)

Smith, A. (1976). *An inquiry into the nature and causes of of the wealth of nations*. Indianapolis: Liberty Classics.

(Original work published 1776) For a good study of the relation between Smith's ethics and his economic theory, see P. Werhane (1991), *Ethics and economics: The legacy of Adam Smith for contemporary capitalism*. Oxford: Oxford Unlversity Press.

Solomon, R. C. (1976). *The passions: The myth and nature of human emotions*. Notre Dame, IN; University of Notre Dame Press. See also R. C. Solomon (1988), *About love*. New York: Simon & Schuster; R. C. Solomon & K. Higgins (Eds.) (1991), *The philosophy of (erotic) love*. Lawrence: University of Kansas Press.

Spinoza, R. (1992). *Ethics* (S. Shirley, Trans.). Indianapolis: Hackett. (Original work published 1677) See also A. Rorty (1991), Spinoza on the pathos of love. In R. C. Solomon & K. Higgins (Eds.), *The philosophy of (erotic) love*. Lawrence: University of Kansas Press; J. Neu (1977, above), Part II.

Stocker, M. (1990). *Plural and conflicting values*. Oxford: Oxford University Press.

Thalberg, I. (1977). *Perception, emotion and action*. New Haven CT: Yale University Press.

Williams, B. (1973). Morality and the emotions. In *Problems of the self*. Cambridge, England: Cambridge University Press.

Wilson, J. R. S. (1972). *Emotion and object*. Cambridge, England: Cambridge University Press.

Wittgenstein, L. (1953). *Philosophical investigations*. London: Routledge & Kegan Paul.

2

History of Emotions: The Issue of Change

PETER N. STEARNS

The focus of historical research on emotion is straightforward: The history of emotions deals with processes of change in emotional standards and emotional experience, or, somewhat more complexly, with emotional continuities amid changing contexts. As part of developing historical understanding of emotional expression, a third focus may apply—seeking to grasp the characteristic emotional styles of a particular period, in and of themselves, as a means of enriching the portrayal of that past time and launching the process of comparing one previous period to another. Ultimately, however, the analytical goals center on change, either in emotions themselves or in the environments in which they operate. Here, correspondingly, is the central justification for adding history to the list of disciplines seriously engaged in emotions research. For if emotions change in significant ways—and historians and others have conclusively demonstrated that they do—then the process must be grappled with as part of evaluating emotional expressions even in the present time. The kinds of alterations to which these expressions may be liable and the past trajectories from which they emanate must be determined. Adding change to the variables involved in emotions research means adding complexity, but it is empirically inescapable and provides an essential perspective for assessing the results of other social research on emotion, such as that emanating from sociology and anthropology.

THE DEVELOPMENT OF EMOTIONS HISTORY

Explicit historical research on emotion is, however, of relatively recent, vintage. Theorists from other social science disciplines provided frameworks for historical assessment long ignored by most historians themselves. Thus Norbert Elias's (1938/1982) classic work on how new levels of "civilization" began to constrain spontaneous emotional expressions, beginning with the Western European aristocracy by the 18th century, focused attention on a key turning point now being widely explored. Until recently Elias's research was more widely utilized by European sociologists dealing with emotion than by any other group. More generally, the constructivist theory of emotion, generated by several social psychologists as well as sociologists, argues that emotions should be interpreted primarily in terms of the social functions they serve; constructivists also correctly note that as social functions frequently change, emotions will shift substantially as well (Averill, 1980, 1982). Some emotions may disappear as part of this process, and others may newly emerge. Here is a richly suggestive historical framework—only rarely, however, fleshed out by detailed historical research, and largely ignored by professional historians. The constructivist view, including the common attention to cultural context as a functional area or as an intermediary between function and emotion, independently affecting ideas about emotional experiences and the vocabularies used to phrase them (Gordon, 1989), in fact tallies closely with recent historical work. However, a formal marriage has yet to occur.

Historians themselves moved into research on emotion hesitantly. The great French social historian Lucien Febvre called over 60 years ago for a "historical psychology" that would "give up psychological anachronism" and "establish a detailed inventory of the mental equipment of the time" (Febvre, 1933/ 1973). His appeal was not quickly heeded. A number of cultural historians dealt with past styles and rituals that had strong emotional components. Johann Huizinga's (1927) masterful portrayal of the late Middle Ages contained a wealth of data relevant to emotions history, and even more limited studies of popular protest or religious life offered important emotional insight into the past periods involved (Stearns with Stearns, 1985). Explicit focus on emotion, however, was lacking. Most historians continued to emphasize the conscious actions and rational decisions of their subjects—particularly, of course, when they dealt with political and diplomatic history, with an eye toward formal policy decisions. Even the advent of social history in the United States, bent on detailing the activities and interests of groups of ordinary people, did not quickly break this mold. Indeed, it could confirm it, as social historians were bent on rescuing ordinary people from accusations of mob impulsiveness and so stressed their transcendent rationality (e.g., in protest situations). Ordinary people may have mental worlds different from those of elites, according to the pioneer social historians, but they are no less careful in choosing methods appropriate to their goals. Emotion, in this formulation, was not a significant variable.

The advent of psychohistory in the 1960s brought attention to the role of emotions in the past, but on a very limited scale. Most psychohistorians, from the great Erik Erikson (1958) to more recent practitioners, have concentrated on biography and have utilized a largely Freudian theoretical framework. They link emotional characteristics to historical developments—thus Erikson translates Luther's tense relationship with his harsh father into Lutheranism's preoccupation with an angry and omnipotent God—but they do not deal with emotional change, and they tend to enmesh emotional factors in a rigid and unchanging psychodynamic. Furthermore, while psychohistorians continue to generate interesting work, their approach has never won wide acceptance within the historical discipline, and (because of pervasive Freudianism) has had a limited reception in other fields as well. Overall, the difficulties of dealing with change and the characteristic inability to go beyond individual case studies have constrained the impact of self-styled psychohistory in emotions research.

It remains true, however, that prior to the development of explicit historical work on emotion, several theories pointed to promising lines of inquiry, and several sociological schools were sketching possible patterns of change over time; a good bit of general cultural history suggested topics in the emotions area and provided a wealth of relevant detail; and psychohistory highlighted the significance of certain kinds of emotional dynamics in the past while again contributing significant evidence. It was psychohistory, for example, that inspired the pioneering study of David Hunt (1970) on parent–child relations in 17th-century France, in turn one of the first direct studies of emotional socialization in the past. It was hardly surprising that as emotions research revived in many disciplines by the late 1970s, historians began to contribute significantly to the agenda.

The direct antecedents of historical research on emotion, however, awaited a final ingredient, provided by the 1970s through the maturation of social history as the leading branch of historical research (a development anticipated, however, in France, as the insight by Lucien Febvre demonstrated). By the 1970s historians throughout the United States and Western Europe increasingly focused not only on the activities and value systems of ordinary people, but also on institutions and behaviors in addition to formal politics, as the central stuff of the past. New topics meant new materials, and also promoted the analysis of change as the dominant mode of historical presentation, displacing the mere narration of political and military events.

From social history, in turn, the issues emerged that led a number of historians to consider emotional patterns as central to their task and that produced increasing confluence with other disciplines dealing with the social contexts of emotional life. Social historians inevitably developed a strong interest in family history. Initially they focused on "objective" features of family organization—size, household composition, marriage age, and the like—where indeed important changes could be traced. Quickly, however, concern about the emotional quality of family relationships began to shape research agendas. Discussion of affective parental ties with children followed, for example, from analysis of the impact of changes in family size. A general linkage emerged between reductions in birth rate and greater affectionate intensity between parents and individual children, although which came first was (and is) not always easy to discern. Other aspects of household composition related to emotional factors. When the property power of older family members began to decline, in a more commercial economy in which independent jobs for younger adults became more abundant, affective links between young adults and older parents might well improve. Finally, efforts to explain changes in marriage patterns—in rates of marriage, ages at marriage, and age ratios between partners—generated attention to the emotional implications of courtship behaviors and subsequent spousal relationships. (For a recent survey of the family history field, see Mintz & Kellogg, 1989.) The social history of emotion—the effort to trace emotional norms in groups of relatively ordinary people and their impact on key institutions of daily life—was born above all from the progressive extension of family history.

By the late 1970s various studies were directly confronting the emotional aspects of family history. Historians working on France, Britain, Germany, and colonial North America uncovered a pronounced increase in familial affection in the late 17th and 18th centuries, contrasting with the more restrained emotional tone seemingly characteristic of families in earlier centuries. John Demos (1970), a historian dealing with colonial New England, noted an effort in 17th-century Plymouth to keep families free from the angry bickering more readily tolerated among neighbors; this effort to control anger was accompanied by the encouragement of conjugal love. European families may have tolerated outbursts of anger as part of appropriate family hierarchy for a slightly longer time—it is possible that in the unsettled conditions of the colonies, preser-

vation of family harmony proved particularly important in North America—but a similar evolution set in throughout much of Western Europe by the 18th century (Stone, 1977; Flandrin, 1979; Trumbach, 1978; Shorter, 1975). Child-rearing methods that had focused on breaking children's wills, reflecting parental anger at animal-like offspring and generating intense if necessarily repressed anger in turn, yielded to greater reliance on affectionate persuasion, though the change was gradual and uneven. Mothers began to be defined as central ingredients of the network of familial affection. Romantic love began to influence courtship and marital expectations; the absence of love even served, by the 18th century, as a valid reason for the dissolution of engagements. On the eve of its decline as an economic unit, the family began taking on important new emotional functions and began to generate new expectations (Leites, 1986). Although the rise of various kinds of love headed the innovation list—one historian (Stone, 1977) described more traditional Western families as possessed of about as much affection as one would expect to find in a bird's nest—other emotions entered in. Most notably, 18th-century family manuals began to urge repression of anger within the family, particularly enjoining men to treat their wives, children, and servants with appropriate decorum. Anger and love did not mix, and love was now becoming more important than anger-implemented maintenance of traditional hierarchies within the household.

While the expansion of familly history began to introduce emotional change as an explicit historical topic—indeed, a central issue in dealing with the rise of new kinds of family relationships in the 17th and 18th centuries—another kind of social history promoted attention to other emotional issues. Here French historians led the way, in contrast to Anglo-Saxon dominance in the pioneering family history studies. A field of "mentalities" research emerged, focusing on deeply held popular beliefs about self, environment, and society, which were expressed more frequently in ritual behavior than in formal declarations of principle. Historians of mentalities probed what ordinary people really meant by their religious observances, often discovering that beneath a Christian veneer a variety of magical ingredients still held sway. Emotional beliefs, or emotional components of other beliefs, increasingly engaged this field of inquiry. Robert Muchembled (1985) and Jean Delumeau (1978, 1989) emphasized the high level of fear characteristic of French peasants from the Middle Ages to the 18th century, expressed in a variety of religious and magical practices and in festival rituals. Anxiety about death, about crop failure, and about violence generated intense community practices that might relieve fears of the outside world. Delumeau, in particular, painted a picture of popular religion dominated by the need to control constantly overspilling fear. Delumeau also argued, however, that as with family emotion, the 18th century saw a pronounced change in popular emotional life: Growing confidence about measures that could control the natural and social environment reduced the need for fear-managing rituals, leading to a shift in religious emphasis and a redefinition of fear that (in a process Delumeau did not himself trace) would lead ultimately to the 20th-century formulation of fear as an interior emotion focused on inward demons.

Mentalities historians also dealt with relationships between elite and popular belief systems. Here too they emphasized a significant change opening up in the early modern period, particularly again in the 17th and 18th centuries. Elite Europeans, increasingly influenced by Renaissance culture, began to look askance at a popular leisure tradition in which they had once willingly shared. A key focus of their dismay was emotional spontaneity—those occasions where emotion generated physical actions, such as crowd frenzy, ribald dances, or dangerously exuberant sports, that now seemed both vulgar and disorderly. Correspondingly, the elite launched a variety of disciplinary and legal measures designed to curb spontaneity, and won some success in denting the traditional festival culture of European peasants and artisans (Burke, 1978; Mitzman, 1987). A historian dealing with colonial Virginia has subsequently traced a somewhat similar process of elite–mass divergence over emotional spontaneity, taking shape in the later 18th century in parts of North America (Isaac, 1982).

In various ways, in sum, analysis of emotional change and its impact had become inescapable by the late 1970s. Without launching a specific subfield concentrating on the history of emotions, social historians of several types were vigorously engaged in dealing with several facets of emotional change, with familial emotions, fear, and spontaneity heading the list. Several topical inquiries, initially directed toward other issues, pointed conclusively both to the existence of substantial emotional change in the past and to the importance of this change in grasping key passages in social history. Attention centered particularly on the early modern period, with demonstrations that in several different ways Europeans and North Americans were changing their emotional rules, or seeing these rules changed, during the 17th and 18th centuries. The link between these findings and Elias's earlier theory about increasing civilized restraint was not immediately drawn, but it soon added a theoretical ingredient to the emerging picture.

A MATURING FIELD

The history of emotions emerged as an explicit and increasingly polished research area during the 1980s. Earlier findings continued to vivify the field, but a number of features were added or redrawn. In the first place, growing numbers of social historians began dealing with the history of emotions in and of itself, rather than as an adjunct to family or mentalities study. Changes in a particular emotion, and the relationship between these changes and other aspects of a historical period, now constitute respectable (if still clearly innovative) historical topics. Social historians also expanded the list of emotions that can be subjected to historical scrutiny. Along with love and fear, anger, jealousy, shame, guilt, grief, disgust, and sadness have received significant historical attention, and interest in augmenting the range of emotions considered as part of research on historical change continues strong.

The contexts in which emotional change can be explored have also been elaborated. Predominant attention, particularly in Anglo-American research, continues to go to family settings and related emotional socialization, but studies of emotional change have now dealt with workplace relations, leisure and its emotional symbolism, and legal standards and uses of the law to reflect new emotional norms.

The maturation of emotions history has also involved growing recognition of a need to modify some of the impulses toward reifying stark contrasts that characterized much of the initial work. Premodern families, for example, are no longer seen as emotionally cold. Affection for children is not a modern invention, nor—despite the fascinating argument of a feminist French historian over a decade ago (Badinter, 1980)—is mother love. Recognition of some biological constants in emotional expressions, and simply more extensive data probes, have modified the earlier picture of sharp premodern–modern emotional dichotomies. Better use of theory has come into play. Historians using Jerome Kagan's findings (1979) on child rearing can understand that evidence of severe physical discipline in the past, once taken as a sign of emotional distancing, is in fact compatible with real affection. Change continues to organize historical research on emotion, but change is now seen as more subtle than was previously the case.

The process of reassessing initial overstatements generated some interesting byways. Some revisionists began to argue that certain emotional relationships do not change; Linda Pollock (1983), most notably, tried to demonstrate that European parents manifested consistent love for their children from the 16th century onward, though in fact her evidence clustered around 1700. In another important variant, Philip Greven (1977; see also the recent extension of the argument, Greven, 1991) posited three basic emotional socialization styles in colonial North America, which have since persisted; change was involved in establishing the initial variety, but thenceforward continuity has prevailed. Angry parents in the 1990s are trapped in the same culture that generated their predecessors in 1750. These approaches have not captured dominant historical attention, however, which continues to emphasize change but in more complex guise.

Love offers a clear illustration of the current approach. Historians now realize that their initial effort to contrast economically arranged marriages with modern romance was overly simple. Economics remains a factor in modern love, and love entered into premodern courtship. The nature and experience of love were different, however. Love in 17th-century Western Europe was less intense, less individually focused, and less physically controlled than would become the norm in the 18th and 19th centuries. The system of arranged marriage led to groups of young men and young women stimulating each other emotionally, for

an individual could not be singled out prior to final arrangement. The 18th-century decline of arranged marriages cut into the group-oriented experience of premarital excitement; this shift soon led to an unprecedented association of love with privacy and with one-on-one intensity. Finally, expressions of love pulled away from a traditional range of vigorous bodily manifestations. Suitors in Wales stopped urinating on their fiancées' robes as a sign of affection; kissing became gentler, biting far less common. The relationship of love and the body, in other words, changed substantially (Gillis, 1985; Leites, 1986; Stearns & Stearns, 1988). This means that a new definition of love—a modern kind of romantic love—did indeed emerge in the late 17th and 18th centuries. The significance of the change is, if anything, enhanced by its fuller definition, even if the complexity increases as well. Similar modifications of initial generalizations about grief (e.g., over infant death) and parent–child affection have generated more subtle, but also richer, definitions of what emotional change entails (Lofland, 1985; Rosenblatt, 1983).

A crucial part of this increased sophistication has resulted from historians' growing recognition of distinctions between emotional standards—the "feeling rules" or emotionology that describes socially prescribed emotional values, and often the criteria individuals themselves use to evaluate their emotional experience—and emotional experience itself. Both topics are important, but they are not the same. The rise of official approval of love in courtship and marriage is genuinely significant—it began to influence legal reactions to marital distress, for example (Griswold, 1986)—but it is not the same thing as a rise of experienced love. The actual experience may have changed less, or at least differently, than the new standards imply. Historians of emotion still try to deal with both aspects of their subject, but in distinguishing between culture and experience they greatly improve their precision.

Finally, maturation of emotions history has involved increasing interaction between historians and other scholars working on the social context of emotion. The revival of attention to emotions research in sociology brought new interest in the issue of emotional change from this camp, inspired to an extent by demonstrated historical work on emotional reformulations over time but augmenting this work as well. American sociologists and social psychologists dealt with a number of changes and patterns in emotional standards in the 20th century, using many of the same materials historians themselves relied upon (Cancian, 1987; Shields & Koster, 1989; Cancian & Gordon, 1988). European sociologists, particularly in The Netherlands, took a somewhat longer view. Relying heavily on the Elias (1938/1982) framework, they dealt with new forms of emotional control in earlier centuries and particularly tried to place 20th-century patterns of emotional management, including a new informality, in the context of earlier shifts (de Swaan, 1981; Wouters, 1991). Finally, although most anthropologists dealing with emotions continued to focus on durable cultural traditions, several major studies, such as Robert Levy's (1973) work on Tahiti, dealt with alterations in emotional expression under the impact of such changes as missionary contact. Historians, for their part, became more aware of relevant work in other fields and more explicitly interested in theories of emotional expression, ranging from Elias's statement (easily assimilable to historical concerns) to Sylvan Tomkins's work (1962–1963); and Peter Gay (1984–1986), essaying an extensive historical survey of the sexual and emotional life of the Victorian bourgeoisie on both sides of the Atlantic, continued to plump for a Freudian approach (applied, however, to group experience).

THE FINDINGS

Growing interest in the history of emotion has generated research in a variety of historical areas, and a handful of classical historians have begun to take up the cause. Several medievalists have contributed explicitly. A substantial literature exists on the rise and subsequent impact of chivalric love (Lantz, 1982). A recent study contrasts this Western impulse with the Orthodox Christian tradition in Eastern Europe, which left less opening for love (Levin, 1989). Other emotions are beginning to receive attention for this period, as the rich vein of research on medieval culture extends to further uses (Morrison, 1988). The literature on emotions history has also been extended actively to scholarship on China. In 1989 Mark Elvin called for "the history

of ideas and emotions," and has advanced his work on this subject in recent publications offering sketches of the emotions in modern China (1989, 1991). A history of Maoism notes the Chairman's need to appeal for emotional reconfiguration on the part of peasants, toward releasing the anger necessary to fuel the revolution he sought (Solomon, 1971). Forthcoming research on the culture toward death in the Middle East promises to provide findings relevant to the history of emotion in this society as well. Although existing examples remain limited, one can expect growing understanding of various facets of emotions history in cultures outside the West, and for periods prior to the last five centuries.

The richest literature on emotions history continues to apply, however, to modern Western history—defined as beginning about 1500 and extending to the present, and as applying to Western Europe and North America. Within this range, three periods command primary attention and generate the most extensive findings, in a pattern that also demonstrates the sporadic bursts rather than the steady development of significant emotional change.

Historical research continues to embellish the picture of a fundamental transformation in emotional standards during the early modern centuries, and particularly the 17th and 18th centuries. Imaginative research on the German peasantry has even discerned some symptoms of emotional change, toward fuller identification of an emotional self, in the century after 1500 (Sabean, 1984). In addition to refinements in the understanding of changes in parental and marital love, and to the ongoing work on fear and spontaneity, historians have added a number of other changes to the early modern transformation model. John Demos (1988), treating New England in the colonial and early national periods, traces a shift from pervasive use of shame in dealing with children and miscreant adults to guilt, from the 18th to the early 19th century. As community cohesion declined, parents had to find new ways to internalize behavioral guidelines; they were able to use newly intense love as the basis for instilling a greatly heightened level of guilt. A comparable shift, toward guilt rather than public shaming, describes innovations in the principles of social discipline and criminal justice in the same period. Carol Stearns (1988), dealing with the 17th and 18th centuries, emphasizes a decline in the acceptability of sadness or melancholia, traditionally acknowledged as an appropriate badge of human baseness and an indirect expression of anger. In England and colonial North America, a growing number of diarists after 1700 began to be able to describe emotions in new detail, to assume that they could be managed as part of developing an individual personality, and to argue that an individual owed those around him or her a normally cheerful demeanor. On yet another front, Alain Corbin (1986) describes a vast transformation in the emotion of disgust, as Frenchmen from the 18th century onward began to manifest intense disgust at a new range of objects and to use the emotion to motivate a variety of new sanitary and cosmetic behaviors and to justify new social distinctions between the washed and the unwashed. Here emotional change is directly linked to altered experience of the senses.

The notion of a substantial redefinition of emotional range, with new meanings and new values placed on a variety of emotions, thus continues to define a growing amount of work on the 17th and 18th centuries. Some of this work amplifies Norbert Elias's insight about a new level of civilization in manners (see also Kasson, 1990), but other findings (e.g., those on guilt and cheerfulness) strike out in newer directions, building on previous research on family emotions and on emotional selfhood.

Research on 19th-century emotions history has become increasingly active, but it lacks the focus of the early modern framework. To some extent, the very notion of a great transformation in the 17th and 18th centuries overshadows findings on the 19th century, as many developments served to amplify and disseminate to new social groups the basic trajectories established earlier. Yet amplification can carry important new messages. American studies on the apotheosis of mother love go well beyond 18th-century findings concerning new expectations for parental affection (Lewis, 1989), and the standards applied to children, in terms of anticipated emotional reward, escalated as well (Zelizer, 1985). Several important studies on the 19th-century version of romantic love similarly point to novel and distinctive features (Stearns, 1989; Lystra, 1989). Love became a virtually religious ideal, involving self-abnegation and worshipful devotion

to the other; 18th-century standards had not sought so much. Jealousy was redefined in this process, as a largely female emotion and a contradiction of proper selflessness in love; older ideas of jealousy in defense of honor fell by the wayside. Grief gained new attention and vast new symbolic expression in Victorian funeral practices (Houlbrooke, 1989). Anger received more explicit condemnation, particularly in the family setting. Gender distinctions urged total suppression of anger on women, but an ability to channel anger toward competition and righteous indignation on men (Stearns & Stearns, 1986).

Victorian emotional patterns thus provided no overall new direction, but they did adjust prior trends to the new sanctity of the family in an industrial world; to new social class divisions; and to new need to define emotional distinctions between boys and girls, men and women. Whereas love was seen as uniting men and women in common emotional goals, negative emotions became highly gender-linked; not only jealousy and anger but also the conquest of fear was redefined to serve purposes of gender identity (Stearns & Haggerty, 1991). Although most current attention is riveted on the new standards urged in 19th-century Western society and within the middle class, spelled out in a surge of new kinds of prescriptive literature, various evidence suggests considerable behavioral impact. Men and women did have, with some frequency, the kind of love experiences now recommended; they did work toward appropriate training of children concerning anger and fear. Still not entirely defined, the 19th century stands as a rich source of materials on emotional history and as the scene of a number of significant modifications in norms and experience.

The 20th century, finally, has received sharper definition from the historical perspective. Several emotions historians, to be sure, trace a variety of oscillations in 20th-century standards without an overarching theme. Some analysis concentrates on the need to refute facile modernization ideas that urge, against virtually all available findings, that the 20th century should be seen simply in terms of increasing openness of emotional expression, as older repressions have gradually fallen away. Significant work also stresses continuities from the 19th century, particularly in the gender-linked quality of certain emotional standards;

women, for example, continue to be held to a particularly self-sacrificing image of love, even as male standards may have changed (Cancian, 1987). A few historians plump for continuity pure and simple, from the 19th or even the 18th centuries (Kasson, 1990; Flandrin, 1979).

Two related approaches focus a number of the most important current findings about the 20th century. The first, emanating particularly from several Dutch sociologists, grapples with the problem of growing emotional informality and apparent liberalization, in a context that continues to insist on a great deal of self-control. Spontaneity has revived, but within strict (if unacknowledged) limits. The general argument is that most Westerners have learned so well the lessons of restraint of violence and of unwanted sexuality that they can be allowed (indeed, must be allowed) a good bit of informal emotional idiosyncrasy as part of personal style. Rules of emotional expression have become more complex, and judgments are made about appropriate emotional personalities on the basis of a variety of individual interactions rather than rigid and hierarchical codes (de Swaan, 1981; Wouters, 1991).

The second approach similarly urges that the 20th century constitutes a period of considerable, and reasonably coherent, change in emotional standards. It focuses on implicit attacks on 19th-century emotional formulas, becoming visible by the 1920s and extending over a transition period of several decades. Hostility to negative emotions has increased. Gender linkages, though by no means absent, has been muted in favor of more uniform standards of emotional control. The importance of managing emotions through talking out rather than active expression has become a dominant theme. Relatedly, reference to embarrassment in front of others has come to supplement guilt and shame as enforcement for emotional normality (Stearns & Stearns, 1986; Stearns, 1989). Amid a host of specific changes, including new emphasis on avoiding rather than mastering fear as part of building character, the dominant theme is a new aversion to undue emotional intensity (Shields & Koster, 1989; Stearns & Haggerty, 1991). The decline of the acceptability of open grief is a key index to the new emotional regime. Even good emotions have dangers; earlier icons of intense emotion, such as the idealized Victorian mother as well as lavish grief, have come in for substantial criticism.

PROBLEMS AND RESPONSES

None of the three chronological focal points of historical research on emotion is entirely worked out. Gaps, disagreements, and issues of synthesis persist. One of the obvious current challenges involves pulling together diverse findings on emotional transformation, even for the early modern period, toward a fuller understanding of relationships among different facets of change. Interpretations of Victorian and 20th-century changes cannot yet rival the longer tradition of research on the early modern transformation, though their greater proximity to the present naturally gives them particular salience for most other emotions researchers. The lack of substantial research on non-Western emotions history limits its theoretical potential and comparative inquiry. Tentative linkages between historical and social science approaches to the topic have yet to be fleshed out; despite their timely rejections of simplistic modernization schemas, American sociologists, for example, continue to emphasize purely 20th-century patterns, sometimes implying an undifferentiated traditionalism before 1900. Emotions history constitutes a relatively new field still, and though it offers important findings concerning three major time periods, there are limits to the established wisdom available.

Furthermore, some obvious problems are endemic to the field. Finding data appropriate for dealing with the emotional standards, and even more the emotional experience, of dead people is no easy task. The distinction between professed values and actual emotions helps. Historical research has become progressively more inventive in finding materials on emotional standards and in interpreting them through nuances of language and choices of metaphor, as well as through explicit message. Changes in word meanings ("temper," "lover") and outright neologisms ("sissy," "tantrum") provide direct testimony. Absence of comment may sometimes prove revealing, as in the avoidance of elaborate jealousy discussions in Victorian culture. Utilization of diary evidence, available in Western society from the 17th century and also in 19th-century Japan (Walthall, 1990), provides insight into internalization of standards and self-evaluations, though there are problems of representativeness. A growing number of historians utilize rituals and various ethnographic evidence to get at emotional expressions in the past (Gillis, 1988). History adds greatly to the cases available for assessing the social contours of emotion, and while its service as laboratory has some undeniable empirical complexities, major strides in data sources continue.

Emotions history also enters researchers into versions of debates important in other social science fields. The results complicate the field, but also allow historical work to contribute to larger issues. Research on emotional change obviously provides yet another confrontation between definitions of basic emotions, biologically predetermined though perhaps variable in target and expression, and emphasis on the cultural preconditions of emotional experience. Like other emotions researchers, historians, as they have gained in theoretical sophistication, participate in these discussions from various vantage points; the fact of significant change in aspects of emotional perception adds a vital dimension to the larger debates, challenging excessive focus on inherent basic responses.

Grasping the emotional arsenal of a past culture involves historians in another set of issues, already familiar in anthropology: Is the task merely to record the emotional language of a past age, or can we legitimately interpret past emotions in light of current categories? Again, dispute has been vigorous, with some historians explicitly renouncing efforts to translate earlier terminology into contemporary parlance even as a means of highlighting differences in time (Clark, 1983), and other agreeing with anthropologists like Melford Spiro in contending that we must translate from one culture to another in order to understand variance or change (Stearns, 1988).

Emotions history also generates some theoretical issues of its own, associated with the focus on tracing change. These issues merit further exploration, not only in history but in other emotions research as historical findings are increasingly taken into account. Problems of timing constitute one example. When emotional standards begin to change in a society, how long does it take for key groups to internalize the changes, at least to some significant extent? Are there generalizable factors that speed or delay the response? For example, advice givers in the United States began early in the 19th century to urge that parents not use fear as a disciplinary tool with children.

But manualists were still arguing against the "bogeyman" style a century later, implying that many parents still held out; and studies of rural areas in the 1930s reveal explicit and only mildly embarrassed use of the ploy. Yet change did come: By the 1950s, most prescriptive literature no longer judged the warnings necessary. The issue is not whether change occurred, but at what pace, and what factors determined the timing. Another instance involves implementation of standards in a more public sphere: Available findings in the 19th and 20th centuries, again in the United States, suggest a three- to five-decade lag between significant middle-class acceptance of new standards (about marital love, jealousy, or grief) and translation of these standards into relevant laws about divorce, jealousy-provoked crime, or grief-related damage suits. Again, can we devise more general models to describe the probable speed of change, at least in modern societies, or will we be confined (as is currently inescapable) to case-by-case judgments? A similar problem arises in dealing with the interaction of dominant prescriptions, issued by leading religious (or, in modern cases, scientific) popularizes, and the effective emotional standards of subcultures (ethnic or social class). Here a vast set of research problems remains virtually untapped, quite apart from generating models of interaction between "hegemonic" values and subsystems. Historians have done much better with middle- and upper-class emotions history than with immigrant or lower-class, but there is no reason not to expect future progress on this second vital front. Here too, the possibility of valid generalizations would greatly simplify analysis, but this stage has not yet emerged.

A second set of historically generated theoretical issues involves the relationship between recreations and emotions. Historical work makes it increasingly clear that cultural expressions—in theater, or reading matter, or ritual, or sports—sometimes serve to train individuals in dominant emotional norms. Middle-class parents in the United States around 1900 believed that boxing was a good way to teach boys to retain and express anger, while confining its intensity to appropriate targets. In other instances, however, culture can be used in reverse fashion, as an outlet for emotions that are proscribed in daily life. Chinese love poems issued from a society highly intolerant of love in actual youth relationships (Goode,

1959). Twentieth-century spectator sports allow men to vent emotions that they know are normally inappropriate, despite greater acceptability in the past. The historical perspective is not the only means of entry into these issues of cultural–emotional relationships, but it provides a growing list of significant and diverse examples.

THE STRENGTHS OF THE HISTORICAL APPROACH

Emotions history, despite the limitations of novelty, has already generated a number of important findings about changes in standards and their relationship to aspects of emotional experience. The direction of changes in three major periods in modern Western history, although by no means fully captured, is becoming increasingly clear. The results in turn add evidence and issues to a number of basic discussions in emotions research, and generate additional theoretical problems associated with the phenomenon of change.

History also permits deeper exploration of the causation operating in the social context of emotions, an area suggested by constructivist theory but not systematically probed. Historical research deals with the factors that induce new emotional formulations, permitting a kind of causation analysis that differs from and is more extensive than that possible in cross-cultural comparisons of relevant variables. In the major cases explored thus far, historians have picked up on the role of shifts in larger beliefs in inducing new emotional standards. For example, the Protestant Reformation encouraged re-evaluation of emotions within the family, while new elite culture prompted reassessment of popular spontaneity. The role of changing expertise in the 20th century provides an opportunity to assess cultural causation of another sort. Economic and organization systems provide the second major strand of causation. Increased commercialization prompted new attention to family emotionality in the early modern period, as relationships among other adults became more competitive (Nelson, 1969). The separation of home and work prompted emotional re-evaluations in the 19th century. Most of the leading judgments on basic shifts in the 20th century point to the impact of new organizational experiences and styles, attendant on the rise of a service

economy, corporate management hierarchies, and mass consumerism. The impact of prior emotional change, in setting standards that gradually affect other facets or other groups, also plays a role in assessments of shifts in emotional perceptions in the 19th and 20th centuries. Definitive statements of causation remain elusive, particularly in terms of assigning priority and precedence to one set of variables over another, but the analytical task has been engaged. It involves evaluations that, though rooted in history, inevitably apply to other social research on emotion as well.

Historical research also encourages renewed attention to the impact of emotion and emotional standards, again in a context of change. Emotions research in other disciplines sometimes assumes that further understanding of emotions themselves constitutes a sufficient end result. The growing group of researchers interested in emotions history certainly seeks to add to this understanding, and accepts it as a major goal. Historians, however, are typically interested in relating one facet of the human experience to others, so it is natural that they seek to discuss the results of emotional change on other aspects of society, whatever the time period involved. The effort to distinguish between emotional standards and outright experience adds to this inclination, for new standards often have measurable impact—on the law, for example—even when basic emotional experience may remain more obdurate.

Historians of emotion have consistently commented on the interaction between emotional change and other facets of family life. History is proving to be a crucial means of improving the articulation between gender and emotion. Because gender is in large measure a cultural construct and varies greatly over time, historical research is central to the determination of the origins and results of particular gender formulas for emotional expression. One of the key findings of researchers dealing with the 19th and 20th centuries thus involves recognizing the central importance of gender distinctions in Victorian emotional prescriptions, and then their reconfiguration beginning in the 1920s. Emotional standards also intertwine with power relationships, even aside from gender. Emotions are used regularly to enforce, and sometimes to conceal, such relationships. Research on emotion in the early modern period deals extensively with the interrelationship between changes in this area and revision of family hierarchies. Research on differences in rates and directions of emotional change, even in the 20th century, provides new insight into the often hidden hierarchies of contemporary social and economic life. It also explains the changing emotional bases for collective protest within the configuration of power—including the decline of emotionally charged protest, the late 1960s excepted, from the 1950s to the present in Western society (Moore, 1978).

Historical research on emotion, gaining momentum from several sources, generates important new data, evaluative tools, and theoretical perspectives for emotions research more generally. It provides prior examples of emotional reassessments and an explicit historical vantage point for evaluating current directions of change. Emotions history, increasingly ensconced in the broader field of social history despite its newcomer status, thus becomes part of an interdisciplinary inquiry into the constituents of emotional experience and the role of emotion in social life. The history of emotions adds challenge and complexity to the study of emotion by introducing the factor of change as a central ingredient. Emotions history also provides many of the tools necessary to deal with the issue of change and to use its analysis toward fuller understanding of the ways in which emotions develop and function.

REFERENCES

Averill, J. R. (1980). A constructivist view of emotion. In R. Plutchik & H. Kellerman (Eds.), Emotion: Theory, research, and experience. Vol. 1. Theories of emotion (pp. 305–339). New York: Academic Press.

Averill, J. R. (1982). Anger and aggression: An essay on emotion. New York: Springer-Verlag.

Badinter, E. (1980). L'Amour en plus: Histoire de l'amour maternel. Paris: Flammarion.

Burke, P. (1978). Popular culture in early modern Europe. New York: New York University Press.

Cancian, F. M. (1987). Love in America: Gender and self development. Cambridge, England: Cambridge University Press.

Cancian, F. M., & Gordon, S. (1988). Changing emotion norms in marriage: Love and anger in U.S. women's magazines since 1900. Gender and Society, 2(3), 303–342.

Clark, S. (1983). French historians and early modern culture. Past and Present, 100, 62–99.

Corbin, A. (1986). The foul and the fragrant: Odor and the French imagination. Cambridge, MA: Harvard University Press.

Delumeau, J. (1978). La peur en Occident, XIVe–XVIIe siècles: Une cité assiégée. Paris: Fayard.

Delumeau, J. (1989). Rassurer et proteger: Le sentiment de sécurité dans l'Occident d'autrefois. Paris: Fayard.

Demos, J. (1970). A little commonwealth: Family life in Plymouth Colony. New York: Oxford University Press.

Demos, J. (1988). Shame and guilt in early New England. In C. Z. Stearns & P. N. Stearns (Eds.), Emotion and social change: Toward a new psychohistory (pp. 69–86). New York: Holmes & Meier.

de Swaan, A. (1981). The politics of agoraphobia: On changes in emotional and relational management. Theory and Society, 10(3), 359–385.

Elias, N. (1982). The history of manners (E. Jephcott, Trans.). New York: Pantheon Books. (Original work published 1938)

Elvin, M. (1989). Tales of the Shen and Xien: Body-personal and heart-mind in China during the last 150 years. Zone, 4, 266–349.

Elvin, M. (1991). The inner world of 1830. Daedalus, 120(2), 33–61.

Erikson, E. (1958). Young man Luther. New York: Norton.

Febvre, L. (1973). A new kind of history. New York: Harper & Row. (Original work published 1933)

Flandrin, J. L. (1979). Families in former times (R. Southern, Trans.). Cambridge, England: Cambridge University Press.

Gay, P. (1984-1986). The bourgeois experience: Victoria to Freud (2 vols.). New York: Oxford University Press.

Gillis, J. R. (1985). For better, for worse: British marriages, 1600 to the present. New York: Oxford University Press.

Gillis, J. R. (1988). From ritual to romance: Toward an alternate history of love. In C. Z. Stearns & P. N. Stearns (Eds.), Emotion and social change: Toward a new psychohistory (pp. 87–122). New York: Holmes & Meier.

Goode, W. J. (1959). The theoretical importance of love. American Sociological Review, 24(1), 38–47.

Gordon, S. L. (1989). The socialization of children's emotion: Emotional culture, competence, and exposure. In C. Saarni & P. Harris (Eds.), Children's understanding of emotion (pp. 319–349). Cambridge, England: Cambridge University Press.

Greven, P. J., Jr. (1977). The Protestant temperament: Patterns of child-rearing, religious experience and the self in early America. New York: Knopf.

Greven, P. J., Jr. (1991). Spare the child: The religious roots of punishment and the psychological impact of physical abuse. New York: Knopf.

Griswold, R. L. (1986). The evolution of the doctrine of mental cruelty in Victorian American divorce, 1790–1900. Journal of Social History, 20, 127–148.

Houlbrooke, R. (Ed.). (1989). Death, ritual and bereavement. New York: Routledge/Chapman & Hall.

Huizinga, J. (1927). The waning of the Middle Ages. London: E. Arnold.

Hunt, D. (1970). Parents and children in history: The psychology of family life in early modern France. New York: Basic Books.

Isaac, R. (1982). The transformation of Virginia, 1740-1790. Chapel Hill: University of North Carolina Press.

Kagan, J. (1979). The growth of the child: Reflections on human development. New York: Norton.

Kasson, J. F. (1990). Rudeness and civility: Manners in nineteenth-century urban America. New York: Hill & Wang.

Lantz, H. R. (1982). Romantic love in the pre-modern period: A social commentary. Journal of Social History, 15, 349–370.

Leites, E. (1986). The Puritan conscience and modern sexuality. New Haven, CT: Yale University Press.

Levin, E. (1989). *Sex and society in the world of the Orthodox Slavs, 900–1700*. Ithaca, NY. Cornell University Press.

Levy, R. I. (1973). *Tahitians: Mind and experience in the Society Islands*. Chicago: University of Chicago Press.

Lewis, J. (1989). Mother's love: The construction of an emotion in nineteenth-century America. In A. E. Barnes & P. N. Stearns (Eds.), *Social history and issues in human consciousness* (pp. 209–229). New York: New York University Press.

Lofland, L. (1985). The social shaping of emotion: The case of grief. *Symbolic Interaction, 8*(2), 171–190.

Lystra, K. (1989). *Searching the heart: Women, men, and romantic love in nineteenth-century America*. New York: Oxford University Press.

Mintz, S., & Kellogg, S. (1989). *Domestic revolutions: A social history of American family life*. New York: Free Press.

Mitzman, A. (1987). The civilizing offensive: Mentalities, high culture and individual psyches. *Journal of Social History, 20*, 663–688.

Moore, B. (1978). *Injustice: The social basis of obedience and revolt*. White Plains, NY: M. E. Sharpe.

Morrison, K. F. (1988). *I am you: The hermeneutics of empathy in Western literature, theology and art*. Princeton, NJ: Princeton University Press.

Muchembled, R. (1985). *Popular culture and elite culture in France, 1400–1750* (L. Cochrane, Trans.). Baton Rouge: Louisiana State University Press.

Nelson, B. (1969). *The idea of usury: From tribal brotherhood to universal otherhood*. Princeton, NJ: Princeton University Press.

Pollock, L. A. (1983). *Forgotten children: Parent–child relations from 1500 to 1900*. Cambridge, England: Cambridge University Press.

Rosenblatt, P. C. (1983). *Bitter, bitter tears: Nineteenth-century diarists and twentieth-century grief theories*. Minneapolis: University of Minnesota Press.

Sabean, D. (1984). *Power in the blood: Popular culture and village discourse in early modern Germany*. Cambridge, England: Cambridge University Press.

Shields, S. A., & Koster, B. A. (1989). Emotional stereotyping of parent in child rearing manuals, 1915–1980. *Social Psychology Quarterly, 52*(1), 44–55.

Shorter, E. (1975). *The making of the modern family*. New York: Basic Books.

Solomon, R. H. (1971). *Mao's revolution and Chinese political culture*. Berkeley: University of California Press.

Stearns C. Z. (1988). "Lord help me walk humbly": Anger and sadness in England and America, 1570–1750. In C. Z. Stearns & P. N. Stearns (Eds.), *Emotion and social change: Toward a new psychohistory* (pp. 39–68). New York: Holmes & Meier.

Stearns, C. Z., & Stearns, P. N. (1986). *Anger: The struggle for emotional control in America's history*. Chicago: University of Chicago Press.

Stearns, C. Z., & Stearns, P. N. (Eds.). (1988). *Emotion and social change: Toward a new psychohistory*. New York: Holmes & Meier.

Stearns, P. N. (1989). *Jealousy: The evolution of an emotion in American history*. New York: New York University Press.

Stearns, P. N., & Haggerty, T. (1991). The role of fear: Transitions in American emotional standards for children, 1850–1950. *American Historical Review, 96*(1), 63–94.

Stearns, P. N., with C. Z. Stearns. (1985). Emotionology: Clarifying the history of emotions and emotional standards. *American Historical Review, 90*(4), 813–836.

Stone, L. (1977). *The family, sex and marriage in England, 1500–1800*. New York: Harper & Row.

Tomkins, S. (1962–1963). *Affect, imagery, consciousness* (2 vols.). New York: Springer.

Trumbach, R. (1978). *The rise of the egalitarian family: Aristocratic kinship and domestic relations in eighteenth-century England*. New York: Academic Press.

Walthall, A. (1990). The family ideology of the rural entrepreneurs in nineteenth-century Japan. *Journal of Social History, 23*, 463–484.

Wouters, C. (1991). On status competition and emotion management. *Journal of Social History, 24*(4), 699–717.

Zelizer, V. (1985). *Pricing the priceless child*. New York: Basic Books.

3

Emotions Inside Out: The Anthropology of Affect

GEOFFREY M. WHITE

In anthropology, as in many disciplines, the last 10 years have seen a rapid expansion of interest in emotion.[1] Even though the subfield of psychological anthropology has a long tradition of research on emotive processes in earlier studies of "culture and personality" (e.g., Benedict, 1934; Bateson, 1958; Geertz, 1976), emotions have now emerged as a central topic for research within the discipline's mainstream (see Lutz & White, 1986, and Levy & Wellenkamp, 1989, for recent reviews). Why is this so, and what are the implications for emotion theory generally? In this chapter I address these questions through a discussion of theoretical developments that are contributing to a reconceptualization of emotion as a thoroughly cultural object of study (see Shweder, 1990 and Chapter 29, this volume).

What, then, are some of the problems and approaches that drive this recent anthropological interest in emotion? And how do cultural approaches to emotion articulate with the perspectives of other disciplines? Given the historical division of labor in social science between psychology as the field concerned with individual phenomena (cognition, percep-

tion, personality, etc.) and anthropology and sociology as the fields dealing with social and interactional processes, anthropologists would seem to be interlopers in the study of emotion—practically the *sine qua non* of the individual. Indeed, until recently, most anthropologists themselves would have agreed with such an assessment.

The identification of emotion as a subject for strictly psychological research, and the disciplinary division of labor itself, are reflections of a Western folk psychology that conceives of persons primarily as autonomous individuals rather than as actors whose subjectivity is continually formed in and through interactions with others. As objective and uncontestable as individuated conceptions of the person may seem to most theorists, comparative research suggests that this orientation is a culturally constituted mode of thought that constrains the development of social-scientific theories of emotions. Furthermore, because such constructions generally presume that actions and motivations spring ultimately from physiological processes of the brain, both academic and popular theories of emotion tend to privilege inner, psychobiological variables over social, semiotic ones. Psychobiological theories of emotion in turn have further epistemological ramifications, such as popular psychological beliefs that emotions constitute a kind of touchstone of the "real" self—an index of the inner realities that code the often unrecognized truths of personal experience. However,

---

[1]In this chapter I am concerned only with recent developments in the study of emotion in sociocultural anthropology. There is also, however, considerable interest in the study of emotion among biological anthropologists (see, e.g., Konner, 1982), including recent moves to bridge the gap between cultural and biological approaches within the discipline (e.g., Worthman, 1992).

the premises of these dominant theories of emotion (both popular and scientific) have themselves become the subjects of a growing anthropological and philosophical critique (Rosaldo, 1980, 1984; Solomon, 1984; de Sousa, 1987; Lutz, 1988; Lutz & Abu-Lughod, 1990; Myers, 1988; White, 1992).

In line with the increasingly reflexive stance of social theory today, the anthropological critique of emotion theory turns the interpretive spotlight back upon assumptions that guide research. Once content with a kind of taxonomic approach in which cultural variations in emotion were interpreted as differences in the expression, construal, or labeling of common emotional processes, comparative research now raises more fundamental questions about the definition of "emotional" across cultures. So long as basic (Western) modes of conceptualizing persons and emotions are taken for granted, the goals of comparative research remain largely a matter of mapping and explaining surface diversity. "Culture" in this context becomes simply a matter of "difference," and cultural research becomes *cross-cultural* in the sense of extending the range of observation for existing paradigms. However, as the interpretive anthropology of the 1970s and 1980s began to produce more and more in-depth ethnographic accounts of the meanings and functions of emotions in non-Western cultures, the paradigms themselves have come under critical scrutiny (see Briggs, 1970; Levy, 1973; Rosaldo, 1980; White & Kirkpatrick, 1985; Myers, 1986; Abu-Lughod, 1986; Doi, 1986; Lutz, 1988; and Lynch, 1990, for examples of ethnographic works that deal centrally with emotions).

Although anthropological research on emotions spans a wide range of approaches (see Lutz & White, 1986), the entry of emotion into the disciplinary mainstream is marked by a heightened concern with the symbolic and interactional construction of emotional meaning. In certain respects, these anthropological concerns converge with constructivist approaches in social psychology (e.g., Averill, 1980; Harré, 1986; Gergen, 1990). It is remarkable that emotions did not become an object of ethnographic interest sooner, insofar as any subject that is widely talked about or "topicalized" in ordinary conversation—as emotion is in many societies—usually becomes a focus for comparative cultural interpretation. I take this as evidence of the force of Western construals of

emotions as essentially irrational and unknowable, and thus unlikely subjects for systematic conceptual and linguistic analysis. It is, however, significant that at the same time as anthropologists have been developing ethnographic interest in emotion, psychologists and linguists have begun to formulate cognitive and semantic models of emotion that focus upon similar interpretive problems (Lakoff & Kövecses, 1987; Kövecses, 1990; Ortony, Clore, & Collins, 1988; Wierzbicka, 1986, 1992).

These developments suggest that there is potential for a convergence of interest between cultural and linguistic–psychological approaches that view emotions as meaning-laden social processes—a possibility that is particularly evident in the renewed interest in Vygotskian perspectives (Wertsch, 1985; Ochs, 1988) and in the emergence of a vigorously interdisciplinary "cultural psychology" (Bruner, 1990; Stigler, Shweder, & Herdt, 1990). However, significant differences continue to separate the various disciplinary approaches to emotion, particularly with regard to their presumed theories of language. Specifically, anthropologists, who focus upon the social and semiotic construction of emotional meaning, remain critical of cognitivist theories, which essentialize definitions of emotion in terms of a small set of discrete universal affects thought to be language-free and grounded in physiology (see Crapanzano, 1989).

Cognitive-psychological approaches to emotion (e.g., Johnson-Laird & Oatley, 1989; Ortony et al., 1988) generally assume that the biological basis of emotion is well described by English emotion words and that the meanings of those same words can be represented in terms of biology. English-language terms are regarded primarily as referential labels for universal feeling states or "basic emotion modes," which are "universally accepted as discriminable categories of direct experience" (Johnson-Laird & Oatley, 1989, p. 90). There is a comforting circularity to all of this: A universal set of core affects can be identified with English emotion words, whose meaning is then referred back to those same affects. Unfortunately, as Wierzbicka (1992) has discussed in some detail, basic emotion words such as *sad* or *angry* are semantically complex and therefore inadequate as "semantic primitives" capable of anchoring translations of emotion cross-culturally. In contrast to referential theories of emotion language, approaches that

I call "discourse-centered" recognize that all language entails culturally specific modes of thought and action, which not only express but *create* the realities they represent. It is this appreciation of the force of conceptual and pragmatic processes to shape emotional experience that has fueled recent critiques of emotion theory (Lutz, 1985; Gergen, 1990).

Discourse-centered definitions of emotion have the effect of decoupling emotions from their essential interiority, broadening the focus of emotional research to include the public arenas of communicative action and shared understanding. Turning the study of emotion "inside out" in this way does not ignore or abandon the biological components of emotion—a strategy that would simply reproduce the old dichotomies of inner and outer, body and mind in a new guise. Rather, the move toward discourse calls attention to the fundamentally meaningful, contingent, and relational nature of emotion as constantly modulating both physiological and social, semiotic processes. The new ethnographies of emotion are sometimes associated with positions of extreme relativism, in which the very possibilities for comparison and generalization are called into question; however, their major thrust has not been to reject the notion of universals, but rather to identify constraints placed upon theory and method by universalizing assumptions, and therefore to redirect methodological strategies. Distinctions between "relativist" and "universalist" postures in the anthropology of emotion are perhaps best regarded as a matter of emphasis and tactics rather than as one of absolute difference.

Before discussing further discourse-centered approaches to emotion, I turn to a brief discussion of the cultural underpinnings of the Western view of emotions as natural facts of individual experience.

ON DENATURALIZING EMOTIONS

Theories of emotion are informed by more basic assumptions about minds, bodies, and persons. Emotion concepts gain much of their facticity from taken-for-granted ways of thinking and talking about personal experience that are rarely made explicit. However, emotions and emotionality *are* frequently noticed and discussed aspects of ordinary life (at least in Western societies), and so are accessible to interpretation as topics of English-language discourse. To do so, as Catherine Lutz (1985, 1988) has done in several eloquent statements, is to expose a certain complicity between popular conceptions and scientific theories. In particular, this collusion has worked to focus attention on the psychobiological aspects of emotion and to marginalize the sociocultural aspects. The relative neglect of emotion as socially and semiotically constituted is reinforced by Western models of the person that define emotion in essentially individual and physical terms (see Geertz, 1983; Gergen, 1990).

What, then, are some of the tacit assumptions that work to naturalize and universalize emotion? Dominant psychobiological paradigms of emotion are supported by common-sense models of the mind that differentiate a realm of bodily affect from a realm of "higher" mentation. This bifurcation of experience is elaborated through networks of dualistic propositions that frame experience in dichotomous terms, such as those represented in the following list of parallel oppositions:

MIND — BODY
COGNITION — AFFECT
THINKING — FEELING
REASON — EMOTION
RATIONAL — IRRATIONAL
CONSCIOUS — UNCONSCIOUS
INTENTIONAL — UNINTENTIONAL
CONTROLLED — UNCONTROLLED

To explicate the implicit schematas that interconnect and align these oppositions in folk psychology would exceed the bounds of this chapter (but see D'Andrade, 1987). It is sufficient to note that these oppositions and others discussed in numerous theories of emotion (e.g., Solomon, 1976; de Sousa, 1987) work to organize our understandings about the nature of thought and emotion through a framework of implicit contrasts and oppositions. However, cross-cultural anthropological research casts doubt upon the status of these oppositions as "given" facts of experience. The suspicion that these dichotomous propositions are as much culturally constructed as "natural" stems from their alignment with one of the most pervasive principles of human classification and categorization: the opposition of NATURE versus CULTURE. Comparative studies show that cultural systems of knowledge and belief everywhere tend to order reality through patterns of binary thought that oppose a realm of the "natural" with one of the "cultural." For Western psychology, the strongly dichotomous mode of thinking about minds and persons tends to naturalize the domain of emotion by aligning it with the realm of nature, conceptualized as unmediated physiological processes that are only secondarily controlled or regulated by human thought and convention (i.e., by "culture").

The opppositions listed above, and the implicit models that support them, have significant implications for the study of emotion. To begin with, "emotion" as a subject of research tends to be located at the intersection of the natural sciences and the social sciences, as evidenced by the substantial tradition of research linking emotions in animals with those in humans—beginning most notably with Darwin (1872/1965), and extended into modern psychology by the work of Ekman and his associates on the facial expression of emotion (e.g., Ekman, 1980, 1984). Biological and ethological investigations of the expression of emotion have produced an impressive array of findings, ranging from the neurophysiological correlates of specific affects to the abilities of human neonates to discriminate facial expressions of emotions only hours after birth. But what is the significance of these findings for theories of human action and consciousness? Answering this question is made problematic by the uncritical application of English-language terms and Western cultural models in the design and interpretation of research. Before taking up problems of translation and interpretation, however, let us consider briefly some of the consequences of the naturalization of emotion for the development of emotion theory.

Although the quest for the natural in human experience may be a valid scientific enterprise, it is an enterprise that is deeply compromised by tacit cultural assumptions. The dichotomous structure of folk psychology and its underlying principle of nature versus culture are consistently reproduced in most of the influential theories of emotion that have conceived of emotional process in terms of dual layers or strata. "Dual-process models," as I refer to them, represent emotions in terms of two layers or phases: A limited number of primary or core affects are then "filtered," "screened," "masked," "amplified," "muted," or otherwise

transformed as they are interpreted and expressed in meaningful interaction and communication. Nearly all the prevailing English-language metaphors for emotional process presume some kind of dual-layer or dual-phase imagery.

Reproducing the opposition of nature and culture, dual-process models permeate popular and scientific theories of human psychology. Examples from academic theories include the psychodynamic distinction between "primary-process" and "secondary-process" thinking, and the Ekman model of emotion (which postulates a set of six core affects that are universally expressed in facial expressions, but are also susceptible to cultural labeling or masking through the operation of "display rules" and other devices). "Culture" in such a theory consists of mental programs that mediate eliciting situations, affects, and appropriate responses. Dual-process models have also extensively influenced anthropological theories of emotion, ranging from the psychodynamic theories used in culture and personality research to Levy's distinction of "primary knowing" and "secondary knowing" (Levy, 1984; Levy & Wellenkamp, 1989). Acknowledging the influence of Ekman's (1980) processual model, Levy characterizes the difference between primary and secondary knowing by distinguishing an initial phase of (unconscious) appraisal and feeling from a secondary phase of cognitive evaluation.

One of the appealing features of dual-process models is that they provide a way of accounting for cultural variation while preserving a set of emotional universals. Thus, Ekman's (1980, 1984) display rules transform universal affects into culturally specific behaviors; Levy's theory allows cultures to variously amplify ("hypercognize") or dampen ("hypocognize") universal affects (Levy, 1984; Levy & Wellenkamp, 1989). Note, however, the inequality or asymmetry between the two layers or types of process, as indicated by the terms "primary" and "secondary." One of the consequences of this asymmetry is to systematically privilege the biological in the definition of emotion. The parameters of emotion theory, the interpretation of specific emotions, and the foci for comparative research are all determined importantly by the primacy of core affects. Once physiological mechanisms are defined as the ultimate arbiters of what constitutes specific emotions, cultural models and communicative practices are relegated to secondary roles as "filters," "screens," or "veneers" that transform the "basic" or "core" emotions into their surface expressions. Philosophical critiques of physiological theories of emotion focus precisely upon this point (Solomon, 1976, 1984; de Sousa, 1987), arguing that particular emotions do not adhere solely in feeling states and facial expressions, but rather consist of socially embedded responses that take on behavioral significance within a field of culturally interpreted person–person and person–situation relations. Comparative research that takes this caution seriously is finding that emotional meaning may vary widely from English-language constructs, particularly in societies where such person–person relations are construed in more relational and collective terms than in most Western societies (e.g., Rosaldo, 1984; White & Kirkpatrick, 1985; Lutz, 1988; Lynch, 1990; Markus & Kitayama, 1991).

THE INTERPRETATION OF EMOTIONAL MEANING

One of the significant methodological liabilities of a naturalized conception of emotion is the tendency to minimize problems of interpretation and translation in coming to terms with emotional meaning—across cultures, but also within English-language communities. Physiological models of emotion collude with referential models of language to suggest that the meanings of basic emotion words and concepts are transparent, deriving from their denotation of universal core affects. As mentioned earlier, the meanings of words such as *anger* or *fear* are assumed to derive from their denotation of feeling states, facial expressions, or (culturally modulated) ethological sequences (e.g., Ekman, 1984; Izard, 1977). Whatever the reference, meaning inheres in a set of conditions that may be specified by close attention to the biology of emotion and its behavioral expressions.

Theories that regard emotion as grounded in a limited set of core affects, and that view emotion language as a set of labels that map onto those affects, find an appealing model in cross-cultural research on the semantics of color terms. The analogy between color terms and emotion words suggests that it might be possible to uncover a universal, evolutionary sequence for the linguistic encoding of basic emotions, similar to that which has been demonstrated for the color lexicon (Kay & McDaniel, 1978). The analogy is encouraged by analyses of facial expressions that find evidence for about six basic affects recognizable in all cultures (Ekman, 1984). With these core affects and their facial expressions as a kind of "etic grid" for categorizing prototypic emotions, it is hoped that cross-cultural investigators might set about eliciting judgments of referential meaning for various emotion lexicons, with the aim of describing the systematic encoding of universal affects. The result might even produce evidence showing an evolutionary ordering for the manner in which emotion lexicons progressively differentiate and encode emotions. So far, however, studies of emotion lexicons in numerous languages have given little evidence for any sort of universal ordering for the linguistic encoding of affect (see Gerber, 1985; Lutz, 1988; Heider, 1991; but cf. Boucher, 1979; White 1980). Even without such evidence, however, some research has been quick to adopt evolutionary assumptions. Numerous comparative psychiatric studies, for example, have proceeded from the assumption that the English emotion lexicon is the pinnacle of evolutionary process (e.g., Leff, 1973).

There are good theoretical reasons for the lack of results showing strong lexical correspondences in the emotion domain of the sort uncovered for color. Emotions are not colors. Unlike color words, which *do* serve largely denotative functions in the identification and discrimination of the visible wavelength spectrum, emotion words carry complex, abstract messages about personal dispositions, social relations, and moral evaluations, among other things. They also do significant performative and interactional work, entering into elaborate "language games" whose significance depends upon the pragmatic functions and contexts of ordinary language. These functions are a particular focus of "discourse-centered" approaches to language.

The assumption that English terms and concepts of emotion are universally applicable has contributed to the relative neglect of cultural models of emotion and problems of translation. The stance typical of earlier personality and culture studies presumed that the meaning and relevance of English-language emotion terms were not problems in describing emotions cross-culturally. In many ethnographies, emotions might be discussed without mentioning local terms and concepts at all. If they were, a local emotion word would simply be followed with a one-word gloss with an English word; the two words were assumed to be semantically similar because of their common denotative referents.

The use of English-language terms to interpret non-Western emotions readily confounds ordinary and scientific language, even though the practice is common in ethnographic writing (White, 1992). Conventions for representing emotions and emotion words in anthropological writing are beset with all kinds of unacknowledged problems of translation. In writing about emotion in non-English-language cultures, at least three distinct usages of English emotion words may be distinguished: (1) as analytical (read "scientific") constructs; (2) as rough translations or glosses of native terms; and (3) as English-language emotion words. In most ethnographic writing, the distinction between the first and third usages is blurred, and the problems of equating the second and third usages are minimized. As analyses of emotion become more explicit about problems of interpretation, I suggest that a word such as "anger" might be placed in double quotes ("anger") to indicate reference to analytical usage, placed in single quotes ('anger') to indicate a gloss of a vernacular term, and italicized (*anger*) when used as the English-language term itself. These distinctions would draw attention to the need to consider local emotional meanings and to differentiate between social-scientific and common-sense concepts of emotion.

Some of the most prominent disagreements in anthropological descriptions of non-Western societies have hinged upon accounts of emotional life. For example, in his well-publicized reassessment of Margaret Mead's (1928) writings about Samoa, Derek Freeman (1983) argued that her portrait of a society characterized by the absence of extreme forms of stress, hostility, or violence had in fact precisely inverted the actual nature of the Samoan ethos, which he described in terms of cultural modes of anxiety, anger, and violence that permeate the society. This argument and its extensive secondary literature demonstrate that (1) emotional lives are full of ambiguities susceptible to multiple interpretations, and that (2) the ambiguity is confounded when English terms

and concepts are applied in other non-English-speaking cultures.

In another recent case of diametrically opposed interpretations of emotional process, Spiro (1984) has argued that Rosaldo's (1980, 1984) claims that the Ilongot of the Philippines do not experience Western "anger" are contraverted by her own evidence. Contrary to Rosaldo's claims for a distinctly Ilongot form of emotional experience, Spiro writes, the absence of expected "angry" responses from the Ilongot simply confirms the operation of well-known principles of denial and displacement associated with "angry" and "hostile" impulses. I have discussed these divergent interpretations elsewhere (White, 1992) and will not go into detail here, except to say that ethnographic disagreements such as this expose the difficulty of obtaining cultural and linguistic data with which to resolve them. Even though Rosaldo's accounts of Ilongot emotion feature an explication of the indigenous emotion *liget* —an emotion that overlaps in certain respects with English *anger*—her ethnography does not give the kind of conceptual or linguistic detail that would allow direct comparison of these emotions.

In recent writings on the interpretation of emotion words and concepts in a variety of languages, Wierzbicka (1986, 1992) has questioned the soundness of ethnographic models that use undefined English-language terms as the focal point for representation. She argues for a semantic metalanguage that could be used to represent and compare the propositional meanings of emotion words across cultures. Taking up the disagreement between Rosaldo and Spiro about the place of "anger" in Ilongot society, she examines the semantics of English *anger* and Ilongot *liget*, and concludes that "the two words embody two entirely different (though overlapping) concepts" (1992, p. 141). Wierzbicka's analysis demonstrates the usefulness of distinguishing which aspects of emotion concepts in different languages are pertinent to one another. Asking whether a particular element of *anger* (such as "the wish to harm an offending other") is part of Ilongot emotional discourse allows a wider range of comparative questions than simply the ethnocentric query of whether the Ilongot do or do not experience *anger*. The fuller account of *liget* given by Rosaldo (1980) suggests that cultural goals connected with male identity, strength, courage, and competitive rivalry could, in themselves, constitute a motivational basis for violent practices without requiring us to draw inferences about displaced hostility. This is not to say that such an account must equate motivation with conscious intention, but only that Ilongot emotional discourse can be represented in terms that are not constrained by Western ethnopsychology and English-language emotion terms.

Ethnographic controversies over the interpretation of emotion in non-Western societies are compounded by the absence of explicit models of English emotion terms and concepts. Only recently has English emotion language been the subject of concerted interpretive research. Here again, the neglect of this important subject probably reflects the collusion between a universalist psychology and a referential semantics that appears to obviate the meanings of English-language emotions. Although there has been some relevant work in recent social-psychological studies (e.g., Sabini & Silver, 1982; Tavris, 1982; and see Davitz, 1969) and cognitive-psychological studies (Ortony et al., 1988), much of the ethnographic spadework on English emotions is being done by linguists (Lakoff & Kövecses, 1987; Kövecses, 1990; Wierzbicka, 1986, 1992). These studies are beginning to describe the cognitive underpinnings of a Western ethnopsychology that draws upon container metaphors to conceptualize the person as a bounded individual, and hydraulic metaphors such as heating and cooling to conceptualize the emotions as physical and mechanistic. As these familiar modes of Western thinking are made explicit, comparative research may begin to articulate points of divergence and convergence in emotional meaning and experience across cultures.

One of the findings that has emerged from linguistic and cognitive investigations of ordinary emotion language is the pervasive, if not universal, presence of event schemas or "scenarios" underlying common-sense understandings of emotion (Lakoff & Kövecses, 1987; Lutz, 1987; White, 1990a, 1990b). Typically, some variant of a scenario that entails a sequence of (SOCIAL) EVENT → EMOTION → (SOCIAL) RESPONSE constitutes the backbone of folk psychological models of emotion. These "prototypic event scenarios" are in line with a broad range of theories that emphasize the so-cial and processual nature of emotional meaning. Event schemas such as the minimal sequence EVENT → EMOTION → RESPONSE have proven useful in exploring common-sense reasoning about social-psychological processes, and comparing the role of emotion concepts across cultures. Although cognitive models such as these run the risk of decontextualizing emotion with strictly representational models of meaning, they work to correct and expand the narrow focus of referential definitions of emotional meaning. Event schemas also suggest means of linking ethnopsychological models of emotion with the interactive scenes that organize and produce emotional experience.

Concern with the conceptual underpinnings of emotional meaning needs to be coupled with the recognition that talk of emotions usually constitutes a moral rhetoric—a way of explaining, evaluating, and directing everyday events (White, 1990a, 1990b). Investigating the conceptual and institutional forces that sustain such talk and make it socially consequential requires a broader study of discourse than has typically been pursued in individual-centered studies of cultural psychology. Ultimately, compensating for "translation" deficiencies will require more than simply improving translations for local emotion terms.

EMOTIONS AS SOCIAL DISCOURSE

Although psychological anthropologists have earlier called for comparative studies of "ethnopsychology" (Hallowell, 1954/1967), what was generally meant by this was a kind of descriptive taxonomy of cultural analogues of Western concepts of emotion and personality. In contrast, the turn toward discourse entails a greater interest in the conceptual and pragmatic functions of language capable of creating diverse social realities. In short, the study of emotional discourse resists reduction to simply the study of *ideas about* emotion (Lutz, 1987, p. 308; White, 1992; see also Shweder, 1990, p. 16). Rather, it involves the study of the meaning-making practices of persons engaged in ordinary talk and interaction.

The increasing number of anthropological studies of emotion reflects the realization that emotion is a widespread, probably universal topic of talk and understanding embedded in the same "socially established structures of meaning" that have always been the subject of ethnographic inquiry. Much of this literature focuses on the meanings and functions of locally constituted emotions (e.g., Lutz & Abu-Lughod, 1990; Lynch, 1990; Watson-Gegeo & White, 1990). Although focusing particularly on language, this work is not about semantics so much as the constitution of emotions in discourse. Here the term "discourse" calls attention to the dialectic relation between model and practice, competence and performance, such that emotion language is not simply representational but works also to shape social relations. Moving away from referential theories of meaning that ask what concepts are coded in emotion terms, discourse-centered approaches attend to the models and practices that make the "work" of emotions possible.

Anthropological research has focused particularly on institutionalized, even ritualized, practices that express and transform the social-emotional problems of everyday life. This includes recognition that language itself constitutes a set of tools for representing and responding to the recurrent dilemmas of social life. For example, the essays in a recent collection of anthropological studies of Pacific island societies (Watson-Gegeo & White, 1990) analyze the culturally patterned means through which those societies deal with interpersonal conflicts through the artful use of talk, especially in meetings defined as occasions for resolving conflicts. These activities frequently involve talk about emotions such as 'anger,' 'sadness,' and 'shame,' which, in these contexts, works to transform problematic emotions and to redefine conflicted relations. These emotional discourses obtain the meaning they do, and have the effects they do, because they invoke cultural understandings about persons and emotions that may have transformative effects. Thus, for example, in my analysis of a practice termed "disentangling" in a Solomon Islands society (White, 1990a, 1990b), I show that talk about emotions has the rhetorical effect of transmuting feelings of 'anger' to those of 'sadness' (White, 1990a). However, the local 'sadness' schema only partially overlaps with the meanings of the English term *sad*. Understanding the emotional processes that unfold in Solomon Islands "disentangling" requires a closer explication of relevant ethno-

psychological understandings, as well as the social practices that make "disentangling" a distinctive type of activity.

I refer to this work on "disentangling" to suggest that it is particularly in the process of talking that emotional experience is intersubjectively validated. In this case, individual and collective emotions obtain cultural meaning because of their role in culturally available "scripts" for communicating and interacting to redefine conflict. In symbolic interactionist terms, these emotions become forceful when they are "externalized" in social contexts where they work to constitute social realities. Whereas earlier anthropological research on emotion often focused on processes of "internalization" (i.e., on the means through which certain aspects of culture obtain motivational valence within individual psyches), we might learn as much about the behavioral force of emotions by asking how emotional meaning is externalized in social situations to become evocative and socially persuasive. Instead of regarding emotions as primarily individual, inner, and private, we might begin to think of emotions as *also* social, outer, and public. By investigating socially organized emotive institutions such as Pacific "disentangling," therapeutic practices, or even gossip sessions (Besnier, 1990), we might begin to observe the dialectic relations between emotions and socially validated understanding.

Discourse-oriented approaches offer a range of methods for analyzing emotions along the lines suggested. Whether focusing on the cognitive organization of emotional understanding (Lutz, 1987), the pragmatics of emotion talk (Crapanzano, 1989; White, 1990b), or the role of emotions in reproducing social relations (Abu-Lughod, 1986), culturally framed discourses situate emotions within a field of purposive talk where their social meanings and effects can be more directly examined. For this reason, discourse approaches face less formidable problems linking emotion with ideology and social institutions than do dual-process models, which begin by dichotomizing personal affective experience and public culture.

Lutz and I have proposed elsewhere (Lutz & White, 1986, p. 427) that a discourse-centered approach to comparative research might frame the parameters of emotions in terms of "a set of problems of social relationship or existential meaning that cultural systems often appear to present in emotional terms" rather than in terms of a given set of psychobiological universals. So, for example, instead of beginning with a concept of "anger" as unmediated core affect, as a response to frustration, or even as a scenario of offense and retribution, we might postulate a generalized model of the problem of real or symbolic violation of cultural codes, and then examine the manner in which the problem is articulated in idioms of emotion—that is, as events and feelings that compel personal response. Such an approach applied to the Ilongot would examine *liget* and the motivational basis of violence in terms of the personal and interpersonal dilemmas posed by culturally constituted challenges to the self, rather than in terms of an *a priori* model of displaced "anger." Comparative research along these lines indicates that we are likely to find substantial convergences in emotional understanding across cultures. Although some of these convergences will articulate with the scenarios of "core emotions" posited in psychobiological theories, other aspects of emotional meaning would not even be perceived if the interpretive apparatus is limited to English emotion terms and their presupposed (Western) models.

CONCLUSION

In a theoretically unified world, the different concerns and methods of psychologists, anthropologists, and emotion researchers in other disciplines would represent a division of labor in which each worked on distinct but related facets of human experience. But this generally has not been the case with respect to the various approaches to human emotions. More often, these disciplinary approaches embody incommensurate assumptions about what the problems are and "where the action is"; about the epistemology of emotion; about its location in the body as opposed to the world of meaningful experience; and about the manner in which emotions exert behavioral force, guiding and motivating social action. Where does one look to find the factors that shape (if not determine) social thought and behavior?

My argument has been that answers to this question have been largely constrained by ethnopsychological assumptions that naturalize emotions by locating them within individual minds and brains, thus privileging psychobiological variables in emotion theory to the detriment of social and semiotic factors (see Geertz, 1983, and Gergen, 1990, for parallel statements on the persuasive force of Western conceptions of the person as individual). The remedy, briefly suggested, is to move the study of emotion "inside out" by giving equal time to the cognitive, linguistic, and sociohistorical processes that produce culturally meaningful emotions with the power to move people and alter relationships. In discussing problems in the interpretation and representation of emotional meaning, I have noted a certain collusion between referential theories of language and essentialist conceptions of emotions as internal feeling states, and have suggested that discourse-centered approaches offer a useful corrective by giving attention to the construction of emotion in cognition, talk and interaction. These approaches, like constructivist theories of emotion, include cultural models, communicative practices, and social-interactional processes as constitutive elements of emotion rather than as secondary or derivative features. Perhaps once we have given some attention to the sociocultural bases of emotion, we might more clearly see how emotions, whether "inside out" or "outside in," are part of the continual negotiations of meaning that make up human social life.

REFERENCES

Abu-Lughod, L. (1986). *Veiled sentiments: Honor and poetry in a Bedouin society*. Berkeley: University of California Press.

Averill, J. R. (1980). A constructivist view of emotion. In R. Plutchik & H. Kellerman (Eds.), *Emotion: Theory, research, and experience. Vol. 1. Theories of emotion*. New York: Academic Press.

Bateson, G. (1958). *Naven* (2nd ed.). Stanford, CA: Stanford University Press.

Benedict, R. (1959). *Patterns of culture*. Boston: Houghton Mifflin. (Original work published 1934)

Besnier, N. (1990). Language and affect. *Annual Review of Anthropology, 19*, 419–451.

Briggs, J. (1970). *Never in anger: Portrait of an Eskimo family*. Cambridge, MA: Harvard University Press.

Bruner, J. (1990). *Acts of meaning*. Cambridge, MA: Harvard University Press.

Boucher, J. (1979). Culture and emotion. In A. Marsella, R. Tharp, & T. Ciborowski (Eds.), *Perspectives on cross-cultural psychology*. New York: Academic Press.

Crapanzano, V. (1989). Preliminary notes on the glossing of emotions. *Kroeber Anthropological Society Papers, 69–70*, 78–85.

D'Andrade, R. G. (1987). A folk model of the mind. In D. Holland & N. Quinn (Eds.), *Cultural models in language and thought*. Cambridge, England: Cambridge University Press.

Darwin, C. (1965). *The expression of the emotions in man and animals*. Chicago: University of Chicago Press. (Original work published 1872)

Davitz, J. R. (1969). *The language of emotion*. New York: Academic Press.

de Sousa, R. (1987). *The rationality of emotion*. Cambridge, MA: MIT Press.

Doi, T. (1986). *The anatomy of self*. Tokyo: Kodansha International.

Ekman, P. (1980). *Face of man: Universal expression in a New Guinea village*. New York: Garland.

Ekman, P. (1984). Expression and the nature of emotion. In K. Scherer & P. Ekman (Eds.), *Approaches to emotion*. Hillsdale, NJ: Erlbaum.

Freeman, D. (1983). *Margaret Mead and Samoa: The making and unmaking of an anthropological myth*. Cambridge, MA: Harvard University Press.

Geertz, C. (1983). "From the native's point of view": On the nature of anthropological understanding. In *Local knowledge: Further essays in interpretive anthropology*. New York: Basic Books.

Geertz, H. (1976). The vocabulary of emotion: A Study of Javanese socialization processes. In R. LeVine (Ed.), *Culture and personality*. Chicago: Aldine.

Gerber, E. (1985). Rage and obligation: Samoan emotions in conflict. In G. M. White & J. Kirkpatrick (Eds.), *Person, self, and experience: Exploring Pacific ethnopsychologies*. Berkeley: University of California Press.

Gergen, K. (1990). Social understanding and the inscription of self. In J. W. Stigler, R. A. Shweder, & G. Herdt (Eds.), *Cultural psychology: Essays on comparative human development*. Cambridge, England: Cambridge University Press.

Hallowell, A. I. (1967). The self and its behavioral environment. In *Culture and experience*. New York: Schocken Books. (Original work published 1954)

Harré, R. (Ed.). (1986). *The social construction of emotions*. Oxford: Basil Blackwell.

Heider, K. G. (1991). *Landscapes of emotion: Mapping three cultures in Indonesia*. Cambridge, England: Cambridge University Press.

Izard, C. E. (1977). *Human emotions*. New York: Plenum Press.

Johnson-Laird, P. N., & Oatley, K. (1989). The language of emotions: An analysis of a semantic field. *Cognition and Emotion*, 3, 81–123.

Kay, P., & McDaniel, C. (1978). The linguistic significance of basic color terms. *Language*, 54, 610–646.

Konner, M. J. (1982). *The tangled wing: Biological constraints on the human spirit*. New York: Holt, Rinehart & Winston.

Kövecses, Z. (1990). *Emotion concepts*. Berlin: Springer-Verlag.

Lakoff, G., & Kövecses, Z. (1987). The cognitive model of anger inherent in American English. In D. Holland & N. Quinn (Eds.), *Cultural models in language and thought*. Cambridge, England: Cambridge University Press.

Leff, J. (1973). Culture and the differentiation of emotional states. *British Journal of Psychiatry*, 123, 299–306.

Levy, R. (1973). *The Tahitians: Mind and experience in the Society Islands*. Chicago: University of Chicago Press.

Levy, R. (1984). Emotion, knowing and culture. In R. A. Shweder & R. LeVine (Eds.), *Culture theory: Essays on mind, self, and emotion*. Cambridge, England: Cambridge University Press.

Levy, R., & Wellenkamp, J. (1989). Methodology in the anthropological study of emotion. In R. Plutchik & H. Kellerman (Eds.), *Emotion: Theory, research, and experience. Vol. 4. The measurement of emotions*. New York: Academic Press.

Lutz, C. A. (1985). Ethnopsychology compared to what?: Explaining behavior and consciousness among the Ifaluk. In G. M. White & J. Kirkpatrick (Eds.), *Person, self, and experience: Exploring Pacific ethnopsychologies*. Berkeley: University of California Press.

Lutz, C. A. (1987). Goals, events and understanding in Ifaluk emotion theory. In D. Holland & N. Quinn (Eds.), *Cultural models in language and thought*. Cambridge, England: Cambridge University Press.

Lutz, C. A. (1988). *Unnatural emotions: Everyday sentiments on a Micronesian atoll and their challenge to Western theory*. Chicago: University of Chicago Press.

Lutz, C. A., & Abu-Lughod, L. (Eds.). (1990). *Language and the politics of emotion*. Cambridge, England: Cambridge University Press.

Lutz, C. A., & White, G. M. (1986). The anthropology of emotions. *Annual Review of Anthropology*, 15, 405–436.

Lynch, O. M. (Ed.) (1990). *Divine passions: The social construction of emotion in India*. Berkeley: University of California Press.

Markus, H., & Kitayama, S. (1991). Culture and the self: Implications for cognition, emotion and motivation. *Psychological Review*, 98, 224–253.

Mead, M. (1928). *Coming of age in Samoa*. New York: Morrow.

Myers, F. R. (1986). *Pintupi country, Pintupi self: Sentiment, place and politics among Western desert aborigines*. Washington, DC: Smithsonian Institution Press.

Myers, F. R. (1988). The logic and meaning of anger among Pintupi aborigines. *Man* (*N.S.*), 23, 589–610.

Ochs, E. (1988). *Culture and language development*. Cambridge, England: Cambridge University Press.

Ortony, A., Clore, G. L., & Collins, A. (1988). *The cognitive structure of emotions*. New York: Cambridge University Press.

Rosaldo, M. Z. (1980). *Knowledge and passion: Ilongot notions of self and social life*. Cambridge, England: Cambridge University Press.

Rosaldo, M. Z. (1984). Toward an anthropology of self and feeling. In R. A. Shweder & R. LeVine (Eds.), *Culture theory: Essays on mind, self, and emotion*. Cambridge, England: Cambridge University Press.

Sabini, J., & Silver, M. (1982). *Moralities of everyday life*. Oxford: Oxford University Press.

Shweder, R. A. (1990). Cultural psychology: What is it? In J. W. Stigler, R. A. Shweder, & G. Herdt (Eds.), *Cultural psychology: Essays on comparative human development*. Cambridge, England: Cambridge University Press.

Solomon, R. C. (1976). *The passions: The myth and nature of human emotions*. Notre Dame, IN: University of Notre Dame Press.

Solomon, R. C. (1984). Getting angry: The Jamesian theory of emotion in anthropology. In R. A. Shweder & R. LeVine (Eds.), *Culture Theory: Essays on mind, self, and emotion*. Cambridge, England: Cambridge University Press.

Spiro, M. E. (1984). Some reflections on cultural determinism and relativism with special reference to emotions and reason. In R. A. Shweder & R. LeVine (Eds.), *Culture theory: Essays on mind, self, and emotion*. Cambridge, England: Cambridge University Press.

Stigler, J. W., Shweder, R. A., & Herdt, G. (Eds.). (1990). *Cultural psychology: Essays on comparative human development*. Cambridge, England: Cambridge University Press.

Tavris, C. (1982). *Anger: The misunderstood emotion*. New York: Simon & Schuster.

Watson-Gegeo, K. A., & White, G. M. (Eds.). (1990). *Disentangling: Conflict discourse in Pacific societies*. Stanford, CA: Stanford University Press.

Wertsch, J. (Ed.). (1985). *Culture, communication and cognition: Vygotskian perspectives*. Cambridge, England: Cambridge University Press.

White, G. M. (1980). Conceptual universals in interpersonal language. *American Anthropologist, 82*, 759–781.

White, G. M. (1990a). Moral discourse and the rhetoric of emotions. In C. A. Lutz & L. Abu-Lughod (Eds.), *Language and the politics of emotion*. Cambridge, England: Cambridge University Press.

White, G. M. (1990b). Emotion talk and social inference: Disentangling in a Solomon Islands society. In K.

Watson-Gegeo & G. M. White (Eds.), *Disentangling: Conflict discourse in Pacific societies*. Stanford, CA: Stanford University Press.

White, G. M. (1992). Ethnopsychology. In T. Schwartz, G. M. White, & C. A. Lutz (Eds.), *New directions in psychological anthropology*. Cambridge, England: Cambridge University Press.

White, G. M., & Kirkpatrick, J. (Eds.). (1985). *Person, self and experience: Exploring Pacific ethnopsychologies*. Berkeley: University of California Press.

Wierzbicka, A. (1986). Human emotions: Universal or culture-specific? *American Anthropologist, 88*, 584–594.

Wierzbicka, A. (1992). *Semantics, culture and cognition*. New York: Oxford University Press.

Worthman, C. (1992). Psyche and Cupid: Investigative syncretism in biological and psychosocial anthropology. In T. Schwartz, G. M. White, & C. A. Lutz (Eds.), *New directions in psychological anthropology*. Cambridge, England: Cambridge University Press.

4

Sociological Models in the Explanation of Emotions

THEODORE D. KEMPER

In primacy of interest, disciplinary seemliness, and volume of empirical work, psychologists "own" the topic of emotions. Yet, given the scope, span, and ramifications of emotion phenomena, other disciplines also legitimately explore affective life. Physiologists relate emotions to anatomical structures and processes; anthropologists link emotions to particular cultural logics and practices; historians view emotions of today in light of emotions of the past; ethologists seek what is phylogenetically given as well as distinctively human in emotions; and sociologists examine how emotions are released, interpreted, and expressed by virtue of the demands and circumstances of human membership in groups. In this chapter, five major sociological models of emotions are presented.

The sociological interest in emotions is manifold, spanning such topics as the emotional foundation of social solidarity in groups, whether small or large (Durkheim, 1912/1954; Goffman, 1967; Collins, 1981, 1990; Scheff, 1988, 1990a); the determination of emotions by outcomes of social interaction (Kemper, 1978, 1991a); the normative regulation of emotional expression and the management of emotional deviance (Hochschild, 1979, 1983; Thoits, 1985, 1990); the socialization of emotions through transfer of meaning to physiological experience (Gordon, 1990; Kemper, 1987); the linkage of emotion to socially derived conceptions of identity and the self (Shott, 1979; Rosenberg, 1990); and the variation in emotional experience according to categories of social organization, such as social class, occupation, gender, race/ethnicity, and the like (Hochschild, 1990; Gordon, 1990). Sociological models of emotion often dovetail with psychological and even physiological approaches to emotion (Kemper, 1978, 1987; Hammond, 1990). But the sociological examination of emotions is valid in its own right.

Put baldly, there can be no individual as the subject of psychological study without the social. Survival itself is socially dependent. The acquisition of any but the most rudimentary abilities and motives is socially determined. The development of a large portion of what we call "personality" is a social product. Even when there is a recognized hereditary contribution (Tellegen et al., 1988; Neubauer & Neubauer, 1990), the socially caused variance in personality and behavior is large. Identity, the self, and self-esteem are social outcomes. Even the capacity of mind to reflect and to rehearse alternative courses of action—that is, the ability to think—is socially given (Mead, 1934). The individual is at all times and everywhere a member of a plurality of groups. Each membership provides him or her with identity, motives, goals, roles, and interaction partners. Threading through, between, and around these elements of the person are emotions.

Notwithstanding that the individual is the locus of emotion—we can measure emotion nowhere but in the individual—the social matrix determines *which emotions are likely to be experienced when and where, on what grounds and for what reasons, by what modes of expression, by whom.* As the social matrix changes, so do all of the parameters of the emotion formula just presented. Sociological models of emotion theorize the social matrix and its parameters. The five sociological models of emotions presented here (Heise & O'Brien, Chapter 34, this volume, offer a sixth) are marked by their scope, substantive diversity, and comprehensiveness. They display the broad range of inquiry that a sociological address to emotions makes possible. (For additional sociological approaches to emotions, see Kemper, 1991b.)

SOCIAL RELATIONS AND EMOTIONS

There can be no argument that social relations produce emotions. Indeed, emotions have an evolutionary function precisely because they allow the individual to adapt to environmental contingencies (Plutchik, 1991), a substantial portion of which entail social relations. If there is an argument, it is over how to characterize the social environment or social relations. Elsewhere (Kemper, 1978; Kemper & Collins, 1990), I have proposed that social relations can be usefully expressed in two dimensions, "power" and "status," and that a very large number of human emotions can be understood as responses to the power and/or status meanings and implications of situations.

Power is understood as a relational condition in which one actor actually or potentially compels another actor to do something he or she does not wish to do. The means of power in a relationship include threatened or actual use of force or deprivation of valued material or symbolic goods and experiences. Noxious behavioral stimuli, including shaking of fists, facial grimacing, raised voice, speech interruptions, and the like, are hallmarks of power use. Lies, deceit, and manipulation also fall within the power category.

Status, on the other hand, is understood as the relational condition of voluntary compliance with the wishes, interests, and desires of another person. One actor accords status to another through acts of recognition of the other's value. These include considerateness, sociability, caring, respect, esteem, and, at its ultimate, love.

Support for the power and status delineation of social relations derives from a large number of factor analyses of interaction in small groups; ethological analyses of primate behavior; studies of cross-cultural roles and behavior; semantic analysis; studies of interpersonal vectors of personality; and the dimensions of learning theory (details in Kemper & Collins, 1990). The weight of evidence for the power and status dimensions of social relationship has led to the surmise that these are perhaps the theoretically optimum dimensions by which any relationship may usefully be characterized.

I have proposed the following implication for emotions: *A very large class of human emotions results from real, anticipated, imagined, or recollected outcomes of social relations.* From the perspective of any actor, an episode of interaction in a social relationship may have the following outcomes: increase, decrease, or no change in the self's power and status *vis-à-vis* the other; and increase, decrease, or no change in the other's power and status *vis-à-vis* the self. Altogether, there are 12 possible outcomes, only 4 of which will occur; that is, both the self's and the other's power and status positions will be affected. Emotions will ensue depending on the particular power and status outcomes, as well as on the factor of "agency"—namely, the attribution of who is responsible for the relational outcome (self, other, or a third party).

The extensive findings obtained in laboratory experiments and surveys support the following conclusions about emotions and power and status outcomes in social relations:

1. *Self's power.* Power increase leads to feelings of security, because one can better protect oneself if necessary from the power incursions of the other, but excess use of power leads to feelings of guilt for having wronged the other, and fear/anxiety concerning the other's possible retaliation. Power decrease leads to feelings of fear/anxiety because the other has greater ability to compel one to do what one does not want to do.

2. *Other's power.* Increase in the other's power has the same effect as decrease of one's own power—namely, fear/anxiety. Decrease in the other's power has the same effect as increase in one's own power—namely, security.

3. *Self's status.* Status increase in the amount felt as deserved leads to satisfaction or happi-

ness/contentment. If the self was the agent, pride is also likely. If the agent was the other or a third party, one will feel gratitude. Increase in status beyond what was expected results in joy, with the corresponding effects of agency, as above. To accept more status than one feels one deserves leads to shame/embarrassment. Decrease in status leads to anger if the agent is the other, shame if the agent is the self, and depression if the situation is deemed irremediable.

4. *Other's status*. One's own emotions in respect to the other's status depend on one's liking for the other. "Liking" is a summary feeling that reflects the degree to which the other has conferred sufficient status on the self and has not used excessive power against the self (Kemper, 1989). If one likes the other, increase in the other's status, regardless of agency, leads to satisfaction. If one dislikes the other, the agent is not likely to be the self. The other or a third party as agent leads to envy or jealousy, depending on whether the other has something one desires, or the other has taken away something of one's own. If one likes the other, and the other's status decreases, agency by the self leads to either guilt or shame, depending on whether one caused the status decrease by use of power or by failing to act according to the standards that apply to one's own level of deserved status. If the agent of the decrease is the other or a third party, one's own feeling is sorrow or pity. If one does not like the other, the other's status decrease where the agent is the self leads to satisfaction. When the agent of the decrease is the other or a third party, the feeling is called *Schadenfreude*—a German term for the satisfaction one feels at the discomfiture of another.

Anticipatory emotions are based on a combination of past relational (power and status) experiences, which affect optimism–pessimism, and one's estimate of present relational conditions, which arouses confidence–lack of confidence. Taken together, the two sentiments give rise to four feelings: optimism + confidence = serene confidence or happiness/contentment; optimism + lack of confidence = guarded optimism or anxiety; pessimism + confidence = grudging optimism or anxiety; and pessimism + lack of confidence = hopelessness or depression.

Within the power–status framework, I have proposed a socialization paradigm for the assumption of the four major negative emo-

tions (guilt, shame, anxiety, and depression) as characteristic moods and personality dispositions. The elements of the model are three dichotomous punishment parameters: type (is it a power-oriented punishment, e.g., physical, or status-oriented punishment, e.g., shaming?); proportionality (is the punishment roughly proportional or excessive with respect to the seriousness of the punished act?); and affection (is the punisher a major source of affection or status?). Tracing the several ($2^3 = 8$) branches of this model leads to a set of eight outcome hypotheses about how each of the negative emotions is socialized as a characteristic personality trait, as well as the usual coping response when the negative emotion is activated. For example, a status-based punishment in proportion to the seriousness of the act socializes shame as a characteristic emotion. If the punisher is also the major source of affection (which one parent is likely to be), coping will be oriented toward compensation of those toward whom the subject acts in a shameful manner. If the punisher (e.g., the other parent) does not control affection, the coping response is hypothesized to be a characteristic hypercritical perfectionism.

Finally, the power–status model affords an insight into love relations and the difference between loving and liking. "Love" can be defined as a relationship in which one actor gives or is prepared to give extremely high amounts of status to another. This definition yields seven different types of love relationships: romantic, brotherly, charismatic, unfaithful, unrequited, adulation by fans, and parent–infant. These differ according to whether one or both actors are conferring extreme amounts of status, and on the power positions of each actor, which are free to vary (power is not excluded from love relations, except in the brotherly and adulation types). Evolution and devolution of love relationships can be understood as outcomes of the dynamics of power and status accord (Kemper, 1978, 1989). The emotion of liking is distinguished from love by the following: Love is experienced when the attributes of one person match the standards of another. The match produces a pleasurable sense of harmony between the self and the other that is labeled "love." Liking, on the other hand, is felt for another who gives adequate status and employs very low power. From this perspective, one can both love and like another person, can not love but like the other, and can like but not love that person (Kemper, 1989).

Although the power–status theory of emotions was derived largely from empirical findings in which social relations could be identified as antecedents of emotions, tests of the theory are scant. Results obtained by Averett and Heise (1988) accord well with the theory, and I (Kemper, 1991a) have found a good fit between the theory and the relational conditions antecedent to four primary emotions (anger, fear, sadness, and joy), about which data were gathered in the eight-nation study conducted by Scherer, Wallbott, and Summerfield (1986).

INTERACTION RITUAL CHAINS: SOURCES OF EMOTIONAL ENERGY

A fundamental question about social life is what keeps a group, whether a society or a marriage, cohesive. One possible answer is coercion. Stronger members force weaker members to remain, usually to serve the stronger ones. From another perspective, self-interest may be used to explain the pattern of continued interaction among group members. In contrast to these explanations, Émile Durkheim (1912/1954) proposed that where coercion and self-interest do not apply, the force of cohesion inheres in shared emotions. Groups cohere because they undertake ritual activities (e.g., of a religious nature), which lead to heightened emotions among the participants. Those who share arousal also respond positively to it, and hence seek the experience again with the same coparticipants. Emotional rewards thus bind us to groups.

This idea was taken further by Erving Goffman (1967), who postulated the ritual nature of *all* interactions, even in dyads. Ordinarily, the enacted ritual is not focused on religious symbols, as in Durkheim's example, but on an equally sacred set of objects— namely, the *self* of each interaction participant. When small-group interactions, which consist mainly of conversation, are successful, they enhance the self of each actor. Although conversation appears to be unstructured, perhaps even random or meandering, Goffman pointed out that talk is strongly guided in the minds of all or most participants by the need to pro-

tect the esteem and standing of all other participants. Ordinarily, this is accomplished without incident. But when the rules fail (a social solecism has occurred), and the integrity of someone's self has been violated (either by his or her own doing or by another's), the result is embarrassment. Indeed, this emotion reveals that the group has failed in its effort to sustain the value of what is often the group's most sacred object—namely, each participant's self.

Goffman detailed the great lengths to which group members are likely to go to preserve themselves and others from embarrassment, including taking people's claims about themselves (except if egregiously questionable) at face value. To challenge a claim is to cause a possible loss of face to the other, but also to oneself, since in addition to denying credibility to another, one has violated the cardinal rule of group coherence—namely, to preserve intact the ritual objects that are the focus of group attention.

Randall Collins (1975, 1981, 1990; Kemper & Collins, 1990) has integrated the ideas of Durkheim and Goffman, along with those of German sociologist Max Weber, into a theory of "interaction ritual chains," designed to explain emotions at the micro (small-group) level but linked to structures at the macro (large-group) level. The key concept for Collins is "emotional energy." This is the biological substrate of the feelings of confidence and enthusiasm that are experienced after successful ritual interaction. Such interaction requires several elements:

1. Group members' attention must be focused on a common object of ritual significance. It may be the self of one or more members, or other symbols of interest (such as the work being done together, or the sports contest all are watching, or the flag being lowered before a massed group at the end of a day).

2. A common emotion is engendered by whatever activities the members are engaged in. In the course of common emotional arousal, members begin to resonate on one another's emotional frequency to the degree that there is physiological entrainment. Each member becomes more and more attuned to the rhythms of talk and action of the other members.

3. The result, over and above all others, is a feeling of solidarity with other members. More often than not, the initial emotion (of step 2 above) is transient. What remains is the

long-term satisfaction of membership. Those who emote together are thus attracted to one another.

Solidarity, according to Collins, is not an abstract notion, but one that is rooted in the body of each participant in the form of emotional energy. The emotional energy derived from such ritual interaction encounters provides the emotional capital with which to undertake other interactions, where one again has the opportunity (if the proper attention has been paid to the requirements of ritual interaction) to renew one's stock of emotional resources or to gain even more of them.

In optimum interaction episodes, all members gain emotional energy because the proper respect has been accorded to the common symbols all hold dear, or to each person's own most cherished symbol (i.e., the self, as discussed above). But interactions are optimum only some of the time. Often only some members come away with surplus emotional energy, while others experience a deficit. Each individual enters the interaction with his or her own stock of emotional energy and other resources attained in prior interactions. Although groups usually try for optimum conditions of interaction, this sometimes fails. For example, a seminar may have too many participants, or a party may have too few. In each case, the proper critical mass for the purposes of the ritual occasion has been missed, and the interaction is likely to be strained, uncomfortable, and unable to mobilize the members into the mutually resonating states that successful groups attain. But beyond these individual or ecological deficits or obstacles to optimum outcomes for members are the power and status conditions, which stratify opportunities for emotional energy. By virtue of their power and status standing in groups, individuals are able to achieve greater or less amounts of emotional resonance with the group and its sacred objects.

Power Interaction

Interactions in the power domain occur between those Collins calls "order givers" and "order takers." The former are the established institutional leaders of the group, the latter their subordinates (e.g., managers and workers, officers and enlisted personnel, teachers and students, government officials and citizens, etc.). In the ritual interactions that these pairs engage in, the order giver is ordinarily more committed to the sacred symbols that are the focus of the interaction—the production schedule, the war strategy, the homework assignment, the tax law. Hence the order giver, who is ordinarily able to enforce his or her view of how the interaction should proceed, is more likely to derive a charge of emotional energy from the interaction. The order taker assists at this process by assenting to the commands of the order giver, and at the same time is likely to lose emotional energy because his or her sacred symbols are being violated or ignored. Order givers thus derive the enthusiasm and confidence to go on to other interaction ritual occasions filled with the expectation of obtaining even more benefits. Together, these chains of ritual interaction in which there is differential power constitute the social class or stratification system of society, with each interaction in the power domain confirming and reinforcing the existing pattern of differential rank and benefits.

Status Interaction

Social life is differentiated not only by the dimension of giving and taking orders, but by membership in groups where one shares identity with others. These include race, ethnicity, gender, social class, occupation, and community (the standard sociological categories), but also peer groups, sociability groups, and transient ad hoc groups with a limited life. Shared identity is the criterion, and membership in and of itself is a basis for emotional energy. This is because each group provides members with a sense of inclusion and access to its sacred symbols. This is status accord, as described above, and is a valued enhancement of self.

But group members differ in the amount of emotional energy they derive from their status group memberships. One consideration is centrality–peripherality. Some members are always present when the group convenes, interacting intensely with many other members. They become sociometric stars, the focus of much interest and attention. Their presence and their conversation are sought, and they come to personify the group's values and interests. Their emotional energy thus constantly recrudesces. Other members are relatively isolated, infrequently in attendance, and little likely to stir interest in other members by their actions or verbal sallies. Such peripheral members derive only the minimal amount of emotional energy from their membership in the group.

Together, power and status constitute a grid of social relations that underlies all social interactions, providing the individual with greater or lesser amounts of emotional resources of a relatively stable nature. Thus, at the high end are the emotions of confidence, enthusiasm, and trust, while at the low end are depression and distrust. Collins (1990) has proposed that the more intense short-term or dramatic emotions, such as fear, anger, joy, and the like, are like spikes superimposed on a tonic or baseline level of emotional energy that is characteristic for the person.

For example, joy is the sharply heightened experience of successful ritual interaction, as when one is participating in a rollicking party among good friends; or when one's team is winning at a sports event; or when one has been recognized by other members as exemplary. Anger is of several kinds. "Dominating" anger is the high-energy aggression of order givers who employ it to overcome obstacles that order takers may put in their way. "Disruptive" anger is manifested by order takers who believe, correctly or otherwise, that they have enough resources to resist the demands of an order giver. "Righteous" anger is felt by those who believe that a sacred symbol has been violated, and thus that the ritual integrity of the group is in peril. Fear is a response to another person's anger, reflecting the expectation that one will be harmed.

According to Collins, these short-term emotions are governed to a great extent by the tide of emotional energy upon which they ride. Those who are high in emotional energy are seldom likely to experience anger, except of the righteous kind. Those low in emotional energy are more likely to experience fear because of their frequent experiences of subordination in the power settings where they are order takers.

Collins's theory offers a lens through which the commonplace interactions of everyday life are seen to pulse with emotion, as well as to provide actors with the emotional voltage required to negotiate further interactions. Some actors are high in emotional potential and others low, and thereby signify their respective places in the overall stratification system of society.

SHAME AND SOCIAL ORDER

Charles Horton Cooley (1902) created the "looking-glass" metaphor by which we understand the sources of self-feeling:

> In imagination we perceive in another's mind some thought of our appearance, manners, aims, deeds . . . and are variously affected by it. A self-idea of this sort seems to have three principal elements: the imagination of our appearance to the other person; the imagination of his judgment of that appearance; and some sort of self-feeling, such as pride or mortification. (p. 184)

Cooley alluded to the process as something like standing before a "looking glass," giving rise to the idea of the "looking-glass self."

For Thomas Scheff (1988, 1990a, 1990b), the emotions that underlie the looking-glass self also underlie social control, which is fundamental to the maintenance of a stable social order. Social control may be external, as in the case of police and other guardians of conformity. Or it may be internal, as when conscience or emotion bar us from doing wrong. For Scheff, the basic mechanism of social control is located in the emotions. He contends that we are continually in a state of either pride or shame with respect to the judgments of others about our adherence to their and society's moral strictures. When we conform, we experience pride; when we deviate, we experience shame. Since pride is a pleasurable emotion and shame unpleasurable, the overall effect is to produce conformity in society, and hence a high degree of social stability. Pride and shame thus ensure social control without the need for external surveillance and regulation.

Although shame is serviceable for society, its constant evocation via the mechanism of the looking glass is not always serviceable for individuals. Indeed, if shame is not discharged or dissipated, it can fester and turn pathological. Yet, if shame is as prevalent as Scheff requires them to be, why is there not more evidence of its presence? To answer this question, Scheff has relied on the work of Lewis (1971), who proposed that there are two forms of shame that go unrecognized by those who experience them. These are "overt, undifferentiated" shame and "bypassed" shame.

According to Lewis, overt, undifferentiated shame is marked by efforts to disguise or hide the shame from others, including the self. It takes the form of speech disruption (stammering, repetition, long vocal pauses), lowered head and averted gaze, blushing, or barely audible speech. This form of shame also tends toward the use of shame-avoidant self-references, including locutions such as "foolish," "inept," "stupid," "incompetent," "insecure," and other terms that do not directly identify shame. On the other hand, in bypassed shame there is no overt disturbance of communication, but rather an obsession with the disturbing incident; this leads to continual internal replay and absorption in the event, to the exclusion of required concentration on presently ongoing events. Notwithstanding, in the bypassed as in the overt form of shame, the emotional pain is present.

The fact that the shame is unacknowledged leads in Scheff's view to continued effects and difficulty. First, although aware of the presence of shame, one may unwittingly become ashamed of one's shame, or angry at oneself for feeling shame, and then ashamed again of this self-directed anger, and so on. Scheff calls this a "shame spiral." Furthermore, the shame–anger spiral may engage two parties, leading to cycles of vengeance, humiliation, and countervengeance, all because the original shame experience was unacknowledged. Scheff contends that even nations may become engrossed in such spirals; he cites the example of the cycle of French and German feelings of shame and consequent motives of revenge, which was inaugurated by the French defeat in the war of 1870 and which ended only in the German defeat in 1945.

But shame is consequential also in everyday contexts and has a particular locus in the socialization experiences of childhood. Scheff has contrasted the widely disparate processes by which children acquire language on the one hand, and mathematical skills on the other. Although highly complex, language is acquired by virtually everyone so that it can be used in a highly functional manner. By contrast, mathematics is not well mastered by many people. What is the difference? Scheff proposes that the socialization of the two skills is ordinarily quite different, especially where shame is concerned.

In respect to language, the parents, who are ordinarily native speakers, are both competent and confident of their own skill in the language, and hence are virtually never ashamed of their technique or prowess in conveying their lessons. Not feeling ashamed themselves, parents are able to teach their offspring without shaming them in turn for committing errors. By contrast, in the transmission of mathematical insight and skill, teachers themselves are not ordinarily as confident of either their knowledge of the fundamental principles, or of the techniques they employ to teach the principles. Often, the result is some degree of shame; this is then transmitted to the children, who then become ashamed of their inability to grasp the materials. Whether overt or bypassed, the shame remains unrecognized and undischarged. The consequence is interference with the cognitive processes that assure learning.

For Scheff, shame is the emotional pivot of social life, since it leads both to conformity and social order as a result of the "looking-glass" process by which actors guide their behavior and to forms of social disorder when the emotion remains submerged and unacknowledged.

EMOTION WORK AND EMOTION MANAGEMENT

An ongoing debate in the social sciences concerns the respective influence of social structure and of culture. The former consists of social arrangements, such as power and status relations; the latter of "conceptions of the desirable" (Kluckhohn, 1951), as detailed in values, norms, and rules. Some sociologists of emotions, such as Kemper and Collins, lean toward social-structural primacy in the determination of emotions; others, such as Arlie Russell Hochschild (1979, 1983, 1989, 1990), Steven Gordon (1990), and Peggy Thoits (1990), lean toward the cultural. The differences between the two approaches are reflected in the degree to which social norms are introduced into the emotional experience to manage or change it.

Hochschild views emotion as having a signaling function—indicating to us where we stand in the world, and defining relationships to others and to our own goals, motives, and interests. Emotional experience is a compound of how we feel, how we wish we felt, how we try to feel, how we classify feelings, and how we express them. How we feel is initially determined by how we appraise the situation, and this is guided to a great extent by social-structural considerations of social class, occupation, gender, race, and similar categories. But almost immediately, cultural considerations enter: There are "feeling rules" and "expression rules," which inform us that what we feel may be inappropriate (too intense or too mild, too long or too brief in duration, suitable or unsuitable for someone with our social identity) or that our manner of expressing our feelings is acceptable or outré. Emotional life, therefore, consists of moments in which a good deal of emotion management necessarily takes place in order to maintain conformity with the normative regime.

Managing emotions requires "emotion work," which includes both "surface acting" and "deep acting." Surface acting is accomplished when an individual purposely puts on a suitable emotion—for example, smiling when he or she feels like crying, in order to swing the feeling away from sadness. Deep acting is done when the individual attempts to change the feeling by changing the determinants of feeling—mainly the mental construction or appraisal that gave rise to the feeling, but also including such underlying somatic elements as muscle tone and heart rate. Hochschild (1983) examined a variety of these emotion management strategies in her study of airline flight attendants. Hochschild found that this occupation requires a good deal of "emotional labor," which is emotion work prescribed as a condition of holding down a job. Flight attendants reported that the burden of emotion suppression or management on the job sometimes led to "emotional numbing" off the job. Hochschild determined that about a quarter of predominantly male jobs and about half of all predominantly female jobs in the U.S. labor force require heavy amounts of emotional labor—that is, the ability to modify or change one's emotions in light of employer requirements.

Hochschild proposed that how and whether or not one chooses to do emotion work is a function of certain ideologies that emerge from and maintain the emotional resonance of social class, gender, occupational, racial, and other identities. Hochschild's major concern has been with gender ideologies, those conceptions of male and female gender role that guide emotional response in situations where gender is salient. Gender ideologies determine the feeling rules that are deemed to apply, and the emotional pathways that allow one to realize the goals of a gender ideology.

In a study of dual-career families with a child, where husbands and wives confronted the need to allocate time and interest to the multiple demands of work and family, Hochschild (1989) found that three gender ideologies prevailed: "egalitarian," "transitional," and "traditional." The first required equal sharing of work at home; the last required that the wife undertake all home burdens; the middle ideology in some way split the differences between the egalitarian and the traditional. Each of these ideologies guided the emotions of their respective holders.

Egalitarian wives in transitional or traditional marriages were filled with resentment, frequently taking the emotional pathway of withdrawal from feelings for their husbands as a preliminary to initiating a change strategy. Egalitarian wives who gave up career opportunities, even if willingly, tended to feel depressed as they reflected on their lost chances. The traditional husband, resisting change, often took the emotional pathway of reducing felt needs so as not to have to accede to his wife's change efforts. In many cases, actual feelings were shown to conflict with the feeling rules that the gender ideology implied, as when a self-declared egalitarian husband nonetheless felt upset if his wife worked.

Hochschild relies on many cognitive elements to explain the creation and display of emotions: culture, norms, rules, and ideologies. These help to define what is emotionally acceptable and whether or not emotion work should be undertaken. A residual concept in this approach is emotional deviance. In data obtained from a college population, Thoits (1990) found that the amount of emotional deviance was just under 20%, with about half the cases reporting guilt or shame over their departure from emotion norms.

Thoits, who shares many of the elements of Hochschild's fundamental approach, has proposed that emotional deviance is likely to occur more frequently under the conditions of multiple role occupancy (e.g., a physician's becoming emotionally involved in the illness of a patient), subcultural marginality (e.g., a "swinging" couple's having to deal with jealousy), occasions of role transition (e.g., postpartum depression in a new mother), and occasions when ceremonial or other rigid rules govern (e.g., feeling sad at a wedding). Emotional deviance ordinarily arouses a felt need to employ emotion management or coping strategies. Thoits (1990) has proposed a typology of these strategies, entailing behavioral and cognitive techniques applied either to the situation evoking the emotion or to physiological, expressive, or labeling aspects of the emotion. For example, a behavioral–expressive strategy might be to engage in hard exercise, or initiate relaxation techniques, or take drugs. A cognitive–situational strategy might be to reinterpret the situational cues, or fantasize an escape, or distract oneself. Where emotional deviance continues, the label of mental illness may be assigned. Thoits (1985) has calculated that nearly half of the 210 disorders described in the *Diagnostic and Statistical Manual of Mental Disorders* (DSM-III; American Psychiatric Association, 1980) are identified by deviant emotions. This suggests that to a significant extent, treatment of mental illness involves the acquisition of techniques of emotion management.

EMOTIONS AND THE SELF

Cognate with Cooley's "looking-glass" metaphor on the development of self-feelings (see above) is the theory of self proposed by American social-behaviorist philosopher George Herbert Mead (1934). Mead proposed that the self is a social creation, formed through the process of "role taking"—that is, mentally putting oneself in the position of another and looking back at oneself as if one were an object. Social experience develops the capacity to take the role of another, and hence to obtain a sense of self. Role taking enables individuals to formulate courses of action by providing advance understanding of how a particular course of action will affect the self. Since language is the main vehicle of role taking, the Meadian approach has been called "symbolic interaction": Role taking is an interactive process that takes place cognitively, rather than in actuality, through the use of language symbols. Another term for the role-taking process and its effects is "reflexivity," which connotes acting back on oneself. Importantly, since role taking or reflexivity is proactive, it empowers the individual as an agent in the self-creation of his or her own emotions. A distinct sociological position on emotions and the self derives from the symbolic-interactionist perspective.

Rosenberg (1990) has proposed that reflexivity is necessarily involved in such fundamental processes as emotional identification, emotional display, and emotional experience. Since emotions do not come readily labeled, there is always, to some degree, a problem of how to identify an emotion. Role taking or reflexivity allows for the interpretation of the ambiguous situational and physiological conditions of the emotional state by attending to three possible identifiers. First is a cause–effect logic that social experience provides and that individuals in a given culture learn to employ to reflect on the meaning of their inner experience (e.g., "My dog died; no wonder I'm so depressed"). Second is the recognition of a social consensus about the situation in the responses of others (e.g. "Everyone at the party is excited; no wonder I'm excited too"). Third are cultural scenarios that provide information about emotions (e.g., "I can't wait until I see her again; I must be in love").

Reflexivity operates also in decisions concerning emotional display, since the intention of display is to persuade others that one is experiencing a given emotion. Although this is fundamentally "impression management," as Goffman (1959) referred to it, the stakes are high. According to Coulter (1986), to fail to show the proper emotion in a given situation is to be accounted morally deficient, or even mentally ill according to the categories of DSM-III (American Psychiatric Association, 1980).

Although emotional experience originates as a direct result of a situation that activates an autonomically based response, reflexivity enters into the process of moderating or managing the experience, or facilitating or inhibiting the likelihood of its occurrence in the first place. Reflexive judgments can be applied to enhancing or changing the initial stimulus conditions for the emotion, or through modifying one's thoughts about those conditions (cf. Hochschild and Thoits, above). In this way, the individual actively partakes in the formation or alteration of the content of emotional experience.

Shott (1979) has applied the role-taking perspective directly to the identification of specific emotions. She differentiates between "reflexive" role-taking emotions and "empathic" role-taking emotions. The former include guilt, shame, and embarrassment. In order to experience these emotions, one must put oneself mentally in the place of another to obtain his or her view of oneself. Guilt entails the other's judgment of moral inadequacy; shame entails the other's unwillingness to accept one's ideal conception of one's action; and embarrassment entails the other's low regard for one's self-presentation. Because these are painful emotions, Shott has hypothesized that they motivate efforts to regain the good opinion of others through a variety of compensatory acts, often of an altruistic nature.

According to Shott, the empathic role-taking emotions are even better at eliciting altruistic behavior. Empathic role taking provides *vicarious* emotional experience, through putting the individual in the place of another who may be suffering and who can be relieved or assisted. Clearly, empathic role taking can also lead to emotional contagion.

AFFECT CONTROL THEORY

Although affect control theory (Heise, 1979; Smith-Lovin, 1990; Smith-Lovin & Heise, 1988) is among the most important sociological models in the explanation of emotion, discussion of this approach is deferred here in favor of Heise and O'Brien's presentation (Chapter 34, this volume).

OTHER MODELS

The efflorescence of interest in emotions among sociologists does not end with the five models detailed in this chapter and in Chapter 34. Those not covered are mainly less comprehensive in scope than the ones presented. These include a contrasociobiological model of how the need for emotional gratification gives rise to systems of stratification (Hammond, 1990); a postmodernist phenomenological analysis of emotions as "lived experience" (Denzin, 1984, 1990); an examination of how emotions are employed as political counters in the micro-interactions that determine social rank (Clark, 1989, 1990); an approach to emotions through the sociology of knowledge (McCarthy, 1989); and a model of the social construction of emotions via "emotion culture" and the socialization process (Gordon, 1989, 1990).

REFERENCES

American Psychiatric Association. (1980). *Diagnostic and statistical manual of mental disorders* (3rd ed.). Washington, DC: Author.

Averett, C., & Heise, D. R. (1988). Modified social identities: Amalgamations, attributions, and emotions. In L. Smith-Lovin & D. R. Heise (Eds.), *Analyzing social interaction: Advances in affect control theory* (pp. 103–122). New York: Gordon & Breach.

Clark, C. (1989). Studying sympathy: Methodological confessions. In D. D. Franks & E. D. McCarthy (Eds.), *The sociology of emotions: Original essays and research papers* (pp. 137–152). Greenwich, CT: JAI Press.

Clark, C. (1990). Emotions and micropolitics in everyday life: Some patterns and paradoxes of "place." In T. D. Kemper (Ed.), *Research agendas in the sociology of emotions* (pp. 305–333). Albany: State University of New York Press.

Collins, R. (1975). *Conflict sociology: Toward an explanatory science.* New York: Academic Press.

Collins, R. (1981). On the micro-foundations of macrosociology. *American Journal of Sociology, 86,* 984–1014.

Collins, R. (1990). Stratification, emotional energy, and the transient emotions. In T. D. Kemper (Ed.), *Research agendas in the sociology of emotions* (pp. 27–57). Albany: State University of New York Press.

Cooley, C. H. (1902). *Human nature and the social order.* New York: Scribner's.

Coulter, J. (1986). Affect and social context: Emotion definition as a social task. In R. Harré (Ed.), *The social construction of emotions* (pp. 120–134). Oxford: Blackwell.

Denzin, N. (1984). *On understanding emotion.* San Francisco: Jossey-Bass.

Denzin, N. (1990). On understanding emotion: The interpretive–cultural agenda. In T. D. Kemper (Ed.), *Research agendas in the sociology of emotions* (pp. 85–116). Albany: State University of New York Press.

Durkheim, E. (1954). *The elementary forms of the religious life.* New York: Free Press. (Original work published 1912)

Goffman, E. (1959). *The presentation of self in everyday life.* New York: Doubleday/Anchor.

Goffman, E. (1967). *Interaction ritual.* Garden City, NY: Doubleday/Anchor.

Gordon, S. (1989). The socialization of children's emotions: Emotional culture, competence, and exposure. In C. I. Saarni & P. L. Harris (Eds.), *Children's understanding of emotion* (pp. 319–349). Cambridge, England: Cambridge University Press.

Gordon, S. (1990). Social structural effects on emotions. In T. D. Kemper (Ed.), *Research agendas in the sociology of emotions* (pp. 145–179). Albany: State University of New York Press.

Hammond, M. (1990). Affective maximization: A new macro-theory in the sociology of emotions. In T. D. Kemper (Ed.), *Research agendas in the sociology of emotions* (pp. 58–81). Albany: State University of New York Press.

Heise, D. R. (1979). *Understanding events: Affect and the construction of social action.* New York: Cambridge University Press.

Hochschild, A. R. (1979). Emotion work, feeling rules, and social structure. *American Journal of Sociology, 85,* 551–575.

Hochschild, A. R. (1983). *The managed heart: The commercialization of human feeling.* Berkeley: University of California Press.

Hochschild, A. R. (1989). *The second shift: Working parents and the revolution at home.* New York: Viking Penguin.

Hochschild, A. R. (1990). Ideology and emotion management: A perspective and path for future research. In

T. D. Kemper (Ed.), *Research agendas in the sociology of emotions* (pp. 117–142). Albany: State University of New York Press.

Kemper, T. D. (1978). *A social interactional theory of emotions*. New York: Wiley.

Kemper, T. D. (1987). How many emotions are there? Wedding the social and the autonomic components. *American Journal of Sociology, 93,* 263–289.

Kemper, T. D. (1989). Love and like and love and *love*. In D. D. Franks & E. D. McCarthy (Eds.), *The sociology of emotions: Original essays and papers* (pp. 249–268). Greenwich, CT: JAI Press.

Kemper, T. D. (1991a). Predicting emotions from social relations. *Social Psychology Quarterly, 54,* 330–342.

Kemper, T. D.. (1991b). An introduction to the sociology of emotions. In K. T. Strongman (Ed.), *International review of studies on emotion* (Vol. 1, pp. 301–349). Chichester, England: Wiley.

Kemper, T. D., & Collins, R. (1990). Dimensions of microinteraction. *American Journal of Sociology, 96,* 32–68.

Kluckhohn, C. (1951). Values and value orientations in the theory of action: An exploration in definition and classification. In T. Parsons & E. A. Shils (Eds.), *Toward a general theory of action* (pp. 388–433). New York: Harper & Row.

Lewis, H. B. (1971). *Shame and guilt in neurosis*. New York: International Universities Press.

McCarthy, D. (1989). Emotions are social things: An Essay in the sociology of emotions. In D. D. Franks & E. D. McCarthy (Eds.), *The sociology of emotions: Original essays and research papers* (pp. 51–72). Greenwich, CT: JAI Press.

Mead, G. H. (1934). *Mind, self and society*. Chicago: University of Chicago Press.

Neubauer, P. B., & Neubauer, A. (1990). *Nature's thumbprint: The new genetics of personality*. Reading, MA: Addison-Wesley.

Plutchik, R. (1991). Emotions and evolution. In K. T. Strongman (Ed.), *International review of studies on emotion* (Vol. 1, pp. 37–58). Chichester, England: Wiley.

Rosenberg, M. (1990). Reflexivity and emotions. *Social Psychology Quarterly, 53,* 3–12.

Scheff, T. (1988). Shame and conformity: The deference-emotion system. *American Sociological Review, 53,* 395–406.

Scheff, T. (1990a). *Microsociology: Discourse, emotion, and social structure*. Chicago: University of Chicago Press.

Scheff, T. (1990b). Socialization of emotions: Pride and shame as causal agents. In T. D. Kemper (Ed.), *Research agendas in the sociology of emotions* (pp. 281–304). Albany: State University of New York Press.

Scherer, K. R., Wallbott, H. G., & Summerfield, A. B. (1986). *Experiencing emotion: A cross-cultural study*. Cambridge, England: Cambridge University Press.

Shott, S. (1979). Emotion and social life: A symbolic interactionist analysis. *American Journal of Sociology, 84,* 1317–1334.

Smith-Lovin, L. (1990). Emotion as the confirmation and disconfirmation of identity. In T. D. Kemper (Ed.), *Research agendas in the sociology of emotions* (pp. 238–270). Albany: State University of New York Press.

Smith-Lovin, L., & Heise, D. (Eds.). (1988). *Analyzing social interaction: Advances in affect control theory*. New York: Gordon & Breach.

Tellegen, A., Lykken, D. T., Bouchard, T. J., Wilcox, K. J., Segal, N. L., & Rich, S. (1988). Personality similarity in twins reared apart and together. *Journal of Personality and Social Psychology, 54,* 1031–1039.

Thoits, P. A. (1985). Self-labeling processes in mental illness: The role of emotional deviance. *American Journal of Sociology, 92,* 221–249.

Thoits, P. A. (1990). Emotional deviance: Research agendas. In T. D. Kemper (Ed.), *Research agendas in the sociology of emotions* (pp. 180–203). Albany: State University of New York Press.

5

Emotions and Their Vicissitudes: Emotions and Psychopathology

ROBERT PLUTCHIK

Psychopathology has been described in many different but interrelated ways. Richard Lazarus (1991), for example, describes psychopathology as involving three different classes of problems. One he calls "dysfunctional neuroses"; these are exemplified by obsessions, anxiety, phobias, and depression. A second he calls "existential problems," characterized by vague feelings of unhappiness, boredom, and lack of meaning in life. The third he describes as a lack of skill for handling such adaptational issues as bereavement, divorce, illness, and handicaps. For Lazarus, the essence of psychopathology is some kind of failure in appraisal and coping, which results in emotional states, ego defenses, and self-deception.

David Shapiro (1989), a psychoanalyst, states that Freud's greatest achievement was the discovery of self-estrangement and its many manifestations. Patients may be caught up by "irresistible impulses" or the need to carry out a ritual against their own will. They may have strong, uncontrollable emotions that are strange to them. They experience conflicts between different emotions—for example, temper outbursts toward important persons in their lives versus the wish for close attachments; feeling humiliated versus feeling furious and needing revenge; wishing to be thought of as generous versus recognizing one's greed or selfishness. All symptoms, in fact, are believed to be the products of conflicts of which the patients are often unaware.

Another well-known psychoanalyst, Sandor Rado (1969), sees psychopathology as an over-reaction of "emergency emotions." For example, fear, rage, and disgust are emergency reactions that attempt to restore the organism to safety through such behaviors as withdrawal, attack, and riddance. Rado suggests that there are four types of miscarried repair mechanisms that underlie most psychopathological behavior. The first is a phobic mechanism that determines avoidance or retreat behaviors. The second is a riddance response evoked by pain. The third is a coercive mechanism related to rage that leads to various types of aggressive behaviors. And the fourth mechanism is self-coercion produced by guilt or shame.

Still another psychoanalyst, Charles Brenner (1975), describes symptoms as "compromise formations." When life events produce emotions such as anxiety or depression that have strong feelings of unpleasure associated with them, ego defenses such as repression or denial are triggered that function to reduce the unpleasant feelings. The result is a compromise between the emotion and the defense, which may be expressed as an avoidance reaction such as a phobia, or a personality trait such as submissiveness. Consistent with this general view is the point made by Bednar, Wells, and Peterson (1989) that the essence of abnormality is avoidance motivated by fear. Edelstein (1990) similarly says that a symptom is a protective device intended to prevent the patient from re-experiencing feelings that were intolerably painful at the time in life when they occurred. He also adds that if a patient has an exceptionally pleasant experience, a symptom (such as alcoholism or drug use) may function to help him recapture these good feelings again and again. Last but not least, Mardi J. Horowitz (1991), another psychoanalyst, describes maladaptive interpersonal patterns as usually containing episodes of strong but irrational emotions.

From a purely descriptive point of view, psychotherapy patients describe their personal problems in several interrelated ways. They may experience certain emotions too often or too strongly—emotions such as depression, anxiety, or anger. The same may be said about other emotions, such as disgust (in the form of blame or hostility), trust (in the form of excessive gullibility), and joy (in the form of mania). The patients would like such emotions reduced in intensity or frequency. In contrast, patients may experience certain emotions too weakly or infrequently. They may complain that they cannot cry, or show affection or love, or get angry, or be assertive. In such cases, the patients would like to increase the frequency or intensity of these emotions.

Sometimes patients describe their problems in interpersonal terms. They experience difficulty in getting along with other people—their spouses, lovers, parents, children, friends, bosses, or coworkers. When such complaints are examined closely, it becomes evident that emotions are at the heart of them as well. Parents make them feel guilty, bosses resentful, children disappointed, lovers anxious. The interpersonal relations apparently trigger emotional reactions that the individuals find difficult to handle. It thus becomes evident why patients are said to suffer from "emotional disorders" or to be "emotionally disturbed."

Another way emotions become part of psychopathology occurs when two or more different emotions are aroused simultaneously, producing severe conflict and possible immobilization of action. This may occur when anger and fear are simultaneously activated, when trust and rejection are in conflict, or when impulses toward independence are in conflict with wishes to be taken care of. The neurotic character has, in fact, been called a personality in conflict (Shapiro, 1989).

One final way in which emotions enter into our ideas about psychopathology has been hinted at in the descriptions above. Almost everyone agrees that the concept of emotion does not apply only to the subjective feelings human adults can describe in words. Emotions also involve a cognitive or appraisal process (Arnold, 1960; Lazarus, 1991), as well as physiological and brain states and impulses to action (Frijda, 1986; Plutchik, 1980). Sometimes a disconnection occurs between different parts of this complex emotional chain of events. Thus, for example, it is possible to have "free-floating anxiety" without an awareness of the source of the anxiety (i.e., without an appropriate cognitive appraisal). It is possible to be depressed without knowing why one is depressed, or angry without being aware of the source of anger. It is even possible to have the physical signs of a panic attack without any subjective feeling of fear or anxiety (Kushner & Beitman, 1990). Psychiatrists also report "masked anxiety" or "masked depression," in which signs of anxiety or depression exist without the individual being aware of them. And "psychosomatic equivalents" are often reported, in which a physical illness appears presumably in place of, or in reaction to, strong emotions (Karasu & Plutchik, 1978). To summarize, emotions are related to psychopathology in four ways: (1) when some emotions are extreme; (2) when some emotions are absent or too limited; (3) when strong emotions are in conflict; and (4) when there are disconnections between such components of the emotion chain as cognitions, feeling, physiology, and behavior. It is important to emphasize that most clinicians believe that no sharp line separates normal from pathological emotional functioning (Brenner, 1975), and all the points made above may be said to reflect the psychopathology of everyday life. It is thus evident that any theory of emotion should have something to say about the initiation and control of emotions as well as methods for changing emotions. A theory of emotion must therefore imply a theory of psychopathology as well as psychotherapy.

The purpose of the present chapter is to provide a brief overview of my psychoevolutionary theory of emotion and to show how ideas from this theory and from evolutionary biology have some relevance for the understanding of emotions and for the practice of psychotherapy.

THE PSYCHOEVOLUTIONARY THEORY OF EMOTIONS: AN OVERVIEW

The theory was first described in a paper in 1958 (Plutchik, 1958), and then elaborated in two books (Plutchik, 1962, 1980) and many papers (e.g., Plutchik, 1970, 1983, 1989, 1990, 1991; Plutchik, Kellerman, & Conte, 1979). It has at least six postulates; these are listed in Table 5.1.

The first postulate—that emotions are communication and survival mechanisms—is a direct reflection of the Darwinian, ethological tradition. Darwin (1872/1965) pointed out that emotions have two functions for all animals. First, they increase the chances of individual survival through appropriate reactions to emergency events in the environment (e.g., by flight). Second, they act as signals of intentions of future action through display behaviors of various kinds (Enquist, 1985).

Evolutionary theory assumes that the natural environment creates survival problems for all organisms that must be successfully dealt with if the organisms are to survive. These problems include, for example, differentially and appropriately responding to prey and predators, foods and mates, caregivers and care solicitors. Emotions may be conceptualized as basic adaptive patterns that can be identified at all phylogenetic levels that deal with these basic issues. Emotions are the ultraconservative evolutionary behavioral adaptations that have been successful (similar to amino acids, DNA, and genes) in increasing the chances of survival of organisms. They have therefore been maintained in functionally equivalent forms through all phylogenetic levels.

The second postulate—that emotions have a genetic basis—stems directly from the psychoevolutionary context. Darwin (1872/1965) first suggested at least four types of evidence one may use for establishing a genetic basis for emotions. First, he noted that some emotional

TABLE 5.1. Basic Propositions of a Psychoevolutionary Theory of Emotions

1. Emotions are communications and survival mechanisms based on evolutionary adaptations.
2. Emotions have a genetic basis.
3. Emotions are hypothetical constructs based on various classes of evidence.
4. Emotions are complex chains of events with stabilizing feedback loops that produce some kind of behavioral homeostasis.
5. The relation among emotions can be represented by a three-dimensional structural model.
6. Emotions are related to a number of derivative conceptual domains.

Note. Reprinted by permission from Plutchik (1990, p. 5).

expressions appear in similar form in many lower animals (e.g., the apparent increase in body size during rage or agonistic interactions, due to erection of body hair or feathers, changes in postures, or expansion of air pouches). Second, some emotional expressions appear in infants in the same form as in adults (e.g., smiling and frowning). Third, some emotional expressions are shown in identical ways by those born blind as by those who are normally sighted (e.g., pouting and laughter). And fourth, some emotional expressions appear in similar form in widely separated races and groups of humans (Ekman & Friesen, 1971; Eibl-Eibesfeldt, 1975).

Recent genetic studies comparing monozygotic and dizygotic twins, cross-adoption studies, and other research methods have revealed hereditary contributions to such temperamental (emotional) qualities as aggressiveness (Fuller, 1986; Wimer & Wimer, 1985), timidity or fearfulness (Goddard & Beilharz, 1985), assertiveness (Loehlin, Horn, & Willerman, 1981), and shyness (Stevenson-Hinde & Simpson, 1982), as well as many others.

Genetic theory indicates that individuals do not inherit behavior per se, but only the structural and physiological mechanisms that mediate behavior. Genes influence thresholds of sensitivity, perceptual preferences, cellular structures, and biochemical events such as enzyme activity. They determine epigenetic rules that act as filters limiting what kind of information is allowed into the system and how the information is to be processed. For example, most animals appear to have auditory detectors "tuned" to signals that are of special significance for their survival (Lumsden & Wilson, 1981). Most, but not all, emotional expressions are based on genetic "templates," or schemas that determine the generality of emotional development and reactions to probable events in the environment (Plutchik, 1983).

The third basic postulate of the psychoevolutionary theory of emotion is that emotions are hypothetical constructs or inferences based on various classes of evidence. The kinds of evidence we use to infer the existence of emotions include (1) knowledge of stimulus conditions; (2) knowledge of an organism's behavior in a variety of settings; (3) knowledge of what species-typical behavior is; (4) knowledge of how an organism's peers react to it; and (5) knowledge of the effect of an individual's behavior on others (Plutchik, 1980). One of the

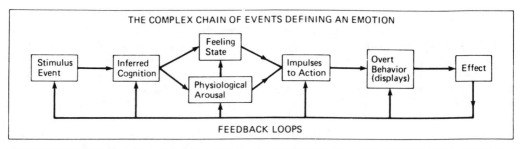

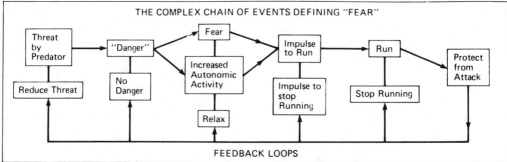

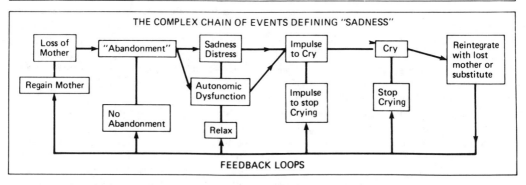

FIGURE 5.1. A schematic description of the chain of events defining an emotion, with illustrations of each link of the chain for the emotions of fear and sadness. It should be emphasized that this differs from a simple chain because of the existence of negative feedback loops. Thus, emotions should be described as homeostatic behavioral feedback systems. Reprinted by permission from Plutchik (1983, p. 224).

more important reasons why emotional states are difficult to define unequivocally is that more than one emotion may occur at the same time. Any given overt display of emotion may reflect such complex states as approach and avoidance, attack and flight, sex and aggression, or fear and pleasure.

The fourth basic postulate of the theory is that emotions are complex chains of events with stabilizing loops that tend to produce some kind of behavioral homeostasis. (Figure 5.1 illustrates this idea.) Emotions are triggered by various events. These events must be cognitively evaluated as being of significance to the well-being or integrity of the individual.

If such a determination is made, various feelings will result, as well as a pattern of physiological changes. These physiological changes have the character of anticipatory reactions associated with various types of exertions or impulses—such impulses, for example, as the urge to explore, to attack, to retreat, or to mate, among others. Depending on the relative strengths of these various impulses, a final vectorial resultant will occur in the form of overt action, which is designed to have an effect on the stimulus that triggered this chain of events in the first place. For example, distress signals by a puppy or the crying of an infant will increase the probability that the mother or a mother substitute will arrive on the scene. The overall effect of this complex feedback system is to reduce the threat or change the emergency situation in such a way as to achieve a temporary behavioral homeostatic balance.

The fifth postulate of the theory is that the relations among emotions can be represented by a three-dimensional structural model shaped like a cone. The vertical dimension represents the intensity of emotions; the circle defines degree of similarity of emotions; and polarity may be represented by the opposite emotions on the circle. This postulate also includes the idea that some emotions are primary and others are derived or blends, in the same sense that some colors are primary and others are mixed (see Figure 5.2). A number of studies have been published showing that the language of emotions can be represented by means of a circle or circumplex (Russell, 1989; Plutchik, 1980; Wiggins & Broughton, 1985; Fisher, Heise, Bohrnstedt, & Lucke, 1985; Conte & Plutchik, 1981). It is important to emphasize that a basic emotion cannot be defined by a single word such as "joy" or "fear."

Basic emotions represent hypothetical dimensions that can be sampled in a number of different ways.

The concept of primary and derived emotions leads to the sixth basic postulate of the theory, which is that emotions are related to a number of derivative conceptual domains. For example, it has been shown that the language of mixed emotions is identical to the language of personality traits. Hostility has been judged to be composed of anger and disgust; sociability is thought to be a blend of joy and acceptance; and guilt is judged to be a combination of joy and fear. Emotional components have been identified for hundreds of personality traits. In addition, there is now clear-cut evidence that personality traits also exhibit a circumplex structure, just as emotions do (Conte & Plutchik, 1981; Russell, 1989; Wiggins & Broughton, 1985).

The idea of derivatives can be extended further. Diagnostic terms such as "depressed," "manic," and "paranoid" can be conceived as extreme expressions of such basic emotions as sadness, joy, and disgust. Several studies have also revealed that the language of diagnoses

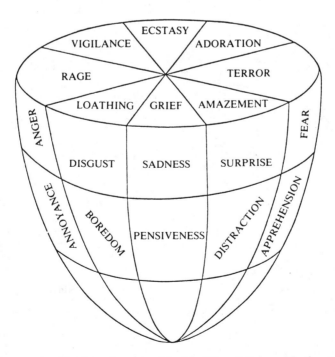

FIGURE 5.2. A representation of a three-dimensional model of the relations among the eight primary emotions, categorized at three different intensity levels. Empirical studies have confirmed the circular or circumplex relations among emotions. Reprinted by permission from Plutchik (1980, p. 157).

also shares a circumplex structure with emotions (Plutchik & Platman, 1977; Plutchik & Schaefer, 1966).

Carrying the notion of derivatives still another step, our research has shown that the language of ego defenses can also be conceptualized as being related to emotions. For example, displacement can be conceptualized as an unconscious way to deal with anger that cannot be directly expressed without punishment. Similarly, projection can be conceptualized as an unconscious way to deal with feelings of disgust with (or rejection of) oneself by attributing this feeling to outsiders. Parallels of this sort have been made for each of the primary emotions and are described in detail in Kellerman (1979) and Plutchik et al. (1979). The concept of derivatives is illustrated more fully in Table 5.2, where the conceptual links among cognitions, affects, behavior, functions, personality traits, diagnoses, and ego defenses are shown. Also added is the domain of coping styles, which I consider to be the conscious derivatives of the unconscious ego defenses. Thus minimization corresponds to denial, substitution to displacement, and mapping to intellectualization. Other derivative domains have also been proposed (Plutchik, 1984, 1989).

There is another general way to describe the psychoevolutionary theory of emotion. The theory consists of three models, which I call the "sequential model," the "structural model," and the "derivatives model." These have already been briefly described in connection with the postulates, but a few more ideas relevant to psychopathology may be added.

SOME IMPLICATIONS OF THE SEQUENTIAL MODEL

If we consider the sequential model, we recognize that certain events trigger the chain of events we call an emotion. But what kind of stimuli act as emotional triggers? A number of studies have shown that very limited classes of events tend to elicit emotions (Blanchard, 1984; Shaver, Schwartz, Kirson, & O'Connor, 1987; Wallbott & Scherer, 1989). They tend to be events that disrupt the equilibrium of the organism at a given moment. These are events that create "emergency" conditions (as Rado, 1969, says) or create existential issues for the individual. Even joyful emotional states can be conceptualized as being related to emergencies. Joy tends to be related to the receiving of nurturance and the accomplishment of goals that enhance personal prestige and power (and thus that increase chances of survival). Joyous occasions are typically connected with gifts, food, courtship, and sex, all of which create issues of acceptance, rejection, and reciprocation (Glantz & Pearce, 1989) for the individual.

A second implication of the sequential model is that most of the elements of the chain are not available to consciousness. Individuals often do not know why they become "emotional"; they are confused about exactly how to label their inner feelings (Plutchik & Ax, 1967); they have little insight into their own physiological states of arousal (Valins, 1966); and they often do not recognize the functions served by their own emotions (Plutchik, 1980). Asking patients *why* they feel some emotion

TABLE 5.2. Emotions and Their Derivatives

Stimulus event	Inferred cognition	Subjective language	Behavioral language	Functional language	Trait language	Diagnostic language	Ego defense language	Coping style language
Threat	"Danger"	Fear	Escape	Protection	Timid	Passive	Repression	Suppression
Obstacle	"Enemy"	Anger	Attack	Destruction	Quarrelsome	Antisocial	Displacement	Substitution
Potential mate	"Possess"	Joy	Mate	Reproduction	Sociable	Manic	Reaction formation	Reversal
Loss of valued individual	"Abandonment"	Sadness	Cry	Reintegration	Gloomy	Depressed	Compensation	Replacement
Member of one's group	"Friend"	Acceptance	Groom	Incorporation	Trusting	Histrionic	Denial	Minimization
Unpalatable object	"Poison"	Disgust	Vomit	Rejection	Hostile	Paranoid	Projection	Fault finding
New territory	"What's out there?"	Expectation	Map	Exploration	Curious	Obsessive–compulsive	Intellectualization	Mapping
Unexpected object	"What is it?"	Surprise	Stop	Orientation	Indecisive	Borderline	Regression	Help seeking

or other almost invariably produces equivocal, confused, or incorrect answers (Plutchik & Plutchik, 1990; Shapiro, 1989; Bednar et al., 1989).

The fact of the limited awareness of the components of the emotion chain emphasizes the point made earlier—that is, that there is no unequivocal way to decide on the existence of a particular emotion. All emotional states are inferences or guesses, based on limited data. The knowledge of the various elements of the chain can only be approximated by evidence from a variety of sources, of which introspective reports are one source, but not necessarily a much better source than any other. Thus, each individual tries to make interpretations not only of the emotions of other people, but also of his or her own emotions. As Greenberg (1990) describes it, our feelings are indicators of our implicit or unconscious judgments of the significance of events. Our own emotions give us information about our reactions to situations that we may not otherwise be aware of, and they reveal to us our needs, concerns, and motives. Our emotions tell us when things feel unfinished, and they imply the need for action. Often unknown to an individual, the action implied is one that will have a chance of returning the individual to a "neutral" or "normal" state—that is, the state he or she was in before some event occurred that triggered the emotional reaction. By a careful and detailed evaluation of an individual's typical emotional reactions, he or she (or we) can determine the individual's real attitudes and wishes.

A further implication of the sequential model also has direct therapeutic relevance. The model implies that the cognition determines the subsequent steps of the emotion chain—that is, the feelings, arousal, preparation for action, display rules used, and (to some extent) outcome. This suggests that if one is able to change one's interpretation of given events, the emotional reactions may be quite different or greatly muted. For example, a woman felt angry, resentful, and depressed because of an alcoholic, abusive husband. When she began to think of him as sick rather than as cruel, she felt less angry and sad and more compassionate. It should not be assumed that events directly determine our emotions. Rather, *interpretations of events* determine what we feel, and to that extent our world of emotions is created by our cognitions (Ellis, 1962; Lazarus, 1991). This does not mean that our cognitions are necessarily conscious; they may include unconscious and defensive processes, so that even cognitions need to be inferred.

SOME IMPLICATIONS OF THE STRUCTURAL MODEL

The structural model assumes that there is a small number of basic emotions whose mixtures or blends produce the many emotions that languages describe. Although different theoreticians disagree on the exact number of primary emotions, they all agree that the number is somewhere between 6 and 10 (Kemper, 1987); I hypothesize that there are 8 (see Figure 5.2). However, there has been some misunderstanding of what is meant by the term "basic emotion." For example, Ortony and Turner (1990) misinterpret this concept as referring only to the particular *words* used by different theoreticians. Thus if one person uses the term "distress" as a basic emotion, and the other uses the term "sadness," Ortony and Turner interpret this to mean that two different emotions are being discussed. It should be evident that such terms are simply convenient, somewhat arbitrary words used to describe a *dimension*. Thus, when I write about "anger" as a basic emotion, I explicitly point out that anger is a moderate level of intensity of a dimension that has multiple levels and multiple connotations. Rage, fury, and irritation are just as primary as anger, and none of these words convey by themselves the variety of cognitions, physiological changes, and display behaviors that also characterize the "destruction" dimension. In fact, a family of words and observations defines each basic emotion.

Another confusion sometimes heard is that the secondary emotions or blends are somehow less important or meaningful than the primary ones. From the point of view of the structural model, *all* emotions are either the eight primary ones or mixtures of the eight primary ones. All emotions, whether primary or secondary, have similar properties: They have adaptive functions for the individual; they need to be inferred from various sources of evidence; they are based on specific cognitions; and they reveal something of an individual's attitudes and motivations.

A further implication of the idea of mixed emotions is that the mixing of emotions necessarily produces some level of conflict. The circumplex or circular model for emotion implies that some blends of emotions involve little conflict and that other blends (of opposites or near-opposites) involve considerable conflict. This model has been used as a basis for the construction of a test of emotions (Plutchik & Kellerman, 1974), which has been widely used and which has revealed systematic differences between patient groups differing in levels of inferred conflict. It is also important to emphasize that the concept of a circular or circumplex ordering of emotions has been empirically confirmed by a number of investigators (Conte & Plutchik, 1981; Daly, Lancee, & Polivy, 1983; Fisher et al., 1985; Wiggins, Trapnell, & Phillips, 1988).

SOME IMPLICATIONS OF THE DERIVATIVES MODEL

All clinicians recognize that at a deep, fundamental level, pathology involves aberrant emotional reactions. What is not so obvious is the precise nature of the vicissitudes of emotional life. One of the most important ideas of the psychoevolutionary theory is the concept of "derivatives." This term is used in three different senses. It can mean that certain human behaviors are seen in lower animals; for example, the sneer of the human may be said to be derived from the snarl of the wolf. It can also mean that certain behaviors seen in adults are derivatives of certain behaviors seen in infants. An example might be the feeding and babyish behaviors sometimes seen between adult lovers. A third meaning of the concept is the idea that certain conceptual domains are derivative of other, more primitive events or concepts. This is the sense in which the term is used here. It means that a number of conceptual domains are systematically related to one another.

Take, for example, the domain of personality. The subject is usually taught in universities as if it had little or nothing to do with emotions. Yet the language of emotions and the language of personality are remarkably similar. An individual can feel depressed or be a depressed person; can feel nervous or be a nervous person; or can feel joyful or be a joyful person. As Allen and Potkay (1981) have pointed out, the difference between emotional states (transient feelings) and personality traits (more enduring dispositions) is arbitrary, and depends often on whether the wording of the instructions of a questionnaire includes the terms "now," "recently," "usually," or "most of the time."

The psychoevolutionary theory has accepted the fundamental identity between emotions and personality traits and has demonstrated (1) the overlap of the language of the two domains (Plutchik, 1980), and (2) the nearly identical circumplex structure of the two domains (Plutchik, 1980; Conte & Plutchik, 1981). It has also shown how traits can be conceptualized as derived from the mixtures of emotions. This is important because the relation is symmetrical; given knowledge of an individual's personality traits, the clinician can work backwards, so to speak, and infer the existence of particular basic emotions and the interpersonal transactions that they imply. The Emotions Profile Index (Plutchik & Kellerman, 1974) is based on this explicit theory. The concept that personality traits can be represented by a circumplex has also received considerable acceptance in the literature (Benjamin, 1987; Kiesler, 1983; Wiggins, 1982).

Let us consider another domain, that of ego defenses. The idea that there exist mental mechanisms such as repression, denial, displacement, and projection was first suggested by psychoanalysts and has become accepted as part of the general body of clinical concepts. Despite this, there is considerable confusion and disagreement on exactly how many defenses there are, how to define them, and what their functions are.

The psychoevolutionary theory attempts to provide explicit answers to such questions. It assumes that ego defenses evolved as methods to handle emotional reactions whose direct expression might otherwise endanger the individual. Thus, for example, a child who is punished by the mother may wish to retaliate, but may be fearful of further punishment or loss of love. The child may unconsciously express his or her anger by hitting a younger sibling, kicking a pet dog, or breaking a toy. One can make the case that each basic emotion has a corresponding ego defense that attempts to deal with it at an unconscious level, in order to avoid further pain or unpleasure. The general idea is that each defense is associated with certain personality traits, with cer-

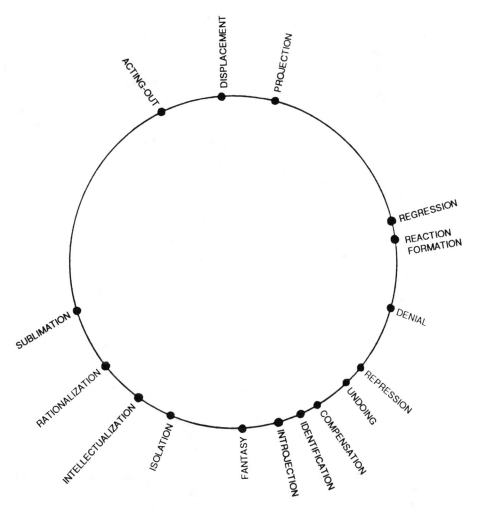

FIGURE 5.3. An approximate circumplex for ego defense concepts, obtained empirically using similarity scaling methods. This shows both the relative similarity and overlap of ego defense concepts, as well as those that are considered to be opposites. Reprinted by permission from Plutchik, Kellerman, and Conte (1979, p. 249).

tain social needs, with a particular mental mechanism, and with a psychological function. For example, projection is associated with people who are critical, fault-finding, and blaming of others. These people's social need is to identify imperfections in other people. The method is to use blame, and the function is to decrease their own feelings of inferiority. The theory therefore implies a set of empirical, testable relations among emotions, personality traits, and ego defenses. It has also been used as the theoretical rationale for the development of tests for the measurement of ego defenses (Buckley, Conte, Plutchik, Wild, & Karasu, 1984; Plutchik & Conte, 1989; Plutchik et al., 1979). It may be added that the theory has guided the construction of a test of

coping styles as well (Conte, Plutchik, Picard, Galanter, & Jacoby, 1991; Plutchik, 1989; Wilder & Plutchik, 1982). Of great interest is the fact that a similarity scaling method for ego defense concepts has produced a circumplex for defenses as shown in Figure 5.3 (Plutchik et al., 1979).

OTHER CLINICAL IMPLICATIONS OF A PSYCHOEVOLUTIONARY APPROACH TO EMOTIONS

Evolutionary considerations suggest that most organisms must deal with certain fundamental problems related to their survival. Social animals, particularly primates, must find their place in a hierarchy or rank order and deal with threats to the positions obtained. They must handle territorial conflicts over what part of the environment belongs to them. They must identify the group members who are part of their own species so that they can interact with them, and they must somehow come to terms with the limited length of an individual life. These four areas of concern are fundamental, in the sense that they all relate in some way to issues of "inclusive fitness"—that is, the likelihood of sexual reproduction and maintenance of one's genes in future generations. I refer to these four survival issues as the problems of "hierarchy," "territoriality," "identity," and "temporality" (Plutchik, 1980, 1983). The following sections provide brief descriptions of these problems, along with some hypotheses about their connections to emotions.

Hierarchy

The concept of hierarchy refers to the vertical dimension of social life. Dominance hierarchies are seen almost universally both in lower animals and in humans. In general, the major expressions of high hierarchical positions are first access to food, to shelter, to comforts, and to sex—that is, the resources needed for both personal and genetic survival.

The vertical organization of social life is reflected in the age relations among people, in some of the relations between the sexes, in economic and military organizations, and in social classes. Generally speaking, hierarchical organizations reflect the facts that some people know more than other people, that some people are stronger or more skillful than others, and that all people vary in affective dispositions. All individuals must face these realities and come to terms with them whether they want to or not, and whether or not they are aware of them.

Of great importance is the fact that an individual's attempt to cope with hierarchical issues implies competition, status conflict, and power struggles. People near the top of a hierarchy tend to feel dominant, self-confident, bossy, and assertive, while those near the bottom feel submissive and anxious (Buirski, Plutchik, & Kellerman, 1978). Depression appears to be related, in part, to perceived downward mobility within a particular hierarchy (Plutchik & Landau, 1973).

Haley (1980) has demonstrated the importance of understanding hierarchical relations in the context of family therapy. He points out that all organizations, including the family, are hierarchical in form, with some members having more authority, power, and status than others. Haley's clinical experience with adolescents has revealed that psychopathology is the result of a malfunctioning organization, and it implies that the task of the therapist is to help change the organization, so that the parents are in charge rather than their offspring.

Territoriality

The second universal conflict area for all individuals concerns the problem of territoriality. In every species, each organism must learn what aspects of the environment and of itself "belongs" to it. From an evolutionary point of view, territories are areas or spaces of potential nourishment necessary for survival, or areas that are safe from attack or predation. Territories may be defined explicitly by scent markings, tree scratches, or boundary lines, or implicitly by the distance one organism allows another to approach before aggression is initiated. Crowding usually generates territorial crises.

Individuals attempting to cope with territorial issues often have feelings of possessiveness, jealousy, and envy. Those who are in possession of some aspect of the environment (including other people) feel in control. In contrast, individuals whose boundaries have been penetrated (or whose possessions have been taken) feel a lack of control. From the point of view of my model of the emotions, I assume that the feelings of control–dyscontrol are basic to the territorial crisis.

Identity

The third major problem that all organisms encounter is the problem of identity. In simplest terms, this refers to the basic question of who we are, or, alternatively, what group or groups we belong to. The issue of identity is a fundamental existential crisis for all organisms because isolated individuals neither propagate nor survive.

In lower organisms, genetic coding mechanisms enable an individual to recognize other individuals of the same species. In humans, however, group memberships are very complex because of the variety of categories one can use to define an identity. The most important criteria of group membership are undoubtedly sex, race, age, religion, occupation, and geography. The fact that these often conflict with one another is one of the reasons for identity crises. Adolescents are particularly prone to crises of sexual identity, while older people are more likely to have to confront crises of religious or occupational identity.

Certain emotions are closely tied to the sense of identity. For those who are part of our group, who share our identity, we feel a sense of belonging or acceptance. We share language, customs, rituals, jokes, and play. We allow hugging, kissing, and (under certain conditions) sexual behavior. The emotion associated with a lack of identity is rejection or disgust. Prejudice against strangers is universal and reflects the sense of danger to survival connected with individuals who are not members of our group. In order to feel comfortable about rejecting someone, we often try to disconnect that person from our group—to dehumanize the person with certain verbal labels, for example. Acceptance and liking versus rejection and hate are the emotional poles connected with the struggle to achieve an identity.

Temporality

The fourth universal problem encountered by all people is the problem of temporality. This word refers to the fact of the limited duration of an individual's life. All organisms have a limited span of life, part of which is spent in infancy, childhood, and adolescence learning fundamental skills about social living. From an evolutionary point of view, the purpose of the acquisition of skills is to enable the individual to survive as long as possible and to become a successful reproducing adult member of a group.

The reality of death creates the inevitability of loss and separation for those who are living. There is a need for social solutions to the problem of loss, since individuals without support from other members of their social group do not survive well or long. During the course of evolution, several solutions have evolved for the problem of loss or separation. One solution is the development of distress signals, which serve as the functional equivalent of cries for help. The second evolutionary solu-

tion for the problem of loss is the evolution of sympathetic or nurturing responses in other members of the social group. It might even be argued that altruism is an extreme form of the nurturing response. In humans, the problem of the limited span of existence has affected the evolution of a series of social institutions that function to deal with death and loss. These include mourning rituals; birth, death, and reunion myths; preparation for an afterlife; and certain aspects of religion.

Emotions also relate to these basic experiences of loss and separation. Sadness is a cry for help that functions to attempt to reintegrate the individual with a lost person or a substitute for the lost person. If the signal of a need for help and nurturance works only partially, it may produce a persistent, long-term distress signal that we call depression. If the cry for help actually works and brings help, it produces an opposite emotion, the emotion of joy. Joy is thus the experience of rejoining or of possession.

From the point of view of existential crises, it thus becomes possible to make inferences from emotions to the existential issues with which an individual is most concerned. For example, someone who is very competitive is probably very much concerned with his or her place in the ladder of life (i.e., with hierarchical issues). Someone who is an obsessive collector and envious of other people's possessions is probably concerned with territorial issues. Someone who is preoccupied with issues of family closeness and loyalty is probably concerned with identity conflicts. And someone who is an avid and anxious reader of the obituary columns is probably concerned with issues of temporality. Obviously, any single concern can be interpreted in more than one way.

Derivatives of the Existential Crises

If we go down a step in the level of abstraction, we recognize that there are many experiences in life that relate directly or indirectly to the existential issues. For example, if we take the problem of hierarchy, we can see that such issues as being assertive, dominant, or in control, being submissive or controlled, and seeking fame and wealth are all related to one another, and all tied to the question of finding one's place in the ladder of life. Similarly, issues concerned with accumulation of posses-

TABLE 5.3. Major Coping Issues Associated with the Existential Crises

Hierarchy	Identity
Becoming dominant	Making friends
Becoming submissive	Courtship, love
Feelings of anger and fear	Marriage, family
	Community, nation
	Feelings of acceptance and rejection
Territorality	Temporality
Having a safe personal space	Dealing with illness
Accumulating possessions	Dealing with death
Feelings of envy and jealousy	Getting or providing social supports
Feelings of control and loss of control	Feelings of gain or loss, joy, or sadness

sions, establishing a personal sense of space or boundaries, and reciprocity (Glantz & Pearce, 1989) are all connected with territorial problems.

Table 5.3 summarizes a set of hypotheses about important problems in life that are related to the four basic existential crises. Problems of coping with dominance and submissiveness relate to hierarchical problems; control issues relate to territorial problems; courtship and love relate to identity issues; and feelings about illness and death relate to the problem of temporality. These issues exist whether or not an individual is aware of them, since they reflect general aspects of the human–environment interaction.

The Problem of Change

To understand psychopathology in terms of emotions is not enough. A general theory of emotions should have implications for the treatment of emotional problems and the reestablishing of normative functioning. This issue has been addressed in several previous publications, and because of limited space it is not explored here (Plutchik, 1961, 1966, 1988, 1990).

To summarize the points made in this chapter, it may be said that the vicissitudes of emotions underlie most of our ideas about the nature of psychopathology. The theory described in this chapter attempts to make the relations between emotions and other domains of pathology (e.g., personality disorders and ego defenses) explicit. It describes the universal crises humans experience in the process of

living and dying, and suggests connections between them and our emotions. It has guided the development of a number of psychometric instruments designed to measure its key dimensions. It has made specific predictions of a novel type that have been largely confirmed (e.g., the circumplex nature of emotions, personality traits, personality disorders, and ego defenses). And it has related its ideas and concepts to that broad and fundamental scientific model, the theory of evolution.

REFERENCES

Allen, B., & Potkay, C. R. (1981). On the arbitrary distinction between states and traits. *Journal of Personality and Social Psychology, 4*, 916–928.

Arnold, M. (1960). *Emotion and personality* (2 vols.). New York: Columbia University Press.

Bednar, R. L., Wells, M. G., & Peterson, S. R. (1989). *Self-esteem*. Washington, DC: American Psychological Association Press.

Benjamin, L. S. (1987). Use of the SASB dimensional model to develop treatment plans for personality disorders: I. Narcissism. *Journal of Personality Disorders, 1*, 43–70.

Blanchard, D. C. (1984). Applicability of animal models to human aggression. In K. J. Flannelly, R. J. Blanchard, & D. C. Blanchard (Eds.), *Biological perspectives on aggression*. New York: Alan R. Liss.

Brenner, C. (1975). Affects and psychic conflict. *Psychoanalytic Quarterly, 44*, 5–28.

Buckley, P., Conte, H. R., Plutchik, R., Wild, K. V., & Karasu, T. B. (1984). Psychodynamic variables as predictors of psychotherapy outcome. *American Journal of Psychiatry, 141*, 742–748.

Buirski, P., Plutchik, R., & Kellerman, H. (1978). Sex differences, dominance, and personality in the chimpanzee. *Animal Behavior, 26*, 123–129.

Conte, H. R., & Plutchik, R. (1981). A circumplex model for interpersonal traits. *Journal of Personality and Social Psychology, 2*, 823–830.

Conte, H. R., Plutchik, R., Picard, S., Galanter, M., & Jacoby, J. (1991). Sex differences in personality traits and coping styles of hospitalized alcoholics. *Journal of Studies on Alcohol, 52*, 26–32.

Daly, E. M., Lancee, W. J., & Polivy, J. (1983). A conical model for the taxonomy of emotional experience. *Journal of Personality and Social Psychology, 45*, 443–457.

Darwin, C. (1965). *The expression of the emotions in man and animals*. Chicago: University of Chicago Press. (Original work published 1872)

Edelstein, M. G. (1990). *Symptom analysis: A method of brief therapy*. New York: Norton

Eibl-Eibesfeldt, I. (1975). *Ethology: The biology of behavior* (2nd ed.). New York: Holt.

Ekman, P., & Friesen, W. V. (1971). Constants across cultures in the face and emotion. *Journal of Personality and Social Psychology, 17*, 124–129.

Ellis, A. (1962). *Reason and emotion in psychotherapy*. New York: Lyle Stuart.

Enquist, M. (1985). Communication during aggressive interactions with particular reference to variation in choice of behavior. *Animal Behavior, 33*, 1152–1161.

Fisher, G. A., Heise, D. R., Bohrnstedt, G. W., & Lucke, J. Z. (1985). Evidence for extending the circumplex model of personality trait language to self-reported moods. *Journal of Personality and Social Psychology*, *49*, 233–242.

Frijda, N. H. (1986). *The emotions*. Cambridge, England: Cambridge University Press.

Fuller, J. L. (1986). Genetics and emotions. In R. Plutchik & H. Kellerman (Eds.), *Emotion: Theory, research, and experience. Vol. 3. Biological foundations of emotion*. New York: Academic Press.

Glantz, K., & Pearce, J. (1989). *Exiles from Eden: Psychotherapy from an evolutionary perspective*. New York: Norton.

Goddard, M. E., & Beilharz, R. G. (1985). A multivariate analysis of the genetics of fearfulness in potential guide dogs. *Behavior Genetics*, *15*, 69–89.

Greenberg, L. (1990, July). Lecture presented at the meeting of the International Society for Research on Emotions, New Brunswick, NJ.

Haley, J. (1980). *Leaving home: The therapy of disturbed young people*. New York: McGraw-Hill.

Horowitz, M. J. (1991). Person schemas. In M. J. Horowitz (Ed.), *Person schemas and and maladaptive interpersonal patterns*. Chicago: University of Chicago Press.

Karasu, T. B., & Plutchik, R. (1978). Research problems in psychosomatic medicine and psychotherapy of somatic disorders. In T. B. Karasu & R. I. Steinmuller (Eds.), *Psychotherapeutics in medicine*. New York: Grune & Stratton.

Kellerman, H. (1979). *Group therapy and personality: Intersecting structures*. New York: Grune & Straton.

Kemper, T. D. (1987). How many emotions are there? Wedding the social and autonomic components. *American Journal of Sociology*, *93*, 263–289.

Kiesler, D. J. (1983). The 1982 Interpersonal Circle: A taxonomy for complementarity in human transactions. *Psychological Review*, *90*, 185–214.

Kushner, M. G., & Beitman, B. D. (1990). Panic attacks without fear: An overview. *Behaviour Research and Therapy*, *28*, 469–479.

Lazarus, R. S. (1991). *Emotion and adaptation*. New York: Oxford University Press.

Loehlin, J. C., Horn, J. M., & Williams, L. (1981). Personality resemblance in adoptive families. *Behavior Genetics*, *11*, 309–330.

Lumsden, C. J., & Wilson, E. O. (1981). *Genes, mind and culture: The coevolutionary process*. Cambridge, MA: Harvard University Press.

Ortony, A., & Turner, T. J. (1990). What's basic about basic emotions? *Psychological Review*, *97*, 315–331.

Plutchik, R. (1958). Outlines of a new theory of emotion. *Transactions of the New York Academy of Sciences*, *20*, 394–403.

Plutchik, R. (1961). Guilt and delinquency: A theoretical analysis. *Journal of Offender Therapy*, *5*, 3–6.

Plutchik, R. (1962). *The emotions: Facts, theories and a new model*. New York: Random House.

Plutchik, R. (1966). Emotions as adaptive reactions: Implications for therapy. *Psychoanalytic Review*, *53*, 105–110.

Plutchik, R. (1970). Emotions, evolution, and adaptive processes. In M. Arnold (Ed.), *Feelings and emotions: The Loyola Symposium*. New York: Academic Press.

Plutchik, R. (1980). *Emotions: A psychoevolutionary synthesis*. New York: Harper & Row.

Plutchik, R. (1983). Emotions in early development: A psychoevolutionary approach. In R. Plutchik & H. Kellerman (Eds.), *Emotion: Theory, research, and experience. Vol. 2. Emotions in early development*. New York: Academic Press.

Plutchik, R. (1984). Emotions: A general psychoevolutionary theory. In K. R. Scherer & P. Ekman (Eds.), *Approaches to emotion*. Hillsdale, NJ: Erlbaum.

Plutchik, R. (1988). The nature of emotions: Clinical implications. In M. Clynes & J. Panksepp (Eds.), *Emotions and psychopathology*. New York: Plenum Press.

Plutchik, R. (1989). Measuring emotions and their derivatives. In R. Plutchik & H. Kellerman (Eds.), *Emotion: Theory, research, and experience. Vol. 4. The measurement of emotions*. New York: Academic Press.

Plutchik, R. (1990). Emotions and psychotherapy: A psychoevolutionary perspective. In R. Plutchik & H. Kellerman (Eds.), *Emotion: Theory, research, and experience. Vol. 5. Emotions, psychopathology, and psychotherapy*. New York: Academic Press.

Plutchik, R. (1991). Emotions and evolution. In K. T. Strongman (Ed.), *International review of studies on emotion* (Vol. 1). New York: Wiley.

Plutchik, R., & Ax, A. F. (1967). A critique of "Determinants of emotional state" by Schachter and Singer (1962). *Psychopathology*, *4*, 79–82.

Plutchik, R., & Conte, H. R. (1989). Measuring emotions and their derivatives: Personality traits, ego defenses, and coping styles. In S. Wetzler & M. Katz (Eds.), *Contemporary approaches to psychological assessment*. New York: Brunner/Mazel.

Plutchik, R., & Kellerman, H. (1974). *Manual of the Emotions Profile Index*. Los Angeles: Western Psychological Services.

Plutchik, R., Kellerman, H., & Conte, H. R. (1979). A structural theory of ego defenses and emotions. In C. E. Izard (Ed.), *Emotions, personality and psychopathology*. New York: Plenum Press.

Plutchik, R., & Landau, H. (1973). Perceived dominance and emotional states in small groups. *Psychotherapy: Theory, Research, and Practice*, *10*, 343–344.

Plutchik, R., & Platman, S. R. (1977). Personality connotations of psychiatric diagnoses. *Journal of Nervous and Mental Disease*, *165*, 418–422.

Plutchik, R., & Plutchik, A. (1990). Communication and coping in families. In E. A. Blechman (Ed.), *Emotions and the family*. Hillsdale, NJ: Erlbaum.

Plutchik, R., & Schaefer, E. S. (1966). Interrelationships of emotions, traits, and diagnostic constructs. *Psychological Reports*, *18*, 399–410.

Rado, S. (1969). *Adaptational psychodynamics: Motivation and control*. New York: Science House.

Russell, J. A. (1989). Verbal measures of emotion. In R. Plutchik & H. Kellerman (Eds.), *Emotion: Theory, research, and experience. Vol. 4. The measurement of emotions*. New York: Academic Press.

Shapiro, D. (1989). *Psychotherapy of neurotic character*. New York: Basic Books.

Shaver, P., Schwartz, J., Kirson, D., & O'Connor, C. (1987). Emotion knowledge: Further exploration of a prototype approach. *Journal of Personality and Social Psychology*, *52*, 1061–1086.

Stevenson-Hinde, J., & Simpson, A. E. (1982). Temperament and relationships. In R. Porter & G. M. Collins (Eds.), *Temperamental differences in infants and young children*. London: Pitman.

Valins, S. (1966). Cognitive effects of false heart-rate feedback. *Journal of Personality and Social Psychology*, *4*, 400–408.

Wallbott, H. G., & Scherer, K. R. (1989). Assessing emotion by questionnaire. In R. Plutchik & H. Kellerman (Eds.), *Emotion: Theory, research, and experience. Vol. 4. The measurement of emotions*. New York: Academic Press.

Wiggins, J. S. (1982). Circumplex models of interpersonal behavior in clinical psychology. In P. C. Kendall & J. N. Butcher (Eds.), *Handbook of research methods in clinical psychology*. New York: Wiley.

Wiggins, J. S., & Broughton, R. (1985). The interpersonal circle: A structural model for the integration of personality research. *Perspectives in Personality*, *1*, 1–47.

Wiggins, J. S., Trapnell, P., & Phillips, N. (1988). Psychometric and geometric characteristics of the Revised Interpersonal Adjective Scales (IAS-R). *Multivariate Behavioral Research*, *23*, 517–530.

Wilder, J. F., & Plutchik, R. (1982). Preparing the professional: Building prevention into training. In W. S. Paine (Ed.), *Job stress and burnout*. Beverly Hills, CA: Sage.

Wimer, R. E., & Wimer, C. C. (1985). Animal behavior genetics: A search for the biological foundations of behavior. *Annual Review of Psychology*, *36*, 171–218.

6

Cerebral Evolution of Emotion

PAUL D. MacLEAN

INTRODUCTION

The purpose of this chapter is to present an analysis of the role played by three major evolutionary developments of the mammalian forebrain in the generation and expression of emotional feelings. Figure 6.1 is a diagram of the phylogenetic hierarchy of the three developments. In evolving to its great size, the human forebrain has retained the anatomical organization and chemistry of three formations that reflect a respective relationship to reptiles, early mammals, and late mammals. In the diagram, the three formations are respectively labeled as "reptilian," "paleomammalian," and "neomammalian." From the standpoint of intercommunication, it appears highly significant that both on the basis of organizational structure and clinical findings, the two evolutionary older formations lack the capacity for verbal communication with the parts of the human brain accounting for speech. The main thrust of the present analysis is that factors related to the evolutionary development of the forebrain of early mammals (the paleomammalian brain or so-called "limbic system") were responsible for the honing of emotional feelings that guide behavior required for self-preservation and the procreation of the species.

Operational Terms

Evolution

In dealing with the subject of the cerebral evolution of emotion, it is essential right at the start to stipulate the sense in which the two words "evolution" and "emotion" are used. An

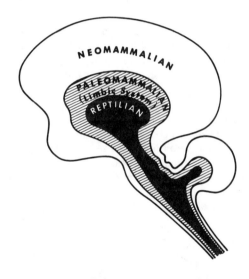

FIGURE 6.1. Symbolic representation of the triune evolution of three main neural assemblies leading to the forebrain of human beings and other advanced mammals. Labeling is placed at the level of the forebrain, where each assembly, respectively, reflects anatomical and biochemical commonalities with reptiles, early mammals, and late mammals. Reprinted by permission from MacLean (1967, p. 377).

illustration from fractal biology about the branching development of life forms serves to exemplify the intended connotation of evolution at either the macro- or microevolutionary level. The branching of the pulmonary bronchial tree, for example, shows a regularity in the proportion and form of the first 10 or so branches that is referred to as "self-similarity." Further on, however, the offshoot branches develop increasing irregularities (West & Goldberger, 1987). Hofstadter (1977) has referred to the increasing complexity as a "sameness-in-differentness." Here this expression is applied symbolically to the descriptive use of the word "evolution." With no pretense of implying knowledge of the underlying mechanisms, the word "evolution" is used to signify the sameness-in-differentness of evolving (literally, "unrolling") fauna and flora.

Emotion

The use of the word "emotion" needs to be explained in terms of the word "affect" which connotes a form of emotional feeling. First, it should be noted that it is the element of subjectivity (self-awareness, consciousness) that most clearly distinguishes psychological from other functions of the brain. Here it may simply be stated that subjectivity is an inseparable quality of the five main classes of psychological information—namely, sensations, perceptions, proclivities (compulsions), affects, and conceptions (thoughts).

Figure 6.2 presents a scheme for the classification of affects. This scheme is dealt with in further detail in a later section, when I describe a clinical condition that provides the best evidence (and, indeed, the only subjective evidence) that the limbic system is basically involved in the experience and expression of emotional feelings. Introspective analysis would indicate that affects are agreeable or disagreeable feelings that "impart subjective information that is instrumental in guiding behavior required for self-preservation and preservation of the species" (MacLean, 1990, p. 425). Only we as individuals have direct access to the experience of affects. The presence of affect in another person or animal must be inferred on the basis of some form of behavior that we identify with our own private, affective feelings. Descartes's (1649/1967) term "emotion" (literally, "a moving out of") is appropriate for denoting the behavioral aspect.

"Behavior" has been defined as any change of an entity with respect to its environment (Rosenblueth, Wiener, & Bigelow, 1943). Affects, on the contrary, like other forms of psychological emanations, exist only as information, and as Wiener (1948, p. 155) has pointed out, "information is information, not matter or energy." The sense of color serves as an example: A perception of a particular color depends on neural activation by photons transmitted at a certain frequency, but there are no known quanta in the entire universe for the color itself (see Cooney, 1991, p. 208). It exists only as an informational product of a "behaving" brain. The same applies to affects and to all other forms of psychological information. This is not to say that the subjective awareness characterizing all psychological functions is an epiphenomenon that, as some would claim, is unnecessary for the performance of our various activities.

In this respect, it is instructive to thumb through a dictionary and estimate how many human activities would drop away without the communication of subjective experience. Although there could hardly be a question more important for solution than the one of how subjective awareness is generated and influences behavior, there remains the important empirical recognition that, like the communication of all information derived from the internal and external environment, the communication of subjective awareness depends on changes of behaving entities with respect to the environment. The invariant dependence on behaving entities for conveying information may be regarded as a law of communication. This realization means that, contrary to what behaviorists and others would contend, subjective phenomena not only are amenable to scientific investigation, but also, in the final

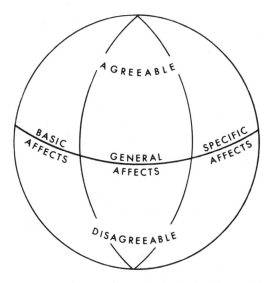

FIGURE 6.2. A global scheme for the classification of affects explained in the text. Reprinted by permission from MacLean (1970, p. 338).

analysis, are the most essential to study for enhancing human understanding. At the same time, it must be admitted that what has been learned thus far about the role of the evolutionarily old cortex in the elaboration of affects, and an undecidable question posed by logical functions of the neocortex, create doubts about certitude of belief in anything—a matter that is considered again at the end of this chapter.

Finally, a statement in regard to what is meant by emotional behavior again requires reference to affects. In Figure 6.2, the central sector is labeled "general affects." These affects are called "general" because, unlike the basic and specific affects to be specified later, they may apply to individuals, situations, or things. They represent what are usually regarded as emotional feelings. In both animals and human beings, the general affects can be identified with six forms of behavior recognized as searching, aggressive, protective, dejected, gratulant (triumphant), and caressive. Associated affects that would characterize these six forms of emotional behavior are desire, anger, fear, dejection, joy, and affection.

Forebrain and Neural Chassis

The forebrain comprises the cerebral hemispheres that are located forward of the midbrain and consist of the diencephalon and telencephalon. Experimentation has shown that reptiles, birds, and mammals deprived of the forebrain show an incapacity for directed behavior, and if uncared for will not survive. Yet many subprimate forms have been shown to retain the capacity for locomotion, as well as bodily mechanisms for such activities as eating, urination, defecation, and copulation. Left alone, however, they resemble an idling mechanism devoid of a driver. In regard to emotional expression, decerebrate preparations with a caudal remnant of the diencephalon can be provoked to display angry behavior, but it is undirected. Importantly, such preparations do not show either grooming or pleasure reactions typical of mammals. In psychological terms, therefore, the forebrain might otherwise be referred to as the "psychencephalon." And in this respect, experimentation would indicate that the telencephalon and diencephalon are as interdependent for psychological processes as are the screen and cone of a television set for the production of a picture.

Mammalian Origins

The evolution of vertebrates can be traced back to the bony fishes. In his book *Our Face from Fish to Man*, Gregory (1927/1967) points out that every one of the 28 bones of the human skull "has been inherited in unbroken succession from the air-breathing fishes of pre-Devonian times" (pp. 20–21). It is relevant to the present subject that fish engage in displays suggestive of emotional expression. In this latter regard, it is also notable that although the forebrain of fish is small compared with the predominant midbrain, its removal results in less aggressive behavior and deficiencies in mating behavior (Noble, 1936).

But in the case of fish, and also the amphibia (in which the forebrain advances to competitive size with respect to the midbrain), there would be no certainty as to which form represents the closest antecedent of mammals. The same would not be true of the reptilian radiation. Nature's invention of the amniote egg made it possible for reptiles to adapt entirely to a terrestrial existence. And as next to be considered, there arose from one of the branches of the stem reptiles (cotylosaurs; see Figure 6.3, panel 1) some advanced mammallike reptiles that can hardly be distinguished from the earliest mammals.

The Mammal-Like Reptiles (Therapsids)

The cactus tree in Figure 6.3, panel 1, depicts the evolutionary radiation of reptiles, with the rightmost branch showing the most primitive mammal-like reptiles (pelycosaurs); these gave rise to a more advanced variety called therapsids because of their having a large temporal opening (apse = arched-over alcove) resembling the temporal fossa of mammals (*therion* = Greek word for "beast," which signifies "mammal" in zoological nomenclature). From about 250 million years ago in mid-Permian times to the mid-Triassic, the mammal-like reptiles were the predominant land fauna. During this period when the earth was still one giant continent known to us by Wegener's (1915) term "Pangaea" (see Figure 6.3, panel 2), the mammal-like reptiles must have roamed every part of it, because their remains have since turned up on every continent.

Most significantly, there were several lines of therapsids showing what is called "direc-

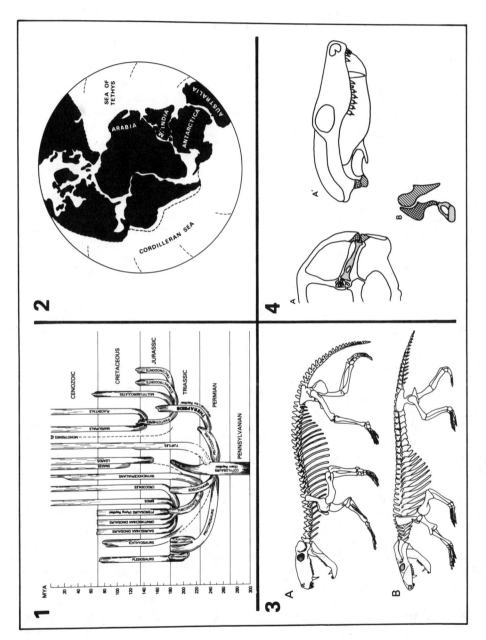

FIGURE 6.3. Illustrations relevant to origin of mammals from mammal-like reptiles (therapsids). (1) Cactus tree, depicting evolutionary radiation of reptiles. Rightmost branch shows therapsid line leading to mammals. (2) Wegener's (1915) "Pangaea." (3) Two carnivorous therapsids illustrating mammal-like features. (4) A and A', therapsid jaw bones (quadrate above and articular below) that became the incus and malleus of the mammalian middle ear (B). Adapted by permission from MacLean (1990, pp. 34 [panel 1], 81 [panel 2], 88 [panel 3], and 94 [panel 4]).

tional evolution" because members of each line were developing similar changes toward a mammalian condition. These changes included the acquisition of a mammal-like posture with the legs supporting the body from underneath (see Figure 6.3, panel 3), and a reduction of the phalangeal formula, with the number of digits corresponding to our five fingers and toes. The jaws and teeth were becoming more mammalian in character, and the development of a secondary palate (hard palate) made it possible to chew and breathe at the same time. And as diagrammed in Figure 6.3, panel 4, two small bones of the reptilian jaw joint—the articular and quadrate—were becoming smaller, as though preparing for their migration to become the malleus and incus of the mammalian ear. Indeed, as one of the most persuasive examples of Haeckl's (1876) statement that ontogeny recapitulates phylogeny, the migration of these two bones can be observed during the development of the human fetus. Moreover, there were tell-tale signs in the fossils that the therapsids were developing from a cold-blooded to a warm-blooded condition.

But what must be emphasized in a separate paragraph is that in the most advanced therapsids, the bony resemblance between them and the earliest mammals became so close that the most reliable distinction has proved to be the continued presence in the jaw joint of two small bones that became the malleus and incus of the mammalian middle ear.

THE REPTILIAN COMPLEX AND THE BASIC ANIMALITY

Given the introductory considerations above, I now deal successively with the three main evolutionary formations of the forebrain, taking into account the part that each plays in contributing to the experience of emotion. For comparative neurobehavioral studies, it is to be noted that there are no existing reptiles directly in line with the mammal-like reptiles. The bony structure of one of the primitive mammal-like reptiles was so lizard-like as to be given the name of *Varanosaurus*—the genus name for the monitor lizard, of which the Komodo dragon is an outstanding example. It is to be emphasized also that the auditory apparatus of the lizard is similar to that found generally in the mammal-like reptiles. For such reasons, lizards were chosen for our neurobehavioral studies on reptiles.

Behavioral Profile of Lizards

For comparative neurobehavioral studies, it is essential to obtain a complete behavioral profile ("ethogram"). An ethogram amounts to a list of (1) elements of a behavior, (2) constructs of behavioral elements, and (3) sequences of constructs. For animal behavior generally, the behavioral profile can be compared to the peaks and subpeaks of two mountain ranges seen from a distance. In one range are all the behaviors observed during the course of an animal's daily master routine and subroutines. Typically, the daily routine is carried out within an animal's domain. The domain usually consists of a home site within a variably sized territory that, in turn, is contained within a home range. The territory may be defended as a place providing water, food, and zones for excreta. The home range provides additional resources but will not be defended. A lizard's master routine usually involves seven activities that are performed regularly every day. Subroutines may be adopted for purposes of courtship; for repeatedly threatening an unwanted intruder; or, say, for engaging in protective rituals.

The other main range of the behavioral profile consists of four main "prosematic" (rudimentary) displays used in social communication. In lizards, these are referred to as (1) signature (self-assertive) displays; (2) courtship displays; (3) challenge (territorial) displays; and (4) appeasement (submissive) displays.

All told, one can identify in lizards more than 25 forms of behavior that are also typical of birds and of mammals.

The Reptilian Complex

What structures of the forebrain might account for the same kinds of behavior appearing in all three classes of terrestrial vertebrates—namely, reptiles, birds, and mammals? Until four decades ago, with Koelle's (1954) development of a stain for cholinesterase, there was extensive disagreement about corresponding structures of the forebrain in reptiles, birds, and mammals. This stain, and the subsequent introduction by Falck, Hillarp, Thieme, and Torp (1962) of a histochemical technique for the demonstration of aminergic systems, proved to be of remarkable value for identifying corresponding structures of the forebrain in all three classes of terrestrial animals. They are of particular value for distinguishing telencephalic structures loosely referred to as belonging to the basal ganglia. Because of their striped appearance, they are referred to as the striatal complex, including the olfactostriatum (nucleus accumbens and olfactory tubercle), corpus striatum (caudate nucleus and putamen), globus pallidus, and satellite collections of gray matter. In a comparative context, I refer to these striatal structures as the "reptilian complex," or for short as the "R-complex."

For close to 100 years, these telencephalic parts of the basal forebrain have been traditionally regarded in neurology as part of the motor systems under the control of the motor areas of the neocortex, having, so to speak, no "mind of their own." This interpretation has persisted in spite of the recognition that bilateral large cavities may exist in these structures without any apparent loss in motor function.

Experimental Findings

Our comparative neurobehavioral studies were designed to test the hypothesis that the R-complex is basically implicated in the orchestration of various forms of species-typical behavior engaged in by the three classes of vertebrates under consideration, but in a manner that is *typical* for any particular species. For example, the various forms of behavior employed for self-preservation and procreation are not specific for any particular species, but are performed in a manner typical for that species.

Monkeys

Since our work on the R-complex was originally performed on squirrel monkeys, I summarize those studies first and then the findings on lizards. We identified two main varieties of squirrel monkeys (genus *Saimiri*), one called Roman because the supraocular patch resembles the shape of a Roman arch, and the other called Gothic because the patch is peak-shaped. In addition to these facial distinctions, the varieties also proved to have identifying behavioral and karyotypic differences. We observed, for example, that the Gothic type would regularly display to its reflection in a mirror, whereas the Roman type generally showed no interest in its reflection. There were three main manifestations of the mirror display that occurred in 80% or more of the displays—namely, vocalization, spreading of one or both thighs, and full genital tumescence. The displays were in every way similar

to those exchanged by Gothic-type monkeys in situations indicative of a greeting display.

Since the mirror display also incorporates the three main manifestations of the aggressive and courtship displays, it provided a desirable means of investigating which parts of the brain were implicated in species-typical behavior, especially as the test excluded variables created by the presence of another monkey. Pre- and postoperative tests were conducted twice a day. Criterion was the performance of the main components of the display in 80% of a succession of 30 trials, usually involving two such sets of preoperative trials and a sufficient series after surgery to assure plateau performance above, at, or below statistically significant levels.

Experiments were completed on more than 120 monkeys. Surgical ablations or electrocoagulations of structures within neocortical and limbic systems were generally ineffective in eliminating or altering the performance of the mirror display. Enduring elimination or significant fragmentation of the display was obtained only when coagulations involved the striatal outflow through the medial segment of the globus pallidus or its projections to the thalamic tegmentum. Lesions involving thalamic nuclei or midbrain pathways known to supply afferents to the corpus striatum were also effective. (See MacLean, 1990, for a detailed summary of these studies.)

Lizards

Subsequently, in testing the effect of forebrain lesions on the territorial display of the green anolis lizard (*Anolis carolinensis*), it was necessary to devise a method that would not interfere with behavioral thermoregulation. Since the optic nerve of the lizard is almost entirely crossed, a lesion could be placed in one hemisphere; then, by covering either eye of the subject, we could observe whether or not it would perform its usual display to a territorial lizard living in the same kind of habitat separated by a removable screen and a glass partition. Under these conditions, we found that the subject performed its usual display when looking with the eye projecting to the control hemisphere, but failed criterion performance when looking with the eye projecting to the side with a lesion involving the paleostriatum. Lesions of the overlying dorsal ventricular ridge or other telencephalic structures were without effect. (See MacLean, 1990, pp. 151–162.)

In summary, the results of experiments on animals as diverse as reptiles and monkeys indicated that the R-complex is basically involved in the orchestration of displays used in social communication.

Master Routine and Subroutines

Except for some of our experiments, I am unaware of any systematic study of brain mechanisms underlying the orchestration of the daily master routine. Our observations on rodents indicate that the R-complex is basically implicated in the complicated cerebration required for linking together the all important functions of the daily master routine (Murphy, MacLean, & Hamilton, 1981).

Clinical case material points to the importance of the corpus striatum with respect to both the master routine and subroutines. In Huntington's disease, which affects primarily the corpus striatum, Caine, Hunt, Weingartner, and Ebert (1978) have observed that an early manifestation is the inability of patients to remember, plan, and organize their daily activities. Although this is not stated, what the authors describe is a failure of their patients to engage in any daily routine. Left alone, they seemed "content to sit and do nothing" for hours at a time. Yet they appeared eager to participate in scheduled activities guided by the staff. Subroutines were also affected early in the course of the disease: A dentist, knowing well the steps of a procedure, could no longer carry it out in the proper sequence; a housewife with long experience in preparing a Thanksgiving dinner could no longer put it all together.

In Sydenham's chorea, there may be a rather diffuse inflammatory condition that is manifested around the walls of the blood vessels of the brain, along with a degeneration of nerve cells "most pronounced in the *caudate nucleus* and *putamen*" (Haymaker, 1956, p. 341). Osler (1894) described the cases of two girls with symptoms of obsessive compulsive behavior as a complication of chorea that involved them in so many oft-repeated rituals as to drastically interfere with everything they did. It was as though the counting compulsions in one case and the touching compulsion in the other became such time-consuming subroutines as to wreck the essential things required in the daily master routine.

Since the availability of various techniques for brain imaging, cases have been reported of large bilateral lesions of the corpus striatum resulting from various conditions. Laplane et al. (1989) have reported a series of eight such cases. In most cases motor disturbances were usually absent or hardly noticeable; rather, the authors give emphasis to a lack of motivation or a loss of drive. But the apparent apathy may have seemed such to an observer, when, in fact, as in the cases described above, it was a manifestation of an inability to pursue a master routine. In four cases there were also compulsive rituals of a time-consuming nature. Since compulsive acts of themselves are notably unaccompanied by emotional feelings, it is significant to point out that in two cases (cases 1 and 6), interruption or prevention of the act provoked a show of anger.

Summarizing Comment

Overall, the available evidence would indicate that the R-complex plays a fundamental role in performing the functions of the basic animality. As has been summarized here, these include principally the orchestration of the daily master routine and subroutines, as well as the performance of four main displays used in social communication. Aside from providing the basic animality, what can be said about the role of the R-complex in emotion? On the basis of introspection, we tend naturally to link the various displays of animals with the expression of emotion. But this can be only a matter of inference, with the problem compounded in the case of the lizard because of the absence of vocalization in this order of reptiles. But with respect to the daily routine and many subroutines of both animals and human beings, it might be proposed that its performance occurs almost automatically, as though propelled by propensities without associated emotion unless the intended acts are thwarted or meet with frustration. The two cases of obsessive compulsive disorder reported in the above-mentioned study by Laplane et al. (1989) could serve as examples of compulsive acts occurring without emotion unless prevented. For such reasons it has been pointed out that, contrary to what some would claim, emotions are often reflectors rather than determinants of action. Phrased metaphorically with respect to the natural propensity to satisfy the necessities of the basic animality, "the reptile does what it has to do."

THE PALEOMAMMALIAN BRAIN (LIMBIC SYSTEM)

In comparing lists of basic behaviors in lizards and mammals, one finds that there are three conspicuously missing in lizards, and this would apply to reptiles in general. There are three cardinal forms of behavior that characterize the evoutionary transition from reptiles to mammals: (1) nursing, in conjunction with maternal care; (2) audiovocal communication for maintaining maternal–offspring contact; and (3) play. Concerning emotion, special emphasis must be given to the separation cry, which perhaps ranks as the most primitive and basic mammalian vocalization—serving originally to help assure maternal–offspring contact and then, as a later development, contact of members of an affiliated group.

It has been said that a sense of separation is a condition that makes being a mammal so painful. The roots of the condition can be traced to the nursing situation, because any prolonged separation of mother and offspring is disastrous. Contrast this situation with that of most lizards, in which the eggs are laid and left to hatch on their own. The young of the African rainbow lizards, for example, must hide and forage in the deep underbrush so as to avoid being cannibalized by their parents or other adult lizards, and the young of the Komodo dragon must take to the trees for the first year of life for the same reason. Hence, unlike mammals, it has survival value for young lizards to be mute and not call attention to themselves.

Brain Changes with Mammalian Evolution

On the basis of the few available brain endocasts, there is evidence that the therapsid cerebrum was more like that of reptiles than of mammals. What cerebral developments accounted for the three new forms of mammalian behavior enumerated above? The first overall perspective was provided by the French neurologist Paul Broca, in a paper published in 1878. As illustrated in Figure 6.4, it was Broca's special contribution to show that a large cerebral convolution, which he called

the great limbic lobe because it "surrounds" the brainstem, is a common denominator in the brains of all mammals. Because of the robust olfactory connections with rostral part of the lobe, he suggested that the functions of the lobe are generally dominated by the olfactory sense. This latter interpretation gained rapid appeal, and by the next decade several textbooks were referring to the entire lobe as the "rhinencephalon."

Since the sense of smell was regarded as unimportant in human beings, the rhinencephalon received little attention in medical instruction. In the scientific literature, mention was made from time to time of the possible role of temporal olfactory structures in different aspects of emotion. For example, in 1919 Elliot Smith, in a Croonian Lecture, suggested that in contrast to other sensory systems, olfactory structures may create an "affective tone" linking anticipation and consummation into one experience, and thereby may provide a germ of memory.

Prior to 1937, however, no author appears to have considered the entire limbic lobe with respect to functions other than olfaction. In that year, Papez, a neurologist and comparative neuroanatomist at Cornell University, published a paper titled "A Proposed Mechanism of Emotion." On the basis of what had been recently learned about the role of the hypothalamus in the expression of emotion, Papez (1937) emphasized that structures of the limbic lobe on the medial wall of the hemisphere were the only ones known to have strong hypothalamic connections. He cited case material to support his proposal that

> the central emotive process of cortical origin may be . . . conceived as being built up in the hippocampal formation and as being transferred to the mammillary body and thence through the anterior thalamic nuclei to the cortex of the gyrus cinguli. The cortex of the cingulate gyrus may be looked on as the receptive region for the experiencing of emotion as the result of impulses coming from the hypothalamic region, in the same way as the area striata is considered the receptive cortex for photic excitations coming from the retina. (p. 728)

The loop formed by these serially connected structures became known as the "Papez circuit" (see Figure 6.6, below).

Over 10 years after the appearance of the Papez paper, Gibbs, Gibbs, and Fuster (1948) published an article that in retrospect must be

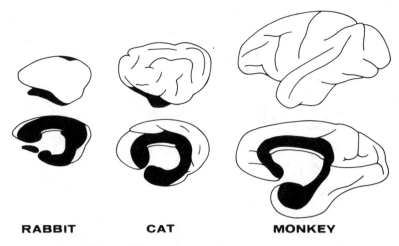

RABBIT   CAT   MONKEY

FIGURE 6.4. Lateral and medial views of three well-known laboratory animals, illustrating, as Broca depicted in the many figures of his 1878 paper, that the limbic lobe has evolved as a common denominator of the mammalian brain. The limbic cortex is shown in black and the neocortex in white. Adapted by permission from MacLean (1954, p. 106).

considered a landmark in the history of neurology and the knowledge of the cerebral substrate of emotion. They drew attention to an ictal condition called psychomotor epilepsy, in which there may be no convulsion, but during which the patient experiences a variety of emotional feelings followed by amnesia and automatisms. With scalp electrodes, they found that in most cases the epileptogenic disturbance appeared to involve the anterior temporal region. That same year, my own research required the recording of electrical activity at the base of the brain. Using an improved type of nasopharyngeal electrodes and newly devised tympanic electrodes, Arellano and I recorded both the standard and basal electroencephalogram (EEG) in a group of patients with psychomotor symptoms, but no localizing signs in previous EEGs (MacLean & Arellano, 1950). In recordings during light sleep (as recommended by Gibbs et al., 1948), the majority of these cases showed spiking activity with maximum amplitude of the spike in recordings from one or the other nasopharyngeal leads. Since the nasopharyngeal electrode is the one nearest the medial aspect of the temporal lobe, we suggested that the focus of the disturbance might be in the hippocampal formation.

Since the hippocampal formation was considered part of the olfactory system, how were we to explain that the symptoms of psychomotor epilepsy included not only a wide range of emotional feelings with viscerosomatic manifestations, but also symptoms involving the

visual, auditory, and somaesthetic systems? It was then that I stumbled upon the Papez paper and had the good fortune to visit him, with the purpose of asking whether he could account anatomically for these same questions. With a specimen of the human brain, he showed by dissection cortical association pathways that could potentially connect visual, auditory, and somatic neocortical areas with the hippocampal gyrus, which in turn connects with the hippocampus. Later, our neuronographic studies in the monkey (Pribram & MacLean, 1953) offered experimental support for such inputs to the hippocampal gyrus, and subsequent neuroanatomical studies gave confirmation to such stepwise connections (e.g., Jones & Powell, 1970; Van Hoesen & Pandya, 1975). Of greater interest, our recordings from single nerve units in squirrel monkeys and our anatomical studies provided evidence of more direct connections via the brainstem, not only for these modalities, but also for interoceptive systems (see MacLean, 1990, for a detailed summary).

Subsequent to my visit to Papez, I wrote a paper citing new experimental and clinical evidence in support of his theory of emotion (MacLean, 1949). Pointing out the possible connections of the visual, auditory, and somatic systems with the hippocampal formation, together with inputs from other extero- and interoceptive systems, I noted that there would be the possibility "for bringing into association not only oral (smell, taste, mouth) sensations, but also impressions from the sex organs, body

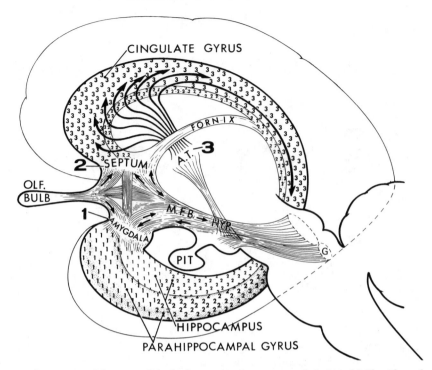

FIGURE 6.5. Three main subdivisions of the limbic system. Large numerals 1, 2, and 3 identify nuclear groups of the respective amygdalar, septal, and thalamo-cingulate divisions. Small numerals overlie limbic cortical areas predominantly interconnected with these respective nuclear groups. See text regarding functions. AT, anterior thalamic nuclei; G, dorsal and ventral tegmental nuclei of Gudden; HYP, hypothalamus; M, mammillary bodies; MFB, medial forebrain bundle; PIT, pituitary; OLF, olfactory. Adapted by permission from MacLean (1973, p. 14).

wall, eye, and ear" (p. 351). The main thesis of the article was that this part of the limbic lobe derives information in terms of emotional feelings and "eludes the grasp of the intellect because its animalistic and primitive structure makes it impossible to communicate in verbal terms" (p. 348). "This situation," I suggested, "provides a clue to understanding the difference between what we 'feel' and what we 'know'" (p. 351). In the title of the paper, I referred to the limbic lobe as the "visceral brain" as a means of reducing the accent on olfactory functions conveyed by the familiar term rhinencephalon. In its 16th-century meaning, "visceral" applies to strong inward feelings and their associated visceral manifestations. The word, however, proved to be subject to misinterpretation because in the modern sense it applies strictly to the viscera. As a way around this, I took advantage of Broca's descriptive word "limbic" and referred to the limbic cortex and its primary brainstem connections as the "limbic system." This explains how this term was introduced into the literature in 1952 (MacLean, 1952).

Functions of Three Main Subdivisions of the Limbic System

The limbic lobe is enveloped by two concentric rings of cortex: (1) an inner ring of the evolutionarily oldest cortex, called archicortex; and (2) an outer ring called mesocortex, because it is transitional between archicortex and neocortex. On the basis of anatomical connections, together with electrophysiological and neurobehavioral findings, the limbic system can be divided into three main subdivisions. In Figure 6.5, the cortical areas of the subdivisions are respectively identified by the overlying numerals 1, 2, and 3. The primary nuclear hub for each division is correspondingly labeled by larger numerals.

Experimental Findings

The following account can give only a brief summary of the extensive experimental work applicable to the three subdivisions in question. Elsewhere, in an illustrated review (MacLean, 1973, 1990) I have given references to some of the most significant contributions.

The Amygdalar Division. The amygdala and the septum provide the nuclear hubs of the correspondingly labeled amygdalar and septal divisions. These nuclear groups can be traced back to fish, where they are located side by side. As illustrated in Figure 6.5, in mammals they are more distantly separated, but retain strong connections with the olfactory apparatus along with those of the brainstem. With respect to emotional behavior, it is first of all noteworthy that electrical stimulation in commonly used laboratory animals elicits angry or defensive forms of behavior. In addition, stimulation induces searching, sniffing, and a wide range of oral responses, including those involved in feeding and alimentation.

As first shown in monkeys by Brown and Schäfer in 1888 and rediscovered by Klüver and Bucy over 50 years later, bilateral temporal ablations including the amygdala and hippocampus induce a reverse effect of the emotional changes seen with stimulation— resulting in a profound vapidity particularly marked by a loss of response to fear-inducing situations (see Klüver & Bucy, 1939). Comparable changes have been observed in human beings. Clinically, it has been recognized since 1900 that bilateral damage or destruction of the hippocampus results in a loss of memory of ongoing experience (anterograde amnesia).

In summary, the experimental findings indicate that the amygdalar division is primarily involved in oral-related behavior as it pertains to feeding and the search for food, as well as the angry and defensive behavior that may be required in obtaining food. In a word, the amygdalar division plays a basic role in functions that ensure self-preservation.

The Septal Division. In contrast to the amygdalar division, the septal division appears to promote primarily procreative functions. At the most basic level, for example, electrical stimulation of the septum near the midline elicits genital tumescence at regular, short latencies in both male and female squirrel monkeys. Genital erection can also be elicited by stimulation in certain parts of the proximoseptal part of the hippocampus in squirrel monkeys and other laboratory animals. In male cats, grooming, pleasure reactions, and other behaviors seen in courtship have also been elicited by electrical or cholinergic stimulation of the proximoseptal part of the hippocampus. In summary, the septal division appears to be primarily concerned with primal sexual functions and behavior conducive to procreation. Apropos of the functions of the third subdivision (described next), it should also be noted that there is evidence in rodents of an incipient involvement of the septum in maternal behavior.

The Thalamocingulate Division. It is the thalamocingulate division that is of primary interest in regard to the evolution of the limbic system in mammals and the development of the above-mentioned family-related triad that distinguishes the transition from reptiles to mammals. This third limbic subdivision, labeled "3" in Figure 6.5, consists of the mesocortical part of the cingulate gyrus and its associated thalamic nuclei. Significantly, there is no definite representation of any part of this division in the reptilian brain. Stamm (1955) appears to have been the first to have made the important observation that ablations of the cingulate cortex interfere with the various acts of maternal behavior. His experiments were performed on rats and have since been confirmed by Slotnick (1967) and others.

We ourselves have confirmed their findings on maternal behavior in another kind of experiment, which involved making cortical lesions in neonatal hamsters. While waiting for these animals to mature, we happened upon a serendipitous finding implicating the cingulate cortex in another constituent of the above-mentioned behavioral triad. Those pups in which the entire neocortex proved to be absent grew and developed normally, manifesting every form of hamster-typical behavior. But unexpectedly and most notably, those with additional absence of the cingulate cortex failed to develop play behavior at the expected time (13th postnatal day) or thereafter (Murphy et al., 1981).

The third element of the family-related triad is audiovocal communication for maintaining maternal–offspring contact. The earliest mammals are presumed to have been tiny, possibly nocturnal animals living on the dark floor of the forest. If so, it is evident how vocalization would have helped to ensure communication. As already mentioned, the separation cry may rank as the earliest and most basic mammalian vocalization, serving originally to help assure contact of the mother with her young, and then, as a later development, contact of members of an affiliated group. The only studies known thus far to have focused on the cerebral representation of the cry have been performed on squirrel monkeys. The results of ablating areas of the medial frontal cortex indicated that a strip of rostral limbic cingulate cortex is necessary for the spontaneous production of the cry in adult monkeys isolated while being tested in a sound-reducing chamber (MacLean & Newman, 1988).

In concluding this summary of experimental findings relevant to the family-related behavioral triad, I should also note that the cortical area involved in the production of the separation cry has been found to receive an innervation from thalamic nuclei known to be involved in the perception of pain. In this respect, it is also most relevant that the cingulate cortex has a high concentration of opiate receptors, and that morphine eliminates the separation cry in monkeys, dogs, and other animals. It is of reciprocal interest that morphine also interferes with maternal behavior.

Clinical Findings

As has been emphasized, the study of the phenomenology of psychomotor epilepsy is more important than anything else in considering the cerebral evolution of emotion. This is because the patients' symptoms provide not only the best evidence, but also the only subjective evidence, that structures of the limbic system play a primary role in the experience of affects. The actual pinpointing of limbic structures in the generation of emotional feelings has derived from observations made during stimulation and recording of the exposed brain in the course of therapeutic neurosurgical procedures. The pre-eminent contributions in this respect were those of Penfield and Jasper (1954) and their colleagues at the Montreal Neurological Institute. Among their findings were those indicative of a slowly progressive scarring process originating in the hippocampus and creeping out to involve the adjacent cortex. The region of damage had a yellowish color and felt rubbery. There was good evidence in many cases that the condition was the result of birth injury. But there are multiple causes of psychomotor epilepsy, including head injury, the affinity of certain viruses for limbic structures, febrile convulsions, and so on. With stimulation at the site of an epileptogenic focus in or near limbic structures, it has been possible to reproduce not only the patient's ictal symptoms, but also the subsequent automatism with its associated amnesia (e.g., Feindel & Penfield, 1954). It is of profound significance that during the associated seizure discharge, the propagating nerve impulses tend to stay within the limbic system. The same situation has been observed in animals, in which a much more extensive mapping has been made of propagating after discharges. Nothing provides a more dramatic demonstration of the integration of the limbic system and the schizophysiology, as it were, between limbic and neocortical functions.

Ictal Affects. In psychomotor epilepsy, the affects experienced during the aura can be explained by reference again to the sphere in Figure 6.2. First of all, it will be recalled that the affects in general have a dual polarity, being either agreeable or disagreeable. The diagram shows the agreeable affects in the northern hemisphere and the disagreeable in the southern. At the equator, there are no neutral affects because by definition affects are either agreeable or disagreeable. This contention is sometimes countered by the statement that some people complain that they are no longer happy or disturbed by anything, but the complaint itself is testimony that the very vacuity of feeling is disturbing. Given this background, one finds that the reported symptoms of patients with psychomotor epilepsy include in one case or another what are denoted in the diagram as "basic," "specific," and "general" affects. The basic affects include agreeable or disagreeable feelings associated with basic bodily needs, such as the feeling of hunger with the need for food; the feeling of thirst with the need for water; and all the feelings conjoined with the need to breathe, to rid the body of waste, to satisfy sexual feelings, and so on. The specific affects are agreeable or disagreeable feelings associated with the special sensory systems, having reference to odors, tastes, somatic feelings, sounds, and visual perceptions. They include the so-called "cultural" affects. The specific affects of the aura provide a powerful illustration of the capacity of limbic mechanisms to affect and modulate the intensity and amplitude of feelings and perceptions: Sounds may seem to grow unusually loud or faint; as in delirium, an extremity may seem swollen to large proportions; things seen may seem near or far.

As explained in the introduction, the general affects are so called because they are feelings that may be associated with things, individuals, or situations. They represent what are usually regarded as emotional feelings. With the aura at the beginning of an epileptic storm, the patient's mind will light up with feelings that in one case or another range all the way from intense fear or terror to ecstasy. The general affects are of six main kinds, which may be designated as (1) feelings of desire; (2) fearful feelings; (3) angry feelings; (4) dejected feelings; (5) gratulant feelings; and (6) feelings of affection. As I note later, gratulant affects include feelings that have profound implications for epistemology. A patient may have Eureka-type feelings of discovery; feelings of revelation; feelings of enhanced reality; convictions that what is being experienced is of the utmost importance, that it's the absolute truth, that it's what the world is all about. *Significantly, these feelings are free-floating, being completely unattached to any particular thing, situation, or idea.*

Finally, the symptoms of psychomotor epilepsy call attention to two indeterminate types of affects. First of all, patients commonly experience a feeling of familiarity or strangeness, or sometimes an alternation of these two opposite feelings, suggesting a cerebral substrate of reciprocal innervation. Since the familiar may be felt as either pleasant or unpleasant, and since the same would apply to feelings of strangeness, neither would fall into the northern or southern hemisphere of the diagram. Rather, they may be compared to the earth's atmosphere, having the capacity to move from one to the other. Second, there are indeterminate affects associated with time and space. For example, patients may report that they have the feeling that time is speeding up or slowing down, or, in regard to space, that a room seems to be of huge proportions.

Ictal Expression of Emotion. During the automatism subsequent to the aura, the unconscious behavior may be in keeping with the remembered feelings of the aura. Following a horrifying feeling of fear or terror, for example, a patient may run screaming to someone for protection. Or after a feeling of anger, there may be angry vocalization and pugilistic behavior, with the arms flailing somewhat like those of a fighting chimpanzee. Or there may be gorilla-like hooting and striking of the chest. An opposite sort of behavior is that of a woman who would walk around her room showing marked affection to anyone present, or that of a 20-year-old woman in whom "each slight seizure was followed by a paroxysm of kissing" (Gowers, 1881).

The question as to what cerebral structures account for crying and laughter continues to be one of the most enigmatic in clinical neurology. Our finding that ablation of the rostral cingulate cortex in adult *Saimiri* monkeys eliminates the spontaneous production of the separation cry made it desirable to review clinical case material in regard to the localization of epileptogenic foci and lesions associated with epileptic crying and laughter, as well as locations where electrical stimulation resulted in these manifestations during neurosurgical intervention. The outcome of the review is too detailed to be described here, but it may be summarized by saying that with respect to both the somatic manifestations and lacrimation, the involved structures were located along the "Papez circuit" diagrammed in Figure 6.6—namely, the *rostral* hippocampal formation and adjacent amygdala; the mammillary bodies (M); the anterior thalamus (A); and the midline fronto-cingulate cortex (MacLean, 1990, pp. 534-538). Under ictal conditions, just as in everyday life, there may be an alternation of crying and laughter, suggesting that these manifestations have an underlying reciprocal innervation.

Ictal Automatisms: Insights into Ontology and Memory. After the beginning of a limbic storm, manifested by the aura, the ictal discharge increases in intensity and spreads further into the limbic system. From the moment of a bilateral spread, the lights go out, so to speak, in the limbic system, and the patient develops automatic behavior that ranges from simple to very complex automatisms. Throughout that entire period there is absolutely no memory for anything that happened. Nevertheless, as illustrated by Jackson's famous Case Z, the patient may be capable of skilled performance and cognitive function depending on the neocortex. Case Z was that of a physician who, during a limbic seizure found to result from a small cavity at the junction of the amygdala and hippocampus, examined a patient, made a correct diagnosis, and wrote a prescription—all with no memory of it afterwards (Jackson & Colman, 1898).

It has been recognized for many years that extensive bilateral damage of the hippocampus

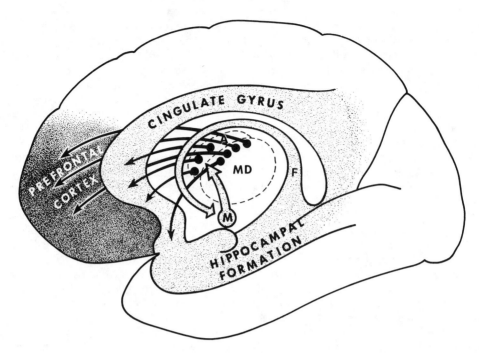

FIGURE 6.6. Diagram of "the Papez circuit" (light shading) for illustrating (1) loci implicated in crying and laughter (see text), and (2) the evolutionary linkage with the granulofrontal neocortex (dark shading). A, anterior thalamic nuclei; F, fornix; M, mammillary bodies; MD, medial dorsal nucleus. Adapted by permission from MacLean (1973, p. 44).

may result in the failure to recall ongoing experience (anterograde amnesia). Why the loss of memory for what happens during the automatism? I have suggested that a bilateral propagation of a limbic seizure amounts to a temporary "functional ablation" of the hippocampus and related structures involved in the registration and retention of ongoing experience.

But why, nevertheless, the loss of memory? Attempting to answer this question requires one further to ask what accounts for a sense of individuality. Without a sense of personal identity, there is, so to speak, no place to deposit a memory. Through introspection, there unfolds the realization that a sense of personal identity depends upon an integration of externally and internally derived experience. Whereas the neocortex receives its information primarily from the exteroceptive systems (somatic, auditory, visual), microelectrode studies have shown that the limbic cortex receives information not only from these systems, but also from the olfactory, gustatory, and visceroceptive systems. It should be emphasized that the hippocampus is a neural network where all these systems converge. Because of the regu-

larity with which they found that automatisms and amnesia occurred with afterdischarges triggered by medial temporal stimulation, Feindel and Penfield (1954) were of the opinion that the hippocampal formation and amygdala are requisite for the registration of memories. Relevant to the retention of neocortical function during limbic seizures, it has been observed experimentally that at the same time there is no change in the configuration of neocortical potentials evoked by natural sensory stimulation (Flynn, MacLean, & Kim, 1961).

Further comment on the significance of this clinical material is deferred until after a consideration of the role of neocortical systems in affective experience and emotional expression.

THE NEOMAMMALIAN BRAIN

Finally, in considering the role of neocortical systems in emotional experience and expression, we run up against another of the most difficult problems requiring neurological explication. Through introspection, we recognize that just as "emotions" can arouse either quiet or tumultuous thoughts, so also can thoughts arouse quiet or tumultuous emotions. But unlike our knowledge about the modular components of our computers, an understanding of the interworking neural systems seems a long way off.

If, as pictured in Figure 6.4, the cortex of the limbic lobe is imagined as a common denominator of the mammalian brain, then the neocortex (shown in white) would compare to an expanding numerator. As we have seen, the phenomenology of psychomotor epilepsy indicates that without a cofunctioning limbic system, the neocortex would fare like a disembodied spirit. In terms of enhancing the possibilities of survival of the animal basically depending on striatal and limbic mechanisms, it is tempting, in computer language, to compare the evolution of the neocortex to the progressive enlargement of a central processor to which an expanding memory and intelligence are added for increasing the chances of survival.

The Prefrontal Cortex

Of all the neocortical areas, the cortex in the forward half of the frontal lobe is most clearly identified with emotional cerebration. This cortex is characterized by a narrow granular layer 4 and is hereafter referred to as the "granulofrontal cortex." The medial dorsal nucleus, with which it is predominantly associated, appears like a great egg in a nest of a large medial group of nuclei that innervate extensive areas of limbic cortex. It is notable that in keeping with this location, a large percentage of its cells have been found to respond to stimulation of the great visceral nerve (vagus). This large medial group lies cupped within a massive group of lateral nuclei that relate exteroceptive systems to most of the remaining neocortex.

If anything positive came out of the medically bleak days of frontal lobotomy, it was the confirmation that the granulofrontal cortex is involved in anticipation and planning. This is a matter of utmost importance for gaining insight into neural mechanisms of emotion, because with its capacity to anticipate and to plan, the frontal cortex affords an endless number of prospects that at the emotional level can induce concern and anxiety or joyful anticipation. Anxiety may be defined as the unpleasant affect associated with the anticipation of the unknown outcome of future events. It was

this symptom that, more than any other, was alleviated by frontal lobotomy.

The granulofrontal cortex has also been credited as a neural substrate of empathic and altruistic feelings. It has been suggested that through its visceral connections (see above), it derives "insight" for the foresight involved in empathic concern for the future welfare of others as well as the self. Apropos of foresight and the requisite capacity to *envision*, it has connections with visual parts of the pulvinar nucleus, as well as strong association connections with visual cortical areas. In regard to empathy ("feeling into"), mention should also be made of its connections with parts of the pulvinar projecting to the somatic cortex. Horton (1976) has accumulated evidence that patients with a defective empathic sense have symptoms comparable to those of a person with parietal lobe dysfunction.

What factors contributed to the evolution of empathic and altruistic feelings? Granted complete ignorance of causative mechanisms, one can only note some of the conspicuous road signs. As has been indicated, lizards must fend for themselves from the day of hatching. They are essentially solitary creatures. A contrary situation is posed by the evolution of nursing, in which the female must assume responsibility for survival of the young. Hence one might say that a sense of caring with its responsibilities originated with nursing. In referring above to Figure 6.6, I have pointed out that the evolving granulofrontal cortex is strongly linked to the thalamocingulate division implicated in the family-related behavioral triad. Through such culminating developments, it might be supposed that a sense of parental responsibility generalizes to other members of the species, becoming what we variously qualify as conscience, empathic concern, and altruism.

In this connection I refer again to crying and laughter, which in many respects deserve to rank along with language as expressive of the human condition. When mammals opted for a family way of life, they set the stage for one of the most distressful forms of suffering—namely, separation, which for human beings commonly reaches an extreme with separation by death. Possible reasons for the painful (and, by definition, affective) nature of the separation cry have been referred to earlier. Physiologically, both the somatic and autonomic manifestations of crying and laughter are of the kind that would rid the body and wash away something noxious. With crying the affect is one of dejection, and with laughing it is one of relief. Although gorillas and chimpanzees display elements of crying and laughter, only human beings are known to shed tears in either circumstance. Why should this be? Just as the use of fire has been discussed as an explanation of the unusually large human cerebrum and great increase of intelligence, so might its product, smoke, be considered in connection with the evolution of the expression of human feelings (MacLean, 1990, p. 556 ff.). There is a hominid association with fire dating back 1.4 million years, and it may have been transported from place to place since the beginning of bipedalism. Only mention can be made here of the numerous prehistory uses of fire, including its uses for warmth and light in caves and elsewhere; for cooking; for ground-fire hunting; for cauterizing wounds; and so on. Since painful stimulation, including the irritation of smoke, is sufficient to elecit tearing, it is evident that the habitual use of fire would have provided abundant opportunities for smoke to induce reflex tearing. Hence, I have suggested that in addition to reflex tearing, it would also have provided countless occasions for psychologically conditioned reflex tearing during activities centering around fire, including the ceremonies involved in disposing of departed loved ones by cremation.

If as in rodents, it is shown in primates that the thalamocingulate division is implicated in play, it would help to explain the close and apparently reciprocal relationship of crying and laughter referred to above. But it has always seemed paradoxical that when we experience the relief and inner rejoicing of seeing an altruistic act, we so often at the same time are prone to misting of the eyes or even crying. Given the mechanisms for reciprocal crying and laughter, is it possible that the seemingly paradoxical manifestations are owing to a high order of generalization, whereby feelings identified with crying situations of childhood compete with those of relief experienced upon parental rescue?

CONCLUDING PERSPECTIVE

It has been said that "something does not exist until you give it a name." But the study of the phenomenology of psychomotor epilespsy would indicate that there is a precondition, and that something does not exist unless it achieves a reality through limbic mechanisms involved in self-awareness and in the registration and recall of ongoing experience.

Given this all-important affective role of the limbic system in a continuing sense of personal being, two other considerations relevant to the respective functions of the limbic and neocortical systems have profound epistemic implications. As I have mentioned, the study of limbic epilepsy indicates that we are dependent on the limbic system for the affective feelings of conviction that we attach to our beliefs, regardless of whether they are true or false. It is one thing to have this primitive, untutored mind to assure us of the authenticity of food or mate, but how can we rely on its judgments for conviction in the truth of our ideas, concepts, and theories? The resulting unresolvable uncertainty is compounded by the artifactual consequences of the logical functions of the neocortex. These are the artifacts owing to the unavoidable self-reference that cannot be purged from logical systems of any complexity. As one critic has commented, the consequence amounts to an endless hall of mirrors of self-reflection (Bronowski, 1966).

There is at least one compensation for the apparent inability of ever extricating ourselves from the resulting mire of ignorance and uncertainty, and this is the satisfaction that can be derived from human values for which there are no measures. For one such value, our eyes may look up to the evolving granulofrontal cortex, which is strongly interconnected with the thalamocingulate division involved in family-related behavior. As I have pointed out, its tie-in with parental concerns may have favored the development of the capacity for altruistic and empathic feelings, and, more than that, the capacity to imagine them as working in future situations. Remarkably, the reaches of the human brain have made it possible for the projection of this concern to generalize not only to one's own progeny, but also to the regional family, the national family, and the world-wide human family. More remarkably still, for the first time in the known history of biology, we are witnessing the evolution of a spirit with a concern for the future suffering and dying of all living things.

Acknowledgments. I wish to thank Susan V. Mann and Alison Stokes MacLean for their technical help in preparing this chapter.

REFERENCES

Broca, P. (1878). Anatomie comparée des circonvolutions cérébrales: Le grand lobe limbique et la scissure limbique dans la série des mammifères. *Revue d'Anthropologie, 1,* 385–498.

Bronowski, J. (1966). The logic of the mind. *American Scientist, 54,* 1–14.

Brown, S., & Schäfer, E. A. (1888). An investigation into the functions of the occipital and temporal lobes of the monkey's brain. *Philosophical Transactions of the Royal Society of London Series B, 179,* 303–327.

Caine, E. D., Hunt, R. D., Weingartner, H., & Ebert, M. H. (1978). Huntington's dementia: Clinical and neuropsychological features. *Archives of General Psychiatry, 35,* 377–384.

Cooney, B. (1991). *A hylomorphic theory of mind.* New York: Peter Lang.

Descartes, R. (1967). The passions of the soul. In E. S. Haldane & G. R. T. Ross (Eds.), *Philosophical works of Descartes* (pp. 332–427). New York: Dover. (Original work published 1649)

Falck, B., Hillarp, N.-A., Thieme, G., & Torp, A. (1962). Fluorescence of catecholamines and related compounds condensed with formaldehyde. *Journal of Histochemistry and Cytochemistry, 10,* 348–354.

Feindel, W., & Penfield, W. (1954). Localization of discharge in temporal lobe automatism. *Archives of Neurology and Psychiatry, 72,* 605–630.

Flynn, J. P., MacLean, P. D., & Kim, C. (1961). Effects of hippocampal afterdischarges on conditioned responses. In D. E. Sheer (Ed.), *Electrical stimulation of the brain* (pp. 382–386). Austin: University of Texas Press.

Gibbs, E. L., Gibbs, F. A., & Fuster, B. (1948). Psychomotor epilepsy. *Archives of Neurology and Psychiatry, 60,* 331–339.

Gowers, W. R. (1881). *Epilepsy and other chronic convulsive diseases: Their causes, symptoms, and treatment.* New York: William Wood.

Gregory, W. K. (1967). *Our face from fish to man.* New York: Hafner. (Original work published 1927)

Haeckel, E. (1876). *The history of creation or the development of the earth and its inhabitants by the action of natural causes.* (2 vols., E. R. Lankester, Trans.). London: King.

Haymaker, W. (1956). *Bings's local diagnosis in neurological diseases.* St.Louis: C. V. Mosby.

Hofstadter, D. R. (1977). *Gödel, Escher, Bach: An eternal golden braid.* New York: Random House.

Horton, P. C. (1976). Personality disorder and parietal lobe dysfunction. *American Journal of Psychiatry, 133,* 782–785.

Jackson, J. H., & Colman, W. S. (1898). Case of epilepsy with tasting movements and "dreamy state"—very small patch of softening in the left uncinate gyrus. *Brain, 21,* 580–590.

Jones, E. G., & Powell, T. P. S. (1970). An anatomical study of converging sensory pathways within the cerebral cortex of the monkey. *Brain, 93,* 793–820.

Klüver, H., & Bucy, P. C. (1939). Preliminary analysis of functions of the temporal lobes in monkeys. *Archives of Neurology and Psychiatry, 42,* 979–1000.

Koelle, G. B. (1954). The histochemical localization of cholinesterases in the central nervous system of the rat. *Journal of Comparative Neurology, 100,* 211–228.

Laplane, D., Levasseur, M., Pillon, B., DuGois, B., Baulac, M., Masoyer, B., Tran Dinh, S., Sette, G., & Baron, J. C. (1989). Obsessive–compulsive and other behavioural changes with bilateral basal gangliar lesions: A neuropsychological, magnetic resonance imaging, and positron tomography study. *Brain, 112,* 699–725.

MacLean, P. D. (1949). Psychosomatic disease and the "visceral brain": Recent developments bearing on the Papez theory of emotion. *Psychosomatic Medicine, 11,* 338–353.

MacLean, P. D. (1952). Some psychiatric implications of physiological studies on frontotemporal portion of limbic system (visceral brain). *Electroencephalography and Clinical Neurophysiology, 4,* 407–418.

MacLean, P. D. (1954). The limbic system and its hippocampal formation: Studies in animals and their possible application to man. *Journal of Neurosurgery, 11,* 29–44.

MacLean, P. D. (1967). The brain in relation to empathy and medical education. *Journal of Nervous and Mental Disease, 144,* 374–382.

MacLean, P. D. (1970). The triune brain, emotion, and scientific bias. In F. O. Schmitt (Ed.), *The neurosciences: Second study program* (pp. 336–349). New York: Rockefeller University Press.

MacLean, P. D. (1973). *A triune concept of the brain and behavior.* Toronto: University of Toronto Press.

MacLean, P. D. (1990). *The triune brain in evolution: Role in paleocerebral functions.* New York: Plenum Press.

MacLean, P. D., & Arellano, Z. A. P. (1950). Basal lead studies in epileptic automatisms. *Electroencephalography and Clinical Neurophysiology, 2,* 1–16.

MacLean, P. D., & Newman, J. D. (1988). Role of midline frontolimbic cortex in production of the isolation call of squirrel monkeys. *Brain Research, 450,* 111–123.

Murphy, M. R., MacLean, P. D., & Hamilton, S. C. (1981). Species-typical behavior of hamsters deprived from birth of the neocortex. *Science, 213,* 459–461.

Noble, G. K. (1936). Function of the corpus striatum in the social behavior of fishes. *Anatomy Records, 64,* 34.

Osler, W. (1894). *On chorea and choreiform affections.* Philadelphia: P. Blakiston.

Papez, J. W. (1937). A proposed mechanism of emotion. *Archives of Neurology and Psychiatry, 38,* 725–743.

Penfield, W., & Jasper, H. (1954). *Epilepsy and the functional anatomy of the human brain.* Boston: Little, Brown.

Pribram, K. H., & MacLean, P. D. (1953). Neuronographic analysis of medial and basal cerebral cortex: II. Monkey. *Journal of Neurophysiology, 16,* 324–340.

Rosenblueth, A., Wiener, N., & Bigelow, J. (1943). Behavior, purpose, and teleology. *Philosophical Science, 10,* 18–24.

Slotnick, B. M. (1967). Disturbances of maternal behavior in the rat following lesions of the cingulate cortex. *Behaviour, 24,* 204–236.

Smith, G. E. (1919). The significance of the cerebral cortex (Croonian Lectures). *British Medical Journal, i,* 796–797; *ii,* 11–12.

Stamm, J. S. (1955). The function of the median cerebral cortex in maternal behavior of rats. *Journal of Comparative Physiology and Psychology, 48,* 347–356.

Van Hoesen, G. W., & Pandya, D. N. (1975). Some connections of the entorhinal (area 28) and perirhinal (area 35) cortices of the rhesus monkey: I. Temporal lobe afferents. *Brain Research, 95,* 1–24.

Wegener, A. J. (1915). *Die Entstehung der Kontinente und Ozeane.* Leipzig: Vieweg.

West, B. J., & Goldberger, A. L. (1987). Physiology in fractal dimensions. *American Scientist, 75,* 354–365.

Wiener, N. (1948). *Cybernetics, or control and communication in the animal and the machine.* New York: Wiley.

II

BIOLOGICAL AND NEUROPHYSIOLOGICAL APPROACHES TO EMOTION

7

Neurochemical Control of Moods and Emotions: Amino Acids to Neuropeptides

JAAK PANKSEPP

INTRODUCTION

Despite the many controversies surrounding the number, nature, and nuances of basic emotions (e.g., see Turner & Ortony, 1992, and accompanying commentaries), neuroscientific evidence strongly supports the existence of a number of genetically ingrained emotional operating systems in the brain (Panksepp, 1982, 1986b, 1989, 1990, 1992b). Neurobiological facts have yet to penetrate psychological conceptions in the field, and prominent investigators still tend to make misleading claims—for example, that "no neural programs . . . have been found for the 'basic' emotions" (Zajonc & McIntosh, 1992, p. 73). Although emotional circuits revealed in "lower" animals are difficult to relate to neuropsychological issues in humans, the translation is not impossible (MacLean, 1990; Panksepp, 1985). Of course, a definitive list of distinct types of emotive processes must remain open until more is known about the functional organization of the human brain, but considerable knowledge exists about the circuitries of rage, fear, separation distress, maternal nurturance, anticipatory eagerness, and various facets of sexuality in other animals. Because of the enormous degree of genetic homology that exists between humans and other mammals, and because of straightforward evolutionary constraints (i.e., evolution can only build on previous solutions), it is likely that these data relate well to the basic facets of the human condition. Indeed, useful connections have been made between ideas derived from animal models and human clinical data and applications (Olivier, Mos, & Slangen, 1991; Panksepp, 1985; Panksepp & Sahley, 1987; Panksepp, Lensing, Bovard, & Leboyer, 1991).

Although our neurochemical understanding of emotions remains in its infancy (Panksepp, 1986a; Baum, Grunberg, & Singer, 1992), the neuroscientific revolution of the past two decades has provided a cornucopia of basic facts that provides many new mechanistic ways to determine how emotions are created in the mammalian brain (Panksepp, 1986b, 1991). In this chapter, I highlight the neurochemical systems that appear to be critical for a substantive psychobiological understanding of emotions. I do not cover the older literature concerning peripheral hormonal factors in emotionality (e.g., Cannon, 1929, to Baum et al., 1992), nor is there space to dwell at length on any one brain system. I also do not attempt to delve into the subtle conceptual and semantic distinctions that burden this field of inquiry, but they have been extensively discussed recently (Ekman & Davidson, in press). To provide a novel entry point into the vast and unintegrated literature relevant to the topic, I first speculate about the mechanistic relationships that exist between basic emotional systems in the brain and rapid-eye-movement (REM) sleep.

EMOTIONS AND DREAMING

An intimate relationship between dreaming and emotionality has been posited by thoughtful observers throughout the ages. Their interdependence is highlighted by the free flow of emotionality in the dream reports of humans, as well as the apparent emotionality of animals during REM sleep. The latter is evident when REM atonia is experimentally reduced through appropriately placed lesions around the locus coeruleus of the brainstem (Sastre & Jouvet, 1979). Such animals act out the oneric states that permeate their dreams, and exhibit a limited number of emotive behavior sequences—rage, fear, exploratory and predatory behavior, and self-grooming. Such animals appear to be spontaneously cycling through genetically preordained psychobehavioral subroutines heavily laden with affective content. What a peculiar "thing," this dreaming process—this spontaneous unreeling of emotionality that mammals exhibit as part of an ancient neural heritage, which may predate what we now deem waking consciousness.

Which Came First . . . Waking or the Dream?

At first glance, the question of whether waking or dreaming came first seems perplexingly obtuse. But it is not. Modern neuroscience suggests that the REM generator is situated in more primitive (i.e., caudal) areas of the brainstem (Hobson, Lydic, & Baghdoyan, 1986; Jouvet, 1972) than the waking apparatus of the ascending reticular activating system (ARAS). For instance, cats that have midpontine, pretrigeminal transections exhibit REM below the cut, but the waking state without any REM above the cut (Moruzzi, 1972). Although we cannot be certain about the temporal history of brain evolution, the traditional perspective that it generally follows a caudorostral trajectory suggests that REM apparatus probably evolved before the classical waking mechanisms of the ARAS, which controls attentional aspects of exteroceptive sensory processing through thalamic nuclei (Steriade & Llinas, 1988). In short, the anatomical evidence suggests that the dream (at least its executive circuitry) evolved before waking. How could this be? A way out of this apparent paradox is to suppose that the ancient REM mechanisms, which still trigger human and animal dreamscapes, originally subserved a form of waking arousal (perhaps a selective form of limbic arousal that was eventually superceded by thalamo-cortical, ARAS-modulated arousal).

The presence of emotionality within REM consciousness may indicate that the REM mechanism orginally promoted and sustained tonic arousal of certain ancient "waking states," perhaps the primal circuits of the basic emotions. When the competitive edge of this type of primitive arousal was compromised by expanding brain evolution, its influence may have come to be restricted to specific occasions and to limited time periods (e.g., to be fully expressed only under tonic inhibitory bondage of REM atonia). By restricting the free flow of emotionality to REM periods, the dreaming process may have emerged to provide a new and subservient background role to waking behavior—the role of sorting, reprocessing, and consolidating important information that had confronted the organism during waking activities. Although emotional systems could still be fully aroused during the new ARAS-controlled form of waking, their more routine role in governing behavioral output may have been to provide a background of affective values for routine life choices (suggesting how subjectivity may have emerged). This scenario suggests a reason why "lower" vertebrates, and even some primitive mammalian species (such as echidnas, the marsupial spiny anteaters that inhabit Australia), have no REM sleep: Their waking activities may still be largely governed by the more ancient arousal system that eventually became the REM generator.

The Role of Brain Research in Understanding Emotions

The distinct emotional "energies" that can inundate the subjective experiences of human beings and the instinctive behaviors of animals probably arise from specific types of neurochemical activities of various subcortical circuits of the brain. The underlying neurodynamics of emotions cannot be revealed simply by a study of the external manifestations of emotions in either humans or animals. They must be revealed through brain research, especially animal brain research (Panksepp, 1991), although better neuroimaging techniques may eventually provide the needed empirical windows into the human brain (see

Zappulla, LeFever, Jaeger, & Bilder, 1991). Existing neurobiological evidence suggests that the basic emotions are instigated by executive systems consisting of longitudinally coursing neural circuits that can simultaneously control a vast amount of brain activity because of their widely distributed effects (Panksepp, 1985, 1989, 1991, 1992b). In this way, many behavioral, physiological, and psychological processes are coherently brought to bear on important life events. In short, it seems that basic emotional systems can arouse distinct forms of waking activity. They are "state control" systems that can interact with many layers of brain activity, via direct neural controls as well as more diffuse paracrine controls (e.g., release of substances into the cerebrospinal fluid [CSF] that can exert widespread nonsynaptic actions at a distance). Because the systems can exert global control over many layers of brain activity, emotions can take as many specific forms as there are types of encephalization in different species, even though many priniciples of deep organization will be conserved. These systems are ideally suited to provide state-specific coding for the formation and retrieval of memory traces. They provide a conceptual substrate for state-dependent and mood-congruent memory effects in humans, even though the physiological details are far from being worked out.

In addition to selecting psychological, behavioral, and physiological responses to deal rapidly with challenging environmental circumstances, emotional systems are surely modulated by many distinct regulatory controls (e.g., those that sustain the intensity and duration of emotive states, providing a multiplicity of neurochemical vectors for each emotional process). Clearly, some neurochemistries serve subsidiary roles, while others directly elaborate executive impulses for specific forms of emotionality. So what do we actually know about the neurochemistries that mediate emotionality? Since the advent of the neuroscience revolution, the possibilities are vast, but definitive evidence remains all too modest. After discussing the small, rapidly acting "classic" neurotransmitters (amino acids and biogenic amines), most of this chapter focuses on the larger and more persistently acting neuropeptides, since they are probably critical for establishing emotion- and mood-specific states in the nervous system.

THE NEUROCHEMISTRIES OF EMOTIONAL ENERGIES

One can seek to analyze the role of various neurochemistries in emotions by using the primary emotions as reference points (e.g., to describe the potential neurophysiological controls of rage, fear, sorrow, anticipatory eagerness, play, lust, pleasure, displeasure, etc). Since I have used that organizational pattern in several past reviews (Panksepp, 1981a, 1982, 1985, 1986a, 1990, 1991), in the present chapter I focus more on the individual chemistries, thereby minimizing redundant coverage. In addition to specific emotions and general mood states, I also include coverage of the role of these chemistries in activation and arousal as well as in some specific regulatory processes (e.g., fluid, energy, salt, temperature, and hormone homeostasis), since they are accompanied by distinct feeling states. In other words, the feelings of hunger, thirst, salt craving, and the various facets of sexuality (Komisaruk, Siegel, Cheng, & Feder, 1986) deserve as much attention from investigators of affective processes as the classic emotions. Since there are now literally thousands of relevant papers for each neurochemical system, to keep within space restrictions I refer liberally to reviews, too often to the exclusion of exhaustive research citations.

Simple Amino Acids

Unmodified neuroactive amino acids, such as glycine, glutamate, and alanine, may have been among the first neurotransmitters that evolved to mediate interneuronal communication. They are especially reasonable choices to signal important resources in the environment (because they are essential bodily nutrients), and thereby to facilitate and inhibit motor patterns that could compete for those resources. For instance, glutamate, which has been widely used as a taste enhancer (especially in Oriental cooking), is the most prolific excitatory neurotransmitter in the brain. It acts on at least three distinct receptor types (kainate, quisqualate, and N-methyl-D-aspartate [NMDA]), which figure heavily in the integration of central sensory and motor processes as well as of higher processes, including affective, memory, and cognitive activities (Farooqui & Horrocks, 1991). The basic motor plans for many emotions may be organized around glutaminergic neural transmission, since a large number of emotional fixed-action patterns can be evoked by local brain application of glutamate receptor agonists.

Glutamate and its analogues administered directly into the brain can precipitate aggressive rage (Bandler, 1988), as well as fear responses and separation-induced distress vocalizations (Panksepp, Normansell, Herman, Bishop, & Crepeau, 1988; Normansell & Panksepp, in press). However, it remains to be clearly demonstrated that these behavioral displays are accompanied by internally experienced affect. It remains possible that glutamate-evoked behaviors reflect pseudoaffective motor displays organized at quite a low level of the neuraxis. However, the ability of NMDA receptor blockade in higher brain areas such as the amygdala to modulate extinction of fear behaviors (Falls, Miserendino, & Davis, 1992; LeDoux, 1992) does suggest that this amino acid contributes to higher psychic processes related to fear.

One end product of glutamate metabolism in the brain is gamma-aminobutyric acid (GABA), the most prolific inhibitory transmitter in the brain. Since both glutamate and GABA evolved early in brain evolution, it is not surprising that they are both implicated in the excitatory and inhibitory control of many primitive emotional processes. GABA probably participates in the inhibitory control of every active psychobehavioral process in the brain, and it figures especially heavily in psychiatric practice in the control of anxiety, through the ability of the benzodiazepine (BZ)-type minor tranquilizers to promote GABA inhibition on fear circuitry (Haefely, 1990; Panksepp, 1990). These agents were first discovered through their ability to control the apparent rage of wild zoo animals, and endogenous molecules that can interact with BZ receptors, such as diazepam-binding inhibitor, remain preeminent proanxiety candidates in the brain (Haefely, 1990). In some species BZs are very effective in reducing separation distress vocalizations, whereas they have very little effect in others (see Panksepp, Newman, & Insel, 1992 for discussion). Since GABA emerges from intermediary energy metabolism (through the GABA shunt that branches off from the Krebs cycle), it can also provide an analogue signal of long-term inhibitory control over feeding circuits (Panksepp & Meeker, 1980), and from that perspective it is not surprising that it

evolved to govern overall brain inhibition. Once enough energy has been acquired, and no emergencies loom on the horizon, the brain should be privy to general inhibition.

Biogenic Amines

Catecholamine systems in the brain—epinephrine (EPI), norepinephrine (NE), and dopamine (DA)—are central representations of the sympathetic nervous system that provide global control over metabolic, sensory, and motor arousal, respectively. NE appears to have a selective influence over sensory arousal (increasing signal-to-noise ratios in cortex), and this becomes especially prominent in high-affect situations. For instance, the NE cells of a feline locus coeruleus are especially responsive to a threatening dog (Jacobs, 1990). By contrast, DA systems have been implicated more in positive psychomotor processes, and they are especially prominent in the mediation of anticipatory eagerness (Panksepp, 1981a, 1986a; Willner & Scheel-Kruger, 1991); certain terminal fields also appear to be critical for the rewarding effects of such psychostimulants as cocaine and the amphetamines (Kuhar, Ritz, & Boja, 1991). Human positive emotionality has been related to heightened DA activity (Depue & Iacono, 1989), and different forms of depression may result from depletions of the individual catecholamine systems, whereas other forms result from depletion of brain serotonin (Willner, 1985).

Although brain indoleamines (i.e., serotonin) have been implicated as potential facilitators of specific emotions such as anxiety, this proposition remains very debatable (for a recent version of the controversy, see Deakin & Graff, 1991, and commentaries). There are a vast number of different receptor systems for this transmitter, which provides the possibility for a great deal of complexity. Although the receptor diversity may reflect behavioral specificities, a compelling general principle is that this system exerts general inhibitory control over many emotive processes (Panksepp, 1982, 1986a).

There are also a variety of trace amines in the brain, such as phenethylamine and histamine; these have remained poorly understood at a behavioral level, and there are only speculations about their functions. In this vein, Liebowitz (1983) entertained the idea that phenethylamine participates in the genesis of love.

Acetylcholine and
Purine Transmitters

Acetylcholine appears to be a key transmitter in mediating arousal and attentional processes in the brain (Napier, Kalivas, & Hanin, 1991; Steriade & Llinas, 1988), and it appears to have a direct influence on certain emotional processes. Rage responses can be precipitated by placement of cholinergic agonists into various areas of the brain, and separation-induced distress vocalizations can be activated by curare (Panksepp, 1989; Panksepp, Siviy, & Normansell, 1985; Panksepp et al., 1988). Cholinergic activity has been implicated in the mediation of punishment and memory in the brain, as well as specific motivational processes (e.g., thirst) and self-stimulation (Napier et al., 1991). In the context of the introductory remarks to this chapter, it is noteworthy that the executive structure of REM sleep in the nucleus reticularis pontis oralis (RPO) is partially cholinergic (Hobson et al., 1986), as is the ARAS–thalamic attentional/waking system (Napier et al., 1991; Steriade, Gloor, Llinas, Lose da Silva, & Mesulam, 1990).

Purine transmitters, such as adenosine, have provided a better understanding of weak mood enhancers such as caffeine, which block this type of neurochemical activity (Dunwiddie, 1986; Snyder, 1985). Adenosine is a natural soporific agent that generally suppresses behavioral activation, and adenosine receptors are especially enriched in the thalamic–neocortical axis, which figures prominently in the elaboration of waking consciousness.

NEUROPEPTIDES
AND EMOTIONS

The discovery of many longitudinally coursing neuropeptide systems in the brain has opened a new chapter in our potential understanding of the chemical coding of behavioral and physiological responses, including those that mediate emotional processes. Some neuropeptides may have executive roles in activating and inhibiting specific emotions, whereas others may have subsidiary roles, such as modulation of the intensity and duration of various integrated responses (Koob, Sandman, & Strand, 1990). For many neuropeptides, there is a harmony between their peripheral and central functions. For instance, insulin stores energy

peripherally and appears to facilitate satiety centrally (Woods & Porte, 1983). As detailed later, oxytocin (OXY) promotes childbirth and feeding peripherally, and maternal tendencies centrally. Throughout this chapter, many similar correspondences are noted. The neuropeptides are covered in five categories: (1) the hypothalamic neuropeptides, which are also posterior pituitary hormones and releasing factors for anterior pituitary hormones (molecules that are extensively represented within neural circuitries of the brain); (2) the anterior pituitary hormones, which are also expressed in brain circuits; (3) the endogenous opioid peptides; (4) gastrointestinal peptides, which have extensive circuitries within the brain; and (5) a variety of miscellaneous neuropeptides that have been discovered in the brain. All of the descriptions are thumbnail sketches, for it is impossible to cover any of the systems in detail.

Access to the detailed literature for many important peptides can be obtained through specialty journals such as *Peptides* and *Regulatory Peptides*, as well as a number of recent issues of the *Annals of the New York Academy of Sciences*. The *Annals* issues include in-depth coverage of substance P (Leeman, Krause, & Lembeck, 1991), cholecystokinin (CCK; Vanderhaeghen & Crawley, 1985), neuropeptide Y (NPY; Allen & Koenig, 1990), thyrotropin-releasing hormone (TRH; Metcalf & Jackson, 1989), bombesin (Tache, Melchiorri, & Negri, 1988), vasoactive intestinal peptide (VIP; Said & Mutt, 1988), corticotropin-releasing factor (CRF) and adrenocorticotropic hormone (ACTH; Krieger & Herbert, 1987), neurotensin (NT; Nemeroff & Prange, 1982), and most recently OXY (Pedersen, Caldwell, Jirikowski, & Insel, 1992). Some specific behavioral changes that can be seen after central neuropeptide administration, such as self-grooming, have also received focused attention (see Colbern & Gispen, 1988), as have the extensive relations to immune processes (O'Dorisio & Panerai, 1990).

Before proceeding to individual neuropeptides, I briefly address the conceptual issue of peripheral versus central mediators of emotionality. Although the James–Lange theory that peripheral autonomic changes precipitate the cascade of events leading to emotionality is no longer credible as a major vector, it deserves some renewed consideration because so many of the neuropeptide chemistries are represented in both brain and viscera, providing many potential avenues for "cross-talk" between central and peripheral processes. Since emotions are characterized by autonomic and thermoperceptive changes too numerous to detail here, it is worth emphasizing that neuropeptides promote a vast diversity of autonomic changes in the body (e.g., Negro-Vilar & Conn, 1988), including changes in body temperature (see Clark & Lipton, 1985; Pittman & Thornhill, 1990) and cardiovascular effects (Gardiner & Bennett, 1989). My aim here is to provide a brief overview of the behavioral effects of neuropeptides that implicate them in the central nervous system control of emotionality, even though this is not meant to rule out a role for peripheral peptides. Although most peripherally secreted neuropeptides have poor access to the brain, some do get in readily. For instance, large peptide hormones such as prolactin gain re-entry to the brain through active uptake mechanisms, and thereby come to modulate brain circuits that control emotive processes (MacLeod, Scapagnini, & Thorner, 1984). Most others, which cannot easily penetrate the brain, may have indirect reafferent influences by modulating peripheral viscerosensory processes that influence arousal circuits of the brain, including noradrenergic (e.g., locus coeruleus) and serotonergic (raphe) cell groups. In short, the newly revealed enteric peptide chemistries (Furness, Bornstein, Murphy, & Pompolo, 1992) provide many potential relations between peripheral and central processes in the modulation of emotionality.

Hypothalamic Neuropeptides

Hypothalamic neuropeptides, some of which control the release of pituitary hormones, play prominent roles in specific emotions. The most evidence presently exists for CRF, OXY, arginine vasopressin (AVP), and luteinizing hormone-releasing hormone (LH-RH), but several other potential key players also deserve mention.

Corticotropin-Releasing Factor

Activation of the pituitary adrenal stress response (ACTH-induced release of glucocorticoids) is triggered by the release of CRF from paraventricular hypothalamic neurons. Nearby CRF neurons, which give rise to intrinsic brain

circuits, course throughout the brainstem, and they instigate a coordinated central stress response that has a major impact on the elaboration of both fear/anxiety and separation distress in the brain (for recent reviews of this vast literature, see Baldwin, Britton, & Koob, 1990; Fisher & Brown, 1990). The key findings are as follows: (1) Central administration of CRF causes motor arousal accompanied by substantial behavioral agitation, which can promote various indices of fear, including freezing, potentiated startle, and increased behavioral responsivity to various stressors (Dunn & Berridge, 1990); (2) CRF can facilitate separation distress calls in primates and birds, even though it does just the reverse for the separation-induced ultrasonic calls of infant rodents—a disparity that may not be as paradoxical as it initially seems (see Panksepp et al., 1992).

The CRF system is likely to be a key player in stress-induced depression and "burnout" in humans. NE from the locus coeruleus has a direct inhibitory influence on CRF neurons, and CRF neurons have excitatory influences on NE systems, which can promote brain NE depletion and thereby psychic depression (for reviews, see Risch, 1991). The genetic expression of CRF in paraventricular neurons is controlled by converging hormonal and neuronal influences (Herman, Wiegand, & Watson, 1990; Young, Mezey, & Seigel, 1986), providing a way for stress experiences to promote semipermanent brain changes that at the psychological level may be experienced as despair. Since early social isolation is a contributory vector to depression, and since CRF can activate the separation response, one intriguing possibility is that early social isolation may facilitate the long-term genetic and neurosecretory activity of the CRF system that precipitates a cascade of events leading from protest to despair—from the experience of separation to the experience of depression (Panksepp, Yates, Ikemoto, & Nelson, 1991; Risch, 1991).

Oxytocin

OXY has emerged as a pre-eminent candidate as a central instigator of maternal behavior (Pedersen, Caldwell, & Brooks, 1990), as well as of nurturant feelings of acceptance and social bonding (Insel, 1992; Panksepp, 1992a). Feelings induced by high brain OXY activity may reduce child abuse, since central administration of OXY reduces infanticide in animal models (McCarthy, 1990). There is increased genetic expression of this system during parturition (Jirikowski, Caldwell, Pilgrim, Stumpf, & Pedersen, 1989) providing, along with central prolactin effects (Bridges, Numan, Ronsheim, Mann, & Lupini, 1990) a potential neurochemical answer to the age-old question "From whence do maternal feelings arise?" Although central OXY activity does not appear to be essential for maintenance of maternal behavior (see Insel, 1992, for a review), insufficient work has been done with long-term extinction paradigms (using OXY antagonists) to determine how well ongoing maternal behavior is sustained without normal OXY activity. In addition to helping generate a feeling of acceptance, OXY also seems to participate in sexual gratification, via facilitation of lordotic responses in the female medial hypothalamus and erectile responses in the male hippocampus and preoptic area (Argiolas & Gessa, 1991). Sexual behavior is promoted in both males and females by centrally administered OXY, and orgasmic responses are characterized by increased OXY release in both males and females (Richard, Moos, & Freund-Mercier, 1991). In these contexts, it comes as little surprise that OXY has remarkably powerful effects in reducing separation distress in a variety of species that have been tested (Panksepp, 1989, 1992a), and that this effect is present in the ancestral hormone vasotocin, which facilitates various sociosexual impulses in reptiles and birds (Moore, 1987). In short, OXY is a prime candidate for mediating feelings of acceptance and social bonding, even though I would add the cautionary note that researchers have had no success yet in obtaining conditioned place preferences in rats as a result of pairings OXY (administered directly into the brain) with specific environments. This peptide could also be studied in humans, since intranasally administered OXY probably gains access to the brain. The ability of this manipulation to modulate socioaffective and sexual moods in humans deserves careful evaluation. Considering the remarkable ability of this peptide to promote erectile responses, intranasal administration may be an effective antidote for certain forms of impotence. Moreover, in lactating mothers there appears to be a correspondence between central and peripheral OXY release, providing a natural model for the analysis of OXY on mood.

Arginine Vasopressin

AVP, the other posterior pituitary peptide (whose main peripheral function is water conservation), also emerged from the evolutionary divergence of vasotocin. But unlike OXY and vasotocin, AVP has no ability to reduce separation distress, nor any ability to facilitate maternal or female sex behavior (although it does promote male sociosexual activities). Although this hormone was originally popularized in a behavioral context as a potential mediator of memory (van Wimersma Greidanus & van Ree, 1990; Van der Hoof, Urban, & deWied, 1989), it probably yields memory-like effects by facilitating arousal (Le Moal et al., 1984; Sahgal, 1984), selective attention, or other nonspecific cognitive processes (Fehm-Wolfsdorf, Bachoholtz, Born, Voigt, & Fehm, 1988). Although it remains possible that AVP does have specific effects on social memories in rats (Dantzer, Bluthe, Koob, & Le Moal, 1987), many of the "memory effects" of AVP following peripheral administration in animals could secondarily arise from aversive autonomic effects. Peripherally administered AVP increases blood pressure (Le Moal et al., 1984), which may be sufficient to serve as the unconditioned stimulus in passive avoidance studies (Ebenezer, 1988). Hedonic properties of centrally administered AVP remain to be adequately evaluated. Indeed, AVP centrally may mediate some type of dynamic emotional effect, since animals that are genetically deficient in vasopressin are behaviorally sluggish and timid (Sokol & Valtin, 1982). In humans, low doses of intranasally administered AVP do produce positive mood changes; this suggests that it may promote attentional and expectancy processes of the limbic system (Fehm-Wolfsdorf & Born, 1991; Snel, Taylor, & Wegman, 1987), perhaps those directly related to evaluating the emotional content of stimuli (Naumann, Bartussek, Kaiser, & Fehm-Wolfsdorf, 1991).

It seems highly likely that AVP may be a specific carrier for male dominance and persistence urges. AVP neural systems are under testosterone control, and castration eliminates approximately half the AVP innervation of the brain (DeVries, Buijs, Van Leeuwen, Caffe, & Swaab, 1985). Male aggressive urges can be promoted by central administration of AVP (Koolhaas, van den Brink, Roozendaal, & Boorsma, 1990) and reduced by AVP antagonists (Potegal & Ferris, 1989). In short, there is a good chance that AVP is a key player in the mediation of heightened tendencies for males to exhibit aggression, and it is possible that the underlying subjective emotional correlate is one of increased irritability and anger.

Low brain AVP levels may contribute to emotional and cognitive disorders (deWied & van Ree, 1989). AVP is reduced in the CSF of some depressed patients (Gjerris, Hammer, Vendsborg, Christensen, & Rafaelson, 1985) and schizophrenic patients (Van Kammen, Waters, & Gold, 1981), and intranasal supplementation has been effective in reversing some of the negative symptoms of schizophrenia (Brambilla et al., 1988; Iager, Kirch, Bigelow, & Karson, 1986). Also, slight improvements in memory search abilities have been observed following AVP in the early stages of Alzheimer's-type dementia (Weingartner et al., 1981).

Luteinizing Hormone-Releasing Hormone

LH-RH prepares the female body for ovulation and promotes spermatogenesis in males (Simon, Birkenfeld, & Schenker, 1990). It is also expressed within certain brain circuits, especially those of the basomedial hypothalamus (Schwanzel-Fukuda & Pfaff, 1989). Considering the evolutionary conservation of function among neuropeptides, it is fitting that this hormone is a key player in facilitation of sexual proclivities (Pedersen et al., 1990). Sexual arousal effects following central administration of LH-RH are generally much clearer in females than in males (Moss & Dudley, 1984), even though male sexuality can also be promoted (Dorsa & Smith, 1981; Pfaff, 1982). The behavioral effects result from actions on the medial preoptic area (Dornan & Malsbury, 1989; Pfaff & Schwartz-Giblin, 1988), but the mood and psychological effects of the neuropeptide remain to be adequately evaluated. It may well prove to be a prime mover of human libido.

Growth Hormone-Releasing Factor

Growth hormone (GH)-releasing factor circuits are restricted to the basomedial hypothalamus, and have a direct role on body energy dynamics (Frohman & Jansson, 1986). Feeding is increased after central adminis-

tration (Feifel & Vaccarino, 1989), but at high doses it also yields intense motor arousal, which may suggest some role in certain types of heightened emotionality (Tannenbaum, 1984). This finding remains to be developed properly.

Somatostatin

Somatostatin was first discovered to be an inhibitor of GH release from the pituitary, but now it is known to be a widely distributed neuronal system throughout the brain that appears to have psychiatric implications (Rubinow, 1986; Vasko & Harris, 1990), with low levels of somatostatin found in the CSF of depressives and anorexics (Agren & Lundqvist, 1984; Davis et al., 1988; Gerner & Yamada, 1982; Paunovic & Popovic, 1989) and elevated levels in manics (Vecsei & Widerlov, 1988). Animal data indicate a variety of effects suggestive of some types of mood changes, including reductions in isolation-induced distress vocalizations (Vilberg, Panksepp, Kastin, & Coy, 1984), and elevated levels of approach and search behaviors in rats, with some agitation (Aponte, Leung, Gross, & Yamada, 1984; Paunovic & Popovic, 1989). Somatostatin also reduces eating (Feifel & Vaccarino, 1990), probably in a normal way, since it can also attenuate the anorexic effect of stress (Shibasaki et al., 1988). It has been suggested that "somatostatinergic projections from the central nucleus of the amygdala . . . may be important in mediating the autonomic responses produced during defense and other 'emotional' behavior" (Higgins & Schwaber, 1983, p. 661).

In addition, somatostatin can facilitate learning (DeNoble, Hepler, & Barto, 1989; Fitzgerald & Dokla, 1989; Romanova, Karganov, Kadar, & Telegdy, 1990; Vecsei, Bollok, Penke, & Telegdy, 1986), and the peptide is depleted in a variety of neurological disorders characterized by cognitive impairments, including schizophrenia and Alzheimer's, Parkinson's, and Huntington's diseases (Gerner & Yamada, 1982; Nemeroff, Youngblood, Manberg, Prange, & Kisel, 1983; Rubinow, 1986; Vecsei & Widerlov, 1988). It is one of the few peptides that is enriched in the thalamocortical axis, especially in reticular nuclei known to control attention (Molinari, Hendry, & Jones, 1987). The effects of this peptide are so broad-ranging (Grabow, Gaumann, & Yaksh, 1989) that it cannot be subsumed under a single principle of action. Although definitive evidence remains scarce, it is sure to be an important player in various aspects of emotionality as well as cognitive processes.

Thyrotropin-Releasing Hormone

TRH was the first neuropeptide to be fully characterized, and it has a very widespread distribution in the brain. This has implicated it as a major factor in the control of autonomic and brain arousal, and deficiencies may be of potential importance in clinical depression (Whybrow & Bauer, 1988). Central administration provokes a variety of behavioral changes, the most prominent of which are increases in activity and "wet-dog" shakes reminiscent of opiate withdrawal (Drust & Crawford, 1982; Katsuura, Yoshikawa, Itoh, & Hsaio, 1984). TRH reduces behavioral indices of depression in animal models (Ogawa et al., 1984); it can alleviate memory deficits in various animal models of dementia (Horita, Carino, Zabawska, & Lai, 1989); and it appears to have some beneficial effects in the treatment of depression and Alzheimer's disease in humans (Mellow et al., 1989). In short, this peptide seems to facilitate arousal processes in a great number of apparently different ways, and it is not clear that a unitary psychobehavioral function can be ascribed to it. Considering that TRH normally sets in motion the chain of events for the metabolic activating effects of thyroxine, and considering the fact that it does have antidepressant effects (Whybrow & Bauer, 1988), one might speculate that it may help facilitate joyful arousal processes such as rough-and-tumble play, but direct empirical evidence is not yet available.

Anterior Pituitary Peptides

Some anterior pituitary peptides, such as α–melanocyte-stimulating hormone (α-MSH) and ACTH have quite extensive brain systems; many others, such as GH , luteinizing hormone (LH), and thyroid-stimulating hormone (TSH), do not appear to have distinct systems within the brain. But even in the absence of distinct brain systems, many of these peptide hormones do have central effects. For instance, prolactin has extensive receptor systems, which have a clear role in promoting various goal-directed behaviors—probably by facilitating brain DA activity, which can promote various affective responses ranging from psychomotor arousal to drug craving (Drago, 1990). In its role of promoting the manufacture of milk, it is gratifying to see that central administration of prolactin can sustain the maintenance of maternal behavior (Bridges et al., 1990). There is reason to believe that short-term exposure to this hormone will promote a positive affective state, whereas long-term exposure may be characterized by dysphoria (MacLeod et al., 1984).

α-Melanocyte Stimulating Hormone

α-MSH given peripherally can facilitate attentional processes in humans, but it is not clear that these are due to direct effects on brain α-MSH receptor systems. They may have these effects by indirect effects on brain catecholamine functions (see Miller, Sandman, & Kastin, 1977, and Sandman, Miller, & Kastin, 1976). Direct central studies in birds indicate that α-MSH can facilitate fear-like freezing, accompanied by a reduction in isolation calls (Panksepp & Abbott, 1990). Accordingly, it has been proposed that the ancestral camouflage functions of this peptide seen in repitles may still be sustained in promoting mammalian fear-induced freezing/hiding responses. This peptide also can produce a characteristic grooming and stretching/yawning syndrome, as do many peptides (Colbern & Gispen, 1988); it remains unclear whether these are simply pseudoaffective motor responses, or whether they reflect some type of specific central affective state.

Adrenocorticotropic Hormone

ACTH has a response very similar to that of α-MSH for both separation distress (Panksepp & Normansell, 1990) and grooming responses (Spruijt & Gispen, 1986). Massive doses given into the periventricular gray can produce explosive jumping in rats, suggestive of a massive intensification of negative affect (Jacquet, 1978). In general, there appears to be little difference between the effects of ACTH and α-MSH, except that the latter appears to be more potent. It should be remembered that both peptides arise from the same segment of the propiomelanocortin (POMC) gene, from which ß-endorphin and several other opioid peptides arise. Indeed, those peptides appear to have effects diametrically opposite to those induced by ACTH and α-MSH, suggesting a yin–yang type of balancing influence on emotional behaviors from this gene family: ACTH and α-MSH promote a state of anxious disaffection, while endorphins promote states of serene satisfaction.

Opioid Peptides

There are three major families of opioid peptides, each emerging from a distinct genetic source and each acting upon distinct receptors: ß-endorphin emerges from the POMC gene and acts on mu receptors; leucine and methionine enkephalins emerge from the pre-proenkephalin gene and act on delta as well as mu receptors; and various dynorphins emerge from the pre-pro-dynorphin gene and act on kappa receptors (Mansour, Khachaturian, Lewis, Akil, & Watson, 1988). The first two peptides have powerful effects in counteracting negative emotions and promoting positive ones, whereas the functions of the third remain more ambiguous.

β-Endorphin

ß-Endorphin, the most powerful opioid presently known to exist in the brain, has more powerful addictive qualities, molecule for molecule, than opiate alkaloids such as heroin. It is found to be desirable partially because it can produce a positive hedonic state, probably through brain mechanisms similar to those mediating psychostimulant addiction (Bechara & van der Kooy, 1989; Wise & Bozarth, 1987), but also because it can quell negative emotionality—ranging from physical pain to emotional pain arising from social loss. Opioids are remarkably effective in quelling separation distress (Panksepp et al., 1985, 1988), but they also can reduce aggression indicative of anger (Siegel & Shaikh, 1992). Perhaps a general principle is that such powerful opioids elaborate pleasurable signals that the system is returning to homeostasis (Panksepp, 1981b). Pleasures as different as those arising from social reunions, sexual orgasms, and gustatory delights may have strong opioid components.

Enkephalins

The enkephalins are much weaker and shorter-acting opioids than the endorphins, and their specific functions are not as clearly established. Perhaps these rapidly acting opioids

participate more in the short-term pleasurable feedback that one gets from the immediate pleasure of various sensation, and it remains possible that these short-acting opioids may be reinforcement transmitters facilitating the development of learned associations (Panksepp, 1986a).

Dynorphins

The dynorphins constitute a class of powerful opioids that act on kappa receptors, which do control pain in the spinal cord, but not to any great extent at supraspinal levels. Brain levels of these peptides are very high, but no clear emotive functions have been established, with behavioral effects such as barrel rolling being prominent behavioral endpoints of central injections. Feeding can be increased with central injections of dynorphins; this raises the possibility that dynorphins are important in arousing feelings of hunger (Morley, Bartness, Gosnell, & Levine, 1986).

Gastrointestinal Peptides: Psychobehavioral Effects

It is noteworthy how many peptides that were initially discovered to modulate gastrointestinal functions have now been discovered in the brain. Although many of them have very clear effects on appetitive and consummatory behaviors, the true brain functions of most remain quite ambiguous. Since emotions have such ramifications on gastrointestinal functions, it is possible that many of them participate in the viscceral experiences of emotions within the brain.

Cholecystokinin

CCK was the first gastrointestinal peptide to find substantial support in the control of behavioral functions in its ability to exert inhibitory control over feeding (Baile, McLaughlin, & Della, 1986; Flood, Silver, & Morley, 1990), but this effect turned out to be largely a peripherally mediated one, since vagotomy could abolish it (Smith, Jerome, Cushin, Eterno, & Simansky, 1981). CCK is now known to be expressed in widespread neural circuits of the brain; unlike many neuropeptides, it is highly enriched in cortical areas (Crawley, 1985; Fallon & Seroogy, 1985) and the central effects of CCK are just beginning to be revealed. CCK has complex effects on loco-motion and pain, partially through interactions with brain DA and opioid systems (Vanderhaeghen & Crawley, 1985). CCK and some of its metabolites appears to exert anxiogenic effects in various animal models (Harro & Vasar, 1991). CCK also modulates sexual receptivity in complex ways, with most of the data suggesting that central administration can facilitate female receptivity when receptivity is low but can reduce it when it is high (Babcock, Bloch, & Micevych, 1988; Bloch, Dornan, Gorski, & Micevych, 1989; Dornan, 1989).

Bombesin

Bombesin, a widely distributed neuropeptide system related to gastrin-releasing peptide (Moody et al., 1988), was first implicated in the inhibitory control of feeding (Morley et al., 1986); it may be especially important developmentally, since the peptides are contained in human breast milk (Takeyama et al., 1991), perhaps to facilitate prolactin and GH release and related maternal behaviors (Telegdy, 1985). Centrally administered bombesin has been found to have a variety of effects that could be related to emotionality. It can produce analgesia (Pert, Moody, Pert, DeWald, & Rivier, 1980), and it may potentiate learning (Flood & Morley, 1988). Intense grooming, with compulsive scratching at the head and neck, stretching, and yawning, have also been produced by bombesin (Colbern & Gispen, 1988), and some have interpreted this as an attempt to block an aversive state produced in the brain by this peptide (Misenberg, Simmons, & Lorens, 1990). The qualitative and adaptive nature of the putative affective state induced by bombesin remains to be elucidated.

Neuropeptide Y

NPY and its related gastric peptide, neuropeptide YY, have a remarkably widespread distribution in the brain and remarkably potent effects on various basic behaviors, including feeding, body temperature, motor activity, and sexual behavior (Kalra & Kalra, 1990). NPY has also been implicated in a variety of psychiatric disorders (Allen & Koenig, 1990). Feeding can be potentiated more by this peptide than any other (Heilig & Widerlov, 1990), and the effect exhibits great species gen-erality (Kulkosky, Glazner, Moore, Low, & Woods, 1989). It appears to facilitate the specific motivation to eat—perhaps the actual experience of hunger (Flood & Morley, 1991)—and it evokes a selective desire for carbohydrates (Stanley, Daniel, Chin, & Leibowitz, 1985). However, it does not produce a general arousal. The peptide decreases spontaneous motor activity, muscle tone, and body temperature (Jolicoeur et al., 1991). It also reduces copulatory behavior in male rats, and it is possible that the gluttony and relative asexuality of certain genetically obese animals are attributable to endogenous elevations of this peptide (Beck, Burlet, Nicholas, & Burlet, 1990a, 1990b).

The potential connection between this peptide and bulimia in humans has been well appreciated (Morley & Blundell, 1988), and recent work has indicated elevated CSF NPY levels in anorexic women, which is not just a secondary consequence of their low weight (Kaye, Berrettini, Gwirstsman, & George, 1990). Although findings in psychiatric patients are not without controversy (Wahlestedt, Kman, & Widerlov, 1989), major depressions may be accompanied by decreased brain NPY levels (Heilig & Widerlov, 1990), and elevated NPY levels may increase vulnerability to schizophrenia (Peters, Van Kammen, Gelernter, Yao, & Shaw, 1990). NPY has also been implicated in memory consolidation, and there is some evidence for modest reductions of NPY in Alzheimer's patients (Morley & Flood, 1990). Clearly, NPY has many important effects for psychological functioning beside the mediation of hunger.

Neurotensin

NT is another peptide that is abundant in both the gastrointestinal tract and the brain; it has been found to participate in the inhibitory control of feeding (Vaughn, Baumeister, Hawkins, & Anticich, 1990). This may reflect a true satiety effect, since NT levels are reduced in hyperphagic obese rats (Beck et al., 1990a), the peptide can also reduce locomotor activity (Nouel, Bubuc, Kitabgi, & Constentin, 1990), and all of these effects may arise via modulation of ventral tegmental DA activity (Shi & Bunney, 1991). NT also reduces pain sensitivity (Levant & Nemeroff, 1988). With regard to neuropathological states, NT may be reduced in schizophrenics (Garver, Bissette,

Yao, & Nemeroff, 1991) and Alzheimer's patients (Benzing, Mufson, Jennes, & Armstrong, 1990). Overall, it would appear that NT might be a mood stabilizer (Levant & Nemeroff, 1988), although clear studies of affective processes remain to be conducted with this intriguing neuropeptide.

Vasoactive Intestinal Peptide

VIP, a gastric peptide with potent vasodilatory properties, has been extensively studied in the physiological context (Christophe, Rosselin, Said, & Yanaihara, 1984; Said & Mutt, 1988), but little is known about its behavioral effects. Central administration of VIP, as of many other peptides, can provoke hyperactivity in rodents (Itoh, Katsuura, & Yoshikawa, 1985). Considering that VIP provokes gastric relaxation (Said & Mutt, 1988), similar to the reflexive relaxation of the stomach that occurs when one starts to eat, and considering that it is represented within somatosensory systems, perhaps it helps mediate the pleasure of sensation. It is possible that the apparent amnestic effects of VIP in aversive situations (Flood, Garland, & Morley, 1990) could be mediated by its ability to counteract aversive states by evoking pleasurable feelings. There are bound to be several interesting affective ramifications for this peptide in the brain.

Galanin

Galanin is a representative of a new family of neuropeptides that has a widespread distribution in human and animal brain (Gentleman et al., 1989, Kohler et al., 1989). It can also induce feeding, especially when placed into the paraventricular nucleus of the hypothalamus, apparently via induction of NE release (Kyrkouli, Stanley, Hutchinson, Seirafi, & Leibowitz, 1990). In addition to being colocalized with serotonin neurons, it is also the only known peptide that coexists with cholinergic ventral forebrain neurons (Crawley & Wenk, 1989); this implicates it in cognitive/memory/arousal control processes, perhaps in an inhibitory way (Napier et al., 1991). Central administration can impair acquisition of spatial memories in rats (Sundstrom, Archer, Melander, & Hokfelt, 1988), and an increase of this neuropeptide has been reported in basal forebrain interneurons of Alzheimer's patients (Beal, MacGarvey, & Swartz, 1990).

Miscellaneous Neuropeptides

Many neuropeptides do not fall into obvious categories, and some deserve mention in the present context. Many, like angiotensin, have been long been known to have very clear behavioral effects, but their potential role in mediating specific affective processes related to regulatory states remains to be widely considered. Indeed, many of these peptides have effects on various consummatory and regulatory behaviors, and they all need to be considered as potential mediators of the specific feelings that accompany various regulatory depletion and repletion states, all of which are accompanied by strong feelings in humans.

Angiotensin was discovered to be a powerful dipsogen, which fits in nicely with its peripheral role in maintaining blood pressure (Johnson & Edwards, 1990). Whether it merely instigates the act of drinking or whether it provokes a central experience of thirst remains a neglected affective question.

Atrial natriuretic factor, a cardiac neuropeptide, helps maintain sodium balance via effects on the kidney (it facilitates urination and sodium excretion in response to increased atrial stretch). It also affects the brain (Steardom & Nathanson, 1987), but little is known of its function. It would be an impressive coincidence if this peptide were found to provide specific inhibitory modulation of salt craving, which is a powerful, albeit not widely recognized, appetitive function of the brain.

Bradykinin helps trigger pain in the periphery, and it has some well-delimited brain circuits (Correa, Innia, Uhl, & Snyder, 1979), which may function more in an antinociceptive than in a pain-instigatory fashion (Ribeiro, Corrado, & Graeff, 1971). Early behavioral studies suggested that it could modify behavioral and autonomic processes (short-acting excitation followed by sedation), suggestive of some role in the control of emotionality (Graeff & Arisawa, 1978), but recent work on the peptide is meager. The development of competitive antagonists for bradykinin (Vavrek & Stewart, 1985) as well as other neuropeptides should help to highlight the mysterious functions of such neuroactive molecules.

Calcitonin gene-related peptide (CGRP) was the first neuropeptide discovered by the use of human logic in the field of molecular biology (as opposed to empirical extraction of molecules from the "brain swamp"). Although calcitonin has been long known to produce a powerful analgesia following central administration (Pecile, Ferri, Braga, & Olgiati, 1975), CGRP acts on different brain systems than calcitonin does (Fischer & Born, 1985), and its function in the brain remains very ambiguous. Perhaps its function could be surmised from its neuroanatomical localization. CGRP receptors are concentrated along the trajectory of the gustatory system through the neuraxis (Skofitsch & Jacobowitz, 1985), and it may serve a key function in some aspect of ingestive behavior—perhaps the mediation of negative taste qualities (Yamamoto et al., 1990) or gustatory disgust. This possibility is supported by the ability of CGRP to reduce feeding; however, it is becoming evident that an enormous number of peptides can produce that effect (Morley et al., 1986), and subtle behavioral tests to evaluate the functional nature of such anorexic effects remain to be widely employed (Siviy & Panksepp, 1985).

Delta sleep-inducing peptide highlights a conundrum that besets the field of neuropeptides and behavior: The first noted behavioral effects of a peptide often tend to pre-empt a more catholic conceptualization of its actual role in the brain. Although this peptide was first highlighted in sleep research (Borbély & Tobler, 1989), it is becoming increasingly clear that it has many other functions; the major one may be to modulate stress responsivity (Graf & Kastin, 1986), bearing out the early finding that this peptide may facilitate an animal's resistance to emotional stress (Sudakov et al., 1983). Whether this effect occurs only with physiological manifestations of stress or with psychological ones as well remains to be elucidated.

Substance P was the first neuroactive peptide to be discovered, and I end this brief overview with this still mysterious peptide. Although it certainly helps modulate pain in the peripheral nervous system and spinal cord, in higher brain circuits it may participate in more subtle functions, such as reinforcement and incentive processes (Panksepp, 1981a; Staubli & Huston, 1985). It, and the several other members of the tachykinin family that are widely distributed in the brain (Hirai & Jones, 1989; Saffroy et al., 1988) may well modulate aspects of mood and emotional behavior; however, such speculations remain to be supported by robust and coherent data bases. This, unfortunately, remains the opera-

tive clause for all too many neuropeptides, for main-line emotion research has yet to penetrate this field effectively. Thus, there are many important findings still in store for us. It is important to remember that each of the neuropeptides has many sides (i.e., potential active sites) and many fragment metabolites that result from enzymatic cleavage (some of which may be bioactive), so a single molecule may eventually yield multiple effects. Indeed, for substance P, some fragments may yield effects via their nitrogen terminal interactions, whereas typically the carboxy-terminal side has mediated most physiological and behavioral effects (Hall & Stewart, 1992). Diversity on both the receptor and transmitter sides of each system appears to be the norm rather than the exception, providing possibilities for extreme functional subtlety within each neuropeptide system that has been discussed.

Modulation of Neuropeptides by Pharmacological Means

Although neuropeptides hold great promise in helping unravel emotional and other psychobehavioral codes in the brain, there are presently few prospects of modulating these systems by means of peripheral pharmacological strategies. With a few exceptions, the various neuropeptide systems do not have receptor antagonists that are effective when given peripherally. (Peptide antagonists have been developed for many systems, but they must be administered directly into the brain.) We simply do not know enough yet about the molecular conformations that yield neurobiological effects, and this kind of knowledge is essential for the design of nonpeptide congeners that could gain access from the periphery to the relevant receptors in the brain. Such molecules will be essential for elucidating the affective functions of neuropeptides in humans. With the eventual development of such molecules, many new psychiatric tools should emerge for the modulation of specific moods and emotions. For brain opioid systems we have long had powerful and reasonably specific receptor antagonists, such as naloxone and naltrexone. Although there was great excitement (and eventually great disillusionment) in the application of these agents in psychiatric practice during the 1970s (Verebey, 1982), it should be emphasized that most suggested applications were based on wild hunches rather than substantive preclinical evidence. On the basis of my own animal work, I have proposed that opiate antagonists should be beneficial in disorders characterized by autistic symptoms (Panksepp, 1981b), and recent clinical work has started to support that conjecture (for a review, see Panksepp, Lensing, et al., 1991). This may be the first neuropeptide manipulation to have a role in psychiatric practice; it suggests the potential practical importance of emotion research in animals. As other nonpeptide agonists and antagonists are developed for the neuropeptides, many other impressive clinical tools are bound to emerge. For instance, CRF and CCK receptor antagonists may help counteract anxiety, panic, and stress. NPY and dynorphin antagonists may be excellent appetite control agents. AVP, OXY, and LH-RH agonists and antagonists may have a role in modulating libido and social emotions.

Other useful strategies will emerge from our developing understanding of the synthetic and degradative enzymes that control the manufacture and destruction of the neuropeptides. We are beginning to understand the posttranslational processing of the various DNA transcripts that eventually yield neuropeptides, and this is bound to yield pharmacological tools of considerable clinical importance.

CONCLUSIONS AND FUTURE PROSPECTS

Considering the vast diversity of neurochemical systems that have been implicated in the control of emotionality, and considering the difficulty in generating definitive work in the field (because of the subjective dimensions inherent in the subject matter), it is not surprising that we presently have more speculation than substance to share with respect to the molecular underpinnings of emotions. Although there is now a realistic basis for the expectation that we can understand moods and emotions at a mechanistic level, there is also reason for concern. The work is proceeding at a snail's pace. What is most desperately needed is a new generation of dedicated investigators interested in the emotions, who are willing to delve into the underlying mechanisms within the brain. It is remarkable that such work has not evolved more rapidly in psychosocial, behavioral, or neuroscience

traditions toward understanding how the brain/ mind operates, but it is historically understandable (Panksepp, 1990): There is no broad agreement yet among the growing cadre of investigators into emotional processes concerning the essential importance and utility of a neurobiological analysis of emotive phenomena.

To return to a key consideration raised at the beginning of this chapter—namely, the possibility that the ancient REM mechanism is a primordial emotional arousal system that was at one time used in the waking state—we have now reached a point where we can appreciate the multiplicity of neurochemical influences that can be incorporated into dreamwork and that probably help determine how internal emotional realities interact with the complexities of the external world. But many important issues have not even been alluded to in the present coverage. For instance, the ability of adrenal and gonadal steroid hormones to modulate the activity of emotional circuits (Joels & de Kloet, 1992), even to the point of controlling gene expression in peptidergic neurons (Young et al., 1986), provides layers of additional control that are just beginning to be fathomed. A separate book could be written about the potential role of other neurohormones, such as melatonin, in arousal and affective processes (Miles, Philbrick, & Thompson, 1989). These chemistries provide many opportunities to establish powerful structure–function relationships that will eventually change our understanding of emotions and modes of thinking about emotional disorders (Ganten & Pfaff, 1988; Risch, 1991). Previous levels of understanding, drawn mainly from behavioral and psychological levels of analysis, will be dramatically highlighted by our understanding of the molecular mechanisms creating the diversity of primary neuroaffective states that can be elaborated by the brain. The ingrained biological values that we experience as moods and emotions are surely triggered by our external experiences, but their essential affective structure is created by the neurochemical dynamics of specific brain circuits. It is clear that neuropeptides are at the heart of many of these systems. At present, many key neurochemical players have been identified, but a great deal of neurobehavioral research is needed to delineate their specific characteristics.

REFERENCES

Agren, H., & Lundqvist, G. (1984). Low levels of somatostatin in human CSF mark depressive episodes. *Psychoneuroendocrinology*, 9, 233–248.

Allen, J. M., & Koening, J. I. (Eds.). (1990). *Annals of the New York Academy of Sciences: Vol. 611. Central and peripheral significance of neuropeptide Y and its related peptides.* New York: New York Academy of Sciences.

Aponte, G., Leung, P., Gross, D., & Yamada, T. (1984). Effects of somatostatin on food intake in rats. *Life Sciences*, 35, 741–746.

Argiolas, A., & Gessa, G. L. (1991). Central functions of oxytocin. *Neuroscience and Biobehavioral Reviews*, 15, 217–231.

Babcock, A. M., Bloch, G. J., & Micevych, P. E. (1988). Injections of cholecystokinin in the ventromedial hypothalamic nucleus inhibits lordosis behavior in the rat. *Physiology and Behavior*, 43, 195–199.

Baile, C. A., McLaughlin, C. L., & Della, F. M. A. (1986). Role of cholecystokinin and opioid peptides in control of food intake. *Physiological Review*, 66, 172–234.

Baldwin, H. A., Britton, K. T., & Koob, G. F. (1990). Behavioral effects of corticotropin-releasing factor. In D. Ganten & D. Pfaff (Eds.), *Current topics in neuroendocrinology: Vol. 10. Behavioral aspects of neuroendocrinology* (pp. 1–14). Berlin: Springer-Verlag.

Bandler, R. (1988). Brain mechanisms of aggression as revealed by electrical and chemical stimulation: Suggestion of a central role for the midbrain periaqueductal grey region. In A. N. Epstein & A. R. Morrison (Eds.), *Progress in psychobiology and physiological psychology* (Vol. 13, pp. 67–154). New York: Academic Press.

Baum, A., Grunberg, N. E., & Singer, J. E. (1992). Biochemical measurements in the study of emotions. *Psychological Science*, 3, 56–60.

Beal, M. F., MacGarvey, U., & Swartz, K. J. (1990). Galanin immunoreactivity is increased in the nucleus basalis of Meynert in Alzheimer's disease. *Annals of Neurology*, 28, 157–161.

Bechara, A., & van der Kooy, D. (1989). The tegmental pedunculopontine nucleus: A brain-stem output of the limbic system critical for the conditioned place preferences produced by morphine and amphetamine. *Journal of Neuroscience*, 9, 3400–3409.

Beck, B., Burlet, A., Nicholas, J. P., & Burlet, C. (1990). Hyperphagia in obesity is associated with a central peptidergic dysregulation in rats. *Nutrition and Behavior*, 12, 806–811.

Beck, B., Burlet, A., Nicholas, J. P., & Burlet, C. (1990b). Hypothalamic neuropeptide Y (NPY) in obese Zucker rats: Implications in feeding and sexual behaviors. *Physiology and Behavior*, 47, 449–453.

Benzing, W. C., Mufson, E. J., Jennes, L., & Armstrong, D. M. (1990). Reduction of neurotensin immunoreactivity in the amygdala in Alzheimer's disease. *Brain Research*, 537, 298–302.

Bloch, G. J., Dornan, A. M., Gorski, R. A., & Micevych, P. E. (1989). Effects of site-specific CNS microinjections of cholecystokinin on lordosis behavior in the male rat. *Physiology and Behavior*, 46, 725–730.

Borbély, A. A., & Tobler, I. (1989). Endogenous sleep-promoting substances and sleep regulation. *Physiological Review*, 69, 605–670.

Brambilla, F., Bondiolotti, G. P., Maggioni, M., Sciatcia, W., Grillo, W., Sanna, F., Latina, A., & Picotti, G. B. (1988). Vasopressin (DDAVP) therapy in chronic schizophrenia: Effects on negative symptoms. *Neuropsychobiology*, 20, 113–119.

Bridges, R. S., Numan, M., Ronsheim, P. M., Mann, P. E., & Lupini, C. E. (1990). Central prolactin infusions stimulate maternal behavior in steroid-treated, nulliparous female rats. *Proceedings of the National Academy of Sciences USA*, 87, 8003–8007.

Cannon, W. B. (1929). *Bodily changes in pain, hunger, fear, and rage.* New York: Appleton-Century-Crofts.

Christophe, J., Rosselin, G., Said, S. I., & Yanaihara, N. (Eds.). (1984). First International Symposium on VIP and Related Peptides [Special issue]. *Peptides*, 5(2).

Clark, W. G., & Lipton, J. M. (1985). Changes in body temperature after administration of amino acids, peptides, dopamine, neuroleptics and related agents: II. *Neuroscience and Biobehavioral Reviews*, 9, 299–371.

Colbern, D. L., & Gispen, W. H. (Eds.). (1988). *Annals of the New York Academy of Sciences: Vol. 525. Neural mechanisms and biological mechanisms and biological significance of grooming behavior.* New York: New York Academy of Sciences.

Correa, F. M. A., Innis, R. B., Uhl, G. Â., & Snyder, S. H. (1979). Bradykinin-like immunoreactive neuronal systems localized histochemically in rat brain. *Proceedings of the National Academy of Sciences USA*, 76, 1489–1493.

Crawley, J. N. (1985). Comparative distribution of cholecystokinin and other neuropeptides: Why is this peptide different from all other peptides? *Annals of the New York Academy of Sciences*, 448, 1–8.

Crawley, J. N., & Wenk, G. L. (1989). Co-existence of glanin and acetylcholine: Is galanin involved in memory processes and dementia? *Trends in Neuroscience*, 12, 278–282.

Dantzer, R., Bluthe, R.-M., Koob, G. F., & Le Moal, M. (1987). Modulation of social memory in male rats by neurohypophyseal peptides. *Psychopharmacology*, 91, 363–368.

Davis, K. L., Davidson, M., Yang, R., Davis, B. M., Siever, L. J., Mohs, R. C., Ryan, T., Coccaro, E., Bierer, L., & Targum, S. D. (1988). CSF somatostatin in Alzheimer's disease, depressed patients, and control subjects. *Biological Psychiatry*, 24, 710–712.

Deakin, J. F. W., & Graeff, F. G. (1991). 5-HT and mechanisms of defence. *Journal of Psychopharmacology*, 5, 305–341.

DeNoble, V. J., Hepler, D. J., & Barto, R. A. (1989). Cysteamine-induced depletion of somatostatin produces differential cognitive deficits in rats. *Brain Research*, 482, 42–48.

Depue, R. A., & Iacono, W. G. (1989). Neurobehavioral aspects of affective disorders. *Annual Review of Psychology*, 40, 457–492.

DeVries, G. J., Buijs, R. M., Van Leeuwen, F. W., Caffe, A. R., & Swaab, D. F. (1985). The vasopressinergic innervation of the brain in normal and castrated rats. *Journal of Comparative Neurology*, 233, 236–254.

deWied, D., & van Ree, J. (1989). Neuropeptides: Animal behaviour and human psychopathology. *European Archives of Psychiatry and Neurological Sciences*, 238, 323–331.

Dornan, W. A., Bloch, G. J., Priest, C. A., & Micevych, P. E. (1989). Micorinjection of cholecystokinin in the medial preoptic nucleus facilitates lordosis behavior in the female rat. *Physiology and Behavior, 45*, 969–974.

Dornan, W. A., & Malsbury, C. W. (1989). Neuropeptides and male sexual behavior. *Neuroscience and Biobehavioral Reviews, 13*, 1–15.

Dorsa, D. M., & Smith, E. M. (1981). Facilitation of mounting behavior in male rats by intracranial injections of luteinizing hormone-releasing hormone. *Regulatory Peptides, 1*, 147–155.

Drago, F. (1990). Behavioral effects of prolactin. In D. Ganten & D. Pfaff (Eds.), *Current topics in neuroendocrinology: Vol. 10. Behavioral aspects of neuroendocrinology* (pp. 263–290). Berlin: Springer-Verlag.

Drust, E. G., & Crawford, I. L. (1983). Comparison of the effects of TRH and D-Ala2-metenkephalinaminde on hippocampal electrical activity and behavior in the unanesthetized rat. *Peptides, 4*, 239–243.

Dunn, A. J., & Berridge, C. (1990). Physiological and behavioral responses to corticotropin-releasing factor administration: Is CRF a mediator of anxiety or stress responses? *Brain Research Reviews, 15*, 71–100.

Dunwiddie, T. J. (1986). The physiological role of adenosine in the central nervous system. *International Review of Neurobiology, 27*, 63–170.

Ebenezer, I. S. (1988). Can vasopressin alone act as an unconditioned stimulus to produce passive avoidance behaviour in rats in a typical memory experiment? *Neuropharmacology, 27*, 903–907.

Ekman, P., & Davidson, R. (Eds.). (in press). *Questions about emotions.* Cambridge, England: Cambridge University Press.

Fallon, J. H., & Seroogy, K. B. (1985). The distribution and some connections of cholecystokinin neurons in the rat brain. *Annals of the New York Academy of Sciences, 448*, 437–447.

Falls, W. A., Miserendino, M. J. D., & Davis, M. (1992). Extinction of fear-potentiated startle: Blockade by infusion of an NMDA antagonist into the amygdala. *Journal of Neuroscience, 12*, 854–863.

Farooqui, A. A., & Horrocks, L. A. (1991). Excitatory amino acid receptors, neural membrane phospholipid metabolism and neurological disorders. *Brain Research Reviews, 16*, 171–191.

Fehm-Wolfsdorf, G., Bachoholtz, G., Born, J., Voigt, K., & Fehm, H. L. (1988). Vasopressin but not oxytocin enhances cortical arousal: An integrative hypothesis on behavioral effects of neurohypophyseal hormones. *Psychopharmacology, 94*, 496–500.

Fehm-Wolfsdorf, G., & Born, J. (1991). Behavioral effects of neurohypophyseal peptides in healthy volunteers: 10 years of research. *Peptides, 12*, 1399–1406.

Feifel, D., & Vaccarino, F. J. (1989). Feeding effects of growth hormone-releasing factor in rats are photoperiod sensitive. *Behavioral Neuroscience, 103*, 824–830.

Feifel, D., & Vaccarino, F. J. (1990). Central somatostatin: A re-examination of its effects on feeding. *Brain Research, 535*, 189–194.

Fisher, L. A., & Brown, M. R. (1990). Corticotropin-releasing factor: Central regulation of autonomic nervous and visceral function. In D. Ganten & D. Pfaff (Eds.), *Current topics in neuroendocrinology: Vol. 10. Behavioral aspects of neuroendocrinology* (pp. 15–32). Berlin: Springer-Verlag.

Fischer, J. A., & Born, W. (1985). Novel peptides from the calcitonin gene: Expression, receptors and biological function. *Peptides, 6*(Suppl. 3), 265–271.

Fitzgerald, L. W., & Dokla, C. P. J. (1989). Morris water task impairment hypoactivity following cysteamine-induced recutions of somatostatin-like immunoreactivity. *Brain Research, 505*, 246–250.

Flood, J. F., Garland, J. S., & Morley, J. E. (1990). Vasoactive intestinal peptide (VIP): An amnestic neuropeptide. *Peptides, 11*, 933–938.

Flood, J. F., & Morley, J. E. (1988). Effects of bombesin and gastrin-releasing peptide on memory processing. *Brain Research, 460*, 208–210.

Flood, J. F., & Morley, J. E. (1991). Increased food intake by neuropeptide Y is due to an increased motivation to eat. *Peptides, 12*, 1329–1332.

Flood, J. F., Silver, A. J., & Morley, J. E. (1990). Do peptide-induced changes in feeding occur because of changes in motivation to eat? *Peptides, 11*, 265–270.

Frohman, L. A., & Jansson, J.-O. (1986). Growth-hormone releasing hormone. *Endocrinological Review, 7*, 223–253.

Furness, J. B., Bornstein, J. C., Murphy, R., & Pompolo, S. (1992). Roles of peptides in transmission in the enteric nervous system. *Trends in Neurosciences, 15*, 66–71.

Ganten, D., & Pfaff, D. (Eds.). (1988). *Current topics in neuroendocrinology: Vol. 8. Neuroendocrinology of mood.* Berlin: Springer-Verlag.

Gardiner, S. M., & Bennett, T. (1989). Brain neuropeptides: Actions on central cardiovascular control mechanisms. *Brain Research Reviews, 14*, 79–116.

Garver, D. L., Bissette, G., Yao, J. K., & Nemeroff, C. B. (1991). Relation of CSF neurotensin concentrations to symptoms and drug response of psychotic patients. *American Journal of Psychiatry, 148*, 484–488.

Gentleman, S. M., Flkai, P., Bogerts, B. Herrero, M. T., Polak, J. M., & Roberts, G. W. (1989). Distribution of glanin-like immunoreactivity in the human brain. *Brain Research, 505*, 311–315.

Gerner, R. H., & Yamada, T. (1982). Altered neuropeptide concentrations in cerebrospinal fluid of psychiatric patients. *Brain Research, 238*, 298–302.

Gjerris, A., Hammer, M., Vendsborg, P., Christensen, N. J., & Rafaelsen, O. J. (1985). Cerebral fluid vasopressin—changes in depression. *British Journal of Psychiatry, 147*, 696–701.

Grabow, T. S., Gaumann, D. M., & Yaksh, T. L. (1989). Electroencephalographic and behavioral assessment of intracerebroventricular somatostatin and a substance P analogue. *Brain Research, 489*, 223–230.

Graeff, F. G., & Arisawa, E. A. L. (1978). Effect of intracerebroventricular bradykinin, angiotensin II, and substance P on multiple fixed-interval fixed-ratio responding in rabbits. *Psychopharmacology, 57*, 89–95.

Graf, M. V., & Kastin, A. J. (1986). Delta-sleep-inducing peptide (DSIP): An update. *Peptides, 7*, 1165–1187.

Haefely, W. E. (1990). The $GABA_A$-benzodiazepine receptor: Biology and pharmacology. In G. D. Burrows, M. Roth & R. Noyes, Jr. (Eds.), *Handbook of anxiety: Vol. 3. The neurobiology of anxiety* (pp. 165–188). Amsterdam: Elsevier.

Hall, M. E., & Stewart, J. M. (1992). The substance P fragment SP(1-7) stimulates motor behavior and nigral dopamine release. *Pharmacology, Biochemistry and Behavior, 41*, 75–78.

Harro, J., & Vasar, E. (1991). Cholecystokinin-induced anxiety: How is it reflected in studies on exploratory behavior? *Neuroscience and Biobehavioral Reviews, 15*, 473–477.

Heilig, M., & Widerlov, E. (1990). Neuropeptide Y: An overview of central distribution, functional aspects, and possible involvement in neuropsychiatric illnesses. *Acta Psychiatrica Scandinavica*, *82*, 95–114.

Herman, J. P., Wiegand, S. J., & Watson, S. J. (1990). Regulation of basal corticotropin-releasing hormone and arginine vasopressin messenger ribonucleic acid expression in the paraventricular nucleus: Effects of selective hypothalamic deafferentations. *Endocrinology*, *127*, 2408–2417.

Higgins, G. A., & Schwaber, J. S. (1983). Somatostatinergic projections from the central nucleus of the amygdala to the vagal nuclei. *Peptides*, *4*, 657–662.

Hirai, T., & Jones, E. G. (1989). Distribution of tachykinin- and enkephalin-immunoreactive fibers in the human thalamus. *Brain Research Reviews*, *14*, 35–52.

Hobson, J. A., Lydic, R., & Baghdoyan, H. E. (1986). Evolving concepts of sleep cycle generation: From brain centers to neuronal populations. *Behavioral and Brain Sciences*, *9*, 371–448.

Horita, A., Carino, M. A., Zabawska, J., & Lai, H. (1989). TRH analog MK-771 reverses neurochemical and learning deficits in medial septal lesioned rats. *Peptides*, *10*, 121–124.

Iager, A. C., Kirch, D. G., Bigelow, L. B., & Karson, C. N. (1986). Treatment of schizophrenia with a vasopressin analogue. *American Journal of Psychiatry*, *143*, 375–377.

Insel, T. R. (1992). Oxytocin: A neuropeptide for affiliation—evidence from behavioral, receptor autoradiographic, and comparative studies. *Psychoneuroendocrinology*, *17*, 3–35.

Itoh, S., Katsuura, G., & Yoshikawa, K. (1985). Hypermotility induced by vasoactive intestinal peptide in the rat: Its reciprocal action to cholecystokinin octapeptide. *Peptides*, *6*, 53–57.

Jacobs, B. L. (1990). Locus coeruleus neuronal activity in behaving animals. In D. J. Heal & C. A. Marsden (Eds.), *The pharmacology of noradrenaline in the central nervous system* (pp. 110–122). Oxford: Oxford University Press.

Jacquet, Y. F. (1978). Opiate effects after adrenocorticotropin or ß-endorphin injections in the periaqueductal gray matter of rats. *Science*, *201*, 1032–1034.

Jirikowski, G. F., Caldwell, J. D., Pilgrim, C., Stumpf, W. E., & Pedersen, C. A. (1989). Changes in immunostaining for oxytocin in the forebrain of the female rat during late pregnancy, parturition and early lactation. *Cell and Tissue Research*, *256*, 411–417.

Joels, M., & de Kloet, E. R. (1992). Control of neuronal excitability by corticosteroid hormones. *Trends in Neurosciences*, *15*, 25–28.

Johnson, A. K., & Edwards, G. L. (1990). The neuroendocrinology of thirst: Afferent signaling and mechanisms of central integration. In D. Ganten & D. Pfaff (Eds.), *Current topics in neuroendocrinology: Vol. 10. Behavioral aspects of neuroendocrinology* (pp. 149–190). Berlin: Springer-Verlag.

Jolicoeur, F. B., Michaud, J. N., Rivest, R., Menard, D., Gaudin, D., Fournier, A., & St.-Pierre, S. (1991). Neurobehavioral profile of neuropeptide Y. *Brain Research Bulletin*, *26*, 265–268.

Jouvet, M. (1972). The role of monoamines and acetylcholine-containing neurons in the regulation of the sleep–waking cycle. In *Ergebnisse der Physiologie: Vol. 64. Neurophysiology and neurochemistry of sleep and wakefulness* (pp. 166–308). Berlin: Springer-Verlag.

Kalra, S. P., & Kalra, P. S. (1990). Neuropeptide Y: A novel peptidergic signal for the control of feeding behavior. In D. Ganten & D. Pfaff (Eds.), *Current topics in neuroen-docrinology: Vol. 10. Behavioral aspects of neuroendocrinology* (pp. 191–222). Berlin: Springer-Verlag.

Katsuura, G., Yoshikawa, K., Itoh, S., & Hsiao, S. (1983). Behavioral effects of thyrotropin releasing-hormone in forntal decorticated rats. *Peptides*, *5*, 899–903.

Kaye, W. H., Berrettini, W., Gwirstsman, H., & George, D. T. (1990). Altered cerebrospinal fluid neuropeptide Y and peptide YY immunoreactivity in anorexia and bulimia nervosa. *Archives of General Psychiatry*, *47*, 543–556.

Kohler, C., Persson, A., Melander, T., Theodorsson, E., Sedvall, G., & Hokfelt, T. (1989). Distribution of galanin-binding sites in the monkey and human telencephalon: Preliminary observations. *Experimental Brain Research*, *75*, 375–380.

Komisaruk, B. R., Siegel, H. I., Cheng, M.-F., & Feder, H. H. (Eds.). (1986). *Annals of the New York Academy of Sciences: Vol. 474. Reproduction: A behavioral and neuroendocrine perspective*. New York: New York Academy of Sciences.

Koob, G. F., Sandman, C. A., & Strand, F. L. (Eds.). (1990). *Annals of the New York Academy of Sciences: Vol. 579. A decade of neuropeptides: Past, present, and future*. New York: New York Academy of Sciences.

Koolhaas, J. M., van den Brink, T. H. C., Roozendaal, B., & Boorsma, F. (1990). Medial amygdala and aggressive behavior: Interaction between testosterone and vasopressin. *Aggressive Behavior*, *16*, 223–229.

Krieger, D., & Herbert, E. (Eds.). (1987). *Annals of the New York Academy of Sciences: Vol. 525. The hypothalmic–pituitary–adrenal axis revisited*. New York: New York Academy of Sciences.

Kuhar, M. J., Ritz, M. C., & Boja, J. W. (1991). The dopamine hypothesis of the reinforcing properties of cocaine. *Trends in Neurosciences*, *14*, 299–303.

Kulkosky, P. J., Glazner, G. W., Moore, H. D., Low, C. A., & Woods, S. C. (1989). Neuropeptide Y: Behavioral effects in the golden hamster. *Peptides*, *9*, 1389–1393.

Kyrkouli, S. E., Stanley, B. G., Hutchinson, R., Seirafi, R. Î., & Leibowitz, S. F. (1990). Peptide–amine interactions in the hypothalamic paravetricular nucleus: Analysis of galanin and neuropeptide Y in relation to feeding. *Brain Research*, *521*, 185–191.

LeDoux, J. E. (1992). Brain systems and emotional memory. In K. Strongman (Ed.), *International review of studies on emotion* (Vol. 2, pp. 23–29). Chichester, England: Wiley.

Leeman, S. E., Krause, J. E., & Lembeck, F. (Eds.). (1991). *Annals of the New York Academy of Sciences: Vol. 632. Substance P and related peptides: Cellular and molecular physiology*. New York: New York Academy of Sciences.

Le Moal, M., Dantzer, R., Mormede, P., Baudel, A., Lebrun, C., Ettenberg, A., van der Kooy, D., Wenger, J., Deyo, S., Koob, G. F., & Bloom, F. E. (1984). Behavioral effects of peripheral administration of arginine vasopressin: A review of our search for a mode of action and a hypothesis. *Psychoneuroendocrinology*, *9*, 319–341.

Levant, B., & Nemeroff, C. B. (1988). The psychobiology of neurotensin. In D. Ganten & D. Pfaff (Eds.), *Current Topics in Neuroendocrinology: Vol. 8. The neuroendocrinology of mood* (pp. 232–262). Berlin: Springer-Verlag.

Liebowitz, M. R. (1983). *The chemistry of love*. Boston: Little, Brown.

MacLean, P. D. (1990). *The triune brain in evolution: Role in paleocerebral functions*. New York: Plenum Press.

MacLeod, R. M., Scapagnini, U., & Thorner, M. O. (Eds.). (1984). *Prolactin: Basic and clinical correlates* (Fidia Research Series, Vol. 1). Padova, Italy: Liviana Press.

Mansour, A., Khachaturian, H., Lewis, M. E., Akil, H., & Watson, J. (1988). Anatomy of CNS opioid receptors. *Trends in Neurosciences, 11*, 308–314.

McCarthy, M. M. (1990). Oxytocin inhibits infanticide in female house mice (*Mus domesticus*). *Hormones and Behavior, 24*, 365–375.

Mellow, A. M., Sunderland, T., Cohen, R. M., Lawlor, B. A., Hill, J. L., Newhouse, P. A., Cohen, M. R., & Murphy, D. L. (1989). Acute effects of high dose thyrotropin releasing hormone infusions in Alzheimer's disease. *Psychopharmacology, 98*, 403–407.

Miller, L. H., Sandman, C. A., & Kastin, A. J. (Eds.). (1977). *Neuropeptide influences on the brain and behavior.* New York: Raven Press.

Metcalf, G., & Jackson, I. M. D. (Eds.). (1989). *Annals of the New York Academy of Sciences: Vol. 553. Thyrotropin-release hormone: Biomedical Significance.* New York: New York Academy of Sciences.

Miles, A., Philbrick, D. R. S., & Thompson, C. (Eds.). (1989). *Melatonin: Clinical perspectives.* Oxford: Oxford University Press.

Misenberg, G., Simmons, W. H., & Lorens, S. Å. (1990). Aversive properties of bombesin in rats. *Pharmacology, Biochemistry and Behavior, 37*, 689–692.

Molinari, M., Hendry, S. H. C., & Jones, E. G. (1987). Distributions of certain neuropeptides in the primate thalamus. *Brain Research, 426*, 270–289.

Moody, T. W., O'Donohue, T. L., Chronwall, B. M., Cuttitta, F., Linden, C. D., Getz, R. L., & Wolf, S. S. (1988). Neurochemistries and pharmacology of bombesin like peptides. In A. Negro-Vilar & P. M. Conn (Eds.), *Peptide hormones: Effects and mechanisms of action* (Vol. 2, pp. 3–14). Boca Raton, FL: CRC Press.

Moore, F. L. (1987). Behavioral actions of neurohypophysial peptides. In D. Crews (Ed.), *Psychobiology of reproductive behavior: An evolutionary perspective* (pp. 61–87). Englewood Cliffs, NJ: Prentice-Hall.

Morley, J. E., Bartness, T. J., Gosnell, B. A., & Levine, A. F. (1986). Peptidergic regulation of feeding. *International Review of Neurobiology, 27*, 207–298.

Morley, J. E., & Blundell, J. E. (1988). The neurobiological basis of eating disorders: Some formulations. *Biological Psychiatry, 23*, 53–78.

Morley, J. E., & Flood, J. F. (1990). Neuropeptide Y and memory processing. *Annals of the New York Academy of Sciences, 611*, 258–272.

Moruzzi, G. (1972). The sleep–waking cycle. In *Ergebnisse der Physiologie: Vol. 64. Neurophysiology and neurochemistry of sleep and wakefulness* (pp. 1–165). Berlin: Springer-Verlag.

Moss, R. L., & Dudley, C. A. (1984). The challenge of studying the behavioral effects of neuropeptides. In L. L. Iversen, S. D. Iversen, & S. H. Snyder (Eds.), *Handbook of psychopharmacology* (Vol. 18, pp. 397–454). New York: Plenum Press.

Napier, T. C., Kalivas, P. W., & Hanin, I. (Eds.). (1991). *The basal forebrain: Anatomy to function.* New York: Plenum Press.

Naumann, E., Bartussek, D., Kaiser, W., & Fehm-Wolfsdorf, G. (1991). Vasopressin and cognitive processes: Two event-related potential studies. *Peptides, 12*, 1379–1384.

Negro-Vilar, A., & Conn, P. M. (Eds.). (1988). *Peptide hormones: Effects and mechanisms of action* (Vol. 2). Boca Raton, FL: CRC Press.

Nemeroff, C. B., & Prange, A. J. (Eds.). (1982). *Annals of the New York Academy of Sciences: Vol. 400. Neurotensin, a brain and gastrointestinal peptide.* New York: New York Academy of Sciences.

Nemeroff, C. B., Youngblood, W., Manberg, P. J., Prange, A. J., Jr., & Kizel, J. S. (1983). Regional brain concentrations of neuropeptides in Huntington's chorea and schizophrenia. *Science, 221*, 972–975.

Normansell, L., & Panksepp, J. (in press). A role for glutamateric systems in the isolation-induced distress calling of domestic chicks. *Psychopharmacology.*

Nouel, D., Dubuc, I., Kitabgi, P., & Constentin, J. (1990). Centrally administered (D-Trp^{11})-neurotensin, as well as neurotensin protected from inactivation by thiorphan, modifies locomotion in rats in a biphasic manner. *Peptides, 11*, 551–555.

O'Dorisio, M. S., & Panerai, A. (Eds.). (1990). *Annals of the New York Academy of Sciences: Vol. 594. Neuropeptides and immunopeptides: Messengers in a neuroimmune axis.* New York: New York Academy of Sciences.

Ogawa, N., Mizunop, S., Mori, A., Nukina, I., Ota, Z., & Yamamoto, M. (1984). Potential anti-depressive effects of thyrotropin releasing hormone (TRH) and its analogues. *Peptides, 5*, 743–746.

Olivier, B., Mos, J., & Slangen, J. L. (Eds). (1991). *Animal models in psychopharmacology.* Basel: Birkhauser Verlag.

Panksepp, J. (1981a). Hypothalamic integration of behavior: Rewards, punishments, and related psychobiological process. In P. J. Morgane & J. Panksepp (Eds.), *Handbook of the hypothalamus: Vol. 3, Part A. Behavioral studies of the hypothalamus* (pp. 289–487). New York: Marcel Dekker.

Panksepp, J. (1981b). Brain opioids: A neurochemical substrate for narcotic and social dependence. In S. Cooper (Ed.), *Progress in theory in psychopharmacology* (pp. 149–175). London: Academic Press.

Panksepp, J. (1982). Toward a general psychobiological theory of emotions. *Behavioral and Brain Sciences, 5*, 407–467.

Panksepp, J. (1985). Mood changes: In P. J. Vinker, G. W. Bruyn, & H. L. Klawans (Eds.), *Handbook of clinical neurology: Vol. 1. Clinical neuropsychology* (pp. 271–285). Amsterdam: Elsevier.

Panksepp, J. (1986a). The neurochemistry of behavior. *Annual Review of Psychology, 37*, 77–107.

Panksepp, J. (1986b). The anatomy of emotions. In R. Plutchik & H. Kellerman (Eds.), *Emotion: Theory, research, and experience: Vol. 3. Biological foundations of emotions* (pp. 91–124). New York: Academic Press.

Panksepp, J. (1989). The neurobiology of emotions: Of animal brains and human feelings. In T. Manstead & H. Wagner (Eds.), *Handbook of social psychophysiology* (pp. 5–26). New York: Wiley.

Panksepp, J. (1990). The psychoneurology of fear: Evolutionary perspectives and the role of animal models in understanding human anxiety. In G. D. Burrows, M. Roth, & R. Noyes, Jr. (Eds.), *Handbook of Anxiety: Vol. 3. The neurobiology of anxiety* (pp. 3–58). Amsterdam: Elsevier.

Panksepp, J. (1991). Affective neuroscience: A conceptual framework for the neurobiological study of emotions. In K. Strongman (Ed.), *International review of studies on emotion* (Vol 1, pp. 59–99). Chichester, England: Wiley.

Panksepp, J. (1992a). Oxytocin effects on emotional processes: Separation distress, social bonding, and relationships to psychiatric disorders. *Annals of the New York Academy of Sciences, 652*, 243–252.

Panksepp, J. (1992b). A critical role for "affective neuroscience" in resolving what is basic about basic emotions. *Psychological Review, 99,* 554–560.

Panksepp, J., & Abbott, B. (1990). Modulation of separation distress by α-MSH. *Peptides, 11,* 647–653.

Panksepp, J., Lensing, P., Leboyer, M., & Bouvard, M. P. (1991). Naltrexone and other potential new pharmacological treatments of autism. *Brain Dysfunction, 4,* 281–300.

Panksepp, J., & Meeker, R. (1980). The role of GABA in the ventromedial hypothalamic regulation of food intake. *Brain Research Bulletin,* 5(Suppl 2), 453–460.

Panksepp, J., Newman, J. D., & Insel, T. R. (1992). Critical issues in the analysis of separation-distress systems of the brain. In K. Strongman (Ed.), *International review of studies on emotion* (Vol. 2, pp. 51–72). Chichester, England: Wiley.

Panksepp, J., & Normansell, L. A. (1990). Effects of ACTH (1-24) and ACTH/MSH (4-10) on isolation-induced distress vocalizations in domestic chicks. *Peptides, 11,* 915–919.

Panksepp, J., Normansell, L. A., Herman, B. , Bishop, P., & Crepeau, L. (1988). Neural and neurochemical control of the separation distress call. In J. D. Newman (Ed.), *The physiological control of mammalian vocalizations* (pp. 263–300). New York: Plenum Press.

Panksepp, J., & Sahley, T. (1987). Possible brain opioid involvement in disrupted social intent and language development of autism. In E. Schopler & G. Mesibov (Eds.), *Neurobiological issues in autism* (pp. 357–382). New York: Plenum Press.

Panksepp, J., Siviy, S. M., & Normansell, L. A. (1985). Brain opioids and social emotions. In M. Reite & T. Fields (Eds.), *The psychobiology of attachment and separation* (pp. 3–49). New York, Academic Press.

Panksepp, J., Yates, G., Ikemoto, S., & Nelson, E. (1991). Simple ethological models of depression: Social-isolation induced "despair" in chicks and mice. In B. Olivier, J. Mos, & J. L. Slangen (Eds.), *Animal models in psychopharmacology* (pp. 161–181). Basel: Birkhauser Verlag.

Paunovic, V. R., & Popovic, V. (1989). The development of dependence to an octapeptide somatostatin analog: Contribution to the study of somatostatin analgesia. *Biological Psychiatry, 26,* 97–101.

Pecile, A., Ferri, S., Braga, P.C., & Olgiati, V. R. (1975). Effects of intracerebroventricular calcitonin in the conscious rabbit. *Experientia, 31,* 332–333.

Pedersen, C. A., Caldwell, J. D., & Brooks, P. J. (1990). Neuropeptide control of parental and reproductive behavior. In D. Ganten & D. Pfaff (Eds.), *Current topics in neuroendocrinology: Vol. 10. Behavioral aspects of neuroendocrinology* (pp. 81–113). Berlin: Springer- Verlag.

Pedersen, C. A., Caldwell, J. D., Jirikowski, G., & Insel, T. R. (Eds.). (1992). *Annals of the New York Academy of Sciences: Vol. 652. Oxytocin in maternal, sexual and social behaviors.* New York: New York Academy of Sciences.

Peters, J., Van Kammen, D. P., Gelernter, J., Yao, J., & Shaw, D. (1990). Neuropeptide Y-like immunoreactivity in schizophrenia: Relationships with clinical measures. *Schizophrenia Research, 3,* 287–294.

Pert, A., Moody, T. A., Pert, C. B., DeWald, L. A., & Rivier, J. (1980). Bombesin: Receptor distribution in brain and effects on nociception and locomotor activity. *Brain Research, 193,* 209–220.

Pfaff, D. W. (1982). Neurobiological mechanisms of sexual motivation. In D. W. Pfaff (Ed.), *The physio-logical mechanisms of motivation* (pp. 287–318). Berlin: Springer-Verlag.

Pfaff, D. W., & Schwartz-Giblin, S. (1988). Cellular mechanisms of female reproductive behaviors. In E. Knobil & J. Neill (Eds.), *The physiology of reproduction* (pp. 1487–1567). New York: Raven Press.

Pittman, Q. J., & Thornhill, J. A. (1990). Neuropeptide mechanisms affecting temperature control. In D. Ganten & D. Pfaff (Eds.), *Current topics in neuroendocrinology: Vol. 10. Behavioral aspects of neuroendocrinology* (pp. 223–242). Berlin: Springer-Verlag.

Potegal, M., & Ferris, C. F. (1989). Intraspecific aggression in male hamsters is inhibited by intrahypothalamic vasopressin-receptor antagonists. *Aggressive Behavior, 15,* 311–320.

Ribeiro, S. A., Corrado, A. P., & Graeff, F. G. (1971). Antinociceptive action of intraventricular bradykinin. *Neuropharmacology, 10,* 725–731.

Richard, P., Moos, F., & Freund-Mercier, M.-J. (1991). Central effects of oxytocin. *Physiological Reviews, 71,* 331–370.

Risch, S. C. (Ed.). (1991). *Central nervous system peptide mechanisms in stress and depression.* Washington, DC: American Psychiatric Press.

Romanova, G. A., Karganov, M. Y., Kadar, T., & Telegdy, G. (1990). The effects of somatostatin and somatostatin antiserum on the retention of passive avoidance behavior after neofrontal decortication in rats. *Physiology and Behavior, 47,* 1035–1036.

Rubinow, D. R. (1986). Cerebrospinal fluid somatostatin and psychiatric illness. *Biological Psychiatry, 32,* 341–365.

Saffroy, M., Beaujouan, J.-C., Torrens, Y., Besseyre, J., Berstrom, L., & Glowinski, J. (1988). Localization of tachykinin binding sites (NK_1, NK_2, NK_3 ligands) in the rat brain. *Peptides, 9,* 227–241.

Sahgal, A. (1984). A critique of the vasopressin–memory hypothesis. *Psychopharmacology, 83,* 215–228.

Said, S. I., & Mutt, V. (Eds.). (1988). *Annals of the New York Academy of Sciences: Vol. 527. Vasoactive intestinal peptide and related peptides.* New York: New York Academy of Sciences.

Sandman, C. A., Miller, L. E., & Kastin, A. J. (Eds.). (1976). *The neuropeptides: Pharmacology, physiological substrates and behavioral effects. Pharmacology, Biochemistry and Behavior,* 5(Suppl. 1).

Sastre, P. J., & Jouvet, M. (1979). Le comportement onirique du chat. *Physiology and Behavior, 22,* 979–989.

Schwanzel-Fukuda, M., & Pfaff, D. W. (1989). Origin of luteinizing hormone-releasing hormone neurons. *Nature, 338,* 161–164.

Shi, W., & Bunney, B. (1991). Neurotensin modulates autoreceptor mediated dopamine effects on midbrain dopamine activity. *Brain Research, 543,* 315–321.

Shibasaki, T., Yamauchi, N., Kato, Y., Masuda, A., Imaki, T., Hotta, M., Demura, H., Oono, H., Ling, N., & Shizume, K. (1988). Involvement of corticotropin-releasing factor in retrain stress-induced anorexia and reversion of the anorexia by somatostatin in the rat. *Life Sciences, 43,* 1103–1110.

Siegel, A., & Shaikh, M. B. (1992). Neurotransmitters and aggressive behavior: Some new perspectives. In K. Strongman (Ed.), *International reviews of studies on emotion* (Vol 1., pp. 5–22). Chichester, England: Wiley.

Simon, A., Birkenfeld, A., & Schenker, J. G. (1990). Gonadotropin releasing hormone (GnRH): Mode of action and clinical applications. A review. *International Journal of Fertility, 35,* 350–362.

Siviy, S. M., & Panksepp, J. (1985). Energy balance and juvenile play in rats. *Physiology and Behavior*, *35*, 435–441.

Skofitsch, G., & Jacobowitz, D. M. (1985). Calcitonin gene-related peptide: Detailed immunohistochemical distribution in the central nervous system. *Peptides*, *6*, 721–745.

Smith, G. P., Jerome, C., Cushin, B., Eterno, R., & Simansky, K. (1981). Abdominal vagotomy blocks the satiety effect of cholecystokinin in rat. *Science*, *213*, 1036–1037.

Snel, J., Taylor, J., & Wegman, M. (1987). Does DGAVP influence memory, attention and mood in young healthy men? *Psychopharmacology*, *92*, 224–228.

Snyder, S. H. (1985). Adenosine as a neuromodulator. *Annual Review of Neuroscience*, *8*, 103–124.

Sokol, H. W., & Valtin, H. (Eds.). (1982). *Annals of the New York Academy of Sciences: Vol. 394. The Brattelboro rat*. New York: New York Academy of Sciences.

Spruijt, B. M., & Gispen, W. H. (1986). ACTH grooming. In D. deWied & C. Ferrari (Eds.), *Central actions of ACTH and related peptides* (pp. 179–187). Padova, Italy: Liviana Press.

Stanley, B. G., Daniel, D. R., Chin, A. S., & Leibowitz, S. F. (1985). Paraventricular nucleus injections of peptide YY and neuropeptide Y preferentially enhance carbohydrate ingestion. *Peptides*, *6*, 1205–1211.

Staubli, U., & Huston, J. P. (1985). Central action of substance P: Possible role in reward. *Behavioral and Neural Biology*, *43*, 100–108.

Steardom, L., & Nathanson, J. A. (1987). Brain barrier tissues: End organs for atriopeptins. *Science*, *235*, 470–473.

Steriade, M., Gloor, P., Llinas, R. R., Lose da Silva, F. H., & Mesulam, M.-M. (1990). Basic mechanisms of cerebral rhythmic activities. *Electroencephalography and Clinical Neurophysiology*, *76*, 481–508.

Steriade, M., & Llinas, R. (1988). The functional states of the thalamus and the associated neuronal interplay. *Physiological Review*, *68*, 649–742.

Sudakov, K. V., Ivanov, V. T., Koplik, E. V., Vedjaev, D. F., Michaleva, I. I., & Sargsjan, A. S. (1983). Delta-sleep inducing peptide (DSIP) as a factor facilitating animals' resistance to acute emotional stress. *Pavlovian Journal of Biological Science*, *18*, 1–5.

Sundstrom, E., Archer, T., Melander, T., & Hokfelt, T. (1988). Galanin impairs acquisition but not retrieval of spatial memory in rats studied in the Morris swim maze. *Neuroscience Letters*, *88*, 332–335.

Tache, Y., Melchiorri, P., & Negri, L. (Eds.). (1988). *Annals of the New York Academy of Sciences: Vol. 547. Bombesin-like peptides in health and disease*. New York: New York Academy of Sciences.

Takeyama, M., Kondo, K., Takayama, F., Kondo, R., Murata, H., & Miyakawa, I. (1991). High concentration of a gastrin releasing peptide-like immunoreactive substance in pregnant human milk. *Biochemical and Biophysical Research Communications*, *176*, 931–937.

Tannenbaum, G. Í. (1984). Growth hormone-releasing factor: Direct effects on growth hormone, glucose, and behavior via the brain. *Science*, *226*, 464-466.

Telegdy, G. (1985). Effects of gastrointesinal peptides on the nervous system. In A. Lajtha (Ed.), *Handbook of neurochemistry: Vol. 8. Neuronal systems* (2nd ed., pp. 217–242). New York: Plenum Press.

Turner, T. J., & Ortony, A. (1992). Basic emotions: Can conflicting criteria converge? *Psychological Review*, *99*, 566–571.

Vanderhaeghen, J.-J., & Crawley, J. N. (Eds.). (1985). *An-nals of the New York Academy of Sciences: Vol. 448. Neuronal cholecystokinin*. New York: New York Academy of Sciences.

Van der Hoof, P., Urban, L. J. A., & deWied, D. (1989). Vasopressin maintains long-term potentiation in rat lateral septum slices. *Brain Research*, *505*, 181–186.

Van Kammen, D. P., Waters, R. N., & Gold, P. (1981). Spinal fluid vasopressin, angiotensin I and II, beta endorphin and opioid activity in schizophrenia: A preliminary evaluation. In C. Perris, G. Strewe, & B. Jansson (Eds.), *Biological psychiatry* (pp. 339–344). Amsterdam: Elsevier/North Holland.

van Wimersma Greidanus, T. B., & van Ree, J. M. (1990). Behavioral effects of vasopressin. In. D. Ganten & D. Pfaff (Eds.), *Current topics in neuroendocrinology: Vol. 10. Behavioral aspects of neuroendocrinology* (pp. 61–80). Berlin: Springer-Verlag.

Vasko, M. R., & Harris, V. (1990). Gamma-aminobutyric acid inhibits the potassium-stimulated release of somatostatin from rat spinal cord slices. *Brain Research*, *507*, 129–137.

Vaughn, A. W., Baumeister, A. A., Hawkins, M. F., & Anticich, T. G. (1990). Intranigral microinjection of neurotensin suppresses feeding in food deprived rats. *Neuropharmacology*, *29*, 957–960.

Vavrek, R. J., & Stewart, J. M. (1985). Competitive antagonists of bradykinin. *Peptides*, *6*, 161-164.

Vecsei, L., Bollok, I., Penke, B., & Telegdy, G. (1986). Somatostatin and (D-TRP, D-CYS)-somatostatin delay extinction and reverse electroconvulsive shock induced amnesia in rats. *Psychoneuroendocrinology*, *11*, 111–115.

Vecsei, L., & Widerlov, E. (1988). Brain and CSF somatostatin concentrations in patients with psychiatric or neurological illness: An overview. *Acta Psychiatrica Scandinavica*, *78*, 657–667.

Verebey, K. (Ed.). (1982). *Annals of the New York Academy of Sciences Vol. 398. Opioids in mental illness: Theories, clinical observations and treatment possibilities*. New York: New York Academy of Sciences.

Vilberg, T. R., Panksepp, J., Kastin, A. J., & Coy, D. H. (1984). The pharmacology of endorphin modulation of chick distress vocalization. *Peptides*, *5*, 823–827.

Wahlestedt, C., Kman, R., & Widerlov, E. (1989). Neuropeptide Y (NPY) and the central nervous system: Distribution effects and possible relationship to neurological and psychiatric disorders. *Progress in Neuropharmacology and Biological Psychiatry*, *13*, 31–54.

Weingartner, H., Kaye, W., Gold, P., Smalleberg, S., Peterson, R., Gillin, J. C., & Ebert, M. (1981). Vasopressin treatment of cognitive dysfunction in progressive dementia. *Life Sciences*, *29*, 2721–2726.

Whybrow, P. C., & Bauer, M. S. (1988). Effects of peripheral thyroid hormones on the central nervous system: Relevance to disorders of mood. In. D. Ganten & D. Pfaff (Eds.), *Current topics in neuroendocrinology: Vol. 8. Neuroendocrinology of mood* (pp. 309–327). Berlin: Springer-Verlag.

Willner, P. (1985). *Depression: A psychobiological synthesis*. New York: Wiley.

Willner, P., & Scheel-Kruger, J. (Eds.). (1991). *The mesolimbic dopamine system: From motivation to action*. Chichester, England: Wiley.

Wise, R. A., & Bozarth, M. A. (1987). A psychomotor stimulant theory of addiction. *Psychological Review*, *94*, 469–492.

Woods, S. C., & Porte, J. D. (1983). The role of insulin as a satiety factor in the central nervous system. In A. J.

Szabo (Ed.), *Advances in metabolic disorders: Vol. 10. CNS regulation of carbohydrate metabolism* (pp. 303–319). New York: Academic Press.

Yamamoto, T., Matsuo, R., Ichikawa, H., Wakisaka, S., Akai, M., Imai, Y., Yonehara, N., & Inoki, R. (1990). Aversive taste stimuli increase CGRP levels in the gustatory insular cortex of the rat. *Neuroscience Letters, 112,* 167–172.

Young, W. S., III, Mezey, E., & Seigel, R. E. (1986). Quantitative in situ hybridization reveals increased levels of corticotropin-releasing factor mRNA after adrenalectomy in rats. *Neuroscience Letters, 70,* 198–203.

Zajonc, R. B., & McIntosh, D. N. (1992). Emotions research: Some promising questions and some questionable promises. *Psychological Science, 3,* 70–74.

Zappulla, R. A., LeFever, F. F., Jaeger, J., & Bilder, R. (Eds.). (1991). *Annals of the New York Academy of Sciences: Vol. 620. Windows on the brain: Neuropsychology's technological frontiers.* New York: New York Academy of Sciences.

8

Emotional Networks in the Brain

JOSEPH E. LeDOUX

INTRODUCTION

Contemporary neuroscientists have available a vast arsenal of tools for understanding brain functions, from the level of anatomical systems to the level of molecules. Localization of a function at the anatomical level is the oldest but also the most basic approach. Until the function in question can be localized to a specific set of structures and their connections, the application of cellular and molecular approaches is the neurobiological equivalent of a search for a needle in a haystack. Fortunately, considerable progress has been made in understanding the anatomical organization of emotion, and this chapter focuses on this work.

IN SEARCH OF THE EMOTIONAL BRAIN

Our understanding of the brain mechanisms of emotion has changed radically over the past 100 years. In the late 19th century, William James (1884) suggested that emotion is a function of sensory and motor areas of the neocortex, and that the brain does not possess a special system devoted to emotional functions. This idea was laid low by studies showing that emotional reactions, but not sensory and motor processes per se, require the integrity of the hypothalamus (Cannon, 1929; Bard, 1929). On the basis of such observations, Papez (1937) proposed a circuit theory of emotion involving the hypothalamus, anterior

thalamus, cingulate gyrus, and hippocampus. MacLean (1949, 1952) then named the structures of the Papez circuit, together with several additional regions (amygdala, septal nuclei, orbito-frontal cortex, portions of the basal ganglia), the "limbic system"; he viewed the limbic system as a general-purpose system involved in the mediation of functions required for the survival of the individual and the species.

MacLean's writings were very persuasive, and for many years the problem of relating emotion to brain mechanisms seemed solved at the level of anatomical systems. However, the limbic system concept has come under fire in recent years. It is now believed that the concept suffers from imprecision at both the structural and functional levels. For example, it has proven impossible to provide unequivocal criteria for defining which structures and pathways should be included in the limbic system (Brodal, 1982; Swanson, 1983). A standard criterion, connectivity with the hypothalamus, extends the limbic system to include structures at all levels of the central nervous system, from the neocortex to the spinal cord. Furthermore, classic limbic areas, such as the hippocampus and mammillary bodies, have proven to be far more important for cognitive processes (e.g., declarative memory) than for emotional processes (e.g., Squire, 1987).

Nevertheless, one limbic area that has been consistently implicated in emotional processes in a variety of situations is the amygdala (e.g., Gloor, 1960; Mishkin & Aggleton, 1981;

Aggleton & Mishkin, 1986; LeDoux, 1987; Rolls, 1986, 1992; Halgren, 1981, 1992). Interestingly, the amygdala was not part of the Papez circuit model and was clearly a second-class citizen, relative to the hippocampus at least, in the limbic system hypothesis. However, the fact that the limbic system hypothesis has survived for so long may be largely attributable to the inclusion of the amygdala (LeDoux, 1992). Otherwise, the relation between emotional functions and classic limbic areas would have been far less prominent over the years.

THE AMYGDALA AS AN EMOTIONAL COMPUTER

The contribution of the amygdala to emotion emerged from studies of the Kluver–Bucy syndrome, a complex set of behavioral changes brought about by damage to the temporal lobe in primates (Kluver & Bucy, 1937). Following such lesions, animals lose their fear of previously threatening stimuli, attempt to copulate with members of other species, and attempt to eat a variety of things that "normal" primates find unattractive (feces, meat, rocks). Studies by Weiskrantz (1956) then determined that lesions confined to the amygdala and sparing other temporal lobe structures produce the emotional components of the syndrome. Weiskrantz proposed that amygdala lesions interfere with the ability to determine the motivational significance of stimuli. A host of subsequent studies have shown that the amygdala is a key structure in the assignment of reward value to stimuli (Jones & Mishkin, 1972; Spiegler & Mishkin, 1981; Gaffan & Harrison, 1987; Gaffan, Gaffan, & Harrison, 1988), in the conditioning of fear to novel stimuli (Blanchard & Blanchard, 1972; Kapp, Frysinger, Gallagher, & Haselton, 1979, 1992; Davis, Kapp, Whalen, Supple, & Pascoe, 1992; Davis, Hitchcock, & Rosen, 1987; LeDoux, 1986b, 1990), in the self-administration of rewarding brain stimulation (Kane, Coulombe, & Miliaressis, 1991; Olds, 1977), and in the elicitation by brain stimulation of a host of behavioral and autonomic responses typical of emotional reactions (Hilton & Zbrozyna, 1963; Fernandez de Molina & Hunsperger, 1962; Kapp, Pascoe, & Bixler, 1984; Iwata, Chida, & LeDoux, 1987). These and other findings have led a number of authors to conclude that the amygdala plays an important role in the assignment of affective significance to sensory events (Geschwind, 1965; Jones & Mishkin, 1972; Mishkin & Aggleton, 1981; Aggleton & Mishkin, 1986; LeDoux, 1984, 1987; Rolls, 1986, 1992; Halgren, 1992). How does the amygdala perform these evaluative functions?

THROUGH-PROCESSING PATHWAYS UNDERLYING STIMULUS EVALUATION BY THE AMYGDALA

Although the amygdala plays a central role in emotion, it is best viewed not as an emotional center but instead as a component of an emotional network. The anatomical inputs from sensory systems to the amygdala, and outputs from the amygdala to motor systems, define its key role in the network and suggest its contribution to emotional processing.

For some time, the amygdala has been known to receive inputs from neocortical association areas of the visual, auditory, somatosensory, and gustatory systems (Whitlock & Nauta, 1956; Herzog & Van Hoesen, 1975; Turner, Mishkin, & Knapp, 1980; Price, Russchen, & Amaral, 1987; Amaral, 1987). These connections are best defined for the visual system, which has become the model system for understanding the role of cortical sensory inputs to the amygdala in emotional processing. Visual information reaching the retina is transmitted over the optic nerve to the dorsal lateral geniculate body (LGd) of the thalamus, to the superior colliculus, and to several other targets. This discussion focuses on the information flow from the LGd, although the other projections also provide significant information.

The LGd receives lemniscal (retinotopic) inputs and relays these to laminae III and IV of primary visual cortex, otherwise known as striate cortex. Striate cortex then projects to prestriate cortex, which in turn projects to inferotemporal cortex (IT) (Ungerleider & Mishkin, 1982). With each step in this sequence, the retinal input undergoes more complex transformations (Gross, 1973). Thus, while neurons in striate cortex extract simple features, such as edges and angles, neurons in IT respond to higher-level characteristics that are best described as global object properties.

The IT is the final stage of visual processing. It is a necessary structure for normal object perception and recognition. Object information processed in IT is transmitted to the amygdala (Turner et al., 1980) and to higher-order (polymodal) association areas of the frontal, temporal, and parietal lobes that integrate information from two or more unimodal systems (Jones & Powell, 1970; Mesulam, Van Hoesen, Pandya, & Geschwind, 1977). Polymodal areas, in turn, project to the amygdala and to the entorhinal cortex, among other areas (Jones & Powell, 1970; Turner et al., 1980). Entorhinal cortex is the main input system to the hippocampal formation (Amaral, 1987), a structure now known to play an essential role in a variety of higher cognitive processes, including declarative memory and spatial thought (e.g., Squire, 1987; O'Keefe & Nadel, 1978; Olton, Becker, & Handleman, 1979). The subiculum is a major output structure of the hippocampus; it projects to entorhinal cortex (closing an intrahippocampal loop), to the amygdala, and to many other forebrain regions (Amaral, 1987; Ottersen, 1982).

The anatomical connectivity of the amygdala thus provides it with inputs from the late stages of modality-specific processing (i.e., IT in the visual system and comparable regions in other sensory systems) inputs from polymodal association cortex; and higher-order, modality-independent inputs from the hippocampus. Behavioral studies have shown that disconnection of the amygdala from modality-specific processing areas produces a Kluver–Bucy syndrome specific to the disconnected modality (Downer, 1961; Horel, Keating, & Misantone, 1975). To the extent that the Kluver–Bucy syndrome reflects an inability to assign emotional significance to sensory events, these results show that the amygdala depends upon inputs from modality-specific cortical areas in evaluating the emotional significance of sensory stimuli. Studies showing that amygdala neurons respond to the hedonic properties of stimuli (Sanghera, Rolls, & Roper-Hall, 1979; Ono, Fukuda, Nishino, Sasaki, & Muramoto, 1983; Nishijo, Ono, & Nishino, 1989), and that amygdala lesions interfere with the ability of animals to learn to associate rewards and punishments with stimuli (Jones & Mishkin, 1972; Spiegler & Mishkin, 1981; Gaffan & Harrison, 1987; Gaffan et al., 1988), support this view. Interestingly, amygdala neurons also respond to complex, socially relevant stimuli (O'Keefe & Bouma, 1969; Jacobs &

McGinty, 1972; Leonard, Rolls, Wilson, & Baylis, 1985; Brothers, Ring, & Kling, 1990), but the extent to which these response properties can be accounted for by simpler trigger features is not known (Bordi & LeDoux, 1992).

An obvious function for the polymodal projections to the amygdala is the provision of a basis for assigning emotional significance to more abstract processes. For example, the amygdala receives projections from the hippocampal formation by way of the entorhinal cortex and the subiculum (e.g., Amaral, 1987; Ottersen, 1982). Given the role of the hippocampus in spatial and contextual processing, it might be expected that projections to the amygdala from the hippocampus might be involved in situations where emotional significance must be assigned to spatial or contextual information. Indeed, recent studies show that lesions of the hippocampus interfere with the acquisition of fear responses to contextual cues without affecting the acquisition of fear reactions to discrete stimuli, presumably by way of hippocampo-amygdala connections (Phillips & LeDoux, 1992; Kim & Fanselow, 1992).

Recent studies have described an additional route of sensory transmission to the amygdala. This route, which involves transmission from sensory thalamus directly to the amygdala without being first transmitted to the neocortex, is best understood in the auditory modality. Auditory inputs are transmitted to the medial geniculate body (MGB) in several parallel systems (see Winer & Morest, 1983). Lemniscal (tonotopic) inputs reach the ventral MGB and are transmitted from there to laminae III and IV of primary auditory cortex. This projection, which makes possible fine auditory discrimination, is equivalent to the DLG projection to striate cortex. Another input system terminates in more medial areas of the MGB. Cells in these areas are not capable of precise stimulus representation, and they project rather diffusely to auditory areas of the cortex and to the amygdala (see LeDoux, Ruggiero, & Reis, 1985; LeDoux, Farb, & Ruggiero, 1990; LeDoux, 1986b). Behavioral studies have shown that the auditory cortex is unnecessary and that the thalamo-amygdala projection participates in the conditioning of emotional responses to simple auditory stimuli (un-discriminated single tones) paired with footshock (LeDoux, Sakaguchi, & Reis, 1984; LeDoux, Sakaguchi, Iwata, & Reis, 1986;

LeDoux, Cicchetti, Xagoraris, & Romanski, 1990; Iwata, LeDoux, Meeley, Arneric, & Reis, 1986). This subcortical sensory input pathway to the amygdala is not peculiar to the auditory system. Behavioral studies have shown that visual cortex is unnecessary but that the amygdala is necessary for the conditioning of emotional responses to a flashing light paired with footshock (LeDoux, Romanski, & Xagoraris, 1989). Although the origin of the subcortical visual input projection to the amygdala is as yet unknown, it clearly exists.

Subcortical sensory inputs to the amygdala may represent an evolutionarily primitive system passed on from early vertebrates that lacked well-developed neocortices (Kudo, Glendenning, Frost, & Masterson, 1986). These inputs were the main sensory transmission routes to the forebrain in such animals. In contemporary mammals, these pathways are clearly in a secondary position with respect to perceptual processing, since they exit the ascending sensory system prior to the neocortex, where object and event information is represented. However, these pathways continue to function as an early warning system, allowing the amygdala to be activated by simple stimulus features that may serve as emotional triggers. This is especially important when rapid responses are required to threatening stimuli (LeDoux, 1986a). In such situations, it may be more important to respond rapidly on the basis of incomplete stimulus information from the thalamus than to wait for a complete object representation from unimodal cortex or more complex cognitive representations from polymodal cortex or hippocampus. The thalamo-amygdala system is several synapses shorter and therefore offers this temporal processing advantage at the expense of perceptual completeness. The thalamo-amygdala system may be of general value in setting up processing in the amygdala, selecting and tuning amygdala neurons, and thus paving the way for more detailed and complete object information to be transmitted from the cortex moments later.

Once the amygdala is activated, it can set into motion a variety of motor systems to control emotional responses appropriate to the meaning of the stimulus (see Kapp et al., 1984; Davis et al., 1987; LeDoux, 1987). For example, projections from the central nucleus of the amygdala to the lateral hypothalamus are important in the expression of autonomic

responses and projections to the central gray in behavioral responses associated with emotional arousal (LeDoux, Iwata, Chicchetti, & Reis, 1988). The central nucleus also projects to forebrain and hypothalamic areas involved in the control of hormonal release by the pituitary gland (Swanson & Sawchenko, 1983), suggesting a possible mechanism for the regulation of hormonal changes associated with emotional arousal and stress.

Although much work on emotional circuitry has been done using aversive conditioning models, amygdala lesions also interfere with certain appetitively conditioned behaviors as well. For example, much of the primate lesion work and physiological recording work has used appetitive conditioning to implicate the amygdala in stimulus–reward association learning (e.g., Jones & Mishkin, 1972; Spiegler & Mishkin, 1981; Gaffan & Harrison, 1987; Gaffan et al., 1988; Sanghera et al., 1979; Ono et al., 1983; Nishijo et al., 1989), and recent studies in rats have shown that amygdala lesions interfere with the formation of conditioned place preferences (Hiroi & White, 1991; Everitt, Cador, & Robbins, 1989).

In summary, the amygdala receives a wide range of inputs about immediately present, imagined, and remembered stimuli. Its anatomical connections suggest that it can be activated by simple features, whole objects, the context in which objects occur, semantic properties of objects, images and memories of objects, and the like. Any and all of these may therefore serve as the critical trigger information for emotional arousal. It is significant that the inputs described are not all randomly distributed throughout the amygdala, which by some accounts can be divided into more than 10 subregions. The inputs mostly terminate in the lateral nucleus. The lateral nucleus is thus the sensory and cognitive gateway to the amygdala. The coalescing of inputs here implies that all of the systems are operating on the same basic set of neurons. This suggests that the opportunity for integation across different classes of inputs is great. At the same time, it also implies that the amygdala is somewhat blind as to the nature of the stimulus that activates it, since primitive sensory features are potentially as capable of activating the emotional system as complex thoughts.

There may be many emotions that do not depend upon the amygdala and its connections. Nevertheless, for many if not most of the

An Emotional Network

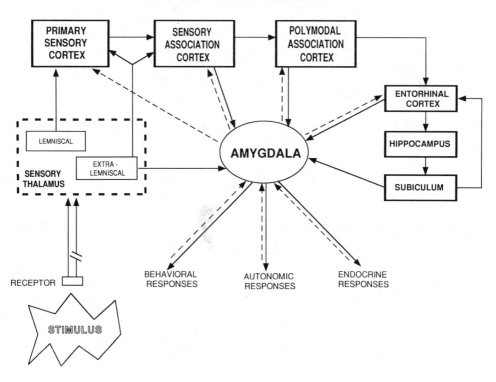

FIGURE 8.1. Proposed model of the role played by the amygdala and its input and output connections in emotional processes.

emotional processes that have been studied in detail, the amygdala and its input and output connections seem to play an important role. (See Figure 8.1 for an illustration of the relevant connections of the amygdala in emotion.)

MODULATORY SYSTEMS

The circuits described do not by any means exhaust the systems involved in emotional functions. Processing in these pathways is influenced by a number of other systems. The contribution of these other systems is best viewed as modulating the processing that occurs in the through-processing systems. Modulating influences arise both from within the brain and from the periphery.

Central Modulatory Systems

It has been known since midcentury that structures in the brainstem play an essential role in maintaining the arousal and arousability of the brain. As originally postulated by Moruzzi and Magoun (1949), the arousal system is located in the brainstem core and is called the ascending brainstem reticular formation (BSRF). Lesions of this system produce a comatose state, whereas stimulation of the system produces cortical electroencephalographic (EEG) patterns similar to those produced by sensory stimulation. The generalized nature of these changes led to the concept that the BSRF mediates "nonspecific" arousal functions. When activated by "specific" sensory systems, the BSRF arouses the cortex, and this aroused condition serves as the background against which specific sensory systems perform attentional, perceptual, mnemonic, emotional, and motivational functions (Lindsley, 1951). When activity in the BSRF is low, forebrain arousal is low and sleep results. The existence of fibers from the BSRF to the thalamus led to the hypothesis that a "nonspecific" thalamo-cortical relay system running in parallel with the specific thalamo-cortical relay functions achieves the cortical arousal functions of the BSRF.

The basic idea that the brainstem mediates nonspecific arousal functions survives today. However, we now have much greater understanding of the anatomy of the brainstem, and can actually point to several distinct systems that work together in the control of arousal (e.g., Hobson & Steriade, 1986). Included are norepinephrine-containing neurons in the locus coeruleus, serotonin-containing neurons in the dorsal raphe nucleus, and cholinergic neurons in the lateral dorsal tegmentum and parabrachial area. The axons of these neurons are highly branched and are distributed to widespread areas of the forebrain, allowing relatively few anatomically discrete, chemically specific neurons to have extensive influence over target neurons throughout the forebrain.

Of particular relevance here is the possible contribution of these nonspecific systems to emotional processing. Presumably, inputs from the nonspecific systems could act to increase attention to and focus attention on emotionally significant stimuli by increasing the level of arousal of neurons in sensory areas of the thalamus, in sensory neocortex, or in the amygdala or other limbic areas. A key question is this: How do these brainstem systems "know" when a stimulus carries emotional significance, and therefore which stimuli deserve to be attended to? The old notion that the nonspecific systems receive collaterals from sensory input systems en route to the neocortex fails to answer this question. It is unlikely that the earliest stages of sensory processing are involved in evaluating the emotional significance of sensory stimuli. It would seem necessary that the nonspecific systems receive inputs, either directly or indirectly, from the forebrain systems known to be involved in the evaluation of the significance of the stimulus. These projections would then activate the brainstem neurons, which in turn would increase the net excitability of forebrain systems (e.g., thalamo-cortical relay nuclei, cortical sensory and association areas, polymodal association cortex, amygdala, so-called limbic cortex, etc.). Projections back to the brainstem from the forebrain would close the loop and could set up feedforward patterns that might play an important role in regulating the intensity and duration of emotional reactions, allowing the emo-

tional reaction, once initiated, to perpetuate itself. In contrast, the quality of the emotional reaction (i.e., whether fear, anger, or joy is elicited by a given stimulus), by this account, is a function of the forebrain evaluative systems involving the amygdala and perhaps other, less well-understood limbic areas. In other words, arousal occurs after, not before, evaluation.

This cursory account hardly does justice to what has been one of the most heavily researched functions of the brain over the past 40 years. The interested reader can find more detail in several excellent reviews of brainstem arousal systems (e.g., Hobson & Steriade, 1986).

Peripheral Modulatory Systems

One of the long-standing controversies in the psychology of emotion involves the extent to which feedback to the brain from the periphery might contribute to emotional functions (e.g., James, 1884; Cannon, 1927; Schachter & Singer, 1962). The goal here is not to survey the current status of this literature (see Frijda, 1986), but instead simply to examine some possible sources of peripheral feedback and their implications for emotional processing.

Several bodily systems are potential sources of feedback to the brain during emotional arousal—the autonomic nervous system, the endocrine system, and sensory nerves in the skin, muscles, and viscera, to name the most obvious ones. The autonomic nervous system is usually divided into sympathetic and parasympathetic divisions. These have somewhat antagonistic functions and act somewhat reciprocally ("somewhat" should be emphasized here, since these systems are no longer thought to be as reciprocal and antagonistic as they once were). For example, consider the actions of the sympathetic and parasympathetic systems in the control of arterial pressure (e.g., Dampney, 1981; Reis, 1984). Increased sympathetic activity causes blood pressure to rise through constriction of the blood vessels. The constriction is a result of increased neural activity in the sympathetic innervation of the blood vessels, but also of the sympathetically mediated release of vasoactive hormones, particularly epinephrine, from the adrenal medulla. The change in the stretch of the blood vessel wall is detected by sensory nerve endings that transmit inputs to the brain in the vagus nerve. These inputs activate medullary neurons in the nucleus of the solitary tract (NTS), which send messages to the heart, by way of the efferent branch of the vagus nerve, to slow down its rate of pumping. This parasympathetic slowing of the heart, known as the baroreceptor reflex, helps to counteract the increase in vasoconstriction, thereby resulting in a lowering of blood pressure.

The amygdala is importantly involved in this scenario. As we have seen, the amygdala is the interface between environmental and mental events on the one hand and mental events and emotional responses (including sympathetic and parasympathetic autonomic responses) on the other. But the story does not stop there. The amygdala also receives messages back concerning the visceral responses it produces. For example, the NTS, which receives viscerosensory inputs from the vagus nerve, projects to the amygdala both directly and by way of the parabrachial nucleus, and amygdala neurons are responsive to changes in blood pressure and heart rate (Cechetto & Calaresu, 1984). These circuits show again how emotional reactions, once started, might perpetuate themselves.

The amygdala may also be an important link in the pathways through which the brain controls the release of pituitary hormones during emotional arousal and stress. In stress, for example, the anterior pituitary gland releases adrenocorticotropic hormone (ACTH), which causes the adrenal cortex to release corticosteroid hormones (e.g., Jacobson & Sapolsky, 1991). The signal causing the pituitary release of ACTH is corticotropin-releasing factor, which originates from pathways in the paraventricular hypothalamus. Neurons in the amygdala project to the paraventricular hypothalamus both directly and by way of the bed nucleus of the stria terminalis (Swanson & Sawchenko, 1983), possibly allowing the amygdala to enter into the chain of events involved in the release of ACTH from the pituitary and corticosteroids from the adrenal cortex. The corticosteriods then feed back to brain areas containing steroid receptors (including the amygdala and hippocampus), and thereby regulate the subsequent release of ACTH. Although most theories of stress hormones emphasize the contribution of receptors in the hippocampus, the amygdala should obviously be considered an important site of action, given its key role in the evaluation of the emotional significance of stimuli and the initiation of emotional reactions.

CONCLUSIONS

The amygdala is an essential brain region in the processing of the emotional significance of environmental events. It evaluates the emotional significance of simple sensory features, complex perceptions, and even abstract thoughts, and controls the expression of emotional reactions. These functions are carried out by pathways that transmit information to the amygdala from the thalamus, neocortex, and hippocampal formation, to name the most well-understood systems. However, the processing in these circuits is regulated or modulated by relatively nonspecific systems, within both the central and the peripheral nervous systems. These modulatory systems, which may account for the greater intensity and longer duration of emotional states (as compared to nonemotional states), are themselves triggered by processing originating in forebrain structures, including the amygdala. The emotional system, in other words, appears to be wired in such a way as to sustain its own activity. These anatomical facts provide biological constraints that may be useful in the generation of theories of emotion.

REFERENCES

Aggleton, J. P., & Mishkin, M. (1986). The amygdala: Sensory gateway to the emotions. In R. Plutchik & H. Kellerman (Eds.), Emotion: Theory, research and experience. Vol. 3. Biological foundations of emotions (pp. 281–299). New York: Academic Press.

Amaral, D. G. (1987). Memory: Anatomical organization of candidate brain regions. In F. Plum (Ed.), Handbook of Physiology: Section 1. The nervous system. Vol. 5. Higher functions of the brain (pp. 211–294). Bethesda, MD: American Physiological Society.

Bard, P. (1929). The central representation of the sympathetic system: As indicated by certain physiological observations. Archives of Neurology and Psychiatry, 22, 230–246.

Blanchard, D. C., & Blanchard, R. J. (1972). Innate and conditioned reactions to threat in rats with amygdaloid lesions. Journal of Comparative and Physiological Psychology, 81, 281–290.

Bordi, F., & LeDoux, J. (1992). Sensory tuning beyond the sensory system: An initial analysis of auditory properties of neurons in the lateral amygdaloid nucleus and overlying areas of the striatum. *Journal of Neuroscience, 12,* 2493–2503.

Brodal, A. (1982). *Neurological anatomy.* New York: Oxford University Press.

Brothers, L., Ring, B., & Kling, A. (1990). Response of neurons in the macaque amygdala to complex social stimuli. *Behavioral Brain Research, 41,* 199–213.

Cannon, W. B. (1927). The James–Lange theory of emotions: A critical examination and an alternative theory. *American Journal of Psychology, 39,* 106–124.

Cannon, W. B. (1929). *Bodily changes in pain, hunger, fear, and rage.* New York: Appleton.

Cechetto, D. F., & Calaresu, F. R. (1984). Units in the amygdala responding to activation of carotid baro- and chemoreceptors. *American Journal of Physiology, 246,* R832–R836.

Dampney, R. A. L. (1981). Brain stem mechanisms in the control of arterial pressure. *Clinical and Experimental Hypertension, 3,* 379–391.

Davis, M. (1992). The role of the amygdala in conditioned fear. In J. P. Aggleton (Ed.), *The amygdala: Neurobiological aspects of emotion, memory, and mental dysfunction* (pp. 255–306). New York: Wiley–Liss.

Davis, M., Hitchcock, J. M., & Rosen, J. B. (1987). Anxiety and the amygdala: Pharmacological and anatomical analysis of the fear-potentiated startle paradigm. In G. H. Bower (Ed.), *The psychology of learning and motivation* (pp. 263–305). New York: Academic Press.

Downer, J. D. C. (1961). Changes in visual gnostic function and emotional behavior following unilateral temporal lobe damage in the "split-brain" monkey. *Nature, 191,* 50–51.

Everitt, B. J., Cador, M., & Robbins, T. W. (1989). Interactions between the amygdala and ventral striatum in stimulus–reward associations: Studies using a second-order schedule of sexual reinforcement. *Neuroscience, 30,* 63–75.

Fernandez de Molina, A., & Hunsperger, R. W. (1962). Organization of the subcortical system governing defense and flight reactions in the cat. *Journal of Physiology, 160,* 200–213.

Frijda, N. (1986). *The emotions.* Cambridge, England: Cambridge University Press.

Gaffan, D., & Harrison, S. (1987). Amygdalectomy and disconnection in visual learning for auditory secondary reinforcement by monkeys. *Journal of Neuroscience, 7,* 2285–2292.

Gaffan, E. A., Gaffan, D., and Harrison, S. (1988). Disconnection of the amygdala from visual association cortex impairs visual reward-association learning in monkeys. *Journal of Neuroscience, 8*(9), 3144–3150.

Geschwind, N. (1965). The disconnexion syndromes in animals and man. Part I. *Brain, 88,* 237–294.

Gloor, P. (1960). Amygdala. In J. Field, H. W. Magoun, & V. E. Hall, (Eds.), *Handbook of Physiology: Section 1. The nervous system. Vol. 2. Neurophysiology* (pp. 1395–1420). Washington, DC: American Physiological Society.

Gross, C. G. (1973). Interotemporal cortex and vision. In E. Stellar & J. M. Sprague (Eds.), *Progress in physiological psychology* (Vol. 5, pp. 77–123). New York: Academic Press.

Halgren, E. (1981). The amygdala contribution to emotion and memory: Current studies in humans. In Y. Ben-Ari

(Ed.), *The amygdaloid complex* (pp. 395–408). Amsterdam: Elsevier/North-Holland.

Halgren, E. (1992). Emotional neurophysiology of the amygdala within the context of human cognition. In J. Aggleton (Ed.), *The amygdala: Neurobiological aspects of emotion, memory, and mental dysfunction* (pp. 191–228). New York: Wiley-Liss.

Herzog, A. G., & Van Hoesen, G. W. (1975). Temporal neocortical afferent connections to the amygdala in the rhesus monkey. *Brain Research, 115,* 57–69.

Hilton, S. M., & Zbrozyna, A. W. (1963). Amygdaloid region for defense reactions and its efferent pathway to the brainstem. *Journal of Physiology, 165,* 160–173.

Hiroi, N. M., & White, E. L. (1991). The lateral nucleus of the amygdala mediates expression of the amphetamine conditioned place preference. *Journal of Neuroscience, 11,* 2107–2116.

Hobson, J. A., & Steriade, M. (1986). Neuronal basis of behavioral state control. In V. B. Mountcastle (Ed.), *Handbook of physiology: Section 1. The nervous system. Vol. 4. Intrinsic regulatory systems of the brain* (pp. 701–823). Bethesda, MD: American Physiological Society.

Horel, J. A., Keating, E. G., & Misantone, L. J. (1975). Partial Kluver–Bucy syndrome produced by destroying temporal neocortex or amygdala. *Brain Research, 94,* 347–359.

Iwata, J., Chida, K., & LeDoux, J. E. (1987). Cardiovascular responses elicited by stimulation of neurons in the central amygdaloid nucleus in awake but not anesthetized rats resemble conditioned emotional responses. *Brain Research, 418,* 183–188.

Iwata, J., LeDoux, J. E., Meeley, M. P., Arneric, S., & Reis, D. J. (1986). Intrinsic neurons in the amygdaloid field projected to by the medial geniculate body mediate emotional responses conditioned to acoustic stimuli. *Brain Research, 383,* 195–214.

Jacobs, B. L., & McGinty, D. J. (1972). Participation of the amygdala in complex stimulus recognition and behavioral inhibition: Evidence from unit studies. *Brain Research, 36,* 431–436.

Jacobson, L., & Sapolsky, R. (1991). The role of the hippocampus in feedback regulation of the hypothalamic–pituitary–adrenocortical axis. *Endocrine Reviews, 12,* 118–134.

James, W. (1884). What is an emotion? *Mind, 9,* 188–205.

Jones, B., & Mishkin, M. (1972). Limbic lesions and the problem of stimulus–reinforcement associations. *Experimental Neurology, 36,* 362–377.

Jones, E. G., & Powell, T. P. S. (1970). An anatomical study of converging sensory pathways within the cerebral cortex of the monkey. *Brain, 93,* 793–820.

Kane, F., Coulombe, D., & Miliaressis, E. (1991). Amygdaloid self-stimulation: A movable electrode mapping study. *Behavioral Neuroscience, 105,* 926–932.

Kapp, B. S., Frysinger, R. C., Gallagher, M., & Haselton, J. (1979). Amygdala central nucleus lesions: Effect on heart rate conditioning in the rabbit. *Physiology and Behavior, 23,* 1109–1117.

Kapp, B. S., Pascoe, J. P., & Bixler, M. A. (1984). The amygdala: A neuroanatomical systems approach to its contribution to aversive conditioning. In N. Butters & L. R. Squire (Eds.), *Neuropsychology of memory* (pp. 473–488). New York: Guilford Press.

Kapp, B. S., Whalen, P. J., Supple, W. F., & Pascoe, J. P. (1992). Amygdaloid contributions to conditioned fear.

In J. P. Aggleton (Ed.), *The amygdala: Neurobiological aspects of emotion, memory, and mental dysfunction* (pp. 229–254). New York: Wiley-Liss.

Kim, J., & Fanselow, M. (1992). Modality-specific retrograde amnesia of fear. *Science, 256,* 675–677.

Kluver, H., & Bucy, P. C. (1937). "Psychic blindness" and other symptoms following bilateral temporal lobectomy in rhesus monkeys. *American Journal of Physiology, 119,* 352–353.

Kudo, M., Glendenning, K. K., Frost, S. B., & Masterson, R. S. (1986). Origin of mammalian thalamocortical projections. I. Telencephalic projection of the medial geniculate body in the opposum (*Didelphis virginiana*). *Journal of Comparative Neurology, 245,* 176–197.

LeDoux, J. E. (1984). Cognition and emotion: Processing functions and brain systems. In M. S. Gazzaniga (Ed.), *Handbook of cognitive neuroscience* (pp. 357–368). New York: Plenum Press.

LeDoux, J. E. (1986a). Neurobiology of emotion. In J. E. LeDoux & W. Hirst (Eds.), *Mind and brain* (pp. 301–354). New York: Cambridge University Press.

LeDoux, J. E. (1986b). Sensory systems and emotion. *Integrative Psychiatry, 4,* 237–248.

LeDoux, J. E. (1987). Emotion. In F. Plum (Ed.), *Handbook of physiology: Section 1. The nervous system. Vol. 5. Higher functions of the brain* (pp. 419–460). Bethesda, MD: American Physiological Society.

LeDoux, J. E. (1990). Information flow from sensation to emotion: Plasticity in the neural computation of stimulus value. In M. Gabriel & J. Moore (Eds.), *Learning and computational neuroscience: Foundations of adaptive networks* (pp. 3–52). Cambridge, MA: MIT Press.

LeDoux, J. E. (1992). Emotion and the limbic system concept. *Concepts in Neuroscience, 2,* 169–199.

LeDoux, J. E., Cicchetti, P., Xagoraris, A., & Romanski, L. R. (1990). The lateral amygdaloid nucleus: Sensory interface of the amygdala in fear conditioning. *Journal of Neuroscience, 10,* 1062–1069.

LeDoux, J. E., Farb, C. F., & Ruggiero, D. A. (1990). Topographic organization of neurons in the acoustic thalamus that project to the amygdala. *Journal of Neuroscience, 10,* 1043–1054.

LeDoux, J. E., Iwata, P., Cicchetti, & Reis, D. J. (1988). Different projections of the central amygdaloid nucleus mediate autonomic and behavioral correlates of conditioned fear. *Journal of Neuroscience, 8,* 2517–2529.

LeDoux, J. E., Romanski, L. M., & Xagoraris, A. E. (1989). Indelibility of subcortical emotional memories. *Journal of Cognitive Neuroscience, 1,* 238–243.

LeDoux, J. E., Ruggiero, D. A., & Reis, D. J. (1985). Projections to the subcortical forebrain from anatomically defined regions of the medial geniculate body in the rat. *Journal of Comparative Neurology, 242,* 182–313.

LeDoux, J. E., Sakaguchi, A., Iwata, P., & Reis, D. J. (1986). Interruption of projections from the medial geniculate body to an archi-neostriatal field disrupts the classical conditioning of emotional responses to acoustic stimuli in the rat. *Neuroscience, 17,* 615-627.

LeDoux, J. E., Sakaguchi, A., & Reis, D. J. (1984). Subcortical efferent projections of the medial geniculate nucleus mediate emotional responses conditioned to acoustic stimuli. *Journal of Neuroscience, 46,* 683–698.

Leonard, C. M., Rolls, E. T., Wilson, F. A. W., & Baylis, G. C. (1985). Neurons in the amygdala of monkeys with responses selective for faces. *Behavioral Brain Research, 15,* 159–176.

Lindsley, D. B. (1951). Emotions. In S. S. Stevens (Ed.), *Handbook of experimental psychology* (pp. 473–516). New York: Wiley.

MacLean, P. D. (1949). Psychosomatic disease and the "visceral brain": Recent developments bearing on the Papez theory of emotion. *Psychosomatic Medicine, 11,* 338–353.

MacLean, P. D. (1952). Some psychiatric implications of physiological studies on frontotemporal portion of limbic system (visceral brain). *Electroencephalography and Clinical Neurophysiology, 4,* 407–418.

Mesulam, M. M., Van Hoesen, G., Pandya, D. N., & Geschwind, N. (1977). Limbic and sensory connections of the inferior parietal lobule (area pg) in the rhesus monkey: A study with a new method for horseradish peroxidase histochemistry. *Brain Research, 136,* 393–414.

Mishkin, M., & Aggleton, J. (1981). Multiple functional contributions of the amygdala in the monkey. In Y. Ben-Ari (Ed.), *The amygdaloid complex* (pp. 409–420). Amsterdam: Elsevier/North-Holland.

Moruzzi, G., & Magoun, H. W. (1949). Brain stem reticular formation and activation of the EEG. *Electroencephalography and Clinical Neurophysiology, 1,* 455–473.

Nishijo, H., Ono, T., & Nishino, H. (1988). Single neuron responses in amygdala of alert monkey during complex sensory stimulation with affective significance. *Journal of Neuroscience, 8,* 3570–3583.

O'Keefe, J., & Bouma, H. (1969). Complex sensory properties of certain amygdala units in the freely moving cat. *Experimental Neurology, 23,* 384–398.

O'Keefe, J., & Nadel, L. (1978). *The hippocampus as a cognitive map.* Oxford: Clarendon Press.

Olds, J. (1977). *Drives and reinforcement.* New York: Raven Press.

Olton, D., Becker, J. T., & Handleman, G. E. (1979). Hippocampus, space and memory. *Behavioral and Brain Sciences, 2,* 313–365.

Ono, T., Fukuda, M., Nishino, H., Sasaki, K., & Muramoto, K.-I. (1983). Amygdaloid neuronal responses to complex visual stimuli in an operant feeding situation in the monkey. *Brain Research Bulletin, 11,* 515–518.

Ottersen, O. P. (1982). Connections of the amygdala of the rat: IV. Corticoamygdaloid and intraamygdaloid connections as studied with axonal transport of horseradish peroxidase. *Journal of Comparative Neurology, 205,* 30–48.

Papez, J. W. (1937). A proposed mechanism of emotion. *Archives of Neurology and Psychiatry, 38,* 725–743.

Phillips, R. G., & LeDoux, J. E. (1992). Differential contribution of amygdala and hippocampus to cued and contextual fear conditioning. *Behavioral Neuroscience, 106,* 274–285.

Price, J. L., Russchen, F. T., & Amaral, D. G. (1987). The limbic region: II. The amygdaloid complex. In A. Bjorklund, T. Hokfelt, & L.W. Swanson (Eds.), *Handbook of chemical neuroanatomy: Vol. 5. Integrated systems of the CNS* (Part 1, pp. 279–388). Amsterdam: Elsevier.

Reis, D. J. (1984). The brain and hypertension: Reflections on 35 years of inquiry into the neurobiology of the circulation. *Circulation, 70*(Suppl. III), 11-31.

Rolls, E. T. (1986). A theory of emotion, and its application to understanding the neural basis of emotion. In Y. Oomur (Ed.), *Emotions: Neural and chemical control* (pp. 325–344). Tokyo: Japan Scientific Societies Press.

Rolls, E. T. (1992). Neurophysiology and functions of the primate amygdala. In J. P. Aggleton (Ed.), *The amyg-*

dala: Neurobiological aspects of emotion, memory, and mental dysfunction (pp. 143–165). New York: Wiley–Liss.

Sanghera, M. K., Rolls, E. T., & Roper-Hall, A. (1979). Visual responses of neurons in the dorsolateral amygdala of the alert monkey. Experimental Neurology, 63, 610–626.

Schachter, S., & Singer, J. E. (1962). Cognitive, social, and physiological determinants of emotional state. Psychological Review, 69, 379–399.

Spiegler, B. J., & Mishkin, M. (1981). Evidence for the sequential participation of inferior temporal cortex and amygdala in the acquisition of stimulus–reward associations. Behavioural Brain Research, 3, 303–317.

Squire, L. R. (1987). Memory: Neural organization and behavior. In F. Plum (Ed.), Handbook of physiology. Section 1. The nervous system. Vol. 5. Higher functions of the brain (pp. 295–371). Bethesda, MD: American Physiological Society.

Swanson, L. W. (1983). The hippocampus and the concept of the limbic system. In W. Seifert (Ed.), Neurobiology of the hippocampus (pp. 3–19). New York: Academic Press.

Swanson, L. W., & Sawchenko, P. E. (1983). Hypothalamic integration: Organization of the paraventricular and supraoptic nuclei. Annual Review of Neuroscience, 6, 269–324.

Turner, B. H., Mishkin, M., & Knapp, M. (1980). Organization of the amygdalopetal projections from modality-specific cortical association areas in the monkey. Journal of Comparative Neurology, 191, 515–543.

Ungerleider, L. G., & Mishkin, M. (1982). Two cortical visual systems. In D. J. Ingle, M. A. Goodale, & R. J. W. Mansfield (Eds.), Analysis of visual behavior (pp. 549–586). Cambridge, MA: MIT Press.

Weiskrantz, L. (1956). Behavioral changes associated with ablation of the amygdaloid complex in monkeys. Journal of Comparative and Physiological Psychology, 49, 381–391.

Whitlock, D. G., & Nauta, W. J. H. (1956). Subcortical projections from the temporal neocortex in Macaca mulatta. Journal of Comparative Neurology, 106, 183–212.

Winer, J. A., & Morest, D. K. (1983). The medial division of the medial geniculate body of the cat: Implications for thalamic organization. Journal of Neuroscience, 3, 2629–2651.

Winer, J. A., & Morest, D. K. (1984). Axons of the dorsal division of the medial geniculate body of the cat: A study with the rapid Golgi method. Journal of Comparative Neurology, 224, 344–370.

9

The Psychophysiology of Emotion

JOHN T. CACIOPPO
DAVID J. KLEIN
GARY G. BERNTSON
ELAINE HATFIELD

The numerous chapters that constitute this handbook testify to the breadth and complexity of the topic of emotion. Human emotion represents psychological phenomena that encompass cognitions (e.g., feelings, memories, appraisals); visceral, humoral, and immunological reactions; gestures, vocalizations, and expressive displays; postural orientations and overt behaviors; or varying combinations of these (e.g., Fridja, 1986; Izard, 1977; Leventhal & Mosbach, 1983). Emotions have been further characterized as being evoked by biologically relevant stimuli and by associated internal or external events, as mobilizing limited attentional and cognitive resources directed toward present or future coping, and as modulating internalized and externalized actions that foster a generally adaptive coping response (Malmo, 1975; Plutchik, 1980). Emotions involve an explicit evaluative categorization of a stimulus into positive and/or negative valence classes, as well as the activation of behavioral dispositions that entail bivalent tendencies toward (e.g., approach, acquisition or consumption, affection) or away from (e.g., avoidance, escape or rejection, withdrawal, repulsion) the stimulus (Berntson, Boysen, & Cacioppo, in press). These dispositions are manifested in the somatic nervous system and, particularly when intense or extended across time, entail the logistical support of the autonomic nervous system. Although cognitive,

social, and developmental factors influence human emotions (e.g., Izard & Malatesta, 1987; Lazarus, 1966), we focus in this chapter on the psychophysiological responses associated with emotions and their likely role in emotional experience.

The embers of scientific interest in the somatovisceral substrates of the emotions (e.g., Darwin, 1872/1873) were fanned by William James's (1884) influential article, "What Is an Emotion?" James's provocative answer to this question was that emotional feelings are consequences rather than antecedents of peripheral physiological changes brought about by some stimulus. James's theory has stimulated debate and research for more than a century. Research on the influence of cognitive appraisals in emotion (e.g., Smith & Ellsworth, 1987; Valins, 1966) and on emotions in the spinal-cord-injured (e.g., Chwalisz, Diener, & Gallagher, 1988) suggests that afferent information from peripheral activity is not a *necessary* condition for emotional experience. James (1884), however, viewed emotions as being multiply determined. For instance, individuals may recall earlier emotional episodes, including their feelings, and in so doing they may re-experience the emotion. If the remembered emotion was weak originally (e.g., it involved little or no somatovisceral activation), re-experiencing the emotion may occur in the absence of significant peripheral bodily disturbances. James

(1884) therefore stated at the outset that "the only emotions I propose expressly to consider here are those that have a distinct bodily expression" (p. 189). James maintained that within this class of emotional phenomena, discrete emotional experiences can be identified with unique patterns of bodily changes, and that the perception of one of these specific patterns of peripheral physiological changes *is* the emotional experience (see Cacioppo, Berntson, & Klein, 1992).

Numerous theories of emotion have been proposed since James (1884), but those dealing with emotions accompanied by significant peripheral physiological changes are bracketed by (1) theories holding that discrete emotional experiences stem from distinct somatovisceral patterns (e.g., Ekman, Levenson, & Friesen, 1983; Levenson, 1988; Levenson, Ekman, & Friesen, 1990), and (2) theories holding that discrete emotional experiences derive from cognitive appraisals initiated by the perception of undifferentiated physiological arousal (e.g., Mandler, 1975; Schachter & Singer, 1962). Because of the centrality accorded to autonomic nervous system (ANS) activity in these theories and to the resurgence of research and debate on emotion-specific ANS activity (e.g., Ekman, 1992; Levenson, 1992; Zajonc & McIntosh, 1992), we begin by examining in some detail the literature on the autonomic differentiation of emotions. We then summarize representative studies and issues in electromyographic (EMG) and electrocortical studies of the emotions. We conclude by outlining a heuristic formulation depicting the possible roles of reafference in emotions that are accompanied by significant somatovisceral changes.

AUTONOMIC ACTIVITY AS A FUNCTION OF EMOTION

James (1884, 1890/1950) suggested that emotions are differentiated by somatovisceral responses, but he did *not* specify what these patterns should be or for what reason particular somatovisceral patterns should be linked to specific emotions. Without theoretical guidance regarding what autonomic responses to measure and why, investigations are reduced to descriptive explorations. Systematic empirical investigations of the autonomic differentiation of the emotions were therefore stimulated

when Arnold (1945) proposed that fear and anger differ autonomically because of their differential involvement of the neurotransmitters epinephrine (fear) and norepinephrine (anger).[1] Wolf and Wolff (1951) subsequently described a patient with a gastric fistula whose stomach could be observed visually. These authors reported that feelings of anxiety were associated with reductions in stomach acidity, blood flow, and motility, whereas feelings of anger were associated with increases in stomach acidity, blood flow, and motility. The epinephrine–norepinephrine hypothesis received additional support when autonomic assessments during realistic manipulations of anger and fear indicated that anger was associated with higher peak diastolic blood pressures (Ax, 1953) and lower heart rate (Schachter, 1957) than fear.[2] Research over the next several decades produced inconsistent results (Funkenstein, King, & Drollette, 1954; see review by Wagner, 1989), and the epinephrine–norepinephrine hypothesis is no longer viewed as plausible.

Conceptual Issues

Most contemporary research on the autonomic differentiation of emotions has been guided by three general hypotheses. The program of research by Ekman, Levenson, and their colleagues has been guided by a variant of James's hypothesis that there is emotion-specific ANS activity:

> Emotion provides a mechanism by which behavior, facial expression, and the *appropriate ANS support* can be quickly matched to the immediate environmental demands. The capacity of the

---

[1]Among the bodily responses following moderate doses of epinephrine are increased heart rate and myocardial contractility (and hence increased cardiac output), vasoconstriction in the cutaneous vascular beds, vasodilation in the vascular beds of the skeletomuscles, and elevated systolic blood pressure. Although moderate doses of norepinephrine have some of the same effects (e.g., vasoconstriction in the cutaneous vascular beds, increased myocardial contractility), vasoconstriction rather than vasodilation is more common in the skeletomuscular vascular beds. Consequently, systemic blood pressure increases and acts to slow heart rate via the baroreceptor reflex.

[2]The data analyzed by Schachter (1957) were a subset of those described by Ax (1953). Nevertheless, the results were not entirely consistent across these investigations. For instance, Schachter (1957) found no differences in diastolic blood pressure between anger and fear.

ANS for supporting a limited number of primary emotional/behavioral pairings is the centerpiece of its evolutionary value in emotion. (Levenson, 1988, p. 40)

The most frequently considered alternative hypotheses have been that (1) discrete emotions are associated with the perception or evocation of increased autonomic activity (e.g., Schachter & Singer, 1962; Mandler, 1975); and (2) the anticipated or realized action requirements of the emotional challenge, rather than emotion per se, determine physiological responses to the stimulus (see, e.g., the discussion by Frijda, 1986; Lang, Bradley, & Cuthbert, 1990). Both of these alternative hypotheses predict that ANS activity is not a function of the emotion per se. For instance, anger is more likely to lead to aggression, and fear to withdrawal. Yet the somatic involvement may be overlapping or equivalent for these emotions. Running may be involved, whether it is to locomote toward a fleeing antagonist to attack in anger, or away from the antagonist in fearful retreat. Measured at the level of the effectors, these emotions may be indistinguishable, even though they differ in terms of goals and outcomes.

Crucial tests among these hypotheses have been hindered by the failure of these hypotheses to make specific empirical predictions and by their not being mutually exclusive. For instance, the important descriptive study by Ekman et al. (1983) renewed interest in the question of emotion-specific ANS activity. Ekman et al. characterized happiness, disgust, and surprise as being associated with lower heart rate in their facial action task than anger, fear, and sadness, and they further discriminated between anger and the latter two emotions in terms of digital skin temperature. However, heart rate and finger temperature did not discriminate between any of these emotions when Ekman et al. (1983) used imagery (i.e., "relived emotion task") to elicit discrete emotions; instead, subsets of the emotions were differentiated by skin resistance level (which did not discriminate between the emotions in the facial action task). Whether or not these data support the hypothesis of emotion-specific ANS activity is unclear, because the mechanism by which discrete emotions are linked to particular ANS changes—or even what set of ANS changes uniquely defines each emotion—has yet to be specified.

The nonexclusivity of the hypotheses derives from research demonstrating that changes in autonomic activity (e.g., heart rate) are influenced by nonemotional factors such as individual differences (e.g., see Cacioppo, Uchino, et al., 1992; Stemmler, 1992) and by anticipated or actual somatic activity (Obrist, Webb, Sutterer, & Howard, 1970), respiration (see Berntson, Cacioppo, & Quigley, 1993), and attention (e.g., orienting; Graham & Clifton, 1966; Lacey, Kagan, Lacey, & Moss, 1963). The influence of specific emotions on ANS activity, therefore, may be difficult to discern, particularly if this influence is weak (Levenson, 1988) or if its effects on the functional output of the ANS are not strictly additive (see Berntson, Cacioppo, & Quigley, 1991).

Finally, whether the intensity and duration of an emotion moderate somatovisceral patterning is a question that warrants more careful investigation (cf. Roberts & Weerts, 1982). For instance, the thresholds and dynamic ranges of somatovisceral responses can vary across effectors (e.g., eccrine sweat glands vs. the heart), making it possible for the same emotion to be associated with additional somatovisceral changes as the intensity of the emotion increases. Furthermore, the somatovisceral and subjective responses to motivational challenges, such as food deprivation or declines in body temperature, are influenced by the magnitude and duration of the challenge. Thus, it may not be sufficient to equate emotions for intensity to identify their psychophysiological signatures if the manifestation of these signatures varies as a function of intensity.

Methodological Issues

In an effort to isolate emotion-specific ANS changes, greater attention over the past decade has been paid to methodological issues (e.g., see Ekman, et al., 1983; Davidson, Ekman, Saron, Senulis, & Friesen, 1990). The following methodological issues are important to consider and are equally applicable to autonomic, somatic, or electrocortical studies of emotion (Davidson et al., 1990):

1. At least two emotions should be compared. Furthermore, because the changes in ANS activity that accompany specific emotions are of interest, it is often important to include baseline measures, nonemotional comparison conditions, and/or manipulations of emotional intensity.

2. Epochs of discrete emotions must be separable. More than one emotion may be elicited by a stimulus, either simultaneously or in close temporal proximity, and this can hinder identification of the physiological substrates of discrete emotions.

3. The epochs of the emotions should be comparable in length and concordant with the time constants on the dependent measures. Ekman (1984) has suggested that most episodes of emotions last less than 4 seconds. Although this view has been disputed (e.g., Frijda, Mesquita, Sonnemans, & Van Goozen, 1991), there is a clear need to ensure that the measurement interval allows the confluence of physiological responses.

4. Independent evidence should be provided that the intended emotion was produced during the epoch.[3] Only if evidence other than the physiological measures of interest is provided can much confidence be placed in any interpretation of the resulting physiological outcomes.

5. Independent evidence should be provided that unintended emotions or confounding variations in motoric and cognitive activity were not present during this epoch.

6. Independent evidence should be provided that the intensity of the elicited emotion was matched across the epochs that were compared. Emotional intensity has long been recognized as a determinant of somatovisceral responses, and differences across emotions in their intensity can mask or masquerade as bona fide physiological differences.

7. The collection of the independent evidence and the physiological measures should be appropriately synchronized to the elicited emotion.

8. The epochs should be of sufficient duration, or the number of epochs within subjects over which aggregation occurs should be sufficient, to produce measures with satisfactory psychometric properties. Developments in psychophysiological instrumentation now make it possible to collect physiological measurements continuously, with consequent improvements in their reliabilities. The benefit of continuous measurements derives from their aggregation within or across epochs. The low reliabilities of physiological measures based on one-shot assessments (e.g., postinduction blood pressure readings; the maximum increase, decrease, or change in a physiological variable) can contribute to measurement variance.

9. Appropriate statistical procedures should be used to examine emotion-specific configurations among the dependent measures, and to protect against spurious findings resulting from multiple dependent measures and comparisons. Procedures such as the Bonferroni correction to protect against Type I errors can be overly conservative when many physiological variables are recorded. In such studies, it may be preferable to include an internal replication (e.g., cross-validation sample) to ensure the reproducibility of significant effects (Cacioppo, Berntsen, & Andersen, 1991).

10. Multiple operationalizations (e.g., eliciting tasks) should be used across, if not within, studies to ensure that results are emotion-specific rather than task-specific.

Table 9.1 lists, in chronological order, published research that has contrasted the effects of at least two discrete emotions on two or more autonomic measures in humans. Included in the far right column is our best determination of which of the preceding 10 methodological desiderata were incorporated.[4] As can be seen in Table 9.1, the emotions of happiness, sadness, anger, fear, disgust, and surprise have been investigated. Note, too, that only the studies by Ekman, Levenson, and their colleagues have compared the effects of more than four emotions on multiple physiological measures. Considerable variation also exists in the procedures used to elicit specific emotions and in the recording epochs used (see Table 9.1). Finally, and as would be expected, methodological and statistical procedures tend to be better in recent than in early studies.

---

[3]A key limitation in the study of emotion is the absence of a generally accepted index of the emotions. Self-reports of emotional experience are sometimes used, but emotions may be more subtle and may vacillate or pass more quickly than self-reports can typically detect. Self-reports are also subject to distortions resulting from social incentives and self-presentational concerns. Prototypical facial expressions of emotions have also been used, but these too can be insensitive. Converging operations, therefore, are often best.

---

[4]Hubert and de Jong-Meyer (1991) studied the emotions of suspense and happiness, each evoked by a film clip. Because it is unclear which emotion to equate with suspense, this study was not included. It should be noted, however, that the inclusion of this study (classifying suspense as fear) increases neither the appearance of consistency in physiological results nor the evidence for the autonomic differentiation of emotions.

TABLE 9.1. Studies Comparing Two or More Physiological Measures as a Function of Two or More Emotions

Study[1]	Manipulations	Dependent variables	Method features[2]
1. Ax, 1953 43 Ss (6 were not affected by one or more of the manipulations and thus excluded from the analyses)	Real-life induction: Fear—short circuit in SCL apparatus/intermittent shock Anger—abusive polygraph operator	Manipulation period (7-minute epoch—5 during manipulation and 2 after) minus baseline in max rises and falls of SBP, DBP, SV, HR, FCT, FT, SCL, EMG, RESP Emotion presence judged by experimenter from interview	1, 3, 4
2. Funkenstein, King, & Drollette, 1954 69 Ss (53 used in analyses)	"Problems situation"[3] manipulation; emotions categorized post hoc as: Anger In (21 Ss), Anger Out (22 Ss), Fear (Anxiety; 9 Ss)[4]	Single measurement at end of problems situation minus baseline of HR (pulse), SBP, DBP, SV, CO, PR Emotion presence and direction judged by raters from taped interview	1, 3, 4, 7, 8
3. Schachter, 1957 48 Ss in three groups: hypertensives, potential hypertensives, and normotensives (the same 15 normotensives as in Ax, 1953)	Real-life manipulation: Fear, Anger—same as Ax, 1953 Pain—cold pressor	Max change during manipulation minus baseline in HR, SBP, DBP, FCT, FT, SCL, EMG, RESP, SV, PR Emotion presence and intensity assessed from judges' ratings of taped verbal, facial, and behavioral responses during manipulations, experimenter notes, and interview after manipulations	1, 3, 4
4. Averill, 1969 54 Ss (males only)	Film manipulation: Sad—Kennedy's assassination Happy (Mirth)—an adaptation of a silent comedy Control—ichthyologists Each preceded by neutral baseline film	Stimulus period (6-minute epoch) minus baseline of max rise, mean, and fall in HR, SBP, DBP, FCT, FT, SCL, FPV, NNSCRs (mean only), RESP (max increase, rate, and irregular[5]—mean only) Vocalization Emotional intensity	1, 3, 4, 9
5. Tourangeau & Ellsworth, 1979 Film effects[6] 128 Ss	Film manipulation: Fear—industrial accidents Sad—boy in orphanage Neutral—flower show Crossed with directed facial action (DFA): Fear, Sad, Neutral, Undirected	Stimulus (2-minute epoch) minus baseline of HR (max rise and fall), SRL (max fall), NNSCRs Emotional intensity Face expression	1, 3, 4, 5, 7
6. Schwartz, Weinberger, & Singer, 1981[7] 32 Ss (with acting experience)	Imagery manipulation[8] of: Happy, Sad, Anger, Fear, Relax, Control	Single measurement following imagery minus baseline of HR, SBP, DBP Emotional intensity self-reported by subject and estimated by experimenter	1, 2, 3, 4, 9
7. Roberts & Weerts, 1982 16 Ss chosen from 351[9]	Imagery manipulation of low and high intensity of: Anger, Fear, and two low-intensity Neutral	Single measurement during imagery minus baseline of HR, SBP, DBP Emotional intensity	1, 2, 3, 4, 5, 6, 7, 9
8. Ekman, Levenson, & Friesen, 1983 8a. Best faces[10,11] 8b. Best imagery[12,13] 16 Ss (actors and scientists who study the face)	DFA and Imagery manipulations of: Fear, Anger, Happy, Sad, Surprise, Disgust	DFA (10-second epoch) or imagery (30-second epoch) minus baseline of HR, FT (right and left), SRL, EMG Emotional intensity Facial expression	1, 2, 3, 4, 5, 7, 8, 9, 10
9. Stemmler, 1989 9a. Real life 9b. Imagery 42 Ss (females only)	Real-life manipulations of: Fear—scary radio play and music, unexpected darkness Anger—abuse during anagrams, induced loud speaking	Standardized reactivity scores[14] of HR, FT, SCL, EMG, MVT (finger and head acceleration), RESP, PTT, FBV, BV Emotional intensity	1, 3, 4, 9, 10

(continued)

TABLE 9.1. (Continued)

Study[1]	Manipulations	Dependent variables	Method features[2]
	Happy—nice experimenter, extra monetary bonus, shorter experiment Imagery manipulation also		
10. Tassinary, Cacioppo, & Green,1989 15 Ss (females only)	DFA manipulation of: Anger, Happy, Control	Stimulus (4-second epoch) minus baseline of SCL, HR Emotional intensity	1, 2, 4, 5, 9
11. Levenson, Ekman, & Friesen, 1990 11a. All faces 11b. Best faces Reports combined results from three experiments: 1. Ekman et al., 1983 2. 16 Ss chosen from 103[15] 3. 30 Ss chosen from 109	DFA manipulation[16] of: Fear, Anger, Happy, Sad, Surprise, Disgust	DFA (10-second epoch) minus baseline of HR, FT, SCL, EMG/MVT[17,18] Emotional intensity Facial expression Task difficulty (in Experiment 2)	1, 2, 3, 4, 5, 7, 8, 9
12. Levenson, Carstensen, Friesen, & Ekman, 1991[19] Best faces/best imagery 20 Ss chosen from 35 (older than 70; 4 on beta blockers)	DFA and imagery manipulation of: Fear, Anger, Happy, Sad, Surprise, Disgust	DRA (10-second epoch) or imagery (15-second epoch—begun when Ss indicated that they felt the emotion) minus baseline of HR, FT, SCL, MVT Emotional intensity Task difficulty Facial expression	1, 2, 3, 4, 5, 7, 8, 9, 10
13. Levenson, Ekman, Heider, & Friesen, 1992 Best faces 46 Ss (males only, from Minangkabau)	DFA and imagery manipulation of: Fear, Anger, Happy, Sad, Disgust	DFA (10-second epoch) minus baseline of HR, FT, SCL, PTT, FPV, RESP (rate and depth) Emotional intensity Task difficulty Facial expression	1, 2, 3, 8, 9

Note. Variable abbreviations: HR, heart rate; SCL, skin conductance level; SRL, skin resistance level; NNSCRs, number of nonspecific skin conductance responses; FT, finger temperature; FCT, face temperature; EMG, muscle activity; MVT, movement; SBP, systolic blood pressure; DBP, diastolic blood pressure; SV, stroke volume; CO, cardiac output; FPV, finger pulse volume; RESP, respiration; PTT, pulse transit time; BV, blood volume.

[1]Because this table includes only studies that compared physiological reactions as a function of two or more emotions, we have not included Sternbach (1962). In this study he did measure physiological responses (SRI, gastric motility, RESP, HR, eyeblink rate, and FPV) of children as a function of a number of emotions—sad, fearful, happy (nice), (and funny) as defined by each subject—elicited by a film stimulus (*Bambi*); however, he compared the physiological responses of the emotions to the prestimulus level and did not perform comparisons between emotions. The only differences reported as significant (through the use of nonparametric tests) were during the sad period, in which he found an increase in skin resistance (a decrease in SCL) and a decrease in eyeblinks, and during the happy (nice) period, in which he found a decrease in gastric motility. Sternbach found "the lack of consistency in direction of autonomic responses rather surprising" (p. 90).

[2]The numbers correspond to the methodological features discussed in the text, representing our best judgment of those features that were possessed by the corresponding study.

[3]Stressor was verbal abuse/provocation from the experimenter while the subject repeated lists of 6–10 digits in reverse order and solved word problems.

[4]Subjects' responses were also categorized as follows: (a) Anger In and Out, (b) No Emotion, (c) Equal Anger and Anxiety, and (d) Miscellaneous. These categories were not included in the statistical analyses because the frequency in each was judged to be too low.

[5]Respiration irregularity—(a) inspiration that was twice the average of the adjacent inspirations, (b) expiration interrupted by inspiration, (c) expiration deviating below the baseline of surrounding breaths.

[6]No significant effects were found for differences in facial expressions during the film. Thus the differences reported in Tables 9.2 and 9.3 are differences due to the emotional effects of the films.

[7]Subjects also exercised and measures were taken following exercise, but those analyses are not included in this table, as they are beyond the scope of this chapter.

[8]Subjects imagined a scene in which they felt the appropriate emotion as they were (in their imagination) exercising on a one-step.

[9]A total of 351 subjects were initially screened with self-report inventories; 34 who scored high (top 10%) on either the anger or the fear/anxiety inventory and scored near the mean on the other were then interviewed to certify that they could produce the appropriate emotional imagery. The 16 final subjects were those who went to the interview and could perform the emotinal imagery task.

[10]"Best faces" denotes the subset of trials during which subjects' facial expressions were rated as being close to prototypic emotion faces.

[11]This amounted to 87% of the directed facial action trials.

[12]"Best imagery" denotes the subset of trials during which subjsects reported feeling the target emotion most strongly.

[13]This amounted to 56% of the imagery trials.

[14]Reactivity scores were derived by (a) obtaining difference scores of the raw score and the current baseline (derived through linear interpolation between the neighboring baseline "anchors"), (b) excluding individual differences by subtracting the subject's overall mean for each variable, and (c) subjecting scores to a McCall normalizing transformation. These scores were then standardized.

[15]Subjects were prescreened for ability to exhibit good voluntary facial muscle control.

[16]Levenson, Carstensen, Friesen, and Ekman (1991) reported that 46 of these subjects also did the imagery task (p. 31).

[17]The report combined 1983 forearm flexor EMG data and 1990 movement (of the subject's chair) sensor data. The intent of the authors was to measure general somatic activity.

[18]Measures of PTT (to ear and to finger), FPA, and REST (rate) were also collected, but were not reported.

[19]Best faces constituted 46% and best imagery constituted 60% of the corresponding trials.

Empirical Outcomes

The results of the investigations identified in Table 9.1 are summarized in Tables 9.2 and 9.3. Given the variation across studies, one might expect to find only moderate consistency in their results. However, a few recent studies, most notably those by Levenson, Ekman, and their colleagues, have used a common set of procedures and measures, making it possible to examine the reproducibility of emotion-specific ANS activity across studies (albeit within one laboratory). Where reproducible effects are found, questions of generalizability can be considered by looking across methods of eliciting the emotion and across laboratories. Table 9.2 follows the format introduced by Zajonc and McIntosh (1992). Differences among emotions on each dependent measure are indicated as in contrast tests. As Zajonc and McIntosh (1992) have noted, perfect distinctiveness among the emotions on a particular measure would result in a different letter within a row, and all entries within a column would be the same (indicating the replicability and generalizability of the result). It is possible that two or more emotions do not differ on a particular measure, but that they do differ in the sets of physiological responses they evoke. Therefore, Table 9.3 summarizes comparisons of the sets of physiological differences between various pairs of emotions.

Several conclusions can be drawn from the cumulative literature on the autonomic differentiation of emotion. First, imagery is not an emotional elicitation procedure that has produced reliably differentiated ANS activity, even though subjects have reported differential emotional experiences (Stemmler, 1989; Zajonc & McIntosh, 1992). It is unclear why this would be the case, unless ANS activity is responsive to the metabolic requirements of the anticipated or realized response to the emotional challenge—a requirement that would tend to be uniformly low in emotional imagery.

Second, there is little evidence for replicable autonomic differences in pairwise comparisons of the emotions on the measures of bodily tension, systolic blood pressure, facial temperature, respiration, skin conductance level, and cardiac stroke volume. For instance, Ekman et al. (1983) reported that skin resistance level decreased (i.e., skin conductance increased) more during sadness than during fear, anger, and disgust. This differentiation was found only when imagery was used to elicit the emotions, however, and this particular pattern has not been replicated. Too few data exist on several other measures (e.g., skin conductance responses, peripheral resistance, cardiac output, finger pulse volume, pulse transit time, body movement) to permit us to draw strong conclusions, leaving only heart rate, diastolic blood pressure, and finger temperature to peruse more closely.

Of 13 pairwise comparisons between discrete emotions, 6 were significant when diastolic blood pressure served as the dependent measure. The strongest result was the tendency for anger to be characterized by high diastolic blood pressure (see Table 9.3), but 4 of 7 comparisons failed to find this effect. The results for finger temperature also provide only tentative evidence for emotion-specific ANS activity. For instance, Table 9.2 summarizes 95 pairwise comparisons involving finger temperature, only 14 (15%) of which were significant. Of these significant comparisons, the most reliable differentiation was found between anger and fear, with anger associated with higher finger temperature than fear in 4 of 11 comparisons (36.4%).

Heart rate has been the best discriminator of the emotions, but it too is far from discriminating consistently or fully among the emotions. Unusually robust findings are evident in the differentiation by heart rate of sadness from disgust (significant in 5 of 6 or 83.3% of the comparisons), anger from disgust (83.3%), and fear from disgust (66.7%). Table 9.2 depicts modest replication rates in the differentiation by heart rate of happiness from anger (5 of 10 comparisons, or 50%, were significant), happiness from fear (44.4%), sadness from surprise (60%), and fear from surprise (60%). The remaining pairwise comparisons show little evidence of reliable differentiation by heart rate.

As modest as most of these replication rates are, there are three reasons to be concerned that these are overestimates. First, the data analyzed by Schachter (1957) were from a subset of the subjects in Ax (1953), and data from Ekman et al.'s (1983) facial action test were part of the data set analyzed by Levenson et al. (1990). Furthermore, studies occasionally involved more physiological measures than those for which results were reported, and double-blind procedures are atypical in this area of research.

Second, the elicitation procedure producing the greatest differentiation of emotions appears

TABLE 9.2. Pairwise Comparisons of Physiological Responses as a Function of Emotion

Heart rate									
Study	Hap	Sad	Ang	Fear	Surp	Disg	Pain	Relx	Cntl
Ax, 1953									
Max rise			A	A					
Max fall			A	B					
Funkenstein et al., 1954			AB	B					
Schachter, 1957[1]									
Max change			B	A			C		
Averill, 1969									
Mean	A	A							A
Max rise	A	B							AB
Max fall	A	A							A
Tourangeau & Ellsworth, 1979									
Max rise		B		A					B
Max fall		B		B					A
Schwartz et al., 1981	B	AB	A	A				C	C
Roberts & Weerts, 1982									
High intensity			A	A					
Low intensity			A	A					
Ekman et al., 1983									
Best faces	B	A	A	A	B	B			
Best imagery	A	A	A	A	A	A			
Stemmler, 1989									
Real life	A		A	A					
Imagery	A		A	A					
Tassinary et al., 1989	A		A						B
Levenson et al., 1990									
All faces	BC	AB	A	A	D	CD			
Best faces	B	A	A	A	B	B			
Levenson et al., 1991									
Best faces/best imagery	AB	A	A	AB	AB	B			
Levenson et al., 1992	BC	AB	A	AB		C			

Finger temperature								
Study	Hap	Sad	Ang	Fear	Surp	Disg	Pain	Cntl
Ax, 1953								
Max fall			A	A				
Max rise			A	A				
Schachter, 1957[1]								
Max change			A	B			C	
Averill, 1969	A	A						A
Ekman et al., 1983								
Best faces[2]	B	B	A	B	B	B		
Best imagery	A	A	A	A	A	A		
Stemmler, 1989								
Real life	A		AB	B				A
Imagery	A		A	A				A
Levenson et al., 1990								
All faces	AB	AB	A	B	AB	AB		
Best faces	B	B	A	B	B	B		
Levenson et al., 1991[3]								
Best imagery/best faces	AB	B	AB	AB	AB	A		
Levenson et al., 1992								
Best faces	A	A	A	A		A		

(continued)

TABLE 9.2. (Continued)

Skin conductance level

Study	Hap	Sad	Ang	Fear	Surp	Disg	Pain	Cntl
Ax, 1953								
Max rise			B	A				
Max fall			A	A				
Schachter, 1957[1,4]								
Max change			B	A			C	
Averill, 1969	A	A						B
Tourangeau & Ellsworth, 1979								
Max rise[5]		A		A				B
Ekman et al., 1983								
Best faces	A	A	A	A	A	A		
Best imagery	AB	A	B	B	AB	B		
Stemmler, 1989								
Real life	A		A	B				
Imagery	A		A	A				
Tassinary et al., 1989	A		A					B
Levenson et al., 1990								
All faces	B	A	AB	A	B	A		
Best faces	B	AB	AB	A	B	A		
Levenson et al., 1991								
Best faces/best imagery	A	A	A	A	A	A		
Levenson et al., 1992								
Best faces	A	A	A	A		A		

EMG

Study	Hap	Sad	Ang	Fear	Surp	Disg	Pain	Cntl
Ax, 1953 (frontalis)								
Number of peaks			B	A				
Max rise			A	B				
Max fall			A	A				
Schachter, 1957[1] (frontalis)			A	A			A	
Ekman et al., 1983								
Best faces	A	A	A	A	A	A		
Best imagery	A	A	A	A	A	A		
Stemmler, 1989								
Extensor digitorum								
Real life	B		A	B				B
Imagery	A		A	A				A
Trapezius								
Real life	A		A	A				A
Imagery	A		A	A				A

Face temperature

Study	Hap	Sad	Ang	Fear	Surp	Disg	Pain	Cntl
Ax, 1953								
Max rise			A	A				
Max fall			A	A				
Schachter, 1957[1]								
Max change			A	A			A	
Averill, 1969	A	A						A
Stemmler, 1989								
Real life	B		A	C				B
Imagery	A		A	A				A

(continued)

TABLE 9.2. (Continued)

Systolic blood pressure

Study	Hap	Sad	Ang	Fear	Surp	Disg	Pain	Relx	Cntl
Ax, 1953									
Max rise			A	A					
Max fall			A	A					
Funkenstein et al., 1954			A[6]	B					
Schachter, 1957[1]									
Max change			A	A			A		
Averill, 1969	B	A							B
Schwartz et al., 1981	A	A	A	A				B	B
Roberts & Weerts, 1982									
High intensity			A	A					
Low intensity			A	A					

Diastolic blood pressure

Study	Hap	Sad	Ang	Fear	Surp	Disg	Pain	Relx	Cntl
Ax, 1953									
Max rise			A	B					
Max fall			A	A					
Funkenstein et al., 1954			A	A					
Schachter, 1957[1]									
Max change			A	A			A		
Averill, 1969	B	A							B
Schwartz et al., 1981	B	BC	A	B				C	BC
Roberts & Weerts, 1982									
High intensity			A	B					
Low intensity			A	A					

Respiration

Study	Hap	Sad	Ang	Fear	Surp	Disg	Pain	Cntl
Ax, 1953								
Max rise			B	A				
Inspiration			A	A				
Respiration amplitude			A	A				
Schachter, 1957[1]								
Max change								
Rate			B	A			C	
Inspiration index[7]			A	A			A	
Averill, 1969								
Mean		A	A					A
Max rise		A	AB					B
Irregular respiration		A	B					B
Levenson et al., 1992								
Best faces								
Rate	B	AB	AB	A		A		
Depth	A	AB	AB	AB		B		

Stroke volume

Study	Hap	Sad	Ang	Fear	Surp	Disg	Pain	Cntl
Ax, 1953								
Max rise			A	A				
Max fall			A	A				

(continued)

TABLE 9.2. (Continued)

Stroke volume

Study	Hap	Sad	Ang	Fear	Surp	Disg	Pain	Cntl
Funkenstein et al., 1954			B[8]	A				
Schachter, 1957[1]								
Max change			B	A			C	

Cardiac output

Study	Hap	Sad	Ang	Fear	Surp	Disg	Pain	Cntl
Funkenstein et al., 1954			B[9]	A				
Schachter, 1957[1]								
Max change			B	A			C	

Finger pulse volume

Study	Hap	Sad	Ang	Fear	Surp	Disg	Cntl
Averill, 1969							
Mean	A	A					A
Max rise	AB	A					B
Max fall	A	A					A
Stemmler, 1989							
Real life	AB		A	C			B
Imagery	A		A	A			A
Levenson et al., 1992	AB	A	B	B		B	

NNSCRs

Study	Hap	Sad	Ang	Fear	Surp	Disg	Cntl
Ax, 1953			A	B			
Averill, 1969	A	A					B
Tourangeau & Ellsworth, 1979		A		A			A

Blood volume

Study	Hap	Sad	Ang	Fear	Surp	Disg	Cntl
Stemmler, 1989							
Finger							
Real life	A		A	A			A
Imagery	A		A	A			A
Head							
Real life	A		A	A			A
Imagery	A		A	A			A

Pulse transit time

Study	Hap	Sad	Ang	Fear	Surp	Disg	Cntl
Stemmler, 1989							
Real life	A		A	A			A
Imagery	A		A	A			A
Levenson et al., 1992	A	B	AB	AB		A	

Body movement

Study	Hap	Sad	Ang	Fear	Surp	Disg	Cntl
Stemmler, 1989							
Finger							
Real life	A		A	A			A
Imagery	A		A	A			A

(continued)

TABLE 9.2. (Continued)

Body movement							
Study	Hap	Sad	Ang	Fear	Surp	Disg	Cntl
Stemmler, 1989 *(continued)*							
Head							
Real life	A		AB	B			A
Imagery	A		A	A			A
Levenson et al., 1990							
All faces	A	A	A	A	A	A	
Best faces	A	A	A	A	A	A	
Levenson et al., 1991							
Best faces/best imagery	B	AB	B	A	B	B	

Peripheral resistance								
Study	Hap	Sad	Ang	Fear	Surp	Disg	Pain	Cntl
Funkenstein et al., 1954[10]			A	B				
Schachter, 1957[1]								
Max change			B	C			A	

Note. Differences in emotions are indicated as contrasts. Emotions with the same letter were not demonstrated to be significantly different. The letters precede alphabetically from the largest mean or difference to the smallest unless otherwise noted. Where no significant difference was reported between two emotions, it was assumed that the difference between them was nonsignificant. Columns to the right of the vertical line are data related to nonemotion states also reported in the study. Abbreviations: Hap, Happiness; Sad, Sadness; Ang, Anger; Surp, Surprise; Disg, Disgust; Relx, Relaxation; Cntl, Control.

[1]Because of a heterogeneity of variance, no comparisons were performed to test the differences among means. The differences in letters, therefore, indicate only rank order differences in the measure when there was a significant F.

[2]Differences are from the temperature of the right finger only. No report was made of the results of the left finger temperature (which was collected separately) or the combined temperature for the best-faces condition.

[3]There was a significant manipulation × emotion interaction.

[4]The changes were all negative. The letter A signifies the smallest negative change and C the largest.

[5]In the study, maximum decrease in SRL was reported. As SRL is the reciprocal of SCL, the direction of the observed relationships were simply reversed so that they would be comparable to the other values.

[6]Anger Out significantly differed from Fear (Anxiety). Anger In did not differ from Anger Out or Fear.

[7]Inspiration/(respiration × respiration rate).

[8]Anger Out was significantly smaller than both Anger In and Fear (Anxiety), which did not differ from each other.

[9]Anger Out was significantly smaller than Anger In, which was smaller than Fear (Anxiety).

[10]Anger Out was significantly greater than Anger In and Fear (Anxiety), which did not differ significantly.

to be Ekman, Levenson, and their colleagues' facial action manipulations, whereby subjects are instructed to contract specific configurations of facial muscles to form prototypical emotional expressions. The subjects actually qualifying for participation in this procedure, however, were highly select, representing either experts in facial behavior (e.g., Ekman et al., 1983) or only about a quarter to a third of subjects prescreened for their ability to contract specific facial muscles and combinations of muscles on command (e.g., Levenson et al., 1990). This may affect the generalizability of their results. Tassinary, Cacioppo, and Geen (1989), for instance, performed no such prescreening in their psychometric study of facial EMG placements, and found that heart rate was elevated similarly by posing expressions of

happiness and anger (which were only two of many facial configurations subjects were instructed to form). Replications of Ekman, Levenson, and their colleagues' research across laboratories would help clarify what particular comparisons are robust, and may aid discovery of the procedural features required to obtain these results.

Third, which emotion has been associated with high versus low heart rate has not always been uniform when comparisons *have* differentiated two emotions. Sadness, for instance, was associated with lower heart rate than happiness in one comparison, but was associated with higher heart rate than happiness in two other comparisons (see Tables 9.2 and 9.3). Furthermore, some experimental reports do not provide sufficient information to enable us

TABLE 9.3. Profile of Physiological Differences between Emotions

		Happiness	Sadness	Anger	Fear	Surprise
Sadness	HR	< 4[1] > 8a,11b = 4[2],6,8b,11a, 12,13				
	FT	= 4,8ab,11ab, 12,13				
	SCL	> 11a = 4,8ab,11b, 12,13				
	EMG	= 8ab				
	MVT	= 11ab,12				
	SBP	> 4 = 6				
	DBP	> 4 = 6				
	RESP	< 4[3] = 4,13				
	FPV	= 1,13				
	FCT	= 4				
	NNSCRs	= 4				
	PTT	< 13				
Anger	HR	> 6,8a,11ab,13 = 8b,9ab,10,12	HR = 6,8ab, 11ab,12,13			

	FT	> 8a,11b
		= 8b,9ab,11a,
		  12,13
			FT > 8a,11b
			  = 8b,11a,12,
			   13			

	SCL	= 8ab,9ab,10,
		  11ab,12,13
			SCL < 8b
			  = 8a,11ab,12
			   13			

	EMG	= 8ab, 9a[5]b > 9a[4]	EMG = 8ab			
	MVT	= 9a[5]b,11ab,12	MVT = 11ab,12			
	SBP	= 6	SBP = 6			
	DBP	> 6	DBP > 6			
	FPV	= 9ab,13	PTT = 13			
	FCT	> 9a = 9b	FPV < 13			
	BV	= 9ab	RESP = 13			
	PTT	= 9ab,13				
	RESP	= 13				

Fear	HR	> 6,8a,11ab
		= 8b,9ab,12,13
			HR > 5[10]
			  = 5[11],6,8ab,
			   11ab,12,13
				HR < 1[12]
				  > 3
				  = 1,2,6,7,
				   8ab,9ab,
				   11ab,12,
				   13		

	FT	< 9a
		= 8ab,9b,11ab,
		  12,13
			FT = 8ab,11ab,
			   12,13
				FT < 3,8a,11ab
				  = 1,8b,9ab,
				   12,13		

	SCL	> 11ab
		< 9a
		= 8ab,9b,12,13
			SCL < 8b
			  = 5,8a,11ab,
			   12,13
				SCL < 9a
				  > 1[13],3
				  = 1[14],8ab,
				   9b,11ab,
				   12,13		

	EMG	= 8ab,9ab	EMG = 8ab	EMG < 1,9a[15]
				  >1[16]
				  = 1,3,8ab,
				   9a[17],9b		

	MVT	> 12 < 9a[6] = 9ab[7],11ab	MVT = 11ab,12	MVT > 12 = 9ab,11ab		
	SBP	= 6	SBP = 6	SBP > 2[18] = 1,2[18],3,6,7		
	DBP	= 6	DBP = 6	DBP < 1[19],6,7[20] = 1[21],2,3,7[22]		
	FPV	< 9a = 9b,13	NNSCRs = 5	FPV < 9a = 9b,13		
	FCT	< 9a = 9b	RESP = 13	FCT < 9a = 1,3,9b		
	BV	= 9ab	FPV < 13	BV = 9ab		
	PTT	= 9ab,13	PTT = 13	SV > 2[23],3 = 1,2		
	RESP	> 13[8] = 13[9]		CO > 2[24],3 = 2[24]		
				RESP > 1[25],3[26] = 1[25],3[27],13		
				PTT = 9ab,13		
				PR < 2,3		
				NNSCRs < 1		

(continued)

TABLE 9.3. (Continued)

		Happiness		Sadness		Anger		Fear		Surprise
Surprise	HR	< 11a = 8ab,11b,12	HR	< 8a,11ab = 8b,12	HR	< 8a,11ab = 8b,12	HR	< 8a,11ab = 8b,12		
	FT	= 8ab,11ab,12	FT	= 8ab,11ab, 12	FT	< 8a,11b, = 8b,11a,12	FT	= 8ab,11ab,12		
	SCL	= 8ab,11ab,12	SCL	< 11a = 8ab,11b, 12	SCL	= 8ab,11ab, 12	SCL	< 11ab = 8ab,12		
	EMG	= 8ab			EMG	= 8ab	EMG	= 8ab		
	MVT	= 11ab,12	EMG	= 8ab	MVT	= 11ab,12	MVT	< 12 = 11ab		
			MVT	= 11ab,12						
Disgust	HR	= 8ab,11ab,12, 13	HR	< 8a,11ab, 12,13 = 8b	HR	< 8a,11ab, 12,13 = 8b	HR	< 8a,11ab,13 = 8b,12	HR	= 8ab,11ab,12
	FT	= 8ab,11ab,12, 13	FT	< 12 = 8ab,11ab, 13	FT	< 8a,11b = 8b,11a,12, 13	FT	= 8ab,11ab,12, 13 = 8ab,12	FT	= 8ab,11ab,12
	SCL	> 11ab = 8ab,12,13	SCL	< 8b = 8a,11ab, 12,13	SCL	= 8ab,11ab, 12,13	SCL	= 8ab,11ab,12, 13	SCL	> 11ab = 8ab,12
	EMG	= 8ab	EMG	= 8ab	EMG	= 8ab	EMG	= 8ab	EMG	= 8ab
	MVT	= 11ab,12	MVT	= 11ab,12	MVT	= 11ab,12	MVT	< 12 = 11ab	MVT	= 11ab,12
	FPV	= 13	FPV	< 13	FPV	= 13	FPV	= 13		
	PTT	= 13	PTT	> 13	PTT	= 13	PTT	= 13		
	RESP	< 13[28] > 13[29]	RESP	= 13	RESP	= 13	RESP	= 13		

Note. Each sign represents the direction of the relationship comparing the emotion on the row to the emotion on the column. The numbers indicate the study (see Table 9.1) that reported the finding. See Table 9.1 for an explanation of the abbreviations.

[1] Max rise.
[2] Max fall and mean.
[3] Irregular respiration was different; mean regular respiration and max rise were the same.
[4] Extensor digitorum.
[5] Trapezius.
[6] Head acceleration in the real-life condition.
[7] Finger acceleration for both the real-life and imagery conditions, and head acceleration for the imagery condition.
[8] Rate.
[9] Depth.
[10] Max rise.
[11] Max fall.
[12] Max fall was different; max rise was not different.
[13] Max rise.
[14] Max fall.

[15] Extensor digitorum.
[16] Includes max increase and decrease.
[17] Trapezius.
[18] Anger Out > Anxiety; Anger In not different from Anger Out or Anxiety.
[19] Max rise.
[20] High intensity.
[21] Max fall.
[22] Low intensity.
[23] Anger Out < Anxiety and Anger in.
[24] Anger Out < Anger In = Anxiety.
[25] Max rise was different; amplitude was the same.
[26] Respiration rate.
[27] Inspiration index.
[28] Depth.
[29] Rate.

to determine whether or which physiological responses during an emotion (or directed facial action) differed from baseline (or nonemotional comparison) conditions. This information may be important in determining the mechanism underlying the autonomic differences that *are* observed. Levenson, Ekman, Heider, and Friesen (1992), who did report sufficient information to examine this issue, found that heart rate was higher in Minangkabau subjects during directed facial expressions of fear, sadness, and anger than during the directed facial expression of disgust, but the mean change score for disgust was not greater than zero. This result raises interesting questions about the reasons for heart rate's not changing during the expression of disgust.

Given these considerations, comparisons that demonstrated the absence of any differentiation may be especially informative about avenues that do *not* warrant further research. For instance, heart rate failed to differentiate happiness from surprise in 4 of 5 comparisons, happiness from disgust in 6 of 6 comparisons, sadness from anger in 7 of 7 comparisons, sadness from fear in 8 of 9 comparisons, anger from fear in 13 of 15 comparisons, and surprise from disgust in 5 of 5 comparisons.

Summary

The research on the autonomic differentiation of emotions is provocative, but the cumulative evidence for emotion-specific autonomic patterns remains inconclusive (Wagner, 1989). Of course, all of the potential elements and patterns of autonomic activity have yet to be examined. More importantly, potential patterns may not be describable by gross measures of end-organ response (e.g., heart rate). A major obstacle in identifying autonomic patterning as a function of emotion, particularly for dually and antagonistically innervated organs such as the heart, is that of the many-to-one mappings that may obtain between underlying neural changes and organ response. Emotional stimuli do not invariably evoke reciprocal activation of the sympathetic and parasympathetic branches of the

ANS. For instance, the presentation of an aversive conditioned stimulus can produce coactivation of the sympathetic and parasympathetic nervous system, with the consequent heart rate response being acceleratory, deceleratory, or unchanged from prestimulus levels, depending upon which activational input was greater (see Berntson et al., 1991). Berntson et al. (1991) recently proposed a theory of autonomic control and modes of autonomic activation that resolves the loss of fidelity in the translation between changes in sympathetic and parasympathetic activation and organ responses. It is possible that emotions (e.g., disgust), or components of emotions (e.g., attention), could be differentiated if the focus were on indices of the sympathetic and the parasympathetic innervation of the viscera, rather than on visceral responses per se. For instance, Quigley and Berntson (1990) found that the deceleratory heart rate response to a low-intensity nonsignal ("orienting") stimulus was small because both parasympathetic and sympathetic activity increased. The acceleratory heart rate response to a high-intensity nonsignal ("defense") stimulus, on the other hand, was larger—not because sympathetic activation was greater than that shown to the low-intensity stimulus, but because parasympathetic activity was unchanged or decreased slightly in response to the high-intensity stimulus.

Whether or not the conditions for and the elements of emotion-specific autonomic patterns of activity can be identified, what does seem clear from this research is that discrete emotional percepts can occur even when the autonomic changes do not fully discriminate the emotions that are experienced. Evidence consistent with this conclusion was provided by Ekman et al. (1983) in the imagery task, where skin resistance level provided only gross distinctions among groups of emotions, despite a careful parsing of epochs of discrete emotional experiences. Recent research on the emotional percepts of patients with lesions at differing points along their spinal cords further suggest that quite different patterns of autonomic afference can be associated with the same emotional experience (e.g., Bermond, Nieuwenhuyse, Fasotti, & Schuerman, 1991; Chwalisz et al., 1988).[5]

If discrete emotional percepts can occur even when the autonomic changes do not fully discriminate the emotions that are experienced, does it necessarily follow that somatovisceral afference plays *no* role in defining these discrete emotional percepts? Cannon's (1927) answer to this question was yes; in his view, autonomic events are too slow, too insensitive, and too undifferentiated to contribute to emotions.[6] Schachter and Singer (1962) revolutionized thinking about emotions when they suggested that undifferentiated autonomic activity *can* subserve discrete emotions. The mechanism by which this was is accomplished, according to Schachter and Singer (1962; Schachter, 1964; see also Mandler, 1975; Reisenzein, 1983), is the arousal of an "evaluative need," which motivates the individual to understand and label cognitively his or her bodily feelings. The consequent attributional processes were thought to produce specific emotional states and influence emotional behavior. There is yet another distinct way in which peripheral bodily reactions may contrib-

---

also be noted that research demonstrating that the emotions experienced by individuals with spinal cord lesions are similar to those experienced by normal individuals does not logically imply that afference plays no role in the generation or shaping of emotional experience. If we let E denote a discrete emotion and we let ϕ denote autonomic afference, we can represent the finding that individuals with spinal cord lesions can experience discrete emotions as the conditional probability $P(E/\text{not-}\phi) > 0$. To infer from this result that $P(E/\text{not-}\phi) = P(E/\phi)$ is speculative, however, because (1) emotions are most likely multiply determined, in which case physiological afference may not be a necessary determinant, while still being a sufficient or contributory determinant; (2) the situations and challenges that individuals with and without spinal cord injuries encounter may differ; and (3) the perspective used by individuals with spinal cord injuries when expressing their feelings in words or along rating scales may change as they adapt to their injuries (e.g., what is meant by the label "intense arousal" or "intense anger" may change).

[6]There is now considerable evidence that is inconsistent with the notion that autonomic activity increases in a general and diffuse manner during emotion. In addition to the data summarized in Tables 9.2 and 9.3, reliable individual and situational stereotypies have been documented (e.g., see reviews by Cacioppo, Uchino, et al., 1992; Lang et al., 1990). Moreover, neural changes within the sympathetic nervous system can be highly fractionated (see Johnson & Anderson, 1990), and different patterns of sympathetic and parasympathetic activity can underlie similar-appearing autonomic responses (Berntson et al., 1991). Hence, by an "undifferentiated" pattern of autonomic response, we mean only that the autonomic responses (from which interoceptive feedback is derived) do not differentiate specific emotions such as fear and anger.

---

[5]The different "patterns" of afference derive from differences in the sites of the lesions. Lower lesions allow afference from more viscera than higher lesions. It should

ute to emotional experience—an active *perceptual* process by which an ambiguous pattern of somatovisceral afference is disambiguated to produce an immediate, spontaneous, and indubitable emotional percept (Cacioppo, Berntson, & Klein, 1992). We briefly discuss this perceptual–emotional process in the final section, but first we review illustrative studies of somatic and electrocortical activity as a function of emotion.

FACIAL ELECTROMYOGRAPHIC AND ELECTROCORTICAL ACTIVITY AS A FUNCTION OF EMOTION

Facial Actions

Contemporary developments in facial expression as a marker of emotion can be traced to Tomkins's (1962) ascription of an instrumental role to facial movement and feedback in the experience of emotion, and to his suggestion that high-speed filming be used to perform microscopic analyses of facial expressions and emotion. These proposals led to important methodological advances in facial coding (e.g., Ekman & Friesen, 1978; Izard, 1971, 1977). Based on research that identified a small set of emotions accompanied by unique configurations of facial actions and labeled reliably across cultures, Ekman (e.g., 1973, 1992b) and Izard (e.g., 1977, 1992) have proposed that there is a small number of *basic* emotions. These basic emotions are hypothesized to be associated with distinctive innate response patterns and neural substrates. Happiness (or joy), sadness, anger, fear, and disgust are generally considered to be basic emotions, but a different five emotions (Fischer, Shaver, & Carnochan, 1990), fewer than five emotions (e.g., Panksepp, 1982), and more than five emotions (e.g., Frijda, 1986; Oatley & Johnson-Laird, 1987) have also been suggested. Recently, Ortony and Turner (1990) have challenged the very premise that there are basic emotions, and they have proposed instead that emotions are constructed from valent and nonemotional component processes. This is an important and continuing debate that will probably have implications for which emotions might be expected to have distinctive psychophysiological substrates (see Ekman, 1992a, 1992b; Izard, 1992; Panksepp, 1992; Turner & Ortony, 1992). That there are a small number

of emotions with panculturally identifiable facial expressions is less controversial, however (e.g., see Ekman, 1989; Izard, 1977).

Not all emotional and affect-laden information processes are accompanied by visually perceptible facial actions, of course, and this has limited the utility of analyses of facial actions in emotions. Approximately 15 years ago, facial EMG began to be used to investigate emotions. As Rinn (1984) noted, overt facial expressions are the result of varied and specific movements of the facial skin and connective tissue caused by the contraction of facial muscles. These movements create folds, lines, and wrinkles in the skin and the movement of facial landmarks, such as the brows and corners of the mouth. Although muscle activation must occur if these facial actions are to be achieved, muscle action potentials in the face can occur in the absence of any overt facial action if the activation of the muscle(s) is weak or very transient, or if the overt response is aborted sufficiently early in the facial action. Facial EMG activity has therefore been especially useful in studies of emotions or emotional processes that are so weak that facial action coding is insensitive (Cacioppo, Tassinary, & Fridlund, 1990).

Representative studies of facial EMG activity as a function discrete emotions are summarized in Table 9.4. Note that most of the research has been conducted by Schwartz and his colleagues, and that emotional imagery has been the dominant method used to study facial EMG responses as a function of discrete emotions. Two distinct conceptualizations of covert facial efference and emotion can be identified in this literature. The first is the "microexpression hypothesis," which posits that emotion-specific covert facial expressions exist even when emotions are of such weak intensity that overt expressions of emotion are absent. According to this hypothesis, the prototypical configuration of facial muscle activity associated with an emotion emerges as visibly distinct expressions of emotion as emotional intensity increases (e.g., Schwartz, Fair, Salt, Mandel, & Klerman, 1976). The "motor recruitment hypothesis," in contrast, posits that facial efference varies only as a function of emotional valence at weak levels of emotional intensity, and that greater emotion-specific differentiation is achieved across the facial muscles at higher levels of emotional intensity (Cacioppo, Petty, & Tassinary, 1989).

TABLE 9.4. Facial EMG Activity as a Function of Discrete Emotions

Study	Emotional imagery	Muscle region				
		CS˙	ZM	LF	M	DAO
Schwartz, Fair, Salt, Mandel, & Klerman, 1976	Happy	−		0	+	+
	Sad	+°		0	0	+
	Angry	+		+	+	+
Schwartz, Ahern, & Brown, 1979[1]	Happy	0	+			
	Sad	+	0			
	Fearful	+	0			
Brown & Schwartz, 1960	Happy	0	+	0	0	
	Sad	+	0	0	0	
	Angry	+	0	0	0	
	Fearful	+	+	0	0	
Smith, McHugo, & Lanzetta, 1986	Happy	0	+			+
	Sad	+	0			+
	Angry	+	0			0

Note. CS denotes the corrugator supercilii muscle region; ZM denotes the zygomaticus major muscle region; LF denotes the lateral frontalis muscle region; M denotes the masseter muscle region; and DAO denotes the depressor anguli oris muscle region. Because EMG activity can vary across muscle regions, comparisons are made across emotions within muscle regions. When only an omnibus F ratio was reported, entries in the table were based to the extent possible on the original authors' description of the results. Entries marked by "+" denote an increase in EMG activity; entries marked by "−" denote a decrease in EMG activity; and entries marked by "0" denote nonsignificant or nominal changes in EMG activity. Where all entries in a column for a study are marked by "0," the omnibus F test was nonsignificant.
[1] Emotions were evoked using reflective questions.
°$p < .06$.

Perusal of Table 9.4 reveals that the most reliable findings are an increase in EMG activity over the corrugator supercilii muscle region during negative emotions, and an increase in EMG activity over the zygomaticus major muscle region during positive and some negative emotions.[7] In especially comprehensive study of facial EMG activity in discrete emotions, Brown and Schwartz (1980) paced 60 subjects through 48 imagery conditions designed to elicit happiness, sadness, fear, and anger at three levels of intensity, while EMG activity was recorded over the corrugator supercilii, zygomaticus major, masseter, and lateral frontalis muscle regions. Results revealed that fearful, angry, and sad imagery were associated with higher EMG activity over the corrugator supercilii muscle regions than was happy imagery. EMG activity over the zygomaticus major region was highest during

happy imagery, but was also elevated during fearful imagery and to a lesser extent during angry imagery. Whether these latter elevations reflect some subjects' engaging in miserable or distress smiling (Ekman, Friesen, & Ancoli, 1980), the pulling of the mouth corners up and back in a sort of silent scream, or "cross-talk" from other muscles of the middle and lower facial regions is unclear. Increasing emotional intensity led to increased EMG activity, particularly over the corrugator supercilii muscle regions during sad, angry, and fearful imagery, and over the zygomaticus major muscle region during happy imagery. Again, EMG activity over the masseter and lateral frontalis muscle regions did not vary significantly. Presumably, if the emotional intensity had been sufficient, distinctive overt facial expressions would have differentiated the negative emotions. Recent evidence further suggests that the activation functions in emotion do indeed differ for different facial muscle regions. For instance, Greenwald, Cook, and Lang (1989) plotted EMG activity along the ordinate and ranked reactions to stimuli along the abscissa such that they ranged from very negative to very positive. They found that EMG activity over the corrugator supercilii

[7] A psychometric study of surface EMG recordings over the depressor anguli oris muscle region, summarized in Cacioppo, Tassinary, and Fridlund (1990), revealed that elevated EMG activity over this region could be attributable to the activation of several different muscles, and that test–retest reliabilities were modest. Therefore, EMG activity over the depressor anguli oris muscle region should be interpreted with caution.

varied linearly and negatively, whereas EMG activity over the zygomaticus major varied in a J-shaped function.

In sum, despite early suggestions that facial EMG patterns are microexpressions of emotion, the evidence for covert emotion-specific facial expressions is less compelling than is the evidence for emotion-specific overt expressions (Ekman, 1980, 1989). Interestingly, developmental studies of overt emotional expressions reveal a pattern similar to that found for weak emotional states. Positive or negative hedonic reactions to olfactory and gustatory stimuli are detectable in neonates (Steiner, 1979), but the identification of distinct patterns of fear, anger, and sadness cannot be coded reliably until the end of the first year (Camras, Malatesta, & Izard, 1991). Fox (1991) further notes that the differentiation of emotions during the first year occurs through the process of addition and integration of new motor patterns associated with approach or withdrawal. Thus, facial EMG activity during low-intensity emotions may reflect a rudimentary bivalent evaluative disposition or motivational tendency rather than discrete emotions.

Anterior Electroencephalographic Asymmetry

Davidson reviews research on electroencephalographic (EEG) activity as a function of emotion in Chapter 10 (this volume). We focus here on a subset of this research indicating that anterior EEG asymmetry differentiates evaluative dispositions rather than discrete emotions per se.

Following Kinsbourne (1978), Davidson (1984) and Fox (1991) have proposed that subcortical and cortical regions provide an important substrate for approach and withdrawal, with the right anterior region subserving a withdrawal system and the left anterior region subserving an approach system. Davidson (1984; Davidson et al., 1990) has further suggested that to the degree that approach and withdrawal are components of different emotions, such emotions should differentially activate the anterior regions of the two cerebral hemispheres. Consistent with this reasoning, studies of discrete emotions and research on individual differences have found that EEG power recorded over the right anterior (frontal) region of the scalp is higher in negative than in positive emotions. In an illus-

trative study, Davidson et al. (1990) exposed subjects to short, emotionally evocative film clips; recorded EEG activity from anterior and posterior regions of the scalp; and coded the facial actions evinced during the films. Subsequently, facial expressions of happiness and disgust were synchronized to the EEG recordings, and hemispheric asymmetry was calculated. Results revealed that expressions of disgust were associated with greater relative left-hemispheric activation than expressions of happiness. Furthermore, this patterning was evident over the anterior but not over the posterior recording sites. Differential anterior EEG asymmetry has not been found as a function of emotions that involve a comparable withdrawal (or approach) component (e.g., Fox & Davidson, 1988; see reviews by Fox, 1991, and Davidson, 1992).

In sum, research indicates that both facial EMG responses and EEG asymmetry vary more strongly as a function of evaluative (positive–negative, approach–withdrawal) disposition than as a function of discrete emotions. The intensity of the emotion may be an important moderating factor, however, at least in the facial EMG research. This is due to evidence that the generation of strong, discrete emotions produces discriminable overt facial expressions (see Camras, Holland, & Patterson, Chapter 14, this volume). Facial EMG and EEG research, therefore, offers more than an avenue for investigating weak emotional states. It also enables investigators to examine the emergence of somatovisceral supports as the intensity of an emotion increases.

AN ORGANIZING FRAMEWORK

Given the multiple determinants of emotions and of physiological activity, it is little surprise that the literature on the psychophysiology of emotion is complex. For instance, emotion-specific ANS activity was thought by James (1884) to underlie the percept of a discrete emotional state. As a result of the *causal* nature of this relationship, the following conditions are implied, at least idiographically (see James, 1890/1950, pp. 447–449): (1) Emotion-specific somatovisceral patterns exist that generate emotional experiences; (2) a somatovisceral pattern begins before the experience of the corresponding emotion; and (3) the somatovisceral pattern is always followed by the experience of the corresponding emotion. Importantly, to the extent that emotional experiences are multiply determined, the experience of a discrete emotion can occur in the absence of the "corresponding" somatovisceral pattern even if somatovisceral afference is an antecedent of the emotion (i.e., $P(E/\Phi) = 1.0$; $P(\Phi/E) \leq 1.0$; see footnote 5 on p. 133 or Cacioppo & Tassinary, 1990). An important implication of this reasoning is that it is more informative to ask under what conditions and for what emotions is differential physiological activity observed than to search for an invariant relationship between emotional experience (or expressions) and physiological response.

Somatovisceral Afference Model of Emotion

These considerations have led to the development of a general framework within which to view the various mechanisms by which somatovisceral afference may influence emotional experience (see Figure 9.1). The somatovisceral afference model of emotion (SAME) specifies psychophysiological conditions under which (1) the *same* pattern of somatovisceral afference leads to discrete emotional experi-

ences, and (2) quite different patterns of somatovisceral afference lead to the *same* emotional experience (Cacioppo, Berntson, & Klein, 1992). A stimulus is depicted in Figure 9.1 as initially undergoing a rudimentary evaluation. This rudimentary evaluation is represented in a central state that determines the initial motivational (e.g., approach–withdrawal) tendency and generates peripheral and central changes. The anterior hemispheric asymmetries found to differentiate motivational dispositions toward the stimulus are consistent with this feature of the model.

Somatovisceral changes are not depicted as being involved in this initial appraisal, but may nevertheless play an important role in the arousal of discrete emotional states. Specifically, the model considers the possibility that somatovisceral activity may range from emotion-specific patterns of activation to completely undifferentiated activation, with ambiguous somatovisceral activation (i.e., partially differentiated activation patterns specific to multiple emotions) falling between these two endpoints along a continuum of somatovisceral patterning (see Figure 9.1, "Somatovisceral Response" column). The nodes along this continuum represent important transitions in the

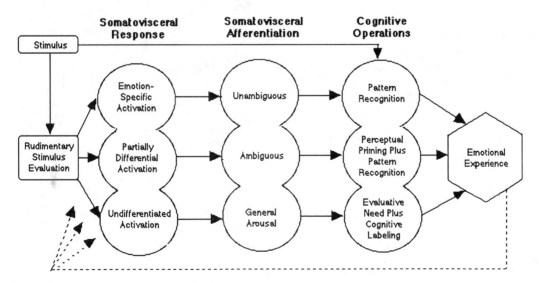

FIGURE 9.1. The somatovisceral afference model of emotion (SAME). The same pattern of somatovisceral activity has been associated with surprisingly different emotions, and the same emotion has been associated with quite different patterns of somatovisceral activity. These results have been viewed as evidence against the importance of somatovisceral afference in emotion. The SAME, depicted here and described in the text, encompasses both of these findings while emphasizing the instrumental role of somatovisceral afference and cognitive–perceptual processes in producing each. Reprinted by permission from Cacioppo, Berntson, and Klein (1992, p. 87).

constitution of the autonomic response, but the openings between these nodes underscores the continuous nature of this dimension. The pattern of somatovisceral activation produces a parallel continuum of somatovisceral sensory input to the brain. The arrows between nodes denote the major pathways for information flow.

In addition to these peripheral events, the emotional significance of the stimulus and the somatovisceral afference undergo more extensive cognitive evaluation in normal adults. Thus, Figure 9.1 also depicts the cognitive operations performed on the somatovisceral afference required to produce discrete emotional states. The extent of the cognitive elaboration of the somatovisceral afference required to produce an emotional experience ranges from simple informational analyses such as pattern recognition (e.g., James's theory of emotion as the perception of discrete patterns of somatovisceral afference) to much more complex attributional analyses and hypothesis testing (e.g., Mandler's theory of emotion), with simple cognitive appraisals of the stimulus and perceptual priming of an emotion schema falling between these two endpoints. The more extensive these cognitive operations, the longer it requires for them to be completed, and consequently the longer it takes for the somatovisceral afference to affect emotional experience. Thus, simple pattern recognition can produce an emotional experience relatively quickly, whereas detailed cognitive appraisals, attributional analyses, and systematic hypothesis testing can take longer.[8] Note that quite different patterns of somatovisceral afference (see Figure 9.1, "Somatovisceral Response" column) can lead to the same emotional experience via three very different psychophysiological mechanisms (see Figure 9.1, "Cognitive Operations" column), whereas the same pattern of somatovisceral afference can lead to discrete emotional experiences by two distinct psychophysiological mechanisms: (1) somatovisceral "illusions" when the afference is ambiguous and an emotion schema has been primed (see below); and (2) cognitive labeling when the perception of the afference is

undifferentiated with respect to an emotion and there is an evaluative need. The former of these mechanisms warrants further comment.

Emotional Percepts as Somatovisceral Illusions

The essential feature of the proposition that discrete emotions can result from "somatovisceral illusions" can be illustrated by analogy, using the ambiguous visual figure depicted in Figure 9.2 (see Cacioppo, Berntson, & Klein, 1992, for a more complete description of the model). Even though there is only one set of visual contours and features in Figure 9.2, top-down processes make it possible for a person looking at this picture to see or experience two very different perceptual images: the face of an Egyptian woman who is located behind a

FIGURE 9.2. An ambiguous figure constructed from overlapping unambiguous elements. The picture depicts (1) the face of an Egyptian woman who is located behind a candlestick, and (2) the right and left profiles, respectively, of identical twins looking at each other. These discrete images are derived from the same sensory information, and although one can switch rapidly between these images, one cannot perceive both images simultaneously. Reprinted by permission from Shepard (1990, p. 58).

---

[8]Feature detection and discriminative processing, of course, occur during complex cognitive appraisals, too, but the proximal cognitive operations that combine with the somatovisceral afference to produce the discrete emotional states are the matters of interest here.

candlestick, and the right and left profiles of identical twins looking at each other. Once these images have been identified, the viewer will find that he or she can alternate quickly between seeing these discrete images, but they cannot both be seen at once. That is, the same visual afference can lead to two different, discrete, and indubitable perceptual experiences.

Ambiguous visual figures such as the one depicted in Figure 9.2 are constructed using elements from two (or more) unambiguous images in such a way that the figure created by overlapping or slightly modifying the elements of the unambiguous images can be interpreted in multiple discrete ways (Sekular & Blake, 1985). Because the same sensory information in an ambiguous figure can produce such strikingly different, immediately obvious, and unambiguous perceptions, Leeper (1935) referred to ambiguous figures as "reversible illusions."

The middle nodes of Figure 9.1 denote the proposal that the active perceptual processes underlying reversible visual illusions are not limited to visual information processing, but can also operate on interoceptive (e.g., visceral) and proprioceptive (e.g., postural, facial, vocal) input.[9] For instance, the architecture of the somatovisceral apparatus is more likely to yield ambiguous afference than is the visual system (Reed, Harver, & Katkin, 1990), and it seems likely that events as important and commonplace as the emotions have cognitive representations that include somatovisceral attributes. Thus, two important features required for the production of somatovisceral illusions are plausibly in place. A unique implication of somatovisceral illusions is that discrete emotions can result from the perception of the *same* somatovisceral input when this input contains somatovisceral attributes of two or more discrete emotions. A second important implication is that these discrete emotional percepts are "reversible" (but can not be blended) as different emotional schemas are serially activated. Thus, just as top-down processes make it possible for people looking at Figure 9.2 to alternate quickly between seeing the face of an Egyptian woman who is located behind a candlestick and the right and left profiles of identical twins looking at each other, they may also make it possible for the person on a ride at an amusement park to alternate rapidly between the states of happy excitement and near-panic fear.

Finally, inspection of Figure 9.1 indicates some of the boundary conditions of these theories. For instance, James's (1884) theory focused on the mechanism outlined in the nodes at the top of the continua, and he did not consider the direct effects of the evaluation of the evocative stimulus on the emotional state. Cannon's (1927) theory of emotion was limited to the direct effects of the evaluation of the evocative stimulus on the rudimentary evaluative processing circuit and on the resulting activation of the viscera. Cognitive labeling theories such as Mandler's theory of emotion have focused more on the mechanism represented in the nodes at the bottom of the continua in Figure 9.1. And the processes underlying discrete emotions as somatovisceral "illusions" are represented by the middle nodes in these continua.

The framework outlined in Figure 9.1 is only heuristic at this point. It remains important to determine what are the moderating variables governing whether discrete, ambiguous, or undifferentiated somatovisceral responses are evoked by an emotional stimulus. Once this is achieved, it may be possible to specify the mechanism by which discrete emotions are linked to particular ANS changes (although the SAME does allow for the possibility that the discriminating features of somatovisceral afferences may be largely somatic in origin). Nevertheless, the model may prove helpful in designing and interpreting data from psychophysiological investigations of emotion, and in identifying moderator variables in emotion, by its explicit recognition of the different forms of somatovisceral activation and potential roles

---

[9]There are limitations to the usefulness of the analogy to visual processes, too. For instance, in the perception of ambiguous visual figures, the stimulus is a visual array outside the body. However, the central nervous system serves to create and interpret both the stimulus and the response to somatovisceral information. In this regard, visual processes are somewhat more like somatic instrumental processes than like visceral processes. Both differ from visceral perception, for instance, in the distinctiveness of the reafference. In the somatic case, the accuracy of response is readily ascertainable and correctable by somatosensory and visual feedback. In the visceral domain, there is no "intended" outcome in the conscious sense (although there are target outcomes in an automatic or homeostatic sense). Hence, visceral perception differs from somatic and visual perception in that there is no discrete criterion (or "correct" perception) for which an individual is consciously looking. For this reason, visceral afference may be particularly prone to misperceptions and "illusions."

of somatovisceral afference in emotion. At the very least, it should diminish the tendency to view the psychophysiological mechanisms underlying emotion in terms of a simple central–peripheral dichotomy.

Acknowledgments. Preparation of this chapter was supported by National Science Foundation Grant No. BNS-8940915 and a National Science Foundation Fellowship.

REFERENCES

Arnold, M. B. (1945). Physiological differentiation of emotional states. *Psychological Review, 52,* 35–48.

Averill, J. R. (1969). Autonomic response patterns during sadness and mirth. *Psychophysiology, 5,* 399–414.

Ax, A. F. (1953). The physiological differentiation between fear and anger in humans. *Psychosomatic Medicine, 15,* 433–442.

Bermond, B., Nieuwenhuyse, B., Fasotti, L., & Schuerman, J. (1991). Spinal cord lesions, peripheral feedback, and intensities of emotional feelings. *Cognition and Emotion, 5,* 201–220.

Berntson, G. G., Boysen, S. T., & Cacioppo, J. T. (in press). Neurobehavioral organization and the cardinal principle of evaluative bivalence. In F. M. Crinella & J. Yu (Eds.), *Brain mechanisms, 1990: Papers in memory of Robert Thompson.* New York: New York Academy of Sciences.

Berntson, G. G., Cacioppo, J. T., & Quigley, K. S. (1991). Autonomic determinism: The modes of autonomic control, the doctrine of autonomic space, and the laws of autonomic constraint. *Psychological Review, 98,* 459–487.

Berntson, G. G., Cacioppo, J. T., & Quigley, K. S. (1993). Respiratory sinus arrhythmia: Autonomic origins, physiological mechanisms, and psychophysiological implications. *Psychophysiology, 30,* 183–196.

Brown, S. L., & Schwartz, G. E. (1980). Relationships between facial electromyography and subjective experience during affective imagery. *Biological Psychology, 11,* 49–62.

Cacioppo, J. T., Berntson, G. G., & Andersen, B. (1991). Psychophysiological approaches to the evaluation of psychotherapeutic process and outcome, 1991: Contributions from social psychology. *Psychological Assessment, 3*(3), 321–336.

Cacioppo, J. T., Berntson, G. G., & Klein, D. J. (1992). What is an emotion? The role of somatovisceral afference, with special emphasis on somatovisceral "illusions." *Review of Personality and Social Psychology, 14,* 63–98.

Cacioppo, J. T., Bush, L. K., & Tassinary, L. G. (1992). Microexpressive facial actions as a function of affective stimuli: Replication and extension. *Personality and Social Psychology Bulletin, 18,* 515–526.

Cacioppo, J. T., Petty, R. E., & Tassinary, L. G. (1989). Social psychophysiology: A new look. *Advances in Experimental Social Psychology, 22,* 39–91.

Cacioppo, J. T., & Tassinary, L. G. (1990). Inferring psychophysiological significance from physiological signals. *American Psychologist, 45,* 16–28.

Cacioppo, J. T., Tassinary, L. G., & Fridlund, A. J. (1990). The skeletomotor system. In J. T. Cacioppo & L. G.

Tassinary (Eds.), *Principles of psychophysiology: Physical, social, and inferential elements* (pp. 325–384). New York: Cambridge University Press.

Cacioppo, J. T., Uchino, B. N., Crites, S. L., Snydersmith, M. A., Smith, G., Berntson, G. G., & Lang, P. J. (1992). The relationship between facial expressiveness and sympathetic activation in emotion: A critical review, with emphasis on modeling underlying mechanisms and individual differences. *Journal of Personality and Social Psychology, 62,* 110–128.

Camras, L. A., Malatesta, C., & Izard, C. (1991). The development of facial expressions in infancy. In R. Feldman & B. Rime (Eds.), *Fundamentals of nonverbal behavior* (pp. 73–105). New York: Cambridge University Press.

Cannon, W.B. (1927). The James–Lange theory of emotions: A critical examination and an alternative theory. *American Journal of Psychology, 39,* 106–124.

Chwalisz, K., Diener, E., & Gallagher, D. (1988). Autonomic arousal feedback and emotional experience: Evidence from the spinal cord injured. *Journal of Personality and Social Psychology, 54,* 820–828.

Darwin, C. (1873). *The expression of the emotions in man and animals.* New York: Appleton. (Original work published 1872)

Davidson, R. J. (1984). Affect, cognition, and hemispheric specialization. In C. Izard, J. Kagan, & R. Zajonc (Eds.), *Emotions, cognition and behavior* (pp. 320–361). Cambridge, England: Cambridge University Press.

Davidson, R. J. (1992). Emotion and affective style: Hemispheric substrates. *Psychological Science, 3,* 39–43.

Davidson, R. J., Ekman, P., Saron, C. D., Senulis, J. A., & Friesen, W. V. (1990). Approach–withdrawal and cerebral asymmetry: Emotional expression and brain physiology, I. *Journal of Personality and Social Psychology, 58,* 330–341.

Ekman, P. (1973). Darwin and cross-cultural studies of facial expression. In P. Ekman (Ed.), *Darwin and facial expression: A century of research in review* (pp. 1–83). New York: Academic Press.

Ekman, P. (1980). Methods for measuring facial action. In K. R. Scherer & P. Ekman (Eds.), *Handbook of methods in nonverbal behavior research* (pp. 45–90). Cambridge, England: Cambridge University Press.

Ekman, P. (1984). Expression and the nature of emotion. In K. Scherer & P. Ekman (Eds.), *Approaches to emotion* (pp. 319–344). Hillsdale, NJ: Erlbaum.

Ekman, P. (1989). The argument and evidence about universals in facial expressions of emotion. In J. Wagner & A. Manstead (Eds.), *Handbook of social psychophysiology* (pp. 143–164). New York: Wiley.

Ekman, P. (1992a). An argument for basic emotions. *Cognition and Emotion, 6*(3/4), 169–200.

Ekman, P. (1992b). A set of basic emotions. *Psychological Review, 99,* 550–553.

Ekman, P., & Friesen, W. V. (1978). *The Facial Action Coding System: A technique for the measurement of facial movement.* Palo Alto, CA: Consulting Psychologists Press.

Ekman, P., Friesen, W. V., & Ancoli, S. (1980). Facial signs of emotional experience. *Journal of Personality and Social Psychology, 39,* 1125–1134.

Ekman, P., Levenson, R. W., & Friesen, W. V. (1983). Autonomic nervous system activity distinguishes among emotions. *Science, 221,* 1208–1210.

Fischer, K. W., Shaver, P. R., & Carnochan, P. (1990). How emotions develop and how they organize development. *Cognition and Emotion, 4,* 81–127.

Fox, N. A. (1991). If it's not left, it's right: Electroencephalogram asymmetry and the development of emotion. *American Psychologist, 46*(8), 863–872.

Fox, N. A., & Davidson, R. J. (1988). Patterns of brain electrical activity during facial signs of emotion in 10-month-old infants. *Developmental Psychology, 24,* 230–236.

Frijda, N. H. (1986). *The emotions.* New York: Cambridge University Press.

Frijda, N. H., Mesquita, B., Sonnemans, J., & Van Goozen, S. (1991). The duration of affective phenomena or emotions, sentiments and passions. In K. T. Strongman (Ed.), *International review of studies on emotion* (Vol. 1, pp. 187–225). Chichester, England: Wiley.

Funkenstein, D. H., King, S. H., & Drollette, M. (1954). The direction of anger during a laboratory stress-inducing situation. *Psychosomatic Medicine, 16,* 404–413.

Graham, F. K., & Clifton, R. K. (1966). Heart-rate change as a component of the orienting response. *Psychological Bulletin, 65,* 305–320.

Greenwald, M. K., Cook, E. W., III, & Lang, P. J. (1989). Affective judgment and psychophysiological response: Dimensional covariation in the evaluation of pictorial stimuli. *Journal of Psychophysiology, 3,* 51–64.

Hubert, W., & de Jong-Meyer, R. (1991). Autonomic, neuroendocrine, and subjective responses to emotion-inducing film stimuli. *International Journal of Psychophysiology, 11,* 131–140.

Izard, C. E. (1971). *The face of emotion.* New York: Appleton-Century-Crofts.

Izard, C. E. (1977). *Human emotions.* New York: Academic Press.

Izard, C. E. (1992). Basic emotions, relations among emotions, and emotion–cognition relations. *Psychological Review, 99,* 561–565.

Izard, C. E., & Malatesta, C. Z. (1987). Perspectives on emotional development: I. Differential emotions theory of early emotional development. In J. Osofsky (Ed.), *Handbook of infant development* (2nd ed., pp. 494–554). New York: Wiley-Interscience.

James, W. (1884). What is an emotion? *Mind, 9,* 188–205.

James, W. (1950). *Principles of psychology* (Vol. 1). New York: Dover. (Original work published 1870)

Johnson, A. K., & Anderson, E. A. (1990). Stress and arousal. In J. T. Cacioppo & L. G. Tassinary (Eds.), *Principles of psychophysiology: Physical, social, and inferential elements* (pp. 216–252). New York: Cambridge University Press.

Kinsbourne, M. (1978). *Asymmetrical function of the brain.* Cambridge, England: Cambridge University Press.

Lacey, J. I., Kagan, J., Lacey, B. C., & Moss, H. A. (1963). The visceral level: Situational determinants and behavioral correlates of autonomic response patterns. In P. H. Kapp (Ed.), *Expression of the emotions in man* (pp. 161–196). New York: International Universities Press.

Lang, P. J., Bradley, M. M., & Cuthbert, B. N. (1990). Emotion, attention, and the startle reflex. *Psychological Review, 97,* 377–395.

Lazarus, R. S. (1966). *Psychological stress and the coping process.* New York: McGraw-Hill.

Leeper, R. (1935). A study of a neglected portion of the field of learning—the development of sensory organization. *Journal of Genetic Psychology, 46,* 41–75.

Levenson, R. W. (1988). Emotion and the autonomic nervous system: A prospectus for research on autonomic specificity. In H. L. Wagner (Ed.), *Social psychophysiology and emotion: Theory and clinical applications* (pp. 17–42). Chichester, England: Wiley.

Levenson, R. W. (1992). Autonomic nervous system patterning in emotion. *Psychological Science, 3,* 23–27.

Levenson, R. W., Carstensen, L. L., Friesen, W. V., & Ekman, P. (1991). Emotion, physiology, and expression in old age. *Psychology and Aging, 6,* 28–35.

Levenson, R. W., Ekman, P., & Friesen, W. V. (1990). Voluntary facial action generates emotion-specific autonomic nervous system activity. *Psychophysiology, 27,* 363–384.

Levenson, R. W., Ekman, P., Heider, K., & Friesen, W. V. (1992). Emotion and autonomic nervous system activity in the Minangkabau of West Sumatra. *Journal of Personality and Social Psychology, 62,* 972–988.

Leventhal, J., & Mosbach, P. A. (1983). The perceptual–motor theory of emotion. In J. T. Cacioppo & R. E. Petty (Eds.), *Social psychophysiology: A sourcebook* (pp. 353–390). New York: Guilford Press.

Malmo, R. B. (1975). *On emotions, needs, and our archaic brain.* New York: Holt, Rinehart & Winston.

Mandler, G. (1975). *Mind and emotion.* New York: Wiley.

Oatley, K., & Johnson-Laird, P. N. (1987). Towards a cognitive theory of emotions. *Cognition and Emotion, 1,* 29–50.

Obrist, P. A., Webb, R. A., Sutterer, J. R., & Howard, J. L. (1970). The cardiac–somatic relationship: Some reformulations. *Psychophysiology, 6,* 569–587.

Ortony, A., & Turner, T. J. (1990). What's basic about basic emotions? *Psychological Review, 97,* 315–331.

Panksepp, J. (1982). Toward a general psychobiological theory of emotions. *Behavioral and Brain Sciences, 5,* 407–467.

Panksepp, J. (1992). A critical role for "affective neuroscience" in resolving what is basic about basic emotions: Response to Ortony and Turner. *Psychological Review, 99,* 554–560.

Plutchik, R. (1980). A general psychoevolutionary theory of emotion. In R. Plutchik & H. Kellerman (Eds.), *Emotion: Theory, research, and experience: Vol. 1. Theories of emotion* (pp. 3–31). New York: Academic Press.

Quigley, K. S., & Berntson, G. G. (1990). Autonomic origins of cardiac responses to nonsignal stimuli in the rat. *Behavioral Neuroscience, 104,* 751–762.

Reed, S. D., Harver, A., & Katkin, E. S. (1990). Interoception. In J. T. Cacioppo & L. G. Tassinary (Eds.), *Principles of psychophysiology: Physical, social, and inferential elements* (pp. 253–294). New York: Cambridge University Press.

Reisenzein, R. (1983). The Schachter theory of emotion: Two decades later. *Psychological Bulletin, 94,* 239–264.

Rinn, W. E. (1984). The neuropsychology of facial expression: A review of the neurological and psychological mechanisms for producing facial expressions. *Psychological Bulletin, 95,* 52–77.

Roberts, R. J., & Weerts, T. C. (1982). Cardiovascular responding during anger and fear imagery. *Psychological Reports, 50,* 219–230.

Schachter, J. (1957). Pain, fear, and anger in hypertensives and normotensives: A psychophysiological study. *Psychosomatic Medicine, 19,* 17–29.

Schachter, S. (1964). The interaction of cognitive and physiological determinants of emotional state. In L. Berkowitz (Ed.), *Advances in experimental social psychology* (Vol. 1, pp. 49–80). New York: Academic Press.

Schachter, S., & Singer, J. E. (1962). Cognitive, social, and physiological determinants of emotional state. *Psychological Review, 69,* 379–399.

Schwartz, G. E., Ahern, G. L., & Brown, S. L. (1979).

Lateralized facial muscle response to positive and negative emotional stimuli. *Psychophysiology, 16*, 561-571.

Schwartz, G. E., Fair, P. L., Salt, P., Mandel, M. R., & Klerman, G. R. (1976). Facial muscle patterning to affective imagery in depressed and nondepressed subjects. *Science, 192*, 489.

Schwartz, G. E., Weinberger, D. A., & Singer, J. A. (1981). Cardiovascular differentiation of happiness, sadness, anger, and fear following images and exercise. *Psychosomatic Medicine, 43*, 343–364.

Sekular, R., & Blake, R. (1985). *Perception*. New York: Knopf.

Shepard, R. N. (1990). *Mind sights*. San Francisco: W. H. Freeman.

Smith, C. A., & Ellsworth, P. C. (1987). Patterns of appraisal and emotion related to taking an exam. *Journal of Personality and Social Psychology, 52*, 475–488.

Smith, C. A., McHugo, G. J., & Lanzetta, J. T. (1986). The facial muscle patterning of posed and imagery-induced expressions of emotion by expressive and nonexpressive posers. *Motivation and Emotion, 10*, 133–157.

Steiner, J. E. (1979). Human facial expression in response to taste and smell stimulation. *Advances in Child Development and Behavior, 13*, 237–295.

Stemmler, D. G. (1989). The autonomic differentiation of emotions revisited: Convergent and discriminant validation. *Psychophysiology, 26*, 617–632.

Stemmler, D. G. (1992). *Differential psychophysiology: Persons in situations*. New York: Springer-Verlag.

Sternbach, R. A. (1962). Assessing differential autonomic patterns in emotion. *Journal of Psychosomatic Research, 6*, 87–91.

Tassinary, L. G., Cacioppo, J. T., & Geen, T. R. (1989). A psychometric study of surface electrode placements for facial electromyographic recording: I. The brow and cheek muscle regions. *Psychophysiology, 26*, 1–16.

Tomkins, S. S. (1962). *Affect, imagery, and consciousness: Vol. 1. The positive affects*. New York: Springer.

Tourangeau, R., & Ellsworth, P. C. (1979). The role of facial response in the experience of emotion. *Journal of Personality and Social Psychology, 37*, 1519–1531.

Turner, T. J., & Ortony, A. (1992). Basic emotions: Can conflicting criteria converge? *Psychological Review, 99*, 566–571.

Valins, S. (1966). Cognitive effects of false heart-rate feedback. *Journal of Personality and Social Psychology, 4*, 400–408.

Wagner, H. (1989). The physiological differentiation of emotions. In H. Wagner & A. Manstead (Eds.), *Handbook of social psychophysiology* (pp. 77–89). New York: Wiley.

Wolf, S., & Wolff, H. G. (1951). *Human gastric function*. New York: Oxford University Press.

Zajonc, R. B., & McIntosh, D. N. (1992). Emotions research: Some promising questions and some questionable promises. *Psychological Science, 3*, 70–74.

10

The Neuropsychology of Emotion and Affective Style

RICHARD J. DAVIDSON

INTRODUCTION

Probably more than any other class of behavior, emotion involves frank biological changes that are frequently perceptible to the individual in whom the emotion arises, and occasionally even visible to an observer (e.g., facial blood flow changes, as in "white with fear"). For much of its relatively short history in scientific psychology, the focus of research on the biological substrates of emotion was mostly on the autonomic changes that accompany emotion in humans or on the subcortical limbic system circuits that mediate specific emotional behaviors in animals. Both of these research endeavors have yielded important insights about the nature of emotion. However, it is clear that in more complex animals, and especially in humans, the cerebral cortex plays an important role in aspects of emotional behavior and experience (Kolb & Taylor, 1990). In particular, anterior cortical regions, which have extensive anatomical reciprocity both with subcortical centers and with posterior cortical circuits, are critically implicated in emotional behavior. These anterior cortical zones are the brain regions that have shown more dramatic growth in relative size over the course of phylogeny, compared with other brain regions (see Luria, 1973, and Jerison, 1973, for reviews).

The focus of this chapter is on asymmetries in anterior cortical function that have been implicated in different forms of emotional behavior. Some of the earliest suggestions regarding the importance of hemispheric asymmetries for emotional behavior resulted from observations on patients with unilateral cortical lesions (e.g., Jackson, 1878). The majority of these reports indicated that damage to the left hemisphere was more likely to lead to what has been termed a "catastrophic-depressive" reaction than was comparable damage to the right hemisphere (e.g., Goldstein, 1939). More recent studies have confirmed this basic observation (e.g., Gainotti, 1972; Sackeim et al., 1982). Of particular importance for the research to be reviewed in this chapter are studies by Robinson and his colleagues (e.g., Robinson, Kubos, Starr, Rao, & Price, 1984). They have reported that it is damage specifically to the left frontal lobe that results in depressive symptomatology. They found that among left-brain-damaged patients, the closer the lesion was to the frontal pole, the more severe the depressive symptomatology. Patients who developed mania subsequent to brain injury were much more likely to have sustained damage to the right hemisphere, sparing the left. These and other observations have provided the basis for our studies of anterior activation asymmetries associated with emotion and affective style.

In the next part of this chapter, I briefly describe the major elements of the theoretical model that motivates the research to be presented. The methods that are common to our studies and the unique methodological requirements of this research are then described. Research on anterior asymmetries associated with the phasic arousal of emotion is presented, followed by a summary of our findings on relations between individual differences in baseline asymmetry and affective reactivity. The chapter ends with a discussion of some unanswered questions posed by this work.

THE ROLE OF
THE CEREBRAL HEMISPHERES
IN EMOTIONAL PROCESSING:
A THEORETICAL ACCOUNT

It is not surprising that there is a fundamental asymmetry in the control of functions related to emotion, in light of speculations concerning the evolutionary advantages of cerebral asymmetry (e.g., Levy, 1972). In searching for the basis of the asymmetry underlying emotion, it is instructive to recall that investigators in comparative psychology (Schneirla, 1959), behavioral neuroscience (Stellar & Stellar, 1985), and child development (Kagan, Reznick, & Snidman, 1988) all agree that approach and withdrawal are fundamental motivational dimensions that may be found at any level of phylogeny where behavior itself is present. In several previous articles (e.g., Davidson, 1984, 1987, 1988; Davidson, Ekman, Saron, Senulis, & Friesen, 1990; Davidson & Tomarken, 1989), I have suggested that the anterior regions of the left and right hemispheres are specialized for approach and withdrawal processes, respectively. The bases upon which this suggestion is made are several:

1. The left frontal region has been described as an important center for intention, self-regulation, and planning (Luria, 1973). The functions that have been ascribed to this area are those that have historically been assigned to the "will," a hypothetical structure of central importance to approach-related behavior.

2. Over the course of ontogeny, an infant or toddler will approach and reach out to objects of interest using its right hand much more often than its left (e.g., Young, Segalowitz, Misek, Alp, & Boulet, 1983). It would be of interest to examine whether episodes of right-handed reaching and grasping are in fact associated with expressive signs of positive affect (e.g., smiling). Right-handed reaching and positive affect are taken to be the collective

manifestation of a brain circuit mediating approach behavior, with the left frontal region serving as a "convergence zone" for this circuit (see Damasio, 1989, for a description of convergence zones, and Davidson, 1992b, for an application of the concept to the frontal emotion circuit).

3. As I have noted above, damage to the left frontal region results in behavior and experience that might best be characterized as a deficit in approach. Patients with damage to this brain region are apathetic, experience loss of interest and pleasure in objects and people, and have difficulty initiating voluntary action (i.e., psychomotor retardation). Thus, hypoactivation in this region should be associated with a lowered threshold for the experience of sadness and depression.

The claim that the right anterior region is specialized for withdrawal is based upon a less extensive but growing corpus of evidence. The most compelling findings are the data on normal humans involving electrophysiological measures of regional hemispheric activation. These findings, which are reviewed in detail in later sections, indicate that during the experimental arousal of withdrawal-related emotional states (e.g., fear and disgust), the right frontal and anterior temporal regions are selectively activated. In addition, subjects with baseline tonic activation in these regions show a propensity to respond with accentuated withdrawal-related negative affect to appropriate emotion elicitors. Such individuals also report greater dispositional negative affect.

Recently, Morris, Bradley, Bowers, Lang, and Heilman (1991) have studied a patient with a right temporal lobectomy, using psychophysiological measures of affective reactivity in response to standardized laboratory elicitors of positive and negative emotion. The resection was performed to remove an arteriovenous malformation in the right temporal lobe and included the anterior portion of the temporal lobe and the whole right amygdala. The stimuli presented to the patient were slides that differed in valence, but that were matched on overall salience. Morris et al. recorded the skin conductance responses to these slide stimuli. They found that the responses to the positive stimuli were equivalent in magnitude to those observed in normals; however, responses to the negative slides were markedly attenuated. Using measures of regional cerebral blood flow derived from positron emission tomography (PET), Reiman, Raichle, Butler, Hercovitch, and Robins (1984) have reported accentuated activation during a resting baseline in a right-hemisphere subcortical site that projects to the amygdala in panic-prone patients. Taken together, these observations suggest a specialization for certain anterior cortical and subcortical right-hemisphere regions in the mediation of withdrawal-related negative affect. Precisely what the differential role of the anterior temporal and frontal regions is in the mediation of the negative affective responding is not clear from the available evidence.

Some of the evidence referred to above is derived from the study of patients with unilateral lesions. Other findings come from the assessment of regional brain activation in neurologically intact subjects. In light of the assumption that lesions result in selective deficits in activation in the lesioned area (e.g., Burke et al., 1982), the findings described above support the following hypotheses regarding the anterior hemispheric substrates of emotion and emotion-related processes. Activation in the left anterior region is associated with approach-related emotions; deficient activation in this region is associated with emotion-related phenomena that might be best described as reflecting approach-related deficits, such as depression; and activation in the right anterior region is associated with withdrawal-related emotions such as fear and disgust and withdrawal-related psychopathology such as anxiety.

Two additional conceptual issues deserve emphasis. The first concerns the subcomponents of emotion that I address in this chapter and in the research described herein. The focus here is on the experience and expression of emotion. The hemispheric substrates of perceiving emotional information are likely to be different from those involved in actual emotional experience. Similarly, the underlying neural controls for the communication of *information about* emotion are likely to be different from those implicated in the experience and expression of *actual* emotion. In this regard it is instructive to note that some investigators have argued for a more general role for the right hemisphere in all emotion (e.g., Borod, Koff, Lorch, & Nicholas, 1986; Etcoff, 1989). However, it is imperative to emphasize that the data upon which this claim is based

come largely from studies of the perception of emotional information (e.g., facial expressions), where the weight of the evidence does indeed suggest that the right *posterior* region is specialized for the perception of emotional information, regardless of valence. This fact underscores the importance of differentiating among different components of emotional functioning, most importantly between the perception of emotion and the experience/expression of emotion. In addition to my own writings on this issue (e.g., Davidson, 1984, 1993), a number of other commentators who have reviewed this literature have reached similar conclusions (e.g., Leventhal & Tomarken, 1986; Silberman & Weingartner, 1986).

The second issue concerns the importance of specifying the hypothesized logical status of the relation between asymmetrical anterior activation and emotion-related processes. Failure to consider this problem has been a source of considerable confusion in previous reviews of this topic (see Davidson, 1993). Although a large number of reports indicate that damage to the left hemisphere, particularly in the anterior regions, results in depressive symptomatology far more frequently than damage to corresponding regions of the right hemisphere, some investigators have underscored the fact that a number of reports have shown no clear difference in the incidence or severity of depressive symptomatology in left- versus right-brain-damaged patients (see review by Gainotti, 1989). In addition to the obvious fact that many of the studies cited by Gainotti (1989) combined patients with both anterior and posterior damage, another crucial point in the interpretation of such data has not been made explicit in most of the reviews on this subject. My colleagues and I have proposed that anterior activation asymmetry functions as a diathesis that predisposes an individual to respond with predominantly positive or negative affect, *given an appropriate emotion elicitor*. In the absence of a specific elicitor, differences in affective symptomatology among individuals with different patterns of anterior activation asymmetry or asymmetry of anterior brain lesions would not be expected. Consistent with this prediction is our observation that whereas baseline anterior asymmetry predicts reactivity to an affective challenge, it is unrelated to measures of the individual's current, unprovoked emotional state (e.g., Davidson &

Fox, 1989; Tomarken, Davidson, & Henriques, 1990; Wheeler, Davidson, & Tomarken, 1993).[1] Thus, in a patient with left anterior damage, depressive symptomatology would be expected only if that patient were exposed to the requisite environmental stresses. Left anterior damage is not in itself sufficient for the production of depressive symptomatology. We would therefore not expect *all* patients with left frontal damage to show depressive symptomatology; only those exposed to an appropriate set of environmental stresses would be expected to show the hypothesized final state.[2]

CEREBRAL PSYCHOPHYSIOLOGICAL METHODS IN THE STUDY OF HEMISPHERIC ASYMMETRY RELATED TO EMOTION AND AFFECTIVE STYLE

Several important considerations apply in the choice of methods to study the regional brain activity that underlies emotion. Many of the core phenomena of emotion are brief and therefore require measures that have a very fast time resolution. Moreover, periods of peak emotional intensity are unpredictable; they can occur at different points in time for different subjects in response to the same emotional stimulus. For example, some facial expressions of emotion are present for as little as 1–2 seconds. An ideal method would be one that could resolve activity as brief as the behavioral manifestations of emotion. It is also important to be able to record physiological activity over much longer time intervals. This is needed when subjects are presented with affect elicitors that last several minutes, requiring physiology to be integrated over the entire period of the eliciting stimulus. In addition, as I describe in detail below, one of the most exciting new areas in psychophysiological research

on emotion is the study of the biological bases of individual differences in emotional reactivity. Such studies often require baseline physiology to be integrated over several minutes in order to obtain a reliable estimate of an individual's characteristic pattern. Thus, with respect to time resolution, the ideal measure would range from subsecond intervals to several minutes.

Another important consideration is related to the first. Data must be stored in a form that will permit post hoc extraction of epochs of varying durations. The capacity for post-hoc data extraction is required so that the physiology coincident with objective measures of emotional state (e.g., facial expressions of emotion) can be examined. In some of the research to be described below, brain activity coincident with the display of spontaneous facial expressions of emotion has been extracted for analysis. Other measures of emotional state might also be utilized in a similar fashion, including vocal indices and on-line self-report. This requirement presupposes the accurate synchronization of the behavioral and physiological data streams. Modern computer and video technology allow for this possibility.

Another essential requirement of any measure of regional brain activity used in the study of emotion is that it be relatively noninvasive. There are three major reasons for this. First, the more intrusive a method, the greater will be the interference with the elicitation of actual emotion. For example, certain types of PET scan protocols are highly intrusive, and it is difficult to override the anxiety that is an inherent side effect of the procedure. It would probably be very difficult to elicit strong positive affect in many subjects undergoing a PET scan. The second important reason for limiting measures of regional brain activation to those that are relatively noninvasive is the need to study individuals over time as they undergo several different emotional states. It is crucial that psychophysiological studies of emotion compare at least two different emotions and a baseline period (see Davidson, Ekman, et al., 1990, for a complete discussion of methodological desiderata in psychophysiological studies of emotion). Such comparisons enable the investigator to determine whether the physiological pattern observed during the emotion period differs from that during baseline, and whether the pattern is simply characteristic of emotion per se (in which case

---

[1]Although baseline anterior asymmetries are unrelated to measures of unprovoked emotional *state*, they are related to individual differences in dispositional mood or emotional *traits* (Tomarken, Davidson, Wheeler, & Doss, 1992). This is discussed in a later section.

[2]One important variable in evaluating the literature on the effects of unilateral lesions is the time from lesion to assessment. With increased time, there should be an increased likelihood of exposure to negative life events, and therefore a higher probability that the individual would show depressive symptomatology.

the pattern associated with each of the two different emotions will not differ) or is emotion-specific. The third reason for preferring relatively noninvasive procedures is the possibility of using them with infants and young children. These age groups are particularly important to study in research on the biological bases of emotion, and the methods used must be appropriate for this population.

In light of the considerations noted above, we have been using scalp-recorded brain electrical activity to make inferences about regional brain activation during the experimental arousal of acute emotions and emotion-related patterns of brain activity during resting baselines. The electroencephalogram (EEG) meets all of the requirements noted above. It is noninvasive; it has a fast time resolution; and it can be effectively synchronized with a behavioral data stream, which permits extraction of data based upon post hoc specification of periods of intense behavioral signs of emotion.

We have used recordings of brain electrical activity to make inferences about regional brain activation in adults, toddlers, and infants, both during baseline periods and in response to a variety of emotion elicitors. We can examine brain activity during very brief epochs of emotion (1 second), provided that periods of the same emotion type occur sufficiently frequently within an individual. To obtain stable estimates of spectral power from which measures of activation are derived, one needs a minimum of approximately 10–15 seconds of activity. The individual epochs themselves can be as brief as 1 second, but their sum must exceed 10 seconds in length (Davidson, 1988; Tomarken, Davidson, Wheeler, & Kinney, 1992). Movement and muscle activity frequently accompany the generation of emotion. We have developed procedures for statistically partialing out the contributions of the muscle activity from the EEG (see Davidson, 1988, for a description of the method, and Henriques & Davidson, 1990, for an application of the method). Finally, we use an electrode cap for EEG recording (Blom & Anneveldt, 1982). Such a cap permits accurate and rapid placement of electrodes and is particularly useful in studies with infants and children, where rapid application of electrodes is essential.

The principal measure extracted from the EEG in the studies I present in the remainder of this chapter is power in the alpha band, which in adults represents activity between 8

and 13 Hz.[3] A wealth of evidence indicates that power in this frequency band is inversely related to activation in adults (e.g., Shagass, 1972). In the studies I describe on infants, we have used power in a lower-frequency band as our dependent measure, since this represents the functional equivalent of adult alpha activity (see e.g., Davidson & Fox, 1989; Davidson & Tomarken, 1989). Our measures of band power are computed from the output of a fast fourier transform, which decomposes the brain activity into its underlying sine wave components.

I now briefly review the findings from several recent studies performed in our laboratory, in which we examined brain activity during the experience/expression of experimentally aroused positive and negative emotion.

ANTERIOR ASYMMETRIES DURING THE EXPERIMENTAL AROUSAL OF APPROACH- AND WITHDRAWAL-RELATED EMOTION

We recently completed a collaborative study with Ekman and Friesen (Davidson, Ekman, et al., 1990), in which adult subjects were exposed to short film clips designed to induce approach-related positive emotion and withdrawal-related negative emotion. Happiness and amusement were the positive, approach-related emotions; disgust was the negative, withdrawal-related emotion. Subjects were presented with two positive and two negative film clips in a darkened room while we videotaped their facial behavior unobtrusively. We also recorded brain electrical activity from the left and right frontal, central, anterior temporal, and parietal regions.

An important consideration in research on emotion is that when two or more emotions are compared for their effects on either physiological or behavioral dependent variables, the intensities of the elicited emotion must be compa-

---

[3]We typically examine power in all frequency bands. However, the majority of variance in task-related and baseline EEG is in the alpha band. Moreover, we have demonstrated that asymmetries in alpha power are more consistently related to both cognitive (e.g., Davidson, Chapman, Chapman, & Henriques, 1990) and affective (e.g., Davidson, Ekman, et al., 1990) processes than are asymmetries of power in other frequency bands.

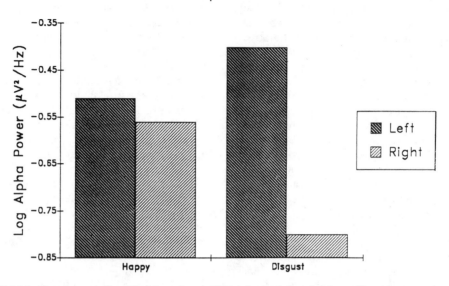

FIGURE 10.1. Mean log-transformed alpha power (μV^2/Hz) for the left and right midfrontal regions (F3 and F4) during happy and disgusted facial expression conditions. More negative numbers indicate less alpha power. The negative numbers are a function of the log transformation. Lower numbers (i.e., more negative) are associated with increased activation. Reprinted by permission from Davidson, Ekman, Saron, Senulis, and Friesen (1990).

rable. If the emotions differ in intensity, then any differences found between them could be attributed to intensity per se, rather than to the qualitative nature of the emotion aroused. Accordingly, our positive and negative films were carefully matched on the intensities of the primary emotion elicited by each (amusement for the positive films and disgust for the negative films), as determined by self-report.

The video record of each subject was coded with Ekman and Friesen's (1978) Facial Action Coding System (FACS). The FACS distinguishes 44 Action Units, the minimal units that are anatomically separable and visually distinctive. Any facial movement can be described in terms of the particular Action Unit(s) that produced it. The scorer identifies the Action Units (such as the one that lowers the brow or pulls the lips' corners up), rather than making inferences about underlying emotional states (such as anger or happiness). FACS scoring of the facial data from this experiment revealed that the two types of expression that occurred with the most frequency were happy expressions in response to the positive film clips and disgust expressions in response to the negative film clips. For each subject, the onset and offset of each happy and disgust expression was identified with the FACS. These times were

then entered into the computer so that brain activity coincident with these expressions could be extracted.

Following removal of eye movement, muscle, and gross movement artifacts the brain activity during periods of happy and disgust facial expressions were Fourier-transformed, and power in different frequency bands was calculated. On the basis of the theory and evidence reviewed above, we hypothesized that the disgust periods would be associated with greater right-sided anterior activation than the happy periods, and that the happy periods would be associated with greater left-sided activation than the disgust periods. Figure 10.1 presents the alpha power data for the frontal leads. As can be seen from this figure, disgust was associated with less alpha power (i.e., *more* activation) in the right frontal lead (F4) than was happiness, while happiness was associated with less alpha power in the left frontal lead (F3) than was disgust. The hemisphere × valence interaction was highly significant ($p <$ .0005). This pattern of greater right-sided activation during disgust than during happiness was also found in the anterior temporal electrodes. Importantly, there were no significant hemisphere × valence interactions in the central or parietal regions, underscoring the specificity of the valence-related asymmetry to anterior brain regions.

We examined frontal asymmetry on an individual-subject basis to determine how consistent the difference was between happy and disgusted epochs. For each subject, we calculated an asymmetry index that expressed the asymmetry of frontal alpha power in a single metric. The index was log right minus log left alpha power. Higher numbers on this index denoted greater relative left-sided activation. We computed this index separately for the happy and disgust periods. We found that every subject showed a lower score on this index during the disgust than during the happy periods. The direction of this difference indicates greater right-sided frontal activation during the disgust than during the happy condition. We also found that there were large differences among individuals in their average asymmetry score (across emotion conditions). The difference between happy and disgust conditions appeared to be superimposed upon subjects' basal levels of asymmetry. In the next part of this chapter, I show how such individual differences in asymmetry are related to characteristic differences in mood and affective reactivity.

In order to examine whether the procedures we used to verify the presence of an emotion (i.e., facial expression) actually made an important difference in uncovering patterns of asymmetry, we performed the type of analysis that is more typical in research on the psychophysiology of emotion. We simply compared all artifact-free EEG epochs extracted from the positive film clips with the comparable epochs extracted from the negative film clips. The epochs used for this analysis were selected independently of the subjects' facial behavior. Although the means were in the expected direction for the frontal leads, with the negative film clips producing more right-sided activation than the positive clips, we found no significant differences between these conditions on any of the measures of asymmetry. The lack of significant effects when the analyses were performed independently of facial behavior suggests that our method of using facial expressivity to flag epochs of peak emotional state was effective. In this study, significant between-condition differences in asymmetry were obtained only when facial expression was used to verify the presence of emotional states. We should note, however, that other studies in our laboratory

(e.g., Davidson & Fox, 1982) and other laboratories (e.g., Ahern & Schwartz, 1985; Tucker, Stenslie, Roth, & Shearer, 1981) have found EEG differences between positive and negative emotional states without using facial expressive measures as an index of peak emotional intensity. Thus, the extraction of data during the presence of discrete facial expressions of emotion does not appear to be *necessary* for the emergence of hemispheric asymmetries relevant to emotion.

We recently completed a study where robust differences in frontal brain asymmetry emerged during approach- and withdrawal-related emotion, in the absence of extraction of epochs based upon facial behavior (Sobotka, Davidson, & Senulis, 1992). In this experiment, we manipulated reward and punishment contingencies in the context of a video-game-like task. The task consisted of a series of 400 trials, presented over the course of two experimental sessions, in blocks of 20 trials each. Half of the trials were potential reward trials, and half were potential punishment trials. Each trial began with the presentation of a fixation point, followed between 2 and 4 seconds later by an arrow. The arrow was in either the "up" or "down" position. An "up" arrow denoted that the trial was a potential reward trial, and a "down" arrow indicated that the trial was a potential punishment trial. Four seconds following the presentation of the arrow stimulus, a square was presented in the center of the screen. This was the imperative stimulus to which the subject was required to respond as quickly as possible. The outcome of each trial was based upon the subjects' reaction time to the imperative stimulus.

There were two possible outcomes on each trial. For reward trials, subjects could either win money or have no change in their earnings. For punishment trials, subjects could either lose money or have no change in their earnings. The amount of money that was won or lost on each trial was always $.25. Subjects were told that they would receive $5 at the beginning of each session, which represented their starting sum of money in the game they were about to play. Subjects were instructed that they could win additional money as well as lose money from the $5 starting amount. They were also told that the amount of money they ended up with following the completion of the game would be theirs to keep. For subjects to win money in the reward trials and stay even (i.e., not lose money in the punishment trials), they were required to have a reaction time that was faster than the median reaction time from the previous block of trials. The computer that acquired the reaction time data thus updated the criterion reaction time on each trial block.

We recorded brain electrical activity from most of the standard 10/20 locations during the performance of the task. Of major interest to us was the frontal brain activity during the preparatory interval between the arrow and imperative stimuli. The EEG during this period was Fourier-transformed, and power in the alpha band was extracted as described in the experiment above. As predicted, we found a significant valence × hemisphere interaction, with greater right frontal activation (i.e., less alpha power) during the punishment than during the reward trials. This interaction was significant in both the midfrontal (F3/F4) and lateral frontal (F7/F8) sites. In both frontal regions, the punishment condition was associated with less alpha power (i.e., more activation) in the right frontal lead than was the reward condition. These data indicate that when reward and punishment contingencies are directly manipulated, frontal brain asymmetry changes in the direction of prediction, with greater right-sided activation present during the punishment condition than during the reward condition. In a series of collaborative studies with Nathan Fox, we have found similar asymmetries in frontal brain activity during the experimental arousal of positive and negative emotions in infants (see Davidson & Fox, 1988, and Fox & Davidson, 1991, for reviews).

We (Sobotka et al., 1992) also examined the contingent negative variation (CNV) during the 4-second preparatory interval. The CNV is a waveform that arises between a warning and imperative stimulus in a reaction time paradigm; it represents a slow negative potential that peaks at the point of responding. No reliable asymmetries were observed in the CNV in this paradigm.

INDIVIDUAL DIFFERENCES IN ANTERIOR ASYMMETRY: A NEURAL SUBSTRATE FOR AFFECTIVE STYLE

In the preceding section, I have noted that although every subject in the Davidson, Ekman, et al. (1990) study showed a difference

in the predicted direction between happy and disgust periods, these emotion-related differences were superimposed upon large individual differences in the overall magnitude and direction of asymmetry. In other research, we have found that subjects' overall (across-task) EEG asymmetry during task performance is highly correlated with their asymmetry during a resting baseline (e.g., Davidson, Taylor, & Saron, 1979) and that anterior asymmetries during resting baselines are stable over time (Tomarken, Davidson, Wheeler, & Kinney, 1992), with test–retest correlations ranging between .66 and .73 for different measures of anterior activation asymmetry. Over the past several years, we have performed a series of studies on both adults and infants that has examined the relation between individual differences in anterior activation asymmetry on the one hand, and dispositional mood, affective reactivity, and psychopathology on the other. I now highlight several components of this research effort.

We began our studies of individual differences in anterior asymmetry by comparing subjects who differed in dispositional depressive mood. We (Schaffer, Davidson, & Saron, 1983) selected subjects on the basis of their scores on the Beck Depression Inventory, and compared a group of high and stable scorers to a group of low and stable scorers on resting frontal asymmetry. We found that the depressed subjects had less left frontal activation than did the nondepressed subjects. We have recently replicated this finding on a group of clinically depressed subjects (Henriques & Davidson, 1991).

An important question concerning these findings with depressives is the degree to which they are state-dependent. Is the decrease in left frontal activation a marker of the state of depression, or is it a more trait-like characteristic that marks an individual's vulnerability to depression? To obtain initial evidence relevant to this question, Henriques and I (Henriques & Davidson, 1990) compared remitted depressives to healthy controls who were screened for lifetime history of psychopathology. The remitted depressives all met Research Diagnostic Criteria (Spitzer, Endicott, & Robins, 1978) for major or minor depression within the past 2 years. All of the remitted depressives were currently normothymic with no depressive symptomatology, and none were currently taking medication for their depression. We examined EEGs during resting baseline conditions. We found that the remitted depressives, like the acutely depressed subjects, had significantly less left frontal activation than the healthy controls. This pattern was found for the anterior electrodes only, again underscoring the specificity of this asymmetry to the anterior cortical regions. Figure 10.2 presents the left- and right-hemisphere alpha power data from each of the regions from which we recorded, for the remitted depressives and healthy controls.

These results indicate that the decreased left anterior activation characteristic of depression remains even when depression is remitted. In turn, these findings suggest that "depressogenic" asymmetry patterns may be a *state-independent* marker that indexes risk for depression. Clearly, to test this hypothesis more comprehensively, a prospective design is required in which subjects are classified on the basis of asymmetry patterns and followed up over time. We would predict that, relative to comparison groups, a higher proportion of subjects who demonstrate decreased left anterior activation would develop subsequent psychopathology.

In three recent studies of adults (Tomarken et al., 1990; Wheeler et al., 1993), we examined the relation between individual differences in anterior asymmetry and reactivity to emotional film clips in normals. We hypothesized that subjects with greater right-sided frontal activation at rest would report more intense negative affect in response to film clips designed to elicit fear and disgust. In both studies, we found that measures of frontal activation asymmetry recorded prior to the presentation of the film clips accounted for significant variance in subjects' self-reports of negative affect in response to the clips. Subjects with greater relative right-sided frontal activation reported more intense negative affect to the clips. It should be noted that the studies included entirely independent groups of subjects and different film clips. In each of the studies, the correlations between frontal asymmetry and positive affect were in the opposite direction, such that greater relative left-sided frontal activation at rest was associated with increased intensity of reports of positive affect in response to film clips designed to elicit happiness and amusement. It is important to note that all of these effects remained significant even when measures of

mood at baseline were statistically partialed out. In other words, frontal asymmetry accounted for significant variance in emotional reactivity to film clip elicitors after the variance accounted for by measures of mood during baseline was statistically removed. This observation strengthens our suggestion that baseline anterior asymmetry is a state-independent measure of affective reactivity, but is itself unrelated to measures of phasic, unprovoked mood.

Baseline anterior asymmetry is related to measures of dispositional mood or affective style. Using the Positive and Negative Affect Scale (Watson, Clark, & Tellegen, 1988), we found that subjects selected on baseline EEG measures to show extreme and stable left frontal activation reported more dispositional positive affect and less dispositional negative affect than their counterparts who showed right frontal activation (Tomarken, Davidson, Wheeler, & Doss, 1992). We have also found that right frontal subjects are immunosuppressed relative to their left frontal counterparts. During a baseline state, right frontal subjects showed significantly less natural killer cell activity than did the left frontal subjects (Kang et al., 1991). In these studies, subjects were selected exclusively on the basis of their baseline frontal EEG asymmetry and then tested on another occasion to obtain measures of dispositional mood and immune function. These studies provide further validity for our suggestion that individual differences in frontal asymmetry reflect important features of affective style.

SUMMARY AND CONCLUSIONS

This chapter has presented an overview of recent research on anterior asymmetries associated with emotion and individual differences in emotional reactivity, psychopathology, and dispositional mood. I have proposed that the anterior regions of the two cerebral hemispheres are specialized for approach and withdrawal processes, with the left hemisphere specialized for the former and the right for the latter. Using electrophysiological measures of regional cortical activation, my colleagues and I have demonstrated that the experimental arousal of approach-related positive affect is associated with left anterior activation, whereas arousal of withdrawal-related negative affect is associated with right anterior activation. In

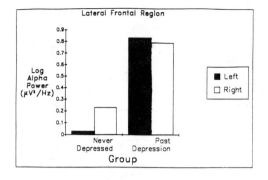

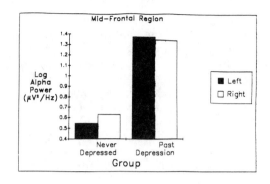

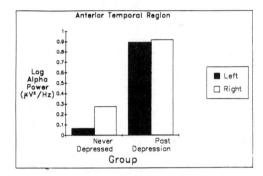

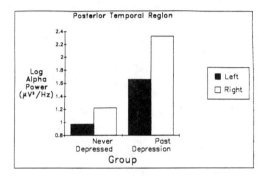

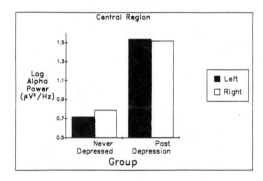

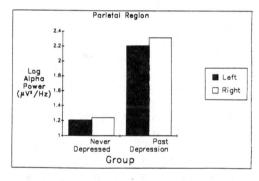

FIGURE 10.2. Mean log-transformed alpha power in left- and right-hemisphere sites from the lateral frontal (F7 and F8), midfrontal (F3 and F4), anterior temporal (T3 and T4), posterior temporal (T5 and T6), central (C3 and C4), and parietal (P3 and P4) regions for subjects with a past depression and for those who were never depressed. Reprinted by permission from Henriques and Davidson (1990).

the second half of the chapter, evidence has been presented indicating that individual differences in patterns of anterior asymmetry are stable over time and predict important features of affective style—an individual's dispositional emotional profile, including characteristic patterns of emotional reactivity as well as mood.

From the data already available, it is clear that asymmetry in the anterior cortical regions is significantly associated with emotion and emotional reactivity. It will be important for future research to characterize both the proxi-

mal and distal causes of this asymmetry. The study of proximal causes will necessarily require the examination of subcortical and neurochemical contributions. Distal causes will inevitably be some combination of heritable and early environmental factors. We have recently developed a primate model of affective lateralization and have found that the benzodiazepine diazepam induces an asymmetrical shift in frontal brain electrical activity in rhesus monkeys (Davidson, Kalin, & Shelton, 1992). This implies that there may be an asymmetrical distribution of benzodiazepine receptors in the frontal cortex. PET has been used to examine this question, and preliminary evidence appears consistent with this suggestion (Abadie et al., 1991). We have every reason to think that future research on this topic will be as exciting and revealing as the recent work has been.

Acknowledgments. The research described in this chapter was supported in part by National Institute of Mental Health (NIMH) Research Scientist Development Award No. MH00875, NIMH Grant Nos. MH40747 and MH43454, and a grant from the John D. and Catherine T. MacArthur Foundation. Portions of this chapter were extracted from Davidson (1992a).

REFERENCES

Abadie, P., Bisserbe, J. C., Boulenger, J. P., Travere, J. M., Barre, L., Petit, M. C., Zarifian, E., & Baron, J. C. (1991). Central benzodiazepine receptors: Quantitative positron emission tomography study in healthy subjects and anxious patients. In M. Briley & S. E. File (Eds.), *New concepts in anxiety* (pp. 203–210). Boca Raton, FL: CRC Press.

Ahern, G. L., & Schwartz, G. E. (1985). Differential lateralization for positive and negative emotion in the human brain: EEG spectral analysis. *Neuropsychologia, 23,* 745–756.

Blom, B. L., & Anneveldt, M. (1982). An electrode cap tested. *Electroencephalography and Clinical Neurophysiology, 54,* 591–594.

Borod, J. C., Koff, E., Lorch, M. P., & Nicholas, M. (1986). The expression and perception of facial emotion in brain-damaged patients. *Neuropsychologia, 24,* 169–180.

Burke, A., Younkin, D., Kushner, M., Gordon, J., Pistone, L., Shapiro, H., & Reivich, M. (1982). Recovery from acute stroke and changes in cerebral blood flow. *Annals of Neurology, 12,* 84.

Damasio, A. R. (1989). The brain binds entities and events by multiregional activation from convergence zones. *Neural Computation, 1,* 123–132.

Davidson, R. J. (1984). Affect, cognition and hemispheric specialization. In C. E. Izard, J. Kagan, & R. B. Zajonc (Eds.), *Emotions, cognition, and behavior* (pp. 320–365). New York: Cambridge University Press.

Davidson, R. J. (1987). Cerebral asymmetry and the nature of emotion: Implications for the study of individual differences and psychopathology. In R. Takahashi, P. Flor-Henry, J. Gruzelier, & S. Niwa (Eds.), *Cerebral dynamics, laterality and psychopathology* (pp. 71–83). New York: Elsevier.

Davidson, R. J. (1988). EEG measures of cerebral asymmetry: Conceptual and methodological issues. *International Journal of Neuroscience, 39,* 71–89.

Davidson, R. J. (1992a). Anterior cerebral asymmetry and the nature of emotion. *Brain and Cognition, 20,* 125–151.

Davidson, R. J. (1992b). Prolegomenon to the structure of emotion: Gleanings from neuropsychology. *Cognition and Emotion, 6,* 245–268.

Davidson, R. J. (1993). Cerebral asymmetry and emotion: Conceptual and methodological conundrums. *Cognition and Emotion, 7,* 115–138.

Davidson, R. J., Chapman, J. P., Chapman, L. P., & Henriques, J. B. (1990). Asymmetrical brain electrical activity discriminates between psychometrically-matched verbal and spatial cognitive tasks. *Psychophysiology, 27,* 528–543.

Davidson, R. J., Ekman, P., Saron, C. D., Senulis, J. A., & Friesen, W. V. (1990). Approach/withdrawal and cerebral asymmetry: Emotional expression and brain physiology. I. *Journal of Personality and Social Psychology, 58,* 330–341.

Davidson, R. J., & Fox, N. A. (1982). Asymmetrical brain activity discriminates between positive versus negative affective stimuli in human infants. *Science, 218,* 1235–1237.

Davidson, R. J., & Fox, N. A. (1988). Cerebral asymmetry and emotion: Developmental and individual differences. In D. L. Molfese & S. J. Segalowitz (Eds.), *Brain lateralization in children: Developmental implications* (pp. 191–206). New York: Guilford Press.

Davidson, R. J., & Fox, N. A. (1989). Frontal brain asymmetry predicts infants' response to maternal separation. *Journal of Abnormal Psychology, 98,* 127–131.

Davidson, R. J., Kalin, N. H., & Shelton, S. E. (1992). Lateralized effects of diazepam on frontal brain electrical asymmetries in rhesus monkeys. *Biological Psychiatry, 32,* 438–451.

Davidson, R. J., Taylor, N., & Saron, C. (1979). Hemisphericity and styles of information processing: Individual differences in EEG asymmetry and their relationship to cognitive performance. *Psychophysiology, 16,* 197.

Davidson, R. J., & Tomarken, A. J. (1989). Laterality and emotion: An electrophysiological approach. In F. Boller & J. Grafman (Eds.), *Handbook of neuropsychology,* (Vol. 3, pp. 419–441). Amsterdam: Elsevier.

Ekman, P., & Friesen, W. V. (1978). *The Facial Action Coding System: A technique for the measurement of facial movement.* Palo Alto, CA: Consulting Psychologists Press.

Etcoff, N. L. (1989). Asymmetries in recognition of emotion. In F. Boller & J. Grafman (Eds.), *Handbook of neuropsychology* (Vol. 3, pp. 363–382). New York: Elsevier.

Fox, N. A., & Davidson, R. J. (1991). Hemispheric specialization and attachment behaviors: Developmental processes and individual differences in separation protest. In J. L. Gewirtz & W. M. Kurtines (Eds.), *Intersections with attachment* (pp. 147–164). Hillsdale, NJ: Erlbaum.

Gainotti, G. (1972). Emotional behavior and hemispheric side of lesion. *Cortex, 8,* 41–55.

Gainotti, G. (1989). Disorders of emotions and affect in patients with unilateral brain damage. In F. Boller & J. Grafman (Eds.), *Handbook of neuropsychology* (Vol. 3, pp. 345–361). Amsterdam: Elsevier.

Goldstein, K. (1939). *The organism.* New York: American Books.

Henriques, J. B., & Davidson, R. J. (1990). Regional brain electrical asymmetries discriminate between previously depressed and healthy control subjects. *Journal of Abnormal Psychology, 99,* 22–31.

Henriques, J. B., & Davidson, R. J. (1991). Left frontal hypoactivation in depression. *Journal of Abnormal Psychology, 100,* 535–545.

Jackson, J. H. (1878). On the affections of speech from disease of the brain. *Brain, 1,* 304–330.

Jerison, H. J. (1973). *Evolution of the brain and intelligence.* New York: Academic Press.

Kagan, J., Reznick, J. S., & Snidman, N. (1988). Biological bases of childhood shyness. *Science, 240,* 167–171.

Kang, D. H., Davidson, R. J., Coe, C. L., Wheeler, R. W., Tomarken, A. J., & Ershler, W. B. (1991). Frontal brain asymmetry and immune function. *Behavioral Neuroscience, 105,* 860–869.

Kolb, B., & Taylor, L. (1990). Neocortical substrates of emotional behavior. In N. L. Stein, B. Leventhal, & T. Trabasso (Eds.), *Psychological and biological approaches* to emotion (pp. 115–144). Hillsdale, NJ: Erlbaum.

Leventhal, H., & Tomarken, A. J. (1986). Emotion: Today's problems. *Annual Review of Psychology, 37,*565–610.

Levy, J. (1972). Lateral specialization of the human brain: Behavioral manifestation and possible evolutionary basis. In J. A. Kriger (Ed.), *The biology of behavior* (pp. 159–180). Corvallis: Oregon State University Press.

Luria, A. R. (1973). *The working brain.* New York: Basic Books.

Morris, M., Bradley, M., Bowers, D., Lang, P., & Heilman, K. (1991, February). *Valence-specific hypoarousal following right temporal lobectomy.* Paper presented at the annual meeting of the International Neuropsychological Society, San Antonio, TX.

Reiman, E. M., Raichle, M. E., Butler, F. K., Hercovitch, P., & Robins, E. (1984). A focal brain abnormality in panic disorder, a severe form of anxiety. *Nature, 310,* 683–685.

Robinson, R. G., Kubos, K. L., Starr, L. B., Rao, K., & Price, T. R. (1984). Mood disorders in stroke patients: Importance of location of lesion. *Brain, 107,* 81–93.

Sackeim, H. A., Greenberg, M. S., Weiman, A. L., Gur, R., Hungerbuhler, J. P., & Geschwind, N. (1982). Hemispheric asymmetry in the expression of positive and negative emotions. *Archives of Neurology, 39,* 210–218.

Schaffer, C. E., Davidson, R. J., & Saron, C. (1983). Frontal and parietal EEG asymmetries in depressed and nondepressed subjects. *Biological Psychiatry, 18,* 753–762.

Schneirla, T. C. (1959). An evolutionary and developmental theory of biphasic processes underlying approach and withdrawal. In M. R. Jones (Ed.), *Nebraska Symposium on Motivation* (pp. 1–42). Lincoln: University of Nebraska Press.

Shagass, C. (1972). Electrical activity of the brain. In N. S. Greenfield & R. A. Sternbach (Eds.), *Handbook of psychophysiology* (pp. 263–328). New York: Holt, Rinehart & Winston.

Silberman, E. K., & Weingartner, H. (1986) Hemispheric lateralization of functions related to emotion. *Brain and Cognition, 5,* 322–353.

Sobotka, S., Davidson, R. J., & Senulis, J. (1992). Anterior brain electrical asymmetries in response to reward and punishment. *Electroencephalography and Clinical Neurophysiology, 83,* 236–247.

Spitzer, R. L., Endicott, J., & Robins, E. (1978). Research Diagnostic Criteria: Rationale and reliability. *Archives of General Psychiatry, 35,* 773–782.

Stellar, J. R., & Stellar, E. (1985). *The neurobiology of motivation and reward.* New York: Springer-Verlag.

Tomarken, A. J., Davidson, R. J., & Henriques, J. B. (1990). Resting frontal brain asymmetry predicts affective responses to films. *Journal of Personality and Social Psychology, 59,* 791–801.

Tomarken, A. J., Davidson, R. J., Wheeler, R. W., & Doss, R. (1992). Individual differences in anterior brain asymmetry and fundamental dimensions of emotion. *Journal of Personality and Social Psychology, 62,* 676–687.

Tomarken, A. J., Davidson, R. J., Wheeler, R. W., & Kinney, L. (1992). Psychometric properties of resting anterior EEG asymmetry: Temporal stability and internal consistency. *Psychophysiology, 29,* 576–592.

Tucker, D. M., Stenslie, C. E., Roth, R. S., & Shearer, S. L. (1981). Right frontal lobe activation and right hemisphere performance decrement during a depressed mood. *Archives of General Psychiatry, 38,* 169–174.

Watson, D., Clark, L. A., & Tellegen, A. (1988). Development and validation of brief measures of positive and negative affect: The PANAS scales. *Journal of Personality and Social Psychology, 54,* 1063–1070.

Wheeler, R. W., Davidson, R. J., & Tomarken, A. J. (1993). Frontal brain asymmetry and emotional reactivity: A biological substrate of affective style. *Psychophysiology, 30,* 82–89.

Young, G., Segalowitz, S. J., Misek, P., Alp, I. E., & Boulet, R. (1983). Is early reaching left-handed? Review of manual specialization research. In G. Young, S. J. Segalowitz, C. M., Corter, & S. E. Trehub (Eds.), *Manual specialization and the developing brain* (pp. 13–32). London: Academic Press.

11

Emotion and Behavior Genetics in Vertebrates and Invertebrates

TERRY R. McGUIRE

Charles Darwin (1872/1965), in his book *The Expression of the Emotions in Man and Animals,* discussed the biological basis of emotion. Darwin believed that emotional expressions could be explained by three principles: (1) the principle of serviceable associated habits, (2) the principle of antithesis, and (3) the principle of actions due to the nervous system. Darwin did not strongly advocate evolutionary explanations for emotional expression. On the contrary, his first two principles were based primarily on learning and habit formation. He believed that some manifestations of emotion serve no useful purpose. Only Darwin's third principle—the direct expression of the nervous system—referred to natural selection.

Darwin specifically discussed the expressions of the stronger emotions—pain, rage, joy, and terror—in terms of biology. For example, during rage the heart rate accelerates, respiration increases, the teeth are clenched, and there are violent muscular actions. The same bodily changes occur during great pain. Despite similar bodily changes, Darwin could easily distinguish between rage and pain. He believed that the coordinated activities of each emotion are an evolutionary legacy.

Darwin was quite cautious in invoking evolution to explain emotional expression. This is not true of many other scholars. Lorenz (1965), in the preface to a new edition of *The Expression of the Emotions in Man and Animals,* attributed to Darwin the idea that "behavior patterns are just as conservatively and reliably characters of species as are the forms of bones, teeth, or any other bodily structures" (p. xiii). Plutchik (1980) defined emotions in terms of their evolutionary history and stated that all emotions "serve an adaptive role in helping organisms deal with key survival issues posed by the environment" (Postulate 3, p. 8). Panksepp (1982) demanded not only that emotions serve an adaptive (and reactive) role, but also that they be hard-wired in the nervous system.

Before the theory of evolution became central to biological thought, it was not necessary to consider animal emotion. If the human species had resulted from special creation, then animals did not have to possess similar behaviors and emotions. On the other hand, if humans had evolved, then it became important to understand what traits humans share with other animals.

Animals probably do have emotions. Darwin was correct in that the coordination between affect production and affect recognition is a legacy of our evolutionary past. Since humans have biologically based emotions, then other animals with which we share recent, common ancestors must have homologous emotions. This is the rationale of comparative psychology, which uses the white rat and other animals for the elucidation of human behavior or for biologically based drug studies.

Experimental psychologists are most familiar with the white rat, and, indeed, the rat, has been extensively studied for emotionality (see below). In fact, most people have little difficulty in ascribing emotions to any mammal. They treat emotion as if it arose in mammals along with suckling the young, endothermy, and hair. MacLean (1970) at least recognizes a primitive, reptilian emotion in his triune brain, so one presumes that he attributes certain emotions to reptiles. Perhaps these theories reflect a backward search for emotion: We first recognize emotion in humans and then search other animals for analogous behaviors. We then claim that the analogous behaviors are emotion units that are stable across species.

I have been interested in individual differences in the behavior and genetics of insects and other invertebrates, though I took little initial interest in emotion. Eventually, I realized that insects show complex behaviors that are neither mechanistic nor learned. For example, food-deprived blow flies (*Phormia regina*) undergo a change in the central nervous system after a single chemosensory hair is stimulated with sucrose. This induced internal state will change the probability of subsequent proboscis extension. This behavior could be considered an "emotion," although such an emotion would not necessarily occur in mammals and would not be noted in a backward, anthropomorphic search. It is my contention that emotion is a necessary function of the nervous system and is ubiquitous in all organisms with a complex nervous system. This will require a definition of "emotion" that is broad enough to cover the range of behavior seen in insects and humans and that is independent of the structure of mammalian nervous systems.

EXISTENCE AND DEFINITION OF ANIMAL EMOTION

A number of scholars have wrestled with the problem of animal emotion. Pieron (1928), for example, believed that emotion governs most animal behavior. Emotion was seen as the organizing principle and was thought to be much more important than cognition: "From the amoeba to man, action is always essentially affective, even when it occurs in the preparatory form which it may assume in the most

highly trained animals, the purely mental form of thought" (p. 285). Tinbergen (1965) acknowledged the possibility that animals have emotion, but he believed that emotion cannot be studied by scientists: "He [the scientist] has to express the cause of what we might interpret as anger in terms of processes that can, in principle, be observed and measured just as well as the behavior itself. In short, he is interested in the machinery of behavior" (p. 14). Tinbergen treated the animal as if emotion did not exist. Although Tinbergen dismissed emotion, he was quite comfortable with other equally nebulous concepts, such as "drive."

Pribram (1980) used a heuristic definition to subdivide feelings into motivations and emotions: Motivations (which include drive states) are active responses or "go" responses, whereas emotions terminate within the organism's body but can stop ongoing behavior. The exception to this is the communicative function of emotions in social situations. Pribram, like Tinbergen, acknowledged the existence of emotion, but defined it in such a way as to make it inaccessible to further study. By contrast, Scott (1980) used a systems theory approach to emotion. He described emotions as aspects of complex, interactional systems of an organism. In his view, emotions arise as part of different behavioral systems. What some researchers would describe as "drives," Scott would describe as "emotions." For example, animals must ingest food to survive. Scott would classify "hunger" as an emotion associated with the ingestive system. Scott's systems theory of emotion allows us to move from a "mammal-centric" viewpoint to a viewpoint that can accommodate emotional behavior in many classes of animals, including fish, reptiles, and insects. Scott believed that emotion is an uncomfortable sensation and that the animal acts to return to a neutral, nonemotional state. None of the above viewpoints allow for emotion as "mood," as well as emotion as a reaction to environmental cues.

I have surveyed a number of recent animal behavior textbooks and confirmed that "emotion" is seldom, if ever, a topic of discussion. Perhaps this is not surprising in view of Tinbergen's (1965) statement. In many ways, however, this oversight reflects that our perception of animal behavior is based on our understanding of machines (automatons) and computers. It was not that long ago that animals were viewed as automatons— little stimulus–response machines—that are absolutely (or relatively) predictable in behavior. Behaviors were thought to be either learned or instinctive. Learning was often reduced to stimulus–response chains. Instinctive behaviors were seen as stereotyped, species-specific, and invariant for all members of the species. Instinctive behaviors might be further divided. One classification scheme divided instinctive behaviors into reflexes, tropisms, taxes and kineses, and more complex instinctive actions. Another scheme divided instinctive behaviors into drives (orientation and search) and consummatory acts (relatively inflexible). It was later necessary to add a third class of behaviors (postconsummatory acts) to account for the variable behavior of animals that cannot be easily ascribed to either drives or consummatory acts.

The animal-as-machine school of thought reached its nadir with the concept of the "fixed action pattern" (FAP; Lorenz & Tinbergen, 1938). FAPs are complex, instinctive behavioral patterns. The FAP is a hydraulic model of behavior. The animal accumulates "nervous energy"; when the energy is sufficiently high, the animal moves around (drive) until it encounters a special "releaser or sign stimulus." This stimulus releases the nervous energy, which then outflows and initiates a complex series of highly stereotyped activities. These activities must run to completion (until nervous energy is exhausted) even if the releaser stimulus is removed. In addition, nervous energy can accumulate until the FAP begins even in the absence of the releaser stimulus. The underlying concept of the FAP is that the behavior of any animal is forced by the combination of internal cues and external stimuli. Emotion has no place in the FAP system, which is entirely stimulus-driven.

The animal-as-machine perspective was partially replaced in the 1970s and 1980s by the animal-as-computer perspective, in which behaviors were viewed as the results of linear brain circuits. Thus, animals have "aggressive circuits," "food centers," "pleasure centers," and so forth. Emotion is allowed, but only if one can find the appropriate neural circuit. The concept of emotional circuits originated with Papez (1937), who suggested that the limbic system plays a critical role in the control of emotional behavior. Others have echoed this belief (see Kupfermann, 1991, for a complete review). Panksepp (1982), for example, defined emotions as necessarily hard-wired. In his version of the animal-as-computer system, emotions are used to react to life-threatening situations. Emotions can be evoked by appropriate stimuli (either external stimuli or direct brain stimulation). The overt behaviors related to emotional expression can be modified by appropriate stimulus–response pairing (learning) or modulated by other linear circuits. In the animal-as-computer model, emotion must be entirely reactive, and there is no place for "mood." When emotion is defined as linear, hard-wired, and reactive, any "feeling" that does not fit this definition cannot be an emotion.

Neither the animal-as-machine perspective nor the animal-as-computer perspective has adequately explained behavior, largely because both are linear models. For example, all animals show some form of movement in their environment. The movement patterns are too complex and variable to be determined by machine-like reflexes, although some attempts have been made to do so (Loeb, 1973). Similarly, locomotion has computer-like aspects in some vertebrates and is controlled by neural circuits with extensive interconnections and feedback loops (Grillner, Wallen, & di Prisco, 1990). Complete understanding of the cellular and neural mechanisms of locomotion, however, does not provide us with complete understanding of locomotion in intact, freely behaving animals.

As long ago as 1961, Breland and Breland, in their paper "The Misbehavior of Organisms," pointed out the limits of linear models of behavior from their own unique perspective. The Brelands had left research to become animal trainers and "to determine if animal psychology could stand on its own feet as an engineering discipline" (p. 681). The Brelands quickly discovered that animals cannot be reduced to stimulus–response machines. Animals are complex organisms whose behavioral repertoire is restricted not by the cleverness of the experimenter but by internal, evolutionary constraints. Even the most carefully designed learning procedures will fail if internal states were not taken into account. Similarly, "emotion" or diffuse internal states may constrain or modify the behavior of animals under many different conditions.

EMOTIONALITY IN INSECTS
AND OTHER INVERTEBRATES

Many researchers argue for the universality of emotion. In most cases, they mean that emotion can be found in most species of mammals; they would not consider that emotion can be found in insects, for example. This is not surprising. I have worked for a number of years on the behavior genetics of insects. At various times I have had to convince individuals outside my field that insects are animals, that insects have behavior, that insects have individual differences in behavior, and that insects can show plasticity in behavior. Some of this plasticity can be attributed to emotion. Pieron (1928) believed that emotional expression is limited to animals at "the higher stages of evolution" (p. 284). Pieron meant insects, mollusks (especially octopi and squids), and crustaceans (crabs and lobsters), in addition to reptiles, amphibians, birds, and mammals. I am in agreement with this view.

As a working definition, I define "emotion" in an invertebrate as a change in the internal systems of the invertebrate so that it is more likely to perform a particular behavior. My definition parallels that of Davis (1985) for "motivation," especially as he applies it to the study of plasticity in the marine mollusk *Pleurobranchaea*. The emotion may be induced by external stimuli (a short-term proximal cause) or by a long-term modulation of an undefined neural mechanisms. Most likely, the emotion will arise as an interaction of internal and external forces. I do not attempt to assign names to these emotions, since there is no way to correlate invertebrate and mammalian emotions. Mammalian emotions we name traditionally by extrapolation from human emotions, although this may ultimately be deceptive.

The "central excitatory state" (CES) was first described by Dethier, Solomon, and Turner (1965). To date, it has been measured in two insects—the blow fly (*Phormia regina*) and the fruit fly (*Drosophila melanogaster*). The CES is a change in the central nervous system of a fly that occurs following stimulation with an excitatory stimulus (e.g., sucrose). In Dethier et al.'s original procedure, water-satiated but food-deprived flies would not respond with proboscis extension to water stimulation. If a single sensory hair was stimulated with sucrose, the fly would then subsequently respond with proboscis extension to water stimulation for a short period of time (less than 2 minutes). The CES is influenced by food deprivation (long-term change), but can only be set up by immediate stimulation. Therefore, the CES is short-term change in the central nervous system of the fly that changes the probability that some behaviors of the fly will occur. There is nothing about this observation per se that would qualify the CES as an emotion. The evidence for this came only after additional work.

In 1981, I (McGuire, 1981) measured reliable individual differences in CES response in a genetically diverse population of flies. I subsequently selected for lines of flies that differed in their CES expression. Selective breeding was done to obtain flies with known CES levels for further analysis of classical conditioning (McGuire & Hirsch, 1977). My selection results were replicated by Tully and Hirsch (1982a), using a slightly modified procedure. Additional breeding analyses showed that the differences between the high- and low-CES lines could be attributed to a single gene (Tully & Hirsch, 1982b). Individual differences in CES had biological correlates, and the level of CES expression could be changed by selection.

Blow flies can be classically conditioned to extend their mouth parts to a neutral (water) or even a slightly inhibitory (salt) stimulus (Nelson, 1971). By selective breeding, we (McGuire & Hirsch, 1977; Hirsch & McCauley, 1977) obtained lines of *Phormia* showing high and low conditioning ability. Genetic analysis showed that the differences between the two selected lines were attributable to at least four genes (McGuire & Tully, 1987).

Individual flies were measured both for conditioning ability and for CES expression. Genetically selected high-CES flies were easily conditioned, and genetically selected low-CES flies were hard to condition (Tully, Zawistowski, & Hirsch, 1982; McGuire, 1983). The same correlation occurred in unselected, wild-type flies. In addition, flies selected for high and low conditioning ability showed corresponding high- and low-CES responses. More importantly, the correlation between CES and conditioning did not disappear in genetically segregating generations. The two behaviors are not independent. High expression of CES seems to be a precondition for fly learning. As an emotion, the presence of high CES changes the probability of subsequent learning.

CES is not merely a general arousal. CES is definitely important for classical conditioning of proboscis extension; it is probably important in a related learning procedure, Pavlovian counterconditioning (McGuire & Schmidt, 1982). However, it is unimportant in classical conditioning involving odors and shock (McGuire, Gelperin, & Tully, 1990). Similarly, CES has no relation to "local food search" or "dance" (McGuire & Tully, 1986; see below). CES levels can be manipulated by drugs (McGuire, 1985; Long, Edgecomb, & Murdock, 1986). The CES is influenced by internal conditions (food deprivation), proximal causes (sucrose concentration), genetic factors, and nervous system factors. The CES work described above suggests that CES is an "emotion" with both immediate reactive functions and long-term "mood" effects, since it changes the probability of subsequent behaviors. (For a description of CES work in *Drosophila melanogaster*, see Vargo & Hirsch, 1982, 1985, 1986).

Courtship in *Drosophila* provides further evidence for an emotion in insects. Female *Drosophila* become receptive to mating 24 hours after emergence from the pupal case. For copulation to occur, receptive females must be courted by males who use a combination of visual and auditory cues (song). Bennet-Clark, Ewing, and Manning (1973) demonstrated that female *Drosophila* could be induced to mate more rapidly if they had been played simulated male song. This excitatory effect decayed over 3 minutes. They hypothesized that the change in female behavior might be attributable to an internal emotional or motivational change analogous to the CES in the blow fly. von Schilcher (1976a, 1976b) extended this work and demonstrated that male courtship song increased the specific courtship activity of males (they showed increased locomotor activity and began to court each other). At the same time, male courtship song decreased both female locomotor activity and the latency to copulation. More recently, Medioni and Manning (1988) showed that males who had courted a female for a few minutes would continue to court for up to 30 minutes after the female had left the courtship chamber. Obviously these flies had undergone some internal state change, probably emotional, which caused short-term changes in their behavior.

Local food search may be another type of emotion. Many hungry insects will search for food (but some are sit-and-wait predators).

Dethier (1957) described a local food search or "dance" that a hungry fly would perform after stimulation with a small drop of sugar. This dance involved profound postural changes, repeated extension and retraction of the proboscis (mouth parts), and changes in the direction of locomotion and the frequency and angle of turns. He believed that this dance might be related to the food dance of honeybees. The food search decays over time, and the duration of the dance is influenced by the amount of deprivation, the concentration of sugar (Dethier, 1957; Nelson, 1977), and genetics (McGuire & Tully, 1986). Similar food search dances have been described for the house fly (*Musca domestica*; White, Tobin, & Bell, 1984) and *Drosophila melanogaster* (Bell, Tortorici, Ruggiero, Kipp, & Tobin, 1985). Ladybird beetles show a similar search pattern when they encounter a single prey item (Nakamuta, 1985). Schal et al. (1983) reported similar short-term search "dances" by male German cockroaches when exposed to the pheromones of female cockroaches. Such search strategies probably maximize the chance of finding desirable resources in patchy environments (see Bell, 1991). That would be the adaptive aspect. Proxially, however, such dramatic changes in activity and posture may also be ascribed to a behavioral change that is "emotional."

Insects and other invertebrates show escape responses, some of which are similar to escape responses seen in vertebrates. Hoy (1989), for example, has reviewed the evidence for startle response in moths, lacewings, crickets, and mantids. Pieron (1927) discussed autogamy in crustaceans and insects. Under conditions of stress, many crabs and insects will amputate their own legs if they are restrained and subsequently exposed to a predator; this is a neurological response. Many cephalopods (octopi and squids) will modify both the color and texture of their skin. A startled octopus will turn pale (Wells, 1962). *Drosophila melanogaster*, if shaken or startled, will show an escape response—they jump up and fly. In flight, a number of behavioral changes become manifest. All *Drosophila melanogaster* when disturbed fly up and toward the light (negative geotaxis and positive phototaxis). *Drosophila* that are not showing an escape response vary in their response to light and gravity (Hadler, 1964a, 1964b; Hirsch & Tryon, 1956). They will reverse their preference during an escape response. For example, Lewontin (1959) demonstrated that *Drosophila pseudoobscura* would uniformly fly to the light if they were shaken or forced to fly. After landing, the light preference reversed, and the flies would slowly move into the dark. I routinely transfer *Drosophila melanogaster* that have been genetically selected for positive geotaxis (orientation and movement toward gravity) by shaking the bottle and having the flies move *up* into a tube. The internal states induced by shaking overrides the strong genetic preferences that occur in other situations.

As a child I used to tease "pincher bugs" (stag beetles) with blades of grass or small twigs. The beetles would rear up on their back legs, spread their mandibles wide, and eventually attack the grass blade/twig or my finger. If this had been a cornered rat, I might have said that the behavior demonstrated both anger and fear. Do insects show anger? One of our common expressions is "mad as a hornet." The defense reactions of hornets or yellow jackets whose nest has been disturbed are almost legendary. Different races of the honeybee (*Apis mellifera*) have different temperaments for defense. Africanized bees from South American are more reactive than most domestic races of bees: They rapidly sting a standard leather ball moving in front of the colony; they leave more stings in the item; and they follow the experimenter much farther from the nest than do races of bees from temperate climates (Collins, Ronderer, Harbo, & Bolton, 1982; W. Rothenbuhler, personal communication, 1975). The defense response is not all-or-none, however (Winston, 1987). Bees moderate their attack according to a variety of factors, including colony size, amount of empty honeycomb, and humidity. They also vary their attack in accordance with experience and predator type: Vertebrates are attacked with biting, hair pulling, and eventually stinging; some insects are attacked with grappling and "balling"; ants are often fanned with the wings and kicked with the legs.

TWENTIETH-CENTURY RESEARCH ON ANIMAL EMOTIONALITY

The current evidence for emotion in invertebrates comes out of a behavior genetic perspective of individual differences and plasticity in behavior. A much more restrictive view

of emotion in animals ("emotionality") came out of the animal-as-machine perspective and remains the basis of the enduring research programs in behavior genetics. There have been hundreds of articles written about emotionality in rats since Calvin Hall's original description in 1934. Each animal was believed to possess a certain amount of emotionality. Emotionality was seen as a function of the autonomic nervous system, and any situation affecting the autonomic nervous system could be used to measure emotionality. Individual differences in emotionality were thought to be influenced by genetic and environmental differences. Hall (1934) originally chose a quite simple measure—defecation of rats in an open-field apparatus.

This famous research strategy has even made its way into the humanities. Robertson Davies (1981), himself an academician, in his novel *The Rebel Angels* introduced the character Dr. Ozias Froats. Dr. Froats spends his very distinguished scientific career studying buckets of human feces to discover the key to human temperament. The fictional "turd skinner" studying human feces and inferring personality is clearly based on the cadre of 20th-century scientists who count rat fecal pellets and infer "emotionality." Although emotionality was first studied in mice and rats, it has transcended the organisms in which it was first measured.

Emotionality in Rats and Mice

Hall (1934) defined "emotionality" as follows: "This state consists of a group of organic, experiential and expressive reactions and denotes a general upset or excited condition of the animal" (p. 385). Emotionality was seen as a unitary characteristic of the organism. As previously stated, emotions were presumed to be a function of the autonomic nervous system, and any stimulation that affected the autonomic nervous system was thought to affect emotionality.

As noted above, Hall accessed the autonomic nervous system by measuring defecation of rats in an open-field apparatus. Rats are nocturnal animals that prefer to be next to walls. Removing a rat from its home cage and placing it in an illuminated open field is somewhat stressful. Rats in such a situation frequently urinate and defecate. Hall believed the number of fecal boli to be correlated with emotionality: The more fecal boli, the more emotional the rat. In addition, Hall observed an inverse correlation between defecation and eating. This observation, he believed, validated defecation as a measure of emotionality, since food ingestion is also a function of the autonomic nervous system. According to Hall (in contrast to Panksepp, 1982, and Plutchik, 1980), emotionality is not adaptive. His highly emotional rats might refrain from eating for extended periods; in fact, one such rat died from starvation.

Hall (1936a, 1936b) further characterized emotionality in rats by looking at food ingestion and ambulation. Hungry rats that were given access to food in an open field were significantly less emotional (measured by defecation) than other rats. Emotionality perseverated unless "derailed" by other stimuli: "If the directive and distractive forces of a need and a goal are lacking from an emotional situation, the animal remains maladjusted to that situation" (1936a, p. 66). Again, Hall emphasized the nonadaptive nature of emotionality. Hall (1936b) also reported that ambulation was negatively correlated with defecation: Highly emotional rats were less mobile.

Hall's studies have been extensively duplicated. Many investigators have looked at the relationship between defecation and a large number of other experimental parameters. I emphasize "duplication" rather than "replication," since most experimenters have changed the size of the open field, the duration of the trials, the handling procedures, and so forth, so that it is very difficult to make comparisons among studies. Most of these studies have been concerned with finding the correlations, if any, between open-field defecation and a series of other behaviors. Just as Hall looked at defecation versus ingestion and ambulation, other investigators have looked at defecation in the open field versus defecation in enclosed mazes, elevated mazes, and runways. Other experimenters have looked at the correlation of open-field behavior with learning. These numerous studies have been amply discussed elsewhere (Fuller & Thompson, 1978; Archer, 1973, 1975; Broadhurst, 1975; Walsh & Cummins, 1976).

Emotionality was one of the first behaviors studied by behavior geneticists. Hall (1951) selectively bred lines of emotional and nonemotional rats in the open field over 12 generations. The number of days over which rats defecated increased significantly in the high-reactive line and decreased in the low-reactive line. Although Hall started a genetic analysis, he did not complete the necessary crosses. The largest effect of Hall's behavior genetic work was to stimulate similar research. In particular, Hall's early work inspired the selection of the Maudsley reactive (MR) and Maudsley nonreactive (MNR) rats (see Broadhurst, 1975; Blizard, 1981); the selection of emotionally reactive mice (DeFries, Wilson, & McClearn, 1970); and, more recently, the selection of emotionally reactive rats in Japan (Kitaoka & Fujita, 1991).

Broadhurst (1960, 1975) selected rats for high and low defecation in an open field (the MR and MNR rats). Approximately 200 albino rats were tested for defecation in an open-field apparatus, and the highest- and lowest-scoring individuals were mated within their families. Thus, Broadhurst both selected and inbred his rats. He obtained a major decrease in defecation but only a moderate increase in defecation. The major use of the MR and MNR strains has been to "fix" emotionality within the two lines. That is, there is little genetic variation within the lines but a large amount of variation between the lines. These genetically different strains have been used to study behavioral, biochemical, or physiological differences that might be correlated with the known emotional differences.

Extensive comparative work with the Maudsley strains has been done (for complete reviews, see Broadhurst, 1975; Archer, 1973; Blizard, 1981). For example, Levine and Broadhurst (1963) reported that MR rats were worse at conditioned avoidance tasks than MNR rats. This observation has not held up in the North American strains of the reactive rats, where MR rats were found to be more efficient on such tasks than the MNR rats (Harrington, 1981). Similarly, Sudak and Maas (1964) reported significant correlations between brain serotonin and emotionality. Again, this correlation did not hold up (Blizard & Liang, 1979). The correlations were probably attributable to chance associations within inbred lines.

It is unsettling that researchers continue to carry out such correlational studies on selected and inbred strains, without actually using the genetic tools that might detect the significance of observed correlations. Elsewhere, I have discussed (McGuire, 1983) multiple reasons why two traits might show strong correlations in wild-type populations or selected or inbred lines. I have also discussed the minimum genetic crosses and analyses that must be carried out to validate those correlations. Without such crosses, one can be fooled into inferring causality from the existence of a chance correlation.

My own work illustrates the problem of chance correlations. I reported (McGuire, 1978) a strong correlation between CES expression and classical conditioning in blow flies (*Phormia regina*) that had been bidirectionally selected for learning ability. The same correlation was found in wild-type flies and in flies that had been bidirectionally selected for CES expression. The correlation remained even in the F_2 generation of crosses between the selected lines when random gene combinations could break up (Tully, et al, 1982; McGuire, 1983). The observed correlation appeared to be attributable to underlying, shared genetic systems. I found a similar correlation between CES expression and local food search in the blow fly (McGuire & Tully, 1987). Food search looked very much like CES: They are induced by the same excitatory stimuli, they show similar rates of decay, and they are similarly affected by food deprivation levels. Furthermore, flies selected for high CES expression showed long dance times, and flies selected for low CES expression showed short dance times. I predicted that CES and dance would prove to be two behaviors associated with the same internal processes. The correlation, however, disappeared in the segregating F_2 generation. The two behaviors were associated in the selected lines by chance. Reports of differences between emotionality and any other behavior, physiological measurement, and/or biochemical or neurochemical reaction in the MR or MNR rats, no matter how compelling, must be validated by appropriate genetic techniques. This same conclusion was recently put forth by van der Staay, Kerbush, and Raaijmakers (1990).

Recent Research in Emotionality in Other Vertebrates

Hall's work with rats in an open field has been adapted for measuring emotionality in other vertebrates, although there is no compelling reason to do so. Most researchers use some aspect of open-field activity, despite the un-

suitability of such measures for the organisms being measured. Others merely acknowledge their dependence on Hall's concept of a unitary emotionality. Open-field defecation and activity are suitable measures of emotionality only in mice (DeFries et al, 1970; Hewitt, Fulker, & DeFries, 1977; Halcomb, Hegmann, & DeFries, 1975; DeFries, Gervais, & Thomas, 1978). Other aspects of open-field activity have been used to assess emotionality in a number of species of birds (see Suarez & Gallup, 1983, for a review). Suarez and Gallup (1983) have called for reinterpreting the generalized concept of emotionality in terms of predator–prey interactions such as tonic immobility and distress calling. Kersten, Meijsser, and Metz (1989) and Meijsser, Kersten, Wiepkema, and Metz (1989) used open-field activity to assess emotionality in rabbits. Dogs and horses have been rated for emotionality using a variety of behavioral and physiological measures, but usually such measurements are not made in the open field (Scott & Fuller, 1965; Searle, 1955; McCann, Heird, Bell, & Lutherer, 1988). Emotionality, as originally described in rats, has become a unitary trait concept that is treated as if it exists independently of the animal in which it is studied or the behavior used to measure it.

BIOLOGICAL BASIS OF EMOTION AND FUTURE RESEARCH

Many studies of emotion have focused upon nervous circuitry in the brain. Many of the researchers have accepted the process of evolution and have then attempted to fit the biological control of emotion into a linear model. For example, Panksepp (1982) defined all emotion in terms of brain circuitry. He required that all emotions be genetically hardwired in the brain and that they be activated in life-threatening situations. This view of emotion is too constrained for the behavior genetics of insects.

The definition of emotion as an adaptive response to life-threatening situations (evolutionarily speaking; Panksepp, 1982) has dictated the types of emotions that can be studied. For example, it leaves out the courtship behaviors described previously. Furthermore, emotions must be inducible in laboratory situations, and they must be objectively measured by present research strategies. In the past, this has usually meant that animal emotion was limited to fear and anger. Reaction to life-threatening situations is obviously essential for personal survival. The concept of the "survival of the fittest," however, refers to reproductive success and not merely personal survival. Gentler emotions—for example, happiness—may be essential for reproductive fitness even if they are too complex to be reduced to a single neural circuit and are nearly impossible to induce in laboratory situations. Biological correlates of emotion do not have to mean linear hard-wiring in the brain. Similarly, evolutionary advantages for an organism do not have to mean easily observable short-term reactions in a laboratory.

I advocate the wider definition of "emotion" as a change in the internal systems of an animal such that it is more likely to perform a particular behavior. This definition allows researchers to study not only neural circuits concerned with emotion, but also the modulation of those circuits and the genetic control mechanisms for emotions.

Neural circuitry is certainly important. A disturbed fly jumps up and flies toward the light and away from gravity. These behaviors are dramatic and reproducible, and can be traced, at least in part, to specific circuits. For example, *Drosophila melanogaster* has a part of the jump reflex in the thorax (Wyman, Thomas, Salkoff, & Costello, 1985). Davis (1985) discusses extensive neural circuits of the carnivorous sea gastropod *Pleurobranchaea* that are involved in various aspects of feeding behavior. Other circuits have been described for vertebrates (see Davis, Jacob, & Schoenfeld, 1989; LeDoux, 1986). Such circuits undoubtedly function in many animals for emotion, and it will be essential to describe them.

Not all emotions, however, can be localized in specific circuits. For example, anger may function in active defense (and thus may be circuit-based), or it may be the organizing emotion in one's own affect. How can one account for emotion as "mood" as opposed to emotion as "reaction"? I suspect that the answer lies in neuromodulators.

In introductory neurobiology, one is introduced to the concept of the synapse. Nervous information travels in a linear fashion by a combination of electrical and chemical messages. There are elaborate circuits, but the overall situation is linear. In recent years, a

number of workers have shown that neuro-modulation is extremely important and that this operates in a nonlinear fashion. For example, Kravitz et al. (1985) have shown that serotonin, octopamine, and proctolin modulate a series of behaviors in the lobster through their effects on abdominal flexion and extension. Evans (1980) discussed the modulating role of a number of monoamines in insects and their effects on behavior. Even well-understood neural circuits are extensively modulated by excitatory and inhibitory substances. Davis (1989), for example, has discussed how the relatively stereotyped mammalian startle reflex is modulated by various neurotransmitters and by emotion (fear). Specific neural circuits may be essential for the expression of a particular behavior, but those circuits may be modulated by emotions.

In future research, it will be profitable to consider that emotions (moods) may act through neuromodulators and may increase or decrease the possibility of certain behaviors. For example, the CES in blow flies increases in strength as a function of food deprivation. Food deprivation may modulate areas in the central nervous system. CES expression can also be modified by selective breeding. Such genetic manipulation may act by changing the number of receptors, the sensitivity of receptors, or the supply of neuromodulators. Finally, CES expression can be modified by drugs that act on various nervous system receptors. Food deprivation, genetic selection, and drugs all probably affect the same neuromodulatory systems. Much of neurobiology has moved from the concept of simple circuits to the concept of neuromodulation (see Davis et al., 1989, for an overview of neuromodulation in vertebrate systems). Behavior is regulated by electrical, synaptic circuits *and* by complex neuromodulatory interactions.

Emotion in the broader sense occurs in a variety of invertebrates. It may be possible to adopt a model systems approach to the study of motivation and emotion. "Many fundamental neurobiological questions simply cannot be addressed in higher animals, owing to the tremendous complexity of the neural circuits underlying even simple behaviors" (Davis, 1985, p. 280). Such a model systems approach has been highly successful in understanding other complex behaviors that were previously thought to be limited to vertebrates (see

Selverston, 1985, for discussions of many model systems). Recent work in molecular genetics has demonstrated that behaviors in invertebrates may be associated with the same genes as behaviors in vertebrates. For example, mutations in the *periodicity* or *per* gene in *Drosophila melanogaster* alter the patterns of daily activity (circadian rhythms). In addition, such mutations may influence learning and courtship. Analogous *per* proteins have been detected in the pacemaker structures of a wide range of organisms, including other insects, a lizard, a frog, a fish, and two mammals—rat and hamster (see Hall, 1990, for a complete review). Similarly, the *Shaker* gene of *Drosophila melanogaster* (which was originally isolated in a behavioral screen) affects potassium channels in the cell. *Shaker* has been cloned and sequenced along with three other potassium channel genes (*Shal*, *Shab*, and *Shaw*). These genes show extensive homology with mouse potassium channel genes and have vindicated the model systems approach for understanding nervous system action (Wei et al., 1990). With the appropriate invertebrate model systems, it should be possible to trace the neural circuits underlying emotion, to identify the complex patterns of neuromodulation, and to look at the genetics of emotional differences. Only after this is accomplished will it be possible to attempt the daunting task of understanding emotion in mammals.

REFERENCES

Archer, J. (1973). Tests for emotionality in rats and mice: A review. *Animal Behaviour, 21,* 205–235.

Archer, J. (1975). The Maudsley reactive and nonreactive strains of rats: The need for an objective evaluation of differences. *Behavior Genetics, 5,* 411–413.

Bell, W. J. (1991). *Searching behaviour: The behavioural ecology of finding resources.* London: Chapman & Hall.

Bell, W. J., Tortorici, C., Ruggerio, R. J., Kipp, L. R., & Tobin, T. R. (1985). Sucrose-stimulated searching behaviour in *Drosophila melanogaster* in a uniform habitat: Modulation by period of deprivation. *Animal Behaviour, 33,* 436–448.

Bennet-Clark, H., Ewing, A. W., & Manning, A. (1973). The persistence of courtship stimulation in *Drosophila melanogaster. Behavioral Biology, 8,* 763–769.

Blizard, D. A. (1981). The Maudsley reactive and nonreactive strains of rats: A North American perspective. *Behavior Genetics, 11,* 469–489.

Blizard, D. A., & Liang, B. (1979). Central serotonergic function and behavior in the Maudsley reactive and nonreactive strains: A reevaluation. *Behavior Genetics, 9,* 413–418.

Breland, K., & Breland, M. (1961). The misbehavior of organisms. *American Psychologist, 16,* 681–684.

Broadhurst, P. L. (1960). Experiments in psychogenetics: Applications of biometrical genetics in the inheritance of behaviour. In H. J. Eysenck (Ed.), *Experiments in psychology: Vol. 1. Psychogenetics and psychopharmacology* (pp. 1–102). London: Routledge & Kegan Paul.

Broadhurst, P. L. (1975). The Maudsley reactive and nonreactive strains of rats: A survey. *Behavior Genetics, 5,* 299–319.

Collins, A. M., Ronderer, T. E., Harbo, J. R., & Bolton, A. B. (1982). Colony defense by Africanized and European honeybees. *Science, 218,* 72–74.

Darwin, C. (1965). *The expression of the emotions in man and animals.* Chicago: University of Chicago Press. (Original work published 1872)

Davies, R. (1981). *The rebel angels.* New York: Viking Penguin.

Davis, M. (1989). Neural systems involved in fear-potentiated startle. In M. Davis, B. L. Jacob, & R. L. Schoenfeld. (Eds.), *Annals of the New York Academy of Sciences: Vol. 563. Modulation of defined vertebrate neural circuits* (pp. 165–183). New York: New York Academy of Sciences.

Davis, M.. Jacob. B. L., & Schoenfeld, R. L. (Eds.). (1989). *Annals of the New York Academy of Sciences: Vol. 563. Modulation of defined vertebrate neural circuits.* New York: New York Academy of Sciences.

Davis, W. J. (1985). Neural mechanisms of behavioral plasticity in an invertebrate model system. In A. I. Selverston (Ed.), *Model neural networks and behavior* (pp. 263–282). New York: Plenum Press.

DeFries, J. C., Wilson, J. R., & McClearn, G. E. (1970). Open-field behavior in mice: Selection response and situational generality. *Behavior Genetics, 1,* 195–211.

DeFries, J. C., Gervais, M. C., & Thomas, E. A. (1978). Response to 30 generations of selection for open-field activity in laboratory mice. *Behavior Genetics, 8,* 3–13.

Dethier, V. G. (1957). Communication by insects: Physiology of dancing. *Science, 125,* 331–336.

Dethier, V. G., Solomon, R. L., & Turner, L. H. (1965). Sensory input and central excitation and inhibition in the blowfly. *Journal of Comparative and Physiological Psychology, 60,* 303–313.

Evans, P. D. (1980). Biogenic amines in the insect nervous system. *Advances in Insect Physiology, 15,* 317–473.

Fuller, J. L., & Thompson, W. R. (1978). *Foundations of behavior genetics.* St. Louis: C. V. Mosby.

Grillner, S., Wallen, P., & di Prisco, G. V. (1990). Cellular network underlying locomotion as revealed in a lower vertebrate model: Transmitter, membrane properties, circuitry and simulation. *Cold Spring Harbor Symposia on Quantitative Biology, 55,* 779–789.

Hadler, N. (1964a). Genetic influence on phototaxis in *Drosophila melanogaster. Biological Bulletin, 126,* 264–273.

Hadler, N. (1964b). Heritability and phototaxis in *Drosophila melanogaster. Genetics, 50,* 1269–1277.

Halcomb, R. A., Hegmann, J. P., & DeFries, J. C. (1975). Open-field behavior in mice: A diallel analysis of selected lines. *Behavior Genetics, 5,* 217–231.

Hall, C. S. (1934). Emotional behavior in the rat: I. Defaecation and urination as measures of individual differences in emotionality. *Journal of Comparative Psychology, 18,* 385–403.

Hall, C. S. (1936a). Emotional behavior in the rat: II. The relationship between need and emotionality. *Journal of Comparative Psychology, 22,* 61–68.

Hall, C. S. (1936b). Emotional behavior in the rat: III. The relationship between emotionality and ambulatory behavior. *Journal of Comparative Psychology*, 22, 345–352.

Hall, C. S. (1951). The genetics of behavior. In S. S. Stevens (Ed.), *Handbook of experimental psychology* (pp. 305–329). New York: Wiley.

Hall, J. C. (1990). Genetics of circadian rhythms. *Annual Review of Genetics*, 24, 659–697.

Harrington, G. (1981). The Har strains of rats: Origins and characteristics. *Behavior Genetics*, 11, 445–468.

Hewitt, J. K., Fulker, D. W., & DeFries, J. C. (1977). Open-field behavior in mice: Generality of results from a diallel analysis of replicate selected lines. *Behavior Genetics*, 7, 441–446.

Hirsch, J., & McCauley, L. A. (1977). Sucessful replication of, and selective breeding for, classical conditioning in the blowfly *Phormia regina*. *Animal Behaviour*, 25, 784–785.

Hirsch, J., & Tryon, R. C. (1956). Mass screening and reliable individual differences in the experimental behavior genetics of lower organisms. *Psychological Bulletin*, 53, 402–410.

Hoy, R. R. (1989). Startle, categorical response and attention in acoustic behavior of insects. *Annual Review of Neuroscience*, 12, 355–375.

Kersten, A. M. P., Meijsser, F. M., & Metz, J. H. M. (1989). Effects of early handling on later open-field behaviour in rabbits. *Applied Animal Behaviour Science*, 24, 157–167.

Kitaoka, A., & Fujita, O. (1991). Behavioral comparisons of the Tsukuba emotional strains of rats (*Rattus norvegicus*) in three types of novel situations. *Behavior Genetics*, 21, 317–325.

Kravitz, E. A., Beltz, B., Glusman, S., Goy, M., Harris-Warrick, R., Johnston, M., Livingstone, M., Scwartz, T., & Siwicki, K. (1985). The well-modulated lobster: The roles of serotonin, octopamine, and proctolin in the lobster nervous system. In A. I. Selverston (Ed.), *Model neural networks and behavior* (pp. 339–360). New York: Plenum Press.

Kupfermann, I. (1991). Hypothalamus and limbic system. In E. R. Kandel, J. H. Schwartz, & T. M. Jessell (Eds.), *Principles of neural science* (3rd ed., pp. 750–768). New York: Elsevier.

LeDoux, J. E. (1986). Neurobiology of emotion. In J. E. LeDoux & W. Hirst (Eds.), *Mind and brain* (pp. 301–356). New York: Cambridge University Press.

Levine, S., & Broadhurst, P. L. (1963). Genetic and ontogenetic determinants of adult behavior in the rat. *Journal of Comparative and Physiological Psychology*, 56, 423–428.

Lewontin, R. C. (1959). On the anomalous response of *Drosophila pseudoobscura* to light. *American Naturalist*, 93, 321–328.

Long, T. F., Edgecomb, R. S., & Murdock, L. L. (1986). Effects of substituted phenylethylamines on blow fly feeding behavior. *Comparative Biochemistry and Physiology*, 83C, 201–209.

Loeb, J. (1973). *Forced movements, tropisms and animal conduct*. New York: Dover.

Lorenz, K. (1965). Preface. In C. Darwin, *The expression of the emotions in man and animals* (1965 edition). Chicago: University of Chicago Press.

Lorenz, K., & Tinbergen, N. (1938). Taxis und Instinkthandlung in der Eirollbewegung der Graugens. *Zeitschrift für Tierpsychologie*, 2, 1–29.

MacLean, P. D. (1970). The triune brain, emotion and scientific bias. In F. O. Schmitt (Ed.), *The neurosciences:* *Second study program* (pp. 336–349). New York: Rockefeller University Press.

McCann, J. S., Heird, J. C., Bell, R. W., & Lutherer, L. O. (1988). Normal and more highly reactive horses: I. Heart rate, respiration and behavioral observations. *Applied Animal Behaviour Science*, 19, 201–214.

McGuire, T. R. (1978). *Behavior-genetic analysis of* Phormia regina: *Conditioning, central excitatory state, and selection*. Unpublished doctoral dissertation, University of Illinois at Urbana–Champaign.

McGuire, T. R. (1981). Selection for central excitatory state (CES) in the blow fly, *Phormia regina*. *Behavior Genetics*, 11, 331–338.

McGuire, T. R. (1983). Further evidence for a relationship between central excitatory state (CES) and classical conditioning. *Behavior Genetics*, 13, 509–515.

McGuire, T. R. (1985). *Octopamine may mediate central excitatory state response in the blow fly* Phormia regina. Paper presented at the annual meetings of the Society for Neuroscience, Dallas, TX.

McGuire. T.R., Gelperin, A., & Tully. T. (1990). Olfactory conditioning of the blow fly *Phormia regina*. *Journal of Insect Behavior*, 3, 49-59.

McGuire, T. R., & Hirsch, J. (1977). Behavior-genetic analysis of *Phormia regina*: Conditioning, individual differences, and selection. *Proceedings of the National Academy of Sciences, USA*, 74, 5193–5197.

McGuire, T. R., & Schmidt, M. K. (1982). The relationship between Pavlovian counterconditioning and central excitatory state (CES) in the blow fly *Phormia regina*. *Behavior Genetics*, 12, 607–608.

McGuire, T. R., & Tully, T. (1986). Food search behavior and its relation to the central excitatory state (CES) in the genetic analysis of the blow fly *Phormia regina*. *Journal of Comparative Psychology*, 100, 52–58.

McGuire, T. R., & Tully, T. (1987). Characterization of genes involved with classical conditioning that produce differences between bidirectionally selected strains of the blow fly *Phormia regina*. *Behavior Genetics*, 17, 97–107.

Medioni, J., & Manning, A. (1988). Age-related perseveration of the precopulatory behaviours in male *Drosophila melanogaster*. *Animal Behaviour*, 44, 76–79.

Meijsser, F. M., Kersten, A. M. P., Wiepkema, P. R., & Metz, J. H. M. (1989). An analysis of the open-field performance of subadult rabbits. *Applied Animal Behaviour Science*, 24, 147–155.

Nakamuta, K. (1985). Mechanism of the switchover from extensive to area-concentrated search behaviour of the ladybird beetle, *Coccinella septempunctata bruckii*. *Journal of Insect Physiology*, 31, 849–856.

Nelson, M. C. (1971). Classical conditioning in the blowfly (*Phormia regina*): Associative and excitatory factors. *Journal of Comparative and Physiological Psychology*, 77, 353–368.

Nelson, M. C. (1977). The blowfly's dance: Role in the regulation of food intake. *Journal of Insect Physiology*, 23, 603–612.

Panksepp, J. (1982). Toward a general psychobiological theory of emotions. *Behavioral and Brain Sciences*, 5, 407–467.

Papez, J. W. (1937). A proposed mechanism of emotion. *Archives of Neurology and Psychiatry*, 38, 725–743.

Pieron, H. (1928). Emotions of animals and man. In M. L. Reymert (Ed.), *Feelings and emotions* (pp. 284–294). Worcester, MA: Clark University Press.

Plutchik, R. (1980). A general psychoevolutionary theory of emotion. In R. Plutchik & H. Kellerman (Eds.), *Emo-*

tion: Theory, research, and experience. Vol. 1. Theories of emotion (pp. 3–33). New York: Academic Press.

Pribram, K. H. (1980). The biology of emotions and other feelings. In R. Plutchik & H. Kellerman (Eds.), *Emotion: Theory, research, and experience. Vol. 1. Theories of emotion* (pp. 246–269). New York: Academic Press.

Schal, C., Tobin, T. R., Surber, J. L., Vogel, G., Tourtellot, M. K., Leban, R. A., Sizemore, R., & Bell, W. J. (1983). Search strategy of sex pheromone-stimulated male German cockroaches. *Journal of Insect Physiology, 25,* 575–579.

Scott, J. P. (1980). The function of emotions in behavioral systems: A systems theory analysis. In R. Plutchik & H. Kellerman (Eds.), *Emotion: Theory, research, and experience. Vol. 1. Theories of emotion* (pp. 35–56). New York: Academic Press.

Scott, J. P., & Fuller, J. L. (1965). *Genetics and the social behavior of the dog.* Chicago: University of Chicago Press.

Searle, J. R. (1955). A factorial study of emotionality in the dog. *Psychological Monographs: General and Applied, 69,* 1–27.

Selverston, A. I. (Ed.). (1985). *Model neural networks and behavior.* New York: Plenum Press.

Suarez, S. D., & Gallup, G. G. (1983). Emotionality and fear in birds: A selected review and reinterpretation. *Bird Behaviour, 5,* 22–30.

Sudak, H. S., & Maas, J. W. (1964). Behavioral–neurochemical correlation in reactive and nonreactive strains of rats. *Science, 146,* 418–420.

Tinbergen, N. (1965). *Animal behavior.* New York: Time–Life Books.

Tully, T., & Hirsch, J. (1982a). Behavior-genetic analysis of *Phormia regina:* I. Isolation of pure-breeding lines for high and low levels of the central excitatory state (CES) from an unselected population. *Behavior Genetics, 12,* 395–415.

Tully, T., & Hirsch, J. (1982b). Behaviour-genetic analysis of *Phormia regina:* II. Detection of a single major-gene effect from behavioural variation for central excitatory state (CES) using hybrid crosses. *Animal Behaviour, 30,* 1193–1202.

Tully, T., Zawistowski, S. A., & Hirsch, J. (1982). Behavior-genetic analysis of *Phormia regina:* III. A phenotypic correlation between the central excitatory state (CES) and conditioning remains in replicated F_2 generations of hybrid crosses. *Behavior Genetics, 12,* 181–191.

van der Staay, F. J., Kerbush, S., & Raaijmakers, W. (1990). Genetic correlations in validating emotionality. *Behavior Genetics, 20,* 51–62.

Vargo, M., & Hirsch, J. (1982). Central excitation in the fruit fly (*Drosophila melanogaster*). *Journal of Comparative and Physiological Psychology, 96,* 452–459.

Vargo, M., & Hirsch, J. (1985). Selection for central excitation in the fruit fly (*Drosophila melanogaster*). *Journal of Comparative Psychology, 99,* 81–86.

Vargo, M., & Hirsch, J. (1986). Biometrical and chromosome analyses of lines of *Drosophila melanogaster* selected for central excitation. *Heredity, 56,* 19–24.

von Schilcher, F. (1976a). The role of auditory stimuli in the courtship of *Drosophila melanogaster. Animal Behaviour, 24,* 18–26.

von Schilcher, F. (1976b). The role of pulse song and sine song in the courtship of *Drosophila melanogaster. Animal Behaviour, 24,* 622–625.

Walsh, R. N., & Cummins, R. A. (1976). The open-field test: A critical review. *Psychological Bulletin, 83,* 482–504.

Wei, A., Covarrubias, M., Butler, A., Baker, K.. Pak, M., & Salkoff, L. (1990). K⁺ currect diversity is produced by an extended gene family conserved in *Drosophila* and mouse. *Science, 248,* 599–602.

Wells, M. J. (1962). *Brain and behavior of cephalopods.* Stanford, CA: Stanford University Press.

Winston, M. L. (1987). *The biology of the honey bee.* Cambridge, MA: Harvard University Press.

White, J., Tobin, T. R., & Bell, E. J. (1984). Local food search in the housefly *Musca domestica* after feeding on sucrose. *Journal of Insect Physiology, 30,* 477–487.

Wyman, R. J., Thomas, J. B., Salkoff, L., & Costello, W. (1985). The *Drosophila* thorax as a model system for neurogenetics. In A. I. Selverston (Ed.), *Model neural networks and behavior* (pp. 513–535). New York: Plenum Press.

12

Multiple-Measure Approaches to the Study of Infant Emotion

NATHAN A. FOX
SUSAN D. CALKINS

INTRODUCTION

Traditionally, research on infant emotion has focused primarily on the expression of emotion, with particular emphasis on charting the developmental course of particular emotions such as anger and fear (Campos, Hiatt, Ramsay, Henderson, & Svejda, 1978; Stenberg, Campos, & Emde, 1983). In recent years, a number of important changes in the field have allowed researchers to broaden the scope of their inquiries. First, vastly improved methodologies for the study of biological components of emotion have led to more detailed and comprehensive descriptions of infant emotional experience. The application of noninvasive psychophysiological procedures for measuring such phenomena as brain electrical activity and cortisol changes have produced a number of important findings, which allow a clearer conception of the relations between emotion and physiology. At the same time, developmental psychology in general has experienced a renewed interest in the study of individual differences in infancy (see Columbo & Fagan, 1990). With respect to the study of infant emotion, this implies examining the phenomenon with special attention both to endogenous infant traits, and to the interaction of these traits with socialization experiences to produce particular patterns of behavior. This approach has led theorists and

researchers to consider emotion, temperament, and social behavior as elements of an emotion system that interact dynamically (Campos, Barret, Lamb, Goldsmith, & Stenberg, 1983). Moreover, recent research on the regulation of emotion demonstrates quite convincingly that infant emotional reactivity is at the core of the infant's personality or temperament, and that the display of affect is a powerful mediator of interpersonal relationships in the first few years of life (Cicchetti, Ganiban, & Barnett, 1991; Malatesta, Culver, Tesman, & Shephard, 1989; Rothbart, 1989; Thompson, 1990).

These two developments in the area of infant emotion—improvements in psychophysiological assessment and analysis, and an interest in infant temperament and its role in developing affiliative relationships—have led to new approaches to the study of infant emotion, ones that consider the interrelation of both behavioral and biological systems. These approaches assume that emotion is neither exclusively expression nor physiology, but a combination of the two that is best captured by behavioral and physiological measures (Davidson & Cacioppo, 1992; Fox & Davidson, 1984). Such perspectives have led to the establishment of programs of research whose aim is to assess as many of these systems as is feasible during the period of infancy, and to observe convergence among them. It is the aim of this chapter to describe the methodologies currently being used in these programs, and to describe some of the early findings.

The chapter is divided into three sections. First, we briefly discuss psychophysiological assessment, with special emphasis on methodologies used in conjunction with infant emotion. Second, we describe some of the research on infant emotion, temperament, and socioemotional development, and discuss the interrelations among these domains as well as the methodological issues associated with each. Finally, we bring together these two areas by reviewing some of the most recent research that has undertaken to assess emotion in infancy with a variety of behavioral and physiological measures.

ISSUES IN PSYCHOLOGICAL MEASUREMENT OF INFANT EMOTION

What Is Being Measured?

The history of psychophysiological measurement in the study of emotion is a long and complex one. In many studies, the measurement of physiological systems has been based on classical theories of emotion and arousal. According to these theories, physiological change either accompanies and intensifies affective experience or is the source of emotion experience itself. Measurement of heart rate is an obvious example. Numerous studies recorded heart rate during different emotion-eliciting situations and interpreted the change in heart rate to reflect the degree to which a subject became aroused by the stimulus. Increases in heart rate were viewed as reflecting arousal, whereas decreases in heart rate or no change were viewed as reflecting lack of arousal. Thus, subjects who exhibited increases in heart rate were thought to be experiencing emotion, while those with little change were not. Emotion experience was seen as a function of the degree to which a subject was aroused by the stimulus.

This unidimensional view of emotion and arousal was replaced by one that specifically interpreted directional heart rate changes within a psychological framework. Graham and Clifton (1966) viewed increases in heart rate as reflecting a defensive response to noxious stimuli and decreases in heart rate as reflecting orienting responses. Changes in heart rate were not thought to reflect general arousal or activation; rather, these changes were linked to specific psychological states. An example from the developmental literature that used these concepts is a study by Campos, Emde, Gaensbauer, and Henderson (1975) in which changes in heart rate in response to stranger approach and maternal separation were reported. Campos et al. (1975) described increases in heart rate that occurred with the increasing proximity of the stranger and with the departure of the mother. Increases in heart rate were interpreted to reflect a defensive emotional response, while decreases were believed to signify orienting, attention, and interest to the novel event.

Contrast this type of study with the research of Ekman and colleagues (and the earlier research of Ax, 1953), who examined specific patterns of autonomic change associated with the expression of certain discrete emotions. The conceptual issue in these studies was to find patterns of autonomic change that were specific to certain emotions. The feeling states of individual emotions were viewed as a function of the different patterns of autonomic change and individual perception of these changes (cf. James, 1890). In a series of studies, Ekman and colleagues reported finding autonomic differentiation among different discrete emotions (Ekman, Levenson, & Friesen, 1983; Levenson, Ekman, & Friesen, 1990).

The majority of these studies—both those focusing on undifferentiated arousal of the autonomic nervous system, and those attempting to identify specific physiological changes associated with discrete emotions—utilized measurement of the autonomic nervous system. As such, these studies recorded changes in the cardiac and vascular systems with measures of heart rate, skin conductance/resistance/potential, skin temperature, blood pressure, and respiration. In general, one or more of these responses were chosen for measurement, and in the best of studies, patterning among these measures was reported (e.g., Ekman et al., 1983).

However, a number of technical issues relevant to these studies and to the research on physiological measurement in general have often been overlooked. Perhaps the most important one is the issue of time course of change of each of these systems. It is clear from the physiological literature that each of the various autonomic responses has quite a different time course, ranging from milliseconds to seconds and in some cases minutes before change in the response can be measured. The fact that each of these systems elicits a different time course of change would seem problematical to the different approaches for study of emotion. For example, if physiological measurement is to describe patterns of arousal, then choice of measure will obviously influence the conclusion as to whether the subject has indeed become aroused by the emotional stimulus or not. Changes in cortisol are only noted some 15 minutes after the eliciting event. If cortisol is measured during an emotion, one may not conclude that the subject has become aroused during that emotion. Similarly, if one is measuring patterns of physiological change during the expression of discrete emotions, the time course for these changes may preclude finding these patterns if ecologically valid expressive responses are utilized. Ekman and colleagues, for example, have been forced to use a task in which subjects hold the facial musculature changes associated with certain emotions (the "directed facial action" task) for long periods of time for just this reason.

The differing time course of physiological systems may also be helpful in understanding certain aspect of emotion experience. Fox (1991) has suggested that the slower-changing autonomic responses associated with the expression of certain discrete emotions may be more closely related to the intensive aspects of the experience than to the central feeling state. Certain emotions may be intensified by the contribution of changing autonomic and visceral tone. Certain emotional states, which last over prolonged periods of time, may do so because of the slow-changing physiological systems that are involved in the expression of the emotion. Of course, the degree to which these states last may be a function of individual differences in physiological lability. To the best of our knowledge, these issues have not been thoroughly explored in the literature, although the time courses of these systems have been well defined.

A parallel issue in the use of multiple physiological measures is the degree to which we understand the connections among different physiological systems. There are a number of levels on which this problem may be approached. Perhaps the most simple and direct one is to record more than one measure

and, given corrections for change because of different time courses, to examine simple bivariate correlations among the measures. If one system goes up in response to or during an emotion, does the other go up or down? Patterning of this nature among systems that share some similarity (e.g., among autonomic measures) has had a long history in psychophysiology. Again, classical approaches emphasizing arousal maintained that there should be a correspondence among physiological systems in their response to emotional stimuli. Physiological arousal should, it was argued, be reflected in multiple measures and should provide change in the same direction for all measures (they should all go up or down together). However, researchers were quick to discover that this is not the case. Indeed, the pioneering work of Lacey and colleagues (Lacey & Lacey, 1970) revealed different directional patterns in autonomic measures all thought to be reflecting arousal. For this reason, simple correlational approaches may not be the ideal strategies for understanding the relations among physiological measures.

Perhaps a more informative strategy is to work toward understanding the particular physiological systems being tapped, and consequently the underlying physiology and anatomy of that system, so that particular patterns of relationship among measures can be interpreted with greater depth and understanding. As an example, consider the research on blood pressure and heart rate. There has been a good deal of work attempting to clarify the physiological mechanisms that relate these two systems, in order to elucidate both the unique nature of each and the manner in which these two systems overlap. The unique feedback systems between blood pressure and heart rate via baroreceptor mechanisms have allowed scientists to understand how blood pressure and heart rate covary. Use of both measures together can illuminate issues regarding the nature of interaction among these physiological systems, rather than just between emotion and a single autonomic index.

Synchrony of Emotion and Physiology

A second issue in the study of multiple response measures of emotion involves the nature of emotion behavior–physiology synchronization. As discussed above, different physiological systems have differing time courses. Measuring more than one system involves understanding the manner in which these different time courses overlap and interact. But what of measurement of the emotion itself? What is its time course, and how does it factor into the pattern that is being described? Again, the history of efforts to answer this question is long and complex. There have been many definitions of emotion and multiple attempts at measurement of emotion. One theoretical position that may be helpful in studying emotion–physiology relationships is presented by Ekman (1984). Emotion, in Ekman's conceptualization, is a fast-occurring event linked directly to changes in facial expression and autonomic activity. The time course of emotion may be viewed on the order of seconds. Feeling states that occur over longer periods of time are thought of as mood states rather than emotions. If one accepts these definitional distinctions, one can begin to find ways to link physiology to emotion behavior. For example, we have utilized facial expression as an anchor in determining the presence of specific central nervous system states in infants. In our studies of brain electrical activity and its relation to emotion, we have synchronized changes in the ongoing electroencephalogram (EEG) to changes in facial expression. This has been possible because the resolution and time course of the EEG are on the order of milliseconds, as are the resolution and time course of facial expressive change. Thus, it is not unreasonable to link the two together; their time changes are compatible.

But what about linking expressive changes to autonomic activity? Again, since most autonomic change is on the order of seconds, it is difficult to find instances of expressive change that match this temporal level. Ekman and colleagues developed the directed facial action task for just this purpose. In this task, a subject is required to move his or her facial muscles into a pattern resembling a discrete emotion. The subject must then hold that expression for a long period of time, so that changes in autonomic activity may be recorded. Although such a pattern is interesting in the abstract and can inform us about the relations between certain behaviors and physiology, its direct relation to ecologically valid changes in facial activity is dubious. Seldom

are facial expressions of discrete emotion in "real life" held for such long periods of time. It is therefore difficult if not impossible in ecologically valid situations to synchronize emotion and autonomic behavior, if emotion is solely defined by the presence of specific facial behaviors.

One can define emotion by the stimulus condition itself. However, the obvious drawback here is that individuals may respond quite differently to the same condition, and if physiology and behavior are linked, one may not find clear relations when differing emotions are elicited across individuals. For example, we have recorded physiology in young infants in response to maternal separation. Not all infants cry at separation or are distressed. Indeed, we have found that the physiology of infants who are distressed is quite different from those who are not upset by this identical stimulus situation. Collapsing data across individual subjects would obscure these differences. As an alternative to either collapsing data across individuals or anchoring emotion to facial expression, which is a fast-changing response, one could interview subjects as to their emotion responses or have subjects rate their individual responses. Subjects could then be grouped by the type of emotion that they report. Alternatively, other response measures of emotion may be used. For example, in the case of infant response to maternal separation, we have grouped infants into those who cry and those who do not cry at this event (e.g., Davidson & Fox, 1989). Interestingly, the discrete facial expression does not discriminate physiological activity within individual infants who cry at separation. We have found, for example, that some infants cry and exhibit anger expressions, while others cry and exhibit distress/sadness. Physiologically (at least with regard to the EEG measures we have utilized), these two subgroups do not differ. Thus, the use of vocal measures of emotion has proved to be more successful in parsing emotion behavior–physiology than have facial expressions of emotion.

Physiological Approaches to the Study of Infant Emotion

Although the study of central and autonomic nervous system substrates of emotion has a long history within the adult personality literature (Davidson, 1984; Porges, 1991), relatively little has been done in the area of infant emotions. Three primary types of measures have been used to study relations between physiology and emotional responsivity to a variety of elicitors: measures of heart rate, brain electrical activity, and adrenocortical activity. Excellent reviews of the use of these three measures in both the adult and child literature are to be found in Fox and Davidson (1984), Porges (1991), and Gunnar (1989; Stansbury & Gunnar, in press). In this section, we briefly describe the application of these measures to the study of infant emotion.

Heart Rate

The use of heart rate measures of emotion has a long and varied history (see Porges, 1991, for a review). Assessment of heart rate among infant populations is a nonintrusive, painless procedure. Whereas methods of collecting heart rate from infants have proven to be relatively straightforward, methods of analyzing it have proven to be more complex. Traditionally, studies examined changes in heart rate (deceleration and acceleration) in response to particular emotion-eliciting events. In particular, a number of studies have examined the changes in heart rate accompanying fear-inducing situations, such as the visual cliff and the approach of an unfamiliar adult (Campos et al., 1978; Emde, Gaensbauer, & Harmon, 1976). These studies were patterned after Graham and Clifton's (1966) reinterpretation of the meaning and significance of directional changes in heart rate. Other studies examined individual differences in heart rate and heart rate variability among different groups of infants and children (Fox & Gelles, 1983; Kagan, Reznick, & Snidman, 1987). Fox and Gelles (1983) found that infants differing in level of heart rate variability also differed in the degree of facial expressivity. Infants with greater heart rate variability were also more expressive. Kagan et al. (1987) found that behaviorally inhibited children displayed faster and less variable heart rates than did behaviorally extroverted children. The authors interpret these differences as reflecting differences in the degree of sympathetic activation between the two groups. A third set of studies has examined individual differences in vagal tone and its relation to emotional reactivity in infancy (Fox, 1989; Porges, Doussard-Roosevelt, &

Portales, 1992; Stifter, Fox, & Porges, 1989; Stifter & Fox, 1990).

The use of the vagal tone measure represents an attempt to quantify the heart rate changes associated with respiration (respiratory sinus arrhythmia). Heart rate increases with respiration and decreases with expiration. In a series of studies, Porges and his colleagues have demonstrated that vagal tone is related to both emotional reactivity and regulation (Porter, Porges, & Marshall, 1988; Stifter et al., 1989). Infants with high vagal tone tend to be more reactive emotionally, and Porges speculates that this responsivity may be predictive of better regulatory ability. Furthermore, developmental changes in vagal tone may be a contributor to normative changes in emotion expression observed during infancy (Porges, 1991).

Electroencephalogram

A second physiological measure that has recently been utilized in the study of infant emotion is the ongoing EEG. The EEG is low-level electrical activity recorded off the scalp. First noticed by Berger (1929), the EEG has been routinely recorded in adults during cognitive tasks and during situations designed to elicit different emotions. The advent of powerful and fast computers made it possible to collect large amounts of EEG data, sample the signal quickly, and spectral-analyze the signal, decomposing it into energy at different frequency bands. Berger (1929) had noticed that the energy in the EEG decreased when patients were attending to the environment. This phenomenon, later described in detail by Lindsley and Wicke (1974), is known as "alpha desynchronization" or "alpha blocking." Greater desynchronization (decreased energy in a frequency band) is associated with increased activation.

Researchers interested in the pattern of activation between the right and left hemispheres have computed ratio scores of the difference in power or energy between the two hemispheres. These ratio or difference scores present relative differences in power and a score reflecting the degree to which one hemisphere or region in a hemisphere exhibits greater activation than a homologous region. There is an extensive literature on EEG asymmetry patterns during verbal versus spatial tasks (Davidson, Chapman, Chapman, & Hen-riques, 1990) and during the expression and perception of different emotions (Davidson, 1984; Fox & Davidson, 1984).

In applying these methods to the study of infant emotion, Fox and Davidson (Davidson & Fox, 1982, 1989; Fox & Davidson, 1986, 1987, 1988) have addressed two issues. The first issue, addressed in their early research, concerns the relation between the experience of a given emotion and the hemispheric acti-vation associated with that emotion experi-ence. In their studies of infants presented with videotaped facial expressions of happiness and sadness, for example, they found that infants displayed greater relative left frontal activation during happy than during sad expressions (Davidson & Fox, 1982). In a study of new-borns, they found that different tastes pro-duced both different facial expressions (inter-est vs. disgust) and different patterns of brain activity (Fox & Davidson, 1986). The second issue addressed in Fox and Davidson's research is whether differences in hemispheric asymmetry are markers for individual differ-ences in emotionality, or temperament in infancy (Davidson & Fox, 1989; Fox & Davidson, 1991). In their study of infants' re-actions to maternal separation, they found that infants who displayed less left-sided activation in the frontal region during a baseline con-dition were more likely to cry at a brief sepa-ration (Davidson & Fox, 1989). Fox and Davidson (1991) argue that infants who show a characteristic right-sided frontal activation may have a lower threshold for negative emo-tion. More recently, this work has been ex-tended to examine differences among behav-iorally inhibited and uninhibited children. Data from the Maryland Infant Study suggest that infants selected for temperamental char-acteristics predictive of inhibition are more likely to exhibit greater relative right frontal activation (Calkins, Fox, & Marshall, 1992).

Adrenocortical Activity

A third physiological measure that has recently been applied to the study of infant emotion is adrenocortical activity as measured in plasma and salivary cortisol. Cortisol is the primary hormone of the adrenocortical system, whose production varies fairly rhythmically during the course of the 24-hour day–night cycle. In addition, however, cortisol levels change in response to both physiological and psychologi-cal elicitors. In using cortisol as a measure of stress or emotional reactivity, then, the aim is to compare changes in cortisol levels from basal to stressor conditions, with consideration of the activity of the system relative to its daily cycle (Stansbury & Gunnar, in press). Mea-surement of adrenocortical activity in infants is further complicated by the developmental changes occurring in the pattern of daily cortisol activity during the first year of life. Nevertheless, recent improvements in the radioimmune assays used to analyze salivary cortisol make this method of obtaining psycho-physiological data from very young infants quite feasible.

In examining the relations between mea-sures of cortisol and emotion, researchers have debated whether observed increases in cortisol reflect reactivity to stress or whether changes in cortisol level reflect reactivity to novelty and uncertainty. The first hypothesis implies that elevations in cortisol levels will be observed consistently in response to stressors producing negative affect, whereas the second hypothesis predicts habituation of the adreno-cortical response once the novelty of the event or stimulus has dissipated (Gunnar, 1990). A third hypothesis recently proposed suggests that control or regulation of the affective response may be the critical factor related to observed changes in cortisol (Stansbury & Gunnar, in press).

Issues and Problems

This brief introduction to the kinds of psycho-physiological measures currently being used with infants to study emotional development raises several issues. First, although these stud-ies have undertaken the study of the biologi-cal component to emotion, it is clear that these emotion responses occur within a social con-text. Responsivity to the approach of a stranger and maternal separations, for example, are not simple biological responses independent of a child's history and experience in dyadic inter-actions. Other systems, such as attachment and/or social learning histories, are at work as well. The emotion the infant displays, then, is a function of both the event and the process of socialization experienced by the infant. The second important issue raised by these stud-ies is that temperamental individuality plays a role in infant behavioral and physiological responsivity. That is, as the recent studies of Fox (1991) suggest, emotions may occur as certain predictable biological events occur in response to particular situational elicitors. Given a certain degree of novelty or stress, certain patterns of biological responsivity may be characteristic responses of an individual. Both pieces of information are critical to the understanding of the relations between physiology and behavior. In the next section, we explore the idea that infant emotions are reflected in both temperament and social behavior.

EMOTION, TEMPERAMENT, AND SOCIAL DEVELOPMENT

Links between Emotion and Temperament, Attachment, and Social Development

The interrelations among emotion, temperament, and social behavior are most dramatically observed in infancy. Infants display a varied repertoire of emotional expressions very early in life (Malatesta et al., 1989), and this repertoire serves as the infants' primary means of communication with their caretakers. Infant expression of emotions and regulation of that expression are key elements in the formation of primary attachments and early social relationships (Thompson, 1990). Infants use distress signals to alert their caretakers to their needs; caretakers become adept at interpreting the infants' signals in order to fulfill those needs. And there are rapid developments in the infants' ability to acquire the necessary skills to regulate their own emotions and monitor their own behaviors. Very young infants are able to use gaze aversion and self-comforting to manage affective experience; as motor and cognitive abilities grow, so too will the range of behaviors infants use to regulate themselves. These developments in self-regulation, which follow a fairly predictable path in infancy and early childhood (Kopp, 1982), are clearly the result of dyadic interactions with the caretakers (Tronick, 1989).

Although there are normative trends in the development of emotion regulation during infancy, there are also individual differences in the way infants learn to regulate affective states and the rate at which this process occurs. Infants bring to the dyadic interactions with caretakers their own personality style, or "temperament." The notion of temperament suggests that infant characteristics are a function of biological predispositions (Rothbart & Derryberry, 1981). Most temperament theorists see emotionality as a core construct, although other traits are measured as well (Bates, 1980; Buss & Plomin, 1984; Carey, 1970). The tendency to be fussy, difficult to soothe, easily distressed by novelty or frustration, and unable to adapt is often tapped by both experimental observations and maternal assessments of infant temperament (Matheny & Wilson, 1981; Rothbart, 1981). Clearly, an infant's tendency to be easily distressed will have an impact on interactions with the caretaker. Furthermore, the infant's success or failure at managing states of emotional reactivity will have implications for future interactions with caregivers, and eventually with others as well. The role of both emotional reactivity and regulation in personality and social development is thus clearly an important one, and one that is influenced not simply by an infant's tendencies, but by a caregiver's input as well. Caregivers vary in the frequency and manner of their attempts to intervene on behalf of their infants. Infants develop styles of interacting with social and nonsocial stimuli that reflect the history of regulatory experiences they have had with caretakers. And these differences in style are likely to be reflected in a variety of settings, including interactions with caretakers, peers, teachers, and unfamiliar events, objects, and people.

Fogel (1982) has suggested that an infant's ability to manage distress predicts three competencies: an ability to self-comfort; less reliance on caregivers; and the development of a sense of security. Alternatively, an inability to tolerate distress may lead to both withdrawn behavior and feelings of insecurity on the part of the infant. The role of a secure attachment in the development of self-regulation seems, then, to be a function of both the infant's own capacity for utilizing necessary mechanisms of affective regulation and the caregiver's ability to meet the regulatory needs of the infant. Attachment theorists use the term "working model" (Bretherton, 1985) to describe the infant's sense of caregiver responsivity. A secure attachment is a function of positive interactions that allow the child to anticipate that regulation needs will effectively be met by the caregiver. An insecure attachment results when regulation needs are not fulfilled, either because the caregiver is neglecting and unavailable, or because the caregiver is inconsistent in meeting the affective needs of the infant. This process is clearly bidirectional, and its success depends on whether an infant is able to elicit the appropriate maternal behaviors to help manage distress and whether the caregiver is competent in fulfilling the role of emotion regulator for the child.

Early reactivity, then, may play a role in the infant's ability to regulate affective states appropriately, so that distress is managed either intrinsically by the infant or extrinsically by the caregiver. In seeking help from the caregiver, the infant is relying on the adult's sensitivity to the signals he or she sends out. Attachment theorists have suggested that insensitivity to infant signals is one component of the kind of behavior that leads to insecure attachments (Ainsworth, Blehar, Waters, & Wall, 1978). Clearly, the caregiver's ability to serve as the regulator of the child's affective state has implications for the child's own developing regulatory abilities. If, as some types of attachment behaviors imply, infants are not provided with satisfactory management of their distress by their caregivers, then the infants may have difficulty in learning the appropriate strategies for affective control (Thompson, 1990).

The critical developments in the experience and expression of affect in the first year of life, then, are not simply limited to changes in the facial and vocal displays of emotion. Temperament plays an important role in both an infant's emotional expressions and a caregiver's responses to those expressions. The role of temperament in infants' reciprocal interactions with caregivers serves to underscore the interrelations among emotion, temperament, and social development, and points to the need to consider these relations in studies of infant emotional development. However, though these conceptual linkages seems strong, the measurement of these separate but interrelated domains may be more difficult.

Measurement Issues in Infant Socioemotional Behavior

There are several technical issues of importance in research using procedures that tap infant emotion in the context of more complex behavior. First, we must consider the issue of what is being measured. That is, in using particular procedures to assess infant temperament, attachment, or social behavior, are we in fact obtaining an accurate assessment of behavior in those domains? A great deal of research on infant social and emotional development has been conducted using relatively few assessment techniques. Of interest is how well these techniques provide information on infant emotional behavior and development.

Assessment of Attachment

One example of a technique designed to assess socioemotional relationships is the method traditionally used to assess attachment in infancy, the Strange Situation (Ainsworth et al., 1978). This procedure is designed to assess the quality of the mother–infant bond, and reflects the history of maternal responsivity to infant signals. The procedure involves a series of separations and reunions designed to elicit the extent to which a child uses the mother as a secure base from which to explore the environment and as a source of comfort in time of stress. The attachment system maintains a balance between exploration and proximity seeking. In moments of duress, when the child feels insecure, the balance shifts from exploring the environment to seeking proximity to the attachment figure. On the basis of infant behaviors observed throughout a series of seven brief episodes, infants are classified as avoidant and insecure (A), secure (B), or resistant and insecure (C). Within each of these three broad classifications, there are subgroups (A1, A2, B1, B2, B3, B4, C1, C2) as well. Infants classified as avoidant/insecure tend not to be upset when they are separated from their mothers, and are conspicuous in their attempts to evade proximity and contact with their mothers during reunions. Conversely, securely attached infants tend to seek proximity and contact with their mothers, and may or may not, depending on their subgroup classification, become upset when the mothers leave. Infants classified as resistant/insecure tend to experience distress at separation, and mix proximity-seeking behaviors with resistant behaviors upon reunion.

The origin of the insecure infant's attachment to the mother can be traced, in part, to the style of sensitivity and responsivity of the mother. Avoidant/insecure infants may have been exposed to angry or controlling mothers, whereas resistant/insecure infants may have mothers insensitive to their signals (Ainsworth et al., 1978). Attachment theorists in the tradition of Ainsworth and colleagues emphasize that the quality of attachment is, to a significant degree, dependent on a mother's sensitivity to her infant. Infant characteristics may influence the parent's behavior, but the direction of influence is, from the attachment theorist's perspective, from parent to infant (Sroufe, 1985).

The Strange Situation has been used by a number of researchers to study the role of secure versus insecure attachment in development. Nevertheless, a number of studies have addressed the question of whether the Strange Situation measures simply the quality of attachment, or the contribution of infant characteristics to the development of that relationship as well (Bates, Maslin, & Frankel, 1985; Belsky, Taylor, & Rovine, 1984; Fox, Kimmerly, & Schafer, 1991; Goldsmith & Alansky, 1987; Miyake, Chen, & Campos, 1985; Vaughn, Lefever, Seifer, & Barglow, 1989). These studies have led to conflicting conclusions. Few studies have found strong links between maternal assessments of temperament and attachment classification. However, several researchers have identified relations between irritability and insecure attachment, and between patterns of behavior exhibited in the Strange Situation and temperament (Connell & Thompson, 1986; Fox et al., 1991; Frodi & Thompson, 1985; Waters, Vaughn, & Egeland, 1980). Fox et al. (1991), for example, found strong relations between the quality of attachment security or insecurity that infants exhibited to mothers and fathers. They argue that these data suggest that an infant's temperament plays an important role in the pattern of behavior exhibited during the Strange Situation and the infant's ultimate attachment classification. Vaughn and colleagues (Vaughn et al., 1992) found, across six separate samples, a modest relation between maternal assessment of infant and child emotionality and security of attachment as assessed by the attachment Q-set. The attachment Q-set has shown convergent validity with the Strange Situation and is considered to be a reliable method of assessing mother–infant attachment.

The use of the Strange Situation or the Q-set as an attachment assessment technique requires, then, clarification of the role played by infant emotionality. We find persuasive the argument that infant emotionality does play a role in the caretaker's ability to regulate the infant's arousal, and that the resulting attachment relationship will, in turn, influence subsequent infant reactivity and regulation across a wide variety of situations. These developments may be observed within the context of the Strange Situation, although other procedures have proven valuable as well. For example, techniques assessing an infant's reactivity to a stranger in the presence of the mother, and the infant's reactivity to other novel events, allow us to consider the way in which the infant balances responsivity of certain events and the regulation of that arousal. These procedures typically involve the use of facial or vocal scoring of the infant's emotional reactivity, and, in the case of reactivity to novelty, assessment of the infant's use of the mother as an affect regulator. Again, however, the issue of what these behaviors reflect in terms of infant emotionality must be addressed. For example, facial expression alone may not reflect the infant's level of distress, whereas vocal distress may. Use of the mother as an affect regulator in response to novelty may reflect a high level of fear, although some infants may be better able to regulate their own distress and not need their mothers' help; their actual level of distress, however, may be quite high.

Assessment of Temperament

Emotionality in infancy has also been assessed via measurements of infant temperament. Efforts to assess endogenous infant traits that may influence subsequent personality development have generated a variety of laboratory and questionnaire techniques. The work of Thomas and Chess and their colleagues (Thomas, Chess, Birch, Hertzig, & Korn, 1963) on the New York Longitudinal Study began the discussion of how to use temperament constructs to measure individual differences among infants. This approach construed temperament in terms of behavioral style, which is thought to be stable over time and to be reflected in the similarity of responses across different emotional elicitors. Various temperament theorists have proposed particular dimensions of temperament, which reflect in general a child's emotionality, activity level, and attention (Buss & Plomin, 1984; Rothbart,

1981; Thomas & Chess, 1977). In addition, these approaches assume a biological component of individual differences. Finally, these approaches are similar in that the measurement of the traits is achieved through the completion of a questionnaire that requires mothers to rate the frequency of particular infant behaviors observed during the previous week.

The measurement of specific temperament dimensions by means of questionnaire techniques has led to a great deal of research concerning the stability of temperament, its convergent validity with observations of behavior, and its role in developing social relationships (see Isabella, Ward, & Belsky, 1985; Worobey, 1986). Two of these issues, stability and convergence, are at the core of the challenge of developing accurate temperament assessment instruments. For if, as the major theoretical positions maintain, temperament is stable, measuring temperament should produce cross-age correlations on the different dimensions. And these assessments should also correlate with observed behavior. Critics of these instruments maintain that maternal report of temperament is biased and ought to be validated by other sorts of information (Isabella et al., 1985; Worobey, 1986). Direct observations of temperament in the home or laboratory have been proposed as a means of validating maternal assessment. These methods are vulnerable to distortion as well, because the period of observation is short and the range of behaviors observed may be constricted. Matheny and colleagues (Matheny, Riese, & Wilson, 1985) have argued in favor of multimethod assessments that include both laboratory and maternal assessments. Such a multimethod approach validates maternal assessment and provides an assessment of temperament that takes into account behaviors observed over the course of several days.

In addition to finding reliable and valid measurement instruments to assess the behavioral component, it seems incumbent upon temperament theorists to try to account for the biological or physiological component as well. That is, if, as temperament theorists propose, temperamental types or characteristics reflect the behavioral manifestation of some underlying biological process, it would be helpful to observe convergent validity of behavior and biology. Moreover, if temperament in fact consists of stable personality characteristics that

will be reflected in a variety of contexts, it seem important to assess temperament with respect to such contexts, with particular emphasis on its role in social interactions. The assessment of temperament, like the assessment of attachment, clearly requires a multimethod approach—one that examines its biological component, and one that takes into account the display of temperament in both social and nonsocial contexts.

Given the obvious intersections among emotion, temperament, and social development, an approach to the study of these domains ought to include multiple behavioral or observational measures; such an approach may provide a more complete picture than a technique that relies on a single measure. In this way, the relative contributions of temperament, attachment, and social responsivity to emotionality may be assessed with respect to one another. Moreover, the strategy of considering multiple indicators of emotion in infancy is further strengthened by application of the types of psychophysiological measures discussed earlier. In the next section, we review recent research that has taken the approach of exploring emotion–physiology relations by studying behaviors reflecting temperament and social behavior as well as emotional displays.

MULTIPLE-MEASURE STUDIES OF INFANT EMOTION

Studies Assessing Autonomic Activity

Several studies relating measures of heart rate to temperament, attachment, and social behaviors have recently been conducted. Using measures of heart period and vagal tone, Porges and colleagues have observed both normative changes and individual differences related to various aspects of behavior. In a recent study of attachment and heart rate activity, a sample of infants was followed from 3 to 13 months, with measures of heart rate collected at each age and attachment assessed at 13 months (Izard et al., 1991). The hypothesis tested was that temperament is related to the quality of the infant's attachment to the mother, and therefore that measures of heart rate, thought to be indicative of temperamental reactivity and regulation, should be related to attachment as well. Their findings indicated that the earliest measures of heart rate variability (at 3, 6, and 9 months) correlated with a continuous variable representing security of attachment. Insecure infants were found to have had higher vagal tone at the earlier ages. Earlier findings that high heart rate variability reflects greater behavioral reactivity to distressing events (Porter et al., 1988) are difficult to support with these data. Among the insecure infants were those who were outwardly distressed by the procedure assessing attachment (insecure/resistant or C infants), as well as those who did not appear distressed (insecure/avoidant or A infants). One explanation for the apparently discrepant findings is that A infants may not display their emotional reactivity during the Strange Situation. It has been suggested that these infants develop defensive mechanisms to mask their emotion during the separation and reunions involved (Cassidy & Kobak, 1988).

A more recent study of temperament and heart rate measures suggests a more complicated interpretation of these attachment findings. Porges has followed a group of infants from the first to the third year of life (Porges et al., 1992). Assessments of temperament included both maternal questionnaires and laboratory observations at 9, 20, and 36 months of age. Again, normative increases in heart rate measures were found across the three ages. Stability of both behavioral measures of difficultness and the heart rate measures was also found. The most interesting finding, however, was that concurrent measures of vagal tone and difficultness did not correlate highly. Rather, earlier measures of vagal tone tended to predict changes in maternal assessments of infant difficultness. Infants with higher vagal tone at 9 months were perceived by their mothers to be less difficult at 36 months than infants with low vagal tone. These findings support Porges's (1991) contention that vagal tone is a reflection of physiological and behavioral regulation. Infants with high heart rate variability, or vagal tone, seem to be responsive to stimuli in a way that assists them in regulating their state. Reports by mothers that these infants became less difficult over time supports the notion that, in fact, they became better able to manage their own emotional reactivity.

These findings of relations between vagal tone and behavioral regulation seem to be in direct contradiction to the attachment study of Izard et al. (1991). Insecure infants with high

vagal tone would appear, in fact, to be displaying poor behavioral regulation in the Strange Situation. What we may be observing, however, is that these infants are reactive but have failed to develop appropriate strategies for behavioral regulation—because, most attachment theorists would argue, of inadequate or unresponsive maternal care. Behavioral regulation is a dynamic process requiring management of distress by both mother and infant. The infant may display the characteristics of an appropriately reactive infant, but may fail to manage that reactivity. If the external regulator fails as well, the child may become insecurely attached.

We have examined a similar hypothesis regarding emotional reactivity and regulation in a longitudinal study (Fox, 1989; Stifter & Fox, 1990; Calkins & Fox, 1992) that assessed the relations among heart rate measures on the one hand and temperament, attachment, and inhibited behavior on the other. Infants were observed at 2 days and at 5, 14, and 24 months of age. Measures of emotional (facial and vocal expressions), behavioral (motor activity and looking behaviors), and physiological (heart period and vagal tone) reactivity to distressing events were taken at 2 days (pacifier withdrawal procedure) and 5 months (arm restraint). At 14 months, measures of quality of attachment were taken with the Strange Situation, and at 24 months, measures of inhibited behavior in the laboratory were collected. Heart rate measures were also recorded at these latter assessment points. In addition, at all ages, maternal assessments of infant temperament were obtained.

In examining these data, Fox (1989) and Stifter and Fox (1990) demonstrated stable individual differences in reactivity during the first year of life. Infants who cried in response to pacifier withdrawal at 2 days were likely to cry in response to arm restraint at 5 months, and were likely to be rated by their mothers as more active. These differences in reactivity were associated with individual differences in autonomic patterning: Infants who cried in the newborn period had a higher vagal tone then did noncriers. Five-month-old infants who cried in response to arm restraint had a higher vagal tone than did noncriers. Infants who cried at both events had higher vagal tone and heart period than those who did not cry at both events, and were rated by their mothers as more distressed by limitations. Fox and

Stifter (1989) have argued that infant negative affect in response to mildly stressful and frustrating events is related to individual differences in vagal tone. However, these infants did not display difficult behavior at later assessments. Indeed, Fox (1989) found that infants displaying high frustrative reactivity in the lab at 5 months were likely to display positive approach and social behaviors toward strangers and novel events at 14 months, compared to those infants who were less reactive to frustration. Moreover, infants from this sample who displayed high heart rate variability across the first three age points demonstrated more sociable and less distressed behavior at 14 months. These findings support the recent finding of Porges et al. (1992) that early reactivity as indexed by high vagal tone may be a sign of good emotional and behavioral regulation.

The stability in autonomic reactivity reported by Stifter and Fox (1990) was confirmed in the later assessments of this same sample (Calkins & Fox, 1992). However, no relations were found between earlier or concurrent measures of heart period and vagal tone, and attachment and inhibition at 14 months and 24 months of age, respectively. Examination of the behavioral data at these later ages did indicate, however, that there was a relation between attachment and temperament. Infants who were insecure/resistant (C) at 14 months of age tended to be inhibited at 24 months of age, whereas infants who were insecure/avoidant (A) at 14 months of age tended to be uninhibited by 24 months. We have also concluded that some types of emotional reactivity may be related to insecure attachments. Emotional reactivity may be influenced by interactions with the parent to produce particular sorts of adaptive or regulatory patterns in early toddlerhood (Calkins & Fox, 1992). Infants whose early distress to frustrations or limits is met with a degree of freedom by their parents may appear to be avoidantly attached, but may in fact be regulating their state of arousal by high amounts of exploratory behavior. Infants whose early distress to novelty is dealt with by parental intervention may be more distressed in the Strange Situation, and may be managing their reactivity by spending large amounts of time in close contact with their parents.

Although our longitudinal study of autonomic reactivity, temperament, and attach-

ment found no relations between heart rate and temperament in the second year of life, Kagan and colleagues have observed such relations (Garcia-Coll, Kagan, & Reznick, 1984; Kagan et al., 1987). For the past 10 years, their research program has focused on the developmental course of inhibited behavior from early infancy through childhood, and has assessed the possible psychophysiological correlates of this behavior. For example, Kagan and colleagues, in two separate samples, have reported associations between heart period and heart period variability, and inhibited behavior observed in the laboratory. Infants with high and stable heart rates tend to be more fearful or reticent during encounters with novel people, objects, and events than infants with low and variable heart rates (Kagan et al., 1987). One important difference, however, between this research and ours (Calkins & Fox, 1992) is that Kagan et al. selected samples of infants that they believed represented the extremes of the population in terms of inhibited behavior, whereas we have reported findings from an unselected sample. The correlations Kagan's group reports are therefore somewhat inflated by the characteristics of the samples.

Kagan and colleagues have recently begun to investigate the origins of these differences in the tendency to develop inhibited versus uninhibited styles of behavior (Kagan & Snidman, 1991). they observed that children who displayed high amounts of negative affect and motor activity in response to novel tended to be fearful at 9 and 14 months of age. Kagan and Snidman argue that these behavioral differences emerge as a function of differential thresholds for arousal, which in turn have their origins in the limbic system. The physiological data presented, in terms of heart rate acceleration to sweet and sour tastes, do suggest that these highly aroused, highly irritable infants may have a lower threshold for arousal to certain kinds of stimuli.

Studies Assessing Adrenocortical Activity

The most recent studies relating adrenocortical activity to such constructs as temperament and attachment are those conducted by Gunnar and colleagues (Gunnar, Manglesdorf, Larson, & Hertsgaard, 1989; Larson, Gunnar, & Hertsgaard, 1991; Malone, Gunnar, &

Fisch, 1985). In one such study, infant response to limb restraint was observed and plasma cortisol levels were obtained (Malone et al., 1985). No effects of the limb restraint on cortisol levels was observed, although the procedure of obtaining the cortisol did elicit behavioral distress, which was related to elevated cortisol levels. Clearly, behavioral distress is associated with increased cortisol production, although in this study limb restraint, observed to cause distress in infants (see Stifter & Fox, 1990), may not have created sufficient stress to elevate cortisol levels.

Gunnar has observed the response of the adrenocortical system in response to other elicitors that have been shown to produce distinct patterns of distress responses in many infants. She and her colleagues have observed the salivary cortisol responses of infants to maternal separations at both 9 and 13 months (Gunnar et al., 1989). During the 9-month assessment, infants were seen in the home first, and assessments were made of temperament. Specifically, each infant's emotional tone was rated by an observer, who also completed scales rating attentiveness, activity, and social behavior. Within 1 week of this assessment, infants were seen in the laboratory for the administration of the Louisville Temperament Assessment (Matheny & Wilson, 1981). This procedure called for a lengthy separation from the mother, which was later scored for emotional tone. At 13 months, infants and mothers returned to the laboratory for assessment of attachment via the Strange Situation. In addition, maternal assessment of infant temperament was obtained.

In examining the data from this study, Gunnar and colleagues observed significant associations between measures of emotional reactivity collected at 9 months and those collected at 13 months. In addition, there were significant associations between salivary cortisol and emotional tone; although the correlations were modest, the pattern of correlations suggests that infants who displayed more positive tone experienced less of an increase in salivary cortisol level from baseline to posttest. And significant relations were found between cortisol levels and emotional response to separation. No relations were found between cortisol levels and attachment classification. The multiple measures collected in this study provide evidence that the adrenocortical response at the end of the first year of life may reflect temperamental or trait-like tendencies toward emotional reactivity. This trait-like tendency may be influencing both physiological and emotional responses to separation at this age (Gunnar et al., 1989). Again, we see evidence that emotional responsivity in infancy is tied to dispositional tendencies that may be observed in an interactional setting, and that may trigger underlying physiological responses.

Studies of Brain Electrical Activity

Although the first research relating brain electrical activity to emotions in infants involved the use of videotaped stimuli (see Davidson & Fox, 1982), more recent research has examined more complex emotion processes. Fox and colleagues, for example, have conducted several studies examining both infants' response to brief maternal separation and their response to unfamiliar adults (Fox, Bell, & Jones, 1992; Fox & Davidson, 1987, 1988). Both are strong affect elicitors by the end of the first year of life, and may continue as such during toddlerhood. And responses to both events may produce individual differences in affective display and approach–avoidance behaviors.

In the first of these studies, Fox and Davidson (1987) observed the responses of 10-month-old infants to the approach of an unfamiliar adult female, the approach and reach of the mother, and departure of the mother from the testing room. Comparisons of the pattern of EEG activation and behavior revealed relations to conditions as well as to individual differences in behavioral response. Greater relative left frontal activation was observed during the mother-reach condition (compared with the mother-enter epoch). And infants who cried at maternal separation showed a larger increase in relative right frontal activation during separation. Interestingly, no association between the stranger-approach epoch and EEG activation was observed. Given the differences between infants who cried to maternal separation and those who did not cry, Fox and Davidson concluded that infants who cry and have greater relative right frontal activation may be displaying a lower threshold to stressful events.

In subsequent analysis of the data from this study, Fox and Davidson (1988) distinguished felt smiles from unfelt (wary) smiles in response to both the mother's and the stranger's approach. Infants were more likely to display felt smiles to the mother and unfelt smiles to the stranger. Moreover, felt smiles were associated with greater relative left frontal activation, whereas unfelt smiles were associated with greater relative right frontal activation. Fox and Davidson (1991) suggest that this pattern of findings may indicate early indications of behavioral regulation in response to emotion-eliciting events.

To provide additional evidence that differences in patterns of brain electrical activity may be a marker for individual differences in temperament, Fox et al. (1992) examined maternal separation data from two separate samples. Study 1 examined infants at ages 14 and 24 months, whereas Study 2 involved monthly assessments of infants from 7 to 12 months. Across both studies, infants exhibiting greater relative right frontal activation were more distressed by maternal separation than those exhibiting greater relative left frontal activation. Among the infants who were observed from 7 to 12 months, there was stability in both the tendency to be distressed by maternal separation and frontal asymmetry. This study provides additional evidence for the hypothesis proposed by Fox (Fox, 1991; Fox & Davidson, 1991) that temperamental differences in tendencies to approach or withdraw from certain elicitors may originate in differences in brain asymmetry; it also underscores the role that the frontal region plays in the regulation of emotion in infancy.

Additional evidence for the role of the frontal lobes in the regulation of affective states in infancy comes from the recent work of Dawson and colleagues (Dawson, Klinger, Panagiotides, Hill, & Spieker, 1992). Dawson's work is notable for its attempt to examine affect across a number of events eliciting both positive and negative affect. She and her colleagues have been especially interested in affective tone and hemispheric differences in infants of mothers exhibiting depressive symptoms. Among the measures collected were (1) several measures of affect across conditions of baseline, affect-eliciting tapes, peek-a-boo, stranger approach, and maternal separation; (2) assessments of temperament; and (3) assessments of maternal characteristics. Although not all the affect measures clearly distinguished infants of mothers with depressive symptoms from those of mothers without such symptoms,

the EEG data did distinguish these groups. Infants of depressive mothers exhibited less relative left frontal activation during a playful interaction (and potential positive elicitor) with their mothers, and did not exhibit the expected greater relative right frontal activation during maternal separation, during which they showed less distress. These findings indicate that the affective differences between mothers with and without depressive symptoms may be reflected both in their interactions with their infants, and in the infants' frontal lobe activity. Such a conclusion supports the evidence that interactions with the caretaker both elicit emotional reactivity and provide a forum for the development of affective regulation.

Dawson has further explored the consequences of disturbances in mother–infant affective synchrony in a study of attachment and brain electrical activity in infants of mothers with depressive symptoms (Dawson, Klinger, Panagiotides, Spieker, & Frey, in press). In addition to the measures collected during the previous study, this study examined behaviors in the Strange Situation, using both the traditional Ainsworth et al. (1978) attachment classification system and a newer classification system that includes the category "disorganized." The findings indicated that more disorganized behavior was observed among infants of mothers with depressive symptoms. No EEG differences were found with respect to either attachment classification system, although an interaction of symptomatology and attachment was found: Reduced left frontal activation was found among securely attached infants of mothers with depressive symptoms.

It is clear from these findings that the relation between attachment and patterns of brain activity may be mediated by other factors. However, a more recent study of ours may provide a clearer picture of these relations (Calkins et al., 1992). The Maryland Infant Study represents a major effort to examine the relations among individual differences in emotional reactivity and regulation, developing socioemotional interactions, and patterns of brain electrical activity. Infants were screened in their homes at 4 months of age; a battery of procedures designed to elicit negative affect, positive affect, and motor activity was used (Kagan & Snidman, 1991). This screening procedure was intended to select infants who would display inhibited behavior and negative affect at later ages. From an initial sample of 200 infants seen at 4 months, 81 infants were selected for follow-up visits at 9 and 14 months. At 9 months, EEG was collected during a baseline procedure, and infant regulatory and affective behavior was coded during a stranger's approach and maternal separation. At 14 months, infant behavior was observed in a series of episodes designed to elicit inhibited versus uninhibited behavior, and mother and infant were observed in the Strange Situation.

The infants who were selected for the follow-up study were clustered into three groups: (1) infants high on motor activity and negative affect and low on positive affect; (2) infants high on motor activity and positive affect and low on negative affect; and (3) infants low on all dimensions. Elsewhere (Calkins et al., 1992), we report a number of behavioral relations that emerged from this study. We found that the infants who were negatively reactive at 4 months tended to use object-oriented regulatory strategies at 9 months and to be inhibited and distressed in the Strange Situation at 14 months. Conversely, infants who were positively reactive at 4 months used person-oriented regulatory strategies at 9 months, and tended to be uninhibited and not distressed in the Strange Situation at 14 months.

Importantly, the data from this study reveal that these behavioral tendencies were accompanied by specific patterns of brain electrical activity. Infants selected at 4 months because they displayed high amounts of negative affect and motor activity exhibited greater relative right frontal activation at 9 months. Infants who displayed high amounts of positive affect and motor activity at 4 months exhibited greater relative left frontal activation. In addition, relations between EEG and attachment classification were observed: Infants classified as insecure/avoidant displayed greater relative right frontal activation, whereas those classified as insecure/resistant displayed greater relative left frontal activation.

Fox points out that these findings are consistent with findings from the adult literature, which demonstrate that adults with resting right frontal asymmetry are more likely to rate video film clips with negative affect than are adults with left frontal asymmetry (Tomarken, Davidson, & Henriques, 1990). These differences in frontal asymmetry may reflect the fact that the left and right hemispheres are differentially specialized for the expression of emotions associated with either approach or withdrawal (Fox, 1991). It is argued that early in life, there is little communication between these two hemispheres, and responses to novel or negative stimuli tend to vary along this approach–withdrawal continuum. With development, there will probably be greater communication between the two hemispheres, and more complex and adaptive responses to stimuli.

The individual-difference tendencies observed in this study have important consequences for social development. As discussed earlier, however, temperamental predispositions toward negative affect and irritability are not the sole predictors of social outcomes. Parental responsivity to these tendencies will influence an infant's responsivity to certain kinds of events. The parents' tendency to comfort versus ignore the infant's displays of emotions will have implications for how the infant will be able to manage emotional responsivity in the absence of parental assistance or feedback. Infant emotional reactivity, then, which appears to be a function of hemispheric differences, has important implications for the development of regulatory mechanisms that will assist the child in a variety of social settings.

CONCLUSIONS

In this chapter, we have adopted the position that emotion is neither a purely behavioral nor a purely physiological phenomenon. This premise, and methodological developments in the study of infancy, have led to attempts to study both behavioral and physiological manifestations of emotion in infancy. Recent attempts to explore dispositions or temperamental types in infancy have added still another dimension to these multiple-measure approaches to the study of emotion. These studies indicate that infant emotion cannot easily be dissociated from such constructs as temperament, attachment, and social development. Moreover, these constructs or systems are linked by emotional reactivity and emotional regulation.

The studies we have reviewed from the past decade have assessed heart rate, brain electrical activity, and adrenocortical activity in infancy. These studies indicate that (1) there are normative changes occurring in these response systems during the first year of life; (2) there are changes in these response systems that are functions of particular emotion or behavior elicitors; and (3) there are individual differences in the reactivity of these response systems, which may be observed in infancy. Importantly, these studies demonstrate the role that this early reactivity plays in the development of systems of behavioral regulation. Observed differences in physiological responses to particular types of elicitors suggest that what we are in fact observing is a complex interactional system involving emotions, physiology, and interactions with caretakers and others. These systems are at the core of an infant's developing regulatory system, which serves to manage emotional and behavioral responses of the infant in addition to, or in lieu of, caretaker regulation.

This review has focused on some of the most recent programs of research collecting multiple measures of infant emotion. Such programs are just beginning to provide a picture of the complex interactions among behavioral and physiological systems that may be observed during infancy Nevertheless, we are encouraged that this direction will provide more data about these processes during the course of the next decade.

Acknowledgment. Support for writing this chapter was provided in part by a grant from the National Institutes of Health (No. HD 17899) to Nathan A. Fox.

REFERENCES

Ainsworth, M. D., Blehar, M. C., Waters, E., & Wall, S. (1978). *Patterns of attachment.* Hillsdale, NJ: Erlbaum.

Ax, A. F. (1953). The physiological differentiation between fear and anger in humans. *Psychosomatic Medicine, 15,* 433–442.

Bates, J. E. (1980). The concept of difficult temperament. *Merrill–Palmer Quarterly, 26,* 299–319.

Bates, J. E., Maslin, C., & Frankel, K. A. (1985). Attachment security, mother–child interaction and temperament as predictors of behavior problems ratings at age three years. In I. Bretherton & E. Waters (Eds.), Growing points in attachment theory and research. *Monographs of the Society for Research in Child Development, 50*(2, Serial No. 209), 167–193.

Belsky, J., Taylor, D. G., & Rovine, M. (1984). The Pennsylvania Infant and Family Development Project: II. The development of reciprocal interaction on the mother–infant dyad. *Child Development, 55,* 706–717.

Berger, H. (1929). Uber das Elektrekephalogramm de Menschen. *Archives fur Psychiatrie und Nervenkrankheit, 87,* 527–570.

Bretherton, I. (1985). Attachment theory: Retrospect and prospect. In I. Bretherton & E. Waters (Eds.), Growing points in attachment theory and research. *Monographs of the Society for Research in Child Development, 50*(2, Serial No. 209), pp. 3–38.

Buss, A. H., & Plomin, R. (1984). *Temperament: Early developing personality traits.* Hillsdale, NJ: Erlbaum.

Calkins, S. D., & Fox, N. A. (1992). The relations among infant temperament, security of attachment and behavioral inhibition at 24 months. *Child Development, 63,* 1456–1472.

Calkins, S. D., Fox, N. A., & Marshall, T. R. (1992) *Behavioral and physiological antecedents of inhibition in infancy.* Manuscript submitted for publication.

Campos, J. J., Barret, K. C., Lamb, M., Goldsmith, H. H., & Stenberg, C. (1983). Socioemotional development. In M. Haith & J. J. Campos (Eds.), *Handbook of child psychology* (4th ed.): Vol. 2. Infancy and developmental psychobiology. New York: Wiley.

Campos, J. J., Emde, R., Gaensbauer, T., & Henderson, C. (1975). Cardiac and behavioral interrelationships in the reactions of infants to strangers. *Developmental Psychology, 11,* 589–601.

Campos, J. J., Hiatt, S., Ramsay, D., Henderson, C., & Svejda, M. (1978). The emergence of fear of heights. In M. Lewis & L. Rosenblum (Eds.), *The development of affect* (pp. 149–182). New York: Plenum Press.

Carey, W. B. (1970). A simplified method of measuring infant temperament. *Journal of Pediatrics, 77,* 188–194.

Cassidy, J., & Kobak, R. R. (1988). Avoidance and its relation to other defensive processes. In J. Belsky & T. Nezworski (Eds.), *Clinical implications of attachment* (pp. 300–323). Hillsdale, NJ: Erlbaum.

Cicchetti, D., Ganiban, J., & Barnett, D. (1991). Contributions from the study of high-risk populations to understanding the development of emotional regulation. In J. Garber & K. A. Dodge (Eds.), *The development of emotion regulation and dysregulation* (pp. 15–48). Cambridge, England: Cambridge University Press.

Columbo, J., & Fagan, J. (Eds.). (1990). *Individual differences in infancy.* Hillsdale, NJ: Lawrence Erlbaum.

Connell, J. P., & Thompson, R. (1986). Emotion and social interaction in the Strange Situation: Consistencies and asymmetric influences in the second year. *Child Development, 57,* 733–748.

Davidson, R. J. (1984). Affect, cognition and hemispheric specialization. In C. E. Izard, J. Kagan, & R. B. Zajonc (Eds.), *Emotions, cognition, and behavior* (pp. 320–361). New York: Cambridge University Press.

Davidson, R. J., & Cacioppo, J. T. (1992). New developments in the scientific study of emotion. *Psychological Science, 3,* 21–22.

Davidson, R. J., Chapman, J. P, Chapman, L. J., & Henriques, J. B. (1990). Asymmetrical brain electrical activity discriminates between psychometrically-matched verbal and spatial cognitive tasks. *Psychophysiology, 27,* 528–543.

Davidson, R. J., & Fox, N. A. (1982). Asymmetrical brain activity discriminate between positive versus negative affective stimuli in human infants. *Science, 218,* 1235–1237.

Davidson, R. J., & Fox, N. A. (1989). Frontal brain asymmetry predicts infants' response to maternal separation. *Journal of Abnormal Psychology, 98,* 127–131.

Dawson, G., Klinger, L. G., Panagiotides, H., Hill, D., & Spieker, S. (1992). Frontal lobe activity and affective behavior of infants of mothers with depressive symptoms. *Child Development, 63,* 725–737.

Dawson, G., Klinger, L. G., Panagiotides, H., Spieker, S., & Frey, K. (in press). Infants of mothers with depressive symptoms: Electroencephalographic and behavioral findings related to attachment status. *Development and Psychopathology.*

Ekman, P. (1984). Expression and the nature of emotion. In K. R. Scherer & P. Ekman (Eds.), *Approaches to emotion* (pp. 319–344). Hillsdale, NJ: Erlbaum.

Ekman, P., Levenson, R. W., & Friesen, W. V. (1983). Autonomic nervous system activity distinguishes between emotions, *Science, 221,* 1208–1210.

Emde, R., Gaensbauer, T., & Harmon, R. (1976). Emotional expression in infancy: A biobehavioral study. *Psychological Issues, 10,* 1–37.

Fogel, A. (1982). Affective dynamics in early infancy: Affective tolerance. In T. Field & A. Fogel (Eds.), *Emotion and early interaction* (pp. 25–58). Hillsdale, NJ: Erlbaum.

Fox, N. A. (1989). Psychophysiological correlates of emotional reactivity during the first year of life. *Developmental Psychology, 25,* 364–372.

Fox, N. A. (1991). If it's not left, it's right: Electroencephalogram asymmetry and the development of emotion. *American Psychologist, 46,* 863–872.

Fox, N. A., Bell, M. A., & Jones, N. A. (1992). Individual differences in response to stress and cerebral asymmetry. *Developmental Neuropsychology, 8,* 165–184.

Fox, N. A., & Calkins, S. D. (1993). Pathways to aggression and social withdrawal: Interactions among temperament, attachment, and regulation. In K. Rubin & J. Asendorpf (Eds.), *Social withdrawal, inhibition and shyness in children* (pp. 81–100). Hillsdale, NJ: Erlbaum.

Fox, N. A., & Davidson, R. J. (1984). Hemispheric substrates of affect: A developmental model. In N. A. Fox & R. J. Davidson (Eds.), *The psychobiology of affective development* (pp. 353–382). Hillsdale, NJ: Erlbaum.

Fox, N. A., & Davidson, R. J. (1986). Taste-elicited changes in facial signs of emotion and the asymmetry of brain electrical activity in human newborns. *Neuropsychologia, 24,* 417–422.

Fox, N. A., & Davidson, R. J. (1987). Electroencephalogram asymmetry in response to the approach of a stranger and maternal separation. *Developmental Psychology, 23,* 233–240.

Fox, N. A., & Davidson, R. J. (1988). Patterns of brain electrical activity during the expression of discrete emotions in ten-month-old infants. *Developmental Psychology, 24,* 230–236.

Fox, N. A., & Davidson, R. J. (1991). Hemispheric asymmetry and attachment behaviors: Developmental processes and individual differences in separation protest. In J. L. Gewirtz & W. M. Kurtines (Eds.), *Intersections with attachment* (pp 147–164). Hillsdale, NJ: Erlbaum.

Fox, N. A., & Gelles, M. (1983). Face-to-face interaction in term and pre-term infants: Facial expression and autonomic variability. *Infant Mental Health Journal, 5,* 192–205.

Fox, N. A., Kimmerly, N., & Schafer, W. (1991). Attachment to mother/attachment to father: A meta-analysis. *Child Development, 62,* 210–225.

Fox, N. A., & Stifter, C. A. (1989). Biological and behavioral differences in infant reactivity. In G. A. Kohnstamm, J. E. Bates, & M. K. Rothbart (Eds.), *Temperament in childhood* (pp. 169–181). New York: Wiley.

Frodi, A., & Thompson, R. A. (1985). Infants' affective responses in the Strange Situation: Effects of prematurity and quality of attachment. *Child Development, 56,* 1280–1291.

Garcia-Coll, C., Kagan, J., & Reznick, J. S. (1984). Behav-

ioral inhibition in young children. *Child Development, 55,* 1005–1019.

Goldsmith, H. H., & Alansky, J. A. (1987). Maternal and infant temperamental predictors of attachment: A meta-analytic review. *Journal of Counseling and Clinical Psychology, 35,* 805–816.

Graham, F. K., & Clifton, R. K. (1966). Heart rate changes as a component of the orienting response. *Psychological Bulletin, 65,* 305–320.

Gunnar, M. R. (1989). Studies of the human infant's adrenocortical response to potentially stressful events. In M. Lewis & J. Worobey (Eds.), *Infant stress and coping* (pp. 3–18). San Francisco: Jossey-Bass.

Gunnar, M. R. (1990). The psychobiology of infant temperament In J. Columbo & J. Fagan (Eds.), *Individual differences in infancy* (pp. 387–409) . Hillsdale, NJ: Erlbaum.

Gunnar, M. R., Manglesdorf, S., Larson, M., & Hertsgaard, L. (1989). Attachment, temperament and adrenocortical activity in infancy: A study of psychoendocrine regulation. *Developmental Psychology, 25,* 355–363.

Isabella, R., Ward, M. J., & Belsky, J. (1985). Convergence of multiple sources of information on infant individuality: Neonatal behavior, infant behavior, and temperament reports. *Infant Behavior and Development, 8,* 283–291.

Izard, C. E., Porges, S. W., Simons, R. F., Haynes, O. M., Hyde, C., Parisi, M., & Cohen, B. (1991). Infant cardiac activity: Developmental changes and relations with attachment. *Developmental Psychology, 27,* 432–439.

James, W. (1890). *Principles of psychology* (2 vols.). New York: Holt.

Kagan, J, Reznick, J. S., & Snidman, N. (1987). Physiology and psychology of behavioral inhibition. *Child Development, 58,* 1459–1473.

Kagan, J, & Snidman, N. (1991). Temperamental factors in human development. *American Psychologist, 46,* 856–862.

Kopp, C. (1982). Antecedents of self-regulation: A developmental perspective. *Developmental Psychology, 18,* 199–214.

Lacey, J., & Lacey, B. (1970). The relationship of resting autonomic acivity to motor impulsivity. *Research Publications of the Association for Research in Nervous and Mental Disease, 36,* 144–209.

Larson, M., Gunnar, M., & Hertsgaard, L. (1991). The effects of morning naps, car trips, and maternal separation on adrenocortical activity in human infants. *Child Development, 62,* 362–372.

Levenson, R. W., Ekman, P., & Friesen, W. (1990). Voluntary facial expression generates emotion-specific autonomic nervous system activity. *Psychophysiology, 27,* 363–384.

Lindsley, D. B., & Wicke, J. D. (1974). The electroencephalogram: Autonomous electrical activity in man and animals. In R. Thompson & M. N. Patterson (Eds.), *Bioelectric recording techniques* (pp. 465–479). New York: Academic Press.

Malone, S., Gunnar, M. R., & Fisch, R. (1985). Adrenocortical and behavioral responses to limb restraint in human neonates. *Developmental Psychobiology, 18,* 435–446.

Malatesta, C. Z., Culver, C., Tesman, J., & Shephard, B. (1989). The development of emotion expression during the first two years of life. *Monographs of the Society for Research in Child Development, 54* (1–2, Serial No. 219).

Matheny, A. P., Riese, M. L., & Wilson, R. S. (1985) Rudiments of infant temperament: newborn to 9 months. *Developmental Psychology, 31,* 486-494.

184 BIOLOGICAL AND NEUROPHYSIOLOGICAL APPROACHES

Matheny, A. P. & Wilson, R. S. (1981). Developmental tasks and rating scales for the laboratory assessment of infant temperament. *JSAS: Catalog of Selected Documents in Psychology, 11*, 81–82.

Miyake, K., Chen, S., & Campos, J. J. (1985). Infant temperament, mother's mode of interaction, and attachment in Japan: An interim report. In I. Bretherton & E. Waters (Eds.), Growing points in attachment theory and research. *Monographs of the Society for Research in Child Development, 50*(Serial No. 209), 276–291.

Porges, S. W. (1991). Vagal tone: An autonomic mediator of affect. In J. Garber & K. A. Dodge (Eds.), *The development of emotion regulation and dysregulation* (pp. 111–128). Cambridge, England: Cambridge University Press.

Porges, S. W., Doussard-Roosevelt, J. A., & Portales, A. L. (1992). *Difficultness and cardiac vagal tone: Stable indices of temperament in infants and toddlers.* Manuscript submitted for publication.

Porter, F., Porges, S. W., & Marshall, R. E. (1988). Newborn pain cries and vagal tone: Parallel changes in response to circumcision. *Child Development, 59*, 495–505.

Rothbart, M. K. (1981). Measurement of temperament in infancy. *Child Development, 52*, 569–578.

Rothbart, M. K. (1989). The early development of behavioral inhibition. In S. Reznick (Ed.), *Perspectives on behavioral inhibition* (pp. 139–158) Chicago: University of Chicago Press.

Rothbart, M. K., & Derryberry, D. (1981). Development of individual differences in temperament. In M. E. Lamb & A. L. Brown (Eds.), *Advances in developmental psychology* (Vol. 1, pp. 37–86). Hillsdale, NJ: Erlbaum.

Stifter, C. A., & Fox, N. A. (1990). Infant reactivity: Physiological correlates of newborn and 5-month temperament. *Developmental Psychology, 26*, 582–588.

Stifter, C. A., Fox, N. A., & Porges, S. W. (1989). Facial expressivity and vagal tone in five- and ten-month-old infants. *Infant Behavior and Development, 12*, 127–137.

Sroufe, L. A. (1985). Attachment classification from the perspective of infant–caregiver relationships and infant temperament. *Child Development, 56*, 1–14.

Stansbury, K., & Gunnar, M. R. (in press). The adrenocortical system and the study of emotion regulation: A multilevel perspective. In N. A. Fox (Ed.), Emotion regulation: Behavioral and biological considerations. *Monographs of the Society for Research in Child Development.*

Thomas, A., & Chess, S. (1977). *Temperament and development.* New York: Brunner/Mazel.

Thomas, A., Chess, S., Birch, H., Hertzig, M., & Korn, S. (1963). *Behavioral individuality in early childhood.* New York: New York University Press.

Thompson, R. A. (1990). Emotion and self-regulation. In R. A. Thompson (Ed.), *Nebraska Symposium on Motivation: Vol. 36. Socioemotional development* (pp. 367–467). Lincoln: University of Nebraska Press.

Tomarken, A. J., Davidson, R. J., & Henriques, J. B. (1990). Resting frontal brain asymmetry predicts affective responses to films. *Journal of Personality and Social Psychology, 59*, 791–801.

Tronick, E. Z. (1989). Emotions and emotional communication in infants. *American Psychologist, 44*, 112–119.

Vaughn, B., Lefever, G. B., Seifer, R., & Barglow, P. (1989). Attachment behavior, attachment security, and temperament during infancy. *Child Development, 60*, 728–737.

Vaughn, B., Stevenson-Hinde, J., Waters, E., Kotsaftis, A., Lefever, G., Shouldice, A., Trudel, M., & Belsky, J. (1992). Attachment security and temperament in infancy and early childhood: Some conceptual clarifications. *Developmental Psychology, 28*, 463–473.

Waters, E., Vaughn, B., & Egeland, B. (1980). Individual differences in infant–mother attachment relationships at age one: Antecedents in neonatal behavior in an urban, economically disadvantaged sample. *Child Development, 51*, 203–216.

Worobey, J. (1986). Convergence among assessments of temperament in the first month. *Child Development, 57*, 47–55.

13

Vocal Expression and Communication of Emotion

JEFFERY PITTAM
KLAUS R. SCHERER

GENERAL INTRODUCTION

Greek and Roman rhetoricians emphasized the central role of vocal communication in the expression of emotion, both felt and feigned, and highlighted the powerful effects of vocal affect expression on interpersonal interaction and social influence (e.g., Cicero's *De Oratore* or Quintilian's *Institutio Oratoria*; see also Scherer, in press-a). Darwin (1872/1965), in his classic work on the expression of emotion in animals and humans, attributed primary importance to the voice as a carrier of affective signals. More recent psychobiological theorizing has elaborated on the various functions of vocal affect communication with respect to major dimensions of intraorganismic states (activity or arousal, valence) and interorganismic relationships (dominance, nurturance), particularly with respect to the communication of reaction and behavioral intention or action tendencies (Cosmides, 1983; Frick, 1985; Scherer, 1981a, 1985). Consistent with this emphasis on vocalization as a powerful instrument in the communication of affect, empirical research in behavioral biology, psychology, and the speech and communication sciences suggests that a large number of different emotional and motivational states are reliably indexed and communicated by acoustic characteristics of the concurrent vocalizations. It is increasingly recognized that affectively toned vocalizations are jointly determined by an externalization of internal states ("push effects") and the requirements of species- or culture-specific normative models for affect signals or displays ("pull effects"; see Scherer, 1985, and Kappas, Hess, & Scherer, 1991, for more detailed discussions of this issue).

There is considerable evidence that emotion produces changes in respiration, phonation, and articulation, all of which determine the parameters of the acoustic signal. Furthermore, there is little doubt that listeners can infer affective state and speaker attitude from that signal. Yet, so far, there is little systematic knowledge about the details of the encoding process (with respect to both externalization of underlying psychophysiological states and realization of culturally determined display characteristics) or the decoding process (with respect to the precise acoustic cues listeners use in inferring speaker state or attitude). This chapter provides a concise overview of the existing literature in this area and points to future research perspectives.

PHONATORY/ACOUSTIC BASES OF EMOTION COMMUNICATION

Physical measures of human speech and vocal sounds are based on three perceptual dimensions: loudness, pitch, and time. The central research concerns are the selection and measurement of appropriate acoustic cues from these dimensions. This section presents a brief introduction to these dimensions and the associated parameters; (see Scherer, 1982, 1989, for a more detailed discussion of voice production and the associated acoustic parameters. Standke, 1992, provides an exhaustive compendium of these measures). One selection criterion that can be adopted is to use acoustic variables and measurement techniques that are relatively long-term, or suprasegmental, since affect is expected to last longer than individual speech segments. Adopting such a criterion does not mean that we must ignore short-term measures related to individual speech sounds, but it does mean that we will often need to aggregate segmental measures over longer time frames. Thus, formant frequencies of vowels can be averaged over many instances of the same vowel to give an overall frequency measure.

Acoustic Variables
Underlying Loudness

Although the simplest variable underlying loudness is amplitude, which is a measure of sound *pressure*, a more useful variable is that of sound *intensity*. Two sounds of the same amplitude but different frequency will require different amounts of energy to produce them, and the sound of higher frequency will sound louder. Given that the voice has energy at many different frequencies, intensity is the more appropriate acoustic variable to use. The unit used as the measure of intensity is the decibel (dB).

Intensity is one of the most difficult acoustic cues to interpret accurately, being dependent on several factors extraneous to the affective state of the speaker. These include distance and spatial orientation of the speaker to the listener or the microphone, and problems related to the calibration of the recorded signal. Despite these issues, both intensity and intensity variability have been shown to be useful acoustic variables in the measurement of affect (in cases where sound recording was properly controlled).

Acoustic Variables Underlying Pitch

One of the most frequently used vocal cues is "fundamental frequency" (F_0) of the vocal signal, measured in hertz (Hz). F_0 is essentially the rate at which the vocal folds vibrate. Basically, it varies continuously and often rapidly, but does so around a base level for each individual. Several types of variability associated with affect can be specified. At a micro level, we sometimes find perturbations in F_0 manifested as fast random fluctuations in period duration. This is known as "jitter." Other pertinent measures based on longer time frames are F_0 range and F_0 variance.

F_0 also has an important linguistic role in the intonation system of languages. As Pierrehumbert (1981) has shown, intonation is dependent not only on longer units such as the overall F_0 contour, but on local F_0 perturbations related to vowel quality. Although studies are scarce, there is some evidence that stress patterns and intonation may play an important role in the communication of affect (Cosmides, 1983; Frick, 1985; Uldall, 1960). Liberman (1978) has pointed to the slight variations in F_0 contour that provide the listener with information about subtle shifts in affect and attitude.

Acoustic Variables Underlying Time

The speech signal consists of temporal sequences of sound and silence. Both may be used in the communication of affect. At first glance, measures of temporal characteristics seem deceptively simple to effectuate. Different emotional states may be characterized by varying utterance length and speech rate, for example. What exactly should count as an utterance, however, is not always easy to determine. Duration of silence is also difficult to quantify. It seems necessary to distinguish between types of silence, such as, on the one hand, the micropauses that occur between words or phrases, and on the other, longer pauses reflecting hesitations. A simple index of silence, formed by the addition of all types of silent time periods, is likely to prove quite meaningless. Similarly, the measurement of speech and articulation rate (independent of pausing) depends on the definition of the segments or units of vocalization in time. In consequence, the determination of temporal characteristics of affective speech is far from trivial.

Acoustic Variables That
Combine Dimensions

In addition to these three individual dimensions, more complex variables can be obtained by combining two of the three dimensions.

Thus, Scherer and Oshinsky (1977) used variations in the "vocal envelope" in studying the attribution of emotional state. This is a measure that combines the amplitude and time dimensions. It refers to the amount of time taken for an auditory signal to reach maximum amplitude (the steepness of "attack"), and the time it takes for it to "decay" to zero amplitude.

Other variables combine frequency and amplitude. Depending on the morphology of the vocal tract and the articulations speakers make, certain frequencies will be dampened or amplified. Maxima of intensity produced by vocal tract resonances are referred to as "formants." Formants are the basis on which we recognize the different vowel sounds in any phonological system. Each vowel is articulated differently, in that it is characterized by a different vocal tract shape. Since the resonances of the vocal tract change as a function of modifications of its length and shape, each vowel is characterized by specific energy concentrations in the frequency domain—the "formants." Phoneticians usually describe each vowel acoustically by using the first three formants (i.e., those lowest in frequency). The higher formants do not vary so much with vowel quality; they seem to relate more to an individual speaker's habitual or transient vocal tract setting. In consequence, the higher formants are potential carriers of affective information. Unfortunately, they are also very difficult to locate and measure, because of their rather low energy.

One highly promising suprasegmental measure is the "long-term average spectrum" (LTAS). This is a composite measure of the distribution of energy in a given frequency range of a sample of continuous speech, averaged over a time period usually of between 30 and 60 seconds. The resulting spectrum is made up of a discrete number of equally spaced points (e.g., 256) across the frequency range. Thus, if a 30-second sample of speech is analyzed over the frequency range 0–5 kHz, an average of the amplitude across that time period is calculated for all 256 points of frequency equispaced in the 5-kHz range. It has been suggested (Li, Hughes, & House, 1969) that after about 30 seconds of continuous speech the LTAS will not change significantly, regardless of how much more speech is analyzed. If the spectrum does stabilize in this way, it is one of the most useful measures of medium-term vocal expression. LTAS should

be calculated separately for the voiced and unvoiced sections of speech, by separately averaging over voiced and unvoiced portions of the speech signal. The voiced LTAS carries more information about the nature of the phonation process, whereas the unvoiced LTAS is more useful to assess features of articulation.

When we hear a voice speaking, acoustic cues reflecting all three dimensions are processed by our auditory system. It is not always clear, however, just what the relationship is between the distal physical cues and the way they are perceived. Even the relationship between the physical variable of F_0 and its proximal representation of pitch is highly complex, because of the effect of a sound's spectral energy distribution and the nonlinearity of pitch perception. The relationship between many of the other acoustic cues and their perceptual counterparts, particularly the more complex measures such as the LTAS, has yet to be explored. It is not clear, for example, how the various parts of the LTAS relate to one another or how they might be used perceptually. The study of these interrelationships is complicated by the large number of values (256 or more) of the LTAS. In many studies the data points are reduced to a few mean values for specified frequency bands (e.g., third-octave bands). Others use advanced multivariate methods to deal with the large quantity of data points (e.g., Pittam et al., 1990, in a study relating affective dimensions to spectral contour). However, even if significant results are found, it is frequently difficult to know exactly what the differences mean (van Bezooijen, 1984; Standke, 1992).

It seems that no single acoustic variable can be successfully harnessed to show how humans communicate emotions vocally. As is indicated in the following section, we need to consider a range of variables.

ENCODING: EVIDENCE ON ACOUSTIC CORRELATES OF EMOTION

The term "encoding studies" is used here to refer to research attempting to measure the acoustic correlates of vocal affect expression elicited through a variety of procedures. Among the major elicitation procedures are portrayals by amateur or professional actors; the induction of real, albeit often rather weak, emotional states in the laboratory; and the surreptitious or unobtrusive recording of naturally occurring affect. Methodologically, encoding studies vary considerably in detail (Scherer, 1986; Wallbott & Scherer, 1986). Among the features that vary among studies are the number and type of speakers, the number and type of emotions studied, the type of stimulus materials or speech samples used, and the nature of the context and the eliciting conditions. Despite this variability, and the methodological differences and problems that result from it, there is quite a bit of convergence in the findings concerning the acoustic cues that correlate with specific affect states.This suggests that there are indeed robust vocal indicators of the emotions. Even where apparent contradictions occur, these may be attributable to different studies' measuring different types of emotion but using the same broad category label. "Anger," for example, seems to cover a range of types from irritation to rage (Scherer, 1986, 1989).

Since space does not allow us to refer to all the relevant work in the literature, we refer the reader to earlier reviews (Frick, 1985; Scherer, 1986), in which most pertinent studies up to those times are discussed and referenced. In the following overview, the number of studies (out of the 39 reviewed in Scherer, 1986) in which a particular effect was found is given in parentheses. Since most parameters were measured in only a few of these studies, the number given does not represent a proportion of the total of studies in which an effect was found (which would imply that the others did not find it). Rather, this number should be considered as an indication of the number of replications. Lack of replication or contradictory results are explicitly mentioned. Scherer and his associates have since conducted two large-scale studies on the acoustic correlates of actor portrayals of emotion, using digital voice analysis. Scherer, Banse, Wallbott, and Goldbeck (1991) report the acoustical correlates for five emotions as portrayed by four professional radio actors; Banse and Scherer (in prep.) present acoustic profiles for the vocal portrayals of 14 emotions as encoded by seven professional theatre actors. If one or both of those studies found the same effect as the studies reviewed in Scherer (1986), the number of studies given in parentheses is followed by an "S" (for successful replication in the Scherer et al. [1991] study) and/or a "B" (for successful replication in the Banse & Scherer

[in prep.] study), respectively. Again, lack of replication is specifically noted (as "not S" or "not B").

1. *Anger*. The frequency domain seems to be particularly important for the encoding of anger, although intensity has also been found to play a vital role. Anger seems to be generally characterized by an increase in mean F_0 (5, S, B) and mean intensity (6, S, B). Some studies, which may have been measuring "hot" anger (most studies do not explicitly define whether they studied "hot" or "cold" anger), also show increases in F_0 variability (2, B) and in the range of F_0 across the utterances encoded (4). Those studies in which these characteristics were not found may have been measuring cold anger. Further anger effects include increases in high-frequency energy (2, S, B) and downward-directed F_0 contours (2). The rate of articulation (4, S, B) usually goes up.

2. *Fear*. There is considerable agreement on the acoustic cues associated with fear. High arousal levels would be expected with this emotion, and this is supported by evidence showing increases in mean F_0 (11, S, B), in F_0 range (4), and in high-frequency energy (3, S, B). Rate of articulation is reported to be speeded up (4, S, B). An increase in mean F_0 has also been found for milder forms of the emotion, such as worry or anxiety (4, not B).

3. *Sadness*. As with fear, the findings converge across the studies that have included this emotion. Decreases in mean F_0 (8, S, B), F_0 range (7), and mean intensity (6, S, B) are usually found, as are downward-directed F_0 contours (5). There is evidence that high-frequency energy (3, S, B) and rate of articulation (5, B) decrease. Most studies reported in the literature seem to have studied the quieter, resigned forms of this emotion, rather than the more highly aroused forms such as desperation, where correlates reflecting arousal are found (Banse & Scherer, in prep.).

4. *Joy*. This is one of the few positive emotions studied, most often in the form of elation rather than more subdued forms, such as enjoyment or happiness. Consistent with the high arousal level that one might expect, we find a strong convergence of findings on increases in mean F_0 (9, S, B), F_0 range (6), F_0 variability (3, S, B), and mean intensity (7, S, B). There is some evidence for an increase in high-frequency energy (3, B, not S), and rate of articulation may also go up (2, S, not B).

5. *Disgust*. As noted by Scherer (1989), the results for disgust tend not to be consistent across the encoding studies. The few that have included this emotion vary in their induction procedures from measuring disgust (or possibly displeasure) at unpleasant films to actor simulation of the emotion. The studies using the former (3) found an increase in mean F_0, whereas those using the latter (2) found the reverse—a lowering of mean F_0. This inconsistency is echoed in the decoding literature.

It is evident even from this brief review that where there is considerable consistency in the findings, it is usually related to arousal. The cues characterizing this dimension appear to be the same regardless of the emotion under investigation, particularly in the case of high-arousal emotions (e.g., fear, anger, or elation). However, this should not be taken as evidence that discrete emotions are not differentiated by vocal cues. There are several reasons why there is as yet little evidence for vocal differentiation of individual emotion states on similar levels of arousal. For one, the number of acoustic cues employed in the majority of studies has been very limited indeed. Many other parameters need to be used, including the more complex measures derived from the spectrum. Also, there is a definite need to differentiate emotional states much more precisely (see Scherer, 1986, 1989). When both of these requirements are met (Banse & Scherer, in prep.), there is a sizable increase in the discriminative power of the acoustic parameters.

Even within a dimensional approach to emotion description, one should go beyond the arousal or activity dimension. Little effort has been made to systematically study the effect on the voice of other emotional dimensions, such as pleasantness and control (Wundt, 1874/1903; Mehrabian & Russell, 1974), even though specific theoretical predictions can be made (Scherer, 1986). Pittam et al. (1990) found evidence that these dimensions were reflected in different frequency bands of the LTAS (see also Pittam, 1987, and Pittam & Millar, 1989, for demonstrations that the LTAS may be used to measure affective dimensions and specific emotions, as well as psychiatric conditions). Other attitudinal dimensions, such as status, solidarity, or benevolence (Giles & Ryan, 1982; Brown, Strong, & Rencher, 1975) may also provide insights into the encoding of affect.

Almost all of the encoding studies to date have attempted to find acoustic correlates for unequivocally labeled affect states. Given the small number of labels for the so-called "basic" emotions that tend to be used, and given the fact that many of these are characterized by relatively high arousal levels, conditions may not be optimally suited to finding clear differentiation. Cosmides (1983) has conducted a study that does not limit encoders to portraying a specific emotion label, but requires them to encode responses in complex emotional situations taken from fiction. Her results show that despite the absence of clear labels, the specificity of the acoustic rendering of different affect situations is far stronger than individual differences in encoding. These results, taken together with the theoretical arguments referred to in the introduction and with the methodological shortcomings of the studies to date, suggest that the vocal expression of emotion may well be as differentiated as the facial expression of emotion. Indirect evidence for this suggestion can be obtained from studies on the number of different emotional states that can be correctly recognized on the basis of vocal portrayals.

DECODING: EVIDENCE FOR THE ABILITY TO CORRECTLY INFER EMOTIONAL STATES FROM THE VOICE

Whereas encoding studies have attempted to provide evidence for the kind of acoustic cues produced as a consequence of emotional portrayal, "decoding studies" are concerned with listeners' ability to correctly recognize or infer speaker affect state or attitude from voice samples, and with the cues that are utilized for this purpose.

Accuracy of Decoding Discrete Emotions

A review of the literature by Scherer (1981a) suggested an average accuracy across the studies reported at that time of about 60% (56% after correction for guessing), which is well above chance (approximately 12%). The studies used to compute this figure did not include those using filtered speech, foreign languages, or abnormal judge populations. The figure is impressive, given that some of the emotions decoded in the studies (such as love, pride, or jealousy) are not part of the set of basic or fundamental emotions.

As Scherer (1986) has pointed out, there is a discrepancy between such high accuracy and the apparent lack of differentiated acoustic cues for discrete emotions. One possibility for this may be the presence of methodological artifacts in the decoding studies. For example, judges are typically asked to choose from a small number of alternatives. Judges may be able to guess, or to form exclusion rules, either of which would result in high accuracy rates. It also seems likely that there is less confusion between emotions that differ in valence or in the arousal levels typically associated with them. When asked to recognize emotions with widely different positions in the underlying dimensional space, judges need to infer only approximate positions on the dimensions to make accurate discriminations. Although all this may provide reasons for the high accuracy, it does not explain it entirely.

More recent work (van Bezooijen, 1984) confirms the earlier estimate on vocal emotion recognition accuracy. In a study of disgust, surprise, shame, interest, joy, fear, sadness, and anger, a mean accuracy of 65% (56% if corrected for chance) was found. Another recent series of studies (reported in Scherer et al., 1991), using five emotions—fear, joy, sadness, anger, and disgust—and different types of listener groups, found a mean accuracy of 56% (45% if corrected for chance). There is good evidence, then, that the overall recognition of emotion from the voice lies at about 50% after correction for chance guessing and sampling error (see also Standke, 1992) —about four to five times what would be expected by chance.

It is instructive to look at the differences between the individual emotions that lie behind these overall accuracy figures. Although it is not possible to compare individual emotions for the large number of studies conducted before the Scherer (1981a) review (the numbers and types of emotions vary too much over studies), a subset of emotions from the van Bezooijen (1984) and Scherer et al. (1991) studies can be directly compared. The respective percentages are given in Table 13.1.

The degree of consistency is surprising, given that the studies were conducted in different countries with different languages (Holland vs. Germany), different types of actors

TABLE 13.1. Comparison of Accuracy Percentages for Individual Emotions in Two Empirical Studies

	Fear	Disgust	Joy	Sadness	Anger
van Bezooijen (1984)					
Raw %	58	49	72	67	74
Corr. %	54	43	69	63	71
Scherer et al. (1991)					
Raw %	52	28	59	72	68
Corr. %	40	09	48	65	60

Note. Corr., corrected for guessing (based on number of response alternatives).

(lay vs. professional), different linguistic material (standard sentences vs. meaningless utterances), different groups of judges (students vs. general population) and so forth. Sadness and anger are best recognized, followed by fear and joy. Disgust is most poorly recognized, with the accuracy barely above chance. It seems possible that sustained episodes of feeling disgust may be rare; rather, it may be communicated by short vocalizations or affect bursts (see Scherer, in press-b). In consequence, neither lay nor professional actors may have sufficient experience to encode disgust correctly in ongoing speech. Similarly, listeners may not have had the experience of hearing such extended disgust portrayals. We need to analyze the recognizability of different emotions separately, rather than that of a whole set. In addition, presentation of confusion matrices may provide a major contribution to the understanding of affect decoding from vocal stimuli, as they tend to show that errors are not randomly distributed and that the patterns of misidentification are quite instructive.

Cross-cultural studies are needed to elucidate the role of language and culture in this inference process. A brief review of the few studies in this area (Frick, 1985) indicates that in some of them at least, accuracy remains high, supporting the idea that the vocal expression of some emotions is universal. In general, a clear picture has not emerged because of the lack of pertinent studies. Scherer, Banse, and Wallbott (in prep.) have used 30 vocal emotion portrayals found to be recognized with better than chance accuracy in an earlier study (Scherer et al., 1991) for comparative judgment studies in different European countries.

Although there are some effects of country on the accuracy of recognition for some emotions, the results generally support the hypothesis of universality of vocal affect expression and inference (see Cosmides, 1983; Scherer, 1985).

Pertinent studies of decoding accuracy are still rare, yet evidence is accumulating that judges are generally able to infer emotions from voice samples with a degree of accuracy that largely exceeds chance. However, there are important differences with respect to the kind of emotion, the nature of the voice and speech sample, and the type of judgment population. Clearly, meta-analyses of decoding studies, including reviews of methodological and theoretical issues, are urgently needed.

Acoustic Cues Used in Inferring Emotional State

If listeners can identify emotions with better than chance accuracy, we need to understand which acoustic cues they perceive and utilize in the process of inference. Scherer (1982) has proposed a Brunswikian lens model aimed at guiding research in this area. There are several issues concerned with the utility of acoustic cues: pertinence (does the cue actually externalize an internal state?), transmission (can the cue be communicated efficiently by the respective modality?), perception (is the distal cue correctly represented proximally?), and attribution (is the state–cue relationship correctly used in inference?).

Since this approach requires measurement operations on at least four levels, there have been only a few attempts to use the complete paradigm. In general, three different approaches have been used:

1. Obtaining acoustic measures, expert judgments, or judgments by trained raters of the distal characteristics of vocal affect expressions, and correlating these with the attributions made by naive listeners asked to infer the underlying emotion or attitude of the speaker. A number of studies have provided information on which vocal characteristics seem to influence the judges' inference, with respect to both extent and direction of cue utilization (Scherer, Koivumaki, & Rosenthal, 1972; Wallbott & Scherer, 1986; van Bezooijen, 1984).

2. Partially masking verbal and vocal cues in speech to allow identification of the information carried by specific cues. Some of the earliest approaches used low-pass filtering to

eliminate the intelligibility of speech, in an effort to study the extent to which vocal cues carry affective information (Kramer, 1964; Starkweather, 1956). Since then, a large number of different techniques have been developed to eliminate, mask, or decompose vocal cues (see Scherer, Feldstein, Bond, & Rosenthal, 1985, for an overview). Using such masking techniques in a systematic research design allows one to determine the extent to which the respective cues are involved in the communication of emotional states (Scherer, Ladd, & Silverman, 1984).

3. Employing electronic sound synthesis procedures. The development of such procedures has provided researchers with techniques that allow systematic experimental manipulation of different acoustic cues in complex factorial designs. Lieberman and Michaels (1962) studied the effect of systematic variations of F_0 and envelope contour on emotion inference. Scherer and Oshinsky (1977) used the Moog synthesizer to study the effects of amplitude variation, pitch level, contour and variation, tempo, envelope, harmonic richness, tonality, and rhythm on emotion attributions to sentence-like sound sequences and musical melodies.

The development of copy synthesis (or resynthesis) techniques allows one to use natural voices and systematically change different cues via digital manipulation of the sound waves. Thus, F_0 level, contour variability and range, intensity, duration, and accent structure of real utterances have been systematically manipulated in factorial designs. The results showed many strong main effects (with a conspicuous lack of interactions) (Bergmann, Goldbeck, & Scherer, 1988; Goldbeck, Tolkmitt, & Scherer, 1988; Ladd, Silverman, Tolkmitt, Bergmann, & Scherer, 1985).

Since the results obtained in these three groups of studies vary considerably (although they are generally noncontradictory), it is not possible to summarize the patterns of utilization in emotion inference studies in the space available. Although all three of the methodological approaches reviewed above can provide important contributions to this area, the third option, using rule synthesis and copy synthesis, represents the state of the art and provides unprecedented possibilities for clean, systematic experimental manipulation.

It has also been shown, however, that the communication of emotion interacts acoustically with the communication of other types of information, such as linguistic meaning, situational context, and personality characteristics. A number of studies have attempted to quantify the nature of that interaction. Thus, Scherer et al. (1984) tested two models of the communication of affect: a covariance model and a configuration model. The former assumes that the communicative systems (e.g., affective and linguistic) are independent of each other. Linguistic meaning and information about speaker state information are expected to be encoded in quasi-parallel vocal channels. Relevant acoustic parameters covary with the strength or intensity of various speaker states. In the configuration model, on the other hand, both verbal and nonverbal information are assumed to be conveyed by different configurations of categorical variables. To date, the evidence in the area of affect communication suggests greater explanatory power for the covariance model (see Ladd et al., 1985; Goldbeck et al., 1988). The relevant cues for emotion recognition evoke continuous attribution on the part of listeners, indicating that they are distributed throughout the whole speech signal, rather than being encoded in categorical packages within the speech signal.

APPLIED RESEARCH ON THE VOCAL INDICATORS OF EMOTION

The studies reviewed above provide the basis for a large number of potential applications —in particular, nonobtrusive diagnosis of affective disturbance and the development of user-friendly computer voice communication systems.

Attempts to use the voice for the diagnosis of psychopathology date to the beginning of this century. Since there is much evidence that affective arousal strongly affects voice production, it is highly probable that affective disturbance will also affect the vocal organs and thus provide acoustic indicator cues in the speech signal. Voice analysis has often been used to diagnose a variety of psychopathological states, particularly depression and schizophrenia (see reviews in Scherer, 1987). Although some of the results are encouraging, major problems are posed by the absence of a clear nosological definition of the disturbance and a frequent lack of sufficient homogeneity in the patient

groups. More promising is the use of voice analysis for continuous monitoring of the development of a patient's affective state in the course of therapy (see Scherer & Zei, 1988; Ellgring & Scherer, submitted). One specific application is the use of voice analysis to track the effect of psychoactive drugs on the development of affect state over time (Helfrich, Standke, & Scherer, 1984).

Another major use of voice analysis is the detection of enduring affective arousal, particularly stress. Given the strong implication of F_0 as an indicator of arousal (see above), one would expect F_0 to rise under stress. This is in fact what has been found in quite a large number of studies (see reviews in Scherer, 1981b; Tolkmitt & Scherer, 1986). The susceptibility of the voice to respond to stress has led to attempts to use the voice as a lie detector. The manifold ethical, scientific, and practical problems, however, require great caution with this approach (Hollien, Geison, & Hicks, 1987).

Over the last decade or so, there has been increasing interest in digital speech processing and its subsequent application in areas such as telephony, speech prostheses, text-to-speech processing, automatic translation, aircraft and spacecraft communication systems, and many security and intelligence applications. Synthesized speech is now commonplace, and voice interaction with a computer will become the rule rather than the exception. Most work in the area is applied, dealing with the ongoing problems of quality (e.g., Pinto, Childers, & Lalwani, 1989), and has been concerned with the segmental (or, to a lesser extent, the suprasegmental) aspects of the speech signal. Speaker affect and attitude have received relatively little attention in this domain (with respect both to the encoding of emotions into the synthesized signal, and to the computer recognition of affectively toned speech). Researchers and practitioners in this area increasingly realize that computers must be able to decode affect while recognizing speech and to put emotional tone into synthesized messages, in order to guarantee greater acceptance of computer speech and to enhance reliability and precision of decoding. It remains to be determined exactly what a computer should need to know to decode the emotional state of a user providing voice input or to produce synthesized speech with appropriate affective tone.

CURRENT RESEARCH PROBLEMS AND PERSPECTIVES FOR THE FUTURE

Emotion Induction and Research Design

The central problem shared with most other approaches to the study of emotion is the difficulty, if not impossibility, of studying real and strong emotions *in situ* or producing such states in the laboratory. Consequently, researchers have either studied emotion portrayals by actors (see Wallbott & Scherer, 1986, and Scherer et al., 1991, for detailed reviews of this type of approach) or used ethically acceptable induction techniques, resulting in relatively weak affect states of the subjects studied. Both approaches entail advantages and disadvantages. Although actor-portrayed emotion states are generally clearly differentiated and of sufficient intensity, it is conceivable that the actors portray, at least in part, socially shared expression prototypes (but see Scherer, 1992, for a discussion of the relationship among stereotypes, prototypes, and archetypes in emotion expression). Induction approaches face the difficulty of ascertaining that the elicitation procedure has actually produced the same emotion in different subjects. This is both methodologically and practically difficult, especially if the intensity is low. Data stemming from these two approaches need to be compared systematically in an effort to determine how much of the acoustic variation in actor emotion portrayals is attributable to theatre conventions or cultural display rules, and how much of what researchers fail to find or replicate in induction studies can be attributed to lack of intensity or clear differentiation of states.

To begin with, the emotion categories studied should not be limited to the "basic" or "fundamental" 4–10 emotions, but should be more clearly differentiated (e.g., "cold" vs. "hot" anger; see Scherer, 1986, and Banse & Scherer, in prep.). In addition, given the prevalence of the activity and valence dimensions in all emotions, it might be useful regularly to obtain appropriate judgments on these dimensions, in order to calibrate the emotion labels used. In other words, if one could compare the respective locations in this two-dimensional space of emotion states studied by two different researchers, one might be able to get clues that could help to explain differences in findings and interpretations. Such a procedure might also contribute to a better understanding of the substratum—the link between physiological processes underlying arousal and valence (see Scherer, 1986) and the voice production process. Finally, recent studies have shown the great importance of gender differences and interindividual variation in emotion encoding in the voice. Much of what looks like lack of replication may well be attributable to inadequate sampling. The same is true of contextual cues (e.g., nature of the respective social situation, audience effects, task demands, etc.), which have all been shown to affect speech. Unless these variables are tightly controlled, it is difficult to expect replication of results.

One possible solution to the difficult task of bringing about greater comparability of studies in this area might consist of a move toward applied settings. In particular, the development of a knowledge base to help computers understand emotionally toned speech and to produce affectively toned synthetic utterances might provide the constraint needed to keep different researchers focused on a similar set of variables and procedures. The automatic inclusion of evaluation procedures to measure the performance of the system is likely to provide a set of comparable measures.

Accuracy in the Recognition of Vocally Expressed Emotion

Many of the studies in the literature are beset by methodological problems with respect to the definition and measurement of accuracy (see Banse & Scherer, in prep.; Frick, 1985; Gallois, in press). In particular, the correction of the accuracy percentages for chance guessing and for the uneven frequency of use of the decoding categories provided is rarely acknowledged. The interpretation of the data needs to be refined to include a more detailed analysis of the differences in accuracy between different emotion states and a consideration of the patterns of errors as shown in the confusion matrices. Furthermore, differences in the research design (e.g., with respect to providing baseline material on "normal" voice or not) need to be taken into account, since these may have strong effects on the nature of the inference process (see Kappas et al., 1991).

Rather than limiting research in this area to studying whether listeners can identify vocally expressed emotions, there should be increased emphasis on identifying which cues are used, to what extent, and in which way in inferring speaker emotion and attitude. Finally, it would be most useful to link the study of encoding and decoding in an integral research design, using the lens model (see above). Such an approach would not only provide an overall analysis of the complete vocal emotion expression and communication process; it would also greatly help to disentangle the different factors that determine accuracy of recognition or lack of it.

Multifactor Determination of Vocal Characteristics

Vocal cues studied in this area are determined by large numbers of biological, linguistic, and sociocultural factors. For example, intensity, F_0, and temporal factors have all been shown to serve linguistic functions, to index individual differences, and to communicate personality characteristics and speaker attitudes, in addition to expressing physiologically mediated affect states and their culturally based display norms. Linguistic data use the same three types of acoustic dimensions used for communicating affect, and as Docherty and Shockey (1988) point out, languages are characterized by much variation in all three. A major advance in research technology would consist of the development of methods allowing for linguistic and speaker-dependent information to be separated during speech analysis and merged during resynthesis.

Three factors likely to be essential in trying to untangle biological, linguistic, and sociocultural determinants are the universality of the expression of emotion; redundancy in the speech signal; and, paradoxically, the variability of the various features in the speech signal. It has been suggested that many aspects of the vocal expression of emotion are universal and even phylogenetically continuous (Cosmides, 1983; Scherer, 1981a, 1985), and although the masking studies referred to above have demonstrated the existence of a considerable amount of redundancy in the speech signal (see also Johnson, Emde, Scherer, & Klinnert, 1986), we do not yet understand how much redundancy there really is or what it signifies in terms of communicative function. Ellman and McClelland (1986) point out that

it is precisely the variability in the speech signal that permits listeners to understand speech in a variety of contexts and spoken by many speakers. Although this may seem paradoxical, it does indicate that the study of vocal emotion communication may well benefit from psycholinguistic work on speech production and perception (and vice versa). Most likely, the close interaction between linguistic and socioaffective information in speech can only be disentangled by close collaboration of the various disciplines concerned.

One of the most difficult matters will be to make progress on the issue of the joint effects of biological push (ex-*pression*) and sociocultural pull (display-driven) effects. Much would be gained if representatives of the more biologically oriented and the more culturally oriented research traditions would each give up their rather extreme claims that emotional expression (or, indeed, emotion) is either mostly biologically or mostly culturally determined. Obviously, both of these factors are operative (Scherer & Wallbott, submitted) and interact strongly. It seems obvious that we will not make any headway without conducting more cross-cultural and cross-species comparison studies.

Finally, it becomes increasingly obvious that we cannot afford to continue to study single modalities, treating facial, vocal, and postural expression as if they were completely separate domains. In many cases, the expression of both stable traits and transient affects, and the display of culturally appropriate signals of reactions and action tendencies (see Frijda, 1986), are encoded in several modalities—vocal, facial, gestural, and postural. Since each expression or signaling modality is differentially affected by the autonomic and somatic nervous systems and is differentially suited for certain messages or certain signal transmission characteristics, we need to study affect expression and communication in the context of a multimodal approach (see Scherer, in press-b).

One of the most urgent needs for change in research strategy in this area, however, concerns the theoretical basis for studies on emotion encoding and decoding with respect to vocalization. Given the large number of factors that affect voice production, a cumulation of empirical studies without clear guidance by theoretically based hypotheses is unlikely to advance our understanding of the phenomenon. Scherer (1986) has suggested an exten-

TABLE 13.2. Predictions of Acoustic Correlates of Major Emotional States

Acoustic parameters	Emotional states											
	ENJ/ HAP	ELA/ JOY	DISP/ DISG	CON/ SCO	SAD/ DEJ	GRI/ DES	ANX/ WOR	FEAR/ TER	IRR/ COA	RAGE/ HOA	BOR/ IND	SHA/ GUI
F_0												
Perturbation	<=	>			>	>		>		>		
Mean	<	>	>	><	<>	>	>	>>	><	><	<	>
Range	<=	>			<	>		>>	<	>>		
Variability	<	>			<	>		>>	<	>>		
Contour	<	>			<	>	>	>>	<	=		>
Shift regularity	=	<						<		<	>	
F_1 mean	<	<	>	>	>	>	>	>	>	>	>	>
F_2 mean			<	<	<	<	<	<	<	<	<	<
F_1 bandwidth	>	><	<<	<	<>	<<	<	<<	<<	<<	<	<
Formant precision		>	>	>	<	>	>	>	>	>		>
Intensity												
Mean	<	>	>	>>	<<	>		>	>	>>	<>	
Range	<=	>			<			>	>	>		
Variability	<	>			<			>		>		
Frequency range	>	>	>	>>	>	>>		>>	>	>	>	
High-frequency energy	<	<>	>	>	><	>>	>	>>	>>	>>	><	>
Spectral noise					>							
Speech rate	<	>			<	>		>>		>		
Transition time	>	<			>	<		<		<		

Note. This table is based on the original predictions published as Table 6 in Scherer (1986, p. 158; adapted by permission). ANX/ WOR, anxiety/worry; BOR/IND, boredom/indifference; CON/SCO, contempt/scorn; DISP/DISG, displeasure/disgust; ELA/JOY, elation/joy; ENJ/HAP, enjoyment/happiness; FEAR/TER, fear/terror; GRI/DES, grief/desperation; IRR/COA, irritation/cold anger; RAGE/HOA, rage/hot anger; SAD/DEJ, sadness/dejection; SHA/GUI, shame/guilt; F_0, fundamental frequency; F_1, first formant; F_2, second formant; >, increase; <, decrease. Double symbols indicate increased predicted strength of the change; two symbols pointing in opposite directions refer to cases in which antecedent voice types exert opposing influences. Symbols printed in boldface indicate predictions that have been supported by empirical research.

sive set of theoretical predictions, based on both emotion theory and recent work on voice production. Many of these predictions have been supported in two recent studies using actor portrayals of emotions (Banse & Scherer, in prep.; Scherer et al., 1991) (see Table 13.2). Further work in this direction, using more naturalistic emotional expressions and the integration of hypotheses concerning sociocultural patterning of the expressions, would greatly strengthen the case.

CONCLUSION

The important role of vocal expression in the communication of emotion has been recognized since antiquity. There is good reason, based on psychobiological principles, to assume phylogenetic continuity and universality for the vocal expression of emotional states and the corresponding inference on the part of listeners. Empirical research has been slow to

accumulate the evidence, particularly with respect to the detailed description of the vocal production mechanisms involved and the resulting changes in the acoustic parameters of vocalization. However, the remarkable technological advances in the area of digital signal analysis have paved the way for research directed toward replication and extension of the promising leads reported in this chapter. There can be little doubt that human listeners are well equipped to accurately decode a relatively large number of highly differentiated emotional states on the basis of vocalization alone. What remains to be done is to link encoding and decoding in an effort at comprehensive description of the expression and communication process, and to disentangle the complex interaction between biological and cultural factors in vocal emotion signaling.

Acknowledgment. We gratefully acknowledge contributions by Rainer Banse and Ursula Scherer.

REFERENCES

Banse, R., & Scherer, K. R. (in prep.). *Vocal profiles of affect: Evidence for 14 emotions.* Manuscript in preparation, University of Geneva.

Bergmann, G., Goldbeck, T., & Scherer, K. R. (1988). Emotionale Eindruckswirkung von prosodischen Sprechmerkmalen. *Zeitschrift für Experimentelle und Angewandte Psychologie, 35,* 167–200.

Brown, B. L., Strong, W. J., & Rencher, A. C. (1975). Acoustic determinants of perceptions of personality from speech. *International Journal of the Sociology of Language, 6,* 11–32.

Cosmides, L. (1983). Invariances in the acoustic expression of emotion during speech. *Journal of Experimental Psychology: Human Perception and Performance, 9,* 864–881.

Darwin, C. (1965). *The expression of the emotions in man and animals.* Chicago: University of Chicago Press. (Original work published 1872)

Docherty, G., & Shockey, L. (1988). Speech synthesis. In M. Jack & J. Laver (Eds.), *Aspects of speech technology* (pp. 144–183). Edinburgh: Edinburgh University Press.

Ellgring, J. H., & Scherer, K. R. (submitted). *Vocal correlates of depression.* Manuscript submitted for publication.

Ellman, J. L., & McClelland, J. L. (1986). Exploiting lawful variability in the speechwave. In J. S. Perkell & D. H. Klatt (Eds.), *Invariance and variability in speech processes* (pp. 360–380). Hillsdale, NJ: Erlbaum.

Frick, R. W. (1985). Communicating emotion: The role of prosodic features. *Psychological Bulletin, 93,* 412–429.

Frijda, N. (1986). *The emotions.* Cambridge, England: Cambridge University Press.

Gallois, C. (1993). The language and communication of emotion. *American Behavioral Scientist, 36,* 309–338.

Giles, H., & Ryan, E. B. (1982). Prolegomena for developing a social psychological theory of language attitudes. In E. B. Ryan & H. Giles (Eds.), *Attitudes toward language variation: Social and applied contexts* (pp. 208–223). London: Arnold.

Goldbeck, T., Tolkmitt, F., & Scherer, K. R. (1988). Experimental studies on vocal communication. In K. R. Scherer (Ed.), *Facets of emotion* (pp. 119–138). Hillsdale, NJ: Erlbaum.

Helfrich, H., Standke, R., & Scherer, K. R. (1984). Vocal indicators of psychoactive drug effects. *Speech Communication, 3,* 245–252.

Hollien, H., Geison, L., & Hicks, J. W., Jr. (1987). Vocal stress evaluators and lie detection. *Journal of Forensic Sciences, 32,* 405–418.

Johnson, W. F., Emde, R. N., Scherer, K. R., & Klinnert, M. D. (1986). Recognition of emotion from vocal cues. *Archives of General Psychiatry, 43,* 280–283.

Kappas, A., Hess, U., & Scherer, K. R. (1991). Voice and emotion. In R. S. Feldman & B. Rimé (Eds.), *Fundamentals of nonverbal behavior* (pp. 200–238). Cambridge, England: Cambridge University Press.

Kramer, E. (1964). Elimination of verbal cues in judgments of emotion from voice. *Journal of Abnormal and Social Psychology, 68,* 390–396.

Ladd, D. R., Silverman, K., Tolkmitt, F., Bergmann, G., & Scherer, K. R. (1985). Evidence for the independent function of intonation contour type, voice quality, and F_0 range in signalling speaker affect. *Journal of the Acoustical Society of America, 78,* 435–444.

Li, K.-P., Hughes, G. W., & House, A. S. (1969). Correlation characteristics and dimensionality of speech spectra. *Journal of the Acoustical Society of America, 46,* 1019–1025.

Liberman, M. V. (1978). *The intonational system of English.* Bloomington: Indiana University Linguistics Club.

Lieberman, P., & Michaels, S. B. (1962). Some aspects of fundamental frequency and envelope amplitude as related to the emotional content of speech. *Journal of the Acoustical Society of America, 34,* 922–927.

Mehrabian, A., & Russell, J. A. (1974). *An approach to environmental psychology.* Cambridge, MA: MIT Press.

Pierrehumbert, J. (1981). Synthesizing intonation. *Journal of the Acoustical Society of America, 70,* 985–995.

Pinto, N. B., Childers, D. G., & Lalwani, A. J. (1989). Formant speech synthesis: Improving production quality. *IEEE Transactions in Acoustics: Speech Signal Processing, 37*(12), 1870–1887.

Pittam, J. (1987) The long-term spectral measurement of voice quality as a social and personality marker: A review. *Language and Speech, 30,* 1–12.

Pittam, J., Gallois, C., & Callan, V. J. (1990). The long-term spectrum and perceived emotion. *Speech Communication, 9,* 177–187.

Pittam, J., & Millar, J. B. (1989). *Long-term spectrum of the acoustics of voice: An annotated and classified research bibliography.* Bloomington: Indiana University Linguistics Club.

Scherer, K. R. (1981a). Speech and emotional states. In J. K. Darby (Ed.), *Speech evaluation in psychiatry* (pp. 189–220). New York: Grune & Stratton.

Scherer, K. R. (1981b). Vocal indicators of stress. In J. Darby (Ed.), *Speech evaluation in psychiatry* (pp. 171–187). New York: Grune & Stratton.

Scherer, K. R. (1982). Methods of research on vocal communication: Paradigms and parameters. In K. R. Scherer & P. Ekman (Eds.), *Handbook of methods in nonverbal behavior research,* (pp. 136–198). Cambridge, England: Cambridge University Press.

Scherer, K. R. (1985). Vocal affect signalling: A comparative approach. In J. S. Rosenblatt, C. Beer, M. C. Busnel, & P. J. B. Slater (Eds.) *Advances in the study of behavior* (Vol. 15, pp. 189–244). New York: Academic Press.

Scherer, K. R. (1986). Vocal affect expression: A review and a model for future research. *Psychological Bulletin, 99,* 143–165.

Scherer, K. R. (1987). Vocal assessment of affective disorders. In J. D. Maser (Ed.), *Depression and expressive behavior* (pp. 57–82). Hillsdale, NJ: Erlbaum.

Scherer, K. R. (1989). Vocal correlates of emotional arousal and affective disturbance. In H. Wagner & A. Manstead (Eds.) *Handbook of psychophysiology* (pp. 165–197). Chichester, England: Wiley.

Scherer, K. R. (1992). On social representations of emotional experience: Stereotypes, prototypes, or archetypes? In M. von Cranach, W. Doise, & G. Mugny (Eds.), *Social representations and the social bases of knowledge* (pp. 30–36). Bern: Huber.

Scherer, K. R. (in press-a). Interpersonal expectations, social influence, and emotion transfer. In P. D. Blanck (Ed.), *Interpersonal expectations: Theory, research, and application.* Cambridge, England: Cambridge University Press.

Scherer, K. R. (in press-b). Affect bursts. In S. H. M. van Goozen, N. E. de Poll, & J. A. Sergeant (Eds.), *Emotions: Essays on emotion theory.* Hillsdale, NJ: Erlbaum.

Scherer, K. R., Banse, R., & Wallbott, H. G. (in prep.). *Cross-cultural comparison of recognition accuracy for vocal emotion expression*. Manuscript in preparation, University of Geneva.

Scherer, K. R., Banse, R., Wallbott, H. G., & Goldbeck, T. (1991). Vocal cues in emotion encoding and decoding. *Motivation and Emotion, 15*, 123–148.

Scherer, K. R., Feldstein, S., Bond, R. N., & Rosenthal, R. (1985). Vocal cues to deception: A comparative channel approach. *Journal of Psycholinguistic Research, 14*, 409–425.

Scherer, K. R., Koivumaki, J., & Rosenthal, R. (1972). Minimal cues in the vocal communication of affect: Judging emotions from content-masked speech. *Journal of Psycholinguistic Research, 1*, 269–285.

Scherer, K. R., Ladd, D. R., & Silverman, K. E. A. (1984). Vocal cues to speaker affect: Testing two models. *Journal of the Acoustical Society of America, 76*, 1346–1356.

Scherer, K. R., & Oshinsky, J. S. (1977). Cue utilization in emotion attribution from auditory stimuli. *Motivation and Emotion, 1*, 331–346.

Scherer, K. R., & Wallbott, H. G. (submitted). *Evidence for universality and cultural variation of differential emotion response patterning*. Manuscript submitted for publication.

Scherer, K. R., & Zei, B. (1988). Vocal indicators of affective disorders. *Journal of Psychotherapy and Psychosomatics, 49*, 179–186.

Standke, R. (1992). *Methoden der digitalen Sprachverarbeitung in der vokalen Kommunikationsforschung*. Unpublished doctoral dissertation, University of Giessen, Germany.

Starkweather, J. A. (1956). Content-free speech as a source of information about the speaker. *Journal of Personality and Social Psychology, 35*, 345–350.

Tolkmitt, F. & Scherer, K. R. (1986). Effects of experimentally induced stress on vocal parameters. *Journal of Experimental Psychology: Human Perception and Performance, 12*, 302–313.

Uldall, E. (1960). Attitudinal meanings conveyed by intonation contours. *Language and Speech, 3*, 223–234.

van Bezooijen, R. (1984). *The characteristics and recognizability of vocal expression of emotions*. Dordrecht, The Netherlands: Foris.

Wallbott, H. G., & Scherer, K. R. (1986). Cues and channels in emotion recognition. *Journal of Personality and Social Psychology, 51*, 690–699.

Wundt, W. (1903). *Grundzüge der physiologischen Psychologie*. Leipzig: Engelmann. (Original work published 1874)

14

Facial Expression

LINDA A. CAMRAS
ELIZABETH A. HOLLAND
MARY JILL PATTERSON

Despite the early work of Darwin (1872/ 1965), considered seminal from a contemporary vantage point, for most of the 20th century psychologists largely rejected the notion that emotions were expressed by means of a set of universal facial expressions (see Ekman, 1982, for a review). Several flawed but extremely influential studies of adults and infants had failed to demonstrate distinctive facial responses in situations designed to elicit different emotions. In addition, anthropologists, in their efforts to promote the notion of cultural relativity, were arguing that the same expression might have radically different meanings in different cultures.

Nevertheless, a minority of researchers, most notably Silvan Tomkins (1962, 1963), remained unconvinced of this wholly relativistic view. During the late 1960s, utilizing Tomkins's theoretical descriptions to guide their choice of facial stimuli, a small group of researchers (Ekman, 1972; Izard, 1971) embarked on a series of expression-recognizing and expression-posing studies in both Western and non-Western cultures (e.g., Japan). Ekman (1972) and his colleagues subsequently extended this work to include preliterate cultures in New Guinea whose members were unfamiliar with Western expressive behavior. These studies produced impressive findings in support of both Tomkins's theory and Darwin's earlier claims, and ushered in a new era of theory and research on emotion and emotional facial expressions.

Regarding emotion theory, both Izard (1977) and Ekman (1972) initially followed Tomkins in proposing that universal recognition of facial expression could only be explained by assuming an underlying innate emotion "program" for each of a number of primary emotions. These affect programs were thought to include automatic neural "messages" to the facial musculature that—*sans* "override" by the voluntary control system in accord with display rules (Ekman & Friesen, 1969)—produce the emotional facial expression. Herein we refer to this proposal as the "efference hypothesis." A second influential principle of Tomkins's theory was the "facial feedback hypothesis." According to this hypothesis, not only does emotion produce facial expression, but facial expression importantly influences emotion.

More recently, Ekman (1989, 1992) and Izard (1991) have suggested that emotions may not always be accompnaied by facial expressions. Thus an empirically based reconsideration of the relationship between emotion and facial expression would be appropriate. Toward this end, in the present chapter, we consider recent research on facial expression in light of the theoretical model and hypotheses described above. We focus on studies of expression production involving adult subjects, referring the reader elsewhere for reviews of the literature on expression recognition (Oster, Daily, & Goldenthal, 1989; Gross & Ballif, 1991; Ekman, 1982) and infant expressive behavior (Camras, Malatesta, & Izard, 1991). After describing new developments in facial coding systems, we briefly examine current knowledge about the neurophysiological basis of facial expression and the issue of emotion lateralization. Subsequently, we review studies relevant to the efference hypothesis and consider several alternative models of facial expression that have recently been proposed. Lastly, we review studies relevant to the facial feedback hypothesis.

FACIAL CODING SYSTEMS

Early studies of emotional expression relied primarily on descriptions provided by Darwin and Tomkins, experimenters' judgments of the emotional content of facial stimuli, and/or ratings of naive observers. More recently, formal coding systems have been developed for measuring facial behavior and identifying emotional expressions. The most comprehensive is Ekman and Friesen's (1978) anatomically based Facial Action Coding System (FACS), which describes facial behavior in terms of its constituent muscle actions. A corollary system, the Emotion Facial Action Coding System (EMFACS; Friesen & Ekman, 1984), specifies a subset of emotion-related facial configurations and is in a continual process of empirically based refinement. Izard and his colleagues have also developed two coding systems: the Maximally Discriminative Facial Movement Coding System (MAX; Izard, 1979) and AFFEX (Izard, Dougherty, & Hembree, 1983). Ekman's and Izard's systems are not completely identical, either in the emotions they include or in the expressions they identify for some emotions. Nevertheless, these systems—especially the comprehensive FACS—have provided us with important tools for the objective description of facial behavior and the study of its relation to emotion.

NEUROPHYSIOLOGY OF EMOTIONAL FACIAL EXPRESSION

The facial musculature is innervated by cranial nerve VII (the facial nerve), consisting of a dual collection of cell bodies (nuclei) in the brainstem, with each nucleus sending its axons to one side of the face. Multiple pathways from both the cortex and subcortical areas lead to the facial nuclei. Although the neurophysiological basis of voluntary facial movement has been well described (Rinn, 1991), the cortical and subcortical connections mediating spontaneous emotional facial expressions are not well understood.

According to LeDoux (1989), emotional significance is assigned to sensory and cortical input by the amygdala, while the hypothalamus is responsible for organized emotional behavior and expression. However, there are few data regarding distinctions among emotions and their corresponding facial expressions. Primarily on the basis of animal research, Panksepp (1986) has described distinct neural subsystems for fear, rage, panic (separation distress), anticipation, and play. But these do not entirely correspond to the basic emotions usually identified by human emotion theorists. In human studies, the amygdala has sometimes been associated with the experience and expression of anger (see review in Buck, 1988), whereas septal stimulation has been reported to produce feelings of pleasure, often with sexual overtones. However, subjects' expressive responses have not been carefully described and may not include the prototypic expressions described in current facial coding systems. Furthermore, distinct subsystems underlying the expression of other emotions, such as sadness, fear, and disgust, have not been identified.

EMOTION LATERALIZATION

In recent years, researchers interested in the neurological basis of emotion have attempted to utilize facial expression to gain insight into the issue of emotion lateralization. Three hypotheses have been proposed in the lateralization literature. According to the right-hemisphere hypothesis, the right hemisphere is the seat of emotion (Borod, Koff, & White, 1983; Campbell, 1978; Sackheim, Gur, & Saucy, 1978; Moscovitch & Olds, 1982; Ley & Bryden, 1982). According to the valence hypothesis, positive emotions are mediated by the left hemisphere, whereas the right hemisphere mediates negative emotions (Dimond, Farrington, & Johnson, 1976; Reuter-Lorenz & Davidson, 1981; Schwartz, Ahern, & Brown, 1979; Tucker, Stenslie, Roth, & Shearer, 1981). According to the approach–withdrawal hypothesis, emotional responses associated with approach behaviors are mediated by the left hemisphere, whereas those associated with withdrawal are mediated by the right hemisphere (Kinsbourne, 1978; see Davidson, 1984, for a review). These three proposals have been investigated primarily in studies of expression asymmetries and hemispheric activation.

Studies of expression asymmetries have argued that lateralized mediation of an emotion will be reflected in more intense expression on the contralateral side of the face. Investigations have utilized both observer judgments and electromyographic (EMG) recording to measure spontaneous and/or posed expressions. Observable facial asymmetries have been assessed by rating or measuring videotapes or still photographs of spontaneous and posed expressions, which are often recorded unobtrusively during conversations. One problem with these studies is that observed asymmetries may reflect a number of factors besides asymmetry in muscle activation (Hager, 1982). Perhaps because of these confounding factors, results of these studies have been inconsistent.

For spontaneous expressions, some investigations have found no asymmetry for most subjects (Ekman, Hager, & Friesen, 1981; Lynn & Lynn, 1938, 1943), whereas others report a preponderance of left-sided asymmetries (Borod et al., 1983; Buck & Duffy, 1980), sometimes modified by sex effects (Borod et al., 1983) and handedness effects (Chaurasia & Goswagmi, 1975; Moscovitch & Olds, 1982). Although their relevance to genuine emotion is questionable, many studies have examined posed (as opposed to spontaneous) emotional expressions. Some studies find no asymmetries (Knox, cited in Borod & Koff, 1984), while others find left-sided asymmetries (Campbell, 1978; Heller & Levy, 1981; Strauss, Moscovitch, & Olds, 1980; Borod, Kent, Koff, Martin, & Alpert, 1988). In support of the valence hypothesis, some investigations find negative expressions to be significantly left-sided (Borod & Caron, 1980; Sackheim & Gur, 1978), whereas positive expressions appear to be less lateralized (Borod & Caron, 1980). Sex differences have also been found (Borod et al., 1983).

Asymmetries in facial expression are measured more directly in studies using EMG measurement techniques. These have generally provided results consistent with both the approach–withdrawal and the valence hypotheses. That is, lateralized responses are found for the zygomatic muscles, with positive emo-

tion conditions (presumably also associated with approach) eliciting greater left-muscle activity than right-muscle activity (Schwartz et al., 1979; Schwartz, Fair, Salt, Mandel, & Klerman, 1976b; Sirota & Schwartz, 1982).

Hemispheric activation (i.e., electroencephalographic or EEG) studies assess differences in cerebral activation during the subjective experience and/or expression of emotion. The results of most EEG studies are also consistent with both the approach–withdrawal and valence hypotheses. Both adults and infants show greater left frontal activation during positive affect episodes (presumably associated with approach), whereas greater right frontal activation is associated with avoidance-related negative affect (Davidson, Schwartz, Saron, Bennett, & Goleman, 1979; Tucker et al., 1981; Fox & Davidson, 1988). However, consistent only with the approach–withdrawal hypothesis, Suberi and McKeever (1977) found angry as well as happy expressions to be associated with increased left-hemisphere activation. These findings were not completely replicated by Davidson, Ekman, Saron, Senulis, and Friesen (1990). Consequently, a modified version of the hypothesis was therein proposed.

In summary, evidence from studies employing minimally biased measurement techniques (EEG and EMG) is generally consistent with both the valence hypothesis and the approach–avoidance hypothesis. Further research is necessary to discriminate between them.

THE EFFERENCE HYPOTHESIS

As described earlier, the efference hypothesis holds that affect programs for discrete emotions produce efference to the facial musculature, generating distinct expressions for each emotion. Many data relevant to the efference hypothesis have been obtained in studies that have examined the relationship between spontaneously produced facial expression and other presumed indices of emotion (e.g., appropriate eliciting stimuli, reports of subjective experience, and autonomic nervous system [ANS] responses). In these studies, three basic methods for measuring facial expression have been employed: observer judgments of emotion, EMG recording, and description of observable facial activity (objective coding).

Because objective coding systems are comparatively recent developments, many investigations have relied on the judgments of observers in identifying emotional facial expressions. Most of these have employed the "encoder–decoder" (also called the "sender–receiver") paradigm. In this procedure, subjects' facial responses to presumably emotion-eliciting stimulus situations are photographed or recorded on videotape. Naive raters (i.e., decoders or receivers) view these responses and make judgments regarding the identity or valence of the stimulus condition or the responders' (i.e., encoders' or senders') emotional reaction. Measures of encoders' subjective experiences and/or their ANS responses may also be obtained.

Consistent with the efference hypothesis, several studies have demonstrated that decoders can accurately identify the category of slide being viewed by encoders (Buck, Savin, Miller, & Caul, 1972); can rate the pleasantness of the encoders' response to the slides (Buck et al., 1972; Buck, Miller, & Caul, 1974; Winton, Putnam, & Krauss, 1984; Zuckerman, Klorman, Larrance, & Spiegel, 1981); can discriminate trials in which the encoders experience shock versus no shock (Lanzetta & Kleck, 1970); can rate the intensity of the shock being experienced by the encoders (Lanzetta, Cartwright-Smith, & Kleck, 1976); and can judge the encoders' evaluation of an odor (Kraut, 1982). However, when discrimination among discrete negative emotions has been required, decoder accuracy has been poor (Wagner, MacDonald, & Manstead, 1986; Motley & Camden, 1988).

Also relevant to the efference hypothesis are encoder–decoder studies examining the relationship between facial expressivity and ANS response. With few exceptions (Zuckerman et al., 1981; Winton et al., 1984), this research has produced fairly consistent findings showing a negative relationship between expressivity and ANS responding across subjects (Jones, 1935; Buck et al., 1972, 1974; Lanzetta & Kleck, 1970). More expressive subjects (as indexed by decoders' accuracy in judging their expressions) tend to produce less extreme ANS responses than do less expressive subjects. This relationship has also been found in the few studies utilizing EMG or direct observation to measure facial expressivity (Vaughan & Lanzetta, 1980; Notarius & Levenson, 1979). In contrast, studies that have involved within-subject comparisons across emotion episodes (Buck et al., 1974; Lanzetta et al., 1976;

Zuckerman, et al., 1981) have found positive relationships between intensity of facial response and ANS reactions. Taken together, these findings have been interpreted as demonstrating both individual differences in emotion response styles and support for the efference hypothesis (Adelman & Zajonc, 1989). According to this view, subjects may be classified as externalizers or internalizers, depending upon the relative intensity of their ANS versus facial responses. However, within each individual, increased emotion produces increased facial efference. Whether this increased efference produces qualitatively distinct discrete emotional expressions has not been determined.

EMG studies of facial expression were originally undertaken to provide a means for measuring emotion when no observable facial expression is produced. In most EMG studies, subjects are asked to imagine themselves in emotion-eliciting situations or are presented with emotion-eliciting slides or videotapes while EMG recordings are made by surface electrodes placed on several sites on the face. These studies have consistently shown that positive versus negative emotion conditions can be differentiated in terms of the accompanying EMG responses. The strongest findings involve the increase of zygomatic muscle activity in pleasant or happy stimulus conditions and the increase of corrugator muscle activity in sad, angry, fearful, or generally unpleasant stimulus conditions (Schwartz, Fair, Salt, Mandel, & Klerman, 1976a, 1976b; Schwartz, Brown, & Ahern, 1980; Sirota, Schwartz, & Kristeller, 1987; Dimberg, 1986, 1988; Fridlund, Schwartz, & Fowler, 1984; Greenwald, Cook, & Lang, 1989; McHugo, Lanzetta, & Bush, 1991; Teasdale & Bancroft, 1977; Cacioppo, Petty, Losch, & Kim, 1986; Cacioppo, Bush, & Tassinary, 1992).

Regarding differentiation among negative emotions, the findings have been inconsistent (e.g., compare Schwartz et al., 1976a, 1976b, 1980; Fridlund et al., 1984; Smith, McHugo, & Lanzetta, 1986; Cacioppo, Martzke, Petty, & Tassinary, 1988). In part, consistent differences among negative emotions may not have been found because of the technical problem of electrode "cross-talk"; minor differences across studies in electrode placement; and/or limitations in the measurement (Tassinary & Cacioppo, 1992) or data analysis techniques (Fridlund & Izard, 1983) employed. However, beyond this, several findings have suggested that some EMG responses may not be minia-ture versions of prototypic emotional expres-sions (Tassinary & Cacioppo, 1992). For example, Schwartz et al., (1980) detected corrugator muscle activity but not frontalis muscle activity in association with fear, al-though both muscles are involved in the prototypic fear expression. Thus EMG stud-ies as well as observer judgment studies have demonstrated that different forms of facial efference can occur in positive versus negative emotion situations, but have not demonstrated distinctions among discrete negative emotions.

Relatively few studies have involved the objective coding of observable facial expressions. However, several studies (Deckers, Kuhlhorst, & Freeland, 1987; Ekman, Friesen, & Ancoli, 1980; Ekman, Malmstrom, & Friesen, 1971; Tassinary, 1985) have yielded evidence consis-tent with the efference hypothesis. For example, Ekman et al. (1980) found positive relationships between subjects' smiling and reports of happi-ness while viewing in private a pleasant video-tape, and between subjects' disgust expressions and reports of disgust while viewing an unpleas-ant videotape. Similarly, Tassinary (1985) found that subjects produced more disgust-related movements in response to strong unpleasant odors than in response to weak unpleasant or strong pleasant odors.

In contrast to the studies described above, other investigations have been interpreted as being inconsistent with the emotion efference hypothesis. Kraut and Johnston (1979) con-ducted three naturalistic observation studies in which they compared persons who were socially engaged with persons not so engaged in their responses to the same nonsocial emo-tion stimulus (e.g., getting a strike while bowl-ing). They reported that solitary subjects sel-dom smiled and that socially engaged subjects smiled at their companions rather than at the presumed source of positive affect (i.e., the bowling pins). Similarly, Chovil (1991) reported that subjects showed few reactive facial grimaces when privately listening to a tape-recorded description of a "close call" (near-accident) situation, but produced an in-creasing number of such facial responses in ex-perimental conditions involving social and/or communicative settings. Brightman, Segal, Werther, and Steiner (1975) and Gilbert, Fridlund, and Sabini (1987) found that decod-ers could not determine whether encoders were smelling or tasting pleasant or unpleas-ant stimuli when the encoders encountered the stimuli in private, but that the decoders were highly accurate in discriminating the stimuli when the encoders were asked to enact their emotional reactions for an audience or were tested in social groups. Fridlund (1991c; Fridlund et al., 1990) found more intense EMG-recorded smiling when subjects generated social as opposed to nonsocial images that were equated for self-reported happiness. These studies have been inter-preted as indicating that facial expressions are social signals rather than expressions of emo-tion (Fridlund, 1991a, 1991b).

Unfortunately, each of the studies described above is critically flawed in one or more of the following respects: (1) It did not determine that the expressers' emotion experiences were equi-valent across the social versus nonsocial condi-tions; (2) it did not distinguish between the felt (emotional) and unfelt (social) versions of some expressions (e.g., smiles; Ekman, Davidson, & Friesen, 1990); and/or (3) it did not demonstrate the complete absence of facial expression dur-ing the nonsocial emotion situations. Thus the findings of these and other studies (e.g., Buck, Losow, Murphy, & Costanzo, 1992; Fridlund, Kenworthy, & Jaffey, 1992; Wagner, 1990; Wag-ner & Smith, 1991) do not disconfirm the effer-ence hypothesis. However, they do suggest that the presence of an audience may importantly influence the intensity of the facial efference.

As suggested above, increased expressive behavior in social as opposed to nonsocial situ-ations does not itself rule out the emotion efference hypothesis. More telling, however, would be studies demonstrating the spontane-ous production of observable facial expressions not predicted by the efference hypothesis. For example, in a recent investigation, Tomarken and Davidson (cited in Davidson, 1992) video-taped clinically defined phobic subjects as they confronted their phobic stimuli in a private setting. Ratings of subjective emotional ex-perience were also obtained. Data analysis showed that subjects produced expressions of disgust rather than expressions of fear or dis-gust–fear blends, although they reported ex-periencing fear and disgust with equal inten-sity. These findings suggest that even when observable facial efference is produced under conditions in which display rules presumably will not be operating, the pattern of efference may not always correspond to the prototypic expressions described for the emotions.

What type of theory might accommodate data such as those produced in Tomarken and Davidson's study? In reviewing the literature on infant expressive behavior (in which similar phenomena have been observed), Camras (1991, 1992; Camras et al., 1991) has proposed that a dynamic systems model might provide a more comprehensive explanation for facial expression data that cannot be easily accommodated by current versions of emotion theory. In contrast to the "top-down" emphasis of such theories, dynamic systems models assert that "bottom-up" influences and synergistic relationships among lower-order behavioral components may be important determinants of behavior. For example, the facial responses to phobic stimuli observed by Tomarken and Davidson may have been determined by the context of the fear situation as much as by the fear itself. In their study, reduction of stimulus input, rather than fleeing or calling for help, was probably the most functionally appropriate response. Such input reduction would be achieved by contraction of the orbicularis oculi (i.e., by squinting the eyes), which might synergistically recruit other muscle actions as part of the spreading defensive reaction described by Peiper (1963). Peiper's generalized defensive reaction strongly resembles some forms of the disgust expression specified by the EMFACS, which was employed by Tomarken and Davidson. Thus in their study, "disgust" expressions were possibly produced because contextual factors—similar to those occurring in classic "disgust" situations—were present and dictated the production of prototypic disgust expressions.

At present, an explicit dynamic systems model of facial expression has not yet been developed. Such a model would most profitably rest on a foundation of empirical data involving objective descriptions of facial behavior in contextually varying emotion situations. The recent advent of a comprehensive objective facial coding system (the FACS) has provided us with a tool for collecting such objective empirical data. Thus future research may enable us to better evaluate the several theoretical models of facial expression that have been proposed.

THE FACIAL
FEEDBACK HYPOTHESIS

According to the facial feedback hypothesis, facial expressions provide proprioceptive, cutaneous (Tomkins, 1984), or vascular (Zajonc, 1985) feedback to the expresser that influences emotional experience. A strong version of the hypothesis asserts that facial expression alone is sufficient to create emotional experience (Ekman, Levenson, & Friesen, 1983); a weaker version asserts that facial feedback enhances emotional experience (Tomkins, 1981). An additional distinction may be made between dimensional and categorical versions of the hypothesis (Winton, 1986; Duclos et al., 1989). The dimensional form states that the movements of the face create dimensional changes in pleasantness and unpleasantness, whereas the categorical version predicts that facial position can produce specific categorical reactions, such as anger, fear, and sadness.

Empirical tests of the facial feedback hypothesis have employed two paradigms. In studies using the exaggeration–suppression paradigm, subjects voluntarily alter their spontaneous expressions by inhibiting or amplifying them. With few reported exceptions (e.g., Deckers et al., 1987), support for the hypothesis has been found in these studies. For example, Lanzetta et al. (1976) found that subjects rated shocks as less painful and showed less skin conductance when attempting to suppress their reactions than when attempting to exaggerate them. Similar findings have been obtained in other studies involving responses to shock (Kleck et al., 1976; Vaughan & Lanzetta, 1981), humorous films (Bush, Barr, McHugo, & Lanzetta, 1989; Cupchik & Leventhal, 1974), pleasant and unpleasant odors (Kraut, 1982), Velten mood induction tasks (Ricceli, Antila, Dale, & Klions, 1989), pleasant and unpleasant videotaped scenes (Zuckerman et al., 1981), and contingency reinforcement schedules (Kleinke & Walton, 1982). However, these studies provide evidence for only the dimensional form of the hypothesis, since distinctions among different negative expressions were not investigated. Furthermore, since emotion stimuli other than facial expressions were used (e.g., shock, films, odors), these studies only support the weaker form of the hypothesis, which states that facial expressions can enhance the experience of emotions produced by other means.

In the muscle induction paradigm, subjects are explicitly instructed to contract the facial muscles believed to be used in emotion expressions or are instructed to perform nonemotion tasks that (arguably) require contraction of these muscles (e.g., Strack, Martin, & Stepper,

1988; Larsen, Kasimatis, & Frey, 1992). Most of these experiments test the weak form of the facial feedback hypothesis, since additional emotion stimuli are presented. However, Duclos et al. (1989) manipulated subjects' facial expressions while the subjects listened to musical tones, and assessed their feelings on four negative and three positive emotion scales. Results were consistent with the categorical version of the hypothesis.

Testing the dimensional version, Laird and his colleagues have evaluated the effects of facial feedback on subjects' self-reports of emotion while writing counterattudinal essays (Rhodewalt & Comer, 1979) or speeches (Duncan & Laird, 1977), viewing humorous stimuli (Laird & Crosby, 1974), recalling emotionally evocative material (Laird, Wagener, Halal, & Szegda, 1982), wearing glasses (Kellerman & Laird, 1982), and viewing emotional slides (Rutledge & Hupka, 1985; Edelman, 1984; McArthur, Solomon, & Jaffe, 1980; Laird, 1974). Laird found individual differences in the effects of facial feedback, which he explains using self-perception theory. That is, Laird (1984) argues that facial feedback effects are found in individuals who pay attention to their own self-produced cues, as opposed to those who do not. Thus, he proposes that the effects of facial feedback are cognitively mediated rather than direct.

Despite Tourangeau and Ellsworth's (1979) initially negative results, Ekman et al. (1983) and Levenson, Ekman, and Friesen (1990) have recently tested the strong categorical form of the facial feedback hypothesis by having subjects contract facial muscles specific to six different emotions (anger, disgust, fear, happiness, sadness, and surprise) and presenting no other emotion stimuli. Different patterns of ANS activity and reports of subjective experience were obtained. These investigators argue that the effects of facial feedback are innate and direct rather than cognitively mediated (Laird, 1984) or peripheral (Tomkins, 1984; Zajonc, 1985).

In summary, support for some form of the facial feedback hypothesis has been found in a number of recent studies. However, the mechanisms by which feedback affects emotion are still in dispute (Izard, 1990; Matsumoto, 1987).

CONCLUSION

Recent research has consistently demonstrated distinctions in the emotion-relevant correlates of positive versus negative facial expressions. However, comparatively few studies have examined distinctions among negative affect expressions, and these have produced less consistent results. In addition, some investigations have raised questions regarding the circumstances under which emotions are accompanied by observable facial expressions. These studies—as well as the work on negative affect differentiation—suggest that the classical affect program model of facial expressions may require modification, or that an alternative model may better represent the data. Lastly, considerable evidence has been accrued in support of the facial feedback hypothesis. However, future research is necessary to clarify the mechanisms by which the effects of facial feedback are produced. Thus recent research has considerably advanced our knowledge about emotional facial expressions, and has simultaneously indicated several lines of investigation that may now be profitably pursued.

REFERENCES

Adelman, P., & Zajonc, R. B. (1989). Facial efference and the experience of emotion. *Annual Review of Psychology, 40,* 249–280.

Borod, J. C., & Caron, H. S. (1980). Facedness and emotion related to lateral dominance, sex and expression type. *Neuropsychologia, 18,* 237–242.

Borod, J. C., Kent, J., Koff, E., Martin, C., & Alpert, M. (1988). Facial asymmetry while posing positive and negative emotions: Support for the right hemisphere hypothesis. *Neuropsychologia, 26,* 759–764.

Borod, J. C., & Koff, E. (1984). Asymmetries in affective facial expression: Behavior and anatomy. In N. A. Fox, & R. J. Davidson (Eds.), *The psychobiology of affective development* (pp. 293–323). Hillsdale, NJ: Erlbaum.

Borod, J. C., Koff, E., & White, B. (1983). Right hemisphere specialization for the expression appreciation of emotion: A focus on the face. In E. Perecman (Ed.), *Cognitive processes in the right hemisphere* (pp. 165–175). New York: Academic Press.

Brightman, V., Segal, A., Werther, P., & Steiner, J. (1975). Ethologic study of facial expressions in response to taste stimuli. *Journal of Dental Research, 54,* L141. (Abstract)

Buck, R. W. (1988). *Human motivation and emotion* (2nd ed.). New York: Wiley.

Buck, R. W., & Duffy, R. J. (1980). Nonverbal communication of affect in brain-damaged patients. *Cortex, 16,* 351–362.

Buck, R. W., Losow, J., & Costanzo, P. (1992). Social facilitation and inhibition of emotional expression and communication. *Journal of Personality and Social Psychology, 63*(6), 962–968.

Buck, R. W., Miller, R. E., & Caul, W. E. (1974). Sex, personality and physiological variables in the communication of affect via facial expression. *Journal of Personality and Social Psychology, 30*(4), 587–596.

Buck, R. W., Savin, V. J., Miller, R. E., & Caul, W. F. (1972). Communication of affect through facial expressions in humans. *Journal of Personality and Social Psychology*, *23*(3), 362–371.

Bush L. K., Barr, C. L., McHugo, G. J., & Lanzetta, J. T. (1989). The effects of facial control and facial mimicry on subjective reactions to comedy routines. *Motivation and Emotion*, *13*(1), 31–52.

Cacioppo, J. T., Bush, L. K., & Tassinary, L. G. (1992). Microexpressive facial actions as a function of affective stimuli: Replication and extension. *Personality and Social Psychology Bulletin*, *18*, 515–526.

Cacioppo, J. T., Martzke, J. S., Petty, R. E., & Tassinary, L. G. (1988). Specific forms of facial EMG response index emotions during an interview: From Darwin to the continuous flow hypothesis of affect-laden information processing. *Journal of Personality and Social Psychology*, *54*(4), 592–604.

Cacioppo, J. T., Petty, R. E., Losch, M. E., & Kim, H. S. (1986). Electromyographic activity over facial muscle regions can differentiate the valence and intensity of affective reactions. *Journal of Personality and Social Psychology*, *50*(2), 260–268.

Campbell, R. (1978). Asymmetries in interpreting and expressing a posed facial expression. *Cortex*, *14*, 327–342.

Camras, L. A. (1991). Conceptualizing early infant affect: View II and reply. In K. Strongman (Ed.), *International review of studies on emotion* (Vol. 1, pp. 16–28, 33–36). New York: Wiley.

Camras, L. A. (1992). Expressive development and basic emotions. *Cognition and Emotion*, *6*(3/4), 269–283.

Camras, L. A., Malatesta, C., & Izard, C. (1991). The development of facial expressions in infancy. In R. Feldman & B. Rimé (Eds.), *Fundamentals of nonverbal behavior* (pp. 73–105). Cambridge, England: Cambridge University Press.

Chaurasia, B. D., & Goswami, H. K. (1975). Functional asymmetry in the face. *Acta Anatomica*, *91*, 154–160.

Chovil, N. (1991). Social determinants of facial displays. *Journal of Nonverbal Behavior*, *15*(3), 141–154.

Cupchik, G. C., & Leventhal, H. (1974). Consistency between expressive behavior and the evaluation of humorous stimuli: The role of sex and self-observation. *Journal of Personality and Social Psychology*, *30*(3), 429–442.

Darwin, C. (1965). *The expression of the emotions in man and animals*. Chicago: University of Chicago Press. (Original work published 1872)

Davidson, R. J. (1984). Affect, cognition and hemispheric specialization. In C. E. Izard, J. Kagan, & R. B. Zajonc (Eds.), *Emotions, cognition, and behavior* (pp. 320–365). New York: Cambridge University Press.

Davidson, R. J. (1992). A prolegomenon to the structure of emotion: Gleanings from neuropsychology. *Cognition and Emotion*, *6*(3/4), 245–268.

Davidson, R. J., Ekman, P., Saron, C. D., Senulis, J. A., & Friesen, W. V. (1990). Approach–withdrawal and cerebral symmetry: Emotional expression and brain physiology, I. *Journal of Personality and Social Psychology*, *58*, 330–341.

Davidson, R. J., Schwartz, G. E., Saron, C., Bennett, J., & Goleman, D. J. (1979). Frontal versus parietal EEG asymmetry during positive and negative affect. *Psychophysiology*, *16*, 202–203.

Deckers, L., Kuhlhorst, L., & Freeland, L. (1987). The effects of spontaneous and voluntary facial reactions on surprise and humor. *Motivation and Emotion*, *11*(4), 403–412.

Dimberg, U. (1986). Facial reactions to fear-relevant and fear-irrelevant stimuli. *Biological Psychology*, *23*(5), 153–161.

Dimberg, U. (1988). Facial electromyography and the experience of emotion. *Journal of Psychophysiology*, *2*, 277–282.

Dimond, S., Farrington, L., & Johnson, P. (1976). Differing emotional response from right and left hemispheres. *Nature*, *261*, 690–692.

Duclos, S. E., Laird, J. D., Schneider, E., Sexter, M., Stern, L., & Van Lighten, O. (1989). Emotion-specific effects of facial expressions and postures on emotional experience. *Journal of Personality and Social Psychology*, *57*(1), 100–108.

Duncan, J., & Laird, J. D. (1977). Cross-modality consistencies in individual differences in self-attribution. *Journal of Personality*, *45*, 191–206.

Edelman, B. (1984). A multiple factor study of body weight control. *Journal of General Psychology*, *110*, 99–114.

Ekman, P. (1972). Universals and cultural differences in facial expressions of emotion. In J. Cole (Ed.), *Nebraska Symposium on Motivation* (Vol. 19, pp. 207–283). Lincoln: University of Nebraska Press.

Ekman, P. (Ed.). (1982). *Emotion in the human face* (2nd ed.). Cambridge, England: Cambridge University Press.

Ekman, P. (1989). The argument and evidence about universals in facial expressions of emotion. In H. Wagner & A. Manstead (Eds.), *Handbook of social psychophysiology* (pp. 143–164). Chichester, England: Wiley.

Ekman, P. (1992). Facial expressions of emotion: New findings, new questions. *Psychological Science*, *3*(1), 34–38.

Ekman, P., Davidson, R., & Friesen, W. (1990). The Duchenne smile: Emotional expression and brain physiology, II. *Journal of Personality and Social Psychology*, *58*, 342–353.

Ekman, P., & Friesen, W. V. (1969). The repertoire of nonverbal behavior: Origins, usage, and coding. *Semiotica*, *1*(1), 49–98.

Ekman, P., & Friesen, W. V. (1978). *Facial Action Coding System: A technique for the measurement of facial movement*. Palo Alto, CA: Consulting Psychologists Press.

Ekman, P., Friesen, W. V., & Ancoli, S. (1980). Facial signs of emotional experience. *Journal of Personality and Social Psychology*, *39*(6), 1125–1134.

Ekman, P., Hager, J. C., & Friesen, W. V. (1981). The symmetry of emotional and deliberate facial actions. *Psychophysiology*, *18*, 101–106.

Ekman, P., Levenson, R. W., & Friesen, W. V. (1983). Autonomic nervous system activity distinguishes among emotions. *Science*, *221*(4616), 1208–1210.

Ekman, P., Malmstrom, E., & Friesen, W. (1971). *Heart-rate changes with facial displays of surprise and disgust*. Unpublished manuscript.

Fox, N. A., & Davidson, R. J. (1988). Patterns of brain electrical activity during facial signs of emotion in ten month old infants. *Developmental Psychology*, *24*, 230–236.

Fridlund, A. J. (1991a). The behavioral ecology and sociality of human faces. *Review of Personality and Social Psychology*, *2*, 90–121.

Fridlund, A. J. (1991b). Sociality of solitary smiling: Potentiation by an implicit audience. *Journal of Personality and Social Psychology*, *60*(2), 229–240.

Fridlund, A. J. (1991c). Evolution and facial action in reflex, social motive, and paralanguage. *Biological Psychology*, *32*, 1–96.

Fridlund, A. J., & Izard, C. (1983). Electromyographic studies of facial expressions of emotions and patterns of emotions. In J. T. Cacioppo & R. E. Petty (Eds.), *Social psychophysiology: A sourcebook* (pp. 243–286). New York: Guilford Press.

Fridlund, A. J., Kenworthy, K., & Jaffey, A. (1992). Audience effects in affective imagery: Replication and extension to dysphoric imagery. *Journal of Nonverbal Behavior, 16*(3), 191–211.

Fridlund, A. J., Sabini, J., Shenker, J., Hedlund, L., Schaut, J., & Knauer, M. (1990). Social determinants of facial expressions during affective imagery: Displaying to the people in your head. *Journal of Nonverbal Behavior, 14*(2), 113–137.

Fridlund, A. J., Schwartz, G. E., & Fowler, S. C. (1984). Pattern recognition of self-reported emotional state from multiple-site facial EMG activity during affective imagery. *Psychophysiology, 21*(6), 622–637.

Friesen, W. V., & Ekman, P. (1984). *EMFACS: Emotion Facial Action Coding System.* (Available from Paul Ekman, Department of Psychiatry, University of California at San Francisco)

Gilbert, A. N., Fridlund, A. J., & Sabini, J. (1987). Hedonic and social determinants of facial displays to odors. *Chemical Senses, 12*, 355–363.

Greenwald, M., Cook, E., & Lang, P. (1989). Affective judgment and psychophysiological response. *Journal of Psychophysiology, 3*, 51–64.

Gross, A., & Ballif, B. (1991). Children's understanding of emotion from facial expressions and situations: A review. *Developmental Review, 11*, 368–398.

Hager, J. C. (1982). Asymmetries in facial expression. In P. Ekman (Ed.), *Emotion in the human face* (2nd ed., pp. 318–352). Cambridge, England: Cambridge University Press.

Heller, W., & Levy, J. (1981). Perception and expression of emotion in right-handers and left-handers. *Neuropsychologia, 19*, 263–272.

Izard, C. E. (1971). *The face of emotion.* New York: Appleton-Century-Crofts.

Izard, C. (1977). *Human emotions.* New York: Plenum Press.

Izard, C. (1979). *The Maximally Discriminative Facial Movement Coding System (MAX).* Newark: Instructional Resources Center, University of Delaware.

Izard, C. E. (1990). Facial expressions and the regulation of emotions. *Journal of Personality and Social Psychology, 58*(3), 487–498.

Izard, C. E. (1991). *The psychology of emotions.* New York: Plenum Press.

Izard, C. E., Dougherty, L., & Hembree, E. (1983). *A system for identifying affect expressions by holistic judgments (AFFEX).* Newark: Instructional Resources Center, University of Delaware.

Jones, H. E. (1935). The galvanic skin response as related to overt emotional expression. *American Journal of Psychology, 47*, 241–251.

Kellerman, J. M., & Laird, J. D. (1982). The effect of appearance on self-perceptions. *Journal of Personality, 50*(3), 296e315.

Kinsbourne, M. (1978). The biological determinants of functional bisymmetry and asymmetry. In M. Kinsbourne (Ed.), *Asymmetrical functions of the brain* (pp. 3–13). New York: Cambridge University Press.

Kleck, R. E., Vaughan, R. C., Cartwright-Smith, J., Vaughan, K. B., Colby, C. Z., & Lanzetta, J. T. (1976). Effects of being observed on expressive, subjective and physiological responses to painful stimuli. *Journal of Personality and Social Psychology, 34*(6), 1211–1218.

Kleinke, C., & Walton, J. (1982). Influences of reinforced smiling on affective responses in an interview. *Journal of Personality and Social Psychology, 42*, 557–565.

Kraut, R. E. (1982). Social presence, facial feedback, and emotion. *Journal of Personality and Social Psychology, 42*(5), 853–863.

Kraut, R. E., & Johnston, R. E. (1979). Social and emotional messages of smiling: An ethological approach. *Journal of Personality and Social Psychology, 37*(9), 1539–1553.

Laird, J. D. (1974). Self-attribution of emotion: The effects of expressive behavior on the quality of emotional experience. *Journal of Personality and Social Psychology, 29*(4), 475–486.

Laird, J. D. (1984). The real role of facial response in the experience of emotion: A reply to Tourangeau and Ellsworth, and others. *Journal of Personality and Social Psychology, 47*(4), 909–917.

Laird, J. D., & Crosby, M. (1974). Individual differences in self-attribution of emotion. In H. London & R. E. Nisbett (Eds.), *Thought and feeling* (pp. 44–59). Chicago: Aldine.

Laird, J. D., Wagener, J. J., Halal, M., & Szegda, M. (1982). Remembering what you feel: Effects of emotion on memory. *Journal of Personality and Social Psychology, 42*(4), 646–657.

Lanzetta, J. T., Cartwright-Smith, J., & Kleck, R. E. (1976). Effects of nonverbal dissimulation on emotional experience and autonomic arousal. *Journal of Personality and Social Psychology, 33*(3), 354–370.

Lanzetta, J. T., & Kleck, R. E. (1970). Encoding and decoding of nonverbal affect in humans. *Journal of Personality and Social Psychology, 16*(1), 12–19.

Larsen, R., Kasimatis, M., & Frey, K. (1992). Facilitating the furrowed brow. *Cognition and Emotion, 6*(5), 321–338.

LeDoux, J. (1989). Cognitive–emotional interactions in the brain. *Cognition & Emotion, 3*(4), 267–289.

Levenson, R. W., Ekman, P., & Friesen, W. V. (1990). Voluntary facial action generates emotion-specific autonomic nervous system activity. *Psychophysiology, 27*, 363–384.

Ley, R. G., & Bryden, M. P. (1982). Consciousness, emotion, and the right hemisphere. In R. Stevens & G. Underwood (Eds.), *Aspects of consciousness* (pp. 215–240). New York: Academic Press.

Lynn, J. G., & Lynn, D. R. (1938). Face-hand laterality in relation to personality. *Journal of Abnormal and Social Psychology, 33*, 291–322.

Lynn, J. G., & Lynn, D. R. (1943). Smile and hand dominance in relation to basic modes of adaptation. *Journal of Abnormal and Social Psychology, 38*, 250–276.

Matsumoto, D. (1987). The role of facial response in the experience of emotion: More methodological problems and a meta-analysis. *Journal of Personality and Social Psychology, 52*(4), 769–774.

McArthur, L. Z., Solomon, M. R., & Jaffe, R. H. (1980). Weight differences in emotional responsiveness to proprioceptive and pictorial stimuli. *Journal of Personality and Social Psychology, 39*(2), 308–319.

McHugo, G. J., Lanzetta, J. T., & Bush, L. K. (1991). The effect of attitudes on emotional reactions to expressive displays of political leaders. *Journal of Nonverbal Behavior, 15*(1), 19–41.

Moscovitch, M., & Olds, J. (1982). Asymmetries in spontaneous facial expression and their possible relation to hemispheric specialization. *Neuropsychologia, 20*, 71–81.

Motley, M. T., & Camden, C. T. (1988). Facial expression of emotion: A comparison of posed expressions versus spontaneous expressions in an interpersonal communication setting. *Western Journal of Speech Communication, 52*, 1–22.

Notarius, C. I., & Levenson, R. W. (1979). Expressive tendencies and physiological response to stress. *Journal of Personality and Social Psychology, 37*(7), 1204–1210.

Oster, H., Daily, L., & Goldenthal, G. (1989). Processing facial affect. In A. Young & H. Ellis (Eds.), *Handbook of research on face processing* (pp. 107–161). Amsterdam: North-Holland.

Panksepp, J. (1986). The anatomy of emotions. In R. Plutchik (Ed.), *Emotion: Theory, research, and experience. Vol. 3. Biological foundations of emotions* (pp. 91–124). New York: Academic Press.

Peiper, A. (1963). *Cerebral function in infancy and childhood* (B. Nagler & H. Nagler, Trans.). New York: Consultants Bureau.

Reuter-Lorenz, P., & Davidson, R. J. (1981). Differential contributions of the two cerebral hemispheres to the perception of happy and sad faces. *Neuropsychologia, 19*, 609–613.

Rhodewalt, F., & Comer, R. (1979). Induced-compliance attitude change: Once more with feeling. *Journal of Experimental Psychology, 15*, 35–47.

Ricceli, P. T., Antila, C. E., Dale, A., & Klions, H. L. (1989). Depression and elative mood inductions as a function of exaggerated versus contradictory facial expressions. *Perceptual and Motor Skills, 68*, 443–452.

Rinn, W. (1991). Neuropsychology of facial expression. In R. Feldman & B. Rimé (Eds.), *Fundamentals of nonverbal behavior* (pp. 3–32). Cambridge, England: Cambridge University Press.

Rutledge, L. L., & Hupka, R. B. (1985). The facial feedback hypothesis: Methodological concerns and new supporting evidence. *Motivation and Emotion, 9*(3), 219–240.

Sackheim, H. A., & Gur, R. C. (1978). Lateral asymmetry in intensity of emotional expression. *Neuropsychologia, 16*, 473–481.

Sackheim, H. A., Gur, R. C., & Saucy, M. C. (1978). Emotions are expressed more intensely on the left side of the face. *Science, 202*, 434–435.

Schwartz, G. E., Ahern, G. L., & Brown, S. L. (1979). Lateralized facial muscle response to positive and negative emotional stimuli. *Psychophysiology, 16*, 561–571.

Schwartz, G., Brown, S., & Ahern, G. (1980). Facial muscle patterning and subjective experience during affective imagery: Sex differences. *Psychophysiology, 17*(1), 75–82.

Schwartz, G. E., Fair, P. L., Salt, P., Mandel, M. R., & Klerman, G. L. (1976a). Facial expression and imagery in depression: An electromyographic study. *Psychosomatic Medicine, 38*(5), 337–347.

Schwartz, G. E., Fair, P. L., Salt, P., Mandel, M. R., & Klerman, G. L. (1976b). Facial muscle patterning to affective imagery in depressed and nondepressed subjects. *Science, 192*, 489–491.

Sirota, A. D., & Schwartz, G. E. (1982). Facial muscle patterning and lateralization during elation and depression imagery. *Journal of Abnormal Psychology, 91*, 25–34.

Sirota, A. D., Schwartz, G. E., & Kristeller, J. L. (1987). Facial muscle activity during induced mood states: Differential growth and carry-over of elated versus depressed patterns. *Psychophysiology, 24*(6), 691–699.

Smith, C. McHugo, G. & Lanzetta, J. (1986). The facial muscle patterning of posed and imagery induced expression of emotion by expressive and nonexpressive posers. *Motivation and Emotion, 10*, 133–157.

Strack, F., Martin, L. L., & Stepper, S. (1988). Inhibiting and facilitating conditions of the human smile: A nonobtrusive test of the facial feedback hypothesis. *Journal of Personality and Social Psychology, 54*(5), 768–777.

Strauss, E., Moscovitch, M., & Olds, J. (1980, June). *Children's Production of Facial Expressions.* Paper presented at the meeting of the International Neuropsychology Society, Italy.

Suberi, M., & McKeever, W. F. (1977). Differential right hemispheric memory storage of emotional and nonemotional faces. *Neuropsychologia, 15*, 757–768.

Tassinary, L. (1985). *Odor hedonics: Psychophysical, respiratory and facial measures.* Unpublished doctoral dissertation, University of Iowa.

Tassinary, L., & Cacioppo, J. T. (1992). Unobservable facial actions and emotion. *Psychological Science, 3*(1), 28–33.

Teasdale, J. D., & Bancroft, J. (1977). Manipulation of thought content as a determinant of mood and corrugator electromyographic activity in depressed patients. *Journal of Abnormal Psychology, 86*(3), 235–241.

Tomkins, S. S. (1962). *Affect, imagery, and consciousness: Vol. 1. The positive affects.* New York: Springer.

Tomkins, S. S. (1963). *Affect, imagery and consciousness. Vol. 2. The negative affects.* New York: Springer.

Tomkins, S. S. (1981). The role of facial response in the experience of emotion: A reply to Tourangeau and Ellsworth. *Journal of Personality and Social Psychology, 40*, 355–357.

Tomkins, S. (1984). Affect theory. In K. Scherer & P. Ekman (Eds.), *Approaches to emotion* (pp. 163-196). Hillsdale, NJ: Erlbaum.

Tourangeau, R., & Ellsworth, P. C. (1979). The role of facial response in the experience of emotion. *Journal of Personality and Social Psychology, 37*(9), 1519–1531.

Tucker, D. M., Stenslie, C. E., Roth, R. S., & Shearer, S. L. (1981). Right frontal lobe activation and right hemisphere performance decrement during a depressed mood. *Archives of General Psychiatry, 38*, 169–174.

Vaughan, K. B., & Lanzetta, J. T. (1980). Vicarious instigation and conditioning of facial expressive and autonomic responses to a model's expressive display of pain. *Journal of Personality and Social Psychology, 38*(6), 909–923.

Vaughan, K. B., & Lanzetta, J. T. (1981). The effect of modification of expressive displays of vicarious emotional arousal. *Journal of Experimental Psychology, 17*, 16–30.

Wagner, H. L., (1990). The spontaneous facial expression of differential positive and negative emotions. *Motivation and Emtotion, 14*, 27–43.

Wagner, H. L., MacDonald, C. J., & Manstead, A. S. R. (1986). Communication of individual emotions by spontaneous facial expressions. *Journal of Personality and Social Psychology, 50*(4), 737–743.

Wagner, H. L., & Smith, J. (1991). Facial expressions in the presence of friends and strangers. *Journal of Nonverbal Behavior, 15*(4), 201–214.

Winton, W. M. (1986). The role of facial response in self-reports of emotion: A critique of Laird. *Journal of Personality and Social Psychology, 50*(4), 808–812.

Winton, W. M., Putnam, L. E., & Krauss, R. M. (1984). Facial and autonomic manifestations of the dimensional structure of emotion. *Journal of Experimental Social Psychology, 20*(3), 195–216.

Zajonc, R. B. (1985). Emotion and facial efference: A theory reclaimed. *Science, 228*, 15–21.

Zuckerman, M., Klorman, R., Larrance, D. T., & Spiegel, N. H. (1981). Facial, autonomic, and subjective components of emotion: The facial feedback hypothesis versus the externalizer–internalizer distinction. *Journal of Personality and Social Psychology, 41*(5), 929–944.

15

Brain Temperature and Subjective Emotional Experience

R. B. ZAJONC
SHEILA T. MURPHY
DANIEL N. McINTOSH

What is it that we feel when we feel happiness, anger, sadness, or disgust? This question of the interface between subjective and bodily states is among the fundamental research questions for the study of emotion. William James's (1890/1950) answer to this question was that we feel the viscera. We feel our own autonomic activity, such as accelerated heart rate, sweating, and digestive processes, derived from the instrumental behaviors triggered by the situation. Thus, James contradicted the common wisdom. In his framework, we do not run because we are afraid, but rather we are afraid because we run; we do not smile because we are happy, but are happy because we smile.

James (1890/1950) was immediately attacked. The first major critique was launched by Sherrington (1906). Using laboratory animals, Sherrington destroyed the afferent pathways of the autonomic nervous system from the shoulders down, yet he found that these animals continued to exhibit normal emotional reactions. These results were taken to mean that the viscera are *not* necessary for the experience of emotion.

Sherrington's (1906) finding provided the foundation for a more severe attack by Cannon (1927). Besides citing Sherrington's work, Cannon made four additional points. First, Cannon noted that the viscera, which James (1890/1950) had regarded as a primary source of emotional experience, are relatively insensitive. Second, he observed that visceral changes (heart rate acceleration, inhibition of digestive activity, sweating, etc.) are not unique to specific emotions, but are present in many emotional states. Moreover, these changes are so diffuse that they cannot discriminate among particular emotions. Third, Cannon cited experiments in which the injection of adrenalin, which produces some of the precise visceral changes mentioned by James, was not sufficient for the elicitation of emotion. Finally, Cannon contended that the viscera are sluggish and incapable of responding in time to be of any use as a feedback mechanism. But this is not entirely true. Many subjective feelings do not occur until much later, very often after the eliciting stimulation and instrumental response have already occurred. For example, we pull our hands away from a hot stove immediately, although we often do not feel pain until later. Frequently, when people are in traffic accidents they first engage all the instrumentally appropriate behaviors: They make sure that no one is hurt, exchange insurance information, and make arrangements for the disabled automobiles to be towed. Often, it is only afterwards that they begin to shake in terror—long after the danger is past.

Over 100 years after James's (1890/1950) assertion, there is now sufficient knowledge about the subjective and bodily processes associated with emotion to enable us to readdress the question: What is it that one feels when one feels happy or sad? We agree with James's contention that emotional expression is not merely a passive signal of what happens internally as a result of an eliciting stimulus, but that facial expression (henceforth referred to as "facial efference"[1] is active and generative. Moreover, we review support for James's conjecture that emotional efference can *precede* and even *produce* subjective feeling.

We do not follow James (1890/1950) unconditionally, however. We disagree with his unnecessarily exclusive position; there is no reason why efference cannot both precede *and* follow subjective states. Furthermore, it must be noted that some criticisms of James were fair and justified. For instance, James's critics were correct in suspecting that the answer to the question of what it is one feels when one feels angry, happy, or sad will not be found by looking at the viscera. Rather, we argue that subjective emotional states can be influenced by all sorts of facial efferents, and we present evidence suggesting that they do so because they are capable of changing hypothalamic temperature. The remainder of this chapter focuses on clarifying the connection among emotional efference, brain temperature, and subjective state.

THE VASCULAR THEORY OF EMOTIONAL EFFERENCE

James's (1890/1950) theory of emotion failed because the process whereby visceral functions influence subjective state was not specified. Just why should heart rate acceleration feel positive or negative, for that matter? There were no theoreticians, except one, who dared to postulate an anatomically and physiologically justified way whereby the valence of subjective emotional experience could be produced by its bodily antecedents. The exception was Israel Waynbaum, an obscure French physician, who sought to explicate the mind–body connection in emotion by focusing on the vascular system of the face and the brain. Waynbaum (1907) argued that facial gestures in general, and emotional gestures in particular, have regulatory and restorative functions for the vascular system of the head. His argument was developed in the following steps: Waynbaum first observed that emotional experiences generally produce a considerable disequilibrium of the vascular process. For example, in fear blood is redistributed to supply skeletal muscles to meet the demands of an incipient flight. Next, he noticed that the main carotid artery is divided at the neck into two arteries: the internal carotid, which supplies blood to the brain, and the external carotid, which supplies the face and skull (see Figure 15.1).

It was this curious anatomic configuration that provided Waynbaum (1907) with his first major clue. Since the blood supply to the brain must remain at a fairly constant level, why does the brain share its supply with the face and skull? In other words, given that the brain cannot tolerate much variation in blood flow, why isn't it supplied directly and independently? Waynbaum conjectured that this anatomical circuit may serve a regulatory function by allowing the facial branch of the main carotid artery to act as a "safety valve" for the brain (*soupape de sûreté pour la circulation cérébrale*; p. 35). More specifically, he speculated that the muscles of the face may act as tourniquets (*ligatures*), pressing facial arteries against the skeletal structure of the face and thus shunting blood away from the brain when there is an oversupply, or, conversely, relaxing pressure and thereby allowing increased flow when the supply is insufficient. Waynbaum further speculated that these regulatory muscular actions of the face—that is, those actions of the face that were commonly classified as emotional expressions—should produce changes in feeling state.

So, like James (1890/1950), Waynbaum (1907) contradicted the common wisdom regarding the order of the emotional sequence. Unlike James, however, Waynbaum proposed a specific physiological process that would make such a sequence plausible. But Waynbaum's idea, embodied in the "vascular theory of emotional efference" (VTEE), were based on turn-of-the-century physiology. Not surprisingly, therefore, several of Waynbaum's as-

---

[1]We use the more neutral term "efference" instead of the pre-emptive term "expression," because the latter implies an untested theory of the emotions according to which the internal state must precede its outward manifestation (Zajonc, 1985).

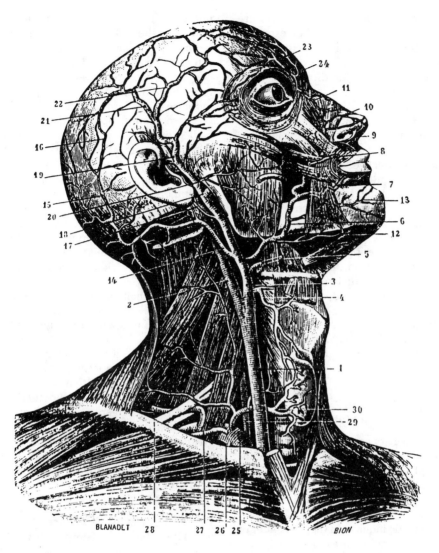

1. Artère carotide primitive droite. — 2. Artère carotide interne. — 3. Carotide externe.
— 4. Thyroïdienne supérieure. — 5. Linguale. — 6. Faciale. — 7. Labiale inférieure. — 8. Labiale supérieure. — 9. Artère de la sous-cloison. — 10. Artère de
l'aile du nez. — 11. Rameau par lequel la branche nasale de l'ophtalmique s'anastomose avec la partie terminale de la faciale. — 12. Artère sous-mentale. — 13. Partie
terminale de la dentaire inférieure. — 14. Occipitale. — 15. Branches terminales ou
cutanées de cette artère. — 16. Anastomose de l'occipitale avec la temporale superficielle. — 17. Auriculaire postérieure. — 18. Origine de la maxillaire interne. —
19. Temporale superficielle. — 20. Transversale de la face. — 21. Branche postérieure
de la temporale superficielle. — 22. Branche antérieure de la même artère. — 23. Artère sous-orbitaire. — 24. Artère frontale interne. — 25. Sous-clavière. — 26. Mam-
maire interne. — 27. Sous-scapulaire. — 28. Scapulaire postérieure. — 29. Vertébrale.
— 30. Thyroïdienne inférieure. [D'après SAPPEY, Anat. topogr., Masson et Cie, édit.]

FIGURE 15.1. Circulatory system of the head. The arteries of interest for Waynbaum's theory are (1) the common carotid, (2) the inernal carotid, and (3) the external carotid. Reprinted from Sappey (1888–1889).

sumptions are questionable and others are outright wrong (Zajonc, 1985). For example, arterial flow is not likely to be affected significantly by the muscular action of the face, because it can be controlled directly by vasodilation and vasoconstriction.

However, much of Waynbaum's (1907) thinking can be useful, and may even be correct, albeit for the wrong reasons. Facial muscles may not have a significant effect on arteries, but they can affect venous flow. Moreover, facial action may alter the temperature of blood entering the brain by interfering with or facilitating the cooling process. These changes in brain temperature, in turn, may have subjective consequences through the release and synthesis of various neurotransmitters. For instance, if a certain facial muscular movement results in changing hypothalamic temperature, then norepinephrine may be either partially blocked or released, causing the individual to experience either calming or excitation. Similarly, if variation in hypothalamic temperature blocks or releases serotonin, the effect may be correspondingly euphoric or depressant.

Brain Temperature and Subjective Emotional States

The connection between emotion and bodily temperature is readily seen in popular metaphors. People are described as being "hot under the collar," "boiling mad," "cool-headed," or as having committed "cold-blooded" murders. Curiously, however, this thermal metaphor has escaped systematic inquiry. In the remainder of this chapter, we describe research that explores some aspects of this metaphor.

When Waynbaum's (1907) VTEE is recast to focus on brain temperature rather than brain blood flow, the following useful hypothesis emerges: Facial action can produce changes in brain blood temperature that influence the release or synthesis of neurotransmitters, which have significant hedonic consequences. Since biochemical processes are temperature-sensitive, emotion-related neurotransmitters are temperature-sensitive as well. To be sure, it remains to be specified precisely which neurotransmitters are vulnerable to temperature changes in different parts of the brain, which are blocked, and which are enhanced. We do not know exactly how emotion-related neurotransmitters and neuroenzymes

interact with local changes in temperature, or how large these temperature changes need to be in order to have significant neurochemical effects. We do know that for some neurochemicals, very little temperature change is required. For example, the major factor that mobilizes the immune system directly is temperature change. Some antigens are released 5,000 times faster when temperature is raised 10°C (Jampel, Duff, Gershon, Atkins, & Durum, 1983; Miller & Clem, 1984). Moreover, evidence has shown that biogenic amines, norepinephrine, dopamine, and acetylcholine are directly implicated in thermoregulation (Lin, 1984). For instance, if alpha- or beta-adrenergic receptor antagonists are injected into the hypothalamus, increased metabolism, cutaneous vasoconstriction, and hypothermia result.

The hypothalamus provides a crucial piece to the puzzle because it is profoundly implicated in *both* temperature regulation and emotion (Corbit, 1969; Dib & Cabanac, 1984; Satinoff, 1964; Satinoff & Shan, 1971). Interestingly, many responses that are involved in thermoregulation are also involved in emotion. Shivering, sweating, and piloerection are all part of the fear response. The hypothalamus is also heavily implicated in the control of aggression, eating, and sex. It is thus highly probable that the hypothalamus plays a pivotal role in the relationship between emotion and temperature.

Breathing, Facial Efference, and Hypothalamic Temperature

A key to the precise nature of the relation between emotion and temperature may be the finding that hypothalamic cooling is hedonically positive (Corbit, 1969, 1973; Dib & Cabanac, 1984). How then does cooling occur? The cooling of the brain relies heavily on heat exchange, whereby venous blood cooled by evaporation exchanges heat with arterial blood entering the brain. Brain temperature is also controlled by the cavernous sinus, a venous configuration that envelopes the internal carotid just before the carotid enters the hypothalamus. The cavernous sinus acts much like a radiator, cooling blood in the course of normal breathing. Thus, the cavernous sinus, the only structure in the body where an artery passes through the interior of a vein, actively participates in the regulation of hypothalamic temperature (see Figure 15.2).

In an elegant experiment, Kluger and D'Alecy (1975) investigated the cooling of the hypothalamus by the cavernous sinus. Using a reversible tracheal canula, they observed rabbits that were breathing either normally through their noses or directly through their tracheas, thus bypassing the upper nasal passage, and therefore also the cavernous sinus. When the rabbits were breathing normally, their hypothalamic temperature was 0.3°C lower than their rectal temperature. When the rabbits were breathing through their tracheas, bypassing nasal airways and thus unable to affect the temperature of the internal carotid, their brain temperature rose to the level of their rectal temperature. The finding that hypothalamic temperature significantly increased when the cavernous sinus was bypassed supports the proposition that it plays a key role in hypothalamic cooling.

If altered temperature can influence the neurochemistry of the brain, then it follows that influencing the cooling capacity of the cavernous sinus (and consequently of the brain) will, in turn, alter an individual's subjective state. One clue to this process can be found in the distress we experience during nasal congestion. Under these conditions, the cooling action of the cavernous sinus is severely restricted; as a result, we feel distinct discomfort. At the chronic end of this continuum are patients who, for a variety of reasons, must breathe through tubes inserted directly into their tracheas, bypassing the cavernous sinus. Many of these patients suffer severe emotional shock (Bendixen, Egbert, Hedley-Whyte, Laver, & Pontoppidan, 1965). Nonetheless, although breathing rate has been used as a measure of emotional excitation for at least 80 years (e.g., Abramowski, 1913), it has never figured as an explanatory concept in theories of emotion.

A second clue to this process can be traced to the fact that although the same air is available through the mouth, 90% of people breathe almost exclusively through their noses. Why?

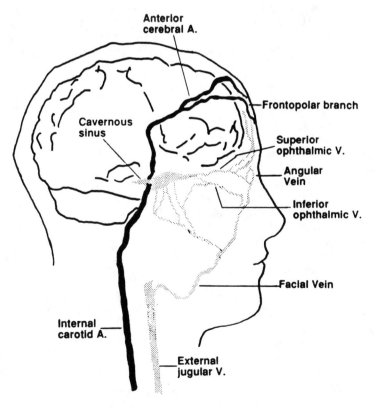

FIGURE 15.2. Location of key elements of vascular system.

Because one cannot cool the brain by breathing through the mouth. Even when nasal breathing is very difficult, people still prefer to take air in through the nose (Drake, Keall, Vig, & Krause, 1988).

Another clue to this process is the fact that facial veins are the only ones that can change the direction of venous flow. They can drain either into the cavernous sinus or into the external jugular vein. Significantly, they change their direction depending on temperature. Very small differences in temperature are sufficient to cause this change; Winquist and Bevan (1980) have shown in *vitro* that changing the temperature just 1°C reverses the direction of the flow in rabbits' facial veins 100%.

Taken together, these clues indicate a mechanism by which physical changes can influence subjective emotional state. In brief, breathing patterns and facial musculature action can control the temperature and the flow in the veins that empty into the cavernous sinus; the cavernous sinus influences brain temperature, which has an effect on subjective feeling state. Here, then, is a means by which physical action can *cause* changes in subjective feeling state. Having specified a means by which bodily changes can influence affective state, we can now describe tests of the hypothesized association.

EVIDENCE FOR THE THEORY

The major problem confronting an experimenter investigating the VTEE is that direct manipulation and measurement of brain temperature are not feasible with humans, and that although such actions are possible with animals, they are incapable of delivering judgments of their subjective states as humans can. The research strategy must therefore combine work with animals (in which invasive procedures are possible, but subjective affective states must be inferred) with research on humans (in whom the temperature manipulation and measurement must be indirect, but subjective judgments can be direct).

The early work on brain temperature indicates that heating may well be aversive (Corbit, 1973). There is less knowledge about the effects of cooling. There is, however, considerable evidence showing strong positive affective consequences that derive from the electrical

stimulation of the hypothalamus. In a recent experiment, Berridge and Valenstein (1991) demonstrated that electrical stimulation of the rat hypothalamus is a pleasurable event that elicits a number of stereotyped behaviors among rats, the most significant being a marked increase in feeding acts. Similar changes in behavior obtained when cooling of the brain is substituted for electrical stimulation would provide more direct evidence in support of the hypothesis that brain cooling is pleasurable. Following this logic, Berridge and Zajonc (1991) sought to determine whether hypothalamic cooling would have the same pattern of effects as electrical stimulation of the hypothalamus. Paralleling the Berridge–Valenstein procedure, they implanted thermodes in the hypothalamus of rats. The hypothalamic temperature was either lowered or raised by 2.5°C, and the rats' reactions to the presence of food were observed. When the hypothalamus was cooled, rats made nearly three times more feeding responses than when it was heated or left at normal temperature. In general, more feeding-linked behaviors were evident during cooling than during heating of the hypothalamus. Figure 15.3 displays feeding behavior changes obtained under temperature manipulation. Note that cooling the hypothalamus has

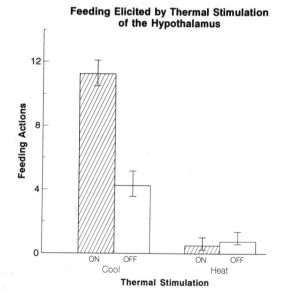

FIGURE 15.3. Feeding behavior changes obtained under temperature manipulation. Reprinted by permission from Berridge and Zajonc (1991).

the same effect on feeding behaviors of rats as does pleasurable electrical stimulation.[2] Thus, if one infers from the Berridge–Valenstein data that electrical brain stimulation is pleasurable, then one must infer from the Berridge–Zajonc data that hypothalamic cooling is pleasurable. Clearly, more research must follow these initial studies before we fully understand the link between affect and hypothalamic temperature.

As mentioned previously, the primary drawback of animal studies is that questions about subjective states are difficult to answer. With human subjects we can access participants' subjective states more directly simply by asking them. This introspective advantage is tempered, however, because the extent of emotional excitation that can be induced in humans in laboratory settings is quite limited. Furthermore, we lose the ability to measure or manipulate brain temperature directly.

Despite these restrictions, a number of studies using humans show that subjective emotional state is associated with changes in temperature. It appears that cooling of the brain "feels" good and heating of the brain "feels" bad. Since direct measures of brain temperature are not possible, proxies must be employed. In the experiments described below, temperature was measured at one or two points on the forehead, midway between the eyebrows and the hairline, and straight above the pupils' position when looking forward. This area is on or near the frontopolar branch of the anterior cerebral artery, which issues from the internal carotid as it enters the brain.[3]

Using forehead temperature and subjective reports allows us to address the question of

---

[2]Why there are no inhibiting effects from heating is not clear. An answer to this question, however, requires a comparison of an electrical stimulation procedure that is comparable to heating and that also inhibits feeding responses. It is not immediately apparent, however, what the nature of such electrical stimulation would be.

[3]Changes in forehead skin temperature are highly correlated with changes in tympanic membrane temperature, which have been shown to be good estimates of changes in brain temperature (see, e.g., Germain, Jobin, & Cabanac, 1987; McCaffrey, McCook, & Wurster, 1975). Although assessing changes on the surface of the tympanic membrane might be a more accurate measure of brain temperature than assessing forehead temperature, resting a temperature probe on the tympanic membrane is quite painful for the subject (Brinnel & Cabanac, 1989). Thus, we have found the forehead to be the best external location for estimating changes in brain temperature.

whether changes in affect influence brain temperature. One prediction of the VTEE is that changes in people's affective states should correspond to changes in their forehead temperatures. When people are feeling positive, their foreheads should display cooling; when they are feeling negative, their foreheads should become warmer. Recent studies in which emotional state is manipulated find these associations. People who are experiencing stress because they believe they have failed miserably on an intelligence test show an increase in forehead temperature of almost 0.5°C (Wolf, 1990). Even the relatively mild affective changes generated by watching clips from an animated children's movie are associated with small but significant forehead temperature changes (McIntosh, Zajonc, Vig, & Emerick, 1991). In this study, subjects watched such movie clips while their forehead temperature was measured and they gave periodic self-ratings of their emotional state. When subjects reported more positive feelings, their temperature was lower than when they reported feeling greater negative emotions.

The VTEE goes beyond predicting that temperature and affect are linked. On the basis of the postulated underlying mechanism, it predicts that nasal breathing will be associated with both temperature and affect. McIntosh et al. (1991) tested these hypotheses by manipulating subjects' affective states with music (either upbeat or sad), while simultaneously measuring their forehead temperatures, breathing patterns, and self-reported affect. Three specific predictions of the VTEE were supported. First, higher temperatures were associated with more negative subjective states. Second, forehead temperature was inversely associated with the volume of air inhaled through the nose (this follows because more air passing through the nose should facilitate cooling of the cavernous sinus and thus the brain). Third, positive affect was related to increases in nasal inhalation, and negative affect was related to decreases in nasal inhalation. With minimal emotional stimulation, small yet significant interrelations among affect, temperature, and nasal breathing predicted by the VTEE were found. This study, however, does not indicate whether changes in nasal breathing do in fact alter temperature and affect.

A more direct test of the influence of temperature on affective reactions was completed by Zajonc, Murphy, and Inglehart (1989). Subjects who believed that they were in a psychophysical study of olfaction were asked to judge the pleasantness of subtle smells delivered to their noses via a small tube. On three critical trials no scent was presented, yet the temperature of the air in the tube was varied (normal, slightly cooled, or warmed), and subjects were asked to rate the smells nevertheless. The results support the VTEE. First, warm air *increased* forehead temperature by about 0.2°C, whereas cool air *decreased* forehead temperature by about 0.1°C. This indicates that brain temperature is influenced by the temperature of the air inhaled via the nose. Second, subjects preferred the "smells" and found them most pleasant when they were presented in association with cool air, and liked "smells" least and rated them least pleasant when they were presented in association with warm air. These data indicate that affective reactions can be caused by changes in temperature.

In the above-described studies, forehead temperature has been viewed as changing in connection with brain cooling caused by nasal breathing. One question is whether such breathing influences skin temperature in general, or, as would be predicted by the VTEE, it influences forehead temperature in particular because of breathing's influence on brain cooling. This issue was addressed by recording changes in dermal forehead and arm temperature for 16 subjects while they pinched their nostrils closed, squeezed a thumb, or breathed normally for 1 minute. The mean dermal temperature change on the forehead when the nose was pinched shut (M = 0.132°C) was significantly larger than when the thumb was squeezed (M = -0.010°C) and during normal breathing (M = -0.002°C). However, there were no significant differences in dermal temperature change on the arm among times when the nose was pinched shut (M = 0.061°C), times when the thumb was squeezed (M = -0.017°C), and normal breathing (M = 0.014°C). Preventing nasal breathing increases forehead temperature but not arm temperature, and forehead temperature is only affected by pinching the nose shut and not by a similar degree of effort made while squeezing the thumb.

Combined, these studies confirm the causal role of nasal breathing in forehead tempera-

ture change—and, by implication, brain temperature change. Forehead temperature can be lowered by inhaling through the nose either cooled air or just more air with a temperature lower than that of the body. Forehead temperature can be increased by inhaling either no air through the nose or inhaling warm air. Furthermore, people's subjective feeling states are related to both breathing and temperature changes of the head. On the whole, then, these data provide consistent evidence that changing brain temperature has affective consequences.

IMPLICATIONS

Facial Efference, Affect, and Temperature

An important implication of the VTEE is that facial action alone—without accompanying emotional excitation—should be able to change subjective states. However, in most studies attempting to relate facial efference to subjective emotional state or its autonomic correlates, the subject is aware that the facial gestures have something to do with emotions. Such confounding can be prevented by eliciting facial efference that is not perceived by the subject as being emotion-related. Phonemic utterance has this quality. For example, the pronunciation of the phoneme *ü* resembles the facial action associated with negative emotions, whereas the pronunciation of the phonemes *e* (as in "cheese") and *ah* resemble facial actions associated with positive emotions. The VTEE predicts that facial efference like that associated with negative emotions should generate negative affect and higher temperatures, whereas facial actions associated with positive emotions should generate positive affect and lower temperatures.

Using this logic, Zajonc et al. (1989) conducted a number of studies in which facial actions that the subjects could not recognize as emotion-related were investigated for their effects on temperature and subjective feeling. In one study, reading stories containing words with many instances of the *ü* sound caused increases in forehead temperature among subjects. Stories containing no instances of *ü* were liked more by the readers than those containing many instances of the phoneme. In further studies, Zajonc et al. (1989) found that having

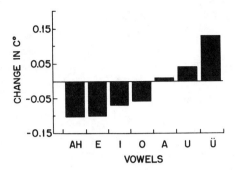

FIGURE 15.4. Changes in forehead temperature for vowel phonemes. Reprinted by permission from Zajonc, Murphy, and Inglehart (1989).

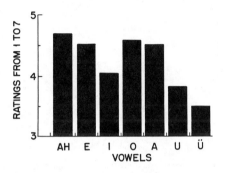

FIGURE 15.5. Pleasantness ratings of vowel phonemes. Reprinted by permission from Zajonc et al. (1989).

subjects simply repeat vowels aloud—and thus perform the facial efferents that accompany positive and negative feeling states—influenced both temperature and feeling state (see Figures 15.4 and 15.5). Voicing the phoneme *ü* was liked least, was associated with the greatest increase in forehead temperature, and put subjects in the most negative mood. This effect held even among German subject, for whom the sound *ü* is quite familiar. Pronouncing the phonemes *e* and *ah* was liked best, produced the greatest decreases in temperature, and put subjects in the best moods. Thus, facial musculature action that is associated with positive and negative feelings states, but that has no emotional meaning to the subject, appears to cause changes in both feeling state and temperature—just what would be expected from the physiological mechanisms we have discussed. James (1890/1950) seems to have been correct in claiming that smiling makes us feel good and that frowning makes us feel bad.

Self-Induced Changes in Feeling State

Since we now know that there are potentially voluntary actions (facial movement and breathing patterns) that influence feeling state, we have a better conceptual handle on several interesting phenomena. Biofeedback, the Lamaze childbirth technique, Qi Chang (a Chinese therapeutic technique that depends on deep nasal breathing), placebo, and meditation are examples of methods used to effect a change in people's feeling states. Analgesic effects on severe pain, for example, were reported for some of these techniques (Fried, 1987, 1990; Jin, 1989; Kojo, 1989; Lundh, 1987; Matthew et al., 1980; Roth, 1989; Yang, Cai, & Wu, 1989). It is quite striking that the literature on these procedures does not offer any ideas about the underlying mechanisms of these dramatic effects.

But these procedures do not work by magic. Something must be happening at the neurophysiological level to reduce pain. The Lamaze technique, Qi Chang, and meditation all involve breathing, and especially deep nasal breathing that is quite likely to augment the cooling action of the cavernous sinus. Biofeedback treatment of migraine headaches involves monitoring changes in finger temperature. The VTEE and the findings from our laboratory suggest that one mechanism by which these practices work is thermoregulation of the brain via changes in facial efference and breathing. The placebo effect, which at times reaches 60% efficiency, may also rely on some action or process that the patient generates. Perhaps people who use these techniques explore various patterns of facial efference and breathing until they find those that produce changes in brain temperature sufficient to alter the release and synthesis of the critical neurotransmitters (say, endorphins). Understanding the actual myogenic processes and their relation to the thermoregulation and neurochemistry of the brain may eventually lead to the discovery of actions people can take to achieve the desired effects.

The VTEE also provides insight into such habitual facial actions as thumb sucking, gum chewing, and fingernail biting. They may all have something to do with the control of brain temperature. For instance, thumb sucking often persists long after it should have extinguished by the absence of the unconditioned reinforcer

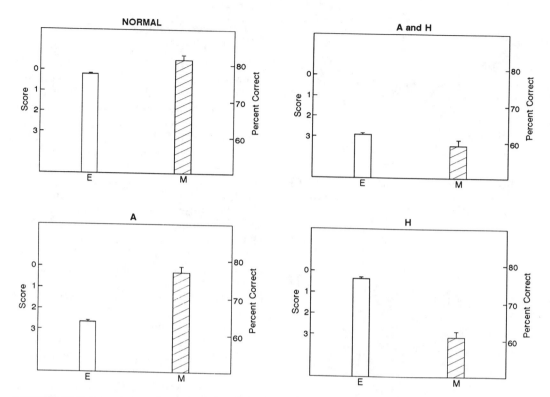

FIGURE 15.6. Dissociation of emotion (E) and memory (M) by lesions of the amygdala and the hippocampal formation. The emotion score was obtained by measuring the responsiveness of monkeys to seven inanimate stimuli that could elicit investigatory or consummatory behavior. The memory score was the score on a delayed nonmatching-to-sample task at a 10-minute delay. Normal, performance by 15 normal monkeys; A and H, performance by two groups of monkeys with damage to both the hippocampal formation and the amygdala (total n = 10); A, performance by two groups of monkeys with damage to the amygdala but not the hippocampal formation (total n = 7); H, performance by two groups of monkeys with damage to the hippocampal formation, associated cortical areas, or both, but not the amygdala (total n = 10). Error bars show the *SEM*. Reprinted by permission from Zola-Morgan, Squire, Alvarez-Royo, and Clower (1991).

(mother's milk). In thumb sucking breathing is possible only through the nose, thus maximizing cooling of the cavernous sinus. Nasal breathing is extremely important for infants because, in contrast to adults, they produce the vast majority of their body heat by the metabolic activity of the brain tissue. This heat must be dissipated, and the cooling of the nasal airways—which can in turn lower the temperature of the blood that enters the brain—is a very important function. These hedonic consequences of nasal breathing may also be responsible for other behaviors, such as gum chewing or fingernail biting.

Affect and Cognition: Two Systems?

Several years ago, the hypothesis was offered that affect and cognition could be in principle separate systems, although they interact on most occasions (Zajonc, 1980). This "primacy of affect" proposal asserts that affective reactions, although in most cases under the influence of cognitive appraisal (Lazarus, 1982), do not *need* a cognitive antecedent. But the evidence for this position was largely indirect.

Recent findings in physiology shed light on this issue. The VTEE offers one possible physiological mechanism by which affect can be altered without cognitive activity. If a change in feeling is possible by a change in breathing pattern or a facial action, no cognitive appraisal is necessary. Furthermore, there is a recent, dramatic neuroanatomic confirmation of the hypothesis that affect and cognition are indeed independent and even separate. Zola-Morgan, Squire, Alvarez-Royo, and Clower (1991) removed monkeys' hippocampus, amygdala, or both, and tested the primates for emotional reactivity and memory functions. Their data, reproduced in Figure 15.6, show quite unambiguously that removing the amygdala destroys affective reactivity but leaves memory functions intact, whereas destroying the hippocampus has the opposite effect. This provides direct evidence for the independence of affect and cognition.

CONCLUSION

One of the longest-standing issues in psychology is the question of how the physical influences the mental, and vice versa. Current emotion research has the promise of answering aspects of this question as it grapples with interrelations among physical, cognitive, and emotional experiences (Zajonc & McIntosh, 1992). Recent evidence supports James's (1890/1950) claim that physical changes can cause emotional changes. Here we have described research about the *process* that makes this influence possible.

Simply put, changes in brain temperature (sometimes quite small ones) influence subjective feeling state—perhaps by facilitating or inhibiting neurochemical processes. Because of the structure of the vascular system, brain temperature can be altered via facial muscular action and nasal breathing patterns. We have described a number of studies that have found support for this theory by demonstrating that the theoretically predicted associations among temperature, affect, and nasal breathing exist. A more complete understanding of the relation between brain temperature and emotion will emerge as work on various aspects of the proposed process is completed—for example, work on thermal influences on specific neurochemical action; the effects of cooling specific brain structures; the types of emotional changes (e.g., motivational vs. evaluative) that are influenced by temperature; and the cognitive consequences of temperature-induced changes in affect.

REFERENCES

Abramowski, E. (1913). Oddech jako czynnik zycia duchowego [Breathing as a factor of psychic life]. In *Prace z psychologii do swiadczalnej* (t. l) [Studies in experimental psychology (Vol. 1). Warsaw: Wende.

Bendixen, H. H., Egbert, L. D., Hedley-Whyte, J., Laver, M. B., & Pontoppidan, H. (1965). *Respiratory care*. St. Louis, MO: C. V. Mosby.

Berridge, K. C., & Valenstein, E. S. (1991). What psychological process mediates feeding evoked by electrical stimulation of the lateral hypothalamus? *Behavioral Neuroscience. 105*, 3–14.

Berridge, K. C., & Zajonc, R. B. (1991). Hypothalamic cooling elicits eating: Differential effects on motivation and pleasure. *Psychological Science, 2*, 184–189.

Brinnel, H., & Cabanac, M. (1989). Tympanic temperature is a core temperature in humans. *Journal of Thermal Biology, 14*, 47–53.

Cannon, W. B. (1927). The James–Lange theory of emotion: A critical examination and an alternative theory. *American Journal of Psychology, 39*, 106–124.

Corbit, J. D. (1969). Behavioral regulation of hypothalamic temperatures. *Science, 166*, 256–258.

Corbit, J. D. (1973). Voluntary control of hypothalamic temperature. *Journal of Comparative and Physiological Psychology, 83*, 394–411.

Dib, B., & Cabanac, M. (1984). Skin or hypothalamus cooling: A behavioral choice by rats. *Brain Research, 302*, 1–7.

Drake, A. F., Keall, H., Vig, P. S., & Krause, C. J. (1988). Clinical nasal obstruction and objective respiratory mode determination. *Annals of Otology, Rhinology and Laryngology, 97*, 397–402.

Fried, R. (1987). Relaxation with biofeedback-assisted guided imagery: The importance of breathing rate as an index of hypoarousal. *Biofeedback and Self-Regulation, 12*, 273–279.

Fried, R. (1990). *The breath connection*. New York: Plenum Press.

Germain, M., Jobin, M., & Cabanac, M. (1987). The effect of face fanning during recovery from exercise hyperthermia. *Journal of Physiological Pharmacology, 65*, 87–91.

James, W. (1950). *Principles of psychology* (2 vols). New York: Dover. (Original work published 1890)

Jampel, H. D., Duff, G. W., Gershon, R. K., Atkins, E., & Durum, S. K. (1983). Fever and immunoregulation: III. Hyperthermia augments the primary in vitro humoral immune response. *Journal of Experimental Medicine, 157*, 1229–1238.

Jin, P. (1989). Changes in heart rate, noradrenaline, cortisol and mood during tai chi. *Journal of Psychosomatic Research, 33*, 197–206.

Kluger, M. J., & D'Alecy, L. B. (1975). Brain temperature during reversible upper respiratory bypass. *Journal of Applied Physiology, 38*, 268–271.

Lazarus, R. S. (1982). Thoughts on the relations between emotion and cognition. *American Psychologist, 37*, 1019–1024.

Kojo, I. (1989). Placebo and imagery. *Medical Hypotheses, 27*, 261–264.

Lin, M. T. (1984). Hypothalamic regulation in the rat: Neurochemical aspects. In J. R. S. Hales (Ed.), *Thermal physiology*. New York: Raven Press.

Lundh, L. G. (1987). Placebo, belief, and health: A cognitive–emotional model. *Scandinavian Journal of Psychology, 28*, 128–143.

Matthew, R. J., Largen, J. W., Dobbins, K., Meyer, J. S., Sakai, F., & Claghorn, J. L. (1980). Biofeedback control of skin temperature and cerebral blood flow in migraine. *Headache, 20*, 19–28.

McCaffrey, T. V., McCook, R. D., & Wurster, R. D. (1975). Effect of head skin temperature on tympanic and oral temperature in man. *Journal of Applied Physiology, 39*, 114–118.

McIntosh, D. N., Zajonc, R. B., Vig, P. S., & Emerick,

S. W. (1991, June). *The vascular theory of emotional efference predicts temperature, affect, and breathing interrelations.* Paper presented at the meeting of the American Psychological Society, Washington, DC.

Miller, N. W., & Clem, L. W. (1984). Temperature-mediated processes in teleost immunity: Differential effects of temperature on catfish *in vitro* antibody responses to thymus-dependent and thymus-independent antigens. *Journal of Immunology, 133,* 2356–2359.

Roth, D. L. (1989). Acute emotional and psychophysiological effects of aerobic exercise. *Psychophysiology, 26,* 593–602.

Sappey, P. (1888–1889). *Traité d'anatomie descriptive.* Paris: Delahaye Lecrosnier.

Satinoff, E. (1964). Behavioral thermoregulation in response to local cooling of the rat brain. *American Journal of Physiology, 206,* 1389–1394.

Satinoff, E., & Shan, S. (1971). Loss of behavioral thermoregulation after lateral hypothalamic lesion in rats. *Journal of Comparative and Physiological Psychology, 77,* 302–312.

Sherrington, C. S. (1906). *The integrative action of the nervous system.* New Haven, CT: Yale University Press.

Waynbaum, I. (1907). *La physionomie humaine: Son mécanisme et son rôle social [The human face: Its mechanism and social function].* Paris: Alcan.

Winquist, R. J., & Bevan, J. A. (1980). Temperature sensitivity of tone in the rabbit facial vein: Myogenic mechanism for cranial thermoregulation? *Science, 207,* 1001–1002.

Wolf, T. (1990). *Effects of music on stress reduction.* Unpublished honors thesis, University of Michigan.

Yang, Z. L., Cai, T. W., & Wu, J. L. (1989). Acupuncture and emotion: The influence of acupuncture anesthesia on the sensory and emotional components of pain. *Journal of General Psychology, 116,* 247–258.

Zajonc, R. B. (1980). Feeling and thinking: Preferences need no inferences. *American Psychologist, 35,* 151–175.

Zajonc, R. B. (1985). Emotion and facial efference: A theory reclaimed. *Science, 228,* 15–21.

Zajonc, R. B., & McIntosh, D. N. (1992). Emotions research: Some promising questions and some questionable promises. *Psychological Science, 3,* 70–74.

Zajonc, R. B., Murphy, S. T., & Inglehart, M. (1989). Feeling and facial efference: Implications of the vascular theory of emotions. *Psychological Review, 96,* 395–416.

Zola-Morgan, S., Squire, L. R., Alvarez-Royo, P., & Clower, R. P. (1991). Independence of memory functions and emotional behavior: Separate contributions of the hippocampal formation and the amygdala. *Hippocampus, 1,* 207–220.

III

BASIC PSYCHOLOGICAL PROCESSES IN EMOTION

16

The Emergence
of Human Emotions

MICHAEL LEWIS

Observation of newborn infants reveals a rather narrow range of emotional behavior. They cry and show distress when pained, lonely, or in need of food and attention. They look attentive and focused on objects and people in their world. They appear to listen to sounds, to look at objects, and to respond to tickle sensations. Moreover, they seem to show positive emotions, such as happiness and contentment. When fed, picked up, or changed, they show relaxed body posture, smile, and appear content. Although they show a wide range of postural and even facial expressions, the set of discrete emotions that they exhibit is rather limited. Yet, in a matter of months—indeed, by the end of the third year of life—these same children display a wide range of emotions. Indeed, some have suggested that by this age almost the full range of adult emotions can be said to exist (Lewis, 1992b). In 3 years, the display and range of human emotions go from a few to the highly differentiated many. In order to understand this rapid development, it is necessary for us to consider the set of issues that will enable a careful articulation of their development. The first issue to be discussed, therefore, is the topic of the topology of emotional features. Embedded within this is a consideration of the development of these features. Finally, the developmental sequence over the first 3 years of life is considered.

THE TOPOLOGY OF EMOTION

In order to talk about developmental issues involved in the study of emotion, it is important that we first make clear what we mean by the term "emotion." "Emotion," like the term "cognition," refers to a class of elicitors, behaviors, states, and experiences. If we do not distinguish among these features of emotion, studying them and their development becomes difficult (see, e.g., Zajonc, 1980; Lazarus, 1982). In this section I discuss emotional states, expressions, and experiences in order to clarify the developmental issues related to emotion.

Emotional States

Emotional states are inferred constructs. These states are defined as particular constellations of changes in somatic and/or neurophysiological activity. Emotional states can occur without the organism's being able to perceive these states. Individuals can be angry as a consequence of a particular elicitor and yet not perceive the angry state that they are in. An emotional state may involve changes in neurophysiological and hormonal responses as well as changes in facial, bodily, and vocal behavior. Two views exist concerning emotional states. According to the first, these states are associated with specific receptors; indeed, they constitute the activation of these receptors

(Izard, 1977; Tomkins, 1962, 1963). In the second, emotional states are not associated with specific receptors and do not exist as specific changes; instead, they are general response tendencies associated with specific cognitions (Mandler, 1975, 1980; Ortony, Clore, & Collins, 1988; Schachter & Singer, 1962).

In the first view, specific emotional states are postulated that have concomitant physiological components and that are expressed in specific facial and bodily behaviors. There is a one-to-one correspondence between an emotion, such as anger, fear, sadness, or happiness, and some internal specific state that matches the emotion. This view of specific emotional states has served, since Darwin's (1872/1965) initial formulation, as the basis of what we believe to be the correspondence between the specific emotions we experience and the functions of our bodies. They are inferred states. Except for bodily and facial expression, no one-to-one correspondence has been found between such inferred physiological changes and emotions. Investigators exploring brain function (Davidson & Fox, 1982) and those looking at specific autonomic nervous system changes (Ekman, 1989) argue for some correspondence between specific internal states and specific emotions. Even so, the evidence for specific states remains lacking.

The nonstate theories, which are cognitive in nature, argue less for a specific correspondence between an internal state and emotions; rather, cognitive activity is seen as the determiner of specific emotions. Either general arousal models, such as that of Schachter and Singer (1962), or cognitive theory models have as their basic tenet a denial of the existence of specific states; instead, emotions are believed to occur as a consequence of thinking (Ortony et al., 1988).

Specific states, having specific stimuli which elicit them, can be found (see Lewis & Michalson, 1983, for a discussion of emotional elicitors and their development). For example, the theory of innate releasing mechanisms (IRMs) suggests that animals will show a fear response, given a particular stimulus event. The argument made here is that there is a direct correspondence between a specific elicitor and a specific state. Watson (1919) argued that there are specific elicitors in infants; for example, fear is produced by a falling sensation or by loud noises. Likewise, attachment theorists argued that children show joy or attachment to the objects that take care of them (Bowlby, 1969). On the other hand, it is quite clear that certain specific emotions can be produced only through cognitive processes. For example, certain elicitors invoke cognitive processes, which in turn may elicit or produce specific emotional states. In such cases, cognition is necessary for the elicitation of a specific state, but may not be the material of that state. Consider the emotion of shame. One must have certain cognitions for shame to occur. Shame occurs when persons evaluate their behavior against some standard and find that they have failed. Moreover, they evaluate their total selves as failures (Lewis, 1992b). Such cognitions can lead to a specific emotional state, which may have specific bodily activity.

The views proposed are quite complex:

1. An emotional state can be elicited in some automatic fashion by certain stimulus events—for example, the case of fear when an animal sees a predator (an IRM).

2. Emotional states are not elicited automatically through some innate "prewiring," but rather through cognitive evaluative processes. Plutchik (1980) and I (Lewis, 1992b) have argued for distinguishing between different emotional states on the basis of the difference between prewired and cognitive evaluation.

3. There are no specific emotional states, but only general arousal, which is interpreted vis-à-vis the events surrounding the arousal (Schachter & Singer, 1962). In this model, there is an emotional state, but it is only a general one.

4. There are no emotional states at all, but only cognitive processes that lead to specific emotions.

These differences have important implications for any theory of emotional development. What is clear is even if there are specific emotional states, they may bear little correspondence to our emotional lives—either emotional expressions or our experience of emotions. So, for example, it may be quite possible to have a specific emotional state but to be unaware of it, ignore it, or even deny it. Likewise, we may have a specific emotional state but may choose not to express it. Thus, for example, I may be angry at my dean for not giving me a raise, but I am not likely to express that anger when I see her. Emotional states, then, are inferred, and whether they are specific, general, or nonexistent awaits further research.

If we hold to the existence of emotional states, then for the most part they must be viewed as transient, patterned alterations in ongoing levels of neurophysiological and/or somatic activity. These alterations imply that there is a constant stream of change. It becomes difficult to imagine, therefore, being awake and not being in some emotional state or at some level of arousal. However, since there need not be any correspondence between the emotional state and emotional experience and expression, there is no reason to assume that we are aware of the states that we are in. This does not mean that these states are not affecting our ongoing behavior—only that they are not apparent (Lewis, 1991).

Development of Emotional States

In a discussion of the developmental issues pertaining to emotional states, two issues need to be addressed. The first concerns the nature of the different states and how they are derived; the second pertains to the developmental course of states once they emerge. For example, if emotional states are viewed as specific, the question of how specific states develop needs to be addressed. Two general models are possible. According to one, specific emotional states are derived from developmental processes. Such processes may be purely maturational, or they may be interactive, involving the organism with its environment. The second model does not depict a role for development in the emergence of specific states; rather, discrete emotional states are assumed to be innate.

In the first model, the infant has two basic states or one bipolar state at birth: a negative or distress state and a positive or satiated state. Subsequent states emerge through the differentiation of this basic bipolar state. Differentiation theories focus on both the modulation of the bipolar state and the general arousal state. Hedonic tone and arousal may be the dimensions necessary to generate specific emotional states. This idea was proposed by Bridges (1932) and is considered a differentiation hypothesis. This theory has been adopted by others, including Spitz (1965), Sroufe (1979), and Emde, Gaensbauer, and Harmon (1976), who have added a contextual dimension to the scheme.

The way in which the interface of arousal and hedonic tone develops into specific emotional states remains speculative. It has been argued that both mother–child interaction and maturation underlie the process of differentia-tion (Als, 1975; Brazelton, Koslowski, & Main, 1974; Sander, 1977). The regulation of the child's state may be the mechanism leading to differentiation. Although some theorists stress that emotional differentiation is determined more by biological than by interactive factors, the combination of the two forces seems most likely. Although such a theory is appealing, the derivation of specific emotional states remains without empirical support.

A much simpler developmental model concerning differentiation can be derived from a purely biological perspective. In such a biological model, undifferentiated emotion becomes differentiated as a function of maturation. According to such a view (see Lewis & Michalson, 1983), the rate of differentiation and the unfolding of differentiated emotion states are programmed according to some physiological timetable. The differentiation of general structures into specific structures is a common process in morphology; there is no reason not to consider such a possibility in emotional development. The most likely explanation of emotional development is the differentiation of emotion states as a function of maturation, socialization, and cognitive development—a topic to which I return shortly. Whatever processes underlie this differentiation, the model is developmental in nature.

An alternative model is that some discrete states are preprogrammed in some sense and need not be further differentiated (Izard, 1978). They exist at birth, even though they may not emerge until a later point in development. The view is unlike the differentiation model in that discrete emotional states do not develop from an original undifferentiated state, but are innate at birth in already differentiated form. In this "discrete-systems model," specific emotion states emerge either in some predetermined order or as needed in the life of the infant. They may co-occur with the emergence of other structures, although they are independent of them. The emotional system essentially operates according to biological directives.

These two models address the conceptual difference between experience and structure found in the arguments of Hume and Kant. In one case, experience produces a structure (Hume, 1739/1888); in the other case, experience is assimilated into innate structures (Kant, 1781/1958). In the study of emotional development, the question that one must address is whether emotional states are preformed and depend only on the development of cognitions, or whether cognitions themselves produce the emotional states or structures. Such a distinction is a rather fine one, but has important theoretical implications. Such a distinction can be seen in the study of fear (Lewis & Rosenblum, 1974). Is each fear state the same as other fear states, regardless of the circumstances, or do fear states differ as a function of the elicitors? For example, is the fear state produced by a loud noise the same as the fear state produced by the association of a doctor's white coat with the pain of a needle? Are emotional states independent of or dependent on particular cognitions? If emotional states are independent, they need not be created by the cognitions.

The first issue in the development of states concerns the origin of discrete emotional states. The second issue focuses on the developmental changes in emotional states once they have emerged. For example, an 8-month-old child may show behaviors reflecting fear at the appearance and approach of strangers, and a 2-year-old child may exhibit fear behaviors when he or she has broken the parents' favorite lamp. Do similar fear states underlie the fear expressions in both cases? Although the elicitors of states and the children's cognitive capacities are different in these two cases, the underlying emotional states may be similar.

Major developmental changes may occur in (1) the events that produce emotional states, (2) the behavioral responses used to reference states, and (3) the cognitive structures of children. Whether the emotional state itself changes as a function of development is difficult to determine. However, there may well be important physiological and neural changes that differentiate young and old organisms. Given that there are important physiological changes that occur over age, the physiological processes associated with emotional states may change over time. If this is the case, then the consistency of an emotion may be more a function of our experience of it than a function of the underlying state. What is clear is that the appearance of particular emotions may be dependent upon new cognitions, as well as the fact that new cognitions may allow for the development of new emotions. The former case can be seen again in the example of fear. Although 1-year-old infants may be fearful of falling off a "visual cliff," they are not fearful of failing an exam or being caught cheating on their income tax. Such fears in an adult are the products of elaborate social and cognitive development. Examples of the latter case—that is, of new emotions produced by new cognitions—are classes of emotions called "self-conscious evaluative emotions." These emotions, such as pride and shame, cannot occur until elaborate cognitive processes have occurred (see Stipek, Recchia, & McClintic, 1992).

Emotional Experiences

Emotional experience is the interpretation and evaluation by individuals of their perceived emotional state and expression. Emotional experience requires that individuals attend to their emotional states (i.e., changes in their neurophysiological behavior), as well as the situations in which the changes occur, the behaviors of others, and their own expressions. Attending to these stimuli is neither automatic nor necessarily conscious. Indeed, emotional experience may not occur because of competing stimuli to which the organism's attention is drawn. For example, consider the following scenario: The car a woman is driving suddenly has a blowout in the front tire; the car skids across the road, but the woman succeeds in bringing it under control and stopping the car on the shoulder. Her physiological state, as well as her facial expression, may indicate that while she is bringing the car under control her predominant emotional state is fear. Because her attention is directed toward controlling the car, however, she is not aware of her internal state or of her expressions. She only experiences fear after she gets out of the car to examine the tire. Emotional experiences thus require people to attend to a select set of stimuli. Without attention, emotional experiences may not occur, even though an emotional state may exist. Many other examples are possible. According to the clinical literature, a patient may be in a particular emotional state (e.g., depression), but may attend to select features of that state (e.g., fatigue), and so may only experience tiredness. Or a patient may not experience pain at the dentist if he is distracted through the use of earphones and loud music.

The emotional experience may not necessarily be conscious, either. If one is willing to distinguish between conscious and unconscious experiences, emotional experiences may occur at different levels of consciousness. Such an analysis forms the basis of much psycho-analytic thought. For example, a man may be in an emotional state of anger. That is, proper measurement techniques would show a pattern of internal physiological responses indicative of anger. Moreover, this person may act toward those objects that or persons who have made him angry in a way suggesting that he is intentionally behaving in response to an internal state of anger. Nonetheless, the person may deny that he feels anger or is acting in an angry fashion. Within the therapeutic situation, this man might be shown that (1) he is angry, and (2) he is responding intentionally as a consequence of that anger. The therapeutic process may further reveal that unconscious processes are operating in a fashion parallel to conscious ones. Defense mechanisms, for example, function at separate levels of awareness. Although awareness may not be at a conscious level, unconscious awareness may still exert powerful effects. Slips of the tongue, accidents, and classes of unintentional conscious behavior may all be manifestations of intentional unconscious awareness (Freud, 1901/1960). Thus, people may experience their internal states and expressions and be aware of this experience, or they may experience them in an unconscious mode in which the conscious perception of the experience is unavailable.

Up until this point, this discussion has assumed the existence of an internal state that is experienced. As some have argued, the experiencing of an emotion does not have to rely upon any internal state at all. In fact, no internal state may exist. For those who do not believe in the construct of a unique set of variables marking a specific state (Ortony et al., 1988), the experience of the state is nothing more than a cognitive construction, utilizing such perceptions as the nature of the experience, past history, the responses of others, and so on. In such a view, emotional experiences are the unique and specific states themselves. From a cognitive-constructive point of view, such a view of emotions is quite reasonable. In fact, clinical data suggest that emotional experiences can occur without specific physiological states. Thus, for example, spinal injury patients who are incapable of receiving neural messages from below the waist report sexually orgasmic experiences, even though no state information is available to them. They construct the experience from their past

knowledge and not from any change in their neurophysiological state.

Emotional experiences occur through the interpretation and evaluation of states, expressions, situations, behaviors of others, and beliefs about what ought to be happening. Emotional experiences are therefore dependent on cognitive processes. Cognitive processes involving interpretation and evaluation are enormously complex and involve various perceptual, memory, and elaborating processes. Evaluation and interpretation not only involve cognitive processes that enable organisms to act on information, but are very much dependent on socialization to provide the content of the emotional experience. The particular socialization rules are little studied and not well understood (see Lewis & Michalson, 1983, and Lewis & Saarni, 1985, for discussions of some of the socialization rules).

Not all theories of emotional experience need be tied to the context, nor do all suggest that there is an underlying emotional state. However, all emotional experience does involve an evaluative interpretive process, including the interpretation of internal states, context, behavior of others, and meaning given by the culture.

Development of Emotional Experiences

The development of emotional experiences is one of the least understood aspects of emotion. Emotional experiences require that the organism possess some fundamental cognitive abilities, including the ability to perceive, discriminate, recall, associate, and compare. Emotional experiences also require a particular cognitive ability—that is, the development of a concept of self. Emotional experiences take the linguistic form "I am frightened" or "I am happy." In all cases the subject and object are the same (i.e., oneself). Until an organism is capable of objective self-awareness (Duval & Wicklund, 1972), the ability to experience may be lacking. Emotional experience requires both general cognitive capacities—something I touch upon below—and the specific cognitive capacity of self-referential behavior, or what I have referred to as "consciousness" (Lewis, 1991a, 1992a, 1992b).

General cognitive processes necessary for an organism to perceive and discriminate elicitors of particular behaviors, whether these be internal or external to them, as well as overt emotional expressions of themselves as well as others, have a developmental course. For example, infants younger than 6 months are generally unable to discriminate between facial patterns and do so on the basis of discrete features (Caron, Caron, & Myers, 1982). Schaffer (1974) demonstrated that children cannot make simultaneous comparisons prior to 7 or 8 months of age. This would suggest that infants are not capable of experiencing emotions prior to this point. Moreover, some emotional experiences may require a higher level of cognitive processing than others, and some are likely to develop earlier than others. For example, fear probably emerges earlier than shame, since the former requires less cognitive and evaluative processing than the latter (Lewis, 1992b).

If emotional experience is the consequence of an evaluation of one's bodily changes, and also of the context and the behaviors of others, then two processes are necessary for most emotional experiences: (1) the knowledge that the bodily changes are uniquely different from other changes; that is, they are internal rather than external; and (2) the evaluation of these changes. The internal–external distinction for emotional development is important, because it addresses the differences between experience and expression. If we believe that facial expression is equivalent to an emotional state or experience, then it is possible to infer an internal event by examining its external manifestation. If, however, we do not subscribe to the view of a one-to-one correspondence between expression and experience, then all we can say is that there is an external manifestation of some unperceived internal event. Emotional experiences, by nature, are internal events. Moreover, the internal and external distinction can only be carried out by a self capable of making the distinction between the self and the other. Such evaluation may involve the process of self-awareness.

Self-awareness is an information-processing and decision-making event related to internal stimuli. It logically requires an organism to possess the notion of agency (Lewis, 1991). The term "agency" refers to that aspect of action that makes reference to the cause of the action—not only who or what is causing the stimulus to change, but who is evaluating it. The stimulus change itself may have the effect of alerting the organism and forcing it to make some type of evaluation. Emotional experience requires that the organism be capable of attending to itself. Thus, the statement "I am happy" implies two things. First, it implies that I have an internal state called happiness, and second, that I perceive that internal state of myself. Until organisms are capable of this cognitive capacity, they should not be capable of emotional experiences (Lewis, 1992a, 1992b; Lewis & Brooks-Gunn, 1978, 1979; Lewis & Michalson, 1983).

This does not mean that infants, prior to acquiring an objective self or consciousness of the self, do not have unique emotional states; they do. What seems reasonable to postulate is that an individual can be in a particular emotional state and yet not experience it. As we have seen in the example of the woman whose car slides off the road, an emotional state can exist without experience; thus, we can imagine an infant's having an emotional state without being able to experience it. This leads to the rather peculiar proposition that a child can be in a state of pain or fear, yet not experience that state, if by "experiencing it" we mean being able to make reference to the self as having that state. In a series of studies, my collaborators and I have demonstrated that the emergence of this self-conscious process does not occur prior to 15 months of age and seems to emerge mostly as a function of maturation in the second half of the second year of life. It is only then that children both can be in a particular emotional state and can be said to experience that state. Moreover, the production of certain states requires self-awareness; therefore, certain emotions are unlikely to occur until this cognitive process emerges (Lewis, Sullivan, Stanger, & Weiss, 1989).

Once the basic cognitive processes that allow for objective self-awareness or consciousness occur, organisms are capable of experiencing emotions. As I have pointed out, they may be capable of experiencing existing emotional states as well as of experiencing emotions that have no internal state, either because internal emotional states do not exist or because the organisms are experiencing a different emotional state than that which exists. The rules that govern how we experience our emotional states or how we create emotional experiences are themselves complex and varied. Clearly, socialization rules are involved on both a cultural and a familial or individual level. For example, in cultures that do not tolerate interpersonal aggression—Japan, for example—the experiencing of anger is culturally inappropriate. It may be the case that Japanese children or adults may act in an angry way and may even have an emotional state of anger. However, since having such a state is inappropriate, they will probably not have the emotional experience of anger. Exactly how the socialization process proceeds so as to influence, modify, alter, or accent emotional experiences is little understood. Clearly, the socialization of emotion involves the socialization of at least all three features of emotion discussed here. It affects the meaning of stimuli and what we allow events to do in terms of acting as elicitors of particular emotions. It affects the dimension of emotional expressiveness, and, finally, it affects the emotional experience.

From an interpersonal and intrapersonal point of view, the socialization rules that act on the experiencing of emotion are somewhat better articulated. Freud's theory of the unconscious and of defense mechanisms addresses this point. Defense mechanisms have as their chief function preventing individuals from experiencing emotions or, alternatively, from having emotions that they do not like to have. For example, denial and repression serve the function of preventing people from having particular emotional experiences that they deem unacceptable. These defense mechanisms prevent certain emotional experiences by not allowing them to become conscious or self-aware. Projection, on the other hand, allows for the experiencing of the emotion—not as the self's experiencing it, however, but as the self's experiencing it in another. As we can see, the major function of each defense mechanism is to provide a means for altering emotional experience.

Emotional Expressions

Emotional expressions are those potentially observable surface changes in face, voice, body, and activity level. Emotional expressions are seen by some as the manifestation of internal emotional states (Ekman & Friesen, 1974). In fact, no single measure of emotional states is more clearly differentiating than emotional expressions. The problem with emotional expressions is that they are soon capable of being masked, dissembled, and in general controlled by the individual. Moreover, emotional expressions are subject to wide cultural and socialization experiences. Thus, the rela-

tionship between expressions and states remains somewhat vague (Lewis & Michalson, 1983). The measurement of emotional expression is reviewed in detail in other chapters, so I spend little time here on the definition of emotional expression except to make several points.

First, emotional expressions tend to be studied in terms of facial expression, and although adults' body postures have been studied (see, e.g., Argyle, 1975), the study of children's emotional expressiveness in terms of body postures and activity has received little attention. Vocalizations are one of the least understood aspects of emotional expression, although they seem to be important conveyors of emotional states. Indeed, vocal expressions are extremely powerful and may have the ability to elicit similar emotional states in others (Fernald, 1989). Vocalization may be much more contagious than facial or bodily expressions. For example, movies are much funnier when one sees them with others who laugh out loud than when one sees them alone. Because of the contagious nature of vocalization, vocial expression may be the target of early socialization efforts. Crying is a case in point. Crying behavior is quickly brought under control as parents socialize their children not to cry when distressed or in need. Locomotion may be another mode of expressing emotions. For example, running away from and running toward an object are locomotive responses associated with negative and positive emotions, respectively. Indeed, it is often infants' moving away from an unfamiliar toy or person, independent of facial expression, that is often used to reference fear (Schaffer, Greenwood, & Parry, 1972).

Although there are some data on emotional expressions in each of the four modalities (facial, postural, vocal, and locomotor), the relations among them have received almost no attention. It seems reasonable to assume that sobering, crying, and running away form a coherent response that reflects the emotional state of fear. The particular modality used to express an emotion may be a function of specific rules of socialization or of a response hierarchy in which one modality has precedence over another. Such a hierarchy may be determined either by a set of biological imperatives or by a set of socialization rules. The use of one or more channels to express a particular emotion may be determined by a complex set of interactions.

One issue of particular interest is the effect on some expressions when one modality is inhibited. Inhibition in a particular modality can be experimentally produced—for example, by preventing a child from moving about. For instance, if children are prevented from running away from an approaching stranger because they are restrained in a highchair, they may express their internal state more intensely through alternative means, such as changes in facial musculature. Another example of the use of differential modalities in expressing emotions occurs in the work on stress. We (Lewis, Ramsay, & Kawakami, in press), for example, found that infants who do not express the emotion of distress when pained are more likely to show large adrenocortical responses. Suomi (1991) and Levine and Wiener (1989) have found a similar phenomenon in non-human primates: Monkeys that do not show loud cries of distress upon being separated from their mothers are much more likely to show higher adrenocortical responses. Thus, the relationship between modalities of expression may play an important role in determining what emotional expressions are presented and how intensely.

Development of Emotional Expressions

The question concerning the development of emotional expressions takes many forms. It is quite clear that discrete emotional expressions can be seen in infants at very young ages. Although there is some discussion as to the number of discrete emotions that are visible (as opposed to mixtures), theories of the development of emotional expression depend upon whether or not emotional expressions are believed to be directly connected to emotional states. Even more central to the issue of the development of emotional expressions is the particular system used to measure them. Because measurement systems for coding expressions other than facial ones are scarce, little is known about the development of other expressions. Thus, most attention has been paid to facial expressions and their development.

Another developmental problem concerns the issue of context. Emotional expressions may be connected to emotional states and to particular elicitors, and the likelihood of observing an emotional expression depends on the nature of the connections. That is, an investigator must know what is likely to make a child afraid in order to produce and measure fear expressions. Since emotional elicitors have a developmental course (Lewis & Michalson, 1983), and emotional expressions are produced by a specific situation, the study of the development of expressions is more complicated than it would seem. The failure to observe an expression in response to a particular elicitor does not constitute grounds for concluding that the expression is not present at that age, since it may appear under other circumstances.

The developmental course of emotional expressions, then, is uncharted. Nevertheless, parents have no difficulty in responding to questions designed to examine their beliefs about when children first express emotions (Pannabecker, Emde, Johnson, Stenberg, & David, 1980). Generally, parents tend to agree about when they think their children first show a particular emotion. It remains, however, to be determined whether their responses are a function of when emotions actually emerge or whether their answers reflect their own belief systems. It is likely that if such questions were asked of parents in different cultures or at different historical times, different results would be obtained. Thus, whereas 87% of American parents see anger in their babies within the first 3 months (Pannabecker et al., 1980), it may be the case that in cultures characterized by less aggression, parents see the emergence of anger somewhat later. The problem with the emergence of emotional expressions and their meaning is quite complicated. The face is an active set of muscles; it is likely to produce combinations that can be measured as reflecting particular emotions.

We are much more inclined to believe that particular emotional expressions reflect a specific underlying state in infants and young children when we see particular faces in particular contexts. Thus, for example, when a child shows a wary or fearful face at the approach of a stranger, we are more apt to credit this face as meaning that the child is in a fear state than if the child shows the same face toward its mother, who is sitting next to it. Recently, my associates and I (Alessandri, Sullivan, & Lewis, 1990; Lewis, Alessandri, & Sullivan, 1990) have observed children's facial responses as they learn a simple task of pulling a string in order to turn on a slide. In the course of their learning, as measured by increases in arm-pulling rate over an observed base rate, we have observed particular emotional expressions that appear appropriate for the particular phase of learning. Thus, for example, the infants show interest when setting about to solve the problem; surprise and joy at the point of discovery; and loss of interest and distress after they have completely mastered the task. Moreover, infants show angry faces when their instrumental responding is interfered with. These faces, expressed in the context of particular situations, lend validating meaning to the connection between facial expression and internal state.

Nevertheless, the question of whether a facial expression truly reflects an emotional state cannot be answered. Indeed, except for phenomenological self-report, it cannot even be addressed in human adults. Adults often make faces that do not reflect the emotional states they report having. Izard (1978) sees an innate connection between emotional expressions and their states. One might think of the developmental process as the connection of expressions to states. Alternatively, there may be no development; there may be, from the start, an innate connection between facial expressions and some underlying internal states (Lewis & Michalson, 1985).

REINTEGRATING EMOTIONAL LIFE

In the preceding discussion, I have focused upon specific features of emotional life. As I have tried to indicate, confusion among these features is apt to lead to nonproductive discussions. Thus, emotions can be considered cognitive if we focus on emotional experiences and can be considered noncognitive if we focus on emotional states. Moreover, in the discussion of "emotion" we have disassembled some of the features that go into emotional life.

The purpose of this discussion has been to see how the developmental process can affect each of these components: state, expression, and experience. Unfortunately, such an analysis does a disservice to the complexity of emotional life. Moreover, it does not allow us to look at developmental issues that may be related to the relationship between various components. Consider the relationship between emotional expression and state. As we (Lewis

& Michalson, 1983) have tried to demonstrate, the relationship between emotional expression and state may well undergo developmental change. It seems reasonable to assume that very early in life, emotional expressions and states may have little correspondence. At some point in development, there appears to be some coherence between emotional states and expressions. States and expressions seem to bear some one-to-one relation to each other; for instance, a child smiling at someone's joke reflects an internal state of amusement or happiness. However, we know that children very quickly learn to dissociate expression from internal states. Children as young as 2½ years of age are quite capable of successfully lying about committing a transgression, through verbal response as well as through facial response (Lewis, Stanger, & Sullivan, 1989). With socialization and further development, the dissociation of expression from internal state takes place. Thus, there is a developmental course in the connection between expression and state. A similar analysis can be made for the coherence between internal state and experience. Earlier in the developmental process, children may have internal states that they do not experience. There may then be a period in which internal states and experiences form some coherence, only to change once again so that experiences of emotion can take place without internal states. These developmental sequences in the coherence between features of emotional life need more careful articulation.

A MODEL OF EMOTIONAL DEVELOPMENT

In the remainder of this chapter, I present a model of the emergence of different emotions over the first 3 years of life. I choose the first 3 years because the majority of adult emotions emerge and develop during this period. This is not to say that past 3 years of age other emotions do not emerge, or that the emotions that have emerged are not elaborated more fully; I suspect that both are the case.

One problem with articulating a model of the emergence of emotional life has to do with the appropriate markers for the emotions. Are we making reference solely to emotional expressions, or are we talking about emotional states or experiences? Given the content of our

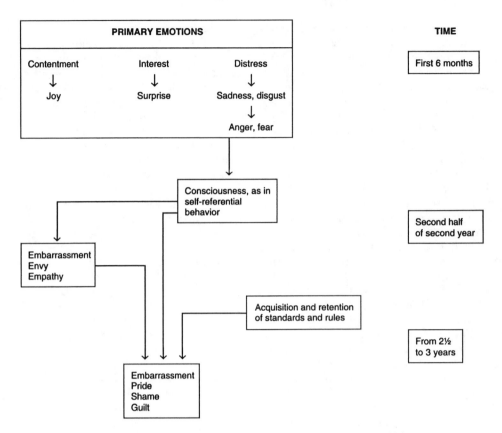

FIGURE 16.1. Development of emotions over the first 3 years of life.

inquiry—namely, the study of the emergence of emotions in the first 3 years of life—we are presented with a difficulty. The ability to observe the emitted behaviors of the child is all that is possible. In order to get at emotional experiences, we need language in the form of "I am sad" or "I am ashamed." Since during this period the language of the child is quite limited, the study of emotional experience is impossible. Likewise, the study of emotional states is difficult to undertake, because "emotional state" is a construct that has not been demonstrated; that is, there has been little success to date in finding unique configurations of neurophysiological events that mark unique emotions in adults, let alone children and infants.

What we are left observing are emotional expression and behavior. However, all does not appear lost, especially if we observe emotional behavior in context. This allows us, at least from the adult meaning system, to assume that the child's expression reflects something

more than a surface manifestation of the emotion. Observation of fear over the approach of a stranger, or joy when a mother appears, allows us to accept that an internal state of fear or joy exists. With these limitations in mind, the following discussion and mapping of emotional development can take place.

Following Bridges (1932), as well as others, we assume that at birth the child shows a bipolar emotional life. On the one hand, there is general distress marked by crying and irritability. On the other hand, there is pleasure marked by satiation, attention, and responsivity to the environment. Attention to the environment and interest in it appears from the beginning of life, and we can place this at the positive pole; or, if we choose, we can separate this, thus suggesting a tripartite division with pleasure at one end, distress at the other, and interest as a separate dimension (see Figure 16.1).

By 3 months, joyful expression emerges. Infants start to smile and appear to show excitement/happiness when confronted with familiar events, such as faces of people they know or even unfamiliar faces. Also by 3 months, sadness emerges, especially in connection with the withdrawal of positive stimulus events. Three-month-old children show sadness when their mothers stop interacting with them. Disgust also appears in its primitive form—a spitting out and getting rid of unpleasant-tasting objects placed in the mouth. Thus, by 3 months, children are already showing interest, joy, sadness, and disgust, and exhibiting these expressions in appropriate contexts.

Anger has been reported to emerge between 4 and 6 months (Stenberg, Campos, & Emde, 1983). Anger is manifested when children are frustrated—in particular, when their hands and arms are pinned down and they are prevented from moving. Recently, however, we (Lewis et al., 1990) have shown anger in 2-month-old infants when a learned instrumental act is removed. This study demonstrates the earliest known emergence of anger. Anger is a particularly interesting emotion, since, from Darwin (1872/1965) on, it has been associated with unique cognitive capacity. Anger is thought to be both a facial and motor/body response designed to overcome an obstacle. Notice that in this definition of anger, the organism has to have some knowledge of the instrumental activity needed to accomplish a goal. For anger to be said to be adaptive, it has to be a response that attempts to overcome a barrier blocking a goal. In some sense, then, means–ends knowledge has to be available, and the demonstration of anger at this early point in life reflects the child's early knowledge acquisition relative to this ability (Lewis, 1991).

Fearfulness seems to emerge still later. Again, fearfulness reflects further cognitive development. Schaffer (1974) has shown that in order for children to show fearfulness, they have to be capable of comparing the event that causes them fearfulness with some other event, either internal or external. Thus, for example, in stranger fear an infant has to compare the face of the stranger to its internal representation or memory of faces. Fear occurs when the face is found to be discrepant with, or unfamiliar relative to, all other faces that the child remembers. Children's ability to show fearfulness, therefore, does not seem to emerge until this comparison ability emerges. Children begin to show this behav-

ior at about 7 to 8 months, although it has been reported by some to occur even earlier, especially in children who seem to be precocious. In the first 8 or 9 months of life, children's emotional behavior reflects the emergence of the six early emotions, called by some "primary emotions" or "basic emotions" (see, e.g., Izard, 1978; Tomkins, 1962).

Surprise also appears in the first 6 months of life. Children show surprise when there are violations of expected events; for example, when infants see a midget (a small adult) walking toward them, they are reported to show interest and surprise rather than fear or joy (Brooks & Lewis, 1976). Surprise can also be seen as a response to discovery, as in an "Aha!" experience. We (Lewis, Sullivan, & Michalson, 1984) found that when children were taught an instrumental arm-pulling response, they showed surprise at the point when they discovered that the arm pull could turn on a slide. Surprise can reflect either a violation or a confirmation of expectancy. Cognitive processes play an important role in the emergence of these early emotions, even though the cognitive processes are limited; this is not so for the next class of emotions.

Figure 16.1 indicates that a new cognitive capacity emerges sometime in the second half of the second year of life. The emergence of consciousness or objective self-awareness (self-referential behavior) gives rise to a new class of emotions. These have been called "self-conscious emotions" and include embarrassment, empathy, and envy. Although little work exists in the development of these emotions, several studies support the emergence of embarrassment at this point in development. We (Lewis, Sullivan, et al., 1989) have shown that the emergence of embarrassment only takes place after consciousness or self-recognition occurs. In a study of children 9–24 months of age, we were able to demonstrate that embarrassment is related to the emergence of self-recognition. Empathy, too, emerges in relation to self-recognition (Halperin, 1989). Although no studies on envy have been conducted, observation of children between 18 and 24 months of age reveals the appearance of envy.

Two points are to be noticed about this class of emotions. First, the observation of these emotions requires measuring not only a facial expression, but bodily and vocal behavior as well. Whereas the earlier emotions can be observed readily in specific facial configurations, these new emotions require measurement of bodily behavior. Embarrassment, for example, is best measured by nervous touching, smiling, gaze aversion, and return behaviors. The second important point related to the emergence of these emotions is that although they reflect self-consciousness, they do not require self-evaluation. The emergence of these self-conscious emotions is related uniquely to the cognitive milestone of paying attention to the self. This topic is taken up in more detail in another chapter (see Lewis, Chapter 39, this volume).

Figure 16.1 also shows a second cognitive milestone, which occurs sometime around 2 years of age. This ability is characterized by the child's capacity to evaluate its behavior against a standard; the standard can be external, as in the case of parental or teacher sanction or praise, or it can be internal, as in the case of the child's developing its own standards. This capacity to evaluate one's behavior in relation to a standard develops in the third year of life. The ability to be able to compare one's behavior to a standard gives rise to another set of emotions. We have called these "self-conscious evaluative emotions"; they include pride, shame, and guilt, among others. These emotions require that a child have a sense of self and be capable of comparing the self's behavior against standards. If children fail vis-à-vis the standard, they are likely to feel shame, guilt, or regret; if they succeed, they are likely to feel pride (Lewis, 1992b). It is important to note that pride and shame are quite different from happiness and sadness. For example, we can win a lottery and feel quite happy about winning the money; however, we would not feel pride because we would not view the winning of the lottery as having anything to do with our behavior. The same is true for failure; we might feel sad if we were not able to do something, but if it was not our fault, then we would not feel shame or guilt. These complex social evaluative emotions make their appearance at about 3 years of age (see Lewis, 1992b; Stipek et al., 1992).

Thus, by 3 years of age, the emotional life of the child has become highly differentiated. From the original tripartite set of emotions, the 3-year-old has come to possess an elaborate and complex emotional system. Although the emotional life of the 3-year-old will continue to be elaborated and will expand, the basic structures necessary for this expansion

have already been formed. New experiences, additional meaning, and more elaborate cognitive capacities will all serve to enhance and elaborate the child's emotional life. However, by 3 years of age, the child already shows those emotions that Darwin (1872/1965) characterized as unique to our species—the emotions of self-consciousness—but which may be present in the great apes as well. With these, part of the major developmental activity has been achieved.

REFERENCES

Alessandri, S. M., Sullivan, M. W., & Lewis, M. (1990). Violation of expectancy and frustration in early infancy. *Developmental Psychology*, 26(5), 738–744.

Als, H. (1975). *The human newborn and his mother: An ethological study of their interaction.* Unpublished doctoral dissertation, University of Pennsylvania.

Argyle, M. (1975). *Bodily communication.* New York: International Universities Press.

Bowlby, J. (1969). *Attachment and loss: Vol. 1. Attachment.* New York: Basic Books.

Brazelton, T. B., Koslowski, B., & Main, M. (1974). The origins of reciprocity: The early mother–infant interaction. In M. Lewis & L. A. Rosenblum (Eds.), *The effect of the infant on its caregiver* (pp. 49–76). New York: Wiley.

Bridges, K. M. B. (1932). Emotional development in early infancy. *Child Development, 3,* 324–334.

Brooks, J., & Lewis, M. (1976). Infants' responses to strangers: Midget, adult and child. *Child Development, 47,* 323–332.

Caron, R. F., Caron, A. J., & Myers, R. S. (1982). Abstraction of invariant face expressions in infancy. *Child Development, 53,* 1008–1015.

Darwin, C. (1965). *The expression of the emotions in man and animals.* Chicago: University of Chicago Press. (Original work published 1872)

Davidson, R. J., & Fox, N. A. (1982). A symmetrical brain activity discriminate between positive versus negative affective stimuli in human infants. *Science, 218,* 1235–1237.

Duval, S., & Wicklund, R. A. (1972). *A theory of objective self awareness.* New York: Academic Press.

Ekman, P. (1989). The argument and evidence about universals in facial expressions of emotion. In J. Wagner & A. Manstead, (Eds.), *Handbook of social psychophysiology* (pp. 143–164). New York: Wiley.

Ekman, P., & Friesen, W. V. (1974). Detecting deception from the body or face. *Journal of Personality and Social Psychology, 29,* 288–298.

Emde, R. N., Gaensbauer, T., & Harmon, R. (1976). Emotional expression in infancy: A biobehavioral study. *Psychological Issues, 10*(1, Whole No. 37).

Fernald (1989). Intonation and communicative intent in mothers' speech to infants: Is the melody the message? *Child Development, 60,* 1497–1510.

Freud, S. (1960). *The psychopathology of everyday life* (A. Tyson, Trans.). New York: Norton. (Original work published 1901)

Halperin, M. (1989, April). *Empathy and self-awareness*. Paper presented at the meeting of the Society for Research in Child Development, Kansas City, MO.

Hume, D. (1888). *A treatise of human nature* (L. A. Selby-Bigge, Ed.). Oxford: Clarendon Press. (Original work published 1739)

Izard, C. E. (1977). *Human emotions*. New York: Plenum Press.

Izard, C. E. (1978). Emotions and emotion–cognition relationships. In M. Lewis & L. A. Rosenblum (Eds.), *The development of affect: The genesis of behavior, Vol. 1* (pp. 389–413). New York: Plenum Press.

Kant, I. (1958). *Critique of pure reason* (N. Kemp-Smith, Trans.). New York: Macmillan. (Original work published 1781)

Lazarus, R. S. (1982). Thoughts on the relations between emotion and cognition. *American Psychologist*, 37, 1019–1024.

Levine, S., & Wiener, S. G. (1989). Coping with uncertainty: A paradox. In D. S. Palermo (Ed.), *Coping with uncertainty: Behavioral and developmental perspectives* (pp. 1–16). Hillsdale, NJ: Erlbaum.

Lewis, M. (1991). Ways of knowing: Objective self awareness or consciousness. *Developmental Review, 11*, 231–243.

Lewis, M. (1992a). The self in self-conscious emotions: A commentary. In D. Stipek, S. Recchia, & S. McClintic Self-evaluation in young children. *Monographs of the Society for Research in Child Development*, 57(1, Serial No. 226), 85–95.

Lewis, M. (1992b). *Shame, the exposed self*. New York: Free Press.

Lewis, M., Alessandri, S., & Sullivan, M. W. (1990). Violation of expectancy, loss of control, and anger in young infants. *Developmental Psychology*, 26(5), 745–751.

Lewis, M., & Brooks-Gunn, J. (1978). Self knowledge and emotional development. In M. Lewis & L. Rosenblum (Eds.), *The development of affect: The genesis of behavior, Vol. 1* (pp. 205–226). New York: Plenum Press.

Lewis, M., & Brooks-Gunn, J. (1979). *Social cognition and the acquisition of self*. New York: Plenum Press.

Lewis, M., & Michalson, L. (1983). *Children's emotions and moods: Developmental theory and measurement*. New York: Plenum Press.

Lewis, M., & Michalson, L. (1985). Faces as signs and symbols. In G. Zivin (Ed.), *Development of expressive behavior: Biology–environmental interaction* (pp. 153–182). New York: Academic Press.

Lewis, M., Ramsay, D. S., & Kawakami, K. (in press). Affectivity and cortisol response differences between Japanese and American infants. *Child Development*.

Lewis, M., & Rosenblum, L. (Eds.). (1974). *The origins of fear: The origins of behavior, Vol. 2*. New York: Wiley.

Lewis, M., & Saarni, C. (Eds.). (1985). *The socialization of emotion*. New York: Plenum Press.

Lewis, M., Stanger, C., & Sullivan, M. W. (1989). Deception in 3-year-olds. *Developmental Psychology*, 25(3), 439–443.

Lewis, M., Sullivan, M. W., & Michalson, L. (1984). The cognitive–emotional fugue. In C. E. Izard, J. Kagan, & R. B. Zajonc (Eds.), *Emotions, cognition, and behavior* (pp. 264–288). New York: Cambridge University Press.

Lewis, M., Sullivan, M. W., Stanger, C., & Weiss, M. (1989). Self-development and self-conscious emotions. *Child Development*, 60, 146–156.

Mandler, G. (1975). *Mind and emotion*. New York: Wiley.

Mandler, G. (1980). The generation of emotion: A psychological theory. In R. Plutchik & H. Kellerman (Eds.), *Emotion: Theory, research, and experience. Vol. 1. Theories of emotion* (pp. 219–244). New York: Academic Press.

Ortony, A., Clore, G. L., & Collins, A. (1988). *The cognitive structure of emotions*. New York: Cambridge University Press.

Pannabecker, B. J., Emde, R. N., Johnson, W., Stenberg, C., & David, M. (1980). *Maternal perceptions of infant emotions from birth to 18 months: A preliminary report*. Paper presented at the International Conference of Infant Studies, New Haven, CT.

Plutchik, R. (1980). *Emotion: A psychoevolutionary synthesis*. New York: Harper & Row.

Sander, L. W. (1977). Infant and caretaking environment: Investigation and conceptualization of adaptive behavior in a system of increasing complexity. In E. J. Anthony (Ed.), *The child psychiatrist as investigator* (pp. 170–183). New York: Plenum Press.

Schachter, S., & Singer, J. E. (1962). Cognitive, social, and physiological determinants of emotional state. *Psychological Review*, 69, 379–399.

Schaffer, H. R. (1974). Cognitive components of the infant's response to strangeness. In M. Lewis & L. A. Rosenblum (Eds.), *The origins of fear: The origins of behavior, Vol. 2* (pp. 11–24). New York: Wiley.

Schaffer, H. R., Greenwood, A., & Parry, M. H. (1972). The onset of wariness. *Child Development*, 43, 165–175.

Spitz, R. A. (1965). *The first year of life*. New York: International Universities Press.

Sroufe, L. A. (1979). Socioemotional development. In J. D. Osofsky (Ed.), *Handbook of infant development* (pp. 462–516). New York: Wiley.

Stenberg, C. R., Campos, J. J., & Emde, R. N. (1983). The facial expression of anger in seven-month-old infants. *Child Development*, 54, 178–184.

Stipek, D., Recchia, S., & McClintic, S. (1992). Self-evaluation in young children. *Monographs of the Society for Research in Child Development*, 57(1, Serial No. 226).

Suomi, S. (1991). Primate separation models of affective disorders. In J. Madden (Ed.), *Neurobiology of learning, emotion and affect* (pp. 195–213). New York: Raven Press.

Tomkins, S. D. (1962). *Affect, imagery, consciousness: Vol. 1. The positive affects*. New York: Springer.

Tomkins, S. D. (1963). *Affect, imagery, consciousness: Vol. 2. The negative affects*. New York: Springer.

Watson, J. B. (1919). *Psychology from the standpoint of a behaviorist*. Philadelphia: J. B. Lippincott.

Zajonc, R. B. (1980). Feeling and thinking: Preferences need no inferences. *American Psychologist*, 35, 151–175.

17

Understanding Emotion

PAUL L. HARRIS

Our emotional lives are complicated by two factors that are frequently ignored in psychology. First, at least beyond the period of early infancy, we not only feel an emotion, we also know that we are feeling an emotion. This self-awareness can be used to report, anticipate, hide, and alter the emotional state. Second, we can identify and understand the emotions that others feel. This other-awareness can be used to upset or comfort the other person; it also has emotional repercussions for the observer, awakening feelings of guilt, apprehension, and gratitude *vis-à-vis* the other.

In this chapter, I trace the development of this dual awareness. I argue that some of its early manifestations reflect a wider body of knowledge about the workings of the mind that children construct, regardless of culture. Having set out the argument, I review various standard approaches to the development of emotional understanding.

INTENTIONALITY

In the first year of life, infants begin to recognize the intentionality of emotional states—the fact that they are often directed at objects or situations in the environment. This is shown most clearly by the phenomenon of social referencing. Confronted by a salient stimulus whose status is uncertain, infants aged about 9 months will look toward a caretaker as if for guidance. Depending on the emotional stance of the caretaker—for example, encouraging or fearful—infants are more or less likely to approach the stimulus (Klinnert, Campos, Sorce, Emde, & Svejda, 1983). This phenom-

enon reveals several features of the infant's early conception of emotion. First, and most obviously, the infant's selective response shows that he or she is able to discriminate between different facial expressions of the caretaker. In addition, the infant is able to respond appropriately to the emotional significance of the expression: to retreat if the caretaker expresses disgust or fear, and to approach if the caretaker expresses encouragement or pleasure. Finally, and of equal importance, is the fact that the caretaker's expression is not simply an inhibitor or releaser of the infant's ongoing action. It operates in a more complex and subtle fashion. Specifically, the infant treats the expression as a comment on a particular object or person in the immediate environment, rather than as a generalized behavioral instruction. Thus, the infant's selective reaction is directed at the object that the adult looks toward when expressing his or her emotion (Hornik, Risenhoover, & Gunnar, 1987). This last feature of social referencing is important because it shows that the infant conceives of another person's emotional stance as an intentional stance—one that is targeted at, and to be glossed as, a comment on a particular object.

In the first year of life, infants resonate appropriately to the emotional expressions of other people, but show little sign of regarding them as states of the other persons that may be initiated or assuaged by their own actions. In short, infants exhibit little tendency to comfort or deliberately upset another person. This starts to change in the second year of life. Although there are important individual differences, infants begin to make rudimentary efforts to comfort a caretaker or sibling who shows obvious signs of distress. For example, they may approach and pat a distressed person, or offer him or her objects (Zahn-Waxler & Radke-Yarrow, 1982). In a parallel fashion, infants start to make deliberate efforts to upset or tease other people in the second year: They may deliberately strike another person, or make off with objects that the other clearly wants (Dunn & Munn, 1985). These various behaviors show that 1- and 2-year-olds think of another person as experiencing an emotional state that they themselves can causally influence. In particular, they exhibit simple efforts to alter the relationship between the other person and the intentional object or target of his or her emotion. Thus, they proffer or withdraw a desired object. They step between warring parents, or they direct their ministrations to the body part of a sibling who has been hurt.

DESIRES AND BELIEFS

Recent research has shown that children aged between 2 and 3 years begin to construe actions in terms of the desires that motivate and guide them. By the age of 4 and 5 years, they also acknowledge that agents do not always pursue their goals with bona fide knowledge of the best means. Children realize that agents select actions in terms of their beliefs—true or false—about how best to attain what they desire (Harris, 1989; Perner, 1991; Wellman, 1990).

This psychological "theory" is also used by children in their understanding of emotion. Insofar as 2- and 3-year-olds regard other people as agents who pursue their own individual goals, they also assume that the emotions these agents experience will be a function of the match between reality and their goals. Thus, children understand that other people will be sad if they do not get what they want, but happy if they do. This very simple conception of emotion is quite powerful. It allows children to realize, for example, that there is nothing inherently joyful or sad in a given outcome; its effect on particular agents may vary sharply. Thus, one person may be pleased to be given milk if that was what he or she wanted, whereas another person may be sad to be given milk if he or she wanted juice instead (Harris, Johnson, Hutton, Andrews, & Cooke, 1989; Yuill, 1984).

By the age of 4 or 5 years, this simple conception is elaborated still further. The child starts to realize that it is not the fit between desire and actual outcome that elicits emotion, but rather the fit between desire and assumed outcome. For example, let us say that the child watches a little drama in which a monkey tricks an elephant: The monkey offers the elephant a can of Coke, Coke being the elephant's favorite drink. Unknown to the elephant, however, but known to the child (who has watched the monkey's prior machinations), the Coke has been tipped out of the can and replaced by milk, which the elephant does not like. The child can now be asked two questions: How does the elephant feel when she first sees the can, before she sips any of the liquid inside with her trunk? And how does she feel after she has taken a sip? Even 3-year-olds can get the second question right, as we would expect from the preceding analysis. Seeing the elephant as an actor with her own distinctive and subjective desires, they realize that she will be sad when she finds out the true contents of the can—the milk that she does not like, rather than the Coke that she enjoys. However, 3- and 4-year-olds have much more difficulty with the first question, which concerns the elephant's emotion prior to her discovery of the monkey's trick. They judge that even at this point she will be sad, as if she somehow knew what the monkey had done. By contrast, many 5-year-olds and almost all 6-year-olds grasp that the elephant's emotion at this point will be based on a false premise: Seeing the can, she will happily anticipate that she is about to enjoy her favorite drink (Harris et al., 1989).

The emergence of this belief–desire conception of emotion appears to be universal among normal children. For example, Baka pygmy children living in a preliterate community in the rain forests of Cameroon exhibit a similar pattern of development to their peers in the West: By 4–5 years of age, they realize that someone will react emotionally not in terms of the actual situation, but in terms of the situation that they mistakenly take to be true (Avis & Harris, 1991).

SOCIAL STANDARDS

The world would be a simpler place if getting what we wanted made us happy and not getting it made us sad. Yet (outside of *laissez-faire* economics) we rarely condone the naked pursuit of self-interest, and its pursuit rarely makes us happy. Young children do not appear to share these qualms. When told simple stories in which the protagonist does something bad (e.g., stealing), but ends up getting what he or she wants (e.g., the marbles belonging to a classmate), then 4- and 5-year-olds judge that the protagonist will be happy. Here again, we find them applying their simple desire model of emotional satisfaction: Getting what one wants brings happiness, and it does so regardless of the cost to others. By contrast, 8-year-olds recognize that such wrongdoing will probably lead to a bad conscience on the part of the perpetrator—he or she will feel guilty (Nunner-Winkler & Sodian, 1988).

One possible explanation for this moral insouciance on the part of young children is that they simply do not know what is right or wrong. However, there is ample research with preschool children showing that this is not the case. In fact, they have a robust appreciation of the wrongness of misdemeanors such as stealing, hitting, and lying: They go so far as to insist that such actions would be wrong even in a culture or environment with no particular rules about such acts (Smetana, 1981).

A more plausible explanation is that young children view their emotional lives in narrowly hedonistic terms: They do not anticipate gaining any emotional satisfaction from conforming to the moral canons they so firmly recognize. Thus, they do not anticipate that a wrongdoer will feel bad or guilty about having violated a moral standard. Conversely, they do not anticipate that someone acting righteously will feel satisfied or proud at having resisted temptation. This neglect of the influence of rules or standards on our emotional lives appears to extend beyond the moral sphere. For example, it is not until 8 years of age that children realize that someone will be proud at having accomplished something that meets or exceeds a social standard. Until that age, they acknowledge that one might feel pride, but only insofar as one's achievement is witnessed by an approving caretaker (Harter & Whitesell, 1989).

Thus, the available evidence suggests that a sea change occurs at about 6 or 7 years of age in young children's conception of the causes of emotion, or rather in their conception of the springs of action. Whereas the preschooler sees an agent as bent on the pursuit of his or her desires, since their satisfaction will bring unalloyed happiness, the 8-year-old realizes that agents are also motivated to meet certain moral and social standards. Securing an otherwise desirable object will not bring happiness if it involves the violation of those social standards; instead, one will feel guilt or shame. Conversely, forgoing an otherwise desirable object may not necessarily lead to sadness, if in so doing one has abided by some social or moral precept.

MIXED EMOTIONS

Hitherto, I have discussed emotional reactions as if they were uncluttered, singular reactions of sadness, fear, shame, and so forth. In fact, the same situation can trigger more than one emotion, and can even provoke emotions of opposite valence. Faced with a new opportunity, we may feel a conjunction of excitement and apprehension; if eventually that opportunity slips through our fingers and is seized by another person, we may end up feeling regret at the opportunity that we have lost, relief at not having to face the challenge that it might have offered, and envy at the person who will go in our stead.

Young children are quite slow to acknowledge this kaleidoscopic aspect of emotion. Whether they are asked to invent or describe episodes (Harter & Buddin, 1987) or to attribute emotions to a story character (Harris, 1983; Meerum Terwogt, Koops, Oosterhoff, & Olthof, 1986), children below the age of 8 or 9 years are inclined to think of emotional reactions as single-valenced. For example, asked about a story character who is asked down into the circus ring to join the clowns, young children are likely to say that the character will be pleased or afraid, but they typically deny that both emotions can be experienced concurrently. By the age of 9 or 10 years, this constraint is set aside; children acknowledge that the same situation can provoke two opposite feelings.

Why do children find it difficult to acknowledge mixed emotions? On the basis of various control procedures, we can rule out some initially plausible hypotheses. For example, it is not the case that young children misconstrue or simplify situations likely to provoke mixed emotions: Asked to retell stories containing such situations, they show quite accurate recall (Harris, 1983). Nor is it likely that young children reject the possibility of mixed feelings because they think of such feelings as mutually exclusive opposites that cannot co-occur in the same person. Even when asked whether different people might feel a single (albeit different) emotion in response to a given situation, younger children tend to deny that it is possible, and to focus exclusively on one of the two possibilities (Gnepp, McKee, & Domanic, 1987).

A more plausible explanation is that young children fail to scrutinize an emotionally charged situation in an exhaustive fashion. Having settled on one feature of the situation, they cease to consider it from a different point of view, even though they know that it contains other features and can describe these features quite accurately if asked. Support for this emphasis on young children's nonexhaustive appraisal strategy comes from a recent training study. Children listened to a story episode that contained two conflicting components; to ensure that they paid attention to each component, they were asked what emotion each component would provoke. Then, at the end of the story, they were asked how the protagonist would feel overall. Many children who had ignored the possibility of mixed feelings at the outset of the study now acknowledged that the protagonist might feel two opposing emotions; moreover, when they were asked about similar episodes in their own lives, they could frequently recollect appropriate examples. Interestingly, this training effect worked for the 6- and 7-year-olds, but was relatively ineffective for younger children, suggesting that an exhaustive appraisal calls for a minimum information-processing capacity (Peng, Johnson, Pollock, Glasspool, & Harris, 1992).

HIDING EMOTION

Do children realize that a person's emotional expression may not correspond to his or her real emotional state? There are two issues involved in answering this question, one conceptual and the other perceptual. We may begin with the perceptual issue. Research with adults shows that their deliberate displays of emotion differ from their spontaneous expressions of emotion. However, the differences are subtle and hard to detect. Not surprisingly, adults are poor at distinguishing a deliberate, strategic display of emotion from its authentic, spontaneous counterpart. Children also have great difficulty in making this perceptual discrimination.

Despite the difficulty in deciding on any particular occasion whether a smile or frown is fake or genuine, children may still have a general conceptual appreciation of the fact that real and apparent emotion need not coincide. Indeed, several experiments show that this insight emerges quite early, typically between 4 and 6 years of age. For example, if children are told stories that contain two critical components—an emotionally charged situation (e.g., tripping and hurting oneself), and an explicit reason for hiding the ensuing emotion (e.g., the likelihood that other children will tease the victim if he or she bursts into tears)—there is a clear age change in their ability to work out the emotional ramifications. Six-year-olds understand that the victim may really feel sad but will try nonetheless to look happy or OK. They also understand that an onlooker will be misled by this display, mistakenly thinking that the victim is not upset. By contrast, 4-year-olds are more likely to collapse the distinction between real and apparent emotion (Gross & Harris, 1988; Harris, Donnelly, Guz, & Pitt-Watson, 1986).

Several additional features of this age change are worth emphasizing. First, it is not restricted to English-speaking children. Japanese children, who grow up in a culture that places considerable emphasis on the appropriate display of emotion even by young children, show a similar age change (Gardner, Harris, Ohmoto, & Hamazaki, 1988). Second, the ability to conceptualise the difference between real and apparent emotion is not a prerequisite for actually deploying display rules under appropriate circumstances. For example, when children unwrap a gift and find that it is disappointing, they will express less overt disappointment in front of the donor than when they open the gift alone (Cole, 1986), even at 4 years of age.

Thus, children can put certain simple display rules into practice before they can understand them. Indeed, this developmental sequence may be necessary. Specifically, children may first need to create a discrepancy between what they actually feel and what they express to others in order to start to conceptualize that discrepancy. The mismatch between actual and expressed emotion may be especially potent if children are alerted to it by the fact that despite their own awareness of what they actually feel, other people react gullibly to their misleading display of emotion. Notice that it would not be easy for the children to discover any discrepancy between real and displayed emotion with respect to other people, because, as noted earlier, it is hard for children to make any perceptual discrimination between a genuine and a simulated expression (Harris & Gross, 1988).

Finally, it is worth emphasizing the revolutionary nature of the child's discovery. The 6-year-old who adroitly distinguishes between real and apparent emotion has discovered the potential privacy of his or her inner emotional life. For the first time, the child can harbor feelings of resentment, anger, and grief, safe (or sorry) in the knowledge that those feelings may be quite unknown to his or her parents or siblings. Of course, children may doubt whether they can successfully hide emotion; for example, adolescents can be quite explicit about such doubts (Harris, Olthof, & Meerum Terwogt, 1981), and some insecure children may overestimate their parents' access to their private feelings (Main, 1991). Nonetheless, the concept of privacy opens up a thicket of possibilities. For the first time, the child can deliberate knowingly about whether to confide or confess. Equally, once the privacy of others' emotions is understood, the child can begin to wonder about the authenticity of other people's professions of happiness, fearlessness, or love. Finally, the child can start to enter complex triangular relationships in which feelings are deliberately hidden from one person following a request (or threat) from another person.

CHANGING EMOTION

We attempt to control our emotions in two ways—by hiding the outward expression of emotion, and by changing the emotional state itself. It has occasionally been suggested that an alteration in the outward expression is sufficient to change the emotional state, but such effects are weak (Matsumo, 1987). Moreover, they are usually achieved under artificially insulated conditions. Specifically, subjects are asked to compose a particular emotional expression in the absence of any counteracting situation. By contrast, in real life, our attempts to compose a particular facial expression have to counteract the influence of the immediate context. For example, "a brave face" is usually composed not in an affectively neutral situation, but in a threatening or dangerous situation.

Given that a mere outward adjustment of our emotional expression is rarely sufficient to change the emotional state itself, we typically resort to techniques that strike at the cause of the emotion rather than at its symptomatic expression. Do young children make this differentiation? In an interview study, children aged 6, 11, and 15 years were asked about the possibility of both hiding and changing their emotion (Harris et al., 1981). Children typically gave different answers to these two questions. With respect to hiding emotion, they emphasized the need to change one's outward behavior. With respect to changing emotion, on the other hand, they focused on the cause of the emotion: They suggested changing either the immediate external situation, or the thought processes sustaining the emotion.

Various studies have shown that there is a gradual shift with age in the balance between these latter two strategies. Younger children concentrate on the need to change the external situation. Older children, in contrast, mention cognitively oriented strategies in addition (Altshuler & Ruble, 1989; Band & Weisz, 1988; Harris & Lipian, 1989). For example, in a study of boys who had just started to live at a new boarding school, a popular technique for warding off homesickness was keeping oneself mentally occupied, thereby leaving no time for thoughts of home (Harris & Guz, 1986).

One plausible explanation for children's increasing emphasis on this technique is that it is part of a wider conceptual change in their understanding of the mind. Specifically, as children get older, they realize that the mind has a limited information-processing capacity. Accordingly, they realize that negative thoughts and the emotions they arouse can be deliberately displaced by positive thoughts and the emotions they arouse. A particularly effective analgesic in the case of painful thoughts is an activity that requires concentration. Even if the activity is not especially enjoyable in itself, it may still serve the function of blocking out painful thoughts. Accordingly, the boarding-school boys sometimes mentioned absorbing intellectual activities (e.g., solving math problems) as a therapeutic technique (Harris, 1989).

REVIEW AND IMPLICATIONS

The evidence reviewed in the preceding sections suggests that children's understanding of emotion is part of a wider conceptual development. A flurry of recent research (Astington, Harris, & Olson, 1988; Harris, 1989, 1991; Perner, 1991; Wellman, 1990) has charted the emergence of the child's so-called theory of mind. Without necessarily subscribing to the notion that children are busy working out a theory concerning the operations of the mind, we can readily acknowledge that children are constructing an increasingly elaborate conception of the way in which a variety of reactions, including emotional reactions, are governed by mental states. During the first year of life, children begin to acknowledge the intentionality of emotion; in the preschool years, emotions are increasingly incorporated into a simple belief–desire psychology. In the school years, this psychological model is refined in various ways as children begin to understand more about the control of emotion, including both the external expression and the internal state itself. We can now begin to consider the implications of these findings for standard theories of emotion and emotion understanding.

Emotion Scripts

A long tradition of work in social cognition, beginning with Borke's pioneering studies (Borke, 1971), has demonstrated that children rapidly work out the type of situations that elicit various emotions—fear, sadness, happiness, guilt, and so forth (Barden, Zelko, Duncan, & Masters, 1980; Harris, Olthof, Meerum Terwogt, & Hardman, 1987). Children are also aware of the typical actions and expressions that accompany a particular emotional state (Trabasso, Stein, & Johnson, 1981).

Given children's facility in building up this knowledge base, it is tempting to conclude that their understanding of each emotion involves a script in which there are slots for the eliciting situation; the subjective state; and the accompanying physiological, behavioral, and expressive symptoms of the emotion. Such an emphasis on script-based knowledge has several advantages. First, it assimilates children's understanding of emotion to a wider body of research on children's understanding of other regular, sequentially organized events (cf. Nel-

son & Gruendel, 1979). Second, it draws attention to the fact that an understanding of emotion calls for a causal understanding of the connections among the sequential components. Third, the script notion is sufficiently flexible that it promises to be of service when we look outside the Western world to children's understanding of emotion in cultures where different emotional themes are prominent (see Lutz, 1987).

Nonetheless, there are problems with a narrow emphasis on script-based understanding. Although it is loosely correct to claim that particular situations arouse particular emotions, closer scrutiny reveals a conceptual difficulty. Specifically, the same situation can elicit different emotions, depending on the appraisal that the actor makes of the situation. To take a simple example, even 3- and 4-year-olds in an experiment described earlier (Harris et al., 1989) realized that the impact of discovering the actual contents of a gift container would depend on whether it matched what the person wanted. Thus, the very same discovery can lead to happiness or sadness, depending on the actor's appraisal. This means, for example, that we cannot write down a list of the situations that elicit happiness, confident in the knowledge that they will have a similar impact on everyone.

A possible solution to this problem is to define the eliciting situation in more abstract terms. For example, we might define situations that provoke happiness as "situations that bring about the fulfillment of an actor's desire." Once we move in this direction, however, we are tacitly recognizing that emotions are very special kinds of scripts. They do not begin with the kind of objective event that we normally associate with scripts (e.g., the action of sitting down at a table may be seen as the first move in the dinner script). Rather, they begin with an event that is inherently psychological, such as an actor's getting what he or she wants. In short, we can apply the script notion to children's understanding of emotion, but its successful application will presuppose an analysis of children's psychological understanding.

A second disadvantage of the script-based approach is that it provides no impetus for the identification of developmental regularities in children's understanding. For example, research described in an earlier section has shown that at about the age of 4–5 years, children start to understand the role of beliefs. This insight appears to generalize across different emotions, including happiness, surprise, and fear (Hadwin & Perner, 1991; Harris et al., 1989. Were children simply acquiring a distinct script for particular emotions, such cross-emotion regularity would not be expected.

The Emotional Unconscious

The traditional approach to the emotional unconscious is to assume that painful feelings are repressed. That such repression occurs is taken for granted by psychoanalytic theory. This is not the place to debate the merits and demerits of the psychoanalytic approach to emotional development. However, it is worth underlining two features of the psychoanalytic approach that contrast with the current approach. First, according to psychoanalytic theory, the child represses painful rather than pleasurable material; only if the latter is associated with threat or guilt is it also subject to repression. Thus, according to psychoanalytic theory, there would be no reason to expect the child to repress feelings of unalloyed joy. Second, the cause of repression is motivational rather than cognitive. Precisely because certain feelings are painful, the child is motivated to banish them from consciousness.

The developmental account that I have described offers a quite different approach to the emotional unconscious. First, it is plausible to suppose that in early infancy a child has emotions and expresses them, but simply lacks the ability to conceptualize his or her emotional experience. Thus, the infant feels and expresses fear or anger, but lacks the conceptual ability to realize that it is in any particular emotional state. Exactly when children start to become aware of their own emotions is, of course, difficult to establish. To the extent that children talk appropriately about their emotions in the second and third year of life (Bretherton & Beeghly, 1982), we can be confident that by that age, if not sooner, they are aware of their emotional states.

Nevertheless, even after this achievement, it is likely that children's awareness remains sharply constrained. I have argued earlier that the appropriate attribution of an emotion depends on an analysis of the actor's beliefs and desires. Consider a child who is trying to make sense of an emotion experienced at some earlier point in time. For example, the child may have been left alone by the caretaker and starts to worry that the caretaker is not going to return. Eventually, the caretaker does return and the anxiety dissipates. The child who seeks to explain his or her feelings to the caretaker may be at a loss, because the belief that caused that anxiety is difficult to reconstruct. There is now considerable evidence that young children have difficulty in acknowledging that someone might hold a false belief. This difficulty occurs not only when a child is invited to diagnose what someone else believes (e.g., the duped elephant in the experiments described earlier), but also when the child attempts to reconstruct what he or she mistakenly believed a few minutes earlier (Gopnik & Astington, 1988; Wimmer & Hartl, 1991).

What exactly might we expect, then, when the child is reunited with his or her caretaker? Theoretically, there are two possibilities. First, the child may remember the fear or distress that was felt during the separation, but (having now abandoned the mistaken belief that the caretaker will not return) may be unable to conceptualize the belief that caused the emotion, and therefore may explain only part of what has happened to the caretaker. Alternatively, in the absence of the ability to reconstruct the belief that caused the emotion, the child may also have difficulty in reconstructing the emotion that it generated. In that case, the child's narrative to the caretaker may be even more sparse. For example, the person looking after the child may explain to the caretaker that the child burst into tears at a certain point; the child, when asked about this, may claim not to remember doing any such thing.

This hypothetical outcome is, of course, similar to the type of outcome that psychoanalytic theory would expect. However, it is important to emphasize that the account I have provided lacks both of the critical elements of the psychoanalytic account. The child's lack of awareness is attributable to cognitive and not to motivational factors. In addition, the reason for the child's lack of awareness has nothing to do with the painfulness of the emotion when it was experienced.

To make this last point very clear, we may consider another hypothetical situation. This time, we may envisage the child separated from its caretaker but playing happily. The caretaker is not expected to return for some time. Suddenly, however, the door opens and the caretaker reappears. The child experiences surprise. Here again, the child needs to reconstruct a mistaken belief (namely, that the caretaker was not about to return) in order to make sense of the surprise that he or she is experiencing. In the absence of the ability to reconstruct that mistaken expectation, we should expect the child to have difficulty in explaining his or her surprise (or even in acknowledging that surprise was felt at all), because once the caretaker is there, the (mistaken) belief that the caretaker is not about to return is abandoned. In this hypothetical example, there is no suggestion that the child is upset when the reunion occurs; if anything, the child is pleasantly surprised that the reunion has occurred earlier than expected. Nonetheless, if the account that I have developed above is correct, we should expect children to have difficulty in conceptualizing any emotion, positive or negative, that is caused by a mistaken belief.

This analysis can even be extended to emotions that are not linked to mistaken beliefs. Recent research has shown that although 3-year-olds find it particularly difficult to reconstruct a belief that they no longer hold, they also have difficulties (albeit less acute) in reconstructing a desire or goal that they no longer have (Baron-Cohen, 1991a; Gopnik & Slaughter, 1991). Consider, for example, a 3-year-old who is upset at having to hand a toy back to a younger sibling; a few minutes later, when the child is happily occupied with some alternative activity, it may be difficult for the child to conceptualize the earlier desire and the emotion that its frustration provoked.

A further example of the same family of difficulties arises with respect to ambivalent or mixed feelings. Recall that without special training, children find it difficult to acknowledge the possibility of experiencing a positive and a negative emotion at the same time until they are approximately 9 or 10 years of age. This difficulty is not attributable to any constraint on the young children's capacity to experience and express mixed feelings. Consider, for example, the extensive research within attachment theory on the group of insecurely attached infants who express an ambivalent emotional reaction to their caretakers on their reunion after separation: Such infants want to approach their mothers, but, at the same time, resist the cuddling or comforting that they offer. It will be many years

before these children can conceptualize the mixed feelings that they express.

In sum, we must distinguish carefully between the emotions that children feel, and the emotions that they can also conceptualize and talk about. Young children will frequently exhibit an easily recognizable emotion; observers may readily identify the beliefs and desires (including the contradictory desires) that lie behind the emotion. For the children themselves, however, it may be difficult to make sense of the emotions that they experience. To conceptualize an emotion requires going beyond the raw experience of the emotion. It needs to be placed in its psychological context. Without that context, children may simply recollect an inchoate feeling and its accompanying overt behavior, with little conscious appreciation of the cause and identity of the emotion. This lack of awareness should not be confused with motivated repression; it occurs because of a cognitive limitation, rather than a defense mechanism.

Individual Differences

Hitherto, I have written about children's understanding of emotion in terms of a relatively stable, age-based sequence, implying that some of the major features of that sequence are to be found universally, in all types of cultures. What role is there for individual differences in such an approach?

First, recent research has shown that those children who encounter problems in understanding the mind exhibit a parallel restriction in their conception of emotion. For example, having established that autistic children have difficulty in conceptualizing beliefs (Baron-Cohen, Leslie, & Frith, 1985), Baron-Cohen (1991b) went on to demonstrate that autistic children have a similar difficulty in understanding belief-based emotions. On the other hand, autistic children show no obvious difficulty (when compared to normal and retarded control groups equated for mental age) in understanding the link between certain familiar situations and particular emotions (Baron-Cohen, 1991b; Tan & Harris, 1991). Since we know from research with normal children that an understanding of belief-based emotions is a later developmental achievement, the implication is that autistic children are delayed in working out the psychological basis for emotion. They reach one of the lower rungs on the ladder, but have difficulty in proceeding further. In short, one obvious way in which individual differences can and do arise is in terms of the rate of progress through the developmental sequence. Severe psychopathology, as in the case of autism, retards progress.

It is unlikely, however, that children vary exclusively in terms of their rate of progress. We may also expect children to show gaps and lacunae rather than a pervasive retardation. Various illustrative studies may be cited. First, there is evidence that emotionally disturbed children (attending special schools) deviate from normal children in their conception of display rules. When they are asked about situations in which it would be appropriate to hide their feelings, such children acknowledge that it would be appropriate to hide one's feelings in at least some situations. Thus, these children understand the basic conceptual point that real and apparent emotion need not coincide. Nevertheless, they apply that insight in a different way from normal children. Normal children recognize that one should hide one's feelings both in order to protect oneself (recall, for example, the story mentioned earlier concerning the child who trips and falls but does not want to be teased for crying) or to protect the feelings of other people (recall the situation of the child who opens a disappointing gift, but manages to smile at the donor). Emotionally disturbed children have particular difficulties with the latter category (Adlam-Hill & Harris, 1988; Taylor & Harris, 1984). One plausible explanation is that they have difficulty in recognizing the impact of their emotions (if expressed) on other people's emotions.

Children also vary in their understanding of strategies for changing as opposed to hiding emotion. For example, Meerum Terwogt, Schene, and Koops (1990) interviewed a group of emotionally disturbed children attending a special school. When asked about strategies for changing emotion, these children were more likely to insist that emotion is an autonomous, inescapable process that cannot be redirected. These studies illustrate how the study of normal development can be used to illuminate abnormal development. Specifically, the study of normal development offers us a set of conceptual benchmarks. We can use these to create a relatively detailed profile of abnormal development. Children who are categorized, for example, as autistic or emotionally disturbed are not abnormal in their entire conceptualization of emotion; rather, they deviate

in specific ways. This circumscribed deviation is helpful from a therapeutic point of view, because it shows where a particular child may need special help, and where the child may enjoy relatively normal development.

REFERENCES

Adlam-Hill, S., & Harris, P. L. (1988). *Understanding of display rules for emotion by normal and maladjusted children.* Unpublished manuscript, University of Oxford.

Altshuler, J. L., & Ruble, D. N. (1989). Developmental changes in children's awareness of strategies for coping with uncontrollable stress. *Child Development, 60,* 1337–1349.

Astington, J. W., Harris, P. L., & Olson, D. R. (Eds.). (1988). *Developing theories of mind.* New York: Cambridge University Press.

Avis, J., & Harris, P. L. (1991). Belief–desire reasoning among Baka children: Evidence for a universal conception of mind. *Child Development, 62,* 460–467.

Band, E. R., & Weisz, J. R. (1988). How to feel better when it feels bad: Children's perspectives on coping with everyday stress. *Developmental Psychology, 24,* 247–253.

Barden, R., Zelko, F., Duncan, S., & Masters, J. (1980). Children's consensual knowledge about the experiential determinants of emotion. *Journal of Personality and Social Psychology, 39,* 968–976.

Baron-Cohen, S. (1991a). The development of a theory of mind in autism: Deviance or delay. *Psychiatric Clinics of North America, 14,* 33–51.

Baron-Cohen, S. (1991b). Do people with autism understand what causes emotion? *Child Development, 62,* 385–395.

Baron-Cohen, S., Leslie, A. M., & Frith, U. (1985). Does the autistic child have a theory of mind? *Cognition, 21,* 37–46.

Borke, H. (1971). Interpersonal perception of young children: Egocentrism or empathy. *Developmental Psychology, 5,* 263–269.

Bretherton, I., & Beeghly, M. (1982). Talking about internal states: The acquisition of an explicit theory of mind. *Developmental Psychology, 18,* 906–921.

Cole, P.M. (1986). Children's spontaneous control of facial expression. *Child Development, 57,* 1309–1321.

Dunn, J., & Munn, P. (1985). Becoming a family member: Family conflict and the development of social understanding in the second year. *Child Development, 56,* 480–492.

Gardner, D., Harris, P. L., Ohmoto, M., & Hamazaki, T. (1988). Japanese children's understanding of the distinction between real and apparent emotion. *International Journal of Behavioral Development, 11,* 203–218.

Gnepp, J., McKee, E., & Domanic, J. A. (1987). Children's use of situational inferences to infer emotion: Understanding emotionally equivocal situations. *Developmental Psychology, 23,* 114–123.

Gopnik, A., & Astington, J. W. (1988). Children's understanding of representational change and its relation to the understanding of the appearance–reality distinction. *Child Development, 59,* 26–37.

Gopnik, A., & Slaughter, V. (1991). Young children's understanding of changes in their mental states. *Child Development, 62,* 98–110.

Gross, D., & Harris, P. L. (1988). Understanding false beliefs about emotion. *International Journal of Behavioral Development*, *11*, 475–488.

Hadwin, J., & Perner, J. (1991). Pleased and surprised: Children's cognitive theory of emotion. *British Journal of Developmental Psychology*, *9*, 215–234.

Harris, P. L. (1983). Children's understanding of the link between situation and emotion. *Journal of Experimental Child Psychology*, *36*, 1–20.

Harris, P. L. (1989). *Children and emotion: The development of psychological understanding*. Oxford: Blackwell.

Harris, P. L. (1991). The work of the imagination. In A. Whiten (Ed.), *Natural theories of mind*. Oxford: Blackwell.

Harris, P. L., Donnelly, K., Guz, G. R., & Pitt-Watson, R. (1986). Children's understanding of the distinction between real and apparent emotion. *Child Development*, *57*, 895–909.

Harris, P. L., & Gross, D. (1988). Children's understanding of real and apparent emotion. In J. W. Astington, P. L. Harris & D. R. Olson (Eds.), *Developing theories of mind*. New York: Cambridge University Press.

Harris, P. L., & Guz, G.R. (1986). *Models of emotion: How boys report their emotional reactions upon entering an English boarding school*. Unpublished manuscript, University of Oxford.

Harris, P. L., Johnson, C. N., Hutton, D., Andrews, G., & Cooke, T. (1989). Young children's theory of mind and emotion. *Cognition and Emotion*, *3*, 379–400.

Harris, P. L., & Lipian, M. S. (1989). Understanding emotion and experiencing emotion. In C. Saarni & P. L. Harris (Eds), *Children's understanding of emotions*. New York: Cambridge University Press.

Harris, P. L., Olthof, T., & Meerum Terwogt, M. (1981). Children's knowledge of emotion. *Journal of Child Psychology and Psychiatry*, *22*(3), 247–261.

Harris, P. L., Olthof, T., Meerum Terwogt, M., & Hardman, C. E. (1987). Children's knowledge of situations that provoke emotion. *International Journal of Behavioral Development*, *10*(3), 319–343.

Harter, S., & Buddin, B. (1987). Children's understanding of the simultaneity of two emotions: A five-stage acquisition sequence. *Developmental Psychology*, *23*, 388–399.

Harter, S., & Whitesell, N. (1989). Developmental changes in children's emotion concepts. In C. Saarni & P.L. Harris (Eds.), *Children's understanding of emotions*. New York: Cambridge University Press.

Hornik, R., Risenhoover, N., & Gunnar, M. (1987). The effects of maternal positive, neutral, and negative affective communications on infants' responses to new toys. *Child Development*, *58*, 937–944.

Klinnert, M., Campos, J. J., Sorce, J., Emde, R. N., & Svejda, M. (1983). Emotions as behavior regulators: Social referencing in infancy. In R. Plutchik & H. Kellerman (Eds.), *Emotion: Theory, research, and experience. Vol. 2. Emotions in early development*. New York: Academic Press.

Lutz, C. (1987). Goals, events, and understanding in Ifaluk

emotion theory. In D. Holland & N. Quinn (Eds.), *Cultural models in language and thought*. Cambridge, England: Cambridge University Press.

Main, M. (1991). Metacognitive knowledge, metacognitive monitoring, and singular (coherent) vs. multiple (incoherent) model of attachment: Findings and directions for future research. In C. Parkes, J. Stevenson-Hinde, & P. Marris. (Eds.), *Attachment across the life cycle*. London: Taristock/Routledge.

Matsumo, D. (1987). The role of facial expression in the experience of emotion: More methodological problems and a meta-analysis. *Journal of Personality and Social Psychology*, *52*, 769–774.

Meerum Terwogt, M., Koops, W., Oosterhoff, T., & Olthof, T. (1986). Development in processing of multiple emotional situations. *Journal of General Psychology*, *11*, 109–121.

Meerum Terwogt, M., Schene, J., & Koops, W. (1990). Concepts of emotion in institutionalized children. *Journal of Child Psychology and Psychiatry*, *31*, 1131–1143.

Nelson, K., & Gruendel, J., (1979). At morning it's lunchtime: A scriptal view of children's dialogues. *Discourse Processes*, *2*, 73–94.

Nunner-Winkler, G., & Sodian, B. (1988). Children's understanding of moral emotions. *Child Development*, *59*, 1323–1338.

Peng, M., Johnson, C. N., Pollock, J., Glasspool, R. & Harris, P. L. (1992). Training young children to acknowledge mixed emotions. *Cognition and Emotion*, *6*, 387–401.

Perner, J. (1991). *Understanding the representational mind*. Cambridge, MA: MIT Press.

Smetana, J. G. (1981). Preschool children's conception of moral and social rules. *Child Development*, *52*, 1333–1336.

Tan, J., & Harris, P. L. (1991). Autistic children understand seeing and wanting. *Development and Psychopathology*, *3*, 163–174.

Taylor, D. A., & Harris, P. L. (1984). Knowledge of strategies for the expression of emotion among normal and maladjusted boys: A research note. *Journal of Child Psychology and Psychiatry*, *24*, 223–229.

Trabasso, T., Stein, N. L., & Johnson, L. R. (1981). Children's knowledge of events: A causal analysis of story structure. In G. Bower (Ed.), *Learning and motivation* (Vol. 15). New York: Academic Press.

Wellman, H. M. (1990). *The child's theory of mind*. Cambridge, MA: MIT Press.

Yuill, N. (1984). Young children's coordination of motive and outcome in judgments of satisfaction and morality. *British Journal of Developmental Psychology*, *2*, 73–81.

Wimmer, H., & Hartl, M. (1991). The child's understanding of own false beliefs. *British Journal of Developmental Psychology*, *9*, 125–138.

Zahn-Waxler, C. & Radke-Yarrow, M. (1982). The development of altruism: Alternative research strategies. In N. Eisenberg-Berg (Ed.), *The development of prosocial behavior*. New York: Academic Press.

18

Tolstoy and the Riddle of Developmental Transformation: A Lifespan Analysis of the Role of Emotions in Personality Development

CAROL MAGAI

JILL HUNZIKER

As many people may know, Lev Nikolaye-vich Tolstoy, the brilliant, self-absorbed Russian novelist, had periodic bouts of depression throughout his life; much of his work conveys an undertone of the unhappiness that the author himself suffered. In later life Tolstoy experienced what appears to have been a major transformation following a particularly intense period of depression. A central idea that haunted him was the ultimate meaning of life. What did it matter, he asked himself, that he had achieved fame? And what difference would it make if his fame were even to exceed that of Pushkin, Shakespeare, and Molière? In a state of great despondency, he contemplated suicide. But Tolstoy had also always had a dread of death, and thus he continued to seek an understanding of, and relief from, his despair. Eventually he turned to a consideration of the working class—people whom he had always idealized—for an answer to his existential dilemma. The working class, he observed, did not seem to trouble themselves with suicidal impulses, and he concluded that the answer resided in their religious faith. Tolstoy joined the Russian Orthodox Church but then left after 3 years, disillusioned with organized religion. He ultimately found meaning in the Gospels, in particular the Sermon on the Mount, and with this as his model he resolved to give away all his worldly goods and live as a peasant—which he did, albeit in his own idiosyncratic way. Tolstoy came to the conclusion that one lived not for the self nor for one's family. One had to divest oneself of worldly connections in order to embrace a more generalized love for mankind. It thus appeared that Tolstoy relinquished a compelling and thorough-going narcissism for a renovated life of self-abnegation and other-directed caring.

How does one make sense of an individual life and transformations in personality patterns? How does current developmental theory deal with the uniqueness of the individual within the context of development? Is personality change real or illusory? To judge from contemporary developmental research, we are still in a veritable Dark Ages in terms of our ability to predict change and/or continuity in the human life course. Nor do we seem to have advanced very far in our understanding of the dynamics of individual development over the lifespan. This lack of progress appears to derive from the sheer complexity of the task, as well as from other factors. One such factor concerns the tendency of our discipline to privilege nomothetic over idiographic approaches to psychological phenomena (Allport, 1937). The nomothetic bias, inherited from the natural sciences and experimental psychology, is geared toward extracting universal principles; however, it also tends to flatten individual differences and hence the opportunity to learn about the dynamics of growth and development. The other major obstacle to tracking the important developmental issues of change and continuity can be attributed to lifespan developmental psychology's virtual neglect of the emotions.

In the present chapter we address the issue of differential personality development over the lifespan, highlighting the role of emotions. We argue that an analysis of emotional organization, particularly in the context of the study of individual lives, will confirm the thesis that emotionally salient moments within the lifespan interact with individual emotional organizations over progressive developmental periods to precipitate both individual continuity and individuation. We begin with a review of general developmental theories and then turn to a consideration of theories that address the emotional content of lives. In the course of this chapter, we hope to merge these understandings with the goal of forwarding a more explanatory model of life course development.

SOURCES OF DEVELOPMENTAL VARIANCE

General Developmental Models

One of the longest-standing developmental debates revolves around the issue of whether the human personality is fundamentally permeable or intransigent to change. Put in contemporary terms, the issue is one of continuity or discontinuity in developmental trajectories. As a general rule of thumb, developmental theories tend to characterize human development as either stage-like or continuous. Stage theories assume that growth is a function of movement from one qualitatively different stage or developmental epoch to another, whereas continuity models view growth as a function of gradual accretion, such that

change is quantitative rather than qualitative. Erikson's (1950) epigenetic model of psychosocial development is somewhat more idiosyncratic, especially in its more recent formulations. His theory is a stage theory much like that of Piaget in its emphasis on qualitative differences at different developmental epochs, but it also emphasizes three other properties that are instructive for a life course analysis.

The first is the notion of what we call "developmental divergence," which contrasts with the more typical universalistic bias found in most stage theories. In universalistic models, the developmental stages are determined by the basic nature of the human organism and its biological inheritance. In more open models such as Erikson's, individuals confront developmental nodes that pose new tasks and potential crises, and that can be resolved in a variety of ways. There are various opportunities for consolidation, regression, or reorganization and growth. This development is thus viewed as a product of a uniquely emergent organism–environment interaction.

The second aspect of Erikson's theory that pertains to our thesis is the suggestion that each developmental transition point can be characterized in terms of the particular kinds of emotions or emotional issues that are galvanized within the transition point. For example, following early infancy, the child will be confronted with the developmental task of achieving success in muscular coordination and bodily control. Muscular maturation sets the stage for experimenting with two social modes: holding on and letting go, either of which can be dealt with by falling prey to hostility on the one hand, or developing benign expectations and attidues on the other. If this nodal developmental period is resolved successfully, the child experiences growing self-confidence and a sense of efficacy. Under less optimal circumstances the child experiences failure, self-doubt, and ultimately shame. In Erikson's system, shame is a by-product of rage turned against the self through repeated exposure to the caregiver's inability to provide adequate positive feedback to the child. Thus, the emotional residues of this developmental stage revolve around varying degrees of self-confidence, rage, and shame. An analysis of each of Erikson's eight stages indicates that different emotions are generated by different developmental tasks, and that the emotional residues of each developmental node tend to be different. Although Erikson was one of the few lifespan developmental psychologists to point to the importance of emotions in psychosocial development, he was not particularly focused on the emotions, and the emotional aspects of the various developmental nodes were not fully elaborated.

The third notable aspect of Erikson's theory is the notion that there is developmental continuity in the midst of change: Personality structure becomes a modification and elaboration of earlier structures, rather than the creation of an entirely new structure. In our own treatment we incorporate each of these three important aspects of developmental theory, but elaborate more fully on the organizational and transformational aspects of emotions. In addition, we include a fourth aspect that is not addressed by Erikson and that we consider important in accounting for individual differences—that of non-normative events.

Other Sources of Developmental Variance

A number of developmentalists have stressed that the human life course is punctuated by non-normative developmental challenges in addition to the expected challenges, and that these events can alter the trajectory of lives in dramatic ways. Losing a parent, contracting a life-threatening illness, winning a lottery, meeting the Prince of Monaco—all are events that might change an individual's life in significant ways. Bandura (1982) has drawn particular attention to what he calls "chance encounters" as formative events; unpredicted social encounters often play an important role in the choice of careers and in the formation of marriages and other partnerships, because they galvanize intense emotions.

In spite of Bandura's insights, chance events in human lives are rarely the focus of research, perhaps because one despairs of ever being able to predict the occurrence of these kinds of phenomena. However, though we cannot predict chance events by definition, it may be possible to gauge the impact that certain types of events may have on individual lives. Bandura's analysis of factors predisposing to the effect of chance encounters in life course change include the following personal factors: social skills that provide access to particular

social milieus; personal susceptibility to social influence; and interpersonal attraction. Note that all of these factors take place in an interpersonal milieu and thus necessarily engender affective products and sequelae. What is missing from Bandura's analysis is the way in which particular kinds of emotional experience influence particular kinds of life choices and thus alter life trajectories.

Transitions and Trajectories

In the time since Erikson's original formulations, other developmentalists have attempted to describe how momentous life events—whether they be normative developmental nodes confronted by almost all individuals as they traverse the life course, or non-normative, unexpected life events such as early widowhood or chance encounters—deflect, undo, or transform earlier developmental trajectories. Developmental crises and transitions appear to offer the opportunity for developmental transformation because they generate psychological disequilibrium. As Caspi and Moffit (1991) point out, most theoretical perspectives on developmental junctures assume that they constitute the periods of time when major reorganizations or discontinuities are most likely to occur. However, there are also a number of studies indicating that developmental transitions often also inspire magnification of basic personality dispositions rather than change (see review by Caspi & Moffit, 1991). Both possibilities (reorganization and magnification), and the processes and dynamics behind them, need to be understood. Indeed, what is missing in most of the research that has studies transitions is an analysis of what it is that gets magnified and produces continuity, and what it is that produces personality transformation and thus discontinuity.

In the present chapter we argue that an individual's unique emotional organization is recruited during moments of crisis and transition to assist coping, and tends to magnify pretransition personality differences. Competing with this tendency is the condition where strong emotions, previously unexperienced because of environmental circumstances or psychological mechanisms of defense, overwhelm the individual and precipitate crisis. In the remainder of this chapter we consider how an individual's emotional organization provides the fundamental superstructure for the interpretation and integration of normative and non-normative developmental crises, and remains at the center of continuity of self. By the same token, we also discuss what it is about emotional experiences that accrue during normative developmental crises, and the emotionally salient experiences of unexpected events and encounters, that may constitute situations of new learning with potential for personality transformation. As a necessary prelude, we first review theory that is most relevant to our consideration of the role of emotions in personality development. As such, a brief overview of attachment theory and discrete-emotions theory is in order.

THEORIES OF EMOTIONAL DEVELOPMENT

There are essentially three bodies of literature that are relevant to the topic of emotional development over the lifespan: psychoanalytic theory, attachment theory, and discrete-emotions theory. The psychoanalytic perspective, which includes the writings of Freud and those of the ego-analytic, object relations, interpersonal, and relational schools, is by nature intrinsically concerned with affect and its products. However, there is also general agreement among the various practitioners of dynamic theory that the psychoanalytic school has failed to produce a systematic theory of affect, much less one that is developmentally informed (although Erikson's psychosocial theory of development does engender discussion of emotional issues, as mentioned earlier). Two other bodies of literature, attachment theory and discrete-emotions theory, offer more systematic treatments of issues that are central to affective development.

Attachment Theory

Attachment theory, as formulated by John Bowlby, represents an attempt to explain the pervasiveness of human social bonds and reactions to their disruptions, and is informed by an unusual theoretical blend of ethology, systems theory, and psychoanalysis. Attachment is viewed as a biologically based, goal-corrected behavioral system oriented toward achieving homeostasis between attachment needs and exploratory drives.

Much of the research following the publication of Bowlby's three-volume work (Bowlby, 1969, 1973, 1980) has tended to focus on how the attachment relationship between infant and caregiver develops over time. Mary Ainsworth and colleagues (Ainsworth, Blehar, Waters, & Wall, 1978) have demonstrated that although all children form attachments, the manner in which a child's attachment needs are achieved can take various forms, and that these relate to personality development. The majority of children form attachments to significant others that are characterized by trust and felt security, which leaves them free to develop an autonomous and flexible sense of self. Two other less optimal outcomes have also been identified in the literature, and are associated with insensitive caregiving. One is the avoidant attachment style, in which a child tends to avoid the caregiver upon reunion following times of distress, and manifests a false independence by appearing not to need the caregiver. The other major insecure attachment style in infants is the ambivalent style, in which a child displays an inconsolability manifested in alternately clinging and rejecting behavior toward the caregiver.

Research on the sequelae of early attachment relationships has emphasized the enduring nature of the bond formed in early infancy, and in continuity of attachment organization over time. Stability of attachment classification is said to be mediated by "internal working models" of the primary attachment relationship, which then generalize to other relationships. The work of Mary Main and colleagues (Main, Kaplan, & Cassidy, 1985) has demonstrated that the majority of children classified as avoidant, secure, and ambivalent retain their classifications into the sixth year of life. The work of adult attachment researchers indicates that adults can also be characterized as either avoidant, secure, or ambivalent in their intimate relationships; moreover, their developmental histories suggest that early experiences with significant others have important developmental consequences that are carried forward in time.

Although attachment theory recognizes that stress releases differential coping in different attachment types, it does not deal specifically with developmental nodes and differential outcomes. Two recent publications by Magai

(Malatesta & Wilson, 1988; Malatesta, 1990) have presented the theoretical framework and supporting data for the argument that emotional biases (particular patterns of discrete emotions) account for the underlying stabilities that have been observed in attachment-related phenomena and other aspects of personality. By the same token, and more significantly for our thesis with respect to developmental change, we also suggest that the emotions galvanized during critical life challenges are pivotal in promoting developmental transformation in attachment relationships, as well as in other spheres of psychological functioning. Although attachment theory embraces an emotional conceptualization of human development, placing affiliative relationships and all that they engender at the center of development, it does not supply us with formulations concerning the role of different emotions in differential development. For this we need to turn to discrete-emotions theory.

Discrete-Emotions Theory

Discrete-emotions theory encompasses the work of a number of writers who espouse the view that the number of basic or primary emotions is limited, and that the different emotions have different properties with implications for feeling, motivation, and behavior. Among the more developmentally oriented writers are Izard (1977) and Tomkins (1962, 1963, 1991). Since Izard's work tends to focus more on the early stages of development, we devote more of our attention to the work of Tomkins, whose writings have more relevance to lifespan issues and differential development. In Tomkins's affect theory, emotions constitute the primary motivational system of humans. Each of the primary emotions (joy, interest, surprise, fear, anger, distress, contempt, disgust, and shame) supplies its own unique kind of motivating information. Fear motivates escape and avoidance behaviors; shyness motivates the defense of privacy; anger motivates the overcoming of obstacles; and so forth. In the course of ontogenesis individuals develop biases or "ideoaffective organizations" around certain emotions, which figure as prominent features of personality and which influence a broad spectrum of behaviors, including information processing and coping strategies. That is, ideoaffective organizations act as selective filters through which incoming information is evaluated for its relevance to the individual's emotion biases; because they engender motivational templates, they also constitute a set of strategies for contending with a variety of conflicts and threats. (See Malatesta & Wilson, 1988, and Malatesta, 1990, for a description of the elicitors of the basic emotions, their motivational properties, and their function within the self and interpersonal systems.)

Tomkins offered a number of formulations about types of affective organization and several models for their elaboration or change over time. He emphasized ideoaffective organizations as both products of socialization and mental elaboration. Although most of his models are variants of the theme that ideoaffective organizations enable and guide the individual throughout life and thus are relatively stable structural features of personality, their activation is context-dependent and thus variable, and it is this aspect that produces occasions for discontinuity. However, as in the case of attachment theory, affect theory does not specify the occasions for developmental change or the mechanisms of change. Although ideoaffective organizations engender coping mechanisms tailored to a variety of environmental threats, Tomkins did not indicate how the various affective organizations he described respond to the kinds of life challenges that inhere in the average expectable life. For this we require some conceptualization of the challenges likely to face the human organism as it develops from birth through maturity.

We also require some conceptualization of how different patterns of early social interaction are instrumental in forging some of the earliest and most enduring personality predispositions. Tomkins acknowledged the importance of the emotional bond between parent and child, but did not elaborate upon the specifics of the attachment relationship and the rationale of its importance as a context for emotional development. What is pivotal in Tomkins's work, however, is recognition that drive (instinct) and affect are two different subsystems of personality and that they serve different functions. According to Tomkins's theory, instinctual behaviors such as drives (and, we would assume, attachment and exploratory behavioral systems) supply various kinds of life-relevant *information*, whereas affect supplies *motivation*. The drive to breathe (need for oxygen) lets the organism know when anoxia is approaching, but it is the affect of fear that mobilizes behavior. Similarly, in this framework, attachment can be seen as involving the "need to become attached," but affect defines the quality of the attachment and causes the child to care, and care in particular ways.

As Ainsworth et al. (1978) have amply documented, there is no such thing as a non-attached child; all children become attached. Attachment researchers have also documented that the quality of attachment may vary from child to child in discriminable ways. We argue here that the central qualitative aspect that varies is affect, and that the particular kind of affect elicited dictates how the attachment needs will be expressed and negotiated. When the infant's safety is jeopardized, fear promotes proximity seeking; when infant attachment behaviors provoke anger in the caregiver, fear promotes avoidance of the caregiver; when infant attachment expectations are violated, anger promotes protest; and so forth. Affect makes the child care about outcomes and care in particular ways, with anxiety, excitement, joy, anger, distress, and shame. With each of the types of caring comes particular motivations and behavior patterns.

Instinct is inflexible and operates in a monolithic way. The affect system, in contrast, has flexibility as its hallmark. Consequently, affect can lend itself to the formation of different kinds of personality. When an infant is faced with frustration of goals, anger is provoked, and different anger-driven behaviors may be tried. The child can protest and cry, bringing caregivers and their own unique behavioral propensities; alternatively, the child can grapple with the frustrating circumstance in another instrumental way, or can give up the goal. When frustration of goals is constant in a child's life, and as behavioral propensities to deal with the frustration evolve, branching begins and precursor personalities are forged. But anger, acknowledged or unacknowledged, remains an organizer in the several different resolutions just described. Anger as a basic predisposition in the personality has ramifying effects for future behavior in many areas, including perception, information processing, and interpersonal relating (see Tomkins, 1963; Malatesta, 1990).

Clearly, then, a consideration of attachment theory combined with affect theory is instructive for an understanding of early personality formation and early developmental branching. Attachment theory addresses the nature of the singularly compelling instinctual drive to become attached to adult members of the species. Affect theory says that individual experiences add emotional content and thus describe the qualitative aspects that inhere in relationships and in personalities.

From the discussion above, we come to the conclusion that a more complete theory of personality development over the life course requires us to think about differential development from the point of view of attachment theory, affect theory, and normative and non-normative life challenges. Both affect theory and attachment theory must be considered in looking at developmental nodes if we are to understand individual differences in inter- and intrapsychic development as it unfolds and is transformed over the life course.

ATTACHMENT, AFFECT, AND THE LIFE COURSE: A SYNTHESIS

Our model of personality development is built around the following elements: affective relationships, emotional biases, normative and non-normative life events, and individual meaning-making.

Beginnings

We start out with the assumption that one of the most fundamental aspects of personality organization revolves around the formation of attachment and the quality of emotional experience that inheres in the relationship. In Erikson's (1950) terms, the first social product of infancy is the achievement of either a state of equanimity (which devolves from the establishment of basic trust in others and ultimately of the self) or one of basic distrust and anxiety. The child for whom the mother has become "an inner certainty as well as an outer predictability" (p. 247) finds that he or she can bear separation from the mother without undue rage and anxiety. Erikson's construct of basic trust has much in common with Bowlby's idea of secure attachment. Both trust and felt security are said to accrue from sensitive caregiving and to act as bulwarks against trauma.

Erikson has little to say about types of nontrusting development and the kinds of specific developmental branching that can occur at this stage. However, attachment research has provided some clues. Malatesta and Wilson's (1988) discrete-emotions analysis of findings from attachment research indicates that the avoidant attachment style revolves around a fear/anger axis. Anxiety about overly intrusive stimulation from insensitive caregiving, as well as anxiety about the overt expression of anger, ensures that a distance is kept from the caregiver and that anger is kept harnessed and hidden so as not to imperil the connection with the caregiver. Under these conditions emotion communication is low, and anger in particular is muted, though there are occasional sudden eruptions of anger that appear unprovoked. Two types of ambivalent organization can also be discriminated (Cassidy & Berlin, in preparation)—one characterized by an overt anger; the other by a more passive, helpless, and withdrawn style, which may be an early forerunner of learned helplessness and a harbinger of a depressive tendency. The developmental origins of these early affective organizations, cast in discrete-emotions terminology, are given in Malatesta and Wilson (1988) and thus are not repeated here.

In summary, attachment experiences in early infancy appear to leave primary emotional residues, which, for the sake of brevity, we identify as emotional cores organized around (1) contentment, (2) wary hostility, (3) anger, and (4) distress/sadness. We furthermore suggest that secondary components of shame are also experienced in wary hostility, anger, and distress/sadness. According to Tomkins's affect theory, the innate releaser of shame is the "incomplete reduction of positive affect," a condition that most certainly obtains when the infant turns to the caregiver in excited joy and interest and finds his or her excitement and pleasure not fully reciprocated. Our own inspection of attachment videotapes of 12-month-olds indicates that shame is a prominent behavioral marker in avoidantly attached and ambivalently attached children.

Although attachment research has emphasized continuity in the way in which the attachment relationship expresses itself, it has had less to say about discontinuities—primarily, we suspect, because it has failed to appreciate the special motivating role of discrete affects and the function that normative and non-normative crises have in instigating strong affects. Here we maintain that as successive developmental tasks are confronted and different kinds of emotion are galvanized, we may expect further elaboration or branching in emotional organization, and thus in personality organization. Let us next consider how each core emotional organization may confront the developmental node expressed by Erikson's second stage of psychosocial development. Before doing so, we point out what the core motivational tendencies consist of in each of the four affective patterns.

1. *Contentment.* Contentment is associated with the motivation to perpetuate good feelings through relatedness to the "good" other, and to engage otherwise in activities that continue to give pleasure. It also tends to reinforce social partners through the contagion of positive affect, such that social bonding is promoted.

2. *Wary hostility.* The central motivations here are to circumvent further arousal of anxiety through avoidance of the understimulating or overstimulating caregiver and through the inhibition of overt expressions of anger. When the individual is frustrated by barriers to goals, he or she dares not express the very anger that might prompt goal-directed aggressivity, which could facilitate removal of barriers. Affect, especially angry affect, tends to be inhibited due to anxiety, because it threatens the relative security of the attachment relationship. Caregivers may interpret this *either* as compliance and submission *or* as detachment, with further differential repercussions for the attachment relationship.

3. *Anger.* In the child whose early affective core is characterized by anger, angry affect is openly expressed, since there is the expectation that at least some protests will be met with satisfaction of needs. Anger does frequently lead to elimination of barriers to goals and satisfaction of needs, and thus anger as a coping strategy is strengthened within the personality.

4. *Distress/sadness.* This emotion tends to immobilize the individual, so that the positive approach that is necessary for the expression and experience of autonomy is kept in abey-

ance. Alternatively, it may also elicit nurturance, empathy, and succor from selected social partners.

Whether or not these primary emotional residues, accruing from early infancy, will consolidate further in personality will depend in part in how caregivers interpret and respond to these behavioral tendencies and on the child's subsequent developmental experiences. Though emotions accruing from the attachment relationship form the initial core of the ideoaffective organization, they do not crystallize for all time at this point, because there will be other significant emotional events as developmental nodes are encountered and other unscheduled challenges occur. The intersection of attachment styles and developmental nodes is the place at which the first branching in personality development can be expected to occur.

Developmental Branching from the First Stage to the Second

As the child leaves early infancy, the developmental question at hand is how the child's inchoate emotional organizations will respond to the developmental task of autonomy versus shame and doubt. Although Erikson (1950) mentions shame and hostility as the prototypical outcomes for an unsuccessful resolution of this stage, other emotional residue can also be engendered. The child's burgeoning sense of self-confidence and desire for autonomy often bring him or her into direct conflict with parental goals. René Spitz (1965) drew attention to the fact that the second year of life heralds a stage of "negativism," which promotes a shift in the nature of the relationship between caregiver and child. Earlier exchanges, typically centered around infant dependency and caregiver solicitude, now give way to frequent conflict of wills as the child seeks to assert his or her autonomy. Such confrontations will require the parent to negotiate with the child (a practice that is more common among Japanese parents than North Americans) or resort to discipline. Maccoby and Martin (1983) note that parental discipline tends to take the form of power assertion (which triggers anger), love withdrawal (which incites fear), or reasoning. Reasoning is sometimes referred to as "induction," but our own analysis of induction items from discipline inventories indicates that

whereas some reasoning statements are relatively neutral, others have the quality of evoking guilt. As such, parent–child conflict, which first emerges during this stage, ushers in a mode of relating that potentially sets the stage for the creation and escalation of guilt and fear, in addition to shame and anger as identified by Erikson. The fear, anger, and shame that are generated during this developmental stage may tend to magnify earlier accretions of fear, anger, and shame derived from experiences of the first stage, or may produce divergence, as may new experiences with guilt. Although one might argue that the emotional cores established in infancy should show continuity, since the child will be interacting with the same caregiver (who will, it is assumed, interact in the same manner with the child and thus prompt similar emotional experiences), an examination of certain anomalies in the attachment literature leads us to question this conclusion.

First, although continuity of attachment classification from one wave of measurement to another is observed for the majority of children, there is still a sizable group of children for whom continuity does not obtain. Stability coefficients for attachment classification tend to be significant in samples comprised mainly of intact middle-class and advantaged families, and are less robust or insignificant in children exposed to harsh circumstances, as found in the Harvard Child Maltreatment Project (Schneider-Rosen, Braunwald, Carlson, & Cicchetti, 1985) and in the Minnesota sample of low-socioeconomic-status mothers (Vaughn, Egeland, Sroufe, & Waters, 1979). Unfortunately, little attempt has been made to account for why some children retain their classification while others shift, except for an occasional and unedifying nod to "environmental stressors." Moreover, it raises the possibility that attachment classifications by and large show stability not so much because they are mediated by the mental furniture of "internal working models," but because relationships remain stable. When relationships shift in the context of larger changes in the social environment, attachments and affective dispositions are also apparently altered. Viewed in this light, the finding of continuity in attachment classification is not as impressive as it might at first seem. It also means that study of the nonconforming cases (those children who show a shift in attachment classification) might be particularly informative with respect to the underlying processes mediating continuity and change.

A second problem involves explaining why adults who show the secure pattern of attachment style can variously present with developmental histories that are positive by usual attachment standards, *or* with histories that seem quite a bit less than optimal. In Main et al.'s (1985) study, infants were classified according to their behavior in the semistructured laboratory protocol called the Strange Situation, and the mothers were classified according to criteria based on an adult attachment interview. Two different types of developmental histories were seen in the secure mothers—one involving largely favorable early experiences; the other involving unfavorable attachment-related experiences in childhood, including loss and rejection. In a replication study of German mothers and children, Grossmann, Fremmer-Bombik, and Grossmann (1988) also identified two types of sensitive mothers of secure children: (1) those who valued attachments and had coherent, integrated memories of supportive childhood experiences with their caregivers; and (2) others who had experienced unresponsive caregiving, including rejection and neglect, but who nevertheless had been able to resolve their conflicting feelings and who had come to value attachments. The authors note that the latter findings constitue somewhat of an enigma. There were few clues from the attachment interviews as to how it was that some of these parents had been able to break the cycle of unsupportive caregiving and to resist transmitting poor parenting patterns. However, the authors mention that supportive spouses may have been partially responsible in some cases; and one individual reported a very stormy adolescence and violent rupture with her parents, which was later resolved.

Although attachment theory recognizes that stress releases differential coping in different attachment types, it does not deal with specific transition points in development. Let us consider the various branching outcomes that may result from the intersection of early emotional organizations of the first stage (trust–mistrust, secure–avoidant–ambivalent) with the emotional by-products of the developmental node of the second stage (autonomy vs. shame and doubt). Here we can only begin to sketch differential developmental pathways, and we rely on some of the formulations from affect theory for guidance.

1. The emotionally contented child faces the inherent conflicts of Erikson's second stage with relative equanimity. He or she has no particular reason to want to fight with the parent about issues of safety, toileting, and individual rights. Therefore, it is likely that the child will comply with most parental enjoinders and restrictions, yet retain enough of his or her self-confidence to test the frontiers of restrictions from time to time, and to engage in creative exploration.

2. In contrast, the warily hostile child will harbor a resentment that will almost guarantee conflict of wills and a further escalation of resentment. Depending on the parent's style of conflict management (power assertion, love withdrawal, reasoning, guilt induction), depending on the magnitude of parental insistence, and depending on the temperamental constitution of the child, the style of wary hostility may erupt into intense tantrums or may be further sequestered in silent, smoldering defiance. The use of power assertion, typically accompanied by anger in the parent, may, through contagion, so magnify the child's latent anger that what had previously been covert becomes overt. In contrast, the use of guilt induction or love withdrawal may heighten the child's underlying anxiety and cause further suppression of anger and further consolidation around anxiety. The use of reasoning may help overcome earlier isolation, fostering a delayed attachment reaction, with a corrresponding abatement in anger and shame.

3. In the anger-prone child, angry power assertion in the parent should readily ignite angry altercation, leading to the dynamic of what Scheff (1987) has called the "interpersonal anger–shame spiral," leading to accentuation of both anger and shame. Since caregivers of ambivalent children tend to show mixed patterns of responsiveness, being available on some occasions and unavailable on others, love withdrawal will only seem like the standard order of the day. The child's experience with on-again, off-again parental attention will lead to alternations between joy and excitement on the one hand, and frustration and anger on the other. Guilt induction may produce anger tinged with guilt. Reasoning may be rehabilitative with the anger-prone child, just as it is with the warily hostile child.

4. In the case of the distress-prone child, there may be meek submission to the parent, and a corresponding failure to flex the muscles of autonomy. With little conflict of wills, there is little need for the parent to exercise power assertion, guilt induction, or love withdrawal. However, submission to parental will and failure to exercise autonomy may ensure that the child remains shame-ridden, as well as passive and depression-prone.

These outcomes would be some of the more predictable patterns to emerge at the intersection of attachment style and this particular node-related emotional juncture, and one largely expects continuities in child emotional organization because of continuities in caretaking style. However, one can easily imagine a host of different outcomes. The parent of the avoidant child, who has been described in the attachment literature as being uncomfortable with the parental role and withholding of affection, as oriented to early independence training, and/or as overstimulating, may respond in a variety of ways to the need to train the child in toileting and independent locomotion. A caregiver who is less than nurturing and sensitive in infancy for reasons other than lack of affection—for example, because the caregiver's work schedule makes the life schedule particularly hectic—may take special satisfaction in training the child to become skilled in matters of personal hygiene and independent navigation, and thus may spend many more hours in nurturing and solicitous interaction. On the other hand, a caregiver who is insensitive to the infant because of a fundamental defect in personality will probably be as cold and negligent with the child in the second stage. Here we are simply proposing that caregiver–child interactions may undergo fundamental transformation because of the nature of the child's developmental stage, as well as because of the parents' emotional needs and life circumstances. This holds as true for different patterns of insecure attachment as for the secure attachment style; an initially secure attachment does not constitute a lifelong inoculation against other emotionally charged encounters and experiences. For example, a son who experienced the unstinting love and attention of a mother in early infancy may experience quite a different affective world when a father returning from active military duty, who is particularly heavy-handed with directives and expectations of compliance, decides to become actively involved in the rearing of his young son. A protracted struggle of wills may then be provoked, resulting in a newly emergent core of angry resentment.

Possibilities for Developmental Branching in Later Stages

The same kinds of multiple opportunities for personality branching can be envisioned at each of the six remaining Eriksonian stages. The warily hostile child may continue to view the world as a place where power struggles are constantly being enacted in various interpersonal arenas. During adolescence and young adulthood, the individual may also continue to have difficulty with intimacy, and thus may invest all his or her energies in work-related accomplishments. Such a personality prototype appears described by the well-known Type A behavior pattern, a personality configuration characterized by hard-driving competitiveness, time urgency, and hostility. Little is known about how the Type A personality copes with the late-life issue of retirement, although retirement has been identified as a transition fraught with a great deal of potential distress. Given a certain degree of economic well-being, an avoidant (warily hostile) man, instead of experiencing retirement as a crisis, may find that he can care for his own self-absorbed needs better than ever and be as contented as a person can be. Under the right conditions he may even turn his well-honed business acumen toward the instruction of others; he may thereby fulfill the mentoring task of an earlier stage of life development, and perhaps even experiment with coming to terms with intimacy. On the other hand, family circumstances may be such that the hostility component and struggle for power will be channeled more acutely into the spousal relationship.

Obviously, there is hardly space in the present chapter to spell out all of the differential developmental trajectories that may be envisioned at these junctures. Let it suffice to indicate that various possibilities can obtain, but that the virtual resolution and consequent consolidation or transformation of emotional biases will be contingent on the emotional product of the transition. What is important to extract from this analysis is that core emotional organizations initially canalize development in terms of how developmental crises and tasks are approached, but also that the actual circumstances of individual lives will play a very considerable role in subsequent development. It is our belief that developmentalists will fail in their endeavors to understand differential development unless they study individual lives, normative and non-normative events, and the role of emotion in transforming experience and socioemotional aspects of the personality. For the most part, this approach is alien to mainstream psychology, which is nomothetic in approach.

Approaches to the study of personality that are exclusively or largely nomothetic bring order to bear on questions of importance but risk oversimplification. The great 20th-century Russian literary and cultural critic Mikhail Bakhtin, commenting on the humanities in general, maintained that the "sad misunderstanding" of all great modern systems such as Freudianism and Marxism is "that truth can only be that sort of truth that is put together out of general moments, that the truth of a proposition is precisely what is repeatable and constant in it" (quoted in Morson, 1991, p. 206). Such systems assume that all phenomena are reducible to generalized descriptions captured by a set of "impersonal laws," which "first abstracts from concrete human actions all that is generalizable, then transforms the abstractions into a system governed by a set of rules, next derives norms from those rules, and finally denies that anything of significance has been left out in the process" (quoted in Morson, 1991, p. 205).

Bahktin was perhaps excessively critical of the generalizing tendency in the humanities, for as Allport (1937) pointed out, the human sciences profit from both the nomothetic and idiographic approaches to knowledge. And yet it is disconcerting to admit that the discipline of developmental psychology is too often content with only that which is normative, generalizable, and predictable, all of which too frequently leads to astonishingly banal conclusions on the nature on development.

One way to advance beyond "impersonal laws" is to introduce more contextualism and more focus on the individual into our developmental models. For emotional development, this means moving beyond models that specify a restricted number of more general outcomes. It means moving to a more complex model permitting permutations based on nodal developmental challenges (normative crises), which can be resolved in a number of individualiz-

ing ways; singular non-normative events; and individual meaning-making. In the present chapter we have considered several theoretical approaches to affect and its development, pointed out their limitations, and suggested a means of conceptualizing development that introduces more degrees of freedom to vary from the general.

It is the individual's emotional organization—the matrix of emotions constituting the individual's personality—that provides the thread of continuity and dictates, in part, the manner in which the individual confronts and resolves developmental crises and tasks. This is not to say that personality does not undergo change over the life course, but we would say that change is only relative to continuity. We believe that developmental transitions do provide the context in which behavioral dispositions are challenged, but that the manner in which they are navigated is not random; it is dictated by adaptive strategies that have their roots in the motivational properties of different kinds of emotions.

AFFECT AND INDIVIDUAL LIVES

The study of individual lives, as recommended by Datan, Rodeheaver, and Hughes (1987), may be one of the best places to discover the developmental principles relevant to emotional development in the life course. In accord with this, we conclude our discussion with an examination of an individual life. In the introduction to this chapter, we have presented a sketch of the novelist Lev Nikolayevich Tolstoy drawn from biography (Steiner, 1904; Wilson, 1988). Here we offer an analysis of his life as interpreted through the theoretical lens of attachment theory and discrete-emotions theory, in order to shed light on the nature of emotional continuity in the context of developmental change.

Throughout his life, Tolstoy desperately sought connection to the world around him—a connection that had eluded him during childhood. Unlike other children, who are able to form stable and enduring attachments to their primary caregivers, Tolstoy was repeatedly thwarted in his attachment longings, beginning with the death of his mother when he was 2 years old. Given the instinctual nature of the attachment behavioral system, we can assume that he formed an attachment to his mother before her tragic death; however, the fact that she died when he was so young suggests that a good deal of her contact with him may have been filled with the distractions of failing health and concerns about maintaining her own connection to the world. Later, after Lev's mother died, his father became central. But then he too died—this time when Lev was 9. When he was 13, an "aunt" who had taken over the responsibility of caring for him also died. This succession of traumatic losses at an early age cannot but have created in Tolstoy a sense of the impermanancy of relationships, as well as great ambivalence with respect to people and life itself.

Tolstoy's more positive yearnings pressed for reassertion of connection, and under the sway of this powerful instinctual urge, he reinvented himself many times throughout his life. He sought connection to the world variously as scholar, soldier, debauched gambler, writer, friend, womanizer, husband, father, nobleman, and peasant, and finally as a self-proclaimed ascetic, with varying degrees of success and failure. Multiple experiences with what he interpreted as failure, along with the conviction that he was physically unattractive, heightened his sense of shame. As Tolstoy navigated the normative developmental nodes as well as those engendered by the experiences to which he opportunistically exposed himself, distress and shame became his primary organizing affects. Secondary features of his emotional organization consisted of a dominating narcissism, which was counteractive to shame, and a powerful drive for discovery, fueled by interest/excitement motives related to a restless and extraordinary intellect. Distress provided a motivating force to find relief from the pain of disconnection, which he sought in his various roles and escapades; however, distress readily degrades into depression when it meets with failure.

For Tolstoy, depressive affect and narcissistic disdain were core elements in his pre-transition personality. The disequilibrium precipitated by the vulnerabilities of the eighth stage of development (ruminations about the life lived and intimations of mortality), heightened in this case by his depressive propensities, made for a real crisis, with the possibilities of change, continuity, and even total annihilation. Though Tolstoy was a depressive

individual, he also harbored a keen dread of death because of the successive losses he had suffered earlier in life. When depression and contemplation of suicide magnified his death anxiety to an intolerable level, Tolstoy searched for a way out. The massive recruitment of anxiety galvanized fear's associated flight-or-fight response. Tolstoy chose to fight. Intense interest in life and the exciting diversions it offered, in combination with fear of the unknown at the abyss of death and the threat of disconnection, propelled Tolstoy to reconstitute himself at the very brink of suicide.

His transformation simultaneously reflected both change and continuity. Many aspects of his life and personality did undergo manifest change. However, in his identification with Jesus as the son of God, in combination with the Russian tradition of the author evolving into sage and prophet at the culmination of a career (Wilson, 1988), Tolstoy's fundamental narcissism was preserved, providing the ultimate thread of continuity in an otherwise idiosyncratically lived life course. His spiritual homecoming also provided the long-sought union with another, more powerful being. From this perspective, Tolstoy's transformation may be viewed as the divergent expression of a lifelong emotional bias at the core of his personality structure, and not the mystifying conclusion of an inexplicable life course.

CONCLUSION

Our treatment of the various issues related to developmental continuity and transformation has necessarily been limited in this chapter. However, we hope that the reader takes away several points from this reading. The first is that a lifespan and biographical perspective can enlarge our sense of what is truly developmental in individual lives. The second is that normative and non-normative life tasks and crises are flashpoints in development and constitute the context for personality transformation and consolidation. Finally, and most importantly, we stress that emotions are the critical motivational forces behind life course individuation. According to Tomkins's formulations, affects *themselves* are innate activators of other affects and thus can instigate change, because each type of affective experience is associated with differential motivation. In our opinion, it is only in the context of understanding the sources and motivating properties of different kinds of affective experience and their interpretation by individuals that we will solve the riddle of developmental transformation.

REFERENCES

Ainsworth, M. D., Blehar, M. C., Waters, E., & Wall, S. (1978). *Patterns of attachment*. Hillsdale, NJ: Erlbaum.

Allport, G. (1937). *Personality: A psychological interpretation*. New York: Holt.

Bandura, W. (1982). The psychology of chance encounters and life paths. *American Psychologist, 37*, 747–755.

Bowlby, J. (1969). *Attachment and loss: Vol. 1. Attachment*. New York: Basic Books.

Bowlby, J. (1973). *Attachment and loss: Vol. 2. Separation: Anxiety and anger*. New York: Basic Books.

Bowlby, J. (1980). *Attachment and loss: Vol. 3. Loss: Sadness and depression*. New York: Basic Books.

Caspi, A., & Moffit, T. E. (1991). Individual differences are accentuated during periods of social change: The sample case of girls at puberty. *Journal of Personality and Social Psychology, 61*, 157–168.

Cassidy, J., & Berlin, L. J. (in preparation). *The insecure/ ambivalent pattern of attachment: Theory and research*. Manuscript in preparation.

Datan, N., Rodeheaver, D., & Hughes, F. (1987). Adult development and aging. *Annual Review of Psychology, 38*, 153–180.

Erikson, E. (1950). *Childhood and society*. New York: Norton.

Grossmann, K., Fremmer-Bombik, R., & Grossmann, K. E. (1988). In R. A. Hinde & J. Stevenson-Hinde (Eds.), *Relationships within families*. Oxford: Clarendon Press.

Izard, C. E. (1977). *Human emotions*. New York: Plenum Press.

Maccoby, E. E., & Martin, J. A. (1983). Socialization in the context of the family. In E. M. Hetherington (Vol. Ed.), *Handbook of child psychology* (4th ed.): *Vol. 4. Social-*

ization, personality, and social development (pp. 1–102). New York: Wiley.

Main, M., Kaplan, N., & Cassidy, J. (1985). Security in infancy, childhood, and adulthood: A move to the level of representation. In I. Bretherton & E. Waters (Eds.), Growing points of attachment theory and research. *Monographs of the Society for Research in Child Development, 50*(1–2, Serial No. 209), 66–104.

Malatesta, C. Z. (1990). The role of emotions in the development and organization of personality. In R. A. Thompson (Ed.), *Nebraska Symposium on Motivation: Vol. 36. Socioemotional development* (pp. 1–56). Lincoln: University of Nebraska Press.

Malatesta, C. Z., & Wilson, A. (1988). Emotion/cognition interaction in personality development: A discrete emotions, functionalist analysis. *British Journal of Social Psychology, 27*, 91–112.

Morson, G. S. (1991). Bakhtin and the present moment. *American Scholar, 60*, 201–221.

Scheff, T. J. (1987). The shame–rage spiral: A case study of an interminable quarrel. In H. B. Lewis (Ed.), *The role of shame in symptom formation* (pp. 109–149). Hillsdale, NJ: Erlbaum.

Schneider-Rosen, K. G., Braunwald, K. G., Carlson, V., & Cicchetti, D. (1985). Current perspectives in attachment theory: Illustration from the study of maltreated infants. In I. Bretherton & E. Waters (Eds.), Growing points of attachment theory and research. *Monographs of the Society for Research in Child Development, 50*(1–2, Serial No. 209), 194–210.

Spitz, R. (1965). *The first year of life*. New York: International Universities Press.

Tomkins, S. (1962). *Affect, imagery, consciousness: Vol. 1. The positive affects*. New York: Springer.

Tomkins, S. (1963). *Affect, imagery, consciousness: Vol. 2. The negative affects*. New York: Springer.

Tomkins, S. (1991). *Affect, imagery, consciousness: Vol. 3. The negative affects: Anger and fear*. New York: Springer.

Vaughn, B., Egeland, B., Sroufe, L. A., & Waters, E. (1979). Individual differences in infant–mother attachment at twelve and eighteen months: Stability and change in families under stress. *Child Development, 50*, 971–975.

Wilson, A. N. (1988). *Tolstoy*. New York: Norton.

19

Positive Affect and Decision Making

ALICE M. ISEN

INTRODUCTION

Most people seem to have a sense that affect (feelings, emotion) can influence their decisions, at least under certain circumstances. However, it is usually assumed that such influence is something irregular or unusual; that only strong and infrequent feelings would have such effects; and that most often only negative feelings such as anger, sadness, or fear would have an impact on thinking processes. Furthermore, most people assume that when affect plays a role in their decision processes, such influences are disruptive and tend to make their decisions "irrational" and less appropriate than otherwise.

Interestingly, however, a growing body of research indicates that even mild and even positive affective states can markedly influence everyday thought processes, and do so regularly. For example, the presence of positive feelings has been found to cue positive material in memory, making access to such thoughts easier and thus making it more likely that positive material will "come to mind" (e.g., Isen, Shalker, Clark, & Karp, 1978; Nasby & Yando, 1982; Teasdale & Fogarty, 1979). This reflects the fact that material in mind is organized and accessible in terms of its positive affective tone, and that people spontaneously use positive affect as a way to organize their thoughts. Thus, far from being an infrequent influence on thought processes, common positive feelings are fundamentally involved in cognitive organization and processing.

Positive affect has also been found to promote creativity in problem solving and negotiation, and both efficiency and thoroughness in decision making (Carnevale & Isen, 1986; Isen, Daubman, & Nowicki, 1987; Isen, Johnson, Mertz, & Robinson, 1985; Isen & Means, 1983; Isen, Rosenzweig, & Young, 1991). Thus, under many circumstances, the influence of mild positive feelings on thinking and decision making has been found to be not only substantial but facilitative, leading to improved decision making and problem solving. How can these two views—people's intuitions and the findings of such studies—be reconciled? Most likely, the resolution is in the details. It is these details that are considered in this chapter.

To put the findings regarding positive affect in context, it should be pointed out first that from the very outset of the work on affect and memory, an asymmetry was noted in the influence of positive and negative affect on memory for compatible material (e.g., Isen et al., 1978; Nasby & Yando, 1982; Teasdale & Fogarty, 1979): Whereas positive affect was found to be an effective retrieval cue for positive material in memory, induced negative affect was not found to be an effective cue for negative material, or was seen to be less effective as a cue for negative material than was positive affect for positive material (e.g., Isen et al., 1978; Teasdale, Taylor, & Fogarty, 1980). Thus, although some authors have reported symmetrical effects of positive and negative affect (e.g., Bower, 1981), it seems likely that those findings may be attributable to something about the type of affect induction employed (e.g., hypnosis with instructions to maintain the state at the induced level), because the preponderance of the studies report asymmetrical findings for positive and negative affect and material—that is, less marked cueing effects for negative than for positive affect (see Isen, 1984, 1985, 1987, 1990, for discussion). This asymmetry may have implications for our understanding of the influence of positive affect itself. Moreover, it suggests that we should not necessarily expect the influence of negative affect on cognitive processing in any task to be the inverse of, or parallel to, that of positive affect.

Even when we are dealing with only positive induced affect, there is reason to expect an asymmetry of influence if the *materials* are affectively valenced (e.g., Isen et al., 1985). The fact that positive affect preferentially cues positive material means that the valence of the material in any cognitive task may well make a difference in the effect of thinking about or performing the task (and, in particular, in positive affect's influence on that effect). That is, as has been found in many studies (and will be discussed more fully later), positive affect may have different effects on the cognitive processing of material of different valence, because it cues positive material as contrasted with other material.

Another matter that involves the valence of the material, and that I discuss in more detail later, is that, all else being equal, positive affect appears to give rise to a motive to try to maintain the positive feeling state (e.g., Isen & Simmonds, 1978). Thus, if there is not a good reason to focus on negative material, people in whom positive affect has been induced may avoid difficult or unpleasant tasks or material, or may choose to work on more pleasant items instead (e.g., Isen & Reeve, 1992). This may be another reason that the impact of positive affect may not be the same for negative material as for other material.

In addition, as we shall see, the impact of positive affect appears to depend on the type of task or decision being made and on specific aspects of the decision situation besides valence of the material. For example, whether the choice is about something interesting or important to subjects, as opposed to uninteresting, trivial, or hypothetical, seems to play a role in determining the precise effect that feel-

ings have (e.g., Isen & Patrick, 1983). People in whom positive affect has been induced have been found to elaborate and think more thoroughly, but usually only about relatively interesting or pleasant (or at least neutral) material (e.g., Isen et al., 1985, 1991; Kraiger, Billings, & Isen, 1989).

Furthermore, these factors (task importance, valence, and the motive to maintain the positive state) may interact to influence the ultimate impact of positive affect: If the task is unimportant and promises to be dull or unpleasant, those in a positive feeling state may decline to work on it or may work on it with as little effort as possible; in contrast, if the material is important to the person, or if there is another reason to work carefully on the task, then positive-affect subjects will do so (Isen et al., 1991; Isen & Reeve, 1992). Consequently, negatively valenced material itself may not produce the same effects in positive-affect subjects across all circumstances; and use of negative material presents a complicating factor that should not be minimized. Thus, the effects of positive feelings will depend on many aspects of the situation, resolved and integrated through the person's judgment and goals in the situation.

In emphasizing the importance of the person's goals and choices (motivation) in determining the impact of positive feelings, I do not mean to imply that the effect can be attributed to a concerted effort to *overcome* some more fundamental tendency to avoid negative material or to avoid systematic processing. Instead, I am emphasizing here the multifacetedness of the influence of positive affect; the flexibility of people who are feeling happy; and the importance of plans, goals, and strategies in people's behavior, even in the context of emotional states.

Another factor that must be considered is that mild positive affect appears to influence the way material is organized in mind—what is seen as related to what—so that the context is different, more complex or rich, for people in whom positive affect has been induced (e.g., Isen & Daubman, 1984; Isen et al., 1985; Isen, Niedenthal, & Cantor, 1992; Kahn & Isen, in press; Kraiger et al., 1989). This is because, as noted earlier, positive affect cues positive material in memory, and positive material is more extensive and diverse than other material (e.g., Cramer, 1968). Thus, the cognitive context is more complex when a person is feeling happy, as a broader range of ideas is cued (Isen et al., 1985). In this way, thoughts that do not usually come to mind in the context of each other do come to mind at the same time, when a person is feeling happy, to form a new and more complex context at that time.

Thus, positive affect appears to influence the context itself, which in its own right has been shown to influence thinking and decision making (e.g., Bransford, 1979; Cramer, 1968; Huber, Holbrook, & Kahn, 1986; Kahneman & Tversky, 1979; Simonson, 1990; Tversky & Kahneman, 1981). This effect, too, can be expected to occur more for certain kinds of tasks, situations, or materials than for others (e.g., it would not be expected with negative material, under most circumstances); thus, the influence of affect on cognitive organization and context needs to be explored.

These points all indicate that the influence of positive affect is complexly determined and will be different in different situations, rather than characterizable by broad, global statements. Determinants of the kinds of tasks that will be affected by feeling states, or the kinds of materials that people experiencing positive affect will prefer, and determinants of the motivations that will guide the behavior of people who are feeling happy, need to be investigated. Although there is still much to be done, some generalizations are emerging from studies on these topics.

A general guideline that can be drawn from this work is that the influence of positive affect on cognitive processes such as judgment and decision making depends on what the affect, together with the task and other aspects of the context, leads the person to think about (e.g., Arkes, Herren, & Isen, 1988; Isen & Geva, 1987; Isen et al., 1985). This in turn depends not only on the impact of affect on memory and on motivation, but also on the context more generally. Moreover, as noted above, context itself is also influenced by affect, through affect's influence on memory and cognitive organization; this, then, can play a role in the way the person sees the situation and the kinds of activities he or she is motivated to undertake.

The impact of affect on thought will thus depend to some extent on particular circumstances and idiosyncratic thought processes of individuals. Yet there are commonalities of thought that can be expected among members of the same culture. For example, any two individuals may have different particular

memories or thoughts associated with positive affect, as with any cognitive category. Yet there will also be some overlap in the thoughts they have categorized in that way (i.e., as "positive"). This would be especially true for members of the same or similar cultures (and there may even be some near-universals that one might expect to be common to all people as components of the positive-affect category). Thus, there are regularities in the data, and there is reason to anticipate the discovery of more.

This chapter presents some of the findings regarding the impact of mild positive affect on thinking and motivation, and explores the processes underlying them and the circumstances under which they are likely to be observed. The focus is on decision making, but in order to understand affect's influence on decisions, it is helpful to consider its impact on cognitive organization (or the way material is thought about and related to other material) and on motivation. This is because organization or context, including the person's goals, plays a crucial role in decision making (e.g., Bransford, 1979; Simonson, 1990; Tversky & Kahneman, 1981). I begin, then, by considering the influence of positive affect on cognitive organization.

POSITIVE AFFECT AND COGNITIVE ORGANIZATION

A growing body of literature indicates that positive affect influences the way in which stimuli are thought about or related to other ideas in mind. For example, studies have shown that people in whom positive affect has been induced in any of a variety of simple ways (e.g., watching 5 minutes of a comedy film, receiving a small bag of candy, or giving associates to positive words) have a broader range of associates, and more diverse associates, to neutral material (Isen et al., 1985).

Similarly, people in such conditions are able to categorize material more flexibly, seeing ways in which nontypical members of categories can fit or be viewed as members of the categories (Isen & Daubman, 1984; Kahn & Isen, in press; Isen et al., 1992). This has been found for items in natural categories, such as those used by Rosch (1975; Isen & Daubman, 1984); for products in the mildly pleasant class of snack foods (Kahn & Isen, in press); and for person types in positive, but not in negative, person categories (Isen et al., 1992). Thus, positive affect has been shown to enable people to see more similarities among items.

It has also been found that if people are specifically asked to focus on differences and find ways in which items differ from one another, positive affect can result in more perceived *difference* as well (Isen, 1987, p. 234; Murray, Sujan, Hirt, & Sujan, 1990). Together, these studies can be interpreted as indicating that positive affect promotes cognitive flexibility: People who are feeling happy become more able to make associations among ideas and see different, multiple relations (similarities *or* differences) among stimuli than people in a neutral feeling state.

It is important to note again in this context that the impact of positive feelings on thought processes, and especially on the results of assigned tasks (such as judgments, ratings, sortings, categorizations, etc.), depends on particulars of the task and the situation. Nonetheless, the effect is regular, predictable, and understandable. If asked to judge similarity among items, people in positive-affect conditions indicate greater similarity than do control subjects; if asked to find differences, they may indicate more difference. As will be explained below, this may not be as irrational as it sounds, nor is it the result of simple response bias.

The process that underlies these effects, as suggested by the word-association findings reported above (Isen et al., 1985), may be that people experiencing positive affect may engage in greater elaboration about the material. Thus, they see more aspects of the items and have more, and more diverse, associations to the items, as those studies reported. Then, as explained by Tversky and Gati (1978) for knowledge about material in general (i.e., not affective material or induced affect in particular), the context supplied by the task (searching for differences vs. searching for similarities) will determine whether this greater elaboration (greater knowledge, in the work by Tversky & Gati) results in a judgment of greater similarity or of greater difference. Those authors found that people rated pairs of items about which they knew more (e.g., the United States and the Soviet Union) as more similar to each other than pairs about which they knew less (e.g., Bolivia and Ceylon) when the task required a similarity judgment, but that people

rated the pairs about which they knew more as more *different* from each other when the task focused attention on differences. Thus, to return to the affect situation, if people in positive-affect conditions have more information (elaboration) about material, more thoughts about it, or more associations to it, then they would be expected to indicate more perceived similarity or difference among the items than control subjects would, depending on the context created by the question posed.

However, as noted in the introduction, an aspect of the context that is critically important in determining the impact that positive affect will have is the nature, including the valence, of the materials being considered. Thus, one cannot expect positive affect to influence the categorization of, or to increase the perceived similarity (or difference) of, *all* stimuli automatically.

To illustrate this point, let us examine the results of a recent study that extended the work on affect's impact on categorization to the area of person categorization (Isen et al., 1992). In that study, subjects were asked to rate the degree to which nonprototypic examples of positive or negative categories of people (e.g., "bartender" as a member of the category "nurturant people," or "genius" as a member of the negative category "unstable people") fit as members of the category. Compared with control subjects, positive-affect subjects rated the weakly related members of the positive categories as fitting better in the category, but this was not observed for the negative person categories. That is, people in the positive-affect condition rated "bartender" as a better exemplar of the category "nurturant people" than did control subjects, but they did not rate "genius" as a better exemplar of the category "unstable people." In accord with results of studies showing that positive affect cues positive material in memory, and enables more ready access to such material and to a broader range of such associates (e.g., Isen et al., 1978, 1985), people in the positive-affect condition could presumably see more positive aspects of the relatively neutral type "bartender"; however, nothing in their affective state would be expected to prompt their seeing the person type "genius" as better fitting a negative superordinate category, in that situation.

This interaction illustrates the importance of the type of material with which the subject is asked to work, in determining the effects of feelings. Although an underlying process (increased elaboration) is postulated to occur, this process is expected to be different for different kinds of material in the situation described. Since positive affect cues positive material, the elaborative process would be expected to occur with positive material (for all subjects) or for positive-affect subjects working with neutral material (see Isen et al., 1985). There is no reason in this situation to expect negative material to be elaborated, or to expect the elaboration of negative material to be facilitated by the induction of a positive affective state.

In addition, as pointed out in the introduction, presentation of sufficiently negatively valenced material may also result in people's not dealing with the material; this tendency may be more notable among people in whom positive affect has been induced, who may be seeking to maintain that positive state (e.g., Isen & Simmonds, 1978). This will probably depend on the degree of negativity in the materials, the importance of the task, and so forth, as noted earlier. It should also be pointed out that if the negative materials are bad enough, they may go so far as actually to overturn the affect induction itself. Moreover (as will be discussed more fully later, in the section on decision making), in a negative frame, where the task requires subjects to focus on possible meaningful loss, people in a positive-affect state may actually have more thoughts about losing than controls (e.g., Isen & Geva, 1987) and may behave conservatively so as to protect themselves from the loss (Isen & Geva, 1987; Isen, Nygren, & Ashby, 1988; Isen & Simmonds, 1978). In the study described here (Isen et al., 1992), however, there was no negative frame (loss or danger) to the task; therefore, such motivational and methodological additional complications were probably not in evidence, and the effect of positive affect simply did not extend to the negative material, as often it does not. However, the point illustrated is that use of negative material in studies of the influence of positive affect can make for complexity in formulating predictions.

A methodological point is worth noting here as well. The interaction observed in the person-categorization study (Isen et al., 1992) between induced affect and the valence of the materials also indicates that the impact of affect on categorization is not an artifact of such processes as response bias, nonsystematic thinking, or reduction in cognitive capacity. This is because the interaction between affect and category valence shows that positive affect influences the categorization of one type of material (positive), but, in comparison with the control group, does not change the way the other type of material (negative) is organized; by contrast, the alternative interpretation (global effects, such as carelessness or reduced cognitive capacity) involves processes that should result in all categories' or stimulus materials' being affected equally.

Compatibly, a study of the impact of positive affect on job perceptions and satisfaction also found that people in whom positive affect had been induced perceived an interesting task that they had been assigned, but not a meaningless one, as richer and more satisfying than did control subjects (Kraiger et al., 1989). Again, this can be seen as reflecting an ability on the part of the positive-affect subjects to see additional associations and aspects of interesting things. At the same time, the interaction with type of task again indicates that a substantive process related to elaboration and thinking, rather than an artifact such as response bias or nonsystematic processing, is responsible for the observed effects.

Another series of studies reflecting affect's influence on cognitive organization indicates that positive affect promotes creative or innovative responding, as would be expected from the kinds of findings described above. Such responding can be seen as involving cognitive flexibility or the ability to put ideas together in new, but useful, ways. For example, people in whom positive affect was induced in any of several ways were better able to solve tasks usually thought to require creativity (Isen et al., 1987). In one of these, the "candle problem" (Duncker, 1945), a person is presented with a candle, a box of tacks, and a book of matches, and is asked to affix the candle to the wall so that it will burn without dripping wax on the table or floor. To solve the problem, the person can empty the box of tacks, tack the box to the wall, and place the candle in it so that it can be lit and won't drip onto the table or floor. Thus, the person must use one of the items (the box) in an unaccustomed way. People in whom positive affect had been induced performed significantly better than controls on this task. A second task that has been used to study the influence of positive affect on cognitive flexibility or creativity is based on the Remote Associates Test (Mednick, Mednick, & Mednick, 1964). In this test, which in its full form was designed to measure individual differences in creativity, subjects are presented with three words and a blank line and are asked to respond with a word that relates to each of the three words given in the problem. An example of a Remote Associates Test item is the following:

MOWER   ATOMIC   FOREIGN   _____

(In this example, POWER would be the correct answer.) Seven items of moderate difficulty are used in the research on the influence of affect. These studies using this dependent measure of cognitive flexibility or creativity also confirm that positive affect increases such ability, and is distinct from negative affect and affectless "arousal" in doing so.

In the studies that examined the influence of negative affect and affectless arousal, negative affect was induced by having subjects view a few minutes of the film *Night and Fog*, a French documentary about the World War II German death camps. People in this condition did not perform better than controls on the Remote Associates Test items (Isen et al., 1987).

Affectless "arousal" was induced by having subjects step up and down on a cinderblock for 2 minutes, so that their heart rates were increased by 66%. Theoretically, arousal should not be expected to increase creativity, since it is thought to facilitate the *dominant* response in a person's response repertoire rather than an innovative one. Nonetheless, its effect was investigated because people sometimes have the hunch that it is "arousal," rather than or as a component of positive affect, that is responsible for the facilitative effect of positive feelings. Results indicated, however, that subjects in this condition did not perform better than controls on the Remote Associates Test (Isen et al., 1987; see also Isen, 1990, and Isen & Daubman, 1984, for discussion). Moreover, reconceptualizations of the "arousal" concept suggest that it may not be a unitary construct and may need to be investigated differently from the way it has been addressed in the past (e.g., Lacey, 1967, 1975; Neiss, 1990; Venables, 1984).

Most recently, tests of these effects of positive feelings on creative problem solving have been extended to include investigation of performance on routine tasks, in order to examine whether there is evidence for an alternative interpretation having to do with effort or global motivation. That is, it is possible that positive affect does not facilitate creative problem solving per se, or seeing connections among things, but rather that it simply raises motivation—that these subjects are simply trying harder. (In some ways, this may be related to the hunches about "arousal," mentioned above, but it can be seen as distinct.) In order to address this alternative interpretation, in some studies we examined positive affect's influence on the performance of two types of routine tasks—circling the letter *a* every time it appeared in pages of randomly ordered letters, and long division—while also examining its influence on creative problem solving, represented by two tasks (the Remote Associates Test and a logical problem-solving task, meant to represent something like scientific creativity). These studies indicated a facilitative influence of positive affect on the Remote Associates Test and the logical problem-solving task, but not on either of the routine tasks, on which performance of the positive-affect subjects and control subjects did not differ (Isen & Berg, 1991). This suggests that it is not just an increase in overall motivation that is responsible for the positive-affect subjects' improved performance on creative tasks.

Another study has found that positive affect, induced by means of receipt of a small gift and by reading funny cartoons, can facilitate the process of negotiation and result in improved outcomes in an integrative bargaining situation (Carnevale & Isen, 1986). An "integrative bargaining" task is one in which, in order to reach the optimal agreement, people must make tradeoffs on different issues, of differing value to them, about which they are bargaining. Reaching agreement on such a task requires seeing possibilities, thinking innovatively, and reasoning flexibly about how tradeoffs might be made. Obvious compromises or simple yielding will not result in satisfactory outcomes (for greater detail, see, e.g., Pruitt, 1983).

In this study, people in the positive-affect condition who bargained face to face were significantly less likely to break off negotiation, and more likely to reach agreement and to reach the optimal agreement possible in the situation, than were face-to-face bargainers in the control condition, in which positive affect had not been induced. They were also less likely to engage in aggressive tactics during the negotiation, and reported more enjoyment of the session (Carnevale & Isen, 1986). And they were better able than control subjects to figure out the other person's payoff matrix (schedule of profit for each component of the agreement) in the negotiation, which differed for the two bargainers. These results support the suggestion that positive affect facilitates a problem-solving approach and improves people's ability to integrate ideas and see ways of relating aspects of situations to one another, in order to come up with a good solution to a problem.

Thus, in summary of this section, positive affect appears to influence the way in which cognitive material is organized—how ideas are related to one another in mind. In particular, it has been found in most situations to give rise to greater elaboration in response to neutral or positive material (but not negative material) and a richer context, which in turn promotes flexibility in thinking. (It should be noted that depending on the task, with positive *material*, although the elaboration effect is occurring, the difference between positive-affect subjects and control subjects may not be apparent: The material itself induces positive affect, and this produces the effect even in the "control" condition. See Isen et al., 1985.)

This means that in any task (that deals with material of neutral or positive valence) undertaken while a person is feeling happy, one should expect unusual and innovative, though reasonable and logical, thoughts and responses. It is a mistake to assume that people in whom positive affect has been induced will think only those arguments and thoughts about the experimental materials that are provided by the experimenters, in the standard way. On the basis of the research reviewed here, we should expect people in the positive-affect condition to think about the materials in a more elaborated, extensive, flexible, responsible, and positive way—provided that the materials are not negative or boring. Thus, in attitude-change studies, for example, people in the positive-affect conditions may think of their own arguments pro or con and may behave accordingly.

In the case of negative material, it is more difficult to predict the behavior of positive-affect subjects. We would expect these subjects not to elaborate the negative material more than controls; in some tasks (e.g., categorization, word association), this will result in their

responses' not differing from those of control subjects (e.g., Isen et al., 1985, 1992). On other tasks, we would expect positive-affect subjects actively to avoid, or show caution with, the materials. Issues related to these distinctions are discussed in the next two sections.

Thus, in sum, positive feelings have been shown to have complex but largely facilitative effects on the thoughts generated, the way these thoughts are organized, and the cognitive context that results, in response to most material. Although ideas are elaborated, and more thoughts (and more nontypical thoughts) come to mind, thinking is flexible, so that both usual *and* unusual aspects and senses of concepts are accessible. And this has a fundamental influence on the performance of many kinds of tasks.

POSITIVE AFFECT AND MOTIVATION

All of the work described thus far indicating that positive affect promotes enjoyment and enrichment of potentially enjoyable, though serious, tasks (e.g., Carnevale & Isen, 1986; Kraiger et al., 1989) suggests that positive affect may influence task motivation (because richer tasks are also more motivating). I have already discussed two other kinds of possible effects of feelings on motivation: one on global motivation or trying harder, and one on specific motivations or direction of effort that may be thought to result from the presence of happy feelings (the tendency to behave so as to maintain the positive state).

Regarding global motivation, recall that there is no evidence as yet to suggest that positive affect simply raises effort on all tasks (e.g., Isen & Berg, 1991). In addition, other studies, such as those investigating the influence of affect on creativity, have reported effects of positive feelings that differ from those resulting from mere "arousal" (e.g., Isen et al., 1987). Therefore, it seems more promising to investigate specific aspects of tasks that are facilitated by positive feelings.

As noted earlier, several reports suggest that positive affect may introduce a motive to maintain the positive state (e.g., Isen & Simmonds, 1978; see also Isen, 1987, for discussion). One early study showed, for example, that people in whom positive affect had been induced (by receipt of a coin in the coin-return slot of a public telephone) were *less* likely than control subjects to help a stranger, when the helping task was one that was portrayed as virtually certain to make them feel depressed (Isen & Simmonds, 1978). This contrasts with the often-obtained finding that in general, people who are feeling happy are more likely than controls to help in any of a variety of ways (e.g., Cunningham, 1979; Isen, 1970; Isen & Levin, 1972). Thus, the results of the study by Isen and Simmonds (1978) were interpreted as indicating that positive affect engenders a motive to avoid loss of the positive state.

On the basis of various studies' results, such a motive would not be expected to be absolute in its effects, nor to result in blind, irrational bias or in distortion of negative stimuli or tasks (e.g., Isen et al., 1985; Isen & Shalker, 1982; Schiffenbauer, 1974). Nonetheless, it can be expected to introduce a tendency to leave more negative topics for another time, or at least to consider doing so. Thus, it could influence responses, or latency of responding, on tasks involving negative material. Such a motive may also be related to positive-affect subjects' relative risk aversion that has been observed under certain circumstances (e.g., Isen & Geva, 1987; Isen et al., 1988; Isen & Patrick, 1983) and that is discussed in the section on decision making.

In parallel, several lines of investigation suggest that positive affect leads to increased enjoyment or pleasure from potentially positive material and situations (e.g., Isen et al., 1978; Kraiger et al., 1989). This work, then, points to two other kinds of motives that appear to be fostered by positive affect: (1) Intrinsic motivation, and (2) variety seeking (stimulation seeking) among safe, enjoyable alternatives.

For example, one series of studies suggests that positive affect promotes variety seeking among safe and pleasant products (Kahn & Isen, in press). Three studies reported that people in whom positive affect had been induced, when given the opportunity to make several choices in a food category (such as soup or snacks), showed more switching among alternatives than controls and included a broader range of items in their choice sets, as long as the circumstances did not make unpleasant or negative potential features of the items salient. In contrast, when a negative but not risky feature (e.g., the possibility that a low-salt product would taste less good than the regular) was salient, there was no difference

between affect groups in variety seeking, the tendency to switch around among the items in making their choices. Thus, there is evidence that positive affect promotes stimulation seeking—that is, enjoyment of variety and of a wider range of possibilities—but only when the situation does not prompt the person to think of unpleasant outcomes.

Another interesting possibility regarding the impact of affect on motivation, suggested by the results of three recent studies, is that positive affect may promote intrinsic motivation (Estrada, Young, & Isen, 1992; Isen & Reeve, 1992). In one study, people in whom positive affect had been induced by receipt of a small bag of candy spent more time, relative to controls, working on a task that promised to be interesting (a puzzle) than on a task on which they could earn money but that promised to be boring and involved time pressure (finding particular combinations of numbers in three pages of randomly ordered numbers during a limited time period). Thus, people in the positive-affect condition appeared relatively less influenced by the extrinsic motivator (money) and more influenced by the intrinsic motivator (interest in the task) than people in the control condition. They also reported more liking for the puzzle task after working on it than did controls, which is another indicator of intrinsic motivation. In this study, subjects were free to choose whichever task they preferred to work on. A follow-up study conceptually replicated this finding, but also showed that when positive-affect subjects knew that the more boring task had to be completed (not for money this time), they were as likely as controls to work on it (Isen & Reeve, 1992).

These findings directly support the observation made earlier that positive affect promotes enjoyment (in particular, enjoyment of tasks in which the subject is interested) and increases the likelihood of engaging in activities that are enjoyable or expected to be fun. They are also compatible with the findings that positive affect increased the perception of task enrichment and satisfaction in regard to interesting jobs (Kraiger et al., 1989). At the same time, they show that people in positive-affect conditions will not avoid work tasks, or more boring, unpleasant, or difficult tasks, if it is clear that those tasks need to be done or if there is some potential benefit in doing them. People who feel good prefer pleasant things and enjoy them more when they do them;

however, relative to control subjects, they do not shirk, irrationally "defend against," or irresponsibly refuse to engage in less pleasant tasks.

Another series of studies, investigating the influence of positive affect on physicians' decision making, suggests that positive affect may influence the relative strength of intrinsic (humanistic), as opposed to extrinsic (money and status), sources of practice satisfaction among physicians (Estrada et al., 1992). That is, relative to a control group, physicians in whom positive affect had been induced (by receipt of candy) attributed greater importance to humanistic sources of satisfaction than to extrinsic sources, on a questionnaire asking about the sources of their satisfaction from practicing medicine. (It should be noted that, overall, the physicians gave higher endorsement to the humanistic motives than to the extrinsic. But the difference was more pronounced in the positive-affect condition.)

It should also be mentioned, in the context of motivations induced by positive affect, that a large body of evidence indicates that under normal circumstances positive affect promotes helpfulness, generosity/responsibility, and friendliness/sociability (see Isen, 1987, for a review and discussion). Of course, as we have seen, this tendency can be overridden by such factors as the potential affective consequences of the helping task (e.g., Isen & Simmonds, 1978), or by other factors, such as dislike of the person or organization in need, that might cause the person not to want to help (e.g., Forest, Clark, Mills, & Isen, 1979). These findings may also indicate that people who are happy may feel more free to behave as they want to behave. Moreover, these latter effects may themselves depend on such factors as the amount of harm that might come to the person in need if the potential helper did not help, and so on (see Isen, 1987, for discussion). The point to be made here is that positive affect in general promotes not selfishness, but a tendency to be kind to both self and others; social connectedness and responsibility; and the ability to see situations from another person's perspective.

Thus, in summary of this section, positive affect appears to produce a variety of behaviors that may be seen as resulting not only from the cognitive effects that have been discussed (increased elaboration and access to positive material, increased integration of concepts and

ability to see connections among ideas, etc.), but also from apparent motivational changes. On the basis of the data presented here, it seems reasonable to propose that positive affect gives rise to two broad classes of motives: (1) enjoyment, interest, and graciousness in neutral or positive situations (or where negatives or uninteresting things can be ignored safely); and (2) self-protection in clearly negative situations in which the person must, for some reason, respond to the negative material. The relevance of these findings for decision making of various kinds is considered in the next section.

POSITIVE AFFECT
AND DECISION MAKING

All of these findings relate to the influence of affect on decision making and suggest that positive affect, in conjunction with the type of task, the framing of the situation, the importance or utility of the task, and other aspects of the situation, may influence decision making of various kinds.

At the outset, it should be noted that the processes described are not postulated to be automatic, but rather are seen as resulting from appraisal of the requirements of the situation. This suggests that processes such as decision making and problem solving may be hierarchically organized rather than monolithic—that before the problem is actually addressed, some command decisions or evaluations may be made regarding how important the task is, what its utility may be, or whether the person has any control over its eventual outcome, as well as what its hedonic consequences may be, how disruptive of ongoing feelings it may prove to be, and so on. These decisions may influence the way in which the problem is addressed. Furthermore, the person may also sometimes go back and re-evaluate such decisions during solving of the task problem.

To state this a bit differently, perhaps the person makes a series of decisions in deciding or solving the problem, and perhaps the first one in the series relates to the domain of the task, with regard to both valence and importance. A helpful way of viewing this first level of decision may be in terms of the framing of the problem. That is, the person may derive a sense of whether this is a situation that is safe, in which he or she can enjoy himself or herself (gain something, share, etc.), or is a situation in which the person must be concerned not to be harmed (not to lose what he or she already has or needs), as well as a sense of what his or her options are.

A conceptualization in terms of the framing of the situation has been useful in the decision-making and risk-taking literature, where differences have been found in people's decisions according to whether the problem was framed as a potential gain or as a potential loss (e.g., Kahneman & Tversky, 1979; Tversky & Kahneman, 1981). Although the parallel may not be exact, a distinction like this (or at least related to safety in contrast to danger) seems to correspond to the two motives resulting from positive affect that have been discussed, and there may be some benefit in thinking about the effects in this way. Issues related to the framing of the experimental situation, and to the possibility of the kind of hierarchical evaluation or decision process proposed, need to be explored more fully in their own right. However, this view may be of some help in understanding the findings that have been obtained.

Risk

One kind of decision that has been studied as a function of positive affect is risk preference (e.g., Arkes et al., 1988; Dunn & Wilson, 1990; Isen & Geva, 1987; Isen et al., 1988; Isen & Patrick, 1983; Isen, Pratkanis, Slovic, & Slovic, 1984). In one series of studies, Dunn and Wilson (1990) suggested that the "illusion of control" effect (the tendency to behave as if one can control random events) might be limited to safe low-cost situations. They noted that positive affect resulting from induced feelings of control promoted wagering where the cost was low but not where the stakes were high.

In another series of studies, people in whom positive affect had been induced were more risk-averse, compared with subjects in control conditions, when the risk situation about which they were reasoning was a realistic one that made them focus on the probability of a real, meaningful loss (e.g., Arkes et al., 1988; Isen & Patrick, 1983; Isen & Geva, 1987). Otherwise, they appeared more risk-prone than controls (Arkes et al., 1988; Isen & Patrick, 1983). For example, when subjects were betting chips representing their credit for participating

in the study, those in whom positive affect had been induced bet less (Isen & Patrick, 1983) and required a higher probability of winning before agreeing to a substantial bet (Isen & Geva, 1987), compared with subjects in control conditions. They also showed more thoughts about losing in a thought-listing task following this assessment. Interestingly, when asked just to indicate their likelihood of taking a risk on a hypothetical task (such as starting up a business in an unstable foreign land), without having to wager anything of value to themselves on their assessment, people in the positive-affect conditions indicated greater riskiness (Isen & Patrick, 1983). Similarly, when people were asked, without an affect induction, to estimate what effect they *thought* positive affect would have on their risk preference, they intuited that it would increase their riskiness (Isen et al., 1984). This difference between response in hypothetical, as contrasted with more real, situations has been noted in the experimental literature before (e.g., Feather, 1959; Slovic, 1969).

The relative risk aversion observed in positive-affect subjects considering real risks can be interpreted in terms of affect maintenance: People who are feeling happy risk losing that state, as well as any tangible stake, if they lose a gamble. Therefore, with more to lose than controls, they are more risk-averse than controls. This interpretation is supported by the results of the study described next, which examined the utility associated with various outcomes, as a function of induced positive affect (Isen et al., 1988).

This study used a technique devised by Davidson, Suppes, and Siegel (1956) to estimate utilities, over a series of gambles, by inference from gambles preferred. Subjects were told that they were wagering fractions of their credit for participating in the study, so that the risk situation was a real one. Affect was induced by means of a small bag of candy. Results showed that in this situation, people in whom positive affect had been induced displayed a greater sensitivity to loss than control subjects, indicating that the same loss had greater negative utility for them than it did for controls (Isen et al., 1988). These results, showing that a loss seems worse to people who are feeling happy, support the suggestion that positive affect may result in a tendency or motive to protect the induced positive state.

Together with the rest of the findings regarding positive affect and risk preference, they illustrate in the area of risk perception (as noted in other areas) that the influence of positive affect does not appear to be simple, but interacts with task and setting characteristics in the situation.

Complex Decision Making

Another type of decision making that has been studied as a function of positive affect is what might be called "complex decision making," in which people are asked to choose the best item from among several alternatives (e.g., to choose a car for purchase) or to solve a complex problem (e.g., to make a medical diagnosis). All of the findings reported thus far suggest that positive affect, in conjunction with other aspects of the task and decision situation, may influence the way people go about making complex decisions, and perhaps even their skill in doing so or their thoroughness in considering alternatives and possibilities. In fact, several interesting effects of feelings on these decision processes have been reported.

Results of two studies suggest that people in whom positive affect has been induced are more efficient in decision making, but at the same time may also be more thorough if the task lends itself to increased effort or care (Isen & Means, 1983; Isen et al., 1991). In the first study, in which positive affect was induced by report of success on a task unrelated to the decision problem, the affect and control groups did not differ in their choices; however, people in the positive-affect condition took significantly less time than those in the control condition to reach a decision (about 11 minutes, in contrast with the control group's average of about 19 minutes). These subjects also displayed significantly less redundancy in their search pattern, compared with controls, and tended significantly more than controls to eliminate unimportant dimensions from consideration (Isen & Means, 1983). In this study the decision task was to choose a hypothetical car for purchase from among six alternatives, differing along nine dimensions (fuel economy, purchase price, etc.).

The second study (Isen et al., 1991) used materials patterned on those of the car-choice experiment, but different in topic. In this study, the subjects were medical students who

had completed their third year of medical training and had finished a rotation in either pediatrics or internal medicine; the task was to choose, from among six descriptions of patients varying with regard to each of nine health-relevant descriptors (e.g., cough, chest X-ray, and so on), the one most likely to have lung cancer. Affect was induced by report of success on a task unrelated to the decision problem or to medicine at all (anagrams). As in the car-choice study, control subjects were shown the task materials but received no performance feedback.

The results of this study were compatible with those of the car-choice study, but particular measures produced different results because of the contextual differences. As had been found in the earlier study, people in the positive-affect condition reached the same answer (a correct one) to the assigned question as did control subjects, but they did so significantly earlier in their protocols. In this study, however, they then went on to do more with the materials—suggesting diagnoses for the other patients, and in some cases thinking about treatments. Their protocols also revealed significantly less confusion and greater integration of information, in the decision process. Thus, in this study the two affect groups did not differ on the specific measures that had been examined in the car-choice study (total time, amount of redundancy in the search, and number of dimensions eliminated). However, this was because those in the positive-affect condition were significantly more likely than controls to go beyond the assigned task and attempt to diagnose the remaining cases or determine treatments for the patients represented in the materials. Consequently, they continued to work on the materials after reaching the decision on the assigned task; they went back over material already considered in solving the original problem; and they did not eliminate any dimensions from consideration completely.

The differences between these two studies, which were designed to use similar materials, illustrate the importance of attention to the specifics of the situation in anticipating the influence of positive affect on particular measures. Although the results of the two studies are conceptually compatible, they indicate differences in particular measures. They also show that understanding the situation from the perspective of the *subject*, rather than from that of the experimenter, is important. Positive-affect participants in both studies were more efficient in reaching a decision; however, the measures that reflected this efficiency were different in the two situations. In the car-choice study, in which there was no point in working with the materials further, positive-affect subjects simply stopped working on the task once the choice was made; thus, total time on task revealed the difference between the groups. In the medical-diagnosis situation, where working with the materials after the decision was made could be interesting and helpful, those in the positive-affect condition went beyond the assigned task and did *more* than control subjects. Thus, their total time on task did not reflect the greater efficiency with which they had solved the assigned task.

These results suggest another possible influence of positive affect on decision making: greater integration of cognitive material. Subjects in the positive-affect condition in the medical-diagnosis study showed significantly less confusion and a significantly greater tendency to integrate material with which they were working. Thus, as has been discussed earlier regarding the cognitive impact of positive affect, it appears that under conditions of positive affect, people integrate material used in decision processes. This enables them to be less overwhelmed by the task, to show less confusion, and to work faster. Then they can either finish sooner, as in the car-choice task, or turn their attention to other details or tasks within the materials, as in the medical-diagnosis situation.

The findings of the medical decision-making study suggest that positive affect may promote not only more efficiency but also more thoroughness in a person's approach to a decision task. It should also be noted, however, that such an effect may be observed only where the materials allow for this possibility. Moreover, compatibly with similar points made earlier in this chapter, this may be true only for material that people experiencing positive affect *want* to think about or in which they are interested. A similar point has been made recently by Forgas (1991), who also found that positive affect increased the efficiency of decision making under some, but not all, circumstances. Results of the medical decision study indicate, notably, that such material includes tasks requiring complex consideration

of serious topics of interest to the subjects, and is not limited to stereotypically "positive" or fun topics.

Heuristics

One question that has arisen recently is whether positive affect results in the use of heuristics, as contrasted with systematic cognitive processing, in decision making and problem solving. Two early studies in our laboratory (cited in Isen, Means, Patrick, & Nowicki, 1982) suggested that positive affect might sometimes promote use of heuristics. Even at that time, however, it was thought that the effect might be limited to certain kinds of situations, and it was suggested that the sparseness of the context (e.g., lack of performance feedback or unexpected testing) might have been playing a role in the observed effect. These ideas were proposed because it was recognized, even then, that the most striking effects of mild positive affect on cognitive processing were facilitative. However, those studies did not actually explore the circumstances under which people experiencing positive affect might be more likely to use heuristics.

At that time, it was suggested that perhaps people in whom positive affect had been induced might rely on heuristic processing *instead of* on systematic processing. This suggestion was based on the assumption that people in whom positive affect had been induced would seek, more than would others, to avoid "cognitive strain" (e.g., Isen et al., 1982). However, the studies were preliminary and did not test those particular propositions (absence of systematic processing, avoidance of "cognitive strain") specifically, either. As the other work reviewed in this chapter has shown, it now appears that the suggestion that positive affect leads to avoidance of "cognitive strain" may be too sweeping.

Furthermore, even if problem simplification does occur, the particular way in which it is accomplished can vary, and it need not involve use of heuristics or nonsystematic thinking. Recent studies suggest, for example, that people in positive-affect conditions integrate material more than those in control conditions do, while nonetheless working systematically on the problem (e.g., Isen et al., 1991). As has been discussed in an earlier paper (Isen, 1987), there is reason to expect processes such as increased differentiation or elaboration, which has been found among people who are feeling happy, to be accompanied by greater integration as well. This is because seeing more dimensions may enable seeing more bases for combination or integration. This kind of two-part process involving both elaboration and integration has been suggested before—in the literature on cognitive style, for example, where it has been related to a style termed "integrative complexity" (e.g., Harvey, Hunt, & Schroder, 1961). It is interesting to note that this style has also been associated with the kinds of flexible processing described here as resulting from positive affect. The greater integration may allow for apparently simplified processing, but this method of simplification is based on elaboration and greater differentiation, better understanding of the issues. Although it may reduce cognitive strain, it may not be the same as use of a heuristic and does not necessarily imply nonsystematic processing. In fact, this kind of processing has been identified in the literature as typical of the way experts, as contrasted with novices, solve problems.

Thus, it can be seen that a person's using a heuristic does not necessarily mean that he or she will not also use systematic processing. But this possibility was not addressed in the earlier studies. Consequently, although those studies showed increased use of heuristics or problem simplification, they do not speak to the matter of whether positive affect reduces systematic processing, because they did not allow discovery of any simultaneous systematic processing that might also have been present.

In sum, there is not substantial evidence in the experimental literature to justify the general conclusion that in most situations, positive affect promotes use of heuristics *as opposed to* systematic processing, or interferes with systematic processing in decision making. Indeed, the preponderance of the evidence suggests just the opposite: that most often positive affect facilitates efficient, but thorough, problem solving.

On the other hand, some studies—for example, in the attitude-change literature—have suggested that positive affect can disrupt systematic processing (or at least can appear to do so), and at least one article has even proposed that this occurs because positive affect drains the limited cognitive capacity store available for performing cognitive functions (Mackie & Worth, 1989). How can these con-

flicting pictures be reconciled? There is insufficient space here to address this question fully; however, a few thoughts on the topic may be appropriate. Again, the resolution may be in the details and specifics of the situations.

For example, many of the differences may come from aspects of the materials used in the studies, and may result from motivational differences engendered by those. As noted throughout this chapter, if boring or unpleasant material is presented to people in positive-affect conditions, and they are not told that it is important to pay attention to those tasks, they may not be motivated to do their utmost in working on them. This may be reflected in the amount of effort or attention they expend on them, or in their latency in beginning to work on them.

Indeed, some variant of this "motivational" interpretation is the argument suggested by a number of authors who start from the premise that positive affect does disrupt systematic processing, but that the disruption comes as a result of insufficient motivation (or insufficient motivation to process systematically), rather than as a result of loss of cognitive capacity (e.g., Bless, Bohner, Schwarz, & Strack, 1990; Kuykendall & Keating, 1990; Smith & Shaffer, 1991).

However, the evidence that, as a rule, mild positive affect disrupts systematic processing actually does not itself seem substantial or convincing. This is because the studies attempting to show this are difficult to interpret, either because they did not include an affect control group (positive and negative affect were contrasted), or because they used materials allowing for an alternative interpretation, such as ones involving negative topics or matters over which subjects have no control (see Schwarz, Bless, & Bohner, 1991, for a review of these studies and a somewhat contrasting view). Further, when evidence for a disruptive influence of positive affect on systematic processing has been obtained, it has been under a severely limited set of conditions (e.g., Mackie & Worth, 1989), and therefore would not justify a sweeping global statement that positive affect decreases systematic processing.

Another problem in interpreting the studies that discuss interference with systematic processing is that such interference has often been inferred indirectly—from the relative effectiveness of weak versus strong arguments in producing attitude change, for example (e.g., Mackie & Worth, 1989). The problem is that attitude change may be reported by subjects for reasons unrelated to their processing of the messages: They may want to be more agreeable, for example, or they may think of good arguments themselves, as noted earlier in this chapter. Consequently, the attitude-change paradigm may not be the best one for assessing the influence of positive affect on the capacity or motivation for systematic cognitive processing.

Thus, the evidence that positive affect per se disrupts systematic processing per se is not yet clear. In cases where it appears to do so, this may be the result of a lack of motivation *for the task presented*; however, this kind of motivational effect is different from one that postulates general interference with motivation to process systematically, or with motivation overall.

This is not to say that positive affect, no matter how intense and no matter what the circumstances, cannot interfere with performance on any task. Certainly it may be true that intensely positive events or interesting good news may sometimes interfere with performance (or may do so for at least certain kinds of tasks). And this may be the source of the sense that people have, as noted at the beginning of this chapter, that affect, even positive affect, is disrupting. For example, news of winning an important prize or victory may distract a person and interfere with performance of a more mundane task. But the reason may be exactly that—that it distracts the person from the other task, or changes what he or she wants to think about—not that it necessarily drains the person's capacity or interferes with systematic cognitive processing, in general. However, this effect would not be unique to positive affect, but would apply to intense negative affect as well or, indeed, to any important or interesting information introduced. In addition, even in the case of intense affect, it may be that the person would not allow a *very important* task to be disrupted. That is, although it might be better not to tell a prize-winning surgeon the news of the prize during a surgery, let us hope that he or she could finish a complicated surgery successfully, even if notified then (and feeling happy about the prize). This, of course, remains to be seen; but in this illustration, in any case, we are speaking of intense positive affect, not the mild affect inductions that have been the subject of this chapter.

Regarding the matter of whether mild, everyday positive affect reduces cognitive capacity, other authors have noted recently that there is not yet substantial enough support to warrant acceptance of that position (e.g., Schwarz et al., 1991). Much of the evidence presented in this chapter further undermines the suggestion that positive affect generally drains a person's cognitive capacity and therefore leaves the person unable to process information clearly or effectively. Furthermore, when the capacity-reduction hypothesis is addressed more fully, proponents of that view will have to delineate the conditions under which capacity-reduction would be expected to occur; in addition, there will have to be differentiation between effects that may stem from distraction and those stemming from true reduction in capacity.

CONCLUSION

In summary of the work presented in this chapter, it seems appropriate to emphasize once again that the influence of affect depends on what it makes the person think about, and that this is determined not by the affective state alone, but by the affect in conjunction with several aspects of the situation that together influence the person's goals, judgments, and expectations.

All else being equal, positive affect tends to promote exploration and enjoyment of new ideas and possibilities, as well as new ways of looking at things. Therefore, people who are feeling good may be alert to possibilities and may solve problems both more efficiently and more thoroughly than controls. However, people who are feeling good respond cautiously in dangerous situations or when caution is otherwise appropriate. They may avoid unpleasant material or situations where possible. However, in situations in which they must think about possible losses, they may be expected to be self-protective and to consider the negative possibilities thoroughly.

Regarding systematic thinking, the most accurate general characterization of the impact of positive affect might be to say that if people who are happy can be expected to want to think about the topic or task that is presented to them (and this will include tasks involving serious topics in which they are competent and interested), then, compared with controls, they will elaborate on the task more and deal with it effectively and efficiently. In contrast, if people in whom positive affect has been induced can be expected to prefer not to focus on the materials or topic (for whatever reason), and there is nothing in the situation that requires, recommends, or alerts them that they should attend to the boring task, then they may not perform that task, may do so with as little effort as possible, or may show reluctance to engage in it. This should not be taken as evidence that positive feelings disrupt systematic thinking as a rule, or that positive-affect subjects *cannot* perform the task. Rather, it only reflects the sensible behavior of free individuals. For, if there is a reason for positive-affect subjects to work on a less preferred task, evidence suggests that they will also do that.

However, these considerations should alert us to the fact that if we expect people to be happy at the time of performing a task, depending on the circumstances we may want to inform them of the importance of the task or the necessity of getting it done, especially if this is not clear from the situation itself. It might be added that this may be more of a necessity in experimental settings, where the meaningfulness of the tasks is not always apparent, than in everyday life.

Thus, common positive feelings seem generally to promote activities that foster enjoyment and maintenance of those feelings, but in rational, responsible, adaptive ways. In addition, they provide many benefits (apart from the happiness inherent in them): They can facilitate creative problem solving, enabling people to come up with solutions to difficult problems that others find extremely hard to solve (while at the same time not detracting from performance on routine tasks, such as long division); and in some instances they enable negotiated solutions to interpersonal disputes. Positive affect has been found to give rise to elaboration and a wide range of cognitive associations in response to neutral stimulus material (while not reducing association to negatively toned words). It increases preference for variety and acceptance of a broader range of options in people's choice sets, when the choice is among safe, enjoyable alternatives, but does not promote risk taking in situations of genuine risk. Happy feeling can lead to efficient and thorough decision making; it stimulates enjoyment of enjoyable tasks and the perception of interesting tasks as even more enriched (but not at the cost of working on less interesting things if these need to be

done). When less interesting or slightly negative things are presented, those things may be deferred if that is an option, but will be addressed effectively if not. Socially, of course, positive affect is known to promote generosity, helpfulness, and responsibility under most circumstances.

This chapter has examined some of the evidence regarding ways in which positive affect influences decision making. Yet much remains to be explored about these relationships, the circumstances under which they occur, and the processes that are involved in producing them. Given the importance of positive feelings in our lives, and the great advantages to social behavior and problem solving that result from people's feeling happy, this seems a worthwhile topic for continued investigation.

Acknowledgments. I wish to thank Mark Chen, John Condry, Jeannette Haviland, Barbara E. Kahn, Carol Krumhansl, and Margaret G. Meloy for their helpful comments on an earlier draft of this chapter.

REFERENCES

Arkes, H. R., Herren, L. T., & Isen, A. M. (1988). Role of possible loss in the influence of positive affect on risk preference. *Organizational Behavior and Human Decision Processes, 42,* 181–193.

Bless, H., Bohner, G., Schwarz, N., & Strack, F. (1990). Mood and persuasion: A cognitive response analysis. *Personality and Social Psychology Bulletin, 16,* 331–345.

Bower, G. H. (1981). Mood and memory. *American Psychologist, 36,* 129–148.

Bransford, J. D. (1979). *Human cognition.* Belmont, CA: Wadsworth.

Carnevale, P. J. D., & Isen, A. M. (1986). The influence of positive affect and visual access on the discovery of integrative solutions in bilateral negotiation. *Organizational Behavior and Human Decision Processes, 37,* 1–13.

Cramer, P. (1968). *Word association.* New York: Academic Press.

Cunningham, M. R. (1979). Weather, mood, and helping behavior: Quasi-experiments in the sunshine Samaritan. *Journal of Personality and Social Psychology, 37,* 1947–1956.

Davidson, D., Suppes, P., & Siegel, S. (1956). *Decision making: An experimental approach.* Stanford, CA: Stanford University Press.

Duncker, K. (1945). On problem-solving. *Psychological Monographs, 58*(Whole No. 5).

Dunn, D. A., & Wilson, T. D. (1990). When the stakes are high: A limit to the illusion-of-control effect. *Social Cognition, 8,* 305–323.

Estrada, C. A., Young, M. J., & Isen, A. M. (1992). Positive affect influences reported source of practice satisfaction in physicians. *Clinical Research, 40*(3), 768A. (Abstract)

Feather, N. T. (1959). Subjective probability and decision under certainty. *Psychological Review, 66,* 150–164.

Forest, D., Clark, M., Mills, J., & Isen, A. M. (1979). Helping as a function of feeling state and nature of the helping behavior. *Motivation and Emotion*, 3(2), 161–169.

Forgas, J. P. (1991). Affective influences on partner choice: Role of mood in social decisions. *Journal of Personality and Social Psychology*, 61, 708–720.

Harvey, O. J., Hunt, D. E., & Schroder, H. M. (1961). *Conceptual systems and personality organization*. New York: Wiley.

Huber, J., Holbrook, M. B., & Kahn, B. (1986). Effects of competitive context and of additional information on price sensitivity. *Journal of Marketing Research*, 23, 250–260.

Isen, A. M. (1970). Success, failure, attention, and reactions to others: The warm glow of success. *Journal of Personality and Social Psychology*, 15, 294–301.

Isen, A. M. (1984). Toward understanding the role of affect in cognition. In R. Wyer & T. Srull (Eds.), *Handbook of social cognition* (Vol. 3, pp. 179–236). Hillsdale, NJ: Erlbaum.

Isen, A. M. (1985). The asymmetry of happiness and sadness in effects on memory in normal college students. *Journal of Experimental Psychology: General*, 114, 388–391.

Isen, A. M. (1987). Positive affect, cognitive processes, and social behavior. In L. Berkowitz (Ed.), *Advances in experimental social psychology* (Vol. 20, pp. 203–253). New York: Academic Press.

Isen, A. M. (1990). The influence of positive and negative affect on cognitive organization: Some implications for development. In N. Stein, B. Leventhal, & T. Trabasso (Eds.), *Psychological and biological approaches to emotion* (pp. 75–94). Hillsdale, NJ: Erlbaum.

Isen, A. M., & Berg, J. W. (1991). *The influence of affect on creative vs. routine tasks*. Unpublished manuscript, Cornell University.

Isen, A. M., & Daubman, K. A. (1984). The influence of affect on categorization. *Journal of Personality and Social Psychology*, 47, 1206–1217.

Isen, A. M., Daubman, K. A., & Nowicki, G. P. (1987). Positive affect facilitates creative problem solving. *Journal of Personality and Social Psychology*, 52, 1122–1131.

Isen, A. M., & Geva, N. (1987). The influence of positive affect on acceptable level of risk: The person with a large canoe has a large worry. *Organizational Behavior and Human Decision Processes*, 39, 145–154.

Isen, A. M., Johnson, M. M. S., Mertz, E., & Robinson, G. F. (1985). The influence of positive affect on the unusualness of word associations. *Journal of Personality and Social Psychology*, 48, 1413–1426.

Isen, A. M., & Levin, P. F. (1972). Effect of feeling good on helping: Cookies and kindness. *Journal of Personality and Social Psychology*, 21, 384–388.

Isen, A. M., & Means, B. (1983). The influence of positive affect on decision-making strategy. *Social Cognition*, 2, 18–31.

Isen, A. M., Means, B., Patrick, R., & Nowicki, G. P. (1982). Some factors influencing decision-making strategy and risk-taking. In M. S. Clark & S. T. Fiske (Eds.), *Affect and cognition: The 17th Annual Carnegie Symposium on Cognition* (pp. 243–261). Hillsdale, NJ: Erlbaum.

Isen, A. M., Niedenthal, P., & Cantor, N. (1992). An influence of positive affect on social categorization. *Motivation and Emotion*, 16, 65–78.

Isen, A. M., Nygren, T. E., & Ashby, F. G. (1988). The influence of positive affect on the subjective utility of gains and losses: It is just not worth the risk. *Journal of Personality and Social Psychology*, 55, 710–717.

Isen, A. M., & Patrick, R. (1983). The effect of positive feelings on risk-taking: When the chips are down. *Organizational Behavior and Human Performance*, 31, 194–202.

Isen, A. M., Pratkanis, A. R., Slovic, P., & Slovic, L. M. (1984). *An influence of affect on risk preference*. Paper presented at the meeting of the American Psychological Association, Washington, DC.

Isen, A. M., & Reeve, J. M. (1992). *The influence of positive affect on intrinsic motivation*. Unpublished manuscript, Cornell University.

Isen, A. M., Rosenzweig, A. S., & Young, M. J. (1991). The influence of positive affect on clinical problem solving. *Medical Decision Making*, 11(3), 221–227.

Isen, A. M., & Shalker, T. E. (1982). Do you "accentuate the positive, eliminate the negative" when you are in a good mood? *Social Psychology Quarterly*, 45, 58–63.

Isen, A. M., Shalker, T., Clark, M. S., & Karp, L. (1978). Affect, accessibility of material and behavior: A cognitive loop? *Journal of Personality and Social Psychology*, 36, 1–12.

Isen, A. M., & Simmonds, S. F. (1978). The effect of feeling good on a helping task that is incompatible with good mood. *Social Psychology Quarterly*, 41, 345–349.

Kahn, B. E., & Isen, A. M. (in press). The influence of positive affect on variety-seeking among safe, enjoyable products. *Journal of Consumer Research*.

Kahneman, D., & Tversky, A. (1979). Prospect theory: An analysis of decisions under risk. *Econometrica*, 47, 263–291.

Kraiger, K., Billings, R. S., & Isen, A. M. (1989). The influence of positive affective states on task perceptions and satisfaction. *Organizational Behavior and Human Decision Processes*, 44, 12–25.

Kuykendall, D., & Keating, J. P. (1990). Mood and persuasion: Evidence for the differential influence of positive and negative states. *Psychology and Marketing*, 7(1), 1–9.

Lacey, J. I. (1967). Somatic response patterning and stress: Some revisions of activation theory. In M. H. Appley & R. Trumball (Eds.), *Psychological stress: Issues in research* (pp. 14–44). New York: Appleton-Century-Crofts.

Lacey, J. I. (1975). Psychophysiology of the autonomic nervous system. In J. R. Nazarrow (Ed.), *Master lectures on physiological psychology*. Washington, DC: American Psychological Association. (Audiotape)

Mackie, D. M., & Worth, L. T. (1989). Processing deficits and the mediation of positive affect in persuasion. *Journal of Personality and Social Psychology*, 57, 27–40.

Mednick, M. T., Mednick, S. A., & Mednick, E. V. (1964). Incubation of creative performance and specific associative priming. *Journal of Abnormal and Social Psychology*, 69, 84–88.

Murray, N., Sujan, H., Hirt, E. R., & Sujan, M. (1990). The influence of mood on categorization: A cognitive flexibility interpretation. *Journal of Personality and Social Psychology*, 59, 411–425.

Nasby, W., & Yando, R. (1982). Selective encoding and retrieval of affectively valenced information. *Journal of Personality and Social Psychology*, 43, 1244–1255.

Neiss, R. (1990). Ending arousal's reign of error: A reply to Anderson. *Psychological Bulletin*, 107, 101–105.

Pruitt, D. G. (1983). Strategic choice in negotiation. *American Behavioral Scientist*, 27, 167–194.

Rosch, E. (1975). Cognitive representations of semantic categories. *Journal of Experimental Psychology: General*, 104(3), 192–233.

Schiffenbauer, A. (1974). Effects of observer's emotional state on judgments of the emotional state of others. *Journal of Personality and Social Psychology, 30*(1), 31–36.

Schwarz, N., Bless, J., & Bohner, G. (1991). Mood and persuasion: Affective states influence the processing of persuasive communications. In M. Zanna (Ed.), *Advances in experimental social psychology* (Vol. 24, pp. 161–199). New York: Academic Press.

Simonson, I. (1990). The effect of purchase quantity and timing on variety-seeking behavior. *Journal of Marketing Research, 27*, 150–162.

Slovic, P. (1969). Differential effects of real versus hypothetical payoffs on choices among gambles. *Journal of Experimental Psychology, 80*, 434–437.

Smith, S. M., & Shaffer, D. R. (1991). The effects of good moods on systematic processing: "Willing but not able, or able but not willing?" *Motivation and Emotion, 15*, 243–279.

Teasdale, J. D., & Fogarty, S. J. (1979). Differential effects of induced mood on retrieval of pleasant and unpleasant events from episodic memory. *Journal of Abnormal Psychology, 88*, 248–257.

Teasdale, J. D., Taylor, R., & Fogarty, S. J. (1980). Effects of induced elation–depression on the accessibility of memories of happy and unhappy experiences. *Behaviour Research and Therapy, 18*, 339–346.

Tversky, A., & Gati, I. (1978). Studies of similarity. In E. Rosch & B. B. Lloyd (Eds.), *Cognition and categorization* (pp. 79–98). Hillsdale, NJ: Erlbaum.

Tversky, A., & Kahneman, D. (1981). The framing of decisions. *Science, 211*, 453–458.

Venables, P. H. (1984). Arousal: An examination of its status as a concept. In M. G. H. Coles, J. R. Jennings, & J. A. Stern (Eds.), *Psychophysiological perspectives: Festschrift for Beatrice and John Lacey* (pp. 134–142). New York: Van Nostrand Reinhold.

20

The Representation and Organization of Emotional Experience: Unfolding the Emotion Episode

NANCY L. STEIN
TOM TRABASSO
MARIA LIWAG

INTRODUCTION

The goal of this chapter is to present a theoretical model that describes how people represent and understand events that lead to emotional reactions and subsequent action. Because the model attempts to depict the unfolding of emotional experience over time, it focuses on both the appraisal and planning processes associated with the evocation of emotion. The theory is characterized by four basic principles:

1. The theory is *knowledge-based and situated*. It describes the informational content that is acquired about emotion, and it specifies the conditions under which particular emotional reactions are elicited. It also describes the planning processes and actions that are carried out in response to events that provoke emotional reactions.

2. The theory is based upon critical assumptions about *human intentionality and goal-directed action*. A fundamental assertion is that the major life task of individuals is to monitor the status of goals and preferences that lead to states of well-being. Our theory describes how people assess and monitor the status of these valued goal states. Moreover, we show how emotions are intimately linked to violations of expectations about the ability to attain/maintain valued states, activities, or objects, or to escape/avoid undesirable states, activities, or objects. Thus, the perception of unexpected changes or novel information about the status of particular goals is a necessary condition for eliciting emotion.

3. The theory describes the *processes* by which the status of goals is monitored so that positive states of well-being can be maintained. Therefore, a description of the temporal and causal properties of the sequence of experiencing and reacting to emotional events becomes central. Moreover, the theory describes how physiological processes interact with cognitive processes to influence thinking during an emotion episode. Here, we describe the focus of attention during a goal-directed episode and the relationship among the focus of attention, physiological processes, and memory for the emotional event.

4. The theory places central importance on both the *appraisal and problem-solving* aspects of emotional experience. Our theory is knowledge-based, and events are always inter-

preted with respect to prior knowledge of situations and plans. Therefore, a one-to-one correspondence does not exist between any one event and the elicitation of a particular emotion, except when knowledge and the general predisposition of individuals are equivalent. Thus, for an emotional response to occur, some type of meaning analysis must be carried out on the precipitating event.

A GOAL-DIRECTED APPROACH TO UNDERSTANDING EMOTIONAL EXPERIENCE

In this section, we present our theory by elaborating upon its four basic tenets. We believe that people's knowledge about goals, the value that these goals hold, and the outcomes associated with goals (e.g., attainment, maintenance, avoidance, escape) are central to the evocation of emotion. By using the word "attainment," we do not mean to cast our approach into a Western cultural orientation toward achievement. What we mean by "attainment" is the ability to be successful at maintaining or reaching a desired outcome, or to be successful at avoiding or escaping from an undesirable outcome. The evocation of desire and the setting of goals are fundamental to all human behavior, including that which occurs in infancy (Lewis, 1990; Willatts, 1990; Mandler, 1984).

Both biological and psychological properties of the human organism constrain knowledge about emotion. Many features of emotional behavior are a function of the architecture, physiology, and processing capacities of human beings. For example, startle responses, responses to novelty, and autonomic nervous system (ANS) arousal at the beginning of an emotional reaction are all regulated and constrained by both anatomical and physiological properties of the nervous system. Moreover, these properties appear to be universal in nature.

Yet much knowledge about emotion is clearly acquired through personal experience, observation, learning, and social interaction. An analysis of the unfolding of emotional experience over time gives us insight, both personally and theoretically, into the relationship between cognition and emotion, the categorical nature of emotions, and the way in which emotions are related to one another. The study of the active, on-line nature of appraisal and

planning processes during an emotional experience, when carried out for the most frequent emotions, also sheds light on developmental and cultural issues surrounding controversies over basic emotions (Stein & Trabasso, 1992).

Conditions That Give Rise to Emotions

The set of dimensions characterizing the appraisal and planning processes that evoke each of the four emotions of happiness, sadness, anger and fear have been described by Stein and her associates (Stein & Jewett, 1986; Stein & Levine, 1987, 1989, 1990; Stein & Trabasso, 1992). The dynamic quality of the appraisal process that leads to different emotional experiences indicates how each emotion is separate from and unique in relation to the other emotions. This dynamism is also indicated in the way emotions share conditions and provides a basis for their similarities and co-occurrences. Unlike Ortony and Turner (1990) as well as Johnson-Laird and Oatley (1989, 1992), who believe that single components can elicit an emotion, we believe that specific goal–outcome combinations must be inferred in order for an emotion to be evoked. Making an inference about the certainty or uncertainty of goal attainment is also crucial for the evocation of an emotional response.

Although the four emotions of happiness, anger, sadness, and fear by no means encompass the spectrum of possible emotion states, we have chosen them for analysis because, along with disgust, we believe that these four emotions represent a set of basic emotions. These emotions can be found in some form in every known culture, despite differences in categorical reference and value judgments about the appropriateness and acceptability of each emotion and its expression. One reason for their basicness is that each of these four emotions corresponds to a particular goal–outcome–goal revision combination that can be used to determine whether or not valued goals have been fulfilled (Stein & Oatley, 1992). Although the language labels that describe emotion states are quite varied, the goal-outcome-goal revision properties of intentional action are not. In fact, the number of possible goal-outcome-goal revision options are quite limited. Moreover, three dimensions (i.e., changes in the status of a goal; the outcomes associated with the change; and a plan to maintain, reinstate, avoid, abandon, or revise a goal), along with a fourth dimension, that of uncertainty (Stein & Jewett, 1986; Stein & Levine, 1987, 1989, 1990), are the dimensions to which attention is first devoted before any emotional reaction is elicited.

Our belief in the importance of goal–outcome–goal revision knowledge arises from certain assumptions about the nature of human behavior. We assume that much of behavior is carried out in the service of achieving and maintaining goal states that ensure survival and adaptation to the environment. A basic tenet underlying this belief (Stein & Levine, 1987, 1990) is that people prefer to be in certain states (e.g., those producing pleasure) and prefer to avoid other states (e.g., those producing pain). A second assumption is that when people experience unpleasant states, they attempt to regulate and change them. One way of achieving this change is to represent a state, called a "goal." A goal can then be used to initiate action or thinking that results in the desired internal state change. Goals are limited and consist of attaining, maintaining, avoiding, or escaping from an internal state.

A critical dimension in defining and describing emotional experience, therefore, focuses on the concept of changing states. Representing and evaluating change with respect to how valued goals have been affected are seen as necessary prerequisites for experiencing and regulating emotion. As such, our theory is oriented toward a specification of the *process* by which changes in goal states are detected and emotions are elicited. We also examine the ways in which emotion-provoking events are represented, the content of these evaluations, and the type of thinking that occurs throughout an emotion episode. Thus, on-line encoding and retrieval processes that are accessed during emotional understanding become germane to our theory, as does a characterization of the temporal-causal sequence of thinking processes (Stein, Trabasso, & Liwag, 1991, in press).

Since we are highlighting the significance of changing conditions, a distinguishing characteristic of emotional experience is an effort to assimilate some type of new information into current knowledge schemes (Mandler, 1975, 1984; Stein & Jewett, 1986; Stein & Levine, 1987, 1990; Stein & Trabasso, 1989, 1992). We contend that people constantly monitor their environment in an effort to maintain preferred states. In order to succeed at this task, procedures analogous to pattern-matching and assimilation are used to analyze and compare incoming data to what is already known. When new information is detected in the input, a mismatch occurs, causing an interruption in current thinking processes. Attention then shifts to the novel or discrepant information. Along with the attentional shift comes arousal of the ANS and a focus on the implications that the new information has for the maintenance of valued goals. Thus, emotional experience is almost always associated with attending to and making sense out of new information.

As a function of attending to new information, *learning* (via content and structural changes in the mental structures used to understand an emotional event) almost always results during an emotion episode. In an effort to understand the consequences of changing conditions upon the status of goals, people are forced to revise and update their beliefs about two dimensions: what the probability is of maintaining goals under a new set of conditions, and whether or not they have plans that will lead to successful goal maintenance. For example, when people fail to maintain or attain a desired goal state, they attend to the conditions that prevented them from being successful; they attend to the consequences of their failure; and they assess the probability of generating a plan of action to overcome goal failure. This sequence characterizes children's emotional responses (Capatides, 1989; Stein & Levine, 1989) as well as parents' descriptions and responses to the children's emotional behaviors (Capatides, 1989; Stein et al., in press).

In updating knowledge about viable conditions that lead to goal success or failure, people may change the *value* they have imputed to a particular set of goals. That is, in attaining or failing to attain a goal, the value associated with that and other goals may increase or decrease in strength. As a result, people often forfeit their goals, or they may intensify their efforts to achieve them, depending upon the new value that these goals now possess.

In privileging intentional action as a core part of our theory, we are assuming that people have a built-in mechanism that allows them to represent *goal–action–outcome* sequences in relationship to the maintenance of goals (Gallistel, 1985; Piaget, 1981; Stein & Levine, 1987, 1990). Individuals are able to infer and represent the causal conditions operating to produce actions that result in certain outcomes, and they are able to use this knowledge to achieve goals. Thus, when a change in goal maintenance occurs, and emotions are experienced, plans are mobilized. Accessing a plan that specifies the conditions necessary to achieve a goal provides an opportunity for coping with goal failure. Similarly, constructing and carrying out a plan enable the maintenance of a goal, once the goal has been achieved.

There are situations, however, where little planning occurs or where plans are not easily available and retrieved. Intense emotional experience often precludes access to certain types of information. Under these conditions, critical inferences about the emotion situation are not made. Thus, the intensity of an emotional experience and the associated sensory and physiological feedback become important variables in predicting the thinking, decision-making, and quality of planning that take place during an emotional experience. Although there are reports that emotional involvement enhances the accuracy of memory for events (Burke, Heuer, & Reisberg, 1992; Goodman, 1991), this is not always the case (Peters, 1991; Rachman, 1978). Depending upon the intensity of the emotional response and the necessity to take action, memory for the external events surrounding the emotion can be diminished or facilitated. The relationship among memory, thinking, and emotion, then, must be stipulated according to the specific circumstances that constrain the experience.

We now review data from studies with very young children as well as adults on changes in emotional awareness and behavior as a function of development. This issue is a thorny one at best; age-related differences can often be accounted for by the amount of knowledge children have acquired or the degree to which they have been exposed to a context rather than by any general process pertaining to development alone. With these qualifications in mind, however, the developmental aspects of emotional experience must be considered.

Developmental Issues

The controversies concerning development revolve around which facets of emotion are considered innate and which are considered learned. A second issue concerns the nature of the transformations that take place in children's knowledge of emotion and the way in which development affects the organization

of emotion. We begin by considering some of the regulatory processes that are present at birth and some that emerge as a result of maturation and experience. Then we advance an analysis of the specific processes and types of knowledge that are acquired and used during emotional experience. Finally, we present data that bear upon the validity of our model, with respect to both developmental and individual differences in emotion knowledge.

The first issue is whether preferences are innate. At birth, the infant's repertoire includes a set of behaviors for responding to different types and intensities of stimulation. Many actions are reflexive in nature (e.g., the startle, orienting, blinking, and sucking reflexes). Some involve an affective reaction specific to the nature of the stimuli. For example, certain events precipitate distress responses, consisting of volatile activity, crying, and particular facial expressions. Other events elicit a quieting response, with the absence of volatile activity and expression. A few researchers have taken these responses as evidence that the infant has innate preferences for being in certain states and innate preferences for avoiding others. For example, Zajonc (1980) argues that initial preferences need no cognitive input for their elicitation, and that they drive all other forms of emotional development.

We do not question the existence and importance of preferences. They are critical to the experience and expression of emotion. However, we take issue with the claim that newborns possess full-blown preferences, such as desires to be in certain states or desires to avoid others. The fact that infants experience pleasure and distress does not mean that they prefer or desire to shift from one state to another. Having preferences requires the ability to represent, remember, compare, and choose between two different states, and to express a desire to orient more toward one state than toward another. In order to carry out this type of thinking, a person must have acquired the ability to represent a state that does not currently exist. Although newborns can demonstrate pleasure or distress in direct response to different events, they have yet to achieve the capacity to represent internal or external states different from those currently directing their behavior.

One reason why young infants experience difficulty in representing hypothetical states such as goals is that they have yet to accumulate the knowledge necessary to construct stable representations of their environment. Creating stable and organized representations permits understanding of the causal constraints that make events predictable. When infants have enough experience of a specific situation and can construct a stable representation of it, they can then begin to mentally link actions with outcomes. They are able to form expectations and learn that certain conditions must be present for specific events, actions, and outcomes to occur. In conjunction with this type of understanding, young infants also learn that their own actions can control or change the conditions that lead to certain outcomes. The result of acquiring an adequate knowledge of the world is that young infants engage in decision making about the value of particular experiences, and determine whether or not to pursue a particular objective.

Although learning of this sort occurs rapidly, it is not present in the newborn infant. The critical period for developmental change appears to be the first 4 to 5 months of life. During this time, several significant cognitive attainments are observed. First, the infant's ability to habituate to different classes of events increases. Evidence of habituation signals that infants can form predictable representations of a phenomenon and that they detect discrepancy (or dishabituate) when novel stimuli are introduced (Lewis, 1990; Alessandri, Sullivan, & Lewis, 1990; Lewis, Alessandri, & Sullivan, 1990). Second, infants attend more systematically to external events, so that they appear to engage consciously in an appraisal process (Stenberg & Campos, 1990; Emde, 1980; Sroufe, 1979). These young infants begin to evaluate an event in terms of how it will affect them. This evaluation requires that an infant understand that a given event results in a specific outcome, and that the outcome results in a particular affective state. If the affective state is aversive or unpleasant, the infant must then be able to represent a state that is not unpleasant. Third, children begin to construct plans that enable them to change their current affective state, and they become more skilled in regulating their motor behavior so that they can carry out and accomplish their plans.

It appears from an analysis of current literature on infant development (e.g., Alessandri et al., 1990; Fernald, 1984; Lewis et al., 1990; Mandler, 1988) that these skills cohere and become integrated during the second to seventh month of life. When infants can bring to bear all of these cognitive and behavioral developments on their encounters with the social world, we would say that a true emotion can be experienced. In making this claim, we are distinguishing between the more general class of affective responses and the more specific class of emotional responses. Affective responses are those that include distress or quieting behaviors where changes in the level of ANS arousal occur without evaluative appraisal. Affective responses are often evoked in direct response to the level, speed, and duration of sensory input from the environment. These affective reactions are seen frequently in the young infant and less frequently in the adult. The important point, however, is that direct sensory responses require little cognitive response and depend upon automatic processes for regulating the quality and quantity of sensory stimulation. Emotional reactions, however, are those that involve higher-order thinking processes as well as input from the sensory and autonomic nervous systems.

PROCESSES UNDERLYING EMOTIONAL EXPERIENCE

In this section, we lay out the processes and components involved in our model of emotional experience and understanding. A necessary feature of our theory is the presence of a representational system that monitors subjective states and bodily reactions. Monitoring is carried out in the service of moving toward states that are beneficial for survival and moving away from environments that are harmful. *The primary function of this system is to access knowledge that allows the evaluation of an event, action, object, or state with regards to its value* (see also Mandler, 1984). This representational system includes information about states that are pleasurable and preferred, and states that are aversive and to be avoided. The system also contains information about the conditions that lead to specific goal states, and it holds information about the relative priority of goals in terms of the necessity for maintaining or avoiding certain states.

Given these properties, the representational system has three essential characteristics. First, it is both hierarchical and sequential in nature. A series of goals can be represented in a superordinate and subordinate fashion. The conditions that elicit each goal can be specified and the connections of goals to one another can be described. Second, preference trees can be constructed; some goals may be accorded more value than others. Third, the system is dynamic in character. Some preferences and some parts of a goal hierarchy (i.e., the conditions specifying the ordering of goals and the links between them) can be changed. As a result of learning and incorporating new information about conditions leading to the attainment of valued goals, the structure of the goal hierarchy may undergo reorganization. Goals that have a high value on one occasion may lessen in value on another, depending upon operating conditions. Similarly, goals that are unfamiliar or lacking in value often strengthen in worth as new connections are made between these goals and other valued familiar goals. The crucial point is that, like all other schemas, value systems are both stable and dynamic. Some parts of the value system can remain constant while other parts can change.

The existence of a value system is fundamental to emotional behavior (Lazarus & Folkman, 1984; Mandler, 1984; Stein & Levine, 1987, 1990) because the system alerts individuals to those situations that bring pleasure and pain. With such a system at work, two primary tendencies exist: the desire to attain or maintain a valued state, and the desire to escape from or avoid an aversive state. As we have previously stated, a value system becomes operative when an individual is in one particular state, imagines the existence of another state, and appreciates that the imagined end state leads to a more pleasurable outcome.

Thus, a second component critical to our model is the ability to detect change in the environment as well as in one's own internal states. Moreover, the change must be assessed with respect to maintaining current values and goal states. Here, we outline the different processes that transpire when emotions are experienced. We begin by describing baseline activities that occur just before the onset of a precipitating event. Four are of interest: (1) the type of ongoing cognitive activity; (2) the level of physiological arousal; (3) the emotional state of the participant; and (4) the type of ongoing overt activity. These variables are significant because our model assumes that an emotional reaction always causes a change

in the first three processes, and often causes a change in overt actions as well (Ekman, 1977, 1992). Thus, our emotion model is a state change model that delineates the physiological, cognitive, and behavioral changes that are triggered by an unexpected precipitating event.

Precipitating events stem from three different sources: the environment (i.e., a physical event, such as a fire or a rainbow), or the action of another person and one's own actions (such as the giving of a gift or the violation of a promise), or the memory of past events. In order for an emotion to occur, the precipitating event must be encoded and accessed during the evaluation process. In the case of recalling an event from memory, the initial encoding has already taken place, but the event must still be accessed and placed in working memory. Then, a meaning analysis has to be performed on the focal information.

The meaning analysis can be broken down into different processes. Of primary interest are those that facilitate the integration of incoming information into current knowledge structures. If we assume that different pattern-matching procedures underlie most attempts to assimilate new information into current knowledge stores, it is important to discriminate between those situations where a match results and those where a discrepancy occurs. If incoming information is congruent with information in existing knowledge schemes, then it is readily assimilated. Under these conditions, individuals are often unaware of the processes associated with encoding and understanding.

Where a mismatch occurs, however, information cannot be immediately integrated into current working schemes. By definition, some of this information is unexpected or novel; that is, some aspect of the incoming information is incongruent with what was expected, given the current state of a person's knowledge. Mismatches interrupt ongoing thinking, give rise to subsequent evaluation processes, and initiate subsequent changes in states of ANS arousal (Mandler, 1975, 1984; Stein & Levine, 1987, 1990). When both ANS arousal and cognitive evaluation take place, an emotional reaction is invoked. As we have stated before, precipitating events often cause ANS arousal, leading to an affective or reflexive response. However, we do not consider these affective responses as belonging to the class of emotional responses, because no evaluation of current goal states is made. It is the conjoint occurrence of ANS arousal and cognitive evaluation that constitutes an emotional experience.

When the evaluation process is initiated, an assessment is first made as to whether an adequate representation of the precipitating event exists. There are many instances where only part of an event is understood because the information is so novel. In these cases, surprise and a sense of curiosity are evoked. This indicates that the first cognitive activity of the individual is to form a representation of the event in the service of understanding the new information. That is, many precipitating events require that new categories be formed or that beliefs be updated so that the event can become known and predictable. *Then* an evaluation can be made as to whether the event has any significance with respect to changing, blocking or facilitating the attainment of goals.

Separating the two processes of representation and evaluation is difficult because of their close temporal proximity. However, forming a representation that has some meaning always precedes the evaluation process. Moreover, different affective reactions should be observed when representations are being constructed than when changes in goal maintenance are being assessed. Surprise, curiosity, and interest are indicative of the creation of new representations, whereas happiness, anger, sadness, and fear are indicative of the assessment of an event with respect to the maintenance of preferred goals. Depending upon the quality of the initial representation, an emotion may be elicited. If a person has encoded enough information about the event to infer that it will directly impinge upon a goal, then the person feels an emotion, despite the fact that the initial representation was incomplete in some sense. If further understanding of the event is necessary to permit an inference about how it will affect a goal, then the emotional response is delayed until such an evaluation can be made.

We provide illustrations of both types of situations: one where further processing must be carried out for an emotion to be experienced, and one where a coherent representation has yet to be formed but the individual has already inferred that the event will impact on a goal. When surprise is felt in close proximity to other emotions, it normally precedes

the other emotions. As an example, we offer part of a dialogue from one of our studies (Stein & Trabasso, 1989) on 5-year-old children. On this occasion, a kindergarten pupil was told that her teacher was going to let all of the children paint as part of their normal classroom activities. The child was then told that she and her classmates could paint every day, and she was asked how she felt about this. Her responses were that she really liked painting (value) and that she felt really happy (emotional response), especially when she got to paint whenever she wanted (goal outcome).

This child was then told that today, right now, when she got through painting, her teacher was going to give her all of the paints to take home. She would be able to paint at home as well as in school. The child was asked to describe her thoughts and feelings in response to this event. She began by saying: "Do you really mean that she [the teacher] is going to let me take all of the paints home? Am I the only one who gets to do this? Is this a present for me? Does she want me to paint every day?"

If we had videotaped the facial expressions of this child, we would have recorded a look of surprise followed by a look of concern as she began to talk. First, she did not quite believe that the teacher would give her a gift, so she displayed surprise in response to this information. Thus, in order for her to form a coherent representation of the event, she first had to determine whether or not it would really happen. If she then believed that this wonderful thing was indeed going to come true, then she needed to reconcile the new information with her prior beliefs.

Here is how she would have attempted to reconcile the two beliefs. If we had interviewed this child at the beginning of the session, before any new information was presented, and asked whether or not she thought her teacher would ever give her a gift of paints, we probably can show that this child judged the event as highly unlikely. The clear majority of all the children in this study (Stein & Trabasso, 1989), in effect, said: "I don't believe it. Can you believe it? Why would she do that?" Apparently, teachers are not thought of as givers of gifts, and this unexpected act of generosity violated children's conceptions of what a teacher usually does. Thus, the first part of the evaluation process in this example was devoted to updating beliefs about what teachers normally think about and do, their reasons for doing such things, and the implications that a teacher's actions have for the future goals and behavior of children. Thus, for the child described above to feel a particular emotion in this context, the child first had to believe that the teacher was indeed giving her a gift and that she could do whatever she wanted with it. Once she accepted these facts, then she expressed happiness verging on joy.

In this example, a child first attempted to discern the truth value associated with a precipitating incident. Then, she tried to understand why the teacher was giving her a paint set and what the teacher wanted her to do with the set. The general act of gift giving was not unfamiliar. Gift giving is common, and is a very pleasurable experience for children (Stein et al., 1991, in press; Trabasso, Stein, & Johnson, 1981). Therefore, the 5-year-old girl encoded the event appropriately when she first heard about it. However, she expressed disbelief because of what was implied by the gift: There could be possible obligations attached. A teacher could give children paint sets for reasons other than the one offered by the experimenter. The little girl was not initially convinced that the stated reason was in fact the one that the teacher had in mind. For this little girl, teachers were not associated with gift giving as much as they were associated with handing out tasks that must be accomplished. Thus, the novel element was the *teacher's act* of giving the children a gift without any conditions attached.

A second illustration of how children dealt with the novel event of a teacher's giving a gift is described. In this instance, a 5-year-old boy expressed happiness when told that he could take his paint set home. When asked why he was happy, he replied that he really preferred to paint at home rather than at school, and taking home the paint set meant that he could paint whenever he wanted to. When asked what he thought about the teacher's gift, he said he didn't quite understand why she would do such a thing. She had never before given the children anything to take home. But the little boy also said that this did not matter because he could still paint at home, no matter what the teacher's reasons were.

In this second case, the little boy immediately made the inference that one of his valued goals would be fulfilled, and he experienced happiness as a result of believing this

to be the case. He also knew that the event leading to goal fulfillment was highly unusual and violated his belief about the conditions under which a desired goal could be attained. However, the little boy did not need to know why this event happened in order for him to experience an emotional reaction. All he needed to believe was that the attainment of a valued goal was certain.

We described the act of dealing with a violation of an expectation in detail for several reasons. First, it is a central part of our representational model. Mandler (1975, 1984) and Scherer (1991) are two other researchers who even speak to the necessity of incorporating novelty or violations of expectations into their models of emotion. However, Scherer does not have a knowledge system component built into his model. Therefore, there is no mechanism in his framework for resolving discrepancies between incoming and prior knowledge. Moreover, Scherer does not distinguish between affective processes and emotional processes, and does not use content representations in modeling the understanding and evaluation processes. We believe, however, that the informational content of evaluations is critical. It is through an explication of the understanding process that we learn how familiar content, via prior knowledge, is combined with novel information to create a violation of expectations during the experience of emotion.

The familiar conjoined with the novel is often the condition that causes the most intense affective and emotional responses (e.g., surprise, shock, or horror). Examples of tragedies are those instances of horrible events (e.g., a plane crash or an earthquake) where the victim loses a loved one and does not believe that such an event could ever happen to him or her. The familiarity of many tragic situations (i.e., knowing that such terrible events could happen and perhaps witnessing the grim reality of others having to cope with such disasters) allows the victim to experience horror or grief. Shock and an air of unreality, however, set in almost simultaneously or even precede the feeling of mourning or terror. The ability to accept the fact that one has been visited by a tragedy and that this cannot be changed is crucial and regulates whether or not the consequences of the event will be processed. If doubt surrounds the occurrence of the event, attention, resources, and effort will be focused first on determining its certainty.

Surprise and interest are different from emotional responses. They indicate an effort to determine meaning and an attempt to understand the implications of novel information in a precipitating event. These affective responses are not directly associated with an evaluation of how a precipitating event affects the accomplishment of goals. Surprise is expressed when expectations are violated and situations go against the norm. As a result, disbelief sets in. Thus, surprise is usually seen in the initial part of an emotion episode and often indicates the amount of discrepancy that the new information carries. Attempts to understand how precipitating events affect valued goals is associated with states of interest or curiosity. However, as soon as the event is understood in terms of its implications for goals, specific emotional responses should be manifested.

We now turn our attention to a description of the processes of thinking and planning associated with the three emotions of happiness, anger, and sadness (see also a similar analysis of fear in Stein & Jewett, 1986). Most investigators (Frijda, 1987; Oatley & Johnson-Laird, 1987; Roseman, 1991; Scherer, 1991) studying the conceptual organization of emotional knowledge have overly simplified the thinking processes associated with emotions. Although emotional responses can indeed be rapid, occurring almost in an automatic fashion (Ekman, 1977), the delay between a precipitating event and an emotion can also be quite long. We know of few on-line processing studies that have actually documented the variations in the time delays of emotional responses, nor do we know of any studies that have described the multiple changes occurring during attempts to understand the meaning of a precipitating event. Although we focus here on only three different emotions, we describe the associated processes of thinking and planning in a detailed fashion.

THINKING AND PLANNING IN SPECIFIC EMOTION CONTEXTS

When we talk about happiness, anger, sadness, or fear, we almost always do so within a particular context. We are angry about something, we fear something, we are happy about something, or we are sad that something has happened. Thus, emotional responses are specific to situations. Although Wierzbicka (1992) questions whether emotions always have causes, we have found that even 3-year-old children (Stein & Levine, 1989; Stein et al., 1991, in press) refuse to talk about emotions unless they can first identify the conditions that caused the emotion. Asserting that people can feel an emotion without being able to identify the cause is not valid evidence to deny the causal structure of emotional knowledge. Mood states, which are longer-lasting than emotional states, are often labeled with the same terms as specific emotional states; upon further questioning, however, adults almost always distinguish, for instance, between a mood state of irritability and an emotion state of anger. Moreover, when both children and adults find themselves in certain physiological states where the causes are not quite apparent, they normally spend the first part of their evaluation of the states trying to determine just what could have caused them to feel a particular way.

Likewise, emotions are often experienced in contexts not only where the individual is striving to understand the past, but where future-oriented behavior is at stake. Thus, in our model of specific emotional reactions, the types of planning and thinking brought to bear upon future behavior are critical. Emotions almost always spring from contexts that are planning and problem-oriented. Even situations where valued goals are permanently blocked have a forward-looking aspect to them. When goals are not longer tenable, strategies for accepting and dealing with the loss must be generated. Learning how to substitute new goals for old ones, and learning how to change and raise the value of old goals that are tenable, require a future orientation and an ability to learn. Thus, the causal inferences made about events that cause the status of goals to change, and the plans formulated to cope with the change in status, are crucial components of the knowledge used to understand and experience specific emotions.

Most of our data are gathered in situations where children and adults are talking about and remembering contexts where different types of emotions have been experienced (Stein & Levine, 1989; Stein & Trabasso, 1989; Stein et al., 1991, in press). However, we also use nonverbal tasks to test our hypotheses about the importance of causal inferences during emotional reactions (Stein et al., in press). Moreover, we include in our analyses the ability to label and make faces, as well as the ability to carry out actions once an emotion is felt. Thus, it is extremely critical for us that convergent methodologies be applied to investigate the nature of the unfolding of the emotion episode.

Happiness

We begin with a description of happiness in order to illustrate how this emotion, as well as the "negative" emotions, depends upon the recognition of discrepant information. For a person to experience happiness, four aspects must be detected or inferred from a precipitating event. First, some aspect of the event must be perceived as novel with respect to the ability to maintain, attain, or avoid a particular goal state. Novelty is normally expressed in the form of a violation of expectation, where a current set of beliefs is challenged and requires updating. Figure 20.1 presents a flow diagram of the processes and decisions that are carried out when happiness is experienced. At the beginning of the episode, attention must shift such that the precipitating event receives full consideration in terms of understanding and identifying it. Second, inferences must be made that the status of a goal has changed, and that this goal has been attained or maintained or an aversive state has been terminated or avoided. Third, an inference must be made about the certainty of attaining or maintaining the goal. That is, the person must believe that goal attainment is certain or that goal attainment has already occurred such that no further obstacles can hinder goal success. And fourth, the person must believe that enjoyment of the goal state or goal maintenance will follow from the outcome.

A prototypic way of thinking about the experience of happiness is to envision the transition from a negative to a positive state. At the beginning of an emotion episode, several features characterize the initial negative state. First, the valued goal under consideration has not as yet been attained, or has been threatened, or an aversive state exists. Second, the current belief state is one in which the person does not envision any certain change in the status of this goal.

For a change in the emotional state to occur, a precipitating event must be perceived to cause or enable the relevant goal to be achieved. Happiness results when the event is encoded and its implications are seen as discrepant from what is known or believed. The fact that the goal has been attained or that goal attainment is virtually guaranteed violates expectations. That is, an event has taken place that forces an alteration in the belief that the focal goal was not attainable. Attention is then focused on whether or not the event was encoded properly, and an appraisal is made about the relative certainty that a particular goal has been attained and will be maintained.

An example from one of our studies (Stein & Trabasso, 1989) illustrates this point. Five-year-old children were initially asked to imagine that their mothers were not going to be able to read them a story before bedtime. They were told that they would just have to go to bed by themselves. Children were then asked (1) how they would feel if this happened to them, (2) how intense their feelings would be (intensity was rated on a 5-point scale), and (3) how sure they would be that their mothers would not read them a bedtime story. In 92% of the cases, the children said that they would feel sad because they would not hear a story and would have to go to bed alone. Their feelings were very intense, averaging 4.5 out of 5 on a rating scale. In rating the certainty of the fact that they were not going to get a story read to them, the average score was 1.5, with 1 being certain that no story would be read and 5 being certain that a story would be read to them. Thus, a negative emotion state had been established, resulting in either sadness or anger.

After answering these questions, children were then told that their mothers had thought about it again, and were going to read them a story after all because the mothers were able to get more of their chores done in time. Children were asked what their first thoughts were about this event. Approximately 96% of the children said they would feel really happy because they loved stories and were glad that their mothers had changed their minds. Thus, for the clear majority of children, there was a rapid shift from believing that goal attainment was at a very low probability (1.5) to believing that they would readily attain their goal (4.5). Moreover, all of the children questioned why their mothers had changed their minds and whether their chores would get in the way of future story-reading situations. Thus, these children were not only happy that they had been successful at attaining a goal state, but they were also planning for the future in terms of maintaining their goal in other contexts.

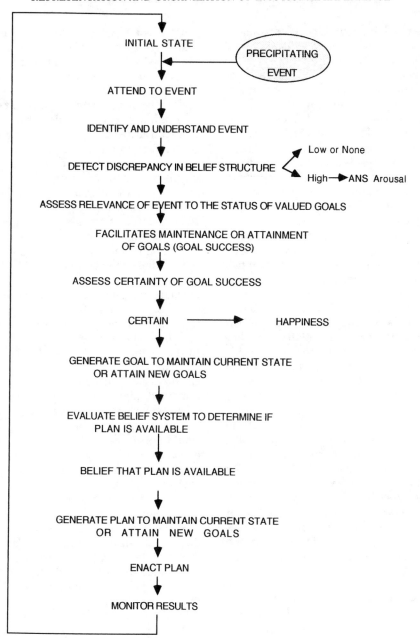

FIGURE 20.1. Flow diagram for happiness.

The flow diagram of happiness shows that as a result of attaining a valued state, the primary goal shifts to one of maintaining that state. If attaining other relevant goals is necessary to maintain the initial state, then people will immediately proceed to do just that. However, the flow diagram in Figure 20.1 indicates that during efforts to maintain the valued state, obstacles frequently arise, and plans are not available to overcome the obstacles. In these cases, negative emotions will be experienced until a plan is found to reinstate the valued goal.

The flow diagram, in conjunction with the data from the Stein and Trabasso (1989) study, illustrates that happiness is expressed when expectations about the probability of goal success are violated. However, children must also update their beliefs about the certainty of goal success if they are to experience happiness. If they are able to change their beliefs, then happiness will be expressed. And when they talk about being happy, children almost always focus on being able to enjoy the activities associated with goal fulfillment. If children do not believe that goal attainment is certain, then they do not express happiness; rather, a low level of anxiety is evoked. Thus, the perception of certainty, along with the perception of goal attainment, maintenance, avoidance, or escape, appear to be necessary to the expression of happiness.

Experiencing happiness does not require that people initially be in a negative emotion state. Individuals can make the transition to a happy state by first being in a more neutral state or by experiencing surprise or interest, signaling the formation of a new representation. However, once they have been successful at constructing a representation where they understand an event, and inferences are made about the success and the certainty of goal attainment, happiness is experienced.

Situations also exist where the experience of happiness intensifies. For example, suppose a person has just achieved an important goal and experiences a state of happiness. Suddenly, another event occurs to ensure the achievement of other valued goals. In this case, the emotion of happiness intensifies. The increase in intensity results from the unexpected attainment of additional desired goals, some of which may be more valued than those originally attained. For example, in the Stein and Trabasso (1989) study, 5-year-old children were told that they were to imagine that their teacher brought a new toy to class every week and that they got an hour to play with it by themselves. Children responded to this initial situation by giving almost unanimously happy responses, with an average of 4.3 on a 5-point intensity rating scale.

The children were then told that the teacher decided that they could take the toy home and keep it, because she knew how much they liked the toy. After expressing their surprise at such an event, 94% of the children manifested happiness about being able to take the toy home. The average intensity rating rose from 4.3 to 4.9. Moreover, when asked whether they were just as happy, more happy, or less happy, after getting the toy to take home, 96% responded that they were more happy. When asked whether or not they expected the teacher to give them a toy, 94% replied that they never thought she would do such a thing. As we showed in our earlier analyses, teachers are not perceived to be the bearers of gifts.

What we have shown so far is that unexpectedly fulfilling goals is sufficient to evoke happiness. Unexpectedly accomplishing additional goals increases the intensity of happiness. The question remains, however, as to whether novelty is *necessary* to induce happiness once inferences have been made about the achievement of a valued goal.

In an attempt to answer this question, we asked the same 5-year-old children to respond to situations where a positive event took place repeatedly. Children were probed about their feelings and expectations the first time the teacher brought a new toy, the second time, and the third time. In all of these instances, the children were told to remember that each time, the teacher brought a different toy. In these situations, 80% of the children gave the same emotional response (happiness) over all three situations, and their intensity ratings remained high and the same (4.5). When asked why they would feel happy, over 98% explained their emotion by saying that they would get to play with a new toy. Thus, the introduction of a new toy each time served to maintain the initial intensity rating of these children.

Children were then asked how they would feel if their teacher brought the same toy to class the first week, the second week, and the third week. In collecting these data, we took care to introduce the events sequentially as they would occur in a realistic setting. Again, 92% of the children said they would be happy the first time, with a mean intensity score of 4.7. After the second trial, 75% said they would be really happy, with a mean intensity score of 3.5. On the third trial, only 20% said they would be really happy, with a mean intensity score of 2.8. Those children who did not express happiness said that they wouldn't feel anything or that they would become bored. Sometimes they got tired of playing with the same toy and needed to switch to another one, and those were the reasons they gave for their affective responses (or lack of a response).

Thus, we propose that when continued exposure to an event results in an emotional response at the same intensity level as the initial response, some degree of novelty is still being processed. However, as people incorporate the novel aspects of a stimulus and build a more stable representation of the event (i.e., the event becomes predictable and responses to it become more automatic), the emotional response decreases in intensity, eventually resulting in a state where attention is no longer focused on the event. These changes are similar to those described in studies of habituation and adaptation to a stimulus, where subjects become immune and almost unaware of certain sensations. Although our studies are still in the preliminary stages of development, they speak to the necessity of considering more seriously the role of repeated exposure in ratings of novelty, predictability, pleasure or pain, emotion, and intensity of felt emotion (see Alessandri et al., 1990, and Lewis et al., 1990, for studies using this methodology). It is in the further study of adaptation phenomena that we will be able to determine whether or not novelty is necessary for the evocation of an emotional response.

Likewise, studying happiness as it occurs naturally, embedded in a sequence of ongoing events, will allow us to ascertain whether or not the thinking processes associated with a happy outcome are qualitatively different from those associated with another emotional outcome. Our model specifies that each emotion results from the perception of a unique combination of goal–outcome states in conjunction with accessing beliefs about possible plans of action. Thus, the evaluation and planning processes relevant to each emotion are distinct. However, this distinctness does not directly imply that new incoming events will be processed any differently, given that a person is in different emotional states at the outset (see Isen, 1987, and Schwarz, 1988, for different points of view). The determining factor will be the perception of some relationship between the current emotional state and the new information. If such a relationship is perceived, then the current emotional state will influence how the new information is processed. If no relationship is perceived, then two things can occur: The new information can provoke a change in emotional state, or the new information can be thrown out and judged as not relevant to current concerns.

Anger and Sadness

Anger and sadness are considered together because of the similarity in the types of events that elicit them: both can be evoked by loss and aversive states. Loss states signal that a person has failed to attain or maintain a desired state, whereas aversive states signal that a person has not been able to avoid or escape an unpleasant state. The prototypic expressions of both anger and sadness are displayed when a person initially believes that a particular goal can be accomplished or that certain standards will be upheld. Anger and sadness also arise when people enter into a situation believing that they can avoid aversive states. To experience either emotion, the status of a goal must shift so that a loss or the transition into an aversive state occurs. Something about the loss or the onset of the aversive state must be perceived as novel or unexpected, and the loss or aversive state must be perceived as certain. Figures 20.2 and 20.3 present the flow diagrams of decisions and evaluations that are made with respect to the experience of anger (Figure 20.2) and sadness (Figure 20.3).

Assessment of certainty with respect to anger and sadness appears problematic at first. Many times we are warned about a major loss that will take place. We discover that a loved one is terminally ill or are told that we may be fired from our job. Neither of these events has yet occurred, and yet when asked how we feel, our answer is often one of extreme sadness or anger. We can explain this emotional reaction, thus: If people believe that nothing can be done about a situation (i.e., no plan of action can prevent the outcome) and that the event is a certain occurrence, then we would say that sadness is experienced. However, the emotional reaction is based upon the *belief* that the occurrence of the event is certain.

Given that anger and sadness are similar in that they are evoked by the same goal outcome pattern, what differentiates them? According to our model (Stein & Levine, 1987, 1989, 1990; Stein & Trabasso, 1992), anger is manifested when a person responds to a loss or aversive state by inferring that an obstructed goal can be reinstated. In other words, people firmly believe that they can somehow initiate a plan to restore the original conditions that existed before a loss or an aversive state occurred. In these circumstances, attention is often focused on understanding the cause of the loss or aversive state, so that an effort can be directed towards changing the conditions that resulted in the undesired state. Thus, anger often carries with it a desire not only to reinstate the goal, but also to remove or

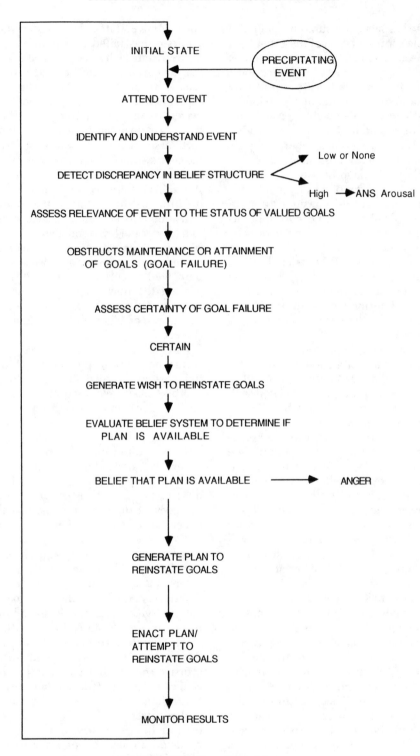

FIGURE 20.2. Flow diagram for anger.

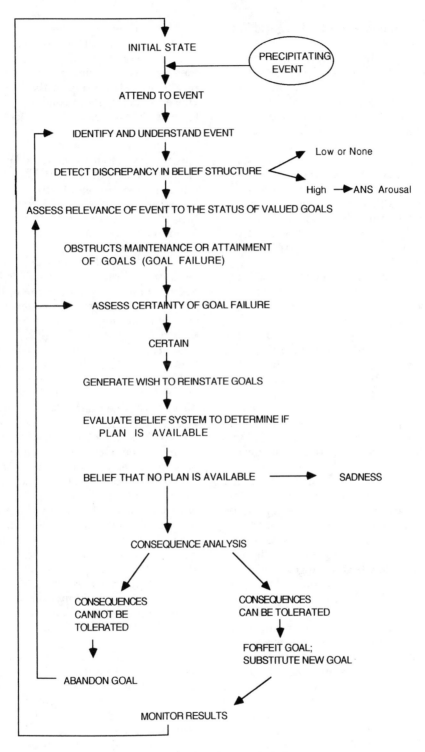

FIGURE 20.3. Flow diagram for sadness.

change the conditions that lead to goal block-age in the first place.

In our analysis, unlike many other analyses of anger (Averill, 1979; Roseman, 1984, 1991; Weiner, 1985), the perception of intentional harm or the presence of an animate agent is not necessary to invoke anger. Anger is expressed because a person experiences an unexpected loss, failure, or aversive state and refuses to accept being in the resultant state. "Refuses" here means that the person believes that somehow the conditions surrounding the loss or aversive state can be changed so that the unpleasant state will no longer exist. Thus, almost any type of loss or aversive state can evoke anger when a belief about goal reinstatement is strongly held.

The intentional-harm component associated with anger may be a function of socialization. In most societies, anger is not condoned because the plan accompanying anger is often destructive and harmful to others. In some societies, actions carried out under the influence of anger are often thought to indicate insanity (Averill, 1979) or the lack of the ability to reason. Therefore certain forms of anger are acceptable only in young children who have not yet been accorded the status of reasoning and thinking beings (Lutz, 1985a, 1985b). However, when children reach the age of 6 or 7, they are taught that anger is a permissible emotion, but only under particular conditions. The distinguishing dimension that is used to teach children when anger can be expressed is directly associated with intentional harm (Lutz, 1985a, 1985b). In fact, in the Ifaluk society that Lutz studied, two different words are used to talk about anger. One refers to anger evoked without reason, and the other refers to justifiable anger caused by an agent who meant intentional harm.

Although sadness and anger are often expressed in response to the same event, sadness is different from anger in two respects. Sadness is experienced when a person believes that a goal cannot be reinstated. Although people who experience sadness often desire to reinstate a failed goal (much as angry people do), the plan of action associated with sadness is one of goal abandonment or goal substitution. Here we make a distinction between the wishes that accompany an emotion and the plans of action that are activated by goal failure. When people suffer devastating losses

such that they no longer have access to a valued state, for instance, the loss of a loved one, they soon realize that no possibility exists for them ever to reinstate their goal (e.g., to regain the relationship in the literal sense). However, under these conditions, the desire to reinstate the goal does not necessarily recede or become less important. Because so many memories are associated with a loved one, the desire to have the valued person back or to interact with him or her again often remains ever-present. A striking example is comedian George Burns's (1988) confession that once a month, when he visited Gracie Allen's grave, he sat and talked to her about everything that was happening to him. He admitted that he had been doing this for 24 years, since Gracie had died. This is, in fact, not uncommon behavior (Worden, 1982). The social ridicule that may go along with it, however, inhibits most people from expressing their real desires and thoughts.

In many instances, the uniqueness of a love object determines whether the desire to reinstate the goal abates. If the love object is deemed irreplaceable, the desire to recreate the original conditions before the loss remains strong. Although this kind of desire seems unrealistic because the focus of attention is on the recreation of conditions that are no longer possible, it can also be put to good use. Recreating previous situations that were highly valued gives the person an opportunity to examine exactly what it was about the situation that proved to be so important. By centering on these critical features, the person can gradually construct wishes and plans to substitute a goal for the permanently blocked goal.

A person may also express wishes and plans to abandon a goal. Many times, goal failure results in such intense distress, as well as sadness, that the goal is abandoned without a desire to reinstate or substitute a similar goal. For example, after many sports competitions, athletes who lose will not try to compete again. They feel that they have given the competition their best shot and interpret their losing as irrevocable under any condition. Thus, the goal to become the top athlete is permanently abandoned, and no future attempts are made.

So far, we have described the evaluation and planning processes associated with anger and sadness. One more phenomenon with respect to these two emotions deserves discussion. Not only do the same events provoke these two emotions, but often *both* emotions are expressed in reaction to a loss or aversive state. In our model, the expression of more than one emotion in response to a precipitating event is not only feasible but increasingly likely, especially as a function of development. The reason for the occurrence of multiple emotions is that a precipitating event can change the probability of attaining or maintaining more than one goal. Anger can be expressed with regard to one goal and sadness in regard to another.

The prototypic context in which both emotions are expressed is one of loss, where the loss is brought about by intentional harm. For example, when Johnny finds out that his friend has deliberately smashed his favorite toy, at least three different emotional responses might be expressed: Johnny might be sad, angry, or both sad and angry. On the one hand, Johnny is sad because his favorite toy has been destroyed, and he feels that it is irreplaceable. Even though he would like the toy fixed, he also knows that repair is impossible, and this makes him sad. On the other hand, Johnny feels really angry because he realizes that his friend has intentionally destroyed the toy. His friend has violated either an unwritten or explicit code about what friends are and are not allowed to do. Moreover, the violation of this code has resulted in direct harm, and Johnny perceives this act as a threat to other important goals. He also feels that his friend may repeat the harmful act in other situations.

Thus, loss caused by an agent intending harm generates changes in the status of several goals. One set of changes focuses on the loss of a valued object and the goals associated with its reinstatement. Another set of changes focuses on the relationship between Johnny and his friend. The violation of the "friendship" code results in the realization that Johnny cannot trust his friend in other situations. Moreover, the fact that his friend has been responsible for breaking the toy evokes a desire to have the friend compensate him in some way. It is interesting to note that anger responses to irrevocable loss often involve getting the harmful agent to engage in some kind of behavior that promotes the substitution of a goal by the injured party. For example, Johnny's response to the loss of his toy may be to demand that his friend reimburse him

for the cash amount of the toy. According to Johnny, the only way the friendship can ever be restored was for his friend to pay for the broken toy. Moreover, his friend will have to "promise" that he will never again engage in another harmful act directed toward Johnny.

There are many instances of anger in which the primary goal of the injured party is simply to destroy the agent who caused intentional harm. However, this is not necessarily the prototypic anger response (Stein & Levine, 1989). For revenge strategies to be initiated, specific inferences must be made about the aggressor. The first concerns the value the victim places on the aggressor. The second concerns the degree of harm the aggressor can still inflict on the victim. If the victim believes that the aggressor will actively seek to carry out harmful acts in the future, and if the victim believes that the aggressor's behavior cannot be changed, then destroying the aggressor or undermining his or her power may emerge as the best solution. Indeed, we can generate many examples of these solutions by examining intense family conflicts, a context where majority of violent acts are committed. In the prototypic anger situation, however, the goal of the victim is to reinstate the original conditions that existed before the loss or aversive state occurred (Stein & Jewett, 1986). The restoration of conditions is oriented towards those that pertain to the loss (if possible) and those that pertain to the relationship that existed between the victim and the aggressor.

In order to test many of these ideas, we (Stein & Levine, 1989) carried out an empirical study with 3- and 6-year-old children as well as a group of college students. The task for all subjects was to respond to several different events by thinking out loud and by answering questions about the causes of three different emotions: happiness, sadness, and anger. The events used to elicit these three emotions were constructed to mirror four different types of goal–outcome relationships: (1) the attainment of valued states; (2) the avoidance of undesirable states; (3) the loss of a valued state; and (4) the failure to avoid an undesired state. Valued states consisted of acquiring or losing a favorite toy car or a puppy. Unpleasant states consisted of having to eat a disliked food (spinach) or being outside when it was very cold. The type of event that caused these states also varied, such that

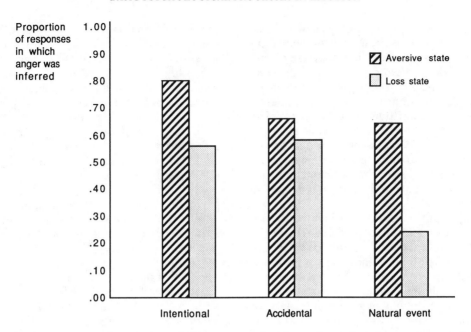

FIGURE 20.4. Proportion of responses in which anger was inferred in each causal condition and in episodes ending in loss and aversive states.

the end states resulted as a function of (1) another person's intentionally causing the outcome, (2) another person's accidentally causing the outcome, or (3) a physical event's causing the outcome.

All subjects were asked a series of questions regarding their feeling states, their first thoughts after the event occurred, the reasons for their feelings, the type of wish they would make in response to coping with the situation, the plans they would carry out, and explanations for their choice of actions. Each subject was therefore guided through all of the parts of an emotion episode related to a causal theory of emotional understanding. Although many investigators have described theoretical constructs for examining the process of emotional experience, the specific processes that are actually carried out with respect to the encoding, representation, and retrieval of information have yet to be described. So we chose to structure our interview to reflect the various processes associated with the sequence of representing and understanding emotional experience.

Figure 20.4 contains the proportion of anger responses reported in each causal condition (physical event, animate agent causing intentional harm, animate agent causing un-

intentional harm) for each type of negative outcome (loss vs. aversive state). Anger was chosen more frequently in all conditions when the episodes ended with an aversive rather than a loss state. The type of causal agent, however, did affect the proportion of anger responses. When an animate agent intentionally or unintentionally caused the story protagonist to suffer a loss, anger responses were more frequent than when a natural event caused the loss. Thus, the mere presence of an animate agent was enough to increase the frequency of anger responses in loss states. When an intentionally harmful agent put the story protagonist into an aversive state, the frequency of anger responses increased significantly in proportion to the frequency in aversive conditions where accidental harm resulted. Thus, the concept of agency is important in ascribing anger to others, but the type of goal failure is also a powerful predictor of anger. Our results are similar to those of Berkowitz and Heimer (1989), who contend that aversive events indeed prime anger, irritation, and hostility across a variety of contexts.

If anger is elicited by the perception that harm has befallen the person and that an unpleasant state exists, then the immediate goal will be to remove the unpleasant state. Desiring a change in the existing conditions should be especially true in situations of an aversive and painful nature. In fact, our results supported this hypothesis. When aversive states resulted and the emotion inferred was one of anger, over 76% of all subjects desired to reinstate the goal. However, the plans of action adopted were often associated with abandoning the goal rather than reinstating it. For example, in one of our scenarios, subjects were told that a protagonist would have to eat spinach for dinner because there was no other food in the house. Under these circumstances, the clear majority of subjects expressed anger at having to eat food that was intensely disliked. On the other hand, most adopted plans of action where the protagonist ate the disliked food. When spinach was all there was to eat, many subjects stated that the thought of not eating anything was worse than eating the spinach. Thus, in actuality, plans to abandon the goal were enacted.

These data strongly suggest that the planning process associated with specific emotions is more complex than originally described. Although anger and sadness carry definite wishes of goal reinstatement, the plans that accompany the two emotions are often constrained by an assessment of how the desired plan of action will affect the achievement of other goals. If the desired plan will result in a more general failure, such that many more goals become unattainable, then the normal plan associated with an emotion will not be enacted. Thus, reasoning about possible conflict among goals becomes an important concern in future work on emotional experience.

Furthermore, what needs to be examined is the effect of repeated anger in situations where the aversive state continues over time. In our study, subjects had to make predictions about other people's behavior when aversive states were experienced at one-time only. For example, our scenarios had a protagonist having to eat spinach because of a snowstorm or because the protagonist's mother forgot to buy a favorite food at the store. Although these aversive states were permanent, in the sense that for the moment subjects chose to tolerate them in order to avoid other unpleasant states, it is unclear what would happen if subjects were exposed to aversive states on a continuing basis. If someone had to eat spinach every day and initially disliked it, the ensuing response might change from one of toleration

to one where specific action was taken to end the aversive state. If no action could be taken, the option of not maintaining other important goals might be made. Under these conditions, anger could easily turn into sadness.

CONCLUDING REMARKS: A GENERAL MODEL OF EMOTION

The approach we are advocating for the study of emotion is one in which the achievement of specific goals is tracked over time. In this way, we can better assess how success or failure in attaining one goal affects the maintenance of other goals. Moreover, the way in which subjects react to repeated success or failure must be examined. Something is learned each time a person succeeds or fails at achieving a goal. We have described decision sequences for evaluating events and generating plans that encompass the specific emotions of happiness, anger, and sadness. Figure 20.5 depicts the flow diagram that can be induced from these specific evaluation and planning sequences. The diagram models the general evaluation and planning sequence related to emotional experience.

The sequence begins on the left side of the figure with the current state of the person involved. A precipitating event then occurs. In order for this event to have any effect, it has to be attended to and perceived. If it is encoded, orienting and attentional arousal is triggered. The person tries to assimilate the event into a prior belief structure. If the content contradicts or is discrepant from what the person believes, then autonomic arousal is evoked. If there is low or no discrepancy, the event is assimilated without arousal. If the event is evaluated as discrepant, however, further understanding of the event and the determination of its relevance for existing goal states must be made.

Three outcomes of relevance determination can be produced: The event can be evaluated as (1) obstructing a goal, (2) facilitating a goal, or (3) not relevant to current goal states. If facilitation or obstruction is present, the person then assesses how certain the goal success or failure is in the circumstances. If it is certain, then a desire is generated to maintain a valued goal or avoid an undesirable state, or a desire is generated to reinstate the goal that failed or escape the state that now exists. To

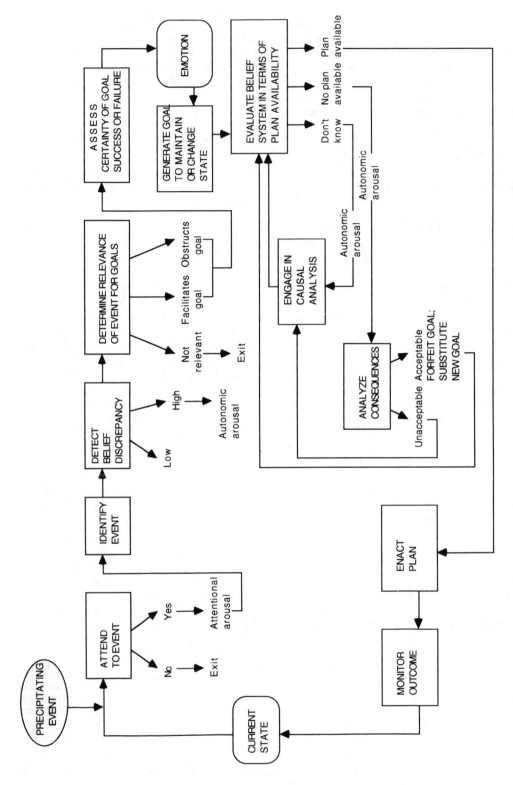

FIGURE 20.5. A general model of the evaluation and planning processes in emotional experience.

do this, a person must determine whether or not a plan is available to achieve the desired goal. There are three possible outcomes here: (1) The plan is available; (2) the plan is not available; or (3) the person does not know any plan.

If a plan is available, then it is enacted, and outcomes of the plan of action are monitored and evaluated with respect to the original goal. If the plan is found not to be available, then autonomic arousal occurs, and the person analyzes the consequences of the goal failure that transpired earlier. If the negative consequences of goal failure are acceptable, then the person may substitute a new goal and abandon the previous one. If, on the other hand, the consequences are unacceptable, then a causal analysis of the situation is made. If the person did not have a plan to begin with, autonomic arousal occurs, and the person engages in causal analysis of the circumstances that have led to changes in goal state. Causal analyses then lead to reassessment of plan availability and/or generation of a new plan. If one becomes available, then it is enacted and monitored with respect to the outcomes of the actions toward goal success or failure.

This model, although developed to account for the evaluation processes and planning sequences of four emotions, should hold over other situations where emotions other than happiness, anger, sadness, and fear are being analyzed. Regardless of the emotion being described, the relevance to personal goals is critical. What differ are the events that provoke the emotions and the plans brought to bear in contending with success or failure.

Acknowledgments. The research reported in this chapter was supported by grants from the Smart Foundation on Early Learning and from the National Institute of Child Health and Human Development (Grant No. HD 25742 to Tom Trabasso and Nancy L. Stein, and Grant No. HD 17431 to Tom Trabasso).

REFERENCES

Alessandri, S., Sullivan, M., & Lewis, M. (1990). Violation of expectancy and frustration in early infancy. *Developmental Psychology, 26*(5), 738–744.

Averill, J. R. (1979). Anger. In H. E. Howe & R. A. Dienstbier (Eds.), *Nebraska symposium on motivation: Vol. 26. Human emotions* (pp. 1–80). Lincoln: University of Nebraska Press.

Berkowitz, L., & Heimer, K. (1989). Aversive events and negative priming in the formation of feelings. In L. Berkowitz (Ed.), *Advances in experimental social psychology* (Vol. 22, pp. 1–37). New York: Academic Press.

Burke, A., Heuer, F., & Reisberg, D. (1992). Remembering emotional events. *Memory and Cognition, 20*(3), 277–290.

Burns, G. (1988). *Gracie: A love story.* New York: Putnam.

Capatides, J. (1989). *Mothers' socialization of children's affect expression.* Unpublished doctoral dissertation. Columbia University.

Ekman, P. (1977). Biological and cultural contribution to body and facial movements. In J. Blacking (Ed.), *Anthropology of the body* (pp. 34–84). London: Academic Press.

Ekman, P. (1992). An argument for basic emotions. *Cognition and Emotion, 6*(3/4), 169–200.

Emde, R. (1980). Levels of meaning in infant development. In W.A. Collins (Ed.), *Minnesota Symposium on Child Psychology* (Vol. 13, pp. 1–38). Hillsdale, NJ: Erlbaum.

Fernald, A. (1984). The perceptual and affective salience of mothers' speech to infants. In L. Feagans, C. Garvey, & R. Golinkoff (Eds.), with M. T. Greenberg, C. Harding, & J. Bohannon, *The origins and growth of communication* (pp. 5–29). Norwood, NJ: Ablex.

Frijda, N. H. (1987). Emotion, cognitive structure, and action tendency. *Cognition and Emotion, 1*, 115–143.

Gallistel, C. R. (1985). Motivation, intention, and emotion: Goal-directed behavior from a cognitive neuroethological perspective. In M. Frese & J. Sabini (Eds.), *Goal-directed behavior: The concept of action in psychology* (pp. 48–66). Hillsdale, NJ: Erlbaum.

Goodman, G. S. (1991). Commentary: On stress and accuracy in research in children's testimony. In J. Doris (Ed.), *The suggestibility of children's recollections* (pp. 77–82). Washington, DC: American Psychological Association.

Isen, A. (1987). Toward understanding the role of affective cognition. In R. S. Wyer & T. S. Srull (Eds.), *Handbook of social cognition* (Vol. 3, pp. 179–236). Hillsdale, NJ: Erlbaum.

Johnson-Laird, P. N., & Oatley, K. (1989). The language of emotions: An analysis of a semantic field. *Cognition and Emotion, 3*(2), 81–123.

Johnson-Laird, P. N., & Oatley, K. (1992). Basic emotions, rationality, and folk theory. *Cognition and Emotion, 6*(3/4), 201–223.

Lazarus, R. S., & Folkman, S. (1984). *Stress, appraisal, and coping.* New York: Springer.

Lewis, M. (1990). The development of intentionality and the role of consciousness. *Psychological Inquiry, 1*(3), 231–247.

Lewis, M., Alessandri, S., & Sullivan, M. (1990). Violation of expectancy, loss of control, and anger expressions in young infants. *Developmental Psychology, 26*(5), 745–751.

Lutz, C. (1985a). Ethnopsychology compared to what? Explaining behavior and consciousness among the Ifaluk. In G. M. White & J. Kirkpatrick (Eds.), *Person, self, and experience: Exploring Pacific ethnopsychologies* (pp. 35–79). Berkeley: University of California Press.

Lutz, C. (1985b). Cultural patterns and individual differences in the child's emotion meaning system. In M. Lewis & C. Saarni (Eds.), *The socialization of affect* (pp. 161–186). New York: Plenum Press.

Mandler, G. (1975). *Mind and emotion.* New York: Wiley.

Mandler, G. (1984). *Mind and body: Psychology of emotion and stress.* New York: Norton.

Mandler, J. (1988). How to build a baby: On the development of an accessible representation system. *Cognitive Development, 3,* 113–136.

Oatley, K., & Johnson-Laird, P. N. (1987). Towards a cognitive theory of emotions. *Cognition and Emotion, 1*(1), 29–50.

Ortony, A., & Turner, T. J. (1990). What's basic about basic emotion. *Psychological Review, 97,* 315–331.

Piaget, J. (1981). *Intelligence and affectivity.* Palo Alto: Annual Reviews.

Peters, D. (1991). The influence of stress and arousal on the child witness. In J. Doris (Ed.), *The suggestibility of children's recollections* (pp. 60–76). Washington, DC: American Psychological Association.

Rachman, S. J. (1978). *Fear and courage.* San Francisco: W. H. Freeman.

Roseman, I. (1984). Cognitive determinants of emotion: A structural theory. In P. Shaver (Ed.), *Review of personality and social psychology: Vol. 5. Emotions, relationships, and health* (pp. 11–36). Beverly Hills, CA: Sage.

Roseman, I. (1991). Appraisal determinants of discrete emotions. *Cognition and Emotion, 5*(3), 161–200.

Scherer, K. (1991). *Toward a dynamic theory of emotion: The component process model of affective states.* Unpublished manuscript, University of Geneva, Geneva, Switzerland.

Schwarz, N. (1988, August). *Happy but mindless.* Paper presented at the symposium "Affect and Cognition," 24th International Congress of Psychology, Sydney, Australia.

Sroufe, A. (1979). Socioemotional development. In J. Osofsky (Ed.), *Handbook of infant development* (pp. 462–516). New York: Wiley.

Stein, N. L., & Jewett, J. (1986). A conceptual analysis of the meaning of negative emotions: Implications for a theory of development. In C. Izard & P. Read (Eds.), *Measuring emotions in infants and children* (Vol. 2, pp. 238–267). Cambridge, England: Cambridge University Press.

Stein, N. L., & Levine, L. (1987). Thinking about feelings: The development and organization of emotional knowledge. In R. Snow & M. Farr (Eds.), *Aptitude, learning and instruction* (Vol. 3, pp. 165–197). Hillsdale, NJ: Erlbaum.

Stein, N. L., & Levine, L. (1989). The causal organization of emotional knowledge: A developmental study. *Cognition and Emotion, 3*(4), 343–378.

Stein, N. L., & Levine, L. (1990). Making sense out of emotion: The representation and use of goal structured

knowledge. In N. L. Stein, B. Leventhal, & T. Trabasso (Eds.), *Psychological and biological approaches to emotion* (pp. 45–73). Hillsdale, NJ: Erlbaum.

Stein, N. L., & Oatley, K. (1992). Basic emotions: Theory and measurement. *Cognition and Emotion, 6*(3/4), 161–168.

Stein, N. L., & Trabasso, T. (1989). Children's understanding of changing emotion states. In C. Saarni & P. L. Harris (Eds.), *Children's understanding of emotion* (pp. 50–77). New York: Cambridge University Press.

Stein, N. L., & Trabasso, T. (1992). The organization of emotional experience: Creating links among emotion, thinking and intentional action. *Cognition and Emotion, 6*(3/4), 225–244.

Stein, N. L., Trabasso, T., & Liwag, M. (1991, April). *Children's and parents' memory for real life emotional events: Conditions for convergence or polarization.* Paper presented at the meeting of the Society for Research in Child Development, Seattle.

Stein, N. L., Trabasso, T., & Liwag, M. (in press). Children's and parents' memory for real life emotional events: Remembering the past and planning for the future. In M. Haith (Ed.), *Future-oriented processes.* Hillsdale, NJ: Erlbaum.

Stenberg, C. R., & Campos, J. J. (1990). The development of anger expressions in infancy. In N. L. Stein, B. Leventhal, & T. Trabasso (Eds.), *Psychological and biological approaches to emotion* (pp. 247–282). Hillsdale, NJ: Erlbaum.

Trabasso, T., Stein, N. L., & Johnson, L. R. (1981). Children's knowledge of events: A causal analysis of story structure. In G. Bower (Ed.), *Learning and motivation* (Vol. 15, pp. 237–282). New York: Academic Press.

Weiner, B. (1985). An attributional theory of achievement motivation and emotion. *Psychological Review, 92*(4), 548–573.

Wierzbicka, A. (1992). Talking about emotions: Semantics, culture, and cognition. *Cognition and Emotion, 6*(3/4), 285–319.

Willatts, P. (1990). The development of problem-solving strategies in infancy. In D. Bjorklund (Ed.), *Children's strategies: Contemporary views of cognitive development* (pp. 23–66). Hillsdale, NJ: Erlbaum.

Worden, J. W. (1982). *Grief counseling and grief therapy.* New York: Springer.

Zajonc, R. (1980). Feeling and thinking: Preferences need no inferences. *American Psychologist, 35,* 151–175.

21

Affect and Personality

LAWRENCE A. PERVIN

A chapter on "Affect and Personality" immediately confronts one with a number of problems. First, it presents two concepts, each of which contains ambiguities and problems in definition. Second, each field is so large that one is faced with difficult decisions concerning what is to be included and what excluded. Finally, related to these problems, one could just as readily include affect as a part of personality as include personality as a part of affect. Which is the superordinate and which the subordinate category? Within the *Handbook of Personality* (Pervin, 1990), for example, there is a chapter on "Emotion and Adaptation" (Smith & Lazarus, 1990), as well as discussion of specific affects in a number of other chapters.

AFFECT WITHIN THE CONTEXT OF THE MAJOR APPROACHES TO PERSONALITY

Definitions of personality have typically contained an emphasis on individual differences and/or an emphasis on the organization of components into a total functioning system (Pervin, 1985, 1992). From the standpoint of the former, most specifically associated with trait theory, one can consider individual differences on specific affects. From the standpoint of the latter (an approach that makes greater sense to me), affects are important in terms of their place in the overall organization of the system. This place may be as central as *the* organizing element or as peripheral as another component of the system associated,

in unspecified ways, with other more significant elements. Building upon this distinction, personality psychologists have historically been concerned with specific affects, such as anxiety and depression. A typical approach might be to develop a questionnaire measure of individual differences in a specific affect (e.g., the Taylor Manifest Anxiety Scale, the Beck Depression Inventory) and then to correlate such scores with performance in other areas. If the period of the 1950s could be described as the decade of "AAA"—"achievement, authoritarianism, anxiety" (Blake & Mouton, 1959)—then the 1980s could perhaps be described as the decade of depression.

In addition, affect has been considered as a part of each of the major theoretical approaches to personality (e.g., psychodynamic, phenomenological/humanistic, trait, cognitive/information-processing). As we shall see, the approaches give varying emphasis to the affect concept, and a specific affect (such as anxiety) is conceptualized in differing ways within each theoretical system. What has been less common in the field—indeed, quite rare—is consideration of affect as central to personality. From this standpoint, the organization of affects would be seen as a central organizing element in the structure of personality (Lewis & Michalson, 1983; Malatesta, 1990). In what follows, attention is given to how affect is considered within the framework of the major theoretical approaches to personality. Attention is then given to how affect might be considered as a central element in the organization of personality.

Psychoanalytic Theory

Affect clearly plays a central role in psycho-analytic theory—perhaps a more central role than in any of the other approaches to be considered. This is true in terms of both the range of affects considered and the role of affect in the total organization.

To turn to the range of affects considered, the index to Fenichel's (1945) *The Psychoanalytic Theory of Neurosis* lists no fewer than 50 terms that might be included in an extensive list of affects, such as "affection," "anxiety," "bashful," "depersonalization," "anxiety," "disgust," "efficacy," "envy," "guilt," "hate," "injured," "intimidated," "jealousy," "loss," "love," "omnipotence," "optimism," "paranoia," "pride," "rage," "revenge," "shame," and "vengefulness." Thus, one can find reference not only to what often are considered the basic or primary affects, but to virtually any affect that might be considered of major significance within any theoretical system! In addition, of course, anxiety plays a major role in almost all aspects of personality functioning, directly or indirectly through the mechanisms of defense. In some ways this is not surprising, given that psychoanalysts spend so much time attending to what patients report and express concerning their feelings. At the same time, as we shall see, not all clinically based approaches to personality are so specific or elaborate in their attention to affect.

Despite the attention given to affect early on in the development of the theory, there is no generally accepted psychoanalytic theory of affect (Greenberg & Mitchell, 1983; Plutchik, 1980; Rapaport, 1971; Rosenblatt & Thickstun, 1977). As with most psychoanalytic concepts, we find conceptual changes over time, a lack of concern with conceptual precision, and varying views among analysts. Among the various conceptualizations of affects have been those of affect as a form of energy, affect as a discharge process, affect as a component of drive representation, and affect as a signal. Such conceptual differences remain, but most analysts agree that cognitive components are important in affective development (Rosenblatt & Thickstun, 1977). In addition, it is likely that most analysts would agree that certain character types are disposed toward experiencing some affects rather than others. Thus, for example, if one considers Erikson's (1950, 1982) psychosocial stages of development, the first three stages are associated with the affects of mistrust, shame, and guilt, respectively. Other analysts emphasize the affects of envy and rage, shame, and guilt for the oral, anal, and phallic character types, respectively.

Another point on which there has been conceptual confusion is the place of affects on the unconscious–conscious dimension. Freud and later analysts struggled with the question of whether affects can be unconscious, or whether, as felt experience, they have to be conscious. One solution to the problem was to consider affects as conscious but affected by unconscious perceptual and other psychic processes. Although this was an important issue for analysts (and still is for current affect theorists), it was secondary to concern with the question of the relation of affect to instinctual drive processes. As on many other issues, analysts are often divided on whether a psychoanalytic conceptualization of affect must be tied to a drive-based, instinct-based model.

Before I conclude this discussion of the psychoanalytic view of affects, it is important to point out that analysts view affect as tied to other components of personality functioning. Such a tie is seen most clearly in the work of Rapaport (1971) on the relation between emotions and memory. Anxiety, of course, was ultimately seen as key to the process of repression. However, Rapaport went beyond this to suggest that emotions organize memories and lend persistence to ideas (e.g., obsessions), in addition to leading to repression. According to him, whether or not a painful emotion such as anxiety leads to repression depends on the intensity and quality of the emotion—a point often forgotten by researchers in this area. Affect also plays a central role in the conceptual efforts of Rosenblatt and Thickstun (1977). These analysts place affect at the center of their theory of motivation as they try to incorporate an information-processing model into psychoanalytic theory.

In recent developments, the trend toward an emphasis on object relations (Greenberg & Mitchell, 1983) and an emphasis on clinical observations as opposed to metapsychology (Klein, 1976; Schafer, 1976; Spence, 1982) have focused interest on affects associated with specific object relationships. However, these developments are not associated with further elaboration of a specific theory of affects.

To summarize the place of affect in psychoanalytic theory, the following can be suggested:

1. There is no developed, generally accepted psychoanalytic theory of affects.

2. Although considered important, affects have typically been viewed as secondary to the drives or instincts. More recent developments in object relations theory and in clinical phenomena as opposed to metapsychology have not been associated with elaboration of a theory of affects.

3. Although analysts are interested in the phenomena of a wide range of affects, greatest attention has been given to anxiety and depression.

4. Although tending to emphasize affect as conscious experience, analysts have emphasized the role of unconscious psychic processes in allowing stimuli to become conscious as felt experience.

Phenomenological Theory: Carl Rogers

One might think that phenomenological theory as represented in the work of Carl Rogers would include a highly articulated theory of affects, because of the attention given to experience and clinical work with clients. What is interesting to discover is that the indexes to some of Rogers's (1951, 1961) most significant work include *no* references to affect terms. In his works there is an emphasis on feelings and experience generally, and positive and negative feelings more specifically, but rarely to any one affect. Illustrative of this approach to experience is Rogers's emphasis on the process of change and growth in the manner of experiencing. "Growth" here means a change in the manner of experiencing the self and the world, from unrecognized, unowned, and fixed feelings to known, accepted, and fluid feelings, rather than a shift in the nature of the affects experienced.

Again, the indexes to Rogers's books are strikingly devoid of references to such important affects as anxiety, depression, guilt, and fear, in contrast with the many references to feeling and meaning. Rogers did have a theory of anxiety, but inconsistencies in it never were eliminated (Pervin, 1993). Originally Rogers suggested that anxiety results from the incongruence between self and experience. The emphasis here was on the state of incongruence thought to result from an incongruence between a negative self-concept and positive experience, as well as from an incongruence between a positive self-concept and negative experience.

This view fit with then-popular models of cognitive dissonance and would continue to be in accord with current social-cognitive models of self-verification (Aronson, 1992; Aronson & Mettee, 1968; Swann, 1990). However, in his discussion of anxiety and defense, Rogers also suggested that people are led to negate experience because of past experiences of states of conditional regard or of negative regard. According to the theory, experiences of unconditional positive regard lead to an openness of experience, whereas experiences of conditional positive regard lead the developing child to protect the self from experiences that might threaten positive regard. Here the emphasis is not so much on consistency as it is on defense against negative self-regard—on what current social-cognitive theorists call "self-enhancement" as opposed to "self-verification" (Swann, 1990). The issue is important not just in relation to Rogers and the affect of anxiety, but because it highlights the contrast between an emphasis on purely cognitive considerations as opposed to one on hedonic value. This contrast has been called the "cognitive–affective crossfire" between self-consistency and self-enhancement (Swann, Griffin, Predmore, & Gaines, 1987).

Finally, it is important to note that Rogers was influenced by Leeper (1948) in his emphasis on emotion as a positive force in maintaining and enhancing the goal-directed behavior of the organism. Such a view was in sharp contrast with the view of emotion as a disorganizing response. However, once more, this said little about the nature of specific emotions or the relevance of these emotions to personality.

Trait Theory

Trait theory represents one of the oldest approaches to personality. Emotions and moods have typically been a part of trait approaches to personality, dating back to the earliest formulations of temperament types. To illustrate their place in two prominent models, we can consider the trait theories of Cattell and Eysenck.

Cattell (1965, 1990) distinguished among "ability" traits "temperament" traits, and "dynamic" traits. Temperament traits relate to the emotional life of the person. Cattell's Sixteen Personality Factor Questionnaire contains evidence of an emphasis on general, stylistic emotional traits as well as on specific emotional traits. An illustration of the former would be the first factor, defining a reserved, detached, cool person as opposed to one who is outgoing, warm-hearted, and easygoing. Illustrations of an emphasis on more specific emotions would be three factors that at their extremes contrast individuals who are low and high on suspicion–jealousy (Factor L), guilt proneness (Factor O), and tension (Factor Q4).

Eysenck's (1982, 1990) approach emphasizes fewer factors (three) than does that of Cattell. The first two of these, introversion–extraversion and neuroticism, are seen as being closely tied to the earlier Greek temperament types (Eysenck, 1975) and include differences along dimensions such as "quiet, unsociable" versus "active, sociable" and "anxious, moody" versus "calm, even-tempered." Like Cattell, Eysenck posits no theory of specific emotions. Rather, attention is given to general genetic and biological considerations (Eaves, Eysenck, & Martin, 1989).

Recently, attention within trait theory has come to focus on the "Big Five" or "five-factor model" (John, 1990; McCrae & John, 1992). The suggestion here is that five factors capture the basic structure of personality across questionnaires, ratings, and cultures. One questionnaire that purports to measure individuals on these five factors, the NEO Personality Inventory (Costa & McCrae, 1985), includes scales for Neuroticism, Extraversion, Openness to Experience, Agreeableness, and Conscientiousness, as well as subscales or facets for the first three scales. Facet subscales for the remaining two scales are being developed. These facet subscales are important, since they go beyond general descriptions of mood and temperament to more specific measures on such affects as anxiety, hostility, depression, and positive emotion. For example, the affects of anxiety, hostility, and depression appear as facet subscales on the Neuroticism scale, whereas warmth and positive emotions appear as facet subscales on the Extraversion scale.

Despite the attention given by Costa and McCrae to emotions as a part of their definition of traits, it can be noted that there is not much elaboration of the connection between emotions and other parts of personality. In addition, there is no theory of the development

of specific emotions. As with other aspects of trait theory, the emphasis is more on description than on explanation.

An alternative current approach to traits is Tellegen's emphasis on the broad dimensions of positive and negative affect/mood (Tellegen, 1985, 1991; Watson & Tellegen, 1985). These fundamental dimensions are seen as being independent rather than as endpoints of a single dimension, and as having important health implications (Watson, 1988; Watson & Clark, 1984; Watson, Clark, & Tellegen, 1984).

Larsen (1991) suggests that emotions be conceived of as trait-like in nature, and distinguishes between the concepts of "emotional content" and "emotional style." Under the former, he includes the typical emotions the person is likely to experience over time; under the latter, he includes how these emotions are typically experienced. Both are considered to exhibit trait-like properties. In considering emotional content, Larsen notes that the findings to date suggest that the most general or primary emotions are positive and negative affect. Picking up on the earlier work of Wessman and Ricks (1966) on mood and personality, Larsen suggests that individuals can be assessed in terms of the construct of "subjective well-being," reflecting the relative amounts of positive and negative emotional content in a person's emotional life. In considering emotional style, Larsen suggests that the major distinction involves "affect intensity," or the level of reactivity and variability of emotional reactivity on the part of the individual. As with subjective well-being, a questionnaire has been developed to assess the construct (Larsen & Diener, 1987).

A recent article by Larsen and Ketelaar (1991) relates work on positive and negative emotional states to the Big Five trait approach and to Gray's (1971, 1987, 1991) psychophysiological theory of personality and emotion. The authors begin by noting a consistent relationship between extraversion and average levels of positive affect, as well as between neuroticism and average levels of negative affect (Costa & McCrae, 1980; Tellegen, 1985). Following McCrae and Costa (1991), they note that such a relationship could be the result of endogenous differences in response to positive and negative emotion stimuli (the "temperamental view"), or the result of life circumstances that determine long-term positive and negative affect and that are influenced by personality (the "instrumental view"). Whereas the effect of personality is direct in the case of the former, it is indirect in the case of the latter. Following a variety of authors (Eysenck, 1967: Gray, 1991; McCrae & Costa, 1991; Strelau, 1983; Tellegen, 1985), Larsen and Ketelaar (1991) have hypothesized that the personality dimensions of extraversion and neuroticism are rooted in biologically based systems that directly promote differential responsivity to positive and negative affect stimuli. In a test of reactivity to positive and negative affect induction procedures, the authors found strong support for the hypothesis. That is, the results were consistent with the hypothesis that extraverts would show greater emotional responsivity to positive mood induction than would introverts, and that neurotic subjects would show greater emotional reactivity to negative mood induction than would stable individuals.

In sum, most trait theorists emphasize traits associated with broad dimensions of mood and temperament. As Plutchik (1980) has noted, trait terms often describe emotional states (e.g., "aggressive," "friendly"), and emotion words are often used to describe individual personalities (e.g., "cheerful," "spiteful"). Thus, it is not surprising that trait theorists would include some recognition of this area of functioning within their descriptive taxonomy. At the same time, two points seem particularly noteworthy. First, attention tends to be given to broad dimensions of mood or temperament rather than to specific affects. Second, as noted, there is no articulated theory of affect per se. Rather, trait theorists tend to rely on principles of genetics and biology/physiology to account for individual differences on these broad dimensions.

Cognitive and Information-Processing Approaches

Cognitive approaches to personality have a long history (does one dare go all the way back to James?), and the literature is both broad and diverse. Perhaps the best place to start is with George Kelly (1955), whose personal construct theory was a forerunner of the cognitive revolution. Kelly's theory was a novel effort to reconstrue the entire field of personality, and a model for approaches that attempt to be both nomothetic and idiographic. Basically, Kelly interpreted all important person-

ality phenomena in terms of the person's construct system. Systematic attention was given to relatively few affects; those that were considered were given new interpretations. For example, anxiety represents the recognition that events with which one is confronted lie outside the range of convenience of one's construct system. Threat represents the awareness of imminent comprehensive change in one's core structure. As I have noted elsewhere (Pervin, 1993), despite efforts to come to grips with the area of human emotions, many interpretations within the context of personal construct theory seem strained; on the whole, human emotions remain an area outside its range of convenience.

The social-cognitive theory of Bandura (1986) is interesting in terms of its historical development. It was initially known as "social learning theory" and gave relatively little attention to cognitive variables; however, Bandura has increasingly worked cognitive variables into the extended development of the theory. At this point, it represents a major approach to personality—perhaps the major current comprehensive theory of personality. Of particular importance for this chapter are Bandura's emphasis on the process of acquiring emotional responses and his discussion of such affects as anxiety and depression.

Considering the former, Bandura suggests that affective responses, like all learned responses, can be acquired through direct experience or through observational learning. The process of learning emotional reactions through observing others is known as "vicarious conditioning" and has been demonstrated in both humans and animals. The process is of particular importance, since it can apparently occur during a brief period of observation; it can be intense and long-lasting; and it can extend to situations different from that in which the emotional reaction was first observed. In terms of the affects of anxiety and depression, Bandura suggests that anxiety is the response to feelings of low self-efficacy in relation to negative outcomes, whereas depression is the response to feelings of low self-efficacy in relation to positive outcomes In addition, depressives are seen as maintaining excessively stringent standards of self-evaluation.

As noted above, Bandura has become increasingly cognitive in his emphasis; in accord with this, he is not sympathetic to positions such as those espoused by Zajonc (1980) and Ekman (1973). He suggests that the extensive similarities in the autonomic correlates of different emotions overshadow any small differences, and that situational instigators are what give emotional specificity to visceral commonality. Finally, he suggests that "social and cognitive factors determine not only what emotions observers are likely to feel, but even whether expressive cues arouse any emotion at all" (1986, pp. 311–312).

Turning to attribution theory, we find a variety of influential approaches to specific emotions as well as to emotion generally. Illustrative of the former would be Seligman's (1975; Peterson & Seligman, 1984) learned helplessness model of depression. Illustrative of the latter would be Weiner's (1985) attributional theory of achievement motivation and emotion. The attributional model of depression has been one of the most influential research models of the past decade. Despite the large amount of important research generated, the role of attributions or explanatory style in depression remains controversial. In fact, the power of purely cognitive explanations of depression has more generally been called into question (see *Psychological Inquiry*, 1992, Number 2).

Finally, Higgins's (1987, 1989) self-discrepancy theory is illustrative of social-cognitive approaches to affect. Higgins suggests that individuals have cognitive representations of standards to meet, called "self-guides." Generally, these self-guides are acquired during the early years of interaction with significant others and take on the properties of chronically accessible constructs—readily available for use with incoming information. The "ideal self" represents attributes that we would ideally like to possess; the "ought self" represents the attributes that we feel we should or ought to possess. According to self-discrepancy theory, failure to meet each of these self-guides has different emotional implications. Thus, failure to reduce the actual–ideal discrepancy is associated with sadness and disappointment, whereas failure to reduce the actual–ought discrepancy is associated with guilt and anxiety.

Starting from a "cold" cognitive position, social-cognitive and information-processing approaches have increasingly turned toward an interest in affect—both in how cognitive processes influence affect and in how affect influences cognitive processes (see Lewis,

Chapter 16; Isen, Chapter 19; Epstein, Chapter 22; Breckler, Chapter 32; and Izard, Chapter 44, this volume). This broadening horizon has been important, and developments are promising. At the same time, it is clear that the range of affects considered has been relatively limited. On the other hand, cognitive approaches that have attempted to account for a broader range of affects have had few ties to the field of personality (Roseman, 1984; Smith & Ellsworth, 1987).

AFFECT AND THE ORGANIZATION OF PERSONALITY

In an illuminating article, Malatesta (1990) has discussed emotions as central organizing axes for personality. Building on the earlier work of theorists such as Tomkins (1962, 1963, 1980), Ekman (1984), Izard (1977), Lewis and Michalson (1983), and Plutchik (1962, 1980), Malatesta has suggested that the emotional organization of the person functions in a trait-like way to bias or predispose the person toward specific perceptions, cognitions, and behavioral responses. Several features of this approach are noteworthy and can be contrasted with some or all of the approaches considered in the preceding section. First, attention is given to a wider range of affects than is considered in most personality approaches to affect. Second, affect is given central status in personality, rather than being an accompaniment or consequence of drives, cognitions, or the like. Third, emphasis is placed on the *organization of personality*—a focus that often has been lost through an emphasis on individual differences. Finally, attention is given both to nomothetic and idiographic concerns—that is, both to general affective processes and to the organization of affects within the individual.

In the remainder of this chapter, I describe a series of research endeavors that focus on affect as central to the organization of personality and on a mix of nomothetic and idiographic foci (Pervin, 1986, 1988, 1992). This research was stimulated by results from the use of a free-response approach to the study of person–situation interaction (Pervin, 1976). These results clearly suggested that people use affect terms to describe not only other people, but situations as well. In addition, the data indicated that people organize their behavior around situations categorized in affective terms. Thus, the data suggested that individuals have patterns of stability and change in their behavior, and that these patterns can be understood largely in terms of the affective meaning of situations for them.

Affects and Drug Abuse

Clinical work in the area of drug abuse suggests that drug abuse is strongly associated with efforts to regulate painful affects, and that abusers who use a variety of drugs also have "drugs of choice" to deal with these painful affects. In a study of drug abuse and the affective meaning of situations, individuals receiving treatment for serious drug abuse problems listed situations in which they used drugs, situations in which they wanted to do so but drugs were not available, situations following the use of drugs, and situations unrelated to drug use (Pervin, 1988a). The situations were specific situations from their daily lives and were generated individually by each subject. Since most subjects abused more than one drug, the list of situations included representative situations associated with each drug. In addition, each subject generated a list of affects he or she might experience. These were combined with a standard list of affects, which the subject rated as strongly relevant, somewhat relevant, or not at all relevant to each of the situations.

The situation × affect ratings data were factor-analyzed to determine whether groups of situations were associated with specific affects for each individual. The data were indeed consistent with the view that people use drugs to deal with painful affects, that certain drugs are generally associated with relief from particular affects, and that individuals involved in polydrug abuse associate particular drugs with relief from specific painful affects. In sum, the data suggested that although all individuals using drugs do so to gain relief from painful affects, and some drugs are generally associated with relief from specific affects, each individual establishes a pattern of preferred drugs to deal with a unique constellation of painful affects.

Affect and Daily Life

In another series of studies, students assessed the role of affect in their lives (Pervin, 1988b). In the first study, students rated the relevance or association of 21 affects to representative situations and people. In addition, each affect was rated in terms of its association with the other 20 affects. The list of affects included 20 standard affects, generated from earlier research, and 1 affect added by each subject as particularly meaningful for him or her. The situations and people were generated by the subject. Of particular interest here was the overall organization of affects across subjects; whether the organization of affects remained stable when subjects considered situations, people, and other affects; and individual differences in the organization of affects.

Some of the conclusions derived from this research were the following:

1. All subjects had a major positive affect factor and a major negative affect factor. For some subjects, one or both of these could be split into two positive and/or negative affect factors, in terms of either the specific affects or what seemed to be an active–passive dimension.

2. The intercorrelations among the affects varied according to whether ratings were made for situations, people, or other affects; that is, the more specific organization of affects seemed to depend on the content being judged.

3. Overall, positive and negative affect were uncorrelated for individuals, although positive and negative affect tended to be negatively correlated in any particular situation; that is, as suggested by other researchers, positive and negative affect appeared to be independent dimensions. However, specific situations were generally associated with either positive or negative affect. This did not preclude, of course, situations with mixed or ambivalent feelings (Emmons, 1989; Emmons & King, 1989).

4. There were large individual differences in the means for the affects, in the rank ordering of affects, in the relationships among affects, and in the kinds of situations that would be associated with specific affects. In addition, for some subjects people seemed more important than situations in determining the organization of affects, whereas for others the reverse appeared to be the case.

In a second study, subjects rated 55 affects (50 standard, 5 generated by each subject) against 20 situations and 20 people. The objective here was to expand the list of affects considered, as well as again to consider the organization of affects in relation to people and situations. The findings here were similar to those reported above. Once more, a major distinction was made between positive and negative affects. Although these factors emerged whether people or situations were being rated, for most subjects the organization of affects varied depending on which stimuli were being assessed.

In a third study, subjects rated 12 affects (standard for all subjects) in terms of their relevance to 30 situations generated by them. The 30 situations included 18 representative of their daily lives and 1 prototypic for them for each of the 12 affects. A list of situation characteristics associated with each affect was also generated by each subject. Thus, a cumulative list of prototypic situations for each affect and a cumulative list of situation characteristics prototypic for each affect were generated. Subjects subsequently rated the prototypicality of each situation on the list for each affect, the next most likely affect they would experience in that situation, and the importance of each situation characteristic for that affect.[1] The interest here was in whether subjects would agree on prototypic situations for each affect, whether subjects would agree on the defining situation characteristics associated with each affect, and whether individuals would differ in the secondary affects associated with situations agreed upon as being prototypic for a specific affect.

The results indicated first that, by and large, the subjects could agree on situations prototypic for the following affects: "love," "happy," "friendship," "trust," "humiliated," "shame–embarrassment," "anxious–tense," "guilty," "disgust," "anger," "sad–depressed," and "envy–jealousy." That is, a situation generated by one subject as prototypic for an affect was rated as high in association for that affect by other subjects. However, there were individual differences in this regard, and some subjects appeared to have highly idiosyncratic notions about prototypic situations for specific affects.

Second, subjects could agree on some situation characteristics as prototypic for each affect, with the prototypicality of these characteristics showing some variation among individuals; that is, though subjects might agree on a set of defining situation character-

istics for an affect, they also might differ in how central each was for the affect. Finally, there were large individual differences in the secondary affects associated with prototypic situations; that is, even if subjects agreed on the primary affect experienced in a prototypic situation, there was substantial variation in the next most likely affect to be experienced in that situation. This again reflected large individual differences in the organization of affects and in the disposition to experience specific affects. It should be reiterated in this regard that individuals might have the same mean rating for experiencing an affect across the situations, but might differ greatly in rating the overall importance of that affect and its relation to other affects in the overall organization of the personality. Thus, for example, two subjects had the same average score for jealousy, but for one subject this affect was low on the list in terms of overall importance (rank of mean scores), while for the other it was one of the most important affects experienced. In addition, jealousy was linked with different affects for the two subjects.

Conclusions

The studies described above have certain elements in common: a concern with the relation of affect to personality; a mix of standard and free-response data; and a mix of nomothetic and idiographic analyses to determine principles that hold for all individuals, as well as patterns that seem unique to the individual. A number of conclusions follow from them.

First, the major categorization appears to be that of positive affects versus negative affects, regardless of whether situations, people, or affects themselves are being considered. However, the association of specific affects with other affects may vary from ratings of situations to ratings of people and from individual to individual. Second, although separate positive and negative affect factors appear, most situations and people are experienced in terms of combinations of affects, including in some cases both positive and negative affects. This is important, because affects are often considered in isolation from one another, and situations are treated as if they elicit one or another specific affect rather than a pattern of affects.

Third, subjects can show good agreement about prototypic situations for affects and about situation characteristics associated with

---

[1]Eliciting the next most likely affect to be experienced in a situation, as well as the most likely one, was suggested by Michael Lewis.

each affect. However, individuals differ in the prototypicality of their situations and in the importance of specific prototypic characteristics for each affect. Finally, individuals differ enormously in mean levels for affects; in rank orderings of importance of affects; and, most importantly, in the pattern or organization of affects in relation to one another. There is virtually no limit as to how individuals will link affects with one another: Jealousy can be linked with love by one person and hate by another; shame can be associated with excitement by one person and depression by another; and love can be linked with relaxation by one person and tension by another. It is this idiosyncratic organization of affects that is suggested to be fundamental for the individual in terms of how people, situations, and events are experienced.

SUMMARY

This chapter has considered the relation between affect and personality—two broad concepts, each with its own diverse literature and conceptual confusions. Every major theory of personality gives some attention to the realm of affect. However, some give surprisingly little attention to this area, and none presents a well-articulated theory of the specific affects and their relation to other aspects of personality functioning. It has been suggested that central to the definition of personality is a concern with pattern and organization. In this regard, affect plays a central role in the organization and patterning of individuals' functioning. People organize their worlds partly in terms of the affects experienced in situations, and show enormous individual differences in their propensity to experience specific affects and patterns of affects. Beyond this, affects show complex relations to behavior. The same affect may be associated with different behaviors in different situations, and different affects may be associated with the same behavior in different situations—the systems concepts of equipotentiality and equifinality, respectively (Pervin, 1978, 1983). Thus, not only is affect central to the organization of personality, but our understanding of its role is complicated by the multiplicity of affects likely to be experienced in any one important situation, and by the complex, multidetermined nature of the relationship between affect and other parts of the personality organization.

REFERENCES

Aronson, E. (1992). The return of the repressed: Dissonance theory makes a comeback. *Psychological Inquiry,* 3, 303–311.

Aronson, E., & Mettee, D. R. (1968). Dishonest behavior as a function of differential levels of induced self-esteem. *Journal of Personality and Social Psychology,* 9, 121–127.

Bandura, A. (1986). *Social foundations of thought and action.* Englewood Cliffs, NJ: Prentice-Hall.

Blake, R. R., & Mouton, J. S. (1959). Personality. *Annual Review of Psychology,* 10, 203–232.

Cattell, R. B. (1965). *The scientific analysis of personality.* Baltimore: Penguin Books.

Cattell, R. B. (1990). Advances in Cattellian personality theory. In L. A. Pervin (Ed.), *Handbook of personality: Theory and research* (pp. 101–110). New York: Guilford Press.

Costa, P. T., Jr., & McCrae, R. R. (1980). Influence of extraversion and neuroticism on subjective well-being: Happy and unhappy people. *Journal of Personality and Social Psychology,* 38, 668–678.

Costa, P. T., Jr., & McCrae, R. R. (1985). *The NEO Personality Inventory manual.* Odessa, FL: Psychological Assessment Resources.

Eaves, L., Eysenck, H. J., & Martin, N. (1989). *Genes, culture, and personality: An empirical approach.* New York: Academic Press.

Ekman, P. (1973). Cross-cultural studies of facial expression. In P. Ekman (Ed.), *Darwin and facial expression: A century of research in review* (pp. 169–222). New York: Academic Press.

Ekman, P. (1984). Expression and the nature of emotion. In K. Scherer & P. Ekman (Eds.), *Approaches to emotion* (pp. 329–343). Hillsdale, NJ: Erlbaum.

Emmons, R. A. (1989). The personal striving approach to personality. In L. A. Pervin (Ed.), *Goal concepts in personality and social psychology* (pp. 87–126). Hillsdale, NJ: Erlbaum.

Emmons, R. A., & King, L. A. (1989). Personal striving differentiation and affective reactivity. *Journal of Personality and Social Psychology,* 56, 478–484.

Erikson, E. H. (1950). *Childhood and society.* New York: Norton.

Erikson, E. H. (1982). *The life cycle completed: A review.* New York: Norton.

Eysenck, H. J. (1967). *The biological basis of personality.* Springfield, IL: Charles C Thomas.

Eysenck, H. J. (1975). *The inequality of man.* San Diego: Edits.

Eysenck, H. J. (1982). *Personality genetics and behavior.* New York: Praeger.

Eysenck, H. J. (1990). Biological dimensions of personality. In L. A. Pervin (Ed.), *Handbook of personality: Theory and research* (pp. 244–276). New York: Guilford Press.

Fenichel, O. (1945). *The psychoanalytic theory of neurosis.* New York: Norton.

Gray, J. A. (1971). The psychophysiological basis of introversion–extraversion. *Behaviour Research and Therapy,* 8, 249–266.

Gray, J. A. (1987). Perspectives on anxiety and impulsivity: A commentary. *Journal of Research in Personality,* 21, 493–509.

Gray, J. A. (1991). Fear, panic, and anxiety: What's in a name? *Psychological Inquiry,* 2, 77–78.

Greenberg, J. R., & Mitchell, S. A. (1983). *Object relations in psychoanalytic theory*. Cambridge, MA: Harvard University Press.

Higgins, E. T. (1987). Self-discrepancy: A theory relating self and affect. *Psychological Review, 94*, 319–340.

Higgins, E. T. (1989). Continuities and discontinuities in self-regulatory and self-evaluative processes: A developmental theory relating self and affect. *Journal of Personality, 57*, 407–444.

Izard, C. E. (1977). *Human emotions*. New York: Plenum.

John, O. P. (1990). The "big five" factor taxonomy: Dimensions of personality in the natural language and in questionnaires. In L. A. Pervin (Ed.), *Handbook of personality: Theory and research* (pp. 66–100). New York: Guilford Press.

Kelly, G. A. (1955). *The psychology of personal constructs* (2 vols.). New York: Norton.

Klein, G. (1976). *Psychoanalytic theory: An exploration of essentials*. New York: International Universities Press.

Larsen, R. J. (1991). Emotion. In V. J. Derlega, B. A. Winstead, & W. H. Jones (Ed.), *Personality* (pp. 407–432). Chicago: Nelson-Hall.

Larsen, R. J., & Diener, E. (1987). Affect intensity as an individual difference characteristic: A review. *Journal of Research in Personality, 21*, 1–39.

Larsen, R. J., & Ketelaar, T. (1991). Personality and susceptibility to positive and negative emotional states. *Journal of Personality and Social Psychology, 61*, 132–140.

Leeper, R. W. (1948). A motivational theory of emotion to replace "emotion as disorganized response." *Psychological Review, 55*, 5–21.

Lewis, M., & Michalson, L. (1983). *Children's emotions and moods*. New York: Plenum Press.

Malatesta, C. Z. (1990). The role of emotions in the development and organization of personality. In R. A. Thompson (Ed.), *Nebraska Symposium on Motivation: Vol. 36. Socioemotional development* (pp. 1–56). Lincoln: University of Nebraska Press.

McCrae, R. R., & Costa, P. T., Jr. (1991). Adding Liebe und Arbeit: The full five-factor model and well-being. *Personality and Social Psychology Bulletin, 17*, 227–232.

McCrae, R. R., & John, O. P. (1992). An introduction to the five-factor model of personality. *Journal of Personality, 60*, 175–216.

Pervin, L. A. (1976). A free-response description approach to the analysis of person–situation interaction. *Journal of Personality and Social Psychology, 34*, 465–474.

Pervin, L. A. (1983). The stasis and flow of behavior: Toward a theory of goals. In M. M. Page (Ed.), *Personality: Current theory and research* (pp. 1–53). Lincoln: University of Nebraska Press.

Pervin, L. A. (1985). Personality: Current controversies, issues and directions. *Annual Review of Psychology, 36*, 83–114.

Pervin, L. A. (1986). Idiographic and nomothetic aspects of affect. In L. Van Langenhove, J. M. DeWaele, & R. Harre (Eds.), *Individual persons and their actions* (pp. 199–217). Brussels: Free University of Brussels.

Pervin, L. A. (1988a). Affect and addiction. *Addictive Behaviors, 13*, 83–86.

Pervin, L. A. (1988b). *Personality and the organization of affects*. Unpublished manuscript, Rutgers University.

Pervin, L. A. (Ed.) (1990). *Handbook of personality: Theory and research*. New York: Guilford Press.

Pervin, L. A. (1993). *Personality: Theory and research* (6th ed.). New York: Wiley.

Peterson, C., & Seligman, M. E. P. (1984). Causal explanations as a risk factor for depression: Theory and evidence. *Psychological Review, 91*, 347–374.

Plutchik, R. (1962). *The emotions: Facts, theories, and a new model*. New York: Random House.

Plutchik, R. (1980). *Emotion: A psychoevolutionary synthesis*. New York: Harper & Row.

Rapaport, D. (1971). *Emotions and memory* (5th ed.). New York: International Universities Press.

Rogers, C. R. (1951). *Client-centered therapy*. Boston: Houghton Mifflin.

Rogers, C. R. (1961). *On becoming a person*. Boston: Houghton Mifflin.

Roseman, I. J. (1984). Cognitive determinants of emotion: A structural theory. In P. Shaver (Ed.), *Review of personality and social psychology* (Vol. 5, pp. 11–36). Beverly Hills, CA: Sage.

Rosenblatt, A. D., & Thickstun, G. T. (1977). Modern psychoanalytic concepts in a general psychology. *Psychological Issues, 11*(Monograph No. 42–43).

Schafer, R. (1976). *A new language for psychoanalysis*. New Haven, CT: Yale University Press.

Seligman, M. E. P. (1975). *Helplessness*. San Francisco: W. H. Freeman.

Smith, C. A., & Ellsworth, P. C. (1987). Patterns of appraisal and emotion related to taking an exam. *Journal of Personality and Social Psychology, 52*, 475–488.

Smith, C. A., & Lazarus, R. S. (1990). Emotion and adaptation. In L. A. Pervin (Ed.), *Handbook of personality: Theory and research* (pp. 609–637). New York: Guilford Press.

Spence, D. P. (1982). *Narrative truth and historical truth: Meaning and interpretation in psychoanalysis*. New York: Norton.

Strelau, J. (1983). *Temperament, personality, and activity*. New York: Academic Press.

Swann, W. B., Jr. (1990). To be adored or to be known? The interplay of self-enhancement and self-verification. In E. T. Higgins & R. M. Sorrentino (Eds.), *Handbook of motivation and cognition: Foundations of social behavior* (Vol. 2, pp. 408–448). New York: Guilford Press.

Swann, W. B., Jr., Griffin, J. J., Predmore, S. C., & Gaines, B. (1987). The cognitive–affective crossfire: When self-consistency confronts self-enhancement. *Journal of Personality and Social Psychology, 52*, 881–889.

Tellegen, A. (1985). Structures of mood and personality and their relevance to assessing anxiety, with an emphasis on self-report. In A. H. Tuma & J. D. Maser (Eds.), *Anxiety and the anxiety disorders* (pp. 681–706). Hillsdale, NJ: Erlbaum.

Tellegen, A. (1991). Personality traits: Issues of definition, evidence, and assessment. In D. Cicchetti & W. Grove (Eds.), *Thinking clearly about psychology: Essays in honor of Paul Meehl* (pp. 55–72). Minneapolis: University of Minnesota Press.

Tomkins, S. S. (1962). *Affect, imagery, consciousness: Vol. 1. The positive affects*. New York: Springer.

Tomkins, S. S. (1963). *Affect, imagery, consciousness: Vol. 2. The negative affects*. New York: Springer.

Tomkins, S. S. (1980). Affect as amplification: Some modifications in theory. In R. Plutchik & H. Kellerman (Eds.), *Emotion: Theory, research, and experience. Vol. 1. Theories of emotion* (pp. 141–164). New York: Academic Press.

Watson, D. (1988). Intraindividual and interindividual analyses of positive and negative affect: Their relation to health complaints, perceived stress, and daily activities. *Journal of Personality and Social Psychology, 54,* 1020–1030.

Watson, D., & Clark, L. A. (1984). Negative affectivity: The disposition to experience aversive emotional states. *Psychological Bulletin, 96,* 465–490.

Watson, D., Clark, L. A., & Tellegen, A. (1984). Cross-cultural convergence in the structure of mood: A Japanese replication and a comparison with U.S. findings. *Journal of Personality and Social Psychology, 47,* 127–144.

Watson, D., & Tellegen, A. (1985). Toward a consensual structure of mood. *Psychological Bulletin, 98,* 219–235.

Weiner, B. (1985). An attributional theory of achievement motivation and emotion. *Psychological Review, 92,* 548–573.

Wessman, A. E., & Ricks, D. F. (1966). *Mood and personality.* New York: Henry Holt.

Zajonc, R. B. (1980). Feeling and thinking: Preferences need no inferences. *American Psychologist, 35,* 151–175.

22

Emotion and Self-Theory

SEYMOUR EPSTEIN

Emotions are of particular interest because they link us to our animal heritage. We register primary emotions, such as fear, anger, sadness, and joy, in a manner that can readily be identified with the corresponding emotions in subhuman animals (Darwin, 1872/1955). Yet here the similarity ends. Humans have complex conceptual systems that both transform emotions and are transformed by them. Emotions in subhuman animals are usually instigated by direct physical stimulation or by threats to bodily needs. A cat displays anger when another cat attempts to usurp its food; it displays fear when a dog does the same. All this is highly adaptive, as the angry cat fights better and the frightened one runs faster. Human anger and fear, on the other hand, are much more likely to be instigated by threats to a person's self-concept than to his or her bodily needs. Words carried in the medium of sound waves that have no capacity to physically injure anything evoke intense emotions in humans because of the meanings people assign to them. An insult or news of a financial disaster—words, and nothing more—are enough to evoke intense emotionally instigated actions, including homicide and suicide. It follows that if we are to understand human emotions, we must understand the "ghost in the machine," the interpreter of words and of events and the director of thoughts and of behavior. In short, we must understand the self-concept.

A cognitive system, by itself, cannot impel action. It can provide a map of means–end relations, but in the absence of motivation to achieve an end, no action will be taken. Because cognitive systems in the absence of motivation are inert, it is necessary to link self-theories to motivation, and to recognize further that motives derive their impelling force from their affective component. It follows that a complete theory of the self must encompass considerations of motivation and emotion.

In this chapter, I examine the relation of the self-concept to emotions and motives. First I present a review of clinical theories of the self, organized according to the basic motives assumed by each. Next, I discuss social-cognitive theories of the self. I end with a presentation of my own theory, which is as much a theory of emotions and motivation as it is a cognitive theory. It provides a broadly integrative framework that is not only compatible with the other theories, but derives interesting synergistic effects from the combination of the basic motives of the other theories.

THEORIES THAT EMPHASIZE THE PLEASURE PRINCIPLE

One of the most widespread assumptions among students of human behavior is that the most fundamental of all motives is the "pleasure principle": the maximization of pleasure and the minimization of pain. Psychoanalytic theory refers to this assumption, and learning theories incorporate it into their conceptualization of reinforcement. Economists endorse the same principle in their assumption that people are motivated to maximize gain and minimize loss.

Two features of Freudian theory are particularly relevant to our interests. One is that in

313

his initial theory, Freud assumed that the pleasure principle is the single overriding source of motivation. The other is that he believed there are two distinct kinds of cognitive processing: a more primitive "primary process" and a more advanced "secondary process."

Although Freud was not particularly concerned with the self as an object of knowledge, he had a great deal to say about the "ghost in the machine," which for him was the ego. Freud (1923/1961, 1933/1964) viewed the ego as an organized and organizing psychic structure encompassing the functions of perception, memory, and thinking. In addition to coping with external reality, the ego's task is to cope with inner reality in the form of drives, impulses, and unconscious wishes. Thus, the ego is a regulator of emotions.

Part of the ego splits off into a superego. The superego represents the internalized moral demands that individuals make on themselves; these are often as irrational and insistent as the demands made by the id, the animalistic, instinctive component of the psyche. The ego's task is to effect reasonable compromises among the conflicting demands of its "three harsh taskmasters"—the id, external reality, and the superego.

The superego is itself divided into two components that have implications for emotions: the conscience, which contains values acquired through punishment and fear, and the ego-ideal, which contains values acquired through rewards and positive sanctions. When an individual fails to meet or anticipates failing to meet the demands of conscience, he or she experiences dysphoric emotions, including guilt, anxiety, and depression. When an individual succeeds in meeting the values of his or her ego-ideal, he or she experiences positive emotions, such as elation and pride.

Although the concept of the pleasure principle reigned supreme in Freud's earlier and more influential theory, he later realized that it was unable to account for certain repetitive phenomena, including the repetitive nightmares of traumatized soldiers and the repetitive enactment of adverse experiences in everyday life. Freud (1920/1955) attributed these phenomena to a "repetition compulsion," a fundamental tendency of the mind to repeat distressing experiences in an attempt at belated mastery. To account for the repetition compulsion, Freud had to radically revise his original theory. He introduced a "death instinct" as the source of the repetition compulsion. This later theory of Freud was so fanciful that it never gained the degree of acceptance of his earlier theory.

It is to Freud's credit that he became aware of the limitations of the pleasure principle. Unfortunately, his solution in terms of a repetition compulsion and a death instinct is based on the wildest of speculations. It will be seen later that a more viable solution is the assumption of a "coherence principle" (i.e., a fundamental motive to maintain the coherence of one's conceptual system).

Freud believed that his crowning achievement was the discovery, through dream analysis, of the primary process, which refers to the principles of operation of the unconscious mind. The primary process is a primitive system that is governed by wish fulfillment. It represents events predominantly in the form of visual images, and its operation is characterized by displacement, condensation, symbolic representation, and a disregard for considerations of space, time, logic, and reality. Operating in the background of consciousness, it influences conscious thought and behavior. In contrast to the primary process, the secondary process operates predominantly at the conscious level, is reality-oriented, and operates according to conventional rules of logic.

It is a credit to Freud's genius that his description of unconscious processes allowed the world to understand in natural terms what previously had been relegated to the spirit world. However, there is good reason to question whether the illogical and unrealistic primary process can help us understand the operation of a self-system that automatically organizes experience and directs behavior in ways that are highly adaptive, at least most of the time. As will be shown later, cognitive–experiential self-theory (CEST) proposes an unconscious system that is ideally suited for this task.

THEORIES THAT EMPHASIZE SELF-ESTEEM

Once a self-concept is formed, the need to view the self favorably becomes as important as the pleasure principle. This becomes readily apparent when one considers that under intense feelings of guilt or shame, people may take their own lives.

William James

William James (1890, 1907) is widely recognized as the father of self psychology. Although he had little use for the concept of the self as agent, or the "I," he believed that the self as object, or the "Me," is of great importance.

James considered the self as object as an extended self that includes everything with which a person is identified. He believed that the self as object is intimately associated with emotions.

> In its widest possible sense, however, *a man's "Me" is the sum total of all that he can call his*, not only his body and his psychic powers, but his clothes and his house, his wife and children, his ancestors and friends, his reputation and works, his lands and horses, and yacht and bank account. All these things give him the same emotions. If they wax and prosper he feels triumphant; if they dwindle and die away, he feels cast down—not necessarily in the same degree for each thing, but in much the same way for all. (James, 1907, p. 177).

A person's overall evaluation of self, or self-esteem, is of particular importance with respect to emotions. Changes in self-esteem are determined not by absolute accomplishment, James concluded, but by the discrepancy between accomplishment and aspiration.

James considered the self to be both differentiated and integrated. The overall self includes three selves. A material self consists of the individual's beliefs and values concerning personal attributes and all with which an individual identifies. A social self includes societal values, internalized because of the individual's desire to receive social approval and to avoid social disapproval. A spiritual self is the person's innermost self, the "felt inner core of one's being."

An interesting but often overlooked contribution of James (1890) is his conviction that there are two kinds of knowledge: knowledge by acquaintance, which is directly derived from experience, and knowledge by description, which is acquired from others. Although James did not relate this conceptualization to his views on the self, it has important implica-

tions for self-theories, for it suggests that there may be two selves, each based on a different kind of knowledge—a possibility I consider later.

Alfred Adler

Adler (1954; Ansbacher & Ansbacher, 1956) proposed the first cognitive theory of personality. Unfortunately, he never received the credit that was his due, because the theory was well ahead of its time. Modern cognitive self-theory is rediscovering Adler without knowing it, and has yet to effect the integration of emotions and motivation with cognition that his theory achieved many years ago.

According to Adler, all individuals construct a belief system and a way of relating to the world, which he called a "style of life." Each person's style of life is fashioned out of the person's manner of coping with inevitable feelings of inferiority that arise out of the condition of being a helpless child. At the center of a person's style of life is a "fictional goal," which guides the individual in his or her attempts to achieve mastery and overcome inferiority. Secure children, who have been raised in an atmosphere of love and respect, have reasonable fictional goals that provide helpful guidelines; those likely to become neurotic have exaggerated fictional goals that they take too seriously and use as rigid standards against which they judge the worth of themselves and others. Neurotics at first take pride in their high standards and use them to feel superior to others. However, the high standards ultimately increase rather than decrease their feelings of inferiority, for the neurotics are unable to meet their own standards. This results in a greater investment in yet more unrealistic goals, which establishes a vicious cycle; as Adler expresses it, the neurotic becomes "nailed to the cross of his fiction" (Ansbacher & Ansbacher, 1956, p. 246). Defensive coping strategies, which Adler referred to as "neurotic safeguards," buttress the neurotic's maladaptive ways of interpreting events and of maintaining his or her maladaptive fictions.

It is evident from the foregoing discussion that emotions and motivation enter into Adler's theory in two important ways. One is that the quest for self-esteem (overcoming feelings of inferiority) provides the incentive for developing a style of life. The other is that once a style of life is developed, it is a major determinant of the emotions that a person experiences. People with adaptive styles of life experience pride, happiness, and positive feelings toward others because they succeed, within reason, in reaching their goals, which are realistic and socially directed. People with maladaptive styles of life experience frustration, anger, and despair as a result of their failure to achieve their goals, which are unrealistic and egocentric, and they therefore fail to gain the social approval that all humans inherently desire.

Gordon Allport

Allport (1955, 1961) like James, had no use for the self as agent. He believed that the word "self" should be used only in hyphenated form, as a descriptor. Also, like James, Allport endorsed the concept of an extended self, for which he used the term "ego-extension." Like James, he also emphasized the importance of the motive of enhancing self-esteem, which he referred to as "ego-enhancement." He believed that ego-enhancement is associated with the need for survival. Overall, Allport's views on the self are largely a recapitulation of those of James, with two notable exceptions. One is that he noted that the discrepancy between actual and desired selves is not necessarily a source of negative affect, but can be a growth-promoting challenge. The other is that he introduced the concept of "functional autonomy" to account for the persistence of certain kinds of behaviors in the absence of positive reinforcement. He believed that such reactions are an extremely important aspect of human behavior, but acknowledged that he was at a loss to account for them. As will be seen later, the principle that eluded him was the same as the one that eluded Freud—namely, the coherence principle.

Karen Horney

Late in her theorizing, Horney (1950) introduced the concepts of an actual and an idealized self. The ideas are very similar to those of Adler, but she carried them further. According to Horney, everyone develops an idealized self-image, which is normally adaptive. As a compensation for feelings of inadequacy, the neurotic develops an exaggerated idealized self-image, which initially enhances self-esteem and is a source of feeling superior to others. Eventually, the idealized image becomes a Frankenstein monster that turns on its creator: The contempt initially directed at others is turned on the self as it becomes apparent that the self can no more achieve the lofty standards than others can. The idealized self-image then becomes the center of the development of a false self, which increasingly displaces the person's true self as the person is forced into defensive strategies to maintain the illusion of superiority. The true self, according to Horney, is the vital part of the personality that strives for fulfillment by reacting spontaneously and realistically to the world. The neurotic inevitably experiences a conflict between the two selves because of the true self's inexorable drive toward expression. Depending on the outcome of the struggle, the individual will remain unhappy, frustrated, and neurotic, or will experience growth, self-acceptance, and increased vitality.

Unfortunately, Horney never defined the true self. Yet there is good reason to suspect that her impressions contain an important insight, for other psychotherapists, including Adler, Jung, Maslow, and Rogers, have come to a similar conclusion about the existence of something akin to a growth principle from a variety of different perspectives. It remains a challenge for self psychologists to identify what Horney sensed in her concept of a true self and to account for a growth principle.

Heinz Kohut

Kohut (1971) was a psychoanalyst who considered self-esteem regulation to be the most central factor in adjustment. It is of such importance, he believed, that the very stability of the self-structure depends on it. A well-functioning self-esteem system is the source of feelings of security and well-being, whereas a poor one is the source of negative emotions, including overwhelming anxiety associated with the fear of disorganization.

Kohut endorsed the concept of an executive self, as indicated by his definition of the self as "the basis of our being an independent center of initiative and perception, integrated with our central ambition and ideals, and with our experience that our body and mind form a unit in space and a continuum in time" (1977,

p. 177). Although that is hardly a useful definition of the self, it does make the point that whatever else Kohut's self is, it is an agentic self, as it plays an important role in initiative.

Kohut studied narcissistic patients who had serious problems in self-esteem regulation, either manifesting grandiose views about themselves or expressing a very low opinion of themselves. According to Kohut, narcissism is the prototypical disorder of our time, which can be attributed to faulty parenting, including rejection, abuse, and overprotection. The result is that there is a failure to satisfy two fundamental needs of the child: the need to be "mirrored," and the need to idealize the parents. Mirroring refers to the parents' responding to the child in a manner that conveys the parents' appreciation of the child's accomplishments. As the result of appropriate mirroring, an ambition pole of the self-structure develops. Through identification with a loved and respected figure, an idealizing pole of the self-structure develops that includes the internalized values of the admired person. Faulty mirroring and idealizing are the sources of various disorders, including an "understimulated" self, characterized by chronic feelings of fatigue, emptiness, and ennui; a fragmenting self, characterized by feelings of vulnerability, anxiety, and disorganization; and an overstimulated self, characterized by grandiose fantasies that generate tension and anxiety, and motivate the individual to avoid attention-eliciting situations that result in such reactions.

Kohut's views are of particular interest for theorists of the self because of his focus on the details of self-esteem regulation and on the consequences of failures in such regulation, including disorganization of the self-structure. Some of Kohut's explanations, to be sure, are unnecessarily complex. The reason why people with "narcissistic wounds" tend both to seek to be admired by others (including their therapists) and to idealize them can be more simply explained by the logic inherent in reflected appraisals: "If you, whom I admire and respect, admire and respect me, then it follows that since I respect your judgment, I must be an admirable person." It is no wonder, then, that people with low self-esteem intuitively seek out such self-correcting relationships.

THEORIES THAT EMPHASIZE RELATEDNESS

Harry Stack Sullivan

According to Sullivan (1953), a child develops a self-system out of the child's desire to please the "mothering one" (i.e., the caretaker). By internalizing the values of the caretaker, the child is able to correct his or her behavioral tendencies in a manner such as to gain approval and avoid disapproval.

The "good me," the "bad me," the "not-me," the "good mother," and the "bad mother" are particularly important internalizations. The good me is an organized network of schemas and associated positive affect derived from rewarding experiences with the caretaker. By internalizing the love of the mothering one toward the child, the child develops self-love and the basis for a high level of self-esteem. The bad me is organized around moderate levels of disapproval. By internalizing negative sanctions toward disapproved behavioral impulses, the child develops a conscience. The not-me serves no constructive function, but is a pathological dissociative reaction involving intense anxiety and disorganization that is produced by the perception of intense disapproval and rejection. When experiences activate the not-me, the individual becomes disorganized and experiences overwhelming anxiety. Sullivan uses the not-me to account for disorganization, dread, and bizarre symptoms in psychosis.

Good and bad mother schemas lay the groundwork for people's attitudes toward others. There is a reciprocal relation between negative attributions directed toward the self and the mothering one. For example, given an unsatisfactory relationship between the two, the child can hold either the self or the mothering one responsible. If the self is held responsible, hostility is directed at the self, and if the mothering one is held responsible, hostility is directed at her, which tends to generalize to other people.

John Bowlby

According to Bowlby (1969, 1988), the child constructs a model of the self and others based on early interactions with significant others. On the basis of laboratory experimentation, he and Ainsworth (Ainsworth & Bowlby, 1991) concluded that children establish three basic kinds of relationships with their caregivers: secure, ambivalent, and avoidant. Infants who are securely attached develop a working model of their mothers as available when they need them, and this schema allows them to be secure in the mothers' absence and to direct their attention to exploring their environments. Children who are ambivalently attached become very distressed in the absence of their mothers and too fearful to attend to unrelated matters. Children with avoidant attachments turn away from their mothers when the mothers return after a brief absence, and although they appear to be unconcerned, they register high arousal levels. Bowlby considered these three kinds of early attachment relationships as important because they are the foundations on which people's model of human relationships are constructed.

Influenced by modern cognitive theory, Bowlby concluded that people evaluate most sensory input rapidly and unconsciously by relating it to stored information, including models of interpersonal relationships. The reason why people are not normally aware of their unconscious evaluations is that such awareness would be inefficient and serve no purpose.

W. R. D. Fairbairn

Fairbairn (1954) is one of a group of object relations psychoanalysts that includes Melanie Klein, Margaret Mahler, Otto Kernberg, D. W. Winnicott, and others. Object relations theorists, to a greater or lesser extent, reject Freud's emphasis on biological factors as the primary motivational force in human behavior, and emphasize instead the need for relationships. I have selected Fairbairn for review here because his theory is the most "pure" object relations theory, in the sense that he emphasizes relationships to the complete exclusion of Freudian drive theory.

Like Melanie Klein before him, Fairbairn emphasized the importance of early mother–child relationships. The course of development if all goes well, according to Fairbairn, is a progression from infantile dependency to mature dependence, better described as "inter-relatedness." At one end of the dimension is the stage of "primary identification," in which the child is unable to distinguish itself from the primary caretaker, and therefore has no sense of self. At the other end, the person is capable of establishing mutually rewarding relationships between equals. In between is a long transitional stage that involves a gradual movement away from infantile dependency toward mature interdependence. Pathological reactions and dysphoric emotions arise as a result of failures to negotiate the transition stage appropriately.

The child copes with the inevitable frustration of dependency needs by developing inner representations of the caregiver and of the self, and by "splitting" the good and bad components of each into separate representations. Here, Fairbairn's thinking is very similar to Sullivan's. According to Fairbairn, it is beyond the child's capacity to conceptualize a parent as a complex individual who has both good and bad characteristics. Maintaining separate images of a good mother and a bad mother is much simpler, and allows the child to relate securely to the good representation without interference from the bad one.

The internalization of the bad "object" (i.e., person) can take one of two forms, depending on whether the mother behaves in a tantalizing, teasing way, or is rejecting in a hostile or withdrawing way. Children in the former situation develop chronic feelings of frustration and/or emptiness, whereas those in the latter situation are characteristically resentful and angry. Self-representations are also split into good and bad components, and the person has representations of these states that parallel the representations of the caretaker.

Excessive splitting is the major source of pathology. The split-off bad representations cannot be corrected because they are removed from conscious control. As a result, they remain as chronic sources of anxiety, despair, and rage that are readily activated by any real or imagined frustration of dependency needs.

THEORIES THAT EMPHASIZE COHERENCE

Erik Erikson

Erikson (1959, 1963, 1968) believed that threats to identity are a major source of pathology. After working with traumatized soldiers, he concluded that the basic source of their difficulties was that their belief systems had been shattered by experiences they could not assimilate. Having been required to behave in ways that violated their deepest values, they lost their sense of identity and suffered from what he referred to as "identity confusion." He found the concept also useful in understanding the problems of Native Americans caught in a clash between cultures, and of adolescents caught between childhood and adult identities.

According to Erikson, a coherent identity provides an individual with a stable sense of self and a frame of reference for making sense of experience. Without it, individuals are unable to function; therefore, when their sense of identity is threatened, they experience high levels of distress. Thus, a great deal of normal behavior can be understood in terms of people's need to maintain and defend their identities, and much maladjusted behavior can be explained by identity confusion.

Phenomenological Psychologists

The phenomenological psychologists include Victor Raimy, Donald Snygg, Arthur Combs, and Carl Rogers, among others. The distinguishing feature of their theories is the assumption that all individuals construct their own reality, a central aspect of which is their views about the self. Having constructed a system for making sense of the world, people's most important motive is to maintain the coherence and stability of their conceptual system. For present purposes, it will suffice to review those aspects of Rogers's (1951, 1959) theory that are most relevant to emotions.

According to Rogers (1951), the organism has one basic tendency and striving—to actualize, maintain, and enhance the experiencing organism" (p. 487). The organism has a natural inclination to develop, grow, and fulfill its potential, which means becoming increasingly autonomous, differentiated, and socialized. The self-system both influences and is influenced by emotions. When the self-system is enhanced, the person experiences positive affect; when it is threatened, the person experiences negative affect. Positive affect in association with an accepting environment facilitates openness and growth of the self-system, whereas negative affect in association with threats to the self-system fosters defensive retrenchment.

People react not to actual events but to their interpretations of events. Even the effects of physical drives, such as hunger and sex, are determined not so much by biological factors as by their perceived significance with respect to maintaining and enhancing the organism. Thus all emotions are influenced by people's interpretive processes, the most important of which involve people's views about themselves.

The self is an organization of conscious, relatively stable beliefs and values about one's person. It is important to distinguish between values acquired directly from experience and those adopted from others. Children may internalize beliefs and values that contradict their own experience because of their desire to please the caretakers on whom they are dependent. Discrepancies between "organic experience" and conscious beliefs are an important source of pathology for two reasons: They are an inherent source of stress and anxiety, and they motivate the use of defenses to maintain the beliefs that are inconsistent with experience. Such defenses restrict the natural operation of the growth principle.

Individuals process events subliminally through a process called "subception." When subliminal perceptions are incongruent with conscious beliefs, the individual experiences anxiety. The perceptions may then be denied, distorted, or accepted. If they are accepted, there will necessarily be a change in the structure of the self. If threats to the self-system continue and defenses are insufficient, disorganization, accompanied by overwhelming anxiety, will ultimately occur.

There is an inherent growth force. In a secure, accepting environment, in which individuals can relax their defenses, they will tend to label their feelings accurately. Their organic and labeled experience will then begin to coincide. Accordingly, their neurosis, will diminish, their dysphoric emotions will be replaced by positive ones, and they will experience an increase in positive feelings toward the self and others.

SOCIAL-COGNITIVE SELF-THEORIES

In contrast to the clinical theories described above, which heavily weight emotional and motivational influences in cognitive processing, social-cognitive theories of the self, in common with Kelly's (1955) personal construct theory, until recently envisioned the self as a strictly cognitive system that goes about its business of cognizing events simply for the sake of doing so. Action properties were attributed to the self by the simple expedient of relabeling preconscious beliefs as "schemas." These theorists failed to realize that knowledge structures by themselves, even those that refer to plans or scripts, cannot account for behavior in the absence of motives for putting the knowledge into action (Westen, 1992).

Much of initial social-cognitive theorizing about the self involved little more than substituting cognitive terms for other terms. For example, "schemas," "working models," "storage," "processing," "storing," and "retrieving" were substituted for previously used terms, such as "beliefs," "theories of reality," "memory," "thinking," "perceiving," "remembering," and "recalling." Some of the early research simply established relations between alternative measures of the same traits or other attributes, labeled one as a schema and the other as a criterion, and claimed that a significant relation between the two measures demonstrated the power of the schema concept e.g., Markus, 1977). Measures of reaction time were said to index the accessibility of constructs in the schema system, while ignoring the consideration that delayed reaction time has long been used as an index of conflict between schemas.

More recently, research and theorizing by social-cognitive self-theorists have become more sophisticated and have resulted in some highly promising findings, with respect to both introducing emotional and motivational variables and examining multiple levels of processing.

Emotional and motivational constructs have been introduced into the theories, based on the assumption that discrepancies between certain components of the self-system (e.g., actual vs. ideal self) and between self- and other-representations (one's own vs. other's standards) can motivate efforts to reduce the discrepancies (e.g., Higgins, 1987; Markus & Nurius, 1986; Tesser, 1991). Of particular interest is the fact that this approach has succeeded in relating specific discrepancies to specific emotions. For example, Higgins (1987) has found that discrepancies between actual and ideal selves are associated with what he refers to as "dejection-related emotions" (e.g., disappointment, dissatisfaction, and sadness), whereas discrepancies between actual and ought selves are associated with "agitation-related emotions" (e.g., fear, threat, and restlessness). Tesser (1991) has predicted the

occurrence of the emotions of jealousy/envy, pride in self, and pride in another as a function of the interaction of three variables: relevance of activity to one's self-conceptualization, relative performance, and psychological closeness to another person who is also being evaluated. Markus has recently introduced motivational and emotional constructs into her self-theory through the medium of "possible selves" (Markus & Nurius, 1986). Some possible selves (such as feared and desired selves) are intrinsically motivating, whereas others (such as representations of past, future, and ideal selves) derive their motivational significance from discrepancies from perceptions of actual selves. Other important research by social-cognitive self-theorists has examined more fundamental motives, such as the need to maintain self-views and the need to enhance them (e.g., Swann, 1990; Tesser, 1988).

Considerable research by social-cognitive psychologists has established that self-relevant schemas are processed automatically, in the absence of conscious awareness (e.g., Bargh, 1990; Bargh & Pietromonaco, 1982; Bargh & Tota, 1988; Bowers & Meichenbaum, 1984; Greenwald & Pratkanis, 1984; Kihlstrom, 1987; Markus & Wurf, 1987; Markus & Nurius, 1986; Nisbett & Wilson, 1977; Strauman & Higgins, 1987; Swann, Hixon, Stein-Seroussi, & Gilbert, 1990; Uleman & Bargh, 1989). These findings have important implications for self-theory, for they suggest that people have different views about themselves at different levels of awareness, and that they therefore may even have different self-theories (Epstein, 1985, 1991a). The task remains for social-cognitive theorists to incorporate these interesting findings into an overall, integrated social-cognitive theory of the self.

AN INTEGRATIVE SELF-THEORY

There are a few recently proposed cognitive–affective theories of personality that incorporate within a single model multiple levels of processing, emotions and motivation, and modern cognitive theory (e.g., Bucci, in press; Epstein, 1973, 1980, 1991b; Horowitz, 1988; Labouvie-Vief, 1982; Labouvie-Vief, Hakim-Larson, DeVoe, & Schoeberlein, 1989; Westen, 1991, 1992). All of these are of considerable interest, but as space limitations preclude a review of all, I concentrate here on my own theory, CEST.[1] Suffice it to note that Bucci, Horowitz, and Westen integrate psychoanalytic with modern cognitive concepts, whereas Labouvie-Vief integrates social-cognitive concepts with a Jungian and Piagetian approach.

CEST asserts that all individuals automatically construct an implicit theory of reality with subdivisions of a self-theory, a world-theory, and connecting propositions. There are three conceptual systems: the rational, experiential, and associationistic systems. For present purposes I emphasize the experiential system, because this it is in this system that an implicit theory of reality that automatically organizes experience and directs behavior resides.

Views on Emotions

Emotions are conceived of in CEST as both influencing and being influenced by a person's implicit theory of reality. They play an important role in the development of a person's conceptual system. Primary emotions (e.g., anger, fear, sadness, joy, affection) are viewed as organized and organizing cognitive–affective systems that provide the nuclei around which expanding networks of constructs develop. They are ready-made cognitive–affective units, or "modules," that organize and direct critical adaptive behavioral patterns (e.g., fighting, fleeing, withdrawing, expressing affection, exploring) before a complex, integrated model of the self and the world has had an opportunity to develop. The overall conceptual system is constructed, in part, by elaborating and integrating these modules. Other concepts about the self and the world are directly acquired because of their affective consequences. In short, people develop conceptual systems because it is emotionally rewarding to do so. It follows that people would not construct a model of the self if it failed to provide them with a net affective gain, which can account for nonorganic cases of childhood autism (Epstein, 1973), and also for the later occur-

rence of schizophrenia in those who abandon a previously somewhat coherent conceptual system (Epstein, 1979a).

Emotions provide the royal road for inferring the schemas in a person's experiential conceptual system. The intensity of an emotional response to an event indicates the degree to which a schema of significance to the individual is implicated. Thus, by observing the kinds of events to which a person responds emotionally, one can map out many of the important schemas in a person's implicit theory of reality (Epstein, 1973, 1983a).

Another way that emotions can be used to detect schemas is through recognition of the cognitions that underlie different emotions (e.g., Beck, 1976; Ellis, 1962; Epstein, 1973, 1979b, 1983a; Lazarus, 1991). On the basis of such information, one can assume that people who are angry much of the time have schemas that others often behave badly and deserve to be punished. By the same token, one can infer that frightened people harbor schemas that danger is ever-present, and that they should be ready to escape; and that sad people have schemas that they have suffered serious losses or are personally inadequate, and that there is nothing they can do about it. Support for such construals has been provided in studies in which subjects kept daily records of the events that preceded their emotions and of the automatic construals of the situations and response options that mediated their emotional responses (Epstein, 1979b, 1983a).

Four Basic Needs and Four Basic Beliefs

A distinguishing feature of CEST is that unlike the other theories, which propose the existence of single basic needs, it assumes that all four basic needs proposed by the other theories are equally important. Included are the need to maximize pleasure and minimize pain; the need to assimilate the data of reality into a stable, coherent conceptual system; the need for relatedness; and the need for self-esteem. Each clinical theory proposes its own basic need and ignores the proposals of the other theories; each assumes it has the one real truth. CEST assumes that since each need is capable of dominating the others, they are all extremely important. Several interesting consequences follow from this approach. One is that it draws attention to four major sources

---

[1]Since its introduction in an article in the *American Psychologist* two decades ago (Epstein, 1973), CEST has undergone considerable development and has been the source of numerous research investigations. The interested reader can consult a number of articles that describe different aspects of the theory and supporting evidence (e.g., Epstein, 1973, 1976, 1980, 1981, 1983a, 1983b, 1984, 1985, 1987, 1989, 1990, 1991a, 1991b, 1991c, 1992, in press; Epstein & Erskine, 1983). Reprints are available on request.

of positive and negative affect, which have obvious important implications for diagnosis and therapy. It also draws attention to the importance of considering the interaction among the four basic needs. It can be inferred that behavior must be a compromise among the needs and that effective adaptation requires a balance to be maintained among them. From this, it follows that the four needs serve as a series of checks and balances against one another. It further follows that a failure to maintain the balance is a source of dysphoric emotions as a result of frustration of some of the needs. Different symptoms are associated with different imbalances (Epstein, 1987, 1991a, in press). An imbalance can arise from overcompensation in response to a threat to any of the needs. For example, if self-esteem is threatened, the need to defend self-esteem may be bolstered at the expense of satisfying the need to maintain a realistic, coherent conceptual system. The result could be an increase in narcissistic symptoms, including delusions of grandeur.

CEST assumes that there are four basic beliefs associated with the four basic needs. In order for individuals to automatically allocate their resources for satisfying the four basic needs, they must intuitively assess the degree to which the needs are being satisfied. Accordingly, they develop beliefs that are relevant to fulfillment of the needs. The following four basic belief dimensions have developed around the four basic needs: the degree to which the world is perceived as benevolent versus malevolent (related to the management of pleasure and pain); the degree to which the world is perceived as meaningful (including predictable and controllable) versus meaningless and chaotic (related to the need to realistically assimilate the data of reality into a coherent, stable conceptual system); the degree to which people are viewed as comforting and trustworthy versus dangerous and undependable (related to the management of relatedness); and the degree to which the self is worthy (including competent and good) versus unworthy (related to the management of self-esteem). A person's automatic self-assessments on these belief dimensions are manifested, respectively, by the degree to which the person is optimistic versus pessimistic, committed versus alienated, trusting versus suspicious, and self-accepting versus self-rejecting.

Since a person's perceptions of his or her positions on the four basic dimensions are among the most fundamental schemas in his or her implicit theory of reality, invalidating any of the schemas has a destabilizing effect on the entire conceptual system. Elsewhere, I have noted that invalidation of such basic beliefs is accompanied by overwhelming anxiety and a tendency to become disorganized, and therefore can account for the conditions that precipitate acute schizophrenic reactions (Epstein, 1979a) and are a source of post-traumatic stress disorder (Epstein, 1987, 1991c).

Because the invalidation of basic beliefs is highly threatening, people have a vested interest in maintaining these beliefs even when they are highly negative, for it prevents disorganization. This realization provides us with an explanation (in common with the phenomenological psychologists) of Freud's repetition compulsion and of Allport's functional autonomy. People repeatedly engage in self-defeating behaviors (repetition compulsion) or maintain maladaptive behaviors in the absence of reinforcement (functional autonomy) not because they have a death instinct or because their behavior is unresponsive to affective consequences, but because they have a fundamental need to maintain the stability of their conceptual systems—a need that, when it cannot be fulfilled, produces intense anxiety. In other words, even a bad conceptual system is better than none, for the alternative is to experience the overwhelming anxiety that is associated with chaos.

Swann (1990) has demonstrated, in a highly creative series of laboratory investigations, that even people's ordinary behavior is motivated by the need to maintain familiar beliefs (even unfavorable ones) about the self. This does not deny the importance of the need to enhance self-esteem, which he and others (e.g., Tesser, 1988) have found may or may not take precedence over the need to maintain familiarity, depending on circumstances. There is also ample evidence that behavior tends to be a compromise between the two needs. In an extensive review of the literature, Taylor and Brown (1988) found widespread support for a tendency in normal individuals to manifest self- and optimism-enhancing biases. Clearly, the amount of enhancement was within acceptable limits, or else the subjects would have had to be tested in a mental institution. Given a compromise between a need for self-enhancement and a need to realistically assimilate the data of experience, it follows that normal individuals can be expected to exhibit modest self-enhancing biases. One can anticipate from CEST that it is possible to demonstrate similar conflicts and compromises between other basic needs, such as between relatedness and self-esteem enhancement, or relatedness and maintenance of familiar self-views. Undoubtedly, the results will differ for different subjects, depending on the relative strengths of their needs; this suggests an interesting area for research.

It is apparent that the assumption that there are four basic needs and four basic belief dimensions opens up new ways of thinking about behavior, and suggests new areas for research. It remains for future research to determine how fruitful this way of thinking will be.

Multiple Levels of Processing

CEST assumes that people apprehend reality by two conceptual systems that operate in parallel: an automatic, experiential system and an analytic, rational system, each operating by its own rules of inference (see Table 22.1).[2] As noted before, James (1890) many years ago proposed two somewhat similar systems, although he did not enumerate their properties. Several related systems have since been proposed by others (e.g., Bucci, in press; Buck, 1985; Labouvie-Vief et al., 1989; Leventhal, 1982; Paivio, 1986; Rosch, 1983; Weinberger & McClelland, 1990).

Of particular interest with respect to emotions, the functioning of the experiential system in CEST is assumed to be mediated by emotions and "vibes," which are more subtle feeling states of which subjects are not always aware. A typical sequence of behavior is that an event occurs; the experiential system scans its memory banks for related events; and vibes from the past events are produced that influence conscious thoughts and behavior. All of

this occurs instantly, automatically, and frequently below the threshold of awareness.

A recent research program exploring the operation of the experiential system has provided evidence in support of the existence of the two systems; has verified some of its rules of operation; and has found that priming people's experiential systems biases the functioning of their rational systems, which has important implications for the degree to which humans are able to think rationally (Epstein, 1991b; Epstein, Lipson, Holstein, & Huh, 1992; Kirkpatrick & Epstein, 1992). The principles of operation of the experiential system, as outlined in Table 22.1, can also account for findings on heuristic processing by social-cognitive psychologists (Epstein et al., 1992; Kirkpatrick & Epstein, 1992; Nisbett & Wilson, 1977; Tversky & Kahneman, 1974, 1981; also see review in Fiske & Taylor, 1991).

Implicit Theories of Reality

Another distinctive feature of CEST is that it assumes that people have integrated implicit theories of reality, rather than more loosely organized sets of schemas or networks of schemas, as is more commonly assumed. By making this broader assumption, CEST is able to account for a number of important phenomena that otherwise remain enigmatic. For example, the elusive "growth principle" of Adler, Jung, Rogers, and Horney can be accounted for by noting that theories grow (become more differentiated and integrated) through the interaction of conceptualization and observation. Moreover, since CEST assumes the existence of two systems, each containing implicit theories of reality, it provides a way of accounting for Horney's true and false selves, and of the importance Rogers attached to a distinction between organic experience and indirect, verbally mediated experience. The true self and the organic experience correspond to the experiential self, and the false self and the indirect, verbally labeled experience correspond to the rational self. According to CEST, the experiential self has evolved over millions of years in contrast to the rational self, which has a relatively brief evolutionary history. Accordingly, the experiential self has a vitality based on its relationships with emotions that is not easily denied; when denied, it is a source of tension that contrib-

---

[2]There is also a third system in CEST—the associationistic system, which is a composite of Freud's and Jung's unconscious. It is viewed not as an adaptive system but as an epiphenomenon, which is not to deny that it can reveal important information. The interested reader can find a discussion of the three systems in Epstein (1983b).

TABLE 22.1. Comparison of the Experiential and Rational Systems

Experiential system	Rational system
1. Holistic	1. Analytic
2. Emotional: Pleasure- and pain-oriented (what feels good)	2. Logical: Reason-oriented (what is sensible)
3. Associationistic connections	3. Cause-and-effect connections
4. Behavior mediated by "vibes" from past experiences	4. Behavior mediated by conscious appraisal of events
5. Encodes reality in concrete images, metaphors, and narratives	5. Encodes reality in abstract symbols, words and numbers
6. More rapid processing: Oriented toward immediate action	6. Slower processing: Oriented toward delayed action
7. Slower to change: Changes with repetitive or intense experience	7. Changes more rapidly: Changes with speed of thought
8. More crudely differentiated: Broad generalization gradient; categorical thinking	8. More highly differentiated: Dimensional thinking
9. More crudely integrated: Dissociative, organized into emotional complexes (cognitive–affective modules)	9. More highly integrated
10. Experienced passively and preconsciously: We are seized by our emotions	10. Experienced actively and consciously: We are in control of our thoughts
11. Self-evidently valid: "Experiencing is believing"	11. Requires justification via logic and evidence

Note. Adapted from Epstein, Lipson, Holstein, and Huh (1992, p. 329).

utes to mental and physical pathology. The inherent impetus of the experiential self to fulfill its needs is the source of the growth principle that has been proposed by others.

The existence of personal theories of reality can account for disorganization of the entire conceptual system. As already noted, acute schizophrenic reactions and symptoms of posttraumatic stress disorder can be attributed to invalidation of basic schemas in a person's implicit theory of reality. This interpretation is consistent with the theoretical views of Lecky (1961), Erikson (1959), Rogers (1959), Horowitz (1976), and McCann and Pearlman (1990).

The concept of a personal theory of reality can also provide a viable explanation of an executive, or agentic, self. Because theories organize experience and direct behavior, they function as executive systems. It is this organization that distinguishes the self as agent from the self as object. Of course, given the assumption that there are two different systems for processing events, it follows that there must be two selves as agents and two selves as objects—one pair residing in the rational system, which is directly available to self-report, and the other residing in the experiential system, which has to be inferred.

The existence of two self-systems, analytic/rational and intuitive/experiential, has impor-

tant implications for the existential consequences of being a human being. It means that we are all caught in an inherent conflict between two aspects of our nature, each of which apprehends reality by its own rules, and neither of which is more valid than the other. If either system defeats the other it also defeats itself, for they share the same body. It follows that the only hope we humans have for achieving equanimity is through effecting a harmonious integration between our two selves.

Acknowledgments. Preparation of this chapter and the research reported in it were supported by National Institute of Mental Health Grant No. MH 01293 and National Institute of Mental Health Research Scientist Award No. 5 K05 MH 00363 to Seymour Epstein.

REFERENCES

Adler, A. (1954). *Understanding human nature.* New York: Fawcett.

Ainsworth, M. D. S., & Bowlby, J. (1991). An ethological approach to personality development. *American Psychologist, 46,* 333–341.

Allport, G. (1955). *Becoming: Basic considerations for a psychology of personality.* New Haven, CT: Yale University Press.

Allport, G. (1961). *Pattern and growth in personality.* New York: Holt, Rinehart & Winston.

Ansbacher, H. L., & Ansbacher, R. R. (1956). *The individual psychology of Alfred Adler: A systematic presentation in selections from his writings.* New York: Harper & Row.

Bargh, J. A. (1990). Auto-motives: Preconscious determinants of social interaction. In E. T. Higgins & R. M. Sorrentino (Eds.), *Handbook of motivation and cognition: Foundations of social behavior* (Vol. 2, pp. 93–130). New York: Guilford Press.

Bargh, J. A., & Pietromonaco, P. (1982). Automatic information processing and social perception: The influence of trait information presented outside of conscious awareness on impression formation. *Journal of Personality and Social Psychology, 43,* 437–449.

Bargh, J. A., & Tota, M. E. (1988). Context-dependent automatic processing in depression: Accessibility of negative constructs with regard to self but not others. *Journal of Personality and Social Psychology, 54,* 925–939.

Beck, A. T. (1976). *Cognitive therapy and the emotional disorders.* New York: International Universities Press.

Bowers, K. S., & Meichenbaum, D. (Eds.). (1984). *The unconscious reconsidered.* New York: Wiley.

Bowlby, J. (1969). *Attachment and loss: Vol. 1. Attachment.* New York: Basic Books.

Bowlby, J. (1988). *A secure base.* New York: Basic Books.

Bucci, W. (in press). *The dual code theory: Psychoanalysis and cognitive science.* New York: Guilford Press.

Buck, R. (1985). Prime theory: An integrated view of motivation and emotion. *Psychological Review, 92,* 389–413.

Darwin, C. (1955). *The expression of the emotions in man and animals.* New York: Philosophical Library. (Original work published 1872)

Ellis, A. (1962). *Reason and emotion in psychotherapy.* New York: Lyle Stuart.

Epstein, S. (1973). The self-concept revisited, or a theory of a theory. *American Psychologist, 28,* 404–416.

Epstein, S. (1976). Anxiety, arousal and the self-concept. In I. G. Sarason & C. D. Spielberger (Eds.), *Stress and anxiety* (pp. 183–224). Washington, DC: Hemisphere.

Epstein, S. (1979a). Natural healing processes of the mind: I. Acute schizophrenic disorganization. *Schizophrenia Bulletin, 5,* 313–321.

Epstein, S. (1979b). The ecological study of emotions in humans. In P. Pliner, K. R. Blankstein, & I. M. Spigel (Eds.), *Advances in the study of communication and affect: Vol. 5: Perception of emotions in self and others* (pp. 47–83). New York: Plenum Press.

Epstein, S. (1980). The self-concept: A review and the proposal of an integrated theory of personality. In E. Staub (Ed.), *Personality: Basic issues and current research* (pp. 82–132). Englewood Cliffs, NJ: Prentice-Hall.

Epstein, S. (1981). The unity principle versus the reality and pleasure principles, or the tale of the scorpion and the frog. In M. D. Lynch, A. A. Norem-Hebeisen, & K. J. Gergen (Eds.), *Self-concept: Advances in theory and research* (pp. 27–37). Cambridge, MA: Ballinger.

Epstein, S. (1983a). A research paradigm for the study of personality and emotions. In M. M. Page (Ed.), *Nebraska Symposium on Motivation: Vol. 31. Personality—Current theory and research* (pp. 91–154). Lincoln: University of Nebraska Press.

Epstein, S. (1983b). The unconscious, the preconscious and the self-concept. In J. Suls & A. Greenwald (Eds.), *Psychological perspectives on the self* (Vol. 2, pp. 219–247). Hillsdale, NJ: Erlbaum.

Epstein, S. (1984). Controversial issues in emotion theory. In P. Shaver (Ed.), *Annual review of research in person-ality and social psychology* (pp. 64–87). Beverly Hills, CA: Sage.

Epstein, S. (1985). The implications of cognitive–experiential self-theory for research in social psychology and personality. *Journal for the Theory of Social Behaviour, 15,* 283–310.

Epstein, S. (1987). Implications of cognitive self-theory for psychopathology and psychotherapy. In N. Cheshire & H. Thomae (Eds.), *Self, symptoms and psychotherapy* (pp. 43–58). New York: Wiley.

Epstein, S. (1989). Values from the perspective of cognitive–experiential self-theory. In N. Eisenberg, J. Reykowski, & E. Staub (Eds.), *Social and moral values* (pp. 3–22). Hillsdale, NJ: Erlbaum.

Epstein, S. (1990). Cognitive–experiential self-theory. In L. A. Pervin (Ed.), *Handbook of personality: Theory and research* (pp. 165–192). New York: Guilford Press.

Epstein, S. (1991a). The self-concept, the traumatic neurosis, and the structure of personality. In D. Ozer, J. M. Healy, Jr., & A. J. Stewart (Eds.), *Perspectives in personality* (Vol. 3A, pp. 63–98). London: Jessica Kingsley.

Epstein, S. (1991b). Cognitive–experiential self-theory: An integrative theory of personality. In R. C. Curtis (Ed.), *The relational self: Theoretical convergences of psychoanalysis and social psychology* (pp. 111–137). New York: Guilford Press.

Epstein, S. (1991c). Cognitive–experiential self-theory: Implications for developmental psychology. In M. Gunnar & L. A. Sroufe (Eds.), *Minnesota Symposium on Child Psychology: Vol. 23. Self-processes and development* (pp. 79–123). Hillsdale, NJ: Erlbaum.

Epstein, S. (1992). The cognitive self, the psychoanalytic self, and the forgotten selves: Comment on Drew Westen's "The cognitive self and the psychoanalytic self: Can we put our selves together?" *Psychological Inquiry, 3,* 34–38.

Epstein, S. (in press). Bereavement from the perspective of cognitive–experiential self-theory. In M. S. Stroebe, W. Stroebe, & R. O. Hansson (Eds.), *Sourcebook of bereavement.* New York: Cambridge University Press.

Epstein, S., & Erskine, N. (1983). The development of personal theories of reality. In D. Magnusson & V. Allen (Eds.), *Human development: An interactional perspective* (pp. 133–147). New York: Academic Press.

Epstein, S., Lipson, A., Holstein, C., & Huh, E. (1992). Irrational reactions to negative outcomes: Evidence for two conceptual systems. *Journal of Personality and Social Psychology, 62,* 328–339.

Erikson, E. H. (1959). Identity and the life cycle: Selected papers. *Psychological Issues, 1,* 5–165.

Erikson, E. H. (1963). *Childhood and society* (2nd ed.). New York: Norton.

Erikson, E. H. (1968). *Identity: Youth and crisis.* New York: Norton.

Fairbairn, W. R. D. (1954). *An object relations theory of the personality.* New York: Basic Books.

Fiske, S. L., & Taylor, S. E. (1991). *Social cognition* (2nd ed.). New York: McGraw-Hill.

Freud, S. (1955). Beyond the pleasure principle. In J. Strachey (Ed. and Trans.), *The standard edition of the complete psychological works of Sigmund Freud* (Vol. 18, pp. 3–64). London: Hogarth Press. (Original work published 1920)

Freud, S. (1961). The ego and the id. In J. Strachey (Ed. and Trans.), *The standard edition of the complete psychological works of Sigmund Freud* (Vol. 19, pp. 3–66). London: Hogarth Press. (Original work published 1923)

Freud, S. (1964). New introductory lectures on psycho-analysis. In J. Strachey (Ed. and Trans.), *The standard edition of the complete psychological works of Sigmund Freud* (Vol. 22, pp. 1–182). London: Hogarth Press. (Original work published 1933)

Greenwald, A. G., & Pratkanis, A. R. (1984). The self. In R. S. Wyer, Jr., & T. K. Srull (Eds.) *Handbook of social cognition* (Vol. 3, pp. 129–178). Hillsdale, NJ: Erlbaum.

Higgins, E. T. (1987). Self-discrepancy: A theory relating self and affect. *Psychological Review, 94*, 319–340.

Horney, K. (1950). *Neurosis and human growth.* New York: Norton.

Horowitz, M. J. (1976). *Stress response syndromes.* New York: Jason Aronson.

Horowitz, M. J. (1988). *Introduction to psychodynamics.* New York: Basic Books.

James, W. (1890). *The principles of psychology* (Vol. 1). New York: Henry Holt.

James, W. (1907). *Psychology: The briefer course.* New York: Holt.

Kelly, G. A. (1955). *The psychology of personal constructs* (2 vols). New York: Norton.

Kihlstrom, J. F. (1987). The cognitive unconscious. *Science, 237*, 1145–1152.

Kirkpatrick, L. A., & Epstein, S. (1992). Cognitive–experiential self-theory and subjective probability: Further evidence for two conceptual systems. *Journal of Personality and Social Psychology, 63*, 534–544.

Kohut, H. (1971). *The analysis of the self.* New York: International Universities Press.

Kohut, H. (1977). *The restoration of the self.* New York: International Universities Press.

Labouvie-Vief, G. (1982). Dynamic development and mature autonomy: A theoretical prologue. *Human Development, 25*, 161–191.

Labouvie-Vief, G., Hakim-Larson, J., DeVoe, M., & Schoeberlein, S. (1989). Emotions and self-regulation: A life span view. *Human Development, 32*, 279–299.

Lazarus, R. S. (1991). *Emotion and adaptation.* New York: Oxford University Press.

Lecky, P. (1961). *Self-consistency: A theory of personality.* Hamden, CT: Shoe String Press.

Leventhal, H. (1982). The integration of emotion and cognition: A view from the perceptual–motor theory of emotion. In M. S. Clark & S. T. Fiske (Eds.), *Affect and cognition: The Seventeenth Annual Carnegie Symposium on Cognition* (pp. 121–156). Hillsdale, NJ: Erlbaum.

Markus, H. (1977). Self-schemata and processing information about the self. *Journal of Personality and Social Psychology, 35*, 63–78.

Markus, H., & Nurius, P. (1986). Possible selves. *American Psychologist, 41*, 954–969.

Markus, H., & Wurf, E. (1987). The dynamic self-concept: A social psychological perspective. *Annual Review of Psychology, 38*, 229–337.

McCann, I. L., & Pearlman, L. A. (1990). *Psychological trauma and the adult survivor: Theory, therapy, and transformation.* New York: Brunner/Mazel.

Nisbett, R. E., & Wilson, T. D. (1977). Telling more than we can know: Verbal reports on mental processes. *Psychological Review, 84*, 231–259.

Paivio, A. (1986). *Mental representations: A dual-coding approach.* New York: Oxford University Press.

Rogers, C. (1951). *Client-centered therapy: Its current practice, implications, and theory.* Boston: Houghton Mifflin.

Rogers, C. (1959). A theory of therapy, personality, and interpersonal relationships, as developed in the client-centered framework. In S. Koch (Ed.), *Psychology: A study of a science* (Vol. 3, pp. 184–256). New York: McGraw-Hill.

Rosch, E. (1983). Prototype classification and logical classification: The two systems. In E. Scholnick (Ed.), *New trends in conceptual representation: Challenges to Piaget's theory* (pp. 73–86). Hillsdale, NJ: Erlbaum.

Strauman, T. J., & Higgins, E. T. (1987). Automatic activation of self-discrepancies and emotional syndromes: When cognitive structures influence affect. *Journal of Personality and Social Psychology, 53*, 1004–1014.

Sullivan, H. S. (1953). *The interpersonal theory of psychiatry.* New York: Norton.

Swann, W. B., Jr. (1990). To be known or to be adored? The interplay of self-enhancement and self-verification. In E. T. Higgins & R. M. Sorrentino (Eds.), *Handbook of motivation and cognition: Foundations of social behavior* (Vol. 2, pp. 408–448). New York: Guilford Press.

Swann, W. B., Jr., Hixon, J. G., Stein-Seroussi, A., & Gilbert, D. T. (1990). The fleeting gleam of praise: Cognitive processes underlying behavioral reactions to self-relevant feedback. *Journal of Personality and Social Psychology, 59*, 17–26.

Taylor, S. E., & Brown, J. D. (1988). Illusion and well-being: A social psychological perspective on mental health. *Psychological Bulletin, 103*, 193–210.

Tesser, A. (1988). Toward a self-evaluation maintenance model of social behavior. In L. Berkowitz (Ed.), *Advances in experimental social psychology* (Vol. 21, pp. 181–227). New York: Academic Press.

Tesser, A. (1991). Emotion in social comparison and reflection processes. In J. Suls & T. Wills (Eds.), *Social comparison: Contemporary theory and research* (pp. 115–145). Hillsdale, NJ: Erlbaum.

Tversky, A., & Kahneman, D. (1974). Judgement under uncertainty: Heuristics and biases. *Science, 185*, 1124–1131.

Tversky, A., & Kahneman, D. (1981). The framing of decisions and the psychology of choice. *Science, 211*, 453–458.

Uleman, J. S., & Bargh, J. A. (Eds.). (1989). *Unintended thought.* New York: Guilford Press.

Weinberger, J., & McClelland, D. C. (1990). Cognitive versus traditional motivational models: Irreconcilable or complementary? In E. T. Higgins & R. M. Sorrentino (Eds.), *Handbook of motivation and cognition: Foundations of social behavior* (Vol. 2, pp. 562–597). New York: Guilford.

Westen, D. (1991). Cultural, emotional, and unconscious aspects of self. In R. C. Curtis (Ed.), *The relational self: Theoretical convergences of psychoanalysis and social psychology* (pp. 181–210). New York: Guilford Press.

Westen, D. (1992). The cognitive self and the psychoanalytic self: Can we put our selves together? *Psychological Inquiry, 3*, 1–13.

23

Emotion and Identity

JEANNETTE M. HAVILAND
PATRICIA KAHLBAUGH

Kohut (1977) described the pervasive disorder of narcissism as one that involves a disorganization of identity. Significantly, narcissism develops when emotions are distorted or denied—not legitimately "mirrored." The search for identity or for the "true inner self" requires the connection of emotion with self-knowledge. This way of looking at emotion and identity reflects an emerging concern with emotion processes in identity formation, change, and maintenance. It also reflects an interest in how social constructs such as individual and group identity create and maintain certain ideas about emotions (Hochschild, 1983; Lutz, 1988; Schweder & LeVine, 1984). Issues of emotion and identity necessarily inform each other and constrain interpretations of each other on a conceptual level as well as on a personal level.

In this chapter, we first describe the perspective on emotion that provides our orientation. Then we describe three ways of organizing personal identity in 20th-century Western culture: (1) identity more rationally dichotomized through consciousness and self-evaluation ("good–bad," "I–me"); (2) identity more empirically compartmentalized as roles, goals, and traits; and (3) identity as a dynamic, creative construct combining the dichotomous and compartmentalized aspects but providing a new *Weltanschauung*. Within each description of an identity construction, we review (a) the place usually and sometimes inevitably assigned to emotion within that construction; (b) the socioideological biases imposed on that construction in connection with emotion; and (c) one or two examples of the changes in theory that have occurred in each construction as new research on emotion has become more fully integrated with that approach.

A PERSPECTIVE ON DIFFERENTIAL EMOTION

Our approach to emotion conceives of different emotions as having separable modes of expression and different functions (Haviland & Kramer, 1991; Haviland & Walker-Andrews, 1992; Izard & Malatesta, 1987; Malatesta, 1990; Tomkins, 1962). For example, in Tomkins's (1962) theory of affect and in theories related to his position, the most basic hypothesis is that different emotions are links between different stimuli and responses, perceived causes and effects, self and others. These links provide contingency between internal events and external events. The "innate scripts . . . connect stimuli and response by imprinting *both* with the same abstract analogic quality and thus amplify both." (Tomkins, 1987, p. 148).

The affects provide "rules for differential resonance to every major abstract profile," according to Tomkins (1987, p. 149). This approach obviously differs from the more social-constructivist approaches in that there is at some level an unconstructed (or, as Tomkins said, "innate") set of emotions or emotion processes. However, as will become apparent, our approach differs from Tomkins's (1962) original theory in that the functions of the basic emotions may be significantly changed in interactions. As the simplest example, a contemptuous smile may not have any of the functions or meanings of smiling at any level. It may also not have any of the functions or meanings of contempt/disgust at any level. When the two emotions interact over time, they may produce something quite different. This "chaotic" element is important in providing a bridge between the discrete-emotions theories and the social-constructivist theories. If one accepts the premise that basic emotions function as systems over time, then the interaction of two or more such systems is likely to produce chaotic developments (Abraham, Abraham, & Shaw, 1990), from which new networks or processes may emerge.

Emotions are not merely reactive responses to designated things or events, but are the metaphoric forms that "resonate" to and unite scenes, experiences, internal cues, and thoughts. This is not to imply that as metaphors they are imaginary or lacking in substance. Just as a narrative or drawing is an identifiable network connecting analogous elements, an emotion functions because it is an analogic process and form. Just as certain cells of the visual system respond to targeted patterns in the environment telling us that "movement" or a "corner" has been detected, certain other patterns respond to sad, fearful, angry (and so forth) sensory patterns with the information that a "sad," "fearful," or "angry" analogue has been detected. The response patterns for the emotion are adapted then for the designated system. So, for "sadness," the slowed, deliberate, rhythmic, and only slowly variable motions and thoughts are analogous.

Emotions as intervening modes of processing information or as responses have little to do with identity or personality when they are so intrapersonally isolated. Responding with anger to a shove in the subway does not necessarily contribute to identity. However, when several "angry–subway" events become interconnected and attract other events, such as "fear–strangers," then they contribute meaning to each other—leading to an abstraction or rule concerning the emotions and the events, settings, people, or ideas. Now issues related to identity arise.

In our affect approach to identity, emotion is the "glue" of identity that creates chunks of experience through processes of emotional magnification and resonance. This emotion rule helps to discriminate parts of identity that are central organizing nodes from skills or ideals. For example, one may be extremely skillful at reading, but may not have emotionally attached this to other parts of life. Reading is therefore not a central aspect of identity. Or one may have an emotionally magnified set of rules for spiritual mysticism, but may find that the system does not provide information about much of one's daily experience. This may thus be a little-used aspect of identity, or it may be forming part of a split-off section of identity. All these aspects of affect theory tantalize us by beginning to describe the dynamics of intrapersonal meaning and emotion.

In this theory of affect, we would argue that an adaptive and recognizable identity would be interconnected with sets of rules that offer usable information about life and that are emotionally dense. The more of what is necessary in one's life is given meaning by a set of rules, the more power that set has in the total identity. Identity constructions may include many or few sets of these information bits × emotions combinations, but affect theory requires that meaningful information about identity be emotionally magnified. Descriptions of the dynamics of the affect system focus on magnification (largely an intrapersonal process) and on resonance (largely an interpersonal process).

Haviland and Goldston (1992) have described two types of emotional magnification that may be useful in identity constructions. On the one hand, a single content issue or theme may be "emotionally elaborated,"—that is, associated frequently with many different emotions. For example, affiliative behavior is emotionally elaborated by adults but not by children; events and objects are more emotionally elaborated by children (see also Stapley & Haviland, 1989). Also, there are significant gender differences in the emotional elaborations of affiliation during adolescence. Adolescent girls relate happiness, anger, fear, shame, and so forth to same-sex and opposite-sex relationships, but adolescent boys relate only happiness to affiliation with any frequency. According to the present definition, affiliation is more emotionally elaborated for adolescent girls because it is associated with diverse emotions. Presumably affiliation is more central in the girls' identities as well. It is not just the frequency of emotional episodes that is important, but the diversity. To emotionally elaborate or magnify content is not merely to decorate it, but is to give that content a particular motivational association of an irresistible nature. The same relationship is capable of being experienced in any emotional state; it is emotionally and cognitively "hot." There is some evidence that such emotionally elaborated roles are difficult to abandon (Tomkins, 1987) and productive of cognitive change (Haviland & Kramer, 1991).

On the other hand, a single emotion can be "content-elaborated," and this has a different significance. For example, if being "exhilarated" is related to death, love, life, thought, and so forth, as it was for Virginia Woolf (Haviland, 1984), then one would argue that exhilaration or qualities of excitement are content-elaborated. Perhaps one would argue that this is a working definition of a personality dimension—that Woolf was a person who needed exhilaration and sought it everywhere. The content elaboration of an emotion produces emotion scripts in which the experience of an emotion is the primary, and sometimes the inflexible, link between different roles or scenes. In this concept, one critical consideration is that the emotion is assumed to have a special role in the individual's identity (see Malatesta, 1990).

The role of emotional magnification has been considered largely as an intrapsychic phenomenon in affect theory. It is somewhat puzzling that the other major emotional process—emotional contagion or resonance—has also frequently been considered to be an intrapsychic phenomenon, although it could be used interpersonally (e.g., Hatfield, Cacioppo, & Rapson, 1992; Haviland & Lelwica, 1987; Hoffman, 1977; Zahn-Waxler & Radke-Yarrow, 1990). The concept of resonance is most often used in affect theories to explain how primitive emotional communication operates. The forms or signs of emotions in oneself or a companion are considered sufficient information to produce or induce emotionally analogous behaviors. So smiling deliberately at oneself aids in intrapersonal resonance with happiness, just as the smile of another will have a similar interpersonal effect. However, the processes of resonance can be conceptually and experimentally expanded to include many social constructions of emotion.

Progress in the study of emotion is just beginning to lead to a comprehension of emotional processes in identity construction. Historically, emotional processes such as magnification or resonance (in their diverse forms) have only been suspected to be primary factors in identity formation. Why were emotions portrayed simply as one of many types of "responses" to important aspects of self, or why were they seen as having a primitive, negative, disorganizing impact on "higher" identity processes?

Sociologists and historians, as well as psychologists, have examined such questions and argue that individual identity issues are complementary to sociocultural identity issues, which—to make a grand circle—are reflected back in scholarly theories (e.g., Simon, 1992). The beliefs and perceptions of individual scholars are not separate from their sources of knowledge. Perceptions or constructions of emotion and identity are reflected in, and themselves reflect, cultural perceptions or constructions. Likewise, scholarly ways of considering personal identity, even theories of identity, are reflections on a larger cultural scale of the processes that occur individually. Emotional processes occurring within a culture influence individual identity constructions at every level and are themselves influenced by such constructions. If individual identities can vary and cultural identities can vary, so also can the uses and functions of emotions. Acknowledging this interactive process, we comment in the remainder of this chapter on the implications of each approach to identity for socioideological positions.

IDENTITY CONSTRUCTIONS AS GESTALTS

In this section we look at identity constructions as gestalts. By "gestalt," we mean that the construct can be figuratively portrayed in terms of the number of elements it is likely to contain and their most likely arrangement. As the figures show, the three general types that we portray differ in the number of elements and then also in the number and type of relationships that are included. What is not immediately obvious from such a figurative approach is that each gestalt either logically requires, or perhaps by accident has happened to impose, particular requirements on the portrayal of emotion, such that the view of emotion and the view of individual identity support each other. Because of this, we examine "the place of emotion" in each approach. To complete the larger picture, although it is not the main purpose of this chapter, we also comment on the group or cultural identity—the "socio-ideological concerns" that are analogous and supportive of the entire approach. Finally, we illustrate the approach with one or two examples.

Although the basic concept of individual identity requires that each person have a singular identity, the complexity of the singular identity and the types of elements that constitute it vary. Reflecting progressive changes in logic and mathematics, as well as in the social sciences, the study of identity has produced models that roughly fit into the three categories presented here.

Dichotomous Identity Constructions

Numerically, the most simple model is dualistic. Some models rather resemble the "yin–yang" symbol, which we use to represent our dichotomous model, the first one (see Figure 23.1). In the dichotomous models, the existence of some component logically requires its opposite or, at the very least, a separable contrast. So if there is a pleasant side, there must be an unpleasant one; if there is an unconscious side, there must be a conscious one; if there is an emotional side, there must be an unemotional or perhaps rational one; if there is an active side, then there must be a passive one; and so forth. Such dichotomous models may have many collections of opposites contained in them; Jung's (1971) personality model has four sets of logically opposed elements, for example. The critical aspect of the dichotomous model is that every element

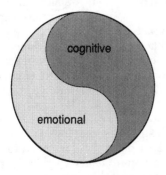

FIGURE 23.1. This illustration of the dichotomous identity shows the broad, undifferentiated "emotion" side of the self contrasted with the "cognition" side of the self.

defined in identity requires and often attracts its opposite. For emotions this has several interesting results. Emotions can be themselves an element requiring an opposite (most usually rationality), but when individual emotions are examined, they also require opposites. Thus happiness requires unhappiness, and so on.

The Place of Emotion

Most traditional dichotomous systems treat emotions as broad, undifferentiated responses that are necessarily contrasted to equally broad and undifferentiated alternatives, such as cognitions. Such approaches have given us theories of "emotionality" in animal behavior (Hall, 1934); theories of bimodal emotional–rational types in personality (Jung, 1971); or, in social psychology, theories of motivational approach–avoidance (Lewin, 1938). However, the dichotomous approaches, because they tend more toward compartmentalism, may also examine specific emotions as opposites of each other (e.g., Schlosberg's [1952] two dimensions of emotion), and thus continue to demonstrate the rationalized, evaluative side of dichotomous systems. Dichotomous systems almost always have evaluative good–bad implications, because the analogy between the dichotomous evaluative approach and any other dichotomy is so obvious and seductive.

Socioideological Concerns

In the dichotomous approaches we see a relationship to two ideas. First, the idea that one part of the self controls the other is similar to the Platonic view of reason as holding the reins on one's emotions (de Sousa, 1987), and is thus congruent with turn-of-the-century approaches to psychology as revisionist philosophy with rational idealism prominent. Second, the distinction between self as experiencer and self as evaluator/interpreter is at the heart of the emotion–cognition dilemma. On the one side, the self is open to the flow of emotion; on the other side, the self reflects on this flow, segmenting it into episodes, sometimes editing it in order to create a coherent picture.

Dichotomous approaches to emotion are compatible with certain ways of looking at identity, both individually and culturally. On the cultural level, historians such as Mitzman (1987) describe the efforts made by "elite" ("high, rational, educated, good") groups of Europeans to constrain the emotional excesses of peasants ("low, emotional, ignorant, bad") in the 17th and 18th centuries. The intellectual association of global emotionality with untutored, undesirable traits may have derived from such historical interludes. In such constructions emotion of any sort is suspect, and the connectionistic (yin–yang) goal in socialization is to harness the emotions and to construct culturally cognized versions of them, such as duty, faith, or patriotism. In this sense, basic emotions as functioning parts of identity have little value.

Dichotomous views of individual identity date from a similar historical time and were dominant at the turn of the last century. Although the culmination of this theory may well have been in G. H. Mead's (1934) work, an earlier version exists in that of William James (1890). In James's dualistic approach to identity, he drew attention to the distinction between the "I" and the "me"—the analytic, rational system versus the automatic, experiential system. This distinction articulates the difference between the subjective self ("I") and the objective self ("me") (see James, 1890, pp. 378–379). This same distinction can be seen even more strongly in Freud's work (e.g., Freud, 1923/1961). If one roughly equates the identity with the id–ego functions, then the id is the originator of activity or the source of motivation, and the ego (with the superego) is the interpreter and evaluator of that activity or motivation. In both examples the interpretation and evaluation of self, which form one's subjective self ("I"), are created in order to control and regulate the "me" or the id. The id, then, is the emotional self, the self that experiences and that motivates. The ego (with the superego) is one's theory of self or one's constructed emotionless social identity. There is no particular requirement in such approaches to identity for different types of emotion; emotionality is quite global. Therefore, questions concerning the different functions of emotions are quite unlikely.

Primarily, the dichotomous position has a tendency to relegate emotions to a primitive—not quite desirable, although necessary—part of the governing self. In research, the stable identity of the adult is studied in terms of its rational components, much as the history of peoples is studied in terms of elite adult leaders. In developmental approaches, the emerging self-conscious (i.e., self-recognizing) identity overtakes the self-experiencing, emotional identity. Only irrational, disturbed, or immature identities deserve being studied in pure emotional terms.

Examples

The dichotomous construction has never been completely absorbed into other constructions, although it has become more compartmentalized and flexible. Even in early theories such as James's, as is implied by the yin–yang model, it has an obvious potential for an interactive quality. Each side of the logical dualism has the potential to inform and influence the other. The interactionist approaches to self proposed by Baldwin (1987/1913), Cooley (1902/1964), or Mead (1934), for example, stressed the interactive quality. These theorists added the interpersonal duality of self–other to other dualisms; they likewise extended the self-evaluative system to visions of the self as evaluated by others and the self as evaluating others, and so forth. A proliferation of good–bad, self–other dichotomies emerged (e.g., "good mother–bad mother"; Sullivan, 1953). However, the dualistic system continued to dichotomize emotion as well as other features. There was still little place for multiple emotions. Since emotions do not always appear to have opposites, nor do they, as a group, always appear to oppose rationality, the dualistic models have presented empirical problems searching for empirical solutions.

To give an example of the dualistic merging into compartmentalization, we consider the modern categorization of two affective disorders, anxiety and depression. Most classifications of mood disorders adhere to the concept that there are at least two classes of negative affect disorders; hence, there is a compartmentalized classification. However, each negative affect disorder contains poorly differentiated negative emotions mixed with other "irrational" symptoms, thus reflecting remnants of the dichotomous approach to emotionality. More importantly, the "cure" for emotional disorders such as depression is cognitive therapy, and that for the anxious/phobic disorders is behavioral therapy. The primitive, undifferentiated, but powerful combinations of negative emotions are disciplined and brought under unified, rational control. There is little recognition that the functional aspects of each negative emotion might be given a place, or that each one might be related to individually differentiated cognitive or perceptual processes (Greenberg & Safran, 1987; Haviland & Goldston, 1992; Schwartz & Clore, 1988).

Recent extrapolations from the dichotomized model used in research on identity have relied on global positive–negative emotional evaluation as part of their method and interpretation. For example, Ogilvie (1987) identifies two (dichotomous) outcomes of emotional interpretation of self: the undesired self and the desired self. The undesired self represents all that we do not wish to become or continue to be—and what we in fact have concretely experienced as the worst part of the self. This definition, of course, still reflects the rational and evaluative point of view, in that even the undesired self is defined within an evaluative ethic. The emotions (negative in this instance) that give the undesired self its meaning act as markers to define the boundaries of self. In the dichotomous mode, we are impelled to move away from the undesired self because of painful negative emotions, even though the same undesired emotions are needed to define the boundaries of identity.

The distinction between good self and bad self, idealized self and actual self in present-day personality research has its roots in the dynamic, clinical work of this century (Adler, 1954; Horney, 1950; Rogers, 1942). Both the modern version (e.g., Ogilvie, 1987) and the early clinical version (e.g., Horney, 1950) of the dichotomized identity acknowledge that the "good" and the "bad" sides of the self use emotion differently. In their descriptions, the undesired self is more closely related to the actual experience of emotion; it is still the emotional side, and it is largely devalued. However, when the dichotomized negative–positive emotions are expanded somewhat and used more broadly as traits, as has occurred in the examples of recent research here, the dichotomized models begin to merge with the compartmentalized models (see also Higgins, 1987).

Compartmentalized Identity Constructions

The empirical problem for emotions that arises in dichotomized approaches seldom occurs in similar fashion for categorical, classification, or compartmentalized approaches. These are in fact the most widespread ways of looking at emotions presently and are presently the most favored modes of examining identity. In the compartmentalized systems—exemplified best by the biological classification strategies (of species, for example)—there are basic groupings that may exist independently of one another. However, it is a major investigatory issue to study their interactions or connections. (In biological classification one examines evolution as a connector among the classifications, for example.) The compartmentalized model is shown in Figure 23.2 as a set (the actual number is only limited empirically, not logically) of identifiable factors, groupings, or basic elements that may interact with one another in interesting manners. The limitation of compartmentalized approaches from the point of view of discrete-emotions theory is that there is no clear way to give each factor or element its own process or way of changing the internal processes of other "compartments." Each compartment is immutable. Each factor is assumed to operate similarly; some attention is paid to its weight, but little attention is paid to the emergence of new components or to the loss over time and circumstances of old ones. Therefore, there is no required, logical organization of the components, as there is in the dichotomous models.

The Place of Emotion

Compartmentalized identity constructions look at identity as a set of relatively independent, interacting factors. Numerically, these constructions are more complex than the dichotomous constructions and tend to be more empirically, less rationally based. In this approach to identity, emotions are usually considered to be traits. In this sense, they are separated from the drive functions and the unconscious functions that flourish in the dichotomous models. Although broadening the dichotomous view by providing multiple traits, the compartmentalized approach to identity traditionally neglects the actual motivational functions of emotions—both magnification and resonance.

This set of compartmentalized theories is supported by a rich tradition in social psychology dating from the middle of this century (e.g., Kelly, 1955; Rosenberg & Jones, 1972). According to the compartmentalized constructions, the internal parameters of an individual's identity consist of multiple roles and traits

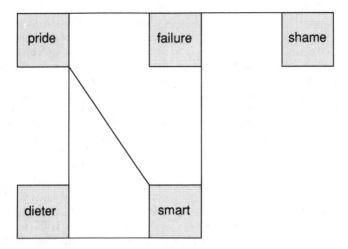

FIGURE 23.2. This illustration of the compartmentalized identity shows emotions as trait types scattered among other traits. Correlative connections are shown forming factors that can then join into a larger identity matrix.

adapted to fit particular life situations. Thus identity is a fairly flexible and pragmatic affair, allowing the individual the opportunity to adapt himself or herself to different situational or person-oriented contexts that arise concurrently as well as developmentally.

One gains insight into identity by examining how people describe themselves in the various compartments of their lives (their activities, characteristics, reactions to situations, and relationships to other people) and by analyzing how these descriptions fall into the various factors (what roles and traits go together and in what situations). Statements such as "I am clever," " I am never guilty," "I am a plumber," and "I am a wife" are all examples of disparate descriptions that can contribute to the structure of one person's identity. Identity is the ordered sum of relationship skills, cognitive skills, feelings, physical abilities, and so forth. These traits are associated with the roles one performs, including relationship roles, work roles, and cultural roles, producing an amalgamated identity or self-structure.

The compartmentalized models, with their implied view of people as autonomous, controlling information processors, tend to neglect the dark, irrational socioemotional combinations common in the evaluative, dichotomous approaches; instead, they give a special place to emotions that promote autonomy, separation, and control. Because of this, when emotion is specifically addressed in these constructions, pride, self-esteem or the lack thereof

(shame), and hostility in the form of self-assertion tend to be emphasized (e.g., Lewis, Sullivan, Stanger, & Weiss, 1989; Schneider, 1977; Sheff, 1988). However, many approaches give no special preference to type of emotion, allowing whatever traits of emotion are offered by an individual a place. Both uses of emotions in defining identity are quite distinct from the dichotomous definitions of emotions as syndromes.

Socioideological Concerns

The compartmentalized person is eminently suited to an autonomous 20th-century culture. To change one's friends or family, to change a job, to change a developmental stage, or to change a global character category, one acquires new traits, reorganizes the old traits, inhibits a few traits. This can be accomplished in a goal-oriented manner (Markus & Nurius, 1986), through the individual's own "self-help" plans, through mandated retraining, or through external organization of environmental demands.

In terms of larger social identities, the compartmentalized identity is closely related to politically anti-class-conscious and socially malleable ideals. Surveys and other "empirical" assessments define political and social groups; there is no acceptance of "natural" sets of elites and *hoi polloi*. If emotion plays a part in identity, it is democratically considered to be one of a multitude of equal trait types—one that can be used or abandoned. One is likely to have "happy" or "ashamed," or, equally, to have "unemotional," as traits right alongside traits such as "attractive" or "clever" or "Republican" or "middle-class." A person is a combination of the "self-made" and "environmentally responsive," but emotional processes have little explicit role in the formation, maintenance, or development of the compartmentalized identity; they are definitely not the "glue" of identity.

Examples

At first glance, the personality and identity theories of modern compartmentalist thinkers may appear to have incorporated emotion. For example, the comprehensive five-factor theory of personality (for an overview, see McCrae & Costa, 1989) includes many emotional items. However, this is only superficial. The five-factor approach, like other compartmentalized theories, is a static presentation with no developmental aspects and no dynamic processes. Each of the factors, as well as each of the trait items composing the factors, is treated without consideration of the possibilities that the traits on one factor may organize certain features of identity in one way and that other traits or factors may have nonequal, very different functions. Factor loadings may indicate something about absolute intensity or frequency, but do not contribute directly to an understanding of dynamic processes or functions. This outcome of compartmentalized approaches leads them to be incompatible with dichotomous approaches, with their opposing elements and different processes (Horney, 1950; Ogilvie, 1987).

A recent developmental approach (Haviland, Davidson, Lancelot, & Reutsch, 1992) has combined a compartmentalized approach with differential affect theory. The research emerged from an Eriksonian (Erikson, 1968; see also Loevinger, 1976) concept of identity. Erikson proposed that the optimal time to form an identity is not in childhood, but in late adolescence. Unlike Freud, who sought the control of undifferentiated affect through Oedipal (ego) identification, Erikson argued that the identification with parents and consequent suppression of negative affect are not the equivalent of attaining an adult identity, but almost the opposite: Childhood identifications form only a potential foundation for identity.

Eriksonian theory (e.g., Marcia, 1966) describes an adolescent identity crisis that proceeds from a very limited "foreclosure" position, in which only roles defined and acceptable in childhood are contained in the identity. This "foreclosure" is followed by trial stages or new categories of behavior, in which new roles are investigated and then used to form a more adult identity structure adapted for the culture of the person's future adult life. Using the compartmentalized model, Haviland et al. (1992) predicted that the interaction of the clusters of roles and traits would change. Roles and emotion traits were gleaned from cross-sectional interviews with children from ages 10 to 18. It was found that childhood roles during childhood were emotionally elaborated with all types of emotion; that is, they were associated with many positive and negative emotions. For children at the beginning of adolescent identity change, only a few *negative* emotions were connected with childhood roles. At this point there were few connections among roles in general, and they were weakly magnified by emotion. There were no complex or hierarchical connecting organizations among the roles. For most middle to late adolescents, disparate, chaotic role–trait clusters of a highly idiosyncratic nature occurred. For example, the most elaborated role might be "me as a dieter" or "me as a Grateful Dead follower." The traditional roles of "son/daughter," "student," or "friend" were not more elaborated than these idiosyncratic roles and were sometimes less elaborated. In young adulthood, again, roles were intricately interconnected and elaborated by all types of emotion.

The Haviland et al. (1992) study suggests that the affect-based approach to identity holds some promise in describing change, as the dichotomous approaches predicted. The emotion traits do not appear to be equal to other traits, but their inclusion or exclusion from compartments in the identity set is related to the complexity and stability of the set connections. This is just another way of saying that the elaboration of roles with emotion is related to the saliency of particular roles in identity. To use the concept of emotional elaboration, identity transformation occurs when the emotional salience or power of childhood roles changes.

In an analysis of Anne Frank's diary, written during her adolescence, a similar change was found in the content that was elaborated with emotion (Haviland & Kramer, 1991). And general survey studies have found consistent developmental change in the events that are emotionally elaborated (Haviland & Goldston, 1992). Although the emotional elaboration of different events across development may be a commonplace notion, the connection of this with identity is a new use for old concepts.

Dynamic Identity Constructions

The final type of model, the dynamic, has had very limited impact in psychology as yet (see Abraham et al., 1990; Levine & Fitzgerald, 1992), although its scientific and philosophical merits have reached beyond the scientific community into the popular press, where the shorthand term for much of the approach is "chaos" (see Gleick, 1987). Dynamic systems or chaotic systems theory is devoted to the elements of motion; it is the science of process rather than state. Whereas both of the models discussed earlier posit static, linear, and additive components changing in their total gestalt because of additive interaction (if they change at all), the dynamic model predicts nonlinear change (i.e., new features emerge nonlinearly) whenever two or more oscillating systems interact (such as oscillations in the system of socioemotional awareness and oscillations in the system of family interaction; see Figure 23.3).

The dynamic model is pictured in Figure 23.3 as a simple example of nonlinear change emerging when a single, tight system (interested emotional awareness of family) begins to encompass too much space and then becomes

attracted to oppositional forces (interested and contemptuous awareness), eventually forming a more complex system. This is the best of the three types of models for beginning to clarify how different emotions can interact to produce emotional behavior that is quite different from what would be predicted for each one independently. It should also be better than the other two for addressing the problems presented by social constructionism in emotion models operating along with resonating, discrete emotional systems.

Dynamic systems theorists look for many processes that will be useful in psychology, such as small effects' becoming larger and vice versa, rather than effects' remaining constant. They also look for the splitting (called "bifurcation" in dynamic systems) of a single system into two systems with different and even opposing properties, rather than linear, cumulative processes.

The Place of Emotion

Emotions may have a more functional place in dynamic constructions; however, the approach is in its infancy and much of the present discussion looks toward the future rather than reviewing a certain past. In the dynamic approach, identity is a product of intersubjective memories, present events, and emotional resonances; all of these change over time, constantly providing new configurations as well as periodic repetitions. Emotional events as motivational systems that help make up identity are likely to have a special role in changing the larger system and in maintain-

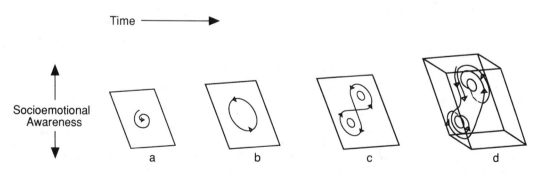

FIGURE 23.3. This illustration of the dynamic identity shows change in the identity system from time (a) to (d). In (a) a small system such as family behavior is attracted to a single emotion such as "interest." In (b) the expanded awareness of "my family" is incorporating more features, some of which are on the boundary and thus very weakly attracted by "interest." In (c) a new attractor such as "contempt" has pulled some of the family features to form an oppositional system. In (d) "interest" and "contempt" as attractors have formed a new family system.

ing it. It is not necessary in dynamic approaches that emotion be a "large" effect, as in constituting a static compartment. An emotional experience may be a periodic effect and small at the origin of the behavior being studied. In dynamic systems theory, such effects are called "butterfly" effects. They are not necessarily reproducible, because the context in which they operate may not be reproducible, but they may nevertheless be critical. For example, this approach is compatible with so-called "unscientific" approaches in psychoanalytic cases, in which nonreproducible systems are modeled as requiring large effects (serious adult disorders) from small occurrences (traumatic, emotionally elaborated childhood events).

To go back to the consideration of affect magnifications and the hypothesis that emotion is the "glue" of identity, one can anticipate that a dynamic approach will be more likely to need information about the "small" processes involved in emotion than will the static dichotomous or compartmentalized approaches. Also the possibility that identity or the emotional elements in it can resonate with one another and with other people's emotions opens up a great many possibilities for crisis and change.

In the sense that dynamic identity approaches can focus on intersubjective identity as aspects of two or more changing systems, there is a clearer need in these conceptualizations for emotions that function to create empathy (attractions) as well as autonomy (bifurcations)—that is, that lead to an attraction of disparate systems as well as clear boundaries and spin-offs. Therefore, they are just as likely to place value on happiness and interest as on sadness, fear, and anger or even shame, pride, and contempt.

Socioideological Concerns

The dynamic approach is part of the *Zeitgeist* in which uniqueness is anticipated, rather than global evaluations or systematic, controlled interactions. It also reflects an appreciation for the importance of small effects on large systems and large effects on small systems. This is the ethos that can argue for preserving seemingly superfluous endangered species on the chaotic off-chance that they will be needed for future biotechnology.

Finally, the dynamic approach is a logical and mathematical outcome of the dichotomous

combined with the compartmentalized approaches. In dichotomous approaches, with their anticipation of attractive and antagonistic sides of identity issues (love–hate relationships, enjoying anger, being self-destructive with self-indulgence, etc.), one detects the seed of the idea for splitting or bifurcations. In the compartmentalized approaches, one detects the seed of the idea that every empirically observed factor, no matter how illogical, has the potential to enter the predictive equations for boundaries and divisions or bifurcations in essential ways.

The importance of more or less independent, oscillating systems in intrapersonal and interpersonal processes appears in feminist and family psychologies, in which meanings arise from interactions that are not present in either system alone and in which minor alterations in the quality of the interactions lead to autonomous meanings (e.g., Chodorow, 1978; Grotevant & Cooper, 1986). In Europe, several of the dynamic clinical psychologies or epistemological philosophies (Foucault, 1973; Kohut, 1971; Miller, 1979; Piaget, 1951) also have qualities similar to the ones described in the dynamic approach, although some of them are fairly teleological (e.g., Piaget, 1951). Empirical approaches to dynamic systems in psychology have begun to appear in the United States (Abraham et al., 1990; Levine & Fitzgerald, 1992; Thelen, 1988), but the ties to identity and emotion are just emerging. The requirement of the dynamic approach leads to the hypothesis that the singularity, predictability, and stability of identity are illusions of sorts. Faith in the predictability of identity is rather like faith in the predictability or stability of weather or stock market reports. The long-term weather reports may tell one about climate and the boundaries on predicting certain types of storms, but they are quite poor at pinpointing specific or singular weather events in time.

Examples

In a way, several lines of research that are emotion-specific anticipate the dynamic approaches. This research has opened the window occasionally to considering the particular emotions of enjoyment/pleasure (Isen, 1990), anger (Dodge & Coie, 1987), sadness (Zahn-Waxler & Radke-Yarrow, 1990), or excitement (Stern, 1985), as well as the various emotions of autonomy (Lewis et al., 1989). In every case, the research demonstrates that approaches to each emotion require consideration of social and cognitive contexts as well as moods, and that different time (developmental and linear) scales affect processes.

With new research on emotional development, there has been a reconstruction of dichotomous interactional approaches, and new related theories have emerged independently. As Stern (1985) has noted, for example, research on the emotional and cognitive capacities of infants has led away from an emphasis on autonomous functions of the self, as well as away from dichotomous psychoanalytic constructions. Stern relies upon research demonstrating that infants and their mothers respond to each other's emotion signals, and seem to change their patterns of response both to regulate the exchange and to regulate their separate experiences. They thereby create new systems of relationships in which the old signals may take on new meanings and functions adapted for the new system.

An example of recent research on the interaction of intrapersonal and interpersonal emotions is Kahlbaugh's work (Kahlbaugh, 1992; Kahlbaugh & Haviland, in press). Adolescents and their parents were videotaped having a family conversation, and their nonverbal behaviors were coded. Younger adolescents (aged 11 to 13 years) showed more hiding, covering, and self-examination (shame behaviors) than older adolescents and children (and more than their parents). They did not diminish the amount of affiliative behavior they displayed; however, it became more coy, and even the affiliation appeared more self-conscious, perhaps controlling. Tomkins (1962) suggested that when people become too excited or too emotional they may cover their faces, using shame to contain excitement. Adolescents, because of changes in cognitive and social awareness, give expanded meaning to old displays, and this expanded meaning includes a self-consciousness and other-consciousness that the adolescents have difficulty modulating.

The young adolescents averted their gaze, played with their hands and hair, and covered their faces. Conceptually similar behaviors have also been reported by Elkind and Bowen (1979) in work on adolescent egocentrism and self-consciousness. Young adolescents are presumed to be more vulnerable to shame both because of changes in interpersonal psycho- social support and because of changes in the intrapersonal experience of emotion related to physical and cognitive changes (e.g., Lynd, 1958). However, there is nothing overtly hostile in the shame–affiliation combination. Obviously, it could be a stable combination; it could resolve itself as a cute, approachable shyness between adolescent and parent. However, the two systems at this developmental age actually occur just before a very different set of nonverbal behaviors seen in the laboratory study. Looking at the next older adolescent group, we get some insight into how the association of shame with affiliation may emerge as one method for attracting even more separating types of displays.

In the laboratory study, slightly older adolescents combined continued shame behavior with strong contempt displays. They were not openly hostile (no clear anger displays in this situation) to their parents, but expressed a fairly contained distancing emotion, contempt. They crossed their arms across their chests, leaned conspicuously back in their chairs, and made rapid disgust facial expressions. Again, they maintained their affiliative behavior. One may use contempt to express superiority and to assert power, thus giving the impression of security. The idea that new adolescent events provide the setting for a bifurcation (first affiliation into affiliation and shame, and then into affiliation, shame, and contempt) in emotional displays is potentially represented in this description. Also, the concept that specific emotions (shame and contempt) can attract each other or compensate for each other is not new. In this example, the displays of shame and contempt are not two types of affiliation display, but are new elements. Nothing in the affiliation display alone anticipates the new systems, but the other systems and the time line can present the model of emerging differentiation. Emotions play a primary, functional role in these interpersonal identity constructions. The power of emotional experiences provides explanations for dynamic interpersonal identity constructions.

OVERVIEW AND SUMMARY

It will have struck the reader that this chapter is compartmentalized and has many dichotomous features as well. It avoids explicit reference to emotional issues relative to the dynamic organization of the chapter. This is significant in the sense that it reflects a continuing emphasis in the history of academic psychology, which requires the compartmentalization and separation of the individual from scholarly reflection; one would be "shamed" to be personally revealing in this context. Even so, the chapter illustrates the position that our personal identities and mass identities, and equally our theories and research on identity, evolve largely out of the history of how our emotions have been responded to, elicited, shaped, and socialized. The fact that there is little concern with the process of constructing the chapter and its dynamic aspects is yet one more example of the hold that the static models have (one is "ashamed" to violate the separation).

Without explicit examination of the role of emotions, the theories and research directed to identity reflect the boundaries of a subconscious status of emotion in personal and mass identity. In the sense that sociologists and anthropologists describe the emergence of sociocultural structure from individual structures, there is a reverse process in which cultural structure dictates the individual. These dichotomous, compartmentalized, and potential dynamic constructions of identity are all truthful constructions, in the sense that they can reflect experience. If there is another level of truthfulness at which unnoted processes act, it may also be the case that we can document a historical and developmental process in identity construction. Erikson (1968) foretold such processes when he suggested that a sense of a consciousness about history and culture did not emerge in identity until late in human history. On a smaller scale, the emergence of an identity that is emotionally integrative and dynamic may have awaited recent interests in emotion and other motivational processes, and vice versa.

REFERENCES

Abraham, F. D., Abraham, R. H., & Shaw, C. D. (1990). *A visual introduction to dynamical systems theory for psychology*. Santa Cruz, CA: Aerial Press.

Adler, A. (1954). *Understanding human nature*. New York: Fawcett.

Baldwin, J. M. (1913). *Social and ethical interpretations in mental development*. New York: Macmillan. (Original work published 1897)

Chodorow, N. (1978). *The reproduction of mothering: Psychoanalysis and the sociology of gender*. Berkeley: University of California Press.

Cooley, C. H. (1964). *Human nature and the social order* (rev. ed.). New York: Schocken Books. (Original work published 1902)

de Sousa, R. (1987). *The rationality of emotion*. Cambridge, MA: MIT Press.

Dodge, K. A., & Coie, J. D. (1987). Social-information-processing factors in reactive and proactive aggression in children's peer groups. *Journal of Personality and Social Psychology, 53*, 1146–1158.

Elkind, D., & Bowen, R. (1979). Imaginary audience behavior in children and adolescents. *Developmental Psychology, 15*, 38–44.

Erikson, E. H. (1968). *Identity: Youth and crisis*. New York: Norton.

Foucault, M. (1973). *The order of things*. New York: Vintage Books.

Freud, S. (1961). The ego and the id. In J. Strachey (Ed. and Trans.) *The standard edition of the complete psychological works of Sigmund Freud* (Vol. 19, pp. 3–66). London: Hogarth Press. (Original work published 1923)

Gleick, J. (1987). *Chaos: Making a new science*. New York: Penguin Viking Press.

Greenberg, L. S., & Safran, J. D. (1987). *Emotion in psychotherapy*. New York: Guilford Press.

Grotevant, H. D., & Cooper, C. (1986). Individuation in family relationships: A perspective on individual differences in the development of identity and role-taking skill in adolescence. *Human Development, 29*, 82–100.

Hall, C. S. (1934). Emotional behavior in the rat: I. Defaecation and urination as measures of individual differences in emotionality. *Journal of Comparative Psychology, 18*, 385–403.

Hatfield, E., Cacioppo, J. T., & Rapson, R. (1992). The logic of emotion: Emotional contagion. In M. S. Clark (Ed.), *Review of personality and social psychology: Vol. 14. Emotional and social behavior* (pp. 151–177). Newbury Park, CA: Sage.

Haviland, J. M. (1984). Thinking and feeling in Woolf's writing: From childhood to adulthood. In C. E. Izard, J. Kagan & R. B. Zajonc (Eds.), *Emotions, cognition, and behavior* (pp. 515–546). Cambridge, England: Cambridge University Press.

Haviland, J. M., Davidson, R., Lancelot, C., & Reutsch, C. (1992). *Paradoxes of adolescent mood, identity development and contraception*. Paper presented at a National Institute of Mental Health workshop on Affective Processes in Adolescence, Rockville, MD.

Haviland, J. M., & Goldston, R. (1992). The agony and the ecstasy: Emotion in narrative. In K. Strongman (Ed.), *International review of studies on emotion* (Vol. 2, pp. 219–247). Chichester, England: Wiley.

Haviland, J. M., & Kramer, D. A. (1991). Affect–cognition relations in an adolescent diary: I. The case of Anne Frank. *Human Development, 34*, 143–159.

Haviland, J. M., & Lelwica, M. (1987). The induced affect response: 10-week-old infants' responses to three emotion expressions. *Developmental Psychology, 23*, 97–104.

Haviland, J. M., & Walker-Andrews, A. (1992). An ecological approach to affect theory and social development. In V. B. Hasselt & M. Hersen (Eds.), *Handbook of social development: A life-span perspective* (pp. 29–49). New York: Plenum Press.

Higgins, E. T. (1987). Self-discrepancy: A theory relating self and affect. *Psychological Review, 94*, 319–340.

Hochschild, A. R. (1983). *The managed heart: The commercialization of human feeling*. Berkeley: University of California Press.

Hoffman, M. L. (1977). Empathy: Its development and

prosocial implications. In C. B. Keasey (Ed.), *Nebraska Symposium on Motivation* (Vol. 26, pp. 169–217). Lincoln: University of Nebraska Press.

Horney, K. (1950). *Neurosis and human growth*. New York: Norton.

Isen, A. (1990). The influence of positive and negative affect on cognitive organization: Some implications for development. In N. Stein, B. Leventhal, & T. Trabasso (Eds.), *Psychological and biological approaches to emotion* (pp. 75–94). Hillsdale, NJ: Erlbaum.

Izard, C. E., & Malatesta, C. Z. (1987). Perspectives on emotional development: I. Differential emotions theory of early emotional development. In J. D. Osofsky (Ed.), *Handbook of infant development* (2nd ed., pp. 494–554). New York: Wiley-Interscience.

James, W. (1890). *The principles of psychology* (Vol. 1). New York: Henry Holt.

Jung, C. C. (1971). *Psychological types*. Princeton, NJ: Princeton University Press.

Kahlbaugh, P. (1992). *Shame and contempt in adolescent family transformations*. Unpublished doctoral dissertation, Rutgers University.

Kahlbaugh, P., & Haviland, J. M. (in press). Nonverbal communication between parents and adolescents: A study of approach and avoidance behaviors. *Journal of Nonverbal Behavior*.

Kelly, G. A. (1955). *The psychology of personal constructs* (2 vols.). New York: Norton.

Kohut, H. (1971). *The analysis of the self*. New York: International Universities Press.

Kohut, H. (1977). *The restoration of the self*. New York: International Universities Press.

Levine, R.., & Fitzgerald, H. E. (Eds.). (1992). *Analysis of dynamic systems in psychology*. New York: Plenum Press.

Lewin, K. (1938). *The conceptual representation and measurement of psychological forces*. Durham, NC: Duke University Press.

Lewis, M., Sullivan, M. W., Stanger, C., & Weiss, M. (1989). Self development and self-conscious emotions. *Child Development, 60*, 146–156.

Loevinger, J. (1976). *Ego development: Conceptions and theories*. San Francisco: Jossey-Bass.

Lutz, C. (1988). *Unnatural emotions: Everyday sentiments on a Micronesian atoll and their challenge to Western theory*. Chicago: University of Chicago Press.

Lynd, H. M. (1958). *On shame and the search for identity*. New York: Harcourt, Brace.

Malatesta, C. Z. (1990). The role of emotions in the development and organization of personality. In R. A. Thompson (Ed.), *Nebraska Symposium on Motivation: Vol. 36. Socioemotional development* (pp. 1–56). Lincoln: University of Nebraska Press.

Marcia, J. E. (1966). Development and validation of ego-identity status. *Journal of Personality and Social Psychology, 3*, 551–558.

Markus, H., & Nurius, P. (1986). Possible selves. *American Psychologist, 41*, 954–969.

McCrae, R. R., & Costa, P. T. (1989). The structure of interpersonal traits: Wiggins's circumplex and the five-factor model. *Journal of Personality, 57*, 17–40.

Mead, G. H. (1934). *Mind, self and society*. Chicago: University of Chicago Press.

Miller, A. (1979). *Prisoners of childhood*. New York: Basic Books.

Mitzman, A. (1987). The civilizing offensive: Mentalities, high culture and individual psyches. *Journal of Social History, 20*, 663–688.

Ogilvie, D. M. (1987). The undesired self: A neglected variable in personality research. *Journal of Personality and Social Psychology, 52*, 379–385.

Piaget, J. (1951). *Play, dreams and imitation in childhood*. London: Routledge & Kegan Paul.

Rogers, C. (1942). *Counseling and psychotherapy*. Cambridge, MA: Riverside Press.

Rosenberg, S., & Jones, R. A. (1972). A method for investigating and representing a person's implicit personality theory: Theodore Dreiser's view of people. *Journal of Personality and Social Psychology, 22*, 372–386.

Schlosberg, H. (1952). The description of facial expressions in terms of two dimensions. *Journal of Experimental Psychology, 44*, 229–237.

Schneider, C. D. (1977). *Shame, exposure and privacy*. Boston: Beacon Press.

Schwartz, N., & Clore, G. L. (1988). How do I feel about it? The informative function of affective states. In K. Fiedler & J. P. Forgas (Eds.), *Affect, cognition and social behavior* (pp. 42–62). Toronto: Hogrefe.

Schweder, R. A., & LeVine, R. A. (Eds.). (1984). *Culture theory: Essays on mind, self and emotion*. Cambridge, England: Cambridge University Press.

Sheff, T. (1988). Shame and conformity: The deference-emotion system. *American Sociological Review, 53*, 395–406.

Simon, H. A. (1992). What is an "explanation" of behavior? *Psychological Science, 3*, 150–161.

Stapley, J., & Haviland, J. M. (1989). Beyond depression: Gender differences in normal adolescents' emotional experiences. *Sex Roles, 20*, 295–308.

Stern, D. (1985). *The interpersonal world of the infant*. New York: Basic Books.

Sullivan, H. S. (1953). *The interpersonal theory of psychiatry*. New York: Norton.

Thelen, E. (1988). Self-organization in developmental processes: Can systems approaches work? In M. Gunnar & E. Thelen (Eds.) *Minnesota Symposium on Child Psychology: Vol. 22. Systems and development* (pp. 77–117). Hillsdale, NJ: Erlbaum.

Tomkins, S. S. (1962). *Affect, imagery, consciousness: Vol. 1. The positive affects*. New York: Springer.

Tomkins, S. S. (1987). Script theory. In J. Aronoff, A. I. Rabin, & R. A. Zucker (Eds.), *The emergence of personality* (pp. 187–216). New York: Springer.

Zahn-Waxler, C., & Radke-Yarrow, M. (1990). The origins of empathic concern. *Motivation and Emotion, 5*, 153–166.

24

Social Construction in Emotions

KEITH OATLEY

INTRODUCTION

Emotions described as "socially constructed" are put together from parts that derive mainly from culture. Repertoires of emotions, according to this approach, are like languages: Although there is no doubt a common basis for language in all human beings, each culture has its own vocabulary, its syntactic forms, its meanings, and its range of pragmatic effects. Comparably, it is argued, each culture has patterns of emotions that are somewhat distinctive, that derive from societal practices, and that convey meanings and effects to members of that culture.

The principal theme of social constructionism is that experience, as well as behavior, is not fixed but protean. Although in everyday life we experience a solid and seamless reality, this reality is largely a social product. This analysis holds for the experience and behavior that we call "emotional." Ideas and experiences that we take to be basic, such as those of self, can differ in different cultures. In the West the self is individualistic, autonomous, the source of action. In many Eastern societies the self is relational, or, as Markus and Kitayama (1991) have said, "interdependent" —derived from belonging to a group. From such basic differences grow differences in emotions. Americans may experience anger when they perceive a threat to their autonomy. For many Asians such threats may not occur, since they neither believe in nor depend on

any such concept—but threats to relatedness may elicit emotions such as anxiety.

The idea of emotions being socially constructed is usually contrasted with biological accounts in which universality is asserted, and continuities of adult emotions with those of nonhuman animals and with those of childhood are pointed out. According to the biological idea, emotions derive from genetically based neural and hormonal programs of response, which include largely involuntary physiological processes, facial expressions, distinctive prosody in speaking, urges to act, and so forth. From the biological perspective emotions are seen as largely fixed, as given, as natural.

One way to see these two approaches is as different theories in competition: Either emotions are socially constructed or they are biological. There is a question, however, as to whether this is a viable way of proceeding at our present level of understanding: Although arguments from either side of a social–biological divide can be readily found, they are often based either on evidence that is ambiguous, or on different working definitions of emotion (which then relate to different kinds of evidence).

The Ambiguity of Evidence

There have been debates about some single pieces of evidence. Consider, for instance, Briggs's (1970) book about the 17 months she spent living with an Inuit family belonging to a group called the Utku. She gives an account of a people who, in contrast to Westerners, encounter the many vicissitudes of Arctic life with calm acceptance and humor. As adults they do not express anger, nor do they use anger in child rearing. This book has been seen by some as evidence for cognitive and social construction. For instance, Solomon (1984) writes that the Utku "do not, as [Briggs's] title *Never in Anger* indicates, get angry. Not only do they not express anger; they do not 'feel' angry, and . . . they do not talk about it. They do not get angry in circumstances that would surely incite us to outrage, and they do not get angry in other circumstances either" (p. 244). Solomon takes the view that, like other emotions, "Anger *is* a kind of interpretation not of a feeling . . . but *of the world* . . . [of] a relationship between oneself and one's situation" (p. 250; emphasis in the original). According to this kind of account, which would be shared by most cognitive theorists of emotion, anger is rare or nonexistent among adult Utku people because they do not interpret their many physical hardships as frustrations. Nor do they see themselves as autonomously separate from other members of their community, and hence they do not experience themselves as being thwarted or let down by others. By contrast, other scholars reading Briggs's book have seen the absence of anger in Utku society differently. For example, Stearns and Stearns (1985) write that "Briggs described how the Utku Eskimo tribe disapproves of anger and seeks to suppress it through socialization. . . . But the study does not prove that the Utku are a people without anger. They regularly sulk when challenged (anger turned inward?), and . . . routinely beat and otherwise abuse dogs" (p. 814). Stearns and Stearns have a model of anger as existing in Utku society, but as capable of being suppressed or diverted.

Each approach offers a view of the world of emotions. In one view, Utku culture is constructed so that anger almost never arises. Anger is not unknown, but it is seen as an attribute of children—and foreigners. In the other view, anger occurs in the Utku as a biological response, but expression is regulated by display rules (Ekman, 1972). Perhaps even phenomenological experience is regulated by feeling rules (Hochschild, 1983).

If one had to choose between social-constructive and biological views, one would not be able to do so confidently on the basis of such examples; plausible alternative explanations exist, but without agreed methodologies for choosing between them. One would have to judge from a much wider gestalt of evidence on emotions. This gestalt has not yet been fully defined, nor has it been subjected to detailed scrutiny from different points of view.

Working Definitions and Differing Evidence

Some of the debate between social constructionists and naturalists revolves around definitions of emotions. Averill (1988) has proposed that emotions are not mere feelings, not mere biological bases: They are complex syndromes, episodic dispositions to behave in a certain kind of way. When we are in love or are angry, we become, during that episode, disposed to act in a way appropriate to that emotion as understood in our society. During an emotion we enter a temporary social role, with its own constitutive and regulative rules. Much of the syndrome or role (what to do and what not to do when in love, when angry, etc.) derives from the social domain. Feelings, bodily disturbances, and the like may be parts of emotion syndromes. They need not invariably be present for the emotion to exist. Ideas that emotions are processes (Frijda, 1986) and that concepts of emotions are based on schematic prototypes (Russell, 1991) are similar, and also define emotions as complexes, made up from parts.

By contrast, those with a biologically based view tend to see an emotion as simpler. Hume (1739/1972), for instance, postulated that emotion is a type of sensation. A modern exponent of Hume's postulate is Zajonc (Zajonc, Murphy, & Inglehart, 1989), who argues that at least some emotions are specific types of sensation experienced as pleasant or unpleasant, and derived from changes of temperature in cerebral blood vessels, which in turn are influenced by contractions of facial muscles. If an emotion is merely such a sensation, there is no place for social influences, beyond inducements to make particular kinds of facial expression.

Other biologists also exclude constructive processes. Darwin, for instance, offered an account of fear as purely given when he described an incident at the London Zoo:

> I put my face close to the thick glass-plate in front of a puff-adder in the Zoological Gardens, with the firm determination of not starting back if the snake struck at me; but, as soon as the blow was struck, my resolution went for nothing, and I jumped a yard or two backwards with astonishing rapidity. My will and reason were powerless against the imagination of a danger which had never been experienced. (Darwin, 1872 /1965, p. 38)

In this example, an emotion and its effect were like a reflex. Darwin saw such processes as actions triggered by specific circumstances, and derived from evolution or individual development. Part of his point was that emotional expressions derive from neural mechanisms operating automatically. His own determination, or indeed any other kind of constructive process working on this basic mechanism, could not alter it.

To give another example: When James (1890) expounded his theory of emotions, he suggested the idea of seeing a bear and running away. Bodily activities of fleeing give rise to the experience of fear. For such incidents, the argument becomes plausible that an emotion *is* the perception of an action of escape and its physiological accompaniments. James, like Hume, argued that the problem of understanding emotions was one of natural science.

But what if James had chosen a different kind of example of an emotion? What if he had chosen falling in love instead of fear? It would have been more difficult to promulgate his theory. However much we may believe that falling in love has a biological basis—perhaps as a response to some kind of releaser pattern; perhaps as an element in an evolutionarily designed courtship ritual that promotes reproduction between genetically fit individuals; perhaps, as Darwin (1872/1965) suggested, because in adulthood an echo is evoked of affectionate interactions of infancy with parents—we know that if we are to understand the emotion of falling in love, something else will be necessary. That "something else" will be from the social domain.

Here then, to contrast with Darwin's and James's examples of the emotion of fear (which can easily seem simple and biological) is one of falling in love, taken from a newspaper report.

On Monday Cpl. Floyd Johnson, 23, and the then Ellen Skinner, 19, total strangers, boarded a train at San Francisco and sat down across the aisle from each other. Johnson didn't cross the aisle until Wednesday, but his bride said, "I'd already made up my mind to say yes if he asked me to marry him." "We did most of the talking with our eyes," Johnson explained. Thursday the couple got off the train in Omaha with plans to be married. Because they would need to have the consent of the bride's parents if they were married in Nebraska, they crossed the river to Council Bluffs, Iowa, where they were married Friday. (Cited by Burgess & Wallin, 1953, p. 151)

This is, of course, unusual; otherwise it would not have been the subject of a newspaper story. But the main way in which it is unusual is that it conforms so closely to a Western cultural ideal. Averill (1985) provides evidence that 40% of an American sample, after reading this newspaper story, said that they had had experiences conforming to the ideal embodied in it. Another 40% said that their experiences of love definitely did not conform to it, basing their responses on any single departure they had felt from the ideal and a generally unfavorable attitude to it—hence also showing that they were influenced by it.

With Darwin's image of recoiling from a striking snake with his "will and reason . . . powerless," or of James's idea of fleeing from a bear (perhaps when walking alone in the wilderness), we easily summon up the idea of a natural emotion, fear, operating now in modern humans as it has done for millions of years in human and nonhuman ancestors. Equally, we can see the social-constructionist argument in the story of Floyd Johnson and Ellen Skinner. Two young people, of an age at which in our culture it is thought appropriate for such events to occur, meet by chance and fall in love. Fantasies are elaborated: "I'd already made up my mind to say yes." Conventions are adopted, apparently directly from Hollywood: "We did most of the talking with our eyes." The emotion propels the two young people to circumvent social constraints of a law forbidding marriage under a certain age, and it accomplishes the social function of providing a justification for themselves and others of changing their social status and living arrangements in a fundamental way.

If an emotion is constructed, it can be analyzed into the components that make it up.

This is the thrust of all cognitive approaches to emotion, from Aristotle and Spinoza to the present day. According to this view, emotions depend on inferences, albeit inferences that are often unconscious and involuntary. The social-constructionist approach, however, has extra components beyond those usually found in cognitive constructionism. The extra components include the prescriptive force that folk theories of emotions have, and the social purposes they accomplish.

Most theorists of emotions who have made any attempt to be comprehensive agree that social influences on emotions are important. It seems best, therefore, at least for the time being, to regard social constructionism and naturalism not as two theories in competition, but as two approaches that are complementary. At some future time, of course, we may see how one kind of explanation is more adequate for some phenomena.

STRONG AND WEAK FORMS OF SOCIAL CONSTRUCTIONISM

Armon-Jones (1986) has described what she calls "strong" and "weak" forms of social constructionism. The strong thesis is that all human emotions are social products, based on beliefs, shaped by language, and derived from culture. They are not modifications of natural states. Taking such an approach, one could consider each element in the story of Floyd Johnson and Ellen Skinner and point out differences from other cultures. One could conclude that such differences are everything, and that similarities between courtship practices in remote peoples are insignificant. Defending this thesis involves arguing that there is no compelling evidence that a human emotion has any connection with states in animals, since it involves cultural beliefs of a kind that an animal simply cannot have. Defending such a thesis can be fun. One can argue, for instance, that the idea of seeing such events as natural is very dear to Western culture. So if we imagine the former Ellen Skinner, aged 19, explaining to her parents what happened, the idea that this was an event of nature goes a long way toward justifying the alteration of previous commitments.

Some theorists come close to defending the strong form of the thesis. For instance, Harré

(1986) has stated, in reviewing evidence from evolutionary theories: "Psychologists have always had to struggle against a persistent illusion that in such studies as those of the emotions there is something *there*, the emotion, of which the emotion word is a mere representation" (p. 4; emphasis in original). The strong view, though it has some of the attractiveness of radicalism, is probably wrong. Much evidence indicates that there is "something there" in an emotion, as well as talk and social practices—something transcultural that precedes language and is not infinitely variable.

The weaker view is preferred by most social constructionists. In the words of Armon-Jones (1986), "It concedes to the naturalist the existence of a limited range of natural emotion responses" (p. 38). Interest in the social-constructionist approach then lies in showing the extent to which emotions, even those taken to be primary, are socially constructed; how this construction occurs; from what components; and for what purposes. This is the thesis explored here.

THE RANGE OF BIOLOGICAL CONSTRAINTS IN EMOTIONS

A good reason for social researchers to characterize the extent to which emotions are socially constructed is that the "limited range of natural emotion responses" conceded by most social constructionists is not agreed by those taking a biological approach. Indeed, a lively current debate focuses on exactly what such natural responses might be. Some theorists, notably Mandler (1990), argue that the only biologically based response is physiological arousal. This is concatenated with a cognitively constructed interpretation of the event that caused the arousal. On another account, prewired emotion subcomponents are given, each elicited by a specific feature of the situation. For instance, eyebrow frowns occur in response to perception of an obstacle, and an increased heart rate occurs in response to making an effort (Smith, 1989). Other components may include an open square mouth with teeth showing in response to desire to aggress, and eyelids raised indicating attention to the visual field (Ortony & Turner, 1990). According to this idea, an emotion is an ensemble of such response subcomponents that may co-occur because there are social situations in which their eliciting elements co-occur (e.g., an obstruction plus the requirement to summon up effort plus the desire to aggress, etc.). One can imagine an emotion constructed from such components and socialized in a particular society, in a particular way, and given a particular name—"anger." If this view (or Mandler's view) turns out to be correct, then, given certain kinds of elicitors, different cultures can construct the entities that are spoken of as emotions rather freely. There would be few constraints on how arousal might be interpreted, or what subcomponents might go together in repeated social situations and be worth forming a specific cultural concept for.

Other theorists do postulate more constraints; in particular, such constraints are inherent in theories of basic emotions. Thus a colleague and I (Oatley & Johnson-Laird, 1987) propose that a basic emotion occurs when the brain enters a particular mode of functioning on recognition of an event relevant to a goal, such as progress toward something one wants, a loss, a frustration, a conflict of goals—but conscious knowledge about what counts as something to want, as a loss, as a frustration, as a conflict, or about which of such events caused the emotion, to whom it is directed, and so forth, is added to the basic emotion mode. This knowledge can be largely culturally determined, and it emerges in the emotion terms used in a culture. A somewhat similar model has been proposed by Berkowitz (1993), based on experimental data of people becoming angry and aggressive when subjected to pains and frustrations. The components of belief (e.g., whom anger should be directed at) may vary widely. Such models, though they involve postulation of a universal biological basis for each emotion, hold such a basis merely as one part of most emotions, and give opportunity for social construction of semantic components.

On yet another kind of account of basic emotions—further along the continuum of biological constraint—what is given biologically is a set of basic emotion types or "families" (Ekman, 1992). Each type is a program of response that can be recognized by its distinctive pancultural facial expression, its physiology, and other attributes. In this view, social variations can still be substantial, but they are confined to changes in intensity, in control of expression, and perhaps in phenomenological experience.

THE FOUNDER OF THE SOCIAL-CONSTRUCTIONIST APPROACH TO EMOTION

Averill argues that H. T. Finck "probably deserves credit for being the first to advance a social-constructionist view of emotion" (Averill, 1985, p. 95). Finck was a music critic for the New York *Evening Post*. He had wide interests, and wrote a treatise on love (Finck, 1887). He argued first that love is a complex of feelings, attitudes, and sentiments; these include an aesthetic appreciation of human form in the person of the loved one, together with impulses to sympathy, solicitude, and self-sacrifice. Second, he argued that not everyone has the talent for love. Like music, it must be cultivated. Third, he argued that love as we know it in the West is of rather recent origin: He exaggerated only somewhat in dating it to 1274, when Dante fell in love with Beatrice.

Finck started by assuming that love is part of human nature, and regarded his third idea as the most original. He later said (Averill, 1985) that he was overjoyed when he discovered this truth that had escaped previous scholars: In ancient Greek, Latin, and Hebrew sources, and in anthropological accounts, love (meaning refined and altruistic love) was never mentioned; thus, it was apparently unknown in earlier times or in other cultures. Averill recounts how William James was among those to review Finck's book. He did so unfavorably. James argued what has become the standard naturalist case: Culture may contribute to damping or inflaming emotions, but it scarcely creates them. In response to such reviews, and thinking that he had omitted to present all the evidence, Finck published a second book of 800 pages, with an abundance of such evidence. Averill judges that although James's influence has been greater, Finck's argument was the better. Culture does not just, as James claimed, affect intensity. Qualitative differences of emotion occur in different cultures and in different eras.

Let me express it like this: Love as we think of it now in the West contains several components, including bodily attraction and altruistic impulses. Though components such as sexual desire and altruism have existed separately for a long time, in different forms and different societies, the construction of these into a recognizable complex is a cultural accomplishment. What we see when we or an acquaintance falls in love, what we imagine in such circumstances, or what we resonate to when read a love story is a complex of parts, including sexual desire, the aesthetic attraction to the other, and the altruism that Finck stressed. The story of Floyd Johnson and Ellen Skinner would have no point if they merely met on a train and later had sexual intercourse. Any sense of what the event might have meant to them, any altruistic impulses that each had for the other, and any rearrangements of long-term personal plans that they made would be inexplicable.

INSIGHTS OF SOCIAL CONSTRUCTIONISM

The social construction of emotions has been explored using a number of methods. I indicate five of them, with some of the insights that have been derived from each.

Cross-Cultural Comparisons

Theoretically, the most informative way to discover the extent to which emotions are socially constructed is to compare different cultures. This is done in two main ways: anthropological research by people from one culture visiting another, and historical study of change in one's own society. Both contemporary anthropology and historical study are methodologically difficult. Not only is there no position outside society from which anyone can view other cultures, but the extent to which we can understand another culture by becoming part of it in imagination or in fact is always partial and open to question. We are always liable to project our cultural preconceptions onto the other culture.

Nevertheless, fruitful comparisons have been made. One way to grasp the variety of emotional ideas and repertoires is to take what Heelas (1986) has called a "Cook's Tour" of cultures as described in anthropological research. He argues that even if there were basic emotions, it is emotion talk that gives meaning to them. In the tour we certainly find a variety of emotional vocabularies. So, among the Chewong (a small group of aboriginal Malaysians), there seem to be just eight words for emotions as found by Howell (1981): "They rarely use gestures of any kind, and their faces register little change as they speak" (pp. 134–135). By contrast, lack of emotional expression during speech would be seen as socially very awkward in the West, and we (Johnson-Laird & Oatley, 1989) found 590 words referring to emotions in English. The emotional atmospheres in societies as different as these are also clearly different. Heelas (1986) argues that in some societies certain kinds of emotions are recognized and talked about a lot, with many distinctions being made. Particular emotions, moreover, act as centers around which significant cultural institutions revolve. He calls these emotions "hypercognized," and asserts that in the West love and guilt are such hypercognized emotions. In other societies, other emotions or dispositions become cultural foci. Examples include fear and shyness among the Chewong; gentleness among the Tasaday (Nance, 1975); *sungkan* among the Javanese, a feeling of respectful politeness and restraint before superiors or unfamiliar people (Geertz, 1959); and so on. In many societies, too, certain emotions are "hypocognized." Depression, for instance, which is common in the West, is not well represented in non-Western experience or vocabularies (Marsella, 1980).

Another method is to try to understand in depth the implicit theories of some particular other culture. To make this understanding available to others, the society must be described in a way such that a reader can, as it were, enter it and share some of its intuitions and vision. We need what Geertz (1973) has called a "thick description"—one that gives the background as to why people interpret things and feel as they do. This has the implication that descriptions of cultures at an indifferent level of literary competence will not do. To create such thick descriptions requires the abilities of a poet or novelist. So, because of Homer, we can enter to some extent into the culture of the preclassical Greeks, where we discover that emotions were not mental and internal, as we in the modern West tend to believe. They were somatized in agitations of the body or its parts (the lungs, the heart, or the guts); they were also externalized, projected outwards in the form of such gods as

Aphrodite, who is lust, or Ares, who is fierce aggression.

One person who has succeeded in giving a "thick description" of a contemporary culture is Lutz (1988). She has written about emotional life on Ifaluk, a tiny Micronesian atoll. Even so, she has done it not by becoming an Ifaluk person, which for her as an adult North American would be impossible. What she has done, building on the method developed (more or less by accident) by Briggs (1970), has been to pay careful attention to her own socialization into Ifaluk society, and to the occasions when her North American assumptions and those of the Ifaluk people did not mesh. Such occasions are the culture shocks of ordinary tourists. They can give rise to embarrassment or worse, but they can also be invaluable pointers to unconscious assumptions of both the host culture and that of the guest. Lutz describes, for instance, how she smiled as she watched a 5-year-old girl dance and make silly faces. A woman with whom Lutz was sitting said, "Don't smile at her— she'll think you are not *song* [justifiably angry]" (p. 167). To show off and be *ker* (happy/excited), as the little girl was being, was to be too pleased with oneself and not to attend to the concerns of others. Such behavior was to be socially disapproved by displays of *song*, which is not anger in the Euro-American individualistic sense, but disapproval, which one is obliged to display if a social rule is broken. For the Ifaluk, children of 6 are able to be socially intelligent. They are able to order their actions primarily with respect to the feelings and concerns of others —mutual concern is the prevailing tone of Ifaluk society. Happiness is not valued, as in North America. Rather, it is disapproved of precisely because it can cause one to disregard others. The woman was explaining to Lutz that the girl was becoming old enough to understand such matters.

On Ifaluk, as in the West, people are very interested in emotions, but they regard them as aspects of relationships, rather than signs of individuality. Lutz has shown that many of the emotions that are salient on Ifaluk need to be thought of as made from parts when described in English. Thus Lutz translates the Ifaluk term *ker* as happiness/excitement. Then there is the concept of *fago,* which Lutz translates as compassion/love/sadness. She goes on to show how this emotion is based on a sense that everyone with whom one is close should be together; the sense that anyone in need should be helped; and the sense that absence of a loved one (which is very likely to cause a person to be needy precisely because that person is away) is likely to give rise to this somewhat sad and affectionate emotion.

The other major method of studying differences between cultures is to study historical materials: narrative literature, diaries, biography. So, for instance, it seems likely that since the 18th century in Europe and North America, there has been an increase in maternal love for children (certainly there has been a growing affirmation of its importance) and a growing focus of emotional life within the home, as the public world has become more individualistic and commercial (Lewis, 1989). But such inferences are problematic: Although one may be helped by some sense of continuity with one's own culture, the materials that constitute evidence are always fragmentary. Those that happen to survive are seldom those one would choose for research purposes.

Prescription

Cultural theories of emotions all seem to have prescriptive qualities. We can ask how appropriate it is, within a culture, for a particular emotion to occur in a particular circumstance. This idea gives rise to a rather wide variety of effects. Thus, socialization practices typically include encouraging some emotions and avoiding others. Then we find exhortations and religious practices for adults who might be tempted toward certain kinds of emotion. We also find gossip and social commentary, praising and blaming others for their emotions. Then there are the various forms of folk medical practices and psychotherapy for those whose emotions have become too hard to cope with.

However widespread such practices might be, it could be argued that they merely embody folk theories about the modifiability of emotions, rather than any direct evidence that emotions can be socially modified. Nevertheless, we can look at these practices themselves and make assessments separately about how successful they are. This domain is an ideal one for historical and cultural study, since from ancient times people have seen emotions as problematic. Prescriptions have been offered for their control and modification, and much writing of this kind remains.

Buddhist writings have been widespread; in them, emotions deriving from attachment to the self and to external things are seen as unwholesome. Even though the cultural base of such teachings is foreign to them, many Westerners have been attracted to Buddhism (see, e.g., Varella, Thompson, & Rosch, 1991, for a treatment linking such ideas to cognitive science).

In Europe a comparable movement, based on the idea of philosophy as a means of saving one's life, gathered momentum with the Stoics, who believed that emotions were diseases of the soul and that they should be extirpated. It has had a persisting influence, with the tradition passing from such early Greek writers as Chrysippus and Xeno to Romans like Cicero and Seneca, and onward to the present (Nussbaum, 1987). The basic idea is a thorough-going constructionist one: Emotions depend on beliefs and interpretations, and hence can be controlled by correct thinking and proper interpretations. For early Stoics, anger was the emotion that was the most important to extirpate.

Now in North America, it turns out, the principal emotion to be avoided is fear. The importance of overcoming fear can be seen in European and North American social history. Stearns and Haggarty (1991) surveyed 84 advice manuals for parents published between 1850 and 1950, as well as popular literature aimed at children. Before the turn of the century three themes stood out: warnings to parents about causing fear in their children (e.g., employing scare tactics for disciplinary purposes), silence on the subject of dealing with childhood fears (which later was to become salient in child-rearing manuals), and boys' stories calculated to inspire courage. A fearful individual was not able to be a good citizen. By the end of the Victorian era a change was already in progress: "Twentieth-century parents were told not only to avoid frightening their children as a disciplinary device but also to master their own emotions lest they give disturbing signals" (p. 75). In Dr. Spock's (1945) manual, childhood fears were presented as somewhat unpredictable and requiring careful management. Parents of 2-year-olds should delay travel plans to avoid inducing anxieties in their children, and fears should be met with reassurance, patience, and affection. By the 1940s also, boys' stories of courage—acting well despite fear—were already dated. Now boys were offered tales of adventure in which

the heroes were tough guys who felt no fear at all, merely determination and perhaps a certain excitement.

Alongside all this there was exhortation. President Franklin Roosevelt, in his 1933 inaugural address, announced: "The only thing we have to fear is fear itself." For those for whom exhortation was ineffective, or those whose upbringing had for some reason not successfully abolished all fear, there was psychotherapy—again aimed largely at fear, now called "anxiety." One of the most compelling results from the social-constructionist point of view is that many forms of psychotherapy do have successful outcomes. On average, both behavioral and psychoanalytically based therapies, typically lasting 12 or so hour-long sessions, successfully decrease measures of anxiety substantially and significantly (Smith, Glass, & Miller, 1980).

Moreover, of all the forms of therapy for depression—a phenomenon that, along with anxiety, has flourished in 20th-century Western cultures—the form based on Stoic principles of thinking "properly" about events liable to provoke depressive moods has been most consistently shown to be effective (Robinson, Berman, & Neimeyer, 1990), and is more successful than antidepressant drugs.

Development of Emotions in Infancy

Studies of socialization practices and their effects in different societies, as opposed to the principles offered to parents, are likely to become increasingly important in deciding the extent to which emotions are constructed. Detailed comparisons are rare, though studies of aspects of emotional development in societies other than Europe and North America are beginning to appear in English-language journals (e.g., Miyake, Chen, & Campos, 1985).

Other methods are also being developed. A recent study of facial expressions by Camras (1992) has challenged the prevailing view that the universality of emotional expressions in adulthood is purely the result of centrally controlled motor programs. Camras analyzed videotape and diary records of emotional episodes of her daughter, Justine, for weeks 4 through 9 of Justine's life. Coding Justine's facial expressions according to a standard infant facial expression coding scheme (AFFEX), Camras found that distress, anger, sadness, fear, and disgust did not emerge as separate expressions, each triggered by an appropriate elicitor. Rather, a composite distress–pain expression often occurred, sometimes when no physical pain was likely (e.g., during bathing, leaning, being moved, or having her pacifier removed). Moreover, the facial expressions characteristic of distress–pain, anger, and sadness were frequently all seen in a single episode of crying.

Camras concludes that at first the different facial expressions of negative emotions occur as expressions of different intensities of a general emotion of distress, rather than as qualitatively different emotions. Then, basing her argument on dynamic systems theory (in which it is postulated that bottom-up feedback from an activity combines with centrally directed action programs), she argues that the distinctive emotion patterns of adulthood may be shaped by a variety of factors. These factors may at first derive from the contexts of movement of infants themselves, and the kinds of actions and perceptions that occur. If Camras is correct, there is nothing to prevent affectionate and other interactions from also affecting the patterning of responses and the habitual shapes of expression that are built up. In other words, it may be the case that even if there are some basic adult emotions, these are really modes of organization that derive from multiple influences, including perhaps some social ones derived from caregiving interactions.

How Emotions Are Constructed in Adulthood

An approach that has been widely influential is that of Hochschild (1983). She studied the process by which emotions are constructed in a particular subcultural setting so that her readers can recognize and look behind the scenes to see how emotional effects are created.

Hochschild's best-known research concerned Delta Air Lines female cabin staff. Though their training involves practicing emergency drills, operating cabin equipment, serving food and so forth, what Hochschild described was how learning to be a Delta flight attendant is a matter of giving a particular kind of emotional performance—performing a role, just as she would in the theater. For the most part the role is to project emotions of pleasurable welcome: "Trainees were asked to think

of a passenger as if he were a 'personal guest in your living room'. The workers' emotional memories of offering personal hospitality were called up and put to use, as Stanislavski would recommend" (Hochschild, 1983, p. 105).

The aim of this training is to induce a certain emotional tone in the passengers. The method is Method acting, perhaps easier and more convincing than merely behaving in a particular way. Work that involves constructing emotions in oneself in order to induce them in others is quite widespread. Hochschild discusses jobs at the interface between a company and the customer; debt collection, for instance, is a kind of inverse of being a flight attendant. "Create alarm" was the instruction of one debt-collecting company's boss (Hochschild, 1983, p. 146). Many traditional "women's jobs" that are not at the customer interface also involve "emotional labor"—perhaps most noticeably the job of being a secretary, which requires cheerfulness, supportiveness, and amiability.

Some 38% of all paid jobs in the United States in 1970 called for substantial amounts of emotional labor, and within the job categories that called for it, women were twice as numerous as men. One need not doubt that the creation of emotions at work serves social purposes—to sell more airline tickets, to persuade the customer, to provide pleasant support for a (usually male) boss, and so on.

Some jobs are free-lance and involve further kinds of induction of emotions. Ellis (1991) discusses a person who worked as an erotic dancer in a strip bar. This woman was also her student, Rambo Ronai, who as part of her research wrote introspective accounts of thoughts and feelings about her dancing work. On the one hand, as for aircraft cabin staff, the job involves adopting a role with its emotional implications. The best way often is to become that role. Rambo Ronai described trying to elicit a smile from a member of the audience or a fellow dancer: "This small evidence of approval and support can be enough to carry me through a whole performance" (cited in Ellis, 1991, p. 131). "At other times . . . I become frightened when large groups of men start yelling and cheering for me too loud. I am painfully aware of my object status. I can feel the fright milk me of my strength. I shrivel up in inside to get away. . . . To combat these feelings I turn off from the crowd" (cited in Ellis, 1991, p. 132). At yet other times she would feel contempt for a customer, though she maintained her sexy smile: ". . . this rotting carcase of wrinkled flesh is no threat. . . . I keep getting angrier and angrier. It escalates exponentially now. But I must act nice, pretty and pleasant" (cited in Ellis, 1991, p. 133).

As well as the theme that is fundamental in many social-constructionist accounts—of describing component feelings that can alternate rapidly or be mixed—here is another theme distinctive to the research that follows from Hochschild's analyses. The assumption of this research is that employees use various techniques in order to deliver the emotional products for which they are paid. These may or may not be their "real" feelings. Here can arise a situation that is painfully problematic. What are the occupational hazards of emotional labor in a society in which the most compelling of all social constructions is of personal individuality? And how does a person cope with these contradictions when a prime index of individual identity is how one "really feels"?

Stated in this form, the sense in which emotions are constructed may seem quite weak. On the one hand, a performance is created that needs merely to have behavioral verisimilitude. On the other hand, there are the person's own feelings, which one can imagine are more real, and which may not be socially constructed at all; they may be evoked by the situation, its threats, its contradictions, its longueurs.

The view that emotions are real insofar as they evoke biologically based programs, and that social roles merely involve demands to control intensity and to regulate displays, might be more conclusive were it not for the analyses of Goffman (1961), who has convincingly argued that we take our very individuality and its emotional tone precisely from the full engagement in the social roles we play—not just at work or in games, but as friend, as parent, as lover. We become different aspects of ourselves in such roles, and experience the emotions that the roles afford. To foster a true self apart from the performance is a maneuver that some people try; however, its effects are not to maintain individuality, but to be disengaged and alienated, suffering a sense of emptiness and pointlessness.

What Emotions Accomplish

One of the principal works of social constructionism is Averill's (1982) book on anger. In

it, he argues that in the West anger functions as a temporary social role, which can be entered in order to adjust social relationships or obligations that would otherwise be fixed. We can see this pattern, Averill argues, in law, which has operationalized certain rules about anger. In extreme cases of anger, killing can occur—and, deriving from Greek and Roman law, American law involves a mental element (i.e., that some homicides are morally more reprehensible than others). So the category of murder carries the most serious penalties, and is applied when a killing was planned or occurred in the course of another crime. Manslaughter has less serious penalties. It is unintentional killing, and it includes killing when angry. But as Averill points out, for the defense of manslaughter while angry to succeed, the emotion must have obeyed certain societal rules. First, there must have been adequate provocation: The event that caused the anger must have been such as would rouse an ordinary person to anger. Second, the killing must have occurred while the perpetrator was actually angry—in the "heat of passion," rather than "in cold blood." Third, it must have been done within a limited period following provocation: The anger must not have had time to cool. And fourth, the killing must have been linked to the provocation: The defense of manslaughter fails if the intent to kill was formed before the incident that aroused the anger.

On the one hand, among all the prohibitions of our society, the prohibition of killing is taken the most seriously. But on the other hand, we can be released from this prohibition under various circumstances. Anger becomes, as Averill says, a temporary social role, in which the solemn rules against any action likely to cause serious bodily harm to another person apply more leniently.

Averill (1982) also studied less extreme instances of anger. He had student and community subjects keep structured diaries in which they each recorded an incident of anger that they experienced, and an incident of irritation. He had other subjects record an incident in which they were the target of another person's anger. Most incidents of anger concerned persons the subjects knew and liked, and the most common motive (for 63% of incidents) was to assert authority or independence, or to improve the subjects' self-image. Despite the fact that most subjects found the anger subjectively unpleasant, 62% of subjects who had become angry and 70% of the targets of anger rated the anger as having been beneficial.

We can conclude, I think, that in the West anger has important social functions. Although we see it as potentially destructive, in its normal occurrence it functions between people to readjust the terms of a long-term relationship. So if in a relationship one person finds that the other has explicitly or implicitly agreed to do something but does not do it—in other words, if the other is not fulfilling expectations—then this is a cause for anger. The incident of anger is also likely to provoke anger in the other; a quarrel occurs, with both entering temporary roles as angry persons. This scenario does often lead to a resolution, in which the terms of the persisting relationship are redefined. Apologies can be made and new intentions formed. Better understandings of each other, leading to more realistic expectations, can occur.

Among the interesting aspects of this kind of analysis is that this role of anger seems peculiar to Western individualistic society. One may hypothesize that two kinds of problems arise for us in the West, precisely because our culture is so individualistic. One is the problem of how any individual can enter into a relationship that will involve close cooperation in many activities and extend long into the future. As discussed in the introduction, the emotion of love serves a function of solving this kind of problem for one kind of relationship, at least to some extent. It allows a person to identify a sexual partner, to interpret feelings, to make commitments, and so forth. A second problem for an individualistic society is how to readjust long-term relationships—and here anger is evidently constructed into an emotion that enables people to enter the role of renegotiators of their relationship, including the possibility that the relationship may be terminated.

CONCLUSION

Social constructionism is at present an approach to understanding emotions rather than a theory, though the approach does contain some fully developed theories of aspects of emotions (e.g., Averill, 1982; Hochschild, 1983). The importance of this approach for understanding emotions is that it offers views below the surface of our emotional interactions, suggests purposes for emotions that

other approaches would find hard to accommodate, and gives form to a question that persistently fascinates us—namely, how appropriate emotions are to circumstances. At some future time, research based on this approach will no doubt make firmer contact with more general cognitive research. As it does so, emotion researchers will be pleased to find how much of importance has been seen by exploring the idea that emotions are not just individual things, but part of the very substance of social interaction.

Acknowledgment. I am grateful to Jim Averill for reading a draft of this chapter and making helpful comments on it.

REFERENCES

Armon-Jones, C. (1986). The thesis of constructionism. In R. Harré (Ed.), *The social construction of emotions* (pp. 32–56). Oxford: Blackwell.

Averill, J. R. (1982). *Anger and aggression: An essay on emotion.* New York: Springer.

Averill, J. R. (1985). The social construction of emotion: With special reference to love. In K. J. Gergen & K. E. Davis (Eds.), *The social construction of the person* (pp. 89–109). New York: Springer-Verlag.

Averill, J. R. (1988). Disorders of emotion. *Journal of Social and Clinical Psychology, 6,* 247–268.

Berkowitz, L. (1993). Towards a general theory of anger and emotional aggression: Implications of a cognitive neo-associationistic perspective for the analysis of anger and other emotions. In R. S. Wyer & T. Srull (Eds.), *Advances in social cognition* (Vol 6). Hillsdale, NJ: Erlbaum.

Briggs, J. L. (1970). *Never in anger: Portrait of an Eskimo family.* Cambridge, MA: Harvard University Press.

Burgess, E. W., & Wallin, P. (1953). *Engagement and marriage.* Philadelphia: J. B. Lippincott.

Camras, L. A. (1992). Expressive development and basic emotions. *Cognition and Emotion, 6,* 269–283.

Darwin, C. (1965). *The expression of the emotions in man and animals.* Chicago: University of Chicago Press. (Original work published 1872)

Ekman, P. (1972). Universals and cultural differences in facial expressions of emotion. In J. Cole (Ed.), *Nebraska Symposium on Motivation* (Vol 19, pp. 207–283). Lincoln: University of Nebraska Press.

Ekman, P. (1992). An argument for basic emotions. *Cognition and Emotion, 6,* 169–200.

Ellis, C. (1991). Emotional sociology. In N. Denzin (Ed.), *Studies in social interaction* (pp. 123–145). Greenwich, CT: JAI Press.

Finck, H. T. (1887). *Romantic love and personal beauty.* London: Macmillan.

Frijda, N. H. (1986). *The emotions.* Cambridge, England: Cambridge University Press.

Geertz, C. (1973). *The interpretation of cultures.* New York: Basic Books.

Geertz, H. (1959). The vocabulary of emotion. *Psychiatry, 22,* 225–237.

Goffman, E. (1961). *Encounters: Two studies in the sociology of interaction*. Indianapolis, IN: Bobbs-Merrill.

Harré, R. (1986). The social constructionist viewpoint. In R. Harré (Ed.), *The social construction of emotions* (pp. 2–14). Oxford: Blackwell.

Heelas, P. (1986). Emotion talk across cultures. In R. Harré (Ed.), *The social construction of emotions* (pp. 234–266). Oxford: Blackwell.

Hochschild, A. R. (1983). *The managed heart: The commercialization of human feeling*. Berkeley: University of California Press.

Howell, S. (1981). Rules not words. In P. Heelas & A. Lock (Eds.), *Indigenous psychologies: The anthropology of the self* (pp. 133–143). London: Academic Press.

Hume, D. (1972). *A treatise on human nature*. London: Fontana/Collins. (Original work published 1739)

James, W. (1890). *The principles of psychology* (2 vols.). New York: Holt.

Johnson-Laird, P. N., & Oatley, K. (1989). The language of emotions: An analysis of a semantic field. *Cognition and Emotion, 3*, 81–123.

Lewis, J. (1989). Mother's love: The construction of an emotion in nineteenth-century America. In A. E. Barnes & P. N. Stearns (Eds.), *Social history and issues in human consciousness* (pp. 209–229). New York: New York University Press.

Lutz, C. A. (1988). *Unnatural emotions: Everyday sentiments on a Micronesian atoll and their challenge to Western theory*. Chicago: University of Chicago Press.

Mandler, G. (1990). A constructivist theory of emotion. In N. L. Stein, B. Leventhal, & T. Trabasso (Eds.), *Psychological and biological approaches to emotion* (pp. 21–43). Hillsdale, NJ: Erlbaum.

Markus, H. R., & Kitayama, S. (1991). Culture and the self: Implications for cognition, emotion and motivation. *Psychological Review, 98*, 224–253.

Marsella, A. J. (1980). Depressive disorder and experience across cultures. In H. C. Triandis & J. Draguns (Eds.), *Handbook of cross-cultural psychology* (Vol 6, pp. 237–289). Boston: Allyn & Bacon.

Miyake, K., Chen, S.-J., & Campos, J. J. (1985). Infant temperament, mother's mode of interaction, and attachment in Japan: An interim report. *Monographs of the Society for Research in Child Development, 50* (Whole No. 209).

Nance, J. (1975). *The gentle Tasaday*. New York: Harcourt Brace Jovanovich.

Nussbaum, M. C. (1987). The Stoics on the extirpation of the passions. *Apeiron, 20*, 129–177.

Oatley, K., & Johnson-Laird, P. N. (1987). Towards a cognitive theory of emotions. *Cognition and Emotion, 1*, 29–50.

Ortony, A., & Turner, T. J. (1990). What's basic about basic emotions? *Psychological Review, 74*, 431–461.

Robinson, L. A., Berman, J. S., & Neimeyer, R. A. (1990). Psychotherapy for the treatment of depression: A comprehensive review of controlled outcome studies. *Psychological Bulletin, 108*, 30–49.

Russell, J. R. (1991). In defense of a prototype approach to emotion concepts. *Journal of Personality and Social Psychology, 60*, 37–47.

Smith, C. A. (1989). Dimensions of appraisal and physiological response in emotion. *Journal of Personality and Social Psychology, 56*, 339–353.

Smith, M. L., Glass, G. V., & Miller, T. I. (1980). *The benefits of psychotherapy*. Baltimore: Johns Hopkins University Press.

Solomon, R. C. (1984). Getting angry: The Jamesian theory of emotion in anthropology. In R. A. Shweder & R. A. LeVine (Eds.), *Culture theory: Essays on mind, self, and emotion* (pp. 238–254). Cambridge, England: Cambridge University Press.

Spock, B. (1945). *The common sense book of baby and child care*. New York: Duell, Sloan & Pearce.

Stearns, P. N., & Haggarty, T. (1991). The role of fear: Transitions in American emotional standards for children, 1850–1950. *American Historical Review, 96*, 63–94.

Stearns, P. N., & Stearns, C. Z. (1985). Emotionology: Clarifying the history of emotions and emotional standards. *American Historical Review, 90*, 813–886.

Varella, F. J., Thompson, E., & Rosch, E. (1991). *The embodied mind: Cognitive science and human experience*. Cambridge, MA: MIT Press.

Zajonc, R. B., Murphy, S. T., & Inglehart, M. (1989). Feeling and facial efference: Implications of the vascular theory of emotion. *Psychological Review, 96*, 395–416.

25

Temperament: Variability in Developing Emotion Systems

H. H. GOLDSMITH

An infant cries vigorously when someone drops a book nearby, calms rapidly when rocked by a babysitter, and later watches a bird on the windowsill for a full 3 minutes. A child is reluctant to approach other children on the playground, can never seem to sit still, and often seems to change moods without any apparent reason. An adult is quick to anger, is easily distracted by outside noises while reading, and seems always to greet friends with a broad smile. Can the concept of temperament provide a framework for organizing and understanding such emotion-related behavioral differences? The existence and vigor of the field of temperament research mean that many investigators judge that the answer to this question is yes. This chapter explains the relation of temperament to emotion and illustrates the scope of current temperament research with a very selective review.

LINKING TEMPERAMENT AND EMOTION

Defining Temperament

Although no single definition is consensually endorsed, most contemporary theorists and researchers would agree that "temperament" is (1) a rubric for individual differences in various behavioral tendencies or traits, (2) most or all of which are present during early life. These traits are (3) relatively stable across significant periods of life and (4) relatively consistent across situations with related incentive values.

Moreover, most researchers believe these individual differences have (5) neurophysiological underpinnings and are partially heritable. Theorists vary in their emphasis on these five properties (Goldsmith et al., 1987).

The concepts of emotion and temperament are linked in the writings of many theorists. Allport (1937) defined temperament as characteristic individual differences in emotional expression, and practically all theorists since have viewed emotional differences among persons as part of the domain of temperament (e.g., Buss & Plomin, 1984; Rothbart, 1989; Strelau, 1987). Other theorists have confined the definition of temperament to emotional differences (Goldsmith & Campos, 1982, 1986; Mehrabian, 1991).

Defining Emotion

Any explication of temperament that refers back to emotion should also define "emotion." Defining emotion in a sentence or so seems injudicious within a handbook devoted to the topic; instead, I allow the definition to unfold as this chapter proceeds. Some initial qualifications are important, however. Emotions most relevant to temperament are called by names such as "joy," "anger," "fear," "sadness," "interest," and "disgust" as opposed to "jealousy," "envy," "guilt," and "pride." The names of even these more basic types of emotions do not refer to unalloyed phenomena. More realistically, a term such as "anger" refers to a family of emotions, as implied by prototype approaches (e.g., Shaver, Schwartz, Kirson, & O'Connor, 1987). There is the anger that derives from frustration; there is the defensive anger that derives from being attacked physically; and there is the vengeful or indignant anger that derives from being attacked psychologically. These different incentive conditions for anger are associated with a class of external signs, action tendencies, and subjective feeling states. However, the link between an incentive condition (such as being insulted) and a response (such as an angry facial expression) is not rigidly reflexive. The larger context of interaction is also important. There is also heterogeneity within classes of responses, such as facial or vocal expressions. For instance, within the class of anger facial expressions, there are both major (e.g., squarish, angular mouth vs. opened mouth with lips stretched tense) and more subtle differences in the appearance of parts of the face. Thus, we may think of a family of anger emotions. The same is true of other emotions. For instance, the family of fear emotions subsumes common language terms such as "scared," "terrified," "wary," and "shy." Contextual elements of fear include novelty and threat in various combinations, and the threat can be directed to the physical self or to more psychological aspects of self such as self-esteem.

Some unity can be restored after this componential dissection of emotion by adopting a functional, or relational, perspective. This perspective casts emotions as processes of establishing, maintaining, or disrupting biologically or socially significant relationships with persons or objects in the environment, either directly or at the representational level (Campos, Barrett, Lamb, Goldsmith, & Stenberg, 1983; Barrett & Campos, 1987).

Further Defining Temperament

However emotions are defined, a view that would probably achieve consensus is that emotionality can be manifested as brief *states*, as longer but still transitory *moods*, and as *traits* or patterns of expression that characterize an individual over significant periods of the lifespan. We may think of temperamental traits such as fearfulness as tendencies to enter a fearful state or to remain in a fearful mood. A similar perspective views temperamental traits as "emotional biases" (Malatesta, 1990). Thus, within the temperament and personality fields, there is little dispute that enduring facets of

emotionality fit a modern trait perspective. Despite its occasional usefulness as a "straw man," a modern trait perspective bears much in common with organizational approaches and systems perspectives on behavior.

There are two key, but qualified, properties that current personality theorists expect of a trait: cross-situational consistency and temporal stability. Cross-situational consistency is not expected across just any set of situations. This property is qualified in at least three ways: If consistency is to be expected, the situations must have common incentive properties; they must afford significant behavioral options; and they must be relevant to individuals' goals. Likewise, temporal stability is only expected between periods of major behavioral reorganization, and the stability is not expected to override other sources of variation. Furthermore, temperamental continuity is sometimes apparent only under conditions of stress, novelty, or other extreme situations (Thomas & Chess, 1977). These two properties of personality traits transfer to temperamental traits, of course, and sometimes a third expectation —that of constitutional (Rothbart, 1989) or genetic (Buss & Plomin, 1984) origins—is added. There is no necessary reason for stable and consistent traits to be rooted in the genetic code, however. Consistencies can inhere in cognitive structures (such as chronically accessible scripts), or can be derived from learning and generalization (as in the case of classically conditioned fears).

Within the general trait perspective just described, there are three broad approaches to sharpening the definition of temperament: (1) in terms of developmental stage (e.g., all aspects of personality that become apparent during infancy); (2) in terms of genetic origins or neurophysiological underpinnings (the genetic or constitutional aspects of personality); or (3) in terms of observable behavioral patterns (Goldsmith et al., 1987). Many definitions—including the ultimate one—employ combinations of the three broad approaches. What should be taken as definitional and what left for empirical determination are matters of metatheoretical preference, potential for encouraging various types of research, and the state of current knowledge.

Levels of Analysis of Temperament

For temperament theory to advance from a stage that is mainly stipulative to a stage more focused on processes, further sharpening is required. For example, Bates (1989) delineated several levels of understanding of temperament. A delineation of levels useful for this chapter specifies genetic, physiological, cognitive, individual behavioral, interpersonal interactional (e.g., familial and peer contexts), cultural, and evolutionary levels. (Despite appearances, these levels do not form a linear sequence. The relation is, in a sense, circular because the evolutionary forces change gene frequencies, thus affecting sources of individuality at the genetic level.) Theoretical statements about temperament would be more precise, and miscommunication could be avoided, if researchers would always specify the level of analysis they have in mind. Also, it would seem fitting if theories posed at, for example, the neurophysiological level were accompanied by studies tapping neurophysiological functioning. Apparent disagreement in the temperament literature sometimes fades when it is realized that the disagreement reflects different levels of analysis. Within a level of analysis, temperament comprises components that form typical—but not necessarily invariant—structures. These structures require explication and measurement. It is this process of explication and measurement at the behavioral level that occupies many contemporary temperament researchers.

Explanations of temperament at one level are inherently incomplete, but it is surely expecting too much consistency of opportunistic evolution that processes operating at different levels should map onto one another in a simple fashion. Hinde (1989), in particular, has warned against the dangers of postulating isomorphisms across levels. Of course, the notion of levels of analysis can easily be overemphasized, because some phenomena cut across levels. Thus, a primary goal of research is to understand each facet of temperament across all levels. Perhaps the issues involved can best be understood with examples from contemporary research.

INVESTIGATION OF TEMPERAMENTAL COMPONENTS AT VARIOUS LEVELS OF ANALYSIS

The Genetic Level

The genetic level of analysis can employ either molecular or quantitative genetic techniques. With recent advances, it is perhaps only

TABLE 25.1. Twin Similarity for Rothbart's Infant Behavior Questionnaire (IBQ)

IBQ scales	Identical R	Fraternal R
Activity Level	.69	.35
Fear	.67	.43
Distress to Limitations	.71	.29
Smiling and Laughter	.72	.66
Soothability	.69	.71
Duration of Orienting	.76	.57

Note. R's are means from Goldsmith (1978, 1986), Goldsmith and Campos (1986), and Goldsmith, Jaco, and Elliott (1986).

slightly premature to apply molecular genetic techniques to complex human temperamental traits. Rather than forecasting this advance, we may turn to quantitative genetic techniques that have been applied widely through the study of different genetic kinships—comparisons of identical with fraternal twins, siblings with one another, parents with offspring, and adoptees with their biological versus adopted families. The assumptions, data-analytic considerations, and implications of these quantitative genetic techniques are beyond the scope of this chapter (see Eaves, Eysenck, & Martin, 1989; Goldsmith, 1989; Loehlin, 1992).

Table 25.1 shows twin similarity pooled from three small studies for the six scales of Rothbart's (1981) Infant Behavior Questionnaire, a leading instrument for assessment of early temperament. Greater identical than fraternal cotwin similarity for the activity and negative affect scales is apparent, and minimal genetic input is implied for the more hedonically positive scales. Other twin studies tend to support moderate heritability for parental report temperament questionnaire scales (e.g., Buss & Plomin, 1984; Cohen, Dibble, & Grawe, 1977; Plomin, 1986), and positive but more equivocal genetic evidence has emerged for laboratory and other observational measures of temperament (e.g., Braungart, Plomin, DeFries, & Fulker, 1992; Goldsmith & Gottesman, 1981; Goldsmith & Campos, 1986; Matheny, 1989; Emde et al., 1992).

Positive evidence of heritability does not necessarily imply that gene action underlies the physiology directly relevant to a temperamental behavioral pattern (Goldsmith, 1988; Tooby & Cosmides, 1990). Direct evidence for this must await molecular genetic studies of temperament. Moreover, heritability established at one developmental period does not necessarily generalize to other periods. In an especially instructive study, Riese (1990) assessed neonatal reactions, most of which might be viewed as temperamental (e.g., irritability, resistance to soothing, activity level, reactivity). No evidence for heritability emerged for any of these characteristics. Does this null finding mean that genes are unimportant for neonatal behavioral reactions? No; it may be that the genes that operate during the neonatal period are fixed in the species.

Concern with genetic input to behavioral variability is not limited to behavioral geneticists. Although ethologists and evolutionary psychologists traditionally deal mainly with genetically coded species-general adaptations, they recognize that important behavioral patterns that vary among species members can also be rooted in the genetic code. In interpreting the theoretical positions of Lorenz, Eibl-Eibesfeldt, and Mayr (who represent classical ethology and evolutionary genetics), Zivin (1989) points out that some genetic programs fully specify the surface form of behavior. Such behavior appears highly ritualized or stereotypic and is relatively rare in humans. Other genetic programs are coded at "deeper levels," and considerable interaction with other programs and environmental input are required before the results of the deeper-level program are apparent at the behavioral surface. We may think of genetic input to temperamental *predispositions* as acting at this deeper level. In one instance of adaptation, a deeper-level program serving the goal of maintaining the integrity of the self in the face of threat or novelty might recruit another genetic program with output of a highly stereotyped fearful facial expression at the behavioral surface. In another instance, the same deeper-level program might recruit other programs more crucially dependent on environmental input, with the resultant behavior being a complex mixture of, say, avoidance and coping. This sort of systems thinking quickly becomes highly abstract, and thus it invites investigation of physiological variables that may reflect, however vaguely, the functioning of some programs "below" the behavioral interface.

The Physiological Level

Neuroendocrine, neuroimmunological, and other biochemical factors are generally regarding as lurking somewhere beneath the behavioral phenotypes of temperament. Similarly, research on peripheral and cortical electrophysiology of emotion is relevant to temperament. The relevance to temperament is obvious: Physiological parameters of emotion expression may be endophenotypes associated with genetic factors in temperament and may also be sources of temporal stability. The breadth of this topic precludes a review in this chapter, but it is treated elsewhere in this volume (see MacLean, Chapter 6; Panksepp, Chapter 7; LeDoux, Chapter 8; Cacioppo, Klein, Berntson, & Hatfield, Chapter 9; Davidson, Chapter 10). However, a few of the important implications for temperament can be mentioned. First, behavioral researchers who may be tempted to look to the physiological level for greater simplicity, lawfulness, and organization are likely to be disappointed. Second, the methodological limitations, the difficulty of demonstrating temporal stability, and the highly interactive nature of development seem every bit as daunting at the physiological level as at the behavioral level (Fahrenberg, 1991). For instance, cortisol levels, which may index the balance of the degree of experienced stress and successful coping, can also be influenced by nutritional, metabolic, immunological, hormonal, and circadian factors (Netter, 1991). Gale and Edwards (1986) list "seven deadly sins" of physiological research that should command the attention of all temperament and emotion researchers who venture into the area.

Third, attempts to find one-to-one correspondences between behavior and physiology are obsolete. For example, in a heuristic attempt to map eight dimensions of temperament to biochemical variables, Netter (1991) suggests that catecholamine levels or other parameters of catecholamine response or turnover are implicated for seven of these eight dimensions. One possible implication is that such broad concepts as global activation, arousal, and threshold of the limbic system are perhaps too vague for fruitful physiological investigation (Derryberry & Tucker, 1991).

A fourth perspective is that evolutionary pressures might well have acted more systematically on behavioral output than on physiological mechanisms, with the various physiological mechanisms being recruited to the service of emotion expression and emotion reception on the basis of availability and utility, rather than according to any more systematic or logical principles.

Despite these and other daunting methodological problems, there is encouraging evidence at the physiological level. A reasonable case can be made that a set of discrete emotions are associated with specific *patterns* of physiological response. However, the number of emotions reliably distinguishable by autonomic nervous system (ANS) function may be fewer than those distinguishable by facial movements, and a discrete-emotions approach may need to be supplemented by dimensional concepts. Dimensions can be useful for characterizing both physiology and behavior. For example, Levenson (1988) points out that the *kind* of ANS activity is too narrow a basis for distinguishing some emotions; *amount, latency,* and *duration* of activity are also likely to be important, such as intensity in physiological explanations. On the behavioral side, researchers studying the electroencephalogram, such as Davidson (1992) and Fox (1991), employ the dimensional concepts of positive and negative affect as the behavioral variables of interest.

A few programmatic efforts to relate physiological functioning to temperament have begun. In four samples, Kagan and colleagues (e.g., Kagan, Reznick, & Snidman, 1988; Kagan & Snidman, 1991) showed that a large proportion of extremely behaviorally inhibited infants and young children exhibited signs of high sympathetic tone in the ANS (high, stable heart rate under defined conditions; pupillary dilation during cognitive tasks). Muscular tension in the vocal cords, urinary catecholamine derivative levels, and morning salivary cortisol levels were other physiological components related to behavioral inhibition measured in the laboratory. Chief components at the behavioral level in this project were shyness in the presence of others and reluctance to approach novel objects. These results gain interpretative weight when considered in the context of an examination of familial resemblance. Kagan, Snidman, Julia-Sellers, and Johnson (1991) interviewed 157 first-degree relatives (parents) and 371 second-degree relatives of children who had been assessed extensively in the laboratory and characterized as either inhibited or uninhibited. Relatives of inhibited children reported themselves as more socially anxious than parents of uninhibited children. From twin and adoption studies (Braungart et al., 1992; Emde et al., 1992; Goldsmith, 1989; Matheny, 1989), we know that inhibition and related behavioral characteristics in infants and toddlers are partially

heritable. Thus, some links across levels have been forged in the study of inhibition.

Another promising approach addresses the effects of the sympathetic–adrenomedullary and pituitary–adrenocortical systems by measurement of peripheral catecholamines and cortisol or cortisol-derived excretion products under theoretically specified conditions (e.g., Tennes, Downey, & Vernadakis, 1977). For instance, Gunnar, Mangelsdorf, Larson, and Hertsgaard (1989) showed that distress-prone temperamental traits were associated with increased salivary cortisol when infants were exposed to strange people or places or separated from their mothers. Gunnar, Marvinney, Isensee, and Fisch (1988) studied children with phenylketonuria, who had to submit to frequent blood sampling. They cried intensely from age 2 to 4 years but tended to cry less by age 5, when large increases in cortisol were noted. These children indicated that they had adopted the rule to act "grown-up or tough." To generalize this finding to a principle, cortisol responses to a stressor become strong when the child recognizes that the culture places constraints on the behavioral expression of distress, but lacks good emotion control strategy. Thus, cortisol production is dependent not only on situational context but also on broader cultural demands. As implied from other perspectives in this chapter, a shift from behavioral to biological levels of explication is not a shift from complex to simpler types of explanations. Much other psychophysiological research also makes the point that rearing conditions can affect physiological systems and development of central nervous system parameters that are often uncritically thought of as "underpinnings" or, less deterministically, "indicators" of temperament.

The foregoing is only a small sample of the large literature on physiology, temperament, and emotion (see Baum, Grunberg, & Singer, 1992; Cacioppo & Tassinary, 1990; Gale & Edwards, 1986; Gray, 1987; and Heller, 1990, for reviews). With the development of improved neuroimaging techniques to facilitate integration of human and animal research, progress in this area may be rapid.

The Cognitive Representational Level

Temperament is not often viewed in cognitive terms. However, several cognitive components are key ingredients of emotion, and it is reasonable to assume that individuals vary in the cognitive components, thus making them relevant to temperament.

The most basic question—one debated at length and with substantial progress in the literature—is the relation of emotion and cognition. An important initial observation is that searching for distinctions between emotion systems and cognitive systems can be taken to reductionistic extremes. Averill (1990) reminds us that the same perceptual, memory, and other psychological mechanisms participate in emotional functions in one context and in cognitive functions in another context. According to most emotion theorists, each family of emotions is associated with an organismic or interpersonal goal and a typical pattern of appraisal (Campos et al., 1983; Lazarus, 1991; Smith & Ellsworth, 1985). For instance, the fear system facilitates the goal of escaping in threatening situations and signals submissiveness that may deflect attack. Of course, these goals and appraisals are not necessarily "cold," conscious, cognitive processes. Indeed, some of these goals and appraisals are early-appearing, species-general characteristics that operate at an automatic level. The cognitive components are probably inherent in infant emotion, but we have no evidence concerning whether these cognitive appraisals are a source of temperamental differences among infants. That is, does infant individuality arise only from differences in reactivity, or do they also arise from appraisal components of emotion or from more complex system properties?

Later in development, individual variability in more complex, self-related cognitive appraisals is well documented (Lazarus, 1991). Indeed, I have proposed that the increasing complexity of self-related cognitions associated with emotional reactions is one of the markers of the imprecise boundary area between the domains of temperament and personality (see my remarks in Goldsmith et al., 1987).

Although the role of cognitive processes in temperament itself remains largely unexplored, the relation of temperamental characteristics to cognitive abilities (conceptualized as a different domain of behavior) has been investigated. Rieser-Danner (1989) lists over 20 studies that have explored some aspect of temperament or emotion in relation to cognition or intelligence. The issue is complicated, be-

cause affect is important in determining cognitive state and is explicitly assessed in some test items (Haviland, 1983). A key problem in the literature has been dealing with such confounds. Given that fearfulness implies reduced exploration, sociability implies increased interaction with others, and interest or persistence implies prolonged engagement with tasks, there is ample rationale for seeking these relations.

The Individual Behavioral Level

Because the individual's behavior is overtly observable, most current investigation of temperament is being carried out at the individual behavioral level. Much of this investigation is a search for coherence, but only limited coherence is evident. Temperamental traits apparently do not override contextual influences in organizing behavior. For instance, a colleague and I demonstrated that fearful distress is *moderately* correlated across the contexts of stranger approach and visual cliff episodes, but that avoidance reactions in these two contexts are independent (Goldsmith & Campos, 1990).

We have proposed that the expressive channels for temperament in infancy are facial, vocalic, gestural and postural, and instrumental. The loci of individual differences involve the parameters of single responses (latency, duration [rise and decay time], peak intensity, etc.) and/or the topography of multiple responses (Goldsmith & Campos, 1986). In this handbook, there is little need for elaboration about these components, because the facial and vocalic channels are the subjects of other chapters (Camras, Holland, & Patterson, Chapter 14, and Pittam & Scherer, Chapter 13, respectively). Gestural and postural components of emotion should not be overlooked as indices of temperament.

What have we learned about temperamental coherence at the level of individual behavior from recent research? The salient stability question has been investigated fairly extensively, and Plomin, DeFries, and Fulker (1988, pp. 101–108) offer a concise review. In the Colorado Adoption Project, year-to-year stability correlations from age 1 to age 4 for parental report of temperament are quite high —mostly in the .50s and .60s. Comparable correlations made by testers on the Infant Behavior Record tend to be lower, often near .20

(Plomin et al., 1988). Another instructive report on stability is that by Matheny (1989), who assessed 130 twin subjects at 12, 18, 24, and 30 months, using three assessment techniques for emotionality/fearfulness. As usual, correlations were higher between adjacent ages; correlations across 6 months averaged a bit over .50, with little variation across methods. (Over longer intervals, parental reports tended to show more stability than laboratory observations, which, in turn, were more stable than testers' ratings.) There are many other studies of temperamental stability, and some allow links with other levels of analysis. For instance, Kagan et al. (1988) compared stability for inhibited behavior and physiological profiles, and we (Goldsmith, McArdle, & Thompson, 1989), using longitudinal twin data, demonstrated that almost all of the (moderate) stability in temperamental reactivity and persistence from ages 4 to 7 years was attributable to stability of genetic effects from age 4. Matheny (1989), in the study cited above, also found much greater identical than fraternal twin similarity in trends across ages, regardless of the assessment technique.

The research just reviewed concerns infants and children, which seems appropriate, given that temperament is often defined developmentally. However, much recent adult personality research addresses similar issues. To cite only one example, Tellegen and colleagues have derived factors of positive affectivity, negative affectivity, and constraint from adult self-report and have interpreted these factors in temperament terms (Tellegen, 1985; Tellegen & Waller, in press; Watson & Tellegen, 1985).

Child temperament research and adult personality research have recently converged in efforts to depict temperament–personality content with a five-factor model (Halverson, Kohnstamm, & Martin, in press). A five-factor model (extraversion/surgency; agreeableness/pleasantness; conscientiousness/dependability; emotional stability; and openness to experience or intellect/culture) seems minimally adequate to represent the trait terms in natural language, at least in English (John, 1990). Several investigations have converged to suggest that, allowing for developmental transformations, a similar set of five factors can be extracted from the item content of parental or teacher report temperament questionnaires (see Halverson et al., in press). As in

the adult personality domain, five factors are unlikely to exhaust what is interesting about early temperament, so premature closure of the issue should be avoided.

The Interpersonal Interactional Level

Emotion is observed in contexts that are usually—some would argue always—interpersonal, either explicitly as others are present or implicitly as others figure into the accompanying appraisal process. Other persons can be contexts, elicitors, targets, or mediators of emotion expression. Thus, the interpersonal level is critical for understanding temperament. Slowly, the field has acknowledged Stevenson-Hinde's (1986) view that behavioral characteristics can be placed on a continuum from the individual to the relational, with few constructs lying at the extremes. Granted that most researchers believe that temperamental constructs lie nearer the individual pole, we may ask what aspects of temperament are more explicitly interpersonal. Frijda (1986) offers one answer: "Emotional experience, at its most prototypical, is . . . in part a felt interaction with the environment . . . something between him and me, or between her and me, or it and me" (p. 249). To say that one is in a particular emotional state is also to describe the state of one's relationships at the moment.

Lazarus (1991) also highlights the interpersonal nature of emotion. He states that "to understand emotions we must spell out the particular person–environment relationships that underlie each of the emotion categories" (p. 124). Lazarus has proposed a "core relational theme" for each emotion state. The theme for anger is "a demeaning offense against me or mine"; for shame, it is "having failed to live up to an ego-ideal"; and for compassion, it is "being moved by another's suffering and wanting to help" (p. 122). Interpersonal themes for a dozen other emotion states are offered by Lazarus (1991). From a psychoanalytic perspective, Luborsky (1984; Luborsky & Crits-Christoph, 1990) has proposed somewhat similar "core conflictual relationship themes," which are applicable to individuals under stress. Although Lazarus's themes apply to states and Luborsky's apply to stable dysfunctional behavioral patterns, it seems likely that a set of similar appraisals would apply to stable but normal variation in emotional experience and expression (temperament). Thus, we are sensitized to the essentially interpersonal nature of temperamental differences. Characteristic variation among individuals in the *tendency* to appraise an offense as demeaning, in the *tendency* to appraise one's behavior as failing to meet the standards of the ego ideal, and in how easily one is moved by another's suffering (to repeat three of Lazarus's themes from above) should lead to temperamental variation in adults. Of course, infants probably do not vary in these appraisals; this may well account for the popularity of the infant as a simpler system for the study of temperament.

Early differences in emotional reactivity probably influence the formation of characteristic relational themes, and once formed, these relational themes shape the further development of temperament as personality traits. However, this line of thinking has not yet inspired empirical investigation by temperament researchers, perhaps because of the difficulty of operationalizing the constructs.

There are more obvious and more easily studied interpersonal facets of temperament. For instance, individuals differ in how sensitive they are to the emotional signals of others, as suggested by the variation observed in studies of social referencing (Bradshaw, Goldsmith, & Campos, 1987). Individuals also differ in how clearly they signal their emotional states to others. It is not difficult to imagine that a child raised in a family where the parents' emotional signals are clearly discernible (and thus interpretable) might develop patterns of emotional expression differing from those of a child raised in a family where these signals are ambiguous. In addition, the degree of emotional positivity and negativity expressed in the family perhaps influences temperamental development, and vice versa (Burrowes & Halberstadt, 1987; Halberstadt, 1991).

The one area in which temperament and interpersonal interaction has been evaluated extensively involves infant temperament and the mother-infant attachment relationship. Unfortunately, research and theorizing about temperament and attachment have hinged too closely on the peculiarities of assessing temperament via parental report and attachment via Ainsworth's "Strange Situation" (Ainsworth, Blehar, Waters, & Wall, 1978). Depending on how the question is conceptualized, what sources of evidence are considered valid, and how the studies are quantified (if at all), reviewers have suggested substantial (Kagan, 1989), minimal (Sroufe, 1985), modest (Goldsmith & Alansky, 1987), and various other interesting associations between temperament (usually negative emotionality) and some components of attachment behavior or types of insecure attachment. We have recently summarized these issues (Goldsmith & Harman, in press).

Finally, the best-known aspect of temperament—difficulty, as elaborated by Thomas and Chess (1977)—is inherently an interactive concept. Temperamental difficulty is not easy to research (Bates, 1980), as both "infant input" and "interactive outcome" are often intertwined in its operational definition. Temperamental difficulty must be understood in the broader framework of person–context relations (e.g., Lerner & Lerner, 1989).

The Cultural Level

The relation of culture and emotion is a reinvigorated research topic (see Shweder, Chapter 29, this volume). What relevance does the topic have to temperament? One domain of research is that of national differences in temperament, the sources of which are difficult to locate in cultural variation, gene pool variation, and/or in the combined action of culture and genetic background. Temperament research has centered on differences in neonatal reactivity, mostly between Orientals and Caucasians. Studies that have uncovered early ethnic differences tend to show that Caucasians are somehow more excitable and less inhibited than Orientals (Freedman, 1974; Kagan, Kearsley, & Zelazo, 1978).

Perhaps a more important topic for future research will be how cultural differences in the construction of self affect the development of temperament. Given that emotion theories practically all entail a role for appraisal of self-relevance, differences in the fundamental nature of self might be expected to lead to temperamental differences as the child matures in the culture. Markus and Kitayama (1991) point out that North Americans in the majority culture tend to stress the uniqueness of the self and to reinforce the difference between self and others. In contrast to this North American emphasis on individuation and assertiveness, Japanese culture emphasizes fitting into the group and being similar to others. This cultural difference between independent and interdependent self-systems should affect the development of temperament and lead to mean differences in certain personality traits between cultures. But, as Markus and Kitayama (1991) also suggest, mean differences in construction of self across cultures should not obscure the differences along the independent versus interdependent dimension within cultures. As other major dimensions of cross-cultural variability are identified, undoubtedly we shall discover that individuals within any one culture differ in their standing on these dimensions.

INTEGRATING COMPONENTS AND LEVELS OF TEMPERAMENT INTO SYSTEMATIC DEVELOPMENTAL APPROACHES

This extensive discussion of components and levels of temperamental individuality has perhaps been overly reductionistic. Lines of causality do not always proceed from the deeper organismic levels to the more observable personal and societal levels. Intertwining of components at different levels is pervasive. How do we regain sight of the whole person? How are the facets of temperament functionally integrated? We can turn to dynamic systems theory for an overall framework for answering this question (Fogel & Thelen, 1987). Dynamic systems theorists view emotions as variable rather than discrete. Emotions are self-organizing processes that are embedded in sequences of actions and that result from dynamic interaction among many constituent elements. These elements include cognitive, motoric, and social components. No rules can be stated that would invariably apply to the expression of emotion (Fogel et al., 1992). The application of systems theory to emotion is in an early stage; thus, it is difficult to derive specific hypotheses from a systems theory perspective that would differentiate it from functional (e.g., Barrett & Campos, 1987), social-constructivist (e.g., Gordon, 1989), and appraisal-based (e.g., Lazarus, 1991) perspectives.

Despite this limitation, a systems perspective is a useful counterbalance to reductionistic tendencies in the field of temperament. It reminds us that developmental processes at each of the levels discussed in this chapter not

only proceed apace but are intimately interrelated. Behavioral properties sometimes viewed as temperamental, such as variability in infant cuddliness, can be understood as emergent system properties. Viewed thus, a degree of cuddliness emerges from a developmental context that perhaps includes the state of infant postural competence, facets of infant reactivity and soothability, experience with being held as a negative reinforcer, and undoubtedly other components.

A property of some systems is sensitivity to initial conditions, and temperament is a prime candidate for an initial condition (where "initial" refers not to presence at birth, but to presence at any time a system becomes organized or undergoes transition). A similar idea is inherent in other developmental approaches to emotionality and temperament, most notably in the study of emotional regulation (Kopp, 1989; Rothbart, 1989). The study of emotional regulation best links the concept of temperament to systems-theory-like approaches. Regulatory processes include attentional allocation, communication with others, self-mediated processes, coping styles, and other processes. Emotional regulatory processes can be considered either as processes internal (or specific) to emotional systems or as other external (or more general) processes that interact with emotion developmentally. At the present stage of knowledge, this definitional issue may not be critical. Ultimately, specificity versus generality of regulatory processes is a matter for empirical determination; in any case, individuals show wide variability in outcome of these processes. At least early in development, such differences are often considered as "temperamental," when the term is used without etiological implications (McCall, 1986; Goldsmith, 1986).

Another tenet of dynamic systems theory is that a process is most fruitfully analyzed at times of transition, when new components may enter the system and when rate-controlling processes of the system may change. If we bear these considerations in mind, it is desirable to define temperament as "variability in developing emotion systems," rather than in more deterministic or reductionistic ways. The proper study of temperament, then, would involve analysis of how individuals negotiate significant transitions. Some significant transitions occur on a daily basis and involve new relations of the self, others, and the object world (e.g., meeting a stranger). Other significant transitions are more pervasive and constitute a new setting for the daily transitions (e.g., starting school). As the individual grows, some consistency probably develops in how these transitions are negotiated, and such consistency is termed "temperamental." In fact, consistency is perhaps most apparent at times of transition, as suggested in the long-term follow-up of subjects by Thomas and Chess (1977).

THE CLASSICAL ISSUES OF TEMPERAMENT RESEARCH

If one compares the outlines of the two recent handbooks on temperament (Kohnstamm, Bates, & Rothbart, 1989; Strelau & Angleitner, 1991) to this chapter, a different impression of temperament research may emerge. By and large, temperament researchers have not spent their effort trying to discern links across the various levels of understanding temperament or trying to discern the system properties that may regulate temperamental development. Rather, temperament researchers have debated the structure of temperament (types vs. dimensions; the nine dimensions of Thomas and Chess vs. the five or so typically identified by others), worked to improve measurement techniques, studied stability (more than change), and related temperament to other aspects of socioemotional functioning. They have also sought to understand the clinical implications of temperamental differences (Carey & McDevitt, 1989; Chess & Thomas, 1984; Maziade, 1989). Many of these issues are not directly related to emotionality, but readers of this handbook who wish to be informed about them might consult the two other handbooks listed above.

CONCLUSION

In the future, temperament research and emotion research are likely to become even more closely related, and perhaps indistinguishable. As temperament research moves into the laboratory and observational arenas, the procedures developed for emotion elicitation are likely to be modified for assessing individual differences—a process that has already begun (e.g., Goldsmith & Rothbart, 1991). Similarly, temperament researchers' concerns for applied issues such as educational adjustment

and behavioral problems are similar to the applied concerns of emotion researchers, so investigation of functional significance should itself force convergence of the fields.

Acknowledgment: Some of the research reported in this chapter was supported by a Research Career Development Award from the National Institute of Child Health and Human Development (No. HD00694).

REFERENCES

Ainsworth, M. D. S., Blehar, M. C., Waters, E., & Wall, S. (1978). *Patterns of attachment: A psychological study of the Strange Situation.* Hillsdale, NJ: Erlbaum.

Allport, G. W. (1937). *Personality: A psychological interpretation.* New York: Holt.

Averill, J. R. (1990). Emotion in relation to systems of behavior. In N. L Stein, B. Leventhal, & T. Trabasso (Eds.), *Psychological and biological approaches to emotion* (pp. 385–404). Hillsdale, NJ: Erlbaum.

Barrett, K. C., & Campos, J. J. (1987). Perspectives on emotional development II: A functionalist approach to emotions. In J. D. Osofsky (Ed.), *Handbook of infant development* (2nd ed., pp. 555–578). New York: Wiley-Interscience.

Bates, J. E. (1980). The concept of difficult temperament. *Merrill–Palmer Quarterly, 26,* 299–319.

Bates, J. E. (1989). Concepts and measures of temperament. In G. A. Kohnstamm, J. E. Bates, & M. K. Rothbart (Eds.), *Temperament in childhood* (pp. 3–26). Chichester, England: Wiley.

Baum, A., Grunberg, N. E., & Singer, J. E. (1992). Biochemical measurements in the study of emotion. *Psychological Science, 3,* 56–60.

Bradshaw, D. L., Goldsmith, H. H., & Campos, J. J. (1987). Attachment, temperament, and social referencing: Interrelations among three domains of infant affective behavior. *Infant Behavior and Development, 10,* 223–231.

Braungart, J. M., Plomin, R., DeFries, J. C., & Fulker, D. W. (1992). Genetic influence on tester rated infant temperament as assessed by Bayley's Infant Behavior Record: Nonadoptive and adoptive siblings and twins. *Developmental Psychology, 28,* 40–47.

Burrowes, B. D., & Halberstadt, A. G. (1987). Self and family-expressiveness styles in the experience and expression of anger. *Journal of Nonverbal Behavior, 11,* 254–268.

Buss, A. H., & Plomin, R. (1984). *Temperament: Early developing personality traits.* Hillsdale, NJ: Erlbaum.

Cacioppo, J. T., & Tassinary, L. G. (Eds.). (1990). *Principles of psychophysiology.* Cambridge, England: Cambridge University Press.

Campos, J. J., Barrett, K., Lamb, M. E., Goldsmith, H. H., & Stenberg, C. (1983). Socioemotional development. In M. M. Haith & J. J. Campos (Vol. Eds.), *Handbook of child psychology* (4th ed.): Vol. 2. Infancy and developmental psychobiology (pp. 783–915). New York: Wiley.

Carey, W. B., & McDevitt, S. C. (Eds.). (1989). *Clinical and educational applications of temperament research.* Berwyn, PA: Swets North America.

Chess, S., & Thomas, A. (1984) *Origins and evolution of behavior disorders.* New York: Brunner/Mazel.

Cohen, D. J., Dibble, E., & Grawe, J. M. (1977). Fathers'

and mothers' perceptions of children's personality. *Archives of General Psychiatry, 34*, 480–487.

Davidson, R. J. (1992). Emotion and affective style: Hemispheric substrates. *Psychological Science, 3*, 39–43.

Derryberry, D., & Tucker, D. M. (1991). The adaptive base of the neural hierarchy: Elementary motivational controls on network function. In R. Dienstbier (Ed.), *Nebraska Symposium on Motivation: Vol. 38. Perspectives on motivation* (pp. 289–342). Lincoln: University of Nebraska Press.

Eaves, L. J., Eysenck, H. J., & Martin, N. (1989). *Genes, culture, and personality*. New York: Academic Press.

Emde, R. N., Plomin, R., Robinson, J., Corley, R., DeFries, J., Fulker, D. W., Reznick, J. S., Campos, J., Kagan, J., & Zahn-Waxler, C. (1992). Temperament, emotion, and cognition at fourteen months: The MacArthur Longitudinal Twin Study. *Child Development, 63*, 1437–1455.

Fahrenberg, J. (1991). Differential psychophysiology and the diagnosis of temperament. In J. Strelau & A. Angleitner (Eds.), *Explorations in temperament* (pp. 317–333). New York: Plenum Press.

Fogel, A., & Thelen, E. (1987). Development of early expressive and communicative action: Reinterpreting the evidence from a dynamic systems perspective. *Developmental Psychology, 23*, 747–761.

Fogel, A., Nwokah, E., Dedo, J. Y., Messinger, D., Dickson, K. L., Matusov, E., Holt, S. A. (1992). Social process theory of emotion: A dynamic systems approach. *Social Development, 1*, 122–142.

Fox, N. A. (1991). If it's not left, it's right: Electroencephalogram asymmetry and the development of emotion. *American Psychologist, 46*, 863–872.

Freedman, D. G. (1974). *Human infancy: An evolutionary perspective*. Hillsdale, NJ: Erlbaum.

Frijda, N. H. (1986). *The emotions*. Cambridge, England: Cambridge University Press.

Gale, A., & Edwards, J. A. (1986). Individual differences. In M. G. H. Coles, E. Donchin, & S. W. Porges (Eds.), *Psychophysiology: Systems, processes, and applications* (pp. 431–507). New York: Guilford Press.

Goldsmith, H. H. (1978). *Behavior genetic analyses of early personality (temperament): Developmental perspectives from the longitudinal study of twins during infancy and early childhood*. Doctoral dissertation, University of Minnesota.

Goldsmith, H. H. (1986). Heritability of temperament: Cautions and some empirical evidence. In G. A. Kohnstamm (Ed.), *Temperament discussed: Temperamental and development in infancy and childhood* (pp. 83–96). Lisse, The Netherlands: Swets & Zeitlinger.

Goldsmith, H. H. (1988). Human developmental behavioral genetics: Mapping the effects of genes and environments. *Annals of Child Development, 5*, 187–227.

Goldsmith, H. H. (1989). Behavior-genetic approaches to temperament. In G. A. Kohnstamm, J. E. Bates, & M. K. Rothbart (Eds.), *Temperament in childhood* (pp. 111–132). Chichester, England: Wiley.

Goldsmith, H. H., & Alansky, J. A. (1987). Maternal and infant temperamental predictors of attachment: A meta-analytic review. *Journal of Consulting and Clinical Psychology, 55*, 805–816.

Goldsmith, H. H., Buss, A. H., Plomin, R., Rothbart, M. K., Thomas, A., Chess, S., Hinde, R. A., & McCall, R. B. (1987). Roundtable: What is temperament? Four approaches. *Child Development, 58*, 505–529.

Goldsmith, H. H., & Campos, J. J. (1982). Toward a theory of infant temperament. In R. N. Emde & R. J. Harmon

(Eds.), *The development of attachment and affiliative systems*. New York: Plenum Press.

Goldsmith, H. H., & Campos, J. J. (1986). Fundamental issues in the study of early temperament: The Denver Twin Temperament Study. In M. E. Lamb, A. L. Brown, & B. Rogoff (Eds.), *Advances in developmental psychology* (Vol. 4, pp. 231–283). Hillsdale, NJ: Erlbaum.

Goldsmith, H. H., & Campos, J. J. (1990). The structure of infant temperamental dispositions to experience fear and pleasure: A psychometric perspective. *Child Development, 61*, 1944–1964.

Goldsmith, H. H., & Gottesman, I. I. (1981). Origins of variation in behavioral style: A longitudinal study of temperament in young twins. *Child Development, 52*, 91–103.

Goldsmith, H. H., & Harman, C. (in press). Temperament and attachment; individual and relationship. *Current Directions in Psychological Science*.

Goldsmith, H. H., Jaco, K. L., & Elliott, T. K. (1986). Genetic analyses of infant and early childhood temperament characteristics. *Behavior Genetics, 16*, 620. (Abstract).

Goldsmith, H. H., McArdle, J. J., & Thompson, B. (1989). Longitudinal twin analyses of childhood temperament. *Behavior Genetics, 19*, 759–760. (Abstract)

Goldsmith, H. H., & Rothbart, M. K. (1991). Contemporary instruments for assessing early temperament by questionnaire and in the laboratory. In J. Strelau & A. Angleitner (Eds.), *Explorations in temperament* (pp. 249–272). New York: Plenum Press.

Gordon, S. (1989). The socialization of children's emotions: Toward a unified constructionist theory. In C. Saarni & P. L. Harris (Eds.), *Children's understanding of emotion* (pp. 319–349). New York: Cambridge University Press.

Gray, J. A. (1987). *The psychology of fear and stress*. Cambridge, England: Cambridge University Press.

Gunnar, M. R., Mangelsdorf, S., Larson, M., & Hertsgaard, L. (1989). Attachment, temperament and adrenocortical activity in infancy: A study of psychoendocrine regulation. *Developmental Psychology, 25*, 355–363.

Gunnar, M., Marvinney, D., Isensee, J., & Fisch, R. O. (1988). Coping with uncertainty: New models of the relation between hormonal, behavioral, and cognitive processes. In D. Palermo (Ed.), *Coping with uncertainty: Biologic, behavioral, and developmental perspectives* (pp. 101–130). Hillsdale, NJ: Erlbaum.

Halberstadt, A. G. (1991). Toward an ecology of expressiveness: Family socialization in particular and a model in general. In R. S. Feldman & B. Rimé (Eds.), *Fundamentals of nonverbal behavior* (pp. 106–160). New York: Cambridge University Press.

Halverson, C. F., Kohnstamm, G. A., & Martin, R. P. (Eds.). (in press). *The developing structure of temperament and personality from infancy to adulthood*. Hillsdale, NJ: Erlbaum.

Haviland, J. M. (1983). Looking smart: The relationship between affect and intelligence in infancy. In M. Lewis (Ed.), *Origins of intelligence: Infancy and early childhood* (pp. 423–449). New York: Plenum Press

Heller, W. (1990). The neuropsychology of emotion: Developmental patterns and implications for psychopathology. In N. L Stein, B. Leventhal, & T. Trabasso (Eds.), *Psychological and biological approaches to emotion* (pp. 385–404). Hillsdale, NJ: Erlbaum.

Hinde, R. A. (1989). Temperament as an intervening variable. In G. A. Kohnstamm, J. E. Bates, & M. K. Rothbart (Eds.), *Temperament in childhood* (pp. 27–33). Chichester, England: Wiley.

John, O. P. (1990). The "Big Five" factor taxonomy: Dimensions of personality in the natural language and in questionnaires. In L. A. Pervin (Ed.), *Handbook of personality: Theory and research* (pp. 66–100). New York: Guilford Press.

Kagan, J. (1989). *Unstable ideas: Temperament, cognition, and self.* Cambridge, MA: Harvard University Press.

Kagan, J., Kearsley, R. B., & Zelazo, P. R. (1978). *Infancy: Its place in human development.* Cambridge, MA: Harvard University Press.

Kagan, J., Reznick, S., & Snidman, N. (1988). Biological bases of childhood shyness. *Science, 240,* 167–171.

Kagan, J., & Snidman, N. (1991) Temperamental factors in human development. *American Psychologist, 46,* 856–862.

Kagan, J., Snidman, N., Julia-Sellers, M., & Johnson, M. O. (1991). Temperament and allergic symptoms. *Psychosomatic Medicine, 53,* 332–340.

Kohnstamm, G. A., Bates, J. E., & Rothbart, M. K. (Eds.). (1989). *Temperament in childhood.* Chichester, England: Wiley.

Kopp, C. B. (1989). Regulation of distress and negative emotions: A developmental view. *Developmental Psychology, 25,* 343–354.

Lazarus, R. S. (1991). *Emotion and adaptation.* New York: Oxford University Press.

Lerner, R. M., & Lerner, J. V. (1989). Organismic and social contextual bases of development: The sample case of adolescence. In W. Damon (Ed.), *Child development today and tomorrow.* San Francisco: Jossey-Bass.

Levenson, R. W. (1988). Emotion and the autonomic nervous system: A prospectus for research on autonomic specificity. In H. Wagner (Ed.), *Social psychophysiology and emotion: Theory and clinical applications* (pp. 17–42). Chichester, England: Wiley.

Loehlin, J. C. (1992). *Genes and environment in personality development.* Newbury Park, CA: Sage.

Luborsky, L. (1984). *Principles of psychoanalytic psychotherapy.* New York: Basic Books.

Luborsky, L., & Crits-Christoph, P. (1990). *Understanding transference.* New York: Basic Books.

Malatesta, C. Z. (1990). The role of emotions in the development and organization of personality. In R. A. Thompson (Ed.), *Nebraska Symposium on Motivation: Vol. 36. Socioemotional development* (pp. 1–56). Lincoln: University of Nebraska Press.

Markus, H. R., & Kitayama, S. (1991). Culture and the self: Implications for cognition, emotion, and motivation. *Psychological Review, 98,* 224–253.

Matheny, A. P. (1989). Children's behavioral inhibition over age and across situations: Genetic similarity for a trait during change. *Journal of Personality, 57,* 215–226.

Maziade, M. (1989). Should adverse temperament matter to the clinician? An empirically based answer. In G. A. Kohnstamm, J. E. Bates, & M. K. Rothbart (Eds.), *Temperament in childhood* (pp. 421–435). Chichester, England: Wiley.

McCall, R. B. (1986). Issues of stability and continuity in temperament research. In R. Plomin & J. Dunn (Eds.), *The study of temperament: Changes, continuities and challenges* (pp. 13–25). Hillsdale, NJ: Erlbaum.

Mehrabian, A. (1991). Outline of a general emotion-based theory of temperament. In J. Strelau & A. Angleitner (Eds.), *Explorations in temperament* (pp. 75–86). New York: Plenum Press.

Netter, P. (1991). Biochemical variables in the study of temperament: Purposes, approaches, and selected findings. In J. Strelau & A. Angleitner (Eds.), *Explorations in temperament* (pp. 249–272). New York: Plenum Press.

Plomin, R. (1986). *Development, genetics and psychology.* Hillsdale, NJ: Erlbaum.

Plomin, R., DeFries, J. C., & Fulker, D. W. (1988). *Nature and nurture in infancy and early childhood.* New York: Cambridge University Press.

Riese, M. L. (1990). Neonatal temperament in monozygotic and dizygotic twin pairs. *Child Development, 61,* 1230–1237.

Rieser-Danner, L. A. (1989). *Cognitive testing in infants: The importance of individual differences in fear.* Unpublished doctoral dissertation, University of Texas.

Rothbart, M. K. (1981). Measurement of temperament in infancy. *Child Development, 52,* 569–578.

Rothbart, M. K. (1989). Temperament and development. In G. A. Kohnstamm, J. E. Bates, & M. K. Rothbart (Eds.), *Temperament in childhood* (pp. 187–248). Chichester, England: Wiley.

Shaver, P., Schwartz, J., Kirson, D., & O'Connor, C. (1987). Emotion knowledge: Further exploration of a prototype approach. *Journal of Personality and Social Psychology, 52,* 1061–1086.

Smith, C., & Ellsworth, P. (1985). Patterns of cognitive appraisal in emotion. *Journal of Personality and Social Psychology, 48,* 813–838.

Sroufe, L. A. (1985). Attachment classification from the perspective of infant–caregiver relationships and infant temperament. *Child Development, 56,* 1–14.

Strelau, J. (1987). Emotion as a key concept in temperament research. *Journal of Research in Personality, 21,* 510–528.

Strelau, J., & Angleitner, A. (Eds.). (1991). *Explorations in temperament.* New York: Plenum Press.

Stevenson-Hinde, J. (1986). Towards a more open construct. In G. A. Kohnstamm (Ed.), *Temperament discussed: Temperament and development in infancy and childhood* (pp. 97–106). Lisse, The Netherlands: Swets & Zeitlinger.

Tellegen, A. (1985). Structures of mood and personality and their relevance to assessing anxiety, with an emphasis on self-report. In A. H. Tuma & J. D. Maser (Eds.), *Anxiety and the anxiety disorders* (pp. 681–706). Hillsdale, NJ: Erlbaum.

Tellegen, A., & Waller, N. G. (in press). Exploring personality through test construction: Development of the Multidimensional Personality Questionnaire. In S. R. Briggs & J. M. Cheek (Eds.), *Personality measures: Development and evaluation* (Vol. 1). Greenwich, CT: JAI Press.

Tennes, K., Downey, K., & Vernadakis, A. (1977). Urinary cortisol excretion rates and anxiety in normal 1-year-old infants. *Psychosomatic Medicine, 39,* 178–187.

Thomas, A., & Chess, S. (1977). *Temperament and development.* New York: Brunner/Mazel.

Tooby, J., & Cosmides, L. (1990). On the universality of human nature and the uniqueness of the individual: The role of genetics and adaptation. *Journal of Personality, 58,* 17–68.

Watson, D., & Tellegen, A. (1985). Toward a consensual structure of mood. *Psychological Bulletin, 98,* 219–235.

Zivin, G. (1989). Innately potentiated communication behaviors. In W. A. Koch (Ed.), *For a semiotics of emotion* (pp. 12–33). Bochum, Germany: Bochumer Beitrage zur Semiotik.

26

Emotion and Illness:
The Mind Is in the Body

HOWARD LEVENTHAL
LINDA PATRICK-MILLER

WHY A CHAPTER
ON EMOTION AND HEALTH?

A large and ever-growing body of epidemiological data links health outcomes such as cardiovascular disease, cancer, and autoimmune
disease to psychosocial variables. Emotional
processes are repeatedly identified as one possible mediator of these associations. There is,
however, a far more important set of issues to
address—specifically, the implications of the
emotion–illness linkages for emotion theory. In
short, looking at emotion through the window
of illness can provide empirical evidence with
respect to issues of major concern to emotion
theorists and can reveal theoretically important
aspects of emotion processes that might otherwise remain hidden.

We have organized our chapter around four
themes or questions that are of importance to
emotion theory, and present data from health
research which suggest specific answers to
these questions. The questions are as follows:

1. Are emotions best represented by a
dimensional or a categorical (i.e., differential)
model? In attempts to cope with the apparently endless variation of verbal and facial
expressions descriptive of emotion, some theorists have suggested lists of discrete or basic
emotions (e.g., see Ekman, 1992; Ekman,
Friesen, & Ellsworth, 1982; Izard, 1991), while
others have suggested that all known emotions
can be described and/or generated by the joint

effects of two or three underlying dimensions
(see Ekman et al., 1982; Russell, 1980). In this
chapter, the relationships of affect to somatic
symptomatology and to disease suggest the
need to retain a differential model of emotion.

2. Is social communication the primary
function of emotion? Some theorists have suggested that emotions have few if any intrapersonal functions, and that emotionally
provocative stimuli will elicit emotional expressions only in the presence of social cues (Fridlund, 1991). The effects of social support on
health reinforce the functions of emotion in
social communication.

3. Are emotions a product of a hierarchically structured processing system (Leventhal,
1984; Leventhal & Scherer, 1987)? We argue
that the importance of the physiological component of affect for health outcomes, and
the debate respecting the interdependence of
emotion and cognition (Lazarus, 1991; Zajonc,
1984), suggest the need for a hierarchically
structured emotion model.

4. Are emotions multicomponent structures
(Ortony & Turner, 1990) that are organized by
neural and non-neural processes? Neural networks are in vogue to account for the integration of the various components of emotional
behavior (i.e., imagery, facial expression, overt
action, etc.; Bower & Cohen, 1982). However,
research in the health area suggests that
endocrine and immune factors may play an
important role in organizing affective states,

and this may require a major overhaul of network models.

Although these questions and issues have been discussed at length by emotion theorists, data from the health domain provide clear reinforcement for some answers and strong discomfirmation for others.

DIMENSIONAL VERSUS CATEGORICAL REPRESENTATIONS OF EMOTION

Watson and his colleagues (Watson & Clark, 1984; Watson & Pennebaker, 1989) have advocated a dimensional approach to emotion and to the relationship of emotion to health indicators. They accept the formulation that positive affect and negative affect are two independent dimensions of emotion rather than opposite poles of a common dimension (Zevon & Tellegen, 1982). Next they review a substantial body of data showing positive correlations between measures of negative affect and reports of somatic symptoms, and they suggest that this correlation is independent of the various components (anxiety, depression, anger) comprising the negative affect pole (Watson & Pennebaker, 1989). From these data, Watson and Pennebaker (1989) and likeminded investigators (Costa & McCrae, 1985) conclude that it is unnecessary to distinguish among the negative affects to establish a causal relationship of affect to disease.

Evidence for a Categorical Approach

Two types of data from health research suggest that it is essential to disaggregate the negative affect pole. The first involves the association of negative affects with somatic symptoms; the second involves the association of negative affects with disease. Although the data support the value of analysis at the level of specific emotions or categories, they do not preclude the utility of dimensional concepts for the analysis of other problems such as the decision to use health care (Taylor, 1991).

Specific Negative Affects and Symptoms

Several studies that have replicated the cross-sectional associations of negative affect measures with somatic symptoms also show that global measures of negative affect have virtually no relationship to changes in somatic symptoms over time (e.g., Spiro, Aldwin, Levenson, & Bosse, 1990). Data from our laboratory, however, show that confirmatory factor analyses separating negative affect into two key constituents (i.e., anxiety and depression) produce a solution that accounts for significantly more variance in emotion ratings than does a global model, and yields a significant positive association of depression with increases in symptoms and no such relationship of anxiety to increases in symptoms (Leventhal, Hansell, Diefenbach, & Leventhal, in prep.). Thus, a differential affect model does a better job than a dimensional model in accounting for *changes* in symptomatology over time.

Our data also show, however, that a global measure of stress (i.e., the accumulation of a large set of negative life events) predicts decisions to utilize health care (Cameron, Leventhal, & Leventhal, in press). Thus, analysis at the level of specific affects may be critical for the prediction of changes in symptoms, whereas analysis at a more global level (i.e., that of general distress) may prove more relevant for higher-order decisions such as using health care.

Affects and the Stress–Disease Relationship

Research on two personality dispositions, Type A behavior pattern and Type C behavior pattern, suggests that it is necessary to differentiate negative affects if we are to understand the mediation of these stress–disease relationships.

Type A Behavior: Hostility and Coronary Disease. The Type A behavior pattern was originally defined by Friedman and Rosenman (1974) as having the four attributes of time urgency, competitiveness, job involvement, and intensity of expression (e.g., explosive speech). Although the epidemiological evidence (Booth-Kewley & Friedman, 1987; Contrada, Leventhal, & O'Leary, 1990; Dembroski, Weiss, Shields, Haynes, & Feinleib, 1978; Matthews, 1988) indicates that the relationship of Type A behavior to coronary disease is robust (2.0 risk ratio for Type A vs. Type B) and replicable in prospective studies (Matthews, 1988), recent research has attempted to decompose and identify the pathogenic components of the Type A pattern. Two sets of issues have emerged in this pursuit. The first involves identifying the Type A components responsible for the physiological and physical (e.g., atherosclerotic) changes that occur over long periods of time and serve as the precursors to acute coronary events (e.g., heart attack) (Kuller, 1979). The second set of issues involves identifying the personality factors and/or the emotional events that may be causally related to the physiological processes responsible for triggering coronary events (e.g., arrhythmias causing sudden death; Kamarck & Jennings, 1991) and creating coronary symptoms (e.g., arterial constriction that may evoke angina; Contrada et al., 1990).

Hostility, an enduring, negative mood state characterized by expressions of irritability and anger (Smith, 1992), has been a candidate for mediation of both the long-term development of atherosclerosis leading to coronary occlusions, and increases in the probability of acute coronary events during environmental crises (Contrada et al., 1990; Kamarck & Jennings, 1991). This linkage has been supported in both cross-sectional and prospective studies (see Smith, 1992; Matthews, 1988).

The precise nature of the association of hostility with cardiovascular disease is unclear because hostility has been measured in different ways and questions about the commonality of the measures have been raised (Smith, 1992). The two most common means of assessment are the ratings of responses during the Type A interview (Dembroski & Costa, 1987) and the Cook and Medley (1954) hostility scale. These instruments appear to measure both the experiential feelings of resentment and expressive aspects of hostility, and to relate the perception of the interpersonal environment as intentionally provoking (see Smith, 1992, p. 141). Earlier interpretations of the Type A pattern (Glass, 1977) suggested that anger and/or hostility emerged as a consequence of feelings of threats. While definition of the hostility construct is not yet complete, the existing data support the need for a differential affect model: Some negative affects such as depressed mood are not predictive of coronary disease (Matthews, 1988), and others, such as anxiety (Matthews, 1988) and somatic exhaustion (Appels, 1990), which are predictive of coronary disease in some studies, are unlikely to predict cardiac outcomes.

Type C Behavior: Depression and Cancer.
The behavioral traits defining the Type C personality are less clearly defined than those of the coronary-prone Type A counterpart. Morris and Greer (1980) conceptualized Type C individuals as "emotionally contained," especially under stress. This conclusion was based on 5- and 10-year follow-up findings that women whose 3-month postdiagnosis adjustment to cancer was rated as either "stoic" or "helpless" had worse outcomes than those rated as having a "fighting spirit" or "denial" (Greer, Morris, & Pettingale, 1979; Pettingale, 1985; Greer, Pettingale, Morris, & Haybittle, 1985). Temoshok reports having proposed a similar constellation (Temoshok & Heller, unpublished, summarized in Temoshok & Fox, 1984), defining the Type C personality or coping style as "cooperative, appeasing, unassertive, patient, unexpressive of negative emotions (particularly anger), and compliant with external authority" (Temoshok, 1987, p. 548).

Although investigators of the Type C behavior pattern have attempted to winnow the toxic trait(s) from this constellation, they have had less success in identifying a mediating affect than the investigators who netted hostility from the Type A sea. Depression, hopelessness–helplessness, repressive coping style, and deficient social support have each been associated somewhat inconsistently with a poorer cancer outcome, hopelessness–helplessness being the least inconsistent (Contrada et al., 1990). Many diverse outcome measures have been utilized in these studies, including cancer diagnosis, patient prognosis at the time of cancer diagnosis, rate of cancer recurrence, years survived, and patient mortality; this variety has no doubt contributed to the inconsistencies of the studies' results. (See Contrada et al., 1990, and Temoshok, 1987, for reviews.)

The proposed physiological mechanism involved in the Type C–cancer relationship has centered on the "learned helplessness" paradigm, in which laboratory animals are exposed to uncontrollable stressors. These "helpless" animals show depletion of brain norepinephrine and activation of the hypothalamic–pituitary–adrenal axis, resulting in the release of corticosteroids into the blood stream. Some of the well-known immunosuppressive effects of corticosterone have been documented in these uncontrollably stressed animals as well: increased growth of implanted tumors (Riley, Fitzmaurice, & Spackman, 1981; Sklar & Anisman, 1979; Visintainer, Volpicelli, & Seligman, 1982; Laudenslager, Ryan, Drugan, Hyson, & Maier, 1983), decreased T-lymphocyte proliferation (Laudenslager et al., 1983), and decreased natural killer (NK) cell activity (Greenberg, Dyke, & Sandler, 1984; see Harbuz & Lightman, 1992, and Levy, Herberman, Maluish, Schlien, & Lippman, 1985, for reviews). Elevation of endogenous opioids has also been observed (Shavit, Lewis, Terman, Gale, & Liebes, 1984). Of these, decreased NK cell activity has been most vigorously pursued as the physiological link between human helplessness–hopelessness and cancer. Although the simplicity of this model (uncontrollable stressor → decreased NK cell activity → cancer) is appealing, it is also deceptive (see Pettingale, 1985) because the variety of cancers and the physiological complexity of their developmental history make identifying a mediational role for emotional factors extremely difficult.

Although the Type C cancer model is not as well validated as the Type A cardiovascular model, the data regarding both the initiation and development of each of these disorders implicate different negative affects, that is, the sympathetic component of hostility–anxiety for coronary disease (Contrada et al., 1982) and the "anterior hypothalamic" component of depression for cancer (hopeless giving up; Asnis & Miller, 1989). Thus, both the previously discussed findings on affect and symptoms, and the relationships of Type A and Type C patterns to disease, support disaggregation of the negative affect pole into at least two different negative emotions.

SOCIAL COMMUNICATION: A SOURCE AND BUFFER OF STRESS

Emotions are social processes. Psychoevolutionary (Plutchik, 1984) and sociological (Kemper, 1984) theorists link categories and dimensions of emotional behavior to specific functions of social organization; for instance, acceptance and rejection are seen as related to group formation and bonding, and anger and fear are viewed as related to hierarchical group structure (i.e., dominance–submission). The data from health research reinforce the emphasis on the social functions of emotion in two ways: They affirm the importance of social factors as sources of life stress, and they show how social factors can buffer or inoculate against stress-induced illness.

Research in the stress–illness area has had three major goals: (1) to confirm the hypothesis that stress does indeed affect illness; (2) to identify relationships between specific types of environmental stress and specific diseases, providing further support for an emotion-specific approach to stress–illness relationships; and (3) to determine whether social support, both instrumental and affective, can ameliorate stress–illness outcomes.

Situational Stress and Illness

Investigators of individual dispositions such as the Type A and Type C patterns recognized that these traits do not exist in a vacuum: The toxic emotional (hence disease-producing) processes associated with them are brought into play by person–environment transactions, which are primarily social. The emphasis on situational factors as elicitors of toxic emotional reactions stems from the writings of two major figures, Walter Cannon and Hans Selye. Cannon cites observations of death-inducing environmental stressors that date back to the 16th century: ". . . an ominous and persistent state of fear can end the life of a man" (1957, p. 188; see also the early work on stress and gastric ulceration by Wolf & Wolff, 1947). Selye (1956), on the other hand, formulated the hypothesis that environmental changes, both positive and negative, produce a general adaptation syndrome that can be disease-inducing. Selye's ideas stimulated Holmes and Rahe (1967) to develop a checklist of life events, the Social Readjustment Rating Scale. The intensity of social changes, as indicated by a numerical value, varies throughout the list from very mild (vacation) to very severe (spouse's death), and is summed to provide a quantitative assessment of life stress (Ruch & Holmes, 1971; Masuda & Holmes, 1989).

The Social Readjustment Rating Scale has also been used to link life stressors to diseases as varied as tuberculosis and diabetes, and has been used in closed populations and communities (see Cohen & Williamson, 1991). The outcomes of these studies have been mixed, some supporting the hypothesis that life events cause illness and others not. The inconsistencies have led to intensive criticism of the use of the Social Readjustment Rating/life events approach: It has failed to account for more than a trivial portion of variance in health outcomes (Rabkin & Streuning, 1976); it has slighted chronic hassles, which may accumulate to produce disease outcomes (Kanner, Coyne, Schaefer, & Lazarus, 1981; see critique by Dohrenwend & Shrout, 1985); it has treated positive and negative changes as equivalent, as suggested by Selye (1956), thus obscuring the role of stress for illness outcomes (Sarason, Sarason, Potter, & Antoni, 1985; Vinokur & Seltzer, 1975); and it has ignored a wide range of factors that may interact to exacerbate or ameliorate stress, the most critical of which are encompassed by the term "social support."

Other approaches to life stress measurement, such as those developed by Cohen, Kamarck, and Mermelstein (1983) (see also Sarason et al., 1985), have shown excellent predictive power for common viral infections. In a recent study by Cohen, Tyrrell, and Stein (1991), a double-blind randomized trial, 394 volunteers were randomly exposed to one of five different viruses or a placebo. Subjects with high stress scores (the subjects were divided into quintiles according to three measures of life stress, including the Social Readjustment Rating Scale) were 3.45 times more likely to become infected by the virus (viral shedding); however, they were no more likely to be judged sick (manifest observable symptoms). These relationships persisted after controlling for a wide range of factors, including two personality traits (self-esteem and optimism), various health behaviors (such as smoking and alcohol consumption), and other opportunities for viral exposure. There were no signs of moderating influence by other factors.

Differing Emotional Outcomes of Threat and Loss

Recent work in the stress–illness arena provides additional support for an emotion-specific approach to stress–illness relationships. Brown and Harris (1978) classify stressors as threats to self, which seem to produce fear and/or anxiety and to precipitate cardiac events (Neilson, Brown, & Marmot, 1989), and significant losses (e.g., death of a spouse or an offspring), which appear to trigger clinical depression and its associated morbidities. These investigators have also shown that positive and/or exciting events can trigger schizophrenic episodes in individuals diagnosed with this disorder. It is worth noting that the two

types of events Brown and Harris identified as antecedents to anxiety and depression, respectively, match the events described by undergraduate subjects as antecedents to these same affects (Shaver, Schwartz, Kirson, & O'Connor, 1987). Thus, highly skilled investigators and naive college subjects have identified the same classes of life events as antecedents to specific emotions and their associated physical and psychological disorders.

Social Support: A Buffer of Life Stress

In their detailed summary of findings from studies of social support, Cohen and Wills (1985) conclude that support has both a main and a buffering effect on health outcomes. Individuals with extensive support are healthier than those without it, as well as less likely to become emotionally distressed or physically ill when they do experience negative life events (Brown & Harris, 1978; Cohen & Wills, 1985).

A test of the hypothesis that social support can buffer the impact of life stress on illness requires evidence for the presence of environmental stress, that is, there must be an emotional distress response to buffer. Support is complex. It can be instrumental, emotional, informational, and/or esteem-oriented (Cohen & Hoberman, 1983; Pearlin, 1985), and it is most effective when it is relevant to the stressor (Gottlieb, 1988). The buffering hypothesis has proven robust when psychological outcomes (e.g., anxiety and depression) are the dependent measures. Studies of physical illness have yielded more equivocal results. Support has been found to serve as a buffer against flare-ups of arthritic conditions during stressful life circumstances (Genest, 1989) and against asthmatic attacks in similar circumstances, but data have failed to show that support can ameliorate other types of stress-induced illness.

The protective role of social contact is illustrated by Smith and colleagues' (Smith, Pope, Sanders, Allred, & O'Keefe, 1988) analysis of the role of social support in ameliorating the toxic impact of hostility on the development of coronary disease. Although atherosclerosis is a relatively self-perpetuating disease, the maintenance of hostility over the many years necessary to develop the life-threatening advanced stages of atherosclerotic disease is a central issue in this emotion–disease relationship. One factor that may be responsible for maintaining this toxic emotional reaction is the stability of the individual's environment. For example, a person may be enmeshed for years, even a lifetime, in a highly competitive, unsupportive work setting in which intensive goal striving is accompanied by a high level of uncertainty respecting performance evaluation. The analysis of Smith and Pope (1990) suggests that the Type A pattern may contribute to this stability, as the Type A individual's rapid and automatic interpretation of situations as competitions and potential attacks on his or her self-esteem produces a set of hostile facial, vocal, and postural reactions, which when perceived by others generate aggressive and avoidant counterresponses. In sum, Type A behavior creates the very environment needed to confirm and sustain a hostile outlook. Moreover, hostile behavior deprives the individual of the instrumental and emotional supports that could reduce the individual's stress and moderate toxic anger. Thus, the physiological components of the hostile activation can ply their toxic trade uninterrupted by the counteractive, systemic reactions elicited by the sharing of positive affects.

Perhaps because they are less able to elicit the interpersonal intimacy that defines the core of support, Type A individuals turn to substance use to regulate their emotional states. Highly hostile individuals report heavier smoking, alcohol and caffeine consumption, and caloric intake than their less hostile peers (Koskenvuo et al., 1988; Scherwitz et al., 1991; Siegler, Peterson, Barefoot, & Williams, 1991). As smoking and obesity are well-known risk factors for the development of coronary disease, hostile individuals may increase their cardiac vulnerability by engaging in these poor health behaviors. In summary, the link of hostility and coronary disease highlights the importance of social factors in emotional communication and the regulation of emotional states.

HIERARCHICAL PROCESSES OF EMOTION: EVIDENCE FROM THE ILLNESS LINK

Our examination of the relationship of emotion to health outcomes points to a multilevel emotional processing system. Two aspects of this system are apparent. First, the system as a whole is multilevel: It includes cognitive, expressive, and instrumental motor reactions, as well as systemic reactions (i.e., endocrine and immune reactions). Specifically, the studies we have reviewed suggest strongly that the subjective and expressive patterns differentiating emotions such as anxiety, hostility, and depression are probably joined to different patterns at the systemic level. Second, studies of emotional reactions to health crises suggest that the cognitive system is itself multilevel, and that emotional responses may be a product of the integrated action of cognitions at a base perceptual level and a higher-order, abstract, or propositional level.

Cognitive, Expressive, and Systemic Levels

Emotion Is a Multilevel Concept

Both early laboratory studies that varied eliciting circumstances (e.g., threat vs. insult) (Schachter, 1957) and more recent studies varying facial expressions (Ekman et al., 1982) suggest reliable linkages among eliciting conditions, subjective emotional states, and physiological (systemic) reaction patterns. The identification of reproducible associations between emotional response patterns and disease (i.e., hostility and anxiety for coronary disease; depression, and hopelessness–helplessness for cancers) lends further support to the hypothesis that each discrete emotion may be associated with an identifiable systemic (autonomic/immune) response pattern. Indeed, the data are of particular significance, as they suggest the need for a persistent association of cognitive, expressive, and systemic components in order for an emotion to affect the occurrence of a chronic illness.

In our view, emotions are integrations of multiple components at the cognitive, subjective, expressive, instrumental, and systemic (autonomic/immune) levels (Leventhal 1979, 1980, 1984), and each discrete emotion represents a unique assembly of components. While the affects of the emotion on health reflect the activity of the entire emotion system, it is the systemic (autonomic/immune) component of the system that is directly disease-inducing. Though the systemic component is an integral part of an emotion, along with the other, more visible (expressive) and verbally accessible (cognitions and subjective moods) levels, different emotions may share one or more systemic components and mediate similar disease outcomes.

The Systemic Level of Discrete Emotions

Investigations of the impact of emotional factors on disease suggest at least three different patterns or prototypic organizations at the level of systemic processes: (1) a *"work–effort"* pattern associated with integrated output of instrumental activity; (2) a *"stress–distress"* pattern associated with cardiac disease risk; and (3) a *"depressed–activity"* pattern linked to depression and immune suppression. The *"work–effort"* pattern is characterized by the readiness for and the subsequent performance of overt action, such as physical exercise; the *"stress–distress"* pattern appears to divide into two contrasting patterns—a readiness to approach and attack, or a readiness to avoid and flee (Gray, 1990). At the systemic level, the stress–distress pattern shows a 300% increase in epinephrine and a 50% increase in norepinephrine, whereas the ratios are the opposite for the work–effort pattern (Dimsdale & Moss, 1986). The differences in autonomic responding seem to be dependent upon the instrumental coping procedure called forth by the individual's situation (a combination of activation and approach or avoidance for stress–distress, vs. activation and energy expenditure for work–effort). Thus, a particular pattern (high epinephrine, lower norepinephrine) of intense autonomic reactivity in the absence of overt action is probably the culprit that creates risk for cardiac disease; it defines the final common point on the direct pathway from "hostility" to the physiological changes inducing atherosclerosis.

The emotional and motor response patterns triggering acute coronary disease events contrast somewhat with those involved in the promotion of atherosclerosis, the underlying condition. Strokes and heart attacks can be generated by intense surges of motor activation and autonomic response, produced either by the stress–distress component that is generated in threatening situations or by the high output levels of the work–effort pattern generated in challenging situations. The increase in heart rate, blood pressure, and so on accompanying these activations can trigger ventricu-

lar fibrillation, resulting in a cardiovascular event (Kamarck & Jennings, 1991). Indeed, even strong positive affects or the abrupt termination of the work–effort response may threaten a compromised system, increasing the risk of a cardiac event and sudden death. The risk-inducing high levels of norepinephrine produced in the abrupt cessation of vigorous exercise are readily avoided by gradual post-exercise tapering of activity (Dimsdale, Alpert, & Schneiderman, 1986).

The depressed-activity pattern is the motor and systemic organization that results when an animal ceases active efforts to cope with an inescapable and uncontrollable stressor, or when an animal receives an immunological challenge (e.g., infectious disease). The former situation is a case of emotion and behavior leading to somatic changes, the latter one of illness leading to changes in emotion and behavior. When the pattern is elicited by an uncontrollable stressor, depletion of brain norepinephrine appears to be the factor causative of disease outcomes ranging from stomach ulceration (Weiss, 1972) to death (Von Holst, 1986); the specific outcome varies as a function of the species and the stressor. The increase of circulating corticosteroids consequent to norepinephrine depletion and activation of the hypothalamic–pituitary–adrenal axis is responsible for many of the immune changes also observed in this activity pattern. Changes in the cellular arm of the immune system include a decrease in macrophage, NK cell, and T-helper lymphocyte activity (Fauci & Dale, 1975; Onsrud & Thursby, 1981; Besodovsky, del Rey, Sorkin, & Dinarello, 1986), including the production of soluble immune factors (e.g., interleukin-1 and interleukin-2 [IL-1, IL-2]; Gillis, Crabtree, & Smith, 1979; Besodovsky et al., 1986). Some of the immune cells that are affected by circulating corticosteroid (e.g., NK cells, macrophages, and monocytes) have the ability, independent of the humoral arm of the immune system, to destroy blood and tissue cells infected with bacteria or oncogenic viruses, as well as mutant cells that have broken away from primary tumor sites. NK cells, specifically, have been hypothesized as the first round of defense against the development of primary tumors and tumor metastases (Herberman & Ortaldo, 1981; Levy et al., 1985). As previously mentioned, decreased NK cell activity is the most commonly hypothesized physiological link in the Type C–cancer model.

When the depressed-activity pattern results from an immunological challenge rather than an unsuccessful attempt to cope with an uncontrollable stressor, it is prompted by the immune signal IL-1 to the hypothalamic–pituitary–adrenal axis (Besedovsky et al., 1983, 1986) and the sympathetic nervous system via corticotropin-releasing factor (CRF) (Sundar et al., 1990). The resulting increase of circulating corticosteroid operates in a negative feedback loop to inhibit the action of several types of immune cells. Although this immune system down-regulation is hypothesized to have potentially hazardous outcomes (e.g., cancer onset or metastasis) when initiated by a hopeless interpretation of an uncontrollable stressor, at the peak of the immune response to an infectious challenge, it appears to work constructively to (1) limit tissue destruction by soluble immune factors (e.g., histamines, prostaglandins, leukitrines); (2) prevent development of autoantibodies and potential autoimmune disorders (e.g., lupus erythematosus, rheumatoid arthritis); and (3) conserve energy (Asnis & Miller, 1989).

Cognition and the Emotion–Disease Relationship

Cognitive factors play a central role in emotion theory as elicitors of emotional states (e.g., Lazarus & Folkman, 1984) and as modifiers of emotional experience (Leventhal & Scherer, 1987; Leventhal & Tomarken, 1986; Mandler, 1975; Schachter & Singer, 1962). Data on the emotional reactions elicited by illness suggest that at least two levels of cognition are involved in the production of these emotional states: a perceptual or schematic level of cognition, which automatically and effortlessly generates short-lived (conditioned) emotional responses, and a conceptual level, which is time-ordered and controlled.

The following two studies are examples of the joint operation of perceptual and conceptual representations of health problems in the generation of emotion. Brownlee, Leventhal, and Balaban (1992) compared autonomic activation (elevated heart rate) in response to self-generated images ("perceptual" cognition) of health crises (having a heart attack, finding a tumor) in comparison to two self-generated control images (exercising, having a calm day).

"Health-vigilant" subjects (i.e., those whose self-concepts led to high scores on measures of somatic self-monitoring and a tendency to interpret somatic signs as indicators of illness) maintained heart rate elevations throughout the imagery period for the health threat scenes, but not for the two control scenes; "not-health-vigilant" subjects' autonomic activity was the same during all scenes as that of the vigilant subjects during the control scenes. As in earlier studies of snake phobics (Lang, 1984), perceptual imagery was critical for the immediate elicitation of affect, but this activation was sustained only when linked to a conceptual framework that defined somatic sensations as threats of illness.

In the second example, Easterling and Leventhal (1989) obtained data on worry about cancer from two groups of women: a group successfully treated for breast cancer 2 to 5 years earlier, and a group of their close friends who had not had breast cancer. On the basis of data showing that illnesses are represented in both an abstract and a concrete form—that is, by a label and by somatic sensations or symptoms (Leventhal & Diefenbach, 1991)—it was hypothesized that both types of cognition would be necessary for the elicitation of disease-based worry. Women from both groups who labeled themselves as vulnerable to cancer reported increased levels of worry about cancer if they perceived themselves as experiencing a large number of general somatic symptoms. The level of worry increased with the number of symptoms experienced. They did not, however, report worry about cancer if they did not experience symptoms. On the other hand, little worry was reported by women who conceptualized their chances of a recurrence as extremely low (low vulnerability to cancer), regardless of how many somatic symptoms they experienced. Not surprisingly, the ex-patients reported more worry about cancer overall than did their friends. Vulnerability beliefs and symptom experiences were unrelated to self-reported daily moods. Thus, two levels of cognitive activity are needed to elicit worry: the perception of symptoms, and self-conception of vulnerability.

The differentiation of the cognitive system into automatic, schema-driven perceptual processing and conceptual or controlled processing suggests an additional facet to understanding how emotional states such as hostility can be maintained over the long periods of time needed to develop a chronic disease such as atherosclerosis or hypertension. As mentioned earlier, the Type A person's aggressive and hostile display may contribute to the creation of a stressful environment and undercut the possibility of positive social support. Given that the Type A person's behavior is based upon a particular set of cognitions, why aren't the cognitions and accompanying hostile, emotional patterns readily changed? The bi-level cognitive model provides an interesting answer. We argue that the expressive (facial, postural, and vocal) reactions associated with hostility are generated by automatic, *schematic* cognitions (Berkowitz, in press), which are elicited by perceptual "cues." Because these expressive reactions communicate hostility, which in turn elicits matching withdrawal and/ or hostile counterreactions from the social environment (Leventhal, 1980, 1984), the social environment's matching behavior will necessarily confirm the hostile person's conceptual view of his or her interpersonal (e.g., work) world. Thus, the automatic, rapid elicitation of expressive reactions by schematic cognitions creates a social context reinforcing the conceptualization that work (or other interpersonal) situations are hostile and threatening. This conceptualization then provides an explanation and justification for the Type A person's acting self-protectively to deter unjust assaults.

Investigations of adaptation to chronic and life-threatening illnesses reveal other facets of the cognitive system involved in the production and control of emotional behavior. Living with a life-threatening chronic disease means living with an immutable, pervasive, internal threat to the self—in other words, the conditions for learned helplessness (Abramson, Seligman, & Teasdale, 1978; Taylor, 1983). When these conditions define the self (i.e., when disease and self overlap), a condition of "hopelessness" results, and depression may be the result (Taylor, 1983). When social and personal conditions allow individuals to perform cognitive, social, and instrumental coping procedures, which enable them to encapsulate or compartmentalize the disease and to view it as a part of but not coextensive with the self, they can retain their individual identity and feelings of control over the disease-free portion of their lives (Nerenz & Leventhal, 1983). Common-sense ideas about

a disease—for instance, whether it is thought of as acute and self-limited, as cyclic or recurrent, or as chronic and life-threatening (Leventhal, Easterling, Coons, Luchterhand, & Love, 1986)—may influence the way the disease is related to the self-system. While the factors resulting in one resolution or another are poorly understood, it is reasonable to assume that they involve multiple levels of cognition and a variety of procedures for self-appraisal (Leventhal, Diefenbach, & Leventhal, 1992; Taylor, 1983). Thus, the procedures used to regulate threat (e.g., maintaining one's self-identity and participation in a close support network) affect whether the individual's emotional state will be one of depression or of flexible vigilance.

EMOTION AND DISEASE AS MULTICOMPONENT PROCESSES

Our review of the data linking emotional factors to disease shows that the linkage is bidirectional: Emotional states appear to play a causal role in the generation of illness, and illness plays a causal role in the generation of emotion. This bidirectional relationship can be seen at both the systemic and cognitive levels; emotion and illness share specific components at each level. Coping failure and depression appear to produce, at the systemic level, a somatic pattern of depressed activity involving corticosteroid-induced immunosuppression implicated in the onset of cancers. A highly similar pattern seems to be elicited by bacterial illness. Specifically, negative mood (anger, anxiety, depression) increases and positive mood (elation, surgency, vigor, social affection) decreases 12 hours after an initial bacterial infection—that is, 36 hours prior to the onset of any somatic symptoms, such as fever (Canter, 1972). It has been hypothesized (Hart, 1988) that this change of affect may well be the result of the initiation of the biological energy conservation process seen in the downregulation of peaked immune response. Phagocytosis of infectious organisms leads to the production of the endogenous pyrogen IL-1. Via the hypothalamus, IL-1 initiates a cascade of neuroendocrine activity, inducing fever, chills, and depressed activity (manifested in fatigue, excessive sleepiness, and anorexia); depressed mood is a likely accompaniment of these somatic changes. Given this mechanism, it is not at all surprising that Aneshensel, Frerichs, and Huba (1984) found that depressed mood appeared 1 to 2 weeks following the onset of common illnesses.

There are, however, many other studies reporting depression following the onset of both non-life-threatening (e.g., rheumatoid arthritis; Genest, 1989) and life-threatening (e.g., cancer, heart failure; Rodin & Voshart, 1986) chronic disease, where affect is initiated by cognitions rather than by the activation of depressed activity. In these cases, it is the cognitive components that are shared by depression and illness that may be critical for the creation of chronic states of depressed mood: The concepts associated with life-threatening chronic disease and those linked to learned helplessness include immutability, pervasiveness, and self-internalization (Abramson et al., 1978; Taylor, 1983).

As our examination of emotion–illness linkages has led us to decompose emotional processes into levels of cognitive, expressive, and systemic processes, and to make further differentiations within each level, we have moved concepts such as fear, anger, and depression to a higher level in the conceptual hierarchy: They are now superordinate labels (some might say "chapter headings") for an underlying set of processes. The factors involved in these processes are determinants of different aspects of the emotion–disease relationship. But having differentiated these emotion concepts and assigned their components the mediating role in the correlation between social-psychological factors and disease, we must confront a basic question as to the mechanism(s) integrating these components into discrete affects.

Traditional Answers to Integration

Both nativist and environmental theories have suggested hypotheses to account for the organization of specific emotions (see Leventhal, 1970, 1980, 1984, 1991). Nativist hypotheses, arising primarily from neo-Darwinian views of expressive behavior (Darwin, 1872/1904), assume that the patterning of emotional displays is innate, and that facial feedback is the source of subjective feeling (Duclos et al., 1989; Tomkins, 1962, 1963) and a key determinant of autonomic response patterns (Ekman, 1992; Levenson, Ekman, & Friesen, 1990). These models have had difficulty dealing with issues such as the low correlation among various measures of affect (Cacioppo et al., 1992), individual differences in their patterning, and the apparent similarities of systemic reactions for affects as different as anger and joy (Schachter & Singer, 1962). On the other hand, cognitive or constructionist models (Ortony & Turner, 1990) account for emotional differentiation in the presence of a dissociation and a presumably homogeneous physiological system by arguing that socially acquired "labels," verbal and situational schemas, define specific emotional states.

Top-Down and Bottom-Up Integration: The Mind Is in the Body

In our view, both neural (cognitive) and humoral (systemic—i.e., endocrine and immune) factors are active in the integration of the components that form our emotions; that is, the organization is both top-down and bottom-up. The primary top-down model derives from computer-based, "network" analogies (Bower & Cohen, 1982; Mandler, 1975). It implies that innate and learned representations and procedures are stored at specific loci, and that the activation of a specific locus in an emotion network spreads via neural communication. The result is an organized interpretive–motor response pattern. The loci may be universal (i.e., yes–no switches capable of storing varied information), or they may be modules that perform specific functions (e.g., speech decoding or speech encoding). It is a model suited for the activation and maintenance of patterning over relatively short time frames (milliseconds to minutes). We believe that a top-down model is both incomplete and fundamentally flawed, as it separates neural and endocrine communication—a distinction which is no longer considered valid. "The major control systems of the body are the nervous and endocrine systems . . . their functional integration is so complete that they are now regarded as one system" (Pettingale, 1985, p. 782).

Communication via endocrine and immune systems, or bottom-up structuring, is extremely complex. The circulating messengers produced by endocrine glands (e.g., epinephrine, norepinephrine, substance P), immune cells (e.g., interleukins, prostaglandins), and other tissue (e.g., cytokines) attach to cell receptor sites on a variety of tissues (e.g., neural, muscle, immune, endocrine) mediating both local and systemic physiological changes. We have proposed that these chemical signals create and/or organize behavioral states (e.g., system states; Leventhal, 1991, in press), and that their activity and regulatory feedback loops play important roles in initiating and sustaining the mood and emotional states that can promote disease. Whereas the effects of some neuroendocrine reactions, including those elicited during encounters with stressful environments, continue for days, weeks, and perhaps months beyond the termination of the visible stressor, others appear only after the stressor is removed (Mason, 1968).

Neuroendocrine modification of the number of receptor sites on targeted tissue also provides for longer-term down-regulation (or up-regulation) of activity within specific organ systems. Thus, a systemic pattern that may be adaptive and protective, such as depressed activity following infection, may have pathological effects when up-regulation of receptor sites maintains this pattern for an extended time frame. As health data require that we conceptualize emotions as self-regulating systems, they remind us that instrumental (coping) procedures (e.g., approach and/or avoidance; Davidson, 1992) are intrinsic parts of the emotion system and play a crucial role in organizing the system, establishing new set points via up- or down-regulation of receptor sites, and generating or ameliorating disease. Therefore, it is an error to identify either the duration or the toxicity of emotional states solely with the cognitive or the overt expressive reactions accompanying them.

CONCLUSION: SELF-REGULATION AND AFFECT–DISEASE RELATIONSHIPS

Assuming that emotional processes are the key factors linking psychosocial factors to disease, we have reviewed data covering both the relationships of psychosocial factors to disease and the relationships of disease to emotion. We selected those themes and data that were useful for defining the mechanisms that mediate or bridge the emotion–disease relationship. In building this bridge we have emphasized the following four features of the emotion system:

1. Emotions must be treated as a differentiated set in order to clarify emotion–disease linkages, though dimensional aspects of emotion (perceiving oneself as distressed) can affect decisions to engage in complex actions, such as calling for medical care.

2. Emotions are embedded in a social framework. Indeed, interpersonal contact (i.e., social support) plays a powerful role in regulating emotional reactions and moderating the effects of stress on health. Social factors are critical for health outcomes because they can directly moderate the toxic effects of emotional distress, and health may suffer further in the absence of a beneficent social context if individuals choose risky behaviors (e.g., substance use) to regulate distress.

3. Emotions are the product of a multilevel system: Processing takes place at the cognitive, feeling, motor (expressive, postural, autonomic), and systemic (endocrine and immune) levels.

4. Every level of the emotion system is itself multicomponent, and the integration of these components is affected from the top down (by neural activity) and from the bottom up (by endocrine activity).

The study of health and emotion involves, however, a vast array of topics and themes in addition to those we have used. Among the omissions, studies of pain stand out. This domain has provided a powerful set of tools for the examination of cognition–affect interactions, including phenomena such as the affective amplification of sensory processes (Leventhal & Everhardt, 1979), the formation of pain memories (Melzack, 1992), and the multilayering of the cognitive system in pain control (Hilgard, 1969).

We believe that detailed examination of the emotion–disease relationship can enrich our view of the components and dynamics of emotion systems. We believe that this domain provides a valuable platform for the study of emotion processes. But it is only one of many such platforms, and a rich and valid understanding of the emotion system will require an integration of views from multiple perspectives.

Acknowledgments. Preparation of this chapter was supported in part by Grant No. AG03501 from the National Institute on Aging. We would like to thank Elaine A. Leventhal, Michael Diefenbach, and Richard Contrada for their helpful comments.

REFERENCES

Abramson, L. Y., Seligman, M. E. P., & Teasdale, J. D. (1978). Learned helplessness in humans: Critique and reformulation. *Journal of Abnormal Psychology*, 87, 49–74.

Aneshensel, C. S., Frerichs, R. R., & Huba, G. J. (1984). Depression and physical illness: A multiwave, non-recursive causal model. *Journal of Health and Social Behavior*, 25, 310–371.

Appels, A. (1990). Mental precursors of myocardial infarction. *British Journal of Psychiatry*, 156, 465–471.

Asnis, G. M., & Miller, A. H. (1989). Phenomenology and biology of depression: Potential mechanisms for neuromodulation of immunity. In A. H. Miller (Ed.), *Depressive disorders and immunity* (pp. 51–64). Washington, DC: American Psychiatric Press.

Berkowitz, L. (in press). Towards a general theory of anger and emotional aggression: Implications of the cognitive–neoassociationistic perspective for the analysis of anger and other emotions. In R. Wyer & T. Srull (Eds.), *Advances in social cognition* (Vol. 6). Hillsdale, NJ: Erlbaum.

Besedovsky, H. O., del Rey, A., Sorkin, E., Da Prada, M., Burri, R., & Honegger, C. (1983). The immune response evokes changes in brain noradrenergic neurons. *Science*, 221, 564.

Besedovsky, H., del Rey, A., Sorkin, E., & Dinarello, C. A. (1986). Immunoregulatory feedback between interleukin-one and glucocorticoid hormones. *Science*, 233, 652–664.

Booth-Kewley, S., & Friedman, H. S. (1987). Psychological predictors of heart disease: A quantitative review. *Psychological Bulletin*, 101, 343–362.

Bower, G. H., & Cohen, P. R. (1982). Emotional influences on learning and cognition. In M. S. Clark & S. J. Fiske (Eds.), *Affect and cognition* (pp. 263–289). Hillsdale, NJ: Erlbaum.

Brown, G. W., & Harris, T. O. (1978). *Social origins of depression*. London: Tavistock.

Brownlee, S., Leventhal, H., & Balaban, M. (1992). Autonomic correlates of illness imagery. *Psychophysiology*, 29, 142–153.

Cacioppo, J. T., Uchino, B. N., Crites, S. L., Snydersmith, M. A., Smith, G., Bernston, G. G., & Lang, P. J. (1992). Relationship between facial expressiveness and sympathetic activation in emotion: A critical review, with emphasis on modeling underlying mechanisms and individual differences. *Journal of Personality and Social Psychology*, 62, 110–128.

Cameron, L., Leventhal, E. A., & Leventhal, H. (in press). Symptom representations and affect as determinants of care-seeking. *Health Psychology*.

Cannon, W. B. (1957). "Voodoo" death. *Psychosomatic Medicine*, 19, 182–189.

Canter, A. (1972). Changes in mood during incubation of acute febrile disease and the effects of pre-exposure psychological status. *Psychosomatic Medicine*, 34, 424–430.

Cohen, S., & Hoberman, H. (1983). Positive events and social support as buffers of life change stress. *Journal of Applied Social Psychology*, 13, 99–125.

Cohen, S., Kamarck, T., & Mermelstein, R. (1983). A global measure of perceived stress. *Journal of Health and Social Behavior*, 24, 385–396.

Cohen, S., Tyrrell, D. A., & Smith, A. P. (1991). Psychological stress and susceptibility to the common cold. *New England Journal of Medicine*, 325, 606–612.

Cohen, S., & Williamson, G. W. (1991). Stress and infectious disease in humans. *Psychological Bulletin*, 109, 5–24.

Cohen, S., & Wills, T. (1985). Stress, social support, and the buffering hypothesis. *Psychological Bulletin*, 98, 310–357.

Contrada, R. J., Glass, D. C., Krakoff, L. R., Krantz, D. S., Kehoe, K., Isecke, W., Collins, C., & Elting, E. (1982). Effects of control over aversive stimulation and Type A behavior on cardiovascular and plasma catecholamine response. *Psychophysiology*, 19, 408–419.

Contrada, R., Leventhal, H., & O'Leary, A. (1990). Personality and health. In L. A. Pervin (Ed.), *Handbook of personality: Theory and research* (pp. 638–669). New York: Guilford Press.

Cook, W. W., & Medley, D. M. (1954). Proposed hostility and pharisaic–virtue scales for the MMPI. *Journal of Applied Psychology*, 38, 414–418.

Costa, P. T., Jr., & McCrae, R. R. (1985). Hypochondriasis, neuroticism, and aging: When are somatic complaints unfounded? *American Psychologist*, 40, 19–28.

Darwin, C. (1904). *The expression of the emotions in man and animals*. London: John Murray. (Original work published 1872)

Davidson, R. J. (1992). Prolegomenon to the structure of emotion: Gleanings from neuropsychology. *Cognition and Emotion*, 6, 245–268.

Dembrowski, T. M., & Costa, P. T., Jr. (1987). Coronary-prone behavior: Components of the Type A pattern and hostility. *Journal of Personality*, 55, 211–235.

Dembroski, T. M., Weiss, S. M., Shields, J. L., Haynes, S., & Feinleib, M. (Eds.). (1978). *Coronary-prone behavior*. New York: Springer-Verlag.

Dimsdale, J. E., Alpert, B. S., & Schneiderman, N. (1986). Exercise as a modulator of cardiovascular reactivity. In K. A. Matthews, S. M. Weiss, T. Detre, T. M. Dembroski, B. Falkner, S. B. Manuck, & R. B. Williams, Jr. (Eds.), *Handbook of stress, reactivity, and cardiovascular disease* (pp. 365–384). New York: Wiley.

Dimsdale, J. E., & Moss, J. (1986). Plasma catecholamines in stress and exercise. *Journal of the American Medical Association*, 243, 340–342.

Dohrenwend, B. P., & Shrout, P. E. (1985). "Hassles" in the conceptualization and measurement of life stress variables. *American Psychologist*, 40, 780–785.

Duclos, S. E., Laird, J. D., Schneider, E., Sexter, M., Stern, L., & Van Lighten, O. (1989). Emotion-specific effects of facial expressions and postures on emotional experience. *Journal of Personality and Social Psychology*, 57, 100–108.

Easterling, D., & Leventhal, H. (1989). The contribution of concrete cognition to emotion: Neutral symptoms as elicitors of worry about cancer. *Journal of Applied Psychology*, 74, 787–796.

Ekman, P. (1992). Are there basic emotions? *Psychological Review*, 99, 550–553.

Ekman, P., Friesen, W. V., & Ellsworth, P. (1982). What emotion categories or dimensions can observers judge from facial behavior? In P. Ekman (Ed.), *Emotion in the human face* (2nd ed., pp. 39–55). New York: Cambridge University Press.

Fauci, A. S., & Dale, D. C. (1975). Alternate-day prednisone therapy and human lymphocyte subpopulations. *Journal of Clinical Investigations*, 55, 22–32.

Fridlund, A. J. (1991). Sociality of solitary smiling: Potentiation by an implicit audience. *Journal of Personality and Social Psychology, 60,* 229–240.

Friedman, M., & Rosenman, R. H. (1974). *Type A behavior and your heart.* New York: Knopf.

Genest, M. (1989). The relevance of stress to rheumatoid arthritis. In R. W. J. Neufeld (Ed.), *Advances in the investigation of psychological stress* (pp. 343–366). New York: Wiley.

Gillis, S., Crabtree, G. R., & Smith, K. A. (1979). Glucocorticoid-induced inhibition of T cell growth factor production: I. The effect on mitogen-induced lymphocyte proliferation. *Journal of Immunology, 123,* 1624–1631.

Glass, D. C. (1977). *Behavioral patterns, stress, and coronary heart disease.* Hillsdale, NJ: Erlbaum.

Gottlieb, B. H. (1988). Marshaling social support: The state of the art in research practice. In B. H. Gottlieb (Ed.), *Marshalling social support: Formats, processes and effects* (pp. 11–52). Newbury Park, CA: Sage.

Gray, J. A. (1990). Brain systems that mediate both emotion and cognition. *Cognition and Emotion, 4*(3), 269–288.

Greenberg, A., Dyck, D., & Sandler, L. (1984). Opponent processes, neurohormones and natural resistance. In B. H. Fox & B. H. Newberry (Eds.), *Impact of psychoendocrine systems in cancer and immunity* (pp. 255–258). Toronto: Hogrefe.

Greer, S., Morris, T., & Pettingdale, K. W. (1979). Psychological response to breast cancer: Effect on outcome. *Lancet, ii,* 785–787.

Greer, S., Pettingale, K. W., Morris, T., & Haybittle, J. (1985). Mental attitudes toward cancer: An additional prognostic factor. *Lancet, i,* 750.

Harbuz, M. S., & Lightman, S. L. (1992). Stress and the hypothalamo–pituitary–adrenal axis: Acute, chronic, and immunological activation. *Journal of Endocrinology, 134,* 327–339.

Hart, B. L. (1988). Biological basis of the behavior of sick animals. *Neuroscience and Behavioral Reviews, 12,* 123–137.

Herberman, R. B., & Ortaldo, J. R. (1981). Natural killer cells: Their role in defenses against disease. *Science, 214,* 24–30.

Hilgard, E. R. (1969). Pain as a puzzle for psychology and physiology. *American Psychologist,* 103–113.

Holmes, T., & Rahe, R. (1967). The Social Readjustment Rating Scale. *Journal of Psychosomatic Research, 11,* 213–218.

Izard, C. E. (1991). *The psychology of emotions.* New York: Plenum Press.

Kamarck, T., & Jennings, J. R. (1991). Biobehavioral factors in sudden cardiac death. *Psychological Bulletin, 109,* 42–75.

Kanner, A. D., Coyne, J. C., Schaefer, C., & Lazarus, R. S. (1981). Comparison of two modes of stress management: Daily hassles and uplifts versus major life events. *Journal of Behavioral Medicine, 4,* 1–39.

Kemper, T. D. (1984). Power, status, and emotions: A sociological contribution to a psychophysiological domain. In K. R. Scherer & P. Ekman (Eds.), *Approaches to emotion* (pp. 369–383). Hillsdale, NJ: Erlbaum.

Koskenvuo, M., Kapiro, J., Rose, R. J., Kesnaiemi, A., Sarnaa, S., Heikkila, K., & Langinvanio, H. (1988). Hostility as a risk factor for mortality and ischemic heart disease in men. *Psychosomatic Medicine, 50,* 330–340.

Kuller, L. H. (1979). Natural history of coronary heart disease. In M. L. Pollock & D. H. Schmidt (Eds.),

Heart disease and rehabilitation (pp. 32–56). Boston: Houghton Mifflin.

Lang, P. J. (1984). Cognition and emotion: Concept and action. In C. E. Izard, J. Kagan, & R. B. Zajonc (Eds.), *Emotions, cognition, and behavior* (pp. 192–228). New York: Cambridge University Press.

Laudenslager, M. L., Ryan, S. M., Drugan, R. C., Hyson, R. L., & Maier, S. F. (1983). Coping and immunosuppression: Inescapable but not escapable shock suppresses lymphocyte proliferation. *Science, 221,* 568–570.

Lazarus, R. S. (1991). Cognition and motivation in emotion. *American Psychologist, 46,* 352–367.

Lazarus, R. S., & Folkman, S. (1984). *Stress, appraisal, and coping.* New York: Springer-Verlag.

Levenson, R. W., Ekman, P., & Friesen, W. V. (1990). Voluntary facial action generates emotion-specific autonomic nervous system activity. *Psychophysiology, 27,* 363–384.

Leventhal, H. (1970). Findings and theory in the study of fear communications. In L. Berkowitz (Ed.), *Advances in experimental social psychology* (Vol. 5, pp. 119–186). New York: Academic Press.

Leventhal, H. (1979). A perceptual–motor processing model of emotion. In P. Pliner, K. Blankstein, & I. M. Spigel (Eds.), *Advances in the study of communication and affect: Perception of emotion in self and others* (Vol. 5, pp. 1–46). New York: Plenum Press.

Leventhal, H. (1980). Toward a comprehensive theory of emotion. In L. Berkowitz (Ed.), *Advances in experimental social psychology* (Vol. 13, pp. 139–207). New York: Academic Press.

Leventhal, H. (1984). A perceptual motor theory of emotion. In L. Berkowitz (Ed.), *Advances in experimental social psychology* (Vol. 17, pp. 117–182). New York: Academic Press.

Leventhal, H. (1991). Emotion: Prospects for conceptual and empirical development. In R. J. Lister & H. J. Weingartner (Eds.), *Perspectives on cognitive neuroscience* (pp. 325–348). New York: Oxford University Press.

Leventhal, H. (in press). A componential, self-regulative systems view of Berkowitz's cognitive–neoassociationistic model of anger. In R. S. Wyer & T. Srull (Eds.), *Advances in social cognition.* Hillsdale, NJ: Erlbaum.

Leventhal, H., & Diefenbach, M. (1991). The active side of illness cognition. In J. A. Skelton & R. T. Croyle (Eds.), *Mental representation in health and illness* (pp. 247–272). New York: Springer-Verlag.

Leventhal, H., Diefenbach, M., & Leventhal, E. A. (1992). Illness cognition: Using common sense to understand treatment adherence and affect cognition interactions. *Cognitive Therapy and Research, 16,* 143–163.

Leventhal, H., Easterling, D. V., Coons, H. L., Luchterhand, C. M., & Love, R. R. (1986). Adaptation to chemotherapy treatments. In B. Andersen (Ed.), *Women with cancer* (pp. 172–203). New York: Springer-Verlag.

Leventhal, H., & Everhardt, D. (1979). Emotion, pain, and physical illness. In C. E. Izard (Ed.). *Emotions and psychopathology* (pp. 263–299). New York: Plenum Press.

Leventhal, H., Hansell, S., Diefenbach, M., & Leventhal, E. A. (in preparation). *Depression, anxiety, energy, and physical symptom reporting among older adults.* Manuscript in preparation.

Leventhal, H., & Scherer, K. R. (1987). The relationship of emotion to cognition: A functional approach to semantic controversy. *Cognition and Emotion, 1,* 3–28.

Leventhal, H., & Tomarken, A. J. (1986). Emotion: Today's problems. *Annual Review of Psychology, 37*, 565–610.

Levy, S. M., Heberman, R. B., Maluish, A. M., Schlien, B., & Lippman, M. (1985). Prognostic risk assessment in primary breast cancer by behavioral and immunological parameters. *Health Psychology, 4*, 99–113.

Mandler, G. (1975). *Mind and emotion.* New York: Wiley.

Mason, J. (1968). A review of psychoendocrine research. *Psychosomatic Medicine, 30*, 576–607, 631–653.

Masuda, M., & Holmes, T. H. (1989). Magnitude estimations of social readjustments. In T. H. Holmes & E. M. David (Eds.), *Life changes, life events, and illness* (pp. 41–49). New York: Praeger.

Matthews, K. A. (1988). Coronary heart disease and Type A behavior: Update on an alternative to the Booth-Kewley and Friedman quantitative review. *Psychological Bulletin, 104*, 373–380.

Melzack, R. (1992). Phantom limbs. *Scientific American, 266*, 120–126.

Morris, T., & Greer, S. (1980). A "Type C" for cancer? *Cancer Detection and Prevention, 3*, 102. (Abstract)

Neilson, E., Brown, G. W., & Marmot, M. (1989). Myocardial information. In G. W. Brown & T. O. Harris (Eds.), *Life events and illness* (pp. 313–342). New York: Guilford Press.

Nerenz, D. R., & Leventhal, H. (1983). Self-regulation in chronic illness. In T. G. Burish & L. A. Bradley (Eds.), *Coping with chronic disease: Research and applications* (pp. 13–37). New York: Academic Press.

Onsrud, M., & Thorsby, E. (1981). Influence of *in vivo* hydrocortisone on some human blood lymphocyte populations: 1. Effect on NK cell activity. *Scandinavian Journal of Immunology, 13*, 573–579.

Ortony, A., & Turner, T. J. (1990). What's basic about basic emotions? *Psychological Review, 97*, 315–331.

Pearlin, L. I. (1985). Social structure and processes of support. In S. Cohen & S. L. Syme (Eds.), *Social support and health* (pp. 43–60). Orlando, FL: Academic Press.

Pettingale, K. W. (1985). Toward a psychobiological model of cancer: Biological considerations. *Social Science and Medicine, 20*, 779–787.

Plutchik, R. (1984). Emotions: A general psychoevolutionary theory. In K. R. Scherer & P. Ekman (Eds.), *Approaches to emotion* (pp. 197–218). Hillsdale, NJ: Erlbaum.

Rabkin, J. G., & Streuning, E. L. (1976). Life events, stress, and illness. *Science, 194*, 1013–1020.

Riley, V., Fitzmaurice, M. A., & Spackman, D. H. (1981). Psychoneuroimmunologic factors in neoplasia: Studies in animals. In R. Ader (Ed.), *Psychoneuroimmunology* (pp. 31–93). New York: Academic Press.

Rodin, G., & Voshart, K. (1986). Depression in the medically ill: An overview. *American Journal of Psychiatry, 143*, 694–705.

Ruch, L. O., & Holmes, T. H. (1971). Scaling of life change: Comparison of direct and indirect methods. *Journal of Psychosomatic Research, 15*, 221–227.

Russell, J. A. (1980). A circumplex model of affect. *Journal of Personality and Social Psychology, 39*, 1161–1178.

Sarason, I. G., Sarason, B. R., Potter, E. H., & Antoni, M. H. (1985). Life events, social support, and illness. *Psychosomatic Medicine, 47*, 156–163.

Schachter, J. (1957). Pain, fear, and anger in hypertensive and normotensives. *Psychosomatic Medicine, 19*, 17–29.

Schachter, S., & Singer, J. (1962). Cognitive, social, and physiological determinants of emotional state. *Psychological Review, 69*, 379–399.

Scherwitz, L. W., Perkins, L. L., Chesney, M. A., Hughes, G. H., Sidney, S., & Manolio, T. A. (1991, March). *Cook-Medley hostility and detrimental health behaviors in young adults: The CARDIA Study.* Paper presented at the meeting of the Society of Behavioral Medicine, Washington, DC.

Selye, H. (1956). *The stress of life.* New York: McGraw-Hill.

Shaver, P., Schwartz, J., Kirson, D., & O,Connor, C. (1987). Emotion knowledge: Further exploration of a prototype approach. *Journal of Personality and Social Psychology, 52*, 1061–1086.

Shavit, Y., Lewis, J. W., Terman, G. W., Gale, R. P., & Liebes, J. C. (1984). Opioid peptides mediate the suppressive effect of stress on natural killer cell cytotoxicity. *Science, 223*, 188–190.

Siegler, I. C., Peterson, G. L., Barefoot, J. C., & Williams, R. B. (1991). Hostility during late adolescence predicts coronary risk factors at midlife. *American Journal of Epidemiology, 136*, 146–154.

Sklar, L. S. & Anisman, H. (1979). Stress and coping factors influence tumor growth. *Science, 205*, 513–515.

Smith, T. W. (1992). Hostility and health: Current status of a psychosomatic hypothesis. *Health Psychology, 11*, 139–150.

Smith, T. W., & Pope, M. K. (1990). Cynical hostility as a health risk: Current status and future directions. *Journal of Social Behavior and Personality, 5*, 77–88.

Smith, T. W., Pope, M. K., Sanders, J. D., Allred, K. D., & O'Keeffe, J. L. (1988). Cynical hostility at home and work: Psychosocial vulnerability across domains. *Journal of Research in Personality, 22*, 525–548.

Spiro, A., Aldwin, C. M., Levenson, M. R., & Bosse, R. (1990). Longitudinal findings from the Normative Aging Study: II. Do emotionality and extraversion predict symptom change? *Journal of Gerontology: Psychological Sciences, 45*, 136–144.

Sundar, S. K., Cierpial, M. A., Kilts, C., Ritchie, J. C., & Weiss, J. M. (1990). Brain Il-1 induced immunosuppression occurs through activation of both pituitary adrenal axis and sympathetic nervous system by corticotrophin-releasing factor. *Journal of Neuroscience, 10*, 3701–3706.

Taylor, S. E. (1983). Adjustment to threatening events: A theory of cognitive adaptation. *American Psychologist, 38*, 1161–1173.

Taylor, S. (1991). Asymmetrical effects of positive and negative events: The mobilization-minimization hypothesis. *Psychological Bulletin, 110*, 67–85.

Temoshok, L. (1987). Personality, coping style, emotion, and cancer: Towards an integrative model. *Cancer Surveys, 6*, 545–567.

Temoshok, L., & Fox, B. H. (1984). Coping styles and other psychosocial factors related to medical status and to prognosis in patients with cutaneous malignant melanoma. In B. H. Fox & B. H. Newberry (Eds.), *Impact of psychoendocrine systems in cancer and immunity* (pp. 258–287). Toronto: Hogrefe.

Tomkins, S. S. (1962). *Affect, imagery, and consciousness: Vol. 1. The positive affects.* New York: Springer.

Tomkins, S. S. (1963). *Affect, imagery, and consciousness: Vol. 2. The negative affects.* New York: Springer.

Vinokur, A., & Seltzer, M. L. (1975). Desirable versus undesirable life events: Their relationship to stress and mental distress. *Journal of Personality and Social Psychology, 32,* 329–337.

Visintainer, M. A., Volpicelli, J. R., & Seligman, M. E. P. (1982). Tumor rejection in rats after inescapable or escapable shock. *Science, 216,* 437–439.

Von Holst, D. (1986). Vegatative and somatic components of tree shrews' behavior. *Journal of the Autonomic Nervous System* (Suppl.), 657–670.

Watson, D., & Clark, L. A. (1984). Negative affectivity: The disposition to experience aversive emotional states. *Psychological Bulletin, 96,* 465–490.

Watson, D., & Pennebaker, J. W. (1989). Health complaints, stress, and distress: Exploring the central role of negative affectivity. *Psychological Review, 96,* 234–254.

Weiss, J. M. (1972). Psychological factors in stress and disease. *Scientific American, 226,* 104–113.

Wolf, S., & Wolff, H. G. (1947). *Human gastric function: An experimental study of a man and his stomach.* New York: Oxford University Press.

Zajonc, R. B. (1984). On primacy of affect. In K. S. Scherer & P. Ekman (Eds.), *Approaches to emotion* (pp. 259–270). Hillsdale, NJ: Erlbaum.

Zevon, M. A., & Tellegen, A. (1982). The structure of mood change: An idiographic/nomothetic analysis. *Journal of Personality and Social Psychology, 43,* 111–122.

27

Moods, Emotion Episodes, and Emotions

NICO H. FRIJDA

DISTINCTIONS AMONG AFFECTIVE PHENOMENA

One of the most common distinctions among kinds of affective phenomena is that between emotions and moods. Moods are usually distinguished from emotions by one of three criteria: longer duration, lower intensity, and diffuseness or globality (e.g., Isen, 1984; Morris, 1989). The three criteria delineate somewhat different sets of phenomena, since they only hang loosely together. There are diffuse affective states of high intensity, such as deep, apathetic depression, and states labeled as moods often last for only a short time (e.g., Mayer, Mambarg, & Volanth, 1988). There are also quite weak emotions, such as a fearful uneasiness that passes before having gained strength. And there are emotional interchanges with a particular event of relatively long duration.

Of the three criteria, "diffuseness" or "globality" is the most interesting. It has been adopted as the main criterion for moods by a number of authors (e.g., Isen, 1984; Ruckmick 1936; Stumpf, 1899). Ruckmick states: "[Mood] has no particular cognitive element. We are often at a loss to say toward whom or what it is directed. . . . There is also generally no cognitive impulse about it. It does not lend itself to any definite action" (1936, p. 72). "Diffuseness" defines a class of affective states that is distinctly set off from emotions. Emotions, by almost general consent, have an object. They are "about" something. One is happy

about something, angry at someone, afraid of something. Emotions, in other words, are "intentional" phenomena; they involve a subject–object relationship. This applies to subjective experience as well as to behavior. Emotional behavior is directed toward or away from, or at least oriented upon, a particular thing.

Moods lack such an object. In fact, according to certain theorists, they are nonintentional mental phenomena (Stumpf, 1899; see Reisenzein & Schönpflug, 1992). The "diffuseness" of moods (i.e., the diffuseness of affective states that makes us classify them as moods) can thus be characterized more precisely by this absence of orientation upon an object. Subjectively, this absence is evident in statements referring to "everything," "anything," or "nothing": "Nothing interests me," "I get mad at anything," "Everything looks rosy" are examples. The absence also features in behavior. There exists "joyful" behavior—behavior that is not focused upon one particular object, but responds to an indifferent variety of these (smiling at this, touching that, looking at that, moving exuberantly with respect to nothing in particular). Likewise, "angry mood" applies to sequences of irritated or angry responses to an unbounded variety of events.

Moods are thus affective states without an object or without a specific object. The latter qualification is added because some affective states have the environment as a whole as their object. In certain anxiety states, the "world" is felt to be an unsafe place, not offering any stability or possibility for control. It is a matter of taste, and not of substantial decision, whether such states are classed as emotions with a diffuse object or as moods (i.e., with no object). A similar choice is offered by panic, as in panic attacks. Catastrophic feelings, by their nature, are global.

The object of an affective state is not the same thing as its cause. Moods, while not having an object, may originate in a specific emotional event involving a specific object. A mood also may be the consequence of a particular emotion. An emotion turns into a mood, or gives rise to a mood, when the focus upon the emotional object is lost and feeling and behavior become diffuse, having no object or unstable, fleeting ones. The subject may know what caused his or her mood, and may nonetheless still be in a mood (i.e., in an unfocused state without an object). He or she may be perfectly aware of the mood's origin—say, an event that angered him or her—and still feel diffusely angry or tend to respond angrily to anybody or anything.

The variety in affective states with a specific object makes a further distinction necessary. The need for that further distinction becomes clearer when one realizes that referring to emotions with the word "state" is confusing; several writers (e.g., Lazarus, 1991) have emphasized that emotions can better be designated as "processes." This is because emotional reactions develop over time and usually consist of sequences of emotional reactions. In these sequences, successive feelings and responses hang together, influence one another, and influence the events that have elicited them. The sequences correspond to emotional "transactions" between the individual and something in the environment. The emotional transaction is a meaningful unit of analysis in describing affective phenomena. Some emotion words tend to refer to such transactions, rather than to individual emotions; "grief" is an example. In fact, when subjects are asked to recall an instance of a given emotion, they tend to report transactions and the sequences these involve. The sequences have an internal structure and usually an extended duration; yet they are considered by the subjects as instances of "an emotion." In one of our studies, subjects were asked to recall instances of an emotion, and to draw a diagram of the course of the emotion over time. In 68% of these instances, the diagrams showed more than one peak, or durations of over 1 hour, or both (Sonnemans, 1991). We call these complex and/or affective phenomena "emotion episodes" (Frijda, Mesquita, Sonnemans, & Van Goozen, 1991).

To summarize, it appears useful to distinguish among emotions, emotion episodes, and moods. The notion of "emotions" can be reserved for object-focused affective processes characterized by only one of the elementary affective phenomena, such as a feeling or mode of action readiness. An "emotion episode" is the sequence of affective processes corresponding to a given person–environment transaction. The notion of "mood" refers to an affective state or process that has no object or only fleeting, shifting objects, or that has the environment as a whole as its object. The nature of all three kinds of affective phenomena can best be further specified in terms of the components found useful when describing emotions.

THE NATURE OF AFFECTIVE STATES

Analysis of Emotion

It has been proposed that emotional experience is built up from a small set of unanalyzable, basic emotional feelings. Other, non-basic emotions then may consist of blends of these basic feelings (Izard, 1977; Plutchik, 1980), or of basic feelings linked to cognitions regarding their origins and consequences (Oatley, 1992; Oatley & Johnson-Laird, 1987). The set of basic feelings may consist of happiness, sadness, fear, anger, and disgust (Oatley, 1992); other investigators (e.g., Ekman, 1982; Izard, 1977) have proposed other sets.

The basic-emotions view of emotional feelings is unsatisfactory for a number of reasons (see Ortony & Turner, 1990). In the present connection I mention two of those reasons. First, the concepts used to label those supposedly elementary feeling qualities are semantically decomposable (Wierzbicka, 1973, 1992). Second, introspective analysis suggests that only affect proper—that is, the experience of pleasantness or unpleasantness—is both unanalyzable and specific for affective experience; only the experience of affect cannot be explicated (Wundt, 1912). Further differences between emotional feelings come from cognitions and bodily sensations.

Spontaneous descriptions of emotional experiences and concepts (Davitz, 1969; Shaver, Schwartz, Kirson, & O'Connor, 1987) allow one to characterize emotional feelings more precisely. Four main components can he distinguished in those descriptions, plus a corollary one (see Frijda, 1986). The four main components are (1) affect; (2) awareness of situational meaning structure, or felt appraisal of events; (3) felt state of action readiness; and (4) felt bodily change. The corollary one is the emotion's "significance."

The notion of "affect" refers to the irreducible aspect that gives feelings their emotional, noncognitive character. Usually, in emotions, one does not experience feelings of pleasantness; rather, one is aware of the pleasant or unpleasant nature of the emotion-eliciting event. In emotions, in other words, affect figures as an aspect of the "felt appraisal of events." Different appraisals can be satisfactorily described in terms of a limited number of dimensions. Apart from pleasantness–unpleasantness, these include certainty–uncertainty, causal agency (by self, other, or the course of events), goal conduciveness or obstructiveness, self-confidence, and controllability (Frijda, Kuipers, & ter Schure, 1989; Ortony, Clore, & Collins, 1988; Roseman, 1991; Scherer, 1984; Smith & Ellsworth, 1985). A particular emotional experience can be represented as a profile of values on such dimensions; these profiles do a reasonable job in differentiating types of experience (or emotion concepts) from one another.

The third component, "felt state of action readiness," refers both to states of activation and to action tendencies. Activation states involve general readiness or unreadiness to enter into contact with the environment or with objects of thought. They reflect the individual's coping resources of the moment. Action tendencies are the tendencies to maintain or modify one's relationship with the environment; each action tendency involves a particular type of relational aim. Modes of action readiness identified by questionnaire research or observation include moving toward, moving away, moving against, hyperactivation, hypoactivation, and competence (Davitz, 1969; Frijda, 1986; Frijda et al., 1989). Forms of action readiness represent the motives for behavior to cope with the emotional event, or else reflect the impossibility of coping (as in apathy). Different emotions tend to involve different kinds of action readiness; strong correlations exist between particular emotion concepts and particular kinds of action readiness (fear and avoidance or self-protection, joy and approach or hyperactivation, etc.; Frijda et al., 1989). Finally, categories of body experience (the fourth component, "felt bodily change") also reliably distinguish among emotions (Rimé, Philippot, & Cisamolo, 1990).

The fifth, the corollary, component of emotional experience is the "significance" of the emotion. Emotional experiences are objects of reflective judgment. They are felt as controllable or uncontrollable, desirable or undesirable, and acceptable or unacceptable; perhaps there are further dimensions. The component is important, in that it controls emotion regulation and also reflects such regulation. Significance in this sense forms part of the experience and categorization of emotions (Frijda, 1986; Mesquita & Frijda, 1992), as well as of that of moods (Mayer & Gaschke, 1988; Mayer, Salovey, Gomberg-Kaufmam, & Blainey, 1991; Morris, 1989).

The notion that emotional experience is built up from various components may seem to conflict with the felt unity and uniqueness of each emotional feeling. I think that the objection is invalid. Every complex notion can give rise to a unitary experience of its sense. The clearest demonstration was provided by the introspective analysis of word meanings, during the research on "imageless thought." One can be aware of the meaning of a given word, in what was called a unitary "thought" (*Gedanke*; Bühler, 1907), without explication of that meaning. The "thought" is the awareness that explication or ostentation can be achieved, and in what direction it can be found.

Several of the components of awareness that I have mentioned represent awareness of processes that occur independently of that awareness. Awareness of bodily change, to a large extent, comes from actual bodily changes that occur anyway; feedback from facial expression or heartbeat presupposes such expression and heartbeat. The same applies to awareness of the state of action readiness. Felt action readiness reflects actual readiness or disinclination for behavior, which may or may not result in manifest behavior, whether one is aware of that readiness or not. The notion of action tendency is equivalent to that of the state of readiness of (defensive, offensive, or appetitive) behavioral systems (Frijda, 1986). Activation states represent the coping resource of the individual at that moment. States of action readiness are hypothetical constructs inferred from from overt behavior as well as from self-report. The constructs do not in the first place refer to inner feelings, but to sets of predictions of past and future appraisals and relational behaviors (e.g., in anger, likelihood of negative evaluation of the event, and/or future avoidance of the object), and of behavior types that are likely to come forth (e.g., in anger, verbal aggression or physical assault if the confrontation persists).

Action readiness has an important aspect that is more or less a criterion for calling a mental process an emotion: control precedence (Frijda, 1986, 1988). One of the main reasons to classify a given mental state as an emotion is that the person's feeling and behavior tend to be controlled by that state, whether he or she wants it or not. Control precedence shows in such things as being preoccupied by the emotional issue; high priority of, and interference by, emotion-relevent behaviors; distraction by relevant stimuli; and indistractibility and persistence during execution of emotion-related actions. A meaningful distinction can be made between "acute" and "less acute" emotions, according to the extent to which control precedence leads to actual behavioral and physiological manifestations of the action readiness concerned (Frijda et al., 1991).

Analysis of Mood

The analysis of mood can closely follow that of emotion, with the differences that derive from its nonintentional or non-object-focused character. Descriptive data on mood have not been collected systematically; analysis must, to a large extent, rely on scattered descriptions.

The major component of moods, obviously, is affect. Analysis of mood self-ratings, to be more extensively discussed in the next section, amply corroborates the common distinction of good moods and bad moods. With respect to affect, moods can be experienced in two quite compatible ways: as states of unfocused pleasant or unpleasant feeling, and as states of lowered thresholds for appraising events as having pleasant or unpleasant aspects to them. Moods thus involve a tuning of the affective evaluation of events. Tuning results in toning down the intensity or quality of events with opposite valence, or in picking out the opposite implications of events that lend themselves

to it. Lowered thresholds for negative affect can he expected to involve an increased threshold for positive affect, and vice versa (although the temporal and intensity ranges within which this would be the case might vary; see the section on the structure of affect). In depressed mood, pleasurable events do not appeal as such, or are experienced with a bitter aftertaste (e.g., Hammen & Glass, 1975). Here is a concrete example of such tuning in depression:

> My farmhouse, my beloved home for thirty years, took on for me . . . an almost palpable quality of ominousness. The fading evening light—akin to that famous "slant of light" of Emily Dickinson's, which spoke to her of death, of chill extinction—had none of its autumnal loveliness, but ensnared me in suffocating gloom. (Styron, 1992, p. 45)

In addition to this, moods can be viewed as appraisal propensities—that is, as states in which the individual tends to see events in a particular way. An anxious mood is one in which almost any event is appraised as a potential threat, or as something one may not be able to deal with; an angry mood is one in which almost any event is perceived as a frustration or offense—as the result of someone else's unfriendly intent. In depressed mood, the world is felt to be barren, devoid of meaning and interest. Generalized appraisal along these dimensions is what distinguishes one unpleasant mood from the other, or is among the major determinants of such distinction. Such a generalized propensity for a particular mode of appraisal can, like affect, be manifested as a generalized tuning to appraise any event whatever in a mood-consonant way, or as a decreased threshold for such appraisal when events ever so slightly lend themselves to it.

In this view, moods are, among other things, modes of appraisal—modes of seeing the world differently. Under that perspective, many of the cognitive changes found with moods are not consequences of moods, but parts of them. Research into these changes is not to be understood as research into the effect of moods upon cognitions, but into the effect of certain aspects of mood (e.g., affect) upon this other aspect, and into the extent of the appraisal change (e.g., whether that change also affects reflected judgment). After all, Styron, in the passage above, knew perfectly well that the ominous light was lovely light at some other time; the explanation of the present ominous-ness did not differ from that of the depressed mood.

Moods are also are diffuse states of action readiness—activation states or action tenden-cies, again without a particular object. Again, these states can be conceived of either as forms of increased readiness, or as lowered thresh-olds for consonant responses, should an event that is appropriate in principle (though per-haps very weak) occur. Moods reflect availabil-ity or inavailability of coping resources (Morris, 1992). An angry mood is a state of heightened readiness to respond angrily (with unfriendli-ness, with a critical answer, or with attribut-ing blame); depressed mood is often a state of listlessness, lack of energy and interest, and the tendency to avoid interpersonal contact. Gen-eralized action tendencies and activation states are the other major features that distinguish different positive or negative moods. As in emotions, appraisal and action readiness in moods are closely linked. The touchiness in an angry mood follows from the appraisal that people are unfriendly, are bothersome, and lack consideration. In this perspective, moods are (among other things) changes in emotional responsiveness and in motivation, and the re-search questions concern the range of these responsiveness and motivational changes.

The description above gives, in my view, a full account of moods. Their lack of an object does not necessarily mean that they lack cog-nitive content. In any case, their lack of object does not imply that they should be considered elementary affective *qualia,* as Oatley (1992) and Oatley and Johnson-Laird (1987) propose. It is true that the appraisals and action readi-ness states in moods, as in emotions, can be viewed as consequences of such *qualia* rather than as aspects of the *qualia* (of the moods themselves), but the supposition appears superfluous. There is no compelling reason to suppose unanalyzable *qualia* where the fea-tures mentioned account perfectly for what-ever phenomenological and functional aspects there are. The experience of moods is ad-equately conceived of as awareness of a global appraisal, and as awareness of one's activation state or action tendency. When ap-plied to behavior, too, the notion of mood is adequately accounted for by the notion of awareness of the environment as appraised, and by that of states of generalized activation and of action tendency.

There is good reason to view moods in this way. As with emotions, discrepancies exist among the various phenomena that give rise to the ascription of moods—that is, among subjective experience, behavior and cognitive changes, and physiological state. Correlations are moderate or low, in moods as well as in emotions. There may be manifest action readi-ness while there is no mood in subjective feel-ing, and vice versa. In the mood literature, the notion of "unconscious moods" has been advanced (Nowlis & Nowlis, 1956; Morris, 1989). The concept is awkward, but the rea-sons for introducing it are perfectly transpar-ent: Changes in behavioral tuning occur that are not accompanied by corresponding feel-ings. Determining the correlations between the various aspects, or operationalizations, of mood is one of the major empirical research issues. Accounting for these correlations is a theoreti-cal issue that can only be considered when examining the causes of each aspect—for in-stance, why and when the causes of mood affect appraisal propensities, and whether they do this by way of affect or directly.

In the discussion above, "affect" is given a central place; after all, I have defined "mood" as an affective state. However, mental states exist that lack affect, but otherwise have the same properties as those indicated: global ap-praisal (e.g., everything is perceived as diffi-cult, every task as a chore) and global state of action readiness (e.g., decreased readiness for action). The properties used for illustration define and describe "tired mood." Whether one wants to consider such states as a subclass of moods or, because of their lack of affect, to place them in a different category is, of course, inconsequential.

Analysis of Emotion Episodes

I have argued that duration is not a meaning-ful characteristic to define a separate class of affective phenomena. Not all affective phe-nomena with durations of more than, say, sev-eral minutes or a quarter of an hour can be meaningfully grouped together. In fact, the durations of moods and emotions or emotion episodes show considerable overlap. Accord-ing to Morris (1989), moods do not last longer than a few hours at most, and experimentally induced moods last between 4 and 15 minutes only (Isen & Gorgoglione, 1983). According to findings by Stone and Neale (1984; see also Neale, Hooley, Jandorf, & Stone, 1987), even the mood alterations caused by serious life events last for no more than a few days. I doubt the validity of these findings, or at least the extent to which they can be generalized. The stated durations may hold for moods as experienced; they are unlikely to hold for moods as defined by changes in emotional tuning.

As regards the duration of emotion episodes, in the study by Sonnemans (1991) the median reported duration of emotion instances was between 3 and 6 hours, and 31% of them were described as having lasted for more than 24 hours. As noted earlier, 68% of these were taken to represent emotion episodes. The durations come from self-reports, which are notoriously unreliable; however, the details of these reports give them some credibility, as they describe emotional incidents of verifiable durations (e.g., being the victim of an attack that lasted for a given length of time, participating in a contest, waiting for an outcome, being upset by an incident occurring at a given hour, and being involved in an incident lasting until an event at a given other hour). So affective events of longer durations can be emotion episodes as well as moods.

Descriptions of emotion episodes can also be obtained from reports by outside observers. Fascinating material was collected and analyzed by Planalp, DeFrancisco, and Rutherford (1990), from the accounts of emotion instances in the reporters' roommates. Their structure and duration appear comparable to those from self-reports.

As I have said earlier, emotion episodes can typically be described as transactions between the subject and a person, object, or contingency in the environment. In such transactions, emotions are accompaniments or outcomes, as well as determinants. Marital quarrels provide clear illustration of the multiple roles of emotions in a transaction.[1] A reproach by one of the contestants elicits distress in the other, who cries during the rejoinder, and whose distress elicits renewed reproach by the first. Transactions usually consist of a number of subevents, and emotional episodes usually consist of a sequence

of different emotions that blend into one another. The sequence follows what actually happens in the transaction (e.g., the reproaches, ripostes, subvictories, and subdefeats in a quarrel), but is also contingent upon the different perspectives that the subject adopts, and that make him or her move from irritation to being upset to anger to compassion to feeling guilty. Sometimes, however, one type of emotion endures; it waxes and wanes over the entire episode. Whatever the structure, emotion episodes (i.e., those sequences here considered as episodes) have an inner coherence that makes them worthy of consideration as emotional units in their own right. This coherence has several sources. One is the person's continuous awareness of dealing with a particular "core relational theme" (Lazarus, 1991), such as a threat, a loss, an offense, an achievement, or a combination of these. Another is the continuous state of emotional engagement. It is, I think, this continuous state of engagement that makes subjects describe an episode as "an emotion" with a beginning, an end, and a changing course of intensity in between. These intensity courses have been represented in graphs showing some intensity increase at onset, and one or several intensity peaks, before a steep or gradual final decline (Sonnemans, 1991). The state of emotional engagement involves enhanced attentional activity, the presence of some emotion, and usually a changing but more or less continuous state of activation (manifested in mental and motor restlessness, disturbed sleep, and perhaps peripheral autonomic arousal). On the whole, emotion episodes tend to be significantly more intense than briefer or simpler emotions on most intensity variables (overall rated intensity, strength of experienced action tendency, magnitude of resulting belief changes, and amount of recurrence in thought); only the self-rated strength of bodily changes is not significantly different from that of simple emotions (Sonnemans, 1991). The finding is particularly interesting, because the rated duration of emotion instances has been found to be independent of intensity indices other than rated overall intensity.

Emotion episodes indicate that emotional processes can best be described in terms of a hierarchical model. The highest level consists of emotional engagement with its overall course of intensity over time, from problem onset to resolution. Within that course of engagement, phases of positive and of negative

---

[1]The data come from self-report accounts of the two participants in each of 24 marital quarrels (unpublished report by Y. Phielix, 1985), and from the analysis of 6 filmed quarrels during marital therapy (unpublished report by J. Kiestra, 1987).

affect may succeed one another. These phases correspond to changes in action readiness at the strategic level, as Lang (1988) has called it—readiness either to accept or to reject the stimulus event. The third level is represented by successive emergence of different appraisals, and by the different more specific forms that action readiness can take, which more or less define particular emotions: threat appraisal and self-protection or withdrawal, which correspond to fear; blameworthiness appraisal and "going against," which correspond to anger; averseness appraisal and rejection, corresponding to disgust; hopelessness appraisal and giving up, corresponding to despair; and the like. At a fourth level, states of action readiness are implemented by specific actions, such as shrieking, reproaching, or sulking within an antagonistic, "angry" phase. Throughout, variations occur in level of activation and bodily arousal. Each lower level presents the various forms that the response at the higher level may take, according to circumstances and changes in perspective. During an episode, different emotions thus succeed or fade over into one another, and emotions may change into moods, to fade out entirely or to be retransformed into emotions.

The notion of emotion episodes has not been extensively employed, and that of emotional transaction has been used only recently, in the work of Lazarus (1991). There are good reasons to grant it more consideration, apart from descriptive ones. One of these is that emotion episodes appear to involve elementary emotional processes with durations in the range of hours to days: energetic processes of activation, cognitive processes of preoccupation, and attentional readiness with relation to a particular issue. Energetic processes of longer duration, such as those responsible for prolonged restlessness, sleep disturbance, and incapacity to concentrate, have hardly been investigated in terms of basic mechanisms. Another reason is the clarification entailed by not automatically classifying every affective reaction of more than a few minutes or hours under the heading of "mood," together with diffuse states of happiness or unhappiness. Furthermore, it provides the analysis of affective phenomena with a slot for those emotional processes stretched out in time that show internal structure and yet possess continuity (as do so many instances of jealousy or anger), and that in some cases even give rise to a particular emotion word (such as "grief"). It draws attention to still another domain in which we are woefully ignorant—the temporal dependence of successive affects, and the nature of higher-order affect variables (such as those here called "affect" and "strategic action readiness"). A final reason is that stress effects are presumably linked to these stretched-out activations, and the stretched-out emotion-focused coping efforts that these episodes call forth. To put it another way, one may hypothesize that stress effects are linked not to individual emotions or to material transactions as such, but to the emotion episodes that these transactions engender.

A Note on the Concept of Mood

Over any given period of time, emotions, moods, and emotion episodes follow one another; emotion episodes themselves consist of successions of various emotions and moods. When asked about their feelings at a given moment or over a given period, people give a sort of summary account, a global assessment, of their emotions, emotion episodes, and moods of that moment or period. Their account may even include an evaluation of their current life prospects. The question "How do you feel?" or "How did you feel last week?", as asked in general mood questionnaires, does not necessarily reflect mood in the sense described above. It is not usually understood as a call for introspection, but as a call for retrospection and perhaps even for prospection. In consequence, care should be taken in generalizing findings concerning mood as an affective process to mood as the summary assessment of one's affective states, and vice versa. In the analyses of mood questionnaires, the word "mood" does not mean the same thing as "mood" in the strict sense of an objectless affective process.

CAUSES AND FUNCTIONS OF AFFECTIVE PHENOMENA

Antecedents and Functions of Emotions and Emotion Episodes

Emotions arise from encounters with events that are appraised as having beneficial or harmful consequences for the individual's concerns (his or her major goals, motives, well-being, or affective sensitivities; Frijda, 1986; Lazarus, 1991; Oatley, 1992; Ortony et al., 1988; Scherer, 1984), under conditions that involve difficulty (Frijda, 1986). Because of this, emotions serve the individual as twofold signals. They signal the occurrence of relevant events, the fact that some relevant issue or concern is at stake; they also signal the state of the individual's estimated coping ability. In addition, they signal to the action system that something should be done about the situation; emotions are motives for dealing with the emotional event. The process of emotion elicitation can be viewed as one in which events are continuously monitored with respect to their possible concern relevance ("primary appraisal"), as well as with respect to difficulties and possibilities in dealing with them ("secondary appraisal"). The process must be supposed to run in parallel with focal cognitive processes, and, by virtue of that, must be able to interrupt the latter when concern relevance is sufficiently high (Frijda, 1986; Oatley, 1992; Ortony et al., 1988; Scherer, 1984).

The antecedents of emotions episodes are, in principle, no different from those of emotions—events of relevance for concerns that involve some measure of difficulty. Emotion episodes can be expected to serve dealing with protracted issues or events; little systematic attention has been devoted so far to the specific causes of emotion duration, but their descriptions suggest that emotion episodes do precisely this. They appear to result either from temporally extended transactions, as opposed to incidental emotionally charged events, or from events that precipitate an enduring emotional problem (e.g., personal loss, harm to the self-image, or threat to material or social security) (Frijda et al., 1991). As noted before, emotion episodes tend to be more intense than briefer or simpler emotions on most intensity variables. Since these intensity variables are found to correlate with the strength and number of concerns at stake in the emotional transaction, the strength and number of concerns involved can be counted among the causes of episodes (Sonnemans, 1991).

Antecedents and Functions of Moods

Systematic literature on the causes of mood is sparse. A survey of the literature suggests that moods can have a multitude of origins—emotionally significant events, hedonically toned stimuli, organismic conditions, and physiologi-

cal processes. They can have external as well as internal origins. The operation of all these antecedents can be plausibly understood from the mechanisms encountered in the preceding analysis of moods. Most antecedents involve changes in the availability of coping resources or the individual's trust in them (Moms, 1992); in addition, and correlated with these latter, are the persistent effects of events and internal conditions upon generalized appraisals and modes of action readiness. I substantiate this assertion here by surveying the various mood antecedents.

Considerable evidence indicates that moods may result from the impact of emotionally significant events. Life events have effects upon mood ratings, upon changes in sense of well-being or life satisfaction, and upon emotional responsiveness to events more or less unrelated to the life events concerned (Stone & Neale, 1984). Personal loss tends to diminish interest in work and one's personal condition for long periods, and to decrease response to positive hedonic stimuli, in addition to inducing feelings of depression (e.g., Parkes, 1972). Depressed moods result not only from personal loss but also from other losses, such as changes in familiar surroundings, even when such changes are to one's advantage (changing jobs, moving house, marriage; Marris, 1974). Traumas and prolonged stress generally entail pronounced mood consequences. Depression, irritability, and angry mood are among the stress syndrome symptoms. In contrast, personal success tends to lead to increases in elated mood and in self-confidence in dealing with other events besides those involved in the initial success.

Emotional events also influence available appraisal and coping resources, either directly or through the changes in appraisal and action readiness. Positive events are activating, as the close link between positive affect and activation demonstrates (Thayer, 1989; Morris, 1992). Loss and other life changes deprive the individual of familiar ways of understanding and dealing with the environment. Prolonged stresses quite obviously tend to drain coping resources. Decrease of coping resources can he expected to facilitate anxious or depressed mood, since both anxiety and depression are responses to events one feels unable to cope with (Abramson, Seligman, & Teasdale, 1978; Mandler, 1984).

Emotionally significant events may induce moods directly, without passing through an emotion or emotion episode, in still other ways, which yet are accounted for by the mechanism indicated: appraisal change, persistence of action readiness, or change in available resources. For instance, emotion may disappear under regulatory efforts and through habituation, while still resources are exhausted and appraisals change. This often seems to occur under prolonged stress. For instance, Grinker and Spiegel (1945), in their study of war pilots, describe how boisterous courage in those pilots gradually gave way to the indifference of masked depression. Apart from the resource consequences, prolonged stress may well directly engender a diffuse, generalized appraisal of threat and uncontrollability, to which each separate event contributes; this appraisal may lead to diffuse feelings of dysphoria or anxiety, and diffuse states of apathy or self-protective withdrawal.

Moods are not only caused by emotionally significant events or by changes in coping resources. It appears that certain external agents can influence mood directly. Odors are an example; certain odors appear to raise or depress mood even when not consciously detected, and they can influence conscious judgments. Zajonc has advanced evidence suggestive of direct mood effects of the temperature of inhaled air: Cool air appears to raise mood and warm air to depress it (Zajonc, Murphy, & Inglehart, 1989). Similarly, certain mood-changing effects of music probably have nothing to do with one's appreciation of that music, but result from some sort of direct effects of the music upon organismic activation; the issue, however, is not easily settled, and the possible mechanisms are unclear. But even in these cases the mechanisms of mood causation need not be essentially different: The mood arises from pleasant or unpleasant events in the (inner or outer) environment.

There is evidence that certain moods may result from purely internal conditions. There exist clear circadian, weekly, and seasonal variations in mood (Clark, Watson, & Leeka, 1989; Thayer, 1989; Wehr & Rosenthal, 1989), as well as monthly changes in women (Schnurr, 1989). An extensive literature exists on the possible biochemical determinants of mood variation in clinical depression and mania (e.g., the so-called catecholamine hypothesis of mood disorder, and the effects of serotonin; Schildkraut, 1978; see Schnurr 1989, for a review). Depressed mood is known to be a side effect of various drugs—for example, reserpine, clomazine, and antihypertensives (see Schnurr, 1989). Morphine induces euphoria. In postpartum blues and premenstrual irritability, too, biochemical influences are likely (Schnurr, 1989; Smith, 1975). Owing to the mentioned interaction of coping ability and the appraisal of events, the boundary between internal conditions and external events in the causation of mood is vague. Even internal events may influence mood not directly, but through some cognitive process involving awareness of available coping resources. For instance, the exhaustion syndrome, consisting of irritable and/or depressed mood, concentration loss, and emotional lability, may result from a direct effect of physical state upon affect or the nervous system; equally plausible, however, is that it results from effects upon coping resources and the person's awareness of them. Similarly, morphine-induced euphoria may result directly from the action of morphine upon whatever biochemical processes are involved in the arousal of positive affect, but it may also be caused by the sense of ease and ability that morphine produces in the first place, and thus by the resulting competence appraisal. Similar interpretations, again, may hold for circadian mood changes and the premenstrual syndrome. The interpretation problems mentioned here are not only relevant for understanding the mood effects of physiological agents. They have a wider bearing upon the discussion of the importance of cognitions in the arousal of emotions (e.g., Zajonc, 1980; Lazarus, 1991); there does not seem to be an easy way to settle the issue.

It is also possible that the biochemical influences upon moods do not constitute determinants in a strict sense, but are agents that facilitate arousal of moods by external events. Whybrow, Akiskal, and McKinney (1984) have advanced the hypothesis that mood disorder results from internally caused failures to regulate external mood influences. Likewise, hormonal changes may weaken normal dampening of mood effects from normal daily events. Quite generally, it is difficult to distinguish variations in emotional phenomena due to variations in sensitivity for elicitors from those due to variations in resources for affect regulation. Interpretation of cultural differences provides examples of this difficulty, and that of the internal mood changes mentioned above provides others. Mood variations due to exhaustion, indeed, can be readily understood as consequences of depletion of resources for affect control, rather than as consequences of mood influences in their own right.

As is well known, arousal of emotions and moods is determined not only by internal and external events, but also by personality variables. There are solid findings in the mood literature that prevalence of positive emotions and moods is correlated with extraversion, and that prevalence of negative affect is correlated with neuroticism, both as defined by questionnaire scores like those on the Eysenck Personality Inventory (e.g., Costa & McCrae, 1980, Diener & Emmons, 1985; Emmons, Diener, & Larsen, 1986; Watson & Clark, 1984; Zevon & Tellegen, 1982). It is uncertain whether such correlations also hold between these personality variables and the occurrence of "moods" in the strict sense; they pertain to indices of "mood" in the sense mentioned earlier (see "A Note on the Concept of Mood," above).

Correlations between personality characteristics and occurrence of emotions are also beginning to be found in other emotion domains. For instance, anger proneness, as assessed from trait questionnaires, is strongly predictive of anger arousal under provocation (Van Goozen, Frijda, & Van de Poll, 1992); trait anxiety correlates with state anxiety under threat; and the like. This domain is only beginning to be explored, and the magnitude of person × event interactions is as yet unclear. Nor is it clear in what way the personality variables influence emotions and moods. Most plausible, however, is that this way is compatible with the analyses given. People may be expected to differ in thresholds for particular emotional response modes, in the readiness with which they appraise events in a particular way, and in resources for coping with particular events. "Sensation seeking," for instance, which (among other things) is the disposition to derive pleasure from risky events and strong stimuli (Zuckerman, 1979), prominently involves the individual's capacity to deal with those risks and stimuli, and with the uncertainties that they entail.

The analysis above indicates that moods may be given a plausible functional interpretation. Moods can be considered to reflect variations in available coping resources, and mood awareness, as Morris (1992, p 264) has recently phrased it, serves as a cue to the individual about the sufficiency of these resources in meeting environmental demands. They also serve to signal variations in the individual's ecology—the general favorableness or unfavorableness of the environment, as appraised. Moods reflect an attunement of the resources to that ecology.

THE STRUCTURE OF AFFECT SPACE

One of the questions in the affect area concerns variety in affects, as well as the structure of that variety. Of course, the variety can be considerable. There are numerous emotion words; their number and nature very considerably from one language to another (Russell, 1991). As to moods, language suggests the difference between "good" and "bad" moods, but also refers to "angry," "arrogant," "insecure," and "tired" moods, among others. Most common emotion words appear acceptable as items in mood adjective checklists, although some emotion words are almost uniquely applicable to emotions (e.g., "jealous"), and others are most readily appraised as referring to moods (e.g., "cheerful," "gloomy"). Concordant with the distinctions made earlier, words more readily rated as referring to emotions appear to possess the semantic feature of focus upon a particular event, and mood words appear to possess the semantic feature of "globality" (see Frijda, 1987).

The structure of affective space has been approached by analyzing the similarity ratings of emotion and mood words (e.g., Gehm & Scherer, 1988; Russell, 1980; Shaver et al., 1987), as well as the frequency of co-occurrence of such words when rating facial expressions (Frijda, 1970) or current mood (Nowlis, 1966, 1970; Sonneville, Schaap, & Elshout, 1985; Thayer, 1978). Cluster analysis of these data produces 6 to 10 clear clusters at the intermediate level of intercorrelations or similarities. These clusters usually correspond to what are often regarded as "basic" emotion categories, such as joyful, fearful and angry affects, plus nonemotional states, such as indifference and fatigue (e.g., Frijda, 1970). When adjective checklists are submitted to factor analysis, about 10 mood factors appear that tend to correspond with the clusters mentioned. The 12 factors obtained by Nowlis (1966) after varimax rotation were as follows: aggression, anxiety, surgency, elation, social affection, sadness, vigor, concentration, fatigue, skepticism, egoism, and nonchalance. Only the first 7 of these factors more or less clearly involve affective states; the others refer to nonemotional states. Lists by Lorr, Daston, and Smith (1967), Sonneville et al. (1985), and Sjöberg, Svensson, and Persson (1979), based on American English, Dutch, and Swedish words, respectively, yielded a similar number of dimensions of a fairly similar nature. There appears to exist a small core of emotion types that regularly appear in analyses like this; only in very remote cultures (e.g., Lutz, 1988) do they fail to show up. The dimensions obtained are usually unipolar; that is, negative correlations are scarce and, when present, quite low, even between such dimensions as "elation" and "sadness." Also, there are nearly always some emotion or mood words that have unstable placements in clusters or factors; "jealousy," "contempt," and "shame" are among them.

In these analyses, the scree lines representing the successive contributions to explained variance almost invariably show a sharp bend after two or three dimensions (e.g.. Frijda, Kroon, & Wiers, 1993; Russell, 1980; Watson & Tellegen, 1985; Zevon & Tellegen, 1982). Oblique rotations and subsequent second-order analyses, as well as multidimensional scaling of similarity judgments of item pairs, also yield two or at most three rather powerful dimensions. The first two dimensions have to do with positive and negative affectivity, and the level of activation. The content of the third dimension, if found, varies between analyses; it is alternatively identified as "potency," "dominance," or "aggression." Cluster analyses clearly reflect the first two dimensions These analyses tend to divide the items into two major clusters, one of which covers most or all unpleasant affects, and the other most or all pleasant affects; the clusters tend to show a low negative correlation (about –.20). Additional clusters contain the nonaffective items (Frijda, 1970; Sonneville et al., 1985). Inconsistencies between the cluster structures in different analyses are mostly attributable to the fact that activation varies independently of affective valence; for instance, anger-type items are sometimes grouped with the positive items, on the basis of activation (Gehm & Scherer, 1988), and sometimes with the other negatively toned items, on the basis of valence (Frijda, 1970).

The analyses thus show the organization of affective space in terms of positive and negative affects, and (primarily from the factor analyses) in terms of degree of activation. The two sets of findings—those identifying 2 or 3 dimensions, and those identifying about 10—are not incompatible. Rather, they may suggest that the linear analysis models are not the most appropriate; partial hierarchical models may be more satisfactory. "In fact, we show that Positive and Negative Affect are hierarchically related to the more numerous and circumscribed 'discrete-emotion' factors posited by other investigators" (Watson & Tellegen, 1985, p. 220). Presumably, within the regions of positive and of negative affect, further, more specific variations exist. These variations appear in part to be attributable to variations in activation, but not wholly so: The difference between, for instance, anger and fear cannot be so explained. One can say that events (or the environment as a whole) are appraised as being of positive or negative (or neutral) valence; if they are appraised as positive or negative, the individual may show weak or strong emotional engagement, as Watson and Tellegen (1985) have aptly termed it. Appraisal of events as being of positive or negative valence is further specified, as Lazarus (1991) has argued, in terms of different appraisal patterns or "core relational themes" —or, as I have argued (Frijda, 1986), in terms of different modes of action readiness.

The organization of affective space in terms of two major dimensions has found strong agreement and has often been replicated (Diener & Emmons, 1984; Russell, 1980; Watson & Tellegen, 1985) Still the precise specification of these major dimensions is not entirely clear, and involves a substantial and theoretically relevant issue: whether positive and negative affect stand in opposition or, rather, are independent dimensions of variation.

One way to describe the organization of affective space is in terms of the two bipolar dimensions of pleasantness–unpleasantness and weak–strong activation. This indeed is the representation of affective space proposed by Russell (1979, 1980), on the basis of the types of data mentioned. The bipolarity of pleasantness–unpleasantness implies the mutual exclusion of these affects. This, however, conflicts with the finding that pleasant and unpleasant mood, when measured by unipolar scales, often show near-zero instead of negative correlations. Such independence has repeatedly in studies of subjective well-being (e.g., Bradburn, 1969; Diener, 1984; Diener & Emmons, 1984) and in the orthogonal "elation" and "sadness" factors (or factors like these) in the analyses of mood adjective scales (e.g., Lorr & Shea, 1979; Nowlis, 1966; Sonneville et al., 1985). It also turns out to be a solid feature in the analysis of the first two factors of mood scale data (Watson & Tellegen, 1985), with interindividual as well as with intraindividual measurements (Zevon & Tellegen, 1982).

These zero correlations were unexpected. It has been suggested that they might be explained by methodological factors (response formats, response biases; Russell, 1979) and, more importantly, by the fact that answers to mood questionnaires usually pertain to a summary of the individual's emotions and mood over a given period. Indeed, Diener and Emmons (1984, Study 4) found that the correlations increased from −.10 to −.57 when the time frame over which mood was assessed was decreased from 3 weeks to "this moment." However, Watson (1988) could not replicate these findings, and obtained correlations between positive and negative affect scales of about −.20, regardless of time frame.

The divergencies and contradictions may be more apparent than real. Watson and Tellegen's notions of Positive and Negative Affect, and those of pleasantness and unpleasantness, or those of positive and negative mood in the strict sense of the word "mood," are not the same. When a two-dimensional plot of the pleasantness–unpleasantness and high–low activation dimensions as obtained by Russell (1980) is rotated by 45 degrees, the independent Positive and Negative Affect factors are obtained. Watson and Tellegen (1985) advocate this rotation because it is regularly found in varimax rotation of the first two mood questionnaire factors, corresponds better with the distribution of mood questionnaire items, provides a plausible structure of affect in presenting dimensions that run from no affect to strong (positive or negative) affect, and provides clear correlations with extraneous data such as personality variables. I have mentioned earlier that Positive Affect in this sense correlates strongly with extraversion, and Negative Affect with neuroticism; these personality variables themselves are uncorrelated. In terms of basic processes, however, Positive Affect and Negative Affect each represent positive and negative affects combined with strong activation or engagement The mood adjectives that anchor the factors at the high end are "active," "elated," "enthusiastic" for Positive Affect, and

"distressed," "fearful," "hostile," "nervous" for Negative Affect the low ends of the two factors are anchored by, respectively, "drowsy," "dull," "sleepy," and "at rest," "calm," "placid," "relaxed." Note that the terms defining low Negative Affect all have positive overtones, and those defining low Positive Affect have negative overtones, as semantic differential ratings will doubtless corroborate. These overtones are not compatible with the position of Tellegen and his collaborators that the two factors are "descriptively bipolar but affectively unipolar" (Zevon & Tellegen, 1982, p. 112). Note also that, although the low ends represent "no engagement" (and thus zero points), they are below zero points with respect to normal, average functioning.

Furthermore, Positive Affect and Negative Affect are not entirely independent. Although their average correlation is only weakly negative, they show strong negative correlations when intense emotions are concerned. Diener and Emmons (1984) found a correlation of −.85 when moments of intense emotion were selected (see also Diener & Iran-Nijad, 1986). Two-dimensional plots of the two factors repeatedly show a curious narrow oval shape, in which the low–low quadrant is empty (items for something like "calm-and-drowsy" do not exist), and the high–high quadrant only has items relatively close to the axes or the origin (few items represent something like "active-and-nervous," the Dutch equivalent of "excited" being the most extreme; Frijda et al., 1993).

One can conclude that the bipolar pleasantness—unpleasantness and unipolar activation or engagement dimensions represent the structure of basic affective processes: One cannot feel both pleasure and displeasure about the same property of the same object at the same time, and one cannot be calm and excited at the same time. These dimensions correspond with the functions of mood outlined in the preceding section, those of signaling the general valence of the ecology, and the individual's available resources for dealing with that ecology. Positive and Negative Affect, in Watson and Tellegen's sense, represent the organization of these basic processes in actually occurring affective reactions. They also suggest that the basic processes of positive and negative affect can be aroused simultaneously and independently, which accords with hypotheses on their anatomical substrates.

CONSEQUENTS OF AFFECTIVE STATES

Affective states are relevant to the individual and his or her environment because they have consequences for behavior and psychological functioning. One of the central questions in the psychology of emotion concerns the nature and extent of these consequences of affective states, as well as the processes that produce them.

One can expect the major consequences of emotions and emotion episodes to be relational and motivational. Curiously enough, little systematic research exists on the actual relationships between emotions and corresponding changes in interpersonal relationships and goal-directed behaviors. No doubt many data can be found scattered in the literature, such as the finding of Sonnemans (1991) in his self-report study that subjects' ratings of the intensity of their emotions was related to the self-rated effect of these emotions upon their conduct of life. At the other end of the range of behavioral complexity, there is experimental evidence that individuals spend more time attending to affect-relevant information than to other information, and have lower thresholds for picking up such information (Williams, Watts, MacLeod, & Mathews, 1988). A systematic search of the literature from this perspective would be a worthwhile undertaking.

Whatever that search will yield, the relationships between emotion and behavior are evidently far from direct. Anger and aggression, for instance, are only loosely linked. According to a self-report study, only a small proportion of anger incidents lead to actual or verbal aggression (Averill, 1982). Obviously, regard for negative response consequences and the various other sorts of emotion regulation form grounds for discrepancies. But Averill's analysis shows how complex the motivational nature and behavioral consequences of specific emotions often are. Anger upon an insult, frustration, and norm transgression of one's child are just not the same, and have dissimilar kinds of consequences.

Emotions, episodes, and moods may all be expected to have more or less nonspecific behavioral and motivational consequences through their associated changes in activation. This second dimension of affect is usually identified with autonomic arousal, but probably is much more often linked to the quite different construct of "arousal 2" (Routten-

berg, 1968), or of "activation" in the sense of tonic readiness for action (Pribram, 1981; see also Thayer, 1989). There is some literature that links emotions to such variables as behavioral amplitude, use of space, interest in one's surroundings, spontaneous initiative, propensity to spend effort, and persistence in goal-directed activity. The latter aspects are regularly mentioned in general mood scales and in depression scales (Beck, 1967; Thayer, 1978; Watson, Clark, & Tellegen, 1988); as we have seen, such items as "alert," "enthusiast," "sullen," or "uninterested" correlate strongly with the affect items proper. Cunningham (1988) found that subjects in whom happy mood was induced by means of the Velten (1968) procedure were more interested in social and physical activities, and engaged more in social interaction, whereas subjects made unhappy were more interested in remaining alone to sit and think. In line with these variations in energy and motivation are performance differences between depressed and normal subjects, such as lower scores on recall tasks, involving slower encoding as well as slower retrieval (Ellis, Thomas, & Rodrigues, 1984; Ellis, Thomas, McFarland, & Lane, 1985). Experimentally induced depressed mood and clinical depression have both been shown to lead to decreased psychomotor speed (e.g., Mayer & Bremer, 1985; Parrott & Sabini, 1990).

Because pleasantness and activation tend to be uncorrelated, certain consequences of emotions and moods will be the same for activated positive and negative affects. Conversely, since mood labels may cover states that vary largely in this regard (as with apathic vs. agitated depression), certain effects may widely differ for a given mood state; agitated depression may well have certain consequences in common with elated states.

The issue of the consequences of emotional activation is linked to a traditional issue in the psychology of emotion: whether emotions are to be considered disorganizing and disturbing (e.g., Hebb, 1949) or organizing and motivating (Leeper, 1948; see also Arnold, 1970). To some extent, the issue was resolved by the hypothesis of the inverted-U curve (Hebb, 1970): Weak emotion (or activation or motivation) leads to low cognitive and motor performance, moderate arousal to optimal performance, and high arousal to performance decrement. Plausible as these generalizations are, the evidence is actually relatively weak (see Näätänen, 1973). Be that as it may, the findings on decreased recall in depressed mood would accord with them, since depressed mood tends to go with low activation (low Positive Affect, in Watson and Tellegen's terms; Hall, cited in Watson & Tellegen, 1985). On the other hand, behavioral interference, as it is involved in high degrees of activation, is more likely to involve arousal in the traditional sense of autonomic arousal (Thayer, 1989).

A large literature exists, most of it relatively recent, about the different effects of pleasant and unpleasant moods upon cognitive processes (Clark, 1986; Morris, 1989). Such effects upon cognitive processes can be expected theoretically, as well as on the basis of common sense and clinical observation. One would expect positive mood to produce a more positive evaluation of one's quality of life, of one's condition and abilities, and of other people, and negative mood to do the opposite. In a sense, it is inappropriate to say that moods "produce" those effects, since positive or negative appraisal is part of what moods are about. The proper research problems would seem to be the extent of the cognitive mood changes, and the processes that bring them about. In any case, it is plausible to expect that mood-inducing conditions produce consonant changes in judgments, and that the intensity of an individual's mood ratings correlates with such changes.

Theoretically, such influences upon cognitive processes are to be expected for various reasons. The first reason is the nature of memory processes. Complex judgments—self-judgments and social judgments in particular—are arrived at with the help of available information. Information may be expected to be more readily available when primed through associations with current affective state, through selective recall of mood-consistent information, and through effects of affect upon selective attention (Bower, 1981, 1991; Forgas & Bower, 1988; Isen, 1984, 1987). In fact, these three possibilities represent three alternative hypotheses in this domain.

Second, affective reactions are sources of information. They carry the global information that the state of the world does or does not conform to one's goals and concerns. This information may well result in the making of attributions about the precise sources of those assessments, namely, the quality of one's conditions and one's coping resources. The less precisely one is aware of what caused one's mood, the more readily such attributions will be made. This is the "feelings-as-information" hypothesis advanced by Schwarz and Clore (1983, 1988; Clore, 1992; Schwarz, 1990).

Third, emotions and moods have further properties—affect, appraisal, state of action readiness, and available coping resources—that are relevant for perception and judgment. Positive emotions and moods are linked to the activation of approach tendencies (e.g., Lang, Bradley, & Cuthbert, 1990), openness to stimulation (e.g., Lacey & Lacey, 1970), and implicit and explicit trust in one's coping resources (Lazarus, 1991). Negative emotions and moods are linked to avoidant and defensive tendencies (Lang et al., 1990), closure to stimulation (Lacey & Lacey, 1970), and selective attention for emotion-relevant information (MacLeod, Mathews, & Tata, 1986; Williams et al., 1988). Furthermore, different affective states can be expected to involve different threshold changes with respect to subsequent affective reactions and judgments, because of their differences in affect and appraisals. The computations involved in evaluative judgments can be expected to include assessment of how one could, or would, be inclined to deal with the relevant contingencies (how one could bear or stand or face risks, explore memory, etc.). Finally, affective states involve particular levels of activation that influence cognitive effort in ways indicated before.

The functional properties of various affective states can be expected to extend to cognitive processing propensities. "If positive affective states inform the individual that his or her personal world is currently an OK place, the individual maybe sees little need to engage in cognitive effort, unless this is required by other currently active goals" (Schwarz, 1990, p. 544). By contrast, in many negative states the individual is motivated to carefully assess features of the current situation. Moods, therefore, may lead to either a "loosening" or a "tightening" of thought processes (Fiedler, 1988). The various information-processing strategies may not be invariably tied to positive and negative emotional states. Important differences among negative states may exist in this regard.

The main experimental findings are briefly summarized here. I begin with those on perception and judgment. Congruent effects of good and bad mood upon evaluative judgments are robust and dependable. Positive moods render them more, and negative moods less, favorable. They have been found in a number of situations: in evaluating satisfaction with one's car or television set after having received an unexpected gift, as compared to controls' not having received a gift (Isen, Shalker, Clark, & Karp, 1978); in rating the pleasantness of slides (Isen & Shalker, 1982), in rating the pleasantness of everyday activities (Cunningham, 1988); and in estimating risks of illness (Johnson & Tversky, 1983) and of the probabilities of future pleasant and unpleasant events (Mayer & Volanth, 1985), all after induction of pleasant or unpleasant mood. Congruence effects are also found in the evaluation of general life satisfaction on rainy and sunny days (Schwarz & Clore, 1983, Studies 1 and 2); attributions of praise or blame to others and self after success or failure (Forgas, Bower, & Moylan, 1990); attractiveness judgments of people (Gouaux, 1971); and other social judgments (see Forgas & Bower, 1988, for a review).

There are also important effects on self-perception. Depressed individuals generally show lower self-esteem, and tend to take less credit for their successes, than nondepressed individuals. "Recent reviews of this literature . . . document an impressive range of different kinds of judgements and perceptions about self that have been shown to be reliably and congruently associated with depressive affect" (Morris, 1989, p. 95). These latter data, however, are ambiguous with regard to the effects of mood upon cognition, since the depressive state may be a consequence rather than a cause of the cognitions. Experimental results indeed are less consistent. Wright and Mischel (1982) found mood congruity only upon self-ratings after failure, and not after success. Baumgardner and Arkin (1988) found attributions to the self only after success, but found this both in good mood (mood congruence) and in bad mood (mood incongruence). Forgas, Bower, and Krantz (1984) obtained consistent mood-congruent self-ratings, and Forgas et al. (1990) found a "positivity bias," that is to say, self-serving internal attribution for success, but only in a good mood. On the other hand, Esses (1989) found congruent changes in self-ratings after performance, in both positive and negative mood.

There is some evidence that moods indeed differ in the information-processing strategies applied, corresponding to the theoretical expectations mentioned. Isen, Daubman, and Nowicki (1987) found that during positive mood thought tends to be more creative, but also more superficial, more holistic, and less analytic, than during negative mood; and Schwarz, Bless, and Bohner (1991) found, as expected, that positive mood tended toward loosening information-processing strategies, and negative mood toward tightening.

Differences in information-processing strategies concern controlled processes. There is some evidence that different affects may differentially influence automatic processes of attention allocation. Anxious mood has been found to lead to enhanced attention for anxiety-relevant stimuli, whereas depressive affect does not appear to influence attention for depression-related ones (MacLeod et al., 1986); however, findings in this domain are as yet unstable and contradictory (see Mogg et al., 1991). Also, anxiety appears to engage attentional resources in general, and to do so more than other negative affects (Eysenck, 1988; Wine, 1971). Anxiety thus may cause performance decrement because of the diversion of attention, whereas depression may do so because of decreased activation or motivation (Cohen, Weingartner, Smallberg, Pickar, & Murphy, 1982). More controlled processes are involved in the influence of affects upon attention to affect-congruous materials, as compared with affect-incongruous materials. Depressed subjects appear to spend more time examining descriptions of their failures than do controls (Roth & Rehm, 1980); after success, subjects spend more time reading descriptions of their positive than of their negative qualities (Mischel, Ebbesen, & Zeiss, 1973); and Forgas and Bower (1987) have found the same in reading about the characteristics of other people.

The various investigations show several interesting features that qualify some of the conclusions and are of theoretical relevance. First, in many experimental studies a positivity bias is found: Subjects in good moods show mood congruity, but those in bad moods do not; they tend not to show such a mood-maintaining bias (e.g., Clark & Isen, 1982; Lewinsohn & Graf, 1973). A similar constellation has been observed in comparisons of depressed individuals with normals. Depressed subjects show "realism" in their self-evaluations, whereas normal subjects tend to amplify such evaluations (Alloy & Abramson, 1979). The interpretations of these findings is complicated, but the asymmetry itself is in line with that found in experimental self-perception studies.

Second, influences of affect upon cognitions occur mostly (or only) with ambiguous and complex target stimulus materials, such as slides that are neither clearly pleasant nor clearly unpleasant (Isen & Shalker, 1982), global judgments of life satisfaction (Schwarz & Clore, 1983), complex social judgments (Forgas & Bower, 1988), or ratings of event probabilities (Johnson & Tversky, 1983).

Third, the effects generally are "nonlocal," in the sense that no relationship obtains between the degree of mood influence and the similarity of the situation to be judged to the mood-eliciting stimulus. For instance, Johnson and Tversky (1983) induced bad mood by having the subjects read a story on death either by cancer, by homicide, or by fire. The induction caused an increase in subjects' worry (compared to that of controls) about the risks of various causes of death, but the degree of increase was not larger for items similar to that of the inducing story than it was for dissimilar items.

Fourth, the effects appear to depend upon whether or not the cause of mood change is salient. This issue has been investigated extensively by Schwarz and Clore (1983, 1988). When conditions are arranged so that a subject can plausibly attribute his or her mood to the induction conditions, congruity effects fail to appear. Such was the case, for instance, when subjects were told that the aim of the study was to assess relationships between mood and the weather (no mood effect upon life satisfaction), or when an arousal transfer manipulation was done immediately after the arousal induction through physical exercise, so that the arousal was clearly attributable to the latter (Cantor, Zillmann, & Bryant, 1975).

Finally, mood incongruity effects are also found on occasion. In a study by Dermer, Cohen, Jacobsen, and Anderson (1979), for instance, imagining a series of negative life experiences led to higher ratings of life satisfaction than imagining a series of positive events. Whether a contrast effect rather than a congruity effect is obtained may depend upon the differential salience of information

content and mood; weak moods may lead to inconguity, and more intense moods to congruity (Strack, Schwarz, & Gschneidiger, 1985).

Considerable experimental attention has been given to the effects of pleasant and unpleasant moods upon memory. Two effects have been investigated: mood state dependence and mood congruity in memory retrieval. "Mood state dependence" refers to the hypothesis that memory performance is improved when both encoding and retrieval occur under the same, as compared to different, mood states. "Mood congruity" refers to congruity between the affective valence of information and the mood under which it is to be recalled; the mood congruity effect consists of superior recall under congruous conditions.

Mood state dependence, first investigated by Bower (Bower, Monteiro, & Gilligan, 1978), is a fragile phenomenon. Studies sometimes find it, but often do not (Blaney, 1986; Morris, 1989; Ucros, 1989). Overall, the phenomenon appears to be a real one (although the size of the effect is modest), and to consist mostly of better recall for materials learned and recalled under positive mood (Ucros, 1989). Mood congruity effects, by contrast, are fairly robust under both positive and negative mood induction. They have been investigated in depressed individuals (within as well as outside the normal range), and after positive or negative mood induction. On the whole, the evidence for the effect is solid in both types of studies.

A large number of studies have used depressed patients and subjects with high scores on depression self-report scales; Blaney (1986) and Morris (1989) offer reviews. Depressed subjects tend to produce significantly poorer recall of pleasant than of unpleasant materials, although this is not always found. Tasks include recall of affectively valenced words, recall of success and failure feedback from previous tasks, and recall of life experiences. Findings of the latter type must again be interpreted with caution, since poorer production of pleasant then of unpleasant recollections may reflect poor life experience rather than a mood effect. However, this does not apply to all studies of this nature. Clark and Teasdale (1982) found recall of positive and negative recollections of depressed patients to be related to diurnal variations in mood; Weingartner, Miller, and Murphy (1982) found that recall of learned materials 4 days after learning in bipolar patients was related to degree of mood change since learning.

In experimental studies with normal subjects, mood-congruent recall has been repeatedly found with a large variety of mood induction procedures. It has most regularly been obtained in studies in which mood at retrieval is varied (rather than mood at encoding), and when the material to be recalled has personal reference for the subject (see Blaney, 1986, and Morris, 1989, for reviews). The importance of self-reference suggests that the most effective condition for mood-congruent recall involves mood state dependence as well, since self-reference is most readily produced by autobiographical memories that, at the time, did produce the corresponding mood (N. Schwarz, personal communication, 1991).

Again, there is a distinct asymmetry of effects: Mood-congruent recall is more regularly found upon positive than upon negative mood induction. In several studies, happy subjects recall more happy materials than controls, but unhappy subjects did not recall more unhappy materials. Similar results were obtained with depressed individuals: They were found to produce fewer positive recollections than negative ones (e.g., Williams & Broadbent, 1986). Negative induction may even lead to mood incongruity effects—that is, better recall of affectively positive stimuli (personal memories, affectively toned words in learned lists) than of affectively negative ones (Parrott & Sabini, 1990).

Both the asymmetry and the incongruity effects are explained by mood management processes—that is, efforts to avoid negative mood or to escape from it (Blaney, 1986; Isen, 1984, 1987; Morris, 1989) Asymmetry in mood–memory effects may, however be more basic than that. There is evidence that, indeed, positive affect does facilitate recall of positive materials, but that negative affect does not facilitate recall of negative materials. What it seems to do is to interfere with the improved recall of positive recollections found under positive affect. Morris (1989, p. 75) cites as evidence that mood congruity effects, when mood is induced by success or failure in some task, appear only when overall success rates are reasonably high (Craighead, Hickey, & DeMonbreun, 1979; DeMonbreun & Craighead, 1977).

Most of the preceding discussion has centered upon mood effects. Similar research with emotions is rare. In fact, there may well be major differences between moods and emotions in effects upon cognitive and memory processes. One would expect the cognitive effects of emotions to be considerably less general, and to be focused upon the emotional event or closely related cognitive contents. On the other hand, one would expect the effects of emotions upon beliefs to be stronger and more enduring than those of moods.

The salience findings by Schwarz and Clore (1983), discussed earlier, provide some pertinent information. Making the mood-eliciting factor more salient focuses affect upon that factor, and may be understood as the transformation of mood into (weak) emotion. Indeed, asking subjects about their emotions, after induction of sad mood, also considerably weakens the mood effects (Keltner & Audrain, 1988). A similar suggestion comes from the delay-of-transfer findings by Cantor et al. (1975): After brief delays between arousal of excitation and transfer stimuli, the excitement is still focused upon its object, which prevents generalization. After transfer, excitement is focused upon the new object and takes the form of the new emotion of sexual excitement or anger, depending upon the stimulus used. More compelling evidence for more specific effects of emotions comes from a study by Gallagher and Clore (1985), in which hypnotically induced fear affected judgments of risk but not of blame, whereas induced feelings of anger affected judgments of blame but not of risk.

The major hypotheses that have been advanced to explain the described effects correspond with the theoretical reasons for expecting such effects, given earlier. The hypotheses involving memory processes have received widest currency. These hypotheses have made use of the network model of memory and recall (Bower, 1981; Bower & Cohen, 1982; Isen, 1984). According to this model, recall results from the activation of elements in a memory network. Activation of an element is supposed to be a function of the activation of associated elements; mood states and emotions function as elements in such a network. When an individual is in a mood or emotional state, that state activates its corresponding memory element, which in turn activates information associated to it; this information may be information that has earlier evoked that particular mood or emotion, or that has been learned when the person was in that mood. The model has wide applicability, in that stored information may be considered essential for all sorts of evaluative tasks, as well as for recall. For instance, when one is asked to evaluate satisfaction with one's television set, such evaluation may use recalled happy experiences with the set, and this recall may be facilitated by current happy mood. The network model has instigated a large body of research, and to a large extent has yielded the predicted results. However, it has to face a number of problems that render it less satisfactory as a comprehensive explanation of affect–cognition effects.

First, in a number of studies, alternative interpretations are possible or likely. Facilitation of recall may often be attributable to priming by the cognitive content of the mood-inducing instructions, or by the previous experience of the subject, rather than by the mood as such. The problem plagues much of affect–cognition research (see, e.g., Williams et al., 1988). Second, the importance of stimulus ambiguity, the nonlocality of effects on judgment, and the positivity bias are difficult to explain from the network point of view. The mood management processes invoked to explain positivity bias are not incompatible with the network model (Isen, 1984); however, they form an additional hypothesis external to the model.

Further problems, more difficult to handle, are the facts (1) that mood-congruent recall is not readily demonstrated with stimuli that do not allow self-referencing or "that do not contact the subject's customary evaluative construct system" (Blaney, 1986, p 236); (2) that it does not occur with unambiguous, well-organized materials (e.g., Fiedler, Pampe, & Scherf, 1986); (3) that there is no relationship between intensity of mood and magnitude of effect (Blaney, 1986); and, most importantly, (4) that the effects can be annihilated by making the mood manipulation salient (Schwarz & Clore, 1988).

This latter finding provides the strength of the "feelings-as-information" explanation (Clore, 1992; Schwarz, 1990; Schwarz & Clore, 1988). This explanation has further merits. One of these is that it can encompass most of the problems just mentioned (e.g., Schwarz & Clore, 1988). Another is that the explanation has been shown to apply to nonaffective feel-

ings, such as feelings of ease of retrieval, feelings of familiarity, and feelings of knowing. Such feelings, too, influence evaluative judgments, and these effects, too, are eliminated by misattributing those feelings to other sources (Clore, 1992).

There is also a more basic merit in the feeling-as-information hypothesis. The network theory of affect influences possesses a deeply unsatisfactory aspect—namely, that affect per se is irrelevant to the explanation Mood is an item of information just like any other. By contrast, the feelings-as-information view starts from the function of affective states—moods as well as emotions—in providing information about the meaning of the environment for the individual. Also, it includes the specific properties of particular moods, such as different cognitive strategies, in its explanation.

One aspect of the feelings-as-information view may be somewhat less convincing, and not necessary for the theory. Mood congruity in judgments is attributed to controlled processes, as opposed to the supposedly automatic processes of facilitation in a network (Schwarz & Clore, 1988). Linked to this is the interpretation that judgment congruence effects result from misattributing the cause of mood, which treats these effects as nonfunctional ones. Perhaps extending the feelings-as-information view so as to include further properties of moods, as suggested earlier, would give a more complete explanation (see also Morris, 1992). The relevance of such properties (changes in appraisal propensities, in appraised competence, in activation) has not been put to a test. However, they would seem to account for most of the data, and particularly for the asymmetry findings. In bad moods, the subject can be expected to be unwilling or unable to pursue happy memories. The information effects upon judgment can be understood as true information effects, not misattributions: They may be the results of actual computations of value combining recalled stimulus properties with available coping resources. These latter should be less, or less available, in depressed than in expansive mood (Russell, 1980; Watson & Tellegen, 1985).

CONCLUDING REMARKS

In this chapter, I have tried to give an overview of some of the major aspects of affective states, and their relations with other psychological processes. I have tried to provide conceptual clarification of the distinctions between the various kinds of affective states. I consider duration and intensity not to be the most profitable basis for distinction between emotions and moods. Rather, "diffuseness" appears as the most consequential difference between these affective states, particularly since it allows more precise analysis in terms of the absence of focus upon a particular object. Also, I consider it useful to draw attention to states of emotional engagement with a particular object that cover larger time spans and that usually involve a succession of several emotions relevant to the same transaction. I have called these states "emotion episodes." They are theoretically relevant because they bring into focus various features of affective response that persist for relatively long durations.

Furthermore, I propose that the study of emotion episodes and moods may profit from the more or less analytical perspective that is becoming current in studies of emotions. In that perspective, emotions are seen as involving appraisal processes and changes in state of action readiness, in addition to affect. Different affective states involve different appraisals and kinds of action readiness. States of action readiness include readiness for specific types of motor and cognitive actions, as well as general activation. Moreover, emotions are seen as evaluative responses to events of personal relevance, and thus as informative concerning such events. This perspective may serve as a more encompassing framework for integrating empirical findings; for achieving a better understanding of the nature of moods, as well as of emotion episodes, the emotional states that cover longer time spans; and for making more detailed predictions about the cognitive and behavioral consequences of moods and episodes.

Acknowledgments. I am grateful to Norbert Schwarz, Joe Sergeant, and Reinoud Wiers for their careful and critical reading of the manuscript, and their helpful comments.

REFERENCES

Abramson, L. Y., Seligman, M. E. P. Teasdale, J. (1978). Learned helplessness in humans: Critique and reformulation. *Journal of Abnormal Psychology*, 87, 49–74.

Alloy, L. B., & Abramson, L. Y. (1979). Judgment of contingency in depressed and nondepressed subjects. Sadder but wiser? *Journal of Experimental Psychology: General*, 108, 441–485.

Arnold, M. B. (1970). Perennial problems in the field of emotion. In M. B. Arnold (Ed.), *Feelings and emotions* (pp. 169–186). New York: Academic Press.

Averill, J. R. (1982). *Anger and aggression: An essay on emotion.* New York: Springer.

Baumgardner, A. H., & Arkin, R. M. (1988). Affective state mediates causal attributions for success and failure. *Motivation and Emotion*, 12, 99–111.

Beck, A. T. (1967). *Depression: Clinical, experimental, and theoretical aspects.* New York: Harper & Row.

Blaney, P. H. (1986). Affect and memory: A review. *Psychological Bulletin*, 99, 229–246.

Bower, G. H. (1981). Mood and memory. *American Psychologist*, 36, 129–148.

Bower, G. H. (1991). Mood congruity of social judgments. In J. P. Forgas (Ed.), *Emotion and social judgment* (pp. 31–53). Oxford: Pergamon Press.

Bower, G. H., & Cohen, P. R. (1982). Emotional influences in memory and thinking: Data and theory. In M. S. Clark & S. T. Fiske (Eds), *Affect and cognition: The 17th Annual Carnegie Symposium on Cognition* (pp. 291–331). Hillsdale, NJ: Erlbaum.

Bower, G. H., Monteiro, K. P., & Gilligan, S. G. (1978). Emotional mood as a context for learning and recall. *Journal of Verbal Learning and Verbal Behavior*, 17, 573–585.

Bradburn, N. M. (1969). *The structure psychological well-being.* Chicago: Aldine.

Bühler, K. (1907). Tatsachen und Problemen zu einer Psychologie der Denkvorgänge. I. Über Gedanken. *Archiv für die Gesamte Psychologie*, 9, 297–365.

Cantor, J. R., Zillman, D., & Bryant, J. (1975). Enhancement of experienced sexual arousal in response to erotic stimuli through misattribution of unrelated residual excitation. *Journal of Personality and Social Psychology*, 32, 69–75.

Clark, D. M., & Teasdale, J. D. (1982). Diurnal variation in clinical depression and accessibility of memories of positive and negative experiences. *Journal of Abnormal Psychology*, 91, 87–95.

Clark, L. A., Watson, D., & Leeka, J. (1989). Diurnal variation in the positive affects. *Motivation and Emotion*, 13, 205–234.

Clark, M. S. (1986). Some effects of everyday moods and possible individual differences in these effects. In R. J. Hockey, A. W. H. Gaillard, & M. G. H. Coles (Eds.) *Energetics and human information processing* (NATO ASI Series, pp. 299–311). Dordrecht, The Netherlands: Nijhoff.

Clark, M. S., & Isen, A. M. (1982). Toward understanding the relationship between feeling states and social behavior. In A. Hastorf & A. M. Isen (Eds), *Cognitive social psychology* (pp. 73–108). Amsterdam: Elsevier/North-Holland.

Clore, G. L. (1992). Cognitive phenomenology: Feelings in the construction of judgment. In L. L. Martin & A. Tesser (Eds.), *The construction of social judgments* (pp. 133–163). Hillsdale, NJ: Erlbaum.

Cohen, R. M., Weingartner, H., Smallberg, S. A., Pickar, D., & Murphy, D. L. (1982). Effort and cognition in depression. *Archives of General Psychiatry*, 39, 593–597.

Costa, P. T., & McCrae, R. R. (1980). Influence of extraversion and neuroticism on subjective well-being: Happy and unhappy people. *Journal of Personality and Social Psychology, 38,* 668–678.

Craighead, W. E., Hickey, K. S., & DeMonbreun, B. G. (1979). Distortion of perception and recall of neutral feedback in depression. *Cognitive therapy and research, 3,* 291–298.

Cunningham, M. R. (1988). What do you do when you're happy or blue? Mood, expectancies, and behavioral interest. *Motivation and Emotion, 12,* 309–332.

Davitz, J. R. (1969). *The language of emotion.* New York: Academic Press.

DeMonbreun, B. G., & Craighead, W. E. (1977). Distortion of perception and recall of positive and negative feedback in depression. *Cognitive Therapy and Research, 1,* 311–329.

Dermer, M., Cohen, S. J., Jacobsen, E., & Anderson, E. A. (1979). Evaluative judgments of aspects of life as a function of vicarious exposure to hedonic extremes. *Journal of Personality and Social Psychology, 37,* 247–260.

Diener, E. (1984). Subjective well-being. *Psychological Bulletin, 95,* 542–575.

Diener, E., & Emmons, R. A. (1984). The independence of positive and negative affect. *Journal of Personality and Social Psychology, 47,* 1105–1117.

Diener, E., & Iran-Nijad, A. (1986). The relationship in experience between different types of affect. *Journal of Personality and Social Psychology, 50,* 1131–1138.

Ekman, P. (Ed.). (1982). *Emotion in the human face* (2nd ed.). New York: Cambridge University Press.

Ellis, H. C., Thomas, R. L., & Rodrigues, I. A. (1984). Emotional mood states and memory: Elaborative encoding, semantic processing, and cognitive effort. *Journal of Experimental Psychology: Learning, Memory, and Cognition, 10,* 470–482.

Ellis, H. C., Thomas, R. L., McFarland, A. D., & Lane, J. W. (1985). Emotional mood states and retrieval in episodic memory. *Journal of Experimental Psychology: Learning, Memory, and Cognition, 11,* 363–370.

Emmons, R. A., Diener, E., & Larsen, R. J. (1986). Choice and avoidance of everyday situations and affect congruence: Two models of reciprocal interactionism. *Journal of Personality and Social Psychology, 51,* 815–826.

Esses, V. M. (1989). Mood as a moderator of acceptance of interpersonal feedback. *Journal of Personality and Social Psychology, 57,* 769–781.

Eysenck, M. (1988). Anxiety and attention. *Anxiety Research, 1,* 9–15.

Fiedler, K. (1988). Emotional mood, cognitive style, and behaviour regulation. In K. Fiedler & J. P. Forgas (Eds.), *Affect, cognition and social behaviour* (pp. 100–119). Toronto: Hogrefe.

Fiedler, K., Pampe, H., & Scherf, U. (1986). Mood and memory for tightly organized social information. *European Journal of Social Psychology, 16,* 149–164.

Forgas, J. P., & Bower, G. H. (1987). Mood effects on person perception judgments. *Journal of Personality and Social Psychology, 53,* 53–60.

Forgas, J. P., & Bower, G. H. (1988). Affect in social and personal judgments. In K. Fiedler & J. P. Forgas (Eds.), *Affect, cognition and social behaviour* (pp. 183–208). Toronto: Hogrefe.

Forgas, J. P., Bower, G. H., & Krantz, S. (1984). The influence of mood on perceptions of social interactions. *Journal of Experimental Social Psychology, 20,* 497–513.

Forgas, J. P., Bower. G. H., & Moylan, S. J. (1990). Praise or blame? Affective influences on attributions for achievement. *Journal of Personality and Social Psychology, 59,* 809–819.

Frijda, N. H. (1970). Emotion and recognition of emotion. In M. B. Arnold (Ed.), *Feelings and emotions: The Loyola Symposium* (pp. 241–250). New York: Academic Press.

Frijda, N. H. (1986). *The emotions.* Cambridge, England: Cambridge University Press.

Frijda, N. H. (1987). Emotion, cognitive structure and action tendency. *Cognition and Emotion, 1,* 115–144.

Frijda, N. H., Kroon, R., & Wiers, R. (1993). *Analysis of mood ratings in four student samples.* Manuscript in preparation.

Frijda, N. H., Kuipers, P., & ter Schure, E. (1989). Relations between emotion, appraisal, and emotional action readiness. *Journal of Personality and Social Psychology, 57,* 212–228.

Frijda, N. H., Mesquita, B., Sonnemans, J., & Van Goozen, S. (1991). The duration of affective phenomena, or emotions, sentiments and passions. In K. Strongman (Ed.), *International review of studies on emotion* (Vol. 1, pp. 187–225). Chichester, England: Wiley.

Gallagher, D. J., & Clore, G. L. (1985, May). *Emotion and judgment: Effects of fear and anger on relevant and irrelevant cognitive tasks.* Paper presented at a meeting of the Midwestern Psychological Association, Chicago.

Gehm, T. L., & Scherer, K. R. (1988). Factors determining the dimensions of subjective emolional space. In K. R. Scherer (Ed.), *Facets of emotion: Recent research* (pp. 99–114). Hillsdale, NJ: Erlbaum.

Gouaux, C. (1971). Induced affective states and interpersonal attraction. *Journal of Personality nnd Social Psychology, 20,* 37–43.

Grinker, R. R., & Spiegel, J. P. (1945). *Men under stress.* Philadelphia: Blakiston.

Hammen, C. L., & Glass, D. R. J. (1975). Depression, activity, and evaluation of reinforcement. *Journal of Abnormal Psychology, 84,* 718–721.

Hebb, D. O. (1949). *The organization of behavior.* New York, Wiley.

Hebb, D. O. (1970). *Textbook of psychology* (3rd ed.). Philadelphia: W. B. Saunders.

Isen, A. M. (1984). Toward understanding the role of affect in cognition. In R. S. Wyer & T. K. Srull (Eds.), *Handbook of social cognition* (Vol. 3, pp. 179–236). Hillsdale, NJ, Erlbaum.

Isen, A. M. (1987). Positive affect, cognitive processes, and social behavior. In L. Berkowitz (Ed.), *Advances in experimental social psychology* (Vol. 20, pp. 203–253). San Diego: Academic Press.

Isen, A. M., Daubman, K. A., & Nowicki, G. P. (1987). Positive affect facilitates creative problem solving. *Journal of Personality and Social Behavior, 52,* 1122–1131.

Isen, A. M., & Gorgoglione, J. M. (1983). Some specific effects of four affect-induction procedures. *Personality and Social Psychology Bulletin, 9,* 136–143.

Isen, A. M., & Shalker, T. E. (1982). The influence of mood state on evaluation of positive, neutral, and negative stimuli: When you "accentuate the positive" do you "eliminate the negative"? *Social Psychology Quarterly. 45,* 58–63.

Isen, A. M., Shalker, T. E., Clark, M. S., & Karp, L. (1978). Positive affect, accessibility of material in memory, and behavior: A cognitive loop? *Journal of Personality and Social Psychology, 36,* 1–12.

Izard, C. E. (1977). *Human emotions*. New York: Plenum Press.

Johnson, E., & Tversky, A. (1983). Affect, generalization and the perception of risk. *Journal of Personality and Social Psychology, 45*, 20–31.

Keltner, D., & Audrain, P. (1988). *Moods, emotions, and well-being judgments*. Unpublished manuscript, Stanford University.

Kiestra, J. (1987). *Ruzies bij paren*. MA thesis, Department of Psychology, University of Amsterdam.

Lacey, J. I., & Lacey, B. C. (1970). Some autonomic–central nervous system relationships. In P. Black (Ed.), *Psychological correlates of emotion* (pp. 205–228). New York, Academic Press.

Lang, P. J. (1977). Physiological assessment of anxiety and fear. In J. D. Cone & R. P. Hawkins (Eds.), *Behavioral assessment: New directions in clinical psychology* (pp. 178–195). New York: Brunner/Mazel.

Lang, P. J. (1988, September 7). *The image of fear: Emotion and memory*. Invited address presented at the Behavior Therapy World Congress, Edinburgh, Scotland.

Lang, P. J., Bradley, M. M., & Cuthbert, B. N. (1990). Emotion, attention, and the startle reflex. *Psychological Review, 97*, 377–395.

Lazarus, R. S. (1991). *Emotion and adaptation*. New York: Oxford University Press.

Leeper, R. W. (1948). A motivational theory of emotion to replace "emotion as disorganized response." *Psychological Review, 55*, 5–21.

Lewinsohn, P. M., & Graf, M. (1973). Pleasant activities and depression. *Journal of Consulting and Clinical Psychology, 41*, 261–268.

Lorr, M., Daston, P., & Smith, I. R. (1967). An analysis of mood states. *Educational and Psychological Measurement, 27*, 89–96.

Lorr, M., & Shea, T. M. (1979). Are mood states bipolar? *Journal of Personality Assessment, 43*, 468–472.

Lutz, C. (1988). *Unnatural emotions: Everyday sentiments on a Micronesian atoll and their challenge to Western theory*. Chicago: University of Chicago Press.

MacLeod, C., Mathews, A., & Tata, P. (1986). Attentional bias in emotional disorders. *Journal of Abnormal Psychology, 95*, 15–20.

Mandler, G. (1984). *Mind and body: The psychology of emotion and stress*. New York: Norton.

Marris, P. (1974). *Loss and change*. New York: Pantheon.

Mayer, J. D., & Bremer, D. (1985). Assessing mood with affect-sensitive tasks. *Journal of Personality Assessment, 49*, 95-99.

Mayer, J. D., & Gaschke, Y. N. (1988). The experience and meta-experience of mood. *Journal of Personality and Sociol Psychology, 55*, 102-111.

Mayer, J. D., Mamberg, M., & Volanth, A. J. (1988). Cognitive domains of the mood system. *Journal of Personality, 56*, 453–486.

Mayer, J. D., Salovey, P., Gomberg-Kaufman, S., & Blainey, K. (1991). A broader conception of mood experience. *Journal of Personality and Social Psychology, 60*, 100–111.

Mayer, J. D., & Volanth, A. J. (1985). Cognitive involvement in the mood response system. *Motivation and Emotion, 9*, 261–275.

Mesquita, B., & Frijda, N. H. (1992). Cultural variations in emotion. *Psychological Bulletin, 112*, 179–204.

Mischel, W., Ebbessen, E. B., & Zeiss, A. M. (1973).

Selective attention to the self: Situational and dispositional determinants. *Journal of Personality and Social Psychology, 27*, 204–218.

Mogg, K., Mathews, A., May, I., Grove, M., Eysenck, M., & Weinman, J. (1991). Assessment of cognitive bias in anxiety and depression using a colour perception task. *Cognition and Emotion, 5*, 221–238.

Morris, W. N. (1989). *Mood: The frame of mind*. New York: Springer-Verlag.

Morris, W. N. (1992). A functional analysis of the role of mood in affective systems. In M. Clark (Ed.), *Review of personality and social psychology: Vol. 13. Emotion* (pp. 256–293). Newbury Park, CA: Sage.

Morrow, G. R., & Labrum, A. H. (1978). The relationship between psychological and physiological measures of anxiety. *Psychosomatic Medicine, 8*, 85–101.

Näätänen, R. (1973). The inverted-U relationship between activation and performance: A critical review. In S. Kornblum (Ed.), *Attention and performance* (Vol. IV, pp. 155–174). New York: Academic Press.

Neale, J. M., Hooley, J. M., Jandorf, L., & Stone, A. A. (1987). Daily life events and mood. In C. R. Snyder & C. E. Ford (Eds.), *Coping with negative life events: Clinical and social psychological perspectives* (pp. 161–189). New York: Plenum Press.

Nowlis, V. (1966). Research with the Mood Adjective Check List. In S. S. Tomkins & C. E. Izard (Eds.), *Affect, cognition and personality* (pp. 352–389). New York, Springer.

Nowlis, V. (1970). Mood, behavior and experience. In M. B. Arnold (Ed.), *Feelings and emotions* (pp. 261–278). New York: Academic Press.

Nowlis, V., & Nowlis, H. H. (1956). The description and analysis of mood. *Annals of the New York Academy of Sciences, 65*, 345–355.

Oatley, K. (1992). *Best laid schemes: The psychology of emotions*. Cambridge, England: Cambridge University Press.

Oatley, K., & Johnson-Laird, P. (1987). Towards a cognitive theory of emotion. *Cognition and Emotion, 1*, 51–58.

Ortony, A., Clore, G., & Collins, A. (1988). *The cognitive structure of emotions*. Cambridge, England: Cambridge University Press.

Ortony, A., & Turner T. (1990). What's basic about basic emotions? *Psychological Review, 97*, 315–331.

Parkes, C. M. (1972). *Bereavement: Studies of grief in adult life*. New York: International Universities Press.

Parrott, W. G., & Sabini, J. (1990). Mood and memory under natural conditions: Evidence for mood incongruent recall. *Journal of Personnlity and Social Psychology, 59*, 321–336.

Phielix, Y. C. (1985). *Het fenomeen ruzie in de partnerrelatie*. MA thesis, Deaprtment of Psychology, University of Amsterdam.

Planalp, S., DeFrancisco, V. L., & Rutherford, D. (1990). *Cues to emotion: Out of the lab and into the world*. Paper, presented at the convention of the International Communication Association, Dublin.

Plutchik, R. (1980). *Emotion: A psychoevolutionary synthesis*. New York: Harper & Row.

Pribram, K. H. (1981). Emotions. In S. B. Filskov & T. J. Boll (Eds.), *Handbook of clinical neuropsychology* (pp. 102–134). New York: Wiley.

Reisenzein, R., & Schönpflug, W. (1992). Stumpfs cognitive–evaluative theory of emotion. *American Psychologist, 47*, 34–45.

Rimé, B., Philippot, P., & Cisamolo, D. (1990). Social schemata of peripheral changes in emotion. *Journal of Personality and Social Psychology, 59,* 38–49.

Roseman, I. (1991). Appraisal determinants of discrete emotions. *Cognition and Emotion, 5,* 161–200.

Roth, D., & Rehm, L. P. (1980). Relationships among self-monitoring processes, memory, and depression. *Cognitive Therapy and Research, 4,* 149–157.

Routtenberg, A. (1968). The two-arousal hypothesis: Reticular formation and limbic system. *Psychological Review, 75,* 51–80.

Ruckmick, C. A. (1936). *The psychology of feeling and emotion.* New York: McGraw-Hill.

Russell, J. A. (1979). Affective space is bipolar. *Journal of Personality and Social Psychology, 37,* 345–356.

Russell, J. A. (1980). A circumplex model of affect. *Journal of Personality and Social Psychology, 39,* 1161–1178.

Russell, J. A. (1991). Culture and the categorization of emotions. *Psychological Bulletin, 110,* 426–450.

Scherer, K. R. (1984). Emotion as a multicomponent process: A model and some cross-cultural data. In P. Shaver (Ed.), *Review of personality and social psychology* (Vol. 5, pp. 37–63). Beverly Hills, CA: Sage.

Schildkraut, J. J. (1978). Current state of the catecholamine hypothesis of affective disorders. In M. A. Lipton, A. DiMascio, & K. E. Killam (Eds.), *Psychopharmacology: A generation of progress* (pp. 1233–1234). New York: Raven Press.

Schnurr, P. P. (1989). Endogenous factors associated with mood. In W. N. Morris, *Mood: The frame of mind* (pp. 35–70). New York: Springer-Verlag.

Schwarz, N. (1990). Feelings as information: Informational and motivational functions of affective states. In E. T. Higgins & R. M. Sorrentino (Eds.), *Handbook of motivation and cognition: Foundations of social behavior* (Vol. 2, pp. 527–561). New York: Guilford Press.

Schwarz, N., Bless, B., & Bohner, G. (1991). Mood and persuasion: Affective states influence the processing of persuasive communications. In M. Zanna (Ed.), *Advances in experimental social psychology* (Vol. 24, pp. 161–199). San Diego: Academic Press.

Schwarz, N., & Clore, G. L. (1983). Moods, misattribution, and judgements of well-being: Informative and directive functions of affective states. *Journal of Personality and Social Psychology, 45,* 513–523.

Schwarz, N., & Clore, G. L. (1988). How do I feel about it? The informative function of affective states. In K. Fiedler & J. P. Forgas (Eds.), *Affect, cognition and social behaviour* (pp. 42–62). Toronto: Hogrefe.

Shaver, P., Schwartz, J., Kirson, D., & O'Connor, C. (1987). Emotion knowledge: Further exploration of a prototype approach. *Journal of Personality and Social Psychology, 52,* 1061–1086.

Sjöberg, L., Svensson, E., & Persson, L.-O. (1979). The measurement of mood. *Scandinavian Journal of Psychology, 20,* 1–18.

Smith, C. A., & Ellsworth, P. C. (1985). Patterns of cognitive appraisal in emotion. *Journal of Personality and Social Psychology, 48,* 813–838.

Smith, S. L. (1975). Mood and menstrual cycle. In E. J. Sachar (Ed.), *Topics in psychoendocrinology* (pp. 19–58). New York, Grune & Stratton.

Sonnemans, J. (1991). *Structure and determinants of emotional intensity.* Doctoral thesis, Department of Psychology, University of Amsterdam.

Sonneville, L. de, Schaap, T., & Elshout, J. J. (1985). Ont-

wikkeling envalidatie van de Amsterdamse Stemmings vragenlijst. *Gedrag, 13,* 13–29.

Stone, A. A., & Neale, J. M. (1984). Effects of severe daily events on mood. *Journal of Personality and Social Psychology, 46,* 137–144.

Strack, F., Schwarz, N., & Gschneidiger, E. (1985). Happiness and reminiscing: The role of time perspective, mood, and mode of thinking. *Journal of Personality and Social Psychology, 49,* 1460–1469.

Stumpf, C. (1899). Über den Begriff der Gemühtsbewegung [On the concept of emotion]. *Zeitschrift für Psychologie und Physiologie der Sinnesorgane, 21,* 47–99.

Styron, W. (1992). *Darkness visible.* London: Jonathan Cape.

Thayer, R. E. (1978). Factor analytic and reliability studies on the Activation–Deactivation Adjective Check List. *Psychology Reports, 42,* 747–756.

Thayer, R. E. (1989). *The biopsychology of mood and arousal.* New York: Oxford University Press.

Ucros, C. G. (1989). Mood state-dependent memory: A meta-analysis. *Cognition and Emotion, 3,* 139–170.

Van Goozen, S., Frijda, N. H., & Van de Poll, N. E. (1992, September). Anger manifestations in an experimental paradigm: Studies in women. In F. Farabollini & S. Parmigiani (Eds.), *From conflict to cooperation: Multidisciplinary studies on aggression in animals and humans* (p. 39). Proceedings of the X World Meeting of the International Society of Research on Aggression (ISRA), Siena, Italy.

Velten, E. J. (1968). A laboratory task for the induction of mood states. *Behaviour Research and Therapy, 6,* 473–482.

Watson, D. (1988). The vicissitudes of mood measurement: Effects of varying descriptors, time frames, and response formats on measuring Positive and Negative Affect. *Journal of Personality and Social Psychology, 55,* 128–141.

Watson, D., & Clark, L. A. (1984). Negative affectivity: The disposition to experience aversive emotional states. *Psychological Bulletin, 96,* 465–490.

Watson, D., Clark, L. A., & Tellegen, A. (1988). Developmenl and validation of brief measures of positive and negative affect: The PANAS scales. *Journal of Personality and Social Psychology, 54,* 1063–1070.

Watson, D., & Tellegen, A. (1985). Towards a consensual structure of mood. *Psychological Bulletin, 98,* 219–235.

Wehr, T. A., & Rosenthal, N. E. (1989). Seasonality and affective illness. *American Journal of Psychiatry, 146,* 829–839.

Weingartner, H., Miller, H., & Murphy, D. L. (1977). Mood-state-dependent retrieval of verbal associations. *Journal of Abnormal Psychology, 86,* 276–284.

Whybrow, P. C., Akiskal, H. S., & McKinney, W. T. J. (1984). *Mood disorders: Toward a new psychology.* New York: Plenum Press.

Wierzbicka, A. (1973). The semantic structure of words for emotions. In R. Jakobson, C. H. Schooneveld, & D. S. Worth (Eds.), *Slavic poetics: Essays in honor of Kiril Taranovsky* (pp. 499–505). The Hague: Mouton.

Wierzbicka, A. (1992). Talking about emotions: Semantics, culture, and cognition. *Cognition and Emotion, 6*(3/4), 285–319.

Williams, J. M. G., & Broadbent, K. (1986). Distraction by emotional stimuli: Use of a Stroop task with suicide attempters. *British Journal of Clinical Psychology, 25,* 101–110.

Williams, M. G., Watts, F. N., MacLeod, C., & Mathews, A. (1988). *Cognitive psychology and emotional disorders*. Chichester, England: Wiley.

Wine, J. D. (1971). Test anxiety and direction of attention. *Psychological Bulletin, 76,* 92–104.

Wright, J., & Mischel, W. (1982). Influence of affect on cognitive social learning person variables. *Journal of Personality and Social Psychology, 43,* 901–914.

Wundt, W. (1912). *Einführung in die Psychologie*. Leipzig: Engelmann. [English translation: *An introduction to psychology* (R. Pintner, Trans.). London: Allen & Unwin.]

Zajonc, R. B. (1980). Thinking and feeling: Preferences need no inferences. *American Psychologist, 35,* 151–175.

Zajonc, R. B., Murphy, S. T., & Inglehart, M. (1989). Feeling and facial efference: Implications of the vascular theory of emotion. *Psychological Review, 96,* 395–416.

Zevon, M. A., & Tellegen, A. (1982). The structure of mood change: An idiographic/nomothetic analysis. *Journal of Personality and Social Psychology, 43,* 111–122.

Zuckerman, M. (1979). *Sensation seeking*. Hillsdale, NJ: Erlbaum.

28

The Experience
of Emotional Well-Being

ED DIENER

RANDY J. LARSEN

In recent decades the field of subjective well-being, addressing topics such as happiness, life satisfaction, and morale, has flourished (see Andrews, 1986; Argyle, 1987; Campbell, Converse, & Rodgers, 1976; Diener, 1984; George & Bearon, 1980; Larson, 1978; Veenhoven, 1984). A distinction has been drawn in the field of subjective well-being between cognitive judgments of one's life (e.g., life satisfaction judgments) and the experience of emotional well-being (Andrews & Withey, 1976). Because the references listed above give a comprehensive overview of the field, the present chapter highlights specific issues that are most relevant to emotional well-being.

When subjective well-being researchers speak of the *experience* of emotional well-being, they choose to evaluate people's emotions from the respondents' perspective. Researchers in this area eschew an objectivist approach that dictates which emotions define well-being. For example, our major concern is not to determine which emotions are "normal" or which emotions are adaptive. Rather, we try to determine what produces the experience of emotional well-being as defined from a respondent's own perspective.

DEFINING AND MEASURING EMOTIONAL WELL-BEING

It should be noted from the outset that the majority of people report positive affect most

of the time, that most people say they are "happy" (e.g., Campbell et al., 1976). When we explore what leads people to evaluate their emotional lives in a positive way, we find that the ratio of pleasant to unpleasant emotions is a central factor. Emotion gives either a pleasant or an unpleasant quality to virtually all of one's waking moments. When people were beeped at random moments, they reported some emotion virtually all of the time (Diener, Sandvik, & Pavot, 1991). Furthermore, we have found that affect has hedonic valence (either a pleasant or an unpleasant quality), which is consistent with the findings of other researchers (e.g., Ortony, Clore, & Collins, 1988; Smith & Ellsworth, 1985; Morgan & Heise, 1988). Thus, some level of affective pleasantness or unpleasantness, albeit often of low intensity, seems to be experienced by most people most of the time. The state of complete hedonic neutrality is certainly the exception rather than the rule.

Given the ubiquity of emotion, it is not surprising that when people evaluate their "happiness," the pleasantness of their affect appears to play a central role. Larsen (1989) found that self-report well-being scales fall at the ends of the pleasantness dimension of the emotion circumplex. Emotional pleasantness has also been found in Diener's laboratory to be a strong predictor of reports of happiness and life satisfaction, outpredicting such factors as physical pleasure, satisfaction with specific life domains, and goal achievement Thus, our results suggest that emotional pleasantness is highly related to global reports of emotional well-being. We begin by defining the experience of emotional well-being as feeling a preponderance of pleasant rather than unpleasant affect in one's life over time.

The Structure of Emotional Well-Being

When the concept of emotional well-being is critically analyzed, a number of questions arise in terms of whether it is a scientifically useful construct:

1. In light of the fact that people's emotions fluctuate constantly, is there a coherent construct of stable and cross-situational emotional well-being? If emotional life changes ceaselessly, does it make sense to study affective well-being?

2. Should discrete, specific emotions be studied rather than global pleasant and unpleasant emotions?

3. Are intense pleasant emotions or prolonged pleasant emotions more important to the experience of emotional well-being?

Momentary versus Long-Term Mood

It is clear from time-sampling and observational studies that human emotions fluctuate a great deal over time (Larsen, 1987). We (Diener & Larsen, 1984) found that people's pleasant emotions at random times in various situations correlated an average of only .10, and their unpleasant emotions also correlated at very low levels. Green, Goldman, and Salovey (in press) found that people's emotions correlated at very low levels on two mornings separated by 2 weeks. Given this instability in mood and emotion, does it make sense to study emotional well-being differences between individuals? Should we instead be studying the situations that cause momentary emotions?

Although emotions fluctuate, they move around a mean level that varies across individuals. That is, life events produce upward and downward shifts in a person's momentary or daily affect, but when moods are averaged over several weeks or months, these shifts average out to reveal the person's mean level of emotion. Individuals differ greatly from one another in their mean level on the pleasant–unpleasant dimension of mood. It is this mean

level that exhibits a degree of stability over time and across situations, and forms the core of emotional well-being (Larsen & Diener, 1985). We and other researchers have found that the stability of well-being is not attributable to artifacts of self-report measurement. For example, persons' emotional well-being as reported by family members correlated .44 with that reported for them by their friends, and this correlation rose to .70 when corrected for the unreliability of the measures (Sandvik, Diener, & Seidlitz, in press). Furthermore, Magnus (1991) found that a person's level of reported emotional well-being correlated .60 over a 4-year interval. Costa and McCrae (1988) found high levels of stability in subjective well-being, even when the measurement came from different sources. And we discovered that individuals' mean levels of unpleasant affect correlated .70 from social to solitary situations, and that their mean levels of pleasant affect correlated .70 from work to recreation situations (Diener & Larsen, 1984).

Thus, there is a coherence in the average emotional life of individuals that transcends the momentary fluctuations in mood. Moreover, this coherent pattern is related to other variables in interesting theoretical ways, thus making long-term emotional well-being an important scientific construct.

Discrete Emotions versus Global Pleasantness

In many scientific studies on affect, discrete emotions such as joy, anger, or anxiety are the focus. Would it be preferable in the field of subjective well-being to study long-term levels of such specific emotions, rather than a broad categorization of emotion in terms of pleasantness and unpleasantness? Although studying long-term average levels of discrete emotions is worthwhile, there are reasons for studying well-being as the global or average level of pleasant and unpleasant emotions. First, situations that produce an unpleasant emotion (such as fear) also often produce other unpleasant emotions (such as anger or sadness) (Polivy, 1981). Second, there is a tendency for individuals who often experience specific unpleasant emotions to experience other unpleasant emotions frequently as well (Diener & Emmons, 1985; Watson & Clark, 1984). Third, in Diener's laboratory it has been found that many of the cognitive and action tendencies that occur with specific emotions are likely to occur with other emotions of the same hedonic valence. Thus, there seems to be some degree of positive covariation among the specific pleasant emotions and among the discrete unpleasant emotions, which justifies study at a more global level. Although the study of specific emotions is valuable, researchers should not overlook the long-term coherence found within the hedonic categories of emotions (e.g., pleasant and unpleasant). There is coherence over time and across specific emotions in these categories, indicating that it is also necessary to study the processes underlying global affective phenomena.

Frequent versus Intense Emotions

Diener, Sandvik, and Pavot (1991) hypothesized that judgments of well-being come primarily from frequently experiencing prolonged pleasant affect and infrequently experiencing unpleasant affect. They found that people who differed in reports of happiness invariably differed in the amount of time they experienced pleasant affect. The intensity of their pleasant emotions, however, was of only secondary importance. Although the intensity of affective experience may be interesting in its own right, research has shown that intensity is unrelated to well-being (Larsen & Diener, 1985; Larsen & Diener, 1987). Diener, Sandvik, and Pavot (1991) argue that intense positive emotions are less important to the experience of long-term emotional well-being because such intense emotions are so rare, and also because they are often counterbalanced by costs. For example, individuals who experience pleasant emotions intensely also have a tendency to experience unpleasant emotions intensely as well (Diener, Larsen, Levine, & Emmons, 1985; Larsen & Diener, 1987). Diener, Colvin, Sandvik, and Allman (1991) showed that intense pleasant emotions often occur because of the same processes that cause intense unpleasant emotions.

Thus, intense pleasant emotions may not be heavily weighted in emotional well-being judgments, because they are fairly rare and are often offset by reversals. For example, a man who wants to really enjoy a football game may get quite invested in his team and "psyched up" on game day. If his team wins, he will experience intense happiness. But he runs the risk of his team's losing, whereupon he may experience intense unhappiness. Life histories or biographies of persons who had intense "highs" often reveal that they had intense "lows" as well (e.g., Elvis Presley, Marilyn Monroe, Vincent van Gogh). Zautra (1991) has found that persons who experience many positive events are also more likely to experience more negative events, and this finding has been replicated (Magnus, Diener, Fujita, & Pavot, 1992). It appears that the life with an occasional intense positive experience, but with a moderate level of pleasant emotional experience most of the time, is likely to lead an individual to evaluate his or her emotional life in a positive way.

Independence of Pleasant and Unpleasant Moods

In terms of the structure of well-being, it has been suggested that pleasant and unpleasant emotions are independent (e.g., Bradburn, 1969; Diener & Emmons, 1985; Zevon & Tellegen, 1982). This implies that a person can feel much pleasant and much unpleasant affect, or not much of either. Furthermore, it has been suggested that certain personality variables may influence one type of affect, but not the other (e.g., Costa & McCrae, 1980; Emmons & Diener, 1985b). For example, Larsen and Ketelaar (1989, 1990) have shown that extraversion predicts responsivity to pleasant (but not unpleasant) stimuli, whereas neuroticism predicts responsivity to unpleasant (but not pleasant) stimuli. The notion of independence between pleasant and unpleasant affect implies that emotional well-being may really represent two different phenomena that must be studied separately.

The independence of the two types of affect has, however, been hotly debated (e.g., Diener, Larsen, et al. 1985; Larsen & Diener, 1992; Watson, 1988). It appears that the degree of independence found depends on the degree to which measurement error is controlled (Green et al., in press), on the time frame sampled (Diener & Emmons, 1985), on the intensity of the emotions sampled (Diener & Iran-Nejad, 1986; Watson, 1988), on the particular emotions sampled (Watson, 1988), and on whether verbal or nonverbal measures are employed (Ketelaar, 1989). Thus, whether pleasantness and unpleasantness should be measured separately or as a single bipolar dimension has not yet been resolved. Although pleasant and unpleasant affect may not be strictly independent, Diener (1991a) has suggested that it is still worthwhile to assess the two separately. There is often enough independent variation that a researcher may uncover a pattern with one type of affect but not with the other.

One structure for emotional well-being is derived from the emotion circumplex (Russell, Lewicka, & Niit, 1989). Although finding several desirable features with circumplex models of emotion, we (Larsen & Diener, 1992) have also criticized this structure on a number of grounds. For one thing, studies using broader samples of emotions than were originally used have failed to find a completely circular structure for emotion (e.g., Morgan & Heise, 1988). Thus, although the circumplex would be extremely useful if it were valid, studies have so far been mixed in supporting it.

In sum, there appears to be some long-term stability in the amounts of pleasant and unpleasant emotions people experience. People experience some level of affect, with its concomitant hedonic tone, virtually all their waking time, but rarely experience intense emotions. It is perhaps for this reason that the amount of time people experience pleasant versus unpleasant affect is weighted heavily when people report their happiness.

Measuring Emotional Well-Being

Emotional well-being has been measured in a large number of studies by means of simple one-time self-reports. Respondents are basically asked, on a single-item or multiple-item scale, how happy they are—for example, on the Satisfaction with Life Scale (Diener, Emmons, Larsen, & Griffin, 1985; Pavot & Diener, 1993) or the Memorial University of Newfoundland Scale of Happiness (Kozma & Stones, 1980). Although Sandvik et al. (in press) have employed a multimethod approach to assessment that does not rely solely on self-reports of emotional experience, no formalized multimethod battery exists. A number of reviews of measures of subjective well-being are available (e.g., Andrews & Robinson, 1991; Larsen et al., 1985).

The evidence to date indicates that self-reports of happiness are surprisingly valid. For example, Sandvik et al. (in press) found strong convergence between self-reports of emotional well-being and interview ratings, peer reports, the average daily ratio of pleasant to unpleasant moods, and memory for pleasant minus unpleasant events. Diener, Sandvik, Pavot, and Gallagher (1991) found that self-reports of emotional well-being do not appear to be contaminated by social desirability. Andrews and Withey (1976) have suggested that about 65% of the variance in self-reports of well-being is valid variance, whereas Sandvik et al. (in press) estimate this number at 50-66%. Another salutary finding is that many measures of well-being show structural invariance across time and across cultural groups (Andrews, 1991; Balatsky & Diener, 1993; MacKinnon & Keating, 1989; Lawrence & Liang, 1988). Pavot and Diener (1992) report that the influence of prior questions on subjective well-being is often minimal.

Despite these encouraging findings, Diener (1991a, 1991b) strongly recommends that multimethod batteries be used to assess emotional well-being. A major limitation of self-report is that it relies exclusively on persons' cognitive labels of their emotions. But emotion is recognized to be a multichannel phenomenon, including physiological, facial, nonverbal, cognitive, behavioral, and experiential components. In order to obtain a complete picture of a person's emotional well-being, it will be desirable to include peer reports, coding of nonverbal behavior, and so forth, in order to assess the full range of emotional responses. In addition, one cannot completely rule out the effects of self-presentation when one compares the self-reported well-being of various groups. Thus, the use of additional methods of measurement is imperative. When the measures converge, one will obtain greater confidence in the results. When the measures diverge, one will gain more complex knowledge of the emotional well-being of the groups being compared.

CORRELATES OF EMOTIONAL WELL-BEING

Because much of the work on subjective well-being has been conducted by sociologists and survey researchers, there exists a plethora of information about the covariation between demographic variables (e.g., age, income, gender) and emotional well-being (Diener, 1984). Age and education show only small correlations with reports of well-being (Diener, 1984), whereas unemployment has sometimes been a strong predictor of unhappiness. Marriage has been a consistent positive predictor of emotional well-being, with married persons reporting greater well-being than the widowed, the divorced, and the never-married (e.g., Glenn & Weaver, 1978; Lawton, Moss, & Kleban, 1984; Tran, Wright, & Chatters, 1991). It should be noted, however, that marriage, like other controllable demographics such as income, may be related to emotional well-being not because it necessarily increases well-being, but rather because people who are happy have a higher probability of marriage (Scott, 1991).

When the well-being literature is examined, it is clear that many demographic variables have been explored in a descriptive way in the absence of a theoretical framework. One exception is the work of Campbell et al. (1976), who present an aspiration–achievement discrepancy model of happiness. According to this theory, because demographics are often related to resources that help individuals attain their aspirations, demographic factors such as income may be related to emotional well-being. Aspirations may, however, rise faster than one's resources.

Another theoretical account of a demographic variable is Fujita, Diener, and Sandvik's (1991) explanation of gender differences in emotional well-being. They note that women and men score similarly in national surveys of global happiness, but that women also consistently report much higher levels of unpleasant affect and suffer from depression at twice the rate of men. Fujita et al. reconcile this paradoxical set of findings by suggesting that in Western cultures, women generally have more intense emotions than do men. They find that women on the average have both more intense pleasant *and* more intense unpleasant emotions. Thus, although women report more unpleasant affect, they report levels of global happiness similar to those of men because the balance or ratio between pleasant and unpleasant emotions is similar for women and for men.

THEORIES ON THE CAUSES OF EMOTIONAL WELL-BEING

A number of minitheories about subjective well-being have been developed. Although none gives a full-blown account of the origins of emotional well-being, each suggests specific factors that can influence long-term emotional experiences.

Personality Dispositions

In correlational research, it has been consistently found that extraversion is associated with elevated pleasant affect, and neuroticism with elevated unpleasant affect (Costa & McCrae, 1980; Emmons & Diener, 1985b; Headey & Wearing, 1989). Experimental studies confirm these findings (Larsen & Ketelaar, 1989, 1991). Although extraversion and neuroticism have been studied most extensively, a number of other traits are also related to emotional well-being (Emmons & Diener, 1985b). For example, Diener and Diener (1993) found that self-esteem correlated .53 with life satisfaction in eight Western countries. Across 31 Western and non-Western countries, however, they found that the size of the relation between life satisfaction and self-esteem depended on the degree of individualism versus collectivism of the country.

One can delve more deeply into the process that relates extraversion to the level of a person's emotional well-being. Research by Pavot, Diener, and Fujita (1990) and Diener, Sandvik, Pavot, and Fujita, (1992) has found that extraverts are happier even when alone, and are happier than introverts whether they live alone or with others, or whether they work in social or nonsocial jobs. Larsen and Ketelaar (1989, 1991) found that extraverts were more susceptible than introverts to a laboratory pleasant mood induction, and that high-neuroticism subjects were more susceptible than stable subjects to an unpleasant mood induction. The propensity for greater well-being on the part of stable extraverts suggests that a broad temperament influence may be at work.

Behavioral genetic work shows that there is a sizable heritability to levels of pleasant and unpleasant affect (Buss & Plomin, 1984). The findings of Ormel (Ormel & Schaufeli, 1991; Ormel & Wohlfarth, 1991) suggest that stable temperamental dispositions may be more powerful than environmental factors in influencing subjective well-being. It is interesting that Tellegen et al. (1988) and Cesa, Baker, and Gosse (1986) both have found a larger heritability for unpleasant than for pleasant affect. This suggests that environmental and situational factors may have a greater influence on pleasant affect, whereas inborn temperament may have a larger influence on unpleasant moods.

A distinction related to personality forms one central focus in the field of subjective well-being—what Diener (1984) has referred to as "top-down" versus "bottom-up" theories of happiness. Top-down theories, such as the propensity model of Stones and Kozma (1986), suggest that emotional well-being stems from the propensity of some people to *interpret* their environment in a positive way, and to react to events with pleasant emotions. In contrast, the bottom-up approach suggests that happiness is the pleasant affect resulting from positive events' happening to individuals. Not surprisingly, evidence supports both top-down and bottom-up effects. For example, Headey, Veenhoven, and Wearing (1991) found causation in both directions for the marriage domain, but found primarily top-down effects in other domains. In contrast, Fujita and Diener (1991) found strong bottom-up effects in several domains when objective predictors were used, but found weaker top-down effects. A number of event studies demonstrate that objective life events can influence emotional well-being, thus supporting the bottom-up approach (e.g., Diener, Magnus, & Fujita, 1992). If researchers are to achieve further progress, the top-down versus bottom-up distinction is in need of a more exact specification of the relevant psychological processes.

Resources

If much of the variation in emotional well-being can be attributed to personality and top-down effects, it would follow that valued assets, such as income, physical attractiveness, social skills, and good health, may be less closely related to happiness than one might suspect. It has been found that income is related to well-being, but that these effects are small in wealthy countries (Diener, Sandvik, Seidlitz, & Diener, 1992; Veenhoven, 1991). Diener and Diener (1993) found that the relation between life satisfaction and financial satisfaction is much stronger in poorer countries. Although common sense suggests that health should covary strongly with emotional well-being, Okun and George (1984) found a small correlation between the two when ob-

jective measures of health were employed. Similarly, Wolsic, and Diener (1992) found that although physical attractiveness is one of the most highly prized resources in Western cultures, it correlates only weakly with subjective well-being. Intelligence shows virtually no correlation with reports of subjective well-being (Diener, 1984; Emmons & Diener, 1985b). Finally, marriage is a resource in Western society and has been found repeatedly to predict emotional well-being, but the relationship is very small (Scott, 1991).

Highly valued resources apparently do not covary strongly with emotional well-being. This casts doubt on a strong form of resource theory—that emotional well-being arises from people's ability to obtain valued cultural goals. It may be, however, that there are so many different resources that no single one is likely to have much effect. Furthermore, it may be that resources do not have a simple linear and direct influence on well-being. For example, some resources may have threshold effects, such that below a certain value a person is unlikely to be happy, but above that value there is no relation between the resource and emotional well-being; rather, well-being now simply becomes a possibility.

Relative-Standards Approaches

It has been hypothesized that a person's level of subjective well-being is determined by comparisons he or she makes with standards. These standards may be based on social comparisons, on the person's aspiration level, on the person's past, or on his or her ideals. It is hypothesized that if people exceed these standards, they will be happy and satisfied, but if they fall short of their standards, they will experience low levels of emotional well-being (e.g., Michalos, 1985). According to this model, happiness does not result directly from objective conditions, but rather from the relation between these objective conditions and relevant standards. For example, William James (1890/1952) hypothesized that happiness is reflected in the ratio of one's accomplishments to one's aspirations. Accordingly, happiness could be increased either by increasing one's accomplishments or by limiting one's aspirations.

Easterlin (1974) adduced evidence to show that the effects of income on happiness are relative. Emmons and Diener (1985a) found that social comparison was an especially strong predictor of satisfaction with various domains, and this finding was replicated by Michalos (1985). Smith, Diener, and Wedell (1989) demonstrated in a controlled laboratory experiment that social comparisons can influence satisfaction. Despite the positive evidence, Veenhoven (1991) has issued a strong rejoinder against relative-standards approaches. Empirical work such as that of Fox and Kahneman (in press) and Fujita and Diener (1991) suggest that social comparisons may not have a causal role in everyday life satisfaction judgments. Work by Diener, Sandvik, Seidlitz, and Diener (1992) indicates that the effects of income on happiness do not depend on expectations, social comparisons, or past conditions.

The debate about the effects of relative standards remains unresolved. On the one hand, it would be hard to deny that people to some extent habituate to their life circumstances (e.g., Lehman, Wortman, & Williams, 1987), suggesting that standards affecting happiness can change. On the other hand, the effects of social comparison and other standards on subjective well-being have not always been found (Diener, Sandvik, Seidlitz, & Diener, 1992). Thus, we need to understand what standards can influence happiness under what conditions.

Emotion Training

Developmental psychologists have noted that parents may differentially reinforce and punish the display of specific emotions in their children (e.g., Halberstadt, 1986; Lewis & Michalson, 1982). In this way, some children may come to evaluate the experience of certain emotions positively and display those emotions openly, and to suppress the experience and display of other emotions. An interesting result of the differential reinforcement and punishment of certain emotions in different groups is that cultural variations in emotional well-being, based on the shaping of emotions, may exist. For example, we have found that those in Asian cultures report being less happy than those in Latin-American cultures (Diener & Suh, 1993). There are a number of possible explanations for this difference, but the pattern of findings makes it seem unlikely that the disparity can be explained solely

as an artifact of self-report. The difference may be attributable to the dislocations and stresses accompanying rapid economic growth, but it may also be attributable to differences in the socialization of emotions in the two regions. For example, Latin cultures may teach the repression or suppression of various unpleasant emotions. How emotional well-being relates to differential socialization of emotions is a fertile area for future research.

Needs and Goals

Diener (1984) has grouped a number of approaches together as "telic theories," because one notion they hold in common is that happiness occurs when a person arrives at some end state. The end state may be set by innate biological drives, as in some need theories (e.g., Maslow, 1954); by psychological needs or motives (Murray, 1938); or by conscious goals (Emmons, 1986). Because needs and goals depend on learning, life cycle, and biological factors, emotional well-being may result from quite different telic states for different people at different times in their lives.

What is the process by which pleasant or unpleasant emotions may result from the reaching of telic states? Note first that reaching some goals (e.g., eating food when one is famished) may be pleasant in itself, independently of any emotional reaction. Thus, the fulfillment of biological needs may lead to an enhanced sense of physical well-being, which may not totally depend on *emotional* well-being.

It also seems, however, that reaching valued end states produces pleasant emotional experiences. Similarly, failing to reach a goal results in the experience of unpleasant affect (Emmons, 1986). It is instructive to note that Emmons has found that conflict between goals is a strong predictor of unpleasant affect. If a person wants things that conflict with each other, the person cannot possibly obtain all the things he or she desires.

There are many intriguing hypotheses about goals and well-being. For example, if a person possesses some desirable state of affairs, such as good health, adaptation or habituation may cause this circumstance to lose its ability to produce pleasant emotions; however, the loss of good health may nevertheless result in strong unpleasant affect. A goal that is obtained but that requires no further action to maintain may lose part or all of its power to produce pleasant emotions. Furthermore, people may gain pleasure from moving toward valued states, even though they have not achieved those states.

Cognitive Theory of Emotional Well-Being

A number of the theories described above may be incorporated into an evaluative–cognitive theory of emotion. According to this approach, affect depends on ongoing evaluations of events happening to the person. Such evaluations may be strongly influenced by the temperament of the individual; early learning may also influence the person's interpretations of many events. But in addition, such evaluations will depend on how much the events meet the person's current goals and needs. If the person interprets events as successfully meeting these goals, he or she will react with pleasant emotions. If the person perceives himself or herself as moving further from the ideal state, he or she will react with unpleasant emotions.

Emotions tell people how they are "faring" with respect to their needs and goals (Epstein, 1984). When a person reaches a goal, however, he or she may come to focus on new challenges. Therefore, the goal state itself may lose its positive power to create pleasant emotions, although its loss often produces unpleasant emotions. In this theory, pleasant and unpleasant emotions are seen as continual feedback about changes in the state of affairs. If that change is positive in terms of a person's goals and outlook, the person will experience emotional well-being. This approach places well-being not only in possessing desired states, but also in the perceived movement toward valued ends. In contrast to adaptation theory, the cognitive approach stresses a change in goals rather than the mere passage of time as the cause of emotional "habituation." Also, unlike the theory of adaptation, the perceived-movement theory holds that people can rise above emotional neutrality because some goals continually recur (e.g., the desire to eat, the need to achieve, or the requirement to clean), and therefore will produce opportunities for continuing pleasant affect. Furthermore, a person may forever acquire entirely new goals and therefore experience movement toward desired end states. If happiness consists primar-

ily of frequent pleasant affect, then achieving many small goals on a daily basis, and infrequently failing to reach goals, may be the road to a happy life.

CONCLUSIONS

Although the field of subjective well-being has developed largely independently of the field of emotion research, a number of interesting observations about affect and emotion can increase our understanding of well-being:

1. When people evaluate their well-being, the ratio of their pleasant to unpleasant emotions over time plays a pivotal role. Emotion seems central to subjective well-being for several reasons. First, people seem to feel some affect during virtually all of their waking life, and all affect seems to have a hedonic valence (either pleasant or unpleasant). Thus, affect carries a large weight in evaluating well-being, because it contributes pleasantness or unpleasantness on a continual basis to personal experience. Second, affect is related to a person's evaluation of life because emotion arises from the evaluations the person makes of events as those events transpire. Thus, a person who interprets his or her life as comprised of desirable events will experience more pleasant than unpleasant emotions over time.

2. The emotion system is reactive to immediate events and the current physiological state of the person. Thus, a person's emotions fluctuate a great deal over time. Nevertheless, there are processes that influence the intermediate- and long-term average pleasantness or unpleasantness of a person's emotional life. For example, people seem to be predisposed by their genetic temperament to experience certain emotions. In addition, personality factors may contribute to the creation of life circumstances that foster pleasant or unpleasant emotional experience (McCrae & Costa, 1991). Thus, there are longer-term factors that produce coherent patterns of affect, and these are subjects for legitimate scientific inquiry.

3. Intense affect, the stock in trade of most psychologists who study emotion, is very rare in the natural daily lives of most adult humans. Most emotions are felt at mild levels (Diener & Iran-Nejad, 1986; Diener, Sandvik, & Pavot, 1991). Because people feel some level of mild emotion virtually all of the time, the frequency and duration of pleasant and unpleasant emo-

tions weigh heavily when a person evaluates his or her emotions and life satisfaction. Although intense emotional experiences are undoubtedly important, their rarity seems to often diminish their long-term impact on well-being.

4. Factors such as income, physical attractiveness, and health have only a modest influence on long-term levels of emotion. Furthermore, people adapt or habituate to events. These findings suggest that the emotion system to some extent adjusts to current circumstances, but the limits of adaptation are not known.

5. Most people report being somewhat happy. Although some theories (e.g., Brickman & Campbell, 1971; Frijda, 1988) suggest that people should be affectively neutral or unhappy most of the time, existing subjective well-being data strongly contradict this prediction (Diener, 1993). Most people report experiencing mild pleasant affect most of the time. Thus, despite a degree of adaptation to long-term circumstances, people are able to derive pleasant emotions from daily living.

6. The correlates of emotional well-being vary in different cultures. For example, self-esteem and financial satisfaction may weakly or strongly covary with life satisfaction (Diener & Diener, 1993). The implication is that to some extent the specific causes of pleasant and unpleasant emotions differ, depending on the life circumstances and culture of the individual.

It is evident that the field of emotional well-being is a land of opportunity for theoretical and empirical work. In answering the question of what produces a happy life, scientists working in this area will further our basic knowledge of emotions.

REFERENCES

Andrews, F. M. (Ed.). (1986). *Research on the quality of life*. Ann Arbor, MI: Institute for Social Research.

Andrews, F. M. (1991). Stability and change in levels and structure of subjective well-being: USA 1972 and 1988. *Social Indicators Research, 25*, 1–30.

Andrews, F. M., & Robinson, J. P. (1991). Measures of subjective well-being. In J. P. Robinson, P. R. Shaver, & L. S. Wrightsman (Eds.), *Measures of personality and social psychological attitudes* (pp. 61–114). San Diego: Academic Press.

Andrews, F. M., & Withey, S. B. (1976). *Social indicators of well-being: America's perception of life quality*. New York: Plenum Press.

Argyle, M. (1987). *The psychology of happiness*. London: Methuen.

Balatsky, G., & Diener, E. (1991). Subjective well-being among Russian students. *Social Indicators Research, 28*, 21–39.

Bradburn, N. M. (1969). *The structure of psychological well-being*. Chicago: Aldine.

Brickman, P., & Campbell, D. T. (1971). Hedonic relativism and planning the good society. In M. H. Appley (Ed.), *Adaptation level theory: A symposium* (pp. 287–302). New York: Academic Press.

Buss, A. H., & Plomin, R. (1984). *Temperament: Early developing personality traits*. Hillsdale, NJ: Erlbaum.

Campbell, A., Converse, P. E., & Rogers, W. L. (1976). *The quality of American life*. New York: Russell Sage Foundation.

Cesa, I. L., Baker, L. A., & Gosse, D. (1986). *Genetic and environmental mediation of the relationship between subjective well-being and depression*. Paper presented at the annual meeting of the Behavioral Genetics Association, Honolulu.

Costa, P. T., & McCrae, R. R. (1980). Influence of extraversion and neuroticism on subjective well-being: Happy and unhappy people. *Journal of Personality and Social Psychology, 38*, 668–678.

Costa, P., & McCrae, R. R. (1988). Personality in adulthood: A six-year longitudinal study of self-reports and spouse ratings on the NEO personality inventory. *Journal of Personality and Social Psychology, 54*, 853–863.

Diener, E. (1984). Subjective well-being. *Psychological Bulletin, 95*, 542–575.

Diener, E. (1991a). *Issues in defining and measuring subjective well-being*. Unpublished manuscript, University of Illinois.

Diener, E. (1991b). *Measuring subjective well-being: Progress and opportunities*. Manuscript submitted for publication.

Diener, E. (1993). *Most people in the United States are satisfied and happy*. Manuscript submitted for publication.

Diener, E., Colvin, C. R., Pavot, W. G., & Allman, A. (1991). The cost of intense positive emotions. *Journal of Personality and Social Psychology, 61*, 492–503.

Diener, E., & Diener, M. (1993). *Self-esteem, financial satisfaction, and family satisfaction as predictors of life satisfaction across 31 countries*. Manuscript submitted for publication.

Diener, E., & Emmons, R. A. (1985). The independence of positive and negative affect. *Journal of Personality and Social Psychology, 47*, 1105–1117.

Diener, E., Emmons, R. A., Larsen, R. J., & Griffin, S. (1985). The Satisfaction With Life Scale. *Journal of Personality Assessment, 49*, 71–75.

Diener, E., & Iran-Nejad, A. (1986). The relationship in experience between various types of affect. *Journal of Personality and Social Psychology, 50*, 1031–1038.

Diener, E., & Larsen, R. J. (1984). Temporal stability and cross-situational consistency of affective, behavioral, and cognitive responses. *Journal of Personality and Social Psychology, 47*, 871–883.

Diener, E., Larsen, R. J., Levine, S., & Emmons, R. A. (1985). Intensity and frequency: Dimensions underlying positive and negative affect. *Journal of Personality and Social Psychology, 48*, 1253–1265.

Diener, E., Magnus, K., & Fujita, F. (1992). *A longitudinal examination of life events and subjective well-being*. Unpublished manuscript, University of Illinois.

Diener, E., Sandvik, E., & Pavot, W. (1991). Happiness is the frequency, not the intensity, of positive versus negative affect. In F. Strack, M. Argyle, & N. Schwarz (Eds.), *Subjective well-being: An interdisciplinary perspective* (pp. 119–139). Elmsford, NY: Pergamon Press.

Diener, E., Sandvik, E., Pavot, W., & Fujita, F. (1992). Extraversion and subjective well-being in a U.S. national probability sample. *Journal of Research in Personality, 26*, 205–215.

Diener, E., Sandvik, E., Pavot, W., & Gallagher, D. (1991). Response artifacts in the measurement of subjective well-being. *Social Indicators Research, 24*, 35–56.

Diener, E., Sandvik, E., Seidlitz, L., & Diener, M. (1992). The relationship between income and subjective well-being: Relative or absolute? *Social Indicators Research, 28*, 253–281.

Diener, E., & Suh, M. (1993). Exploring subjective well-being in Pacific Rim countries. *Social Indicators Research*. Manuscript in preparation.

Easterlin, R. A. (1974). Does economic growth improve the human lot? Some empirical evidence. In P. A. David & W. R. Melvin (Eds.), *Nations and households in economic growth* (pp. 98–125). Stanford, CA: Stanford University Press.

Emmons, R. A. (1986). Personal strivings: An approach to personality and subjective well-being. *Journal of Personality and Social Psychology, 51*, 1058–1068.

Emmons, R. A., & Diener, E. (1985a). Factors predicting satisfaction judgments: A comparative examination. *Social Indicators Research, 16*, 157–168.

Emmons, R. A., & Diener, E. (1985b). Personality correlates of subjective well-being. *Personality and Social Psychology Bulletin, 11*, 89–97.

Epstein, S. (1984). Controversial issues in emotion theory. In P. Shaver (Ed.), *Review of personality and social psychology: Vol. 5. Emotions, relationships, and health* (pp. 64–88). Beverly Hills, CA: Sage.

Fox, C. R., & Kahneman, D. (in press). Correlations, causes and heuristics in surveys of life satisfaction. *Social Indicators Research*.

Frijda, N. H. (1988). The laws of emotion. *American Psychologist, 53*, 349–358.

Fujita, F., & Diener, E. (1991). *On the comparative versus absolute value of resources for well-being*. Manuscript in preparation, University of Illinois.

Fujita, F., Diener, E., & Sandvik, E. (1991). Gender differences in negative affect and well-being: The case for emotional intensity. *Journal of Personality and Social Psychology, 61*, 427–434.

George, L. K., & Bearon, L. B. (1980). *Quality of life in older persons: Meaning and measurement*. New York: Human Sciences Press.

Glenn, N. D., & Weaver, C. N. (1978). A multivariate, multisurvey study of marital happiness. *Journal of Marriage and the Family, 40*, 269–281.

Green, D. P., Goldman, S., & Salovey, P. (in press). Measurement error masks bipolarity in affect ratings. *Journal of Personality and Social Psychology*.

Halberstadt, A. G. (1986). Family socialization of emotional expression and nonverbal communication styles and skills. *Journal of Personality and Social Psychology, 51*, 827–836.

Headey, B., Veenhoven, R., & Wearing, A. (1991). Top-down versus bottom-up theories of subjective well-being. *Social Indicators Research, 24*, 81–100.

Headey, B., & Wearing, A. (1989). Personality, life events, and subjective well-being: Toward a dynamic equilibrium model. *Journal of Personality and Social Psychology, 57*, 731–739.

James, W. (1952). *The principles of psychology*. Chicago: Encyclopedia Britannica. (Original work published 1890)

Ketelaar, T. (1989). *Examining the dimensions of affect in the domain of mood-sensitive tasks*. Unpublished master's thesis, Purdue University.

Kozma, A., & Stones, M. J. (1980). The measurement of happiness: Development of the Memorial University of Newfoundland Scale of Happiness (MUNSCH). *Journal of Gerontology, 35*, 906–912.

Larsen, R. J. (1987). The stability of mood variability: A spectral analytic approach to daily mood assessments. *Journal of Personality and Social Psychology, 52*, 1195–1204.

Larsen, R. J. (1989, August). *Personality as an affect dispositional system*. In L. A. Clark & D. Watson (Chairs), *Emotional bases of personality*. Symposium conducted at the meeting of the American Psychological Association, New Orleans.

Larsen, R. J., & Diener, E. (1985). A multitrait–multimethod examination of affect structure: Hedonic level and emotional intensity. *Personality and Individual Differences, 6*, 631–636.

Larsen, R. J., & Diener, E. (1987). Affect intensity as an individual difference characteristic: A review. *Journal of Research in Personality, 21*, 1–39.

Larsen, R. J., & Diener, E. (1992). Promises and problems with the circumplex model of emotion. In M. S. Clark (Ed.), *Review of personality and social psychology: Vol. 14. Emotional and social behavior* (pp. 25–59). Newbury Park, CA: Sage.

Larsen, R. J., Diener, E., & Emmons, R. A. (1985). An evaluation of subjective well-being measures. *Social Indicators Research, 17*, 1–18.

Larsen, R. J., & Ketelaar, T. (1989). Extraversion, neuroticism, and susceptibility to positive and negative mood induction procedures. *Personality and Individual Differences, 10*, 1221–1228.

Larsen, R. J., & Ketelaar, T. (1991). Personality and susceptibility to positive and negative emotional states. *Journal of Personality and Social Psychology, 61*, 132–140.

Larson, R. (1978). Thirty years of research on the subjective well-being of older Americans. *Journal of Gerontology, 33*, 109–125.

Lawrence, R. H., & Liang, J. (1988). Structural integration of the Affect Balance Scale and the Life Satisfaction Index A: Race, sex, and age differences. *Psychology and Aging, 3*, 375–384.

Lawton, M. P., Moss, M. S., & Kleban, M. H. (1984). Marital status, living arrangements, and the well-being of older people. *Research on Aging, 6*, 323–345.

Lehman, D. R., Wortman, C. B., & Williams, A. F. (1987). Long term effects of losing a spouse or child in a motor vehicle crash. *Journal of Personality and Social Psychology, 52*, 218–231.

Lewis, M., & Michalson, L. (1982). The measurement of emotional state. In C. E. Izard (Ed.), *Measuring emotions in infants and children* (pp. 178–207). Cambridge, England: Cambridge University Press.

MacKinnon, N. J., & Keating, L. J. (1989). The structure of emotions: Canada–United States comparisons. *Social Psychology Quarterly, 52*, 70–83.

Magnus, K. B. (1991). *A longitudinal analysis of personality, life events and subjective well-being*. Unpublished honors thesis, University of Illinois.

Magnus, K. B., Diener, E., Fujita, F. & Pavot, W. (1992).

Personality and events: A longitudinal analysis. Manuscript submitted for publication.

Maslow, A. H. (1954). *Motivation and personality.* New York: Harper.

McCrae, R. R., & Costa, P. (1991). Adding *Liebe und Arbeit*: The full five-factor model and well-being. *Personality and Social Psychology Bulletin, 17,* 227–232.

Michalos, A. C. (1985). Multiple discrepancies theory (MDT). *Social Indicators Research, 16,* 347–413.

Morgan, R. L., & Heise, D. (1988). Structure of emotions. *Social Psychology Quarterly, 51,* 19–31.

Murray, H. A. (1938). *Explorations in personality.* New York: Oxford University Press.

Okun, M. A., & George, L. K. (1984). Physician- and self-ratings of health, neuroticism and subjective well-being among men and women. *Personality and Individual Differences, 5,* 533–539.

Ormel, J., & Schaufeli, W. B. (1991). The stability and change in psychological distress and their relationship with self-esteem and locus of control: A dynamic equilibrium model. *Journal of Personality and Social Psychology, 60,* 288–299.

Ormel, J., & Wohlfarth, T. (1991). How neuroticism, long-term difficulties, and life situation change influence psychological distress: A longitudinal model. *Journal of Personality and Social Psychology, 60,* 744–755.

Ortony, A., Clore, G. L., & Collins, A. (1988). *The cognitive structure of emotions.* New York: Cambridge University Press.

Pavot, W., & Diener, E. (1992). The affective and cognitive context of self-reported measures of subjective well-being. *Social Indicators Research, 28,* 305–324.

Pavot, W., & Diener, E. (1993). A manual for the Satisfaction with Life Scale. *Psychological Assessment.*

Pavot, W., Diener, E., & Fujita, F. (1990). Extraversion and happiness. *Personality and Individual Differences, 11,* 1299–1306.

Polivy, J. (1981). On the induction of emotion in the laboratory: Discrete moods or multiple affect states? *Journal of Personality and Social Psychology, 41,* 803–817.

Russell, J. A., Lewicka, M., & Niit, T. (1989). A cross-cultural study of a circumplex model of affect. *Journal of Personality and Social Psychology, 57,* 848–856.

Sandvik, E., Diener, E., & Seidlitz, L. (in press). The assessment of well-being: A comparison of self-report and nonself-report strategies. *Journal of Personality.*

Scott, C. (1991). *Marriage, personality, and well-being.* Unpublished doctoral dissertation, University of Illinois.

Smith, C. A., & Ellsworth, P. C. (1985). Patterns of cognitive appraisal in emotion. *Journal of Personality and Social Psychology, 48,* 813–838.

Smith, R. H., Diener, E., & Wedell, D. (1989). The range–frequency model of happiness applied to temporal and social comparisons. *Journal of Personality and Social Psychology, 56,* 317–325.

Stones, M. J., & Kozma, A. (1986). Happiness and activities as propensities. *Journal of Gerontology, 41,* 85–90.

Tellegen, A., Lykken, D. T., Bouchard, T. J., Wilcox, K. J., Segal, N. C., & Rich, S. (1988). Personality similarity in twins reared apart and together. *Journal of Personality and Social Psychology, 54,* 1031–1039.

Tran, T. V., Wright, R., & Chatters, L. (1991). Health, stress, psychological resources, and subjective well-being among older blacks. *Psychology and Aging, 6,* 100–108.

Veenhoven, R. (1984). *Conditions of happiness.* Dordrecht, The Netherlands: Reidel.

Veenhoven, R. (1991). Is happiness relative? *Social Indicators Research, 24,* 1–34.

Watson, D. (1988). The vicissitudes of mood measurement: Effects of varying descriptors, time frames, and responses found on measures of positive and negative affect. *Journal of Personality and Social Psychology, 55,* 128–141.

Watson, D., & Clark, L. A. (1984). Negative affectivity: The disposition to experience aversive emotional states. *Psychological Bulletin, 96,* 465–490.

Wolsic, B., & Diener, E. (1992). *Physical attractiveness and well-being.* Unpublished manuscript, University of Illinois.

Zautra, A. J. (1991, August). *Small events are not always hassles: Sometimes they are worse.* Paper presented at the 99th Annual Convention of the American Psychological Association, San Francisco.

Zevon, M. A., & Tellegen, A. (1982). The structure of mood change: An idiographic/nomothetic analysis. *Journal of Personality and Social Psychology, 43,* 111–112

29

The Cultural Psychology of the Emotions

RICHARD A. SHWEDER

Great, deep, wide and unbounded, the ocean is nevertheless drunk by underwater fires; in the same way, Sorrow is drunk by Anger.
(Translation of an unidentified Sanskrit stanza from India in the early Middle Ages; Gnoli, 1956, p. 35)

In recent years there have been several major reviews of contemporary research on similarities and differences in emotional meanings across cultural groups (Good & Kleinman, 1985; Kleinman & Good, 1985; Lutz & White, 1986; Marsella, 1980; Mesquita & Frijda, 1992, Russell, 1991; Scherer, Wallbott, & Summerfield, 1986; Shweder & LeVine, 1984; Shweder, 1991; White & Kirkpatrick, 1985). There have also been several books and essays defining the character of a new or renewed interdisciplinary field for cross-cultural research on the emotions, which is coming to be known as "cultural psychology" (e.g., Bruner, 1990; Cole, 1988, 1990; Howard, 1985; LeVine, 1990; Lutz, 1985a; Markus & Kitayama, 1991, 1992; Peacock, 1984; Shweder, 1990, 1991; Shweder & Sullivan, 1990, 1993; Stigler, Shweder, & Herdt, 1990). For a discussion of the historical antecedents of cultural psychology, see Jahoda (1993). In anthropology, the two most notable forums for research on the cultural psychology of the emotions are the journals *Ethos: Journal of the Society for Psychological Anthropology*, and *Culture, Medicine and Psychiatry*.

The major goals of cultural psychology are to spell out the implicit meanings that give shape to psychological processes, to examine the distribution of those meanings across ethnic groups and temporal–spatial regions of the world, and to identify the manner of their social acquisition. Related goals are to reassess the principle of psychic unity or uniformity, and to develop a credible theory of psychological diversity or pluralism.

One hallmark of cultural psychology is the idea that a "culture" consists of meanings, conceptions, and interpretive schemes that are activated, constructed, or brought "on-line" through participation in normative social institutions and practices (including linguistic practices) (see, e.g., D'Andrade, 1984; Geertz, 1973; LeVine, 1984; Miller, Potts, Fung, Hoogstra, & Mintz, 1990; Shweder, 1991; Shweder & Much, 1987). According to this view, a culture is the subset of possible or available meanings that, by virtue of (informal or formal, implicit or explicit, unintended or intended) enculturation, has become active in giving shape to the psychological processes of individuals in a society.

A second hallmark of cultural psychology is the idea that interpretation, conceptualization, and other "acts of meaning" can take place rapidly, automatically, and un-self-consciously.

Indeed, it is assumed that "acts of meaning" (e.g., the judgment that the human body may become polluted or desanctified because it is a temple for the soul; or that illness is a means of empowerment because it unburdens a person of accumulated spiritual debts; or that shyness, shame, modesty, and embarrassment are good emotions because they are forms of civility) can take place so rapidly, automatically, and un-self-consciously that from the point of view of an individual person they are indistinguishable from "raw" experience or "naked" consciousness itself (see, e.g., Geertz, 1984, on "experience-near" concepts; Kirsh, 1991, on "thought in action"; and Nisbett & Wilson, 1977, on the unconscious "knowing more than we can tell"; see also Fish, 1980). According to this view, many rapid, automatic, and un-self-conscious psychological processes are best understood not as "pure," "fundamental," or "intrinsic" processes, but rather as content-laden processes, which are contingent on the implicit meanings, conceptual schemes, and interpretations that give them life (Shweder, 1990; Stigler, 1984; Stigler, Chalip, & Miller, 1986; Stigler, Nusbaum, & Chalip, 1988).

In the context of the study of the emotions, the intellectual agenda of cultural psychology can be defined by four questions:

1. What is the generic shape of the meaning system that defines an experience as an emotional experience (e.g., anger, sadness, or shame) rather than as an experience of some other kind (e.g., muscle tension, fatigue, or emptiness? (See, e.g., Harré, 1986a, 1986b; Lakoff, 1987; Levy, 1984a, 1984b; Shweder, in press; Smedslund, 1991; Solomon, 1976, 1984; Stein & Levine, 1987; Wierzbicka, 1986, 1992).

2. What particular emotional meanings (e.g., Pintupi *watjilpa*, Balinese *lek*, Oriya *lajya*, Ifaluk *fago*, American "happiness") are constructed or brought "on-line" in different ethnic groups and in different temporal–spatial regions of the world? (See, e.g., Abu-Lugod, 1985, 1986; Appadurai, 1985; Briggs, 1970; Geertz, 1959; Gerber, 1985; Lutz, 1982, 1985b, 1988; Miller & Sperry, 1987; Myers 1979a, 1979b; Parish, 1991; Rosaldo, 1980, 1983, 1984; Schieffelin, 1976, 1983, 1985a, 1985b; Stearns & Stearns, 1988; Swartz, 1988; Wierzbicka, 1986, 1990; Wikan, 1984, 1989.)

3. To what extent is the experience of various states of the world (e.g., "loss," "goal blockage," "status degradation," "taboo violation") "emotionalized" (e.g., as sadness, anger, fear,

or guilt) rather than "somatized" (e.g., as tiredness, chest pain, or appetite loss) in different ethnic groups and in different temporal–spatial regions of the world? (See, e.g., Angel & Guarnaccia, 1981; Angel & Idler, 1992; Angel & Thoits, 1987; Kleinman, 1986; Levy, 1984a, 1984b; Shweder, 1988.)

4. Precisely how are emotionalized and somatized meanings brought "on-line," socialized, enculturated, or otherwise acquired? More specifically, what is the role of everyday discourse and social interpretation in the activation of emotionalized and somatized meanings? (See, e.g., Bruner, 1990; Garvey, 1992; Miller & Sperry, 1987; Miller et al., 1990; Miller, Mintz, Hoogstra, Fong, & Potts, 1992; Miller & Hoogstra, 1992; Ochs & Schieffelin, 1984; Schieffelin & Ochs, 1986; Shweder & Much, 1987).

Any comprehensive review of answers to these questions would have to address hundreds of years of theoretical arguments, empirical sightings, and philosophical reflections in the literatures of several different civilizations (see Dimock, 1974; Harré, 1986a, 1986b; Kakar, 1982; Kleinman, 1986; Rorty, 1980; Shixie, 1989; Solomon, 1976; Veith, 1978). In this chapter my aim is simply to formulate the first two of those questions in ways that seem promising, provocative, and stimulating of future interdisciplinary research.

I start the discussion, however, in the 3rd century A.D. in India, with a relatively detailed examination of a Sanskrit text (the "Rasādhyāya" of the *Nāṭyaśāstra*) that was written relatively close to the beginning of the historical record of systematic human self-consciousness about the emotions. It is through an analysis of this venerable text that I address some contemporary concerns. The "Rasādhyāya" is a useful intellectual pole star on which to concentrate a discussion of the cultural psychology of the emotions, for three reasons: (1) The text, although ancient, compares favorably with any contemporary treatise on the subject of the symbolic character of emotional experience; (2) the text, although famous among Sanskritists and scholars of South Asian civilization, is hardly known at all by emotion researchers in anthropology and psychology; and (3) the text provides the opportunity for an object lesson about the universally appealing yet culturally revealing character of all accounts about what is "basic" to the emotional nature of human beings.

THE BASIC EMOTIONS
OF THE "RASĀDHYĀYA"

In Sanskrit the word for "existence" and the word for "mental state" (*bhāva*) are the same, and mental states are said to "bring into existence the essence of poetry" (Gnoli,1956, p. 63). So one should not be surprised to discover that between the 3rd and 11th centuries A.D., Hindu philosophers of poetics and drama, interested in human emotions as objects of aesthetic pleasure, posited the existence of eight (or nine) basic emotions (*sthāyi-bhāva*)— four of which they viewed as primary—and developed a relatively detailed account of the symbolic structures that give them shape and meaning.

There is no standard English translation of the Sanskrit terms for the eight (or nine) postulated basic emotions. Indeed, there is no agreement about whether they should be translated as "emotions," as "mental states," or as "feelings," or about whether they should be translated as "basic," "dominant," "permanent," "universal," "natural," or "principal" emotions (or mental states or feelings). The eight basic (or dominant) emotions (or mental states or feelings) are variously translated as follows: (1) sexual passion, love, or delight (*rati*); (2) amusement, laughter, humor, or mirth (*hāsa*); (3) sorrow (*śoka*); (4) anger (*krodha*); (5) fear or terror (*bhaya*); (6) perseverance, energy, dynamic energy, or heroism (*utsāha*); (7) disgust or disillusion (*jugupsā*); and (8) amusement, wonder, astonishment, or amazement (*vismaya*). Some early medieval commentators mention an additional basic (or dominant) emotion (or mental state or feeling), (9) serenity or calm (*sama*). To simplify my exegesis, I refer to the eight (or nine) as "basic emotions," and I label them "sexual passion," "amusement," "sorrow," "anger," "fear," "perseverance," "disgust," "wonder," and "serenity." Of the eight (or nine) basic emotions, four are privileged as primary basic emotions: sexual passion, anger, perseverance, and disgust (with serenity sometimes substituted or linked to disgust as a primary basic emotion).

The canonical Sanskrit text on the emotions, attributed to Bharata, is the sixth chapter, the "Rasādhyāya," of the *Nāṭyaśāstra*, a book about drama. Ancient and medieval Hindu thought specialized in "psychological" topics concerned with the nature of consciousness. Much of Sanskrit philosophy elevated the human mind

and body to the status of sacramental objects, and was disinclined to draw sharp oppositions among the material, the sensate, the conscious, the poetic, and the divine. In Sanskrit drama the primary aim of the aesthetic experience was psychological as well: indeed, it was the symbolic representation of emotional states per se that set the stage for aesthetic and revelatory experience (see Dimock, 1974). The famous sixth chapter of the *Nāṭyaśāstra* is about the narrative structure (the causes, consequences, and concomitants) of eight basic emotional states and the most effective means (via facial expression, voice, posture, setting, character, action, and physiological response) of their representation in the theatre.

The *Nāṭyaśāstra* was probably written some time between the 3rd and 5th centuries A.D. The most famous explication and commentary on the text—itself a critique of earlier explications and commentaries, and the source of our knowledge of the earlier commentaries—derives from the 10th- and 11th-century Kashmiri Brahman philosopher, Abhinavagupta (partial translations and contemporary commentaries can be found in Masson & Patwardhan, 1970, and Gnoli, 1956; see also Dimock, 1974, and Keith, 1924).

One major concern of the text and commentaries is to define the nature and significance (both aesthetic and theological) of a certain elusive metaemotion called *rasa*. *Rasa* means "to taste," "to savor," or "to sample," but when the term is used to refer to the grand metaemotion of Hindu aesthetic experience it is usually translated as aesthetic "pleasure," "enjoyment," or "rapture." It is a pleasure that lasts only as long as the dramatic illusion that makes *rasa* a reality. Because it is possible for members of the audience who witness a drama (the *rasiki*) to experience enjoyment or pleasure (*rasa*) even from the apprehension of negative emotional states (disgust, fear, anger, sorrow), which in other circumstances one might want to avoid or repress, Abhinavagupta and others reasoned that *rasa* must be an autonomous metaemotion, a *sui generis* form of consciousness.

A second major concern of the text and commentaries is to differentiate eight (or nine) varieties, colors, or flavors of *rasa*, each related to one of the eight (or nine) basic emotions. There is no standard English translation of the Sanskrit terms for the eight (or nine) *rasa*. They are variously translated as (1) the erotic or love (*sṛṅgara*) (the *rasa* of sexual passion); (2) the comic (*hāsya*) (the *rasa* of amusement); (3) the compassionate or pathetic (*karuṇa*) (the *rasa* of sorrow); (4) the furious or fury (*raudra*) (the *rasa* of anger); (5) the heroic (*vīra*) (the *rasa* of perseverance); (6) the terrifying or terror (*bhayānaka*) (the *rasa* of fear); (7) horror, the loathsome, the odious, or the disgusting (*bībhatsa*) (the *rasa* of disgust); (8) the marvelous, the awesome, admiration, or wonder (*adbhuta*) (the *rasa* of wonder); and (9) the quietistic or calm (*śānta*) (the *rasa* of serenity). When viewed from the perspective of their relationship to the eight (or nine) basic emotions of everyday life, the eight (or nine) flavors of *rasa* (the pleasure of the terrifying, the delight of horror, etc.) are sometimes translated as the eight (or nine) "sentiments" or "moods" of the theatre.

A third major concern of the text and commentaries is to give an account of the precise relationship between the eight (or nine) *rasa* and the eight (or nine) basic emotions (*sthāyibhāva*) to which they are said to correspond. Is the relationship one of identity, such that, for example, the audience's experience of the *rasa* of fear is itself a real everyday experience of fear? Or is the experience of the *rasa* of fear a mere simulation, imitation, or pretense of everyday fear? Or is it perhaps an intensification or amplification of the basic emotion? Ultimately, the idea is advanced that the experience of the *rasa* of a basic emotion is something entirely different from the experience of the basic emotion itself.

Instead, the relationship of the eight (or nine) *rasa* to the eight (or nine) basic emotions is akin to the relationship of an intentional state to its intentional object. To experience *rasa* is to experience the pleasure or enjoyment (an intentional state) that results from the dramatically induced perception of the hidden or unconscious generic symbolic structures (the intentional objects) that lend shape and meaning to the basic emotions in everyday life. To paraphrase Bharata, in drama the basic emotions are brought to a state of *rasa*. This happens to the very extent that their implicit symbolic codes are revealed and savored (or tasted) as objects of pleasure and as a means of self-consciousness and transcendence.

According to this line of reasoning, then, what "flavors" or "colors" the eight or nine *rasa* and distinguishes them from one another is that each has a different intentional object, one of the eight (or nine) basic emotions, which are

thought to be possessed by all human beings at birth. Nevertheless, there is still something common to all the flavors of *rasa*. It is the pleasure, enjoyment, delight, or rapture that comes from being artfully transported out of time, place, and the immediacies of personal emotional experiences—beyond "the thick pall of mental stupor which cloaks one's own consciousness" (Gnoli, 1956, p. 53)—into the hidden depths of the soul, where one perceives, tastes, and savors the transcendental or impersonal narrative forms that are immanent or implicit in the most deeply rooted modes of human experience.

Thus, viewed generically, all *rasa* possess that quality of pleasure or enjoyment that comes from the tasting of a transcendent form that had previously been hidden from the consciousness it had organized. It is this *sui generis* experience of delight, viewed as an intentional state aimed at the basic emotions as its intentional object, that explains how even disgust, anger, fear, and sorrow can be objects of pleasure when they present themselves as objects of aesthetic encounter. Thus viewed, what is common to the *rasa* is a metaemotion, the feeling of delight that comes from the clear apprehension of the symbolic forms implicit in ordinary emotional experience. This line of reasoning is suggestive of a parallel type of analysis of "empathy." Empathy may be viewed as a metaemotion motivated by its own characteristic source of enjoyment or pleasure, which makes it possible to be responsive to another person's negative emotional states such as sorrow or guilt. By this analysis, empathic sorrow or guilt is not the same as the direct or secondary experience of sorrow or guilt. Instead, it is a dignifying experience precisely because, as a witness to someone else's emotional experience, one is transported out of oneself. It is as if empathy is also a metaemotion, but of a middle scale. It is less detached than the experience of *rasa*, which comes from witnessing the generic symbolic structure that lends shape and meaning to a basic emotion; yet it is more detached than the experience of a basic emotion itself, which is the unwitnessed and all too immediate experience of everyday personal life. (For an account of the psychology of empathy, see Hoffman, 1990.)

Having summarized, however hazardously and incompletely, a few key elements of the "Rasādhyāya" and subsequent commentaries, I would now like to ask two questions about text. What does the "Rasādhyāya" reveal about the symbolic structure of emotional experience? And what does it reveal about itself as a cultural account of what is "basic" to human emotional experience? I treat the last question first.

THE WONDER OF THE SANSKRIT EMOTIONS: A CULTURAL ACCOUNT

Contemporary emotion researchers are likely to find the account of the basic emotions in the "Rasādhyāya" both familiar and strange. If we compare the Sanskrit list of nine (eight plus one) basic emotions (sexual passion, amusement, sorrow, anger, fear, perseverance, disgust, wonder, and serenity) with Paul Ekman's well-known contemporary list of nine (six plus three) basic emotions (anger, fear, sadness, happiness, surprise, disgust, interest, shame, and contempt), which he derives from the analysis of everyday facial expressions (Ekman, 1980, 1984), the two lists are not closely coordinated, although they are not totally disjunctive either.

Richard Schechner (1988, pp. 267–289), in his book *Performance Theory*, actually presents a series of photographs of facial expressions that he claims are iconic representations of the nine *rasa* of the *Nāṭyaśāstra*. This, of course, is a rather risky thing to do. The *Nāṭyaśāstra* never abstracts out facial expressions as the key markers of the basic emotions, but rather treats them as one element in an array of constituents; and there is every reason to believe that in Hindu drama facial expressions unfold dynamically in a sequence of movements, which are not easily frozen into a single frame. Nevertheless, Schechner posits direct analogies between six of his facial expressions for the *rasa* and the six facial expressions from Ekman's primary scheme—equating, for example, Ekman's representation of the face of surprise with the face for the *rasa* of wonder (*adbhuta*) and Ekman's representation of the face of happiness with the face for the *rasa* of sexual passion (*sṛṅgara*). Schechner thinks he sees a universal pattern reflected in the two schemes. He states, "Humankind has countless gods, but I would be very surprised if there were not some agreement concerning the basic emotions" (1988, p. 266).

In my view, several of Schechner's equations are dubious. For example, in Ekman's photo of the face of surprise, the mouth is wide open; it is not similar to the mouth of the *rasa* of wonder, which is closed and faintly suggestive of a smile. (The mouth is closed in all of the facial expressions of the *rasa*, which may be related to a cultural evaluation concerning the vulgarity of an open mouth.) And in Ekman's photo of the face of happiness, the eyes are directly frontal; they are not similar to the eyes of the *rasa* of sexual passion, where the gaze is conspicuously averted to one side, perhaps suggestive of secrecy or conspiracy. More importantly, because Schechner's equation of American "happiness" with Sanskrit "sexual passion" seems peculiar from the start, it should also be noted that Ekman's photo of the face of happiness bears no resemblance to the face of the *rasa* of amusement (*hāsya*), which is the *rasa* one might have intuitively expected to be connected to the Western conception of "happiness."

I strongly doubt that most Anglo-Americans could spontaneously generate accurate descriptions for the majority of the nine facial icons of the *rasa* displayed in Schechner's book. (Curiously, one of the faces that my U.S. graduate students seem to identify without much difficulty is the Sanskrit face of serenity, which as far as I know is not a basic emotion on any Western list. In informal experiments conducted in class, they also converge in their responses to faces of fear, disgust, and sorrow, but not in their responses to the others.) Indeed, I believe one can plausibly argue that happiness, surprise, and most of the basic emotions on Ekman's list do not have close analogues among the basic emotions of the "Rasādhyāya," and any sense of easy familiarity with the Sanskrit list is more apparent than real.

As I read the "Rasādhyāya" and commentaries, three of the nine basic emotions (anger, fear, and sorrow) are genuinely familiar, in the sense of possessing an equivalent shape and meaning for medieval Hindus and contemporary Anglo-Americans. Of course, to acknowledge those three points of dense similarity is not to suggest that those three emotional meanings must be cross-cultural universals. Wierzbicka (1992; see also 1990), for example, an anthropological linguist and polyglot who specializes in the study of semantic universals and the language of the emotions, has brought to a halt facile claims about translation equivalence by arguing quite cogently that "sadness," as understood in European and Anglo-American conceptions of the emotions, is not an empirical universal and is neither lexicalized, important, nor salient in most of the languages of the world. She claims that from the point of view of the study of the linguistic semantics of emotion terms around the world, there are no basic or universal emotions.

Nevertheless, anger, fear, and sorrow are easy to recognize in the "Rasādhyāya." Sorrow, for example, is said to arise from misfortune, calamity, and destruction, and from "separation from those who are dear, [their] downfall, loss of wealth, death and imprisonment." "It should be acted out by tears, laments, drying up of the mouth, change of color, languor in the limbs, sighs, loss of memory, etc." (Masson & Patwardhan, 1970). Sorrow is said to be accompanied by other mental states, including world-weariness, physical weariness, lifelessness, tears, confusion, dejection, and worry.

Anger and fear are also easy to recognize in the text. Anger, for example, is said to arise from provocative actions, insult, lies, assault, harsh words, oppression, and envy. The actions accompanying it include beating, splitting open, crushing, breaking, hitting, and drawing blood. "It should be acted out by red eyes, furrowing of the brows, biting one's lips and grinding one's teeth, puffing the cheeks, wringing the hands, and similar gestures." It is accompanied by other mental states, including an increase in determination or energy, rashness, violence, sweat, trembling, pride, panic, resentment, and stuttering (see Masson & Patwardhan, 1970, pp. 52–53).

For three of the nine basic emotions described in the "Rasādhyāya," it is easy to recognize the underlying script, to see the self in the other, and to arrive at a cross-cultural and transhistorical agreement about what is basic in emotional functioning (at least for them and us). Yet as one moves beyond sorrow, anger, and fear to disgust, amusement, wonder, perseverance, sexual passion, and serenity, the way in which consciousness is partitioned or hierarchically structured into basic and nonbasic states in the "Rasādhyāya" seems less and less familiar, despite any initial appearances to the contrary.

Thus it becomes clear upon examination of translations of the relevant Sanskrit texts and the commentaries that medieval Hindu "disgust" partitions its domain somewhat differently than we do. Hindu disgust includes aspects of horror and disillusionment (and world-weariness associated with the quest for detachment, transcendence, and salvation) that are not easily reducible to contemporary Anglo-American nausea, although nausea is mentioned as one of the two major subtypes of disgust. Horror at the sight of blood is the other major subtype of the domain. Medievel Hindu disgust is, as my colleague McKim Marriott has suggested, more like a domain of the loathsome; it gathers together within its territory a broad range of human responses to the ugly, the nasty, and the odious, and is thereby far more inclusive than our domain of disgust.

It becomes clear that medieval Hindu "wonder" is not contemporary Anglo-American "surprise," but rather a state of mind closer to admiration than to startle or shock. For Hindu wonder has less to do with a sudden violation of expectations and more to do with one's reactions to the opportunity to witness divine, heavenly, or exalted feats, events, or beings (including, e.g., the feats of a juggler). It is even possible to do such witnessing with one's mouth closed, as long as the eyes are wideopen!

It also becomes clear that medieval Hindu "amusement" (which includes contemptuous, indignant, or derisive laughter at the faults and inferior status of others) is not contemporary Anglo-American "happiness," which has celebratory implications. Indeed, happiness, shame, indignation, arrogance, and some contempt-like emotions are explicitly mentioned in the "Rasādhyāya" for inclusion among 33 nonbasic ("accompanying") mental states. Thus it seems reasonable to assert that the basic emotion designated by medieval Hindu philosophers as "amusement" is not adequately translated as "happiness" or as "contempt." (It should be noted that although the text provides little basis for determining equivalence of meaning for the terms used to translate the 33 nonbasic mental states, there is good reason to doubt that "shame" and "happiness" have the same implications and associations or play the same psychological role in India as they do in the contemporary United States. See Menon & Shweder, in press, and Shweder, in press, on the positive qualities of shame in India, where it is a virtue associated with civility, modesty, and an ability to rein in one's destructive powers in support of the social order rather than with the diminishment of the ego; see also Parish, 1991, and below.)

It also becomes clear upon examination of the text that medieval Hindu "perseverance" is not contemporary Anglo-American "interest"; rather, it is deeply connected to heroic determination and a willingness to engage in acts requiring endurance and self-sacrifice. In the context of the early medieval Hindu scriptures, when the Hindu goddess Durga (or Kali) endured trials and tribulations yet persisted in a seemingly hopeless battle against uncountable demons in an effort to save the world, her efforts are said to have displayed the heroic *rasa* of perseverance. Mere interest had very little to do with it; she would probably rather have been doing something else (see below).

In sum, the two lists of nine basic human emotions truly overlap at only three points. All the other apparent points of similarity (amusement as happiness, Hindu disgust as Anglo-American disgust, wonder as surprise, perseverance as interest) turn out to be merely apparent; and for several of the emotions (sexual passion, serenity, shame, contempt) there is not even an illusion of transcultural equivalence. In the end, most of the items can not be easily mapped across the two lists.

There are other ways in which the "Rasādhyāya" presents us with a somewhat unfamiliar portrait of the way consciousness is organized. One has to do with the way the text divides the basic emotions into *primary* basic emotions and *secondary* basic emotions. According to the text and commentaries, the four primary basic emotions are sexual passion, anger, perseverance, and disgust. The four secondary basic emotions are amusement, sorrow, wonder, and fear. The ninth basic emotion, serenity, is sometimes viewed as a primary basic emotion and either substituted for disgust or associated with disgust (through a causal sequence which begins with horror and revulsion over attachments in the world, and ends with the serenity of ego alienation, detachment, and salvation).

In commenting on this scheme, it is perhaps worth noting in passing that Sigmund Freud might find much of value in a conception that treats sexual passion and anger (and perseverance and disgust) as the deepest aspects of human experience. One wonders whether Freud would have interpreted perseverance and disgust as analogues to the life and death instincts. More notable, however, is the fact that the primary basic emotions are primary primarily because they are the emotions associated in classical and folk Hindu thought with the four worthy ends or goals of life. One of those goals of life—pleasure (*kāma*)—is linked to sexual passion. A second goal—control, autonomy, and power (*artha*)—is linked to anger. A third goal—social duty and moral virtue (*dharma*)—is linked to perseverance. The fourth and perhaps highest goal—salvation or the attainment of divinity (*moksha*)—is linked to disgust and/or serenity. In other words, presupposed by this famous formulation about the organization of human emotions are a special theory of morality and human motivation, and a specific way of life. Thus it is hardly surprising that this particular medieval South Asian conception of the hierarchical structuring of consciousness into basic versus nonbasic emotions and primary basic versus secondary basic emotions should seem somewhat strange to emotion researchers in North America.

There is yet another way in which the "Rasādhyāya" presents us with an unfamiliar portrait of the organization of consciousness. For the eight or nine items on the Sanskrit list are bound to seem like a disparate and anomalous collection, at least from the point of view of Anglo-American folk and academic conceptions about how to partition consciousness into kinds of mental states (see D'Andrade, 1987). Indeed, one might expect Anglo-American emotion researchers to recoil at the very suggestion that the Sanskrit list is really a list of "basic emotions" at all. Anglo-American folk and academic psychology do not really classify serenity, wonder, sexual passion, amusement, or perseverance as definitive or clear examples of "emotions" (see Shaver, Schwartz, Kirson, & O'Connor, 1987). Sexual passion would probably be classified as a motive or, alternatively, as a nonemotional feeling. Serenity might be classified as a nonemotional feeling or a state of mind, although not as a motive. Perseverance would probably be classified as a quality of will or agency, or perhaps a formal property of motivation. Amusement and wonder seem to be none of the above. Indeed after reading the text and commentaries and the various nonequivalent translations of *bhāva* and *rasa* (are they mental states, emotions, feelings, moods, sentiments, or what?), one might begin to suspect that in the "Rasādhyāya" one is faced with a somewhat different conception of how to partition a person into parts and how to divide consciousness into kinds. Here, however, I would suggest that one must proceed with caution.

It is of course possible (indeed, likely) that in some ways the "Rasādhyāya" presupposes a partitioning of the person into parts that is not coordinate with our own conception of the person, and that this is why it is so hard to settle on any single translation equivalent for the Sanskrit *bhāva* and *rasa*. This is a familiar kind of translation problem, and it is encountered even across European languages and subcultures. Wierzbicka (1989), for example, has analyzed in detail the many distortions of meaning that occur when the Russian word *duša* is translated into English. *Duša* is a lexical item signifying a key Russian cultural concept that has to do with the partitioning of a person into parts. It is typically translated into English as "soul," or alternatively as "mind" or "heart" or "spirit." None of those lexical mappings is adequate, because none of those English words signifies the full and equivalent set of meanings associated with *duša*—for example, as Wierzbicka notes (1989, p. 52), that it is one of two parts of the person; that one cannot see it; that because of this part, things can happen in a person that cannot happen in anything other than a person; that these things can be good or bad; that because of this part, a person can feel things that nothing other than a person can feel; that other people can't know what these things are if the person doesn't say it; that a person would want someone to know what these things are; and that because of this part a person can be a good person and feel something good toward other people.

Similar issues concerning variations in the organization of consciousness arise in connection with the research of Steven Parish (1991) on conceptions of the mental life among the South Asian Hindu Newars of Nepal (see also Appadurai, 1990; Brenneis, 1990). For the Newars, mental states such as memory, desire, feeling, thought, and emotion, which we would spatially differentiate between the head and the heart (and perhaps the gut and the skin), are all thought to be located together in the heart; this heart of the mental life is thought to be animated by a god, who makes perception and experience possible. Consequently, for the Newars "the efforts of individuals to monitor their inner life often draw on the sense of a divine agency," and it is believed

that "a person sees because the god sees through his or her eyes" (Parish, 1991, p. 316). So it would be surprising, indeed, if the set of meanings associated with the Sanskrit terms *rasa* and *bhāva* could be easily mapped onto the set of meanings associated with any single English term or phrase, such as "emotion," "feeling," "mood," "sentiment," "mental state," or "consciousness." I look forward to the day when Sanskritists do for the concept signified by the term *bhāva* what Wierzbicka has done for the concept signified by the Russian word *duša*.

For the time being, however, I am not going to try to solve the very deepest of questions about the partitioning of the person into parts and the division of consciousness into kinds. Instead, I am going to argue that it is helpful enough to know what the text tells us. What the "Rasādhyāya" tells us is that in drama the *sthāyi-bhāva* (I continue calling them "basic emotions") are brought to a state of *rasa*. More importantly, however, what the text tells us is that the *rasa* are nothing more than the union of three script-like or narrative components:

1. The determinants, causes, or eliciting conditions (*vi-bhāva*), which include all the background information, settings, events, and action tendencies that might make manifest some state of the world and one's relationship to it (e.g., forced separation from something one cherishes; finding oneself powerless in the face of danger).

2. The consequences (*anu-bhāva*), which include eight types of involuntary somatic responses (sweating, fainting, weeping, etc.), and various action tendencies (abusing the body, brandishing weapons) and expressive modes (bodily movement, voice tone, facial expression)—for example, wailing and tears.

3. The "accompanying" mental states (*vyabhicari-bhāva*), which are something like a 33-item symptom list of secondary side effects, including emotions, feelings, and cognitive states; some of these effects are weariness, reminiscence, panic, envy, dreaming, confusion, sickness, shame, and even death.

In other words, in the "Rasādhyāya" one finds a relatively elaborate account of the symbolic structures that give shape and meaning to a selected subset of mental experiences, which because they have been privileged for symbolic elaboration have become transformed into "basic" mental experiences for that culturally constituted world.

THE SYMBOLIC STRUCTURE
OF THE EMOTIONS

The strategy adopted in the "Rasādhyāya" is to define a basic emotion by the implicit symbolic structure that gives shape and meaning to that emotion (its *rasa*—the intentional object of aesthetic pleasure in the theatre) and then to define that symbolic structure by resolving it into its determinants, consequences, and accompanying side effects. This strategy is directly parallel to various contemporary approaches to the cultural psychology of the emotions.

One aspect of this symbolic (or, as some would call it, "cognitive," "interpretive," or "intentional") approach is the view that kinds of emotions do not exist independently of our implicit representations of them and thus are not kinds of things like plants or animals. Instead, they are (*rasa*-like) interpretive schemes of a particular script-like, story-like, or narrative kind, which give shape and meaning to the human experience of those conditions of the world that have a bearing on the self. The elements that are proposed as slots in the story may vary slightly from scholar to scholar, although most of the slots in use today can be found in the "Rasādhyāya."

Mesquita and Frijda (1992; see also Ellsworth, 1991; Frijda, 1986; Lewis, Wolan-Sullivan, & Michalson, 1982; Lewis, 1989; Stein & Levine, 1987), for example, parse each emotion script into a series of slots including "antecedent events," "event coding" (type of condition of the world), "appraisal" (judged implications for the self and well-being), "physiological reaction patterns," "action readiness," "emotional behavior," and "regulation." Elsewhere (Shweder, in press), I have suggested a parsing of emotion scripts into slots such as "self-involving conditions of the world" (e.g., loss and gain, protection and threat), "somatic feelings" (e.g., muscle tension, pain, dizziness, nausea, fatigue, breathlessness), "affective feelings" (e.g., agitation, emptiness, expansiveness), "expressive modes" (e.g., face, posture, voice), and "plans for self-management" (e.g., to flee, to retaliate, to celebrate, to invest). (See also Shweder, 1991, where a slot is provided in the emotion narrative for variations in "social regulation" or the normative appropriateness of certain emotions' being experienced or expressed.)

The primary assumption of the symbolic approach is the same as the approach of the

"Rasādhyāya"—namely, that the "emotion" (e.g., sadness, fear, or love) is not something independent of or separable from the conditions that justify it, from the somatic and affective events that are ways of feeling or being touched by it, from the actions it demands, or the like. The "emotion" is the whole story: a kind of somatic event (fatigue, chest pain, goose flesh) and/or affective event (panic, emptiness, expansiveness) experienced as a perception of some antecedent conditions (death of a friend, acceptance of a book manuscript for publication, a proposition to go out to dinner) and their implications for the self (e.g., as loss, gain, threat, possibility), and experienced as well as a social judgment (e.g., of vice or virtue, sickness or health) and as a kind of plan for action to preserve one's self-esteem (attack, withdraw, confess, hide, explore). The "emotion," one is tempted to argue, is the entire script. It is the simultaneous experience of all the components, or, perhaps more accurately, the unitary experience of the whole package deal.

A second aspect of the symbolic approach is the view that for the sake of comparison and translation, any "emotion" is decomposable into its narrative slots. From this point of view, to ask whether people are alike or different in their emotional functioning (or whether emotion words in different languages are alike or different in their significations) is really to ask several more specific questions:

1. Are they alike or different in their somatic experiences (e.g., muscle tension, headaches, etc.)? (the somatic phenomenology question)

2. Are they alike or different in their affective experiences (e.g., emptiness, calm)? (the affective phenomenology question)

3. Are they alike or different in the antecedent conditions of those somatic and affective experiences (e.g., infertility, job loss, winning the lottery)? (the environmental determinants question)

4. Are they alike or different in the perceived implications of those antecedent conditions for the self (e.g., irreversible loss, fame and recognition)? (the self-appraisal question)

5. Are they alike or different in the extent to which showing or displaying that state of consciousness has been socially baptized as a vice or virtue or as a sign of sickness or health? (the social appraisal question)

6. Are they alike or different in the plans for the self-management of self-esteem that get

activated as part of the emotion script (e.g., celebration, withdrawal from social contacts)? (the self-management question)

7. Are they alike or different in the iconic and symbolic vehicles used for giving expression to the whole package deal (e.g., facial expressions, voice, posture, and action)? (the communication question)

Given this type of decomposition of the definition of an emotion to its constituent narrative slots, the issue of translation equivalence becomes a matter of pattern matching, as one tries to determine whether the variables in each of those slots are linked in similar ways across cultures.

"BITE YOUR TONGUE": THE CASE OF HINDU *LAJYA*

For example, the contemporary Hindu conception of *lajya* has recently been explicated for two communities in South Asia—the Newars of Bhaktapur in Nepal (Parish, 1991) and the Oriyas of Bhubaneswar in Orissa, India (Menon & Shweder, in press; Shweder, in press)—and, as spelled out below, there is even more to be said about *lajya* than can be found in these two accounts. *Lajya* is often translated by bilingual informants and dictionaries as "shame," "embarrassment," "shyness," or "modesty"; yet, as should become obvious from the following bit of cultural exegesis, every one of these translations is problematic or fatally flawed.

For starters, *lajya* is something one deliberately shows or puts on display the way Anglo-Americans might show "gratitude," "loyalty," or "respect." It is a state of consciousness that has been baptized in South Asia as a supreme virtue, especially for women, and it is routinely exhibited in everyday life (e.g., every time a married woman covers her face or ducks out of a room to avoid direct affiliation with those members of her family she is supposed to avoid). Parish (1991, p. 324) describes it as both an emotion and a moral state. It is by means of their *lajya* that those who are civilized uphold the social order—by showing perseverance in the pursuit of their own social role obligations; by displaying respect for the hierarchical arrangement of social privileges and responsibilities; by acting shy, modest, or deferential and not encroaching on the

prerogatives of others; by covering one's face, remaining silent, or lowering one's eyes in the presence of superiors. Like gratitude, loyalty, or respect, *lajya*, which is a way of showing one's civility and commitment to the maintenance of social harmony, is judged in South Asia to be a very good thing.

Although *lajya* may be experienced by both men and women, it is an emotion and a virtue associated with a certain feminine ideal. It is talked about as a lovely ornament worn by women. *Lajya* is the linguistic stem for the name of a local creeper plant (a "touch-me-not"), which is so coy that upon the slightest contact it closes its petals and withdraws into itself. To say of a woman that she is full of *lajya* is a very positive recommendation. Here is one reason why.

Perhaps the most important collective representation of *lajya* in various regions of eastern India is the tantric icon portraying the mother goddess Kali, brandishing weapons and a decapitated head in her 10 arms, eyes bulging and tongue out, with her foot stepping on the chest of her husband, the god Siva, who is lying on the ground beneath her. On the basis of interviews with 92 informants, Usha Menon and I have been examining the meaning of this icon and its significance for our understanding of *lajya* (Menon & Shweder, in press).

The gist of the story, as it is narrated by local experts, is that once upon a time the male gods gave a boon to a minor demon, Mahisasura, to the effect that he could only be killed at the hands of a naked female. They thereby turned Mahisasura into a major demon who was able unimpeded to terrorize all the male gods. In order to destroy the demon, the male gods pooled all their energy and powers and created the goddess Durga, and armed her with their own weapons. On their behalf they sent Durga into battle against Mahisasura, but they neglected to tell her about the boon. She fought bravely but could not kill the demon; he was too strong and clever. In desperation Durga appealed for guidance from an auspicious goddess, who let her in on the secret. As one informant narrated the story:

So Durga did as she was advised to [she stripped], and within seconds after Mahisasura saw her [naked], his strength waned and he died under her sword. After killing him a terrible rage entered Durga's mind, and she asked herself, "What kinds of gods are these that give to demons such boons, and apart from that what kind of gods are these that they do not have the honesty to tell me the truth before sending me into battle?"

Durga felt humiliated by her nakedness and the deceit. She decided that such a world with such gods did not deserve to survive; she therefore took on the form of Kali and went on a mad rampage, devouring every living creature that came in her way. The gods then called on Siva, Kali's husband, to do something to save the world from destruction at the hands of the mother goddess. Siva lay in her path as she came tramping along, enraged. Absorbed in her wild dance of destruction, Kali accidentally stepped on Siva and placed her foot on her husband's chest, an unspeakable act of disrespect. When she looked down and saw what she had done, she came back to her senses—in particular to her sense of *lajya*, which she expressed by biting her tongue between her teeth. She reined in her anger and became calm and still. To this day in Orissa, India, "Bite your tongue" is an idiomatic expression for *lajya*; it is the facial expression used by women as an iconic apology when they realize, or are confronted with the fact, that they have failed to uphold social norms.

One moral of the story is that men are incapable of running the world by themselves, even though they are socially dominant. They rely on women to make the world go round. Yet in a patriarchal society, men humiliate women by the way they exploit female power, strength, and perseverance. This leads to anger and rage in women, which is highly destructive of everything of value and must be brought under control, for the sake of the social order. *Lajya* is a salient ideal in South Asia because it preserves social harmony by helping women to swallow their rage.

If we decompose *lajya* into its constituent narrative slots, it becomes apparent just how hazardous it can be to assume that one can render the emotional meanings of others with terms from our received English lexicon for mental states. (See Geertz, 1984, p. 130, on the difficulties of translating the Balinese term *lek*. Balinese *lek* seems much like Hindu *lajya*. Geertz notes that "'lek' has been variably translated and mistranslated" and that "'shame'

is the most common attempt." He tries to render it as "stage fright.") Hindu *lajya* does not map well onto words such as "shame," "embarrassment," "shyness," "modesty," or "stage fright." An analysis of the constituents of *lajya* helps us see why.

From the perspective of social appraisal and self-appraisal, for example, to be full of *lajya* is to be in possession of the virtue of behaving in a civilized manner and in such a way that the social order and its norms are upheld. It is not a neurosis, and it does not connote a reduction in the strength of the ego. Indeed, *lajya* promotes self-esteem. Of course, to be perceived or labeled as someone without *lajya*—as someone who encroaches on the station of others, or fails to live up to the requirements of his or her own station—is unpleasant and arousing. Parish notes that to feel *lajya* is sometimes associated with blushing, sweating, and altered pulse (1991, p. 324), but I suspect that such a somatic phenomenology is a feature of the anxiety provoked by the social perception of the absence of *lajya* and is not definitive of *lajya* itself. For to experience *lajya* is to experience that sense of virtuous, courteous, well-mannered restraint that led Kali to rein in her rage.

The environmental determinants of *lajya* as a sense of one's own virtue and civility are as varied as the set of actions that are dutiful and responsible, given one's station in life in a world in which all people are highly self-conscious about their social designation (see Geertz, 1984, for a brilliant attempt to capture the dramatic qualities of such a world). They include events that Anglo-Americans would find familiar (not being seen naked by the wrong person in the wrong context), as well as many events that might seem alien or strange (never talking directly to one's husband's elder brother or to one's father-in-law; never being in the same room with both one's husband and another male to whom he must defer).

From the perspective of self-management, South Asian *lajya* may appear at first glance to be similar to Anglo-American "shame" or "embarrassment." It activates a habit or routine that sometimes results in hiding, covering up, and withdrawing from the scene. Yet what is really being activated by *lajya* is a general habit of respect for social hierarchy and a consciousness of one's social and public responsibilities, which in the context of South

Asian norms may call for avoidance, silence, withdrawal, or other deferential, protective, or nonaggressive gestures and actions.

Finally, let us consider the semantic structure of "shame" and *lajya* in the minds of informants. When middle-class Anglo-American college students are presented with the triad of terms "shame–happiness–anger" and asked, "Which is most different from the other two?", they are most likely to respond either that "happiness" or "shame" is most different from the other two, perhaps on the grounds that "shame" and "anger" go together because they are both unpleasant feelings; or that "happiness" and "anger" go together because they are both ego-expanding emotions. Neither response is typical of responses in the South Asian community where I work, where *lajya* (shame?) and *suka* (happiness?) are thought to go together in the triad test, and *raga* (anger?), perceived as destructive of society, is the odd emotion out. Here something seems to be amiss in the translation process. Something may well have been amiss in most past attempts to equate emotions across languages and across local cultural worlds (see Wierzbicka, 1992).

In sum, as we enter a new era of collaborative research among anthropologists, psychologists and physiologists, concerned with similarities and differences in emotional functioning on a worldwide scale, a major goal for the cultural psychology of the emotions will be to decompose the emotions (and the languages of the emotions) into constituent narrative slots. It is to be hoped that by means of the decomposition of the symbolic structure of the emotions, it will be possible to render the meaning of other people's mental states without assimilating them in misleading ways to an *a priori* set of lexical items available in the language of the researcher (e.g., rendering Hindu *lajya* as English "shame").

It is one of the great marvels of life that across languages, cultures, and history, it is possible, with sufficient knowledge, effort, and insight, to truly understand the meanings of other people's emotions and mental states. Yet one must also marvel at one of the great ironies of life—namely, that the process of understanding the consciousness of others can deceptively appear to be far easier than it really is, thereby making it even more difficult to achieve a genuine understanding of "otherness." Thus, in the end, this discussion of the cultural psychology of the emotions and medi-

tation on the venerable "Rasādhyāya" of the *Nāṭyaśāstra* are really pleas for a decomposition of emotional states into their constituent narrative slots (environmental determinants, somatic phenomenology, affective phenomenology, self-appraisal, social appraisal, self-management strategy, and communication codes). Unless we take that step, we will continue to be prone to the bias that the emotional life of human beings is "basically" the same around the world. The truth may well be that when it comes to "basic" emotions, we all (medieval Hindus and contemporary Anglo-Americans, Pintupis and Russians, Eskimos and Balinese, etc.) are not only basically alike in some ways, but can be basically different from one another as well.

Acknowledgments. Some ideas for this chapter were developed while I was a Visiting Scholar at the Russell Sage Foundation, and with the support of the Health Program of the John D. and Catherine T. MacArthur Foundation. I am grateful to Eugene Gendlin, Usha Menon, and Steven Parish for their helpful comments on the manuscript.

REFERENCES

Abu-Lughod, L. (1985). Honor and the sentiments of loss in a Bedouin society. *American Ethnologist, 12,* 245–261.

Abu-Lughod, L. (1986). *Veiled sentiments: Honor and poetry in a Bedouin society.* Berkeley: University of California Press.

Angel, R., & Guarnaccia, P. (1981). Mind, body and culture: Somatization among Hispanics. *Social Science and Medicine, 12*(28), 1229–1238.

Angel, R., & Idler, E. L. (1992). Somatization and hypochondriasis: Sociocultural factors in subjective experience. *Research in Community and Mental Health, 7,* 71–93.

Angel, R., & Thoits, P. (1987). The impact of culture on the cognitive structure of illness. *Culture, Medicine and Psychiatry, 11,* 465–494.

Appadurai, A. (1985). Gratitude as a social mode in South India. *Ethos, 13,* 236–245.

Appadurai, A. (1990). Topographies of the self: Praise and emotion in Hindu India. In C. Lutz & L. Abu-Lughod (Eds.), *Language and the politics of emotion* (pp. 92–112). New York: Cambridge University Press.

Brenneis, D. (1990). Shared and solitary sentiments: The discourse of friendship, play and anger in Bhatgaon. In C. Lutz & L. Abu-Lughod (Eds.), *Language and the politics of emotion* (pp. 113–125). New York: Cambridge University Press.

Briggs, J. L. (1970). *Never in anger: Portrait of an Eskimo family.* Cambridge, MA: Harvard University Press.

Bruner, J. S. (1990). *Acts of meaning.* Cambridge, MA: Harvard University Press.

Cole, M. (1988). Cross-cultural research in the socio-historical tradition. *Human Development*, 31, 137–157.

Cole, M. (1990). Cultural psychology: A once and future discipline? In J. J. Berman (Ed.), *Nebraska Symposium on Motivation: 1989. Cross-cultural perspectives.* Lincoln: University of Nebraska Press.

D'Andrade, R. G. (1984). Cultural meaning systems. In R. A. Shweder & R. A. LeVine (Eds.), *Culture theory: Essays on mind, self, and emotion* (pp. 88–119). Cambridge, England: Cambridge University Press.

D'Andrade, R. G. (1987). A folk model of the mind. In D. Holland & N. Quinn (Eds.), *Cultural models in language and thought.* Cambridge, England: Cambridge University Press.

Dimock, E. C. (1974). *The literatures of India.* Chicago: University of Chicago Press.

Ekman, P. (1980). Biological and cultural contributions to body and facial movement in the expression of emotions. In A. Rorty (Ed.), *Explaining emotions* (pp. 73–101). Berkeley: University of California Press.

Ekman, P. (1984). Expression and the nature of emotion. In K. Scherer & P. Ekman (Eds.), *Approaches to emotion* (pp. 319–343). Hillsdale, NJ: Erlbaum.

Ellsworth, P. (1991). Some implications of cognitive appraisal theories of emotion. *International Review of Studies of Emotion*, 1, 143–161.

Fish, S. (1980). *Is there a textbook in this class? On the authority of interpretive communities.* Cambridge, MA: Harvard University Press.

Fridja, N. (1986). *The emotions.* Cambridge, England: Cambridge University Press.

Garvey, C. (1992). Introduction: Talk in the study of socialization and development. *Merrill–Palmer Quarterly*, 38(1), iii–viii.

Geertz, C. (1973). *The interpretation of culture.* New York: Basic Books.

Geertz, C. (1984). From the native's point of view. In R. Shweder & R. LeVine (Eds.), *Culture theory: Essays on mind, self, and emotion* (pp. 123–136). Cambridge, England: Cambridge University Press.

Geertz, H. (1959). The vocabulary of emotion: A study of Javanese socialization processes. *Psychiatry*, 22, 225–236.

Gerber, E. R. (1985). Rage and obligation: Samoan emotions in conflict. In G. M. White & J. Kirkpatrick (Eds.), *Person, self and experience: Exploring Pacific ethnopsychologies* (pp. 121–167). Berkeley: University of California Press.

Gnoli, R. (1956). *The aesthetic experience according to Abhinavagupta.* Rome: Istituto Italiano per Il Medio ed Estremo Oriente.

Good, B. J., & Kleinman, A. M. (1985). Culture and anxiety: Cross-cultural evidence for the patterning of anxiety disorders. In A. H. Tuma & J. D. Maser (Eds.), *Anxiety and the anxiety disorders.* Hillsdale, NJ: Erlbaum.

Harré, R. (1986a). An outline of the social constructionist viewpoint. In R. Harré (Ed.), *The social construction of emotions* (pp. 2–14). Oxford, England: Basil Blackwell.

Harré, R. (Ed.). (1986b). *The social construction of emotions.* Oxford: Basil Blackwell.

Hoffman, M. L. (1990). Empathy and justice motivation. *Motivation and Emotion*, 14(2).

Howard, A. (1985). Ethnopsychology and the prospects for a cultural psychology. In G. M. White & J. Kirkpatrick (Eds.), *Person, self and experience: Exploring Pacific ethnopsychologies* (pp. 401–420). Berkeley: University of California Press.

Jahoda, G. (1993). *Crossroads between culture and mind: Continuities and change in theories of human nature.* Cambridge, MA: Harvard University Press.

Kakar, S. (1982). *Shamans, mystics and doctors.* Boston: Beacon Press.

Keith, A. B. (1924). *The Sanskrit drama.* London: Oxford University Press.

Kirsh, D. (1991). Today the earwig, tomorrow man? *Artificial Intelligence*, 47, 161–184.

Kleinman, A. (1986). *The social origins of distress and disease.* New Haven, CT: Yale University Press.

Kleinman, A., & Good, B. (Eds.). (1985). *Culture and depression: Studies in the anthropology and cross-cultural psychiatry of affect and disorder.* Berkeley: University of California Press.

Lakoff, G. (1987). *Women, fire and dangerous things: What categories reveal about the mind.* Chicago: University of Chicago Press.

LeVine, R. A. (1984). Properties of culture: An ethnographic view. In R. A. Shweder & R. A. LeVine (Eds.), *Culture theory: Essays on mind, self, and emotion* (pp. 67–87). Cambridge, England: Cambridge University Press.

LeVine, R. A. (1990). Infant environments in psychoanalysis: A cross-cultural view. In J. Stigler, R. Shweder, & G. Herdt (Eds.), *Cultural psychology: Essays on comparative human development* (pp. 454–476). New York: Cambridge University Press.

Levy, R. I. (1984a). Emotion, knowing and culture. In R. A. Shweder & R. A. LeVine (Eds.), *Culture theory: Essays on mind, self, and emotion* (pp. 214–237). Cambridge, England: Cambridge University Press.

Levy, R. I. (1984b). The emotions in comparative perspective. In K. R. Scherer & P. Ekman (Eds.), *Approaches to emotion* (pp. 397–412). Hillsdale, NJ: Erlbaum.

Lewis, M. (1989). Cultural differences in children's knowledge of emotional scripts. In C. Saarni & P. L. Harris, (Eds.), *Children's understanding of emotion* (pp. 350–374). New York: Cambridge University Press.

Lewis, M., Wolan-Sullivan, M., & Michalson, L. (1982). *The cognitive-emotional fugue* (Research and Clinical Center for Child Development, Annual Report). Sapporo, Japan: Hokkaido University.

Lutz, C. (1982). The domain of emotion words on Ifaluk. *American Ethnologist*, 9, 113–128.

Lutz, C. (1985a). Ethnopsychology compared to what Explaining behavior and consciousness among the Ifaluk. In G. M. White & J. Kirkpatrick (Eds.), *Person, self and experience: Exploring Pacific ethnopsychologies* (pp. 35–79). Berkeley: University of California Press.

Lutz, C. (1985b). Depression and the translation of emotional worlds. In A. Kleinman & B. Good (Eds.), *Culture and depression: Studies in the anthropology and cross-cultural psychiatry of affect and disorder* (pp. 63–100). Berkeley: University of California Press.

Lutz, C. (1988). *Unnatural emotions: Everyday sentiments on a Micronesian atoll and their challenge to Western theory.* Chicago: University of Chicago Press.

Lutz, C., & White, G. (1986). The anthropology of emotions. *Annual Review of Anthropology*, 15, 405–436.

Markus, H. R., & Kitayama, S. (1991). Culture and the self: Implications for cognition, emotion and motivation. *Psychological Review*, 98, 224–253.

Markus, H. R., & Kitayama, S. (1992). The what, why and how of cultural psychology: A review of Shweder's *Thinking through cultures. Psychological Inquiry*, 3(4).

Marsella, A. J. (1980). Depressive experience and disorder across cultures: A review of the literature. In H. Triandis & J. Draguns (Eds.), *Handbook of cross-cultural psychology* (Vol. 6, pp. 237–289). Boston: Allyn & Bacon.

Masson, J. L., & Patwardhan, M. V. (1970). *Aesthetic rapture: The Rasādhyāya of the Nāṭyaśāstra.* Poona, India: Deccan College.

Menon, U., & Shweder, R. A. (in press). Kali's tongue: Cultural psychology and the power of "shame" in Orissa, India. In H. Markus & S. Kitayama (Eds.), *Culture and the emotions.* Washington, DC: APA Publications.

Mesquita, B., & Fridja, N. H. (1992). Cultural variations in emotion. *Psychological Bulletin, 112,* 179–204.

Miller, P., & Hoogstra, L. (1992). Language as tool in the socialization and apprehension of cultural meanings. In T. Schwartz, G. M. White, & C. A. Lutz (Eds.), *New directions in psychological anthropology.* Cambridge, England: Cambridge University Press.

Miller, P., Mintz, J., Hoogstra, L., Fung, H., & Potts, R. (1992). The narrated self: Young children's construction of self in relation to others in conversational stories of personal experience. *Merrill–Palmer Quarterly 38*(1), 45–67.

Miller P., Potts, R., Fung, H., Hoogstra, L., & Mintz, J. (1990). Narrative practices and the social construction of self in childhood. *American Ethnologist, 17,* 292–311.

Miller, P., & Sperry, L. (1987). Young children's verbal resources for communicating anger. *Merrill–Palmer Quarterly 33,* 1–31.

Myers, F. R. (1979a). Emotions and the self: A theory of personhood and political order among Pintupi aborigines. *Ethos, 7,* 343–370.

Myers, F. R. (1979b). The logic and meaning of anger among Pintupi aborigines. *Man, 23,* 589–610.

Nisbett, R. E., & Wilson, T. D. (1977). Telling more than we can know: verbal reports on mental processes. *Psychological Review, 84,* 231–259.

Ochs, E., & Schieffelin, B. (1984). Language acquisition and socialization: Three developmental stories. In R. Shweder & R. LeVine (Eds.), *Culture theory: Essays on mind, self, and emotion* (pp. 276–320). Cambridge, England: Cambridge University Press.

Parish, S. (1991). The sacred mind: Newar cultural representations of mental life and the production of moral consciousness. *Ethos, 19*(3), 313–351.

Peacock, J. L. (1984). Religion and life history: An exploration in cultural psychology. In E. M. Bruner (Ed.), *Text, play and story: The construction and reconstruction of self and society.* Washington, DC: American Ethnological Society.

Rorty, A. (Ed.). (1980). *Explaining emotions.* Berkeley: University of California Press.

Rosaldo, M. Z. (1980). *Knowledge and passion: Ilongot notions of self and social life.* Cambridge, England: Cambridge University Press.

Rosaldo, M. Z. (1983). The shame of headhunters and the autonomy of self. *Ethos, 11,* 135–151.

Rosaldo, M. Z. (1984). Toward an anthropology of self and feeling. In R. A. Shweder & R. A. LeVine (Eds.), *Culture theory: Essays on mind, self, and emotion* (pp. 137–157). Cambridge, England: Cambridge University Press.

Russell, J. A. (1991). Culture and the categorization of emotions. *Psychological Bulletin, 110*(3), 426–450.

Schechner, R. (1988). *Performance theory.* London: Routledge & Kegan Paul.

Scherer, K. R., Wallbott, H. G., & Summerfield, A. B. (Eds.). (1986). *Experiencing emotion: A cross-cultural study.* Cambridge, England: Cambridge University Press.

Schieffelin, B., & Ochs, E., (Eds.). (1986). *Language and socialization across cultures.* Cambridge, England: Cambridge University Press.

Schieffelin, E. L. (1976). *The sorrow of the lonely and the burning of the dancers.* New York: St. Martin's Press.

Schieffelin, E. L. (1983). Anger and shame in the tropical forest: On affect as a cultural system in Papua New Guinea. *Ethos, 11,*181–191.

Schieffelin, E. L. (1985a). The cultural analysis of depressive affect: An example from New Guinea. In A. Kleinman & B. Good (Eds.), *Culture and depression: Studies in anthropology and psychiatry of affect and disorder* (pp. 101–133). Berkeley: University of California Press.

Schieffelin, E. L. (1985b). Anger, grief and shame: Toward a Kaluli ethnopsychology. In G. M. White & J. Kirkpatrick (Eds.), *Person, self and experience: Exploring Pacific ethnopsychologies* (pp. 168–182). Berkeley: University of California Press.

Shaver, P., Schwartz, J., Kirson, D., & O'Connor, C. (1987). Emotion knowledge: Further exploration of a prototype approach. *Journal of Personality and Social Psychology, 52*(6), 1061–1086.

Shixie, L. (1989). Neurasthenia in China: Modern and traditional criteria for its diagnosis. *Culture, Medicine and Psychiatry, 13,* 163–186.

Shweder, R. A. (1988). Suffering in style [Review of *the social origins of distress and disease* by A. Kleinman]. *Culture, Medicine and Psychiatry, 12,* 479–497.

Shweder, R. A. (1990). Cultural psychology: What is it? In J. Stigler, R. Shweder, & G. Herdt (Eds.), *Cultural psychology: Essays on comparative human development* (pp. 1–43). New York: Cambridge University Press.

Shweder, R. A. (1991). *Thinking through cultures: Expeditions in cultural psychology.* Cambridge, MA: Harvard University Press.

Shweder, R. A. (in press). "You're not sick, you're just in love": Emotion as an interpretive system. In P. Ekman & R. Davidson (Eds.), *Fundamental issues and questions about emotion.* New York: Oxford University Press.

Shweder, R. A., & LeVine, R. A. (Eds.). (1984). *Culture theory: Essays on mind, self, and emotion.* Cambridge, England: Cambridge University Press.

Shweder, R. A., & Much, N. C. (1987). Determinations of meaning: Discourse and moral socialization. In W. Kurtines & J. Gewirtz (Eds.), *Social interaction and socio-moral development* (pp. 197–244). New York: Wiley.

Shweder, R. A., & Sullivan, M. A. (1990). The Semiotic Subject of Cultural Psychology. In L. A. Pervin (Ed.), *Handbook of personality: Theory and research* (pp. 399–416). New York: Guilford Press.

Shweder, R. A., & Sullivan, M. A. (1993). Cultural psychology: Who needs it? *Annual Review of Psychology, 44,* 497–523.

Smedslund, J. (1991). The pseudoempirical in psychology and the case for psychologic. *Psychological Inquiry, 2*(4), 325–338.

Solomon, R. C. (1976). *The passions.* Garden City, NY: Doubleday/Anchor.

Solomon, R. C. (1984). Getting angry: The Jamesian theory of emotion in anthropology. In R. A. Shweder & R. A. LeVine (Eds.), *Culture theory: Essays on mind, self, and emotion* (pp. 238–254). Cambridge, England: Cambridge University Press.

Stearns, C. Z., & Stearns, P. N. (Eds.). (1988). *Emotion and social change: Toward a new psychohistory.* New York: Holmes & Meier.

Stein, N., & Levine, L. J. (1987). Thinking about feelings: The development and organization of emotional knowledge. In R. E. Snow & M. J. Farr (Eds.), *Aptitude, learning and instruction* (Vol. 3, pp. 165–197). Hillsdale, NJ: Erlbaum.

Stigler, J. (1984). "Mental Abacus": The effect of abacus training on Chinese children's mental calculation. *Cognitive Psychology, 16,* 145–176.

Stigler, J., Chalip, L., & Miller, K. (1986). Culture and mathematics learning. *Review of Research in Education, 15,* 253–306.

Stigler, J., Nusbaum, H., & Chalip, L. (1988). Developmental changes in speed of processing: Central limiting mechanisms on shell transfer. *Child Development, 59,* 1144–1153.

Stigler, J., Shweder, R. A., & Herdt, G. (Eds.). (1990). *Cultural psychology: Essays on comparative human development.* New York: Cambridge University Press.

Swartz, M. J. (1988). Shame, culture, and status among the Swahili of Mombasa. *Ethos, 16,* 21–51.

Veith, I. (1978). Psychiatric foundations in the Far East. *Psychiatric Annals, 8*(6), 12–41.

White, G. M., & Kirkpatrick, J. (Eds.). (1985). *Person, self and experience: Exploring Pacific ethnopsychologies.* Berkeley: University of California Press.

Wierzbicka, A. (1986). Human emotions: Universal or culture-specific? *American Anthropologist, 88,* 584–594.

Wierzbicka, A. (1989). Soul and mind: Linguistic evidence for ethnopsychology and cultural history. *American Anthropologist, 91*(1), 41–58.

Wierzbicka, A. (1990). The semantics of emotions: Fear and its relatives in English. *Australian Journal of Linguistics (Special Issue on the Semantics of the Emotions), 10*(2), 359–375.

Wierzbicka, A. (1992). Talk about emotions: Semantics, culture and cognition. *Cognition and Emotion, 6*(3/4), 285–319.

Wikan, U. (1984). Shame and honour: A contestable pair. *Man, 19,* 635–652.

Wikan, U. (1989). Illness from fright or soul loss: A North Balinese culture-bound syndrome? *Culture, Medicine and Psychiatry, 13,* 25–50.

IV

SOCIAL PROCESSES
RELATED TO EMOTION

30

Socialization of Emotion

CAROLYN SAARNI

The topic for this chapter presents a peculiar contradiction. On the one hand, we know generally what is meant by the "socialization of emotion"—namely, how people come to feel as they do as a result of their relationships over time with others. On the other hand, both concepts, "socialization" and "emotion," are multifaceted and hence problematic when it comes to specifying more clearly what is entailed in the socialization of emotion. To make the matter even more complicated, cross-cultural research on emotion socialization suggests that "emotions can be seen as both the medium and the message of socialization. Their uniqueness, and their crucial importance for understanding development, lies in this dual and encompassing role" (Lutz, 1983, p. 60). Thus, even as we may observe emotional development *in the child*, those who interact with the child are communicating their own emotions *to the child*, often elicited by their evaluation of the child's emotional behavior. Given the conceptual social–emotional–relational melange created by this reciprocity of emotional processes, I begin by taking an author's prerogative to narrow what I intend to describe under the rubric of socialization of emotion (which obviously includes my biases). The reader is also referred to Lewis and Saarni (1985), Garber and Dodge (1991), Halberstadt (1991), Ratner and Stettner (1991), and Thompson (1990), among others, for additional consideration of what is involved in the socialization of emotion.

WHAT IS SOCIALIZED?

Lewis and Michalson (1983) have proposed looking at emotion as consisting of five components: emotional elicitors, emotional receptors, emotional states, emotional expression, and emotional experience. Each of these can be seen as the "target" of socialization processes; however, important as the individual components may be as objects of socialization's influence, so too are the linkages among these emotion components as targets of socialization (e.g., depending on the social context surrounding the emotional elicitor, emotional expression may not be veridical to what is felt as the emotional state). Consider the following example, which demonstrates all of these components:

Heather (age 11) was accustomed to exploring tide pools along the northern California coast. One winter day her father and uncle were washed off a rocky cliff by a "rogue" wave, and a major emergency ensued because of rough seas, a strong current, and the very cold temperature of the water. Fortunately both survived, but Heather was exposed to a variety of emotional experiences *in relationship to others* that contributed to significant emotional learning on her part. Contrary to her earlier beliefs about the ocean, she now viewed it as potentially fear-provoking (i.e., its emotion-eliciting character had changed from benign to dangerous as a result of her involvement in the emergency); relative to emotional receptors, we can only infer that some degree of enhanced scanning for potential danger may have resulted. Her emotional state was initially extreme fear and distress, and afterwards relief. She also witnessed the physical effects of hypothermia, as well as considerable laceration and bruising, and associated these effects with an internal state of fear. The emotional expressions of others around her ranged from fear to panic, from sorrow to anguish, from the grim earnestness of the rescuers to the weak smiles of the rescued. Later she saw emotional exchanges of chagrin on the part of the rescued, as well as gentle reproach from the rescuers (not to mention the spouses involved!). Her emotional experience, as she reflected upon it later that evening, was a mixture of extreme fear, sadness, anxiety, and happiness.

Granted, this was a rather harrowing way to learn about how emotion occurs and is dealt with in emergency situations, but it gives us a template with which we can examine how children (and adults, for that matter) are exposed to emotion-eliciting circumstances; learn about the emotions involved; and subsequently incorporate that learning into their own emotional "map" of when to feel, what to feel, how to express feelings, and whom to express them to. I now examine each of Lewis and Michalson's (1983) components of emotion in greater detail, relative to how each is influenced by socialization. Then I discuss how socialization processes influence emotion, with an emphasis on the social construction of emotional experience (the reader is undoubtedly now aware of my biases). Folk theories of emotion are also addressed, in that they are also shaped by socialization, particularly with regard to how emotions and social relations are integrated. Lastly, I briefly consider individual differences in the socialization of emotion, with an emphasis on maladaptive outcomes in the child or young adult when the socialization of emotion goes awry. The reader is also referred to the other chapters in this volume that address the topic of individual differences in emotion processes, many of which stem from different patterns and histories of emotion socialization.

COMPONENTS OF EMOTION

Emotional Elicitors

"Emotional elicitors" are the stimuli that are appraised as causes of our emotional responses, and they clearly reflect considerable social influence, in that our culture determines to a great extent what are viewed as "typical" causes for particular categories of emotion (e.g., see Russell, 1991, for a review of culture and emotion categorization). Thus, gustatory pleasure at the prospect of eating a lizard does not seem especially plausible for me, but in some other parts of the world, a person might be quite pleased at the invitation to dine on

such a delicacy. Even within a given culture, there may be considerable variability in what is viewed as a situational elicitor of an emotional response; for that matter, there appears to be variability attributable to one's age group, which also interfaces with the social construction of causes for emotions.

As an illustration of differences across age groups, Lewis (1989) found that a majority of preschool children thought they would feel sad if lost in a store, whereas a majority of adults expected children of that age group to feel afraid if lost in a large store. Although there could have been some degree of misunderstanding of emotion labels by the child respondents, it does not seem likely, given the exhaustive work of Dunn, Bretherton, and Munn (1987) and Bretherton, Fritz, Zahn-Waxler, and Ridgeway (1986), among others, who have analyzed young children's discourse on emotions and found them to be impressively sophisticated by 3 to 4 years of age in our culture's emotion lexicon. Different normative expectations exist for different age groups relative to what sort of emotion is likely to be felt in particular situations (e.g., consider what constitutes "fun" for young adolescents vs. what is "fun" for 40-year-olds). The important point for investigators is to remain aware of this variability and not to construct rigid coding schemes that fail to take into account this fluid construal of expectations regarding emotion elicitation.

Emotional Receptors

"Emotional receptors" are hypothesized structures that create the interface between the emotion-eliciting situation and the individual. Arousability, attention behaviors (e.g., scanning or vigilance), and temperament may all play a role in emotional receptors, and indeed may be implicated in individual differences in emotional responsiveness. Investigations of arousal or temperament in conjunction with emotional development have only recently been conducted (e.g., Bugental, 1985; Eisenberg, Fabes, Schaller, Miller, et al., 1991; Fox, 1989). Other research examining temperament and emotional intensity of responding (e.g., Derryberry & Rothbart, 1988; Larsen & Diener, 1987) suggests that these variables mediate social influence in important ways. For example, an infant with a "difficult temperament" and a low threshold for reacting with intense negative emotion affects the social–emotional interaction it receives from its caregivers, who, in turn, draw upon their own particular repertoire of strategies of emotional responding and coping in dealing with the "difficult" infant.

Emotional States

"Emotional states" refer to the bodily changes that co-occur with emotional responding. Biochemical, neurological, and physiological activity can be examined for patterns associated with different emotions (e.g., Levenson, Ekman, & Friesen, 1990) or arousal more generally (e.g., Stemmler, 1989). Eisenberg and Fabes (1990, 1991) have found that children exhibiting personal distress when confronted by another's distress were more aroused physiologically (higher skin conductance) than those who showed sympathetic concern toward the distressed individual. In other studies, Eisenberg, Fabes, and their collaborators have found complex patterns of parental attitudes toward children's emotionally expressive displays, parental modeling of sympathetic responses, and gender of child to be related to whether the child was likely to respond with personal distress as opposed to sympathetic concern when faced with distressed others (e.g., Eisenberg, Fabes, Schaller, Carlo, & Miller, 1991). Thus, the somatic activity associated with emotional states can be indirectly influenced by social experience. In some cases, caregivers may even try directly to influence the external manifestation of emotion-related somatic activity, as when a parent notices the pallor or hyperventilation of a badly frightened child and offers coping suggestions, reassurance, or a reframing of the emotion-eliciting situation (e.g., "Try to breathe slowly and deeply so you'll feel better; it just looks dangerous when the rollercoaster goes down the hill fast, but you're safely strapped in"). However, Pollack and Thoits (1989) found that teacher/therapists at a school for emotionally disturbed children almost never directly commented on children's somatic sensations that might have been reasonably inferred as accompanying the children's assorted emotional experiences in the school setting (e.g., butterflies in one's stomach or pounding heart). The teacher/therapists' most frequent verbal interpretation about emotions to the children was to link a situational cause with an emotion label (e.g., addressed to an angry child: "Sometimes kids get mad when their moms are late to pick them up," p. 26).

Emotional Expression

Socialization affects emotional expression in significant ways: In all cultures, children learn rules or guidelines for where and when to express what emotion with which people. When children alter their external expression of their feelings, they are often attempting to bring their expressive behavior into accordance with cultural or subcultural beliefs about what is appropriate or socially desirable under certain circumstances. These beliefs about what expressions of emotions are socially desirable or appropriate are referred to as "display rules," in that there is considerable social consensus or predictability about what sort of facial expression is displayed.

Ekman and Friesen (1975) introduced four prototypical strategies for characterizing how adults in our culture may modify their emotional behavior when they attempt to put display rules into practice. These display rule strategies include "minimization," which is tantamount to miniaturizing the display of one's genuine feelings; "maximization," which is an exaggerated expression of how one really feels; "masking," which is adopting a neutral expression or "poker face"; and "substitution," which entails expressing an emotion that is altogether different from what one actually feels. These expressive strategies have been observed in children (e.g., Cole, 1985; Saarni, 1984, 1992), and although their order of emergence does not appear to be fixed, minimization and maximization are thought to appear first in children's expressive strategy repertoires. Figuring out how to make a substitution or how to go poker-faced may require somewhat more complexity of thought and greater command of facial musculature, and it is sometimes assumed that children will demonstrate these expressive strategies somewhat later. However, what is astonishing is that minimization and maximization may already be occurring in the second year of life and perhaps even earlier (e.g., an 18-month-old boy may cry exaggeratedly when his older sibling teases him, in order to dramatize his apparent distress for the purpose of bringing a parent to his aid). What this suggests is that human beings are remarkably responsive to social influence when it comes to modification of their emotionally expressive behavior. An additional important implication is that early in life, emotional expression becomes increasingly subject to self-control or volition, although there may be limits as to what degree expressive behavior is controllable when emotion is very intense.

Emotional Experience

Lewis and Michalson (1983) view "emotional experience," the last component of emotion, as the most cognitive one. It requires access to a language of and about emotion; it takes into account knowledge about emotion, and assumes increasing insight into one's emotional processes as one matures. Thus, reflection upon the self's affective experience is implied, as well as being able to infer emotional responses in others (see Harris & Saarni, 1989, and Saarni & Harris, 1989, for relevant reviews of children's understanding of emotion).

Understanding one's emotional experience reflects the influence of socialization, in that inherent in the construction of emotional experience are cultural meaning systems (Lutz, 1983). Lutz argues that cultural values are embedded in the socialization of beliefs about emotional experience, and the transmission of these cultural values constitutes a parental goal insofar as parents attempt to socialize and guide their children toward culturally desirable ways of feeling and behaving.

Ethnographers and observers in natural settings have often collected information about how socializing agents (parents, teachers) use an emotional lexicon to interpret emotional experience to children. As mentioned earlier, Pollack and Thoits (1989) found that explicit verbal linkages between situational cause and resulting emotion characterized the emotion statements most frequently used by teachers in a therapeutic school. Miller and Sperry (1987) found that mothers used emotion language to specify the greater legitimacy (or acceptability) of some emotional responses over others relative to social context (e.g., retaliatory anger was encouraged toward provoking peers but severely discouraged toward adults, even if the adults had behaved in a provoking fashion). Russell's (1991) comprehensive cross-cultural comparison of emotion language categories provides one of the most incisive analyses of how emotion concepts can be viewed as

systems of representational scripts: The meaning of any one emotion concept is related to a network of concepts within which it is integrated. Thus, emotional experience will reflect this acquired network of concepts, which provides the growing child with scripts for representing his or her own emotional responses within a multidimensional matrix of causes, goals, values, social relations, and beliefs about emotion management (including both internal emotional regulation and expressive control).

Summary

Those aspects of emotion that are the clearest targets of socializing influence appear to be emotional elicitors, emotional expression, and emotional experience. Certainly these last two components of emotion have the most developmental research associated with them. These last two components also provide people with the greatest communicative access to one another's emotional processes: Emotional expression is meaningful and informative to interactants, and emotional experience permits the verbal description and exchange of emotional processes to others. The influence of socialization on emotional receptors and states is more ambiguous, but these aspects of emotion may be viewed as embedded in a system of scripts. The cultural scripts include the meaningfulness of emotional elicitors, which in turn influence what sorts of receptors "discern" the emotionally meaningful event and subsequently result in a somatic or emotional state response.

PROCESSES OF EMOTION SOCIALIZATION

Processes of emotion socialization are embedded in relationships, and the emotional dynamics of these relationships mediate the form and quality of emotion socialization in the individual child. For example, an involved and warmly attentive mother may have the intended effect when she directly instructs her disappointed son not to hurt Grandpa's feelings by showing disappointment upon receiving from Grandpa a set of old records for his birthday. The parent may suggest to the son that he should smile and say thank you to Grandpa for his well-meaning, albeit misguided, intentions, instead of showing his disappointment over receiving used records. In contrast, a harsh, emotionally distant parent may give the same directive, but either the child does not attend or transforms the directive into what is being modeled (i.e., brusque emotional remoteness). The child then responds to Grandpa with a frown, accompanied by a curt tone of voice, and does not take into account the potential effect of this expressive behavior on Grandpa's feelings.

The preceding example illustrates what Ratner and Stettner (1991) call "intersubjectivity," which they have argued is necessary for emotion socialization (from a Vygotskian perspective). They contend that intersubjectivity consists of

> both cognitive and affective coordination between the participants and the representation of this coordination enables the re-enactment of the interaction as an internal symbolic dialogue in other contexts. . . . When the child experiences a particular emotion, previous interactions in which the emotion was experienced will be activated (e.g., Bower, 1981) and parents' responses (e.g., verbal statements or rules, physical contact, facial expressions, and tone of voice) to the child's emotional expressiveness will be re-experienced. (p. 17)

What I conclude from this perspective is that emotions, beliefs (i.e., representations), and relationships are inextricably intertwined in emotional development and more specifically in the socialization of emotion. At the beginning of this chapter, I have quoted Catherine Lutz's comment about emotion being both the medium and the message in emotion socialization, and this viewpoint appears very relevant to understanding what intersubjectivity is all about.

Similar to Miller and Sperry's (1987) theoretical interpretation of their ethnographic research on the socialization of anger and aggression in a particular Baltimore community, Ratner and Stettner also distinguish between socialization "instruction" (or what is presented by the parents and/or other cultural agents, such as schools and television, as the "message" or content of what is to be transmitted to the child) and socialization "acquisition" (which is what the child actually internalizes and subsequently performs behaviorally). The preceding example of two different outcomes to the same directive given by two different sorts of parents to children about

not expressing disappointment over an unwanted gift illustrates how children may actually acquire rather different beliefs about how to adapt emotional expression to social contexts. However, I suspect that the majority of our empirical research does not delineate exactly what is intended by socializing agents and what is actually acquired by the child in terms of emotion learning.

Methods of Socialization

Children learn about emotional elicitors, emotional states, emotional expression, and emotional experience by means of direct instruction, contingency learning, imitation, identification with role models, and communication of expectancies, which are briefly described below (for elaboration, see Saarni, 1985, 1989, or Saarni & von Salisch, 1993).

Didactic teaching and contingency learning are direct methods of socialization. Illustrating contingency learning particularly well is a study carried out by Malatesta and Haviland (1982). They videotaped mothers interacting with their young infants, and found that during the period of a few months mothers' positive expressive responses reinforced the display of positive behavior in their infants, whereas the display of negative expressive behavior declined during this period. Malatesta and Haviland also found an interesting sex difference: Baby boys received more expressive matching behavior from their mothers, and daughters received a greater variety of expressive reactions from their mothers. Although this study is provocative for how emotional expression may be directly socialized, what we cannot determine is whether the infants' emotional state was affected or whether only their negative emotional expression was "dampened" in its intensity.

Another broad category of socialization is indirect influence. By "indirect," I am referring to those processes of influence that feature temporal or situational factors intervening between the initial elicitor and subsequent emotional experience. Imitation, identification, and social referencing are all examples of indirect socialization. Social referencing in particular has attracted considerable attention in recent investigations of emotional development. It refers to the process whereby an infant derives the "appropriate" emotional meaning of an otherwise ambiguous situation through observing how the caregiver responds expressively in the situation (Feinman & Lewis, 1983; Sorce, Emde, Campos, & Klinnert, 1985). It is likely that for older children and adults, social referencing is used more often in an imitative fashion: They may mimic the emotional expression of others when they are in an emotionally ambiguous situation, but they may not necessarily recreate the corresponding internal emotional state. However, for infants there does appear to be more of a correspondence between the subsequent expressive behavior displayed and the internal emotional state.

The last sort of socialization influence to be mentioned here is expectancy communication (for elaboration, see Saarni, 1985). Emotional responses may be influenced by others' communicated beliefs or expectations about how one is likely to feel in some situation. The communication can be verbal or nonverbal. The process begins with a suggestion's being offered (again, verbally or nonverbally) about the anticipated emotional reaction; to the degree to which that suggested emotional response appears credible to the listener, he or she will be more likely to scan his or her subsequent emotional experience for features that match this suggestion. When there is a good match between the prior suggestion and the subsequent emotional response, then the suggestion is validated and begins to be used by the listener as a personal expectancy. In other words, what was once "outside" the listener begins to be internalized as an "inside" expectancy for how the listener is likely to feel in similar future situations.

Readers may notice that this expectancy communication process bears considerable similarity to hypnotic communication, and one could also contend that parents are the "original hypnotists" in terms of how emotion beliefs and expectancies are passed on to children as suggestions for how to feel in situation X, Y, or Z. The mass media also play a similarly hypnotic role in suggesting how children will feel in a particular situation, with advertising perhaps being the most notoriously blatant purveyor of such emotion suggestions.

Folk Theories of Emotion

Also socialized in the individual is the culture's (or subculture's) folk theory or naive psychology about how emotion "works." We tacitly acquire such folk theories—not only about emotion, but also about social relations, the self, and even the nature of thought—as we mature and are socialized within a particular cultural context. Such naive theories of emotion function as internal guides or "working models" for both understanding *and* facilitating social exchange that is mediated by emotion processes. A metalevel understanding of emotion that is embedded within a "working model" or naive theory of emotion may be important in order for children to comprehend more complex emotional transactions between people, such as in the vignette presented at the beginning of this chapter describing 11-year-old Heather's exposure to her father's and uncle's chagrin at "needing" to be rescued.

Lutz (1987) has presented a view of folk theories of emotion that emphasizes social roles and relationships as integral to emotional experience. Her term, "ethnotheories of emotion," refers to implicit and pragmatic guidelines and beliefs held by individuals for facilitating and understanding ordinary social–emotional transactions. She also emphasizes that ethnotheories of emotion are open-ended and subject to change. This feature is a key one, for as children mature, their naive theory for how emotion "works" changes as well (recall the previously cited research by Lewis, 1989, on age group differences about what young children would feel if they were lost in a store). Lutz further observes that ethnotheories of emotion typically include two different kinds of goals. "Action tendency goals" refer to the motivating value of an emotion for the individual to undertake some sort of action (e.g., to run away if afraid), and "disclosure goals" or "attribution goals" refer to the degree of social acceptability surrounding an emotional experience that one has (e.g., in the United States it is often more socially acceptable for a woman to report somewhat ambiguously to others that she felt upset than to say that she felt angry; the reverse may hold true for men, and indeed, Fuchs & Thelen [1988] report that boys said they were unlikely to disclose that they felt sad).

Research on children's understanding that certain emotions tend to go hand in hand with particular motives and behavioral sequelae has been undertaken by Gnepp (1989a, 1989b) and Stein and Trabasso (1989), among others. Children's awareness of the social acceptability of certain emotional experiences and expressive behaviors has been examined (Saarni, 1979a, 1979b, 1988a, 1989, 1990) in terms of what they report as socially appropriate expressions of emotion, which include not expressing any emotion at all under some circumstances.

Cognitive Mediation of Emotions

One of the more prominent aspects of Western culture's views of how emotion "works" is the emphasis on cognitive mediation of emotion or appraisal (e.g., Lazarus, 1991). What do we know about children's acquisition of this belief—namely, that emotion results from one's own cognition (as opposed to one's kinship system, dream spirits or ghosts, or bodily illness)? I would argue that one of the corollaries to this Western folk theory belief about emotions as stemming from one's thoughts, images, and the like is our culture's emphasis on emotion as an *internal*, individual experience, as opposed to several other cultures' emphasis on emotion as an *interactive* experience (see Heider, 1984, for further discussion). However, given that we are focusing on the socialization of emotion in children reared in Western cultures, let us look at how children acquire this specific facet of Western folk theory of emotion.

I have found the cognitively oriented work undertaken by Harris and his colleagues to be especially descriptive and useful for examining children's developing belief that emotions are connected to how and what one thinks. In a series of studies, Harris and his collaborators investigated how children (both English and Dutch) made sense of their own and others' emotional experience (e.g., Harris, 1985, 1989; Harris & Gross, 1988; Harris & Lipian, 1989; Harris & Olthof, 1982; Harris, Olthof, & Meerum Terwogt, 1981). Their most recent data suggest that in the preschool years children are already able to conceptualize emotional experience as stemming from "mental" causes. That is, they demonstrate in their understanding of others' experience that the perspective or belief held by the other is significantly involved in determining how the other feels (i.e., that emotional elicitors are *constructed*). As they move through middle childhood, children begin to invoke mental factors as well for how to *change* emotional experience. For example, Harris and Lipian (1989) interviewed children in boarding schools to find out how the children thought they could alleviate such negative feelings as homesickness and sadness. Older children (age 10) were much more likely to cite such strategies as distraction, focusing on something positive, reinterpreting the situation, and so forth. Younger children (age 6) tended to restrict their strategies to suggestions about how to change the situation, rather than looking inward to seeing whether and how they might alter their internal experience. This greater reliance by the older children on internal, mental states as part of the "emotional package" (i.e., the folk theory of emotion) reflects several critical features of emotion, among them what cues are used to identify emotions reliably; how emotional expression is regulated; whether emotion moderates other psychological domains, such as memory and beliefs; and, importantly, how to cope with negative emotions.

Developmental Models

To account for children's progressive acquisition of this mental mediation of emotional experience, Harris and Olthof (1982) suggest three developmental models, which are not to be viewed as mutually exclusive. The first is the "solipsistic model," which posits that children observe that they can identity their own emotional responses more reliably by examining their own attributions (i.e., mental state) than by relying on any particular situation they may be in. To illustrate, by the time of school entry a child normally knows that children are usually happy at their own birthday celebrations. However, it can occur that children also experience a disappointment in the course of a birthday party and are no longer happy in that situation (e.g., they did not get what they wanted, a noncustodial divorced parent does not show up as a child had hoped, etc.). Such children will report that they are unhappy, despite its being their birthday celebration; that is, the children's mental attributions are more reliable than looking to the customary situational elicitor for ascertaining what they feel.

The second model is the "behavioral model," which emphasizes that children draw their data for determining where emotions come from by observing others rather than themselves. Children undoubtedly notice that certain situations and people's reactions to them have some degree of correspondence. However, as they mature, children may also observe that not all people react the same way to a given situation, and that a given reaction can occur in a seemingly noneliciting situation. The children might then come to attribute such an emotional reaction to a person's internal mental state rather than to an external situation.

The third developmental model is the "sociocentric model," which contends that the verbal community is the impetus for children to begin orienting themselves to a more mentalistic view of emotional experience. The child's linguistic community can presumably direct the child's attention to the covert, internal aspects of emotional experience in the absence of immediate situational and/or behavioral contexts. The child acquires as a result of this verbal "instruction" the belief that emotions both have their source in and can be modified by the self's cognitive constructions (e.g., evaluations, beliefs, reinterpretations, intentional distractions, etc.). Several investigators have studied preschool children's exposure to and involvement in conversations about emotional experiences; the general result has been that, given the redundant cues provided by both verbal and nonverbal emotional communication, young children tacitly acquire a great many "rules" by which emotions are linked to eliciting circumstances and coordinated with social transactions (e.g., Beeghly, Bretherton, & Mervis, 1986; Brown & Dunn, 1991; Dunn, Brown, & Beardsall, 1991).

INDIVIDUAL DIFFERENCES IN EMOTION SOCIALIZATION

There is an ever-growing body of research on individual differences in emotion processes, much of which is reviewed in the other chapters in this volume. The major kinds of individual differences usually examined relative to the socialization of emotion are gender differences (e.g., Eisenberg & Lennon, 1983; Fuchs & Thelen, 1988), temperament and/or personality differences (e.g., Goldsmith & Campos, 1982; Rothbart, Ziaie, & O'Boyle, 1992), cultural differences (e.g., Gordon, 1989; Lutz, 1983), and those differences stemming from pathology-inducing circumstances (e.g., Camras, Grow, & Ribordy, 1983; Cicchetti & Carlson, 1989; Feldman, Philippot, & Custrini, 1991; Lewis & Miller, 1990; Zabel, 1979).

More subtle differences, such as to what degree parents are controlling or accepting of children's emotionally expressive behavior and to what degree parents talk about emotion in the family, have been less easily and less consistently determined as having a *direct* effect on children's subsequent emotional behavior or emotional understanding (e.g., Cassidy, Parke, Butkovsky, & Braungart, 1992; Dunn et al., 1991; Eisenberg, Fabes, Schaller, Carlo, & Miller, 1991; Eisenberg, Fabes, Carlo, & Karbon, 1992; Saarni, 1988b). What appears to occur relative to these parenting differences is that other variables (such as family structure, presence of siblings, and level of maternal education, in addition to temperament, gender role, dysfunctional circumstances, and so forth) mediate or influence how parenting differences translate into observable outcomes in children's emotional socialization. Thus, the sources of more subtle individual differences in emotional socialization are likely to be difficult to unravel, because of their embeddedness in unique developmental histories. Furthermore, insofar as emotional and social development are inextricably intertwined, social events and emotional experiences interact mutually in the socialization of emotion (e.g., Saarni, 1989).

Differences in Emotional Competence

Elsewhere, I have described the kinds of "skills" needed for emotional competence in our culture (Saarni, 1990), and I have defined emotional competence as the demonstration of self-efficacy in the context of emotion-eliciting social transactions. One can also think of individual differences in emotion socialization as being played out in differential acquisition of these skills of emotional competence. I reprint the skills below,[1] for what I would like to examine next is when the socialization of emotion contributes to maladaptive outcomes in the child or young adult. These maladaptive outcomes can be viewed as incomplete or distorted versions of the skills of emotional competence.

Components and Skills of Emotional Competence
 1. Awareness of one's emotional state, including the possibility that one is experiencing mul-

---

[1]Reprinted by permission from Saarni (1990, pp. 117–118). Copyright 1990 by the University of Nebraska Press.

tiple emotions, and at even more mature levels, awareness that one might also not be consciously aware of one's feelings owing to unconscious dynamics or selective inattention.

2. Ability to discern others' emotions, based on situational and expressive cues that have some degree of cultural consensus as to their emotional meaning.

3. Ability to use the vocabulary of emotion and expression terms commonly available in one's (sub)culture.

4. Capacity for empathic involvement in others' emotional experiences.

5. Ability to realize that inner emotional state need not correspond to outer expression—either in oneself or in others.

6. Awareness of cultural display rules.

7. Ability to take into account unique personal information about individuals and apply it when inferring their emotional state, which may be discrepant from cultural expectations for what would commonly be experienced in some emotion-eliciting situation.

8. Ability to understand that one's emotional-expressive behavior may affect another and to take this into account in one's self-presentation strategies.

9. Capacity for coping adaptively with aversive or distressing emotions by using self-regulatory strategies that ameliorate the intensity or duration of such emotional states (e.g., "stress hardiness").

10. Awareness that the structure or nature of relationships is in part defined both by the degree of emotional immediacy or genuineness of expressive display and by the degree of reciprocity or symmetry within the relationship; for example, mature intimacy is in part defined by mutual or reciprocal sharing of genuine emotions, whereas a parent–child relationship may entail asymmetric sharing of genuine emotions.

11. Capacity for emotional self-efficacy: individuals view themselves as feeling, overall, the way they want to feel. That is, emotional self-efficacy means that one accepts one's emotional experience, whether unique and eccentric or culturally conventional, and that this acceptance is in alignment with one's beliefs about what constitutes desirable emotional "balance." In essence, one is living in accord with one's *personal* naive theory of emotion when one demonstrates emotional self-efficacy.

It is unlikely that a person growing up with an intact and normal nervous system will be utterly incapable of the first six emotional competence "skills." The last five may not be especially well developed in many individuals, as they are more dependent on the concep-

tual complexity available to the individual; their underdevelopment in a person probably contributes to that person's acting toward others in a highly egocentric fashion (skills 7, 8, and 10). Underdevelopment of skills 9 (ability to cope with aversive feelings) and 11 (generally feeling in accord with one's expectancies) probably contributes to individuals' experiencing their emotions as outside of their control, as though the emotions are happening to them. Such people have considerable difficulty in stressful situations and may often feel overwhelmed. In extreme cases, dissociation of self and emotion may occur; for example, severe sexual and physical abuse in childhood has been found to contribute to such dissociation (Courtois, 1988).

Dysfunctional Socialization of Emotion

Evidence from a number of significant studies suggests that socialization does contribute to distorted or immature development of emotional functioning. As a result of dysfunctional and/or pathological relationships with caregivers, children's emotional functioning becomes disorganized and maladaptive (for general reviews, see Lewis & Miller, 1990); thus, such children's potential for emotional competence is compromised. Relative to the specific skills of emotional competence listed above, young abused children have been shown to have deficits in their ability to use the vocabulary of emotion (Cicchetti & Beeghly, 1987). Zabel (1979) found that emotionally disturbed school-age children evidenced deficits in decoding others' emotional states, and Feldman, White, and Lobato (1982) determined that emotionally disturbed adolescents had difficulty in *both* encoding and decoding emotional states. These two studies (among others) suggest that emotional disturbance manifests itself in an impaired awareness of, and limited ability to express, specific emotions in oneself, as well as difficulty in discerning emotions in others. The capacity for empathic involvement in others' emotional experiences has been shown to be limited in delinquent children and youths (e.g., Magid & McKelvey, 1988).

Skills 5 and 6—the ability to distinguish internal emotional state from external expression, and awareness of cultural display rules—have been relatively infrequently studied in conjunction with clinic-referred children or youths. However, Harris (1989) describes a couple of studies he and his associates carried out with emotionally disturbed boys attending special schools in England. What they found was that compared to matched normals, the disturbed boys were less likely to entertain the idea of modifying or concealing the genuine expression of their emotion, and they seemed particularly insensitive to adopting a display rule strategy in order to protect the feelings of another. Harris's comment is appropriate here:

> The child who adopts a display rule to protect another person's feelings is not just saying: I do not *want* you to *know* how I *feel* but is anticipating the emotional repercussions of that knowledge and effectively saying: I do not *want* you to be *saddened* by *knowing* how I *feel*. (1989, p. 145)

His comment firmly anchors the ability to differentiate internal emotional experience and external emotional expression in processes of social development as well. Thus, the child who grows up within relationships (intra- and extrafamilial) that are fragmented, abusive, chronically conflictual, and pervaded by despair is targeted for a socialization of emotion that is likely to result in that child's experiencing relative degrees of emotional *in*competence and concurrent deficits in social competence.

SUMMARY

The perspective taken in this chapter on the socialization of emotion has been one that emphasizes the social construction of emotional meaning and experience. I have begun by describing how Lewis and Michalson's (1983) structural model of emotion as consisting of components can be used descriptively for examining how socialization contributes to developmental change in each emotion component. Next I have discussed several broad categories of socialization processes—namely, direct and indirect processes, and those based on expectancy and belief communication ("intersubjectivity"). How children acquire their culture's folk theory or theories of emotion has also been considered. Lastly, individual differences in emotion socialization have been discussed as representing variable and complex developmental social–emotional histories. Maladaptive

individual differences in emotional functioning are conceptualized as stemming from either deficits in emotional competence or immaturity in acquiring the "skills" of emotional competence.

REFERENCES

Beeghly, M., Bretherton, I., & Mervis, C. (1986). Mothers' internal state language to toddlers: The socialization of psychological understanding. *British Journal of Developmental Psychology, 4,* 247–260.

Bower, G. H. (1981). Mood and memory. *American Psychologist, 36,* 1129–1148.

Bretherton, I., Fritz, J., Zahn-Waxler, C., & Ridgeway, D. (1986). Learning to talk about emotion: A functionalist perspective. *Child Development, 57,* 529–548.

Brown, J. R., & Dunn, J. (1991). "You can cry, mum": The social and developmental implications of talk about internal states. *British Journal of Developmental Psychology, 9,* 237–256.

Bugental, D. B. (1985). Unresponsive children and powerless adults: Cocreators of affectively uncertain caregiving environments. In M. Lewis & C. Saarni (Eds.), *The socialization of emotions* (pp. 239–261). New York: Plenum Press.

Camras, L., Grow, J. G., & Ribordy, S. (1983). Recognition of emotional expression by abused children. *Journal of Clinical Child Psychology, 12,* 325–328.

Cassidy, J., Parke, R., Butkovsky, L., Braungart, J. (1992). Family–peer connections: The roles of emotional expressiveness within the family and children's understanding of emotions. *Child Development, 63,* 603–618.

Cicchetti, D., & Beeghly, M. (1987). Symbolic development in maltreated youngsters: An organizational perspective. *New Directions for Child Development, 36,* 47–68.

Cicchetti, D., & Carlson, V. (Eds.). (1989). *Child maltreatment: Theory and research on the causes and consequences of child abuse and neglect.* New York: Cambridge University Press.

Cole, P. M. (1985). Display rules and the socialization of affective displays. In G. Zivin (Ed.), *The development of expressive behavior* (pp. 269–287). New York: Academic Press.

Courtois, C. (1988). *Healing the incest wound: Adult survivors in therapy.* New York: Norton.

Derryberry, D., & Rothbart, M. (1988). Arousal, affect, and attention as components of temperament. *Journal of Personality and Social Psychology, 55,* 958–966.

Dunn, J., Bretherton, I., & Munn, P. (1987). Conversations about feelings states between mothers and their young children. *Developmental Psychology, 23,* 132–139.

Dunn, J., Brown, J., & Beardsall, L. (1991). Family talk about feeling states and children's later understanding of others' emotions. *Developmental Psychology, 27,* 448–455.

Eisenberg, N., & Fabes, R. (1990). Empathy: Conceptualization, assessment, and relation to prosocial behavior. *Motivation and Emotion, 14,* 131–149.

Eisenberg, N., & Fabes, R. (1991). Prosocial behavior and empathy: A multimethod, developmental perspective. In P. Clark (Ed.), *Review of personality and social psychology.* (Vol. 12, pp. 34–61). Newbury Park, CA: Sage.

Eisenberg, N., Fabes, R., Carlo, G., & Karbon, M. (1992). Emotional responsivity to others: Behavioral correlates and socialization antecedents. *New Directions for Child Development, 55,* 57–73.

Eisenberg, N., Fabes, R., Schaller, M., Carlo, G., & Miller, P. A. (1991). The relations of parental characteristics and practices to children's vicarious emotional responding. *Child Development, 62,* 1393–1408.

Eisenberg, N., Fabes, R., Schaller, M., Miller, P. A., Carlo, G., Poulin, R., Shea, C., & Shell, R. (1991). Personality and socialization correlates of vicarious emotional responding. *Journal of Personality and Social Psychology, 61,* 459–470.

Eisenberg, N., & Lennon, R. (1983). Sex differences in empathy and related capacities. *Psychological Bulletin, 94,* 100–131.

Ekman, P., & Friesen, W. V. (1975). *Unmasking the face.* Englewood Cliffs, NJ: Prentice-Hall.

Feinman, S., & Lewis, M. (1983). Social referencing and second order effects in ten-month-old infants. *Child Development, 54,* 878–887.

Feldman, R. S., Philippot, P., & Custrini, R. (1991). Social competence and nonverbal behavior. In R. S. Feldman & B. Rimé (Eds.), *Fundamentals of nonverbal behavior* (pp. 329–350). New York: Cambridge University Press.

Feldman, R. S., White, J. B., & Lobato, D. (1982). Social skills and nonverbal behavior. In R. S. Feldman (Ed.), *Development of nonverbal behavior in children* (pp. 259–277). New York: Springer-Verlag.

Fox, N. A. (1989). Psychophysiological correlates of emotional reactivity during the first year of life. *Developmental Psychology, 25,* 364–372.

Fuchs, D., & Thelen, M. (1988). Children's expected interpersonal consequences of communicating their affective states and reported likelihood of expression. *Child Development, 59,* 1314–1322.

Garber, J., & Dodge, K. A. (Eds.). (1991). *The development of emotion regulation and dysregulation.* New York: Cambridge University Press.

Gnepp, J. (1989a). Children's use of personal information to understand other people's feelings. In C. Saarni & P. L. Harris (Eds.), *Children's understanding of emotion* (pp. 151–180). Cambridge, England: Cambridge University Press.

Gnepp, J. (1989b). Personalized inferences of emotions and appraisals: Component processes and correlates. *Developmental Psychology, 25,* 277–288.

Goldsmith, H. H., & Campos, J. (1982). Toward a theory of infant temperament. In R. Emde & R. Harmon (Eds.), *The development of attachment and affiliative systems* (pp. 161–193). New York: Plenum Press.

Gordon, S. L. (1989). The socialization of children's emotions: Emotional culture, competence, and exposure. In C. Saarni & P. L. Harris (Eds.), *Children's understanding of emotion* (pp. 319–349). Cambridge, England: Cambridge University Press.

Halberstadt, A. G. (1991). Toward an ecology of expressiveness: Family socialization in particular and a model in general. In R. S. Feldman & B. Rimé (Eds.), *Fundamentals of nonverbal behavior* (pp. 106–160). New York: Cambridge University Press.

Harris, P. L. (1985). What children know about the situations that provoke emotion. In M. Lewis & C. Saarni (Eds.), *The socialization of affect* (pp. 161–185). New York: Plenum Press.

Harris, P. L. (1989). *Children and emotion: The development of psychological understanding.* Oxford: Basil Blackwell.

Harris, P. L., & Gross, D. (1988). Children's understanding of real and apparent emotion. In J. W. Astington, P. L. Harris, & D. R. Olson (Eds.), *Developing theories of mind* (pp. 295–314). Cambridge, England: Cambridge University Press.

Harris, P. L., & Lipian, M. S. (1989). Understanding emotion and experiencing emotion. In C. Saarni & P. L. Harris (Eds.), *Children's understanding of emotion* (pp. 241–258). Cambridge, England: Cambridge University Press.

Harris, P. L., & Olthof, T. (1982). The child's concept of emotion. In G. Butterworth & P. Light (Eds.), *Social cognition* (pp. 188–209). Brighton, England: Harvester Press.

Harris, P. L., Olthof, T., & Meerum Terwogt, M. (1981). Children's knowledge of emotion. *Journal of Child Psychiatry and Psychology, 22,* 247–261.

Harris, P. L., & Saarni, C. (1989). Children's understanding of emotion: An introduction. In C. Saarni & P. L. Harris (Eds.), *Children's understanding of emotion* (pp. 3–24). Cambridge, England: Cambridge University Press.

Heider, K. (1984, November). *Emotion: Inner state versus interaction.* Paper presented at the meeting of the American Anthropological Association, Denver.

Larsen, R. J., & Diener, E. (1987). Affect intensity as an individual difference characteristic: A review. *Journal of Research in Personality, 21,* 1–39.

Lazarus, R. (1991). *Emotion and adaptation.* New York: Oxford University Press.

Levenson, R. W., Ekman, P., & Friesen, W. (1990). Voluntary facial action generates emotion-specific autonomic nervous system activity. *Psychophysiology, 27,* 363–385.

Lewis, M. (1989). Cultural differences in children's knowledge of emotional scripts In C. Saarni & P. L. Harris (Eds.), *Children's understanding of emotion* (pp. 350–374). Cambridge, England: Cambridge University Press.

Lewis, M., & Michalson, L. (1983). *Children's emotions and moods: Developmental theory and measurement.* New York: Plenum Press.

Lewis, M., & Miller, S. (Eds.). (1990). *Handbook of developmental psychopathology.* New York: Plenum Press.

Lewis, M., & Saarni, C. (Eds.). (1985). *The socialization of emotions.* New York: Plenum Press.

Lutz, C. (1983). Parental goals, ethnopsychology, and the development of emotional meaning. *Ethos, 11,* 246–262.

Lutz, C. (1987). Goals, events, and understanding in Ifaluk emotion theory. In D. Holland & N. Quinn (Eds.), *Cultural models in language and thought* (pp. 290–312). New York: Cambridge University Press.

Magid, K., & McKelvey, C. (1988). *High risk: Children without a conscience.* New York: Bantam.

Malatesta, C. Z., & Haviland, J. M. (1982). Learning display rules: The socialization of emotion expression in infancy. *Child Development, 53,* 991–1003.

Miller, P., & Sperry, L. L. (1987). The socialization of anger and aggression. *Merrill–Palmer Quarterly, 33,* 1–31.

Pollack, L., & Thoits, P. (1989). Processes in emotional socialization. *Social Psychology Quarterly, 52,* 22–34.

Ratner, H., & Stettner, L. (1991). Thinking and feeling: Putting Humpty Dumpty together again. *Merrill–Palmer Quarterly, 37,* 1–26.

Rothbart, M., Ziaie, H., & O'Boyle, C. (1992). Self-regulation and emotion in infancy. *New Directions for Child Development, 55,* 7–23.

Russell, J. A. (1991). Culture and the categorization of emotion. *Psychological Bulletin, 110,* 426–450.

Saarni, C. (1979a). Children's understanding of display rules for expressive behavior. *Developmental Psychology, 15,* 424–429.

Saarni, C. (1979b, March). *When not to show what you feel: Children's understanding of the relations between emotional experience and expressive behavior.* Paper presented at the meeting of the Society for Research in Child Development, San Francisco.

Saarni, C. (1984). An observational study of children's attempts to monitor their expressive behavior. *Child Development, 55,* 1504–1513.

Saarni, C. (1985). Indirect processes in affect socialization. In M. Lewis & C. Saarni (Eds.), *The socialization of emotions* (pp. 187–209). New York: Plenum Press.

Saarni, C. (1988a). Children's understanding of the interpersonal consequences of dissemblance of nonverbal emotional-expressive behavior. *Journal of Nonverbal Behavior, 12*(4, Pt 2), 275–294.

Saarni, C. (1988b). *Psychometric properties of the Parent Attitude Toward Children's Expressiveness Scale (PACES).* Unpublished manuscript, Sonoma State University.

Saarni, C. (1989). Children's understanding of strategic control of emotional expression in social transactions. In C. Saarni & P. L. Harris (Eds.), *Children's understanding of emotion* (pp. 181–208). Cambridge, England: Cambridge University Press.

Saarni, C. (1990). Emotional competence: How emotions and relationships become integrated. In R. Thompson (Ed.), *Nebraska Symposium on Motivation: Vol. 36. Socioemotional development* (pp. 115–182). Lincoln: University of Nebraska Press.

Saarni, C. (1992). Children's emotional-expressive behaviors as regulators of others' happy and sad states. *New Directions for Child Development, 55,* 91–106.

Saarni, C., & Harris, P. L. (Eds.). (1989). *Children's understanding of emotion.* Cambridge, England: Cambridge University Press.

Saarni, C., & von Salisch, M. (1993). The socialization of emotional dissemblance. In M. Lewis & C. Saarni (Eds.), *Lying and deception in everyday life* (pp. 106–125). New York: Guilford Press.

Sorce, J., Emde, R., Campos, J., & Klinnert, M. (1985). Maternal emotional signaling: Its effects on the visual cliff behavior of 1-year-olds. *Developmental Psychology, 21,* 195–200.

Stein, N., & Trabasso, T. (1989). Children's understanding of changing emotional states. In C. Saarni & P. L. Harris (Eds.), *Children's understanding of emotion* (pp. 50–80). Cambridge, England: Cambridge University Press.

Stemmler, G. (1989). The autonomic differentiation of emotions revisited: Convergent and discriminant validation. *Psychophysiology, 26,* 617–632.

Thompson, R. A. (1990). Emotion and self-regulation. In R. A. Thompson (Ed.), *Nebraska Symposium on Motivation: Vol. 36. Socioemotional development* (pp. 367–467). Lincoln: University of Nebraska Press.

Zabel, R. (1979). Recognition of emotions in facial expressions by emotionally disturbed and nondisturbed children. *Psychology in the Schools, 16,* 119–126.

31

Gender and Emotion

LESLIE R. BRODY
JUDITH A. HALL

The interrelated ideas that women are more emotional and more emotionally expressive than men, as well as more expressive of particular kinds of emotions than men, are common in popular culture. These ideas exist in fiction and drama, as well as in popular surveys (Shields, 1986) and child-rearing manuals (Shields & Koster, 1989). Insofar as these stereotypes are linked to a gender-linked division of labor and life tasks along instrumental and socioemotional lines, they are likely to be universal as well.[1]

In fact, Deaux and Major (1987) argue that gender stereotypes themselves may be critical in bringing about gender-stereotypic behavior, and Hall and Briton (1993) argue that expectancies and behaviors probably exert strong bidirectional influences. Deaux and Major hypothesize that in any interaction, participants have a set of gender-stereotypic beliefs about themselves and their partners; these may or may not be activated to influence behavior, depending on the context, the attributes of their partners, and the goals they have in the interaction. The data we review suggest that there are indeed clearly held stereotypes of greater female expressivity, greater expression of sadness and fear by females, and greater expression of anger by males. These stereotypes in and of themselves may be self-fulfilling prophecies that lead to actual behavior, and vice versa.

But these stereotypes, as well as the actual behaviors that they imply, deserve much elaboration. As many authors have observed, efforts to ascribe generalized qualities to males and females as groups are bound to be theoretically simplistic and empirically unsound (Brody, in press; Shields, 1987, 1991; Deaux & Major, 1987). Logic suggests and research confirms, that gender differences in emotion-related behaviors are influenced by situational and contextual variables, task characteristics, age, and culture.

Culture and context become particularly important when emotions are viewed from a functionalist perspective (i.e., a view that emotions are adaptive for both interpersonal and intrapersonal goals). Since such goals vary widely for males and females—depending on, among other things, age, culture, socialization history, and socioeconomic status—it is not surprising both that gender differences in emotion are widely documented, and that these gender differences are sometimes inconsistent, varying as a function of these same factors. Interpersonal goals that may differ for males and females include culturally and socially prescribed gender roles (e.g., the role of a child caretaker vs. a provider); intra-

Author Note: We are listed in alphabetical order in recognition of our equal contributions to this chapter.

[1]In this chapter we use the word "gender" arbitrarily to refer to biological sex, to culturally determined psychological and behavioral differences between males and females, and to attributes stereotypically connoting maleness and femaleness. Some writers (e.g., Unger, 1979; Shields, 1990) argue for a distinction between the terms "sex" and "gender," based on an analysis of causal influences. Though we acknowled the importance of studying the multiple determinants of observed differences, we believe that such a semantic distinction involves prejudging the causes of the differences, and therefore we do not draw a distinction between these terms.

personal goals that may differ for males and females include the extent to which conflict and anxiety are minimized and the types of self-schemas that are maintained. Intrapersonal goals can certainly be influenced by the nature of an individual's underlying biological disposition, (including temperament and neuropsychological processes), both of which may also vary for males and females, although the quality and extent of such differences are hotly debated (see Bleier, 1991).

The quality of expressed emotions may also reflect enduring personality dispositions that become habitual patterns through repeated interpersonal interactions, leading to certain interpersonal expectancies (Malatesta, 1990). The mutual expression of emotions within interpersonal dyads can serve as communication signals, and the parents' empathic responses to such signals by the infant may be the fundamental process through which the infant's self is developed (the "self-in-relation") (Jordan, 1986; Stern, 1985). If caretakers attempt to shape their children in accordance with the demands of the larger culture (Ruddick, 1982), which presents very different standards for female than for male development, then parents may be empathic to different emotional signals in their sons versus their daughters. Differing patterns of interaction may shape male versus female emotional development, and consequently the development of the male versus the female self, in very different ways.

The purpose of the present chapter is to summarize research and theory concerning gender differences in emotional experience, emotional expression, and nonverbal communication behaviors relating to emotion. In reviewing these topics, we document both stereotypes and actual behavior patterns. In addition, we summarize evidence for socialization and developmental processes, including the development of verbal language and gender roles, that may underlie gender differences in these domains. In our chapter we concentrate on research on normal populations of children and adults.

EXPERIENCE OF EMOTIONS

Stereotypes

Though for analytic purposes there is obvious merit in separating the experience of an emotion from its expression, not all research permits a clear distinction. This is particularly evident in masculinity–femininity scales and other measures of gender stereotypes that include "emotional" in their item content; the term "emotional" implies both experience and expression. Though interpretation of this word has its ambiguities, there is no ambiguity about its gender connotation: "Emotional" is always classified as feminine or more typical of females (e.g., Spence, Helmreich, & Stapp, 1975; Antill, 1987).

Research that specifically asks subjects to differentiate experience from expression finds that people believe gender differences in emotional experience to be considerably weaker than corresponding differences in expression. Johnson and Shulman (1988) asked subjects to read descriptions of behavior and to rate how intensely an emotional reaction would be experienced by a typical male or female friend, or how extremely the given emotion would be displayed. Females were rated as more intense on both experience and display, but the difference between males and females was greater for display. Fabes and Martin (1991) asked subjects to rate the frequency with which imaginary persons varying on gender and age would experience or express a list of emotions. Differences for experience were fewer and weaker than differences for expression. Out of six emotions, only for love was there a gender difference, with females said to experience love more often than males. However, on the expression of emotion there were pervasive differences.

These two studies introduce another important distinction: The frequency of experiencing an emotion is not synonymous with the intensity with which it is experienced. The Johnson and Shulman (1988) study, which used intensity ratings, found stronger evidence for gender differences in experience than did the Fabes and Martin (1991) study, which used frequency ratings. But both studies found that subjects believed expression differences to be larger than experience differences.

Self-Descriptions

With self-descriptions, various sources of bias are always to be considered. In the case of gender-linked attributes, the main concern is that subjects' self-descriptions will be biased, consciously or unconsciously, by their knowledge of gender stereotypes (Brody, in press). Also, since women are more willing to talk about their emotions than men are, this also may bias the pattern of results; though we do not review the literature on verbal self-disclosure here, it is consistent with the gender differences in expression reviewed here (see, e.g., Dindia & Allen, 1992; Reis, Senchak, & Solomon, 1985; Snell, Miller, & Belk, 1988). With these reservations in mind, the following summary is offered.

Allen and Haccoun's (1976) study on undergraduates' self-rated emotional experience highlights the frequency–intensity distinction. When asked how they would "feel inside" in response to four emotions, subjects manifested no overall gender difference on frequency, but did on intensity of feeling, with females reporting greater intensity for three of the four emotions (fear, sadness, and joy).

The most extensive evidence for greater panemotional affect intensity in females comes from the work of Diener and his colleagues. Fujita, Diener, and Sandvik (1991) found that college females reported greater intensity of experiencing both positive and negative emotions. Observers well acquainted with the subjects, who responded as they thought the subjects would, produced the same pattern of results. Diener, Sandvik, and Larsen (1985) measured affect intensity in subjects ranging from 16 to 68 years of age. Females were higher on affect intensity (both positive and negative affects) and on extreme variations in mood than males, and there was no age × gender interaction. More strongly felt and more volatile emotions are therefore characteristic of females over a large portion of the lifespan.

Consistent with females' generally greater intensity of affect, Brody (in press) found that self-rated emotional reactions to written scenarios were more intense for females across a range of emotions, including annoyance, disgust, sadness, warmth, happiness, hurt, fear, nervousness, and anger (though for some of these there were interactions with the gender of the protagonist in the scenario).

Although the finding of generally greater affect intensity in females is well established, consideration of particular kinds of affect is also instructive. First we consider positive affect. In Rehm's (1978) study, subjects rated their mood daily for 2 weeks; females had significantly more positive mood. In the study by Fujita et al. (1991), females reported spending a greater percentage of time in a positive affective state. As noted above, Allen

and Haccoun (1976) found greater female intensity for joy, and Brody (in press) found females to respond with more intensity for warmth and happiness.

Relevant to our discussion of positive affect is the literature on positive well-being and happiness. Women tend to rate themselves higher on these constructs (e.g., Matlin & Gawron, 1979; Wood, Rhodes, & Whelan, 1989), though in the Wood et al. review this was the case only for married samples. Related constructs measured by self-report instruments also suggest greater positive affect in women. For example, females score higher on interpersonal trust, a positively toned attitude (Johnson-George & Swap, 1982); they also report liking others more and having more emotional closeness in relationships (Reis et al., 1985; Hall, 1984).

Women's apparently more positive outlook is captured in their more rosy interpretations of people and events—a tendency that has been called the "Pollyanna" effect. Warr's (1971) review of this literature found that women were more prone to see the good in others. As one recent example, Taylor and Hinds (1985) found, in a laboratory experiment, that females gave more positive adjective ratings to their partners.

Negative emotions present a less consistent picture of gender differences. Females generally exceed males on self-reports of emotions that are intropunitive (shame, guilt, sadness, fear, and anxiety). Using a behavioral self-report inventory, Tangney (1990) found that females reported more shame- and guilt-based experiences than did males. Stapley and Haviland (1989) found that adolescent girls reported more shame (combining over frequency, duration, and intensity). Sadness is also reported more by females (Stapley & Haviland, 1989; Brody, in press). The latter is consistent, of course, with higher rates of subclinical and clinical depression in females. Fear and nervousness were reported as more intense by women in Brody and Flanagan's (1992) study, as well as in many other self-report studies (e.g., Brody, Hay, & Vandewater, 1990). For these emotions cultural differences have been shown: Sommers and Kosmitzki (1988) found that German men and women did not report differences in fear.

Empathy can also be thought of as a dysphoric affect, since the experience is often one of distress felt vicariously in response to another's plight. Females, both children and adults, experience more empathy than do males when self-report measures are used (Eisenberg & Lennon, 1983).

In contrast, outward-directed negative affect seems to be felt more by males than by females. Stapley and Haviland (1989) studied 5th- through 11th-graders and found, using a composite of frequency, intensity, and duration of experience, that males reported experiencing more contempt than females. However, Brody (in press) found no gender difference in the intensity of contempt reported by adult males and females. For anger experience, gender differences are often minimized or reversed in favor of males. Averill (1983) found no gender difference on either frequency or intensity of anger experience reported by college students and community residents, nor did Allen and Haccoun (1976) for college students. Wintre, Polivy, and Murray (1990 found anger differences that varied with age and the nature of the eliciting circumstances. Brody (in press), using self-reported intensity of reactions to written scenarios, found greater reports of anger by women toward imaginary male protagonists but not toward female ones.

It may seem paradoxical that females report experiencing more positive *and* negative emotions—for example, better subjective well-being and more depression. Diener and Emmons (1985) showed that within short time frames, positive and negative emotions occur in inverse proportion to each other. However, over longer stretches they become independent: How often one feels positive emotion is not predictable from how often one feels negative emotion. Moreover, the intensity of experiencing positive feelings is *positively* correlated with the intensity of experiencing negative emotions (Diener, Larsen, Levine, & Emmons, 1985). These findings would tell us that results pertaining to gender can be expected to vary, depending on the response format and the mix of emotions represented in a given study (Fujita et al., 1991).

EXPRESSION OF EMOTION

In the expressive domain, a greater variety of measurement approaches is seen. Here we make distinctions among stereotypes, self-reports, and observational data, and we also draw the distinction, where possible, between global expressiveness on the one hand and specifically verbal or nonverbal expressiveness on the other. Nonverbal communication skills related to emotion are also taken up in this section.

Stereotypes

As mentioned earlier, global measures often obscure the difference between experience and expression; clearly, the common finding that females are rated as more "emotional" implies outward expression as well as inward experience. When "masculinity" and "femininity" are measured on separate scales (e.g., Spence et al., 1975), the entire "feminine" scale is often called "expressive," in contrast to the "masculine" scale, which is often called "agentic" or "instrumental." However, "expressive" in this context subsumes item content that is more diverse, including, for example, the traits "considerate," "gentle," and "understanding." In addition to this loose terminology, one can also note that many items that are stereotypic of males also imply expression, but of different qualities—for example, expression or self-confidence, hostility, or pride.

In terms of overall emotional expression, the stereotype definitely points to women as more expressive, as in Johnson and Shulman's (1988) study. Stereotypes about specific emotions show remarkable correspondence with data on experience of emotion. Birnbaum and Croll (1984) asked working-class parents, middle-class parents, and college students to report their beliefs about expression of anger, fear, sadness, and happiness in "typical" boys and girls. Working-class parents believed that males expressed anger more often and more intensely than females, and fear less often and less intensely, and also believed that these were desirable differences. They also thought that females expressed sadness more often. College students believed that anger was expressed more often and more intensely by males, and sadness less often and less intensely, but did not indicate that these differences were desirable. All three groups indicated more acceptance of anger in boys.

Birnbaum (1983) found that children aged 3–5 believed that males expressed anger more, while females expressed fear, sadness, and happiness more. In the Fabes and Martin (1991) study described earlier, subjects rated adolescent and adult females as expressing love, sadness, and fear more frequently than males in those age groups, and anger less often, with no difference on happiness and surprise. Subjects did not perceive gender differences in younger groups.

In all of the studies mentioned so far, "expression" was globally defined. Specifically *nonverbal* expression was asked about by Briton and Hall (1992). College students believed that females had more expressive faces and voices, smiled and laughed more, gazed more, had more expressive hands, and were more skilled in the sending and receiving of nonverbal cues. They did not believe that there was a difference in the frequency of frowning.

Self-Descriptions

Among Ross and Mirowsky's (1984) married sample, women reported crying in the previous week more than men did. Balswick and Avertt's (1977) undergraduate females reported greater frequency of showing love, happiness, and sadness than the males did, but not greater frequency of hate. Allen and Haccoun's (1976) undergraduate females reported greater intensity of expression than the males for fear, sadness, joy, and anger, but the difference for anger was the weakest. Similarly, Dosser, Balswick, and Halverson's (1983) self-reports showed females to express love, sadness, and happiness more frequently than males, but there were much weaker effects for anger.

Using a multi-item instrument, Zuckerman and Larrance (1979) gathered self-reports of nonverbal expressiveness. These items, which emphasized spontaneous (unplanned) facial and vocal expressions, produced substantial gender differences: As might be expected, college females described themselves as more expressive than their male peers reported themselves to be.

Observational Data

Again, a methodological point is in order. Because observers are typically not blind to the gender of those they are observing, stereotype-based bias is a possible problem. When target gender is manipulated, bias is a concern; for example, the same infant may be rated as more fearful and happy if perceived as female, but more angry if perceived as male (Condry & Condry, 1976).

Observational studies of nonverbal expressiveness find females to be considerably more expressive overall (Hall, 1984). Gender differences are also found with the "slide-viewing paradigm" (Buck, 1984), in which people are shown affectively arousing slides or films while their faces are videotaped surreptitiously. Judgments of these tapes reveal that the content of the stimulus is easier to judge from females' than from males' faces, but only after early childhood. Buck (1984) has found that among preschoolers. spontaneous facial expression accuracy shows little relation to gender; consistent with this, there is evidence that facial expressiveness and expression skill decrease over time among young boys, while increasing in girls. Buck's research reveals a gender difference on the so-called "internalizer–externalizer" dimension, a term used to describe the inverse relation between spontaneous facial signs of affect on the one hand and internal physiological arousal on the other (Buck, 1984). Males tend to be internalizers, females externalizers.

Research on deliberate, or posed, emotional communication finds that women's faces are more accurately judged, a finding unlikely to be subject to stereotype bias; however, data on accuracy of vocal emotion expression are extremely inconsistent. Though women's voices are more expressive in terms of pitch variation and other acoustic variables, their ability to express particular emotions on demand via the voice is not, on average, superior to men's (Hall, 1984). Overall, research does not indicate any consistent pattern of gender differences in accuracy of communication for particular emotions.

Behaviors that imply emotion show gender differences, but a full range of relevant behaviors has not been studied. Research is largely limited to the sexes' tendencies to smile and laugh; on these, females very consistently exceed males except in childhood, where differences have not emerged (Hall, 1984). Gender differences in smiling are also moderated by situational factors, such as situational anxiety (Hall & Halberstadt, 1986). Other facial behaviors indicative of emotion are less studied; females clearly weep more than males do, but for other negative emotions (e.g., anger or fear) there are few data. Birnbaum and Croll(1984) observed children aged 2–4 watching a film; boys showed more anger, while girls showed more fear and happiness (no difference was found for sadness).

Other nonverbal behaviors provide insight into the kinds of interpersonal messages characteristically conveyed by men and women. Women use more expressive hand gestures and nod more; their gazing and interpersonal spacing tendencies, reviewed by Hall (1984), also suggest that women prefer more intimate, affectively immediate communication with others.

DECODING OF EXPRESSIVE CUES

The final category of gender difference findings we summarize concerns males' and females' abilities to recognize or decode affective expressions sent by others. Since this topic has been extensively reviewed (Hall, 1978, 1984), we only highlight the findings here. In reviews summarizing 75 and 50 independent studies, respectively, Hall (1978, 1984) concluded that females are superior to males at identifying affect from nonverbal cues of face, body, and voice. In at least 80% of all retrieved studies, females scored higher. Notably, the gender difference was relatively invariant across the gender of the stimulus person, tasks, different ages of the subjects being tested, and cultures. Results have been remarkably similar in the literature at large and for 133 diverse samples tested with the Profile of Nonverbal Sensitivity (PONS; Rosenthal, Hall, Dimatteo, Rogers, & Archer, 1979). For the PONS, subject age × subject gender interactions are not apparent, and females' advantage (which is greatest for facial cues) is also evident cross-culturally.

Recent evidence suggests that there may be an exception to women's superior decoding skills where expressions of anger are concerned; here, women appear to read the facial cues less accurately than men do, especially when the encoder is male (Rotter & Rotter, 1988; Wagner, MacDonald, & Manstead, 1986).

AN OVERVIEW IN RELATION TO GENDER ROLES

The data we have reviewed are surprisingly consistent in indicating that in this culture, females are both stereotyped to be and in fact are more intensely expressive of both positive and some negative emotions (as indicated both by self-report and by objective judges); that they report themselves to experience a wider variety of emotions than do males; and that they are superior to males at recognizing and decoding affective expressions in others from nonverbal face, body, and voice cues. In some contexts, females have been found to be relatively weaker than are males in both expressing and recognizing anger and other outer-directed emotions (e.g., contempt). Males have also been found to report more pride in the self than do women, and fewer of the intropunitive affects (e.g., shame, embarrassment, guilt, and anxiety). The data on greater female expressivity are more convincing for intensity than for frequency, and seem somewhat stronger for expression than for experience, although the two are difficult to disengage. It is important to note that these effects may be culturally and situationally specific. Although we have not focused on developmental research studies documenting gender differences in nonverbal affect recognition and emotional expressiveness, studies on children corroborate the literature we have reviewed (see Brody, 1985 and in press, for reviews of additional developmental studies).

These findings are consistent with the perspective that gender differences in emotion are adaptive for the differing roles that males and females play in this culture (see also Eagly, 1987). Thus, the emotions that women display more (warmth, happiness, shame, guilt, fear, and nervousness) are related to affiliation, vulnerability, and self-consciousness, and are consistent with women's lower social status and power, lower physical aggression, and their traditional gender roles (including child caretaking and social bonding, which necessitate being able to read the emotion signals of others). Greater male anger, pride, and contempt are consistent with the male role of differentiating and competing with others, in which the goals are the minimization of vulnerability in order to maximize the chances of success. It should be noted that although the gender differences we have reviewed are consistent with various etiological theories based on gender role differences, including status and power differences between men and women, this does not imply that any gender role variables actually cause gender differences in emotion (see Hall, 1987). In particular, much recent evidence suggests that the relations among status, power, and emotional decoding and expressiveness abilities are quite complicated, with the direction of the relations among these variables not always consistent with models positing that status differences produce differences in emotional functioning (Brody & Flanagan, 1992; Hall & Halberstadt, 1992; Vrugt & Kerkstra, 1984).

As Brody (in press) has argued, the direction of gender differences for specific emotions (e.g., that men express more anger but less shame than women do) is consistent with the idea that each sex is socialized to adapt to differing gender roles. In fact, there is a great deal of accumulating evidence for systematic relationships between gender roles and emotional expressiveness, especially for personality attributes related to gender role, such as being communal and nurturant versus agentic. Studies have shown that more feminine individuals (defined by stereotypic personality traits) report more emotional expressiveness than do masculine individuals, including more fear, anxiety, sadness, nervousness, hurt, warmth, and love; that they amplify negative affect in general; and that they are more intimate in the content of their self-disclosures (Bander & Betz, 1981; Brody, et al., 1990; Dillon, Wolf, & Katz, 1985; Ganong & Coleman, 1985; Ingram, Cruet, Johnson, & Wisnicki, 1988; Lewis & McCarthy, 1988; Narus & Fischer, 1981; Orlofsky &Windle, 1978). More feminine individuals are also more skilled in expressing emotions via face and voice (Zuckerman, Defrank, Spiegel, & Larrance, 1982). In the few studies that have looked at the relative contribution of biological sex versus gender role, gender role has made the more significant contribution (Brody et al., 1990).

There is also accumulating evidence that behavioral gender roles (e.g., the amount of child care individuals do and the types of occupations in which they are engaged) are also systematically related to emotional functioning. Risman (1987) found that mothers and fathers who interacted more with their children reported higher intimacy and levels of feminine stereotyped traits than did mothers or fathers who interacted less. Brody and Flanagan (1992) found that men who did more stereotypic female household tasks (e.g., laundry, child care, and meal preparation) reported greater nervousness, whereas women who did more household tasks stereotypically associated with men (e.g., yardwork) reported less nervousness and fear. For both men and women, traditionally female occupations (nursing, teaching) were associated with increased reported fear toward both men and women. Interestingly, Brody (in press) found that a group of working women with traditional attitudes toward women's roles reported the highest levels of fear and nervousness, especially toward men, than did groups of men and women with other types of gender roles. These women also reported higher levels of anger and gratitude toward men than toward women. All of these data suggest, as is consistent with Risman's (1987) work, that the differing roles men and women play shape their daily experiences, which in turn shape their affective experiences. Of course, the reverse may also be true: Those individuals with certain types of affective predispositions may choose certain gender-stereotypic occupations and tasks to perform (e.g., those who are more fearful may choose more feminine stereotypic occupations).

Some theorists have argued that gender-stereotypic traits (e.g., nurturance), and possibly emotional expressivity itself, are biologically based (Lewis, 1985), and a heritability index for gender-related personality traits has been estimated at 20–26% (Ahern, Johnson, Wilson, McClearn, & Vandenberg, 1982). Thus gender-role-related traits and behaviors, including and in relation to emotional expressivity, may not be attributable solely to socialization practices. For example, those individuals who are more biologically predisposed to be nurturing might choose to do more human service work. However, there is also exciting and growing evidence that gender differences in emotion are indeed socialized by peers, by parents, and through language; we discuss this in the next section.

EXPLAINING GENDER DIFFERENCES

The Role of Peer Socialization

Sex-differentiated peer interaction patterns are widespread throughout development and noteworthy for the effects they may have on emotional functioning. Hall (1987), drawing on the work of Maltz and Borker (1982), argues that differences in male and female peer play may in fact account for the intergenerational socialization of gender differences in emotional functioning. Girls' play tends to occur in small, intimate groups, which minimize hostility and overt conflict and which attempt to maximize cooperation and agreement. Boys' play tends to occur in larger, status-oriented groups, which maximize conflict, aggression, and hostility, including criticism and teasing of others. Both Paley's (1984) and Tannen's (1990) descriptions of nursery school children's play vividly portray girls' tendencies to maintain affiliation and social bonding, often at the expense of individual needs, and boys' tendencies to emphasize competition and self-promotion (played out as superhero fantasies), often at the expense of cooperation and affiliation. These differing types of interactions would certainly foster different emotional skills: Girls would become adept at reading both verbal and nonverbal emotional signals, at expressing and communicating their feelings, and at minimizing anger; boys would become adept at maximizing their hostility and anger and at minimizing emotions having to do with vulnerability, guilt, fear, and hurt. Tannen (1990) points out that one-downsmanship (or downswomanship!)—that is, trying to equalize a relationship by pointing out one's own flaws and one's partner's assets—is an attempt by women to promote affiliation and bonding. Self-denigrating types of peer interactions are typical of female peer interactions; they are certainly consistent with the evidence we have reviewed that women express more intropunitive emotions than do males. (Intropunitive emotions may protect the feelings of others and therefore promote affiliation.) Thus, sex-differentiated patterns in peer interaction may play a large role in producing and maintaining the gender differences in emotional functioning we have reviewed above.

Further evidence for the power of peer interactions in affecting emotional development comes from data by Brody (in press) showing that males express more warmth when the target of their affection is women, whereas women express more anger when the target of their rage is men. This suggests the interesting possibility that gender differences in the expressivity of these two emotions (anger and warmth) are attributable to the fact that both men and women often interact in sex-differentiated situations, women spending more time in the company of other women and

men spending more time in the company of other men. Since it tends to be less socially acceptable to express anger toward women and warmth toward men (Blier & Blier-Wilson, 1989; Brody, in press), then women (who spend less time in the company of men) may learn to express less anger overall, and men (who spend less time in the company of women) may learn to express less warmth overall. Consistent with these results are data from nonverbal studies, which indicate more extreme gender differences when people interact with their own gender. When with the opposite gender, males and females each appear to accommodate to the other's behavioral style (Hall, 1984). Data showing gender differences as a function of the gender of the participant in the interaction implicate sex-differentiated peer interaction patterns as a possible etiology.

Familial Socialization Influences

In addition to peer socialization, there is of course familial socialization, including mother–child and father–child emotion interaction patterns, which researchers have found to differ greatly for boys and girls. A growing and consistent body of literature indicates that in this culture, parents both discuss emotions more with their daughters than with their sons (with the exception of anger and other outer-directed emotions, such as disgust), and also display a wider range of emotions to their daughters than to their sons. It also seems that fathers have characteristically different interaction patterns with both sons and daughters than do mothers, and may serve as objects of identification for their sons. Fathers use more demands than do mothers, more threats, and more pejorative language, especially with their sons (e.g., "you ding-a-ling"). They also interrupt the speech of their children more than mothers do and speak to them in more cognitively demanding language (Gleason, 1989). These patterns are quite similar to the male peer interaction patterns we have discussed above, and seem adaptive to a competitive role. In recent research by Fuchs and Thelen (1988), first-, fourth-, and sixth-grade children all reported that they would be more likely to express their feelings of anger and sadness to their mothers than to their fathers.

Research on mother–infant interaction with infants ranging in age from 2½ to 22 months

(Malatesta, Culver, Tesman, & Shepard, 1989) indicated that girls were exposed to a wider range of emotions than were boys, especially in a play session as opposed to conditions of child distress. Malatesta and Haviland (1982) found that mothers of 3- to 6-month-olds smiled more at their daughters than at their sons. Similarly, Parnell (1991) found that mothers displayed more positive affects to their 32-month-old daughters than to their same-aged sons, whereas 14-month-old daughters displayed both more positive and more negative affects and 32-month old-daughters displayed more positive affects to their mothers than did same-aged sons.

Some intriguing data on gender differences in the neonatal period may contribute to the gender differences in socialization we have reviewed. Cunningham and Shapiro (1984) found that infant boys were judged to be more intensely emotionally expressive than were infant girls, even when judges were misinformed about the actual sex of the infant. These provocative results suggest that girls may have to amplify their emotional expressions in order to be better understood; that is, they may have to learn to work harder at communicating their inner states, because their expressions are initially not well understood. This may partially account for female superiority at expressing and decoding affect later in development, since girls may have to learn to recognize the expressions of others in order to make sure that their own expressions are being understood. It would also help to explain why mothers display less affect to their sons (i.e., perhaps they are trying to contain the emotional expressivity of their sons), and why data have indicated that mothers are better able to match their sons' than their daughters' expressions (Tronick & Cohn, 1989).

These gender differences in socialization in the early infancy period are followed by gender differences in the preschool period. When given wordless storybooks to "read" to their preschool sons and daughters, fathers used more emotion words in creating stories for their daughters than for their sons, avoiding only the word "disgust"; mothers avoided using the term "angry" when creating a story for their daughters. Father–daughter dyads used the highest frequency of emotion words, compared to mother–son, mother–daughter, and father–son dyads (Greif, Alvarez, & Ulman, 1981; Schell & Gleason,1989). In other studies, mothers used more emotion words when interacting with their 18- to 24-month-old daughters than with their same-aged sons (Dunn, Bretherton, & Munn, 1987); in recounting shared memories, they also used more positive than negative emotion words with their preschool daughters, while using equal numbers of positive and negative emotion words with their preschool sons (Fivush, 1989). Consistent with Greif et al.'s (1981) results was Fivush's finding that mothers never spoke about anger with their daughters and did not attribute related dysphoric emotions to the daughters themselves; they also spoke more about sadness with their daughters than with their sons. Another provocative finding was that with daughters mothers discussed the emotion state itself, whereas with sons they elaborated on the causes and consequences of the feeling (processes associated with control over emotion), rather than the experience of the emotion itself.

Consistent with gender differences in the family socialization of preschoolers' emotions is a study of teacher–preschooler interactions (Botkin & Twardosz, 1988). The study found that teachers at day care centers smiled more and were more physically affectionate to girls than to boys, thus possibly giving girls more opportunities to learn about affection as a reciprocal process.

There is little research on family interaction and socialization of emotion during the school-age period. In one of the few provocative studies in this area, Fuchs and Thelen (1988) found that school-aged girls expected mothers to react more positively to the expression of sadness than to the expression of anger. School-aged boys reported that they were less likely to express sadness than were girls. They also expected that their mothers and fathers would be less likely to act warmly toward them after they expressed sadness. Fuchs and Thelen (1988) interpret their data to mean that sadness is encouraged among females and discouraged among males; conversely, anger seems to be discouraged among girls. Both findings are consistent with the preschool research.

These studies on the socialization of emotion all suggest that girls are encouraged to learn to express feelings through words and facial expressions (except anger, disgust, and related emotions, such as contempt), whereas boys are discouraged from learning to express feelings through words or facial expressions (with the possible exception of anger). Alternatively, perhaps boys never learn to substitute words for (or use words in addition to) the physiological or behavioral expression of feeling. Support for the idea that boys use different modalities for the expression and experience of their feelings, especially for emotions related to aggression, comes not only from the internalizing–externalizing data mentioned above (which indicate that males may physiologically experience emotions but may not show them in their verbal or facial expressions), but also from data on gender differences in emotion-coping strategies. Several studies have indicated that boys use more retaliatory and aggressive strategies to cope with anger than do girls (Eagly & Steffen, 1986; Fabes & Eisenberg, 1991; Whitesell, Robinson, & Harter, 1991). One can interpret this to mean that boys learn to act on their feelings, rather than to talk about them or to experience them fully.

The Role of Language

Brody (in press) argues that gender differences in the socialization of emotional expressiveness may be partly attributable to gender differences in the development of verbal language, with girls developing verbal language earlier and maintaining a language superiority throughout development (Gleason, Hay, & Cain, 1989). She cites psychoanalytic writers, who have long theorized that words can substitute for actions, a process Selma Fraiberg (1959) terms "word magic." That is, children who can learn to say "I'm angry" will be less likely to hit, bite, or use other behavioral means for the expression of anger. Since girls do learn verbal language earlier than boys do (Gleason et al., 1989)—perhaps because of subtle neuropsychological differences (one theory centers around the extent of cerebral lateralization), or perhaps because of socialization influences—it may be that in learning language earlier, girls learn to curb aggressive behavioral modes of emotional expression more readily than boys do.

Of the four modes of emotional expression, including physiological means, behavioral acting out, facial expressions and other nonverbal cues, and verbal expressions (which usually reflect a more conscious awareness of affect),

females primarily use the latter two while males primarily use the former two. The two modes used primarily by females (verbal and facial expressions) are more representative of communication signaling (with verbal expressions reflective of symbolic processes) than are the two modes used primarily by males (physiological processes and behavioral acting out). Verbal and facial expressions are also more likely to maintain social bonding and the social order than are physiological processes and behavioral acting out, and thus are consistent with stereotypic feminine gender roles.

In one of the few studies to address the relationship between affective expression and language in infancy, Bloom and her colleagues (Bloom & Capatides, 1987; Bloom, Beckwith, & Capatides, 1988) indeed found that infants who learned words earlier in development showed no change from earlier levels of nonverbal affective expression; however, those who learned words later in development increased their levels of nonverbal affective expression over their earlier levels. The sample in this study was too small to permit an analysis of gender differences in these patterns. However, it is entirely possible that the later language learners tend to be boys, who, in the process of learning to verbalize more slowly, may also learn to increase the frequency and intensity of their nonverbal expression of feelings (possibly through both behavioral and physiological means) in order to communicate their needs. This may be especially true of feelings related to anger and aggression.

Stern (1985) further posits that with the emergence of verbal language, the communication of shared experiences and meanings becomes possible, and the infant becomes publicly accountable for experiences that were once private. He goes on to hypothesize that nonverbal experiences, which are private, may become deniable both to others and to the self, merging into the unconscious. We may hypothesize that girls become more accountable to others for their internal feeling states because of an emphasis on the verbalization of feelings. Lewis (1985) similarly argues that females' language superiority may facilitate attachments to others (as well as the vocal or nonharmful control of the infant). In contrast, boys, for whom the verbalization of affects is de-emphasized, may become largely unconscious of their emotional states, both in themselves and in others.

Thus, as Brody (in press) posits, it may be that a transactional developmental model (reciprocal dyadic or systems interactions varying over time) may well explain the gender differences we see in emotional expression and nonverbal recognition. In their interactions with their sons and daughters, caretakers may bring to bear the influence of their own gender role stereotypes, as well as their own gender-differentiated interaction patterns (possibly shaped by peer, school, and familial influences). These patterns may well be unconscious, as discussed by Hall (1987). Furthermore, their sons and their daughters may interact differently with them from early on. Their sons' emotional expressions may be more intense, and hence easier for them to interpret and match. They may wish to constrain their sons' expressiveness, both in accordance with the gender role norms of the culture and as an adaptive response to their sons' initial temperament. Their daughters may verbalize more and display their emotions less intensely through facial expressions and behaviors. Parents may adapt to their daughters' initial temperament by displaying more emotions to their daughters in order to encourage their facial expressivity. Parents may also talk to their daughters about emotions more, again both in accordance with the gender role norms of the culture and in response to their daughters' early verbal facility. Thus, parents may bring their own gender role stereotypes to bear on their interactions with their children, partly in response to the subtle neuropsychological and genetic differences between their sons and their daughters. Whatever the origins, it seems that males and females learn to use affect language differently, which "inevitably structures" their experience of reality (Hare-Mustin & Marecek, 1988).

CONCLUDING THOUGHTS

In reviewing the literature in preparation for this chapter, we were repeatedly surprised by the consistency of the literature across several types of data. For example, gender stereotypes in emotional functioning were frequently borne out by systematic data on actual patterns of behavior; gender differences in peer and family socialization patterns matched later gender differences documented in emotional expression, experience, and recognition (to an almost unprecedented extent, in our experience); and gender differences in the intensity and frequency of specific emotions (e.g., anger vs. sadness) were documented across several different types of emotional functioning, including recognition, expression, and experience.

The evidence indicates that females are superior to males both at recognizing feelings in others and at verbally and facially expressing a wide variety of feelings themselves. Anger and some other outer-directed emotions (e.g., contempt and disgust) sometimes appear as exceptions to this general pattern. Gender differences in such emotions may be situationally, and perhaps culturally, specific.

Gender differences in emotional functioning are undoubtedly partly rooted in peer and family socialization patterns, in which a wider variety of emotions are displayed to and discussed more with infant and preschool girls than with boys, and in which intimate peer relationships are normative for girls whereas hierarchical, status-oriented peer relationships are normative for boys. The gender differences we have documented are also consistent with (and have been found to be related to) the differing gender roles that males and females play in this culture. We have further suggested that they may be attributable to the early verbal language superiority of females, which may set up a transactional pattern whereby parents verbalize about emotions more to their daughters than to their sons. Females may thus tend to become more publicly accountable for their feelings, whereas males may tend to deny emotions, both to others and perhaps even to themselves.

NEW DIRECTIONS FOR RESEARCH

First, we would like to point out that in this culture emotional functioning cannot be generalized across the two sexes, and that research on emotion should always incorporate gender as a consideration. Further research in several areas would help to illuminate our understanding of the relation between gender and emotion. The bidirectional nature of the relation between gender-based stereotypes about emotion and actual emotional functioning could be productively elaborated (Hall & Briton, 1993).

Cross-cultural research would help us to understand the universality versus cultural specificity of the gender differences we have reviewed. In particular, cross-cultural explorations of gender differences in peer, family, and teacher emotion socialization patterns would be especially interesting. Although the literature on gender differences in emotion socialization has only just begun to be developed, it has already borne a great deal of fruit, and more research in this area seems especially worthwhile. Prospective longitudinal studies of the socialization of gender differences in emotion, though costly, would provide a new source of data about the developmental processes that may be at work in producing the findings we have reviewed.

Research on individual differences in emotional functioning within each gender, assessed in relation to other personality variables (such as gender role or language capabilities), would help us to better understand the origins and extent of gender differences. Furthermore, it would be helpful for research to try to address in meaningful ways the thorny issue of the relationship between emotional expression and emotional experience. The facial feedback hypothesis would suggest that people's facial expressions directly affect their experience of emotion (Strack, Stepper, & Martin, 1988). A study of how facial feedback might serve to amplify or constrain the frequency or intensity of individual women's and men's emotional experiences would be a fascinating area for further study.

REFERENCES

Ahern, F. M., Johnson, R. C., Wilson, J. R., McClearn, G. E., & Vandenberg, S. G. (1982). Family resemblances in personality. *Behavior Genetics, 12,* 261–280.

Allen, J. G., & Haccoun, D. M. (1976). Sex differences in emotionality: A multidimensional approach. *Human Relations, 29,* 711–722.

Antill, J. R. (1987). Parents' beliefs and values about sex roles, sex differences, and sexuality: Their sources and implications. *Review of Personality and Social Psychology, 7,* 294–328.

Averill, J. R. (1983). Studies on anger and aggression: Implications for theories of emotion. *American Psychologist, 38,* 1145–1160

Balswick, J., & Avertt, C. P. (1977). Differences in expressiveness: Gender, interpersonal orientation, and perceived parental expressiveness as contributing factors. *Journal of Marriage and the Family, 39,* 121–127.

Bander, R. S., & Betz, N. E. (1981). The relationship of sex and sex role to trait and situationally specific anxiety types. *Journal of Research in Personality, 15,* 312–322.

Birnbaum, D. W. (1983). Preschoolers' stereotypes about sex differences in emotionality: A reaffirmation. *Journal of Genetic Psychology, 143,* 139–140.

Birnbaum, D. W., & Croll, W. L. (1984). The etiology of children's stereotypes about sex differences in emotionality. *Sex Roles, 10,* 677–691.

Bleier, R. (1991). Gender ideology and the brain: Sex differences research. In M. Notman & C. Nadelson (Eds.), *Women and men: New perspectives on gender differences* (pp. 63–73). Washington, DC: American Psychiatric Press.

Blier, M. J., & Blier-Wilson, L. A. (1989). Gender differences in self-rated emotional expressiveness. *Sex Roles, 21,* 287–295.

Bloom, L., Beckwith, R., & Capatides, J. (1988). Developments in the expression of affect. *Infant Behavior and Development, 11,* 169–186.

Bloom, L., & Capatides, J. B. (1987). Expression of affect and the emergence of language. *Child Development, 58,* 1513–1522.

Botkin, D., & Twardosz, S. (1988). Early childhood teachers' affectionate behavior: Differential expression to female children, male children, and groups of children. *Early Childhood Research Quarterly, 3,* 167–177.

Briton, N. J., & Hall, J. A. (1992). *Perceived gender differences in nonverbal communication.* Manuscript submitted for publication.

Brody, L. R. (1985). Gender differences in emotional development: A review of theories and research. *Journal of Personality, 53,* 102–149.

Brody, L. R. (in press). On understanding gender differences in the expression of emotion: Gender roles, socialization and language. In S. Ablon, D. Brown, E. Khantzian, & J. Mack (Eds.), *Human feelings: Explorations in affect development and meaning.* New York: Analytic Press.

Brody, L. R., & Flanagan, L. (1992). *Gender role stereotypic occupations, personality attributes, household behaviors and fear in women and men.* Manuscript submitted for publication.

Brody, L. R., Hay, D., & Vandewater, E. (1990). Gender, gender role identity and children's reported feelings toward the same and opposite sex. *Sex Roles, 3,* 363–387.

Buck, R. (1984). *The communication of emotion.* New York: Guilford Press.

Condry J., & Condry, S. (1976). Sex differences: A study of the eye of the beholder. *Child Development, 47,* 812–819.

Cunninghan, J., & Shapiro, L. (1984). *Infant affective expression as a function of infant and adult gender.* Unpublished manuscript, Brandeis University.

Deaux, K., & Major, B. (1987). Putting gender into context: An interactive model of gender-related behavior. *Psychological Review, 94,* 369–389.

Diener, E., & Emmons, R. A. (1984). The independence of positive and negative affect. *Journal of Personality and Social Psychology, 47,* 1105–1117.

Diener, E., Larsen, R. J., Levine, S., & Emmons, R. A. (1985). Intensity and frequency: Dimensions underlying positive and negative affect. *Journal of Personality and Social Psychology, 48,* 1253–1265.

Diener, E., Sandvik, E., & Larsen, R. J. (1985). Age and sex effects for emotional intensity. *Developmental Psychology, 21,* 542–546.

Dillon, K. M., Wolf, E., & Katz, H. (1985). Sex roles, gender, and fear. *Journal of Psychology, 119,* 355–359.

Dindia, K., & Allen, M. (1992). Sex differences in self-disclosure: A meta-analysis. *Psychological Bulletin, 112,* 106–124.

Dosser, D. A., Jr., Balswick, J. O., & Halverson, C. F., Jr. (1983). Situational content of emotional expressions. *Journal of Counseling Psychology, 30*, 375–387.

Dunn, J., Bretherton, I., & Munn, P. (1987). Conversations about feeling states) between mothers and their children. *Developmental Psychology, 23*, 132–139.

Eagly, A. H. (1987). Sex differences in social behavior: A social-role interpretation. Hillsdale, NJ: Erlbaum.

Eagly, A. H., & Steffen, V. J. (1986). Gender and aggressive behavior: A meta-analytic review of the social psychological literature. *Psychological Bulletin, 100*, 309–330.

Eisenberg, N., & Lennon, R. (1983). Sex differences in empathy and related constructs. *Psychological Bulletin, 94*, 100–131.

Fabes. R. A., & Eisenberg, N. (1991, April). *Children's coping with interpersonal anger: Individual and situational correlates.* Poster presented at the biennial meeting of the Society for Research in Child Development. Seattle.

Fabes, R. A., & Martin, C. J. (1991). Gender and age stereotypes of emotionality. *Personality and Social Psychology Bulletin, 17*, 532–540.

Fivush, R. (1989). Exploring sex differences in the emotional content of mother–child conversations about the past. *Sex Roles, 20*, 675–691.

Fraiberg, S. (1959). *The magic years.* New York: Scribner's.

Fuchs, D., & Thelen, M. (1988). Children's expected interpersonal consequences of communicating their affective state and reported likelihood of expression. *Child Development, 59*, 1314–1322.

Fujita, F., Diener, E., & Sandvik, E. (1991). Gender differences in negative affect and well-being: The case for emotional intensity. *Journal of Personality and Social Psychology, 61*, 427–434.

Ganong, L., & Coleman, M. (1985). Sex, sex roles and emotional expressiveness. *Journal of Genetic Psychology, 146*, 405–411.

Gleason, J. (1989). Sex differences in parent–child interaction. In S. Philips, S. Steele, & C. Tanz (Eds.), *Language, gender, and sex in comparative perspective* (pp. 189–199). Cambridge, England: Cambridge University Press.

Gleason, J. B., Hay, D., & Cain, L. (1989). Social and affective determinants of language acquisition. In M. L. rice & L. Schiefelbusch (Eds.), *The teachability of language* (pp. 171–186). Baltimore: Paul H. Brookes.

Greif, E., Alvarez, M., & Ulman, K. (1981, April). *Recognizing emotions in other people: Sex differences in socialization.* Paper presented at the biennial meeting of the Society for Research in Child Development. Boston.

Hall, J. A. (1978). Gender effects in decoding nonverbal cues. *Psychological Bulletin, 85*, 845–857.

Hall, J. A. (1984). *Nonverbal sex differences: Communication accuracy and expressive style.* Baltimore: Johns Hopkins University Press.

Hall, J. A. (1987). On explaining gender differences: The case of nonverbal communication. *Review of Personality and Social Psychology, 7*, 177–200.

Hall, J. A., & Briton, N. J. (1993). Gender, nonverbal behavior, and expectations. In P. D. Blanck (Ed.), *Interpersonal expectations: Theory, research and applications.* Cambridge, England: Cambridge Unviersity Press.

Hall, J. A., & Halberstadt, A. G. (1986). Smiling and gazing. In J. S. Hyde & M. C. Linn (Eds.), *The psychology of gender: Advances through meta-analysis* (pp. 136–158). Baltimore: Johns Hopkins University Press.

Hall, J. A., & Halberstadt, A. G. (1992). *"Subordination" and sensitivity to nonverbal cues: A study of married, working women.* Manuscript submitted for publication.

Hare-Mustin, R. T., & Maracek, J. (1988). The meaning of difference. *American Psychologist, 43*, 455–464.

Ingram, R., Cruet, D., Johnson, B., & Wisnicki, K. (1988). Self-focused attention, gender, gender role, and vulnerability to negative affect. *Journal of Personality and Social Psychology, 55*, 967–978.

Johnson, J. T., & Shulman, G. A. (1988). More alike than meets the eye: Perceived gender differences in subjective experience and its display. *Sex Roles, 19*, 67–79.

Johnson-George, C., & Swap, W. C. (1982). Measurement of specific interpersonal trust: Construction and validation of a scale to assess trust in a specific other. *Journal of Personality and Social Psychology, 43*, 1306–1317.

Jordan, J. (1986). *The meaning of mutuality* (Work in Progress No. 23). Wellesley, MA: Stone Center Working Papers Series.

Lewis, E. T., & McCarthy, P. R. (1988). Perceptions of self-disclosure as a function of gender-linked variables. *Sex Roles, 19*, 47–56.

Lewis, H. B. (1985). Depression vs. paranoia: Why are there sex differences in mental illness? *Journal of Personality, 53*, 150–178.

Malatesta, C. Z. (1990). The role of emotions in the development and organization of personality. In R. Thompson (Ed.), *Nebraska Symposium on Motivation: Vol. 36. Socioemotional development* (pp. 1–55). Lincoln: University of Nebraska Press.

Malatesta, C. Z., Culver, C., Tesman, J., & Shepard, B. (1989). The development of emotion expression during the first two years of life. *Monographs of the Society for Research in Child Development, 50*(1–2, Serial No. 219).

Malatesta, C. Z., & Haviland, J. M. (1982). Learning display rules: The socialization of emotion expression in infancy. *Child Development, 53*, 991–1003.

Maltz, D. N., & Borker, R. A. (1982). A cultural approach to male–female miscommunication. In J. Gumperz (Ed.), *Language and social identity* (pp. 195–216). Cambridge, England: Cambridge University Press.

Matlin, M. W., & Gawron, V. J. (1979). Individual differences in Pollyannaism. *Journal of Personality Assessment, 43*, 411–412.

Narus, L. R., & Fischer, J. L. (1981). Sex roles and intimacy in same and other sex relationships. *Psychology of Women Quarterly, 5*, 444–455.

Orlofsky, J. L., & Windle, M. T. (1978). Sex role orientation, behavioral adaptability and personal adjustment. *Sex Roles, 4*, 801–811.

Paley, V. G. (1984). *Boys and girls: Superheroes in the doll corner.* Chicago: University of Chicago Press.

Parnell, K. (1991). *Toddler interaction in relation to mother and peers.* Unpublished doctoral dissertation, Boston University.

Rehm, L. P. (1978). Mood, pleasant events, and unpleasant events: Two pilot studies. *Journal of Consulting and Clinical Psychology, 46*, 854–859.

Reis, H. T., Senchak, M., & Solomon, B. (1985). Sex differences in the intimacy of social interaction: Further examination of potential explanations. *Journal of Personality and Social Psychology, 48*, 1204–1217.

Risman, B. J. (1987). Intimate relationships from a microstructural perspective: Men who mother. *Gender and Society, 1*, 6–32.

Rosenthal, R., Hall, J. A., DiMatteo, M. R., Rogers, P. L.,

& Archer, D. (1979). *Sensitivity to nonverbal communication: The PONS test.* Baltimore: Johns Hopkins University Press.

Ross, C. E., & Mirowsky, J. (1984). Men who cry. *Social Psychology Quarterly, 47,* 138–146.

Rotter, N. G., & Rotter, G. S. (1988). Sex differences in the encoding and decoding of negative facial emotions. *Journal of Nonverbal Behavior, 12,* 139–148.

Ruddick, S. (1982). Maternal thinking. In B. Thorne & M. Yalon (Eds.), *Rethinking the family* (pp. 76–94). New York: Longman.

Schell, A., & Gleason, J. B. (1989, December). *Gender differences in the acquisition of the vocabulary of emotion.* Paper presented at the annual meeting of the American Association of Applied Linguistics, Washington, DC.

Shields, S. A. (1986). Are women "emotional"? In C. Tavris (Ed.), *Everywoman's emotional well being* (pp. 131–147). New York: Doubleday.

Shields, S. A. (1987). Women, men, and the dilemma of emotion. *Review of Personality and Social Psychology, 7,* 229–250.

Shields, S. A. (1990). Conceptualising the biology–culture relationship in emotion: An analogy with gender. *Cognition and Emotion, 4,* 359–374.

Shields, S. A. (1991). Gender in the psychology of emotion: A selective research review. In K. I. Strongman (Ed.), *International review of studies on emotion* (Vol. 1, pp. 227–245). Chichester, England: Wiley.

Shields, S. A., & Koster, B. A. (1989). Emotional stereotyping of parents in child rearing manuals, 1915–1980. *Social Psychology Quarterly, 52,* 44–55.

Snell, W. E., Jr., Miller, R. S., & Belk, S. S. (1988). Development of the Emotional Self-Disclosure Scale. *Sex Roles, 18,* 59–73.

Sommers, S., & Kosmitzki, C. (1988). Emotion and social context: An American–German comparison. *British Journal of Social Psychology, 27,* 35–49.

Spence, J. T., Helmreich, R., & Stapp, J. (1975). Ratings of self and peers on sex role attributes and their relation to self-esteem and conceptions of masculinity and femininity. *Journal of Personality and Social Psychology, 32,* 29–39.

Stapley, J. C., & Haviland, J. M. (1989). Beyond depression: Gender differences in normal adolescents' emotional experiences. *Sex Roles, 20,* 295–308.

Stern, D. (1985). *The interpersonal world of the infant.* New York: Basic Books.

Strack, F., Stepper, S., & Martin, L. (1988). Inhibiting and facilitating conditions of the human smile: A nonobtrusive test of the facial feedback hypothesis. *Journal of Personality and Social Psychology, 54,* 768–778.

Tangney, J. P. (1990). Assessing individual differences in proneness to shame and guilt: Development of the Self Conscious Affect and Attribution Inventory. *Journal of Personality and Social Psychology, 59,* 102–111.

Tannen, D. (1990). *You just don't understand.* New York: Ballantine Books.

Taylor, D. A., & Hinds, M. (1985). Disclosure reciprocity and liking as a function of gender and personalism. *Sex Roles, 12,* 1137–1153.

Tronick, E., & Cohn, J. (1989). Infant–mother face to face interaction: Age and gender differences in the coordination and occurrence of miscoordination. *Child Development, 60,* 85–92.

Unger, R. K. (1979). Toward a redefinition of sex and gender. *American Psychologist, 34,* 1085–1094.

Vrugt, A., & Kerkstra, A. (1984). Sex differences in nonverbal communication. *Semiotica, 50,* 1–41.

Wagner, H. L., MacDonald, C. J., & Manstead, A. S. R. (1986). Communication of individual emotions by spontaneous facial expressions. *Journal of Personality and Social Psychology, 50,* 737–743.

Warr, P. B. (1971). Pollyanna's personal judgments. *European Journal of Social Psychology, 1,* 327–338.

Whitesell, N. R., Robinson, N. S., & Harter, S. (1991, April). *Anger in early adolescence: Prototypical causes and gender differences in coping strategies.* Poster presented at the biennial meeting of the Society for Research in Child Development, Seattle.

Wintre, M. G., Polivy, J., & Murray, M. (1990). Self predictions of emotional response patterns: Age, sex, and situational determinants. *Child Development, 61,* 1124–1133.

Wood, W., Rhodes, N., & Whelan, M. (1989). Sex differences in positive well-being: A consideration of emotional style and marital status. *Psychological Bulletin, 106,* 249–264.

Zuckerman, M., DeFrank, R. S., Spiegel, N. H., & Larrance, D. T. (1982). Masculinity–femininity and encoding of nonverbal cues. *Journal of Personality and Social Psychology, 42,* 548–556.

Zuckerman, M., & Larrance, D. T. (1979). Individual differences in perceived encoding and decoding abilities. In R. Rosenthal (Ed.), *Skill in nonverbal communication: Individual differences* (pp. 171–203). Cambridge, MA: Oelgeschlager, Gunn & Hain.

32

Emotion and Attitude Change

STEVEN J. BRECKLER

Emotion-related functioning plays a central role in the persuasion process. Attitudes are often established and changed by repeated associations between an attitude object and a state of affective or emotional arousal. Emotional appeals are common in advertising and political rhetoric, and such appeals can produce changes both in one's feelings associated with an attitude object and in one's beliefs about it. The affective component of attitude can be changed even by persuasive communications that depend primarily on logical or "rational" argumentation. And recent research suggests that a message recipient's mood during exposure to a persuasive communication can influence that person's ability or motivation to scrutinize the information.

This chapter begins with a review of how emotions have been considered in models of attitude structure and change. Emotions form an integral component of attitude structure, and models of attitude change specify several ways in which emotions may participate in the persuasion process. The chapter then turns to a review of the empirical literature on emotions and attitude change. Research in this area has been active, and benefits from a variety of theoretical and empirical approaches. The chapter concludes with suggestions for future research and theoretical integration.

EMOTION IN MODELS OF ATTITUDE STRUCTURE AND CHANGE

Emotion in the Structure of Attitudes

An attitude is generally defined as "a learned predisposition to respond in a consistently favorable or unfavorable manner with respect to a given object" (Fishbein & Ajzen, 1975, p. 6). Some definitions accord relatively little status to emotion-related processes, such as McGuire's (1985) definition of attitudes as "responses that locate objects of thought on dimensions of judgment" (p. 239). Other theorists assign a central role to emotional functioning, such as Petty and Cacioppo (1981), who define attitude as "a general and enduring positive or negative feeling about some person, object, or issue" (p. 7).

The structure of individual attitudes has been the focus of recent theoretical and empirical attention (see McGuire, 1989; Pratkanis, Breckler, & Greenwald, 1989; Zanna & Rempel, 1988). Central to many of the recent treatments is the classic tripartite model of attitude structure, according to which attitudes consist of affective, cognitive,[1] and behavioral components (Katz & Stotland, 1959; Rosenberg & Hovland, 1960). Several studies provide empirical support for the three-component distinction (e.g., Breckler, 1984; Kothandapani, 1971; Ostrom, 1969). Other studies have focused more specifically on the affect–cognition distinction, demonstrating that the two attitude components enjoy unique relationships with behavior (Breckler & Wiggins, 1989b; Millar

---

[1] I prefer to use the term "evaluative" instead of "cognitive" to emphasize that this component of attitude refers to judgments *about* an attitude object. The term "cognition" in this context is misleading, because in its broadest sense cognition includes emotion-related functioning (see Breckler & Wiggins, 1989a, 1989b). For purposes of this chapter, I use the term "cognition" (as most attitude theorists continue to do), with the understanding that I am referring more narrowly to thoughts, beliefs, and propositions about an attitude object.

& Tesser, 1986, 1989; Wilson & Dunn, 1986) and that affect and cognition play distinct roles in the persuasion process (Breckler & Wiggins, 1991; Millar & Millar, 1990).

The tripartite model, and the affect–cognition distinction in particular, suggest that attitudes can be represented in multiple forms (see Breckler & Wiggins, 1989a). Thus, the cognitive component of attitude represents thoughts, beliefs, and judgments about an attitude object, whereas the affective component represents emotional experiences and feelings aroused by an attitude object (Breckler & Berman, 1991). According to this view, affective experience does not necessarily depend on verbalized knowledge (see Breckler & Wiggins, 1989a; Buck, 1985; Zajonc, 1980; Zajonc & Markus, 1982, 1984).

Attitudes can differ in the extent to which they are based on affective versus cognitive components (see Millar & Millar, 1990). In developing a typology of attitudes, Katz and Stotland (1959) distinguished between "affective associations" and "intellectualized attitudes." Affective associations develop when an attitude object has been paired with some form of need satisfaction; such associations can be independent of a person's belief systems and knowledge structures. In contrast, intellectualized attitudes develop out of a need to understand, organize, and integrate information about one's world in a realistic and coherent fashion.

A person's attitude toward a given object typically (but not necessarily) includes a mixture of both affective and cognitive components. People are generally motivated to maintain some degree of consistency between the various elements of an attitude (e.g., Insko & Schopler, 1967; Rosenberg, 1965). Katz and Stotland (1959) assumed, however, that the affective component of attitude has some priority over the cognitive component. That is, an inconsistency between affect and cognition is most readily resolved by changes in cognitive structure rather than by a change in affect.

Emotion in Models
of the Persuasion Process

Most persuasion research derives from the Yale message-learning approach (Hovland, Janis, & Kelley, 1953), according to which a persuasive communication is most effective when its recipient *attends* to and *comprehends*

the message, *yields* to the advocated position, and *remembers* the conclusion. Cognitive response theory (Greenwald, 1968; Petty, Ostrom, & Brock, 1981) suggests that recipient-generated thoughts are the critical determinants of attitude change, and that such thoughts need not be related to message content. Although other approaches have been taken to the study of attitude change (see Petty & Cacioppo, 1981), the majority of them are based on theories that emphasize some aspect of information processing (Eagly & Chaiken, 1984).

Research on the persuasion process is currently dominated by two models: the "elaboration likelihood model" (ELM; Petty & Cacioppo, 1986) and the "heuristic–systematic model" (HSM; Chaiken, Liberman, & Eagly, 1989). Both models share the fundamental assumption that people want to hold correct, valid, and accurate attitudes. When a message recipient is motivated to scrutinize a persuasive communication, and when the situation permits issue-relevant thinking and elaboration, attitude change is achieved through a change in cognitive structure. This process is defined as "systematic processing" by the HSM and as "central-route persuasion" by the ELM, and is most applicable in the case of intellectualized attitudes.

It is often the case that message recipients are not strongly motivated to scrutinize or engage in deep elaboration of the arguments in a persuasive communication: The issue may be perceived as unimportant, or the message recipient may not want to expend the necessary cognitive effort. The situation can also interfere with message-relevant thought, as often happens when the message recipient is distracted or occupied with other tasks. Nevertheless, features of the persuasion setting may provide a basis for attitude change. For example, message recipients can rely on simple inferential rules or heuristic devices to make attitudinal judgments without having to engage in deep processing of message content. Thus, by applying the simple rule that "Experts can be trusted," a message recipient can decide to accept arguments attributed to experts and to reject arguments attributed to nonexperts. This form of attitude change is defined by the HSM as "heuristic processing" and by the ELM as "peripheral-route persuasion," but it is still most applicable in the case of intellectualized attitudes.

The ELM identifies additional mechanisms through which peripheral-route persuasion can be achieved, such as the repeated pairing of an attitude object with an affectively arousing stimulus. In these cases, attitude change may occur in the absence of issue-relevant thought and without the use of judgmental heuristics. Thus, the ELM can also be applied in the case of affective associations, which are changed by new associations rather than by a modification of cognitive structure (Katz & Stotland, 1959).

Petty, Gleicher, and Baker (1991) identify multiple potential roles for affect in the persuasion process (see also Cacioppo & Petty, 1989; Petty, Cacioppo, & Kasmer, 1988; Petty, Cacioppo, Sedikides, & Strathman, 1988). Under conditions that promote systematic processing or elaboration, affect can play two distinct roles. First, one's affective responses to the attitude object or advocated position may serve as information, to be scrutinized and considered along with other relevant information in the setting. Second, affective or emotional processes that are coincidentally aroused in the persuasion setting may influence the nature, course, or extent of issue- and message-relevant thought (see Isen, 1984). Under conditions that discourage or prevent systematic processing or elaboration, Petty et al. (1991) suggest that affective responses can serve as simple peripheral cues. Thus, positive affect should promote more favorable attitudes and negative affect less favorable attitudes.

RESEARCH ON EMOTION AND ATTITUDE CHANGE

Classical Conditioning

Attitudes are frequently established and changed by repeated pairings of the attitude object with an affectively arousing stimulus or event. Mass media advertising offers numerous illustrations: Consumer products are often and consistently paired with pleasant scenes, uplifting music, and desirable social images. It is hoped that, over time, the presentation of an initially neutral or even a disliked product will begin to elicit a favorable affective response. Affective associations rather than intellectualized attitudes (Katz & Stotland, 1959) appear to be the primary targets for classical conditioning procedures.

An early experiment on classical conditioning of attitudes was reported by Razran (1940),

who presented a number of sociopolitical slogans as subjects were enjoying a free lunch or as subjects were inhaling putrid odors. After five to eight of these conditioning trials, the subjects were asked to rate their personal approval for each slogan. Compared to pretest measures, slogans that had been associated with a free lunch showed increases in approval, and those that had been paired with unpleasant odors showed decreases in approval.

Staats and Staats (1958) conducted the classic experiments in this area. The conditioned stimuli (CSs) were national names ("Dutch," "Swedish") or personal names ("Tom," "Bill"), and the unconditioned stimuli (USs) were evaluatively loaded words (e.g., "happy," "ugly"). The CS names were presented visually, followed by one of the US words read aloud by the experimenter. The subjects were assigned the task of learning both the visually and the auditorily presented words. One CS was paired with evaluatively favorable words on 18 trials, and the other CS was paired with evaluatively unfavorable words on 18 trials. The remaining 72 trials involved pairings of other names with affectively neutral words (e.g., "chair"). When subjects were later asked to rate the pleasantness of each CS name, the name was rated as more pleasant when it had been paired with favorable rather than unfavorable US words.

Page (1969) suggested that this evaluative conditioning effect was an artifact of demand characteristics. Page reported an experiment in which evaluative conditioning occurred only when subjects were aware of the CS-US contingency and when they had some basis for knowing the expected results. Staats (1969) discounted the experimental demand explanation, and several studies have effectively demonstrated that evaluative conditioning does not depend on demand awareness (e.g., Berkowitz & Knurek, 1969; Insko & Oakes, 1966; Zanna, Kiesler, & Pilkonis, 1970; Zellner, Rozin, Aron, & Kulish, 1983; but see Page & Kahle, 1976). The importance of contingency awareness, however, has not been so easily resolved. Some experiments indicate that awareness of the CS-US contingency is required for evaluative conditioning to occur (e.g., Insko & Oakes, 1966; Allen & Janiszewski, 1989), although it is not clear that this contradicts a classical conditioning explanation (Staats, 1969). Other recent experiments, however, suggest that evaluative conditioning may not depend on contingency awareness (Baeyens, Eelen, & van den Bergh, 1990; Krosnick, Betz, Jussim, & Lynn, 1992; Martin & Levey, 1978; but see Shanks & Dickinson, 1990).

The emerging picture is that attitudes can be classically conditioned, and that the process depends on relatively simple affective mechanisms (Eagly & Chaiken, 1993). Indeed, several recent studies indicate that evaluative conditioning procedures are most effective when the attitude object is novel (rather than familiar) and when knowledge about the attitude object is not well integrated in memory (e.g., Shimp, Stuart, & Engle, 1991). In these cases, classical conditioning procedures appear to cause a change in attitudes that is best described as peripheral-route persuasion (Petty & Cacioppo, 1986). Along these lines, Cacioppo, Marshall-Goodell, Tassinary, and Petty (1992) paired words and pronounceable nonwords (CSs) with mild electric shocks (USs). The CSs were selected for each subject so that both the word and the pronounceable nonword were initially rated at the midpoint of a 9-point pleasant–unpleasant scale. Results showed an evaluative conditioning effect for both words, but the effect was clearly stronger for the pronounceable nonword.

Fear and Threat Appeals

Persuasive communications are often designed to scare people into compliance with an advocated course of action. This approach is commonly used to promote healthful behaviors (e.g., "If you exercise regularly, eat a balanced diet, and don't smoke, then the chances of developing heart disease, obesity, and lung cancer are greatly reduced"). Public safety communications warn about the undesirable consequences of failing to wear seatbelts; insurance companies relate the tragic stories of parents who compromised their own children's welfare by failing to purchase life insurance; and manufacturers of home alarm systems dramatize the horror and sense of violation that occurs when one's home has been burglarized.

Theory and research on fear appeals can be traced to the Yale persuasion researchers, who used a "drive model" to explain the effects of fear arousal on attitude change (Hovland et al., 1953; Janis & Feshbach, 1953, 1954). According to the drive model, people are motivated to avoid or reduce unpleasant emotions that are aroused by threatening communications. Message acceptance will be reinforced and should be accompanied by a change in attitude if rehearsal of the advocated position helps to ameliorate the aversive emotional state. The advocated position may be rejected, however, if its acceptance does not sufficiently diminish or remove the perceived threat, if the level of arousal is so intense that it interferes with message comprehension, or if the threat is so great that it elicits a defensive avoidance response.

In an elaboration of the drive model, Janis (1967) suggested that a family of inverted-U-shaped curves describes the relationship between level of fear arousal and probability of message acceptance. According to the "family-of-curves model," the likelihood of message acceptance increases with increasing fear arousal until the arousal reaches some optimal level, after which message acceptance decreases with further increases in fear arousal. As Janis (1967) described it, a central problem for research was to identify the content, situational, and predispositional factors that determine the optimal level of arousal.

The drive model was consistent with Janis and Feshbach's (1953) experiment, in which mild versions of a fear appeal were found to be more effective than a strong and vivid appeal. However, additional research on fear appeals failed to support the family-of-curves model, suggesting instead that increasing fear generally produces greater message acceptance (Higbee, 1969; Sutton, 1982). The family-of-curves model was also criticized because of its silence on what determines the optimal level of arousal and because of the difficulty associated with disconfirming an inverted-U-shaped function (Leventhal, 1970).

In an effort to improve upon the drive model, Leventhal (1970) proposed a "parallel-response model" to explain the effects of fear communications. According to this model, people can respond in a number of distinct and potentially independent ways to the perception of an environmental threat or danger. In particular, the parallel-response model distinguishes between "adaptive behaviors" and "emotional behaviors." Adaptive behaviors are associated with "danger control," which includes the development of favorable attitudes toward the advocated position, evaluations of alternative instrumental actions, and decisions to take protective action. Emotional behaviors are associated with "fear control," which includes avoidance reactions and other efforts to control the aversive arousal.

The parallel-response model (Leventhal, 1970) indicates that adaptive responses to a perceived threat do not necessarily depend on emotional arousal. Adaptive and emotional responses are often correlated, but this occurs because both classes of behavior are in response to a common source of environmental stimulation and not because one causes the other. Thus, the effectiveness of a fear appeal depends primarily on danger control (i.e., motivating the message recipient to control the perceived threat). Fear control processes may disrupt or interfere with adaptive behavior; they may facilitate adaptive responding; or they may have no adaptive significance with regard to the perceived threat.

An important contribution of the parallel-response model is its distinction between danger control and fear control. In particular, the process of danger control suggests that a message recipient can extract information from a fear appeal, evaluate the efficacy of advocated coping responses, and act accordingly. "Protection motivation theory" (Rogers, 1975; Rogers & Mewborn, 1976) helped to formalize this view by offering an expectancy–value analysis of fear appeals. Rogers (1975) suggested that fear appeals communicate three important categories of information: (1) severity of the threat, (2) likelihood of the threat's occurrence, and (3) efficacy of the advocated protective response. Thus, a fear appeal will be most effective when a threat is depicted as severe and as likely to occur, but as one that can be effectively avoided. According to this view, emotional arousal (fear) has a direct influence on perceived severity of threat, but it does not directly influence attitudes or behavior (Rogers, 1983).

"Response efficacy" appears to be an important component of the danger control process. Recipients of a fear appeal must be convinced that the advocated coping response is an effective way to reduce or avoid the perceived threat. In addition, however, message recipients must be convinced that they are capable of performing the recommended action. Beck and Frankel (1981) refer to this as "personal efficacy," and Rogers (1983) now includes "self-efficacy" in a revised version of protection motivation theory.

Theorists have been quick to dismiss the drive model, offering to replace it with models that emphasize parallel responses (Leventhal, 1970), protection motivation (Rogers, 1975, 1983; Tanner, Hunt, & Eppright, 1991), or subjective expected utilities (Sutton, 1982; Sutton & Eiser, 1984). What is most noteworthy about this theoretical evolution is that emotional arousal is no longer viewed as having any direct influence on attitudes or behavior. Fear arousal may have a moderating effect on perceived severity of a threat, but in some cases it may reflect nothing more than a coincidental response to a persuasive communication.

It is possible that theorists have been too eager in assigning fear a subordinate role in the persuasion process. The main effect is regularly obtained: Increasing fear is associated with greater attitude change. Although the drive model's postulated reinforcement mechanism has not been supported in research, other features of the drive model may offer important insight in accounting for the fear–persuasion relationship (Eagly & Chaiken, 1993). Most importantly, fear arousal may influence one's ability or motivation to scrutinize message content, and may therefore be a significant determinant of systematic or central-route processing versus heuristic or peripheral-route processing (Gleicher & Petty, 1992; Jepson & Chaiken, 1990).

Other Forms of Emotion-Arousing Communications

Research on fear appeals represents the largest concentrated effort to understand the persuasive impact of emotion-arousing communications. Clearly, persuasive communications are often designed to arouse emotions other than fear. It is not unusual for appeals to elicit excitement, joy, anger, or disgust. Nevertheless, research on emotion-arousing communications has focused primarily on fear, to the exclusion of other discrete or fundamental emotions (see Izard, 1977; Plutchik, 1984; Tomkins, 1984). A general exception is research on advertising, but even here the focus is at the level of "feeling effects" or "warmth" engendered by advertising, rather than on a discrete emotional response (e.g., Aaker, Stayman, & Hagerty, 1986; Batra, 1986; Mitchell, 1988).

Roseman, Abelson, and Ewing (1986) introduced an "emotional resonance hypothesis" to help understand the effects of emotional appeals in political communication. According to the resonance hypothesis, the most effective appeals are those that arouse emotions matching or resonating with the emotional proclivity of the message recipient. Roseman et al. reported three studies that provided partial support for the hypothesis. For example, appeals to pity seemed to work best for audiences who were disposed to feel pity. However, not all of the discrete emotions examined by Roseman et al. (hope, fear, pity, anger) showed evidence in support of the resonance hypothesis.

Emotional versus Rational Appeals

It is natural to ask whether appeals based on emotion are any more or less effective than appeals based on well-reasoned and coherent arguments. Instances of both approaches are easily found in consumer product advertising. Image-based ads associate desirable personal, social, and emotional images with a product, even though the image may have nothing to do with the product itself. In contrast, quality-based ads establish the utility of a product by emphasizing its features and attributes. Of course, the two approaches are not mutually exclusive, and it is common for a single product to be advertised using both approaches (either separately or in combination).

Surprisingly little research has examined the relative effectiveness of emotional versus rational appeals. In two early studies, Knower (1935, 1936) developed emotional and logical appeals on the topic of prohibition (note the dates of his articles!). Two appeals (one emotional and one logical) favored prohibition, and two other appeals (one emotional and one logical) opposed prohibition. The message recipients were divided on the basis of pretest attitude measures into two groups: those who favored prohibition ("dry" subjects) and those who opposed it ("wet" subjects). All subjects then received a counterattitudinal appeal, with half getting the emotional version and half the logical version. The logical appeal was more effective than the emotional appeal for dry subjects, whereas the emotional appeal was more effective than the logical appeal for wet subjects. The interaction suggests that characteristics of the message recipient may determine whether an emotional or rational approach is more effective.

More recently, Snyder and DeBono (1985) identified "self-monitoring" as a personality characteristic that could potentially determine the relative impact of image-oriented versus quality-oriented appeals. The high self-monitor is a person who is especially sensitive to situational cues in interpersonal settings, and who uses those cues as a guide to behavior; the low self-monitor is a person who uses internal cues and personal attributes (attitudes, feelings, values) as a guide to behavior (Snyder, 1974, 1979). Snyder and DeBono (1985) found that high self-monitors were more responsive to appeals based on image, whereas low self-monitors were more responsive to appeals that emphasized quality.

Millar and Millar (1990) and Edwards (1990) related differences in the structural basis of attitude to the relative impact of emotional versus rational appeals. As already noted, a distinction is commonly made between affective and cognitive components of attitude (Katz & Stotland, 1959; Rosenberg & Hovland, 1960). Millar and Millar (1990) suggested that a person's expressed attitude may be based primarily on affect or primarily on cognition, depending on which attitude component is most salient at the time. Millar and Millar hypothesized and found that affectively based attitudes are more susceptible to rational than to emotional appeals, and that cognitively based attitudes are more susceptible to emotional than to rational appeals. Edwards (1990) reached a different conclusion, finding that affectively based attitudes were more strongly influenced by an affective than by a cognitive appeal, and that cognitively based attitudes were influenced equally by affective and cognitive appeals.

Pallak, Murroni, and Koch (1983) used the distinction between heuristic and systematic processing to compare the attitudinal consequences of emotional versus rational appeals. Pallak et al. hypothesized that emotionally toned messages enhance the salience of the communicator, and as a result will encourage heuristic rather than systematic processing. Rationally toned messages, in contrast, are expected to invite systematic rather than heuristic processing. Pallak et al. had subjects read either an emotionally toned or a rationally toned endorsement for a certain brand of aspirin. The message was attributed either to an attractive or to an unattractive source. Acceptance of the emotionally toned message was influenced by source attractiveness, indicating reliance on a heuristic cue. In contrast, source attractiveness did not influence acceptance of the rationally toned message. Additional results indicated that the rational message was processed systematically rather than heuristically.

Mood and Persuasion

It is common for people to be experiencing a good or bad mood during receipt of a persuasive communication. Television advertising may be imbedded within a stream of programming that engenders either a negative mood (such as reports on the evening news about violent crimes) or a positive mood (such as a situation comedy). Exposure to magazine advertising or newspaper editorials may be surrounded by stories and headlines that arouse mild positive or negative affective states. Radio advertising is typically preceded by music that may make the listener feel good, relaxed, or energetic. And exposure to messages on billboards or subway placards often occurs when the message recipient is experiencing some tension or nervousness because of especially heavy traffic or a noisy and polluted environment.

These situations differ from cases of classical conditioning in two important ways. First, although mood is aroused in the persuasion setting, the source of that arousal is independent of the communication itself. Second, the particular mood that happens to accompany a persuasive communication may not be reliably associated with that message on repeated exposure or in different contexts. Indeed, very different moods may be experienced during receipt of the same message on separate occasions. Thus, if coincidentally experienced mood influences the persuasive impact of a communication, it is likely to do so through mechanisms other than classical conditioning.

The ELM (see above) helps to identify a potentially important way in which affect may participate in the persuasion process (Petty et al., 1991). A good mood (compared to a neutral mood) has been hypothesized to increase one's reliance on judgmental heuristics and to reduce systematic processing of complex information (see Isen, 1984). Thus, being in a good mood should reduce the likelihood of message elaboration or central-route persuasion, and should increase the likelihood of heuristic processing or peripheral-route persuasion. Several studies support this hypothesis.

Worth and Mackie (1987) examined the persuasive impact of a message having to do with acid rain. In one group of subjects, a positive mood was established before exposure to the communication; mood was not manipulated in another condition, presumably leaving those subjects in a neutral mood. The message was attributed either to an expert or to a nonexpert source, and contained either nine strong or nine weak arguments. Subjects who were in a good mood were influenced by source expertise but not by argument strength. In contrast, neutral-mood subjects were influenced by argument strength but not by source expertise. Thus, being in a good mood appeared to decrease systematic processing of message content and to increase the reliance on a heuristic cue.

Bless, Bohner, Schwarz, and Strack (1990) found a compatible pattern of results. Subjects were presented with a counterattitudinal advocacy in favor of increasing student services fees. Some of the subjects were in a happy mood and some in a sad mood, and the message contained either 11 strong or 11 weak arguments. Sad subjects were more persuaded by the strong than by the weak arguments. In contrast, happy subjects were influenced equally by the strong and weak arguments (unless specifically instructed to focus on message content). In a second experiment, Bless et al. distracted some of the subjects as they were listening to the communication. Distraction is known to interfere with systematic processing of message content (Osterhouse & Brock, 1970). Happy subjects showed little sensitivity to argument strength, whether they were distracted or not. Sad subjects were more heavily influenced by strong arguments, but only when they were not distracted. Thus, being in a good mood and being distracted were functionally similar: Both reduced the likelihood of systematic processing and message elaboration.

Two distinct explanations can be offered for the result that positive mood reduces the likelihood of elaboration. One possibility is that a good mood reduces one's *ability* to engage in systematic processing of complex information. Positive affect increases the accessibility of positive information from memory, increases the complexity of cognitive content, and promotes a broader and more integrated organization of knowledge (Isen, 1987). All of this presumably consumes cognitive capacity, leaving the message recipient less able to devote the cognitive resources needed to elaborate on a persuasive communication. Another possibility is that a good mood reduces one's *motivation* to engage in systematic processing. People may avoid cognitive effort that threatens their good feelings (Isen, 1984), or they may interpret positive affect as indicating that systematic processing is not necessary to deal effectively with current environmental exigencies (Schwarz, 1990).

It is not yet clear whether positive affect reduces systematic processing because of a reduction in ability, a reduction in motivation, or both. In support of the reduction-in-motivation hypothesis, Schwarz, Bless, and Bohner (1991) point out that people in a good mood *can* engage in message elaboration when they are specifically instructed to evaluate argument quality (Bless et al., 1990, Experiment 1). Similarly, Innes and Ahrens (1991) found that subjects who were in a good mood did not show a reduced capacity for systematic processing, but rather seemed less motivated to think critically about message content.

In support of the reduction-in-ability hypothesis, Mackie and Worth (1989) found that positive affect reduced systematic processing only when subjects were given limited time to scrutinize the message; when exposure time was not restricted, subjects in a good mood chose to view the message for longer durations than did neutral-mood subjects, and they showed clear signs of systematic processing. In another experiment, Worth, Mackie, and Asuncion (cited in Mackie & Worth, 1991) gave one group of subjects an incentive by stressing to them the importance of evaluating the message thoroughly and completely, and by offering a reward (money) in proportion to the accuracy of their performance. As in the previous experiments, positive affect reduced systematic processing. Importantly, this effect was found even for those subjects who were strongly motivated by the incentives to give careful consideration to message content.

The effects of mood on persuasion may also depend on when the message recipient's mood is aroused. Bless, Mackie, and Schwarz (1992) found that positive and negative moods *at the time of message encoding* produced the pattern of results described previously: Strong argu-

ments were more persuasive than weak arguments, but only for subjects who were in a bad or a neutral mood rather than a good mood during receipt of the persuasive communication. In contrast, subjects who were in a neutral mood at the time of encoding were more heavily influenced by the strong arguments when they were in a good rather than a bad mood *at the time of attitude assessment.* Bless et al. (1992) suggest that the same underlying processes can explain both results. In particular, positive moods produce a simplification of cognitive processing tasks. At the time of encoding, a good mood reduces the likelihood of systematic processing and message elaboration. Thus, the message recipient is less likely to be sensitive to message quality. At the time of attitude assessment, a good mood reduces the likelihood of retrieving details about the message and one's cognitive responses to it. Instead, message recipients are induced to rely on simple evaluative summaries, which generally tend to produce more extreme judgments (Judd & Lusk, 1984).

Dissonance Arousal and Attitude Change

People sometimes do or say things that are inconsistent with their own attitudes. They may take a counterattitudinal position for the sake of argument (playing the devil's advocate), because someone has asked or instructed them to do it (a debate), or for purposes of self-presentation or self-gain (a political campaign). Counterattitudinal behavior produces "cognitive dissonance" when an actor must assume personal responsibility for the action, perceives the attitude and behavior as personally important and relevant, and anticipates negative and irrevocable consequences as a result of the action (Brehm & Cohen, 1962; Cooper & Fazio, 1984; Festinger, 1957). Cognitive dissonance is assumed to be an aversive experience, and people are generally motivated to reduce or eliminate it (Festinger, 1957). One way to reduce cognitive dissonance is to change one or more of the dissonant cognitive elements. Thus, cognitive dissonance often leads to attitude change.

An important line of research examines the question of why people are motivated to reduce cognitive dissonance. One possibility is that people change their attitudes in an effort to reduce *arousal* (regardless of its hedonic value). Cognitive dissonance is accompanied by heightened physiological arousal (Croyle & Cooper, 1983; Elkin & Leippe, 1986; Losch & Cacioppo, 1990), and substantial indirect evidence suggests that cognitive dissonance produces effects on performance similar to those produced by other sources of arousal (Kiesler & Pallak, 1976). In addition, attitude change does not occur when the actor is given an opportunity to misattribute dissonance-induced arousal to another source (Pittman, 1975; Zanna & Cooper, 1974; Zanna, Higgins, & Taves, 1976), or when the actor is given a sedative (Cooper, Zanna, & Taves, 1978).

Another possibility is that cognitive dissonance produces attitude change because people are motivated to reduce *negative affect* (regardless of degree of arousal). In a refinement of the misattribution procedure, Higgins, Rhodewalt, and Zanna (1979) offered subjects an opportunity to misattribute their dissonance-induced affect to a pill that was described as causing either tension, pleasant excitement, unpleasant sedation, or relaxation. Attitude change was attenuated when subjects believed the pill caused tension or unpleasant sedation, but not when the pill was thought to cause pleasant excitement or relaxation. Similarly, Losch and Cacioppo (1990) found a diminution of dissonance-induced attitude change when subjects could misattribute their affect to tension, but not when they could misattribute their affect to pleasant excitement. Losch and Cacioppo also measured subjects' nonspecific skin conductance responses as an indicator of sympathetic activity. Compared to subjects in the low-choice condition, high-choice subjects exhibited increased arousal immediately following the attitude-discrepant decision. Importantly, this elevation in arousal occurred regardless of the source for potential misattribution. Thus, it appears that dissonance-induced attitude change happens because people are motivated to reduce negative affect rather than to reduce nonspecific arousal.

Affective and Cognitive Responses to Persuasive Communications

The dependent variable in most persuasion experiments is a single-item self-rating of agreement with an attitudinal position. The implied unidimensionality stands in contrast to the theoretical and empirical distinction between affective and cognitive components of attitude (Breckler, 1984; Breckler & Wiggins, 1989b; Katz & Stotland, 1959; Kothandapani, 1971; Ostrom, 1969; Rosenberg & Hovland, 1960). It is reasonable to expect that a single persuasive communication can have unique effects on affect and cognition, especially when the message includes elements of both rational and emotional appeals. Along these lines, a colleague and I (Breckler & Wiggins, 1991) found that persuasive communications on the topic of legalized abortion had distinct and independent effects on self-report measures of the affective and cognitive components of attitude.

Recipient-generated cognitive responses to a persuasive communication appear to mediate attitude change under conditions of central or systematic processing (see Petty & Cacioppo, 1986). The content and favorability of cognitive responses is determined partly by features of the persuasion context and partly by the message recipient's own precommunication attitude (Greenwald, 1968). Focusing on the recipient's attitude as a source for cognitive responses, we (Breckler & Wiggins, 1991) found that the favorability of listed thoughts was more strongly related to the affective than to the cognitive component of precommunication attitude. Thus, it appears that one's thoughts in response to a persuasive communication may be influenced by affective predispositions toward the issue.

Measurement problems have created a significant obstacle to studying emotion-related functioning in attitude research (Breckler & Berman, 1991; Breckler & Wiggins, 1989a). Indeed, the methods most commonly used to assess attitudes are better suited for measuring the cognitive than the affective component (e.g., semantic differential scales, equal-appearing interval scales, and cognitive response protocols). Although attitude researchers have occasionally used nonverbal measures (e.g., Hess, 1965; Westie & DeFleur, 1959), such efforts have not been generally successful. A notable exception has been the recent application of facial electromyographic (EMG) measurement in the study of affective and cognitive responses to persuasive communications (see Cacioppo & Petty, 1981).

Specific patterns of facial expression appear to be associated with each of the primary emotions (see Hager & Ekman, 1983; Izard, 1971). Even activity in the face that is too small to be visibly detected may participate in emotional episodes (Fridlund & Izard, 1983). The EMG provides a method for measuring and quantifying such covert changes in the facial musculature (Schwartz, Fair, Salt, Mandel, & Klerman, 1976), and these measures can reveal both the direction and the intensity of affective responses (Cacioppo, Petty, Losch, & Kim, 1986). Cacioppo and Petty (1979) measured facial EMG activity in several areas of the facial musculature while subjects anticipated and then received either a proattitudinal, a counterattitudinal, or a neutral communication. The patterns of facial EMG activity indicated that affective responses were more positive during receipt of a proattitudinal or neutral message than during receipt of a counterattitudinal message. In addition, the facial EMG measures were only weakly correlated with the favorability of listed thoughts. Thus, persuasive communications appear to have unique and distinct effects on the affective and cognitive components of attitude.

CONCLUSION

Models of attitude change have evolved primarily from the Yale message-learning approach, with an emphasis on the dynamics of intellectualized attitudes. The ELM and the HSM clearly allow multiple roles for affect in persuasion (see Petty, et al., 1991), but these models are not strongly grounded in emotion theory (Breckler & Wiggins, 1989a). Future research may benefit by considering how characteristics of persuasive appeals interact with different fundamental or discrete emotions (e.g., Roseman et al., 1986). Additional insight might also be gained by using attitude measures that preserve more information about affective and emotional representations, such as facial EMG (Cacioppo & Petty, 1979) and voice quality measures (Scherer, 1986).

I hope that this chapter reflects the excitement and vibrancy of research on emotion and attitude change. Contemporary persuasion research is clearly moving beyond the effects of rational appeals on verbally expressed attitudes by considering the role of mood in the persuasion process, by relating message characteristics to the structural basis of attitudes, and by developing new methods for nonverbal measurement of attitudinal responses. Perhaps this marks the beginning of a new era of persuasion research that will embrace the emotional dynamics of social attitudes

Acknowledgments. Preparation of this chapter was supported by National Science Foundation Grant No. BNS-86-57093. I thank Kari Edwards, Anthony G. Greenwald, Paula M. Niedenthal, and especially Elizabeth C. Wiggins for commenting on earlier drafts.

REFERENCES

Aaker, D. A., Stayman, D. M., & Hagerty, M. R. (1986). Warmth in advertising: Measurement, impact, and sequence effects. *Journal of Consumer Research, 12,* 365–381.

Allen, C. T., & Janiszewski, C. A. (1989). Assessing the role of contingency awareness in attitudinal conditioning with implications for advertising research. *Journal of Marketing Research, 26,* 30–43.

Baeyens, F., Eelen, P., & van den Bergh, O. (1990). Contingency awareness in evaluative conditioning: A case for unaware affective–evaluative learning. *Cognition and Emotion, 4,* 3–18.

Batra, R. (1986). Affective advertising: Role, processes, and measurement. In R. A. Peterson, W. D. Hoyer, & W. R. Wilson (Eds.), *The role of affect in consumer behavior* (pp. 53–85). Lexington, MA: Lexington Books.

Beck, K. H., & Frankel, A. (1981). A conceptualization of threat communications and protective health behavior. *Social Psychology Quarterly, 44,* 204–217.

Berkowitz, L., & Knurek, D. A. (1969). Label-mediated hostility generalization. *Journal of Personality and Social Psychology, 13,* 200–206.

Bless, H., Bohner, G., Schwarz, N., & Strack, F. (1990). Mood and persuasion: A cognitive response analysis. *Personality and Social Psychology Bulletin, 16,* 331–345.

Bless, H., Mackie, D. M., & Schwarz, N. (1992). Mood effects on attitude judgments: Independent effects of mood before and after message elaboration. *Journal of Personality and Social Psychology, 63,* 585–595.

Breckler, S. J. (1984). Empirical validation of affect, behavior, and cognition as distinct components of attitude. *Journal of Personality and Social Psychology, 47,* 1191–1205.

Breckler, S. J., & Berman, J. S. (1991). Affective responses to attitude objects: Measurement and validation. *Journal of Social Behavior and Personality, 6,* 529–544.

Breckler, S. J., & Wiggins, E. C. (1989a). On defining attitude and attitude theory: Once more with feeling. In A. R. Pratkanis, S. J. Breckler, & A. G. Greenwald (Eds.), *Attitude structure and function* (pp. 407–427). Hillsdale, NJ: Erlbaum.

Breckler, S. J., & Wiggins, E. C. (1989b). Affect versus evaluation in the structure of attitudes. *Journal of Experimental Social Psychology, 25,* 253–271.

Breckler, S. J., & Wiggins, E. C. (1991). Cognitive responses in persuasion: Affective and evaluative determinants. *Journal of Experimental Social Psychology, 27,* 180–200.

Brehm, J. W., & Cohen, A. R. (1962). *Explorations in cognitive dissonance.* New York: Wiley.

Buck, R. (1985). Prime theory: An integrated view of motivation and emotion. *Psychological Review, 92,* 389–413.

Cacioppo, J. T., Marshall-Goodell, B. S., Tassinary, L. G., & Petty, R. E. (1992). Rudimentary determinants of attitudes: Classical conditioning is more effective when prior knowledge about the attitude stimulus is low than high. *Journal of Experimental Social Psychology, 28*, 207–233.

Cacioppo, J. T., & Petty, R. E. (1979). Attitudes and cognitive response: An electrophysiological approach. *Journal of Personality and Social Psychology, 37*, 2181–2199.

Cacioppo, J. T., & Petty, R. E. (1981). Electromyograms as measures of extent and affectivity of information processing. *American Psychologist, 36*, 441–456.

Cacioppo, J. T., & Petty, R. E. (1989). The elaboration likelihood model: The role of affect and affect-laden information processing in persuasion. In P. Cafferata & A. Tybout (Eds.), *Cognitive and affective responses to advertising* (pp. 69–89). Lexington, MA: Lexington Books.

Cacioppo, J. T., Petty, R. E., Losch, M. E., & Kim, H. S. (1986). Electromyographic activity over facial muscle regions can differentiate the valence and intensity of affective reactions. *Journal of Personality and Social Psychology, 50*, 260–268.

Chaiken, S., Liberman, A., & Eagly, A. H. (1989). Heuristic and systematic information processing within and beyond the persuasion context. In J. S. Uleman & J. A. Bargh (Eds.), *Unintended thought* (pp. 212–252). New York: Guilford Press.

Cooper, J., & Fazio, R. H. (1984). A new look at dissonance theory. In L. Berkowitz (Ed.), *Advances in experimental social psychology* (Vol. 17, pp. 229–266). Orlando, FL: Academic Press.

Cooper, J., Zanna, M. P., & Taves, P. A. (1978). Arousal as a necessary condition for attitude change following induced compliance. *Journal of Personality and Social Psychology, 36*, 1101–1106.

Croyle, R. T., & Cooper, J. (1983). Dissonance arousal: Physiological evidence. *Journal of Personality and Social Psychology, 45*, 782–791.

Eagly, A. H., & Chaiken, S. (1984). Cognitive theories of persuasion. In L. Berkowitz (Ed.), *Advances in experimental social psychology* (Vol. 17, pp. 267–359). Orlando, FL: Academic Press.

Eagly, A. H., & Chaiken, S. (1993). *The psychology of attitudes*. Fort Worth, TX: Harcourt Brace Jovanovich.

Edwards, K. (1990). The interplay of affect and cognition in attitude formation and change. *Journal of Personality and Social Psychology, 59*, 202–216.

Elkin, R. A., & Leippe, M. R. (1986). Physiological arousal, dissonance, and attitude change: Evidence for a dissonance–arousal link and a "don't remind me" effect. *Journal of Personality and Social Psychology, 51*, 55–65.

Festinger, L. (1957). *A theory of cognitive dissonance*. Stanford, CA: Stanford University Press.

Fishbein, M., & Ajzen, I. (1975). *Belief, attitude, intention, and behavior: An introduction to theory and research*. Reading, MA: Addison-Wesley.

Fridlund, A. J., & Izard, C. E. (1983). Electromyographic studies of facial expressions of emotions and patterns of emotions. In J. T. Cacioppo & R. E. Petty (Eds.), *Social psychophysiology: A sourcebook* (pp. 243–286). New York: Guilford Press.

Gleicher, F., & Petty, R. E. (1992). Expectations of reassurance influence the nature of fear-stimulated attitude change. *Journal of Experimental Social Psychology, 28*, 86–100.

Greenwald, A. G. (1968). Cognitive learning, cognitive response to persuasion, and attitude change. In A. G. Greenwald, T. C. Brock, & T. M. Ostrom (Eds.), *Psychological foundations of attitudes* (pp. 147–170). New York: Academic Press.

Hager, J. C., & Ekman, P. (1983). The inner and outer meanings of facial expressions. In J. T. Cacioppo & R. E. Petty (Eds.), *Social psychophysiology: A sourcebook* (pp. 287–306). New York: Guilford Press.

Hess, E. H. (1965). Attitude and pupil size. *Scientific American, 212*(4), 46–54.

Higbee, K. L. (1969). Fifteen years of fear arousal: Research on threat appeals, 1953–1968. *Psychological Bulletin, 72*, 426–444.

Higgins, E. T., Rhodewalt, F., & Zanna, M. P. (1979). Dissonance motivation: Its nature, persistence, and reinstatement. *Journal of Experimental Social Psychology, 15*, 16–34.

Hovland, C. I., Janis, I. L., & Kelley, H. H. (1953). *Communication and persuasion*. New Haven, CT: Yale University Press.

Innes, J. M., & Ahrens, C. R. (1991). Positive mood, processing goals and the effects of information on evaluative judgment. In J. P. Forgas (Ed.), *Emotion and social judgments* (pp. 221–239). Oxford: Pergamon Press.

Insko, C. A., & Oakes, W. F. (1966). Awareness and the "conditioning" of attitudes. *Journal of Personality and Social Psychology, 4*, 487–496.

Insko, C. A., & Schopler, J. (1967). Triadic consistency: A statement of affective–cognitive–conative consistency. *Psychological Review, 74*, 361–376.

Isen, A. M. (1984). Toward understanding the role of affect in cognition. In R. S. Wyer & T. K. Srull (Eds.), *Handbook of social cognition* (Vol. 3, pp. 179–236). Hillsdale, NJ: Erlbaum.

Isen, A. M. (1987). Positive affect, cognitive processes, and social behavior. In L. Berkowitz (Ed.), *Advances in experimental social psychology* (Vol. 20, pp. 203–253). San Diego, CA: Academic Press.

Izard, C. E. (1971). *The face of emotion*. New York: Appleton-Century-Crofts.

Izard, C. E. (1977). *Human emotions*. New York: Plenum Press.

Janis, I. L. (1967). Effects of fear arousal on attitude change: Recent developments in theory and experimental research. In L. Berkowitz (Ed.), *Advances in experimental social psychology* (Vol. 3, pp. 166–224). New York: Academic Press.

Janis, I. L., & Feshbach, S. (1953). Effects of fear-arousing communications. *Journal of Abnormal and Social Psychology, 48*, 78–92.

Janis, I. L., & Feshbach, S. (1954). Personality differences associated with responsiveness to fear-arousing communications. *Journal of Personality, 23*, 154–166.

Jepson, C., & Chaiken, S. (1990). Chronic issue-specific fear inhibits systematic processing of persuasive communications. *Journal of Social Behavior and Personality, 5*, 61–84.

Judd, C. M., & Lusk, C. M. (1984). Knowledge structures and evaluative judgments: Effects of structural variables on judgmental extremity. *Journal of Personality and Social Psychology, 46*, 1193–1207.

Katz, D., & Stotland, E. (1959). A preliminary statement to a theory of attitude structure and change. In S. Koch (Ed.), *Psychology: A study of a science* (Vol. 3, pp. 423–475). New York: McGraw-Hill.

Kiesler, C. A., & Pallak, M. S. (1976). Arousal properties of dissonance manipulations. *Psychological Bulletin, 83*, 1014–1025.

Knower, F. H. (1935). Experimental studies of changes in attitudes: I. A study of the effect of oral argument on changes of attitude. *Journal of Social Psychology*, 6, 315–347.

Knower, F. H. (1936). Experimental studies of changes in attitudes: II. A study of the effect of printed argument on changes in attitude. *Journal of Abnormal and Social Psychology*, 30, 522–532.

Kothandapani, V. (1971). Validation of feeling, belief, and intention to act as three components of attitude and their contribution to prediction of contraceptive behavior. *Journal of Personality and Social Psychology*, 19, 321–333.

Krosnick, J. A., Betz, A. L., Jussim, L. J., & Lynn, A. R. (1992). Subliminal conditioning of attitudes. *Personality and Social Psychology Bulletin*, 18, 152–162.

Leventhal, H. (1970). Findings and theory in the study of fear communications. In L. Berkowitz (Ed.), *Advances in experimental social psychology* (Vol. 5, 119–186). New York: Academic Press.

Losch, M. E., & Cacioppo, J. T. (1990). Cognitive dissonance may enhance sympathetic tonus, but attitudes are changed to reduce negative affect rather than arousal. *Journal of Experimental Social Psychology*, 26, 289–304.

Mackie, D. M., & Worth, L. T. (1989). Processing deficits and the mediation of positive affect in persuasion. *Journal of Personality and Social Psychology*, 57, 27–40.

Mackie, D. M., & Worth, L. T. (1991). Feeling good, but not thinking straight: The impact of positive mood on persuasion. In J. P. Forgas (Ed.), *Emotion and social judgments* (pp. 201–219). Oxford: Pergamon Press.

Martin, I., & Levey, A. B. (1978). Evaluative conditioning. *Advances in Behaviour Research and Therapy*, 1, 57–102.

McGuire, W. J. (1985). Attitudes and attitude change. In G. Lindzey & E. Aronson (Eds.), *Handbook of social psychology* (3rd ed., Vol. 2, pp. 233–346). New York: Random House.

McGuire, W. J. (1989). The structure of individual attitudes and attitude systems. In A. R. Pratkanis, S. J. Breckler, & A. G. Greenwald (Eds.), *Attitude structure and function* (pp. 37–69). Hillsdale, NJ: Erlbaum.

Millar, M. G., & Millar, K. U. (1990). Attitude change as a function of attitude type and argument type. *Journal of Personality and Social Psychology*, 59, 217–228.

Millar, M. G., & Tesser, A. (1986). Effects of affective and cognitive focus on the attitude–behavior relation. *Journal of Personality and Social Psychology*, 51, 270–276.

Millar, M. G., & Tesser, A. (1989). The effects of affective-cognitive consistency and thought on the attitude-behavior relation. *Journal of Experimental Social Psychology*, 25, 189–202.

Mitchell, A. A. (1988). Current perspectives and issues concerning the explanation of "feeling" advertising effects. In S. Hecker & D. W. Stewart (Eds.), *Nonverbal communication in advertising* (pp. 127–143). Lexington, MA: Lexington Books.

Osterhouse, R. A., & Brock, T. C. (1970). Distraction increases yielding to propaganda by inhibiting counterarguing. *Journal of Personality and Social Psychology*, 15, 344–358.

Ostrom, T. M. (1969). The relationship between the affective, behavioral and cognitive components of attitude. *Journal of Experimental Social Psychology*, 5, 12–30.

Page, M. M. (1969). Social psychology of a classical conditioning of attitudes experiment. *Journal of Personality and Social Psychology*, 11, 177–186.

Page, M. M., & Kahle, L. R. (1976). Demand characteristics in the satiation–deprivation effect on attitude conditioning. *Journal of Personality and Social Psychology*, 33, 553–562.

Pallak, S. R., Murroni, E., & Koch, J. (1983). Communicator attractiveness and expertise, emotional versus rational appeals, and persuasion: A heuristic versus systematic processing interpretation. *Social Cognition*, 2, 122–141.

Petty, R. E., & Cacioppo, J. T. (1981). *Attitudes and persuasion: Classic and contemporary approaches*. Dubuque, IA: William C. Brown.

Petty, R. E., & Cacioppo, J. T. (1986). The elaboration likelihood model of persuasion. In L. Berkowitz (Ed.), *Advances in experimental social psychology* (Vol. 19, pp. 123–205). Orlando, FL: Academic Press.

Petty, R. E., Cacioppo, J. T., & Kasmer, J. A. (1988). The role of affect in the Elaboration Likelihood Model of persuasion. In L. Donohew, H. E. Sypher, & E. T. Higgins (Eds.), *Communication, social cognition, and affect* (pp. 117–146). Hillsdale, NJ: Erlbaum.

Petty, R. E., Cacioppo, J. T., Sedikides, C., & Strathman, A. J. (1988). Affect and persuasion: A contemporary perspective. *American Behavioral Scientist*, 31, 355–371.

Petty, R. E., Gleicher, F., & Baker, S. M. (1991). Multiple roles for affect in persuasion. In J. P. Forgas (Ed.), *Emotion and social judgments* (pp. 181–200). Oxford: Pergamon Press.

Petty, R. E., Ostrom, T. M., & Brock, T. C. (Eds.). (1981). *Cognitive responses in persuasion*. Hillsdale, NJ: Erlbaum.

Pittman, T. S. (1975). Attribution of arousal as a mediator in dissonance reduction. *Journal of Experimental Social Psychology*, 11, 53–63.

Plutchik, R. (1984). Emotions: A general psychoevolutionary theory. In K. R. Scherer & P. Ekman (Eds.), *Approaches to emotion* (pp. 197–219). Hillsdale, NJ: Erlbaum.

Pratkanis, A. R., Breckler, S. J., & Greenwald, A. G. (1989). *Attitude structure and function*. Hillsdale, NJ: Erlbaum.

Razran, G. H. S. (1940). Conditioned response changes in rating and appraising sociopolitical slogans. *Psychological Bulletin*, 37, 481. (Abstract)

Rogers, R. W. (1975). A protection motivation theory of fear appeals and attitude change. *Journal of Psychology*, 91, 93–114.

Rogers, R. W. (1983). Cognitive and physiological processes in fear appeals and attitude change: A revised theory of protection motivation. In J. R. Cacioppo & R. E. Petty (Eds.), *Social psychophysiology: A sourcebook* (pp. 153–176). New York: Guilford Press.

Rogers, R. W., & Mewborn, C. R. (1976). Fear appeals and attitude change: Effects of a threat's noxiousness, probability of occurrence, and the efficacy of coping responses. *Journal of Personality and Social Psychology*, 34, 54–61.

Roseman, I., Abelson, R. P., & Ewing, M. F. (1986). Emotion and political cognition: Emotional appeals in political communication. In R. R. Lau & D. O. Sears (Eds.), *Political cognition* (pp. 279–294). Hillsdale, NJ: Erlbaum.

Rosenberg, M. J. (1965). Some content determinants of intolerance for attitudinal inconsistency. In S. S. Tomkins & C. E. Izard (Eds.), *Affect, cognition, and personality* (pp. 130–147). New York: Springer.

Rosenberg, M. J., & Hovland, C. I. (1960). Cognitive, affective, and behavioral components of attitude. In M. J. Rosenberg, C. I. Hovland, W. J. McGuire, R. P.

Abelson, & J. W. Brehm (Eds.), *Attitude organization and change: An analysis of consistency among attitude components* (pp. 1–14). New Haven, CT: Yale University Press.

Scherer, K. R. (1986). Vocal affect expression: A review and a model for future research. *Psychological Bulletin, 99,* 143–165.

Schwartz, G. E., Fair, P. L., Salt, P., Mandel, M. R., & Klerman, G. L. (1976). Facial muscle patterning to affective imagery in depressed and nondepressed subjects. *Science, 192,* 489–491.

Schwarz, N. (1990). Feelings as information: Informational and motivational functions of affective states. In E. T. Higgins & R. M. Sorrentino (Eds.), *Handbook of motivation and cognition: Foundations of social behavior* (Vol. 2, pp. 527–561). New York: Guilford Press.

Schwarz, N., Bless, H., & Bohner, G. (1991). Mood and persuasion: Affective states influence the processing of persuasive communications. In M. Zanna (Ed.), *Advances in experimental social psychology* (Vol. 24, pp. 161–199). San Diego, CA: Academic Press.

Shanks, D. R., & Dickinson, A. (1990). Contingency awareness in evaluative conditioning: A comment on Baeyens, Eelen, and van den Bergh. *Cognition and Emotion, 4,* 19–30.

Shimp, T. A., Stuart, E. W., & Engle, R. W. (1991). A program of classical conditioning experiments testing variations in the conditioned stimulus and context. *Journal of Consumer Research, 18,* 1–12.

Snyder, M. (1974). The self-monitoring of expressive behavior. *Journal of Personality and Social Psychology, 30,* 526–537.

Snyder, M. (1979). Self-monitoring processes. In L. Berkowitz (Ed.), *Advances in experimental social psychology* (Vol. 12, pp. 85–128). New York: Academic Press.

Snyder, M., & DeBono, K. G. (1985). Appeals to image and claims about quality: Understanding the psychology of advertising. *Journal of Personality and Social Psychology, 49,* 586–597.

Staats, A. W. (1969). Experimental demand characteristics and the classical conditioning of attitudes. *Journal of Personality and Social Psychology, 11,* 187–192.

Staats, A. W., & Staats, C. K. (1958). Attitudes established by classical conditioning. *Journal of Abnormal and Social Psychology, 57,* 37–40.

Sutton, S. R. (1982). Fear-arousing communications: A critical examination of theory and research. In J. R. Eiser (Ed.), *Social psychology and behavioral medicine* (pp. 303–337). Chichester, England: Wiley.

Sutton, S. R., & Eiser, J. R. (1984). The effect of fear-arousing communications on cigarette smoking: An expectancy–value approach. *Journal of Behavioral Medicine, 7,* 13–33.

Tanner, J. F., Hunt, J. B., & Eppright, D. R. (1991). The protection motivation model: A normative model of fear appeals. *Journal of Marketing, 55,* 36–45.

Tomkins, S. S. (1984). Affect theory. In K. R. Scherer & P. Ekman (Eds.), *Approaches to emotion* (pp. 163–195). Hillsdale, NJ: Erlbaum.

Westie, F. R., & DeFleur, M. L. (1959). Autonomic responses and their relationship to race attitudes. *Journal of Abnormal and Social Psychology, 58,* 340–347.

Wilson, T. D., & Dunn, D. S. (1986). Effects of introspection on attitude–behavior consistency: Analyzing reasons versus focusing on feelings. *Journal of Experimental Social Psychology, 22,* 249–263.

Worth, L. T., & Mackie, D. M. (1987). Cognitive mediation of positive affect in persuasion. *Social Cognition, 5,* 76–94.

Zajonc, R. B. (1980). Feeling and thinking: Preferences need no inferences. *American Psychologist, 35,* 151–175.

Zajonc, R. B., & Markus, H. (1982). Affective and cognitive factors in preferences. *Journal of Consumer Research, 9,* 123–131.

Zajonc, R. B., & Markus, H. (1984). Affect and cognition: The hard interface. In C. E. Izard, J. Kagan, & R. B. Zajonc (Eds.), *Emotions, cognition, and behavior* (pp. 73–102). Cambridge, England: Cambridge University Press.

Zanna, M. P., & Cooper, J. (1974). Dissonance and the pill: An attribution approach to studying the arousal properties of dissonance. *Journal of Personality and Social Psychology, 29,* 703–709.

Zanna, M. P., Higgins, E. T., & Taves, P. A. (1976). Is dissonance phenomenologically aversive? *Journal of Experimental Social Psychology, 12,* 530–538.

Zanna, M. P., Kiesler, C. A., & Pilkonis, P. A. (1970). Positive and negative attitudinal affect established by classical conditioning. *Journal of Personality and Social Psychology, 14,* 321–328.

Zanna, M. P., & Rempel, J. K. (1988). Attitudes: A new look at an old concept. In D. Bar-Tal & A. W. Kruglanski (Eds.), *The social psychology of knowledge* (pp. 315–334). Cambridge, England: Cambridge University Press.

Zellner, D. A., Rozin, P., Aron, M., & Kulish, C. (1983). Conditioned enhancement of humans' liking for flavor by pairing with sweetness. *Learning and Motivation, 14,* 338–350.

33

Studying Emotion in Social Interaction

JOHN MORDECHAI GOTTMAN

INTRODUCTION

This chapter begins with a review of observational research on families and marriages. This area has an interesting history from the standpoint of emotion theory, because the data from this research made it clear that the study of emotion in families was imperative. Here is an example of a field that did not begin with an interest in emotion, but was compelled to study emotion by the results of the research. The field was then faced with practical problems of how best to conceptualize and measure emotion within the context of studying naturalistic social interaction. Unfortunately, the emotion field has little guidance to offer.

Next, this chapter discusses the practical problems of studying emotion in social interaction, and demonstrates that in resolving them, a number of theoretical issues were also posed for emotion theory itself. These practical issues lead naturally to a reconceptualization of emotion that both borrows from laboratory research and contributes to it. In conclusion, we can also see the limitations of studying emotion in the marital and family context; that is, we can see what is missing from an analysis of family systems that relies solely on emotion.

HISTORY OF EARLY OBSERVATIONAL WORK ON FAMILIES AND MARRIAGES

In the 1960s, the first decade of studying family interaction, emotion was not even suggested as important. That may seem surprising, but the early family systems theorists (e.g., Bateson, Jackson, Haley, & Weakland, 1956) suggested studying what they called the "structure" of communication. They were not sure which variables would prove important in analyzing this idea of "structure." For example, in the new journal *Family Process*, early family research by Jay Haley (e.g., Haley, 1964) examined the predictability of speaking turns. Haley hypothesized that dysfunctional families would have a nonrandom speaking turn matrix (e.g., defined by how often father follows mother), whereas in normal families this matrix would be closer to random. Despite Haley's gallant attempts at an operational definition of "structure," for the most part the idea became like a Christmas tree, decorated over time with more and more attractive metaphors.

What metaphors did general systems theorists devise in discussing the "structure" of communication? Defined most broadly, they suggested that every message has three components: its content component, which they suggested was "digital"; its nonverbal component, which they suggested was "analogic"; and its "command" component, which was left unspecified (see Watzlawick, Beavin, & Jackson, 1968). In this breakdown of a message, the content component was presumed to be linguistic and semantic; the nonverbal component (eventually to be mistakenly equated with emotion) was presumed to qualify the semantic component in an unspecified way (e.g., providing the double-bind aspect by contradicting the content); and the command aspect was presumed to be related to power or status. Coding systems were subsequently designed with this model in mind (e.g., Rogers & Farace, 1975), but after a series of early failures, the general sytems approach to studying families has remained largely nonempirical.

Another insight into the fact that emotion made itself important in the study of family interaction is provided by a classic small study by Soskin and John (1963). About 30 years ago, these investigators built a 3-pound audio radio transmitter with a foot-long antenna that projected from the upper lid of a backpack, and gave it to a vacationing married couple so that their conversation could be recorded. The sound was transmitted to a radio tower at the resort. The unit could be disconnected when the couple wanted privacy. They offered the couple a free vacation at the resort if they would agree to have their every word monitored by the two researchers. Soskin and John tape-recorded the conversations and typed out what the couple said verbatim. It will be instructive to consider the analyses Soskin and John undertook, in order to get some idea of the vast array of possibilities of what to observe in a couple's conversation, and how investigators were finally led to study emotion.

From the many excerpts of conversation Soskin and John collected for several days, they identified many methods of analysis. They computed such variables as the total talking time and the distribution of utterance durations. They categorized each statement made in a number of ways and made up exotic new names for their categories. For example, they distinguished some statements as "Informational" (e.g., "Thats a Modigliani") and others as "Relational" messages ("Oh, I like that") or "Expressive" statements ("Ouch!"). They also had some fairly exotic categories, such as "Excogitative" statements ("Hmm-m-m what have I done wrong here?"), "Signones" (messages reporting the speaker's present physical or psychological state, such as "I'm cold"), "Metrones" (appraising and valuing statements, such as "What a fool I've been"), "Regones" (regulative statements designed to influence the partner's behavior, such as "Why don't you do it right now?"), and "Structones" (factual statements, such as "I weigh 181 pounds").

Soskin and John's attempts at description were quite elaborate. In what they called their "Dynamic" analysis, they described the message according to "state," "locus–direction,"

and "bond." The state contained affective information in a six-interval scale (a state of joy, glee, high pleasure; a state of satisfaction, contentment, liking; a state of ambivalence, mild apprehension; a state of mild apprehension, dislike, frustration, disappointment; a state of pain, anger, fear, grief; or a state of neutrality). Locus–direction contained nine subcategories, scored in terms of primary effect (e.g., wants, wishes, and self-praise were one subcategory), and bonds indexed the degree of intimacy the speaker was willing to tolerate in the relationship.

When investigators go to these great lengths to invent not only new categories but a new language for the categories, it is a sure sign that they think they are on to something important. Certainly there was a great deal of excitement about the naturalistic nature of their methods. However, at the end of all their laborious coding and analysis of these conversations, what really seemed to surprise Soskin and John was just how dull their conclusions were. For example, the main conclusion of what they called their "Ecological" analysis was how little time the husband (Jock) spent alone. In what they called the "Structural" analysis, they noted a great deal of variability in Jock's talking time across different episode types, such as breakfast and planning with the wife (Roz); they noted that the longer utterances were predominantly Structones (i.e., factual exchange). They concluded that Jock was a highly gregarious individual. They finally decided that this kind of conclusion was hardly likely to lead to profound insights into the structure of conversation or marriage. Part of their surprise lay in the realization that, rather than being separate components, emotion and the structure of interaction were intricately connected in everyday marital interaction. For example, in the "Functional" analysis 1,850 messages were analyzed. They were surprised that a very small proportion of these messages involved exchanging information. Nearly two-thirds of the messages were classified as what they called "relation changing" (i.e., affective messages).

They were also struck by the gender differences in the interaction with respect to emotional expression. They found that Roz produced a significantly higher proportion of emotion-venting messages than her husband, both in the cabin and in the rowing incident. To summarize, Soskin and John found that expressed emotion was central to the interaction, and they noted a possible gender difference in this couple with respect to affect. They also concluded that Roz produced significantly more emotion-venting messages in private than she did in public situations, while Jock's output was relatively low throughout.

Intuitively, Soskin and John knew that they ought to describe something about two aspects of the marital interaction: the "structure" of the interaction and the affective component of the interaction. For Roz and Jock, they tried to capture these two aspects of the marital interaction with their observational coding systems. They found their Dynamic analyses most interesting. However, they were puzzled by the fact that their codes and their analytic methods did not capture the interaction as well as they could do by summarizing the action in plain, nonpsychologized English. Using an anecdotal account, they obtained a very clear description of the thoughts, feelings, and action of a short segment of interaction. But they felt that their quantitative coding categories failed to capture all this subtlety.

It is clear that there were two dimensions that Soskin and John thought important intuitively—namely, affect and power. However, they were disappointed with their ability to get at these two dimensions. For example, at one point in their chapter they wrote, "As with locus–direction shift, the assessment of affective state changes met with only marginal success" (p. 270). They continued, "neither the locus–direction scoring nor the affective state scoring adequately conveys Jock's practice of scattering a series of mildly provocative messages throughout an episode as, for example, his persistence in the rowing episode in urging Roz to row farther out into the lake despite her growing apprehensiveness" (p. 272). Put simply, the investigators *knew intuitively* what was going on that was important in the interaction, but their measurement and analytic methods prevented them from getting at their intuitions.

After the 1960s, observational research on marital interaction began from a different quarter, that of the behavioral marital therapists. They focused on how a couple resolved disagreements—a set of social acts known as "problem solving." The idea of the new therapy was that marital discord could be resolved by appropriate social learning. They were strongly influenced by behavioral approaches to improving parenting (e.g., see Patterson, 1982),

and they emphasized dimensions such as specificity in problem solving, not emotion. For example, the first observational system applied to marriage (the Marital Interaction Coding System, or MICS; Hops, Wills, Patterson, & Weiss, 1972) had one category called "negative solution." Negative solution involves the husband's or wife's stating desired changes as what behaviors they wish to see less of in the relationship (e.g., "I wish you'd stop insulting my mother") instead of what behaviors they wish to see more of (e.g., "I wish you'd be nicer to my mother"). This was an attempt to deal with the phenomenon of global disaffection and negative attribution in distressed marriages.

Interestingly, the MICS was designed so that all interaction could be coded. However, when it came down to analyzing the data, investigators almost always combined their data into a positive category and a negative category. Without an emotion theory as a basis for the design of the observational categories, this was a difficult proposition. Not all of the codes fell neatly into "positive" or "negative." For example, is expressing disagreement negative, or is it a good thing to express one's views? Is agreement positive, or is it merely compliance? Decisions about how to classify the codes were made, although they were made arbitrarily, without justification, and the decisions were not consistent across studies. But some codes carried over from the parent–child context nicely into the marital; for example, like children, spouses also whine, and like parents and children, they insult each other. Whining and insults seemed more clearly negative.

THE COUPLES INTERACTION SCORING SYSTEM

Ekman, Friesen, and Ellsworth (1972), in their classic book *Emotion in the Human Face*, lamented the difficulty of scoring emotion in human interaction. They also suggested that a disadvantage of studying emotion in the context of naturalistic interaction is that one has little control of the stimulus. Emotions come fast and furious; they come in varying blends and intensities; and one is never sure whether one is studying the effects of person A's expression of emotion X, or person B's previous or simultaneous expression of emotion Y. Yet this is the context in which emotion expression and experience primarily take place (unless one is interested in emotional expressions of people when they are alone—i.e., their expressions to themselves).

In my own work on marital interaction, a paper by Goldfried and D'Zurilla (1969) was particularly influential. They argued that social skills training intervention programs ought to be built empirically, by discovering the differences in behavior of competent and incompetent populations—in particular, their differing strategies in coping with problematic situations. In this approach the would-be therapy designer is like an ethologist, who studies behavioral variety and classifies the behavior of different populations. Also, the salient situations must be empirically defined.

In marital interaction, the situation selected was conflict and its resolution, or problem solving. This decision was largely based on historical precedent. When a couple arrives for therapy, the therapist usually asks, "What's the problem?", thus assuming that there is a problem that must be solved. Other approaches are easily imagined (e.g., marital distress is a problem in loving), but this focus on conflict and its resolution is the one currently universally accepted. With the salient situation selected, another step was the design of a good observational system.

On the basis of behavior exchange theory (Thibaut & Kelley, 1961), couples were instructed to take turns at speech, and a physical device (called a "talk table") was used to rate the positivity–negativity of the intended impact of every message sent and the actual impact of every message received. This method made it possible to consider a variety of models of communicational competence (Gottman et al., 1976). For example, one definition of competent communication was that it was perceived as positive in impact (high payoffs, low costs); another was that intent simply matched impact, regardless of valence; another was that intentions were generally positive; and so on. This interpretation of behavior exchange theory implied an emphasis on the couple's perception of the positivity or negativity of their communication.

As part of this behavior exchange approach, couples were videotaped, and an observational coding system (the Couples Interaction Scoring System, or CISS) was designed, influenced by general systems theorists and also by social psychologists and others who studied nonverbal communication (Argyle, 1969; Knapp, 1972; Mehrabian, 1972). My students C. Notarius, H. Markman, and I reasoned that emotional communication among humans must be considered part of the entire signal system. As such, language cannot be ignored. We adopted the general systems idea of dismantling a message into its components, and used the two components of content and affect. We could neither obtain interobserver reliability about power, nor be sure we knew what we were measuring with that component. Eight summary categories describing what people say when they engage in marital conflict resolution (e.g., giving information about a problem, expressing an opinion about a problem, proposing a solution, summarizing self, summarizing other, metacommunication, etc.) were obtained. For the affect component, cues from face, voice, and body that previous literature had suggested were related to the positivity or negativity of emotion were selected. For example, cues of fear/tension were "non-ah" speech disturbances. A separate group of observers coded content and affect for each speech unit (a semantic unit we called the "thought unit"). This coding required verbatim transcripts and was quite slow; however, reliability was quite high (see Gottman, 1979).

Part of the problem that had to be solved in following the Goldfried and D'Zurilla (1969) recommendation was developing methods for sequential analysis. The hypotheses of competence were always of the form "When he does this, she tends to do that." Cumbersome forms of these methods had already been devised using information theory and Markov models, and had been applied to marriage by Raush, Barry, Hertel, and Swain (1974), but a streamlined approach to discovering sequences with fewer data awaited the invention of lag sequential analysis (Sackett, 1979). The application of lag sequential analysis to these sequences led to a detailed analysis of the precise social skills deficits of unhappily, compared to happily, married couples. This information led to an empirically derived therapy program, which had significant but modest results in our laboratory in three studies. This general method produced reasonably consistent results (see Gottman, 1979, for a summary; see also Schaap, 1982). One of the major conclusions of this line of research was that emotional expressions are extremely important in understanding function and dysfunction in marital communication.

However, there were serious limitations to the way affect was coded by the CISS. The Ekman and Friesen (1978a) conceptualization of specific and discrete facial affects, which underlies the anatomically based Facial Action Coding System (FACS), challenged the idea that all negative emotions are the same. Ekman has argued throughout his career that there is a great need for specificity to understand the function of emotions in interaction.

USING FORMAL CODING SYSTEMS TO MEASURE SPECIFIC AFFECTS

I will begin by discussing the coding of emotion using only facial movement. The methodological advance that the FACS represented was remarkable. The objective description of facial movements made possible by using numbered Action Units (AUs) to represent facial muscle groups made dialogue about emotional marital interaction behavior far more precise and less a matter of subjective impression. In subsequent research, Robert Levenson and I used a wide variety of observational methods. We employed microanalytic observational systems (Ekman & Friesen's [1978b] Emotion Facial Action Coding System, or EMFACS); macroanalytic observational systems (my Specific Affect Coding System, or SPAFF); and coding systems that were less specifically designed to study emotion, but more focused on communicative skill or problem-solving ability (coding of visual gaze direction, the MICS, the CISS, and my new Rapid Couples Interaction Scoring System, or RCISS).

What Is an Emotion?

In this work, Levenson and I took a "dustbowl empirical" approach to the coding of emotion. Our view of the literature on emotion was that, unfortunately, more theory than data had been generated, and more heat than light was the result. Thus, we reasoned that while it might be useful to employ (for example) a neo-Darwinian orientation to emotion in terms of facial expression from a *measurement* standpoint, this orientation to emotion did not have to be taken as religious dogma. We argued that the usefulness of a particular theoretical orientation would ultimately lie in the goodness of the numbers that it generated.

An example may help clarify this "dustbowl empirical" approach. A Darwinian perspective, exemplified by Ekman and Friesen and by Izard, would admit a potential candidate (e.g., "pride" or "worry") as an emotion only if it satisfied the criteria of cross-cultural universality in recognition and production. Ekman and Friesen have other criteria with respect to timing and behavioral flexibility (vs. stereotypy) that have led them to suggest that the startle is a reflex rather than an emotion, and that depression is a mood state, not an emotion (Ekman, Friesen, & Simons, 1985). Hence, the investigator needs to consider what to code as an emotion. Are "pride" and "worry" emotions? If not, ought they to be ignored? One could argue that it does not make sense to ignore some action as emotional just because it is not cross-culturally universal. One could argue that one ought not to care whether it is a universal action. The argument is simply that an action ought to be taken as emotional if in this culture, at this time, cultural informants can reliably tell us that this action means, say, "sadness." Feld (1982) studied the Kaluli culture and noted that they employ vestiges of the musical sounds of tropical birds that surround them to denote their own feelings. Hence, a Kaluli who says, "My mother-in-law is coming for a visit," and feels sad about it will say the sentence with one set of musical notes and intonation; if the feeling is excitement, the person will employ another set of notes. Only a competent Kaluli observer can decode these feelings. Hence, one can ask this question: Is it important to code culture-specific behaviors as emotional if they appear to have that function in that culture? The issue is a practical issue: Does one employ a specific-features approach to coding emotion (as represented by the FACS), or does one employ a cultural-informants system?

Our approach to these and other issues in emotion theory has been empirical. We have employed two observational coding systems—one based on a cultural-informants approach (the SPAFF), and one based on cross-culturally universal actions (the EMFACS). If there is a horse race, the test between the two is empirical: Which gives us better information in terms of some criterion we are concerned about? But, there is really no horse race. The issue between microanalytic and macroanalytic systems, between physical-features and cultural-informants approaches, as a dialectic—a discourse that is enriched by having both systems represented in the research program.

This highlights a particular bias. For the most part, the research program our work represents is not interested in emotion, but in marriage. If emotion is informative about marriage, then emotion is part of the research program. It turns out that emotion can tell us a great deal about marriage. Over time, it has also become clear to me that although a general positive–negative emotion categorization can be extremely useful in describing distressed marriages, it is probably not going to be adequate for describing in detail what goes wrong in an ailing marriage. There is a need for greater specificity.

Problems in Using Only Facial Behavior in Coding Marital Interaction

There are some inherent problems with employing only facial codes to study emotion in marital interaction. I consider each of these here.

Toward Whom Is the Emotion Expressed?

First, there is the question of toward whom the emotional expression is addressed. Is it toward the self, toward another person or thing not present but talked about, or toward the partner? Wouldn't we expect different physiological reactions if, for example, contempt is directed toward another person rather than toward the self? One would think so, since self-contempt probably has an entirely different function than does contempt directed at another person. Another example of this issue will dramatize the point. If two people are angry at each other, we might expect a physiological profile characteristic of anger. However, suppose that both people are angry at the same incompetent repairman who has worked on their house. This turns out to be a moment of solidarity and affection in the marriage, a "we against others" moment. Wouldnt we expect a physiological response more like that of affection? Yet in both cases people are experiencing and expressing anger. What does this mean theoretically?

The distinction about toward whom the emotion is addressed also turns out sometimes to be not so easy to make. For example, say the wife hates the husband's friends and expresses strong disgust toward them. Is she also disgusted with her husband when he is with these friends, or disgusted with him for his choice of friends? It is not clear toward whom the emotion is addressed in this kind of exchange.

The FACS Does Not Provide an Emotion Code

When using the FACS, one winds up with a set of specific AUs. If the investigator is interested in using emotion words to summarize the data (e.g., how often was the husband angry?), this is a serious drawback. This problem is not solved with the more rapid EMFACS. The problem is that what Ekman and Friesen refer to as an "emotion dictionary" is not yet written. One must currently rely on Friesen to make these judgments, and the investigator cannot summarize Friesen's methods for a particular emotion judgment as a simple rule. This makes using facial expressions with the FACS an extremely cumbersome approach for studying emotion. Izard's observational systems have taken a stand on a facial dictionary, although some of the decision rules are questionable (e.g., "square mouth" as an anger code may include a raised upper lip, characteristic of disgust). The problem is quite complex, because not enough is yet known to create the facial dictionary, and because Ekman and Friesen are quite correctly cautious. Still, an investigator interested in using facial coding to make emotion judgments is in a quandary.

There Are Theoretical Problems with the Level of Analysis

The fundamental idea of physical features is questionable. The assumption is that there exists a codebook for looking up any nonverbal behavior and deciphering its meaning. Even if such a codebook exists theoretically, it would take a lifetime to devise it. An example from my work is a pregnant woman in her seventh month on one videotape. The spouses were discussing her jealousy of the women in her husband's car pool. The husband was quite irritated by the wife's jealousy and said so. At one point she appealed to him for affection with a gesture reminiscent of Ingrid Bergman in *Casablanca*. She leaned her cheek on her shoulder, looked up softly at her husband, and said, "You're always going on and on about the women in your car pool." He responded appropriately with affection and validation: He said, "Honey, none of those women are as attractive to me as you are right now." This was the right thing to say. Yet let us consider the wife's behavior in appealing for affection and support. If one had an itch on the cheek and used the shoulder to scratch it, the wife's behavior would be similar, except for parameters of cheek-to-shoulder speed and the time course of the cheek resting on the shoulder. Do we wish to make such distinctions in these parameters microanalytically? If we do, how many variables would we need? And how would we get the data into the proper form relating to emotions and not cheek-to-shoulder velocity?

In attempting to describe marital interaction, one realizes the level of description that is of interest. One does not want to have data descriptive of the sequences of physical features displayed in precise detail. For example, one does not wish to have summary codes to read something like this: "Husband shows zygomatic major contraction on face accompanied by contraction of the cheek raiser muscle, with shift downward in vocal fundamental frequency, decrease in amplitude, voice in a major key, and rapid inhalation and exhalation of breath with 'hut hut' vocalizations." Instead, one wishes to say that the husband laughed. This is not a facetious point. One wishes description at the following level: "Wife fearful and tense, followed by husband's contempt, followed by wife's sadness." Hence the unit of measurement of interest in coding marital interaction is the emotion judgment in *specific* emotion categories, without regard for precisely which cues coders use to arrive at these judgments.

One basic issue each investigator needs to decide in emotion research is the level of description desired for obtaining the data. In research on marital interaction, it is probably more important to know someone was sad, and not exactly how this sadness is displayed. There can be many actors for one script. Hamlet's soliloquy "To be or not to be . . ." can be delivered in an infinite number of valid ways, yet the general message is quite clear in all of them. What general conclusion does the investigator wish to extract from the message? If it is an emotion state, is it important to know exactly how this emotional state information was conveyed?

Yet this line of reasoning leads to a dilemma. How can one be sure that coders took advantage of the great progress that has been made in the study of physical features in describing emotion? What if some coders are blind to some kinds of cues? How does one cope with the lack of uniformity in the coders' sensitivity? One can ensure that all coders have a minimum base of knowledge about those specific features that are reasonably reliable in the making of emotional judgments. They have to be trained on what is currently known. However, these physical features should only be considered *illustrative*, not exhaustive. The coders should be told, "This is one way that people get angry. Learn to recognize the lips pressed together or less red showing in the upper lip. Be sensitive to these cues is the message, but recognize the fact that this is not the only way that people show their anger."

Scherer (1974) used a Moog synthesizer to generate sounds that were speech-like. Actually, they were not speech, and he systematically varied pitch level, pitch variation, pitch contour, amplitude level and variations, and tempo. He then asked people to rate these segments on 10-point scales for the following emotions: interest, sadness, fear, happiness, disgust, anger, surprise, elation, and boredom. He was able to discover, for example, which set of cues predicted judgments of anger. Scherer discovered that extreme variation in amplitude (volume) was seen as active and potent, and as most indicative of the emotions of fear and anger. What is the problem with employing Scherer's findings in coding emotion from the vocal channel? It is probably true that when people raise their voices and speak in an even tempo, they are likely to be angry. But this is by no means the only way that people communicate their anger. Imagine, for example, that a wife has said, "This year we are going to paint the house with your bonus money"; imagine that in response the husband looks away, is silent for a while, and then glares at her, *lowers* the pitch and volume of his voice, and says, "The hell we are." This form of constrained anger can be quite menacing, and a great deal of anger can be communicated in this manner.

Once one abandons a physical-features approach, the issue becomes one of being sure of what one is actually measuring. This is an issue of the coding system's construct validity.

It is a critical issue, and it illustrates why there must always be a dialectic between microanalytic and macroanalytic systems.

Why Rely on Just the Face?

Clearly, emotion is communicated in channels other than the face. The voice, and even the content of speech, can convey emotional information. People would not write plays if the words alone did not convey emotion. An enormous amount of emotional information is also conveyed by vocal qualities of speech. Unfortunately, there is as yet no equivalent of the FACS for the voice. Nonetheless, specific cues in the voice can be coded reliably by observers, such as shifts away from fundamental frequency, or tension indexed by a shift from a chest to a head register (see Scherer, 1984). Similarly, the context of the interaction, the way people hold their bodies, and paralinguistic (Knapp, 1972) and extralinguistic (see Knapp, 1972, Ch. 10) aspects of communication can convey emotional information. Thus, careful thought will reveal that the initial assumption of the CISS (i.e., that emotions are conveyed through only the nonverbal channels) was wrong. It is clear that the script also communicates emotion. To illustrate this fact, here is an example of a husband and wife talking about the events of their day.

> H: You'll never guess who I saw today at the Hour House—Frank Dugan!
> W: So, big deal, you saw Frank Dugan.
> H: Don't you remember I had that argument with him last Wednesday?
> W: I forgot.
> H: Yeah.
> W: So I'm sorry I forgot. All right?
> H: So it is a big deal to see him.
> W: Oh, brother, here we go again.
> H: You don't have to look at me that way.
> W: Whadda ya want me to do, put a paper bag over my head?
> H: Well, how was *your* day, *honey?*

Here we can see that the words themselves are quite capable of conveying emotion.

The Cross-Cultural Universality Criterion May Be Wrong

At first, it seems ideal to restrict one's definition of what an emotion is in several ways.

Ekman (personal communication, 1980) has suggested limiting "emotion" to those aspects of emotion that are cross-culturally universal in recognition and production, and also including criteria of timing and flexibility. The latter criteria rule out depression as a psychopathology and not an emotion; long-term sadness or "the blues" as a mood state and not an emotion; and the startle response as too stereotyped to be an emotion (it is more like a reflex).

However, in coding emotion in interaction, these criteria prove to be far too restrictive. Feld's (1982) book is important in this regard. A great deal of emotional information is communicated in culturally specific ways. As described above, Feld noted that the Kaluli use vestiges of specific tropical bird sounds to convey emotional meanings. Only a competent Kaluli informant can detect this information. Because it is not cross-culturally universal does not imply that it is not useful emotional information. We believe that emotion in the stream of natural social interaction is conveyed by a nonadditive gestalt of information, which is detectable by competent cultural informants. In practice, it is wise to employ cultural informants who have also been trained to recognize the important physical features (e.g., who can read the face using the FACS), but who view them as only *examples* of how emotion may be expressed.

To state this point another way, one may expect that contempt, for example, may be conveyed somewhat differently in London than in Sumatra. However, the physiological effects of expressing contempt or receiving a contemptuous message may be the same in both places. Why would one wish to ignore valid information simply because it is specific to a particular culture? This decision would be like studying Chinese couples and hiring coders who understand no Chinese. Their ability to code would be quite limited. These considerations have led me to one major deviation from a FACS or physical-features approach, and this deviation is the use of a cultural-informants system.

There Is a Need for a Gestalt Approach in Coding Emotion

A hidden assumption in coding different components or channels of a message (the face, the voice, content, etc.) is that such a dismantling makes sense. Usually, investigators have assumed something even more restrictive—namely, that the emotional information in different channels is additive when one attempts to reconstruct the whole message's emotional content. The physical-features approach thus has an implicit "additive-channel assumption," which assumes that specific features *add* emotional information to a substrate of "emotion-neutral" language. Without such an assumption, techniques such as high-frequency voice filtering would not make sense. In a voice-filtering approach, the investigator assumes that content can be filtered out electronically and that what is left is the emotional or paralinguistic component. However, it is easy to show that physical paralinguistic features *interact* with language to convey emotional meaning. For example, consider the paralinguistic cue of stress; if the word "soon" is stressed in "I'd like this as soon as possible," it conveys impatience; if the word "possible" is stressed, it conveys the opposite. How, then, is it possible that emotion can be reliably coded using electronically filtered speech? The answer is probably that when speech is electronically filtered, reliability in emotion coding is probably obtained at the expense of coding most speech units as emotionally neutral.

If we add other cues in addition to voice stress, the situation becomes extremely complex, and the additive-channel assumption has to fall. Ekman (1984) has suggested other ways in which voice and speech are related that he proposes are not emotional. He has called these facial movements such things as "underliners," "batons," and "emblems." However, there may actually be instances in which these facial cues provide emotional "color" to what is being said. Another example is the ways in which voice and face are often related. They cannot necessarily be separated, analyzed separately, and then mixed together again, as the additive-channel model would have us believe. A cogent illustration is provided by the observation of L. Camras (personal communication, 1980) that the brow raise (AUs 1 + 2) is usually accompanied by a rising pitch contour. This is usually accompanied by excitement and some verbal messge of anticipation (e.g., "My supervisor is coming tomorrow to take a look at what I've accomplished on this project so far"). Camras observed that if the same message is accom-

panied by brow lowering (AU 4), there is usually a lowering of pitch and expressed worry. Brow, pitch, and emotional meaning are intricately connected. The reader can try the experiment of attempting to violate these patterns (raising the brows and lowering the pitch while saying with worry, "My supervisor is coming tomorrow to take a look at what I've accomplished on this project so far," and then lowering the brows and saying the same thing with increasing pitch and happy excitement); it is a bit like trying to pat one's head and rub one's stomach at the same time.

When we drop the criterion of cross-cultural universality in recognition and production, we are confronted with questions of what to exclude or include in the category of emotion. For example, should Camras's examples be included? What about "whine"? Is it to be included in sadness, as Tomkins (1963) suggested (it is like crying, he said)? My approach is to code all these behaviors as if they were emotions, and then to assess their function empirically (antecedents, consequences, contexts, prediction, and other validity criteria) across a series of investigations. This is ultimately the correct approach to dealing with the problem of knowing what one is measuring.

Other Issues: Context and Intensity

Ekman and Friesen's EMFACS is very interesting for a variety of reasons. First, it is an attempt to speed the coding of facial movement; it takes only three times real time to code a tape with the EMFACS. Second, it is an initial attempt to provide a facial dictionary, although Ekman and Friesen feel that their first attempts at this were inadequate. Third, it tries to confront the notion that some AUs can constrain the expression of other AUs, so that there can be categories such as constrained anger, smiling, or sadness. This is one of the basic ideas in Uta Hagen's (1975) approach to acting. She pointed out that we know that people are drunk through their attempts to act sober; we know that people are hot through their attempts to get cool. She suggested that opposites in conflict are essential in powerful acting. What is missing is as important as what is there. In a similar way, the context of interaction provides additional information about the meaning of an emotional message; for example, if a spouse has just been threatening, a simple agreement and silence following the threat may be resigned sadness. There are also issues of the intensity of the affect. For example, do we get anger physiology as anger becomes more intense? Or do we get diffuse physiological arousal as intensity increases?

THE SPECIFIC AFFECT CODING SYSTEM (SPAFF)

One major goal of the SPAFF (Gottman & Krokoff, 1989) is performing sequential analysis of emotions. "Sequential analysis" is concerned with detecting sequences of emotion codes that occur contingently far greater than one would expect by chance alone. With the current coding procedures, we also obtain duration and timing information. A large manual and training audiotapes are available, and this section provides only a brief summary of the coding system. Other investigators of marital interaction have also moved toward coding specific emotions (e.g., Biglan, Lewin, & Hops, 1990).

Live interactions or videotapes are coded with the SPAFF, which is a cultural-informants coding system in which a team of coders considers a gestalt consisting of verbal content, voice tone, context, facial expression, gestures, and body movement. This system dismantles affect into specific positive and negative affects. The following are the SPAFF positive affect categories: (1) interest; (2) affection; (3) humor; (4) validation; and (5) excitement/joy. The negative affect codes are (1) anger; (2) belligerence; (3) domineering; (4) contempt; (5) disgust; (6) tension/fear/worry; (7) sadness; (8) whining; and (9) defensiveness. There are also four listener codes: (1) neutral listener; (2) positive listener; (3) negative listener, and (4) stonewalling, which is listener withdrawal from interaction. To assess interobserver reliability, the average kappa coefficient of reliability, which controls for agreement by chance, was computed. The average kappa was equal to .64 for wives and .62 for husbands for the entire SPAFF; this is an acceptable level for kappa (see Bakeman & Gottman, 1986).

In my own research program, I am concerned about the slowness of coding interaction and wish to follow large samples of couples longitudinally (and hence repeatedly). Hence, I have been working on rapid versions of the SPAFF for the past 2 years. Three versions of the SPAFF currently exist. Two versions are used with a specific piece of software that uses both a videocassette recorder and a computer (the Video Coding System, designed by James Long). The third version is used with a computer that simultaneously acquires physiological data on-line. The most detailed version, and the slowest (about 10 hours of coding for 15 minutes of tape), is SPAFF MICRO, which permits any two blends (primary and secondary affect); specifies toward whom the affect is directed (self, partner, other); provides an intensity code; and provides a specific set of listener affects as well. On the other hand, SPAFF MACRO only permits two specific blends (experimentally determined as the most frequently used blends across studies); they are anger/defensiveness and affection/humor. It also ignores the "toward whom" dimension. (A decision rule is employed: If they are both negative toward the same thing, it is coded affection; otherwise, affect is only coded if it is addressed to the partner.) SPAFF MACRO seems to take a bit less time (about 6 hours per 15-minute interaction). The fastest version of the SPAFF is the Affect Wheel, which codes the interaction in real time; two observers, one who codes the husband and one the wife, are used. The Affect Wheel was designed by Al Ross of the Instrument Development Laboratory at the Child Development and Mental Retardation Center of the University of Washington. The Affect Wheel permits two intensity ratings for every affect except neutral, does not allow blends, and avoids the "toward whom" issue in the same way that SPAFF MACRO does. The Affect Wheel also has surprise as separate from excitement/joy, and there are two valences to surprise, positive and negative. The SPAFF has been successfully imported (with good on-site reliability and good intersite informal agreements on its use) to a different laboratory (M. Forgatch of the Oregon Social Learning Center), to code parent–child as well as marital and adult confidant interactions.

Why Emotions Must Be Qualified within the Marital Interaction Context

Previous observational systems for coding emotional expression have not been designed for studying social interaction. Within the context of social interaction, greater specification and differentiation of emotional behaviors in terms of their social function are both possible and necessary. The SPAFF makes some differentiations of emotional expression in terms of their social functions. We code three forms of anger, which vary in intensity: (1) pure anger (e.g., "Don't you ever do that again!"); (2) belligerent anger, which is a provocative form of anger (e.g., "What are you gonna do about it if I go on a drinking binge with Jim?"); and (3) domineering anger, which is a form of anger designed to squelch a response rather than provoke it (an example is condescending or threatening lecturing of one's partner, such as "How many times have I told you that we do not have a problem with finances? My investments simply preclude a savings account. Let me go over it again . . ."). At the more extreme end, we have what are generally considered the "hostile" emotions of contempt and disgust, which are derision and rejection (respectively) of the partner (e.g., contempt can be a direct insult or intimation that the partner is incompetent).

Although anger must be differentiated, some emotions are more elusive in our context. We have found that fear is difficult to define and code with validity in the context of marital interaction. When it is coded as an expression of tension (an example is what is called a "non-ah" speech disturbance, such as a phrase repetition) or an expression of worry, it does not validly discriminate happy from unhappy marriages across studies. Perhaps this is because couples' tension may result from the invasive experimental configuration itself. However, fear in the context of marital interaction can reliably be measured as defensiveness, which is a form of self-protection (e.g., denial of responsibility for a problem), or as the listener's withdrawal from interaction—a behavior we call "stonewalling," because the listener presents a stone wall to the speaker. In marital interaction, sadness is either directly expressed, or indirectly expressed by whining.

Positive affects must be differentiated far more than is possible with the face. In the marital interaction context, examples of positive affect are interest, humor, affection, joy, and validation (which is an acknowledgment of the validity of the partner's feelings).

Is Coding in Real Time the Correct Way to Code Emotion?

How fast should coders be required to decode? Issues of coding speed are both practical and theoretical problems. First, the practical problem: Most observational coding is very slow. As noted above, Al Ross and I have developed a real-time computer-assisted coding system (the Affect Wheel) for coding emotion in marital interaction. This system has produced reasonable levels of reliability, and it has predicted important criterion variables (e.g., in a recent study, parents' marital interaction as coded with the Affect Wheel at Time 1 was able to predict the teacher's ratings of their child's behavior problems in school 3 years later; Katz & Gottman, 1992). To accomplish this feat, the coders have to be very highly trained. This training time is essential for them to be able to see details, and then to give rapidly formed first impressions. For example, it takes a while to learn how to see things in the face, and then it takes longer for this learning to become automatic. The theoretical issue accompanies the practical issue: Since people do not decode facial expressions in normal interaction by going over a videotape many times, one may question the validity of a method of forming emotion judgments that is so different from the normal processes people employ in their everyday behavior. An empirical approach would suggest doing both types of coding (slow and fast), and deciding what information is missed in the prediction of some important criterion variable by a rapid coding speed.

It is interesting to speculate about how emotion ought to be coded. Although increased coding speed was motivated by practical concerns, it could be the case that coding at a macro level at the speed at which signals are normally sent in interaction will pick up precisely those cues that emotional communication was designed to send. In other words, a practical innovation may lead to an understanding of emotional communication. It may be the case that emotional signals in real time are processed by particular regions of the brain that have to do with automatic scanning for danger and other cues important for survival (e.g., the amygdala; see LeDoux, 1986). Slowing down the coding process may introduce the kinds of thinking and decision making in observers that avoid precisely those parts of the brain responsive to emotional cues in real time. For example, slowing things down may introduce the kind of effortful processing of information that automatically puts coding emotion into a cognitive realm other than that usually involved in the processing of emotion.

A caveat is in order here: Once emotion judgments in real time have proven themselves empirically, it may be very important to go back and code specific features slowly so that we can try to determine more precisely what was being measured in a real-time system. Although the coding manual tells observers what to look for, and inter- and intraobserver reliability must be established and maintained, this does not insure that the observers are measuring what the coding manual instructed them to detect. The more microanalytic systems can play a role in ensuring the purity of the theoretical constructs that the more rapid and more macroanalytic systems purport to measure. Thus, there needs to be a continual dialectic between macro and micro levels of measurement.

PRELIMINARY FINDINGS OF IMPORTANCE FOR THE FIELD OF MARITAL AND FAMILY RELATIONSHIPS

The following discussion is based on two research collaborations—one with Robert Levenson, and the other with Lynn Fainsilber Katz. It seems remarkable that in all the literature on divorce, only four longitudinal studies have tried to predict which couples would remain married and which would dissolve their marriages over time (Gottman & Levenson, 1992). With couples who had been married an average of 5 years, Levenson and I discovered that it was possible to predict the longitudinal course of marriages by using specific affect codes obtained at Time 1. When we coded only facial expressions, using Ekman and Friesen's (1978b) EMFACS, we found that disgust expressions by the wife predicted marital separation over 4 years ($r = .51$); in couples who later separated, the wife expressed disgust on her face more often than once a minute, whereas the rate was far lower for couples who did not separate. With the SPAFF we found that couples who progressed on a cascade toward divorce were more defensive, more contemptuous, and more negative as listeners (stonewalling) than stable couples. These results suggest that there may be a cascade of processes tapped by specific affects that predict dissolution at various stages of the marriage.

Katz and I (Katz & Gottman, 1992) have studied the effect of the parents' marital interaction on the child's emotional development. Two specific marital interaction patterns were identified by cluster analysis. One was a symmetrical mutually hostile pattern (best indexed by the wife's contempt), and the other was an asymmetrical pattern in which the wife was angry and the husband was withdrawn (which we called the pursuer–distancer pattern). The marital interaction samples were collected when the children were 5 years old. Three years later, once the children were in the early elementary school years, their teachers filled out Child Behavior Checklists on the children, and on all the same-sex children in their classes. The mutually hostile pattern predicted externalizing behavior problems in the children (e.g., aggressiveness), whereas the pursuer–distancer pattern predicted internalizing problems (e.g., depression).

SUMMARY

It is clear that there are some advantages to studying emotion in the context of naturalistic social interaction, and in particular in close relationships, which are likely to generate a great deal of emotion in the laboratory. Although there are difficulties inherent in this endeavor, consideration of the methodological problems leads to insights that stretch current thinking about the nature of emotion. The paradigm has already led to challenges in our current thinking on the physiology of emotion, as well as insights within the field of close relationships. Future research may benefit from combining laboratory and naturalistic procedures.

REFERENCES

Argyle, M. (1969). *Social interaction*. Chicago: Aldine.

Bakeman, R., & Gottman, J. M. (1986). *Observing behavior sequences: From systematic observation to sequential analysis*. New York: Cambridge University Press.

Bateson, G., Jackson, D. D., Haley, J., & Weakland, J. (1956). Toward a theory of schizophrenia. *Behavioral Science, 1*, 251–264.

Biglan, A., Lewin, L., & Hops, H. (1990). A contextual approach to the problem of aversive practices in families. In G. R. Patterson (Ed.), *Depression and aggression in family interaction* (pp. 43–58). Hillsdale, NJ: Erlbaum.

Ekman, P. (1984). Expression and the nature of emotion. In K. P. Scherer & P. Ekman (Eds.), *Approaches to emotion* (pp. 319–344). Hillsdale, NJ: Erlbaum.

Ekman, P., & Friesen, W. V. (1978a). *The Facial Action Coding System (FACS)*. Palo Alto, CA: Consulting Psychologists Press.

Ekman, P., & Friesen, W. V. (1978b). *EMFACS7: Emotional coding of facial action*, Unpublished manual, University of California at San Francisco.

Ekman, P., Friesen, W. V., & Ellsworth, P. (1972). *Emotion in the human face: Guidelines for research and an integration of findings*. Elmsford, NY: Pergamon Press.

Ekman, P., Friesen, W. V., & Simons, R. C. (1985). Is the startle reaction an emotion? *Journal of Personality and Social Psychology, 49*, 1416–1426.

Feld, S. (1982). *Sound and sentiment: Birds, weeping, poetics and song in Kaluli expression*. Philadelphia: University of Pennsylvania Press.

Goldfried, M. R., & D'Zurilla, T. J. (1969). A behavioral-analytic model for assessing competence. In C. D. Spielberger (Ed.), *Current topics in clinical and community psychology* (Vol. 1, pp. 111–138). New York: Academic Press.

Gottman, J. M. (1979). *Marital interaction: Experimental Investigations*. New York: Academic Press.

Gottman, J. M., & Krokoff, L. (1989). Marital interaction and marital satisfaction: A longitudinal view. *Journal of Consulting and Clinical Psychology, 57*, 47–52.

Gottman, J. M., & Levenson, R. W. (1985). A valid procedure for obtaining self-report of affect in marital interaction. *Journal of Consulting and Clinical Psychology, 53*, 151–160.

Gottman, J. M., & Levenson, R. W. (1992). Marital processes predictive of later dissolution: Behavior, physiology and health. *Journal of Personality and Social Psychology, 63*, 221–233.

Gottman, J. M., Notarius, C., Markman, H., Bank, S., Yoppi, B., & Rubin, M. E. (1976). Behavior exchange theory and marital decision making. *Journal of Personality and Social Psychology, 34*, 14–23.

Hagen, U. (1975). *Respect for acting*. New York: Holt.

Haley, J. (1964). Research on family patterns: An instrument measurement. *Family Process, 3*, 41–65.

Hops, H., Wills, T. A., Patterson, G. R., & Weiss, R. L. (1972). *The Marital Interaction Coding System (MICS)*. Unpublished manuscript, University of Oregon, Eugene.

Katz, L. F., & Gottman, J. M. (1992). *Patterns of marital conflict predict children's internalizing and externalizing behaviors*. Unpublished manuscript, University of Washington, Seattle.

Knapp, M. (1972). *Nonverbal communication in human interaction*. New York: Holt, Rinehart & Winston.

LeDoux, J. (1986). A neurobiological view of the psychology of emotion. In J. LeDoux & W. Hirst (Eds.), *Mind and brain: Dialogues between cognitive psychology and neuroscience* (pp. 75–88). New York: Cambridge University Press.

Mehrabian, A. (1972). *Nonverbal communication*. New York: Aldine-Atherton.

Patterson, G. R. (1982). *Coercive family process*. Eugene, OR: Castalia.

Raush, H. L., Barry, W. A., Hertel, R. K., & Swain, M. A. (1974). *Communication, conflict, and marriage*. San Francisco: Jossey-Bass.

Rogers, L. E., & Farace, R. V. (1975). Analysis of relational communication in dyads: New measurement procedures. *Human Communication Research, 1*, 222–239.

Sackett, G. P. (1979). The lag sequential analysis of contingency and cyclicity in behavioral interaction research. In J. D. Osofsky (Ed.), *Handbook of infant development* (pp. 623–649). New York: Wiley.

Schaap, C. (1982). *Communication and adjustment in marriage*. Lisse, The Netherlands: Swets & Zeitlinger.

Scherer, K. R. (1974). Acoustic concomitants of emotional dimensions: Judging affect from synthesized tone sequences. In S. Weitz (Ed.), *Nonverbal communication* (pp. 105–111). New York: Oxford University Press.

Scherer, K. R. (1984). On the nature and function of emotion: A component process approach. In K. R. Scherer & P. Ekman (Eds.), *Approaches to emotion* (pp. 293–317). Hillsdale, NJ: Erlbaum.

Scherer, K. R., & Ekman, P. (Eds.). (1984). *Approaches to emotion*. Hillsdale, NJ: Erlbaum.

Soskin, W. F., & John, V. P. (1963). The study of spontaneous talk. In T. Barker (Ed.), *The stream of behavior* (pp. 21–46). New York: Appleton-Century-Crofts.

Thibaut, J. W., & Kelley, H. H. (1961). *The social psychology of groups*. New York: Wiley.

Tomkins, S. S. (1963). *Affect, imagery, and consciousness: Vol. 2. The negative affects*. New York: Springer.

Watzlawick, P., Beavin, J. H., & Jackson, D. D. (1968). *Pragmatics of human communication: A study of interactional patterns, pathologies and paradoxes*. New York: Norton.

34

Emotion Expression in Groups

DAVID R. HEISE
JOHN O'BRIEN

Face-to-face encounters are a primary arena for the display and feeling of those intense, ephemeral, and situated affective experiences we call "emotions." Emotions, as much as interpersonal transactions, reflect the social structure and the encompassing culture of participants involved in interaction, and emotions help manifest that structure and culture from moment to moment. A sociology of emotions that deals with these themes emerged in the 1980s (Kemper, 1990a; Thoits, 1989).

EMPIRICAL EVIDENCE

Earlier sociologists, beginning with Bales (1950), systematically observed groups in laboratories and found that a substantial proportion of group interaction is devoted to the socioemotional issues of expressing affect and dealing with tension (Hare, 1976, Ch. 3, reviews the work). Simultaneously, field studies of liking and disliking in natural groups showed that interpersonal sentiments collate into informal social structures (Hare, 1976, Ch. 7— a discovery that is still being explored in the burgeoning field of social network analysis (e.g., Burt, 1982; Knoke & Kuklinski, 1982; Bradley, 1987).

Ethnomethodologists (sociologists concerned with the methods by which people create, maintain, and heed implicit cultural rules) demonstrated emotional commitments to common understandings in social relationships by having a group participant purposely violate some mundane, shared understanding. For example, one breaching experiment required students to spend from 15 minutes to an hour acting as boarders in their own homes: "They were instructed to conduct themselves in a circumspect and polite fashion. They were to avoid getting personal, to use formal address, to speak only when spoken to" (Garfinkel, 1967, p. 47). Though a fifth of the assignments were not completed because the students were afraid to carry through or because their families refused to take their performance seriously, the remaining four-fifths of the students found emotions rampant:

> Reports were filled with accounts of astonishment, bewilderment, shock, anxiety, embarrassment, and anger, and with charges from various family members that the student was mean, inconsiderate, selfish, nasty, or impolite. Family members demanded explanations: What's the matter? What's gotten into you? Did you get fired? Are you sick? What are you being so superior about? Why are you mad? Are you out of your mind or are you just stupid? One student acutely embarrassed his mother in front of her friends by asking if she minded if he had a snack from the refrigerator. "Mind if you have a little snack? You've been eating little snacks around here for years without asking me. What's gotten into you?" One mother, infuriated when her daughter spoke to her only when she was spoken to, began to shriek in angry denunciation of the daughter for her disrespect and insubordination and refused to be calmed by the student's sister. (Garfinkel, 1967, p. 48)

Some families tried to connect with the students' behavior as a joint comedy routine, but they soon gave up in irritation and exasperated anger. Other families accounted for the students' behavior in terms of a mood or a prior misfortune; they became angry when the students did not accept help in dealing with the problem. Sometimes nasty interpersonal schisms developed that could be repaired only by revealing the experiment.

Purposely breaching a norm distresses the actor at least as much as observers. Milgram (1974) sensitively related the feelings of a person asking passengers on a New York subway for their seats—a demonstration of breaching that he had assigned to his students, and then decided to do himself. Waves of emotion accompanied his experience and continued until the interpersonal situation was over. At first, Milgram nearly quit because of his unexpected apprehension and intense emotional reaction. It was only through the urging of a student observer that he finally did approach a man and say, "Excuse me, sir, may I have your seat?"

> A moment of stark anomic panic overcame me. But the man got right up and gave me the seat. A second blow was yet to come. Taking the man's seat, I was overwhelmed by the need to behave in a way that would justify my request. My head sank between my knees, and I could feel my face blanching. I was not role-playing. I actually felt as if I were going to perish. Then the third discovery: as soon as I got off the train, at the next station, all of the tension disappeared. (Milgram, 1974, p. 72)

Gregory's (1982) study of intentional breachers showed that people cope with the severe anxiety generated by rule breaking through rationalizations that normalize their actions to themselves, and through public accounts that normalize their actions to others, including tacit accounts such as Milgram's sinking head and blanched face. Garfinkel (1967, pp. 68–70) noted changes in emotion with habitual rule breaking. For example, student breachers who had to bargain for standard-priced merchandise just once were more distressed than student breachers beginning a series of six bargaining episodes. Distress declined with repetition, so most students with a sequence of trials actually looked forward to and enjoyed the assignment by the third epi-

sode, and some resolved to continue similar behavior in the future.

Breaching experiments showed that bland expressions and reserved miens, to be seen in audiences confronting heinous events in the mass media, are misleading indicators of how people emotionally respond to interpersonal deviance. In face-to-face situations, even trifling violations of mores generate intense emotions—for observers and perpetrators alike. The breaching studies reveal "a definite and strong relationship between common understandings and social affects" (Garfinkel, 1967, p. 50).

Breaching of norms usually provokes negative emotions, but other studies show that interpersonal relationships are the primary medium for people to express positive emotions as well. Records from observational studies in laboratories (Hare, 1976, Table 4) show that tension releases (laughing, displaying satisfaction) constitute about 6% of all events in groups. Brandstatter (1983) found that housewives reported their most positive moods when others were present, especially family and friends. Kraut & Johnston (1979) studied smiling in several different settings, and found that displays of happiness were correlated with the presence of people to see it, even though the basis for happiness might be a personal achievement. For example, bowlers who made a strike often did not smile until they turned to face their friends. Recordings of social interactions also reveal frequent occurrences of laughter, even in serious, task-oriented situations. For example, Grimshaw (1989, Appendix A) provided an accurate transcription of discourse by four professors during the *in camera* segment of a dissertation defense—the part devoted to discussion of the candidate's graduate career, dissertation, and career prospects. Twelve minutes of serious discussion were interspersed with 26 instances of laughs or chuckles (often by multiple people), which amounts to a laugh about every half minute on the average.

The correlation between emoting and socializing provides the empirical basis for supposing that emotions are intertwined with the maintenance and alteration of social relationships, and with the cultural understandings that gird social events. Emotionality in groups also encourages investigating how emotions synchronize social interaction and foster group unity. We turn now to reviewing some theoretical formulations concerned with these themes.

SOCIAL CONSTRUCTIONISM

Social constructionists approach the interpenetration of emotions and sociocultural phenomena by understanding the expression of emotions as intelligent conduct, contrived according to cultural rules so as to effect desired interpersonal outcomes. In this perspective, displays of emotion are not uncivilized eruptions coming from deep within individual psyches, but rather amount to sophisticated social discourse that is employed to influence others.

Representative of this kind of theorizing is Schieffelin's (1983) analysis of the systematic use of anger, grief, and shame among the Kaluli people in Papua New Guinea—a study that expands on Goffman's (1967) analyses of the function of emotion displays in self-presentation. Among the Kaluli, anger and grief are ways of entreating others, while shaming is employed as a way of obstructing appeals. First, let us consider anger; it is an assertive posture used to provoke, intimidate, excite, and inspire others.

> A man whose expectations have been frustrated or who has suffered wrong or injury at the hands of others does not usually suppress his annoyance. Rather he is likely to orchestrate his anger into a splendid frightening rage, projecting himself with threats and recriminations against his (often equally angry) opponent . . . (Schieffelin, 1983, p. 183)

Anger implies that the person has suffered a loss of some kind and legitimately is entitled to redress. Accordingly,

> an angry man is not only intimidating, he is also a figure of pathos for the Kaluli, and a display of anger is frequently meant to be a forceful plea for support. . . . Thus anger attains a particular rhetorical force, a certain kind of measure and legitimacy, and a set of implications, from the way it is situated in the scenario of reciprocity. (pp. 186–187)

A Kaluli can also attain influence with friends and relatives by posturing as needy, vulnerable, and dependent, in order to appeal to sentimentality and compassion:

> [G]rief is the extreme posture of vulnerability and appeal. Given meaning, like anger, within the Kaluli sense of reciprocity, grief represents a picture of a person reduced to powerlessness and vulnerability by devastating loss, a figure of great pathos, one who is in principle entitled to redress. Powerful in rage, men are reduced to a particular helplessness in grief, weeping in a hysterical and uncontrolled manner. (p. 187)

A display of grief insinuates that a person, who is incapacitated in seeking justified compensation for a loss, awaits redress from goodhearted others who in one way or another are able to help. The appeal is largely to others' sense of justice, though among the Kaluli grief achieves some of its persuasiveness from the implicit danger that grief can turn into rage.

Faced with forceful interpersonal rhetorics, such as anger and grief, as means of commandeering one's energies and resources, Kalulis depend on shame as a tool to help preserve their own interests. A Kaluli may question another's rights to something lost, attempting to evoke shame over illegitimate claims:

> The phrasing of the challenge as a rhetorical question aims to avoid a confrontation or clash of wills and risk of anger, and throws the one to whom it is directed on the defensive. Moreover, for an assertive move, the question "Is it yours?" implies that the request for the object amounts to a kind of potential theft that suggests the threat of retaliation in line with the Kaluli's sense of reciprocity. (p. 188)
>
> Shame is revealed here as a situation as much as a private emotion: both its existence and meaning are products of interaction, not loss of reputation or a sense of right and wrong. . . . The legitimacy of one's basic posture of assertion or of appeal has been removed. (p. 189)

Thus, Kaluli emotions form a nonverbal system of interpersonal communication, used in negotiating culturally normative rights and obligations: "[They] are socially located and have a social aim. To this degree they are located not only in the person, but in the social situation and interaction which, indeed, they help construct" (Schieffelin, 1983, pp. 190–191). Being declarations of mind for social consumption, public displays of emotion may not reveal what a person really feels. Asked what other persons feel about an event, a Kaluli informant typically replies, "'I don't know. How is one to know what another man feels?' . . . [or that they] *acted as if* they were angry (happy, dismayed, etc.)'" (p. 184; italics Schieffelin's).

The Kalulis' use of anger, grief, and shame has parallels in industrial societies, and Westerners engage in the calculated use of emotional displays no less than New Guineans. Clark (1990) has identified a number of strategies by which emotion presentations keep others in their place and allow an individual to gain or recover status; Heise (1989) has presented an alternative approach to these issues. Moreover, because emotion displays in everyday social affairs articulate underlying ideologies that some people want legitimated, sophisticated expressions of emotion have turned into a form of labor that individuals market in capitalist societies (Hochschild, 1979, 1983, 1990); we return to the issue of commercial emotion work in a later section.

SOCIAL DETERMINISM

Social determinists approach the interpenetration of emotions and sociocultural phenomena by understanding emotions as authentic, involuntary responses that occur during social interactions. Emotions emerge from the operative social structure in a situation, and emotions allow people to sense that structure, as well as the social consequences of actions. Moreover, because displays of emotion broadcast a person's subjective appraisals to others, emotions contribute tacitly to sharing views about social structure and to synchronization of action and feeling within a group.

Kemper's deterministic framework (Kemper, 1978, 1981, 1990b; Kemper & Collins, 1990) posits that people in social interaction are arrayed along two relational dimensions. First, a person, Ego, has a degree of "status" that is determined by Alter's esteem for Ego and that determines the extent to which Alter is likely to engage in unconditional acts of regard for Ego. A person with high status realizes other people's ideals, so that the others voluntarily and spontaneously function on that person's behalf. Second, Ego has a degree of "power" in a relationship that is a net outcome of Alter's dependency on Ego and that determines the likelihood that Alter will perform as Ego wills, conditional on Ego's surveillance of Alter and on Ego's foiling Alter's power plays. A person with power is seen as resourceful by

others, so others function on that person's behalf strategically as a way of sustaining their own objectives, trying to consolidate control over the resources held by the powerful person.

Emotions arise as interpersonal events affirm and change individuals' levels of status and power. Events affirming social status and power yield "structural" emotions that characterize the nature of the relationship. For example, acting in such a way as to affirm another's exalted status yields emotions related to love, and Kemper (1972) has identified different kinds of love-related emotions. The variations are related to the power of the loved person and the status and power of the lover (e.g., a feeling of "romantic" love arises when both have high status and high power; "brotherly" love arises when both have high status and low power).

"Consequent" emotions occur during social interaction as events change social structure, as people distribute responsibility for these changes, and as they compare structural changes to their anticipations. Increases or decreases in status or power of self or of other lead to specific emotions, as discussed by Kemper in Chapter 4 of this volume. According to Kemper (1981, p. 338), "particular social stimulus keys fit particular locks to produce particular emotions." This explains why people may feel a different emotion than the one they socially display: They interpret the personal implications of interaction and feel the appropriate emotion even if they are constructing a culturally or ideologically suitable emotional display that advances their rational interests.

Another branch of social determinism focuses on simultaneous emotional arousal within a collectivity, as a result of rituals involving cultural symbols (e.g., a flag, the word "democracy," the presence of a baby, etc.), or as a result of emotional contagion (Hatfield, Cacioppo, & Rapson, 1992). Early social analysts (e.g., LeBon, 1895/1960) thought that emotional contagion in crowds swept away individual rationality and substituted emotion-based goal seeking and synchronization of action. However, McPhail's (1991) extensive observational studies of crowds suggest that contagion phenomena are rare in those crowd situations where they are supposed to thrive; emotion contagion may occur mainly in collective situations where conditions encourage altered states of consciousness (Prince, 1982).

Durkheim (1912/1954) proposed that rituals hold society together by producing sacred objects and moral constraints, and Collins (1975, 1981, 1990) has expanded on Durkheim's theme by proposing that a common emotional mood generated in rituals creates social solidarity and diffuses charismatic emotional energies that preserve and disseminate normative group patterns. Profaning a symbol usually elicits anger and conflict between groups or between group factions, but reaffirming symbols generates positive emotion and synchronization within a group. Collins holds that the inherent emotionality of even commonplace interaction rituals is the glue that holds society together and the driving force that mobilizes social change (Collins, 1981).

SOCIAL INTERACTIONISM

Social interactionists approach the interpenetration of emotions and sociocultural phenomena by understanding that emotions are both constructed and determined. "The interactionist model points to a certain paradox; a feeling is what happens to us. Yet it is also what we do to make it happen" (Hochschild, 1990, p. 120). Emotions erupt during social interaction. Then they are judged for suitability according to cultural and ideological standards, and are managed to effect culturally acceptable displays that yield social accord.

Affect control theory (Heise, 1977, 1979, 1986; Smith-Lovin & Heise, 1988; Smith-Lovin, 1990; MacKinnon & Heise, in press) proposes that people construct and understand social action so as to have important cultural meanings affirmed by impressions generated in manifest behavior. People credit themselves and others with specific identities during social encounters. They then engage in physical and mental work so that events create impressions that maintain sentiments attached to their identities, as well as to other categories of action (i.e., behaviors, settings, and personal conditions—emotions included).

Sentiments for all categories of action can be measured quantitatively on three culturally universal dimensions of affective meaning (Osgood, May, & Miron, 1975): "evaluation" (the extent to which things seem good vs. bad); "potency" (impressions of powerfulness vs. powerlessness); and "activity" (impressions of activation vs. tranquility). The same dimensions serve for measuring transient impressions of people, behaviors, settings, and personal conditions, as generated by particular events. The theory proposes that people seek experiences in which transient evaluation–potency–activity impressions, created by an event, match their pre-existing sentiments as much as possible. Since research indicates that the impressions generated by an event are transformations of feelings that exist before the event (Smith-Lovin, 1987), people seek experiences that transform current feelings into new, sentiment-confirming feelings.

In affect control theory, emotions are momentary personal states that reflect how events affect people. The emotion depends on the current impression of the person, and on how that impression compares to the sentiment attached to the person's identity. For example, a person may feel overwhelmed or anxious if made to seem bad and weak, but a more extreme response (feeling ashamed, desperate, or depressed) is to be expected if the person has a particularly good and powerful role in a group.

Affect control theory has an empirical base and can be implemented mathematically in a computer program (Heise & Lewis, 1988) that allows prediction of the probable emotions resulting from events. For example, in an analysis where one person is identified as a father and the other as a daughter, we can specify that the father educates the daughter (a behavior predicted by the affect control model). The theory predicts that the father then will feel generous, secure, or forgiving while the daughter feels humble, relaxed, or touched. Forcing the daughter to disobey the father leads to predictions that the daughter must be feeling irate, angry, or anxious, and that the father feels melancholy, apprehensive, or shocked. These particular analytic outcomes are based on sentiments measured in the southern United States, and predictions would be different with sentiment measurements from other cultures. The affect control simulation system currently allows analyses to be conducted for U.S., Canadian, Irish, German, and Japanese interactants.

People protect their pre-existing sentiments both through their own conduct and through their interpretations of others' conduct. To continue the father–daughter example, the father may exonerate the daughter who has disobeyed him, and his action will thus begin to reaffirm pre-existing sentiments about fathers and daughters. Alternatively, according to analyses, he may begin to see his daughter as greedy, manipulative, or mean—reconceptualizations that match pre-existing sentiments to the girl's behavior. Thus, in affect control theory, a socially undesirable emotion can be changed by implementing a new event that will replace the unwanted emotion with a different emotion, or by reinterpretating a past event so that the emotion produced by the original interpretation is replaced by another emotion.

Thoits's (1990) typology of emotion management techniques includes implementation of new events and reinterpretation of past events as ways of managing emotions through reconstruction of the situations that evoke the emotions. Thoits notes that emotions can also be managed directly by manipulating accompanying physiology (as with drugs), by performing or fantasizing expressive gestures for desired emotions, or by recategorizing one's affective sensations in terms of a desired emotion.

Spontaneous eruptions of emotion arise from appraising security, control, and stimulation with reference to a personal identity, and the consequent emotion may not accord with emotion norms appropriate to a publicly negotiated identity (Heise & MacKinnon, in press). The personal and the normative systems unite when group members are deeply committed to their group identities; in this case, people spontaneously emote and act according to group norms in order to experience affirmation of self through the reflected appraisals of others (Burke & Reitzes, 1991). The two systems diverge when a person maintains multiple definitions of a situation simultaneously, and the actor's deepest commitment is to an identity other than the public identity. In that case, emotion management is required to prevent the display of emotions appropriate to the private identity, and to authenticate one's supposed commitment to the public identity.

Hochschild's (1983) study of emotion work among flight attendants illustrates how people have to manage emotions in order to hide tacit definitions of a situation and their alienation from the public definitions of the situation. In the heyday of friendly airline service, attendants were instructed to treat passengers as if they were family members and friends in their own living rooms, and the attendants—deeply committed to their prestigious roles—were able to do so and to gain satisfaction from their work. "When feelings are successfully commercialized, the worker does not feel phony or alien; she feels somehow satisfied in how personal her service actually was" (Hochschild, 1983, p. 136). However, as airlines began encountering financial problems in the early 1970s and demanded more cost-efficient flying, attendants had to work longer shifts and cope with more people. Then deregulation of airlines dropped the price of tickets and brought more difficult passengers on board (e.g., children, frightened elderly persons, people unacquainted with airplane travel) and further increased the workload for attendants. Hochschild (1983) summarizes the consequences as follows:

> When an industry speed-up drastically shortens the time available for contact between flight attendants and passengers, it can become virtually impossible to deliver emotional labor. In that event, the transmutation of emotion work, feeling rules, and social exchange will fail. Company claims about offering a smile "from the inside out" (Delta) will become untenable. The living room analogy will collapse into a flat slogan. The mosaic of "as if" techniques will fall to pieces, and deep acting will be replaced by surface displays that lack conviction. (p. 121)

Nowadays airlines demand overwhelming housework and serving from flight attendants, leaving little time for pleasantries. The ideal of the friendly attendant is still advertised by airlines, but attendants have little commitment to this role, which they express with superficial smiles. Their commitment is to a job with lowered status, in which they see passengers as crowds of strangers—a job that yields private feelings of estrangement, even hostility, as they do their work.

HOLONOMIC EMERGENCE THEORY

Some sociologists (Bradley, 1987; Gregory, 1990; O'Brien, 1989, in press) propose that sociocultural structures emerge from interplays of individual psyches within aggregates of people. In this view, seemingly separate psychological processes, including affective ones, complement one another (Stephenson, 1986a, 1986b), and the complementation leads to the manifestation of emergent sociocultural structures. Alterations in one psychological process can cause changes in the emergent structures, and thereby reflect back on the same or other psychological processes. The basic metaphor for emergence is a holograph, applied to sociocultural phenomena as Pribram (1971a, 1971b, 1982) applied the model to mind–brain organization.

Bradley (1987) has used a holographic paradigm to understand why some informal groups regenerate the same social structure after virtually every member has been replaced, and other groups disintegrate under the same conditions. He postulates that informal charismatic groups organize almost instantly according to the capacity of their members to stimulate, and accept, positive affect (love). On the other hand, formal groups organize through cognitive rule making and through power relations involving negative affect. Group instability correlates with the degree of overreliance on either love or power as the primary organizing mechanism. In effect, group survival requires balancing positive bonds and power relations based tacitly on negative emotions. Whether this happens or not depends on whether a group's composition includes individuals disposed to project each kind of bond. Bradley concludes that group emergence, organization, and survival all relate to affective processes.

O'Brien (in press) uses the semantic differential technique in connection with a holonomic model to assess whether individuals apply basic distinctions in ways that project normative culture in their social groups. The particular distinctions studied by O'Brien form a highly interrelated complex for most people in Western cultures (Needham, 1972, 1978): high, low; right, left; man, woman; God, Satan; good, bad; can do, cannot do. O'Brien assesses the kinds of evaluative complexes that groups and individuals maintain by obtaining ratings of each of the 12 signs on six bipolar scales made from the sign pairs. A sign is meaningfully related to a distinction when it receives a non-neutral rating on the scale corresponding to the distinction.

The relationship of the complexes to decision making and emotion is examined by comparing the complexes of conventional people to those with alcohol impairment (i.e., those hospitalized for substance abuse treatment and those convicted of driving under the influence of alcohol). The findings show that these affective meaning complexes are pronounced and stable for years among most people, but less stable for alcoholics; that they are different in character for conventional people than for alcoholics; and, that the capacity to maintain one's meaning complex in the face of a distressing emotional experience declines for people with less pronounced complexes, especially alcoholics. The interpretive thesis is that individuals' affective meaning complexes resonate with or suppress each other during social interaction, leading to emergent norms reflecting the composition of the group. When alcoholics are present, their peculiar complexes project interactionally into altered group norms, which may be different from general cultural norms. This can trigger inappropriate decision making, unorthodox behavior (e.g., drunken driving), and distressing affective experiences. And distressing affective experiences arising from unorthodox group norms can further incapacitate alcoholics' affective meaning systems as a basis for generating orthodox culture.

Explication of the holonomic metaphor and empirical testing of its basic assumptions are still in progress. However, the approach offers a novel perspective on how sociocultural structures emerge from and predispose individual thoughts, feelings, and actions: a classic issue for social scientists studying groups and collectivities.

A CHALLENGE
FOR THE FUTURE

During decades of research based on laboratory studies, participant observation, and ethnographic projects, sociologists accumulated extensive evidence that interpersonal dynamics are laden with emotional processes. Attempts to organize the data have produced a rich body of sociological theory that relates affect to social processes and social organization.

Currently sociologists are returning to empirical study to test and refine their theories. Kemper (1991) found that his power–status model could account successfully for more than two-thirds of emotion episodes self-reported by some of the respondents in an eight-nation study of emotions (Scherer, Wallbott, & Summerfield, 1986). Lynn Smith-Lovin and her students are empirically testing affect control theory (Robinson & Smith-Lovin, 1992), and at the time of this writing they are demonstrating high levels of success for affect control theory's predictions of emotions in social encounters described in vignettes.

The challenge now is to develop sensitive measures of emotion for studying rapid changes in affect that occur during social interaction in natural groups. One approach is to employ the latest in sound–image recording technology and to code nonverbal emotional expressions (Scherer & Ekman, 1982), drawing especially on Ekman and Friesen's (1978) explication of facial expressions. Meaningful sociological analyses of emotion also require assessing people's definitions of situations and their appraisals of events; such meanings might be tapped by replaying recordings for participants and eliciting their interpretations of what was happening during social interaction. It remains to be seen whether social psychologists can develop less costly, labor-intensive, and intrusive techniques for assessing emotions and operative meanings in group encounters.

Acknowledgments. We gratefully acknowledge help from Peggy Thoits in structuring this chapter and from Neil MacKinnon in articulating some ideas.

REFERENCES

Bales, R. F. (1950). *Interaction process analysis: A method for the study of small groups.* Cambridge, MA: Addison-Wesley.

Bradley, R. T. (1987). *Charisma and social structure.* New York: Paragon.

Brandstatter, H. (1983). Emotional responses to other persons in everyday life situations. *Journal of Personality and Social Psychology, 45,* 871–883.

Burke, P. J., & Reitzes, D. C. (1991). An identity theory approach to commitment. *Social Psychology Quarterly, 54,* 239–251.

Burt, R. S. (1982). *Toward a structural theory of action: Network models of social structure, perception, and action.* New York: Academic Press.

Clark, C. (1990). Emotions and micropolitics in everyday life: Some patterns and paradoxes of "place." In T. D. Kemper (Ed.), *Research agendas in the sociology of emotions* (pp. 305–333). Albany: State University of New York Press.

Collins, R. (1975). *Conflict sociology: Toward an explanatory science.* New York: Academic Press.

Collins, R. (1981). On the microfoundations of macrosociology. *American Journal of Sociology, 86,* 984–1014.

Collins, R. (1990). Stratification, emotional energy, and the transient emotions. In T. D. Kemper (Ed.), *Research agendas in the sociology of emotions* (pp. 27–57). Albany: State University of New York Press.

Durkheim, E. (1954). *The elementary forms of the religious life.* New York: Free Press. (Original work published 1912)

Ekman, P., & Friesen, W. V. (1978). *Manual for the Facial Action Coding System.* Palo Alto, CA: Consulting Psychologists Press.

Garfinkel, H. (1967). *Studies in ethnomethodology.* Englewood Cliffs, NJ: Prentice-Hall.

Goffman, E. (1967). *Interaction ritual.* Garden City, NY: Doubleday/Anchor.

Gregory, S. W., Jr. (1982). Accounts as assembled from breaching experiments. *Symbolic Interaction, 5,* 49–63.

Gregory, S. W., Jr. (1990). Analysis of fundamental frequency reveals covariation in interview partners' speech. *Journal of Nonverbal Behavior, 14,* 237–251.

Grimshaw, A. D. (1989). *Collegial discourse: Professional conversation among peers.* Norwood, NJ: Ablex.

Hare, A. P. (1976). *Handbook of small group research* (2nd ed.). New York: Free Press.

Hatfield, E., Cacioppo, J. T., & Rapson, R. (1992). The logic of emotion: Emotional contagion. In M. S. Clark (Ed.), *Review of personality and social psychology: Vol. 14. Emotional and social behavior* (pp. 151–177). Newbury Park, CA: Sage.

Heise, D. R. (1977). Social action as the control of affect. *Behavioral Science, 22,* 163–177.

Heise, D. R. (1979). *Understanding events: Affect and the construction of social action.* New York: Cambridge University Press.

Heise, D. R. (1986). Modeling symbolic interaction. In S. Lindenberg, J. S. Coleman, & S. Nowak (Eds.), *Approaches to social theory* (pp. 291–309). New York: Russell Sage Foundation.

Heise, D. R. (1989). Effects of emotion displays on social identification. *Social Psychology Quarterly, 52,* 10–21.

Heise, D. R., & Lewis, E. (1988). *Introduction to interact* [Computer program and documentation]. Dubuque, IA: William C. Brown.

Heise, D. R., & MacKinnon, Neil J. (in press). Affective control in social behavior. In R. K. Shelly (Ed.), *Emergent structure, interaction, and affect.* Albany: State University of New York Press.

Hochschild, A. R. (1979). Emotion work, feeling rules, and social structure. *American Journal of Sociology, 85,* 551–575.

Hochschild, A. R. (1983). *The managed heart: The commercialization of human feeling.* Berkeley: University of California Press.

Hochschild, A. R. (1990). Ideology and emotion management: A perspective and path for future research. In T. D. Kemper (Ed.), *Research agendas in the sociology of emotions* (pp. 117–142). Albany: State University of New York Press.

Kemper, T. D. (1972). Power, status, and love. In D. R. Heise (Ed.), *Personality and socialization* (pp. 180–203). Chicago: Rand McNally.

Kemper, T. D. (1978). *A social interactional theory of emotion.* New York: Wiley.

Kemper, T. D. (1981). Social constructionist and positivist approaches to the sociology of emotions. *American Journal of Sociology, 87,* 336–362.

Kemper, T. D. (Ed.). (1990a). *Research agendas in the sociology of emotions*. Albany: State University of New York Press.

Kemper, T. D. (1990b). Social relations and emotions: A structural approach. In T. D. Kemper (Ed.), *Research agendas in the sociology of emotions* (pp. 207–237). Albany: State University of New York Press.

Kemper, T. D. (1991). Predicting emotions from social relations. *Social Psychology Quarterly*, 54, 330–342.

Kemper, T. D., & Collins, R. (1990). Dimensions of micro-interaction. *American Journal of Sociology*, 96, 32–68.

Knoke, D., & Kuklinski, J. H. (1982). *Network analysis*. Beverly Hills, CA: Sage.

Kraut, R. E., & Johnston, R. E. (1979). Social and emotional messages of smiling: An ethological approach. *Journal of Personality and Social Psychology*, 37, 1539–1553.

LeBon, G. (1960). *The psychology of the crowd*. New York: Viking. (Original work published 1895)

MacKinnon, N. J., & Heise, D. R. (in press). Affect control theory: Delineation and history. In J. Berger & M. Zelditch, Jr. (Eds.), *Theoretical research programs: Studies in theory growth*. Stanford, CA: Stanford University Press.

McPhail, C. (1991). *The myth of the madding crowd*. New York: Aldine/de Gruyter.

Milgram, S. (1974, June). An interview with Carol Tavris. *Psychology Today*, pp. 70–73.

Needham, R. (1972). *Belief, language, and experience*. Oxford: Basil Blackwell.

Needham, R. (1978). *Primordial characters*. Charlottesville: University Press of Virginia.

O'Brien, J. D. (1989). *Culture and agency: A "unit" approach*. Paper presented at the meeting of the American Sociological Association, San Francisco, CA.

O'Brien, J. D. (in press). *A holographic minimum unit model for culture, cognition–emotion and social action*. Lewiston, NY: Edwin–Mellon Press.

Osgood, C. H., May, W. H., & Miron, M. S. (1975). *Cross-cultural universals of affective meaning*. Urbana: University of Illinois Press.

Pribram, K. H. (1971a, September). The brain. *Psychology Today*, pp. 44–48; 88–90.

Pribram, K. H. (1971b). *Languages of the brain: Experimental paradoxes and principles in neuropsychology*. Englewood Cliffs, NJ: Prentice-Hall.

Pribram, K. H. (1982). What the fuss is all about. In K. Wilber (Ed.), *The holographic paradigm and other paradoxes: Exploring the leading edge of science* (pp. 27–34). Boulder, CO: Shambala.

Prince, R. (Ed.). (1982). Shamans and endorphins [Special issue]. *Ethos*, 10(4).

Robinson, D. & Smith-Lovin, L. (1992). Selective interaction as a strategy for identity maintenance: An affect control model. *Social Psychology Quarterly*, 55, 12–28.

Scherer, K. R., & Ekman, P. (Eds.). (1982). *Handbook of methods in nonverbal behavior research*. New York: Cambridge University Press.

Scherer, K. R., Wallbott, H. G., & Summerfield, A. B. (Eds.). (1986). *Experiencing emotion: A cross-cultural study*. Cambridge, England: Cambridge University Press.

Schieffelin, E. L. (1983). Anger and shame in the tropical forest: On affect as a cultural system in Papua New Guinea. *Ethos*, 11, 181–191.

Smith-Lovin, L. (1987). Impressions from events. *Journal of Mathematical Sociology*, 13, 35–70.

Smith-Lovin, L. (1990). Emotion as the confirmation and disconfirmation of identity: An affect control model. In T. D. Kemper (Ed.), *Research agendas in the sociology of emotions* (pp. 238–270). Albany: State University of New York Press.

Smith-Lovin, L., & Heise, D. R. (1988). *Analyzing social interaction: Advances in affect control theory*. New York: Gordon & Breach.

Stephenson, W. (1986a). William James, Niels Bohr, and complementarity: I. Concepts. *Psychological Record*, 36, 519–527.

Stephenson, W. (1986b). William James, Niels Bohr, and complementarity: II. Pragmatics of a thought. *Psychological Record*, 36, 529–543.

Thoits, P. A. (1989). The sociology of emotions. *Annual Review of Sociology*, 15, 317–342.

Thoits, P. A. (1990). Emotional deviance: research agendas. In T. D. Kemper (Ed.), *Research agendas in the sociology of emotions* (pp. 180–203). Albany: State University of New York Press.

35

Emotion and Change Processes in Psychotherapy

LESLIE S. GREENBERG

PSYCHOTHERAPEUTIC APPROACHES TO EMOTION

Psychotherapists have long concerned themselves with working with people's emotions. Theories of psychotherapy, however, have unfortunately failed to produce adequate theories of emotional functioning or comprehensive means of assessing emotion in therapy. Emotion for too long fell into the background in attempts at understanding dysfunction and therapeutic change. Despite the lack of attention (until very recently) to the emotions in psychotherapy, a number of propositions on the role of emotion in therapy have appeared in the psychotherapy literature over the years.

Although psychoanalysis was originally developed (Breuer & Freud, 1893–1895/1955) out of an appreciation of the neglected role of emotion in human affairs, Freud (1910/1957) and subsequent analytic theorists never really developed a systematic, comprehensive theory of emotion. Affect has therefore played a variety of different roles in psychodynamic theory and therapy. Initially, the strangulation of affect was seen as the main cause of hysteria, with abreaction as the cure (Breuer & Freud, 1893–1895/1955). As Freud developed his biologically based theorizing, he viewed affect as some form of psychic energy, and affects came to be regarded as drive derivatives with no independent status of their own. Freud (1910/1957) thereby lost sight of the crucial importance of affects as a fundamental aspect of human functioning. Wilhelm Reich (1942) continued to emphasize abreaction and the sustained expression of emotion throughout therapy as an important curative factor.

Ego psychologists (Fenichel, 1945; Rapaport, 1953) shifted their focus from affects as drive derivatives to a discussion of the relations between the ego and affects. They emphasized the problems caused by traumatic affects (especially anxiety and overwhelming of the ego), and the importance of the taming of affects. Object relations theorists, on the other hand, began emphasizing the role of feelings in object relations (Klein, 1937/1981). Sandler and Sandler (1978), for example, argued that affects are not exclusively tied to drives, but are a function of the relationship between the self and its internal objects (representations of others). Kernberg (1982) saw affects as the earliest experiences both with oneself and with others, and as providing links between self-representations and object representations. In this view, drives are thus derivatives of affects.

In psychodynamic practice, current perspectives emphasize the curative effects of the affective experience of conflicts in the transference with the therapist. Either transference interpretations or corrective emotional experience with the therapist are then seen as mutative (Eagle, 1984). In these views, fully experiencing affective responses in the context of a therapeutic relationship is seen as a prerequisite for correcting distortions of the object world. Within the practice of more modern object relations, self-psychological (Kohut, 1977), and interpersonally oriented (Sullivan, 1953) dynamic therapies, affect is seen as connecting the organism with its environment through both action tendencies and communication. Affective experience and expression are seen as being centrally involved in need satisfaction, and the owning of disclaimed action tendencies is seen as therapeutic (Schafer, 1983; Eagle, 1984).

In summary, in the classical psychoanalytic view emotions were seen generally as drive-related and as needing to be discharged or tamed, whereas in object relations, self-psychological, and interpersonal approaches emotions are seen as the building blocks of the self and as linking the person to others. Modern developments in psychodynamic therapy have led to a greater emphasis on the acknowledgment of disavowed affect and the owning of disclaimed action tendencies as important to therapeutic change (Eagle, 1984).

In the behavioral perspective, emotions have been treated fundamentally as learned emotional behaviors, and behavior therapists have focused on the clinical problem of modifying maladaptive emotional behavior. Fear and anxiety have received the greatest amount of attention from behavior theorists, and the views derived from their study have tended to become paradigmatic of behavioral views of emotion. Two major themes have dominated behavioral views of emotion. In one, the individual is viewed as a *tabula rasa* who learns emotional responses in relation to environmental contingencies (Skinner, 1953). In the other, emotion is viewed as stemming, at least in part, from innate propensities or predispositions (Rachman, 1978). In both perspectives, anxiety reduction is seen as the key to therapy; this has led to treatment strategies involving deconditioning, gradual exposure, or flooding. More recently, attempts have been made to explain the modification of fear as involving emotional processing (Rachman, 1980; Foa & Kozak, 1986). In this perspective, "emotional processing" is the modification of emotional memory by the incorporation of corrective information. Repeated exposure to fear situations—be it gradual or total, imaginal or *in vivo*—has been a key ingredient in the behavioral approach to the treatment of anxiety. Thus in the behavioral perspectives, the need for modification of maladaptive emotional responses is stressed.

In the cognitive approaches, affect has predominantly been seen as a postcognitive phenomenon. Cognitive–behavioral theory holds that the meaning of an event determines the emotional response to it (Beck, 1976; Ellis, 1962). Constructs such as "automatic thoughts," "irrational beliefs," and "self-statements" have been posited as mediating between events and emotional responses to events. Some cognitive–behavioral theorists have begun to question the assumption of the causal priority of cognition (Beck & Emery, 1985; Guidano & Liotti, 1983; Mahoney, 1984), but most cognitive approaches to working with emotion still emphasize the elimination of emotional responses to faulty cognitions by rationally challenging beliefs, by presenting schema-inconsistent evidence, and by providing self-instructional training. Mahoney (1991), however, has recently contrasted a constructivist position (which incorporates emotion as a fundamental aspect of meaning construction) with a rationalist approach (which elevates reason above emotion).

Experiential and humanistic therapies, in contrast to cognitive and behavioral views, have always regarded emotion as an essential component of human meaning and as an important motivator of behavior. In this tradition, emotions are conceptualized neither as expressions of instinctual impulses nor as learned responses; rather, affect is seen as an orienting system that provides the organism with adaptive information (Greenberg & Safran, 1987a).

In client-centered therapy, "experiencing," defined as" everything occurring within the organism that is currently available to awareness (Rogers, 1959), has been a central construct. "To experience" means to receive the impact of sensory and physiological events occurring in the moment. Rogers (1959) defined "feeling" as a complex cognitive–affective unit composed of emotionally toned experience and its cognized meaning. He claimed that therapeutic change involves experiencing fully in awareness feelings that in the past were denied awareness or distorted.

In gestalt therapy (Perls, Hefferline, & Goodman, 1951), although the experience and expression of emotion is regarded as of critical importance to change, there has been little systematic theory about its role in the therapeutic process. In this view, emotion is regarded as the organism's direct, evaluative, immediate experience of the organism–environment field. It is not mediated by thoughts and conceptual judgments, but is rather a vital regulator of action. Emotion is seen as furnishing the basis of awareness of what is important to the organism and as energizing action; however, it is thought that emotions are often interrupted before they enter awareness or organize action. Gestalt therapists see avoidance of painful feelings and the fear of unwanted emotion as the core of many problems (Perls et al., 1951).

In the experiential approaches, feelings are thus valued aspects of experience, not something to be expelled or discharged. The goal of therapy is not to get rid of feelings, but to increase awareness of emotional experience so that it is available as orienting information in dealing with the environment, and to help clients become aware of and responsive to the action tendencies toward which feelings prompt them. Treatment involves empathic responding to client experiencing (Rogers, 1957) or the creation of experiments to increase awareness of both emotional experience and processes that interrupt such experience (Perls, 1973).

The views discussed above reflect a wide range of different perspectives on the role of emotions in human functioning and in therapy. Although there is a clinical literature on emotion, this literature has suffered from two major limitations. The first is that, lacking a comprehensive theory of emotion, each tradition has tended to adopt a narrow, singular view of emotion. The second, as indicated by the sparseness of the literature, is that emotion has never been given the central role it deserves in an understanding of dysfunction and therapeutic change.

Emotion has been treated by different therapies either as irrational, as destructive, as an epiphenomenon, or as an aspect of adaptive biological functioning. Clearly, all of these are possible. If a comprehensive understanding of emotion in therapy is to be attained, a more differentiated, multifaceted view of emotion and its function in the process of change is required. No single therapeutic perspective has encompassed all of emotional functioning in therapy, and unnecessary disagreements and conceptual confusion have arisen because different investigators have focused on different affective phenomena without being aware of it (Greenberg & Safran, 1987a, 1987b).

CURRENT VIEWS OF EMOTION

One of the views of emotion most useful for understanding emotions in psychotherapy is that of emotion as an action tendency. In this perspective, emotions are relational action tendencies that act to establish, maintain, or disrupt a relationship with the environment in the form of a readiness to act (Frijda, 1986; Arnold, 1970). These emotions are most noticeable as changes in action readiness. Emotions that can easily be characterized in terms of action readiness and facial expression correspond to what are often called "primary" or "fundamental" emotions (Ekman, 1984). More complex emotions (e.g., pride and jealousy) are defined more clearly by the situation, story, or script. They have no characteristic facial features and no expression or action tendencies.

Emotion, according to Frijda (1986), results from an encounter between an event and the individual concern to which the event is relevant. This view implicates motivation in emotion. Concerns, needs, or goals in this view, however, are not drive-like, pushing for release; rather, they are highly stimulus-sensitive and involve a behavioral potential in the form of an increased readiness to act. Motivation is thus the elicitation of behavior systems by appropriate stimuli. In this view of motivation, the things we need or desire are provided both by nature and by experience. Emotion and motivation are thus highly interlinked, and it is best not to separate them but to think of a combined emotion–motivation system.

Another important view of emotion arises from network theories of emotion, which focus on how emotions generate meaning. A number of recent network theories of emotion construe emotional experience as resulting from a synthesis of different levels of processing (Leventhal, 1984; Lang, 1984). The product of this synthesis is emotion and is available to us as a constant readout of information relevant to adaptation. Thus our feelings are an ongoing source of feedback to us about our automatic reactions to situations. Emotions generate important information about the meaning of events, and they motivate behavior in a potentially adaptive fashion. It is therefore important to recognize and attend to what we are feeling, because we get information about our physiological readiness to act.

In this view, automatic associative processes are dominant at first in the generation of emotional experience, and govern initial primary reactions (which are based on only simple appraisal). Automatic responses, however, are rapidly followed by more complicated emotional responses. These more developed emotional experiences are constructed as the mind brings various sensory ideational and memorial inputs together, guided by a prototype. My colleagues and I have termed this high-level integrative structure an "emotion scheme" (Greenberg, Rice, & Elliott, 1993), and we see these internal, emotionally based mental models as the primary targets of therapeutic change.

Tacit unconscious processes are thus centrally involved in generating emotion. In addition, it is important to note that although emotions organize us for action, they do not lead directly to action. Action results from the preattentive integration of a number of levels of information processing, plus conscious planning and goal setting.

WHY IS EMOTION IMPORTANT IN PSYCHOTHERAPY?

Emotion is important in therapy for the following reasons:

1. *Emotion makes schemes accessible.* Central to our argument concerning the importance of emotion in psychotherapy is the idea that the experience of emotion is an indicator that a schematic emotion network has been activated and is running. Network analyses of emotion, which view emotion as consisting of a variety of components, suggest that eliciting any one component can evoke other parts of the network. Activation of any one component automatically spreads to other components, increasing the probability of the whole network's becoming conscious (Lang, 1984); if a sufficient number of components are primed, the whole network is activated. This automatic evocation of parts of the network becomes important in the practice of therapy where the goal is to evoke underlying cognitive–affective structures. This notion of the priming of schemes begins to make sense of nonlinear, nonrational styles of therapeutic intervention. Evocation of emotion is not a simple linear or conceptual process; it is more primarily an experiential process involving the shifting of attentional allocation to different elements of experience until the scheme is evoked and emotional experience is generated by it.

2. *Emotion is an orienting and meaning-producing system.* If emotion signifies what is of concern, provides information about people's reactions to situations, and is thus fundamentally an adaptive orienting system, then people ignore their feelings at their peril. If people are organized to avoid their feelings, they rob themselves of information that helps them to orient themselves in the environment and aids problem solving. When people's emotional responses to situations are problematic or dysfunctional, they have lost their orienting system, and their primary reactive system has gone awry. Therapy needs to help clients access the information provided by the emotion system to orient themselves, or to become aware when the system is dysfunctional.

If people's emotional response information is no longer adaptive to their current situation, they will respond dysfunctionally. People's life experience leads to the development of complex affective schematic structures, which essentially store their experienced reactions to situations plus the salient features of the eliciting situations. When these emotion schemes are activated in a new situation, they generate the responses to the previous situation. People may react with anger or fear to authority if they have experience of being harshly disciplined, or with anger when others come too close if they were sexually abused. This is when emotional restructuring is called for.

3. *Emotion is a regulatory system.* Regulation is an essential component of the emotion process. Emotion, behavior, and experience are the products of excitation of an action tendency on the one hand and inhibition of that same tendency on the other. What is observed or felt depends upon the balance between the two. It is a dual-control system involving letting go and restraint. There are thus two potential problems in the system: the possible presence of unwanted emotions, and the possible absence of desired emotions. It is important to recognize that emotion literally means "from motion." Trying to stop emotion is like trying to stop a stream; a flood may be the result. Problems thus emerge from (a) suppression and (b) indulgence or overreaction. People do not only have emotions; they also manage them, and they need to find a balance between expression and control. Therapy thus

needs to address two quite different major arenas—one involving self-expression and the other self-control.

4. *Awareness of elicitors provides personal clarity and control.* If an emotional reaction or an organized response occurs without any awareness of the elicitors, people are left feeling puzzled by their emotional state. When there is an automatic cueing of an idiosyncratic emotion scheme, and the cued scheme is more self-relevant than situation-relevant, then the response may not seem to fit the situation. Thus people may automatically appraise neutral situations or statements as rejections or as threats to their competence or knowledge; they may feel insecure, inexplicably shaky, or devalued and unappreciated. They may automatically respond with fear or sadness but may not know why.

For example, in making a public presentation a person may automatically or rapidly attend to specific audience cues during the talk as criticism or boredom, resulting in feelings of being devalued and unappreciated. The person automatically responds with sadness/distress at the loss of esteem. In conscious processing, however, the person has not clearly symbolized the cues that elicited this response; thus, his or her conscious conceptual view does not contain this information, but a view that everything went well. The person is, however, left with feelings of depression. By contrast, if people can symbolize their own appraisals and emotional reactions in consciousness, they feel more in control of their experience and can begin to deal with their inner experience. Without this awareness, they are confused and stuck in their reactions. Therefore, in therapy, closely tracking the quality of clients' feeling reactions to problematic situations enables them to become aware of the meaning the stimuli had for them, their experienced reality at the moment the response was triggered, and their actual response.

5. *Emotion identifies where to focus.* In addition to tracking the quality of clients' feelings in the world, clinicians need to use clients' current emotions to grasp what is personally important to the clients (motivation) and what clients believe about themselves at the core (cognition). Emotion is thus the central means for accessing cognition and motivation. When clients talk in therapy, emotion indicates to therapists what clients are involved in, and therefore when and where to focus to get at what is centrally of concern to them and at their at core beliefs about themselves.

6. *Emotion controls action.* In addition, because of what Fridja (1986) has termed the "control precedence" of emotion (i.e., the fact that emotion controls action), if change is desired it is important that therapists pay attention to helping clients achieve a living connection between thought and emotion. People must experience what they think and say in order to effect action. One of the most frequent clinical observations is that behavior governing cognitions seems to change most when a cognition is accompanied by emotion. When people feel what they say and think, the confusion disappears and they become clear. They are then connected to their internal resources, and they are confident that what they say is valid and are more likely to act.

AFFECTIVE ASSESSMENT

Assessment of ongoing client process is of great significance in working with emotional processes in psychotherapy. There is a need, however, to make clinical distinctions among different types of affective expression. Before a therapist chooses whether to access, stimulate, modify, or bypass different expressions, a "process diagnosis" (Rice & Greenberg, 1984; Greenberg, 1986) needs to be made; that is, the current type of processing in which the client is engaged needs to be determined. On the basis of this assessment of the client's current state, the therapist needs to intervene so as to direct the client's internal processing in ways that will change the client's emotional state.

We have suggested (Greenberg & Safran, 1984, 1987a, 1989) that for the purpose of intervention, distinctions initially need to be made at least among the following four broad categories of emotional expression: (1) adaptive primary emotions, (2) secondary emotions, (3) instrumental emotions, and (4) maladaptive primary emotions. I consider each of these in turn.

1. *Biologically adaptive primary affective responses.* These experiences provide information to the organism about responses to situations. Emotions such as anger at violation, sadness at loss, and fear in response to danger provide adaptive action tendencies to help organize appropriate behavior. Anger mobi-

lizes people for fight, fear for flight, and sadness for recovery of that which is lost and for reparative grieving. These emotions are often not initially in awareness, and need to be accessed and intensified in therapy and used as aids to problem solving.

2. *Secondary reactive emotional responses.* These are often problematic and are not the organism's direct responses to the environment. Rather, they are secondary to some underlying, more primary generating process, or are reactions to primary responses' being thwarted. Defensive or reactive responses, such as crying in frustration when angry or expressing anger when afraid, are secondary emotional responses to underlying emotional processes. In addition, emotions such as fear in response to anticipated danger or hopelessness in response to negative expectations are secondary emotional responses to underlying cognitive processes. Secondary reactive responses of these types are not to be focused on or intensified in therapy; rather, they are to be bypassed or explored in order to access underlying processes. Secondary emotions are generally readily available to awareness and often are part of the presenting problem.

3. *Instrumental emotional responses.* These are emotional behavior patterns that people have learned to use to influence others. They are emotions that are expressed in order to achieve some intended effect, such as crying in order to evoke sympathy or expressing anger in order to dominate. Instrumental expressions of this type are not information about responses to situations, but attempts to influence. In therapy these expressions are best bypassed, confronted, or interpreted, rather than explored or differentiated to access adaptive information.

4. *Learned maladaptive primary responses.* Examples of these responses to the environment include fear to harmless stimuli and anger in response to caring. As I have suggested above, although the emotional response system generally plays an adaptive role in human functioning, maladaptive responses can be learned as a function of trauma or strongly negative environmental contingencies in childhood. These emotions then need to be accessed in therapy, but they need to be modified rather than to be used for orientation.

Assessing the type of emotion being expressed in therapy thus provides the clinician with a notion of what to do when. Primary and maladaptive expressions, as opposed to secondary and instrumental expressions, need to be accessed in therapy, albeit for different purposes. Primary adaptive emotion is accessed for its orientation information, whereas maladaptive emotion is accessed to make it more amenable to modification and restructuring. Secondary and instrumental expression are bypassed and often dampened in order to get at underlying experience.

GENERAL PRINCIPLES OF EMOTIONALLY FOCUSED INTERVENTION

Elsewhere, we (Greenberg & Safran, 1987a) have outlined the following general principles of intervention for working with emotion: (1) directing attention to inner experience; (2) refocusing attention on inner experience; (3) focusing on the present; (4) analyzing expression; (5) intensifying experience; (6) symbolizing experience; and (7) establishing intents. These seven principles are based on a distillation of the essential therapist operations involved in the practice of emotionally focused interventions by expert practitioners (Gendlin, 1981; Greenberg & Safran, 1987a; Perls et al., 1951; Rice & Greenberg, 1984; Rogers, 1959). They are principles of therapeutic process that guide the moment-by-moment interventions of the therapist, in an approach to therapy that is highly attuned to shifts in the ongoing experiential process in the client.

In order for these principles and the style to be effective, therapists need to create particular types of relationship contexts that will support the intense inner concentration needed for focusing on emotion. Therapists need to establish good therapeutic alliances (Bordin, 1979) with their clients—alliances in which the emotional bonds between them will promote the exploration of the clients' internal experience. Without a relationship bond in which clients feel accepted, safe, and supported, they will not enter into exploration of their feelings.

In addition to this sense of acceptance in the "safe enough" environment, what seems necessary for a good working alliance is clients' sense that they are working together with their therapists to overcome the obstacles in their paths, and that they feel hopeful or optimistic that what they are doing in therapy will help (Alexander & Luborsky, 1986; Greenberg & Pinsof, 1986). In order to promote affective work in therapy, clients thus need to feel that they are in agreement with their therapists on the goals of therapy, and that the affective tasks they are engaged in are relevant to these goals (Bordin, 1979; Horvath & Greenberg, 1986).

A therapist, in addition to establishing a collaborative and empathically attuned relationship, guides a client's information processing in particular ways at particular times according to the principles above, in order to deepen experience and promote the generation of new meaning. Directing attentional allocation in order to symbolize tacitly generated emotional experience is the key intervention process. Emotion is accessed by directing the client to *attend* to his or her internal experience. The therapist can direct the client's attention by directly suggesting that the client attend to what he or she is feeling, or by asking "What are you experiencing?", or by directing a response at the client's internal experience (e.g., "I hear some sadness as you say this"). If and when the client moves attentional allocation away from his or her internal experience, the therapist *refocuses* the client's attention inward to attend to bodily felt experience (Gendlin, 1981). Refocusing involves noticing when the client deflects from a description of an internal experiential track, and redirecting him or her to this inner track. The focus in accessing affect is predominantly on what is occurring in the *present* in the client's experience. In addition to focusing on current bodily felt experiences, the therapist carefully analyzes the manner of verbal and nonverbal *expression* as it is occurring, and directs attention to or provides feedback about this expression in order to promote the client's awareness of current experience. Emerging experience is *intensified* by increasing the client's level of arousal, accessing memories, and encouraging active expression in order to make the experience more vivid and clear. Finally, the therapist works with the client toward *symbolizing* in awareness current experience and *stating intentions* based on needs or wants. The latter two principles serve to promote the creation of new meaning and to provide a sense of direction for action.

The seven general principles describe a style of therapeutic intervention that, guided as it is by the emerging experience of the moment, is inherently nonlinear. The therapist responds to the client's expressions of the moment—a sigh, a gesture, a poignant phrase, a tone of voice, or a vivid memory fragment—in order to help prime and evoke the underlying network. Rather than interpreting or exploring purely at the level of meaning, the therapist is attempting to help the client bring into awareness and develop certain implicit affectively laden information from the expressive motor and schematic levels, as well as the conceptual level. Thus the therapist jumps from one level to another, priming the network until sufficient stimulus material has been provided to evoke the network. The therapist first works to evoke affect; once feelings are experienced vividly, in the moment, the process shifts to a more symbolic form of processing in order to generate meaning.

TYPES OF THERAPEUTIC INTERVENTION PROCESSES

Three major types of emotionally focused intervention processes can be extracted from the theory and practice of psychotherapy: (1) acknowledging emotion; (2) evoking and intensifying emotion; and (3) restructuring emotion schemes.

Acknowledging Emotion

In the first group of processes, therapists help clients attend to what they are feeling. One method is to *direct* the clients to attend to what is being felt. This in the long run provides response tendency information. The point here is that emotion cannot serve its biologically adaptive function in the complex human environment if emotionally toned experience is not attended to with accuracy and immediacy.

People can attend to different levels of emotion. Training clients to be aware of their feelings includes training them to pay attention to different aspects of their experience— to sensations, expressive actions, primary emotions, complex felt senses of meaning/feeling, and needs and wants. When attending to bodily sensations, clients begin to experience actual tension, aches, temperature, and the like; when attending to expressive motor actions, they become aware of gestures, movements, vocal quality, and facial expression.

Attention to discrete primary emotions leads to conscious awareness of feelings of sadness, anger, fear, disgust, and joy. When attending to complex feelings and felt meanings, clients come to differentiate a perplexing inner felt sense into complex meanings, such as feeling "humiliated" or "over the hill," as well as to differentiate complex sensory and expressive motor experience into feeling "hollow inside" or "drained." It is the idiosyncratic meaning of complex relational emotions and their meanings that needs to be attended to. This is often helped by identifying the stimuli that trigger the emotions, as well as by attending to the bodily sense. Finally, in symbolizing needs/wants or organismic concerns, clients attend to the action tendency associated with the emotion. This disposition to action is the clearest aspect of emotions and always needs to be identified, as it provides the directional tendency in emotional experience.

Empathic attunement to clients' feelings and empathic responding to these feelings is a second major method of facilitating clients' attention to inner experience and acknowledging of emotion. Empathic confirmation plays an important therapeutic role in solidifying the clients' highly subjective, unsure felt sense. When a feeling first emerges into a client's awareness, it is vague and the client is unsure. When it is empathically understood by another, this acts to confirm that the feeling is real, and the client becomes more confident in his or her own experience. With therapeutic development, the unsure felt sense progresses from a state of relative globality and lack of differentiation to one of increased differentiation, articulation, and integration— for instance, from a sense of "I feel bad," to "I feel afraid," to "I feel afraid of losing face if you are present to observe me," to the want "I prefer you not to be present." One client, in confronting his abusiveness to his wife, described the process of differentiation as follows: At first he seemed to have an overwhelming large ball of confused, mixed feelings. With the help of therapy, he could now recognize this as a lot of small balls of separate, different feelings (e.g., anger, fear, or sadness), which he now could manage a lot more readily.

Evoking and Intensifying Emotions

Evoking emotions in therapy leads to a number of change processes:

1. When emotions are experienced, they lead to the *accessing of core cognitions*. It is only when clients feel hopeless that their core organizing beliefs become available. For example, it is only when clients are truly experiencing their pain that they may be able to say, "I feel like a failure," or "I feel so unlovable." In marital therapy, when one partner actually feels the fear of being abandoned, only then do beliefs about being unlovable emerge. Emotion therefore leads to accessing "hot" cognitions (Greenberg & Safran, 1987a).

2. Emotion when experienced leads to *action*. A person who feels angry, sad, or joyous will act accordingly. Emotion thus motivates behavior, and its evocation or intensification can be used to change behavior. Thus anger will promote assertive action and can help overcome fear.

3. Emotion when expressed leads to *further processing and to completion*. In situations such as loss or trauma, or the persistence or return of intrusive signs, there has been incomplete processing of emotional reactions, and the action tendencies have been interrupted. Failure to fully express emotional experience can interfere with the ability to allocate processing capacity optimally to other tasks. In the safety of the therapeutic situation, clients need to access traumatic or painful memories and to relive, re-experience, and fully express their interrupted emotions. Surrendering to emotion lets it run its course. This allowing of emotion follows a "release–relief–recovery" sequence (Greenberg & Safran, 1987a; Nichols & Efran, 1985).

Emotional Restructuring

The third group of procedures accounts for possibly the most important goal of emotionally focused intervention. In order to achieve the goal of emotional restructuring, *relevant activating information* must first be made available to the emotion scheme in a fashion that will evoke the internal structure. Here paying attention to body sensation, expressive movement, images, and other immediately evocative aspects of emotional experience, rather than purely conceptual aspects (memory and symbolizing), is important. Priming sufficient nodes of the emotion network gets it activated and running.

Second, *novel information* must be made available to the emotion scheme—information that is new and incompatible with existing elements in the emotion structure—in order for a new scheme and a new memory to be formed. It is unclear at present whether change is brought about by modifying the old scheme or making a new scheme more accessible. Once a new scheme is formed, there are new automated reactions. Newness comes as well from affective synthesis of new meanings guided by the new scheme.

Restructuring of emotion schemes can occur when new information is made available from a number of different sources. Thus restructuring can be achieved when external and/or internal dialectical contradictions are resolved; when new organismic information about needs and concerns becomes available; when new, more developed adult processing capacity is brought to bear on childhood experience; when greater attentional capacity is made available in the current in-therapy situation, enabling more information to be synthesized; or when dysfunctional beliefs in the scheme are changed.

CONCLUSIONS

Therapy is an ideal laboratory for studying emotion processes. A number of possible research questions immediately suggest themselves. Research on what emotional processes lead to what kind of change would illuminate how change occurs in treatment. Establishing when it is therapeutic to intensify or promote expression of emotion and when it is therapeutic to dampen, modify, or control emotion would be highly relevant to enhancing treatment and improving our understanding of therapeutic change. In addition, the development of reliable means of assessing affective processes (primary, secondary, instrumental, and maladaptive emotions), based on differential patterns of action readiness and eliciting situations, would be most helpful to practice and research. The empirical investigation of these and many other questions on emotional processes in psychotherapy will greatly advance our understanding of the psychotherapeutic enterprise.

REFERENCES

Alexander, L., & Luborsky, L. (1986). The Penn Helping Alliance Scales. In L. S. Greenberg & W. M. Pinsof (Eds.), *The psychotherapeutic process: A research handbook* (pp. 325–366). New York: Guilford Press.

Arnold, M. (1970). *Feelings and emotion.* New York: Academic Press.

Beck, A. T. (1976). *Cognitive therapy and the emotional disorders.* New York: International Universities Press.

Beck, A. T., & Emery, G. (1985). *Anxiety disorders and phobias.* New York: Basic Books.

Bordin, E. (1979). The generalizability of the psychoanalytic concept of the working alliance. *Psychotherapy: Theory, Research, and Practice, 16,* 252–260.

Breuer, J., & Freud, S. (1955). *Studies on hysteria.* In, J. Strachey (Ed. and Trans.), *The standard edition of the complete psychological works of Sigmund Freud* (Vol. 2, pp. 1–305). London: Hogarth Press. (Original work published 1893–1895)

Eagle, M. (1984). *Recent developments in psychoanalysis.* New York: McGraw-Hill.

Ekman, P. (1984). Expression and the nature of emotion. In K. R. Scherer & P. Ekman (Eds.), *Approaches to emotion* (pp. 319–343). Hillsdale, NJ: Erlbaum.

Ellis, A. (1962). *Reason and emotion in psychotherapy.* New York: Lyle Stuart.

Fenichel, O. (1945). *The psychoanalytic theory of neurosis.* New York: Norton.

Foa, E., & Kozak, M. (1986). Emotional processing of fear: Exposure to corrective information. *Psychological Bulletin, 99,* 20–31.

Freud, S. (1957). *Five lectures on psycho-analysis.* In J. Strachey (Ed. and Trans.), *The standard edition of the complete psychological works of Sigmund Freud* (Vol. 11, pp. 3–56). London: Hogarth Press. (Original work published 1910)

Frijda, N. H. (1986). *The emotions.* Cambridge, England: Cambridge University Press.

Gendlin, E. T. (1981). *Focusing.* New York: Bantam.

Greenberg, L.S. (1986). Change process research. *Journal of Consulting and Clinical Psychology, 54,* 4–9.

Greenberg, L. S., & Pinsof, W. M. (Eds.). (1986). *The psychotherapeutic process: A research handbook.* New York: Guilford Press.

Greenberg, L. S., Rice, L. N., & Elliott, R. (1993). *Facilitating emotional change: The moment-by-moment process.* New York: Guilford Press.

Greenberg, L.S., & Safran, J. D. (1984). Integrating affect and cognition: A perspective on the process of therapeutic change. *Cognitive Therapy and Research, 8,* 559–578.

Greenberg, L. S., & Safran, J. D. (1987a). *Emotion in psychotherapy: Affect, cognition, and the process of change.* New York: Guilford Press.

Greenberg, L. S., & Safran, J. D. (1987b). Emotion, cognition and action. In H. Eysenck & I. Martin (Eds.), *Foundations of behavior therapy* (pp. 295–314). New York: Plenum Press.

Greenberg, L. S., & Safran, J. D. (1989). Emotion in psychotherapy. *American Psychologist, 44*(1), 19–29.

Guidano, V. F., & Liotti, G. (1983). *Cognitive processes and emotional disorders.* New York: Guilford Press.

Horvath, A., & Greenberg, L. S. (1986). The development of the Working Alliance Inventory. In L. S. Greenberg & W. M. Pinsof (Eds.), *The psychotherapeutic process: A research handbook* (pp. 529–556). New York: Guilford Press.

Kernberg, O. F. (1982). Self, ego, affects and drives. *Journal of the American Psychoanalytic Association, 30,* 893–917.

Klein, M. (1981). Love, guilt an reparation. In R. Money-

Kyrle (Ed.), *The writings of Melanie Klein* (Vol.1, pp. 306–343). London: Hogarth Press. (Original work published 1937)

Kohut, H. (1977). *The restoration of the self.* New York: International Universities Press.

Lang, P. J. (1984). Cognition in emotion: Concept and action. In C. E. Izard, J. Kagan, & R. B. Zajonc (Eds.), *Emotions, cognition and behavior* (pp. 192–226). New York: Cambridge University Press.

Leventhal, H. (1984). A perceptual–motor theory of emotion. In L. Berkowitz (Ed.), *Advances in experimental social psychology* (Vol. 17, pp. 117–182). New York: Academic Press.

Mahoney, M. (1984). Integrating affect and cognition: A comment. *Cognitive Therapy and Research, 8,* 585–589.

Mahoney, M. (1991). *Human change processes.* New York: Basic Books.

Nichols, M., & Efran, J. (1985). Catharsis in psychotherapy: A new perspective. *Psychotherapy: Theory, Research, and Practice, 22,* 46–58.

Perls, F. S. (1973). *The Gestalt approach and eye-witness to therapy.* Palo Alto, CA: Science & Behavior Books.

Perls, F. S., Hefferline, R., & Goodman, P. (1951). *Gestalt therapy.* New York: Dell.

Rachman, S. (1978). *Fear and courage.* San Francisco: W. H. Freeman.

Rachman, S. (1980). Emotional processing. *Behaviour Research and Therapy, 18,* 51–60.

Rapaport, D. (1953). On the psychoanalytic theory of affects. *International Journal of Psycho-Analysis, 34,* 177–198.

Reich, W. (1942). *The function of the orgasm.* New York: Orgone Press.

Rice, L. N., & Greenberg, L. S. (1984). *Patterns of change: Intensive analysis of psychotherapy process.* New York: Guilford Press.

Rogers, C. (1957). The necessary and sufficient conditions of therapeutic personality change. *Journal of Consulting Psychology, 21,* 95–103.

Rogers, C. (1959). A theory of therapy, personality, and interpersonal relationships, as developed in the client-centered framework. In S. Koch (Ed.), *Psychology: A study of a science* (Vol. 3, pp. 184–256). New York: McGraw-Hill.

Sandler, J., & Sandler, A. (1978). On the development of object relationships and affects. *International Journal of Psycho-Analysis, 59,* 285–296.

Schafer, R. (1983). *The analytic attitude.* New York: Basic Books.

Skinner, B. F. (1953). *Science and human behavior.* New York: Macmillan.

Sullivan, H. S. (1953). *The interpersonal theory of psychiatry.* New York: Norton.

V

SELECT EMOTIONS

36

Fear and Anxiety as Emotional Phenomena: Clinical Phenomenology, Evolutionary Perspectives, and Information-Processing Mechanisms

ARNE ÖHMAN

> Very softly down the glade runs a waiting, watching shade
> And the whisper spreads and widens far and near
> And the sweat is on thy brow, for he passes even now—
> He is Fear, O Little Hunter, he is Fear!
>
> On thy knees and draw the bow; bid the shrilling arrow go;
> In the empty, mocking thicket plunge the spear;
> But thy hands are loosed and weak, and the blood has left thy cheek—
> It is Fear, O Little Hunter, it is Fear!
>
> Now the spates are banked and deep; now the footless boulders leap—
> Now the lightning shows each littlest leaf-rib clear—
> But thy throat is shut and dried, and thy heart against thy side
> Hammers: Fear, O little Hunter—this is Fear!
>
> (Kipling, 1895/1983, pp. 176–177)

INTRODUCTION

Fear and anxiety provide recurrent themes for humans pondering their existential predicament. For example, in a theological version, anxiety has been interpreted as resulting from "divine disconnection"—the experience of being separated from God's grace. In existential philosophy, on the other hand, the distress of anxiety is seen as something positive—as the mark of a person exercising his or her freedom and responsibility to choose an authentic life. In a clinical context, the vicissitude of anxiety has been understood as the key to the dynamics of psychopathology, whether it is conceptualized in terms of a learnable drive supporting escape and avoidance, or as the target of psychologically distorting defense mechanisms.

The ubiquity and controversial status of anxiety have made it a central topic for research and reflection. Thus, there is a truly voluminous literature on the psychology of anxiety (see Barlow, 1988, for an admirably comprehensive review), only a tiny fraction of which can be represented in this chapter. Its point of departure is that fear and anxiety are emotional phenomena, the elucidation of which has much to gain from being informed by the psychology of emotion. Conversely, empirical data on the clinical phenomena of fear and anxiety provide a rich testing ground for theories of emotion. My first purpose is to describe the emotional phenomena of fear and anxiety from a clinical perspective. Clinical data, particularly as distilled in diagnostic criteria, reflect real experiences and behavior observed or reported in real-life situations, often with the reliability of the observations ascertained. My discussion includes a review of psychophysiological findings, and an analysis of the stimulus contexts that set the stage for the phenomena of fear and anxiety. The issue here is whether there are several forms of anxiety and fear or whether different manifestations originate from a common source. The second part of the chapter is devoted to a discussion of the theoretical structures that are needed to understand the phenomena of anxiety. The theoretical perspective derives from information-processing psychology emphasizing the nonconscious mechanisms, which I believe are pivotal in understanding fear and anxiety. The concluding section discusses some of the implications of this theoretical perspective.

THE PHENOMENA OF ANXIETY AND FEAR

The Basic Components of Anxiety and Fear

Providing pertinent descriptions of the experiential aspects of emotion is a privilege of poets. The Kipling poem quoted at the beginning of the chapter portrays the phenomena of fear and anxiety very accurately. The experiential side consists of "an ineffable and unpleasant feeling of foreboding" (Lader & Marks, 1973) ("Very softly down the glade runs a waiting, watching shade"), and it is associated with bodily changes including both somatic ("thy hands are loosed and weak") and autonomic ("thy throat is shut and dried, and thy heart against thy side/Hammers") manifes-

tations. The relevant behavioral dimensions are escape and avoidance (e.g., Lang, 1984). These three aspects of fear and anxiety—subjective experience as reflected in verbal reports, physiological responses, and avoidance behavior—should not be taken as alternative indicators of an inferred unitary state of anxiety, presumably isomorphic with experience, but as dissociable components of a loosely coupled anxiety response (Lang, 1968, 1978).

Distinguishing Fear and Anxiety

According to the glossary of the Diagnostic and Statistical Manual of Mental Disorders, third edition, revised (DSM-III-R; American Psychiatric Association [APA], 1987), the term "anxiety" denotes "apprehension, tension or uneasiness that stems from the anticipation of danger, which may be internal or external" (p. 392). It is suggested that anxiety differs from fear in lacking a recognizable external source of the threat, but both fear and anxiety are said to include the same manifestations: "motor tension, autonomic hyperactivity, apprehensive expectation, and vigilance and scanning" (p. 392).

However, as eloquently argued by Epstein (1972), external stimuli are insufficient to distinguish fear and anxiety. He concluded that fear is related to action, and particularly to escape and avoidance. However, when the action is blocked or thwarted (e.g., because the situation is uncontrollable), fear is turned into anxiety. In Epstein's view, then, "*fear* is an avoidance motive. If there were no restraints, internal or external, fear would support the action of flight. *Anxiety* can be defined as unresolved fear, or, alternatively, as a state of undirected arousal following the perception of threat" (Epstein, 1972, p. 311; italics added). This is the distinction between fear and anxiety that I adhere to in this chapter, when a distinction is needed.

Varieties of Fear/Anxiety

One of the dimensions given for fear/anxiety in the DSM-III-R is that it may be focused on an external sources, as in phobias, or it may be situationally unfocused, as in free-floating anxiety. Furthermore, fear/anxiety may come in episodic panic attacks (i.e., as sudden emotional surges dominated by physical symptoms, sometimes with and sometimes without clear precipitants), or it may be a more or less constant preoccupation with more or less reasonable threats and dangers. As these descriptions imply, fear/anxiety may be regarded both as an emotional state, evoked in a particular context and having a limited duration, and as a personality trait, characterizing an individual across time and situations (e.g., Spielberger, 1972). The differences between clinical and normal fear/anxiety include that the former is more recurrent and persistent; that its intensity is far above what is reasonable, given the objective danger or threat; that it tends to paralyze individuals and make them helpless and unable to cope; and that it results in impeded psychosocial or physiological functioning (e.g., Lader & Marks, 1973).

Factor-analytic work on both observed and self-reported symptoms of fear/anxiety agree in suggesting a division between "somatic overreactivity" (as manifested in, e.g., sweating, flushing, shallow breathing, and reports of heart palpitations, instestinal discomforts, and aches and pains) and "cognitive or psychic anxiety" (including, e.g., intrusive and unwanted thoughts, worrying, ruminations, restlessness, and sometimes feelings of muscle tension) (e.g., Buss, 1962; Fenz & Epstein, 1965; Schalling, Cronholm, & Åsberg, 1975).

CLINICAL MANIFESTATIONS OF ANXIETY AND FEAR

In a very influential reconceptualization of anxiety, Klein (1981) has argued that there are two distinct forms of anxiety: panic attacks and anticipatory anxiety. Although the empirical basis for this claim has been effectively called into question (e.g., Margraf, Ehlers, & Roth, 1986a, 1986b), it has been highly heuristic for research, and it has had an enormous impact on the diagnosis and treatment of anxiety. Therefore, any current treatment of the topic must consider this distinction.

Clinical Varieties of Anxiety

Recurrent panic attacks are at the top of the diagnostic hierarchy for anxiety disorders in the DSM-III-R (APA, 1987). A "panic attack" is defined as the sudden and spontaneous occurrence of at least 4 of the 13 symptoms listed in the first column of Table 36.1. A diagnosis of panic disorder requires at least four such panic attacks in the preceding 4-week period. Usually, the panic disorder is coupled with agoraphobia—that is, with fear of being in "places or situations from which escape might be difficult (or embarrassing) or in

TABLE 36.1. Symptoms of Anxiety in the Anxiety Disorders of DSM-III-R

Panic disorder	Social and simple phobias	Post-traumatic stress disorder	Generalized anxiety disorder
Shortness of breath	Feeling panicky	Difficulty falling or staying asleep	Trembling, twitching, or feeling shaky
Dizziness, unsteady feeling, or faintness	Sweating	Irritability or outbursts of anger	Muscle tension, aches, or soreness
Palpitations or tachycardia	Tachycardia	Difficulty concentrating	Restlessness
Trembling and shaking	Difficulty breathing	Hypervigilance	Easy fatigability
Sweating		Exaggerated startle	Shortness of breath
Choking		Enhanced physiological reactivity to relevant stimuli	Palpitations or tachycardia
Nausea or abdominal distress			Sweating or cold, clammy hands
Depersonalization or derealization			Dry mouth
Numbness or tingling sensation			Dizziness or lightheadedness
Flushes (hot flashes) or chills			Nausea or abdominal distress
Chest pain or discomfort			Flushes (hot flashes) or chills
Fear of dying			Frequent urinations
Fear of going crazy or doing something uncontrolled			Trouble swallowing ("lump in throat")
			Feeling keyed up or on edge
			Exaggerated startle response
			Difficulty concentrating or blank mind
			Trouble falling or staying asleep
			Irritability

which help might not be available in the event of a panic attack" (APA, 1987, p. 238). As a consequence of the fear, the person is restricted with regard to travel, and needs a trusted companion in order to endure the phobic situations without excessive fear. However, some patients can be diagnosed with panic disorder without any agoraphobic symptoms, and some agoraphobics have never experienced spontaneous panic attacks.

Phobias come next in the diagnostic hierarchy. In contrast to panic attacks, where the emphasis is on symptoms, phobias are defined primarily in terms of the avoided situations. Thus, social phobics show excessive and unreasonable fear of situations involving potential critical scrutiny by others, or in situations where they risk being embarrassed or humiliated. Specific phobics, on the other hand, fear and avoid circumscribed situations such as small animals or heights, even though they recognize that the fear is excessive and unreasonable. The few experienced symptoms of a phobic response that are given in DSM-III-R are listed in the second column of Table 36.1. Note that one of the listings, "Feeling panicky," is a cover for an unclear number of the symptoms of a panic attack (first column).

When the anxiety originates in the experience of an event that is "outside the range of usual human experience and that would be markedly distressing to almost anyone" (APA, 1987, p. 250), post-traumatic stress disorder (PTSD) may be diagnosed, provided that the traumatic event is persistently re-experienced (e.g., in the form of "flashbacks"), that stimuli or events associated with the trauma are persistently avoided, and that the person feels generally numbed with regard to emotions. Common anxiety symptoms experienced by persons suffering from PTSD are listed in the third column in Table 36.1. Two of these are required for a PTSD diagnosis.

If the manifest anxiety is not episodic, as in panic, or is not tied to specific eliciting situations, as in phobias or PTSD, the remaining diagnostic option is generalized anxiety disorder. In generalized anxiety disorder, the person has been bothered by excessive anxiety and worry (apprehensive expectations) about two or more life circumstances for a period of at least 6 months. "Worry" may be defined as relatively uncontrollable, distressing chains of thoughts and images (Borkovec, Robinson, Pruzinsky, & DePree, 1983). Worries appear to involve primarily thoughts rather than images, and more so in generalized anxiety patients than in controls (Borkovec & Inz, 1990). Craske, Rapee, Jackel, and Barlow (1989) had generalized anxiety patients and normal controls self-monitor their worries over a 3-week period. Patients reported more worrying over the past month than controls (61% vs. 18% of the time). Patients worried more about illness/health/injury and less about finances than controls, and they rated their worries as less controllable, less realistic, and less capable of being voluntarily interrupted. Whereas 40% of the worries reported by generalized anxiety patients lacked a clear precipitant, this was true for only 12% of the worries reported by controls. Thus the patients' worries appeared less controllable and more self-driven and ruminative than those of the controls. Although worry is central to a DSM-III-R diagnosis of generalized anxiety disorder, it is not sufficient. To be transformed into anxiety, worry must be combined with somatic symptoms (Mathews, 1990) or some of the other anxiety symptoms listed in the fourth column of Table 36.1.

For completeness, obsessive-compulsive disorder should also be mentioned. No anxiety symptoms are listed for this disorder, the essential features of which are "recurrent obsessions or compulsions sufficiently severe to cause marked distress, be time-consuming, or significantly interfere with the person's normal routine, occupational functioning, or usual social activities or relationships with others" (APA, 1987, p. 245).

How Many Forms of Clinical Anxiety Are There?

When the symptoms of anxiety characterizing the different anxiety disorders are listed side by side as in Table 36.1, there is a striking overlap among them. It is clear that these clinical symptoms can easily be subsumed under the headings of "somatic overreactivity" versus "cognitive/psychic anxiety," as noted earlier. The somatic symptoms seem to be dominant in panic and in phobic responses, whereas cognitive symptoms are more prevalent in PTSD and particularly in generalized anxiety disorder. Nonetheless, many symptoms are shared between the two putatively different types of anxiety in panic and generalized anxiety syndromes. Thus, it is clear that there are important similarities between the two types of anxiety postulated by Klein (1981).

At the descriptive level, the empirical literature does not allow a strong conclusion on this issue. All the panic symptoms listed in Table 36.1 occur with very high frequencies (80–90%) in patients diagnosed with panic disorders, with fear of dying, palpitations, trembling, shortness of breath, and dizziness rated as the most intense ones (Barlow & Craske, 1988). However, equally high frequencies of these symptoms were reported from patients with phobias, obsessive compulsive disorder, generalized anxiety disorder, and even a major depressive episode (Barlow et al., 1985), most of whom reported anxiety episodes fulfilling the criterion of at least four symptoms for a panic attack. It was only when the frequency criterion (at least four attacks during the last 4 weeks) was applied that the panic disorder group was clearly distinguished from the others. Taking the overall fewer symptoms endorsed by the other groups into considerations, Barlow et al. (1985) did not find any differences between panic patients and other patients in the rated severity of symptoms.

In contrast to generalized anxiety patients, who typically recognized their anxiety symptoms as unreasonable, panic patients engaged in cognitions of going crazy, having a heart attack, dying, and fainting when experiencing their symptoms (Rapee, 1985). Borden and Turner (1989) examined the differences between panic disorder and other anxiety disorder patients in a more sophisticated way by using covariance analysis to control for overall level of anxiety. With state and trait anxiety as covariates, the panic patients scored above other patient groups on a general panic factor, and they specifically exceeded the generalized anxiety patients on feeling suddenly scared for no reason, thoughts of death or dying, and feeling that something bad would soon happen.

In an effort to examine potential differences between stimulus-elicited and spontaneous panic, Barlow et al. (1985) compared patients who had never experienced a spontaneous panic attack with two groups experiencing both cued and spontaneous panic and a pure panic group. Dizziness and fear of going crazy or losing control were significantly more prevalently reported during spontaneous than during cued panic, but again the between-group differences in rated severity of the symptoms were minimal. Similar results were reported by Rapee, Sanderson, McCauley, and Di Nardo (1992). In a second study, these authors were able to use a within-subject design to compare unexpected panic attacks with specific stimulus-elicited fear responses in patients having dual diagnoses of panic disorder and phobias. Palpitation, sweating, trembling, dizziness and hot–cold flashes were frequently (70–80%) reported both in panic and specific fear. The only differences between responses pertained to fear of dying, fear of going crazy/losing control, and numbness/tingling sensations, which were reliably more frequently reported during panic attacks.

Mellman and Davis (1985) examined flashback experiences in PTSD patients, a majority of whom were Vietnam veterans, and reported that the flashbacks met DSM-III (APA, 1980) criteria for a panic attack. Thus, more than about 70% of the patients reported shortness of breath, palpitations, dizziness, faintness, sweating, trembling, and fear of loss of control. Granted the interpretational hazards of lactate infusions (Margraf et al., 1986b), it is still very interesting that this commonly accepted method of evoking panic in panic patients (see review by van den Hout, 1988) elicited PTSD-like flashbacks in PTSD patients (Rainey et al., 1987).

This review of the literature suggests that the symptoms related to panic in the DSM-III-R (APA, 1987) occur with similar frequency and severity in all anxiety disorders. Thus, if symptoms were the only basis for diagnosis, there would be little reason to give panic a privileged position. The most consistent difference between panic patients and other anxiety patients does not seem to pertain to symptoms per se, but to the interpretation of the symptoms. Thus, reported fears of dying, going crazy, or losing control have provided the best differentiation of panic patients in several studies (Barlow et al., 1985; Borden & Turner, 1989; Rapee et al., 1992). Taken together, the data seem to fit a model that regards panic attacks, phobic responses, and flashback-generated anxiety in PTSD patients as exemplars of state anxiety, because the responses are limited in time and appear to have clear physiological correlates. Generalized anxiety disorder, on the other hand, appears to be an exemplar of trait anxiety (Rapee, 1991): Cognitive symptoms of anxiety play a more prominent role, and it is more stable over time.

The communality among phobic responses, PTSD anxiety, and panic attacks is further underscored by psychophysiological data. After a rapid initial surge in the direction of sympathetic activation in phobics confronted with the feared object (e.g., Fredrikson, 1981; Hare & Blevings, 1975), there are more lasting elevations of heart rate and blood pressure, as well as increases in the secretion of catecholamines and cortisol from the adrenals (Fredrikson, Sundin, & Frankenhaeuser, 1985; Nesse et al., 1985). Similar responses are exhibited by PTSD-diagnosed veterans exposed to battlefield noises (Blanchard, Kolb, Gerardi, Ryan, & Pallmeyer, 1986; Pallmeyer, Blanchard, & Kolb, 1986) or instructed to relive combat experiences in imagery (Pitman, Orr, Forgue, de Jong, & Claiborn, 1987; Pitman, Orr, Forgue, Altman, & de Jong, 1990). Panic patients, finally, show similar sympathetically dominated elevations during spontaneous panic attacks recorded in the laboratory (Cohen, Barlow, & Blanchard, 1985; Lader & Mathews, 1970) or during ambulatory monitoring of physiological activity (Freedman, Ianni, Ettedgui, & Puthezhath, 1985), as well as when they are confronted with agoraphobic situations in a real-life setting (Woods, Charney, McPherson, Gradman, & Heninger, 1987). Of particular interest is an ambulatory monitoring study by Pauli et al. (1991) demonstrating relationships between perceived heart rate changes, actual changes in heart rate, and experienced anxiety in panic patients.

However, as shown by Taylor and colleagues (Taylor, Telch, & Havvik, 1982–1983; Taylor et al., 1986), panic can occur without heart rate changes; and as demonstrated by Pauli et al. (1991) heart rate changes, even if perceived, do not invariably lead to panic. Thus, physiological responding is neither a necessary nor a sufficient factor for an anxiety response. This conditional relation between the experience of fear and the physiological responses is highlighted in "panic attacks without fear" (Kushner & Beitman, 1990)—that is, patients showing a symptomatology fulfilling diagnostic criteria of panic (e.g., in terms perceived physiological symptoms), but yet not interpreting them in terms of fear and anxiety. Again, we are reminded that fear is not a homogeneous and fixed entity with invariable relations to surface manifestations in terms of verbal reports, behavior, and physiological responses, but a loosely interwoven network of responses that are only partially correlated with one another (Lang, 1968, 1978).

Thus, when comparing the physiological responses seen in phobics exposed to their feared object with those seen in PTSD patients exposed to relevant traumatic scenes for the disorder, and with physiological responses during panic attacks, one is much more struck by the similarities than by the differences. The most data are available for heart rate, and for this measure large increases are associated with the anxiety response across the diagnostic categories. Therefore, there seems to be no compelling reason, either in terms of symptoms or in terms of the associated physiological responses, to regard panic anxiety as different from other forms of high-intensity state anxiety. Rather, it is tempting to view panic, phobic fear, and the intense anxiety exhibited by PTSD patients reminded of their trauma as the activation of one and the same underlying anxiety response. Barlow (1988) has used the terms "alarms," "false alarms," and "learned alarms" to discuss unconditioned fear/anxiety responses, spontaneous panic, and learned fears and phobias, respectively.

The anxiety or alarm response, furthermore, may profitly be viewed as an

adaptation that evolved to facilitate flight from life-threatening danger. The sudden increase in the rate and strength of cardiac contractions sends extra blood to the muscles, while the gut feels empty and the skin blanches and becomes cool as blood is shunted elsewhere. Rapid and deep breathing increases blood oxygen content. Cooling sweat is secreted, muscles tighten and tremble, and the endocrine system prepares for catabolism (Nesse, Cameron, Curtis, McCann, & Huber-Smith, 1984; Mason, 1968). Intense mental activity is focused on planning escape. When the overwhelming urge to flee is translated into action, all effort is concentrated on escape. The direction of flight is towards home and trusted kin, a behavioral pattern typical of animals that rely on homes and kin for protection. (Nesse, 1987, p. 77S)

Viewed from this evolutionary perspective, it is not the fear/anxiety response in itself that is malfunctional and maladaptive, but the fact that it is triggered in a malfunctional context, as in phobias (see Öhman, Dimberg, & Öst, 1985), or that it may have a dysfunctionally low threshold, as in panic (Klein, 1981; Nesse, 1987). Furthermore, the full response may be more or less completely triggered in different situations, depending upon the situational context and the overt defense responses it affords (in terms of, e.g., flight, attack, or submission). For example, active escape may be much more functional in animal phobia than in social phobia, which may account for some of the differences between these two types of disorders (Öhman et al., 1985).

The relationship between the state anxiety response seen in phobia, PTSD, and panic on the one hand, and the background trait anxiety observed, for example, in generalized anxiety disorder on the other hand, remains an open question. Whereas phobics seldom differ from controls in resting levels of autonomic activity (e.g., Hare & Blevings, 1975; Lader, 1967), panic patients often (e.g., Margraf et al., 1986b) but not invariably (e.g., Freedman et al., 1985) show high resting heart rates. Similarly, PTSD patients often show high resting heart rates (Blanchard et al., 1986; Pallmayer et al., 1986; Pitman et al., 1987), although this is not invariably true (Pitman et al., 1990). This tendency toward high resting autonomic levels could be viewed as suggesting high levels of trait anxiety in these patient groups. Although early studies not using DSM-III criteria found elevated tonic autonomic levels in anxiety state patients (e.g., Lader, 1967), recent studies using DSM-III-R criteria to delineate generalized anxiety disorder did not find higher resting levels in skin conductance and heart rate in patients than in controls (Hoehn-Saric, McLeod, & Zimmerli, 1989). However, resting electromyographic (EMG) activity levels (frontalis and gastrocnemius) were higher in patients than in controls. The EMG levels remained higher in patients during laboratory tasks, whereas their autonomic responses were smaller and more restricted in range than those of controls. Thus, Hoehn-Saric et al. (1989) concluded that generalized anxiety was associated with enhanced muscle tension and constriction of autonomic responding. High levels of muscle tension across many EMG sites were also reported by Fridlund, Hatfield, Cottam, and Fowler (1986) for highly trait-anxious subjects. However, a more detailed analysis revealed that the high EMG levels could be attributed to uncorrelated bursts of activity in many muscle groups, which prompted the authors to attribute their finding to agitation rather than to tension, concluding that "the muscu-

lar activity we observed in anxious subjects serves to activate and not defend or immobilize" (Fridlund et al., 1986, p. 234). Thus, the limited evidence that exists suggests that the psychophysiology of generalized anxiety disorder is quite distinct from the other anxiety disorders, in that it seems more directed at the muscular than at the autonomic system.

THE SITUATIONAL CONTEXT OF FEAR AND ANXIETY

Traumatic Situations

Fear or alarm is exhibited in a multitude of more or less obviously threatening situations. In some respects, the situational dimension appears most important and simple in PTSD, because, in a sense, this disorder involves "rational" fear in response to very intense stimuli—that is, situations that would be overwhelmingly distressing to anyone, because they more or less explicitly threaten survival. The DSM-III-R (APA, 1987) stipulates that the situation should be "outside the range of usual human experience" (p. 250). Thus, relatively common distressing experiences such as simple bereavement or marital conflict would not be sufficient. Rather, the situation must be life-threatening to oneself or to close kin; it may involve natural catastrophes, such as floods or hurricanes destroying one's home or community; or it may involve seeing others being seriously injured or killed as a result of an accident or physical violence. One may be exposed to the trauma alone, as in a rape or an assault, or in a group, as in military combat. Some events, such as torture, frequently result in PTSD, whereas others, such as natural disasters or car accidents, only occasionally result in the disorder (APA, 1987).

Breslau, Davis, Andreski, and Peterson (1991) reported a fairly high prevalence of exposure to traumatic events in a metropolitan U. S. sample of young adults (aged 20–30 years). About 40% reported at least one traumatic experience, and the most common traumas were sudden injury/serious accident, physical assault, and seeing someone seriously hurt or killed. About a quarter of those exposed met DSM-III-R criteria for PTSD. Sudden injury/serious accident was followed by a low rate of PTSD (11%), whereas women who had been raped had a very high rate of PTSD (80%). The risk for PTSD among those exposed to traumas were higher for females, for persons high in neuroticism, for those who had experienced early separations, and for those with a pre-existing anxiety disorder or with a family history of anxiety and antisocial behavior. Another study examining female crime victims (Kilpatrick et al., 1989) reported that crime-related PTSD was particularly likely for those exposed to the combination of a completed rape, a threat to life, and physical injury. Victims with all of these three features were 8.5 times as likely to develop PTSD as victims exposed to none of these factors. Thus, it appears clear that PTSD results from an interaction between situational and personal factors.

Commonly Feared and Potentially Phobic Situations

The threat involved in situations resulting in PTSD is so severe that, for survival reasons, people should show an adaptive and dramatic defense response of the type that previously was postulated to underlie anxiety responses. However, people fear many other situations that, at least on the surface level, seem much more innocuous. Nevertheless, survival considerations, either presently or in an evolutionary perspective, are relevant for most situational dimensions of human fears. Arrindell, Pickersgill, Merckelbach, Ardon, and Cornet (1991) provided an extensive review of studies factor-analyzing questionnaire data on self-reported fear. After applying strict methodological criteria, they accepted 25 out of 38 published studies for their own analysis. They found that the 194 factors and components identified in these studies could be classified into a structure involving four factors. The first factor was "fears about interpersonal events or situations." It included fears of criticism and social interaction, rejection, conflicts, and evaluation, but also interpersonal aggression and display of sexual and aggressive scenes. The second factor was "fears related to death, injuries, illness, blood, and surgical procedures." This factor had a quite heterogeneous content, incorporating fears of illness, diseases, and disabilities; complaints about physical and mental problems; fears of suicide, homosexuality, and sexual inadequacy; and fears losing control. Finally, it incorporated fears of contaminations, syncope, or other threats to physi-

cal health. The third factor, "fear of animals", included common domestic animals; other small, often harmless animals; and creeping and crawling animals such as insects and reptiles. Finally, "agoraphobic fears" was the fourth factor. It involved fear of entering public places (such as stores or shopping malls) and crowds, but also fear of closed spaces (such as elevators, tunnels, theaters, or churches). Furthermore, it involved fears of traveling alone in trains or buses, crossing bridges, and entering open spaces.

All these four factors represent situations of relevance for human evolution (see Seligman, 1971). Human history is replete with examples of how social conflicts that have escalated out of control provide a potentially deadly danger, not to speak of the social threat in terms of the defeat and humiliation they may involve (Öhman, 1986). Thus, it comes as no surprise that social interactions are sometimes feared. For fear of death and illness, and associated bodily conditions, there is no need to elaborate the potential survival threat. Although many animals are friendly and sought as companions, there is no question that animals as predators have provided recurrent threats in the evolution of humankind, and it is reasonable to give reptiles a privileged position as the prototypical predators (Öhman, 1986; Öhman et al., 1985). Finally, agoraphobic fears center on the lack of security inherent in separation from safe bases and kin, and the avoidance of places associated with panic and feelings of discomfort.

It is immediately seen that the factors isolated by Arrindell et al. (1991) correspond to four prominent types of phobia: social phobia, blood phobia, animal phobia, and agoraphobia. Furthermore, the second factor incorporates fears often encountered in panic disorder, such as fears or syncope, and in obsessive compulsive disorder, such as contamination.

Departing from a preparedness perspective on phobias (Seligman, 1971), my colleagues and I (Öhman et al., 1985) have argued that these fear factors may be taken to reflect basic behavioral systems, which have been adaptively shaped by evolution. In particular, we have suggested that social fears resulted from a dominance–submissiveness system, the adaptive function of which was to promote social order by means of facilitating the establishment of dominance hierarchies. Animal fears, on the other hand, are attributed to a predatory defense system, originating in the fear of reptiles by early mammals, and prompting rapid escape from potential predators. These basically adaptive systems are held to be compromised into producing social and animal phobias when the fear response they engender becomes conditioned to stimuli that actually are harmless in the ecology of modern human existence. The basic argument is that evolution has equipped humans with a propensity to associate fear with situations that threatened the survival of their ancestors (Seligman, 1971). The propensity must be based in the genes, and thus genetic variation can be expected. Hence, although humans in general are prepared to acquire some fears (e.g., snake fears) easily, some individuals must be more prepared than others. We have tested these ideas (see reviews by McNally, 1987; Öhman, 1993) in autonomic conditioning experiments primarily comparing acquisition and resistance to extinction of skin conductance conditioning to potentially phobic (e.g., snakes, spiders, angry faces) and neutral (e.g., flowers, mushrooms, neutral faces, or friendly faces) stimuli. The general, but not invariable, finding has been that responses conditioned to potentially phobic stimuli show enhanced resistance to extinction, compared to responses conditioned to neutral stimuli (McNally, 1987; Öhman, 1993). Examples of data on skin conductance responses from a single cue conditioning paradigm are given in Figure 36.1.

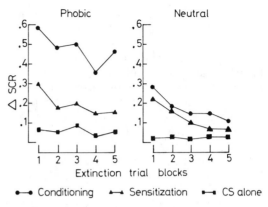

FIGURE 36.1. Extinction of skin conductance responses (SCRs) in subjects who were conditioned to potentially phobic stimuli (pictures of snakes; left panel) or neutral stimuli (pictures of houses; right panel) by receiving them paired with electric shock (unconditioned stimulus). Control subjects received the pictures and the shocks unpaired ("Sensitization") or were only exposed to pictures ("CS alone"). It is obvious that potentially phobic conditioned stimuli resulted in much larger resistance to extinction than did neutral conditioned stimuli.

Panic Stimuli

Biologically oriented theories of panic (e.g., Klein, 1981; Sheehan, 1982) suggest that panic attacks are spontaneous or endogenously originated. Thus, one of the essential characteristics of panic has been held to be that it lacks an eliciting stimulus. However, when prospectively assessed, naturally occurring panic attacks typically appear to have precipitants, such as arguments with family members or problems at work (Freedman et al., 1985) or ideations of threat and fear (Hibbert, 1984).

Perceiving spontaneously occurring heart rate increases was associated with anxiety in more than 70% of panic patients, but in none of the controls; also, the more intense the anxiety, the larger and more sustained the heart rate change (Pauli et al., 1991). Laboratory means of eliciting panic, such as lactate infusion, CO_2 inhalation, or hyperventilation, have in common the fact that they produce bodily changes that can be perceived by the subject. Indeed, Klein (1993) has developed a new and comprehensive theory of panic: He interprets it as the response to a misfiring, biologically evolved "suffocation alarm" system, which produces respiratory distress, hyperventilation, and an urge to escape situations lacking useful air for breathing.

These bodily stimuli, however, are insufficient to produce panic. According to an influential formulation by Clark (1986, 1988), it is only when the bodily stimulation is combined with a catastrophic cognitive interpretation (e.g., an impending heart attack or suffocation) that panic is elicited. Thus, cognitive interpretations may create a vicious circle: The catastrophic interpretation results in more intensely perceived threat and more apprehension; further bodily sensations feed further catastrophic interpretations; and so on (see Pauli et al., 1991). If the symptoms are not given a catastrophic interpretation, however, they may not be associated with fear but with interpretations in terms of bodily problems, as in "panic without fear" (Kushner & Beitman, 1990). The fact that the most consistent symptomatic differences between panic and other anxiety patients pertain not to symptoms but to interpretation of symptoms, such as fears of dying, going crazy, or losing control, is what one would expect from the cognitive perspective (Barlow et al., 1985; Borden & Turner, 1989; Rapee et al., 1992).

This review suggests that the phasic responses of increased state anxiety seen in phobia, PTSD, and panic typically have identifiable eliciting stimuli. However, whereas those stimuli are externally and easily confirmed by observers in the two former disorders, they are internal and often not recognized even by the person experiencing the anxiety attack in the case of panic. Nevertheless, what all the situations associated with fear and anxiety have in common is that they provide some level of threat to the well-being of the person or his or her kin, either in a contemporary or an evolutionary perspective. I now turn to a theoretical perspective, in which all types of anxiety responses are viewed as primarily rooted in information-processing mechanisms evolved to discover and evaluate potential threats (both external and internal), and often operating outside of awareness.

THEORETICAL PERSPECTIVE: THE ROLE OF UNCONSCIOUS PROCESSES IN ANXIETY AND FEAR

So far, I have provided what may be termed a stimulus–response analysis of anxiety and fear. Thus, I have argued that fear/anxiety is rooted in defense responses, which have evolved because they were functional devices to keep people away from potentially deadly contexts. Furthermore, these defenses have been tied to situations involving survival threats, either directly or indirectly, through evolutionary considerations. However, a stimulus–response analysis is by necessity incomplete, because it does not specify the mechanisms whereby a fear stimulus evokes a response.

A Functional Perspective on Anxiety

Evolved defense responses would be of little use unless they were appropriately elicited. Thus, to function adequately, they require a perceptual system that can effectively locate threat. Clearly, false negatives (i.e. failing to elicit defense to a potentially hazardous stimulus) are more evolutionarily costly than false positives (i.e., eliciting the response to a stimulus that is in effect harmless). Whereas the former are potentially lethal in an evolutionary perspective, the latter, even though distressing to the individual, merely represent wasted energy. Thus, the perceptual system is likely to be biased in the direction of a low threshold for discovering threat. Indeed, this provides an evolutionary perspective on why there are anxiety disorders. To be absolutely sure that defense is elicited when life is at stake, the system is biased sometimes to evoke defense in actually nonthreatening contexts. Such responses, of course, seem unnecessary and unreasonable, and may be understood as "irrational anxiety" by both observers and the person. Thus, if anxiety is not (as claimed by existential philosophers) the price paid for the freedom to choose an authentic life, it may be the price paid for our existence in the sense that it reflects something central to our evolution.

Effective defense must be quick; consequently, there is a premium for early detection of threat. Furthermore, threat stimuli must be detected wherever they occur in the perceptual field, independently of the momentary direction of attention. Coupled with the bias toward false positives, these factors mean that discovery of threat is better based on a quick, superficial analysis of stimuli wherever they are than on an effortful, detailed, and complete extraction of the meaning of one particular stimulus. Thus, the functional, evolutionary perspective suggests that the burden for the discovery of threat should be placed on early, parallel-processing perceptual mechanisms, which define threat on the basis of relatively simple stimulus features.

The neuroarchitecture of such a system has indeed been described by LeDoux (1990b). In an extensive series of studies of the neural control of auditorily elicited conditioned emotional responses in the rat, he and his coworkers have demonstrated a direct neural link from auditory nuclei (medial geniculate body) in the thalamus to the "significance evaluator" and "fear effector system" in the lateral and central amygdala, respectively. This monosynaptic link provides immediate information to the amygdala of gross features of emotionally relevant auditory stimuli. Thus, it bypasses the traditionally emphasized thalamo-cortical pathway, which gives full meaning to the stimulus, and the cortico-amygdala link, which is presumed to activate emotion. It is described as a "quick and dirty" transmission route: It "probably does not tell the amygdala much about the stimulus, certainly not much about Gestalt or object properties of the stimulus, but it at least informs the amygdala that the sensory receptors of a given modality have been activated and that a significant stimulus may be present" (LeDoux, 1990a, p. 172), so that the amygdala can start early activation of defense responses. It is explicitly stated that this system is adaptively biased toward false positives rather than false negatives, because it is less costly to abort falsely initialized defense responses than to fail to elicit one when the threat is real. This system provides a neural basis for Zajonc's (1980) somewhat startling slogan that "affect precedes inference" in the generation of emotion (LeDoux, 1989).

Automatic Information-Processing Routines to Discover Threat

Elsewhere (Öhman, 1986, 1987, 1992; Öhman, Dimberg, & Esteves, 1989), I have developed a theoretical perspective on the generation of emotion which is consistent with the functional scenario discussed above. Starting from a model of the activation of orienting responses (Öhman, 1979), I have adhered to a distinction between "automatic" and "controlled" or "strategic" information processing (e.g., Posner, 1978; Schneider, Dumais, & Shiffrin, 1984; Shiffrin & Schneider, 1977) to argue that many perceptual channels can be automatically and simultaneously monitored for potential threat. When stimulus events implying threat are located by the automatic system, attention is drawn to the stimulus, as the control for its further analysis is transferred to the strategic level of information processing. The switch of control from automatic to strategic information processing is associated with activation of physiological responses, particularly the orienting response (Öhman, 1979).

Automatic processing can thus occur in parallel across many different sensory channels without loss of efficiency. It is involuntary, in the sense that it is hard to suppress consciously once it is initiated; it does not interfere with

focal attention; it is not easily distracted by attended activities; and it is typically not available for conscious introspection (Schneider et al., 1984). Controlled or strategic information processing, on the other hand, is governed by intentions. It is resource- or capacity-limited, in the sense that interference is marked between strategically controlled tasks; it works sequentially rather than in parallel; it requires effort; and it is more readily available to consciousness (Schneider et al., 1984).

This conceptualization suggests that the automatic sensory monitoring processes have a capacity for sensory events vastly exceeding that of the controlled or strategic processes. Thus, they can keep track of a large number of channels, only one of which can be selected for strategic processing. Sensory messages have to compete for access to the strategic processing channel for complete sensory analysis. Given the survival contingencies implied by potential threats in the external and internal environment, it is a natural assumption that stimuli implying some degree of threat should have selection priority for strategic processing. This theoretical analysis suggests that anxiety and fear may be activated from unconscious stimulus analysis mechanisms, as a correlate to the selection of the threatening stimulus for further conscious, controlled processing. Because threatening stimuli are located by automatic perceptual mechanisms, the person is not necessarily aware of the eliciting stimuli, which may result in episodes of anxiety. Thus, what appear from the inside to be "spontaneous" episodes of anxiety may in fact be the result of unconscious stimulation.

Experimental Test of the Model: Unconscious Activation of Phobias

Backward Masking

The central theoretical tenet of this model is that responses of anxiety and fear can be elicited after only a very preliminary, unconscious analysis of the stimulus. Thus, its empirical examination requires a means of presenting fear stimuli outside of the subject's awareness. Such a means is provided by backward masking. Seminal work by Marcel (1983) demonstrated that subjects appeared to process backwardly masked target stimuli for semantic meaning, even though the intervals between targets and masks were selected to preclude conscious perception of the targets. These effects have been replicated by other investigators (e.g., Balota, 1983; Fowler, Wolford, Slade, & Tassinary, 1981), and backward masking has been regarded as the potentially most fruitful avenue to unconscious perception (Holender, 1986). Thus, if fear stimuli were presented backwardly masked to fearful subjects, and still elicited physiological responses suggesting activation of fear/anxiety, the theoretical notions advanced here would receive experimental support.

Unconscious Phobic Responses

A colleague and I reported such an experiment (Öhman & Soares, in press). Out of a total sample of about 800 individuals answering questionnaires on specific fears, we selected subjects who feared (above the 95th percentile) snakes but not spiders (below the 50th percentile), or vice versa. A control group was selected to fear neither stimulus. The subjects were exposed to series of pictures of snakes and spiders, with pictures of flowers and mushrooms serving as controls. In the first series, presentations were effectively masked (see Öhman & Soares, 1993) by similar pictures that had been randomly cut to pieces, randomly reassembled, and rephotographed. Thus, they were grossly similar to the target stimuli in colors and texture, but they lacked any recognizable central object. A pilot experiment using a forced-choice procedure ascertained that both fearful and nonfearful subjects consistently failed to identify the target with the masking parameters used. Thus, the masks interrupted presentation of the target stimuli after 30 milliseconds of exposure and remained on for 100 milliseconds during the masked presentation series. In the following series of presentation, the stimuli were presented nonmasked. Skin conductance responses were measured as the physiological dependent variable; in addition, the subjects rated the stimuli for arousal, valence, and control/dominance during separately presented masked and nonmasked rating series.

As shown in Figure 36.2, the results were clear-cut. The upper panels show skin conductance responses to masked (a) and nonmasked (b) presentations of the stimuli. It is evident that the fearful subjects responded specifically to their feared stimulus, but did not differ from controls for the other stimulus categories, independently of masking. Thus, the enhanced

responding to the feared stimulus cannot be attributed to conscious perception. Exactly parallel data were obtained for all three rating dimensions; that is, the fearful subjects rated themselves as more disliking, more aroused, and less in control when exposed to masked presentations of their feared stimulus. Thus, these data confirm that an unconscious stimulus analysis is sufficient to trigger phasic anxiety responses.

The lower panels of Figure 36.2 show data from spontaneous skin conductance responses, a measure closely related to generalized anxiety (e.g., Lader, 1967). Again, the results show enhanced responding in the fearful groups compared to the control group, independently of masking. Thus, unconscious exposure to the feared stimuli had effects on anxiety outlasting the specific responses to the stimuli. In other words, it is suggested that nonaware exposure to the feared stimulus resulted in generalized anxiety among fearful subjects.

Conditioning of Unconscious Effects

The data presented in Figure 36.2 provide strong support for the notion of anxiety as elicitable after only preliminary, preattentive, automatic and unconscious analyses of the stimulus. One question raised by these findings concerns the origin of this effect: What is the mechanism whereby fearful subjects acquire these preattentively controlled responses to their feared stimuli? Addressing this question, we (Öhman & Soares, 1993; Soares & Öhman, 1993a, 1993b) demonstrated that Pavlovian conditioning to nonmasked presentations of fear-relevant stimuli (snakes and spiders) in normals resulted in conditioned skin conductance responses that survived backward masking. Conditioning to fear-irrelevant stimuli (flowers and mushrooms), on the other hand, resulted in more elusive responses that were abolished by masking. Similar data were obtained for another class of fear-relevant stimuli, angry faces, which were masked by neutral faces (Öhman et al., 1989). Furthermore, we (Esteves, Dimberg, Parra, & Öhman, 1993) reported that skin conductance responses could be conditioned to masked fear-relevant, but not to masked fear-irrelevant, stimuli. That is, after conditioning to masked angry or happy faces, subjects showed enhanced responding to subsequent nonmasked presentations of angry but not happy faces.

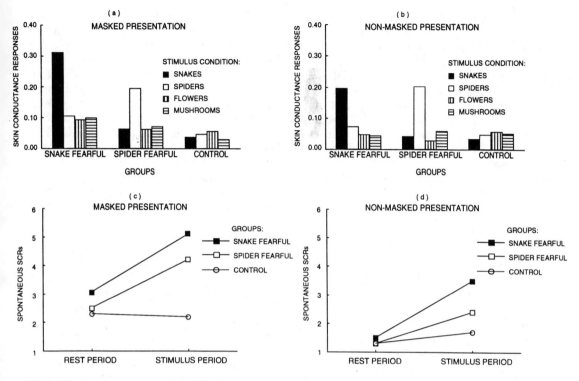

FIGURE 36.2. Upper panels (a and b) show skin conductance responses from snake-fearful, spider-fearful, and nonfearful controls to effectively masked (a) and nonmasked (b) presentations of pictures of snakes, spiders, flowers, and mushrooms. Fearful subjects showed elevated responding to their feared stimulus even if it was prevented from entering conscious perception by backward masking (a). Lower panels (c and d) show spontaneous skin conductance responses (SCRs) in the intervals between stimulation. Whereas controls did not change from rest during stimulation, the fearful subjects showed enhanced spontaneous responding, suggesting that they became anxious after both masked (c) and nonmasked (d) presentations of feared stimuli.

Thus, not only could emotional responses be elicited to masked stimuli, but they could also be learned to such stimuli, provided that they were evolutionarily fear-relevant.

On the basis of an extensive analysis of the available literature, I have concluded (Öhman, 1992) that these types of preattentive effects are best interpreted in terms of the ability of biologically fear-relevant stimuli to directly access physiological responses as they automatically capture attention. Thus, consistent with LeDoux's (1990b) findings, I have argued that the effects can more plausibly be attributed to some gross and relatively simple features of the stimuli than to a complete analysis of their meaning.

The theory, in combination with the data we have reported (Öhman & Soares, 1993, in press; Soares & Öhman, 1993a, 1993b) provides a good account of animal phobias, which may be extended to social phobias (Öhman

et al., 1989; Esteves et al., 1993). Because phobic stimuli have direct, automatic access to the physiological arousal system, phobics perceive their bodies in full-swing responding when they consciously locate a phobic stimulus in the surroundings. Consequently, the fear becomes experienced as inevitable and uncontrollable. This account therefore provides a viable explanation for the "irrationality of phobias"—that is, the dissociation between conscious considerations and fear that is typical of phobias (APA, 1987) (see Öhman & Soares, 1993).

Processing Biases in Anxiety

Mathews, MacLeod, Eysenck, and coworkers (see review by Mathews, 1990) have developed an impressive program of research on cognitive functions in anxiety, focused on the proposition that the processing of mood-congruent information is facilitated (Bower, 1981). In the case of anxiety, this means that an anxious mood activates memory information centered on threat, which in turn facilitates processing of threat-related information. Thus, Mathews (1990) has suggested that "anxiety and worry are associated with an automatic processing bias, initiated prior to awareness, but serving to attract attention to environmental threat cues, and thus facilitating the acquisition of threatening information" (p. 462). It should be apparent that this view is consistent with the functional perspective on anxiety presented above.

Selective Attention Bias in Generalized Anxiety Disorder

To test this theory, Mathews and MacLeod (1986) had generalized anxiety disorder patients and controls verbally "shadow" (read aloud) stories presented to one ear (the attended channel), while series of unconnected words were presented to the other ear (the rejected channel). At the same time, they were required to respond to visually presented probes by pressing a key. Some series of the words presented to the rejected channel involved threat (e.g., "injury," "disaster," "disease," "accident"), whereas others served as emotionally neutral controls, matched for word length and frequency of occurrence in the language. When questioned after the experiment, the subjects typically remained unaware that words had been presented in the rejected channel, and they did not perform above chance levels in forced-choice recognition tests on threat and control words. Nevertheless, anxious subjects slowed their reaction times to the probes when they occurred with threat as compared to nonthreat words in the rejected channel, whereas the controls did not discriminate these conditions. Similar data were reported by MacLeod, Mathews, and Tata (1986), who used a visual selective attention task.

The basic result was again replicated by MacLeod and Mathews (1988) for medical students high and low in trait anxiety. They were tested twice, in periods with or without examination stress, to examine the relative contributions of trait and state anxiety to the previously demonstrated attentional biases. Trait anxiety appeared to carry the main burden of the bias effect, but the interaction between trait and state anxiety also played a

role. Thus, as examination time approached and state anxiety increased, high-trait-anxious subjects showed an increased bias to respond faster to examination-relevant threat words, whereas low-trait-anxious subject showed an increased bias away from these words. Thus, trait anxiety was associated with a general attentional bias in the direction of discovering threat, and with rising state anxiety this bias became more specifically geared towards threats associated with the anticipated stressful events. Low-trait-anxious subjects, on the other hand, in general showed a bias away from threat, and as their state anxiety rose before examination, this avoidance bias came to center on threat associated with the impending stress. This is consistent with the concepts of trait and state anxiety. The former is presumably generalized across situations, and thus it is associated with a general bias to discover threat. State anxiety, on the other hand, should be more dependent on the situation, and thus it is more associated with situationally relevant threats.

The data presented by Mathews, MacLeod, and coworkers (see Mathews, 1990, and Dalgleish & Watts, 1990 for further reviews) are not easily summarized in a comprehensive formula, in part because the data appear somewhat inconsistent. This impression is perhaps more apparent than real, however, because to a considerable extent it reflects the commendable use of a wide assortment of different information-processing paradigms. Despite this variety, the results appear to concur in delineating an anxiety-related processing bias, which may be attributed to a selective attention effect of preattentive origin. Thus, peripherally presented threat appears to capture attention, independently of the current focus of attention. As attention is then automatically switched to the threat, there is competition for processing resources, which is manifested as impeded performance in ongoing, resource-demanding tasks. These effects appear related to enduring characteristics of the person—that is, to trait anxiety (MacLeod & Mathews, 1988; MacLeod & Rutherford, 1992; Mathews, May, Mogg, & Eysenck, 1990). However, there is also an interaction with state anxiety, albeit of a somewhat unclear nature. Sometimes it has been attributed to enhanced generalized distractibility (Mathews et al., 1990), sometimes it has been related to generalized threat (MacLeod & Rutherford, 1992), and sometimes it has been linked to specific threats related to current stress (MacLeod & Mathews, 1988).

The Role of Expectancy and Controlled Processing in Anxiety

So far, all the explanatory burden in the discussion of mechanisms of anxiety has been put on early, automatic and preattentive processing. However, it is clear that these mechanisms are as insufficient to account for anxiety as they are to account for any emotional phenomenon. Thus, theories of emotion have traditionally stressed the role of controlled processing in the generation of emotion (e.g., Lazarus, Kanner, & Folkman, 1980; Mandler, 1975, 1984; Schachter & Singer, 1962). With regard to anxiety, for example, it was noted in the discussion of the stimulus conditions for panic that bodily cues did not elicit attacks unless they were coupled with catastrophic interpretations (e.g., Clark, 1986, 1988). Thus, to approach a complete mechanism-oriented account of anxiety, it is necessary to consider controlled or strategic information processing.

No Panic with Explanation of Symptoms

Anecdotal data reported by Rapee (1986) illustrate the role of cognitions in panic. Although 80% of his panic patients reported a marked similarity between panic and the symptoms they experienced after hyperventilation, none of them panicked. When questioned, they attributed the lack of panic attacks to the fact that they knew what was causing the symptoms, and that they were in a safe place in case they should panic. Rapee, Mattick, and Murrell (1986) formally tested the hypothesis that a readily available explanation for bodily symptoms would save panic patients from attacks. They compared panic patients and social phobics who were given an explanation or no explanation for the physiological effects of CO_2 inhalation. The groups did not differ in reported symptoms, regardless of the explanation given. However, panic patients given no explanation reported more intense symptoms, more intense panic, and more similarity to a "natural" panic attack. In addition, they reported a higher frequency of catastrophic thoughts (e.g., "I am going to die").

The explanation given had no effect on the social phobics, who experienced little panic in any of the explanation conditions. Thus, these results show that panic patients are more vulnerable to anxiety attacks than social phobics when given CO_2 inhalation, and that a readily available explanation of the symptoms can abort the panic attacks. Relating to one of the classical issues in the study of emotion (see Schachter & Singer, 1962), the findings of Rapee et al. (1986) show that unexplained arousal is particularly effective in prompting negatively valenced emotional experience (see Marshall & Zimbardo, 1979; Maslach, 1979).

Effects of Expectations of Control over Symptoms

The role of cognitions in aborting panic was further elucidated by Sanderson, Rapee, and Barlow (1989). Again, CO_2 inhalation was used to induce panic in panic disorder patients. All patients were instructed that they might experience a range of physical sensations, and a range of emotional states "from relaxation to anxiety" as a result of CO_2 administration. Furthermore, they were all informed that they would be able to adjust the CO_2 mixture by manipulating a dial if (and only if) a designated light was illuminated. However, they were urged to stay with the experimenter-selected mixture, because that would facilitate assessment. In effect, the dial could not affect the CO_2 mixture, and none of the subjects tried to use it. The light was illuminated for half of the subjects, who thus were given an illusion of control. Subjects in this group reported a much stronger belief in control over CO_2 symptoms than did those in the no-illusion group. Ten subjects panicked during inhalation, 8 of whom were in the no-illusion group. Subjects in this group also reported more symptoms, higher intensity of symptoms, more catastrophic cognitions, and larger similarity of their response to naturally occurring panic attacks than the subjects in the illusion-of-control group. The quite dramatic effect of perceived control over symptoms reported in this study is in accordance with the prominent place of "fear of losing control" in the symptomatology of panic attacks (Barlow et al., 1985; Borden & Turner, 1989; Rapee et al., 1992). Furthermore, it highlights the importance of cognitions in the elicitation of panic.

The Role of Physiological Feedback in Panic

The data reviewed so far suggest that panic results from a misattribution of physiological sensations, with emphasis on their potentially catastrophic consequences. The data have primarily dealt with the panic-inhibitory effects of correct attribution of bodily symptoms to a more or less controllable external source. However, if the misattribution process is focal, then *false beliefs* about physiological activation should also prompt panic, regardless of the actual physiological changes (Valins, 1972). This hypothesis was tested by Ehlers, Margraf, Roth, Taylor, and Birbaumer (1988). They gave panic patients and controls feedback about their heart rate by having each heartbeat trigger a tone pip. After a baseline period without feedback, there was a true-feedback period during which the actual heart rate was fed back to the subjects. However, unknown to the subjects, at the end of the true feedback period, control of the feedback was transferred to the experimenter, who produced a 50-beat increase in heart rate over a 30-second period, mimicking the heart rate of an intense panic attack (Cohen et al., 1985; Lader & Mathews, 1970). When subjects who realized that the feedback was false were excluded, the alleged increase in heart rate produced large increases in rated anxiety and excitement, as well as in skin conductance level, in patients but not in controls. Furthermore, whereas the controls showed a significant decrease in heart rate and blood pressure from true to false feedback, the panic patients showed increases. Thus, in support of the hypothesis, it appeared that the false feedback of a heart rate increase was sufficient to induce an anxiety attack in the patients, whereas the controls appeared more or less unaffected by this manipulation.

Bodily Sensations and Expectancy of Anxiety in Normals

It appears from the data considered in this section that anxiety patients have not only a bias to attend to threat in the environment, but also a bias to expect some types of stimuli to signal impending doom; in accordance with this expectation, it would seem, they react with anxiety and panic to these cues. Because all the studies reviewed so far have used panic patients as subjects, one may wonder whether the effects reported are specific to them, or whether normals could be made with appropriate expectancy inductions to respond like panic patients. If this were possible, the conclusion that it actually is the expectancy that is critical would be much strengthened.

Such an experiment was reported by van der Molen, van den Hout, Vroemen, Lousberg, and Griez (1986). They exposed normal volunteers to lactate infusion or placebo in balanced order. Lactate infusion is a well-established method for experimentally inducing anxiety, and has been specifically related to panic (see Margraf et al., 1986b, and van den Hout, 1988, for excellent reviews). Half of the subjects were instructed that "the infusions might cause unpleasant bodily sensations similar to those experienced during periods of anxiety" and that "they might experience anxious effects" (van der Molen et al., 1986, p. 678). The other half of the subjects were told that the infusion would evoke feelings of "pleasant tension, such as those experienced during sports, watching an exciting movie, etc." (van der Molen et al., 1986, p. 678). The subjects rated their emotional state from −100 (very anxious tension) to +100 (very pleasant excitement). The instructions had no effect in the placebo condition, which resulted in neutral emotional ratings. With lactate infusion, however, subjects instructed to expect aversive symptoms and anxiety rated their state as quite negative (−64.3), whereas the subjects expecting positive affect showed variable ratings averaging out as emotionally neutral. Thus, the results demonstrated that the interaction between bodily cues as induced by lactate infusion, and expectancy of aversive effects, was critical in inducing anxiety. Neither infusion nor instruction per se was sufficient to induce anxiety. Thus, this result is quite persuasive support for the argument that expectations of negative affect and catastrophic consequences are critical determinants of anxiety and panic attacks, as claimed by cognitive theorists (e.g., Clark, 1986, 1988).

THEORETICAL INTEGRATION

To sum up, I have argued that anxiety originates in biologically evolved defense systems, which are presumably responsible both for acute attacks of increased state anxiety, and for

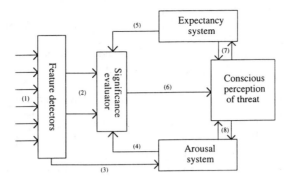

FIGURE 36.3. An information-processing model of the generation of anxiety. See text for explanations.

more enduring and stable levels of trait anxiety. These defenses are served by information-processing mechanisms centered on the determination of threat and operating at several loci of information processing. In this section, a somewhat speculative integration of the information processing mechanisms is presented. It is pictorially represented in Figure 36.3.

Feature Detectors

Stimulus information (1 in Figure 36.3) reaches feature detectors, which provide a preliminary segregation of the stimulus before the information is passed on (2) to the significance evaluation system. The important part of this system for alarm/anxiety/fear is that some stimulus features may be directly connected to the arousal system. Thus, it is assumed that the alarm reaction, which may eventually surface as an anxiety response, is started to be recruited immediately when the perceptual system encounters a sign of a survival-relevant stimulus. The feature detectors under discussion here are assumed to operate primarily on physical input. That is, they do not yet interact with memory to provide meaning to the stimulus; rather, they help to preliminary segregate the stimulus inflow and to direct attention toward potentially relevant areas (e.g., Posner, 1980). Primary examples of stimulus features that may directly trigger the arousal system include high intensity and rapid rise times, provoking startle.

In attentional terms, this system may be set to discover potential threat in the environment by a filtering mechanism, giving priority to biologically important stimuli (see Öhman, 1992, for documentation of this point). Such stimuli, then, have the dual effect of immedi-

ately activating the arousal system (3) and being selected for preferential treatment by the significance evaluation system (2), which passes information directly on to the conscious perception system (6).

There are good data available to suggest that a mechanism of this type is operating in phobias (Öhman & Soares, in press) and that it may result from conditioning (Öhman & Soares, 1993; Öhman et al., 1989). It may also be speculated that this mechanism is operating in panic attacks. Barlow et al. (1985) reported clinical impressions suggesting that panic attacks are "usually associated with mild exercise, sexual relations, sudden temperature changes, stress, or other cues that alter physiological functioning in some discernible way, albeit outside the patient's awareness" (p. 327). If we accept Klein's (1993) argument that panic reflects the activation of an alarm system evolved to respond to suffocation hazard and prompting rapid escape from potentially deadly locations, it appears reasonable to presume that critical cues for this system would activate feature detectors that are sensitive to specific bodily stimuli. These stimuli would result in either unconditioned activation (e.g., increased CO_2 concentration in the inhaled air, lack of oxygen) or they would reflect conditioned activation of alarm (e.g., heart rate increases). In both cases, however, the process would rapidly and automatically trigger the arousal system, independently of the person's awareness of the threat stimulus. A similar argument can perhaps be made for PTSD, where the eliciting event is so threatening that it provides traumatic conditioning to associated cues, which in this way may acquire power to activate the arousal system automatically. Few data are available to support the conditioning scenario postulated here for panic disorder or PTSD; however, it is clear that a severely traumatic event (such as a failure to get air) is an extremely efficient unconditioned stimulus for persistent conditioned fear responses (Sanderson, Laverty, & Campbell, 1963).

The Significance Evaluator

The significance evaluator automatically assesses stimuli for relevance. In contrast to the feature detectors, which are selective for input in terms of a stimulus set or a filtering mechanism, this system operates by a response set or a pigeon-holing mechanism (Broadbent, 1970). That is to say, its selection is "top-down" or schema-driven, in the sense that it is set by the expectancy system (5) to look for particular categories of input. This implies that its operation is predicated on a full-meaning analysis of the stimuli. This is the locus of the bias to discover threat, studied by Mathews, MacLeod, and coworkers (e.g., Mathews, 1990; see review above). Thus, as part of interrelated memory systems, memorial representations of moods (Bower, 1981) or emotional responses (Lang, 1984) may prime memory areas focused on threat; as a result, the expectancy system sets the significance evaluator to respond to threat words, for example. When threat words are discovered, the conscious perception system (6) is called, and this call may result in competition with other ongoing tasks, such as responding to visual probes (MacLeod et al., 1986; Mathews & MacLeod, 1986). Such competition implies that the significance evaluator requires cognitive resources, and thus that it is at least partly a controlled processing system. Nevertheless, it operates preattentively, without any necessary conscious access (Öhman, 1988, 1992; see also Spinks & Kramer, 1991). Thus, it is assumed that there is controlled processing that is not consciously available.

The significance evaluator has been viewed as central to the elicitation of orienting responses (Bernstein & Taylor, 1979; Öhman, 1979). As the significance evaluator activates the conscious perception channel (through 6) so that the eliciting stimulus (e.g., the threat) is consciously perceived, an orienting response is elicited through activation of the arousal system (8). It should perhaps be explicitly noted that the view presented here, associating the orienting response with conscious perception (Öhman, 1992), represents a change

from my previous view (Öhman, 1979), which assumed that orienting responses were activated by a direct link from the significance evaluator to the arousal system. The basic argument for this change is that backward masking, which blocks the target stimulus from entering conscious perception (i.e., path 6), also blocks skin conductance responses to significant conditioned stimuli, unless they are biologically fear-relevant. Biologically fear-relevant conditioned stimuli, on the other hand, are presumed to activate the arousal system through path 3, and thus skin conductance responses to such stimuli survive masking (see Öhman, 1992). The important implication for anxiety is that nonconscious discovery of potential threat through the significance evaluator does not result in activation of the arousal system unless it results in conscious perception of threat. Thus, the enhanced skin conductance responses to relevant threat words presented in the rejected channel of a shadowing task for obsessive compulsive subjects (Foa & McNally, 1986) should be attributed to switches of attention between channels (Dawson & Schell, 1982; Trandel & McNally, 1987). Similarly, enhanced skin conductance responses to relevant threat words presented against a noisy background to PTSD veterans should be attributed to conscious perception (McNally et al., 1987).

The Arousal System

Although the significance evaluator is assumed to have no effect, or only a weak effect, on the arousal system, this latter system is assumed to be able to "tune up" the significance evaluator (4). Thus, increased arousal is assumed to enhance the biases of the significance evaluator, perhaps in a way analogous to the multiplicative relation between drive and habit in Hullian learning theory. This assumption explains the effect of state anxiety on attentional bias (MacLeod & Mathews, 1988; MacLeod & Rutherford, 1992; Mathews et al., 1990).

The arousal system also provides critical input to the conscious perception system, which has been taken as the distinctive feature of emotional experience (Mandler, 1975). For example, the studies by Ehlers et al. (1988) and Pauli et al. (1991) demonstrated the power of such perceived input to generate anxiety in anxiety-prone individuals. However, it is important to note that the relationship between the arousal system and the conscious perception system is bidirectional. Thus, as threat and danger are consciously perceived, the arousal system is recruited to provide metabolic support for the more or less vigorous coping actions that may become necessary.

Although the arousal system is presented as a unitary system here, this is, of course, a gross oversimplification. The core of the system is Cannon's (1929) emergency reaction—that is, a sympatho-adrenal mobilization of bodily resources for vigorous action—but the character of the resulting physiological response is modulated by stimulus factors, available action alternatives, and the particular action chosen, as well as by characteristics of the individual (see Berntson, Cacioppo, & Quigley, 1991, for an updated and sophisticated analysis of autonomic nervous system control of physiological responses).

The Expectancy System

The expectancy system relies on the organization of emotion in memory. Following Lang (1979, 1984), it is assumed that memory for emotional episodes can be represented by interconnected nodes comprising stimulus, response, and meaning information. Such networks can be activated by matching input information, but because nodes are assumed to coactivate one another within the network, a partial match involving only a few nodes is sufficient to put the system into an activated state. However, the more complete the match, the stronger the activation (Lang, 1984). When activated, the system can be viewed as biasing the significance evaluator to respond to information matching active memory nodes (5). Furthermore, such matching provides information for the conscious perception system, which in turn keeps the memory foundation of the expectancy system in continual activation—maintaining, as it were, the bias to discover threat. In agreement with Mathews (1990), it is assumed that this biasing of the significance evaluator occurs at a nonconscious level of information processing.

However, the expectancy system has a dual role in generating fear and anxiety. Not only does it bias the processing of incoming information, but it also provides the context for the interpretation of inputs to the conscious perception system (see Mandler, 1975, 1984). At this level, the influence of the expectancy system occurs at a consciously reportable level,

where it is more appropriate to use the term "expectancy" than in the case of biasing the significance evaluator. Thus, interpretation of input from the significance evaluator (5) and the arousal system (8) by the conscious perception system occurs in continuous interaction with the expectancy system and its associated memory. This is the basis for the effects of expectancies on panic that have been discussed previously.

Perceived Threat and Coping

The conscious perception system is merely an aspect of a much broader system, whether we call it the "mind" elucidated as the "cognitive–interpretive system" (Mandler, 1975), "consciousness" (Posner, 1978), "control processing" (Schneider et al., 1984), or the "central capacity-limited channel" (Öhman, 1979). For present purposes this system has two central functions: (1) to integrate information input from the arousal system, the significance evaluator, and the expectancy system; and (2) to select an action alternative to cope with the perceived threat. When Epstein's (1972) distinction between anxiety and fear is adhered to, the latter function becomes critical for deciding the emotional effect of the perceived threat. If its nature is such that avoidance or escape provide successful coping with the threat, the result is fear. If there is no such possibility, or if attempted escape is interfered with, the result is anxiety (Epstein, 1972).

CONCLUDING DISCUSSION

To recapitulate, it has been argued that responses of fear and anxiety originate in an alarm system shaped by evolution to protect creatures from impending danger. This system is biased to discover threat, and it results in a sympathetically dominated response as a support of potential flight or fight. This response system can be triggered from three different levels of information processing, the first two of which are inaccessible to introspection. The first level concerns a direct link to an arousal system from elementary feature detectors geared to respond to biologically relevant threats. Thus, the arousal system becomes collaterally and automatically activated with the activation of further information-processing stages, whose functioning may be influenced by the arousal. The second level concerns a schema-driven nonconscious bias to discover threat in the environment, which delivers information to conscious perception, but has no effect or only a weak effect on physiological arousal. The third level concerns the direct effect of expectancy and physiological arousal on the cognitive–interpretive activity resulting in perceived threat. In this concluding section of the chapter, some implications of this view of anxiety are discussed.

The Nature of the Unconscious Effects

Freud (e.g., 1900/1953), of course, believed that anxiety has an unconscious origin, residing in the interaction between bodily and instinctual energies on the one hand, and various psychological defense mechanisms on the other. Similarly, according to the present scheme, unconscious activation of bodily systems in interaction with an interpretive conscious system plays a pivotal role in the generation of anxiety. Indeed, the correspondence with classic psychodynamic notions can be pushed a step further by noting that the present scheme, in a way, does not operate with one but with two different types of unconscious. Thus, Freud distinguished between what might be termed a "drive unconscious" and a "repressed unconscious" (see Power & Brewin, 1991), which in some respects would correspond to the unconscious effects of the feature detectors and the significance evaluator, respectively, in the present model. Furthermore, in some other respects the former would correspond to the "collective unconscious" postulated by Jung (1953) to encompass the cumulative experience of the human species. In the model (Figure 36.3), this role is played by feature detectors, which have been shaped to respond particularly strongly to features associated with recurrent threats to well-being in the evolution of humankind. Elsewhere (Öhman, 1986), I have suggested that reptiles provided an archaic prototype for threats emanating from predation pressure, and that this may explain the human tendency to equip the embodiments of evil with bestial features. Thus, Jung's notion of "archetypes" can, in fact, be reinterpreted in terms of biological preparedness (e.g., Seligman, 1971).

The other mechanism of nonconscious bias for responding to threat, residing in the significance evaluator and the expectancy system, suggests some of the Freudian notions of the unconscious. Because this bias represents schema-driven effects dependent on memorial organization (e.g., Lang, 1984), it will reflect the individuals unique personal experience. Thus, depending on the history of the individual, he or she may respond to some potential threat cues rather than others. Furthermore, what is extremely threatening to one individual may be completely innocuous to another, because the corresponding memorial node may not be connected to nodes in memory structures related to threat. Thus, effects similar to those of the classical Freudian defenses may be interpretable in these terms. Furthermore, one may even argue that the schema-driven unconscious threat-biasing system may sometimes be pitted against the feature-driven detection system in a way strongly reminiscent of the interactions between defenses and drives in psychoanalytic theory. For example, if bodily cues activate the arousal system, but the significance evaluator is biased against responding to these cues in terms of threat, then something similar to the phenomenon seen in patients with "panic without fear" (Kushner & Beitman, 1990) should result. However, whether this should be viewed as anxiety counteracted by defenses, or simply as lack of anxiety, appears a moot point. The important insight here is rather that phenomena similar to those described by psychoanalysts are readily interpretable in terms of the current model (see Power & Brewin, 1991, for further discussion of the communality between traditional psychoanalytic theories and contemporary cognitive theories). These interpretations, furthermore, are preferable to the psychoanalytic ones because they are backed up by a scientific literature based on rigorous theorizing and controlled data, rather than based on anecdotal observations from uncontrolled case studies (see Grünbaum, 1984).

The Relationship between Fear and Anxiety

The model depicted in Figure 36.3 implies that there are in effect two types of anxiety, which both differ from fear. Following Lang (1984), emotions can be viewed as action sets—as readinesses to respond in particular ways. Fear, then, is viewed as an emotional response related to avoidance and escape. Although such responses may be primed by the feature detectors and the significance evaluator, which may recruit metabolic support for vigorous action, the eventual overt responses are taken to occur after conscious perception of the threat. When such responses are blocked, fear is changed into anxiety (Epstein, 1972). However, if anxiety is construed as "unresolved fear" or "undirected arousal" related to perceived threat (Epstein, 1972), then the model implies that there is a more basic type of anxiety than the one resulting when avoidance motives become frustrated. This type of anxiety results from the unconscious input to the conscious perception system from the significance evaluator and the arousal system. Because the source of this input is not necessarily available to consciousness, the resulting state of undirected arousal is experienced as anxiety, or perhaps more precisely as "undirected alarm." The person knows that something is wrong, but cannot pinpoint any clear reason for it. Anxiety in this sense, then, is entirely dependent on the unconscious mechanisms, whereas the anxiety resulting from interference with avoidance is more readily appraised at the conscious level as originating in the external world or in personal shortcomings.

The "alarm" or "primary" anxiety may be channeled or "resolved" into fear, if escape is selected as the action option after a complete conscious and controlled processing of the stimulus situation. Normally, of course, the eliciting stimulus is consciously perceived simultaneously with the arousal of anxiety, as attention is directed to the preattentively located threat. It is only when the attention shift fails to locate the stimulus that preattentively elicited unconscious anxiety is left in the system without any apparent stimulus for its explanation. This may occur when the stimulus is very faint and thus fails to be perceived; when the preattentive mechanisms falsely locates a threat that is not confirmed by controlled processing; or when several more or less simultaneous stimuli (e.g., emanating from the body) mask one another. In any of these cases, an emotional state perhaps best characterized as "anxious alarm" should be the experienced result, and this state should be clearly different from anxiety generated by failed escape or avoidance.

Implications for Anxiety Disorders

The model depicted in Figure 36.3 permits the various anxiety disorders to be viewed as resulting from different emphases within the same information-processing structures.

As already noted, phobias and panic disorder are taken as resulting from the automatic activation of the arousal system by specific features located by the feature detectors. This activation provides a surge of physiological arousal, cues from which become available to the conscious perception system. Therefore, these two types of disorders should be similar in the sense that they both reflect increases in sympathetically mediated arousal. However, whereas the information reaching the conscious perception system from the arousal system is quite similar in phobias and panic disorder, the information arriving via the significance evaluator is radically different. In the case of a phobia, the source of the physiological arousal is attributed to some factor in to external world; in the case of panic, the arousal is attributed to an enemy from within. As everyone who has considered security management knows, the former case is much easier to handle than the latter. An external enemy can be met with barricades, attack, or defensive withdrawal, depending on situational factors and the relative balance of power between the threatened and the threatener. In phobias, this balance is typically interpreted as supporting flight. However, an enemy within has crossed the defensive barricades, which makes the impending danger acute. Flight is not an option, and the risk of being overwhelmed and of capitulation become acute. Therefore, catastrophic interpretations of the situation are readily invited. In this way, both the similarities and the differences in symptomatology between phobias and panic disorder can be accounted for.

If Klein's (1993) interpretation of panic as the result of an alarm system responding to suffocation threat is accepted, then a route to the understanding of agoraphobia is opened. In agoraphobia the suffocation alarm may be conditioned to environmental cues, which then become avoided. However, if the alarm response rather is conditioned to bodily cues, such as heart rate increases, then the person may end up with apparently spontaneous panic attacks, without obvious situational triggers.

In PTSD, there is an original trauma that totally recruits the individual's defense responses, often for quite protracted periods of time and at overwhelming intensities (e.g., in combat). As a result, cues may be conditioned to recruit the arousal system automatically, as in phobia and panic. In PTSD, however, the subsequent stage—cognitive preoccupation with the trauma, partly mediated through the expectancy system and the significance evaluator—appears to take on a more prominent role than in phobias and panic disorder, leading to physiological activation not only automatically but also through conscious mediation (via worries and ruminations).

Generalized anxiety disorder, finally, appears to lack arousal activation via the feature detectors; it seems to be primarily driven by the expectancy system and the bias to discover threats (Rapee, 1991). The physiological effects that are needed to turn the worry into anxiety (Mathews, 1990) are likely to be recruited through activation of the arousal system from the cognitive perception system. Thus, in this disorder the expectancy–significance–perception loop appears to play the primary role and the nonconscious activation of arousal a secondary role in the problem.

The perspective provided here views phobias and panic disorders as physiologically driven, and generalized anxiety disorder as a cognitively driven, with PTSD at a somewhat intermediate position between the two groups. Thus, within a unitary theoretical frame, it is possible to deal quite effectively with important aspects of the different anxiety disorders. However, whereas this account appears quite successful in dealing with the symptomatology of the disorders, it is relatively silent on the issue of etiology. Conditioning is given a role in several disorders—and, elaborated as biologically prepared learning, it may be decisive for phobias (Öhman et al., 1985)—but there is at present no information in the model to suggest why some persons develop panic disorder and others generalized anxiety disorder. In particular, the origin of the cognitively driven ruminations in generalized anxiety disorder remains a mystery.

Anxiety, Emotion, and Cognition

If the interaction between physiological cues and cognitive interpretive activity is taken as the hallmark of emotional phenomena (e.g., James, 1884; Mandler, 1975), then fear and anxiety as described in this chapter are *prima facie* emotional phenomena. Thus, it has been documented that bodily cues provide some of the most important experienced symptoms in fear and anxiety, and that measurable physiological responses are prominent correlates of fear and anxiety both in the laboratory and

when ambulatorily monitored in everyday life. There are good data suggesting that perceived bodily changes are critical to anxiety attacks (e.g., Pauli et al., 1991), but it is equally clear that such bodily changes are neither necessary nor sufficient for anxiety to be experienced. The anxiety is typically evoked in particular types of situations, the nature of which is such that an evolutionary origin appears a quite straightforward interpretation of their potency.

With regard to theory, an interactional perspective stresses the inextricable interplay among physiological activation, cognitive processes, and emotional responding from the very moment an effective stimulus makes contact with the relevant sensory organ. Thus, it is clear that some emotional effects occur immediately upon presentation of an effective stimulus (LeDoux, 1990b; Öhman & Soares, in press), providing some justification for the claim that "affect precedes inference" (Zajonc, 1980). However, it is equally clear that cognitions stemming from nonconscious biases play pervasive roles in the interpretation of threats (e.g., Mathews, 1990), in the volitional appraisal of the stimulus, and in deliberations about potential response alternatives. Thus, as a final point, the literature reviewed in this chapter is taken to suggest that it is hardly meaningful to ask oneself whether cognition is necessary for emotion. We appear to have reached a stage in the knowledge of fear and anxiety at which the meaningful question is *how* the interaction between emotion and cognition occurs, and some tentative answers to this fundamental question may already be at hand.

Acknowledgment. Preparation of this chapter was supported by grants from the Swedish Council for Research in the Humanities and Social Sciences. Address communications to: Arne Öhman, Department of Clinical Neuroscience and Psychiatry, Karolinska Hospital, Box 60500, S-104 01 Stockholm, Sweden.

REFERENCES

American Psychiatric Association (APA). (1980). *Diagnostic and statistical manual of mental disorders* (3rd ed.). Washington, DC: Author.

American Psychiatric Association (APA). (1987). *Diagnostic and statistical manual of mental disorders* (3rd ed., rev.). Washington, DC: Author.

Arrindell, W. A., Pickersgill, M. J., Merckelbach, H., Ardon, M. A., & Cornet, F. C. (1991). Phobic dimensions: III. Factor analytic approaches to the study of common phobic fears: An updated review of findings obtained with adult subjects. *Advances in Behaviour Research and Therapy*, 13, 73–130.

Balota, D. A. (1983). Automatic semantic activation and episodic memory encoding. *Journal of Verbal Learning and Verbal Behavior*, 22, 88–104.

Barlow, D. H. (1988). *Anxiety and its disorders: The nature and treatment of anxiety and panic*. New York: Guilford Press.

Barlow, D. H., & Craske, M. G. (1988). The phenomenology of panic. In S. Rachman & J. D. Maser (Eds.), *Panic: Psychological perspectives*. Hillsdale, NJ: Erlbaum.

Barlow, D. H., Vermilyea, J., Blanchard, E. B., Vermilyea, B. B., Di Nardo, P. A., & Cerny, J. A. (1985). The phenomenon of panic. *Journal of Abnormal Psychology*, 94, 320–328.

Bernstein, A. S., & Taylor, K. W. (1979). The interaction of stimulus information with potential stimulus significance in eliciting the skin conductance orienting response. In H. D. Kimmel, E. H. van Olst, & J. F. Orlebeke (Eds.), *The orienting reflex in humans*. Hillsdale, NJ: Erlbaum.

Berntson, G. C., Cacioppo, J. T., & Quigley, K. S. (1991). Autonomic determinism: The modes of autonomic control, the doctrine of autonomic space, and the laws of autonomic constraint. *Psychological Review*, 98, 459–487.

Blanchard, E. B., Kolb, L. C., Gerardi, R. J., Ryan, P., & Pallmeyer, T. P. (1986). Cardiac response to relevant stimuli as an adjunctive tool for diagnosing posttraumatic stress disorder in Vietnam veterans. *Behavior Therapy*, 17, 592–606.

Borden, J. W., & Turner, S. M. (1989). Is panic a unique emotional experience? *Behaviour Research and Therapy*, 27, 263–268.

Borkovec, T. D., & Inz, J. (1990). The nature of worry in generalized anxiety disorder: A predominance of thought activity. *Behaviour Research and Therapy*, 28, 153–158.

Borkovec, T. D., Robinson, E., Pruzinsky, T. & DePree, J. A. (1983). Preliminary exploration of worry: Some characteristics and processes. *Behaviour Research and Therapy*, 21, 9–16.

Bower, G. H. (1981). Mood and memory. *American Psychologist*, 36, 129–148.

Breslau, N., Davis, G. C., Andreski, P., & Peterson, E. (1991). Traumatic events and posttraumatic stress disorder in an urban population of young adults. *Archives of General Psychiatry*, 48, 216–222.

Broadbent, D. E. (1970). Stimulus set and response set: Two kinds of selective attention. In D. M. Mostofsky (Ed.), *Attention: Contemporary theory and analysis*. New York: Appleton-Century-Crofts.

Buss, A. H. (1962). Two anxiety factors in psychiatric patients. *Journal of Abnormal and Social Psychology*, 65, 426–427.

Cannon, W. B. (1929). *Bodily changes in pain, hunger fear, and rage*. New York: Appleton-Century-Crofts.

Clark, D. M. (1986). A cognitive approach to panic. *Behaviour Research and Therapy*, 24, 461–470.

Clark, D. M. (1988). A cognitive model of panic attacks. In S. Rachman & J. D. Maser (Eds.), *Panic: Psychological perspectives*. Hillsdale, NJ: Erlbaum.

Cohen, A. S., Barlow, D. H., & Blanchard, E. B. (1985). Psychophysiology of relaxation-associated panic attacks. *Journal of Abnormal Psychology*, 94, 96–101.

Craske, M. G., Rapee, R. M., Jackel, L., & Barlow, D. H. (1989). Qualitative dimensions of worry in DSM-III-R

generalized anxiety disorder subjects and nonanxious controls. *Behaviour Research and Therapy*, 27, 397–402.

Dalgleish, T., & Watts, F. N. (1990). Biases of attention and memory in disorders of anxiety and depression. *Clinical Psychology Review*, 10, 589–604.

Dawson, M. E., & Schell, A. M. (1982). Electrodermal responses to attended and nonattended significant stimuli during dichotic listening. *Journal of Experimental Psychology: Human Perception and Performance*, 8, 315–324.

Ehlers, A., Margraf, J., Roth, W. T., Taylor, C. B., & Birbaumer, N. (1988). Anxiety induced by false heart rate feedback in patients with panic disorder. *Behaviour Research and Therapy*, 26, 1–11.

Epstein, S. (1972). The nature of anxiety with emphasis upon its relationship to expectancy. In C. D. Spielberger (Ed.), *Anxiety: Current trends in theory and research* (Vol. 2). New York: Academic Press.

Esteves, F., Dimberg, U., Parra, C., & Öhman, A. (1993). *Nonconscious associative learning: Pavlovian conditioning of skin conductance responses to masked fear-relevant facial stimuli*. Manuscript submitted for publication.

Fenz, W. D., & Epstein, S. (1965). Manifest anxiety: Unifactorial or multifactorial composition. *Perceptual and Motor Skills*, 20, 773–780.

Foa, E. B., & McNally, R. J. (1986). Sensitivity to feared stimuli in obsessive–compulsives: A dichotic listening analysis. *Cognitive Therapy and Research*, 10, 477–485.

Fowler, C. A., Wolford, G., Slade, R., & Tassinary, L. (1981). Lexical access with and without awareness. *Journal of Experimental Psychology: General*, 110, 341–362.

Fredrikson, M. (1981). Orienting and defensive responses to phobic and conditioned stimuli in phobics and normals. *Psychophysiology*, 18, 456–465.

Fredrikson, M., Sundin, Ö., & Frankenhaeuser, M. (1985). Cortisol excretion in specific phobias. *Psychosomatic Medicine*, 47, 313–319.

Freedman, R. R., Ianni, P., Ettedgui, E., & Puthezhath, N. (1985). Ambulatory monitoring of panic disorder. *Archives of General Psychiatry*, 42, 244–255.

Freud, S. (1953). The interpretation of dreams. In J. Strachey (Ed.) *The standard edition of the complete psychological works of Sigmund Freud* (Vols. 4 and 5). London: Hogarth Press. (Original work published 1900)

Fridlund, A. J., Hatfield, M. E., Cottam, G. L., & Fowler, S. C. (1986). Anxiety and striate-muscle activation: Evidence from electromyographic pattern analysis. *Journal of Abnormal Psychology*, 95, 228–236.

Grünbaum, A. (1984). *The foundation of psychoanalysis: A philosophical critique*. Berkeley: University of California Press.

Hare, R. D., & Blevings, G. (1975). Defensive responses to phobic stimuli. *Biological Psychology*, 3, 1–13.

Hibbert, G. A. (1984). Ideational components of anxiety: Their origin and content. *British Journal of Psychiatry*, 144, 618–624.

Hoehn-Saric, R., McLeod, D. R., & Zimmerli, W. D. (1989). Somatic manifestations in women with generalized anxiety disorder. *Archives of General Psychiatry*, 46, 1113–1119.

Holender, D. (1986). Semantic activation without conscious identification in dichotic listening, parafoveal vision, and visual masking: A survey and appraisal. *Behavioral and Brain Sciences*, 9, 1–66.

James, W. (1884). What is an emotion? *Mind*, 9, 188–205.

Jung, C. G. (1953). Two essays on analytical psychology. In *Collected works* (Vol. 7.) New York: Pantheon.

Kilpatrick, D. G., Saunders, B. E., Amick-McMullan, A., Best, C. L., Veronen, L. L., & Resnick, H. S. (1989). Victim and crime factors associated with the development of crime-related post-traumatic stress disorder. *Behavior Therapy, 20*, 199–214.

Kipling, R. (1983). *The second jungle book*. London: Macmillan. (Original work published 1895)

Klein, D. F. (1981). Anxiety reconceptualized. In D. F. Klein & J. Rabkin (Eds.), *Anxiety: New research and changing concepts*. New York: Raven Press.

Klein, D. F. (1993). False suffocation alarms and spontaneous panics: Subsuming the CO_2 hypersensitivity theory. *Archives of General Psychiatry*.

Kushner, M. G., & Beitman, B. D. (1990). Panic attacks without fear: An overview. *Behaviour Research and Therapy, 28*, 469–479.

Lader, M. H. (1967). Palmar skin conductance measures in anxiety and phobic states. *Journal of Psychosomatic Research, 11*, 271–281.

Lader, M., & Marks, I. (1973). *Clinical anxiety*. London: Heinemann.

Lader, M., & Mathews, A. (1970). Physiological changes during spontaneous panic attacks. *Journal of Psychosomatic Research, 14*, 377–382.

Lang, P. J. (1968). Fear reduction and fear behavior: Problems in treating a construct. In J. M. Shlien (Ed.), *Research in psychotherapy* (Vol. 3). Washington, DC: American Psychological Association.

Lang, P. J. (1978). Anxiety: Toward a psychophysiological definition. In H. S. Akiskal & W. L. Webb (Eds.), *Psychiatric diagnosis: Explorations of biological predictors*. New York: Spectrum.

Lang, P. J. (1979). A bio-informational theory of emotional imagery. *Psychophysiology, 16*, 495–512.

Lang, P. J. (1984). Cognition in emotion: Concept and action. In C. E. Izard, J. Kagan, & R. B. Zajonc (Eds.), *Emotions, cognition, and behavior*. New York: Cambridge University Press.

Lazarus, R. S., Kanner, A. D., & Folkman, S. (1980). Emotions: A cognitive–phenomenological analysis. In R. Plutchik & H. Kellerman (Eds.), *Emotion: Theory, research, and experience. Vol. 1. Theories of emotion*. New York: Academic Press.

LeDoux, J. E. (1989). Cognitive–emotional interactions in the brain. *Cognition and Emotion, 3*, 267–289.

LeDoux, J. E. (1990a). Fear pathways in the brain: Implications for a theory of the emotional brain. In P. F. Brain, S. Parmigiani, R. J. Blanchard, & D. Mainardi (Eds.), *Fear and defence*. London: Harwood.

LeDoux, J. E. (1990b). Information flow from sensation to emotion: Plasticity in the neural computation of stimulus value. In M. Gabriel & J. Moore (Eds.), *Learning and computational neuroscience: Foundations of adaptive networks*. Cambridge, MA: MIT Press.

MacLeod, C., & Mathews, A. (1988). Anxiety and the allocation of attention to threat. *Quarterly Journal of Experimental Psychology, 40A*, 653–670.

MacLeod, C., Mathews, A., & Tata, P. (1986). Attentional bias in emotional disorders. *Journal of Abnormal Psychology, 95*, 15–20.

MacLeod, C., & Rutherford, E. M. (1992). Anxiety and the selective processing of emotional information: Mediating roles of awareness, trait and state variables, and personal relevance of stimulus materials. *Behaviour Research and Therapy, 30*, 479–491.

Mandler, G. (1975). *Mind and emotion*. New York: Wiley.

Mandler, G. (1984). *Mind and body: Psychology of emotion and stress*. New York: Norton.

Marcel, A. (1983). Conscious and unconscious perception: An approach to the relations between phenomenal experience and perceptual processes. *Cognitive Psychology, 15*, 238–300.

Margraf, J., Ehlers, A., & Roth, W. T. (1986a). Biological models of panic disorder and agoraphobia: A review. *Behaviour Research and Therapy, 24*, 553–567.

Margraf, J., Ehlers, A., & Roth, W. T. (1986b). Sodium lactate infusions and panic attacks: A review and critique. *Psychosomatic Medicine, 48*, 23–51.

Marshall, G. D., & Zimbardo, P. G. (1979). Affective consequences of inadequately explained physiological arousal. *Journal of Personality and Social Psychology, 37*, 970–988.

Maslach, C. (1979). Negative emotional biasing of unexplained arousal. *Journal of Personality and Social Psychology, 37*, 953–969.

Mason, J. W. (1968). Overall hormonal balance as a key to endocrine functions. *Psychosomatic Medicine, 30*, 791–808.

Mathews, A. (1990). Why worry? The cognitive function of anxiety. *Behaviour Research and Therapy, 28*, 455–468.

Mathews, A., & MacLeod, C. (1986). Discrimination of threat cues without awareness in anxiety states. *Journal of Abnormal Psychology, 95*, 131–138.

Mathews, A., May, J., Mogg, K., & Eysenck, M. (1990). Attentional bias in anxiety: Selective search of defective filtering? *Journal of Abnormal Psychology, 99*, 166–173.

McNally, R. J. (1987). Preparedness and phobias: A review. *Psychological Bulletin, 101*, 283–303.

McNally, R. J., Luedke, D. L., Besyner, J. K., Peterson, R., Bohm, K., & Lips, O. J. (1987). Sensitivity to stress-relevant stimuli in posttraumatic stress disorder. *Journal of Anxiety Disorders, 1*, 105–116.

Mellman, T. A., & Davis, G. C. (1985). Combat-related flashbacks in posttraumatic stress disorder: Phenomenology and similarity to panic attacks. *Journal of Clinical Psychiatry, 46*, 379–382.

Nesse, R. M. (1987). An evolutionary perspective on panic disorder and agoraphobia. *Ethology and Sociobiology, 8*, 73S–83S.

Nesse, R. M., Cameron, O. G., Curtis, G. C., McCann, D. S., & Huber-Smith, M. J. (1984). Adrenergic function in panic anxiety patients. *Archives of General Psychiatry, 41*, 320–332.

Nesse, R. M., Curtis, G. C., Thyer, B. A., McCann, D. S., Huber-Smith, M. J., & Knopf, R. F. (1985). Endocrine and cardiovascular responses during phobic anxiety. *Psychosomatic Medicine, 47*, 320–332.

Öhman, A. (1979). The orienting response, attention, and learning: An information processing perspective. In H. D. Kimmel, E. H. van Olst, & J. F. Orlebeke (Eds.), *The orienting reflex in humans*. Hillsdale, NJ: Erlbaum.

Öhman, A. (1986). Face the beast and fear the face: Animal and social fears as prototypes for evolutionary analyses of emotion. *Psychophysiology, 23*, 123–145.

Öhman, A. (1987). The psychophysiology of emotion: An evolutionary–cognitive perspective. *Advances in Psychophysiology, 2*, 79–127.

Öhman, A. (1988). Nonconscious control of autonomic responses: A role for Pavlovian conditioning? *Biological Psychology, 27*, 113–135.

Öhman, A. (1992). Orienting and attention: Preferred preattentive processing of potentially phobic stimuli. In

B. A. Campbell, H. Haynes, & R. Richardson (Eds.), *Attention and information processing in infants and adults: Perspectives from human and animal research.* Hillsdale, NJ: Erlbaum.

Öhman, A. (1993). Stimulus prepotency and fear: Data and theory. In N. Birbaumer & A. Öhman (Eds.), *The organization of emotion: Cognitive, clinical and psychophysiological perspectives.* Toronto: Hogrefe.

Öhman, A., Dimberg, U., & Esteves, F. (1989). Preattentive activation of aversive emotions. In T. Archer & L.-G. Nilsson (Eds.), *Aversion, avoidance, and anxiety.* Hillsdale, NJ: Erlbaum.

Öhman, A., Dimberg, U., & Öst, L.-G. (1985). Animal and social phobias: Biological constraints on learned fear responses. In S. Reiss & R. R. Bootzin (Eds.), *Theoretical issues in behavior therapy.* New York: Academic Press.

Öhman, A., & Soares, J. J. F. (1993). On the automaticity of phobic fear: Conditioned skin conductance responses to masked phobic stimuli. *Journal of Abnormal Psychology, 102.*

Öhman, A., & Soares, J. J. F. (in press). Unconscious anxiety: Phobic responses to masked stimuli. *Journal of Abnormal Psychology.*

Pallmeyer, T. P., Blanchard, E. B., & Kolb, L. C. (1986). The psychophysiology of combat-induced post-traumatic stress disorder in Vietnam veterans. *Behaviour Research and Therapy, 24,* 645–652.

Pauli, P., Marquardt, C., Hartl, L., Nutzinger, D. O., Hölzl, R., & Strian, F. (1991). Anxiety induced by cardiac perceptions in patients with panic attacks: A field study. *Behaviour Research and Therapy, 29,* 137–145.

Pitman, R. K., Orr, S. P., Forgue, D. F., de Jong, J. B., & Claiborn, J. M. (1987). Psychophysiologic assessment of posttraumatic stress disorder imagery in Vietnam combat veterans. *Archives of General Psychiatry, 44,* 970–975.

Pitman, R. K., Orr, S. P., Forgue, D. F., Altman, B., & de Jong, J. (1990). Psychophysiologic responses to combat imagery of Vietnam veterans with posttraumatic stress disorder versus other anxiety disorders. *Journal of Abnormal Psychology, 99,* 49–54.

Posner, M. I. (1978). *Chronometric explorations of mind.* Hillsdale, NJ: Erlbaum.

Posner, M. I. (1980). Orienting and attention. *Quarterly Journal of Experimental Psychology, 32,* 3–25.

Power, M., & Brewin, C. R. (1991). From Freud to cognitive science: A contemporary account of the unconscious. *British Journal of Clinical Psychology, 30,* 289–310.

Rainey, J. M., Aleen, A., Ortiz, A., Yeragami, V., Pohl, R., & Bereliou, R. (1987). A laboratory procedure for the induction of flashbacks. *American Journal of Psychiatry, 144,* 1317–1319.

Rapee, R. M. (1985). Distinctions between panic disorder and generalised anxiety disorder: Clinical presentation. *Australian and New Zealand Journal of Psychiatry, 19,* 227–232.

Rapee, R. M. (1986). Differential response to hyperventilation in panic disorder and generalized anxiety disorder. *Journal of Abnormal Psychology, 95,* 24–28.

Rapee, R. M. (1991). Generalized anxiety disorder: A review of clinical features and theoretical concepts. *Clinical Psychology Review, 11,* 419–440.

Rapee, R. M., Mattick, R., & Murrell, E. (1986). Cognitive mediation in the affective component of spontaneous panic attacks. *Journal of Behavior Therapy and Experimental Psychiatry, 17,* 245–253.

Rapee, R. M., Sanderson, W. C., McCauley, P. A., & Di Nardo, P. A. (1992). Differences in reported symptom profile between panic disorder and other DSM-III-R anxiety disorders. *Behaviour Research and Therapy, 30,* 45–52.

Sanderson, R. S., Laverty, R. S., & Campbell, D. (1963). Traumatic conditioned responses acquired during respiratory paralysis. *Nature, 196,* 1235–1236.

Sanderson, W. C., Rapee, R. M., & Barlow, D. H. (1989). The influence of an illusion of control on panic attacks induced via inhalation of 5.5% carbon dioxide-enriched air. *Archives of General Psychiatry, 46,* 157–162.

Schachter, S., & Singer, J. (1962). Cognitive, social, and physiological determinants of emotional state. *Psychological Review, 69,* 379–399.

Schalling, D., Cronholm, B., & Åsberg, M. (1975). Components of state and trait anxiety as related to personality and arousal. In L. Levi (Ed.), *Emotions: Their parameters and measurement.* New York: Raven Press.

Schneider, W., Dumais, S. T., & Shiffrin, R. M. (1984). Automatic and control processing and attention. In R. Parasuraman & D. R. Davies (Eds.), *Varieties of attention.* Orlando, FL: Academic Press.

Seligman, M. E. P. (1971). Phobias and preparedness. *Behavior Therapy, 2,* 307–320.

Sheehan, D. V. (1982). Panic attacks and phobias. *New England Journal of Medicine, 307,* 156–158.

Shiffrin, R. M., & Schneider, W. (1977). Controlled and automatic human information processing: II. Perceptual learning, automatic attending, and a general theory. *Psychological Review, 84,* 127–190.

Soares, J. J. F., & Öhman, A. (1993a). Backward masking and skin conductance responses after conditioning to non-feared but fear-relevant stimuli in fearful subjects. *Psychophysiology.*

Soares, J. J. F., & Öhman, A. (1993b). Preattentive processing, preparedness, and phobias: Effects of instruction on conditioned electrodermal responses to masked and non-masked fear-relevant stimuli. *Behaviour Research and Therapy, 31,* 87–95.

Spielberger, C. D. (1972). Anxiety as an emotional state. In C. D. Spielberger (Ed.), *Anxiety: Current trends in theory and research* (Vol. 1). New York: Academic Press.

Spinks, J., & Kramer, A. (1991). Capacity views of human information processing: Autonomic measures. In J. R. Jennings & M. G. H. Coles (Eds.), *Handbook of cognitive psychophysiology. Central and autonomic nervous system approaches.* Chichester, England: Wiley.

Trandel, D. V., & McNally, R. J. (1987). Perception of threat cues in post-traumatic stress disorder: Semantic processing without awareness? *Behaviour Research and Therapy, 25,* 469–476.

Taylor, C. B., Sheikh, J., Agras, W. S., Roth, W. T., Margraf, J., Ehlers, A., Maddock, R. J., & Gossard, D. (1986). Ambulatory heart rate changes in patients with panic attacks. *American Journal of Psychiatry, 143,* 478–482.

Taylor, C. B., Telch, M. J., & Havvik, D. (1982–1983). Ambulatory heart rate changes during panic attacks. *Journal of Psychiatric Research, 17,* 261–266.

Valins, S. (1972). The perception and labelling of bodily changes as determinants of emotional behavior. In P. Black (Ed.), *Physiological correlates of emotion.* New York: Academic Press.

van der Molen, G. M., van den Hout, M. A., Vroemen, J.,

Lousberg, H., & Griez, E. (1986). Cognitive determinants of lactate-induced anxiety. *Behaviour Research and Therapy*, 24, 677–680.

van den Hout, M. A. (1988). The explanation of experimental panic. In S. Rachman & J. D. Maser (Eds.), *Panic: Psychological perspectives*. Hillsdale, NJ: Erlbaum

Woods, S. W., Charney, D. S., McPherson, C. A., Gradman, A. H., & Heninger, G. R. (1987). Situational panic attacks: Behavioral, physiological and biochemical characterization. *Archives of General Psychiatry*, 44, 365–375.

Zajonc, R. B. (1980). Feeling and thinking: Preferences need no inferences. *American Psychologist*, 35, 151–175.

37

The Development of Anger and Hostile Interactions

ELIZABETH A. LEMERISE
KENNETH A. DODGE

The resurgence of scientific interest in emotions has been associated with a change from the view that emotions are maladaptive and disruptive to a new emphasis on their adaptive and functional significance (e.g., Averill, 1982; Campos, Barrett, Lamb, Goldsmith, & Stenberg, 1983; Lazarus, 1991; Malatesta, 1982). In this chapter, we are consistent with this trend and address both the adaptive and maladaptive aspects of anger and hostile interactions. The main focus of the chapter is on the developmental course and socialization of anger and hostile interactions in infants and young children; both common developmental patterns and individual differences are discussed.

As Averill (1982) pointed out, the relation between anger and aggression is not clear-cut. Sometimes aggression can be an expression of anger, but in other cases it may serve dominance and instrumental functions (Dodge, 1991a). Nor does anger lead inevitably to aggression. However, the literature on anger and hostile interactions in infants and children contains relatively few studies of anger per se. Therefore, it has been necessary to fill some of the gaps in the literature by considering studies of aggression, as well as studies of emotions in general. This does not mean that we consider aggression to be equivalent to anger; nor do we suggest that anger and other emotions are interchangeable.

THE FUNCTIONAL SIGNIFICANCE OF ANGER

Along with joy, surprise, fear, disgust, and distress or sadness, anger has been seen as a primary human emotion (Campos et al., 1983) that has evolved to enhance the adaptation and survival of the species (e.g., Izard, 1977). Anger serves a variety of adaptive functions, including the organization and regulation of internal physiological and psychological processes related to self-defense and mastery, as well as the regulation of social and interpersonal behaviors (Averill, 1982; Izard & Kobak, 1991; Klinnert, Campos, Sorce, Emde, & Svejda, 1983; Lewis, Sullivan, Ramsay, & Alessandri, 1992; Sroufe, Schork, Motti, Lawroski, & LaFreniere, 1984; Stenberg & Campos, 1990). Thus, anger is seen both as an energizer and organizer of behavior, *and* as a social signal that regulates interpersonal behaviors.

Even though anger (as well as other emotions) can serve to regulate interpersonal behavior, anger itself also comes to be regulated in an interpersonal context through socialization by caregivers and the larger social context. Every culture has "display rules" for anger (Malatesta, 1982; Averill, 1982). The socialization of these "display rules" can be observed quite early in the first year of life (e.g., Malatesta & Haviland, 1982; also, see below). The individual has to learn when, to whom, and how to express anger in culturally acceptable ways.

Problems in the modulation and expression of anger have been implicated in failures in social interaction. Anger has been shown to bias social information processing (as well as to occur as a function of biased processing), making reactively aggressive responses to others more likely. Reactive (or angry) aggression, in turn, is a major correlate of social rejection by the peer group (Dodge & Coie, 1987; Dodge, 1991a, 1991b). Children's exposure to chronic high levels of anger and arousal has been linked to patterns of anger and noncompliance toward parents and to interactions with peers that are both more negative and at a lower level of complexity (e.g., Gottman & Katz, 1989; Katz & Gottman, 1991).

Difficulty in the modulation of anger is also associated with maladaptive internal regulation that, if chronic, becomes reflected in the development of psychopathology (Dodge & Garber, 1991; Garber, Braadfladt, & Zeman, 1991; Izard & Kobak, 1991; Stenberg & Campos, 1990) and disease. For example, high levels of chronic angry affect, cynical beliefs, and aggressive behavior in early adulthood are known to predict mortality over a 30-year period, with the major cause of this mortality being coronary heart disease (Barefoot, Dodge, Peterson, Dahlstrom, & Williams, 1989). Thus, difficulties in the modulation and regulation of anger have been linked to a variety of maladaptive outcomes. More favorable outcomes are associated with the ability to express anger in a socially constructive way without becoming highly aroused.

THE DEVELOPMENTAL COURSE OF ANGER

When Is Anger First Displayed?

The question of when infants first show clear signs of anger has been the topic of considerable debate. One of the problems in studying this question has been the difficulty researchers have had in finding a situation that can reliably elicit anger. A number of situations may elicit anger, but anger is not an inevitable response to these situations. Likewise, the situations that elicit anger may well change across age. Thus, finding a situation that elicits anger in 2-year-olds but not in 6-month-olds does not mean that 6-month-olds are incapable of experiencing or producing anger. Another difficulty has in-

volved finding a response measure that unequivocally and consistently denotes anger and can be assessed independently of the eliciting circumstances. This debate was largely unresolved until the advent of research on facial expressions of emotion demonstrated that the facial expression of anger could be recognized consistently across cultures. The objective scoring techniques developed in this research have been used with video records to examine the development of anger and other emotions. Infants have been seen as ideal subjects for this work, because they are presumably less likely to dissemble or modify their facial expressions for a video camera (see Stenberg & Campos, 1990, for a review).

Using the above-described techniques, researchers have begun to study the emergence of the anger facial expression in infants. Research in this area is still relatively scarce (see Stenberg & Campos, 1990, for suggestions for further study). Evidence comes from two sources: (1) cross-sectional studies of infants' responses to frustration (removal of an object) and to physical restraint (Stenberg, Campos, & Emde, 1983; Stenberg & Campos, 1990); and (2) a longitudinal study of infants' responses to inoculations (Izard, Hembree, & Huebner, 1987).

Even though infants of all ages studied display negative facial expressions, there are developmental changes in the facial expressions themselves, as well as in how they are directed. Stenberg and Campos (1990) have found that clear facial and vocal expressions of anger in response to restraint are displayed by 4- and 7-month-olds. The facial expressions of 1-month-olds are negative, though undifferentiated, and their negative vocalizations are not as clearly related to the onset of restraint. Observing reactions to inoculations, Izard et al. (1987) have reported similar findings on infants studied longitudinally between 2 and 19 months of age. Infants' initial reactions to pain consist of a physical distress response, but beginning at 4 months, an anger response is also observed. The proportion of time that infants display an anger expression increases with age, particularly between 7 and 19 months. By 19 months, 25% of infants show *only* an anger response to inoculation.

The emergence of clear anger expressions at 4 months has been explained as reflecting infants' acquired (though relatively primitive) understanding of the means–end relation and expanded capacity for voluntary behavior (e.g.,

Izard, 1978; Campos et al., 1983; Stenberg & Campos, 1990). In other words, it is presumed that the expression of anger requires an understanding that one can act intentionally to cause harm. As these cognitive and motor abilities become more sophisticated, changes in the expression and direction of anger should be seen. Data on developmental changes in the direction of anger expressions tend to support this analysis (Stenberg & Campos, 1990). One-month-olds' relatively undifferentiated negative expressions do not appear to be displayed in a directionally selective way. Older infants are more likely to direct their initial head movements toward the source of restraint (either toward an experimenter or an experimenter's hands) than are 1-month-olds. After the onset of an initial negative facial expression, 7-month-olds are more likely to look at their mothers, whereas 4-month-olds are more likely to look at the experimenter or, more specifically, at the experimenter's hands (the immediate source of restraint). One-month-olds are more likely to look at nonsocial and irrelevant targets. Similar results have been found for negative vocalizations. These results are interpreted as supporting both a change in infants' understanding of the cause of the frustration and an increasing tendency for anger expressions to be displayed in a socially targeted fashion, perhaps reflecting expectations about mothers as a source of assistance and comfort (Stenberg & Campos, 1990).

Data on the emergence of clear expressions of anger indicate that infants' cognitive abilities may well be an important component of this response. Anger is first clearly expressed at the age that infants should have at least a rudimentary understanding of the means–end relation. However, it should be pointed out that there are no available data demonstrating that an appreciation of the means–end relation is *necessary* to an expression of anger in the situations that have been studied. It is also possible that situations that elicit anger may facilitate or accelerate the consolidation of causal understanding because of the salience of those situations. The "infant" state of this literature certainly precludes any resolution of the cognition–emotion debate (e.g., Lazarus, 1981; Zajonc, 1980).

What Elicits Anger?

During infancy, anger expressions have been observed in response to physical restraint (e.g.,

Stenberg & Campos, 1990); interference with an infant's activity, such as removing a teething biscuit or rattle (Stenberg et al., 1983); and physical pain (Izard et al., 1987). Anger expressions also have been observed for most, but not all, infants during extinction in a contingency learning task (Lewis, Alessandri, & Sullivan, 1990; Lewis et al., 1992). Patterns of emotions during extinction have been found to be independent of responding during the learning portion of the task, and they predict responding during relearning. Infants who display anger during extinction later show both the highest levels of interest and joy facial expressions and the highest levels of the arm pull operant required in the task. Infants who display just sadness during extinction show the lowest levels of responding for interest and joy facial expressions and for arm pulls. Thus, anger during extinction appears to facilitate relearning—an example of anger as an energizer of adaptive behavior. Lewis et al. (1992) hypothesize that the individual differences observed may reflect temperamental differences among infants, and that these differences may be early precursors of mastery and learned helplessness orientations.

After the first year of life and before preschool age, empirical data on eliciters of anger are relatively rare, despite the universally shared image of the tantrum-prone "terrible twos." Goodenough's (1931) classic monograph remains unchallenged as a comprehensive, empirical investigation of children's naturally occurring anger. She reported on the situations during which angry outbursts were most often observed by mothers. Approximately 40% of the outbursts reported by these mothers occurred in the context of some caretaking activity; dressing and mealtime were the contexts in which more than half of these outbursts took place. Another 40% of the outbursts took place in the context of play, but because of methodological problems, the exact proportion of outbursts occurring during social play was difficult to determine. The remaining 20% of the outbursts occurred across several contexts; the majority of these occurred when the children were unoccupied. Goodenough also classified episodes in terms of the immediate conditions or stimuli precipitating the angry outburst. For infants and children up to 3 years of age, objections to routine caretaking activities (e.g., feeding, bathing, dressing) and conflicts with adults on other matters comprised proportionally more of the outbursts, whereas for children 3 years of age and older, social conflicts, particularly with peers, were the major instigators of angry outbursts (though conflicts with adults persisted). Across all contexts and causes, angry outbursts peaked in frequency during the second year and declined thereafter; these outbursts were observed more frequently in boys than in girls. There was also a developmental change in the expression of the outbursts, with younger children's outbursts being more extreme and undifferentiated energy discharges, and older children showing both an increasing tendency to use less violent and more symbolic forms of expression and to direct the outburst to a social target.

Beginning with the preschool period, the research literature on peer relations, though much of it is not *directly* concerned with anger and hostile interactions, provides some information about developmental changes, particularly in aggressive behavior. Even though aggressive behaviors comprise a smaller proportion of all interactive behaviors as children get older, their frequency increases up until 4 years of age, after which they decline (Hartup, 1983; Parke & Slaby, 1983). Disputes among 4-year-olds are most often about possessions and space (Hartup, 1983; Parke & Slaby, 1983), but there is evidence that the social significance of the disputed items contributes to the conflict. For example, children have been observed to fight over objects for which there are available duplicates, and children often do not use the very items they have fought over (Hay & Ross, 1982). Whereas instrumental (object-oriented) aggression decreases and all forms of aggression are less frequent after 4 years of age, the incidence of verbal, person-directed, or hostile aggression (insults, teasing) increases (Hartup, 1983).

Preschoolers' angry conflicts have been studied in detail by Fabes and Eisenberg (1992a, 1992b), using naturalistic observation techniques. Children were observed over the course of 3 months in a day care context, and their spontaneous angry provocations and reactions were recorded and coded. In addition, children's social competence was evaluated through teacher and peer ratings. These authors found that the vast majority of angry conflicts (86%) occurred with peers; the rest were with adults. They found no sex differences in the number or type of angry conflicts. Conflicts over material possessions were the most

frequent contexts for anger, supporting the contention that instrumental goals are the major function of anger for children of this young age.

HOW DO OTHERS REACT TO THE CHILD'S ANGER?

Parental Socialization of Anger

Research has demonstrated that in the context of face-to-face interaction, parents respond differentially to infants' emotion expressions (e.g., Frodi, Lamb, Leavitt, & Donovan, 1978; Malatesta, Culver, Tesman, & Shepard, 1989; Malatesta, Grigoryev, Lamb, Albin, & Culver, 1986; Malatesta & Haviland, 1982). Parents' socialization goals appear to involve the encouragement of positive emotion and the modulation of negative emotion. As such, parents have been observed to model mostly positive facial and vocal expressions of emotion when interacting with their infants; negative emotion expressions are observed rarely. Infants' positive emotions are more likely to be matched by parents, whereas negative emotions, including anger, are likely to be responded to with a different emotion (e.g., concern, interest, sadness) or to be ignored by parents. Over time, infants' emotion expressions become less labile and more positive, resembling those of the parents. Later in the first year and in the second year of life, infants can be observed to use expressions that signify dampening of negative emotion, such as wrinkled brow, compressed lips, and lip biting; use of these expressions is associated with the earlier and concurrent parental display of the same expressions (Malatesta et al., 1989; Malatesta-Magai, 1991).

Information about parental socialization of anger in more varied and/or more naturalistic contexts is relatively scarce. Goodenough (1931) reported a change with the age of the children in how middle-class mothers reported handling children's angry outbursts. Mothers of younger children (under 2–3 years) were more likely to employ coaxing, diversion of attention, ignoring, and physical restraint in response to outbursts. With increasing age, ignoring continued to be used with girls, whereas boys received both more attention and more power-assertive measures (e.g., bribery, threats, spanking, isolation, and deprivation of privileges) in response to their angry outbursts. More recent findings (Radke-Yarrow &

Kochanska, 1990) also indicate both developmental changes and sex differences in mothers' responses to anger. With increasing age, mothers are less likely to respond supportively and affectionately to toddlers' anger and are more likely to tell the children that the anger is inappropriate and that the children should stop expressing anger. Boys' anger is more likely to elicit some form of maternal attention, and boys are more likely to be rewarded for anger. Girls' angry behavior, on the other hand, is more likely to elicit ignoring or a command to stop. Radke-Yarrow and Kochanska (1990) have interpreted these findings as consistent with cultural stereotypes concerning the male and female expression of anger.

Thus, as children move from infancy to toddlerhood, parents become less permissive of anger and aggressive behavior. Individual differences in how mothers handle toddlers' difficult behaviors have been associated with differences in their children's emotional responding and behavior. Crockenberg (1985) has reported that mothers who respond to toddlers with anger have children who are more likely to persist in angry, noncompliant behavior and who are less likely to show empathic responding to the distress of others. Mothers who respond to children's actions with other emotions (e.g., sadness, pain, fear) have children who are more likely to comply and respond empathically to others. Such empathic responding has been hypothesized to be an important inhibitor of angry/aggressive behavior (Miller & Eisenberg, 1988). Furthermore, it appears that there are some home environments in which angry interactions are relatively pervasive. For example, frequencies of expressed anger for different family members have been reported to be correlated moderately and positively (Radke-Yarrow & Kochanska, 1990). Such a home environment would seem to make more empathic and optimal interpersonal behavior on the part of both children and parents less probable. Even though it is difficult to ascertain the direction of influence (parent to child vs. child to parent) in such families, data on the effects of children's difficult temperament suggest that temperamental difficulty does not inevitably lead to nonoptimal outcomes; however, when social support to these families is low, the risks are raised considerably (Crockenberg, 1981).

As children get older, language plays an increasingly important role in the socialization of anger and other emotions, as well as in the children's own self-regulation. Parents help to provide emotion labels for children's experiences, and use language to communicate cultural and subcultural norms for the expression of emotion, including anger (e.g., Camras, 1985; Lutz, 1985; Malatesta & Haviland, 1985; Michalson & Lewis, 1985; Miller & Sperry, 1987). For example, Karniol and Heiman (1987) have found that even though elementary school children report feeling equivalently angry at provocations from peers and from adults, they say they would retaliate aggressively only if the provocation came from a peer, reflecting their acquired knowledge of cultural norms regarding the acceptable display of anger.

The socialization of anger involves direct action on the part of the parents (through reward, punishments, and direct tuition), as well as more indirect effects (Lewis & Saarni, 1985). For example, parental sensitivity in responding to infants' signals in the first year has been linked to children's later accuracy in labeling facial expression of emotion (Tesman & Malatesta-Magai, 1991). Miller and Sperry (1987) studied the socialization of anger and aggression in an urban, working-class sample and found direct and indirect influences of the social context on young children's (as young as 2½ years) communication and justification of anger. They found that parents, other adults, and older children took an active role in teaching toddlers, and that they also modeled relevant behaviors.

In summary, parental socialization of anger, as well as other emotions, begins with the earliest face-to-face interactions parents have with their children. As children reach the toddler stage, parents become less permissive of angry behavior and exert their influence in a number of direct and indirect ways; children's responses to these efforts also influence the parents. Individual differences in children's expression, labeling, and regulation of anger, as well as other emotions, are best thought of as the result of a transaction between the characteristics of the children (e.g., temperament) and parental socialization efforts.

Peers as Socializers of Anger and Aggression

Peers can act as both elicitors and reinforcers of angry and aggressive behaviors; peer reactions to angry and aggressive behaviors have been shown to have both short- and long-term consequences for children's behavior and peer relations. For example, children's angry and aggressive responses to others tend to elicit similar behavior in return; in fact, angry, threatening actions tend to escalate conflicts (Dodge & Frame, 1982). In contrast, giving in to an attacker tends to terminate the encounter, but this response also makes it more likely that the attacker will repeat the aggressive behavior in the future (Parke & Slaby, 1983; Patterson, Littman, & Bricker, 1967). Thus, the expression of angry and aggressive behaviors among peers comes to be interpersonally regulated. Evidence from naturalistic observations of children's groups indicates that over time, a dominance hierarchy comes to regulate the expression of aggression (e.g., Strayer, 1980).

Even though in certain cases angry and aggressive behavior may be associated with short-term, material gains (e.g., Patterson et al., 1967), the long-term consequences of continued aggressive and antisocial behavior can include rejection by the peer group (e.g., Dodge, 1991b; Dodge & Coie, 1987; Fabes & Eisenberg, 1992a; Parke & Slaby, 1983). This state of affairs is complicated by the fact that rejected children come to perpetuate their status, because of information-processing biases that serve to maintain their aggressive response styles. Dodge and Somberg (1987) have presented evidence, based on children's reasoning about hypothetical situations, that social information processing by aggressive children may be particularly vulnerable to the effects of emotional arousal. Under conditions of threat to the self, aggressive boys are more likely to attribute hostile intent to peers than are nonaggressive boys; hostile attributions, in turn, make aggressive responding more likely, and this type of behavior often leads to rejection by peers (Dodge, 1985).

Research conducted with preschool children illustrates the social costs of anger in peer interaction (Fabes & Eisenberg, 1992a, 1992b). Children who become angry easily and are highly aroused are less likely to respond to provocations in constructive, nonaggressive ways and are more likely either to seek revenge or to escape the situation. Children who become less aroused and angry when provoked are more likely to cope by defending themselves in a nonaggressive fashion (Fabes

& Eisenberg, 1992b). These differences in coping are meaningfully related to peer acceptance and teacher ratings of competence: Children who are popular with their peers and are rated as socially competent by their teachers are less likely to become involved in angry situations. However, when they do become involved in angry situations, they are more likely to deal with the provocation in a nonaggressive, though direct, fashion that tends to preserve the relationship (Fabes & Eisenberg, 1992a).

In summary, the peer group has an important influence on angry and aggressive behavior, but its influence operates in a variety of ways. In some contexts, angry and aggressive behavior can be associated with short-term reward, such as obtaining (or defending) a desired possession. There is even some long-term gain in this situation, because resisting a peer is associated with a lowered probability of further attacks by that peer (Patterson et al., 1967). However, the long-term consequences of continued angry and aggressive behavior also include rejection by the peer group; in this way, the peer group acts to enforce cultural norms concerning anger and aggression. Children who have difficulty regulating their anger and inhibiting their aggression will, in the long run, lose the approval of the peer group. Children who can regulate their arousal seem to be able to deal with anger provocation in a more socially constructive way that is associated with better acceptance by the peer group.

HOW DOES THE CHILD REACT TO ANGRY BEHAVIOR IN OTHERS?

The angry behavior of other people also plays a role in the socialization of anger. Crockenberg (1985) has demonstrated that angry behavior directed toward a child is likely to be associated with angry, noncompliant behavior and less empathic responding on the part of the child. Crockenberg (1985) has suggested that such interchanges may interfere with the child's acquisition of more prosocial and empathic responding and with more optimal patterns of parenting in the mother, because of patterns of interactions that are similar to what Patterson (1982) termed "coercive cycles."

A related issue concerns the impact on the child of witnessing "background anger" (Cummings, Iannotti, & Zahn-Waxler, 1985)—that is, angry behavior that is not directed toward the child but to which the child is exposed. It has been hypothesized that exposure to anger and aggression in the home may be an important influence on children's developing antisocial behavior through social learning, modeling, and threatening effects (Cummings et al., 1985; Dodge, 1985; Dodge, Pettit, McClaskey, & Brown, 1986). There is a growing literature on the effects of exposure to background anger (e.g., Cummings, 1987; Cummings, Ballard, & El-Sheikh, 1991; Cummings et al., 1985; Cummings, Vogel, Cummings, & El-Sheikh, 1989; Cummings, Zahn-Waxler, & Radke-Yarrow, 1981; Klaczynski & Cummings, 1989; Radke-Yarrow & Kochanska, 1990). From these studies, a number of developmental trends and individual differences can be discerned.

Background anger, both in the home and in laboratory simulations, has been shown to have a negative emotional impact on children and adolescents. Children as young as a year appear to become emotionally upset by others' angry interactions; they may stare or "freeze," look concerned, frown, or show signs of distress (whimpering or crying). Children who are a little over a year old have been reported to engage in "social referencing" (e.g., Klinnert et al., 1983) of their mothers when exposed to angry interactions (Radke-Yarrow & Kochanska, 1990). Slightly older toddlers (between 16–18 months and older), particularly those exposed to higher levels of angry conflicts in the home, have been observed to engage in some kind of "flight" (e.g., covering the ears, leaving the room) or "fight" (intervening physically and/or verbally) reaction (Cummings et al., 1981; Radke-Yarrow & Kochanska, 1990). Children of this age have also been reported to engage in imitation of some aspect of the parents' angry behavior (see Radke-Yarrow & Kochanska, 1990), though evidence obtained from maternal records of children's reactions to anger does not indicate that children's immediate responses to anger are usually aggressive. The data available from maternal records do not permit an evaluation of whether more delayed effects occur (Cummings et al., 1981; Radke-Yarrow & Kochanska, 1990).

Cummings et al. (1985) followed up the naturalistic research reported above with a laboratory study on the effects of background anger on 2-year-olds. Pairs consisting of a target child and a familiar peer, accompanied by the target child's mother, came to the laboratory for a play session on two separate occasions. The sessions took place in a "home-like" setting (living room with attached kitchenette); there were toys for the children, and the mother was not an active participant in the children's play. During each session, the children witnessed an angry conflict between two female confederates.

These researchers found that children's immediate reactions to this angry conflict resembled the distress reactions reported by mothers in the naturalistic studies (Cummings et al., 1981; Radke-Yarrow & Kochanska, 1990). Increases in aggression toward the peer occurred in the period following the adults' angry conflict. Aggressive responding after the adult conflict particularly high during later periods, indicating a cumulative effect of background anger. Children who could be classified as high in aggression on other measures showed more high-intensity aggression and more extended conflicts following the adult conflict than did children who could be classified as moderate or low in aggression. Exposure to background anger has also been associated with heightened aggressive responses to hypothetical situations for first- and third-grade boys (Klaczynski & Cummings, 1989).

Cummings et al. (1985) also found sex differences in children's responses to the adult conflict: Girls were more distressed than boys *during* the conflict, whereas boys were more aggressive with the peer *after* being exposed to the adult conflict. Overall, higher levels of distress during the conflict were associated with lower levels of aggression afterwards, suggesting that distress (a more empathic response) may inhibit the expression of anger/aggression (e.g., Crockenberg, 1985; Miller & Eisenberg, 1988).

Using the same kind of paradigm, Cummings (1987) investigated the effects of background anger on 4- and 5-year-olds, who showed a similar pattern of heightened arousal and emotional responding during the adult conflict and increased verbal aggression afterwards. Distinct coping styles during the conflict were found as well, and these styles of coping were related to children's behavior and verbal reports after the conflict. Over a third of children exhibited both positive and negative emotions during the adult conflict (they were called an "ambivalent" group). These children had the highest levels of postconflict verbal and physical aggression; they also reported feeling both happy and aroused or disregulated. Almost half showed signs of distress, such as "freezing" and facial expressions of concern (a "concerned" group); these children reported feeling sad and wanting to mediate or intervene in the adults' fight. About one in seven children showed no behavioral evidence of an emotional response during the conflict (an "unresponsive" group); they reported feeling angry during the conflict and trying to hide their feelings. The remaining few were unclassifiable.

Cummings et al. (1989, 1991) have also used other procedures to assess children's reactions to anger. In one paradigm, children watched videotaped depictions of different types of angry and friendly interactions (see Cummings et al., 1989, for details of the various situations depicted) and then were interviewed concerning their perceptions, feelings, and coping strategies. With advancing age across the years 4 through 9, children perceived hostile (physical) aggression and unresolved aggression as being increasingly negative; across ages 9 through 19, these negative perceptions persisted. From ages 4 to 9, children increasingly said that they would try to intervene in the conflict and seemed to be increasingly upset by the events around them. With advancing age into the adolescent years, however, negative emotional responses declined; adolescents, like younger children, perceived the anger around as negative, but they did not report as strong negative emotional responses as the younger children did. This pattern may reflect an increasing ability to modulate negative arousal in adolescence.

Sex differences have been found in responses to background anger, but these differences are difficult to interpret. Among children younger than 9, boys respond with more anger than do girls. In adolescence, boys report more sadness, and girls report more anger.

In summary, exposure to background anger is associated with negative emotional arousal at all ages that have been studied. Toddlers and preschoolers who witness angry confrontations are likely to show an increase in aggressive responding afterwards. School-age children become increasingly likely to say that they would try to intervene in the conflict, but the effects of angry conflicts on actual behavior are not known. Among adolescents, it appears that responses are less disrupted by angry conflicts than is true for younger children, indicating growing emotional regulation.

SUMMARY AND CONCLUSIONS

The available evidence indicates that anger makes its appearance very early in development. Averill (1982) characterized anger as being primarily an *interpersonal* emotion, and, indeed, it appears that anger can be understood primarily from its interpersonal functions (Campos, Campos, & Barrett, 1989). Even though there are gaps in our knowledge, the interpersonal nature of the modification and regulation of anger is apparent even in the earliest months of life. In children as young as 4 months of age, anger is a well-defined response to goal-blocking stimuli. Four-month-old infants' experience of anger seems somewhat less interpersonal than it will be just a few months later; 7-month-olds clearly direct their anger displays at a *social* target. As children become even more socially aware during the preschool and school years, their emotional responses (including anger) to distressing environmental stimuli become stronger. In later years, skills of emotion regulation are associated with dampening of these emotional responses and increasing control.

Parents act as major socializers of anger. Infants reference their parents to determine when it is acceptable and appropriate to display anger. Parents, in turn, teach children appropriate means of expressing anger and alternative response repertoires to anger-inducing situations. Peers socialize anger as well, by rejecting children who display anger at inappropriate times or in inappropriate ways. As children get older, they become more socially involved and aware, and thus experience more inducements to anger; however, increasing skills of emotion regulation are evidenced in the acquisition of control.

The normal socialization process is not always successful. Deviant development of extreme anger and/or chronic aggressive behavior is fostered by chronic environmental conditions of exposure to stress (such as background anger) and by failures of socializing agents to teach skills of social information processing and emotion regulation.

Virtually every scientist reviewed here has lamented the dearth of scientific evidence on anger and its development. Although it is certainly unfortunate that we know comparatively little, it is also true that the development of anger and of its control are is likely to be the subjects of increasing scientific inquiry in the future.

Acknowledgment. We would like to thank Anne Wannemuehler for her assistance in the preparation of this chapter.

REFERENCES

Averill, J. R. (1982). *Anger and aggression: An essay on emotion.* New York: Springer-Verlag.

Barefoot, J. C., Dodge, K. A., Peterson, B. L., Dahlstrom, W. G., & Williams, X. B. (1989). The Cook–Medley Hostility Scale: Item content and ability to predict survival. *Psychosomatic Medicine, 51,* 46–57.

Campos, J. J., Barrett, K., Lamb, M. E., Goldsmith, H. H., & Stenberg, C. (1983). Socioemotional development. In M. M. Haith & J. J. Campos (Vol. Eds.), *Handbook of child psychology* (4th ed.): *Vol. 2. Infancy and developmental psychobiology* (pp. 783–915). New York: Wiley.

Campos, J. J., Campos, R. G., & Barrett, K. C. (1989). Emergent themes in the study of emotional development and emotion regulation. *Developmental Psychology, 25,* 394–402.

Camras, L. (1985). Socialization of affect communication. In M. Lewis & C. Saarni (Eds.), *The socialization of emotions* (pp. 141–160). New York: Plenum Press.

Crockenberg, S. (1981). Infant irritability, mother responsiveness, and social support influences on the security of mother–infant attachment. *Child Development, 52,* 857–865.

Crockenberg, S. (1985). Toddlers' reactions to maternal anger. *Merrill–Palmer Quarterly, 31,* 361–373.

Cummings, E. M. (1987). Coping with background anger in early childhood. *Child Development, 58,* 976–984.

Cummings, E. M., Ballard, M., & El-Sheikh, M. (1991). Responses of children and adolescents to interadult anger as a function of gender, age, and mode of expression. *Merrill–Palmer Quarterly, 37,* 543–560.

Cummings, E. M., Iannotti, R. J., & Zahn-Waxler, C. (1985). Influence of conflict between adults on the emotions and aggression of young children. *Developmental Psychology, 21,* 495–507.

Cummings, E. M., Vogel, D., Cummings, J. S., & El-Sheikh, M. (1989). Children's responses to different forms of expression of anger between adults. *Child Development, 60,* 1392-1404.

Cummings, E. M., Zahn-Waxler, C., & Radke-Yarrow, M. (1981). Young children's responses to expressions of anger and affection by others in the family. *Child Development, 52,* 1274–1282.

Dodge, K. A. (1985). Attributional bias in aggressive children. *Advances in Cognitive–Behavioral Research and Therapy, 4,* 73–110.

Dodge, K. A. (1991a). The structure and function of reactive and proactive aggression. In D. Pepler & K. Rubin (Eds.), *The development and treatment of childhood aggression* (pp. 201–218). Hillsdale, NJ: Erlbaum.

Dodge, K. A. (1991b). Emotion and social information processing. In J. Garber & K. A. Dodge (Eds.), *The devel-*

opment of emotion regulation and dysregulation (pp. 159–181). New York: Cambridge University Press.

Dodge, K. A., & Coie, J. D. (1987). Social-information-processing factors in reactive and proactive aggression in children's peer groups. *Journal of Personality and Social Psychology, 53,* 1146–1158.

Dodge, K. A., & Frame, C. L. (1982). Social cognitive biases and deficits in aggressive boys. *Child Development, 53,* 620–635.

Dodge, K. A., & Garber, J. (1991). Domains of emotion regulation. In J. Garber & K.A. Dodge (Eds.), *The development of emotion regulation and dysregulation* (pp. 3–11). New York: Cambridge University Press.

Dodge, K. A., Pettit, G. S., McClaskey, C. L., & Brown, M. M. (1986). Social competence in children. *Monographs of the Society for Research in Child Development, 51*(2, Serial No. 213).

Dodge, K. A., & Somberg, D. R. (1987). Hostile attributional biases among aggressive boys are exacerbated under conditions of threat to the self. *Child Development, 58,* 213–224.

Fabes, R. A., & Eisenberg, N. (1992a). Young children's coping with interpersonal anger. *Child Development, 63,* 116–128.

Fabes, R. A., & Eisenberg, N. (1992b). Young children's emotional arousal and anger/aggressive behaviors. In A. Fraczek & H. Zumkley (Eds.), *Socialization and aggression* (pp. 85–102). Berlin: Springer-Verlag.

Frodi, A. M., Lamb, M. E., Leavitt, L. A., & Donovan, W. L. (1978). Fathers' and mothers' responses to infant smiles and cries. *Infant Behavior and Development, 1,* 187–198.

Garber, J., Braadfladt, N., & Zeman, J. (1991). The regulation of sad affect: An information processing perspective. In J. Garber & K. A. Dodge (Eds.), *The development of emotion regulation and dysregulation* (pp. 208–240). New York: Cambridge University Press.

Goodenough, F. L. (1931). *Anger in young children.* Minneapolis: University of Minnesota Press.

Gottman, J. M., & Katz, L. (1989). Effects of marital discord on young children's peer interaction. *Developmental Psychology, 25,* 373–381.

Hartup, W. W. (1983). Peer relations. In E. M. Hetherington (Vol. Ed.), *Handbook of child psychology* (4th ed.): *Vol. 4. Socialization, personality, and social development* (pp. 103–196). New York: Wiley.

Hay, D. F., & Ross, H. S. (1982). The social nature of early conflict. *Child Development, 53,* 105–113.

Izard, C. E. (1977). *Human emotions.* New York: Plenum Press.

Izard, C. E. (1978). On the development of emotions and emotion–cognition relationships in infancy. In M. Lewis & L. A. Rosenblum (Eds.), *The development of affect* (pp. 384–413). New York: Plenum Press.

Izard, C. E., Hembree, E. A., & Huebner, R. R. (1987). Infants' emotion expressions to acute pain: Developmental change and stability of individual differences. *Developmental Psychology, 23,* 105–113.

Izard, C. E., & Kobak, R. R. (1991). Emotions system functioning and emotion regulation. In J. Garber & K. A. Dodge (Eds.), *The development of emotion regulation and dysregulation* (pp. 303–321). New York: Cambridge University Press.

Karniol, R., & Heiman, T. (1987). Situational antecedents of children's anger experiences and subsequent responses to adult vs. peer provokers. *Aggressive Behavior, 13,* 109–118.

Katz, L. F. & Gottman, J. M. (1991). Marital discord and child outcomes: A social psychophysiological approach. In J. Garber & K. A. Dodge (Eds.), *The development of emotion regulation and dysregulation* (pp. 129–155). New York: Cambridge University Press.

Klaczynski, P., & Cummings, E. M. (1989). Responding to anger in aggressive and nonaggressive boys. *Journal of Child Psychology and Psychiatry, 30,* 309–314.

Klinnert, M. D., Campos, J. J., Sorce, J. F., Emde, R. N., & Svejda, M. (1983). Emotions as behavior regulators: Social referencing in infancy. In R. Plutchik & H. Kellerman (Eds.), *Emotion: Theory, research, and experience. Vol. 2. Emotions in early development* (pp. 57–86). New York: Academic Press.

Lazarus, R. S. (1981). A cognitivist's reply to Zajonc on emotion and cognition. *American Psychologist, 36,* 222–224.

Lazarus, R. S. (1991). *Emotion and adaptation.* New York: Oxford University Press.

Lewis, M., Alessandri, S. M., & Sullivan, M. W. (1990). Violation of expectancy, loss of control, and anger expressions in young infants. *Developmental Psychology, 26,* 745–751.

Lewis, M., & Saarni, C. (1985). Culture and emotions. In M. Lewis & C. Saarni (Eds.), *The socialization of emotions* (pp. 1–17). New York: Plenum Press.

Lewis, M., Sullivan, M. W., Ramsay, D., & Alessandri, S. M. (1992). Individual differences in anger and sad expressions during extinction: Antecedents and consequences. *Infant Behavior and Development, 15,* 443–452.

Lutz, C. (1985). Cultural patterns and individual differences in the child's emotional meaning system. In M. Lewis & C. Saarni (Eds.), *The socialization of emotions* (pp. 37–53). New York: Plenum Press.

Malatesta, C. (1982). The expression and regulation of emotion: A life span perspective. In T. Field & A. Fogel (Eds.), *Emotion and early interaction* (pp. 1–24). Hillsdale, NJ: Erlbaum.

Malatesta, C., Culver, C., Tesman, J. R., & Shepard, B. (1989). The development of emotion expression during the first two years of life. *Monographs of the Society for Research in Child Development, 54*(1–2, Serial No. 219).

Malatesta, C., Grigoryev, P., Lamb, C., Albin, M., & Culver, C. (1986). Emotion socialization and expressive development in preterm and fullterm infants. *Child Development, 57,* 316–330.

Malatesta, C., & Haviland, J. (1982). Learning display rules: The socialization of emotion expression in infancy. *Child Development, 53,* 991–1003.

Malatesta, C., & Haviland, J. M. (1985). Signals, symbols, and socialization: The modification of emotional expression in human development. In M. Lewis & C. Saarni (Eds.), *The socialization of emotions* (pp. 89–116). New York: Plenum Press.

Malatesta-Magai, C. (1991). Development of emotion expression during infancy: General course and patterns of individual difference. In J. Garber & K. A. Dodge (Eds.), *The development of emotion regulation and dysregulation* (pp. 49–68). New York: Cambridge University Press.

Michalson, L., & Lewis, M. (1985). What do children know about emotions and when do they know it? In M. Lewis & C. Saarni (Eds.), *The socialization of emotions* (pp. 117–139). New York: Plenum Press.

Miller, P., & Eisenberg, N. (1988). The relation of empathy to aggressive and externalizing/antisocial behavior. *Psychological Bulletin, 103,* 324–344.

Miller, P., & Sperry, L. L. (1987). The socialization of anger and aggression. *Merrill–Palmer Quarterly, 33,* 1–31.

Parke, R. D., & Slaby, R. G. (1983). The development of aggression. In E. M. Hetherington (Vol. Ed.), *Handbook of child psychology* (4th ed.): *Vol. 4. Socialization, personality, and development* (pp. 547–641). New York: Wiley.

Patterson, G. R. (1982). *Coercive family process.* Eugene, OR: Castalia.

Patterson, G. R., Littman, R. A., & Bricker, W. (1967). Assertive behavior in children: A step toward a theory of aggression. *Monographs of the Society for Research in Child Development, 32*(5, Serial No. 113).

Radke-Yarrow, M. & Kochanska, G. (1990). Anger in young children. In N. L. Stein, B. Leventhal, & T. Trabasso (Eds.), *Psychological and biological approaches to emotion* (pp. 297–310). Hillsdale, NJ: Erlbaum.

Sroufe, L. A., Schork, E., Motti, F., Lawroski, N., & LaFreniere, P. (1984). The role of affect in social competence. In C. E. Izard, J. Kagan, & R. B. Zajonc (Eds.), *Emotions, cognition, and behavior* (pp. 289–319). New York: Cambridge University Press.

Stenberg, C. R., & Campos, J. J. (1990). The development of anger expressions in infancy. In N. L. Stein, B. Leventhal, & T. Trabasso (Eds.), *Psychological and biological approaches to emotion* (pp. 297–310). Hillsdale, NJ: Erlbaum.

Stenberg, C. R., Campos, J. J., & Emde, R. N. (1983). The facial expression of anger in seven month old infants. *Child Development, 54,* 178–184.

Strayer, F. F. (1980). Social ecology of the preschool peer group. In A. Collins (Ed.), *Minnesota Symposium on Child Psychology* (Vol. 13, pp. 165–196). Hillsdale, NJ: Erlbaum.

Tesman, J. R., & Malatesta-Magai, C. (1991, April). *Affective labeling of facial expressions of emotion in fullterm and preterm children.* Paper presented at the meeting of the Society for Research on Child Development, Seattle.

Zajonc, R. B. (1980). Feeling and thinking: Preferences need no inferences. *American Psychologist, 35,* 151–175.

38

Sadness

CAROL ZISOWITZ STEARNS

"Sadness" is an elusive concept, for even in our own language "sad" once meant dignified and steadfast, while at the same time implying satiation and perhaps weariness (*Compact Edition of the Oxford English Dictionary*, 1971, p. 2617). Early English words such as "sorrowful," "piteous," and "aggrieved" appeared in situations similar to those where we would use "sad," but clearly none is entirely equivalent; moreover, as we shall see, many languages today offer no full translation for "sad." The meaning of sadness, then, may be more mysterious than we realize if we think of it as a "basic" emotion.

Sadness has not been well studied. Whereas other so-called "basic" emotions (such as anger and shame) have received book-length investigation by scholars, and even emotions no one calls "basic" (such as jealousy) have merited the same, sadness remains, so to speak, sadly neglected. The reader may object that there is a vast literature on depression and also on grief; however, though these are both cousins of sadness, they are not sadness. The brilliant synthetic effort *Culture and Depression* (Kleinman & Good, 1985), has raised the question of the relationship between sadness and depression, but for the most part the book deals with the latter. Although there is controversy over whether and to what extent depression is a universal biological disorder, and to what extent it is a culturally determined state or set of behaviors, most of the authors agree (implicitly or explicitly) that depression is an ongoing dysphoric state; that it is regarded as an illness or at least as deviant; and that it precludes the experience of positive emotions for

long periods of time. The upsurge of interest in the study of emotion in the last decade, from which the present volume derives, centers on the normal and functional aspects of emotion, not on psychopathology. Thus, I undertake the task of exploring sadness—a transient, normal emotion, no more to be subsumed under depression than happiness would be under mania, or fear under generalized anxiety disorder. Insofar as the literature on depression sheds light on sadness, it is considered, but it is not a central focus.

Similarly, there is a huge literature on grief, largely influenced by John Bowlby's three-volume work *Attachment and Loss* (see especially Bowlby, 1980), and the seminal book by Peter Marris, *Loss and Change* (1974); however, for three reasons, studying grieving is not the same as studying sadness. First, the grief literature tends to assume rather than to investigate the relationship between situations and emotions. Grieving is conceptualized as following upon loss. My task here, on the contrary, is to pose the question "Why and when are people sad?", not to assume that sadness always comes after loss. Second, the grief literature recognizes that emotions other than sadness, such as anger, come with grieving, so that the study of grief is not the study of the single emotion of sadness. Finally, the grief literature focuses on mechanisms and rituals for dealing with loss. The behaviors in these mechanisms interest students of emotion, but for most of us emotion implies an inner state as well as a set of behaviors, so that the study of sadness must be related to but more than the study of grief mechanisms.

Although there is no major synthetic work on sadness, a number of disciplines offer work that is germane to the subject. I start with psychology, which grapples in the most straightforward way with the emotion, and then turn to history and anthropology in order to test some of the claims for universality implied by the psychologists. I then attempt to synthesize the work of the divergent disciplines, and to suggest avenues for further investigation and collaboration.

PSYCHOLOGICAL APPROACHES

A promising approach to understanding sadness comes from those psychologists who think, in Darwinian terms, of the function of emotion as enabling and motivating us to respond adaptively. Heavily influenced by the work of Silvan Tomkins and Paul Ekman on basic emotions, many psychologists in the late 1970s and 1980s have attempted to delineate the differences between the negative emotions by studying the situations or cognitions that lead us, consciously or unconsciously, to choose a specific emotion. In addition, the psychologists have assumed that by learning which emotion is appropriate to which appraisal of a situation, more can be concluded about the differing "functions" of each emotion (Folkman, Lazarus, Dunkel-Schetter, DeLongis, & Gruen, 1986). These studies have usually asked subjects to describe events that would lead to a list of "basic" emotions, including sadness, named by the investigators. However, more sophisticated studies have described types of situations or appraisals the investigators feel are important as independent variables, and then asked the subjects to describe emotions they would feel in each case (Ellsworth & Smith, 1988). Other studies have approached the question of function directly by asking subjects what they do when they experience various emotions, including sadness.

What have these studies concluded about the nature of sadness? All concur in seeing sadness as an emotion experienced in the face of an event described as unpleasant; characteristically, sadness is seen as a response to a goal lost or not attained (Ellsworth & Smith, 1988; Camras & Allison, 1989; Shaver, Schwartz, Kirson & O'Connor, 1987). After agreeing that sadness is a negative emotion,

the studies attempt to distinguish it from other negative emotions. For the most part, there is a consensus that sadness is distinguished from fear by being a response to an event that has already taken place, whereas fear anticipates an event to come. There is some indication that what distinguishes sadness from guilt is the judgment that the self is not responsible for the problem. Anger is seen as the emotion chosen if another person is responsible, whereas sadness arises when nobody is at fault. The studies show however, that the negative emotions anger, guilt, and sadness are often felt together, and that a judgment about agency cannot always explain the choice of sadness versus anger or guilt, or why some individuals tend to pick one emotion and some another. Particularly in distinguishing anger from sadness, there is some murkiness as to which emotion is chosen when someone else is responsible for a misfortune, but it is someone over whom the subject has no control. Similarly, it is not clear that anger is seen as a legitimate emotion when someone else is responsible for a problem if that person has done nothing considered unjust or wrong. In such cases, some subjects may feel anger while others feel sadness, so that it remains mysterious why and in what circumstances people need to recognize an injustice in order to feel angry. And of course there are subjects who admit to anger in the sense of frustration, even when it is clear to them that there is no person responsible for their problem. The psychologists have demonstrated, then, that a judgment about agency is important in our choice of the particular emotion of sadness, but have by no means thoroughly explained that choice.

Some psychologists are less convinced that a determination about agency is the crucial appraisal that governs sadness. Roseman (1991) argues that it is the degree of surprise that an outcome was not better that predicts sadness as opposed to anger. Ellsworth and Smith (1988) also take account of expectations in distinguishing resignation from sadness: Resignation is seen as a response when the bad outcome is perceived as having been inevitable, whereas sadness comes when the situation might have been reversible. Stein and Levine (1990) see the difference as a plan for action: An angry person thinks he or she can replace a lost goal, while a sad one accepts the loss. Neither distinction about degree of disappointment or plan of action, however, explains unequivocally the differences between the negative emotions or allows us to predict which emotion will be picked by which subjects in which cases. Psychologists have made a promising start, then, in attempting to understand the difference between sadness and other negative emotions, but have been unable to answer all their own questions.

Apart from the issue of distinguishing sadness from other emotions, American psychologists, in their effort to clarify the "function" of sadness, have been interested in whether it is an emotion correlated with an increase or a decrease in attention. The bulk of the work seems to indicate that sadness impairs attention to tasks (Potts, Camp, & Coyne, 1989). Ellsworth and Smith (1988) have seen sadness as associated with a lowering of attention, because the emotion is seen as not being caused by another agent, and so attention is focused inward. However, they also do note that sadness is sometimes named as an emotion experienced when one would want to attend closely, and they offer no clear explanation of the discrepancy (p. 295). They imply that there also may be some self-protectiveness in low-attention sadnesses, which may function to shut out an unpleasant situation (pp. 294–295). Psychologists are unable to tell us definitively, then, that the function of sadness is either to lower or to raise attention levels toward the outside world.

There seems to be more agreement, however, that sadness focuses the person on himself or herself. Hochschild (1983) and Stein and Jewett (1986) characterize it as a "me" emotion rather than an "it" emotion; they reason that the focus in sadness is on the consequences to the self of not achieving its goals, as opposed to say, anger, where the focus is on the external cause or frustration. The function of self-focus in sadness is seen as providing the individual with feedback on how well things are going, probably in order to allow the person to pay more effective attention to the pursuit of his or her goals (Stein & Jewett, 1986; Pyszczynski & Greenberg, 1987). Decreased attention to the outside conserves energy, so that the person may focus on solving the problem (Cunningham, 1988). For those who see sadness this way, there is a tendency to minimize the avoidant behaviors or self-gratifying behaviors that ensue from sadness. For example, despite the fact that his

subjects named listening to music as the second most likely thing they would do if sad, and taking a nap as the fourth, Cunningham (1988) still sees sadness as having the function of fostering constructive self-examination (p. 320).

Intricately connected to the question of whether the function of sadness is to focus a person inward so that he or she can solve problems is the possibility that a function of sadness may be to cue others that the individual needs help. Cunningham's (1988) evidence does not support this; his subjects chose to be alone when sad (p. 320). Ellsworth and Smith (1988) do see sadness's function as a call for help, but admit that there is a problem in their inability to explain how often sadness leads to withdrawal from social situations (p. 298). They also raise the problem that too much sadness may become a drain on others, and thus dysfunctional. Some psychologists solve this problem of distinguishing between cueing help and triggering rejection by calling emotions that elicit help "normal sadness," but those that elicit rejection "depression" (Swallow & Kuiper, 1987). However, the difficulties in reconciling a position assuming that each emotion has a specific function with the empirical data revealing that sadness sometimes turns a person inward, but sometimes, quite conversely, helps him or her attain external aid, or (complexity compounded) sometimes leads him or her to seek help that is not forthcoming, have not been fully addressed.

There are several reasons for the limitations of the dominant psychological approach to sadness. First, the studies flow from the assumption that there are discrete, basic emotions, each of which has a function. This works when subjects are forced in experimentation to describe situations in which they would feel one discrete emotion named by the investigators; yet, when subjects are allowed to name their own feelings, they almost always come up with a blend of emotions. This makes it difficult to say that emotions have clearly discrete functions. Second, since there is the assumption of universality of emotional response in the functional approach, there is no mechanism in these experiments to account for differences among individuals, though the results show that individuals vary widely in their choice both of the emotion of sadness and of the behavior that follows from the emotion. Third, although these studies attempt to elucidate the function of emotion, they tell us only half the story, since they study the individual who feels the emotion rather than how observers respond to his or her feeling. There is no way, for example, that we can determine whether the function of sadness is to elicit help simply by asking people what they do when they feel sad. We need to be looking at how others respond to sadness if we are to determine its social function; however, none of the experiments discussed above has done this even in a laboratory, and certainly not in natural settings. Fourth, since the studies are based on the subjects' descriptions of themselves, they may really be telling us more about emotion rules or emotionology in our own culture than about the inner experience of basic emotion. Since the studies focus almost entirely on American college students, they are unacceptably culture-bound. The possibility that sadness may be different in other contexts is not considered, and the opportunity for understanding American assumptions more clearly by investigating them from other perspectives is lost.

ANTHROPOLOGICAL AND HISTORICAL APPROACHES

The psychological experiments I have described are unquestionably valuable in raising important questions about sadness. They force us to think about the difference between sadness and other negative emotions; they raise good questions as to what sadness does to our level of attention and as to what behaviors result from sadness. However, because of the problems raised above, it is essential to turn to anthropology and history in order to learn more about sadness. What the psychologists have done is to provide us with an invaluable structure—a set of hypotheses through which we can make sense of the anthropological and historical material.

Perhaps the least questioned hypothesis of American psychologists has been that sadness is a negative emotion felt in response to events viewed as unpleasant. Several studies challenge that view. Catherine Lutz (1988b) has studied the Ifaluk, a society of some 430 people who live on an island in the Pacific. In observing their emotion words, although she finds none that is the exact equivalent of our "sadness," she notes their interest in *fago*—an emotion most often felt in the face of distress

of another person, which Lutz translates as approximating "compassion/love/sadness." It is plain that feeling *fago* can be painful, but it is also clear that people take pride in their ability to feel *fago*, which implies that they are calm and gentle. *Fago* is linked with generosity and maturity, and the people noted to feel it most are often those such as chiefs or benevolent spirits, who are especially respected. Capacity to feel *fago*, then, implies power. Thus to assert one's *fago* is to claim to be a good person (Lutz, 1985), and is clearly not experienced entirely as a negative emotion.

My own work on sadness in premodern England and America reveals a sadness different from *fago*, but one also highly valued. In my study based on emotions as expressed in 17th-century diaries, the subjects associated sadness in the face of difficulty with patience, wisdom, and humility—all highly esteemed qualities—and thus were pleased to note their sadness. To be doleful was sometimes seen as the opposite of being sinful, so that one diarist even suggested that God "allowed of no joy nor pleasure, but of a kind of melancholy demeanor and austerity" (quoted in Stearns, 1988, p. 51). Melancholia as a subject of admiration fascinated many intellectuals in this period (MacDonald, 1981, p. 150 ff.).

Kleinman and Good (1985) have noted that in many Asian societies, sadness is highly valued and associated with a step in the direction of salvation. In Iran and Sri Lanka, the ability to experience it marks a person's depth (Good, Good, & Moradi, 1985; Obeyesekere, 1985). Modern Americans, of course, have our own pleasurable sadness in the mixed emotion of nostalgia. It appears, then, that sadness is not always an unalloyedly negative emotion. Though in all these cases it is experienced in the face of problems, the experience itself connotes some pleasure and pride, and is not unmixedly negative. Lest it be argued that the basic emotion of sadness is still negative even though the experience is valued positively, we must keep in mind that we have no evidence that the basic emotion is ever experienced separately from the evaluation.

Another hypothesis is that the single most important factor differentiating sadness from other emotions is a judgment about agency. If another person is considered the cause, then the response is anger; if it is seen as someone's own fault, the response is guilt or shame. Let us look at the sadness–anger differentiation.

SADNESS 551

Two kind of situations would argue against the hypothesis: those in which a person causes the problem but the response is sadness, and those in which no person causes the problem but the response is anger. Both situations arise clearly in the evidence from outside modern America. Jean Briggs (1970), who has studied the emotional responses of the Utku, a small Inuit (Eskimo) society, mentions no word for sadness; her closest equivalent is *hujuujaq,* which most often implies loneliness. She tells us, however, that the Utku also use the word to describe their response to another person's lying or stealing, and that in that sense it connotes hostility. She feels they label such responses *hujuujaq* rather than words that connote primarily anger, however, because overt anger is so strictly forbidden in their society. Hence, in linguistic terms, they do not clearly differentiate between anger and sadness by employing one word to label a response to a problem caused by a person, and a different word for one with no human cause (pp. 352–355).

My study of early Anglo-American responses to disappointment similarly reveals that most diarists called responses to problems created by others sadness, not anger (Stearns, 1988). Mistreatment by an employer, theft, victimization by gossip, familial quarrels—all these could be described by the diarist in labeling his or her response as grief or sadness.

Other studies reveal cultures in which, although no human agency is clearly responsible for a misfortune, responses resemble what we call "angry." Michelle Rosaldo (1980), in her study of the head-hunting practices of the Ilongot, a Philippine warrior society, notes that the murders are sometimes seen clearly as avenging specific wrongs. However, when asked their motives, her subjects would also speak of *uget*—it is unclear whether she wants to translate this as "bad feeling" or "grief," but at any rate it implies a weight or burden to be borne until one finds a victim (by no means necessarily the agent of the wrong) and slashes off his or her head. She is explicit that killing comes not just when people must seek vengeance, but also when people feel the need to cast off heavy weights from their hearts. Edward Schieffelin (1976, 1985b) has described similar reactions among the Kaluli of New Guinea, who deal with loss by becoming angry and displaying this in a ceremony in which dancers who sing and wail about loss are then burned in anger by the observers. The loss can be through death or departure of a loved one; it does not have to have been caused by a person in order to evoke this response. A wrong or a loss may lead to furious stamping, yelling, and a wish for redress (Schieffelin, 1985a), even if it is not clear that some individual is responsible.

Catherine Lutz's Ifaluk have a word, *nguch,* for frustration not caused by another person. Someone may feel *nguch,* say, after getting tired of grating coconut for 3 hours (Lutz, 1985). Relatedly, one may feel *tang,* which implies frustration in the face of a personal misfortune one cannot redress (Lutz, 1988b, p. 157). Lutz feels these words cluster closer to *song,* which is like anger, than to *fago,* which is more like sadness. Thus it seems that what the Ifaluk feel when disappointed, even though it is nobody's fault, seems to them more like anger than sadness.

Another complex case arises in the Bedouin community of Awlad 'Ali, studied by Lila Abu-Lughod (1986). Here, children are socialized to attribute misfortunes to misdeeds of others, so that mothers usually respond to crying children by asking "Who did it?" rather than "What's the matter?" People are trained to respond in a hostile mode even to entirely inevitable losses, so that, for instance, a woman losing her hair may say something equivalent to "God willing, it won't return" or "Good riddance." Thus, there is abundant anger even when misfortune's cause is clearly not another person. However, Abu-Lughod informs us that the Bedouins express a sad reaction to the very same events in their poetry, and in this poetry, grieving is acknowledged not only for inevitable disappointments but also for those engendered by others. A deserted spouse, for example, will use words and metaphors for sad emotions in his or her poetry. Thus, the anthropologist finds here that the differentiation between the two emotions is not at all a question of deciding what caused the problem, but rather of knowing when, to what audience, and in what sort of language it is appropriate to feel one or the other. The cross-cultural evidence, then, does not support the notion that what universally differentiates sadness from other emotions is a cognition about agency.

Another issue with which American psychologists have grappled, in the effort to determine a function for sadness, is the seeming contradiction between the sad person's tendency to turn inward in order to find solace or solve problems, and the tendency to turn outward, cueing others that he or she needs help. Clearly, sadness in modern America causes both behaviors. Looking at other cultures may help us understand why we are puzzled by the duality in sadness, and also why we find some of the behaviors of both those who seek help and those who turn inward problematical. Let us start with sadness as a motivator to seek help. There has been some puzzlement that a sad individual does not in fact always get the help he or she needs, and may even repel others. In simple societies, we often see a more unalloyed expectation that a sad person will receive compassion and aid. Lutz (1988b) notes that in the face of death, or a loss of important possessions because of natural disasters, the Ifaluk speak in terms of recognition of a general vulnerability and emphasize a collective sadness and response. *Tang lanal*, which means literally "cry inside," is what a person who deserves help but does not get it may feel, and this is somewhat akin to *song*, or justifiable anger. In other words, a person who is sad can expect that others should help (Lutz, 1985). As noted earlier, Briggs's (1970) Inuit subsume most sadness under the word *hujuujaq*, which they define as "loneliness." Thus, when one is distressed for no apparent reason, or even when one is cold, wet, or mosquito-bitten, one may be described as *hujuujaq*. That a word meaning "lonely" is used in these cases does seem to imply that the fundamental problem in sadness is that one needs something from others. The most common cure for such feelings is to seek out company. Logically, the Inuit expect a compassionate and protective response to the sadness of others, and have a word for that response in *naklik*, which is akin to the *fago* or compassionate response expected among the Ifaluk. Schieffelin (1985a), likewise, notes that among the Kaluli sadness has an assertive sense, in that it demands a helpful response from observers.

Many grief theorists have commented on the ritualized ceremonies simple societies employ to enable the group to join with and help the individual who is bereft. The intent of these comments is to critique modernized societies, which do not help the individual with loss. What is not noted, however, is that the simple societies often demarcate quite sharply the situations in which sadness is acknowledged.

Robert Levy (1973) has observed that the Tahitians have no word equivalent to our "sadness." They have a vocabulary for grief and lamentation, but not for a generalized sadness. Lutz (1988b) also finds the Ifaluk to be without a word that connotes our sadness in the sense of global loss or hopelessness. Her explanation is that through the word *fago* the Ifaluk take a general responsibility to help one another, whereas with "sadness" we blame the individual or chastise the victim. Another way to think of this, however, is that simple societies do not acknowledge diffuse sadness, in part because there is an expectation that the group should aid the individual with problems. Losses for which the group has scripts, such as death, illness, loss of love, loss by natural disaster, and loneliness, are acknowledged. However, losses for which there are no scripts, such as a generalized sense of meaninglessness or loss of self-esteem, are simply not recognized. Lutz (1986) does not tell us what happens when someone feels *niyefiyef*, or regret or anger at the self, but this emotion is not seen by the Ifaluk as resembling sadness. Her Ifaluk will *fago* a person who is transiently embarrassed or even drunk, but a person who has drawn difficulties on himself or herself may also be the object of anger or laughter. It is not clear what their response would be to unhappiness that has no clear cause, nor does Lutz explicitly discuss this, but we have no reason to feel from the anthropological studies that help would always be forthcoming.

In simple societies, then, individuals may be socialized to minimize pain for which there are no scripted solutions. Thus, Briggs's (1970) Inuit are embarrassed to be the object of too much concern, or *naklik*, which is for children, not adults. A woman explained to Briggs that she didn't tell the anthropologist of her son's death, lest she make her sad, which would in turn make the woman "sadder still and sorry for myself" (p. 325). We see here the sense that sadness demands a sad response, but also that one should suppress sadness—in part lest one be too demanding, which is unacceptable. Unfortunately, Briggs does not tell us the word in which this woman expressed "sorry for myself," but in her glossary there seems to be no such single word; this fits with Levy's (1973) observation in Tahiti that what we call "sadness" may be hypocognized in some societies. Briggs also found that her Inuit informants became quite angry and rejecting with her when she suffered a kind of diffuse sadness or depression for which they had no scripted response. Abu-Lughod's (1986) Bedouin lend support to the notion that societies develop mechanisms to limit demands on their help. She feels that anger rather than sadness is often a response to loss, in part because the sad person asks for help, which is considered a weakness in an adult. Children, not adults, are allowed to express vulnerability. However, sadness is expressed as long as it is indirect and to some extent depersonalized and intellectualized (i.e., in poetry). Writing the poetry is used to soothe the self, and does not necessarily demand a response from the listener. However, listeners often do show and express empathic concern. This seems to be possible, in part, because that response is not demanded directly.

Two historical studies have demonstrated a transition from a more traditional position, in which scripted sadnesses are clearly acknowledged and expected to elicit help, to a more modern stance, in which the sadness of others is seen as an annoyance. In a book on the history of tears in France, Vincent-Buffault (1991) has described a transition from the 18th century, in which collective tears were enjoyable and there was a heavy emphasis on the virtue of compassion, to the 19th century, in which tears showed an absence of self-mastery and were better suppressed. Anger at the crying person was expressed in the belief that there was something not genuine about those who cried too readily. A dignified and respected sadness would be self-contained, and quite clearly would not demand solace from others. One social dictionary she quotes defined tears as "water too often ill-employed, for it remedies nothing. Resources which women have in their command to hide an infidelity or demand a cashmere shawl . . . weapons which they employ" (cited in Vincent-Buffault, 1991, p. 148). We see in this quotation the modern assumption that individuals should help themselves, as well as anger at the help seeker, whose cries were described as false "weapons." My own work on the increasing distaste for sadness in 17th- and 18th-century England and America (Stearns, 1988) illustrates a similar change. In the earlier period, much sadness was expressed, and there were many frank tears. The crier, a private diarist, was not looking to others for aid, but in every case did expect some succor from God. It was all right to

be sad because help was available, even if it was not help from another person. The later effort to maintain good cheer seems to have coincided with the notion that one had to take care of one's own difficulties rather than lean on external help, even the help of the Almighty. Many historians have described a modernizing process in which there was increasing anger at and unwillingness to aid the unfortunate (MacFarlane, 1970; Lindemann, 1990). This has been demonstrated most clearly in an increasing distaste for charity and condemnation of the poor, but it seems germane as well to changing attitudes toward the sad.

It appears, then, that how societies think about sadness has something to do with how they think about help. In societies more collective than our own, sadnesses are often viewed as deserving a response, but such societies limit their obligation by the absence of vocabulary for or recognition of sadnesses for which a collective response is not expected. In societies that have other mechanisms for limiting the demands of the sad individual on the group, such as the shaming mechanisms by which the Bedouin contain complaint, or the guilt mechanism through which modern Americans tell individuals to take care of themselves, there may be more possibility of speaking about different kinds of sadness. In all cases, the discourse about sadness—implicit in simpler cultures, more explicit in our own—is also a discourse about the demarcation between what is the individual's responsibility and what is the group's (Wellenkamp, 1992). The puzzlement of American functionalists about whether the "purpose" of sadness is to elicit help, and their difficulty in the face of evidence that sadness in our culture often leads to rejection, are themselves expressions of that discourse. Labeling a person who requires too much help as deviant or "dysfunctional" assuages our own guilt in not wishing to help. The distinction between "sad" and "depressed" constitutes in some sense a tool to demarcate the dividing line between situations when we are on the one hand, or are not on the other, willing to offer succor.

In addition to their interest in how sadness leads the individual to seek help, American psychologists have explored and been puzzled by how sadness works to turn the individual inward. We find it functional if people are motivated by sadness to solve their problems, but are troubled by those who withdraw too far from social contacts, and those who, refusing to solve their problems, either find soothing avoidant behaviors or become apathetic. Other cultures, as we shall see, also grapple with these issues, and how they think about them may help us understand ourselves. Jane Wellenkamp (1992), in a study of the Toraja, an Indonesian agricultural people, has divided societies into those that are more egalitarian, encouraging assertiveness and therefore discouraging sadness, and those that are more hierarchical, encouraging postures of appeal and sadness. Here a slightly more complex scheme will be suggested, in which attitudes toward help and appeal are taken into consideration, but also a variety of solutions flowing from gradations in attitudes about passivity. Most, though not all, cultures have great fears regarding passivity; there seem to be three types of cultural solutions to the problem of passivity created by sadness. Traditional societies that tolerate high levels of aggression strive to transform sadness into anger; traditional societies that are less tolerant of aggression seem to minimize sadness and emphasize goal substitution; modern societies are likely to minimize sadness by goading the individual to solve his or her problem. All three types are examined here.

Rosaldo's (1980) Ilongot are an example of the first case. They describe symptoms akin to what we would label "depression" among those who are upset but inactive. She tells us that among the Ilongot "affliction in these instances leaves one ill, distressed, or helpless, humiliated but unable to redress imbalance, sick but too weak to cast off a disease . . . the . . . heart is . . . distracted. . . . Impotent to act, it dwells on its deficiencies . . . fails to find a reasonable course of action" (p. 48). She also speaks of the "'weight', grief or dizziness . . . and sickness" (p. 48) that are associated with withdrawal and passivity. All this the Ilongot see as unfocused energy, which is cured by the activity of head hunting. Happiness is the opposite of feeling weighted down; she says that it suggests activity and sociality, and "has little to do with quietness, tranquility, or peace" (pp. 52–53). Schieffelin's (1985a) Kaluli are similarly anxious about the dangers of passivity, and therefore transform sadness into the active stance of aggression whenever possible. They have no word for passive sadness; the two words for grief imply either compassion, or an active grief for a misfortune, which has a ritualized response (p. 171).

Abu-Lughod's (1986) Bedouin use metaphors of death, illness, drowning, and apathy for describing sadness. There is a sense of danger to the self in sadness, of self-dissolution; a weeping man may he counseled, "Pull yourself together." Sadness implies weakness and vulnerability, and is associated with being a child or female. Men respond angrily to losses, even to death, in part to avoid the danger that is seen in the sad stance. The anthropologist tells of a man so upset by being deserted by his wife that he moped around and begged her to come back. The general response of his peers was that he was an idiot and would have been better off had he beaten her. To allow himself to be sad and vulnerable was to relinquish control. People would no longer fear him. Anger, not sadness, maintains selfhood.

In simple cultures that are less friendly to aggression, sadness is also seen as a danger because of its association with passivity. Levy (1973, 1984) found his Tahitian subjects eager to seal off grief quickly, and implies that this was because they found a danger in sadness, which was associated with fatigue, lacking drive, or feeling heavy or subdued. He explains that they do not have a word equivalent to our "sadness"; in part this is because sadness is not seen as an emotion, in that it is not felt by the self, but rather is the result of an outside difficulty that subdues the self. Tahitians, he believes, depend on a sense of drive and energy to get the work of the world done, and are worried about flagging enthusiasm and apathy. Although they do not condone aggression, they feel it is important to do something about bad feelings rather than to withdraw. They advise mistreated parties to talk to those who have wronged them, because anger held in can lead to weakness and loss of drive: "It's as if your head isn't right" (Levy, 1973, p. 285). All these problems can be cured by taking an active, social stance and confronting the wrongdoer—not to do him or her violence, but to settle the situation verbally.

Like the Tahitians, the Inuit studied by Briggs (1970) lack a word equivalent to our "sadness." Briggs observed behavior, particularly in her Inuit adoptive father, that seemed to be the equivalent of a kind of fatigued, aloof withdrawal, but tells us that this sort of behavior is largely ignored rather than discussed or labeled. *Qiquq*, a word meaning "clogged up," is applied sometimes to such behaviors, but not freely used for those who are respected. It may be used to describe clogged holes or nipples, but also silent withdrawal, with a sense of imminent tears. It is considered childish to behave this way. A person distressed by the bad behavior of someone else may admit to feeling *hujuujaq*, but since this word implies loneliness, it propels the person who feels it into a social stance and away from the social withdrawal condemned in *qiquq*. Like the Tahitians, the Inuit try not to let themselves get too sad about problems for which there is no solution. The acceptable feeling is *ayuqnaq*, which implies resignation, calm, and a refusal to get too upset.

Levy (1984) has raised the question of why cultures hyper- or hypocognize emotions. Emotions that are considered problems may be labeled and dealt with through suppression, or unlabeled and dealt with through repression or other unconscious mechanisms, such as denial or conversion. In all the simple cultures discussed, diffuse sadness seems to be viewed as a problem, in that it withdraws the person from society and undermines activity. In those cultures such as the Kaluli, Ilongot, and Bedouins, which are fairly tolerant of aggression, there seems to be more explicit recognition of the problem of sadness, because the problem can be treated by a not entirely unconscious transformation of the sadness into anger. For those cultures less accepting of anger, such as the Inuit and the Tahitians, there is some sense of the potential for illness in too much bad feeling. Therefore, people are counseled to get over their sadness quickly, and there seems to be some effort to deny that intense sadness exists.

There are some cultures that embrace a passive rather than an active stance, and these seem more accepting of sadness than those described above. This was certainly true of the 17th-century diarists I studied (Stearns, 1988): They were proud of their sadness, because it implied patience and humility. In the face of adversity, a sad demeanor enabled them to renounce anger and to turn to God to right their wrongs. To be angry was considered unacceptable, because it implied pride, which was ungodly. However, passivity was not seen as problematic, as it is by the Inuit or Tahitians. I have discussed elsewhere (Stearns, 1988) the utility of dignifying the passive

position in a highly stratified complex society in which the vast majority of people must be socialized to be obedient and to suppress initiative. It would be worth exploring whether the passivity implied in some of the Asian religions' high valuation of sadness is connected with similar social structures. For now, though, I wish to emphasize that societies that transform sadness into anger or repress sadness seem to be those societies that value initiative and activity (such as the Ilongot, Kaluli, and Bedouin), or that at least fear withdrawal and passivity (such as the Inuit or Tahitians). Conversely, the transformation of anger into sadness appears to be associated with the devaluing of active, initiating positions. In all these cases, sadness is valued or not, depending on how the society feels about passivity.

The choice of emotions, then, is not mainly determined by a judgment about agency, as the attributionists have argued. Attribution of agency is often, in fact, culturally determined, as in the Bedouin readiness to find someone to blame for all misfortunes. Attribution, then, is the dependent variable; the independent variables are deeply held cultural assumptions about what sort of personalities and behaviors are valuable, what kind of people or responses are valuable or dangerous (Hofstede, 1984). This view can be used to explain otherwise inexplicable American data. For instance, Stein and Jewett's (1986) failure to separate anger and sadness definitively along the criteria of whether the person who caused the harm did it intentionally is clearer when we look at the particular situations that made the children feel each emotion. In four cases in which a person deliberately interfered with a child's wish, differing proportions of children expressed anger and sadness, but much more sadness was expressed when the interferer was someone over whom the child could have little control (a teacher) and much more anger when it was a peer (pp. 253–255). The authors fail to note this, because they think of agency of harm as a generalizable attribute. However, it should be clear by now that the distinction between sadness and anger has something to do with a sense of when aggressive responses are or are not acceptable, and this is probably true in modern America as well as elsewhere.

However, unlike many of the societies discussed above, our society does not always make a conscious clear association of "sad" and "passive," at least for adults. Here, an active sadness may be envisioned that in some sense asserts the self. The sad person is counseled to figure out what is troubling him or her, and to do something about it. Perhaps this is possible for us because we look to the individual, not the group, to solve problems. Since we do not tolerate aggression as do the Kaluli, Ilongot, or Bedouins, we describe some situations they would see as cause for anger, as cause for sadness. For instance, in the face of death or loss of love, we do not justify violence as a solution. Unlike the Tahitians or Inuit, however, we are able to label and recognize diffuse sadness, because we are less worried about an individual's social withdrawal. We think that individuals on their own may find solutions; they need not be passive. Even for us, though, some sense remains of the lurking dangers of passivity. This appears in the very way in which American psychologists analyze data about the behaviors flowing from sadness. It is notable that Shaver et al. (1987), in looking for a basic sadness, do not notice the cultural meaning of the fact that their subjects differentiate what they do when sad (namely, become active) from what they claim others do (namely, sink into apathy). They explain this difference as resulting from cognitive distortion. They do not explain the logic behind the distortion, which is that we project the "bad" passive response onto others and claim the "good" active response for ourselves; unlike 17th-century Americans, who valued passivity, we cannot afford to socialize the majority of our population to lack initiative or to depend on higher forces for succor. We are too large and complex a society, however, to tolerate unchecked anger (Stearns & Steams, 1986). In some sense, we resemble the Inuit and Tahitians in fearing both the poles of passivity and aggression, and are like them in wanting people to get over sadness quickly. It is possible, though, that we cognize and label sadness more freely than they do, because we do have more of a sense that individuals who are conscious of their problems can find solutions. We do like individuals to concentrate on themselves and to be introspective, because we feel that this enables them to find answers. Emphasis on individuals' ability to solve their own problems also allows us, as discussed above, to feel less guilty about our refusal to offer help and our wish to label help seekers as dysfunctional. In less individualistic societies, which expect more solutions to come from group consensus and activity, too much introspective

brooding and interest in the self may feel dangerous in that they are potentially antisocial. Sadness that comes from a clear problem and for which the group is willing to offer help will be recognized; individual sadnesses, for which the group does not feel obligated to offer help, may be hypocognized or ignored.

DISCUSSION

The anthropological and historical literature addresses many of the issues raised by American psychologists, and refines them considerably. We learn from this literature that sadness is not always an unalloyedly negative emotion. We learn also that the extent to which a society recognizes and values sadness is related to the society's views about aggression, about individual versus collective responsibility, and about activity versus passivity. We learn, finally, that a lack of conclusiveness about the function of sadness manifested in the psychologists' experiments may have something to do with ambivalence on the part of both the investigators and their subjects, and indeed on the part of modern North Americans in general, regarding all these issues.

The complexities introduced by the evidence from other cultures does return us to our early question of whether, indeed, it is reasonable to assume that there is some basic and universal emotion represented by our word "sadness." Silvan Tomkins (1984), one of the fathers of the idea of discrete affects, was himself unable to differentiate a qualitative difference between the neuronal firings of sadness and anger, concluding only that anger was a more intense form of sadness (p. 173 ff.). Although he could distinguish the other affects from one another on the basis of the pattern of neuronal firing, he could not do this for sadness and anger. On a superficial level, the studies of Paul Ekman and others on the universal recognition of facial expressions, including sadness, across cultures would seem to indicate that there is a universal sadness. However, there are problems in this conclusion. For one, Ekman's studies rely on a response not only to stories describing situations, but also to words describing an emotion (Ekman, Friesen, & Ellsworth, 1972, p. 160). Since he glosses over the whole problem of translation discussed by later anthropologists (Heelas, 1986), we cannot be certain what "sadness" means in the various cultures, but it is fairly clear that the translators chose words implying resignation rather than fighting. The faces identified, then, do not necessarily convey an internal universal response to situations, but rather convey a plan for action or behavior. In the sense that emotion means an appraisal of a situation leading to a particular behavior, Ekman's work does show some universal cross-cultural recognition of what behaviors may be expected from what faces. It does not show, however, that there is a universal basic and discrete feeling of sadness. Rather, it indicates that there is a universally recognized possible response to distressing situations that implies passivity or appeal rather than a fight. And indeed, since as Ekman himself well knows (Ekman & Friesen, 1975), faces may deceive us as to inner states, it makes intuitive sense that we read faces to tell us what behaviors to expect rather than what we or others feel.

Another type of evidence that has been used to argue for a basic affect of sadness is the crying of infants. If newborns display distinct affective states, it is difficult to think of these as anything but basic. However, although there is certainly evidence that infants make distinctly different kind of cries (Demos, 1986) and that mothers respond to them differently (Huebner & Izard, 1988), it is not clear that sadness is clearly differentiated in an infant's cry in the early months (Emde, 1984), or that the different kinds of cries correspond neatly to the difference that adults understand between sadness and anger (Tomkins, 1991, p. 113). In fact, since Ekman himself thinks of distress as more fundamental than sadness, and has stated that the face of sadness is more muted than a crying face (Ekman & Friesen, 1975), it would be difficult to say that there is a face/cry of an infant that corresponds to Ekman's basic sad face, and that supports the notion of an innate sadness as distinct from anger.

Why, then, do we have words for a variety of negative emotions? This can be explained best if we keep in mind Tomkins's (1962) general argument that the function of emotion is to allow us a certain plasticity and adaptability in adjusting to our world. When we are disappointed, there are several things we can do. We can fight; we can seek help from others or attempt to rectify the situation ourselves; or we can withdraw into inactivity. Clearly, the choice of what action to take will affect our biological response. There is evidence that what we call "sad" in modern America is asso-

ciated with a kind of slowing of the body, a feeling of inactivity, and a sense of sluggishness or weakness, and that indeed it is hard to continue to feel "sad" when moving (Schwartz, Weinberger, & Singer, 1981; Shields, 1984; Averill, 1969; Shaver et al., 1987). This corresponds with work showing that the vocalizations of sadness are considered smaller, softer, and slower than those of anger (Scherer, 1982), and with Tomkins's (1991) notion that patterns of movement cause as well as respond to affect. It is also a way of thinking about affect that may unify the distinction Stern (1985) makes between "categorical" and "vitality" affects. Using the idea of vitality affect, we can think of sadness as slowness, sluggishness, passivity, softness, and drawing in, compared to the loud explosiveness of anger. The distinction, then, is not one of appraisal but one of activity (Frijda, 1987). The choice to withdraw in the face of difficulty does seem to be in the universal repertory of biological response; it is evident in early life in some animal species (Averill, 1968), and though not apparent in the human neonate, it is certainly universal in humans at later ages.

All functioning societies must offer individuals a variety of solutions to deal with goal blockage and goal loss. We use the word "sadness," most characteristically to describe the slow, sluggish type of response, although we sometimes also use it to describe the help-seeking response. Other societies, depending on the parameters described above (views of aggression, individualism vs. collectivism, and activity vs. passivity), may use different words. The words that are used and the distinctions that are made, as well as those that are glossed over, tell us about each society's values and each society's anxieties as it considers the advantages and disadvantages of the many different sorts of responses people may make when they don't get what they want (Lutz, 1988a).

Since I am arguing that what is basic is distress, not sadness, is there a way to explain the function of distress? Grief and loss theorists (Bowlby, 1980; Marris, 1974; Mahler, 1961; Averill, 1968) have felt that distress functions to help people become more aware of what they value, in part to motivate them to conserve what is important, and more particularly to motivate them to maintain attachment to others. Tomkins (1963) also had such an explanation for the problem of human suffering. I am skeptical that it would be possible to operationalize such a hypothesis, though certainly it seems intuitively appealing. What I wish to emphasize, here, though, is that this notion is a notion about distress and grief, which encompass both sadness and anger, and perhaps guilt and shame. It supports the notion that the emotions in natural settings are usually blended, and that what distinguishes them is not intrinsic, basic function. It is consonant with the observations that there is no general agreement about what are the basic affects, and that sadness is not on every such list, as well as with the argument that there is a lack of utility in the whole concept of sorting out basic emotions. Indeed, it may be more useful to think in terms of a repertory of human responses and cognitions related to, but not corresponding in a one-to-one fashion to, biological states or vitality affects (Ortony & Turner, 1990).

These difficulties with "basic affect" revive, of course, the possibility that the psychoanalytic concept of "drive" may have some utility in explaining emotions. Sadness appears closely related to anger, and the choice of how and when to express one or the other expresses attitudes toward aggressive impulses (Cohen, 1990; Freud, 1972). Sadness is also related to frustration of the drive for attachment (Bowlby, 1980), and the choice of how and when to express it reflects defenses relating to dependency needs. In Kohutian terms, sadness may follow upon a threat to the image of the self, the drive to maintain that image being fundamental. Defenses against sadness, like those against other affects, are influenced both by cultural training and by the idiosyncrasies of the individual. They range over a wide gamut from entirely unconscious to explicitly understood and elaborated. Affect theorists, coming from a tradition in rebellion against psychoanalysis, may have been too quick to ignore the utility of the psychoanalytic concepts of drive, defense, and the unconscious in explaining emotion.

POSSIBILITIES FOR
THE FUTURE

Where will future studies of sadness take us? This depends in part on the interests of those doing the studies, and three general areas emerge. Those interested primarily in contemporary America must become more exquisitely sensitive to the nuances of language. How so-

cieties cluster and label words shows a great deal of how they think about feelings (Lutz, 1986). Why do we cluster so many meanings under the label "sad"? The attributionists indicate that for us agency is a more salient distinction than any other, for they discover words for shame, anger, and guilt, but not words that clearly distinguish different sorts of sadness. It may be that this is an artifact, based on the investigators' embrace of the old lists of basic emotion words, and that in natural American contexts we as frequently employ words that acknowledge other distinctions. We do have "neediness," which expresses a wish for help, and "depressed," which in popular language often expresses withdrawn sadness. But we have no clear words to distinguish between sadness that leads to avoidant or self-soothing behaviors, and sadness that which leads to problem solving. "Coping" implies problem solving but without the sadness. Since these distinctions are important to us, it would be worth exploring why we have no clear words for them. Investigations along these lines would also shed light on the minor but puzzling question of why the attribution studies reveal a use of "sadness" that encompasses many different sorts of behavior, whereas in the biologically oriented studies (Shields, 1984; Schwartz et al., 1981; Averill, 1969) Americans seem to equate the word with a particular withdrawn, choked-up, slowed response. We need to know more about how Americans think about sadness in terms of the problems (discussed above) of attitudes toward help, aggression, and passivity. Studies that would answer these questions fully must be done in natural settings, not laboratories.

Historians and anthropologists will want more general studies of the relationship between culture and sadness than those focusing simply on modern America. Although we now have a great deal of information about sadness in our own culture and in a few simple traditional cultures, we need to know much more about sadness in complex but non-Western cultures. This may be particularly enlightening in helping us to understand sadness in societies where passivity is highly valued. We also need more investigations of how and when societies change their use of sadness as they modernize; these of course, must be historical studies.

Finally, some investigators will want to know more about the universal qualities of what we call "sadness." Cross-disciplinary work will be essential here. Although psychologists have been hampered by the confines of American laboratories, anthropologists would benefit from more attention to their colleagues in psychology. It is interesting to know, for instance, that in many societies there is no word for nonscripted sadnesses that have no clear cause. However, the fact that there is no word for a situation does not mean that it does not exist. It is a mistake to ignore, as Lutz has done, the nonverbal evidence for affect, and with it the indications of psychodynamic conflict (Gerber, 1985; Levy & Wellenkamp, 1989). To understand sadness better, anthropologists not only must focus on the situations they have seen as emblematic or typical of their subjects, but also must ask what happens in all the sorts of situations that the psychologists hypothesize, and particularly what happens when people's reactions seem discordant with their own rules. Several questions remain unanswered. Are there variants in the amount of distress felt in different societies? In societies that stress angry responses, is there less sadness than in contemporary America? In societies that stress goal substitution or that offer comfort to the individual, meeting his or her dependency need, is there less withdrawn sadness than here, or is there a sadness that is simply ignored? These questions are part of the larger question as to whether the sluggish, withdrawn response we label "sadness" is indeed "basic." It is notable that Americans describe feeling "choked up" when sad (Shields, 1984), and that Tomkins (1984) noted a decrease in vocalization as an indication of "backed-up" affect—that is, affect constrained by socialization. Indeed, Tomkins felt that all societies must limit the expression of the full cries of distress and anger. There is evidence of a sad, withdrawn response in other animals (Averill, 1968), but one wonders for aggressive humans, who enter the world with loud tears, whether sadness in the sense of choked-up withdrawal is basic biologically, or is basic only in the sense of being a socially necessary universal. Evidence that sad people are physiologically activated, and yet hold still and behave sluggishly (Averill, 1969; Schwartz et al., 1981), leads one to suspect that there may be something puzzling or even "unnatural" about sadness. This, in turn, raises the question of the relationship between sadness and depression. The latter is often viewed as

an inability to feel emotion, and depressed people often cry less instead of more than others, because affect is suppressed. To the extent that sadness implies withdrawal rather than crying to get help, is a sad response most common in societies that are also most prone to depression? Are sadness and depression rarer in societies more tolerant of affect expression? What sorts of conditions create such societies? To answer these questions well, we will need the cooperation not only of psychologists, anthropologists, and historians, but also of biologists, linguists, sociologists, psychiatrists, and psychoanalysts.

REFERENCES

Abu-Lughod, L. (1986). *Veiled sentiments: Honor and poetry in a Bedouin society.* Berkeley: University of California Press.

Averill, J. R. (1968). Grief: Its nature and significance. *Psychological Bulletin, 70*(6), 721–748.

Averill, J. R. (1969). Autonomic response patterns during sadness and mirth. *Psychophysiology, 5*(4), 399–414.

Bowlby, J. (1980). *Attachment and loss: Vol. 3. Loss: Sadness and depression.* New York: Basic Books.

Briggs, J. L. (1970). *Never in anger: Portrait of an Eskimo family.* Cambridge, MA: Harvard University Press.

Camras, L. A., & Allison, K. (1989). Children's and adults' beliefs about emotion elicitation. *Motivation and Emotion, 13*(1), 53–70.

Cohen, D. J. (1990). Enduring sadness: Early loss, vulnerability, and the shaping of character. *Psychoanalytic Study of the Child, 45,* 157–178.

Compact Edition of the Oxford English Dictionary. (1971). New York: Oxford University Press.

Cunningham, M. R. (1988). What do you do when you're happy or blue? Mood, expectancies, and behavioral interest. *Motivation and Emotion, 12*(4), 309–331.

Demos, V. (1986). Crying in early infancy: An illustration of the motivational function of affect. In T. B. Brazelton & M. W. Yogman (Eds.), *Affective development in infancy* (pp. 39–73). Norwood, NJ: Ablex.

Ekman, P., & Friesen, W. V. (1975). *Unmasking the face.* Englewood Cliffs, NJ: Prentice-Hall.

Ekman, P., Friesen, W. V., & Ellsworth, P. C. (1972). *Emotion in the human face.* Elmsford, NY: Pergamon Press.

Ellsworth, P. C., & Smith, C. A. (1988). From appraisal to emotion: Differences among unpleasant feelings. *Motivation and Emotion, 12*(3), 271–302.

Emde, R. N. (1984). Levels of meaning for infant emotions: A biosocial view. In K. R. Scherer & P. Ekman (Eds.), *Approaches to emotion* (pp. 77–107). Hillsdale, NJ: Erlbaum.

Folkman, S., Lazarus, R. S., Dunkel-Schetter, A., DeLongis, A. & Gruen, R. J. (1986). Dynamics of a stressful encounter: Cognitive appraisal, coping, and encounter outcomes. *Journal of Personality and Social Psychology, 50*(5), 992–1003.

Freud, A. (1972). Comments on aggression. In *The writings of Anna Freud* (Vol. 8, pp. 151–175). New York: International Universities Press.

Frijda, N. H. (1987). Emotion, cognitive structure, and action tendency. *Cognition and Emotion, 1*(2), 115–143.

Gerber, E. R. (1985). Rage and obligation: Samoan emotion in conflict. In G. M. White & J. Kirkpatrick (Eds.), *Person, self, and experience: Exploring Pacific ethnopsychologies* (pp. 121–167). Berkeley: University of California Press.

Good, B. J., Good, M. D., & Moradi, R. (1985). The interpretation of Iranian depressive illness and dysphoric affect. In A. Kleinman & B. Good (Eds.), *Culture and depression* (pp. 369–428), Berkeley: University of California Press.

Heelas, P. (1986). Emotion talk across cultures. In R. Harré (Ed.), *The social construction of emotions* (pp. 234–266). Oxford: Basil Blackwell.

Hochschild, A. R. (1983). *The managed heart: The commercialization of human feeling.* Berkeley: University of California Press.

Hofstede, G. (1984). *Culture's consequences: International differences in work related values.* Beverly Hills, CA: Sage.

Kleinman, A., & Good, B. (Eds.). (1985). *Culture and depression.* Berkeley: University of California Press.

Huebner, R., & Izard, C. E. (1988). Mothers' responses to infants' facial expressions of sadness, anger, and physical distress. *Motivation and Emotion, 12*(2), 185–195.

Levy, R. I. (1973). *Tahitians: Mind and experience in the Society Islands.* Chicago: University of Chicago Press.

Levy, R. I. (1984). The emotions in comparative perspective. In K. R. Scherer & P. Ekman (Eds.), *Approaches to emotion* (pp. 397–412). Hillsdale, NJ: Erlbaum.

Levy, R. I., & Wellenkamp, J. C. (1989). Methodology in the Anthropological Study of Emotion. In R. Plutchik & H. Kellerman (Eds.), *Emotion: Theory, research, and experience. Vol. 4. The measurement of emotions.* (pp. 205–232). New York: Academic Press.

Lindemann, M. (1990). *Patients and paupers: Hamburg 1700–1830.* New York: Oxford University Press.

Lutz, C. (1985). Depression and the translation of emotional worlds. In A. Kleinman & B. Good (Eds.), *Culture and depression* (pp. 63–100), Berkeley: University of California Press.

Lutz, C. (1986). The domain of emotion words on Ifaluk. In R. Harré (Ed.), *The social construction of emotions* (pp. 267–288). Oxford: Basil Blackwell.

Lutz, C. (1988a). Ethnographic perspectives on the emotion lexicon. In V. Hamilton, G. H. Bower, & N. H. Frijda (Eds.), *Cognitive perspectives on emotion and motivation* (pp. 399–419). Dordrecht, The Netherlands: Kluwer.

Lutz, C. (1988b). *Unnatural emotions: Everyday sentiments on a Micronesian atoll and their challenge to Western theory.* Chicago: University of Chicago Press.

MacDonald, M. (1981). *Mystical Bedlam.* Cambridge, England: Cambridge University Press.

MacFarlane, A. (1970). *Witchcraft in Tudor and Stuart England: A regional and comparative study.* New York: Harper & Row.

Mahler, M. S. (1961). On sadness and grief in infancy and childhood. *Psychoanalytic Study of the Child, 16,* 332–349.

Marris, P. (1974). *Loss and change.* New York: Pantheon.

Obeyesekere, G. (1985). Depression, Buddhism, and the work of culture in Sri Lanka. In A Kleinman & B. Good (Eds.), *Culture and depression* (pp. 134–152). Berkeley: University of California Press.

Ortony, A., & Turner, T. J. (1990). What's basic about basic emotions? *Psychological Review, 97*(3), 315–331.

Potts, R., Camp, C., & Coyne, C. (1989). The relationship between naturally occurring dysphoric moods, elaborative encoding, and recall performance. *Cognition and Emotion, 3*(3), 197–205.

Pyszczynski, T., & Greenberg, J. (1987). Self-regulatory perseveration and the depressive self-focusing style: A self-awareness theory of reactive depression. *Psychological Bulletin, 102*(1), 122–138.

Rosaldo, M. Z. (1980). *Knowledge and passion: Ilongot notions of self and social life.* Cambridge, England: Cambridge University Press.

Roseman, I. J. (1991). Appraisal determinants of discrete emotions. *Cognition and Emotion, 5*(3), 161–200.

Scherer, K. R. (1982). The assessment of vocal expression in infants and children. In C. E. Izard (Ed.), *Measuring emotions in infants and children* (pp. 127–163). Cambridge, England: Cambridge University Press.

Schieffelin, E. L. (1976). *The sorrow of the lonely and the burning of the dancers.* New York: St. Martin's Press.

Schieffelin, E. L. (1985a). Anger, grief, and shame: Toward a Kaluli ethnopsychology. In G. M. White & J. Kirkpatrick (Eds.), *Person, self, and experience: Exploring Pacific ethnopsychologies* (pp. 168–182). Berkeley: University of California Press.

Schieffelin, E. L. (1985b). The cultural analysis of depressive affect: An example from New Guinea. In A. Kleinman & B. Good (Eds.), *Culture and depression* (pp. 101–133). Berkeley: University of California Press.

Schwartz, G. E., Weinberger, D. A., & Singer, J. A. (1981). Cardiovascular differentiation of happiness, sadness, anger and fear—following imagery and exercise. *Psychosomatic Medicine, 43*(4), 343–364.

Shaver, P., Schwartz, J., Kirson, D., & O'Connor, C. (1987). Emotion knowledge: Further exploration of a prototype approach. *Journal of Personality and Social Psychology, 52*(6), 1060–1086.

Shields, S. A. (1984). Reports of bodily change in anxiety, sadness, and anger. *Motivation and Emotion, 8*(1), 1–21.

Stearns, C. Z., & Stearns, P. N. (1986). *Anger: The struggle for emotional control in America's history.* Chicago: University of Chicago Press.

Stearns, C. Z. (1988). "Lord help me walk humbly": Anger and sadness in England and America, 1570–1750. In C. Z. Stearns & P. N. Stearns (Eds.), *Emotion and social change: Toward a new psychohistory* (pp. 39–68). New York: Holmes & Meier.

Stein, N. L., & Jewett, J. L. (1986). A conceptual analysis of the meaning of negative emotions: Implications for a theory of development. In C. Izard & P. B. Read (Eds.), *Measuring emotions in infants and children* (Vol. 2, pp. 238–267). Cambridge, England: Cambridge University Press.

Stein, N. L., & Levine, L. J. (1990). Making sense out of emotion: The representation and use of goal structured knowledge. In N. L. Stein, B. Leventhal, & T. Trabasso (Eds.), *Psychological and biological approaches to emotion* (pp. 45–73). Hillsdale, NJ: Erlbaum.

Stern, D. N. (1985). *The interpersonal world of the infant.* New York: Basic Books.

Swallow, S. R., & Kuiper, N. A. (1987). The effects of depression and cognitive vulnerability to depression on judgments of similarity between self and other. *Motivation and Emotion, 11*(2), 157–167.

Tomkins, S. A. (1962). *Affect, imagery, and consciousness: Vol. 1. The positive affects. New* York: Springer.

Tomkins, S. A. (1963). *Affect, imagery, and consciousness: Vol. 2. The negative affects.* New York: Springer.

Tomkins, S. A. (1984). Affect theory. In K. R. Scherer & P. Ekman (Eds.), *Approaches to emotion* (pp. l63–195). Hillsdale, NJ: Erlbaum.

Tomkins, S. A. (1991). *Affect, imagery, and consciousness: Vol. 3. The negative affects: Anger and fear.* New York: Springer.

Vincent-Buffault, A. (1991). *The history of tears: Sensibility and sentimentality in France* (T. Bridgeman, Trans.). New York: St. Martin's Press.

Wellenkamp, J. C. (1992). Variation in the social and cultural organization of emotions: The meaning of crying and the importance of compassion in Toraja, Indonesia. In D. D. Franks & V. Gecas (Eds.), *Social perspectives on emotion* (Vol. 1, pp. 189–216). Greenwich, CT: JAI Press.

39

Self-Conscious Emotions: Embarrassment, Pride, Shame, and Guilt

MICHAEL LEWIS

In Chapter 16, I have suggested a model for the emergence of emotional life in the first 3 to 4 years of life. Here, I focus on a unique set of emotions that emerge late and that require certain cognitive abilities for their elicitation. Whereas the emotions that appear early, such as joy, sadness, fear, and anger, have received considerable attention, this set of later-appearing emotions has received relatively little attention. There are likely to be many reasons for this. One reason is that these self-conscious emotions cannot be described solely by examining a particular set of facial movements; they necessitate the observation of bodily action more than facial cues (Darwin, 1872/1965).

A second reason for their neglect is the fact that there are no clear, specific elicitors of these particular emotions. Happiness, for example, can be elicited by seeing a significant other, and fear can be elicited by the approach of a stranger; however, there are few specific situations that will elicit shame, pride, guilt, or embarrassment. These self-conscious emotions are likely to require classes of events that can only be identified by the individuals themselves. Consider pride. What kinds of elicitors are necessary for pride to take place? Pride requires a large number of factors, all having to do with cognitions related to the self. Pride occurs when one makes a comparison or evaluates one's behavior *vis-à-vis* some standard, rule, or goal (SRG) and finds that one has

succeeded. Shame or guilt, on the other hand, occurs when such an evaluation leads to the conclusion that one has failed.

The elicitation of self-conscious emotions involves elaborate cognitive processes that have, at their heart, the notion of self. Although some theories—psychoanalysis, for example (see Freud, 1936/1963, and Erikson, 1950)—have argued for some universal elicitors of shame, such as failure at toilet training or exposure of the backside, the idea of an automatic, noncognitive elicitor of these emotions does not make much sense. Cognitive processes must be the elicitors of these complex emotions (Lewis, 1992a). It is the way we think or what we think about that becomes the elicitor of pride, shame, guilt, or embarrassment. There may be a one-to-one correspondence between thinking certain thoughts and the occurrence of a particular emotion; however, in the case of this class of emotions, the elicitor is a cognitive event. This does not mean that the earlier emotions, those called "primary" or "basic," are elicited by noncognitive events. Cognitive factors may play a role in the elicitation of any emotion; however, the nature of the cognitive events is much less articulated and differentiated in the earlier ones (Plutchik, 1980).

In order to explore these self-conscious emotions, we need first to articulate the role of self in their elicitation. Following this, an attempt at a working definition through a cognitive–attributional model is presented. The chapter focuses on shame, pride, guilt, and embarrassment, although other self-conscious emotions could be included—for example, jealousy, empathy, and envy.

THE ROLE OF SELF

Recently, there has been an attempt to clarify those specific aspects of self that are involved in self-conscious emotions—in particular, the self-conscious *evaluative* emotions (Lewis, 1992b). Self-conscious evaluative emotions first involve a set of standards, rules, or goals (SRGs). These SRGs are inventions of the culture that are transmitted to children and involve their learning of, and willingness to consider, these SRGs as their own. This process of incorporating SRGs has been discussed recently by Stipek, Recchia, and McClintic (1992). What is apparent from the work of Stipek et al. is that the process of incorporation starts quite early in life. SRGs imply self-evaluation, for it would make little sense if we had SRGs but had no evaluation of our action in regard to them.

Having self-evaluative capacity allows for two distinct outcomes: We can evaluate our behavior and hold ourselves responsible for the action being evaluated, or we can hold ourselves not responsible. In the attribution literature, these outcomes have been called an "internal attribution" and an "external attribution," respectively (Weiner, 1986). If we conclude that we are not responsible, then evaluation of our behavior ceases. However, if we evaluate ourselves as responsible, then we can evaluate our behavior as successful or unsuccessful *vis-à-vis* the SRGs. The determination of success or failure resides within the individual and is based on the nature of the SRG that is set. For example, if a student believes that only receiving an A in an exam constitutes success, then receiving a B represents a failure for that student; on the other hand, a B may be considered a success by another. Still another type of cognition related to the self has to do with the evaluation of oneself in terms of specific or global attributions. "Global self-attributions" refer to the whole self, whereas "specific self-attributions" refer to specific features or actions of the self (see Dweck & Leggett, 1988; Weiner, 1986).

The need for cognitive elicitors having to do with the self was known to Darwin (1872/

1965). Darwin not only described the basic, primary, or early emotions, but also dealt with the self-conscious emotions. Darwin saw these latter emotions as involving the self, although he was not able to distinguish among the various types (see also Tomkins, 1963, and Izard, 1979, for similar problems). For example, Darwin believed that blushing, which could be a sign of either shyness, embarrassment, or shame and guilt, was caused by how we appear to others; as he put it, "the thinking about others, thinking of us . . . excites a blush" (Darwin, 1872/1965, p. 325). His observation in regards to blushing indicates his concern with two issues: the issue of appearance and the issue of consciousness. He repeatedly made the point that these emotions depend on sensitivity to the opinion of others, whether good or bad. Thus, he emphasized the distinction between emotions that require opinion or thought of others, and emotions that do not suggest that two different kinds of cognitive processes are involved.

The distinction between self-conscious emotions and primary or basic emotions remains one of concern. The idea that there is a basic set of emotions grows out of the idea of human instincts or propensities. If they are basic, prewired, or genetically given, they have to be limited in number. Although we recognize an enormous variety of emotions, the existence of each one as necessitating unique and discrete "wiring" is too burdensome a characterization of the nervous system. Instead of positing this complex set of emotions, many have argued that there is only a select number of basic, primary, or pure emotions (see Ortony, Clore, & Collins, 1988, and Oatley & Johnson-Laird, 1987, for a contrary view). In order to resolve this problem in regard to self-conscious emotions, we might instead make the distinction between emotions that involve few or simple cognitive processes and emotions that involve complex cognitive processes (Darwin, 1872/1965; Plutchik, 1980).

TOWARD A WORKING DEFINITION

A most difficult task is to try to distinguish among the different types of self-conscious emotions (e.g., embarrassment, shyness, shame, and guilt). As Darwin's analysis makes clear, all of these emotions are likely to produce blushing. Since Darwin viewed blushing as a human species-specific behavior, he also viewed these emotions as unique to humans as well. However, blushing occurs with any one of these emotions, so it is clear that blushing will do us little good in distinguishing among them.

One can turn to the psychoanalytic literature; however, its focus on guilt rather than shame (see Broucek, 1991, and Morrison, 1989, for exceptions) makes this literature suspect. For example, Freud (1905/1953) discussed the function of guilt but said little about shame. For Freud, the superego—the mechanism by which the standards of the parents are incorporated into the self, specifically via the child's fear that the parents will respond to transgression by withdrawal of love or even by punishment—is the initial source of the feeling of guilt. Freud's discussion of guilt in relationship to the superego is similar to his discussion of guilt in relation to the instinctual drives and their expression. For Freud, anxiety or fear is translatable directly into guilt. The two stages in the development of the sense of guilt related to the superego are (1) the fear of authority and (2) the fear of the superego itself, once the authority standards are incorporated. In the well-developed superego, the sense of guilt arises not only when a violation is committed, but even when a violation is being anticipated.

The guilt that Freud focused on is not a guilt related to the whole self, but rather a guilt related to one's action (see Lewis, 1992a, for this distinction). For Freud, guilt is a specific and focused response to a transgression that can also be rectified by abstinence and penance. Freud's focus on guilt, not shame, can also be found in his discussion of psychopathology. It is to be found in the overdeveloped sense of guilt resulting from an overdeveloped ego. Within normal functioning, the superego condemns the ego; this condemnation, in turns, give rise to normal guilt. When Freud did mention shame, he usually did so in the context of drives and impulses that require restriction. So, for example, in discussing the abandon impulses having to do with the erogenous zones, he stated that these impulses

would seem in themselves to be perverse—that is, to arise from erogenic zones, and to derive their activity from instincts which, in view of the direction of the subjects' development, can arouse only unpleasant feelings. They [the impulses]

consequently evoke opposing mental forces [reacting impulses] which, in order to suppress this displeasure affectively, build up the mental dams of . . . disgust, shame and morality. (Freud, 1905/1953, p. 178)

More recently, Erikson (1950) has discussed shame, but he had no more success in distinguishing between shame and guilt than the earlier psychoanalysts. Erikson turned more to the Darwinian view when he suggested that shame arises when "one is completely exposed and conscious of being looked at, in a word, self-conscious" (1950, pp. 223–224). Again, this self-consciousness is an undifferentiated state of being—that is, shame, shyness, embarrassment, and guilt. Erikson tried to differentiate these terms but was not completely successful. For example, he discussed "visual shame" versus "auditory guilt," but did not develop these confusing concepts. I imagine that the reference to visual shame is based on Darwin's theory that shame derives from being looked at, and that in feeling shame, one wishes to hide one's face and to disappear. Although Erikson held to a more interactional view, one involving self and self-consciousness, he also indicated that the conditions necessary for feeling shame include being in an upright and exposed position. As he stated, "Clinical observation leads me to believe that shame has much to do with a consciousness of having a front and a back, especially a 'behind'" (Erikson, 1950, pp. 223–224). Erikson believed that shame is related to specific body acts, in particular toilet functions.

Erikson's familiar theory of ego challenges offered the clearest view of the differentiation between shame and guilt, their place in human life, and events likely to elicit them. Erikson's second challenge was autonomy versus shame and doubt. Autonomy is the attempt of the child to achieve, to do for itself—an attempt that is related to a developing sense of the self. Achieving muscular control, including control of the elimination of body waste, is the challenge of socialization and development at this life stage. Shame and doubt arise during this stage as the counterpoints to autonomy, the successful achievement. In other words, shame and doubt arise from the child's inability to fully control bodily functions. It is only after this basic ego task that the third ego task, initiative versus guilt, becomes significant. Here Erikson suggested that guilt has a reparative function. Erikson's developmental sequence indicated a recognition that shame and guilt are different emotions—that shame precedes guilt, and that they are associated in counterpoint with different ego tasks.

There is very little agreement as to the specific elicitors of shame, guilt, and embarrassment. Many events are capable of eliciting any one of them. No particular stimulus event has been identified as the trigger for shame or guilt. It would be easier to understand these self-conscious emotions if we could specify the class of external events likely to elicit them. If it were true that shame and guilt are similar to anxiety and that they reflect the subject's fear of uncontrollable impulses, then we could consider the causes of shame to be sexual or aggressive impulses. Alternatively, if we could prove that situations having to do with toilet or genital functions are likely to elicit shame, or if we could prove that the way we appear physically or how we behave in front of others may automatically elicit embarrassment, we could then specify situations that would help us to define these self-conscious emotions and increase our understanding of what causes them. There is no such clear cause-and-effect pattern, no event that can be used consistently as an elicitor of each of these self-conscious emotions.

Alternative theories having to do with self psychology are necessary. To anticipate the argument, let me state a few broad requirements. Success or failure *vis-à-vis* an SRG is likely to produce a signal to the self that results in self-reflection (see Mandler, 1975, for a discussion of events likely to cause self-reflection). This cognitive reflective process gives rise to self-attribution and to the specific emotions accompanying the different types of self-attribution. The importance of such a view resides in three important factors. First, the model does not attempt to specify what constitutes success or failure, or how the person goes about evaluating success or failure. Second, the model does not specify any particular SRG. In other words, it is not clear whether there are any specific stimuli that uniquely contribute to any of the self-conscious emotions. Third, the model assumes that self-attributions leading to specific emotions are internal events that reside in people themselves, although the SRGs are taught by others.

Although this model is based on a phenomenological and cognitive–attributional model, I do not mean to suggest that the self-conscious emotions are epiphenomenological or deserve "lower status" than the cognitive–attributional processes themselves. These self-conscious emotions may have discrete and specific locations, as well as specific processes that are themselves "bodily" in nature. The cognitions associated with these emotions may serve simply as elicitors of specific emotions in the same way as do other stimuli, such as the social behavior of others, loud noises, or sudden and uncontrolled events. The important point here is that specific emotions can be elicited through a variety of attributions. The idea that cognitions can lead to emotions has been poorly received by some, who believe that this idea implies that cognitions have real status whereas emotions are epiphenomenological (Schachter & Singer, 1962). I mean to give emotions the same status as cognitions. Just as cognitions can lead to emotions, emotions can lead to cognitions. The theory implies no status difference.

A COGNITIVE–ATTRIBUTIONAL THEORY

Figure 39.1 presents a structural model for defining various self-conscious emotions. In the figure, A, B, and C represent cognitive processes that serve as stimuli for these emotions.

SELF-CONSCIOUS EVALUATIVE EMOTIONS

FIGURE 39.1. Structural model for the elicitation of self-conscious evaluative emotions. Reprinted by permission from Lewis (1992c, p. 7).

Standards, Rules, and Goals

The first feature of the model has to do with the SRGs that govern our behavior. All of us have beliefs about what is acceptable for others and for ourselves in regard to actions, thoughts, and feelings. This set of beliefs, or SRGs, constitutes the information one acquires through culturalization in a particular society. SRGs differ across different societies, across groups within societies, across different time epochs, and among individuals of different ages. The standards of our culture are varied and complex, yet each of us knows at least some of them. Moreover, each of us has a unique set. To become a member of any group requires that we learn them. I can think of no group that does not have SRGs, or in which violation of SRGs does not lead to negative sanctions. These SRGs are acquired through a variety of processes. They are prescribed by the culture at large, as well as by the influences of specific groups, such as family and peers.

It is safe to claim that by the age of 1 year, children are beginning to learn the appropriate action patterns reflecting the SRGs of the culture. By the second year of life, children show some understanding about appropriate and inappropriate behavior (Heckhausen, 1984; Kagan, 1981). Recent work indicates that by the beginning of the third year of life children already have SRGs and seem to show distress when they violate them (Heckhausen, 1984; Lewis, Alessandri, & Sullivan, 1992; Stipek, 1983). The acquisition of SRGs continues across the lifespan; however, some emerge early.

Evaluation

The evaluation of one's actions, thoughts, and feelings in terms of SRGs is the second cognitive–evaluative process that serves as a stimulus for self-conscious emotions. Two major aspects of this process are considered; the first has to do with the internal and external aspects of evaluation. For the model to work in describing the process of eliciting emotions, internal evaluation, as opposed to either no evaluation or external evaluation, is necessary. Individuals differ in their characteristic evaluative response. Moreover, situations differ in the likelihood that they will cause a particular evaluative response. The second consideration has to do with how individuals make a determination about success or failure in regard to any specific standard.

Internal versus External Evaluation

Within the field of attributional studies, the problem of internal versus external attribution has received considerable attention (Weiner, 1986). People violate SRGs but often do not attribute the failure to themselves. They may explain their failure in terms of chance or the actions of others (Seligman, 1975; Seligman et al., 1984). Internal and external evaluations are functions both of situational factors and of individual characteristics. There are people who are likely to blame themselves no matter what happens. Dweck and Leggett (1988), in studying causes of success and failure within academic fields, found that many children blamed their success or failure on external forces, although there were as many who were likely to evaluate success and failure in terms of their own actions. Interestingly, strong sex differences emerged: In academic achievement, boys were more apt to hold themselves responsible for their success and others for their failure, whereas girls were apt to hold others responsible for their success and themselves for their failure.

Success or Failure

Another feature of the self-evaluation process has to do with the socialization of what constitutes success or failure. Once one has assumed responsibility (internal evaluation), exactly how one comes to evaluate an action, thought, or feeling as a success or a failure is not well understood. This aspect of self-evaluation is particularly important because, as we can see from Figure 39.1, the same SRGs can result in radically different feelings, depending upon whether success or failure is attributed to oneself.

Many factors are involved in producing inaccurate or unique evaluations of success or failure. These include early failures in the self-system leading to narcissistic disorders (see Morrison, 1989), harsh socialization experience, and high levels of reward for success or punishment for failure (see Lewis, 1992a). The evaluation of one's behavior in terms of success and failure is a very important aspect of the organization of plans and the determination of new goals and new plans.

Attribution about Self

Another attribution in regard to the self has to do with "global" or "specific" evaluations about the self (Beck, 1967, 1979; Seligman, 1975). "Global" attribution refers to an individual's propensity to focus on the total self. Thus, for any particular behavior violation, some individuals, some of the time, are likely to focus on the totality of the self; they use such self-evaluative phrases as "Because I did this, I am bad (or good)." Janoff-Bulman's (1979) distinction between "characterological" and "behavioral" self-blame is particularly relevant here.

On such occasions, the focus is upon the self, both as object and as subject. The self becomes embroiled in the self, because the evaluation of the self by the self is total. There is no way out. The focus is not upon the individual's behavior, but upon the total self. There is little wonder that in using such global attribution one can think of nothing else, and one becomes confused and speechless (H. B. Lewis, 1971). Because of this, one is unable to act and is driven from the field of action into hiding or disappearing.

"Specific" attribution refers to individuals' propensity in some situations, some of the time, to focus on specific actions of the self. That is, their self-evaluation is not global, but specific. It is not the total self that has done something wrong or good; instead, particular behaviors are judged. At such times as these, individuals will use such evaluative phrases as "What I did was wrong, and I mustn't do it again." Notice that for such occurrences, the individual's focus is not on the totality of the self but on the specific behavior of the self in a specific situation, in interaction with objects or persons. Here the focus is on the actions of the self or the effect on other selves.

Global versus specific self-focus may be a personality style. Global attributions for negative events are generally uncorrelated with global attributions for positive events. It is only when positive or negative events are taken into account that relatively stable and consistent attributional patterns are observed. Some individuals are likely to be stable in their global and specific evaluations; under most conditions of success or failure, these subjects are likely to maintain a global or specific posture in regard to self-attribution. In the attribution literature, such dispositional factors are thought to have important consequences upon a variety of fixed "personality patterns." So, for example, depressed individuals are likely to make stable global attributions, whereas non-depressed individuals are less likely to be stable in their global attributions (Beck, 1979).

In addition to the dispositional factors relating to specific or global attributions, there are likely to be situational constraints as well. Some have called these "prototypic situations." That is, although there are dispositional factors, not all people all the time are involved in either global or specific attributions. Unfortunately, these situational factors have not been well studied. It seems reasonable that certain classes of situations should be more likely than others to elicit a particular focus, but exactly what classes of stimuli are likely to elicit global or specific attributions remain unknown (see Lewis, 1992a).

MAKING SENSE OF THE MODEL

Given these three sets of activities—(1) the establishment of one's SRGs, (2) the evaluation of success or failure of one's action in regard to these, and (3) the attribution about the self—it is now possible to see how these factors bear on some self-conscious emotional states. It is important to point out that this model is symmetrical in relation to positive and negative self-conscious emotions. Because of this, it focuses not only upon shame and guilt, but upon the other side of the axis, hubris and pride. It is the cognitive–evaluative process of the organism itself that elicits these states. The immediate elicitors of these self-conscious emotions are cognitive in nature.

The model distinguishes among four emotional states. Notice that shame is a consequence of a failure evaluation relative to the SRGs when the person makes a global evaluation of the self. Guilt is also the consequence of a failure evaluation; however, the focus is on the self's specific action. A parallel exists as a consequence of success. When success is evaluated and the person makes a global attribution, hubris (pridefulness)[1] is the resulting emotion; when success is evaluated and the person makes a specific attribution, pride is the resulting emotion. With these definitions, I move to a discussion of shame, guilt, hubris, and pride. In addition, embarrassment and shyness are discussed.

Shame

Shame is the product of a complex set of cognitive activities: individuals' evaluation of their actions in regard to their SRGs and their global self-evaluation. The phenomenological experience of the person having shame is a wish to hide, disappear, or die (H. B. Lewis, 1971; Lewis, 1992a). It is a highly negative and painful state that also results in the disruption of ongoing behavior, confusion in thought, and an inability to speak. The physical action accompanying shame is a shrinking of the body, as though to disappear from the eye of the self or the other. Because of the intensity of this emotional state, the global attack on the self-system, all that individuals can do when presented with such a state is to attempt to rid themselves of it. However, since it is a global attack on the self, people have great difficulty in dissipating this emotion. When shamed repeatedly, people do employ strategies to rid

themselves of this feeling, including a variety of disassociative behaviors (see Lewis, 1992a).

Shame is not produced by any specific situation, but rather by an individual's interpretation of an event. Even more important is that shame is not related necessarily to the event's being public or private. Although many hold that shame is a public failure, this need not be so. Failure, attributed to the whole self, can be either public or private. Shame may be public, but it is as likely to be private. Each of us can think of private events when we say to ourselves, "I'm ashamed of having done that." Shame can center around moral action as well. Thus, when persons violate some moral SRG, they are ashamed.

Guilt

The emotional state of guilt or regret is produced when individuals evaluate their behavior as a failure but focus on the specific features or actions of the self that led to the failure. Unlike the focus in shame on the global self, the focus in guilt is on the self's actions and behaviors that are likely to repair the failure. From a phenomenological point of view, individuals are pained by their failure, but this pained feeling is directed to the cause of the failure or the object of harm. Because the cognitive–attributional process focuses on the action of the self rather than on the totality of self, the feeling that is produced—guilt—is not as intensely negative as shame and does not lead to confusion and to the loss of action. In fact, the emotion of guilt always has associated with it a corrective action that the individual can take (but does not necessarily take) to repair the failure. Rectification of the failure and preventing it from occurring again are the two possible corrective paths. Whereas in shame we see the body hunched over itself in an attempt to hide and disappear, in guilt we see an individual moving in space as if trying to repair an action (see Barrett & Zahn-Waxler, 1987). The marked postural differences between guilt and shame are helpful both in distinguishing these emotions and in measuring individual differences. We might point to blushing as a measure also distinguishing guilt from shame; however, because of the variability in the likelihood of individuals to blush, the use of blushing is not an accurate index.

---

[1] I use here the Greek term "hubris" to differentiate what I mean from "pride," because of the general confusion in the use of the term "pride." As I have warned before, the usage issues associated with these emotions render careful analysis most difficult. Not only do we have the problems of differentiating shame from guilt, embarrassment, and shyness, but we also have the difficulty of distinguishing between different kinds of pride. We can think of two uses of the term "pride." On the one hand, we can think of pride in one's accomplishment—the pride one feels in being successful in fulfilling a particular goal and activity. We recognize this in our discussions of achievement motivation and of how children learn to feel proud about their achievements in terms of a particular SRG. On the other hand, we can also use the term "pride" to indicate a negative emotional state. One speaks of the "proud man" or the "proud woman" with some disdain. The Bible speaks of pride going before a fall, and throughout the Old and New Testaments, we have examples of how false pride brings down a man. The story of Job is but one example of pride and the Lord's abhorrence of it. It is clear that the term "pride" carries a surplus of meaning, and that if we are to make any headway at all, we need to distinguish between specific pride and global pride. I have done so here by the use of the term "hubris" to represent global pride and "pride" to represent specific achievement.

Because in guilt the focus is on the specific, individuals are capable of ridding themselves of this emotional state through action. The corrective action can be directed toward the self as well as toward the other; thus, unlike shame, which is a melding of the self as subject and object, in guilt the self is differentiated from the object. As such, the emotion is less intense and more capable of dissipation.

There are levels of this negative state, having to do with the ease or availability of corrective action. In some cases, corrective action may not be as readily available as in others. In all cases, however, there is an attempt at corrective action. Should the corrective action not be forthcoming, either in thought, feeling, or deed, it is possible that a guilt experience can be converted into one of shame (H. B. Lewis, 1971). Here, then, is another difference between shame and guilt. We can be ashamed of our guilty action, but we cannot be guilty over being ashamed, suggesting a levels difference and a directional difference in the experiencing of these emotions. The emotion of guilt lacks the negative intensity of shame. It is not self-destroying, and as such can be viewed as a more useful emotion in motivating specific and corrective action. However, because it is less intense, it may not convey the motivation necessary for change or correction.

Hubris

Hubris is defined as exaggerated pride or self-confidence often resulting in retribution. As noted above (see footnote 1), it is something dislikeable and to be avoided. Hubris is a consequence of an evaluation of success in regard to one's SRGs where the focus is on the global self. In this emotion, the individual focuses on the total self as successful. Hubris is associated with such descriptions as "puffed up"; in extreme cases, it is associated with grandiosity or with narcissism (Morrison, 1989). In fact, "hubristic" is defined as "insolent" or "contemptuous." Unlike shame, it is highly positive and emotionally rewarding—that is, the person feels good about the self.

Hubris is, however, an emotion difficult to sustain because of its globality; there is no specific action that precipitates the feeling. Because such a feeling is alluring yet transient, people prone to hubris derive little satisfaction from the emotion. Consequently, they seek out and invent situations likely to repeat this emo-

tional state. They can do this either by altering their SRGs or by re-evaluating what constitutes success in their actions, thoughts, or feelings.

From the outside, other people observe an individual who is experiencing hubris with some disdain. Hubristic people have difficulty in their interpersonal relations, since their hubris is likely to interfere with the wishes, needs, and desires of others, in which case there is likely to be an interpersonal conflict. Moreover, given the contemptuousness associated with hubris, the other persons are likely to be shamed by the nature of the actions of the person having this emotion. The three problems associated with hubris, therefore, are that (1) it is a transient but addictive emotion; (2) it is not related to a specific action, and therefore requires altered patterns of goal setting or evaluation of what constitutes success; and (3) it interferes with interpersonal relationships because of its contemptuous and insolent nature.

Pride

The emotion I have labeled "pride" is the consequence of a successful evaluation of a specific action. The phenomenological experience is joy over an action, thought, or feeling well done. Here, the focus of pleasure is specific and related to a particular behavior. In pride, the self and object are separated, as in guilt. Unlike shame and hubris, where subject and object are fused, pride focuses the organism on its action; the organism is engrossed in the specific action that gives it pride. Some investigators have likened this state to achievement motivation (see, e.g., Heckhausen, 1984; Stipek et al., 1992)—an association that seems particularly apt. Because this positive state is associated with a particular action, individuals have available to themselves the means by which they can reproduce the state. Notice that, unlike hubris, pride's specific focus allows for action. Because of the general use of the term "pride" to refer to "hubris," "efficacy," and "satisfaction" (see footnote 1), the study of pride as hubris has received relatively little attention. Dweck and Leggett (1988) have approached this problem through the use of individuals' implicit theories about the self, which are cognitive attributions that serve as the stimuli for the elicitation of the self-conscious emotion of mastery.

EMBARRASSMENT
AND SHYNESS

In the discussion to this point, it is clear that one can differentiate, from a behavioral as well as a phenomenological point of view, shame and guilt. There are, however, two further emotions that tend to be confused with these two—embarrassment and shyness.

Shyness

Izard and Tyson (1986) consider shyness to be sheepishness, bashfulness, a feeling of uneasiness or psychological discomfort in social situations, and oscillation between fear and interest or between avoidance and approach. In this description, shyness is related to fear and is a nonevaluative emotion centered around the individual's discomfort response to others. Such a description fits Buss's (1980) notion of shyness as an emotional response elicited by experiences of novelty or conspicuousness. For Buss, shyness and fear are closely related and represent a fearfulness toward others. A way of distinguishing shyness from shame is that it appears much earlier than either shame or guilt.

Such an approach to shyness seems reasonable because it fits with other notions relating the self to others, or what we might call the "social self." Eysenck (1954) has characterized people as social and asocial by genetic disposition, and recently Kagan, Reznick, and Snedman (1988) have pointed out the physiological responses of children they call "inhibited." These inhibited or shy children are withdrawn, are uncomfortable in social situations, and appear fearful. Shyness may be a dispositional factor not related to self-evaluation. Rather, it may simply be the discomfort of being in the company of other social objects—in other words, the opposite of sociability (Lewis & Feiring, 1989).

Embarrassment

For some, embarrassment is closely linked to shame (Izard, 1979; Tomkins, 1963). The most notable difference between embarrassment and shame is the intensity level. Whereas shame appears to be an intense and disruptive emotion, embarrassment is clearly less intense and does not involve the disruption of thought and language that shame does. Second, in terms of body posture, people who are embarrassed do not assume the posture of one wishing to hide, disappear, or die. In fact, their bodies reflect an ambivalent approach and avoidant posture. Repeated looking and then looking away, accompanied by smiling behavior, seem to index embarrassment (see Edelman, 1987; Geppert, 1986; Lewis, Stanger, & Sullivan, 1989). Rarely in a shame situation do we see gaze aversion accompanied by smiling behavior. Thus, from a behavioral point of view, these two emotions appear to be different.

Phenomenologically, embarrassment is less clearly differentiated from shame than from guilt. People often report that embarrassment is "a less intense experience of shame." Situations similar to those that invoke shame are found to invoke embarrassment, although, as I have mentioned, its intensity, duration, and disruptive quality are not the same. It is important to differentiate two types of embarrassed behavior, since this may help us distinguish embarrassment from shame: (1) embarrassment as self-consciousness and (2) embarrassment as mild shame.

Embarrassment as Self-Consciousness

In certain situations of exposure, people become embarrassed. It is not related to negative evaluation, as is shame. Perhaps the best example is the case of being complimented. One phenomenological experience of a speaker who appears before an audience is that of embarrassment caused by the positive comments of the introduction. Consider the moment when the speaker is introduced: The person introducing the speaker extols his or her virtues. Surprisingly, praise, rather than displeasure or negative evaluation, elicits embarrassment!

Another example of this type of embarrassment can be seen in reactions to public display. When people observe someone looking at them, they are apt to become self-conscious, look away, and touch or adjust their bodies. Women being observed will often adjust or touch their hair; men are less likely to touch their hair, but may adjust their clothes or change their body posture. In few cases do the observed people look sad. If anything, they appear pleased by the attention. This combination—gaze turned away briefly, no frown, and nervous touching—looks like this first type of embarrassment.

A third example of embarrassment as exposure can be seen in the following experiment: When I wish to demonstrate that embarrassment can be elicited just by exposure, I announce that I am going to point randomly to a student. I repeatedly mention that my pointing is random and that it does not reflect a judgment about the person. I close my eyes and point. My pointing invariably elicits embarrassment in the student pointed to.

In each of these examples, there is no negative evaluation of the self in regard to SRGs. In these situations, it is difficult to imagine embarrassment as a less intense form of shame. Since praise cannot readily lead to an evaluation of failure, it is likely that embarrassment resulting from compliments, from being looked at, and from being pointed to has more to do with the exposure of the self than with evaluation. Situations other than praise come to mind, in which a negative evaluation can be inferred, although it may not be the case. Take, for example, walking into a room before the speaker has started to talk. It is possible to arrive *on time* only to find people already seated. When walking into the room, eyes turn toward you, and you may experience embarrassment. One could say that there is a negative self-evaluation: "I should have been earlier; I should not have made noise (I did not make noise)". I believe, however, that the experience of embarrassment in this case may not be elicited by negative self-evaluation, but simply by public exposure.

Embarrassment as Mild Shame

The second class of embarrassment, which I call "embarrassment as mild shame," seems to me to be related to a negative self-evaluation. The difference in intensity can probably be attributed to the nature of the failed SRG. Some SRGs are more or less associated with the core of self; for me, failure at driving a car is less important than is failure at helping a student. Failures associated with less important and central SRGs result in embarrassment rather than shame. If this analysis is correct, then it is possible that each of the four self-conscious emotions has a milder or less intense form.

It may well be that embarrassment may not be the same as shame. From a phenomenological stance, they appear very different. On the other hand, there is the possibility that embarrassment and shame are in fact related, and that they only vary in intensity. It is safe to say that, as a working definition, there appear to be at least two different types of embarrassment.

CONCLUSION

The study of self-conscious emotions has only recently begun. The model outlined here offers an opportunity to consider and to define carefully some of the self-conscious emotions. Unless we develop a more accurate taxonomy, we will be unable to proceed in our study of these emotions. Given the renewed interest in emotional life, it is now appropriate to consider these more complex emotions, rather than the more "primary" or "basic" ones. Moreover, as others have pointed out, these self-conscious emotions are intimately connected with other emotions, such as anger and sadness (see, e.g., H. B. Lewis, 1971; Lewis, 1992a; Morrison, 1989). Finally, given the place of self-evaluation in adult life, it seems clear that the self-conscious evaluative emotions are likely to stand in the center of our emotional life (Dweck & Leggett, 1988; Heckhausen, 1984).

REFERENCES

Barrett, K. C., & Zahn-Waxler, C. (1987, April). *Do toddlers express guilt?* Poster presented at the meeting of the Society for Research in Child Development, Toronto.

Beck, A. T. (1967). *Depression: Clinical, experimental, and theoretical aspects.* New York: Harper & Row.

Beck, A. T. (1979). *Cognitive therapy and emotional disorders.* New York: Times Mirror.

Broucek, F. J. (1991). *Shame and the self.* New York: Guilford Press.

Buss, A. H. (1980). *Self-consciousness and social anxiety.* San Francisco: W. H. Freeman.

Darwin, C. (1965). *The expression of the emotions in man and animals.* Chicago: University of Chicago Press. (Original work published 1872)

Dweck, C. S., & Leggett, E. L. (1988). A social-cognitive approach to motivation and personality. *Psychological Review, 95,* 256–273.

Edelman, R. J. (1987). *The psychology of embarrassment.* Chichester, England: Wiley.

Erikson, E. H. (1950). *Childhood and society.* New York: Norton.

Eysenck, H. J. (1954). *The psychology of politics.* London: Routledge & Kegan Paul.

Freud, S. (1936). *The problem of anxiety.* New York: Norton.

Freud, S. (1953). Three essays on the theory of sexuality. In J. Strachey (Ed. and Trans.), *The standard edition of the complete psychological works of Sigmund Freud*

(Vol. 7, pp. 123–231). London: Hogarth Press. (Original work published 1905)

Freud, S. (1963). *The problem of anxiety* (H. A. Bunker, trans.) New York: Norton. (Original work published 1936)

Geppert, U. (1986). *A coding system for analyzing behavioral expressions of self-evaluative emotions.* Munich: Max-Planck-Institute for Psychological Research.

Heckhausen, H. (1984). Emergent achievement behavior: Some early developments. In J. Nicholls (Eds.), *The development of achievement motivation* (pp. 1–32). Greenwich, CT: JAI Press.

Izard, C. E. (1977). *Human emotions.* New York: Plenum Press.

Izard, C. E. (1979). *The Maximally Discriminative Facial Movement Coding System (MAX).* Newark: Instructional Resources Center, University of Delaware.

Izard, C. E., & Tyson, M. C. (1986). Shyness as a discrete emotion. In W. H. Jones, J. M. Cheek, & S. R. Briggs (Eds.), *Shyness: Perspectives on research and treatment* (pp. 147–160). New York: Plenum Press.

Janoff-Bulman, R. (1979). Characterological versus behavioral self-blame: Inquiries into depression and rape. *Journal of Personality and Social Psychology, 37,* 1798–1809.

Kagan, J. (1981). *The second year.* Cambridge, MA: Harvard University Press.

Kagan, J., Reznick, J. S., & Snedman, N. (1988). Biological bases of childhood shyness. *Science, 240,* 167–171.

Lewis, H. B. (1971). *Shame and guilt in neurosis.* New York: International Universities Press.

Lewis, M. (1992a). *Shame, the exposed self.* New York: Free Press.

Lewis, M. (1992b). The self in self-conscious emotions. In D. Stipek, S. Recchia, & S. McClintic, Self-evaluation in young children. *Monographs of the Society for Research in Child Development, 57*(1, Serial No. 226), 85–95.

Lewis, M. (1992c, April). Shame, the exposed self. *Zero to Three,* pp. 6–10.

Lewis, M., Alessandri, S. M., & Sullivan, M. W. (1992). Differences in shame and pride as a function of children's gender and task difficulty. *Child Development, 63,* 630–638.

Lewis, M., & Feiring, C. (1989). Infant, mother, and mother–infant interaction behavior and subsequent attachment. *Child Development, 60,* 146–156.

Lewis, M., Stanger, C., & Sullivan, M. W. (1989). Deception in three-year-olds. *Developmental Psychology, 25,* 439–443.

Mandler, G. (1975). *Mind and emotion.* New York: Wiley.

Morrison, A. P. (1989). *Shame: The underside of narcissism.* Hillsdale, NJ: Analytic Press.

Oatley, K., & Johnson-Laird, P. N. (1987). Toward a cognitive theory of emotions. *Cognition and Emotion, 1,* 29–50.

Ortony, A., Clore, G. L., & Collins, A. (1988). *The cognitive structure of emotions.* New York: Cambridge University Press.

Plutchik, R. (1980). A general psychoevolutionary theory of emotion. In R. Plutchik & H. Kellerman (Eds.), *Emotion: Theory, research, and experience. Vol. 1. Theories of emotion* (pp. 3–33). New York: Academic Press.

Schachter, S., & Singer, J. E. (1962). Cognitive, social, and physiological determinants of emotional state. *Psychological Review, 69,* 379–399.

Seligman, M. E. P. (1975). *Helplessness: On depression, development, and death.* San Francisco: W. H. Freeman.

Seligman, M. E. P., Peterson, C., Kraslow, N., Tanenbaum, R., Alloy, L., & Abramson, L. (1984). Attributional style and depressible symptoms among children. *Journal of Abnormal Psychology, 39,* 235–238.

Stipek, D. J. (1983). A developmental analysis of pride and shame. *Human Development, 26,* 42–54.

Stipek, D. J., Recchia, S., & McClintic, S. (1992). Self-evaluation in young children. *Monographs of the Society for Research in Child Development, 57*(1, Serial No. 226).

Tomkins, S. S. (1963). *Affect, imagery, and consciousness: Vol. 2. The negative affects.* New York: Springer.

Weiner, B. (1986). *An attributional theory of motivation and emotion.* New York: Springer-Verlag.

40

Disgust

PAUL ROZIN
JONATHAN HAIDT
CLARK R. McCAULEY

North Americans do not eat cockroaches. We are likely to explain our revulsion to eating or even touching a cockroach by saying that cockroaches are dirty and carry disease, but this explanation is inadequate. Most of us will decline to drink our favorite juice if a dead cockroach has been dipped in our glass, even if the cockroach has been sterilized (Rozin, Millman, & Nemeroff, 1986). Our emotional reaction depends upon a remarkably abstract cognition: We do not even suggest that we can taste the essence of cockroach that contaminates the juice. North Americans do not eat cockroaches because cockroaches are disgusting. The problem for psychology is to learn more about what it means to say that something is disgusting, and to learn why some things are disgusting and others are not.

Our analysis of disgust elicitors in North Americans, in association with development of a scale of disgust sensitivity, has identified seven domains of disgust elicitors: certain foods or potential foods; body products; certain animals; certain sexual behaviors; contact with death or dead bodies; violations of the exterior envelope of the body, including gore and deformity; and poor hygiene. In addition, direct or indirect contact with unsavory human beings (interpersonal contamination) and certain moral offenses, such as stealing from a blind beggar, are often described as disgusting (Haidt, McCauley, & Rozin, 1992). Although all of these domains involve negative or unpleasant events, there are many kinds of negative events, such as rights violations or fear elicitors, that are not disgusting. The focus of this chapter is an attempt to make sense of this varied set of elicitors—that is, to describe the meaning of disgust within both developmental and cultural contexts.

We will argue for a path of development in individuals and cultures that extends from the presumed origin of disgust as a rejection response to bad tastes, to the full range of elicitors described above. We distinguish disgust from fear on the grounds that fear is primarily a response to actual or threatened harm to the body, whereas disgust is primarily a response to actual or threatened harm to the soul. Given the centrality of the soul in the understanding of disgust, we claim that although disgust has a precursor in nonhuman animals, it is the only one of the six or seven "basic" emotions that has been completely transformed in the human condition, making it a uniquely human emotion along with such emotions as guilt, shame, and embarrassment.

The review of disgust that we are about to present is based primarily on research by scholars from the United States, Canada and Western Europe, and is based on the emotion of disgust as experienced in those cultures. This is an extremely narrow base for what appears to be a universal emotion that is strongly influenced by culture. Indeed, there are reasons to believe that disgust would be highly elaborated and different from "Western" disgust among Hindu Indians, especially

in consideration of the central role that interpersonal contamination plays in Hindu social
organization (Marriott, 1968; Appadurai,
1981). When one considers that there are currently more living Hindu Indians than there
are people in all of North and South America,
the magnitude of this omission becomes clear.
We believe that there are many commonalities across culture, especially with respect to
what we call "core disgust," but recognize that
the range of elicitors—and in particular, the
expansion of elicitors into the social domain—
is quite variable.

DEFINING DISGUST

There are two classic papers describing disgust, published some 70 years apart. The first,
a chapter in Darwin's *The Expression of the
Emotions in Man and Animals* (1872/1965)
defined disgust as referring to "something revolting, primarily in relation to the sense of
taste, as actually perceived or vividly imagined;
and secondarily to anything which causes a
similar feeling, through the sense of smell,
touch and even of eyesight" (p. 253). Darwin
related disgust not only to the experience of
revulsion but to a characteristic facial expression. The second paper, by psychoanalyst
Andras Angyal (1941), held that "disgust is a
specific reaction towards the waste products
of the human and animal body" (p. 395).
Angyal related the strength of disgust to the
degree of intimacy of contact, with the mouth
as the most sensitive focus. Both of these
papers are rich in insights and intuitions about
disgust, and deserve repeated reading.

Tomkins's (1963) description of disgust
expanded on Angyal's idea that disgust is a
reaction to unwanted intimacy. According to
Tomkins, disgust is "recruited to defend the
self against psychic incorporation or any
increase in intimacy with a repellent object"
(p. 233). Our own definition of disgust, or what
we call "core disgust" in this chapter, derives
from those of Darwin, Angyal, and Tomkins:
"Revulsion at the prospect of (oral) incorporation of an offensive object. The offensive
objects are contaminants; that is, if they even
briefly contact an acceptable food, they tend
to render that food unacceptable" (Rozin &
Fallon, 1987, p. 23).

All of these definitions, and many others,
focus on the mouth and real or imagined

ingestion. Tomkins (1963, 1982) held that of
all the emotions, disgust has the clearest linkage to a specific motivation (hunger), and
functions to oppose this motive. Ekman and
Friesen (1975) see disgust as an aversion that
centers on oral rejection. Wierzbicka (1986)
defines disgust as feeling bad about another
person's action. This feeling is "similar to what
one feels when one has something in one's
mouth that tastes bad and when one wants to
cause it to come to be out of one's mouth"
(p. 590). The English term "disgust" itself
means "bad taste," and the facial expression of
disgust can be seen as functional in rejecting
unwanted foods and odors. The most distinct
physiological concomitant of disgust—nausea—is a food-related sensation that inhibits
ingestion. There is thus considerable reason to
believe that the mouth and eating are at the
core of disgust (Rozin & Fallon, 1987).

Nevertheless, it must be acknowledged that
the centrality of food and eating in the emotion of disgust is far from established at this
time. Indeed, there have been important
attempts to understand disgust without focusing on food and eating. Freud (1905/1953) saw
disgust as a means to rein in the polymorphous
sexuality of childhood and channel it to the
narrow class of acceptable adult objects. However, in harmony with Angyal, Freud (1910/
1957) also saw disgust as a means of curbing
the coprophilic impulses of childhood. Some
investigators have preferred to see disgust as
primarily a defense against infection; in this
view, disgust promotes cleanliness, especially
distancing from soft bacteria generating things
(Izard, 1977; Plutchik, 1980; Frijda, 1986;
Davey, 1992). Any animal is likely to profit by
reducing contact with decaying organic matter. Renner (1944) relates disgust particularly
to the strong human desire for clean skin.

DISGUST AS A BASIC EMOTION

A chapter on disgust in a *Handbook of Emotions* suggests in itself that disgust holds a special place among hundreds of possible emotions. There is much debate now as to whether
there are such things as basic emotions
(Ortony & Turner, 1990; Ekman, 1992), and
there are reasonable arguments on both sides.
However, it is clear that if there are basic
emotions, then disgust is one of them. Disgust
is on almost every list of basic emotions that

has at least four emotions in it, from Darwin's onwards (see, e.g., the table of emotion categorizations in Ortony, Clore, & Collins, 1988, p. 27). Disgust emerges as a basic emotion whether the primary criterion is facial (e.g., Darwin, 1872/1965; Ekman & Friesen, 1975), semantic (Johnson-Laird & Oatley, 1989), or eclectic (Izard, 1977; Scherer, 1992).

Disgust is relatively unique among the basic emotions in that it is specifically related to a particular motivational system (hunger) and to a particular part of the body (mouth). Disgust also plays a special role among the basic emotions in that it is a primary means for internalization of cultural prohibitions; that is, it is a major means of socialization. In this regard, it is similar to emotional reactions such as guilt, shame, and embarrassment. Finally, disgust should be of special interest to psychologists because it is relatively easy and ethical to elicit in experimental situations.

Criteria for qualification as a "basic" emotion vary. Perhaps the most clearly articulated set of conditions has been offered by Ekman (1992), and disgust meets these criteria about as well as any of the other "basic" emotions (which almost always include anger, fear, sadness, disgust, and happiness). In accord with Ekman's nine criteria, disgust involves (1) a universal signal (expression), (2) a comparable expression in other animals, (3) an emotion-specific physiology, (4) universal antecedent events, (5) coherence in response systems, (6) quick onset, (7) brief duration, (8) automatic appraisal mechanism, and (9) unbidden occurrence. We consider here in more detail a set of four properties thought to be essential to the concept of emotion.

Behavioral Component

Disgust is manifested as a distancing from some object, event or situation, and can be characterized as a rejection.

Physiological Component

Two types of physiological changes have been associated with disgust. One distinguishes disgust from other emotions: Only disgust is associated with a *specific* physiological state. This physiological state, nausea, is typically measured by self-report. As a quick review of one's own personal experience will indicate, nausea is neither a necessary nor a sufficient

condition for the experience of disgust, but it is clearly correlated with disgust. Another specific physiological aspect of disgust has been suggested by Angyal (1941), who pointed to increased salivation (itself associated with nausea and as a response to bad tastes) as a concomitant of disgust.

In spite of a large literature devoted to the search for physiological signatures of different emotions, we know of no experimental studies of the relation of disgust to nausea or salivation. Rather, the study of the physiological side of disgust has been limited to the more or less standard set of autonomic responses explored by psychophysiologists (heart rate, blood pressure, galvanic skin response [GSR]). In this limited arena, it appears that disgust is associated with parasympathetic response. As with other negative emotions, the GSR is increased in disgust; however, in accord with the parasympathetic flavor of disgust, and in contrast to the negative emotions of anger and fear, heart rate is stable or decreased (Levenson, Ekman, & Friesen, 1990; Levenson, 1992). Disgust may also be associated with changes in finger temperature (Zajonc & McIntosh, 1992) and in right frontal area brain activation (Davidson, 1992).

Expressive Component

The expressive component of disgust has been studied almost entirely with reference to the face. The characteristics of the "disgust face" have received particular attention from three researchers: Darwin (1872/1965), Izard (1971), and Ekman (Ekman, 1972; Ekman & Friesen, 1975). Although there is a family of facial movements that are related to disgust, authors are not in complete agreement about a prototypical disgust face. Thus, Darwin emphasized the gape (in the Facial Action Coding System [FACS; Ekman & Friesen, 1978], the gape is Action Unit [AU] 26), but also refers to retraction of the upper lip (AU 10) and, to some extent, the nose wrinkle (AU 9), dropping of the mouth corners (AU 15), and a few other movements. Izard (1971) also emphasizes the gape (AU 26) and the upper lip retraction (AU 10), with some associated movements; Ekman and Friesen (1975) focus on lip retraction (AU 10) and nose wrinkle (AU 9), along with a raising of the lower lip (AU 17).

What is clear from all of these accounts is that the activity centers around the mouth and nose, and that the movements tend either to discourage entry into the body (e.g., nose wrinkle, lower lip raise) or to encourage discharge (gape or tongue extension). With regard to the first function, Darwin (1872/1965) noted that "As the sensation of disgust primarily arises in connection with the act of eating and tasting, it is natural that its expression should consist chiefly in movements around the mouth" (p. 257). But Darwin also recognized the discharge function of the disgust expression by hypothesizing that disgust is a phylogenetic residue of the vomiting system. Any functional analysis of disgust expressions is thus complicated by the fact that disgust can be viewed as both a rejection of incorporated substances (hence the gape; Plutchik, 1980) and as an avoidance of such incorporation by closing the vulnerable aperture (the nose wrinkle or raised lower lip).

Qualia

Qualia, the mental or feeling component of emotion, may be at once the most central component of disgust and the most difficult to study. The qualia of disgust is often described as revulsion. Johnson-Laird and Oatley (1989), in their semantic analysis of emotions, identify disgust as one of five basic or primitive emotions on the grounds that only these five can exist as pure qualia, without a referent. That is, it is possible to say, "I feel disgust (fear, sadness), but I don't know why." We question whether this interesting criterion actually applies to disgust, for, unlike sadness, it seems to us to require a referent (Ortony & Clore, 1989).

ORIGINS OF DISGUST

Infrahuman Origins

In keeping with our supposition that disgust originates as food rejection is Darwin's (1872/1965) claim that it is the phylogenetic residue of a voluntary vomiting system. Note that Darwin indicates the gape as the primary facial indicant of disgust. Gaping in response to distasteful foods or foods associated with upper gastrointestinal illness has been reported in a number of animals, including coyotes, wolves, blue jays, and red-tailed hawks (reviewed in Garcia, Rusiniak, & Brett,

1977). The laboratory rat (Rattus norvegicus) shows a distinct gaping response, which has been studied in detail, to both innately distasteful bitter substances and other foods that have been paired with nausea (Grill & Norgren, 1978). The gape presumably serves to promote egress from the body, of either the contents of the mouth or those of the stomach. Although it is surely true that the gaping response is quite general to distasteful foods, we know of no direct evidence for this response in nonhuman primates. Indeed, in a review of facial expressions in nonhuman primates, Chevalier-Skolnikoff (1973) notes that "Contrary to Darwin's expectations, no counterpart to human disgust has been distinguished in monkeys" (p. 82). This same paper reports that primate facial expressions are linked to appropriate behaviors that relate to a number of other human emotions.

As already noted, it is possible that cleanliness of the body or nest, rather than food rejection, is the precursor of human disgust. Primates and many other mammals spend a great deal of time in grooming and related activities, and this activity is presumably selected for in terms of reduction of parasite load and microbial infection. Avoidance of feces or other decaying organic matter could be accounted for as an adaptation with the same function. Thus one might assume that decay is at the heart of disgust, insofar as animals may avoid spoiled food, spoilage in the nest, feces, or vomit.

There are some problems with this view, however. Feces ingestion is not uncommon in primates or other mammals, and has been implicated as an adaptive means of replenishing the gut flora (Barnes, 1962). Furthermore, although there are suggestions that at least some animal species prefer fresh to spoiled food (Steininger, 1950), it is not clear that there is a general aversion to spoiled foods. Although Plutchik (1980) sees disgust as a rejection response related to cleaning, vomiting, and defecating, there is just not very good evidence for a strong or reliable aversion to these entities or activities in nonhuman animals. In short, we are inclined to associate ourselves with the good company of Darwin (1872/1965) and hold that the bulk of evidence supports his claim that "The term 'disgust,' in its simplest sense, means something offensive to the taste" (p. 256).

Disgust Precursors in Infancy

In parallel with the results from rats and other animals, there appears to be an innate and present-at-birth rejection of bitter substances in humans, accompanied by a gape (Peiper, 1963; Steiner, 1979). Peiper (1963) presented evidence that strong stimulation in a particular modality (visual, oral, olfactory) would generate a face in the newborn that would close the appropriate sensory entry point, with some radiation to other sense organs. Hence bright lights would cause eye closing, strong odors would cause nostril closing (wrinkling—AU 9), and strong tastes would elicit mouth closing. Of course, because the oral receptors actually physically capture the offending stimulus, a ridding response (gaping) may be more appropriate than a closing off.

The bitterness–gape link (Steiner, 1979) surely exists in newborns, but the linkage is much more statistical than categorical. Thus, Rosenstein and Oster (1988), in careful measurements using the FACS (Ekman & Friesen, 1978) on the videotaped responses of newborns to various tastants, reported a gape in 75% of infants in response to bitterness (quinine), and a similar gape in response to sourness (citric acid) in 50% of infants (each infant was tested twice for each tastant, and occurrence of a specific response on either occasion was scored as presence in the percentages cited here). On the other hand, lip purses (AU 18) occurred in 33% of infants in response to quinine, and 89% in response to citric acid. Hence there was a mixture of gapes and lip purses (and a few other facial movements) in response to both bitter and sour stimulation. There was also some confusion by raters who viewed the videotapes and guessed which of the four basic tastants had been presented. This same confusion occurs in adults viewing photographs of purse or gape faces made by adults, and assigning appropriate situations (e.g., eating something bitter, eating something sour) to them (Rozin, Ebert, & Lowery, 1992). Overall, however, there is no doubt, as Steiner (1979) pointed out, that the predominant response to bitterness is a gape (AU 26 or 27).

So far as we know, there is no sense of offensiveness or rejection outside of the sensory realm in either infants or nonhumans, and hence no gape elicitors other than certain negative tastes. Disgust seems to be a cultural acquisition—a supposition confirmed by Malson's (1964/1972) review of some 50 feral humans, none of whom showed any sign of disgust.

CORE DISGUST

Disgust as a Category of Food Rejection

Disgust has been described as one of four categories of food rejection, the others being distaste (rejection motivated by bad sensory properties), danger (motivated by fear of harm to body), and inappropriateness (culturally classified as not edible) (Rozin & Fallon, 1980; Fallon & Rozin, 1983; Rozin, 1984). Disgust is differentiated from danger and distaste in that the basis for rejection is ideational (knowledge of the nature or origin of an elicitor). Disgust differs from the category of inappropriateness (e.g., paper, marigolds, and sand) in that disgusting potential foods are thought to be offensive and contaminating. Of the four categories of food rejection, it appears that the only rejection category that has any innate exemplars is distaste (e.g., bitterness). The danger category emerges in the first few years of life, and disgust breaks off from distaste at some later point, perhaps between 4 and 8 years, for American children (Rozin, Hammer, Oster, Horowitz, & Marmara, 1986; Rozin, Fallon, & Augustoni-Ziskind, 1986). If we consider the defining characteristics of core disgust to be (1) linkage to food and eating, (2) sense of offensiveness, and (3) contamination sensitivity, then it seems unlikely that a clear disgust category exists before age 5 or 6 (but see Siegal, 1988, for evidence of an early appearance of contamination sensitivity). Thus, although 3-year-olds typically reject feces as food, it is not clear that this rejection is any different from a distaste, or a distaste combined in some way with a sense of danger.

Origins of Disgust: Feces and Decay

For adults, feces seems to be a universal disgust substance (Angyal, 1941; Rozin & Fallon, 1987), with the odor of decay as perhaps the most potent sensory attribute associated with disgust. It is also conceivable that vomit is a primary substance for disgust. Since feces, vomit, and decay are probably associated with disease vectors, it would be reasonable to suppose that there would be an innate rejection of such things; however, as we have indicated above, none seems to be reliably present in nonhuman animals. Similarly, children do not show rejection of feces early in life. Rather— and here we have some sympathy with the psychoanalytic view—it appears that the infant may be attracted to feces, and that disgust is a powerful cultural force that turns this attraction into aversion (Freud, 1910/1957; Jones, 1912/1948).

Nor do children show early rejection of decay odors. Although Steiner (1979) reports an infant gape response to decay odors, this type of response seems absent in older children, suggesting that the result reported by Steiner may have been a reaction to sensory irritation. Studies of children's reactions to odors suggest that there are no innately negative nonirritant odors, and that a rejection of decay odors (without a referent object present) appears somewhere between 3 and 7 years of age (Petó, 1936; Stein, Ottenberg, & Roulet, 1958; Engen & Corbit, 1970). However, in keeping with the general trend in developmental research to discover earlier onsets of behaviors with more sensitive testing, Schmidt and Beauchamp (1988) have recently reported rejection of adult disgust odors in 3-year-olds. Still, the balance of evidence argues against a natural rejection of decay odors, which would parallel the innate aversion to bitter tastes in humans and other animals.

Toilet Training

Given the centrality of toilet training in psychoanalytic theory, and the fact that toilet training is one of the earliest arenas for socialization, it is surprising how little is known about the process. Although children do not seem to have an aversion for feces before toilet training (Rozin, Hammer, et al., 1986), it is not clear whether the feces avoidance that appears subsequently should be characterized as disgust, as opposed to avoidance or distaste. In the period following toilet training, feces does not seem to have contaminating properties (Fallon, Rozin, & Pliner, 1984), but children do develop an aversion for substances resembling feces (e.g., mud, dirt, and mushy substances) and sometimes a marked concern for cleanliness (Senn & Solnit, 1968; Ferenczi, 1914/1952). There may be a latency period be-

tween completion of toilet training and the emergence of feces as a particularly negative disgust substance some years later. Despite the uncertainties just noted, it does seem likely that the process of toilet training, with all of the attendant negative affect toward feces from significant others, plays an important role in the development of disgust.

Processes Accounting for the Spread of Response from Feces in Young Children

We believe that there is a spread of rejection responses following toilet training and the rejection of feces, but little is known about the mechanisms and events that account for this spread. Rozin and Fallon (1987) categorize these processes as "primary" (meaning that a new rejection is learned from the reactions of others or from some new information) and "secondary" (meaning that the acquisition is related to an existing disgust substance).

Primary acquisition usually depends on a response to the display of disgust in another person, preferably an admired or identified-with person (Tomkins, 1963). Tomkins suggested two ways in which a facial (or other) display of disgust could be transmitted. A disgust response in the observer may be induced by the disgust display in others (a form of empathic conditioning; Aronfreed, 1970), or by the observer's voluntary imitation of the disgust display in others. Tomkins assumed that the production of a disgust face in the observer induces the emotion of disgust in the observer. Both of these mechanisms require some process of either conditioning or cognition; either mechanism may be operative, but there is no direct evidence for either. The more widely studied phenomenon of social referencing may form a basis for such learning (Klinnert, Campos, Sorce, Emde, & Svejda, 1983). It is almost certain that social transmission plays a major role in the creation of primary disgusts. A model for such a process is provided in Mineka and Cook's (1988) demonstration of the "transfer" of snake fear from one monkey to another when a monkey without a snake fear observes the reaction of a snake-fearing monkey to a snake.

Secondary disgusts also may occur by two pathways (Rozin & Fallon, 1987). One is generalization, based on similarity, from existing disgust substances such as feces (Ferenczi,

1914/1952; Tomkins, 1963; Darwin, 1872/1965). For example, Jamieson (1947) describes a woman who got asthma attacks when changing diapers. The attacks subsequently generalized to sweat, Limburger cheese odor, and rotting seaweed. Another pathway is evaluative conditioning (Martin & Levey, 1978; Baeyens, Crombez, Van den Bergh, & Eelen, 1989; Rozin & Zellner, 1985), a form of Pavlovian conditioning in which a valenced entity (an unconditioned stimulus—e.g., an already disgusting entity) is paired with a previously neutral entity, with the result that the neutral entity (the conditioned stimulus) changes in valence in the direction of the unconditioned stimulus. There are suggestions that such pairings in the laboratory (e.g., between a favored juice and a cockroach) can induce aversion (Rozin, Millman, & Nemeroff, 1986).

There are also abundant anecdotal reports of such pairings. Perhaps the first comes from Darwin (1872/1965) himself, who referred to spread of response by habit and association, and offered an example from his own experience. He was cleaning a bird skeleton, and the smell of the rotted flesh on it made him retch. On subsequent days, when he handled clean skeletons of the same type, they made him retch. Other examples include development of aversion to M&Ms after hearing that the outside shell was made of fly droppings; dislike of spaghetti after having had a hand placed in what was described as a bowl of worms in a "haunted" house and later discovering that it was spaghetti; and dislike of red meat after cutting into a piece of rare meat and seeing blood spurt out (Rozin, 1986). These are all examples of acquired aversions mediated by disgust elicitors, but it is important to recognize that these acquired aversions may not qualify as disgust—that is, may not show the characteristics (e.g., contamination) that differentiate disgust from distaste or danger.

Properties and Acquisition of Core Disgust

By the definition we have offered for core disgust, three components are requisite for the occurrence of the emotion: (1) a sense of oral incorporation (and hence a linkage with food or eating); (2) a sense of offensiveness; and (3) contamination sensitivity. We now consider each, in terms of the nature of the component, its requisites, and its development.

Oral Incorporation

Rozin and Fallon have noted (1987) that the mouth is the principal route of entry of material things into the body, and hence can be thought of as the gateway to the body. Since putting external things into the body can be thought of as a highly personal and risky act, the special emotion associated with ingestion is understandable (Rozin, Nemeroff, Gordon, Horowitz, & Voet, 1992). The mouth can be viewed as a kind of Mach Band phenomenon—that is, an area of special vulnerability on the body outside–inside border, where there is marked contrast in affective response depending on which side of the border an object lies. The aversion response to an offensive entity in the mouth is usually stronger than response to the same entity on the body surface near but not inside the mouth, or inside the stomach (Rozin, Nemeroff, et al., 1992).

The threat of oral incorporation is framed by a widespread belief that one takes on the properties of the food one eats ("You are what you eat"). This belief has been thought to be characteristic primarily of members of traditional cultures. James Frazer (1890/1922) in *The Golden Bough*, noted: "The savage commonly believes that by eating the flesh of an animal or man, he acquires not only the physical but even the moral and intellectual qualities which are characteristic of that animal or man" (p. 573). Keith Thomas (1983) notes that "you are what you eat" was a common belief in Europe some centuries ago. In fact, this idea is consistent with common sense, since it is our general experience that when two things combine (in this case, a food and a person), the product has resemblances to both. Nemeroff and Rozin (1989) have found evidence for this belief in North American college students, when it was elicited indirectly by use of the Asch impressions technique. Students reading about a culture of boar eaters rated the members of the culture as more boar-like than students who read about a culture that is identical, except that the members are turtle eaters.

Offensive Entities: Animals and Their Products

Angyal (1941) held that the center of disgust is animal (including human) waste products, which he saw as debasing. It is hard to avoid the conclusion that waste products have a special role in disgust. Body products are usually a focus of disgust, and are central to the related anthropological concept of pollution (Douglas, 1966; Meigs, 1978, 1984). There is widespread historical and cultural evidence for aversion to virtually all body products, including not only feces, vomit, and urine, but most particularly blood (especially menstrual blood). For example, blood pollution at birth was a central aspect of ancient Greek religion (Parker, 1983).

In accord with Angyal's (1941) suggestion of an animal focus for disgust, Rozin and Fallon (1987) have proposed that the elicitor category for core disgust is animals and their products as potential foods. Surveys of North American students suggest that the word "disgust" is occasionally applied to potential foods other than animals or their products; however, these foods (e.g., broccoli) rarely have the contamination property of core disgust elicitors (Rozin & Fallon, 1980, 1987; Fallon & Rozin, 1983). Soler (1973/1979) argues that animal food prohibitions, such as those of the ancient Hebrews, should be seen as the rule, and that ingestion of a few animals or of specific animal parts is the exception. Thus, Adam and Eve began as vegetarians, and it was only after the flood that animals were allowed by God into the human diet.

Almost all cultures eat a very small subset of potential animal foods. In American culture, we avoid almost all invertebrates (except a few shellfish and mollusks), virtually all reptiles and amphibians, and all but a small subset of the possible birds and mammals. Furthermore, we tend to avoid the viscera, head, and a number of other parts of the few edible mammals that we do consume. And as Angyal (1941) pointed out, in many cultures some care is taken to disguise the animal origin of animal food by cutting, chopping, and other culinary preparations, as well as by having names for animal foods (e.g., "pork," "beef," in English) that are distinct from the corresponding animal names.

Animal prohibitions or taboos vary cross-culturally. The designated animals need not be disgusting, but a disgust orientation is informative as an account of many taboos. Some animals are considered intrinsically disgusting, either because they bear some resemblance to body products such as mucus (e.g., slugs, worms), or because they are commonly in contact with rotting animal flesh, feces, or other human wastes (e.g., flies, cockroaches, rats, vultures, and other scavengers). Many other animals are considered disgusting as potential foods. Carnivorous land animals eat raw or decaying animal flesh, and produce putrid feces. They are therefore disgusting at both ends. Herbivores are much less likely to be prohibited cross-culturally. Even the hunter gatherer !Kung bushmen, who eat a much wider variety of species than we do, reject rodents, carnivores, and most insects (Howell, 1986). Food prohibitions based on association and similarity are common, as among the Hua of Papua New Guinea (Meigs, 1984). Hua adolescent males must avoid any food that is red, wet, slimy, or hairy; that comes from a hole; or that is in any other way construed to resemble menstrual blood or female genitalia.

Two other categories of animal food prohibitions deserve mention. Animals that are in some sense close to humans, either in appearance (e.g., other primates) or by virtue of a relationship with humans as pets, are rarely eaten. And finally, there is a group of anomalous animals that seem to produce a mixture of fear (danger) and disgust (e.g., spiders and snakes). These animals are feared, though they are not particularly harmful. Davey (1992) offers evidence that the aversion to these animals is based on disgust/disease avoidance, rather than fear of harm.

Contamination

The contamination response (e.g., the rejection of a potential food if it even briefly contacted a disgusting entity) appears to be powerful and universal among adults. North American college students reject liked beverages after they have briefly contacted a sterilized cockroach (Rozin, Millman, & Nemeroff, 1986), and virtually all North Americans surveyed reject foods that have been handled or bitten by either unsavory or disliked persons (Rozin, Nemeroff, Wane, & Sherrod, 1989). Although this aversion is typically justified as an avoidance of disease transfer, removal of this possibility (e.g., by sterilizing the offending dead cockroach) typically has only a small effect. The contamination property of disgust was commented upon, in passing, by both Darwin (1872/1965) and Angyal (1941) in their classic works.

The idea of contamination is quite sophisticated in requiring a separation of appearance and reality. There is no sensory residue of past contamination in a contaminated entity; it is the history of contact that is critical (see Rozin & Nemeroff, 1990, for further discussion). Furthermore, contamination implies some conception of invisible entities (e.g., traces of cockroach) that are the vehicle of contamination. Both the notion of invisible entities and appearance as distinct from reality are cognitive achievements of considerable abstraction, and seem to be absent in young children (Piaget & Inhelder, 1941/1974; Flavell, 1986). This cognitive limitation may be the principal barrier to a full childhood representation of disgust. The cognitive sophistication of disgust puts it in the company of other uniquely human emotions such as pride, shame, and guilt, which also do not assume an adult-like form until the age of 7 or 8 (Harris, 1989).

Rozin and his colleagues have found that a clear contamination response to disgusting contacts with a favored beverage (e.g., dog feces or a grasshopper as contaminants in milk or juice) does not appear until about 7 years of age in North American children (Fallon et al., 1984; Rozin, Fallon, & Augstoni-Ziskind, 1985, 1986). However, Siegal (1988), using more sensitive procedures, has reported contamination responses in Australian children by 4 years of age, and recent studies of children's conceptions of the disappearance of solute in the process of dissolving suggests that there is some effective sense of invisible particles by age 4 or 5 in North American children (Rosen & Rozin, in press).

Rozin and his colleagues have also suggested that contagion effects may be instances of the sympathetic magical law of contagion (Tylor, 1871/1974; Frazer, 1890/1922; Mauss, 1902/1972), which essentially holds that "once in contact, always in contact" (Rozin & Fallon, 1987; Rozin & Nemeroff, 1990). Although this law was proposed to account for thought patterns in traditional cultures, it also appears in a wide range of domains for adult North Americans (Rozin et al., 1989).

A second law of sympathetic magic, the law of similarity, accounts for some other aspects of disgust. The law of similarity, also dating from Tylor, Frazer, and Mauss (see Rozin & Nemeroff, 1990, for a review), basically holds that if things are superficially similar, then they resemble each other in a deep sense as well. In other words, it holds that appearance, roughly speaking, is reality. It accounts for the frequent observation that objects that look like something disgusting, but are known not to be, are often treated as disgusting. Thus, we find that many North American college students are reluctant to consume imitation dog feces that they know is made out of chocolate fudge (Rozin, Millman, & Nemeroff, 1986), and many North Americans say they would be reluctant to consume a favorite beverage stirred by a brand-new comb or contaminated with a plastic replica of an insect (Rozin et al. 1989).

The law of contagion as applied to disgust is potentially crippling; everything we might eat or touch is potentially contaminated. We deal with this problem in a number of ways. First, contamination rules are developed in some cultures, such as the explicit rules limiting contamination in the Hebrew dietary system (Grunfeld, 1982). These rules—for example, the rule that there is a minimal contamination below which a contaminated food remains kosher—provide ritualistic relief but not necessarily psychological relief of a sense of contamination (Nemeroff & Rozin, 1992).

Most often, framing is the strategy that can keep potential contamination out of consideration—as when we do not think of the people in the kitchen who prepare our food in a restaurant; or the animal that was the source of our meat; or the fact that our body contains a host of disgusting substances, including feces, urine and saliva (see discussion in Rozin & Fallon, 1987). Indeed, as Allport (1955) noted (confirmed in the survey data of Rozin, Millman, & Nemeroff, 1986), we are disgusted by our own saliva as soon as it leaves our body, as when we reject drinking a glass of water that we have just spit into. Our framing solution fails when the source of contamination/disgust is too salient. Thus, although we normally handle money without thinking of who touched it before us, this strategy would inadequately protect us in the case of a dollar tendered by a vagrant.

ANIMAL-ORIGIN DISGUST AND BEYOND

Our discussion of disgust up to this point has focused on issues surrounding food and eating. We have presented core disgust as an oral defense in relation to potential foods, body products, and some animals. We now consider some other domains of disgust elicitors.

Sex, Hygiene, Death, and Body Envelope Violation

We recently asked a number of North American respondents to list the things they thought were disgusting. Their lists included exemplars of the three core disgust domains (food, body products, and animals) but also these five additional domains: sexual acts, hygiene, death, violations of the body envelope (e.g., gore, amputations, surgery), and sociomoral violations (e.g., liars, racists, and Nazis). In the course of developing a scale to measure disgust sensitivity across these eight domains (Haidt, McCauley, & Rozin, 1992) we discovered that reactions to all of the domains were intercorrelated, except for the sociomoral violations. That is, people who were easily disgusted by food items were also more bothered by incest, rats, and amputations. Table 40.1 gives the seven items that are most predictive of total score on the final 32-item Disgust Scale (which included four items in each of seven domains other than socio-moral violations). Note that five of the seven domains are represented among the top seven items, demonstrating the conceptual heterogeneity of disgust elicitors. Items from the remaining two domains, food and envelope violations, also showed respectable correlations with total score, and the best item from each of those two domains is given at the bottom of Table 40.1.

Thus, we observe a spread of the focus of threat from just the mouth to contact with the body in general, and even offensive sights (Table 40.1). This spread is captured in a psychoanalytic treatment of disgust: "In summary, any modality that represents a means of entry into the self or body—the mouth, the nose, the skin, the eyes—seems to play a part in the disgust experience" (Miller, 1986, p. 300). Even more striking is the spread of disgust elicitors beyond the domains of core disgust, in particular the importance of death as an elicitor of disgust. Two of the top seven items in Table 40.1 concern death.

In various versions of the Disgust Scale, we noted with some surprise the particularly high correlation with total score for items dealing with death (see Table 40.1). The involvement of death in disgust may be of particular note, because it may relate to the importance of decay odor as a disgust elicitor. Furthermore, it suggests a more general construal of disgust

within a psychoanalytic framework. Rather than as a defense against coprophilia or sexuality, disgust, a universal emotion, can be understood as a defense against a universal fear of death by humans.

Becker (1973) has argued that the most important threat to the psyche is not infantile sexuality, but the certainty of death. Only human animals know they are to die, and only humans need to repress this threat. In this framework, disgust can be viewed as a rejection of thoughts or experiences that might suggest human mortality.

An intriguing Asian perspective on the relation of death and disgust comes from a study of Sri Lankan Buddists by Obeyesekere (1985). With the aim of producing disgust at sensory pleasure, initiates will meditate over an actual corpse in 10 states of decay. In the lay tradition, something of the same sort is done in the imagination; meditation emphasizes the putrescence of the body, with a focus on the body as a vessel containing feces.

A Theory of Disgust: Avoidance of Reminders of Animal Origins

These speculations about death lead naturally to an overarching description of disgust elicitors: Anything that reminds us that we are animals elicits disgust (Rozin & Fallon, 1987). An examination of the seven domains of disgust elicitors we have identified suggests that disgust serves to "humanize" our animal bodies. Humans must eat, excrete, and have sex, just like animals. Each culture prescribes the proper way to perform these actions—by, for example, placing most animals off limits as potential foods, and most people off limits as potential sexual partners. People who ignore these prescriptions are reviled as disgusting and animal-like. Furthermore, humans are like animals in having fragile body envelopes that, when breached, reveal blood and soft viscera; and human bodies, like animal bodies, die. Envelope violations and death are disgusting because they are uncomfortable reminders of our animal vulnerability. Finally, hygienic rules govern the proper use and maintenance of the human body, and the failure to meet these culturally defined standards places a person below the level of humans. Insofar as humans behave like animals, the distinction between humans and animals is blurred, and we see ourselves as lowered, debased, and (perhaps

TABLE 40.1. Nine Items from the Disgust Scale and Their Correlations with Total Score

Rank	Correlation w/total score	Domain	Item
1	.57	Body products	You see a bowel movement left unflushed in a public toilet.
2	.54	Body products	While you are walking through a tunnel under a railroad track, you smell urine.
3	.53	Death	Your friend's pet cat dies, and you have to pick up the dead body with your bare hands.
4	.52	Animals	You are walking barefoot on concrete, and you step on an earthworm.
5	.50	Death	It would bother me tremendously to touch a dead body.
6	.48	Sex	You hear about an adult woman who has sex with her father.
7	.47	Hygiene	You discover that a friend of yours changes underwear only once a week.
.	.	.	.
.	.	.	.
.	.	.	.
13	.42	Food	I might be willing to try eating monkey meat, under some circumstances.
14	.42	Envelope violations	You see someone accidentally stick a fishing hook through his finger.

Note. Data from Haidt, McCauley, and Rozin (1992).

most critically), mortal (see also discussion in Haidt, McCauley, & Rozin, 1992).

Consistent with this description, Rozin and Fallon (1987) have suggested that "Humans see themselves as quite distinct from (and superior to) other animals and wish to avoid any ambiguity about their status by accentuating the human–animal boundary." (p. 28) Tambiah (1969) emphasizes the importance of this distinction for humans, and points to the paradox of human fascination for and aversion to animals. Ortner (1973) notes that the one body product that does not reliably elicit disgust is tears, and these are seen as uniquely human. DesPres (1976), in a gripping account of the psychology of the Holocaust, notes that the dehumanization of the inmates, so that guards as well as inmates thought of the inmates as animals, facilitated participation in mass executions. He points out that those inmates who went to great lengths to preserve their humanity—that is, refused to behave like animals, and washed themselves ritually (even if only with dirty water)—were the individuals most likely to survive. And Leach (1964) has pointed out that animal words are used as insults in many cultures. In general, the ethnographic literature is filled with references to the fact that humans consider themselves better than animals, and they work to maintain a clear animal–human boundary. Violations of

that boundary—for example, treating an animal as a person in a pet relationship—are rather rare cross-culturally.

Keith Thomas (1983), in *Man and the Natural World*, provides much material for a history of disgust in describing human reactions to animals. He documents a pre-Darwinian increase in sensitivity to the relation of man and nature that occurred in England from the 16th to the late 18th centuries. This sensitivity included an extreme concern with human uniqueness, and concern for maintaining animal–human boundaries (as manifested in opposition to animals as pets; rejection of certain styles of eating, sex, and evacuation; and a concern for cleanliness). Inferior humans were seen as animal-like.

We turn now to discussion of some issues specific to three of the domains of disgust that we have identified as reminders of our animal origins. For each of these domains, the issue concerns a possible broadening of our understanding of the domain.

Body Envelope Violations and Deformity

Disgust elicitors that we have identified with the domain of body envelope violations include gore, body parts, and deformity. Gore and body parts are clearly reminders of our animal origins, but the fact that deformity can be disgusting calls for some additional discussion. Why should the sight of the stump of a missing hand be disgusting? One account emphasizes the importance of deviance or departure from a body ideal as an occasion of disgust. Angyal (1941), once again, touched on this issue; he referred to an aspect of disgust as "uncanniness," using as examples supernumerary limbs or mutilated parts. Tomkins (1963) also included deviation from a norm in his conception of disgust.

The most systematic account of this conception of disgust comes from Mary Douglas's (1966) classic work of anthropology, *Purity and Danger*. She relates pollution to a sense of violation of accepted categories, sometimes described as matter out of place. This easily accounts for the disgust response to deformity, and can be extended to "deviant" sex acts, gore (internal body in the outside world), and body products (in the ambiguous state of both inside and outside the body). This provocative formulation surely has something to contribute to psychological theories of disgust, but it cannot account for some of the most commonplace elicitors of disgust, such as rats and cockroaches.

Hygiene and Interpersonal Contamination

Hygiene violations capable of eliciting disgust include contact with dirt and germs (e.g., dirt under the fingernails, a restaurant chef with the flu, or unwashed hands before eating). But disgust at sipping soda from another's glass or aversion to wearing used clothing points to a very large and important category of disgust that is perhaps not adequately comprehended under the category of hygiene. Sensitivity to interpersonal contamination is an enormous phenomenon.

The fact that direct or indirect contact with other people can elicit disgust was noted by Darwin (1872/1965). Furthermore, Angyal (1941) noted that other persons, as receptacles for waste products, are potentially disgusting. The reluctance of many North Americans to buy or wear used clothing is certainly a phenomenon of interpersonal contamination. In Hindu India, interpersonal contagion, mediated primarily by contacts with food, is a major feature of society and a major basis for the maintenance of the caste system (Appadurai, 1981; Marriott, 1968).

We have found widespread evidence in the United States for aversion to contact with possessions, silverware, cars, and rooms used by strange or otherwise undesirable persons (Rozin et al., 1989; Rozin, Markwith, & McCauley, 1992). We have analyzed this interpersonal aversion into four separately identifiable components: strangeness, disease, misfortune, and moral taint (Rozin, Markwith, & McCauley, 1992). Thus, a sweater worn once by a healthy stranger and then laundered is less desirable than an unworn sweater for most of the North American students we have surveyed (aversion to strangeness). This negativity is substantially enhanced if the stranger has had a misfortune (e.g., an amputated leg), a disease (e.g., tuberculosis), or a moral taint (e.g., a conviction for murder).

We are not sure at this point whether the phenomena of interpersonal contagion just described are expressions of disgust. If they are, however, it is not clear why indirect contact with other human beings should remind us of our animal nature in the same way or to the same degree as death, body envelope violation, food and eating, sex, body products, or hygiene. Of course, contact with other people does open us to contact with their body products: their sweat, their saliva, their mucus, and traces of their urine and feces. But laundering and even sterilizing things used by others reduce the contamination effect only very slightly in our studies, and this fact makes it more difficult to understand interpersonal contamination simply in terms of potential contact with body products.

In the early development of our Disgust Scale (Haidt, McCauley, & Rozin, 1992), quite a few interpersonal contagion items were included, such as reactions to wearing a sweater previously worn by someone with AIDS, shaking hands with strangers, wearing used clothing, touching doorknobs in public buildings, and feeling funny about handling money. These items did not appear on the final version because they did not correlate highly with the total disgust score. However, it remains possible that interpersonal contagion is an important domain of disgust, and one that is to some extent independent of the other domains.

Sexual and Other Moral Violations

When we elicited lists of disgusting things from North American informants (Haidt, McCauley,

& Rozin, 1992), we found many instances referring to moral offenses. Many of these items had some sexual content (e.g., homosexuality, pornography, incest), and are thus easily assimilable to the animal-reminder view of disgust. Deviance from the narrow class of "normal" heterosexuality is often seen as unnatural, inhuman, and therefore disgusting. Indeed, items about sexual morality and the proper pairing of sexual partners have been consistently good as predictors of total score on the Disgust Scale.

However, the word "disgusting" is often used as a synonym for "immoral" in situations that do not seem to be reminders of our animal origins. Thus our subjects have told us that Nazis, people who steal from beggars, and lawyers who chase ambulances are all disgusting. It is our guess that moral offenses involving some reminder of our animal nature (e.g., incest) are more likely to be labeled "disgusting" than are offenses of a uniquely human sort (e.g., fraud). A lawyer who chases ambulances might be described by English speakers as "disgusting," but we must be careful that we are not witnessing a casual usage or metaphorical extension of the word. It would be a mistake to define the emotion of disgust simply in terms of the referents of the word, but it would also be a mistake to ignore these referents.

These moral offenses on the fuzzy fringe of disgust may, as we have said, share some of the animal–nature theme that we have attributed to the rest of disgust. They may also share another property—contamination—with disgust. Indirect contact with people who have committed moral offenses (such as murders) is highly aversive, more so than similar contact with someone with a serious illness (Rozin, Markwith, & McCauley, 1992). In our research on contamination, one of the most potent stimuli we have discovered is Adolf

Hitler's sweater. Yet, in our attempt to link the various elicitors of disgust under one conceptual umbrella, we must be cautioned by the fact that the nonsexual moral offense items in the earlier forms of the Disgust Scale did not show substantial correlations with reactions to the seven domains of disgust (Haidt, McCauley, & Rozin, 1992).

We speculate that what unites the domain of morally disgusting actions is that they reveal a lack of normal human social motivation. People who betray friends or family, or who kill in cold blood, are seen as inhuman and revolting; criminal acts with "normal" human motivations, such as robbing banks, are seen as immoral but not disgusting. This kind of disgust may represent a more abstract set of concerns about the human–animal distinction, focusing not on the human body, but on the human body-politic—that is, the human as a member of a cooperating social entity.

The Cultural Evolution of Disgust

We have suggested a course of cultural evolution and development of disgust, summarized in Table 40.2. The proposed origin is the rejection response to bad-tasting foods, even though bad taste ultimately has little to do with the emotion of disgust. However, oral rejection remains the focus of disgust reactions, in what we have called "core disgust." Eating, animals, and body products are the elicitors for core disgust.

A further expansion of the conception and domain of elicitors, in both cultural evolution and perhaps development, involves reminders of our animal origins beyond the elicitors of core disgust. Elias (1978), in *The History of Manners*, a treatment of the development of manners in Europe from medieval to more modern times, describes this expansion as follows: "... people, in the course of the civiliz-

TABLE 40.2. Proposed Pathway of Expansion of Disgust and Disgust Elicitors

	Disgust stage				
	Distaste	Core	Animal origin	Interpersonal contamination	Moral
Function	Protect body	Protect body and soul	Protect body and soul	Protect body, soul, and social order	Protect social order
Elicitors	Bad tastes	Food/eating, body products, animals	Sex, death, hygiene, envelope violations	Direct and indirect contact with strangers or undesirables	Certain moral offenses

ing process, seek to suppress in themselves every characteristic that they feel to be 'animal'" (p. 120). From the prohibitions mentioned in etiquette books of the 15th century, Elias surmises that people must have regularly engaged in a variety of activities that we now consider disgusting. Readers were entreated not to blow their noses with the same hand that they used to hold the meat, not to greet a person while urinating or defecating, and not to return tasted morsels to the general dish.

In the major expansion of disgust, animal functions or properties relating to sex, death, a fragile body envelope, and poor hygiene become disgust elicitors. We have further suggested that human concern about being distinct from animals, the new focus of disgust, centers on our desire not to share the property of mortality with animals.

We have identified two other sets of elicitors of disgust that are problematic for the "avoidance of the reminders of animal origins" view. One is interpersonal contamination, and the other is moral offenses. These may be linked to the animal–human distinction. However, they may also be independent accretions to the disgust system; that is, they may become offensive for reasons independent of the prior focus of disgust, but may access the already present rejection system of disgust.

This model suggests what might be called an opportunistic accretion of new domains of elicitors, and new motivations, to a rejection system that is already in place. A parallel to this model in evolutionary biology is the concept of preadaptation (Mayr, 1960). Mayr suggests that the major source of evolutionary "novelties" is the co-opting of an existing system for a new function. The classic example is the conversion of a jaw articulation in more primitive vertebrates into the middle-ear ossicles found in mammals. Preadaptation can operate either to replace an original function, or to accrete new functions to an existing system. Both of these processes seem to be a work in disgust. We suggest that in both cultural evolution and individual development, as in biological evolution, preadaptation plays an important role, and can be described as the accessing of previously inaccessible systems for a wider range of activities, functions, or elicitors (Rozin, 1976).

This account of the cultural evolution of disgust, and the invocation of the process of preadaptation, is supported by a recent study of the components of the disgust facial expression (Rozin, Ebert, & Lowery, 1992). In a study in which North American subjects matched situations to pictures of specific facial expressions, the nose wrinkle (AU 9) and gape (AU 26) were identified primarily with elicitors of core disgust. The raised upper lip (AU 10) was more associated with animal origin, interpersonal contamination, and moral disgust. If the raised upper lip is the newer expressive component, this result suggests preadaptation; as disgust expands to the moral domain, it incorporates a facial expressive associated with anger (baring the upper teeth) and, hence, moral violations.

DISGUST AS A MORAL EMOTION

Like anger and contempt, disgust can be a moral reaction to other people, implying that their actions or character have violated normative standards. We think of these three emotions as forming a continuum of moral response. The moral nature of anger is most obvious, captured in definitions going back to Aristotle, who defined it as a response to unjustified insult or transgression, including an impulse toward revenge (Aristotle, 1941; Sabini & Silver, 1983). At the other end of the continuum, core disgust appears to have nothing to do with morality, arising more from a phylogenetic disposition to be wary of potentially harmful or distasteful food. But as disgust becomes elaborated, it becomes a more general feeling of revulsion, even to sociomoral violations, and it begins to shade into anger. We propose that contempt is the middle ground between anger and disgust.

Anger and disgust are on almost all lists of basic emotions, whereas the status of contempt is less clear. There are arguments that contempt has a clear, universally recognized face (Ekman & Friesen, 1986), and hence may qualify by at least one criterion as a basic emotion. Darwin (1872/1965) associates scorn/disdain (including contempt) with the unilateral lip raise (AU 10), a subcomponent of the disgust and anger responses; Ekman and Friesen (1986), in both American and cross-cultural studies, implicate the unilateral smirk (AU 14). They note that this expression, and perhaps the unilateral AU 10 as well, are uniquely human expressions. Russell (1991b) and Izard and Haynes (1988) have taken issue with Ekman's claim, with the result that the status of the unique contempt expression is now uncertain (Ekman, O'Sullivan, & Matsumoto, 1991).

Darwin (1872/1965, p. 253) says that "extreme contempt, or as it is often called loathing contempt, hardly differs from disgust." Darwin noted the similarities in the facial expression of these two emotions, and concluded that contempt is a way of declaring that a despised person is disagreeable to behold and smells offensive. Tomkins (1982) sees both disgust and contempt as originally auxiliary drive mechanisms to the hunger drive, respectively involved with mouth and nose. Thus contempt appears to harness the oral–nasal rejection response of disgust, and to apply it to people whose behavior or character one finds offensive. A crucial component of contempt is the belief that the other person is base and inferior to oneself. Izard (1977) describes contempt as an expression of a need to feel stronger or better than another, with superiority as the predominant feeling. Similarly, Ekman and Friesen (1975) hold that contempt can only be felt for people, and that it includes an element of condescension.

Disgust, contempt, and anger often occur together. Izard (1977) refers to disgust, contempt, and anger as the "hostility triad," one of these always being the next most salient emotion when one of the others is stimulated. In an extensive recent cross-cultural study of emotional responses in 37 different cultures, Scherer and Wallbott (1992) report on the actual experiences related by subjects to illustrate each of a set of emotion words. Responses for disgust and anger were similar, and disgust stories were rated high on the dimension of perceived immorality.

Shweder (1990) offers a theory of moral judgment that may help clarify the role of emotions in morality. He proposes that three codes of ethics underlie the morality of most cultures. The first code, called the "ethics of autonomy," encompasses issues of rights and justice. This is the most fully elaborated code in Western societies, and philosophers and psychologists have at times claimed that rights and justice are the whole of morality (e.g., Rawls, 1971; Kohlberg, 1971). Aristotle's definition of anger makes it clear that anger is the response to violations of this code of ethics. A second code, called the "ethics of divinity," focuses on the self as a spiritual entity and

seeks to protect that entity from degrading or polluting acts. As should be clear by now, disgust is precisely the emotion that guards the sanctity of the soul as well as the purity of the body. A third code is more problematic for an emotional analysis. It is called the "ethics of community," and it focuses on issues of duty, hierarchy, and the proper fulfillment of one's social roles. What is the emotional reaction to a person who, for example, betrays his or her group or tries to usurp authority? We propose that the emotional reaction is contempt. Hence we see a rough match between Shweder's three moral codes, and what we call the three moral emotions.

Shweder's theory offers an account of the substantial variation in the domain of morality found cross-culturally (see also Shweder, Mahapatra, & Miller, 1987). Some cultures, such as Hindu India, have highly elaborated the ethics of divinity, and therefore see issues of purity and pollution as central to morality. Middle-class North Americans, on the other hand, see little connection between morality (justice and rights) and matters of personal hygiene. Cultures should therefore differ in the degree to which disgust is related to moral judgment. Haidt, Koller, and Dias (1992) asked North Americans and Brazilians of higher and lower socioeconomic status about a number of actions that were disgusting yet harmless, including incestuous kissing, eating one's dead pets, and eating a chicken one has just had sex with. They found that North Americans of high socioeconomic status separated their emotional reactions from their moral judgments, whereas other groups were more likely to condemn disgusting actions, even when they were harmless.

INDIVIDUAL DIFFERENCES IN DISGUST SENSITIVITY

The Measurement and Extent of Individual Differences

In one of the few studies of individual differences in disgust sensitivity, Templer, King, Brooner, and Corgiat (1984) constructed a 26-item scale to measure attitudes towards body products and body elimination (e.g., "The smell of other persons' bowel movements bothers me"). They found that scores were higher (attitudes were more negative) among an inpatient psychiatric population than among a normal population. Even among normals, high scorers also scored higher on various measures of psychopathology, including neuroticism and obsessiveness, suggesting a link between anxiety and disgust sensitivity. Templer et al. also found that females scored higher than males, and that less educated subjects scored higher than more highly educated subjects.

Research with our final 32-item Disgust Scale (Haidt, McCauley, & Rozin, 1992) confirms and extends these findings. We too have found a relationship between anxiety and disgust sensitivity: Scores on the Disgust Scale were positively correlated with measures of neuroticism (Eysenck & Eysenck, 1975) and, more specifically, with fears about death and dying (Boyar, 1964). The Disgust Scale showed its highest correlation (inverse, $r = -.50$) with a measure of sensation seeking (Sensation Seeking, Form V; Zuckerman, 1979), suggesting that disgust may act as a brake or counterweight to the urge to seek out new foods, activities, and adventures. The largest and most consistent demographic difference on the Disgust Scale related to gender. In our North American samples, covering a broad range of social classes, women always scored higher than men, typically by almost one standard deviation.

Past research directed at understanding modes of transmission of disgust sensitivity has been hampered by the lack of a psychometrically validated scale. The only measures that were available were Templer et al.'s (1984) body elimination scale and an unvalidated scale of contamination sensitivity (focusing on disgust in a contagion context) developed by Rozin, Fallon, and Mandell (1984). The Contamination Scale (24 items) was given to University of Pennsylvania students and their parents, and mid-parent–child correlations ranged between .30 and .60, with a correlation of .52 for the total scale score (Rozin et al., 1984). This significant mid-parent–child correlation for the full Contamination Scale was confirmed in a study in Britain ($r = .33$; Davey, Forster, & Mayhew, in press). These substantial correlations are much higher than correlations for individual food preferences (ranging between 0 and .30) from the same U.S. sample that generated the .30 to .60 correlations for disgust/contamination. That is, the family resemblance pattern for disgust/contamination sensitivity is more in line with correlations

obtained for values (e.g., attitudes to abortion) than with those for preferences (Rozin, 1991). It seems reasonable to attribute the parent–child resemblance in disgust sensitivity to social transmission in childhood. This presumption is supported by evidence for minimal heritability in a twin study using a short (5-item) version of the Contamination Scale used by Rozin et al. (1984): Monozygotic twins showed a correlation of .29 on this scale, while dizygotic twins showed a correlation of .24 (Rozin & Millman, 1987).

Children have ample opportunities to observe and be informed about their parents' attitudes and responses in disgust situations. We cannot, at this time, indicate what experiences may be more or less critical in the developing sense of disgust. The focus of earlier research was the Freudian link between toilet training and anal character. No convincing evidence has been presented in support of this relation (Orlansky, 1949). However, one study (McClelland & Pilon, 1983) does offer some support for the much more plausible link between toilet training and concern for cleanliness and neatness. Parents' ratings of the severity of toilet training of their children when the children were 5 years of age correlated .31 with standards of neatness for that same child 26–27 years later. Of course, the same parental (and perhaps child) characteristics that produced different severities of toilet training were no doubt manifested in other parent–child interactions, so that this promising finding does not directly implicate toilet training as a source of individual differences in disgust sensitivity.

CONCLUSION

Our analysis suggests a cultural evolution of disgust that brings it to the heart of what it means to be human. We propose that disgust, originally evolved as a rejection response to bad tastes, develops into a much more abstract and ideational rejection of potential foods. Included in this oral-centered rejection are body products and animals as potential ingestants. This core disgust, already suggestive of threat to the soul as opposed to danger to the body, then expands to include other reminders of our animal nature. In addition to the animal processes of eating and excretion, disgust can be elicited by other demonstrations of our animality: sex, death, gore, and violations of the body envelope. We see this animal-origin disgust as the central concept in elaborated disgust, and suggest that fear of the animal properties of mortality and associated decay replaces the original motive of avoidance of bad taste. Further expansions of the domains of disgust, depending on the culture, may include interpersonal contamination and an association between disgust and immoral actions. At this most fully elaborated level, the disgust system may have lost both its original connections to bad taste and its intermediate value of avoiding reminders of animal origin and death. The range of disgust may expand to the point that the exemplars have in common only the fact that we want nothing to do with them. At this level, disgust becomes a powerful form of negative socialization and an abstract moral emotion. We have presented a skeleton of evidence in support of this analysis, but there are many alternatives and points of difficulty. Nonetheless, we hope that we have built on the seminal work of Darwin and Angyal to develop a fuller conception of disgust.

Acknowledgment. We thank the Whitehall Foundation for supporting some of the research reported in this chapter and the preparation of this chapter.

REFERENCES

Allport, G. W. (1955). *Becoming: Basic considerations for a psychology of personality*. New Haven, CT: Yale University Press.

Angyal, A. (1941). Disgust and related aversions. *Journal of Abnormal and Social Psychology, 36*, 393–412.

Appadurai, A. (1981). Gastro-politics in Hindu South Asia. *American Ethnologist, 8*, 494–511.

Aristotle. (1941). Rhetoric. In R. McKeon (Ed.), *The basic works of Aristotle* (W. Rhys Roberts, Trans.) (pp. 1325–1454). New York: Random House.

Aronfreed, J. (1970). The socialization of altruistic and sympathetic behavior: Some theoretical and experimental analysis. In J. Macaulay & L. Berkowitz (Eds.) *Altruism and helping behavior* (pp. 103–126.) New York: Academic Press.

Baeyens, F., Crombez, G., Van den Bergh, O., & Eelen, P. (1988). Once in contact always in contact: Evaluative conditioning is resistant to extinction. *Advances in Behavior Research and Therapy, 10*, 179–199.

Barnes, R. H. (1962). Nutritional implications of coprophagy. *Nutrition Reviews, 20*, 289–291.

Becker, E. (1973). *The denial of death*. New York: Free Press.

Boyar, J. (1964). *The construction and partial validation of a scale for the measurement of the fear of death*. Ann Arbor, MI: UMI Dissertation Information Service.

Chevalier-Skolnikoff, S. (1973). Facial expression of emotion in nonhuman primates. In P. Ekman (Ed.), *Darwin and facial expression: A century of research in review* (pp. 11–90). New York: Academic Press.

Darwin, C. R. (1965). *The expression of the emotions in man and animals*. Chicago: University of Chicago Press. (Original work published 1872).

Davey, G. C. L. (1992). *Attitudes to animals: Relationship between self-reported fear and characteristics associated with disgust*. Manuscript submitted for publication.

Davey, G. C. L., Forster, L., & Mayhew, G. (in press). Familial resemblance in disgust sensitivity and animal phobias. *Behaviour Research and Therapy*.

Davidson, R. J. (1992). Emotion and affective style: Hemispheric substrates. *Psychological Science, 3*, 39–43.

DesPres, T. (1976). *The survivor*. Oxford: Oxford University Press.

Douglas, M. (1966). *Purity and danger*. London: Routledge & Kegan Paul.

Ekman, P. (1972). Universals and cultural differences in facial expressions of emotion. In J. K. Cole (Ed.), *Nebraska Symposium on Motivation: 1971* (Vol. 19, pp. 207–283). Lincoln: University of Nebraska Press.

Ekman, P. (1992). An argument for basic emotions. *Cognition and Emotion, 6*, 169–200.

Ekman, P., & Friesen, W. V. (1975). *Unmasking the face*. Englewood Cliffs, NJ: Prentice-Hall.

Ekman, P., & Friesen, W. V. (1978). *Facial Action Coding System: A technique for the measurement of facial movement*. Palo Alto, CA: Consulting Psychologists Press.

Ekman, P., & Friesen, W. C. (1986). A new pan-cultural facial expression of emotion. *Motivation and Emotion, 10*, 159–168.

Ekman, P., O'Sullivan, M., & Matsumoto, D. (1991). Confusions about context in the judgment of facial expression: A reply to "The contempt expression and the relativity thesis." *Motivation and Emotion, 15*, 169–176.

Elias, N. (1978). *The history of manners: Vol. 1. The civilizing process* (E. Jephcott, Trans.). New York: Pantheon Books. (Original work published 1939)

Engen, T., & Corbit, T. E. (1970). *Feasibility of olfactory coding of noxious substances to assure aversive responses in young children* (Final Report, Contract No. PH 86-68-162, ICRL-RR-69-6). Washington, DC: U.S. Department of Health, Education and Welfare.

Eysenck, H. J., & Eysenck, S. B. G. (1975). *Eysenck Personality Questionnaire*. San Diego: Educational and Industrial Testing Service.

Fallon, A. E., & Rozin, P. (1983). The psychological bases of food rejections by humans. *Ecology of Food and Nutrition, 13*, 15–26.

Fallon, A. E., Rozin, P., & Pliner, P. (1984). The child's conception of food: The development of food rejections with special reference to disgust and contamination sensitivity. *Child Development, 55*, 566–575.

Ferenczi, S. (1952). The ontogenesis of the interest in money. In S. Ferenczi (Ed.), *First contributions to psychoanalysis* (E. Jones, Trans.) (pp. 319–331). London: Hogarth Press. (Original work published 1914)

Flavell, J. (1986). The development of children's knowledge of the appearance–reality distinction. *American Psychologist, 41*, 418–425.

Frazer, J. G. (1922). *The golden bough: A study in magic and religion* (abridged ed., T. H. Gaster, Ed.). New York: Macmillan. (Original work published 1890)

Freud, S. (1953). Three essays on the theory of sexuality. In J. Strachey (Ed. and Trans.), *The standard edition of the complete psychological works of Sigmund Freud* (Vol. 7, pp. 123–231). London: Hogarth Press. (Original work published 1905)

Freud, S. (1957). Five lectures on psycho-analysis. In J. Strachey (Ed. and Trans.), *The standard edition of the complete psychological works of Sigmund Freud* (Vol. 11, pp. 3–56). London: Hogarth Press. (Original work published 1910)

Frijda, N. H. (1986). *The emotions.* Cambridge, England: Cambridge University Press.

Garcia, J., Rusiniak, K. W., & Brett, L. P. (1977). Conditioning food-illness aversions in wild animals: Caveat canonici. In H. Davis & M. B. Hurwitz (Eds.), *Operant–Pavlovian interactions* (pp. 273–311). Hillsdale, NJ: Erlbaum.

Grill, H. J., & Norgren, R. (1978). The taste reactivity test: I. Oro-facial responses to gustatory stimuli in neurologically normal rats. *Brain Research, 143,* 263–279.

Grunfeld, D. I. (1982). *The Jewish dietary laws: Vol. 1. Dietary laws regarding forbidden and permitted foods, with particular reference to meat and meat products* (3rd ed.). London: Soncino Press.

Haidt, J., Koller, S. H., & Dias, M. G. (1992). *Affect, culture, and the morality of harmless offenses.* Manuscript submitted for publication.

Haidt, J., McCauley, C. R., & Rozin, P. (1992). *A scale to measure disgust sensitivity.* Manuscript submitted for publication.

Harris, P. (1989). *Children and emotion.* Oxford: Basil Blackwell.

Howell, N. (1986). Feedbacks and buffers in relation to scarcity and abundance: Studies of hunter-gatherer populations. In R. Scofield (Ed.), *Beyond Malthus* (pp. 156–187). Cambridge, England: Cambridge University Press.

Izard, C. E. (1971). *The face of emotion.* New York: Appleton-Century-Crofts.

Izard, C. E. (1977). *Human emotions.* New York: Plenum Press.

Izard, C. E., & Haynes, O. M. (1988). On the form and universality of the contempt expression: A challenge to Ekman and Friesen's claim of discovery. *Motivation and Emotion, 12,* 1–16.

Jamieson, H. C. (1947). Asthma due to the odor of urine, feces, and sweat. *Annals of Allergy, 5,* 234–235.

Johnson-Laird, P. N., & Oatley, K. (1989). The language of emotions: An analysis of a semantic field. *Cognition and Emotion, 3,* 81–123.

Jones, E. (1948). Anal-erotic character traits. In *Papers on psychoanalysis* (pp. 413–437). Boston: Beacon Press. (Original work published 1912)

Klinnert, M. D., Campos, J., Sorce, J., Emde, R. N., & Svejda, M. (1983). The development of social referencing in infancy. In R. Plutchik & H. Kellerman (Eds.), *Emotion: Theory, research, and experience. Vol. 2. Emotions in early development* (pp. 57–86). New York: Academic Press.

Kohlberg, L. (1971). From is to ought: How to commit the naturalistic fallacy and get away with it in the study of moral development. In T. Mischel (Ed.), *Psychology and genetic epistemology* (pp. 151–235). New York: Academic Press.

Leach, E. (1964). Anthropological aspects of language: Animal categories and verbal abuse. In E. Lenneberg (Ed.), *New directions in the study of language* (pp. 23–64). Cambridge, MA: MIT Press.

Levenson, R. W. (1992). Autonomic nervous system differences among emotions. *Psychological Science, 3,* 23–27.

Levenson, R. W., Ekman, P., & Friesen, W. V. (1990). Voluntary facial action generates emotion-specific autonomic nervous system activity. *Psychophysiology, 27,* 363–384.

Malson, L. (1972). *Wolf children* (E. Fawcett, P. Ayrton, & J. White, Trans.). New York: Monthly Review Press. (Original work published in French, 1964)

Marriott, M. (1968). Caste ranking and food transactions: A matrix analysis. In M. Singer & B. S. Cohn (Eds.), *Structure and change in Indian society* (pp. 133–171). Chicago: Aldine.

Martin, I., & Levey, A. B. (1978). Evaluative conditioning. *Advances in Behavior Research and Therapy, 1,* 57–102.

Mauss, M. (1972). *A general theory of magic* (R. Brain, Trans.). New York: Norton. (Original work published 1902)

Mayr, E. (1960). The emergence of evolutionary novelties. In S. Tax (Ed.), *Evolution after Darwin: Vol. 1. The evolution of life* (pp. 349–380). Chicago: University of Chicago Press.

McClelland, D. C., & Pilon, D. A. (1983). Sources of adult motives in patterns of parent behavior in early childhood. *Journal of Personality and Social Psychology, 44,* 564–574.

Meigs, A. S. (1978). A Papuan perspective on pollution. *Man, 13,* 304–318.

Meigs, A. S. (1984). *Food, sex, and pollution: A New Guinea religion.* New Brunswick, NJ: Rutgers University Press.

Miller, S. B. (1986). Disgust: Conceptualization, development, and dynamics. *International Review of Psychoanalysis, 13,* 295–307.

Mineka, S., & Cook, M. (1988). Social learning and the acquisition of snake fear in monkeys. In T. R. Zentall & B. G. Galef, Jr. (Eds.), *Social learning: Psychological and biological perspectives* (pp. 51–74). Hillsdale, NJ: Erlbaum.

Nemeroff, C., & Rozin, P. (1989). "You are what you eat": Applying the demand-free "impressions" technique to an unacknowledged belief. *Ethos: The Journal of Psychological Anthropology, 17,* 50–69.

Nemeroff, C., & Rozin, P. (1992). Sympathetic magical beliefs and kosher dietary practice: The interaction of rules and feelings. *Ethos: The Journal of Psychological Anthropology, 20,* 96–115.

Obeyesekere, G. (1985). Depression, Buddhism, and work of culture in Sri Lanka. In A. Kleinman & B. Good (Eds.), *Culture and depression* (pp. 134–152). Berkeley: University of California Press.

Orlansky, H. (1949). Infant care and personality. *Psychological Bulletin, 46,* 1–48.

Ortner, S. B. (1973). Sherpa purity. *American Anthropologist, 75,* 49–63.

Ortony, A., & Clore, G. L. (1989). Emotions, moods, and conscious awareness: Comment on Johnson-Laird and Oatley's "The language of emotions. An analysis of a semantic field." *Cognition and Emotion, 3,* 125–137.

Ortony, A., Clore, G. L., & Collins, A. (1988). *The cognitive structure of emotions.* Cambridge, England: Cambridge University Press.

Ortony, A., & Turner, T. (1990). What's basic about basic emotions? *Psychological Review, 97*, 315–331.

Parker, R. (1983). *Miasma: Pollution and purification in early Greek religion.* Oxford: Clarendon Press.

Peiper, A. (1963). *Cerebral functions in infancy and childhood.* New York: Consultants Bureau.

Petó, E. (1936). Contribution to the development of smell feeling. *British Journal of Medical Psychology, 15*, 314–320.

Piaget, J., & Inhelder, B. (1974). From conservation to atomism. In J. Piaget & B. Inhelder, *The child's construction of quantities* (pp. 67–116). London: Routledge & Kegan Paul. (Original work published 1941)

Plutchik, R. (1980). *Emotion: A psychoevolutionary synthesis.* New York: Harper & Row.

Rawls, J. (1971). *A theory of justice.* Cambridge, MA: Harvard University Press.

Renner, H. D. (1944). *The origin of food habits.* London: Faber & Faber.

Rosen, A. (1992). *Children's identification of embarrassment and disgust in everyday situations.* Unpublished doctoral dissertation, University of Pennsylvania.

Rosen, A., & Rozin, P. (in press). Now you see it now you don't: The preschool child's conception of invisible particles. *Developmental Psychology.*

Rosenstein, D., & Oster, H. (1988). Differential facial responses to four basic tastes in newborns. *Child Development, 59*, 1555–1568.

Rozin, P. (1976). The evolution of intelligence and access to the cognitive unconscious. In J. A. Sprague & A.N. Epstein (Eds.), *Progress in psychobiology and physiological psychology* (Vol. 6, pp. 245–280). New York: Academic Press.

Rozin, P. (1984). The acquisition of food habits and preferences. In J. D. Matarazzo, S. M. Weiss, J. A. Herd, N. E. Miller, & S. M. Weiss (Eds.), *Behavioral health: A handbook of health enhancement and disease prevention* (pp. 590–607). New York: Wiley.

Rozin, P. (1986). One-trial acquired likes and dislikes in humans: Disgust as a US, food predominance and negative learning predominance. *Learning and Motivation, 17*, 180–189.

Rozin, P. (1991). Family resemblance in food and other domains: The family paradox and the role of parental congruence. *Appetite, 16*, 93–102.

Rozin, P., Ebert, R., & Lowery, L. (1992). *Varieties of disgust faces and the structure of disgust.* Manuscript submitted for publication.

Rozin, P., & Fallon, A. E. (1980). Psychological categorization of foods and non-foods: A preliminary taxonomy of food rejections. *Appetite, 1*, 193–201.

Rozin, P., & Fallon, A. E. (1987). A perspective on disgust. *Psychological Review, 94*(1), 23–41.

Rozin, P., Fallon, A. E., & Augustoni-Ziskind, M. (1985). The child's conception of food: The development of contamination sensitivity to "disgusting" substances. *Developmental Psychology, 21*, 1075–1079.

Rozin, P., Fallon, A. E., & Augustoni-Ziskind, M. (1986). The child's conception of food: Development of categories of accepted and rejected substances. *Journal of Nutrition Education, 18*, 75–81.

Rozin, P., Fallon, A. E., & Mandell, R. (1984). Family resemblance in attitudes to food. *Developmental Psychology, 20*, 309–314.

Rozin, P., Hammer, L., Oster, H., Horowitz, T., & Marmara, V. (1986). The child's conception of food: Differentiation of categories of rejected substances in the 1.4 to 5 year age range. *Appetite, 7*, 141–151.

Rozin, P., Markwith, M., & McCauley, C. R. (1992). *The nature of aversion to indirect contact with another person: AIDS aversion as a composite of aversion to strangers, infection, moral taint and misfortune.* Manuscript submitted for publication.

Rozin, P., & Millman, L. (1987). Family environment, not heredity, accounts for family resemblance in food preferences and attitudes. *Appetite, 8*, 125–134.

Rozin, P., Millman, L., & Nemeroff, C. (1986). Operation of the laws of sympathetic magic in disgust and other domains. *Journal of Personality and Social Psychology, 50*, 703–712.

Rozin, P., & Nemeroff, C. J. (1990). The laws of sympathetic magic: A psychological analysis of similarity and contagion. In J. Stigler, G. Herdt, & R. A. Shweder (Eds.), *Cultural psychology: Essays on comparative human development* (pp. 205–232). Cambridge, England: Cambridge University Press.

Rozin, P., Nemeroff, C., Horowitz, M., Gordon, B., & Voet, W. (1992). *The borders of the self: Contamination sensitivity and potency of the mouth, other apertures and body parts.* Manuscript submitted for publication.

Rozin, P., Nemeroff, C., Wane, M., & Sherrod, A. (1989). Operation of the sympathetic magical law of contagion in interpersonal attitudes among Americans. *Bulletin of the Psychonomic Society, 27*, 367–370.

Rozin, P., & Zellner, D. A. (1985). The role of Pavlovian conditioning in the acquisition of food likes and dislikes. *Annals of the New York Academy of Sciences, 443*, 189–202.

Russell, J. A. (1991). The contempt expression and the relativity thesis. *Motivation and Emotion, 15*, 149–168.

Sabini, J., & Silver, M. (1983). *Moralities of everyday life.* Oxford: Oxford University Press.

Scherer, K. (1992). *Toward a dynamic theory of emotion: The component process model affective states.* Manuscript submitted for publication.

Scherer, K. R., & Wallbott, H. G. (1992). *Emotions are universal and culture dependent: I. Biopsychological patterning.* Manuscript submitted for publication.

Schmidt, H., & Beauchamp, G. (1988). Adult-like odor preferences and aversions in three-year-old children. *Child Development, 59*, 1136–1143.

Senn, M. J. E., & Solnit, A. J. (1968). *Problems in child behavior and development.* Philadelphia: Lea & Febiger.

Shweder, R. A. (1990). In defense of moral realism: Reply to Gabennesch. *Child Development, 61*, 2060–2067.

Shweder, R. A., Mahapatra, M., & Miller, J. G. (1987). Culture and moral development. In J. Kagan & S. Lamb (Eds.), *The emergence of moral concepts in young children* (pp. 1–82). Chicago: University of Chicago Press.

Siegal, M. (1988). Children's knowledge of contagion and contamination as causes of illness. *Child Development, 59*, 1353–1359.

Soler, J. (1979). The semiotics of food in the Bible. In R. Forster & O. Ranum (Eds.), *Food and drinking history* (E. Forster & P. M. Ranum, Trans.). (pp. 126–138). Baltimore: Johns Hopkins University Press. (Original work published 1973)

Stein, M., Ottenberg, P., & Roulet, N. (1958). A study of the development of olfactory preferences. *Archives of Neurology and Psychiatry, 80*, 264–266.

Steiner, J. E. (1979). Human facial expressions in response to taste and smell stimulation. In H. W. Reese & L. P.

Lipsitt (Eds.), *Advances in child development and behavior* (Vol. 13, pp. 257–295). New York: Academic Press.

Steininger, F. von. (1950). Beitrage zur Soziologie und Sonstigen Biologie der Wanderratte. *Zeitschrift für Tierpsychologie, 7,* 356–379.

Tambiah, S. J. (1969). Animals are good to think and good to prohibit. *Ethnology, 8,* 423–459.

Templer, D. I., King, F. L., Brooner, R. K., & Corgiat, M. (1984). Assessment of body elimination attitude. *Journal of Clinical Psychology, 40,* 754–759.

Thomas, K. (1983). *Man and the natural world.* New York: Pantheon Books.

Tomkins, S. S. (1963). *Affect, imagery, consciousness: Vol. 2. The negative affects.* New York: Springer.

Tomkins, S. S. (1982). Affect theory. In P. Ekman (Ed.), *Emotion in the human face* (2nd ed., pp. 353–395). Cambridge, England: Cambridge University Press.

Tylor, E. B. (1974). *Primitive culture: Researches into the development of mythology, philosophy, religion, art and custom.* New York: Gordon Press. (Original work published 1871)

Wierzbicka, A. (1986). Emotions: Universal or culture-specific? *American Anthropologist, 88,* 584–594.

Zajonc, R. B., & McIntosh, D. N. (1992). Emotions research: Some promising questions and some questionable promises. *Psychological Science, 3,* 70–74.

Zuckerman, M. (1979). *Sensation seeking.* Hillsdale, NJ: Erlbaum.

41

Love and Attachment Processes

ELAINE HATFIELD
RICHARD RAPSON

On March 30, 1981, less than 2 hours before John W. Hinckley, Jr., shot President Ronald Reagan, Hinckley scrawled a final plea to the actress Jodie Foster, with whom he was obsessed:

Dear Jodie,

There is a definite possibility that I will be killed in my attempt to get Reagan. It is for this very reason I am writing you this letter now.

As you well know by now I love you very much. Over the past seven months I've left you dozens of poems, letters and love messages in the faint hope that you could develop an interest in me. Although we talked on the phone a couple of times I never had the nerve to simply approach you and introduce myself. Besides my shyness, I honestly did not wish to bother you with my constant presence. I know the many messages left at your door and in your mailbox were a nuisance, but I felt that it was the most painless way for me to express my love for you. . . .

Jodie, I would abandon this idea of getting Reagan in a second if I could only win your heart and live out the rest of my life with you, whether it be in total obscurity or whatever.

I will admit to you that the reason I'm going ahead with this attempt now is because I just cannot wait any longer to impress you. I've got to do something now to make you understand, in no uncertain terms, that I am doing all of this for your sake! By sacrificing my freedom and possibly my life, I hope to change your mind about me. This letter is being written only an hour before I leave for the Hilton Hotel. Jodie, I'm asking to please look into your heart and at

least give me the chance, with this historical deed, to gain your respect and love.

I love you forever,
John Hinckley

(quoted in Caplan, 1984, pp. 46–48)

Of course, passionate love rarely leads to murderous fantasies. However, the power of love has sparked social psychologists' and emotions researchers' interest in passionate and companionate love and the attachment processes which shape them.

DEFINITIONS

Most scientists distinguish between two forms of love—"passionate love" and "companionate love." Fischer, Shaver, and Carnochan (1990) point out that all emotions possess a number of components:

[Emotions are] . . . organised, meaningful, generally adaptive action systems. . . . [They] are complex functional wholes including appraisals or appreciations. patterned physiological processes, action tendencies, subjective feelings, expressions, and instrumental behaviors. . . . [However,] none of these features is necessary for a particular instance of emotion. Emotions fit into families, within which all members share a family resemblance but no universal set of features. (pp. 84–85)

They contend that there are five prototypic emotions: two positive emotions (love and joy) and three negative ones (anger, sadness, and fear). They, too, distinguish two kinds of love: passionate love (which they label "infatuation") and companionate love (which they label "fondness"). Other researchers have proposed more elaborate typologies of the varieties of love (Sternberg, 1988; Hendrick, (1989).

Passionate love (sometimes called "obsessive love," "infatuation," "lovesickness," or "being in love") is an intense emotion. Elsewhere, we have defined it as follows:

> A state of intense longing for union with another. Reciprocated love (union with the other) is associated with fulfillment and ecstasy. Unrequited love (separation) is associated with emptiness, anxiety, or despair. Passionate love is a complex functional whole including appraisals or appreciations, subjective feelings, expressions, patterned physiological processes, action tendencies, and instrumental behaviors. (Hatfield & Rapson, 1993, p. 5)

The Passionate Love Scale was designed to assess the cognitive, physiological, and behavioral indicants of such a "longing for union" (Hatfield & Sprecher, 1986).

Companionate love (sometimes called "true love" or "conjugal love") is a far less intense emotion. It combines feelings of deep attachment, commitment, and intimacy. We have defined it as follows:

> The affection and tenderness we feel for those with whom our lives are deeply entwined. Companionate love is a complex functional whole including appraisals or appreciations, subjective feelings, expressions, patterned physiological processes, action tendencies, and instrumental behaviors. (Hatfield & Rapson, 1993, p. 9)

Psychologists have used a variety of scales to measure companionate love. For example, Berscheid and Hatfield (1978) focused on subjects' subjective appraisals (attitudes). More recently, Sternberg (1988) has assumed that companionate relationships possess little passion but a great deal of commitment and intimacy; thus, he assessed companionate love by measuring commitment and intimacy (Sternberg, 1986). Berscheid (1983) focused on assessing how "entwined" or linked couples' organized action sequences were.

Researchers have proposed that both passionate and companionate love can be understood, in part, by examining the mother–child attachment experiences on which they are based. Researchers interested in passionate love have tended to focus on infants' attachments (as the prototype of later passionate attachments); researchers interested in companionate love have tended to focus on parental attachments (as the prototype of companionate love). Of course, love relationships can involve both passionate and companionate love.

PASSIONATE LOVE

The Evolutionary Soil of Passionate Love

The Triune Brain

In the 1940s, MacLean (1986) proposed that in the course of evolution, humans have ended up with a brain that possesses a "triune structure." The brain is thought to consist of three different types of brains, layered one upon the other. The oldest brain is basically reptilian. It is primarily concerned with the preservation of the self and the species. The second brain, the neomammalian brain or limbic system, is inherited from the early mammals and evolved to facilitate mother–child relationships. Such emotions as desire, affection, ecstasy, fear, anger, and sadness all derive from activities in the limbic system. The third brain, the late mammalian/early primate brain or neocortex, is inherited from the late mammals and early primates. Not until the neocortex evolved did symbolic or verbal information become important in shaping emotional experience and expression.

Love in Primates

Rosenblum and Plimpton (1981) point out that even primates may experience a primitive form of passionate love. In some species, infant primates must possess a "desire for union" if they are to survive. Separation often means death. Thus, infants are prewired to cling to their mothers. Should a brief separation occur, infants quickly become frantic and begin searching for their mothers. If the mothers return, the infants are joyous—they cling to them and/or bound about in excitement. If the mothers do not return, the infants eventually abandon all hope of contact, despair, and die. The experience Rosenblum and Plimpton describe, with its alternating lows and highs, certainly sounds much like passionate love's "desire for union." Fervent attachments seem not to be unique to humans.

Love in Children

Ainsworth (1989) and Bowlby (1969, 1973, 1980) carried out extensive studies of the process of attachment, separation, and loss in children. They found that infants and toddlers react to separation in the same way as do their primate ancestors.

There is some evidence that children experience passionate love very early. Bell (1902) interviewed 1,700 Indiana teachers and observed 800 children; he concluded that children could experience "sex-love" as early as 3½ years of age. Easton and Hatfield (cited in Hatfield, Schmitz, Cornelius, & Rapson, 1988) developed the Childhood Love Scale, a children's version of the Passionate Love Scale. They interviewed more than 200 boys and girls, ranging in age from 4 to 18, about their romantic feelings. Their results made it clear that Bell was right—even the youngest of children were capable of passionate love. Subsequent research (Hatfield, Brinton, & Cornelius, 1989) has made it clear that when children are anxious or fearful, they are especially vulnerable to passionate love.

Of course, passionate love becomes very powerful when children enter puberty. Perhaps this is because teenagers experience the return of old separation anxieties during the period; perhaps they are under unusual stress as they go through the agonies of adolescence. Neurophysiologists remind us that passionate love may also be fueled by pubescent hormonal changes (Gadpaille, 1975; Money, 1980). In any case, puberty and sexual maturity may well bring a new depth to passion.

Love in Adults

Recently, Shaver and Hazan (1988) have proposed that romantic love should be conceived of as a form of attachment. Children's early patterns of attachment should influence their adult attachments. For example, children are likely to become securely attached to their mothers if they are allowed to be both affectionate *and* independent. Such children should mature into secure adults who are comfortable with intimacy and are able to trust and depend on those they care for. Children may become

anxious/ambivalent if they have learned to be clingy and dependent, or fearful of being smothered and restrained, or both. Such children should become anxious/ambivalent adults who fall in love easily, who seek extreme levels of closeness, and who are terrified that they will be abandoned. Their love affairs are likely to be short-lived. The avoidant child (who has been abandoned early on) may well become an avoidant adult who is uncomfortable getting too close and has difficulty depending on others. The authors have amassed considerable support in favor of this formulation.

Using the same logic, Bartholomew (1990) has proposed that adults' attachment styles should fall into one of four patterns, depending on their self-image (positive or negative) and their image of the other (positive or negative): (1) Men and women who have a positive self-image and a positive image of others should be capable of becoming securely attached to others; (2) those with low self-esteem and a positive regard for others should be preoccupied with intimate relations; (3) those who have a negative self-image and a negative image of others should be fearful of becoming close to others; and (4) those who have a positive self-image and a negative image of others should be dismissing of or detached from others. Bartholomew has found evidence in support of this typology. Hindy, Schwarz, and Brodsky (1989) tested the notion that children who receive inconsistent love and affection will be "at risk" in their love relationships. They gave men and women a battery of tests designed to determine the stability of their childhoods. (How stormy was the marriage between their parents? Did they get a divorce?) Then they asked subjects about their own romantic histories. (Did they often fall passionately in love? Or did they go out of their way to avoid entanglements? How jealous were they? When their love affairs fell apart, did they sink into deep depression?) They found that young men and women whose parents had been inconsistent in their love and nurturance were more "addicted" to love *or* more afraid of it than was the case with those who came from more secure backgrounds.

The Antecedents of Passionate Love

If passionate love is rooted in childhood attachments, certain types of people, caught up in certain types of situations, should be especially vulnerable to passion. Anything that makes adults feel as helpless and dependent as they were as children—anything that makes them fear separation and loss—should increase their passionate craving to merge with others. There is some evidence to support these speculations.

Low Self-Esteem

Reik (1949) was on of the first to propose that when self-esteem is threatened, individuals will be more likely to fall prey to passionate love. Hatfield (1965) conducted an experiment to test the hypothesis that when self-esteem has been bruised, subjects should be unusually receptive to the love and affection offered by others. As predicted, women whose self-esteem was threatened were most attracted to a potential romantic partner. (Other theorists have also found a link between low self-esteem and passionate love. See Jacobs, Berscheid, & Hatfield, 1971; Bartholomew & Horowitz, 1991.)

Dependency and Insecurity

A number of theorists have observed that people who are dependent and insecure (or who are caught up in affairs that promote such feelings) are especially vulnerable to passionate love. Berscheid and her associates (Fei & Berscheid, 1977) have argued that passionate love, dependency, and insecurity are tightly linked. When people are passionately in love, they are painfully aware of how dependent they are on those they love; dependency naturally breeds insecurity. In an ingenious experiment, Berscheid, Graziano, Monson, and Dermer (1976) found clear evidence in support of these contentions.

Anxiety

Numerous theorists, beginning with Sigmund Freud (1910/1953), have proposed that passionate love is fueled by anxiety and fear (Hatfield, 1971a, 1971b; Hatfield & Rapson, 1987; Carlson & Hatfield, 1992). This makes sense; passionate love and anxiety are closely related both neuroanatomically and chemically (Kaplan. 1979; Liebowitz, 1983). Researchers have demonstrated that anxious individuals are especially prone to seek passionate love relationships (Solomon & Corbit, 1974; Peele,

1975). In a series of studies, Hatfield et al. (1989), for example, found that adolescents of Caucasian, Chinese, Japanese, Korean, and mixed ancestry who were either momentarily or habitually anxious were especially vulnerable to passionate love.

Neediness

Social psychologists have found that acute deprivation does seem to set the stage for passionate love. Stephan, Berscheid, and Hatfield (1971) tested the simple hypothesis that when people are sexually aroused, their minds wander, and soon their dazzling fantasies lend sparkle to drab reality. They proposed that when men are sexually aroused, they should have a greater tendency to see women as sex objects. Hence, they should tend to exaggerate two of their dates' traits: their sexual desirability and their sexual receptivity. They found that they were right. As predicted, the more aroused the men, the more beautiful they thought their dates. In addition, the more aroused they were, the more likely they were to assume that their dates would be sexually receptive. Unaroused men judged their dates-to-be as fairly "nice" women. Aroused men suspected that they were probably "amorous," "immoral," "promiscuous," "willing," "unwholesome," and "uninhibited."

The Consequences of Passionate Love

The previous sections, dealing with the *roots* of love, have painted a somewhat dismal picture. We have focused on the bruised self-esteem, the dependence, and the insecurity that make people hunger for love. Here, we would normally point out that when people attain love (or imagine that they might), they experience intense happiness and excitement. Why would people long for love unless they enjoyed receiving it?

The Rewards of Passionate Love

Surprisingly, we have been able to find little survey or experimental research documenting the delights of passionate love; nonetheless, interviews with lovers and insights derived from works of fiction suggest that lovers may experience at least four kinds of rewards:

1. *Moments of exultation.* When love is realized, lovers may experience moments of passionate bliss.

2. *Feeling understood and accepted.* When men and women are loved, they sometimes feel fully understood, loved, and accepted.

3. *Sharing a sense of union.* Lovers may feel a sense of union with their beloved.

4. *Feeling secure and safe.* Lovers may feel safe and secure when they are with someone they love.

5. *Transcendence.* When people fall in love, they are sometimes able to transcend their former limitations.

The Costs of Passionate Love

Of course, love has its costs too. When hopes are dashed or relationships fall apart, people's self-esteem is often shattered; they feel lonely and miserable; and they may experience intense jealousy.

Why Is Passion So Passionate?

There are probably two main reasons why passionate love is often such an overpowering experience. First, passionate love is a basic emotion; for our ancestors, union was a life-and-death matter. Second, passionate feelings are mixed with other intense emotional experiences—joy, jealousy, loneliness, sadness, fear, and anger. The resulting emotional mixtures are often explosive combinations. Researchers have proposed that such emotional blending can produce especially strong emotional experiences/reactions. Let us review evidence in support of the "cross-magnification" hypothesis.

Shaver, Wu, and Schwartz (1991) interviewed young people in the United States, Italy, and the People's Republic of China about their emotional experiences. In all cultures, men and women identified the same emotions as basic or prototypic. These were joy/happiness, love/attraction, fear, anger/hate, and sadness/depression. They also agreed as to whether the various emotions should be labeled as positive experiences (such as joy) or negative ones (such as fear, anger, or sadness). They agreed completely, that is, except about one emotion—love. The U.S. and Italian subjects tended to equate love with happiness; both passionate and companionate love were assumed to be intensely positive experiences.

Chinese students, however, had a darker view of love. In Chinese there are few "happy love" words; love is associated with sadness. They associated passionate love with such idiographs (words) as "infatuation," "unrequited love," "nostalgia," and "sorrow love." Shaver et al.'s students from the East and West never did come to an agreement as to the nature of love. The Eastern and Western groups continued to regard each other's visions of love as "unrealistic."

In this chapter, we take a complex view of the nature of passionate love. We would argue that, in fact, even in North American culture passionate love is usually a mixed blessing. As the definition of love indicates, passionate love *is* sometimes a joyously exciting experience, sparked by exciting fantasies and rewarding encounters with the loved one. But that is only part of the story. Passionate love is like any other form of excitement. By its very nature, excitement involves a continuous interplay between elation and despair, thrills and terror. Think, for example, of the mixed and rushed feelings that novice skiers experience. Their hearts begin to pound as they wait to lurch onto the ski lift. Once they realize they have made it, they are elated. On the easy ride to the top, they are still a bit unnerved. Their hands shake and their knees tremble, but they slowly begin to relax. Moments later they look ahead and realize it is time to push off the lift. The landing looks icy and steep. Their rush quickly turns to panic. They can't turn back. They struggle to get their feelings under control. They jump off the lift, elated and panicky—it is hard to tell which. Then they start to ski downhill, experiencing as they go a wild jumble of powerful emotions. Eventually, they arrive at the bottom of the hill, elated, relieved. Perhaps they feel like crying. Sometimes they are so tired they are flooded with waves of depression. Usually, they get up, ready to try again. Passionate lovers experience the same roller-coaster rush of feelings—euphoria, happiness, vulnerability, anxiety, panic, despair. The risks of love merely add fuel to the fire.

Sometimes men and women become entangled in love affairs where the delight is brief, and pain, uncertainty, jealousy, misery, anxiety, and despair are abundant. Recent social-psychological research makes it clear that passionate love, which thrives on excitement, is linked to a variety of strong emotions—both positive and negative. Tennov

(1979) interviewed more than 500 lovers. Almost all of them took it for granted that passionate love (which Tennov labeled "limerence") is a bittersweet experience.

Hatfield (Carlson & Hatfield, 1992) has argued that such emotional mixtures sometimes produce the most intense explosions of feeling. Logically, when people are exposed to a variety of emotional stimuli, their emotions can interact in three different ways. First, sometimes people are able to identify the ebb and flow of their separate emotions. In such cases, they experience a series of distinct emotions, or emotional blends. Secondly, sometimes incompatible emotions may "cancel" one another out. Finally, people most often experience emotional cross-magnification. Passionate love, for instance, may actually be intensified by the shyness, anxiety, jealousy, or anger the other sparks in us. It is easy to identify such instances of emotional spillover in our daily lives. When we have been frenetically rushing around all day, we often end up snapping at a friend over some trifle. What would normally be slight irritation has exploded into rage; we have to remind ourselves (or *be* reminded) to "settle down." Or we trip on the threadbare carpet and save ourselves just in time from hurtling down the stairs. We dissolve in a fit of giggles. What's so funny about almost being killed? Our sense of the absurd has been magnified by our fear and relief.

Hatfield argued that in life such emotional spillover effects can have powerful consequences. Most intense emotional experiences involve such blends of emotions. This may not be pure coincidence. Perhaps emotions (especially positive emotions) have a better chance to rise to a fever pitch when several emotional units are activated. Love may be more intense than usual when it is fueled by ecstasy *and* jealousy, insecurity *and* fear of loss. The death of a mate may be especially hard for the survivor to bear when combined with guilt about the way he or she treated the deceased. Add grief and anger at the loss to that guilt, and the darkness deepens. Mixtures of emotions most certainly can fuel passion.

Evidence That Both Pleasure and Pain May Fuel Passion

Passion and the Positive Emotions. Our definition of passionate love states that "Recipro-

cated love (union with the other) is associated with fulfillment and ecstasy." No one doubts that love is such a "high," that the joys of love generally spill over and add sparkle to everything else in life. What has been of interest to psychologists is the converse of this proposition: that the adrenalin associated with a wide variety of highs can spill over and make passionate love more passionate.

A number of carefully crafted studies make it clear that various positive emotions—amusement (White, Fishbein, & Rustein, 1981), erotic excitement (Istvan & Griffitt, 1978; Istvan, Griffitt, & Weider, 1983; Stephan et al., 1971), or general excitement (Zuckerman, 1979)—can all intensify passion.

Passion and the Negative Emotions. In defining passionate love, we have also observed: "Unrequited love (separation) is associated with emptiness, anxiety, or despair." The world has noted that the failure to acquire or sustain love is an extraordinarily painful experience. Psychologists, along with most other writers, report the panic, loneliness, and eventual despair that people feel when they are separated from those they love (Peplau & Perlman, 1982).

By now, psychologists have amassed considerable evidence for the proposition that people are especially vulnerable to love when their lives are turbulent. For example, Dutton and Aron (1974), in a duo of studies, discovered a close link between fear and sexual attraction. By now there is a great deal of experimental and correlational evidence for the intriguing contention that, under the right conditions, a variety of awkward and painful experiences— anxiety and fear (Brehm, Gatz, Goethals, McCrimmon, & Ward, 1978; Dienstbier, 1978; Hoon, Wincze, & Hoon, 1977; Riordon & Tedeschi, 1983), embarrassment (Byrne, Przybyla, & Infantino, 1981), the discomfort of seeing others involved in conflict (Dutton, 1979), jealousy (Clanton & Smith, 1987), loneliness (Peplau & Perlman, 1982), anger (Barclay, 1969; Driscoll, Davis, & Lipsetz, 1972), horror (White et al., 1981), and even grief—can all deepen passion.

The evidence, then, suggests that various states of arousal can spill over and influence one another. Although most of us assume that we love the people we do in *spite* of the suffering they cause us, it may be that, in part, we love them *because* of the pain they cause.

Love seems to flourish when it is nurtured by a torrent of good experiences, as well as a sprinking of unsettling, irritating, and even painful ones.

Passion and Emotionally Neutral Arousal. Research indicates that passion can even be stirred by excitation transfer from such emotionally neutral hut physically arousing experiences as riding an exercise bicycle (Cantor, Zillman, & Bryant, 1975) or jogging (White et al., 1981).

COMPANIONATE LOVE

Theorists who tried to explain the origins of companionate love have generally taken an evolutionary approach. Plutchik (1980), for one, argues that emotional "packages" are inherited, adaptive patterns of emotional experience, physiological reaction, and behavior. At every phylogenetic level, organisms face the same problems: If they are to survive and reproduce, they must find food, avoid being killed, and take advantage of reproductive opportunities. Many theorists believe that companionate love is built on the ancient circuitry evolved to ensure that mammals and primates mate, reproduce, and care for the young. Recently, neuroscientists, anthropologists, and developmentalists have begun to learn more about companionate love. They have begun to study the subjective feelings, expressions, patterned physiological processes, and action tendencies associated with this form of love's ancient heritage.

The Chemistry of Companionate Love

Neuroscientists know very little about the biological bases of companionate love and tenderness; researchers have just begun to speculate. Recently, neuroscientists have identified a hormone, oxytocin, which seems to promote affectionate, close, intimate bonds (Caldwell, Jirikowski, Greer, & Pedersen, 1989) and sexual and reproductive behavior (Pedersen, Caldwell, Jirikowski, & Insel, 1991). Carter, a zoologist, (quoted in Angier, 1991), observes: "It [oxytocin] facilitates tactile contact between animals, and that's an early step in the development of social attachment" (p. B8). Oxyto-

cin also promotes more intense bonds between mothers and infants; it increases mothers' eagerness to nurture their young. Finally, oxytocin appears to increase contact between same-sex pairs as well (Angier, 1991, p. B8).

The Look, Posture, Sounds, and Behaviors of Companionate Love

Some theorists have argued that love's ancient beginnings can be read today in the looks, postures, sounds, and behaviors of companionate love.

The Look of Love

Emotions researchers have found that the universal emotions—joy, love, sadness, fear, and anger—are associated with certain characteristic facial expressions. In recent research, scientists have tried to pinpoint the facial expressions associated with joy and love. For example, Hatfield, Costello, Schalekamp, Hsee, and Denney (1991) found that people were able to distinguish facial expressions of love from expressions of joy, sadness, fear, and anger. Exactly how the subjects did this is not yet known. The authors have speculated that perhaps when men and women are experiencing companionate love, they take on the expression mothers often instinctively display when they are happily, tenderly gazing at their young infants: They gaze downward (at the infants), their faces soften, and a slight, tender smile plays about their lips. (Bloch, Orthous, & Santibañez-H., 1987, have proposed the same hypothesis; they provide some suggestive evidence in support of this contention.)

The Posture of Love

Morris (1971) observes:

> These, then, are our first real experiences of life—floating in a warm fluid, curling, inside a total embrace, swaying to the undulations of the moving body and hearing the beat of the pulsing heart. Our prolonged exposure to these sensations in the absence of other, competing stimuli leaves a lasting impression on our brains, an impression that spells security, comfort and passivity. (p. 12)

After birth, Morris contends, mothers instinctively try to recreate the security of the womb. Mothers kiss, caress, fondle, and embrace their infants; they cradle them in their arms. In the womb, neonates hear the steady drumbeat of their mothers' hearts beating at 72 beats per minute. After birth, mothers instinctively hold their babies with their heads pressed against the mothers' left breasts, closest to their hearts. When their infants fret, mothers unconsciously rock them at a rate of between 60 and 70 rocks per minute, the rate that is most calming to infants. Morris points out: "It appears as if this rhythm, whether heard or felt, is the vital comforter, reminding the baby vividly of the lost paradise of the womb" (1971, p. 14). Of course. in adulthood, these same kisses, tender caresses, and embraces continue to provide security for men and women—who are unconscious of the early origins of these behaviors.

The Sounds of Love

Finally, French psychophysiologist Bloch and her colleagues (1987) argue that not just joy, but passionate love ("eroticism") and companionate love ("tenderness") are associated with different breathing patterns and sounds. Mothers often coo or croon softly with their mouths held near their infants' heads. Bloch et al. have speculated that such tender maternal sounds become the forerunners of the breathing patterns and sounds associated with love. They studied the basic emotions of joy, love/eroticism, love/tenderness, fear, anger, and sadness, and discovered that the breathing patterns associated with eroticism and tenderness are somewhat different:

> In *eroticism*, the principal feature of sexual activation is an even breathing pattern which increases in frequency and amplitude depending on the intensity of the emotional engagement; inspiration occurs through a relaxed open mouth. The face muscles are relaxed, and the eyes are closed or semi-closed. In the female version of the erotic pattern, the head is tilted backwards, and the neck is exposed. (p. 6)

On the other hand, in tenderness,

> The breathing pattern is of low frequency with an even and regular rhythm; the mouth is semiclosed, the relaxed lips forming a slight smile. Facial and antigravitational muscles are very relaxed, eyes are open and relaxed, and the head is slightly tilted to the side. The postural attitude is one of approach. Vocalization includes a humming type lullaby sound. (p. 6)

Behavioral Indicators of Love

Finally, anthropologist Eibl-Eibesfeldt (1971), in *Love and Hate*, observes that primate mothers and infants reveal their close bonds in certain characteristic behaviors. In infancy, human mothers and their infants express their feelings for each other in much the same way. And in adulthood, men and women in all cultures cannot help showing their companionate love in the same ways they did as infants. For instance, newborn infants rhythmically rotate their heads from side to side as they root for their mothers' nipples. An adult, playfully nuzzling a loved one, often finds himself or herself using motions, gestures, and rhythms from the distant past—holding the loved one's head in his or her hands, or rubbing his or her lips against the loved one's cheek with a sideways movement of the head. Eibl-Eibesfeldt graphically illustrates the kissing, mutual feeding, and embracing that bond people together.

Parent–Child Coordination

Mothers and fathers differ in how well attuned they are to their infants' rhythms. Usually, both mother and child are in control of their interaction. The baby's needs must shape the general structure in which the interaction occurs; the mother then has the opportunity to regulate the tempo of the interaction. If she speeds up, she will reduce the baby's level of communication; if she slows down, she can expect a higher level of communication and engagement (Stern, 1974).

Sometimes, parents are not able to shape themselves to their infants' needs. When an infant turns its head, needing to cut down the level of stimulation that it is receiving, a young mother may panic: "The child doesn't like me. What did I do wrong?" She may intrusively force herself on the baby, looking for reassurance, but overwhelming the infant still further. A father, in an effort to play, may frighten a child with too much noise and movement. Or the parents may give the infant too little attention. They may be bored, uninterested, or distracted. They both may be exhausted from trying to keep house and from their careers outside the home. Generally, infants respond to such lack of interest by trying to rouse their caretakers. If that proves to be impossible, they eventually withdraw completely. We might expect such parental intrusion or indifference to have a profound impact upon children's strategies for dealing with their subsequent love relationships. Such experiences may well shape their eagerness and willingness to get close to others, as well as their ability to balance closeness and distance, intimacy and independence.

CONCLUSIONS

In sum, then, researchers have proposed that both passionate and companionate love can be understood, in part, by examining the mother–child attachment experiences on which they are based. Researchers interested in passionate love have tended to focus on infants' attachments to their mothers (as the prototype of later passionate attachments); researchers interested in companionate love have tended to focus on parental attachments to their infants (as the prototype of companionate attachments). Of course, love relationships can involve both passionate and companionate love. In this chapter, we have reviewed research in support of these contentions.

REFERENCES

Ainsworth, M. D. S. (1989). Attachments beyond infancy. *American Psychologist, 44*, 709–716.

Angier, N. (1991, January 22). A potent peptide prompts an urge to cuddle. *The New York Times*, pp. B5–B8.

Barclay, A. M. (1969). The effect of hostility on physiological and fantasy responses. *Journal of Personality, 37*, 651–667.

Bartholomew, K. (1990). Avoidance of intimacy: An attachment perspective. *Journal of Social and Personal Relationships, 7*, 147–178 .

Bartholomew, K., & Horowitz, L. M. (1991). Attachment styles in young adults: A test of a four-category model. *Journal of Personality and Social Psychology, 61*, 226–244.

Bell, S. (1902). A preliminary study of the emotion of love between the sexes. *American Journal of Psychology, 13*, 325–354.

Berscheid, E. (1983). Emotion. In H. H. Kelley, E. Berscheid, A. Christensen, J. H. Harvey, T. L. Huston, G. Levinger, E. McClintock, L. A. Peplau, & D. R. Peterson (Eds.), *Close relationships* (pp. 110–168). San Francisco: W. H. Freeman.

Berscheid, E., Graziano, W., Monson, T., & Dermer, M. (1976). Outcome dependency: Attention, attribution, and attraction. *Journal of Personality and Social Psychology, 34*, 978–989.

Berscheid, E., & Hatfield, E. (1978). *Interpersonal attraction* (2nd ed.). Reading, MA: Addison-Wesley.

Bloch, S., Orthous, P., & Santibañez-H., G. (1987). Effector patterns of basic emotions: A psychophysiological method for training actors. *Journal of Social and Biological Structures, 10*, 1–19.

Bowlby, J. (1969). *Attachment and loss: Vol. 1. Attachment.* New York: Basic Books.

Bowlby, J. (1973). Affectional bonds: Their nature and origin. In R. Weiss (Ed.), *Loneliness: The experience of emotional and social isolation* (pp. 38–52). Cambridge, MA: MIT Press.

Bowlby, J. (1980). *Attachment and loss: Vol. 3. Loss: Sadness and depression.* New York: Basic Books.

Brehm, J. W., Gatz, M., Goethals, G., McCrimmon, J., & Ward, L. (1978). Psychological arousal and interpersonal attraction. *JSAS: Catalogue of Selected Documents in Psychology, 8.* (Ms. No. 1724)

Byrne, D., Przybyla, D. P. J., & Infantino, A. (1981, April). *The influence of social threat on subsequent romantic attraction.* Paper presented at the meeting of the Eastern Psychological Association, New York.

Caldwell, J. D., Jirikowski, G. F., Greer, E. R., & Pedersen, C. A. (1989). Medial preoptic area oxytocin and female sexual receptivity. *Behavioral Neuroscience, 103*, 655–662.

Cantor, J., Zillman, D., & Bryant, J. (1975). Enhancement of experienced sexual arousal in response to erotic stimuli through misattribution of unrelated residual excitation. *Journal of Personality and Social Psychology, 32*, 69–75.

Caplan, L. (1984, July 2). Annals of law: The insanity defense. *The New Yorker*, pp. 45–78.

Carlson, J. G., & Hatfield, E. (1992). *Psychology of emotion.* Fort Worth, TX: Harcourt Brace Jovanovich.

Clanton, G., & Smith, L. G. (Eds.). (1987). *Jealousy.* Lanham, MA: University Press of America.

Dienstbier, R. A. (1978). Emotion–attribution theory: Establishing roots and exploring future perspectives. In H. E. Howe & R. A. Dienstbier (Eds.), *Nebraska Symposium on Motivation* (Vol. 26, pp. 237–306). Lincoln: University of Nebraska Press.

Driscoll, R., Davis, K. E., & Lipsetz, M. E. (1972). Parental interference and romantic love: The Romeo and Juliet effect. *Journal of Personality and Social Psychology, 24*, 1–10.

Dutton, D. (1979). *The arousal–attraction link in the absence of negative reinforcement.* Paper presented at the meeting of the Canadian Psychological Association, Toronto.

Dutton, D., & Aron, A. (1974) . Some evidence for heightened sexual attraction under conditions of high anxiety. *Journal of Personality and Social Psychology, 30*, 510–517.

Eibl-Eibesfeldt, I. (1971). *Love and hate.* New York: Holt, Rinehart & Winston.

Fei, J., & Berscheid, E. (1977). *Perceived dependency, insecurity, and love in heterosexual relationships: The eternal triangle.* Unpublished manuscript, University of Minnesota.

Fischer, K. W., Shaver, P. R., & Carnochan, P. (1990). How emotions develop and how they organize development. *Cognition and Emotion, 4*, 81–127.

Freud, S. (1953). Contributions to the psychology of love: A special type of choice of objects made by men. In E. Jones (Ed.), *Collected papers of Sigmund Freud* (Vol. 4, pp. 192–202). London: Hogarth Press. (Original work published 1910)

Gadpaille, W. (1975). *The cycles of sex.* New York: Scribner's.

Hatfield, E. (1965). The effect of self-esteem on romantic liking. *Journal of Experimental Social Psychology, 1*, 184–197.

Hatfield, E. (1971a). Passionate love. In B. I. Murstein (Ed.), *Theories of attraction and love* (pp. 85–99). New York: Springer.

Hatfield, E. (1971b). *Studies testing a theory of positive affect.* Proposal for National Science Foundation Grant No. 30822X.

Hatfield, E., Brinton, C., & Cornelius, J. (1989). Passionate love and anxiety in young adolescents. *Motivation and Emotion, 13,* 271–289.

Hatfield, E., Costello, J., Schalekamp, M., Hsee, C., & Denney, C. (1991). *The effect of vocal feedback on emotional experience/expression.* Unpublished manuscript, University of Hawaii.

Hatfield, E., & Rapson, R. L. (1987). Passionate love/sexual desire: Can the same paradigm explain both? *Archives of Sexual Behavior, 16,* 259–278.

Hatfield, E., & Rapson, R. L. (1993). *Love, sex, and intimacy: Their psychology, biology, and history.* New York: HarperCollins.

Hatfield, E., Schmitz, E., Cornelius, J., & Rapson, R. L. (1988). Passionate love: How early does it begin? *Journal of Psychology and Human Sexuality, 1,* 35–52.

Hatfield, E., & Sprecher, S. (1986). Measuring passionate love in intimate relations. *Journal of Adolescence, 9,* 383–410.

Hendricks, C. (Ed.). (1989). *Close relationships.* Newbury Park, CA: Sage.

Hindy, C. G., Schwarz, J. C., & Brodsky, A. (1989). *If this is love why do I feel so insecure?* New York: Atlantic Monthly Press.

Hoon, P. W., Wincze, J. P., & Hoon, E. F. (1977). A test of reciprocal inhibition: Are anxiety and sexual arousal in women mutually inhibitory? *Journal of Abnormal Psychology, 86,* 65–74.

Istvan, J., & Griffitt, W. (1978). *Emotional arousal and sexual attraction.* Unpublished manuscript, Kansas State University.

Istvan, S., Griffitt, W., & Weider, G. (1983). Sexual arousal and the polarization of perceived sexual attractiveness. *Basic and Applied Social Psychology, 4,* 307–318.

Jacobs, L., Berscheid, E., & Hatfield, E. (1971). Self-esteem and attraction. *Journal of Personality and Social Psychology, 17,* 84–91 .

Kaplan, H. S. (1979). *Disorders of sexual desire.* New York: Simon & Schuster.

Liebowitz, M. R. (1983). *The chemistry of love.* Boston: Little, Brown.

MacLean, P. D. (1986). Ictal symptoms relating to the nature of affects and their cerebral substrate. In R. Plutchik & H. Kellerman (Eds.), *Emotion: Theory, research, and experience. Vol. 3. Biological foundations of emotion* (pp. 61–90). New York: Academic Press.

Money, J. (1980). *Love and love sickness.* Baltimore: Johns Hopkins University Press.

Morris, D. (1971). *Intimate behaviour.* London: Triad/ Grafton Books.

Pedersen, C. A., Caldwell, J. D., Jirikowski, G., & Insel. T. R. (1991, May 19–22). *Oxytocin in maternal, sexual and social behaviors.* Paper presented at the meeting of the New York Academy of Sciences, Arlington, VA.

Peele, S. (1975). *Love and addiction.* New York: Taplinger.

Peplau, L. A., & Perlman, D. (1982). *Loneliness.* New York: Wiley-Interscience.

Plutchik, R. (1980). *Emotion: A psychoevolutionary synthesis.* New York: Harper & Row.

Reik, T. (1949). *Of love and lust.* New York: Farrar, Straus.

Riordan, C. A., & Tedeschi, J. T. (1983). Attraction in aversive environments: Some evidence for classical conditioning and negative reinforcement. *Journal of Personality and Social Psychology, 44,* 683–692.

Rosenblum, L. A., & Plimpton, L. A. (1981). The infant's effort to cope with separation. In M. Lewis & L. Rosenblum (Eds.), *The uncommon child* (pp. 225–257). New York: Plenum Press.

Shaver, P. R., & Hazan, C. (1988). A biased overview of the study of love. *Journal of Social and Personal Relationships, 5,* 474–501.

Shaver, P. R., Wu, S., & Schwartz, J. C. (1991). Cross-cultural similarities and differences in emotion and its representation: A prototype approach. In M. S. Clark (Ed.), *Review of personality and social psychology* (Vol. 13, pp. 175–212). Newbury Park, CA: Sage.

Solomon, R. L., & Corbit, J. D. (1974). An opponent process theory of motivation: I. The temporal dynamics of affect. *Psychological Review, 81,* 119–145.

Stephan, W., Berscheid, E., & Hatfield, E. (1971). Sexual arousal and heterosexual perception. *Journal of Personality and Social Psychology, 20,* 3–101.

Stern, D. N. (1974). Mother and infant at play: The dyadic interaction involving facial, vocal, and gaze behavior. In M. Lewis & L. A. Rosenblum (Eds.), *The effect of the infant on its caregiver* (pp. 105–121). New York: Wiley.

Sternberg, R. J. (1986). *Construct validation of a triangular theory of love.* Unpublished manuscript, Yale University, New Haven, CT.

Sternberg, R. J. (1988). Triangulating love. In R. J. Sternberg & M. L. Barnes (Eds.), *The psychology of love* (pp. 119–138). New Haven, CT: Yale University Press.

Tennov, D. (1979). *Love and limerence.* New York: Stein & Day.

White, G. L., Fishbein, S., & Rustein, J. (1981). Passionate love and the misattribution of arousal. *Journal of Personality and Social Psychology, 41,* 56–62.

Zuckerman, M. (1979). *Sensation seeking: Beyond the optimal level of arousal.* Hillsdale, NJ: Erlbaum.

42

Exhilaration and Humor

WILLIBALD RUCH

THE EMOTION OF EXHILARATION

The study of the emotion of exhilaration originated in the study of positive affective responses to humor. "Exhilaration" was introduced as an emotion construct aimed at integrating the various responses occurring at the levels of behavior, physiology, and emotional experience (Ruch, 1990a). A prior concept, the so-called "humor response," was too narrowly defined and did not adequately represent the affective nature of the response to humor. Typically, the term "humor response" denoted the perception of a stimulus as funny, sometimes also including such overt responses as smiling and laughter. However, the physiological changes occurring, as well as other elements of emotional experience, were not covered. Furthermore, the term "humor response" is misleading, in that it gives the impression that exhilaration is a response unique to humor; this might have resulted from the failure to investigate humor in the context of other stimuli yielding similar responses, such as tickling or nitrous oxide (Ruch, 1990b).

The term "exhilaration" is of Latin origin (*hilaris* means "cheerful") and is used here in its original sense to denote the process of making cheerful or the temporary rise in cheerful state. Whereas in contemporary dictionaries "to exhilarate" is also defined as "to make cheerful, laugh, merry, glad, or joyous," it also means "to enliven" or "to make excited." Some definitions give even more emphasis to the "excitement" component than to the "cheerfulness" component, and in common

language the meaning of the term is sometimes restricted to the high end of the excitement continuum. However, as the term is used here, the excitement component is de-emphasized. Although high levels of excitement are involved in strong exhilaration (e.g., in an outburst of laughter at a very arousing joke revealed by a surprising and clever punch line), intermediate and low levels of excitement can also occur. Thus, although the present definition of "exhilaration" may deviate slightly from the understanding of this term in common language, the term is preferred to other related terms. The shortcomings of potential alternative terms, such as "amusement" or "mirth," are discussed by McGhee (1979).

Wundt's (1874/1903) descriptive dimensions of feelings may help to characterize exhilaration. In his three-dimensional model containing the axes pleasantness–unpleasantness, excitation–quietness, and strain–relaxation, exhilaration might be described as a pleasurable, relaxed excitation. Within taxonomies of emotion categories, exhilaration may be seen as a facet of the positive emotion of happiness (or joy). Within the family of positive emotions, exhilaration may be the one most strongly aligned with laughter; whereas empirical studies of happiness rarely report its occurrence, laughter is an inevitable response category in humor studies.

Exhilaration should be separated conceptually from cheerfulness as a mood state or a more tonic change in mood. A cheerful mood is characterized by a longer duration, less fluctuation in intensity, and greater independence from an eliciting stimulus. Single incidents of exhilaration are of short duration and have a marked timing; typically, there is a more or less steep onset, a pronounced apex, and a generally less steep offset. Although conceptually different, exhilaration and the state of cheerfulness should be studied together, since it can be hypothesized that there is a reciprocal relationship between them. A cheerful state facilitates the induction of exhilaration, and an accumulation of exhilaration responses may lead to longer-lasting changes in the level of cheerfulness. Also, if the induction of exhilaration fails (e.g., when a joke is told that is perceived as tasteless), the cheerful state may be lowered.

Thus, "exhilaration" may be defined as an emotion construct denoting a temporary increase in a cheerful state that is observable in behavior, physiology, and emotional experience, and that occurs in response to humor, but also to other stimuli.

DESCRIPTION OF EXHILARATION

Behavior

Exhilaration may be observed in facial behavior, gestures, and posture. Whereas milder forms of exhilaration are reflected only in facial displays, body movements and changes in gesture or posture also occur at more intense levels of exhilaration.

Smiling

The smile of exhilaration is produced by the contraction of two pairs of facial muscles: the zygomatic major and the orbital part of the orbicularis oculi. The action of the former muscle produces the facial appearance perceived as "smiling"; it pulls the lip corner obliquely up and back, and deepens the furrow running from the nostril to the lip corner. The orbicularis oculi muscle lifts the cheeks upward and draws the skin toward the eyes from the temple and cheeks. It narrows the eye opening and may cause "crow's feet" wrinkles to appear at the outer corner of the eye opening (Ekman & Friesen, 1982). Although electromyographic (EMG) studies show that both muscles are typically involved in the smile of exhilaration, in smiles of lower intensity the facial display may contain only signs of contraction of the zygomatic major muscle (Ruch, 1990a).

Several facial changes occur in reactions that are on the borderline between a big smile and a laugh. The lips can be opened or not, the teeth may be shown or not, and the jaw can be opened or not. Sometimes there is an audible expulsion of air or a single-syllable "ha" vocalization. The air usually escapes through the mouth, but if the jaw is not opened it does so through the nose.

Laughing

The contraction of the zygomatic major and the orbicularis oculi (pars orbitalis) muscles also forms the core of the laughter of exhilaration. The exact number of additional muscles involved in laughing is not yet known. However, the following muscles have been shown to enhance EMG activity during laughing: levator labii superioris, risorius, mentalis, depressor anguli oris, and orbicularis oris (Sumitsuji, 1967). Activity of the buccinator and depressor labii inferioris muscles is also likely. The actions of some muscles are coordinated with respiration and vocalization. Their contraction (as well as relaxation) helps to let the air stream out through the mouth. Such actions include the opening of the lips and jaw, a radial opening of the mouth, and perhaps also a stretching of the lower jaw. Some researchers claim that during laughing every facial muscle is innervated to some degree (Dearborn, 1900; Heller, 1902); this has been shown for the masseter (Santibañez-H. & Bloch, 1986), the chewing muscle whose relaxation initially helps to lower the jaw.

Gesture and Posture

With increasing intensity of laughter, movements of the trunk and the limbs may occur, as well as changes in posture. They were described in detail by Darwin (1872), Hall and Allin (1897), and others. However, we are still lacking a comprehensive description of laughter—one that separates elements of the expressive pattern from merely associated secondary movements and from attempts to regulate the intensity of the emotion. Some movements serve other actions. For example, throwing back the head facilitates the expulsion of air through the throat. Other gestural and postural changes, such as the vibrations of the trunk and shoulders, simply reflect effects of the forced respiration movements of the diaphragm and abdominal muscles.

While phasic discharges (albeit of low intensity) from the muscles of the arm (brachioradialis) and the legs (rectus femoris) can be observed during laughter (Santibañez-H. & Bloch, 1986), there is generally a lowering of muscle tonus (Paskind, 1932). This may cause the laughing person to hold on to something, sit down, or (primarily in children) lie down on the floor (Hall & Allin, 1897). Clinical studies report a complete loss of muscle tension during laughing (e.g., in narcolepsy). Also, incontinence may occur. Bloch, Orthous, and Santibañez-H. (1987) postulate that two dimensions of posture discriminate between different emotions—namely, tension–relaxation and approach–avoidance. Whereas both laughing and crying are displayed in a relaxed posture, they are separated by the second dimension; the former is characterized by approach and the latter by avoidance.

Smiling and laughter typically represent different levels of intensity of exhilaration; Laughing occurs at higher levels of exhilaration, and smiling is typical of lower levels. Also, different intensities of smiling reflect different degrees of exhilaration. As compared to smiling, laughter is accompanied by a stronger contraction of the zygomatic major muscle, is of longer duration, and is shown at jokes judged by the person laughing to be funnier (Ruch, 1990a; Sumitsuji, Inoue, Tanaka, & Takahashi, 1986). Also, laughter always gradually fades out as a "smile" and may also be preceded by it (Pollio, Mers, & Lucchesi, 1972). This occurs smoothly rather than abruptly, and thus underscores the assumption of a quantitative relationship between smiling and laughing. Within a single laughing act, the duration of the actual vocalization period(s) is rather short; the purely facial stages (especially in the offset of the facial action) constitute roughly two-thirds of the total duration.

Exhilaration smiles rarely last longer than 4 seconds, and single acts of laughter seldomly exceed 7 seconds (Ruch, 1990a). EMG recordings yield longer durations, however, since (especially in the offset of the facial actions) slight contractions of the muscles go undetected by observational methods.

Physiology

Exhilaration, especially in its more intense forms, has several response components. Among them, disruption of the normal breathing pattern and the emission of sounds are the most characteristic features. It is the vocalization component that gave laughter its name; the verb "laugh" ("hlehhan," in Old English) is of echoic (sound-imitating) origin. The study of the neurophysiological conditions of exhilaration covers the brain structures involved and the neurohormonal activity.

Respiration

A respiration cycle consists of inspiration, inspiration pause, expiration, and expiration pause. There are approximately 14 such cycles per minute during resting periods, and the duration of expiration (including the pause) exceeds the duration of inspiration (inspiration–expiration ratio = .60). During laughter the respiration rate remains within the boundaries of the resting state; however, the predominance of expiration over inspiration increases. The inspiration–expiration ratio during laughter (Feleky, 1916, .30; Bloch, Lemeignan, & Aguilera, 1991, .38) is lower than in any other emotional state studied.

Whereas the respiration muscles during exhaling are normally passive, there is a forced expiration during laughter. The depth of respiration increases, mainly because of the stronger expiration, but also because of a deeper inspiration. The amplitude during laughter may be up to 2.5 times higher than the amplitude during resting respiration. The characteristic elements of laughter, the "ha-ha" cycles, occur during expiration and are produced at a low lung volume (Bright, Hixon, & Hoit, 1986) but a high transdiaphragmatic pressure (Agostoni, Sant'Ambrogio, & Portillo Carrasco, 1960). Normally these cycles are initiated around functional residual capacity (i.e., at the lung volume after a normal expiration) and terminate close to residual volume (i.e., the air volume remaining in the lung after maximal expiration) (Bright et al., 1986; Lloyd, 1938). These saccadic movements are superimposed on the normal expiration movement and are of low amplitude and high frequency. Most likely they are due to the contraction of the diaphragm (Agostoni et al., 1960) and the abdominal muscles (Santibañez-H. & Bloch, 1986).

Vocalization

In an early survey on laughter, Hall and Allin (1897) found that the sounds emitted during laughter are extremely diverse, including all vowels and many consonants, but also voiceless laughter. The sound most generally emitted was described as "he-he" passing over to "ha-ha." A similar range of vowels can be expected for the laughter of exhilaration, since the facial expression of exhilaration (lip corners backward and upward) and the widely opened mouth (to let the air stream out) leave little room for articulation. Variations may exist with respect to the degree of the vertical opening of the mouth, resulting in a change of the vowel from /e/ (slightly opened mouth) to /a/ (widely opened mouth). Indeed, Habermann (1955) reports that the laughter of exhilaration is most frequently based on an /a/, but also on /ɑ/ and /ɛ/, or on fluent changes between them. The occurrence of other vowels (such as *o* or *u*) appears to be incompatible with a free expression of exhilaration and may indicate other emotional qualities—attempts to regulate the intensity of exhilaration, or a comment on its expression.

Laughter frequently begins with the initial sound /h/ (Habermann, 1955). This unvoiced palatal sound is produced when air is pressed up from the lungs and passes a not (fully) closed glottis. The closure of the vocal fold is prerequisite for the vibration of the vocal chords and the production of a voiced sound. There are approximately seven such "ha" syllables during laughter at a rate of five per second (Boeke, 1899; Mowrer, LaPointe, & Case, 1987; Provine & Yong, 1989). Because of the lack of articulation, there may be more syllables per second than during normal speech. The pitch of the laughing sounds is characteristic, too. The early study by Boeke (1899) revealed that there is an increase in level and variation of fundamental frequency (F_0) (which is a major determinant of perceived pitch) during laughter as compared to speech.

Cardiovascular and Electrodermal Activity

Characteristic cardiovascular changes and fluctuations in electrodermal activity (EDA) can also be observed during laughter, perhaps triggered by the altered respiration pattern. Heitler (1904) was the first to report an acceleration of the heart rate. These changes are more pronounced than during other emotional responses (Santibañez-H. & Bloch, 1986), but last only for the duration of the laughing act (Fry & Savin, 1988). Smiling is not usually accompanied by respiration changes; however, a heart rate increase of 5 beats per minute has

been observed during spontaneous smiling in infants (Emde, Campos, Reich, & Gaensbauer, 1978), and an increase of 2.5 beats per minute has been noted during voluntary smiling in adults (Levenson, Ekman, & Friesen, 1990). Diastolic and systolic blood pressure both increase during laughter (Fry & Savin, 1988). Peripheral blood volume has also been shown to change between a smile and a laugh (Sumitsuji et al., 1986). There are massive changes in EDA during laughter (Averill, 1969; Hagfors, 1970). However, EDA changes also occur during funny scenes when subjects are not laughing, suggesting that they cannot be fully accounted for by the respiration changes.

Hecker (1873) observed that pupil dilation occurs during laughter induced by tickling, as well as humor. The "brightening" of the eyes was described by Darwin (1872) and Piderit (1858). Lacrimation (tearing) may also occur, perhaps more frequently in females and in younger ages. However, lacrimation during laughter remains to be studied.

Some insights regarding the neurophysiological basis of exhilaration come from studies of pathological laughter (excessive laughter, epileptic laughter, forced laughter), microcephalic children, intracranial stimulation, brain-damaged patients, and hemisphere differences in normals. Reviews of the literature indicate that many brain regions are involved in the production of the exhilaration response (Duchowny, 1983; Müller & Müller, 1980; Ruch, 1990a).

Various hypotheses regarding the effects of laughter on endocrine secretion have been proposed in the last few years. These hypotheses include, for example, effects on immune functioning, release of hormones, catecholamines, or endorphins (e.g., Berk et al., 1989; Dillon, Minchoff, & Baker, 1985; Levi, 1965). Some of these hypotheses are supported by preliminary data; however, conclusive evidence is still missing.

Experience

A systematic analysis of the experience of exhilaration is still lacking. However, as with other emotions, the awareness of one's own actions and action tendencies, of physiological changes, and of the feeling structure must be considered, along with the awareness of the situation's meaning structure and the perception of stimulus properties of the exhilaration-inducing stimulus.

Dimensions of Feeling

The description of exhilaration as a pleasurable, relaxed excitation suggests that all three of Wundt's (1874/1903) dimensions contribute to the feeling state. Most elicitors of exhilaration may also induce unpleasurable states; for example, both humor and tickling can be aversive. However, if the induction of exhilaration is successful, the resulting state will typically be a highly pleasurable one. Exhilaration is a state we enjoy being in. The excitation component of the feeling state relates to the perception of intensity of the behavior activated and its physiological concomitants. As noted in the introduction, exhilaration is not restricted to the high end of the excitement continuum, but also occurs at intermediate and low levels of excitement. Finally, the experience of exhilaration is characterized by relaxation. During laughter there is a relaxed posture and a typically lowered muscle tone, associated with a reduced readiness to respond attentively or with planned behavior to changes in the surroundings. The laughing person has been described as abandoning himself or herself to the body response (Plessner, 1941), and as being in an unprotected state (Zutt, 1939). Crile (1915) noted that one never sees purposeful acts and laughter together; laughter and goal-oriented behavior are incompatible (Apter & Smith, 1977).

Thus, in contrast to negative emotions such as anger or anxiety, the excitation during laughter occurs at a relaxed basis. The physiological changes occurring during laughter do not prepare the individual for "fight or flight;" in this respect, they are more or less purposeless. This is noteworthy, since several studies report that the physiological changes during laughter usually exceed the ones for the other emotions studied (Feleky, 1916; Hagfors, 1970; Santibañez-H. & Bloch, 1986). In contrast, happiness—at the level of smiling—appears to be accompanied by the smallest physiological changes, compared to the other emotions studied (Levenson et al., 1990).

Whereas there are low levels of strain during the emotional response, a buildup of strain or tension and its abrupt relief may precede the release of exhilaration (Sroufe & Waters, 1976; Wilson, 1979). In humor, attention is paid to the eliciting event, and it is processed seriously until it is discovered that it is "just fun." The sudden annulment of seriousness (Frijda, 1986) and disengagement from prior problem-solving-like activity may be related to the feeling of "lightness" ascribed to amusement or exhilaration (Lyman & Waters, 1986).

The definition of exhilaration as a temporary rise in cheerful state underscores the fact that the intensity of the emotional experience changes over time. Typically, there is a sudden and intense increase in cheerfulness, followed by a more or less pronounced plateau and a prolonged fading out of the emotional tone.

Perception of Stimulus Properties

Finally, the perceived properties of the eliciting stimulus also contribute to the experience. In the case of humor, individuals are confronted with a stimulus that contains incongruous, contradicting, or opposing elements. This incongruity—for instance, the final part of a punch line—is unexpected and initially perplexing. Some effort is required to discover that the incongruity makes sense from another perspective, and even after this discovery various degrees of incongruity usually remain. Such terms as "funny," "humorous," "comical," or "witty" are used to denote the perceived properties of stimuli causing us to engage in such playful processing of incongruity. The second meaning of the term "funny," as "strange," "odd," "curious," or "puzzling," underscores the fact that incongruity does not exclusively lead to exhilaration.

Traditionally, humor research focused on the perception of qualities of the stimulus. Therefore, the subjects were typically asked to judge the degree of "funniness" of a stimulus rather than the degree of exhilaration or amusement induced by it. Studies show that these two judgments do correlate very highly with each other, but there may be also conditions (e.g., in repeated exposure experiments) where stimulus-based and emotion-based judgments diverge (Ruch, 1990a).

Emotional Experience, Behavior, and Physiology

Exhilaration behavior, physiological changes, and emotional experience are positively intercorrelated; that is, increased intensity in one component of exhilaration goes along with increased intensity in the other two components. At the behavioral level, the intensity ranges from an invisible or barely visible contraction of the zygomatic major and orbicularis oculi muscles, through various degrees of smiling, single expulsions of air, and a fully developed laughing pattern, to the most extreme forms of laughter. The intensity of emotional experience and the complexity of physiological changes should vary accordingly. The data obtained so far support this assumption (e.g., Averill, 1969; Ruch, 1990a; Sumitsuji et al., 1986). For example, for any individual studied there is a highly consistent pattern in the amount of smiling/laughing the person displays in response to a set of jokes and cartoons, and the funniness ratings (as an index of the experience of exhilaration) given (Ruch, 1990a). The average correlation of .70 may underestimate the strength of this relationship. However, the form of this relationship varies from individual to individual. For example, whereas the minimal funniness of a joke necessary to induce smiling is low for individuals in a cheerful mood, a noncheerful individual displays smiling only at jokes perceived to be very funny (Ruch, 1990a). Not surprisingly, the computation of a correlation *across* individuals varying in cheerful mood yields low to moderate coefficients, which, according to McGhee (1977), typically range between .30 and .40. Other factors, such as intoxication with alcohol (Weaver, Masland, Kharazmi, & Zillmann, 1985), the presence of others, or personality variables, may have a similar moderating effect—which, however, should not be ascribed to a discordant response pattern.

ANTECEDENTS

Exhilaration can be elicited by a variety of stimuli. The induction of exhilaration normally is imbedded in a more or less complex situation, and therefore several social and physical factors may influence the success of the induction. Furthermore, organismic factors may also facilitate or inhibit the release of exhilaration; these factors may relate to temporal states or to habitual traits.

Elicitors of Exhilaration

Humor

Humor (in the form of jokes, cartoons, funny stories or films, comedy, parody, practical jokes, music, pantomime, etc.) is a reliable elicitor of exhilaration. However, humor itself is not an emotion (McGhee, 1979). In experi-

mental studies, slides with cartoons or videotapes with funny films are generally used. The use of jokes and cartoons as an induction procedure, as compared to tapes, allows for better control over both the actual eliciting event and the quality of the responses induced. Furthermore, because of their brevity, many stimuli can be used, and a taxonomy-based selection allows a reduction in the variance reflecting differential humor preference. However, the degree of exhilaration induced is usually lower than that obtained by funny videos.

Numerous theories have been proposed to explain the perceived funniness of humor (for a review, see Keith-Spiegel, 1972). Structural properties as well as content contribute to the exhilarating effects of humor. However, these key ingredients cannot be varied independently of each other in intact jokes or cartoons. Therefore, beginning with Ertel (e.g., Ehrenstein & Ertel, 1978), the experimental verification of the effects of structure and content in humor has been undertaken with "artificial" humor stimuli. This may take, for example, the form of sequences of words deviating from proper grammatical sequences (Ehrenstein & Ertel, 1978), adjective-noun pairs varying in semantic distance (Godkewitsch, 1974), computer-drawn caricatures with various degrees of exaggeration (Rhodes, Brennan, & Carey, 1987), or a weight-judging paradigm (Deckers, 1993). In studies of intact jokes, one can undertake a differential priming of the two meanings of a key word in a joke (Wilson, 1979), or a priming of the theme of the jokes to follow (Goldstein, Suls, & Anthony, 1972).

Such studies demonstrate the importance of an intermediate degree of incongruity. Although incongruity is a necessary condition for humor, it is not a sufficient one. Sheer incongruity may also lead to puzzlement and even to aversive reactions. To account for this, such variables as the resolution of the incongruity (Suls, 1972), the acceptance of unresolvable incongruity, or the "safeness" of the context in which the incongruity is processed (Rothbart, 1976) have been proposed. Adding sexual content to humor or increasing the salience of the joke themes has been shown to increase funniness (Ehrenstein & Ertel, 1978; Goldstein et al., 1972). However, personality variables also influence the extent to which structural and content properties are optimal for the induction of exhilaration (Ruch, 1992).

Tickling

According to Hecker (1873) and Wundt (1874/ 1903), tickling is the most common elicitor of laughter other than humor. Chimpanzees also show a facial display, a respiration pattern, and vocal sounds comparable to those associated with human laughter when being tickled or expecting to be tickled.

From their survey on laughter, Hall and Allin (1897) concluded that the areas where children are most ticklish are the following: soles of the feet, under the arms, the neck, under the chin, the waist and ribs, and the cheeks. Whereas tickling is done manually in natural settings, in experimental studies the application of a tickle stimulus is undertaken by means of a feather, a brush (Hecker, 1873), a wad of cotton (Ruggieri & Milizia, 1983), or a constructed apparatus (Weisskrantz, Elliot, & Darlington, 1971). The typical feeling during tickling does not appear immediately after the onset of stimulation, but only after a period of latency in which the tactile sensation is present. This is followed by a variable phase of a pleasurable tickle sensation, which may change again into a phase of merely tactile sensation (Ruggieri & Milizia, 1983). The unpredictability of the pattern of the stimulation plays a critical role in the perception of tickle; self-application of a tickle stimulus is less effective, since the person has a plan about the movements to be carried out, which then corresponds to the perceived stimulation (Weisskrantz et al., 1971). The tickle perception also habituates after repeated application of the stimulus (Hecker, 1873; Weisskrantz et al., 1971).

Nitrous Oxide

Nitrous oxide (N_2O, the "laughing gas") is a colorless, nonflammable gas that has a sweet, almost mentholated taste. Even before it began to be used as an anesthetic, its exhilarating, laughter-inducing effects were known and offered for public entertainment. William James (1882) described its effects and the frequent occurrence of elation, laughter, or the urge to laugh. These effects were also reported in more recent experimental studies (Harris, Zucker, & Lynn, 1974; Steinberg, 1956). The effects last for the duration of the time the gas is inhaled. The concentration of N_2O can be varied experimentally by mixing it with O_2. Despite these optimal properties for experi-

mentation, N_2O has not yet been used as an induction procedure in experiments studying exhilaration.

Even at doses too low to induce laughter, N_2O produces some effects that are typically ascribed to laughter, such as muscle relaxation and the appearance of delta and theta waves in the electroencephalogram (Pozzessere et al., 1982). The study of the uptake of N_2O in various regions of the brain was proposed for answering the question of the location of a "laughing center" (Niethammer, 1983).

Other Stimuli and Situations

Exhilaration may also occur in response to other stimuli and situations. The laughter of others can be exhilarating itself; exhilarated laughter is catching. Exhilaration may occur during various forms of motor play (e.g., dancing, running, jumping, or chasing), although as McGhee (1979) points out, these states are not experienced as humorous. Exhilaration may accompany the breaking of taboos, or doing something that is forbidden or secret (Hall & Allin, 1897; McGhee, 1979). As with other emotions, imagination of exhilarating events or their retrieval from memory may release the emotion; these techniques have been tried out already (Bloch et al., 1987; Prerost, 1989), and might be used as experimental induction procedures.

More work must be completed to find the elicitors of exhilaration most suitable for experimental purposes. It has to be considered that the exhilarating potential of any given stimulus differs from individual to individual, and across different ages or developmental levels (e.g., Sroufe & Waters, 1976).

Facilitating and Inhibiting Factors
Social Influence

The induction of exhilaration may be moderated by a variety of social factors. The effectiveness of humor may depend on who tells the jokes and whether this person is liked or not. The moderating effect of the personal relationship upon reactions to the source of stimulation may even be stronger in the case of a tickle stimulus. In general, the presence of a "play signal" (McGhee, 1979) facilitates the induction of exhilaration. It communicates to the recipient that a message should be received in a playful rather than a serious mode.

Several experiments have examined audience effects on humor-induced smiling and laughter (Chapman, 1983). The variables studied include the presence of a laughing versus a nonlaughing model, seating position, proximity, crowding, eye contact, age difference between subjects, and whether groups of strangers or friends were tested. Several of these factors have been quite powerful in enhancing the frequency or duration of smiling and laughing. However, no separation of different sorts of smiles and laughter was undertaken. The increased frequency of smiling in the presence of a laughing model, for example, may have been attributable to the appearance of "false" smiles (Ekman & Friesen, 1982).

Social factors are effective in facilitating the induction of exhilaration even when reduced to a minimal intensity. Several studies show that the mere presence of another person is sufficient to facilitate humor-induced smiling and laughter (Chapman, 1983). However, this effect was found to be restricted to individuals in a cheerful mood (Ruch, 1990a). Maybe an implicit (physically not present) audience is sufficient to facilitate exhilaration. Subjects tested solitarily smile more when they assume that a friend is also taking part in the same experiment in another room (Fridlund, 1991), and "canned laughter" (simulating a laughing audience) added to tape-recorded jokes increases exhilaration behavior (Chapman, 1973). However, accumulation of facilitating factors does not have summative effects; subjects accompanied by a mirthful confederate displayed less humor-induced laughter when "canned laughter" was present than when it was absent (Donoghue, McCarrey, & Clement, 1983).

Situational cues may also inhibit the expression of exhilaration or of certain forms of exhilaration by activating "display rules." Display rules are acquired during socialization, and they tell the individual when, where, and with whom exhilaration may be expressed. For example, most people learn that it is not appropriate to exhibit exhilaration at the misfortunes of others; in solemn places; or during religious ceremonies and rites, dignified addresses, and other serious occasions. Also, such rules may dictate that mild exhilaration may be displayed, but intense forms should be avoided. Thus, social regulations concerning the expression of emotions may apply to positive as well as to negative emotions.

Psychoactive Drugs and Alcohol

Alcohol and psychoactive drugs such as hallucinogens, opiates, and stimulants also affect the threshold for induction of exhilaration (Raulin, 1900; Siegel & Hirschman, 1985; Stearns, 1972). They may have facilitating or inhibiting effects, depending on the dose. Intoxication induced by these substances may lead to elation or euphoric mood. In this state of intoxication, even negligible or minimal stimuli may become potent elicitors of exhilaration, and the degrees of exhilaration induced in this state typically cover the high end of the intensity continuum.

Little is known about intoxication-induced exhilaration. Siegel and Hirschman (1985) note that laughter is perhaps the most conspicuous and yet most ignored feature of intoxication with psychoactive drugs. Since the laughter is often inappropriate, it is considered silly and not worthy of serious attention. The most frequent references to drug-induced laughter are found in the cannabis literature. The early study by Stoll (1947) on small doses of LSD documents the appearance of euphoric mood, exhilaration, and laughter triggered by minimal stimuli during the use of this drug. Similar effects have been postulated for alcohol (Stearns, 1972), but they lack experimental verification. Alcohol does not seem to raise the frequency of humor-induced exhilaration responses, but appears instead to increase the relative proportion of laughter among all exhilaration responses exhibited (Ruch, 1990a). Alcohol may alter the preference for type of humor preferred (Weaver et al., 1985).

Mood and Personality

The success of the induction of exhilaration also depends on temporal and habitual organismic factors. Among the temporal organismic factors, such physiological variables as degree of sympathetic arousal, health status, or exhaustion may moderate the effectiveness of the stimulus. Moreover, being in a goal-oriented state (Apter & Smith, 1977), thoughtful, or preoccupied with serious problems may increase the threshold for the induction of exhilaration.

A cheerful mood facilitates the induction of exhilaration. Subjects' level of state cheerfulness, assessed immediately before the induction stage, predicted frequency, threshold, and intensity of humor-induced exhilaration behavior in two studies (Ruch, 1990a). State cheerfulness turned out to be a better predictor of exhilaration than other closely related (e.g., elation) or broader (e.g., positive affectivity) positive mood states. Negative mood states did not predict exhilaration. Cheerfulness also moderated the effects of intoxication with alcohol on the induction of exhilaration. However, state cheerfulness is only predictive of exhilaration if another person is present in the room (even when engaged in a different activity), and has no predictive power during solitary situations (Ruch, 1990a).

Personality characteristics may facilitate the induction of exhilaration as well. Everybody is in a cheerful state now and then. However, individuals differ with respect to the frequency, duration, and intensity of occurrence of these states. Such habitual differences might be best accounted for by a "cheerfulness" trait, which can be subsumed under the higher-order temperament dimension of extraversion–introversion (Eysenck & Eysenck, 1985). Research remains to be initiated on the predictive power of trait cheerfulness; however, extraversion has been shown to predict frequency and intensity of humor-induced exhilaration behavior (Ruch, 1990a).

EFFECTS OF EXHILARATION

On the one hand, exhilaration is the outcome of the combined effects of a stimulus and of facilitating factors. On the other hand, its appearance may in turn have effects on the organism and the social environment. However, since in present research humor is generally used to induce exhilaration, these effects are typically attributed to humor rather than to (humor-induced) exhilaration. Such attributions neglect the possibility that most of the effects are contingent on the successful induction of exhilaration, and that presentation of humor may also lead to indifferent or even negative affective states.

If the induction of exhilaration is successful, the individual is in a state of pleasurable, relaxed excitation. This state is incompatible with a variety of states differing in one or more of the Wundtian dimensions (i.e., with states characterized by unpleasantness, quietness, and/or strain/tension). Hence fostering the appearance of exhilaration may help to miti-

gate, suppress, interrupt, or even permanently replace a variety of negative states. For example, humor and laughter have been used in the counterconditioning of anger responses (Smith, 1973) and in systematic desensitization of fear (Ventis, 1973). Other hypotheses postulate that humor and laughter buffer stress, reduce discomfort or pain, lower tension, or are otherwise beneficial for mental and physical health. Some of these effects have been ascribed to postulated neurohormonal changes occurring during laughter, such as the release of endorphins or the enhancement of immunocompetence.

As noted earlier, the accumulation of exhilaration responses may lead to longer-lasting elevation of cheerful mood. Sharing humor and laughter is considered to strengthen the in-group bonds and to facilitate communication. The successful use of humor can induce a relaxed atmosphere in the group. Furthermore, the value of humor and its exhilarating effects has been discussed in a variety of fields. For example, humor is applied in mass media advertising, in the industrial selling process, at work, in the classroom, in textbooks, in the promotion of learning and creativity, in psychotherapy and counseling, in health visiting, in the health professional–patient interaction, and so on.

The belief that humor and exhilaration are beneficial for humans is documented in sayings, proverbs, and folk wisdom. Potential health benefits have also been mentioned in scientific writings for a long time. More recently, Cousins's (1979) claim to have cured himself of a normally terminal disease by heavy doses of laughter and Vitamin C has helped to spread such beliefs in the general public. However, the scientific research has only begun (e.g., Martin & Lefcourt, 1983) and is starting to absorb much activity in contemporary humor research.

CONCLUDING REMARKS

Because of its recent conceptualization, exhilaration has not been studied as intensively as other emotions. Hence several basic issues have not yet been resolved and are open for investigation. However, exhilaration provides a common basis for various phenomena of different disciplines that have hitherto been studied in isolation. Specifically, it ties the study of humor into general emotion research. It adds another facet to the positive emotions, which are treated in a less differentiated way than the negative emotions. Finally, the promotion of the emotion of exhilaration may raise the level of awareness for phenomena in different fields that have previously been overlooked or not considered worthy of scientific enquiry.

Acknowledgments. I would like to thank Lambert Deckers, Paul McGhee, and Don Mowrer for their helpful comments on an earlier version of this chapter. Preparation of this chapter was supported in part by a Heisenberg Grant from the German Research Council. This chapter is based on my Habilitation thesis submitted to the School for Nature Sciences at the University of Düsseldorf.

REFERENCES

Agostoni, E., Sant'Ambrogio, G., & Portillo Carrasco, H. del. (1960). Elettromiografia del diaframma e pressione transdiaframmatica durante la tosso, lo sternuto ed il riso. *Rendiconti: Accademia Nazionale dei Lincei, Roma, Classe di Scienze Fisiche, Matematiche e Naturali, 28,* 493–496.

Apter, M. J., & Smith, K. C. P. (1977). Humour and the theory of psychological reversals. In A. J. Chapman & H. C. Foot (Eds.), *It's a funny thing, humour* (pp. 95–100). Oxford: Pergamon Press.

Averill, J. R. (1969). Autonomic response patterns during sadness and mirth. *Psychophysiology, 5,* 399–414.

Berk, L. S., Tan, S. A., Fry, W. F., Napier, B. J., Lee, J. W., Hubbard, R. W., Lewis, J. E., & Eby, W. C. (1989). Neuroendocrine and stress hormone changes during mirthful laughter. *American Journal of the Medical Sciences, 296,* 390–396.

Bloch, S., Lemeignan, M., & Aguilera, N. (1991). Specific respiratory patterns distinguish among human basic emotions. *International Journal of Psychophysiology, 11,* 141–154.

Bloch, S., Orthous, P., & Santibañez-H., G. (1987). Effector patterns of basic emotions: A psychophysiological method for training actors. *Journal of Social and Biological Structures, 10,* 1–19.

Boeke, W. (1899). Mikroskopische Phonogrammstudien. *Pflügers Archiv für die Gesamte Physiologie des Menschen (und Tieres), 76,* 497–516.

Bright, K. E., Hixon, T. J., & Hoit, J. D. (1986). Respiration as a laughing matter. In D. L. F. Nilsen (Ed.), *Proceedings of the 1985 Conference of Western Humor and Irony Membership Serial Yearbook (WHIMSY IV)* (pp. 147–148). Tempe: Arizona State University, Department of English.

Chapman, A. J. (1973). Funniness of jokes, canned laughter and recall performance. *Sociometry, 36,* 569–578.

Chapman, A. J. (1983). Humor and laughter in social interaction and some implications for humor research. In

P. E. McGhee & J. H. Goldstein (Eds.), *Handbook of humor research* (Vol. 1, pp. 135–157). New York: Springer.

Cousins, N. (1979). *Anatomy of an illness as perceived by the patient.* New York: Norton.

Crile, G. W. (1915). *The origin and nature of the emotions.* Philadelphia: W. B. Saunders.

Darwin, C. (1872). *The expression of the emotions in man and animals.* London: John Murray.

Dearborn, G. V. N. (1900). The nature of the smile and laugh. *Science, 11,* 851–856.

Deckers, L. H. (1993). On the validity of a weight-judging paradigm for the study of humor. *Humor, 6,* 43–56.

Dillon, K. M., Minchoff, B., & Baker, K. H. (1985). Positive emotional states and enhancement of the immune system. *International Journal of Psychiatry in Medicine, 15,* 13–17.

Donoghue, E. E., McCarrey, M. W., & Clement, R. (1983). Humour appreciation as a function of canned laughter, a mirthful companion, and field dependence: Facilitation and inhibitory effects. *Canadian Journal of Behavioural Science, 15,* 150–162.

Duchowny, M. S. (1983). Pathological disorders of laughter. In P. E. McGhee & J. H. Goldstein (Eds.), *Handbook of humor research* (Vol. 2, pp. 89–108). New York: Springer.

Ehrenstein, W. H., & Ertel, S. (1978). Zur Genese des Lustigkeitseindrucks. *Psychologische Beiträge, 20,* 360–374.

Ekman, P., & Friesen, W. V. (1982). Felt, false, and miserable smiles. *Journal of Nonverbal Behavior, 6,* 238–252.

Emde, R. N., Campos, J., Reich, J., & Gaensbauer, T. J. (1978). Infant smiling at five and nine months: Analysis of heart rate and movement. *Infant Behavior and Development, 1,* 26–35.

Eysenck, H. J., & Eysenck, M. W. (1985). *Personality and individual differences: A natural science approach.* New York: Plenum Press.

Feleky, A. (1916). The influence of the emotions on respiration. *Journal of Experimental Psychology, 1,* 218–241.

Fridlund, A. J. (1991). Sociality of solitary smiling: Potentiation by an implicit audience. *Journal of Personality and Social Psychology, 60,* 229–240.

Frijda, N. (1986). *The emotions.* Cambridge, England: Cambridge University Press.

Fry, W. F., & Savin, W. M. (1988). Mirthful laughter and blood pressure. *Humor, 1,* 49–62.

Godkewitsch, M. (1974). Correlates of humor: Verbal and nonverbal aesthetic reactions as functions of semantic distance within adjective–noun pairs. In D. E. Berlyne (Ed.), *Studies in the new experimental aesthetics* (pp. 279–304). Washington, DC: Hemisphere.

Goldstein, J. H., Suls, J. M., & Anthony, S. (1972). Enjoyment of specific types of humor content: Motivation or salience? In J. H. Goldstein & P. E. McGhee (Eds.), *The psychology of humor* (pp. 159–171). New York: Academic Press.

Habermann, G. (1955). *Physiologie und Phonetik des lauthaften Lachens.* Leipzig: Barth.

Hagfors, C. (1970). The galvanic skin response and its application to the group registration of psychophysiological processes. *Jyväskylä Studies in Education, Psychology and Social Research,* (Vol. 23). Jyväskylä, Finland: Jyväskylän Yliopisto.

Hall, G. S., & Allin, A. (1897). The psychology of tickling, laughing, and the comic. *American Journal of Psychology, 9,* 1–41.

Harris, L., Zucker, R. A., & Lynn, E. J. (1974). Some effects of nitrous oxide on fear. *Journal of Psychedelic Drugs, 6*, 29–41.

Hecker, E. (1873). *Die Physiologie und Psychologie des Lachens und des Komischen.* Berlin: Dümmler.

Heitler, M. (1904). Pulskurve, während des Lachens aufgenommen. *Zentralblatt für innere Medizin, 25*, 17–18.

Heller, H. V. (1902). *Grundformen der Mimik des Antlitzes.* Vienna: Anton Schroll.

James, W. (1882). Subjective effects of nitrous oxide. *Mind, 7*, 186–208.

Keith-Spiegel, P. (1972). Early conceptions of humor: Varieties and issues. In J. H. Goldstein & P. E. McGhee (Eds.), *The psychology of humor* (pp. 4–39). New York: Academic Press.

Levenson, R. W., Ekman, P., & Friesen, W. V. (1990). Voluntary facial action generates emotion-specific autonomous system activity. *Psychophysiology, 27*, 363–384.

Levi, L. (1965). The urinary output of adrenalin and noradrenalin during pleasant and unpleasant emotional states. *Psychosomatic Medicine, 27*, 80–85.

Lloyd, E. L. (1938). The respiratory mechanism in laughter. *Journal of General Psychology, 19*, 179–189.

Lyman, B., & Waters, J. C. E. (1986). The experiential loci and sensory qualities of various emotions. *Motivation and Emotion, 10*, 25–37.

Martin, R. A., & Lefcourt, H. M. (1983). Sense of humor as a moderator of the relation between stressors and moods. *Journal of Personality and Social Psychology, 45*, 1313–1324.

McGhee, P. E. (1977). Children's humour: A review of current research trends. In A. J. Chapman & H. C. Foot (Eds.), *It's a funny thing, humour* (pp. 199–209). Oxford: Pergamon Press.

McGhee, P. E. (1979). *Humor: Its origin and development.* San Francisco: W. H. Freeman.

Mowrer, D. E., LaPointe, L. L., & Case, J. (1987). Analysis of five acoustic correlates of laughter. *Journal of Nonverbal Behavior, 11*, 191–199.

Müller, D., & Müller, J. (1980). *Lachen als epileptische Manifestation.* Jena, East Germany: Gustav Fischer.

Niethammer, T. (1983). Does man possess a laughter center? Laughing gas used in a new approach. *New Ideas in Psychology, 1*, 67–69.

Paskind, H. A. (1932). Effect of laughter on muscle tone. *Archives of Neurology and Psychiatry, 28*, 623–628.

Piderit, T. (1858). *Mimik und Physiognomie.* Detmold, Germany: Meyer.

Plessner, H. (1941). *Lachen und Weinen.* Bern, Switzerland: Francke.

Pollio, H. R., Mers, R., & Lucchesi, W. (1972). Humor, laughter, and smiling: Some preliminary observations of funny behaviors. In J. H. Goldstein & P. E. McGhee (Eds.), *The psychology of humor* (pp. 211–239). New York: Academic Press.

Pozzessere, G., Pierelli, F., Rizzo, P. A., Gerono, A., Niethammer, T., Morocutti, C., & Timsit-Berthier, M. (1982). Electrophysiological measures (CNV-EEG) and nitrous oxide at low doses in man. *Italian Journal of Neurological Sciences, 3*, 211–214.

Prerost, F. (1989). Humor as an intervention strategy during psychological treatment: Imagery and incongruity. *Psychology, 26*, 34–40.

Provine, R. R., & Yong, Y. L. (1991). Laughter: A stereotyped human vocalization. *Ethology, 89*, 115–124.

Raulin, J. M. (1900). *Le rire et les exhilarants.* Paris: Baillière.

Rhodes, G., Brennan, S., & Carey, S. (1987). Identification and ratings of caricatures: Implications for mental representations of faces. *Cognitive Psychology, 19*, 473–497.

Rothbart, M. K. (1976). Incongruity, problem-solving and laughter. In A. J. Chapman & H. C. Foot (Eds.), *Humour and laughter: Theory, research and applications* (pp. 37–54). Chichester, England: Wiley.

Ruch, W. (1990a). *Die Emotion Erheiterung: Ausdrucksformen und Bedingungen.* Unpublished Habilitation thesis, University of Düsseldorf, Germany.

Ruch, W. (1990b, August). Exhilaration: The emotional response to humour. In W. Ruch (Chair), *Innovations in psychological humour research.* Symposium conducted at the Eighth International Humour Conference, Sheffield, England.

Ruch, W. (1992). Assessment of appreciation of humor: Studies with the 3 WD humor test. In C. D. Spielberger & J. N. Butcher (Eds.), *Advances in personality assessment* (Vol. 9, pp. 27–75). Hillsdale, NJ: Erlbaum.

Ruggieri, V., & Milizia, M. (1983). Tickle perception as micro-experience of pleasure: Its phenomenology on different areas of the body and relation to cerebral dominance. *Perceptual and Motor Skills, 56*, 903–914.

Santibañez-H., G., & Bloch, S. (1986). A qualitative analysis of emotional effector patterns and their feedback. *Pavlovian Journal of Biological Science, 21*, 108–116.

Siegel, R. K., & Hirschman, A. E. (1985). Hashish and laughter: Historical notes and translations of early french investigations. *Journal of Psychoactive Drugs, 17*, 87–91.

Smith, R. E. (1973). The use of humor in the counterconditioning of anger responses: A case study. *Behavior Therapy, 4*, 576–580.

Sroufe, L. A., & Waters, E. (1976). The ontogenesis of smiling and laughter: A perspective on the organization of development in infancy. *Psychological Review, 83*, 173–189.

Stearns, F. R. (1972). *Laughing. Physiology, pathophysiology, psychology, pathopsychology and development.* Springfield, IL: Charles C Thomas.

Steinberg, H. (1956). 'Abnormal behaviour' induced by nitrous oxide. *British Journal of Psychology, 47*, 183–194.

Stoll, W. A. (1947). Lysergsäure-diäthylamid, ein Phantastikum aus der Mutterkorngruppe. *Schweizer Archiv für Neurologie und Psychiatrie, 60*, 279–323.

Suls, J. M. (1972). A two-stage model for the appreciation of jokes and cartoons: An information-processing analysis. In J. H. Goldstein & P. E. McGhee (Eds.), *The psychology of humor* (pp. 81–100). New York: Academic Press.

Sumitsuji, N. (1967). Electromyographic studies on the facial expression. *Psychiatria et Neurologia Japonica, 69*, 1101–1119.

Sumitsuji, N., Inoue, T., Tanaka, M., & Takahashi, K. (1986). A peculiar changes in the plethysmogram following the human laughing act. *Electromyography and Clinical Neurophysiology, 26*, 263–272.

Ventis, W. L. (1973). Case history: The use of laughter as an alternative response in systematic desensitization. *Behavior Therapy, 4*, 120–122.

Weaver, J. B., Masland, J. L., Kharazmi, S., & Zillmann, D. (1985). Effect of alcoholic intoxication on the appreciation of different types of humor. *Journal of Personality and Social Psychology, 49*, 781–787.

Weisskrantz, L., Elliot, J., & Darlington, C. (1971). Preliminary observations on tickling oneself. *Nature, 230*, 598–599.

Wilson, C. P. (1979). *European monographs in social psychology: Vol. 16. Jokes: Form, content, use and function.* London: Academic Press.

Wundt, W. (1903). *Grundzüge der Physiologischen Psychologie* (Vol. 2). Leipzig: Engelmann. (Original work published 1874)

Zutt, J. (1939). Über das Lachen, das Weinen und das Gähnen. *Allgemeine Zeitschrift für Psychiatrie und ihre Grenzgebiete, 110*, 224–231.

43

Happiness

JAMES R. AVERILL
THOMAS A. MORE

A chapter on happiness in a handbook of emotions would seem to require little justification. When asked to give examples of emotion, or to rate the representativeness of emotional concepts, the proverbial person in the street typically places "happiness" at or near the top of the list (Averill, 1975; Fehr & Russell, 1984; Shaver, Schwartz, Kirson, & O'Connor, 1987). Moreover, our folk model of happiness (e.g., as represented linguistically in metaphors and metonymies) shares many features in common with folk models of other emotions (Kövecses, 1991). Yet most theoretical discussions of emotion avoid happiness. The reasons are multiple; we mention two.

Whereas most emotions are well-circumscribed reactions to specific events, happiness is a way we evaluate life as a whole, or significant aspects of life (such as family and work) that have a broad impact on life as a whole. Because happiness involves such global evaluations, its scope is correspondingly broad. More than most emotional concepts, it represents a "fuzzy set" without clear boundaries —indeed, without even a clear center or prototype (Kövecses, 1991; Strasser, 1977; Tatarkiewicz, 1976). Seeking clarity, therefore, theorists often refer to "joy," a more delimited concept than "happiness" (e.g., Shaver et al., 1987; Izard, 1977). That strategy, however, merely substitutes a part for the whole. Happiness may include episodes of joy as well as other positive emotions, such as contentment, but happiness cannot be equated with any of these. Indeed, happiness does not even exclude moments of struggle, turmoil, and pain.

Breadth of scope does not account entirely for the neglect of happiness by emotion theorists; happiness also has depth of meaning that seems to mock analysis. In his book *Happy People*, Freedman (1978) recounts the difficulty his research assistant had when interviewing people with respect to happiness. When interviewed in groups, people joked and trivialized the topic; when interviewed in private, they grew serious but stopped talking. The research assistant concluded that it would be easier to ask people about the intimate details of their sex lives than about what makes them happy. Why might this be so? The answer, we believe, lies in the close link between happiness and values. With few possible exceptions (e.g., anxiety), all emotions involve valuative judgments. In fear, we evaluate a situation as threatening; in anger, as an affront; in joy, as a benefit; in sadness, as a loss; and so forth (Frijda, 1986; Lazarus, 1991). Happiness, however, is special in this regard. As already noted, happiness involves an evaluation of life as a whole, or at least of significant aspects of life, such as work and family. Happiness thus touches upon our deepest strivings— our goals, ideals, and competencies. Happiness is not prized simply because it "feels good." For many people happiness is itself the highest good, the *summum bonum* of classical theory. This is why, when part of a meaningful endeavor, even pain and suffering can contribute to happiness. To talk about happiness—seriously and not trivially—we must drop all pretenses and admit our shortcomings as well as our successes. That makes happiness difficult to discuss, not just for the average person, but for emotion theorists as well.

To overcome the twin difficulties of breadth and depth, researchers often speak of "subjective well-being." Measures of subjective well-being typically include avowed (self-reported) happiness, as well as measures of satisfaction and morale (Andrews & Robinson, 1991). (Note that people can be relatively satisfied without being happy; they are, in a sense, "resigned"; Michalos, 1986). A great deal of empirical research has accumulated relating subjective well-being to various social and demographic variables. Although we touch upon that research in the discussion that follows (see Diener & Larsen, Chapter 28, for a detailed review), in this chapter we are concerned with "happiness" as a theoretical construct, and not with "subjective well-being" as a broad descriptive category.

To summarize these introductory comments, we follow the lay conception of happiness as an emotion, recognizing the multifaceted nature of that conception. Episodes of happiness may last for minutes or days, and may be punctuated by moments of sadness and despair as well as joy and gladness. Although we conceive of happiness as an episodic state, its connotations are nevertheless global. With happiness, the implication is that things are right with the world, even if, as is sometimes the case, temporary hardships must be endured.

APPROACHES TO UNDERSTANDING HAPPINESS

We consider three general approaches to understanding happiness, namely, happiness in relation to (1) systems of behavior, (2) enabling mechanisms, and (3) personality characteristics. By "systems of behavior," we mean coordinated patterns of responses "designed" to achieve some goal or fulfill some function; by "enabling mechanisms," we mean the inner workings that allow a system to fulfill its functions; and by "personality characteristics," we mean traits and abilities assessed without regard to function or inner workings (Averill, 1992).

Most recent research relevant to happiness has focused on enabling mechanisms and personality characteristics. Theoretically, however, systems of behavior have precedence: Without such systems, there would be no enabling mechanisms or characteristics of which to speak. Historically, too, systems of behavior have been the traditional focus of discussions of happiness.

HAPPINESS IN RELATION TO SYSTEMS OF BEHAVIOR

Over 25 years ago, Wilson (1967) observed that little theoretical progress has been made in understanding happiness since the time of the ancient Greeks. That is something of an overstatement. Nevertheless, anyone seriously interested in the topic of happiness is well advised to begin with Aristotle's (ca. 330 B.C./ 1947) brief discussion in *Nicomachean Ethics*. It is sometimes suggested that the Greek concept of *eudaemonia*, of which Aristotle spoke, is not equivalent to our own concept of happiness. As Vlastos (1985) demonstrates, however, the two concepts are quite comparable. Such comparability is not coincidental. The analyses of happiness by Aristotle and other ancient Greek philosophers, particularly the Stoics and Epicureans, have influenced Western thought for over two millennia.

> Each animal is thought to have a proper pleasure, as it has a proper function; viz. that which corresponds to its activity. If we survey them species by species, too, this will be evident; horse, dog, and man have different pleasures, as Heracleitus says, "asses would prefer sweepings to gold"; for food is pleasanter than gold to asses. (*Nicomachean Ethics*, 1176a3).

This quotation from Aristotle introduces what we term "biological systems of behavior." Biologically, the highest good is preservation of the species. Most higher species achieve this through survival of the individual and his or her contribution to the gene pool. The major biological systems ("instincts," such as attachment, sex, and aggression) contribute more or less directly to the survival of the species. When they are functioning optimally, the animal may be said to be happy (see Novak & Suomi, 1988, for an application of this principle to the well-being of nonhuman primates).

Biological systems at this global level can, in turn, be divided into "part-instincts" and elementary responses, such as fixed action patterns. Elementary responses that contribute to survival are typically experienced as pleasurable—for example, the sweet taste of ripe fruit, the pleasure of sexual orgasm.

Optimally functioning biological systems contribute to, but are not sufficient for, happiness in human beings. We are social animals that cannot survive outside of society. Happiness among humans must therefore take into account social as well as biological systems of behavior. To quote Aristotle (1947) once more:

> Any chance person—even a slave—can enjoy the bodily pleasures no less than the best man; but no one assigns to a slave a share in happiness—unless he assigns to him also a share in human life. For happiness does not lie in such occupations, but . . . in virtuous activities. (*Nicomachean Ethics*, 1177a5)

"Virtuous activity" refers to behavior that furthers societal goals, and the ultimate goal of societies—like that of species—is preservation. The preservation of society may be achieved through many subsidiary goals, which vary from one society to another. The important point is that a society defines as virtuous those behaviors vital to its survival, and condemns as vices those that are detrimental. For the well-socialized individual who has internalized the goals and values of society, happiness thus becomes associated with virtuous activity. In the extreme, *true* happiness has been equated with virtue; that is, a happy life and a virtuous life are considered identical, for both are, from a social perspective, the best life possible.

Aristotle ridiculed this "identity thesis" with the rather obvious retort: "Those who say that the victim on the rack or the man who falls into great misfortune is happy if he is good, are . . . talking nonsense" (*Nicomachean Ethics*, 1153b19). Nevertheless, as we have just seen, Aristotle did postulate virtue as a necessary if not a sufficient condition for happiness. Bertrand Russell (1945, 1950), for one, scorned even this more modest proposal, arguing that it "appeals to the respectable middle-aged, and has been used by them . . . to repress the ardours and enthusiasms of the young" (1945, p. 173). Russell would link happiness primarily to psychological systems of behavior.

By "psychological systems," we mean patterns of behavior that help preserve and enhance a person's self (as opposed to the species or society). The self is here conceived of as a set of concepts or propositions about who one is as an individual and one's relation to the world. "Self-actualization" (i.e., preservation and enhancement of a sense of self) has been proposed by many theorists as a major—if not *the* major—motivation behind much of human behavior.

Although the roots of the self are to be found in our biological and social heritage, promotion of the self often comes into conflict with biological and social needs. Thus, the martyr may sacrifice health and even life to preserve a sense of self, and the rebel may reject social values in favor of self-determined norms. Given the appropriate circumstances, we are all martyrs or rebels to some degree, for neither biological constraints nor social practices fully determine our behavior.

With these observations as background, we now provide a more formal account of systems of behavior and their relation to happiness. A system of behavior is a set of responses organized with respect to some goal or end state. Behavioral systems can be distinguished in terms of both principles of organization (biological, social, and psychological) and levels of organization or degree of complexity (Averill, 1990). Biological principles refer to information encoded in the genes; social principles, to the norms and values of society; and psychological principles, to cognitive schemas or knowledge structures. Figure 43.1 illustrates this organization, with separate hierarchies for biological, social, and psychological systems. The base of each hierarchy represents the multitude of elementary processes that constitute systems. The apex represents the most inclusive unit (suprasystem) that can be analyzed from a given perspective: the species in the case of biological systems, society in the case of social systems, and the self in the case of psychological systems.

Needless to say, the system hierarchies depicted in Figure 43.1 are abstractions. Like the concave and convex sides of an arc, they can be distinguished in theory, not in practice.

The relation of systems of behavior to happiness can be stated in five propositions:

1. Happiness is associated with the optimal functioning of behavioral systems at each level in a hierarchy.

Levels of Organization

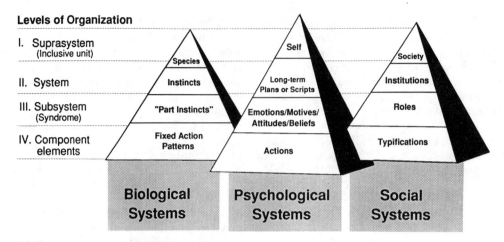

I. Suprasystem (Inclusive unit)
II. System
III. Subsystem (Syndrome)
IV. Component elements

Species — Instincts — "Part Instincts" — Fixed Action Patterns

Self — Long-term Plans or Scripts — Emotions/Motives/Attitudes/Beliefs — Actions

Society — Institutions — Roles — Typifications

Biological Systems   **Psychological Systems**   **Social Systems**

FIGURE 43.1. Three systems hierarchies organized according to biological, social, and psychological principles. Adapted by permission from Averill (1990, p. 389).

2. Happiness at one level in a hierarchy is informed or given meaning by higher-order systems, and is given substance or content by lower-order systems.
3. Among the higher-order systems, those that comprise the social order are the most important for happiness.
4. Maximizing one kind of system (biological, social, or psychological) may involve some sacrifice of the others.
5. Because of personal incapacities and environmental constraints, happiness is relative to the individual and the situation.

These five propositions relate to five traditional debates concerning the nature of happiness.

First, is happiness an end in itself or a characteristic of behavior pursued for other ends? For example, do people engage in activities in order to be happy, or are people happy because they engage in activities that successfully lead to goals other than happiness (fame, fortune, or whatever)? In a classic paper, Duncker (1941) explored both sides of this issue in great detail, at least for elementary pleasures. Our own position follows from Proposition 1: Happiness is associated with the optimal functioning of behavioral systems. People do seek happiness, but not necessarily for its own sake. From a systems point of view, happiness is a characteristic of activities well performed. These activities differ from one species to another, from one society to another, and from one individual to another;

however, if the proper goal or function of an activity is eliminated, the associated happiness soon becomes vacuous.

A second issue traditionally distinguishing theories is whether happiness consists of the sum of momentary pleasures (a bottom-up approach), or whether pleasures contribute to happiness only when informed by higher-order principles (a top-down approach). From a systems perspective, this is a pseudoissue, for both bottom-up and top-down approaches are legitimate and necessary when analysis involves a hierarchy (see Proposition 2). To proceed from the bottom up, happiness at the most elementary level is related to simple sensory pleasures and associated responses, such as smiling and laughing. (We ignore for the moment the possibility that happiness may include unpleasurable as well as pleasurable activities.) At a slightly more complex level, we may speak of particular but relatively short-term joys and contentments (e.g., reading a good book). These, in turn, may be integrated into more enduring states of happiness (e.g., with respect to work or family). A life without its share of elementary pleasures could hardly be regarded as happy. But, conversely, to constitute happiness, momentary pleasures must be subsumed within broader systems of behavior. That is, an adequate analysis of happiness must also proceed from the top down. Coming from a very different perspective (operant conditioning), Skinner (1986) has made a similar point with respect to the role of reinforcement in the acquisition and maintenance of behavior. Divorced from meaningful behavior, many reinforcers are now used for the pleasures they afford; however, like junk food, they titillate the senses without providing real nourishment.

A third traditional problem has been to explicate the relation of happiness to values, and to provide a proper place for nonmoral (value-free) sources of happiness. According to Proposition 3, happiness is centrally related to social systems of behavior and the values embodied in those systems. This accounts for the close link, so often emphasized by ethical theorists, between happiness and virtue. But biological systems also contribute to happiness (in a nonmoral sense), as do psychological systems. The relative importance of biological, social, and psychological principles may vary, depending on the person and situation. For the hedonist, biological principles may predominate; for the saint or patriot, social principles; and for an individualist like Bertrand Russell (see the quotation above), psychological principles. In general, however, social principles are the most fundamental. Human beings are born relatively "world-open," with few highly developed biological instincts. Society provides a second nature that, in reality, becomes our first (Averill, 1980, 1991). The individualist in pursuit of self-fulfillment may reject some of society's values in favor of others, but only sociopaths subordinate all social values to their own biological and psychological needs. Indeed, individualism is itself a value, encouraged by some societies more than others.

A fourth traditional debate is whether happiness consists of tranquility, or whether it necessarily involves some conflict and struggle. According to Proposition 4, optimizing any one set of functions (biological, social, or psychological) typically involves sacrificing others. Society restricts our biological propensities, and what is most fulfilling from an individual (psychological) perspective may be counter to the common good, whether biological or social. Ultimately, happiness involves compromise among competing demands and hence cannot be equated with tranquility, which connotes a state of minimal rather than optimal functioning. As H. L. Mencken (1930) satirically observed, if we take tranquility as our ideal, then a hog is happier than a human, and a bacillus happier than a hog. Optimal functioning, by

contrast, implies an active and often conflictive engagement in the world.

Finally, can happiness be defined objectively, or must we settle for a subjective definition, with each individual the arbiter of his or her own happiness? In analyzing the concept of *eudaemonia*, Aristotle (ca. 330 B.C./ 1947) presumed that happiness is an objective state of affairs—namely, the perfection of one's potentials as a rational, fully functioning human being. A slave could not be happy, according to Aristotle, for a slave could never achieve his or her potentials; neither, presumably, could a person who is physically or mentally handicapped. There are good reasons for rejecting Aristotle's objective but absolute standard (see Kraut, 1979). Unfortunately, most current investigators go to the opposite extreme, adopting not only relative criteria, but subjective ones as well. As Grichting (1983) put it, "We are not prepared to second-guess our subjects as to what they mean by happiness" (p. 247). Proposition 5 implies that happiness can be both objective *and* relative. Individuals differ in their capacities to achieve goals, and environmental constraints limit accomplishments. Therefore, when we speak of the optimal functioning of behavioral systems, we mean in relation to a person's capacities and situation. What is optimal for one person, and hence conducive to happiness, need not be optimal for another.

The importance of considering objective (even if relative) standards for the evaluation of happiness is illustrated by a thought experiment proposed by Nozick (1989). Imagine an "experience machine" that can, by activating relevant neural circuits, produce any set of feelings you might desire. You want pleasure? Friendship? Success? Just dial them on the machine. Anything you might want, you can experience—not just momentarily, but for as long as, and in whatever variety, you wish. Assuming that all your physiological needs were also met, so that you remain in perfect health, would you choose to spend the rest of your life attached to such a machine?

Kraut (1979) has presented a similar but more realistic thought experiment. Suppose that you were voted the most popular student in high school. It was, you believed at the time, a well-deserved recognition. You have never again felt so happy as you did upon receiving that honor. The next day, however, you discovered that the award was a cruel hoax; you were actually the laughingstock of the school. Looking back on the day when you falsely believed in the reality of the award, would you now consider it among the happiest days of your life?

As these exercises imply, happiness can be illusory and subject to reevaluation. Objective standards exist against which avowed happiness can be assessed—and sometimes found wanting.

HAPPINESS IN RELATION TO ENABLING MECHANISMS

A major point we wish to make in this chapter is the importance of distinguishing between systems of behavior and enabling mechanisms. As just described, a systems approach to happiness concerns the origins and functions of behavior; a mechanistic approach, by contrast, concerns the inner workings that make happiness possible. Any one system of behavior may require a variety of enabling mechanisms, and, conversely, any one enabling mechanism may enter into a variety of different systems.

In one sense, analyses in terms of behavioral systems and enabling mechanisms represent little more than a convenient division of labor. Both approaches are important and necessary (Averill, 1992). However, simply to leave the matter at that risks blurring an important fact: In current theory and research, the division is heavily biased in favor of mechanism. The reasons are both philosophical and practical.

Philosophically, the current emphasis on mechanism over function stems from the Scientific Revolution of the 16th and 17th centuries; rightfully or wrongly, it pervades our current scientific worldview. If Aristotle promoted the earlier "nonscientific" view, the British empiricist Locke presaged the modern "scientific" approach, at least as far as happiness is concerned. For Locke, happiness can be reduced to a mechanical combination of pleasures, and maximal happiness is the greatest quantity of pleasure a person is capable of experiencing over time. Gone is the Aristotelian emphasis on happiness in relation to fulfillment of function, and on behavior interpreted in terms of ends and virtues (see Murray, 1988, p. 36 ff.).

Practically, the current emphasis on mechanism reflects "the preference for scientific

action at the expense of scientific thought" (Natsoulas, 1991, p. 342). We have already noted that emotion theorists tend to ignore happiness; not so, empirical researchers. The latter, however, seldom attempt to define happiness except in terms of their assessment instruments, which are usually self-report measures of "avowed happiness" or "subjective well-being." If people say they are happy, the reasoning goes, then presumably they are happy, whatever that might mean. By permitting each participant to define happiness in his or her own terms, the investigator can get on with the business of research—for example, investigating the psychological and social correlates of avowed happiness. Theoretical questions concerning the nature of happiness per se can conveniently be set aside, or even dismissed as meaningless. A systems approach provides no such luxury.

Enabling mechanisms, like behavioral systems, can be analyzed from biological, social, and psychological perspectives, and we continue our discussion in terms of that threefold division. In a consideration of enabling mechanisms, however, another division is also helpful—namely, that between intrinsic and extrinsic mechanisms. Strictly speaking, it is not the mechanism that is intrinsic or extrinsic, but the mode of activation. "Intrinsic" refers to mechanisms activated as part of an ongoing system of behavior; "extrinsic" refers to mechanisms activated irrespective of their relation to behavioral systems. A brief discussion of biological enabling mechanisms introduces this distinction in concrete terms.

Biological enabling mechanisms consist of physiological systems (particularly the endocrine and central nervous systems and their subdivisions), to the extent that their operation is under genetic control. The biological mechanisms for happiness include, among other things, pleasure centers of the brain; specialized circuitry in the left frontal lobes (which appear to be involved in positive emotional experiences); endorphins and other naturally occurring opioids; and the like. Such mechanisms are discussed in detail in Section II of this handbook (especially Chapters 7–10). We do not consider them further here, except to reiterate a point made earlier: To produce happiness and not just momentary pleasures, the activation of biological mechanisms must be associated with meaningful patterns of response (systems of behavior). When activated extrinsically (e.g., by means of drugs), the net result is often a vague sense of dissatisfaction, no matter how pleasurable the immediate experience.

The distinction between intrinsic and extrinsic mechanisms is less obvious, but no less important, in the case of social enabling mechanisms. Roughly speaking, social enabling mechanisms are the organizations—public and private, formal and informal—that help make society "run." Intrinsic social mechanisms are organizations that foster engagement in systems of behavior (whether biological, psychological, or social). Extrinsic social mechanisms are organizations that provide goods independent of a person's behavior.

In the United States, a small body of law has grown up around the notion, written into the Declaration of Independence and adopted by some state constitutions, that the pursuit of happiness is an "unalienable right" (Jones, 1953). Not everyone agrees with this sentiment. C. S. Lewis, in an article published in *The Saturday Evening Post* (1963/1982), asserted that "a right to happiness doesn't, for me, make much more sense than a right to be six feet tall, or to have a millionaire for your father, or to get good weather whenever you might want to have a picnic" (p. 42). Lewis was particularly concerned about the way licentiousness, greed, and selfishness are sometimes justified in the name of happiness. By contrast, Murray (1988) argues that the primary purpose of government is, in fact, to enable its citizens to pursue happiness. The difference between Lewis and Murray is based, in part, on their conception of happiness. For Lewis, happiness is little more than feeling good, to which no one has an unalienable right. For Murray, happiness is the highest good; and anyone who confuses licentiousness, say, with the highest good simply does not know the meaning of happiness. But the difference between Lewis and Murray also has to do with the kinds of social mechanisms they oppose or advocate. The kinds of mechanisms mentioned by Lewis (e.g., having a millionaire for a father) are primarily extrinsic; the kinds favored by Murray are primarily intrinsic.

Adopting an explicitly Aristotelian stance, Murray (1988) argues that social policy should nurture associations ("little platoons") among individuals. The most vital of these little platoons center around the family, neighborhood, and workplace. Even the least talented and gifted among us can be a good parent, neighbor, and worker. And, as ample empirical research suggests, it is primarily with respect to family, friends, and work that happiness is in fact achieved (Argyle, 1987; Bradburn, 1969; Campbell, Converse, & Rodgers, 1978; Veenhoven, 1984). The catch, according to Murray, is that to afford happiness, group endeavors must be meaningful; they must require some effort; and group members must feel responsible for their own success and failures. If government eliminates any of these requirements (e.g., through the establishment of an impersonal bureaucracy), opportunities for happiness are correspondingly diminished.

Murray's "little platoons" can be considered intrinsic social mechanisms, in that they facilitate systems of behavior as defined in the previous section. Extrinsic social mechanisms, by contrast, provide goods and services without regard to an individual's own performance. State-supported lotteries provide a good example of an almost purely extrinsic social mechanism. Contrary to what might be expected, winning a large amount of money in a lottery has little enduring influence on self-reported happiness (Brickman, Coates, & Janoff-Bulman, 1978). Actually, this should not be too surprising. Unless winners use their newfound wealth to pursue activities that are intrinsically more rewarding than prior activities, there should be no long-term increase in happiness.

Similar considerations apply to other governmental programs (e.g., unemployment compensation, welfare, and food stamps) in which recipients are unable to take credit for the benefits they receive. Most such programs are designed as short-term measures to alleviate temporary hardships over which the individual has little control. Like winning a lottery, they cannot provide long-term happiness, no matter how generous the compensation.

More permanent extrinsic mechanisms can be found in most societies, such as inherited wealth, aristocracies, and caste systems. Questions of fairness aside, these can create as many problems as they solve, because of the unfavorable social comparisons they may produce. Moreover, with the exception of the extremes of poverty and privation, socioeconomic variables such as income, housing, and the like show little relationship to avowed happiness. As long as we deal with extrinsic social mechanisms, the pursuit of happiness may be, as Brickman and Campbell (1971) suggest, a task to rival that of Sisyphus.

Most social organizations can be either intrinsic or extrinsic, depending on the circumstances and the attitudes of the individuals involved. This is perhaps most evident with respect to work. For many people, work occupies such a central position in their lives that it is critical to their happiness. To the extent that a job is intrinsically rewarding, it will facilitate happiness. But many jobs are undertaken primarily for the money they provide—an extrinsic reward. To make matters worse, we sometimes label certain jobs as "dead-end," thus implying they have no intrinsic value. But as Csikszentmihalyi (1991) has documented, some people have the ability to turn even the most routine tasks into challenging occupations, thus deriving intrinsic rewards from their efforts.

When work is unfulfilling, for whatever reason, many people look to leisure activities to find opportunities for self-expression. In addition to government organizations, such as public parks, libraries, and museums, a multi-billion-dollar industry has arisen in the private sector to meet the needs for leisure; manufacturers of sporting goods and hobby supplies, gambling casinos, movie theaters, amusement parks, and private hunting clubs are only a few examples. Like the workplace, organizations that facilitate leisure activities can be classified as either intrinsic or extrinsic, depending on the type of behavior they encourage. For example, organizations that support hobbies (manufacturing and retail outlets, clubs, etc.) are intrinsic social mechanisms, to the extent that they offer challenges that contribute to individual growth. By contrast, much of the entertainment industry can be classified as extrinsic: Passively watching television, for example, often fails to engage the individual in meaningful thought or activity, no matter how enjoyable the experience may be at the moment.

Volunteer and philanthropic organizations also deserve brief comment. These can be distinguished from work in that they are "not for profit," and from leisure in that they are "not for fun." Previously, we have argued that the exercise of moral values is a key component of social systems of behavior and hence of happiness. For many people, volunteer organizations provide the main opportunity for virtuous expression. Visiting hospitals, aiding the poor, leading youth groups, serving on boards and advisory committees, donating time and expertise to charitable and civic organizations, participating in food co-ops—such activities contribute to happiness in significant ways, for they allow people to *be* good, not just look (or feel) good.

We turn now to psychological enabling mechanisms. These, too, can be divided into intrinsic and extrinsic varieties, depending on their mode of activation. As explained previously, intrinsic mechanisms are activated in support of systems of behavior, whereas extrinsic mechanisms operate relatively independently of an ongoing system.

The self is the most inclusive unit in the psychological systems hierarchy (see Figure 43.1). When psychological systems function optimally, the self is enhanced and happiness is facilitated. Self-esteem is, in fact, one of the best predictors of avowed happiness (for a review, see Diener, 1984).

Central to a person's sense of self are long-term plans and goals. We might thus define intrinsic psychological mechanisms as those processes that directly support purposive or goal-directed behavior. The three most important such mechanisms are (1) the setting of challenging but realistic goals, (2) belief in one's ability to achieve desired goals, and (3) adequate feedback with respect to progress. Each of these mechanisms has been the object of considerable research (Locke & Latham, 1990; Bandura, 1989), but only the first two have been directly related to happiness. (The relevance of the third, appropriate feedback, is intuitively obvious.)

With regard to goal setting, Kekes (1982) has argued persuasively that "a man is extremely unlikely to have a happy life without having a more or less clearly formed view about what his life should be" (p. 361). His arguments are logical (i.e., an analysis of the concept of happiness); however, ample psychological research supports the notion that purpose and direction are fundamental to happiness (e.g., Emmons, 1986; Maslow, 1968; Ryff, 1989). Goal-setting strategies are also important components of many happiness enhancement programs (e.g., Fordyce, 1981). One commonly advised strategy is to lower aspirations and to focus on short-term rather than on long-term goals. For many people, the advice is not unreasonable, for they are so fixated on grandiose future goals that they are unable to enjoy the present. However, the strategy has obvious limitations: Lowered aspirations and short-range goals can lead to an impoverished sense of self. Pleasure without purpose is no prescription for happiness.

With regard to self-efficacy beliefs, people who lack confidence in their ability to achieve goals are unlikely to undertake challenging activities. Not surprisingly, therefore, both a belief in personal control over outcomes and the degree of perceived choice in one's life are positively related to happiness (e.g., Abbey & Andrews, 1986; Deci & Ryan, 1985).

Most recent research on happiness has concerned extrinsic rather than intrinsic psychological mechanisms (although, as stated earlier, the dividing line between intrinsic and extrinsic mechanisms is not absolute, but depends on the context). We refer, in particular, to the set of mechanisms encompassed by "gap theories" (e.g., Michalos, 1986; Parducci, 1968; Smith, Diener, & Wedell, 1989; Wills, 1981). According to gap theories, people judge their own happiness by comparing their actual condition or performance against some standard. If the comparison is favorable, happiness is facilitated; if it is unfavorable, happiness is impaired. Such mechanisms are "extrinsic" to the extent that the comparison is activated for reasons that are only tangentially related to the behavior being evaluated (as when a person judges his or her performance, not on its merits, but in comparison to the performance of another).

Michalos (1985, 1986) has described six different gap theories, which address the discrepancies between (1) what one wants and what one has, (2) actual and ideal conditions, (3) actual conditions and expectations, (4) actual conditions and best past conditions, (5) what one has and what others have, and (6) a personal attribute and an environmental attribute. In one study, Michalos found that three of these gap-theoretic variables (1, 4, and 5) accounted for 38% of the variance in self-reported happiness with life as a whole. Sociodemographic variables (age, sex, housing, health, etc.) had little explanatory power over and beyond these three variables. After reviewing 41 other studies that tested gap-theoretic hypotheses, 90% of which were successful, Michalos (1986) concluded that "even a cautious reading of the evidence indicates that we are on the right track with such theories" (p. 72).

There are, however, four problems with gap-theoretic explanations of happiness. First, perceiving a gap can lead to a variety of outcomes, depending on the person and the circumstances. This has been most thoroughly investigated for social comparison—the perceived gap between what one has and what others have. Under some conditions, a downward comparison seems favorable ("I am better off than many"); under other conditions, an upward comparison seems favorable ("If others can succeed, so can I"); and of course, there are a host of potential reference groups and possible dimensions along which comparisons can be made (see Wood, 1989, for a review). Given a choice, people will generally choose a comparison that makes them feel good, while ignoring other possible comparisons.

Second, gap-theoretic variables, by themselves, have little explanatory power. Downward social comparison offers an example: Why should personal satisfaction be increased by a favorable contrast between oneself and others who are less fortunate? The following are only three possibilities: (1) The comparison may focus attention on one's own good fortune; (2) the comparison may mitigate negative emotions, such as envy, anger, and frustration; and (3) to the extent that the discrepancy is perceived as deserved, the comparison may increase self-esteem. In short, on further analysis, gap-theoretic variables may be reduced to non-gap mechanisms.

Third, as we increase the number of relevant gaps (cf. the six mentioned by Michalos), the possible combinations and interactions among them become unmanageable. To take only one possible interaction as an example, the gap between what one wants and what one has may be either exacerbated or mitigated by the gap between what one has and what others have. If progress is to be made, it seems that reduction to more fundamental mechanisms is not only possible but necessary.

Fourth, even in a relatively molar analysis, gap-theoretic variables represent only one class of mechanism that might account for differences in happiness. Simple sensory pleasures, for example, do not always presume the existence of some prior discrepancy. The same is true of more complex constituents of happiness—for example, the enjoyment of the company of others, a sense of accomplishment in a job well done, and so forth. These reflect mechanisms that are intrinsic to the proper functioning of systems of behavior (see our previous discussion of intrinsic mechanisms).

HAPPINESS IN RELATION TO PERSONALITY CHARACTERISTICS

People differ in their capacities for happiness. This brings us to a third major body of research—namely, the relation of happiness to personality characteristics. To begin with, it is important to note that personality characteristics can be assessed without knowledge of underlying mechanisms (biological, social, or psychological). For example, we do not need to know the causes of introversion–extraversion before we can measure the trait and relate it to individual differences in happiness. Moreover, two people can be equally extraverted, say, but for different reasons.

Recent research suggests that five broad dimensions are sufficient to characterize much of personality: introversion–extraversion, neuroticism (or negative affectivity), openness to experience, agreeableness, and conscientiousness (Digman, 1990; McCrae, 1992). People who score high on extraversion and low on neuroticism also tend to report greater happiness (Costa & McCrae, 1980; Emmons & Diener, 1985; Larsen & Ketelaar, 1989). Openness to experience, the third of the "Big Five" traits, seems related to the intensity of emotional reactions, both positive and negative, and is relatively independent of overall ratings of happiness (Costa & McCrae, 1984; McCrae & Costa, 1991). Agreeableness (the fourth dimension) and conscientiousness (the fifth dimension) also make contributions to self-reported happiness over and above the contributions of the other three dimensions. Among 429 adults, McCrae and Costa (1991) found that the five factors together accounted for 19% to 25% of the variance in self-reported happiness, depending on whether the personality ratings were made by the subjects themselves or by their spouses.

Self-reported happiness has been related to other, more specific personality traits, such as energy level, but space does not allow a review of that vast literature (see Argyle, 1987; Diener, 1984; Veenhoven, 1984). The major theoretical questions concerning all such associations are: Why? And under what conditions? Two general approaches to these questions are possible, one in terms of enabling mechanisms and the other in terms of behavioral systems. These approaches may overlap, especially when the focus is on intrinsic rather than extrinsic mechanisms, and the trait is narrowly defined (e.g., energy level). For analytic purposes, however, it is helpful to distinguish between them.

With regard to the first approach, the same or similar mechanisms may facilitate both a particular personality characteristic and happiness, thus accounting for the relation between the two. For example, extraverts may be inherently less sensitive to punishment or aversive stimulation (a biological mechanism); they may be more engaged in convivial activities (a social mechanism); or they may be more prone to make favorable comparisons between self and others (a psychological mechanism). These examples are hypothetical, although not entirely without empirical support. At the present time, however, the actual mechanisms that help mediate the observed relation between extraversion (and other broadly defined personality traits) and happiness are little understood. (For relevant data, see Emmons & Diener, 1986; Headey & Wearing, 1989; Hotard, McFatter, McWhirter, & Stegall, 1989; Larsen & Ketelaar, 1989).

The second general approach to the relation between personality and happiness focuses on systems of behavior, as opposed to enabling mechanisms. On the personality side of the equation, this approach bears some semblance to the act–frequency conception in which traits are treated as summary categories for sets of discrete and representative behavioral acts (Buss & Craik, 1984). On the emotional side of the equation, happiness is, as we have discussed in an earlier section, associated with the optimal functioning of behavioral systems. Behavioral systems also comprise representative behavior acts. However, what is optimal for one individual may not be optimal for another, depending on their respective capacities. This last point requires that we expand the notion of personality characteristics beyond a simple act–frequency conception.

In personality theory as well as everyday discourse, it is common to distinguish between temperamental traits (such as introversion–extraversion) and ability traits (such as intelligence). The distinction, however, is not as clear cut as is commonly assumed (Wallace,

1966; Willerman, Turner, & Peterson, 1976). Both kinds of traits—temperamental as well as ability—can be regarded as capacities to act in ways representative of the trait. For example, extraverts are typically more adroit in social situations than are introverts, whereas introverts have a greater capacity for solitary activities than do extraverts. To the extent that individuals differ in their capacities to act in characteristic ways, it makes little sense to ask whether extraverts, say, are happier than introverts in an absolute sense, and, if so, by what mechanism. The more appropriate question is this: What behavioral systems are most characteristic of extraversion, and under what conditions do they find optimal expression? Similar considerations apply to the other "Big Five" personality traits mentioned earlier, each of which reflects a combination of strengths and weaknesses.

In short, there may be no set or absolute connection between broadly defined personality characteristics (capacities) and happiness. This does not mean that personality research is irrelevant to an understanding of happiness. On the contrary, such research is necessary if we are to temper the presumed relation between happiness and behavioral systems to fit the individual case.

CONCLUDING OBSERVATIONS

Discussing happiness in a brief chapter is a formidable task, for no other topic has been the subject of more debate and controversy over the centuries. We have outlined three approaches to the study of happiness (systems of behavior, enabling mechanisms, and personality characteristics), and within that framework, we have attempted to illustrate how some traditional issues concerning happiness are amenable to empirical research. Other approaches to the study of happiness are possible. For example, considerable recent research has been devoted to the effects, as opposed to the causes and correlates, of happiness (e.g., the effects of positive mood on recall and creative problem solving). We cannot review that research here (see Isen, 1990; Schwarz & Bless, 1991). We therefore conclude with one final observation. Is happiness the *summum bonum* of classical theory? Our definition of happiness in terms of the optimal functioning of behavioral systems would seem

to imply a positive answer. What could be better than optimal functioning? But we must remember that optimizing one function entails sacrifices in others. Happiness can never be complete, except for fleeting moments before balance must be restored. And perhaps that is for the best: "But a lifetime of happiness! No man alive could bear it: it would be hell on earth" (Shaw, 1905/1963, p. 527).

Acknowledgments. Preparation of this chapter was supported in part by Grant No. 23-133 from the Forest Service, U.S. Department of Agriculture. Thanks are due to Carol Thomas-Knowles for her assistance in reviewing the literature on happiness.

REFERENCES

Abbey, A., & Andrews, F. M. (1986). Modeling the psychological determinants of life quality. In F. M. Andrews (Ed.), *Research on the quality of life* (pp. 85–116). Ann Arbor: University of Michigan, Institute for Social Research.

Andrews, F. M., & Robinson, J. P. (1991). Measures of subjective well-being. In J. P. Robinson, P. R. Shaver, & L. W. Wrightsman (Eds.), *Measures of personality and social psychological attitudes* (pp. 61–114). New York: Academic Press.

Argyle, M. (1987). *The psychology of happiness.* London: Methuen.

Aristotle. (1947). Nicomachean ethics (W. D. Ross, Trans.). In R. McKeon (Ed.), *Introduction to Aristotle* (pp. 300–543). New York: Modern Library.

Averill, J. R. (1975). A semantic atlas of emotional concepts. *JSAS: Catalog of Selected Documents in Psychology, 5,* 330. (Ms. No. 1103)

Averill, J. R. (1980). On the paucity of positive emotions. In K. R. Blankstein, P. Pliner, & J. Polivy (Eds.), *Assessment and modification of emotional behavior* (pp. 7–45). New York: Plenum Press.

Averill, J. R. (1990). Emotions as related to systems of behavior. In N. L. Stein, B. Leventhal, & T. Trabasso (Eds.), *Psychological and biological approaches to emotion* (pp. 385–404). Hillsdale, NJ: Erlbaum.

Averill, J. R. (1991). Emotions as episodic dispositions, cognitive schemas, and transitory social roles: Steps toward an integrated theory of emotion. In D. Ozer, J. M. Healy, Jr., & A. J. Stewart (Eds.), *Perspectives in personality* (Vol. 3a, pp. 139-167). London: Jessica Kingsley.

Averill, J. R. (1992). The structural bases of emotional behavior: A metatheoretical analysis. In M. S. Clark (Ed.), *Review of personality and social psychology* (Vol. 13, pp. 1–24). Newbury Park, CA: Sage.

Bandura, A. (1989). Human agency in social cognitive theory. *American Psychologist, 44,* 1175–1184.

Bradburn, N. M. (1969). *The structure of psychological well-being.* Chicago: Aldine.

Brickman, P., & Campbell, D. T. (1971). Hedonic relativism and planning the good society. In M. H. Appley (Ed.), *Adaptation-level theory* (pp. 287–302). New York: Academic Press.

Brickman, P., Coates, D., & Janoff-Bulman, R. (1978). Lottery winners and accident victims: Is happiness relative? *Journal of Personality and Social Psychology, 36*, 917–927.

Buss, D. M., & Craik, K. H. (1984). Acts, dispositions, and personality. In B. A. Maher & W. B. Maher (Eds.), *Progress in experimental personality research* (Vol. 13, pp. 241–301). Orlando, FL: Academic Press.

Campbell, A., Converse, P. E., & Rodgers, W. L. (1976). *The quality of American life: Perceptions, evaluations, and satisfactions*. New York: Russell Sage Foundation.

Costa, P. T., Jr., & McCrae, R. R. (1980). Influence of extraversion and neuroticism on subjective well-being: Happy and unhappy people. *Journal of Personality and Social Psychology, 38*, 668–678.

Costa, P. T., Jr., & McCrae, R. R. (1984). Personality as a lifelong determinant of well-being. In C. Malatesta & C. Izard (Eds.), *Affective processes in adult development and aging* (pp. 141–157). Beverly Hills, CA: Sage.

Csikszentmihalyi, M. (1991). *Flow: The psychology of optimal experience*. New York: Harper Collins.

Deci, E. L., & Ryan, R. M. (1985). *Intrinsic motivation and self-determination*. New York: Plenum Press.

Diener, E. (1984). Subjective well-being. *Psychological Bulletin, 95*, 542–575.

Digman, J. M. (1990). Personality structure: Emergence of the five-factor model. *Annual Review of Psychology, 41*, 417–440.

Duncker, K. (1941). On pleasure, emotion, and striving. *Philosophy and Phenomenological Research, 1*, 391–430.

Emmons, R. A. (1986). Personal strivings: An approach to personality and subjective well-being. *Personality and Social Psychology, 51*, 1058–1068.

Emmons, R. A., & Diener, E. (1985). Personality correlates of subjective well-being. *Personality and Social Psychology Bulletin, 11*, 89–97.

Emmons, R. A., & Diener, E. (1986). Influence of impulsivity and sociability on subjective well-being. *Journal of Personality and Social Psychology, 50*, 1211–1215.

Fehr, B., & Russell, J. A. (1984). Concept of emotion viewed from a prototype perspective. *Journal of Experimental Psychology: General, 113*(3), 464–486.

Fordyce, M. W. (1981). *The psychology of happiness*. Fort Myers, Fl: Cypress Lake Media.

Freedman, J. L. (1978). *Happy people*. New York: Harcourt Brace Jovanovich.

Frijda, N. H. (1986). *The emotions*. Cambridge, England: Cambridge University Press.

Grichting, W. L. (1983). Domain, scope and degree of happiness. *British Journal of Social Psychology, 22*, 247–260.

Headey, B., & Wearing, A. (1989). Personality, life events, and subjective well-being: Toward a dynamic equilibrium model. *Journal of Personality and Social Psychology, 57*, 731–739.

Hotard, S. R., McFatter, R. M., McWhirter, R. M., & Stegall, M. E. (1989). Interactive effects of extraversion, neuroticism, and social relationships on subjective well-being. *Journal of Personality and Social Psychology, 57*, 321–331.

Isen, A. M. (1990). The influence of positive and negative affect on cognitive organization. In N. L. Stein, B. Leventhal, & T. Trabasso (Eds.), *Psychological and biological approaches to emotion* (pp. 75–94). Hillsdale, NJ: Earlbaum.

Izard, C. E. (1977). *Human emotions*. New York: Plenum.

Jones, H. M. (1953). *The pursuit of happiness*. Cambridge, MA: Harvard University Press.

Kekes, J. (1982). Happiness. *Mind, 91*, 358–376.

Kövecses, Z. (1991). Happiness: A definitional effort. *Metaphor and Symbolic Activity, 6*, 29–46.

Kraut, R. (1979). Two conceptions of happiness. *Philosophical Review, 88*, 167–197.

Larsen, R. J., & Ketelaar, T. (1989). Extraversion, neuroticism, and susceptibility to positive and negative mood induction procedures. *Personality and Individual Differences, 10*, 1221–1228.

Lazarus, R. S. (1991). *Emotion and adaptation*. New York: Oxford University Press.

Lewis, C. S. (1982, April). We have no right to happiness. *The Saturday Evening Post*, pp. 42–44. (Original work published 1963)

Locke, E. A., & Latham, G. P. (1990). *A theory of goal setting and task performance*. Englewood Cliffs, NJ: Prentice-Hall.

Maslow, A. H. (1968). *Toward a psychology of being* (2nd ed.). New York: Van Nostrand Reinhold.

McCrae, R. R. (Ed.). (1992). The five-factor model: Issues and application [Special issue.]. *Journal of Personality, 60*(2).

McCrae, R. R., & Costa, P. T., Jr. (1991). Adding *Liebe und Arbeit*: The full five-factor model and well-being. *Personality and Social Psychology Bulletin, 17*, 227–232.

Mencken, H. L. (1930). Editorial: Comfort for the ailing. *American Mercury, 19*, 288–289.

Michalos, A. C. (1985). Multiple discrepancies theory (MDT). *Social Indicators Research, 16*, 347–413.

Michalos, A. C. (1986). Job satisfaction, marital satisfaction, and the quality of life. In F. M. Andrews (Ed.), *Research on the quality of life* (pp. 57–84). Ann Arbor: University of Michigan, Institute for Social Research.

Murray, C. (1988). *In pursuit of happiness and good government*. New York: Simon and Schuster.

Natsoulas, T. (1991). The concept of consciousness$_2$: The personal meaning. *Journal for the Theory of Social Behaviour, 21*, 339–367.

Novak, M. A., & Suomi, S. J. (1988). Psychological well-being of primates in captivity. *American Psychologist, 43*, 765–773.

Nozick, R. (1989). *The examined life*. New York: Simon & Schuster.

Parducci, A. (1968). The relativism of absolute judgements. *Scientific American, 219*, 84–90.

Russell, B. (1945). *A history of Western philosophy*. New York: Simon & Schuster.

Russell, B. (1950). *The conquest of happiness*. New York: Liveright.

Ryff, C. D. (1989). Happiness is everything, or is it? Explorations on the meaning of psychological well-being. *Journal of Personality and Social Psychology, 57*, 1069–1081.

Schwarz, N., & Bless, H. (1991). Happy and mindless, but sad and smart? The impact of affective states on analytic reasoning. In J. P. Forgas (Ed.), *Emotion and social judgments* (pp. 55–71). Oxford: Pergamon Press.

Shaver, P., Schwartz, J., Kirson, D., & O'Connor, C. (1987). Emotion knowledge: Further exploration of a prototype approach. *Journal of Personality and Social Psychology, 52*, 1061–1086.

Shaw, G. B. (1963). Man and superman. In G. B. Shaw, *Complete plays with prefaces* (Vol. 3, pp. 483–686). New York: Dodd, Mead. (Original work published 1905)

Skinner, B. F. (1986). What is wrong with daily life in the Western world? *American Psychologist, 41*, 568–574.

Smith, R. H., Diener, E., & Wedell, D. H. (1989). Intrapersonal and social comparison determinants of happiness: A range-frequency analysis. *Journal of Personality and Social Psychology, 56*, 317–325.

Strasser, S. (1977). *Phenomenology of feeling* (R. E. Wood, Trans.). Pittsburgh: Duquesne University Press.

Tatarkiewicz, W. (1976). *Analysis of happiness*. Warsaw: Polish Scientific.

Veenhoven, R. (1984). *Conditions of happiness*. Dordrecht, The Netherlands: D. Reidel.

Vlastos, G. (1985). Happiness and virtue in Socrates' moral theory. *Topoi, 4*, 3–22.

Wallace, J. (1966). An abilities conceptions of personality: Some implications for personality measurement. *American Psychologist, 21*, 132–138.

Willerman, L., Turner, R. G., & Peterson, M. A. (1976). A comparison of the predictive validity of typical and maximal personality measures. *Journal of Research in Personality, 10*, 482–492.

Wills, T. A. (1981). Downward comparison principles in social psychology. *Psychological Bulletin, 90*, 245–271.

Wilson, W. (1967). Correlates of avowed happiness. *Psychological Bulletin, 67*, 294–306.

Wood, J. V. (1989). Theory and research concerning social comparisons of personal attributes. *Psychological Bulletin, 106*, 231–248

44

Organizational and Motivational Functions of Discrete Emotions

CARROLL E. IZARD

THEORETICAL FRAMEWORK

Five broad assumptions provide the theoretical framework for this chapter. First, the emotions system constitutes the primary motivational system for human behavior (Tomkins, 1962; Izard, 1971). Second, each of the discrete emotions serves distinct functions in the way it organizes perception, cognition, and actions (behavior) for adaptation, coping, and creative endeavors and in the way it contributes to behavioral development (Izard, 1978). Third, emotion–behavior relations begin to develop early and remain stable over time (Izard, 1977; Plutchik, 1980); although the repertoire of specific responses for a given emotion changes as development proceeds, the new responses are complementary to the ones that remain and functionally similar to those that disappear. Fourth, the capacity of emotions to organize, motivate, and sustain particular sets of behaviors contributes to the development of personality. And fifth, individual differences in emotion activation thresholds and in the frequency and intensity with which particular emotions are experienced are major determinants of specific traits and broad dimensions of personality.

The foregoing assumptions represent a discrete-emotions approach, which is distinguished from the view that emotion can be understood in terms of certain broad dimensions such as pleasantness and arousal/activation. In my opinion, these positions can be viewed as complementary rather than contradictory (cf. Watson & Tellegen, 1985), but the issue of the structure of the emotion(s) system requires further discussion and research. The issue is pertinent to the understanding of the role of emotions in organizing and motivating behavior and in the development of personality.

Do emotions operate as two or three broad dimensions, or as 7 or 11 separate and distinct units? This fundamental question in emotion theory has concerned scientists since the beginnings of psychology as a discipline. Indeed, some of the progenitors of psychology and emotions theory enunciated opposing views.

Darwin (1872/1965) described a dozen or so discrete emotions and argued that the expressions of some of these emotions evolved from functional systems. In his theory, the expressions that characterize certain of the discrete emotions are patterns of movement that served adaptive functions in evolution. Darwin made his arguments along this line clear and prominent in his book on emotions, but he did not highlight or emphasize the notion that emotion expressions continue to serve adaptive functions in contemporary life. However, a careful reading of his work shows that he believed that the expressions of the emotions continue to be useful mechanisms. Darwin's description of the role of expressions includes what psychologists label as "adaptive functions."

Darwin identified two adaptive functions of emotion expressions: social communication and the regulation of emotion experiences. Regarding the first function, he said that the mother's smile of approval or frown of disapproval starts the child on the right path. Regarding the second function, he said that suppressing the expression of an emotion attenuates the experience of that emotion, and that the free and full expression of an emotion amplifies the emotion experience. In his statements about the evolution and adaptive functions of the emotions, Darwin was clearly talking about discrete emotions. He gave specific and anatomically detailed descriptions of unique and separate emotion expressions.

In contrast to Darwin, Spencer (1890) conceptualized emotions as dimensions of consciousness. Wundt (1897) extended Spencer's ideas and maintained that all emotion feelings can be explained in terms of three dimensions: pleasantness–unpleasantness, relaxation–tension, and calm–excitement. Variations of this approach were enunciated later by a number of highly influential investigators (Duffy, 1941; Lindsley, 1951; Schlosberg, 1941; Woodworth, 1938). As a result of their efforts and a psychology that was largely controlled by behaviorism, the dimensional approach to the study of emotion was dominant in psychology until about the fourth quarter of the 20th century.

Well before discrete-emotions theories gained a more or less equal footing with dimensional theories, Tomkins (1962, 1963) wrote a brilliant exposition of his affect theory that identified eight separate emotions. At the same time, Plutchik (1962) published the early version of his theory, and he too described eight discrete emotions. Although he used different labels, most of his eight map directly onto those of Tomkins. Tomkins's and Plutchik's functionalist approach tied their work to the Darwinian tradition, and had immediate appeal to a few psychologists who were open to the possibility that a bioevolutionary perspective might offer new insights on emotions and their role in developmental processes, personality, social relations, cognition, and actions (e.g., Ekman, 1972; Izard, 1971). It was at least 20 years after the appearance of the volumes by Tomkins and Plutchik, however, that discrete-emotions theories began

having a significant impact on the field and guiding the work of a significant number of researchers.

Currently, a number of emotion researchers consider the discrete-emotions and dimensional approaches as complementary rather than as contradictory. Even investigators who have developed discrete-emotions theories or subscribe to this position sometimes resort to a methodology that derives from the dimensional approach (e.g., Izard, 1972; Lang, 1984). A major reason for doing this is that on average it is easier to obtain reliable measures at the level of broad dimensions, such as valence (pleasantness–unpleasantness) or positive and negative emotionality, than at the level of discrete emotions. In the language of psychometrics, indices of discrete emotions are primary factors and indices of broad dimensions are secondary factors; hence the greater stability of the latter (Izard, Haynes, Libero, & Putnam, in press; Watson & Clark, 1992). Nevertheless, it is possible to obtain reliable indices of discrete emotions (Izard, 1972), and these have been found useful in analyzing traits of personality, as well as anxiety, depression, hostility, and other affective–cognitive structures (Blumberg & Izard, 1985, 1986; Izard, 1972; Watson & Clark, 1992).

Numerous reviews have concluded that there is impressive research supporting the hypothesis of unique and universal expressions for at least seven discrete emotions (Izard, 1971; Ekman, Friesen, & Ellsworth, 1972). Most developmental theorists acknowledge the existence of discrete emotions (e.g., Campos & Barrett, 1984; Cicchetti, 1990; Emde, 1980). There is also a rapidly growing body of literature based on concepts and measures of discrete emotion experiences. This research has come from a number of different theoretical orientations—attribution theory (Weiner, 1985), appraisal theory (Smith & Ellsworth, 1985), cognitive–motivational theory (Harris, 1989; Roseman, 1984; Roseman, Weist, & Swartz, in press), and differential-emotions theory (Libero & Izard, 1992).

Despite the substantial body of evidence that testifies to the validity and usefulness of the concepts of discrete emotions, they are a long way from having gained universal acceptance by emotion theorists and researchers; they are even further from acceptance in the cognitive sciences and neuroscience. This is so even though research has shown that different discrete emotions have different effects on perceptual and cognitive processes (e.g., Bower & Gilligan, 1984). In the present chapter, I present evidence and arguments in support of discrete-emotions concepts and variables. I do this by attempting to answer two questions about a sample of specific emotions. First, does this discrete emotion have functions that can be readily understood as providing an adaptive advantage in evolution? Second, does this specific emotion continue to serve functions that facilitate development, adaptation, and coping? Finally, I try to show that a principal function of the emotions system is that of organizing and motivating characteristic patterns of responses or traits of personality.

In order to discuss the functions of emotions, it is necessary to be clear about what is meant by the term "emotion" and by a few other key emotion-related concepts. Despite the sizable and growing body of literature on emotion theory, the lack of widely accepted definitions makes it necessary to draw some conceptual boundaries. The following definitions from differential-emotions theory (Izard, 1977; Izard & Malatesta, 1987) establish the terminology for this chapter.

An emotion is a particular set of neural processes instigating efferent processes that may or may not lead to an observable expression, but that always lead to a unique conscious experience. The subjective experience may or may not be accessible through cognitive processes or the language system. Thus emotion has three levels or aspects—neural, expressive, and experiential—and the term "emotion" refers to all three components operating as an integral system. When data relate to only one component, that component is identified specifically as "neural activity," "emotion expression" (efferent processes), or "emotion experience."

In infants, the efferent processes in emotion activation typically lead to expressive behavior. However, as a function of both maturation and socialization, the relations between the neural activation process and expressive behavior change with development (Izard, Hembree, & Huebner, 1987). As children gain more mastery over the somatic muscles of expression, and as socialization proceeds, children learn to regulate and modify emotion expressions and expressive styles. Eventually, observable expression in some situations may be completely inhibited or dissociated. Because feedback from expressive behavior contributes to the activation and regulation of emotion experiences (Laird, 1974), the child's learning to regulate emotion expressions is part of the process of learning to regulate emotion experiences (Izard, 1990).

In differential-emotions theory, emotion experience is defined as a quality of consciousness. It is defined in terms of emotion processes. It can be described as a feeling or motivational state that may include an action tendency or feeling of action readiness. Emotion experience proper does not include cognition; however, emotion experience is cue-producing, and, as such, it normally recruits the cognitive system.

An emotion experience does not recruit cognitive processes in random fashion. The quality of consciousness that is joy recruits cognitive and motoric responses that are appropriate to joy as a motivational state. Similarly, the feeling/motivational state of sadness recruits cognitive and motoric responses congruent with that state, and so on for anger and the other discrete emotions (Bower, 1987; Izard, Wehmer, Livsey, & Jennings, 1965). When an emotion feeling/motivational state recruits cognition that guides an effective action (suitable response), the groundwork is laid for the development of an adaptive affective–cognitive structure. An "affective–cognitive structure" is an association or bond between emotion experience and cognition. It is the most common type of mental structure, the fundamental building block of mind and memory.

Indeed, what many emotion theorists call "emotion" or "emotion experience" is probably pretty close to the present concept of affective–cognitive structure. Virtually all research on emotion experience has relied on verbal self-report. This means that what is measured is the cognitive content associated with a particular emotional experience. Results are described as though we have indexed emotion experiences; it would be more accurate to say that we have assessed affective–cognitive structures.

Making a clean break between motivation and cognition, and in particular between the subjective experience of emotion and the cognition that it recruits, has a number of implications for theory and empirical research (Izard, 1992). For example, it invites us to explore the possibility that unconscious motivation may be an emotion experience (motivational/feeling state, action tendency) that is not cognitively tagged or articulated. Therefore, it is not possible to access this emotion experience through the language system.

Another important consequence of separating emotion experience proper from cognition is that it makes it easier to formulate hypotheses about the role of cognition in emotion activation. A recent review has suggested that there are multiple systems of emotion activation, some cognitive and some noncognitive (Izard, 1992). The view of separate systems for emotions and cognition also invites clearer hypotheses regarding emotion–cognition relations. If cognition is viewed as part of emotion experience per se, then it becomes more difficult to examine cause–effect relations among cognitive and emotion processes. The position that an emotion experience is essentially a motivational/feeling state and an action tendency, a direct product of neural processes, allows us to conceptualize appraisal/evaluative processes as independent determinants of emotions and other cognitive processes as consequences.

The foregoing conceptual framework guides the following discussion of the adaptive functions of discrete emotions in evolution and development. Because of space limitations, the discussion is limited to the emotions of joy, sadness, anger, disgust, shame, and fear. Each of these emotions serves at least one distinct function. Furthermore, some emotions serve a common function in different ways.

THE ADAPTIVE FUNCTIONS OF DISCRETE EMOTIONS IN EVOLUTION AND DEVELOPMENT

The Functions of Joy

The joy experience is different from sensory pleasure, but the latter often leads to the former, as when the culmination of sexual or postprandial pleasure increases intimacy and leads to enjoyable social interaction. Openness is often heightened in such situations, and openness can contribute to the strengthening of social bonds. Social bonds and the social support they provide constitute a highly adaptive mechanism that can easily be conceived as an advantage in evolution and development. In species in which the young experience a

long period of dependency, a strong social bond between parent and offspring is essential to survival (Hamburg, 1963; Mellen, 1981). No other emotion serves this function so effectively, providing significant benefits at little or no cost.

A distinct function of joy is served by its expression. It has the capacity to operate as a universally recognizable signal of readiness for friendly interaction. By the principles of contagion, empathy, and facial feedback, joy expression can contribute to the well-being of the social surround (Izard, 1990; Lelwica & Haviland, 1983; Tomkins, 1962). Joy also has recuperative powers and can serve as an antidote to stress (Tomkins, 1962). Although not specifically identifying joy, Lazarus and his colleagues have argued that positive emotions function as "breathers" in relieving stress, and that they sustain coping in taxing situations (Lazarus, Kanner, & Folkman, 1980).

The Functions of Sadness

Sadness, like joy, can also strengthen social bonds. For example, on the loss of a loved one, families and friends come together and emotional ties are renewed. The breaking of a tie through death is a compelling reminder of the value of family, friendships, and community. A review by Averill (1968) suggests that in the course of evolution, grief, by strengthening communal bonds, increased the probability of surviving. Although several emotions may be involved in grief, sadness is the dominant one.

A unique function of sadness is its capacity to slow the cognitive and motor systems. In one study, mothers' facial and vocal expressions of sadness during face-to-face mother–child interactions increased sadness expressions and significantly decreased exploratory play in their 9-month-old infants (Termine & Izard, 1988). Because play is the principal and virtually continuous activity of healthy infants and children, the slowing of play behavior dramatically demonstrates this function of sadness.

The sadness-induced slowing of mental and motor activity can have adaptive effects. The slowing of cognitive processes may enable a more careful look for the source of trouble, and deeper reflection on a disappointing performance or a failure that instigated the sadness (see Tomkins, 1963). This slower and more deliberate scrutiny of the self and the circumstances may help the individual gain a new perspective—one that facilitates plans for a better performance in the future. Such plans and the anticipation of another attempt may ameliorate the sadness.

Sadness also communicates to the self and to others that there is trouble (Tomkins, 1963). A sad expression, particularly on the face of a friend or loved one, is likely to generate empathic sadness in the observer. The sadness one feels with (or for) a friend increases the likelihood that one will feel sympathy and lend a helping hand (Moore, Underwood, & Rosenhan, 1984). Thus sadness may often be the key emotion in the personal distress that plays a key role in empathic, sympathetic, and altruistic behavior (see Eisenberg & Strayer, 1987).

The Functions of Anger

In the colorful language of Tomkins (1991), the principal function of anger is to make bad matters worse and increase the probability of an anger response. He hastens to add that this need not be an aggressive response, acknowledging (as do most emotion theorists) that there is no necessary connection between anger and aggression (cf. Averill, 1983). This insightful description of the function of anger does not consider the possibility that the anger expression itself may serve important functions.

Indeed, anger expression may prevent aggression. Such is the case when the alpha male in a primate colony casts a hard stare at a challenger (Chevalier-Skolnikoff, 1973), or when a parent does the same to inhibit a fight between two children. Furthermore, the effects of anger expression toward another adult may even truncate the anger-related response of the angry individual. This may be the case if the anger expression elicites an immediate sad expression and apology from the other person.

A unique function of anger is that of mobilizing and sustaining energy at high levels. Other emotions, even the positive emotions of interest and joy, mobilize energy and sustain goal-directed activity, but not at a similar intensity. Intense interest/excitement can speed mental and motor functions and sustain them for long periods, but interest is no match for anger in directing bodily resources to the muscles of action (Cannon, 1929). No other emotion can equal the consistency and vigor

of anger in increasing and sustaining extremely high levels of motor activity. It is no coincidence that coaches in contact sports, aided greatly by the media, foster a little anger (and contempt) for opposing coaches and players.

The Functions of Disgust

From an evolutionary perspective, it is easy to conceive of disgust as motivating animals to keep the nest clean and maintain an environment sufficiently sanitary for survival. Most mammals and birds do in fact maintain a tidy niche. Animals that excrete their waste without regard to the locale usually lead a nomadic existence. Disgust continues to function in contemporary life as a motive for environmental cleanliness as well as bodily hygiene.

All the functions of all the emotions probably serve both biological and psychological purposes, directly or indirectly. The notion of a division of functions is not meant to suggest a sharp dichotomy, but in the case of disgust some functions can be readily identified as serving biological purposes—the eliciting of nausea and the avoidance of contaminated substances. Although protracted high levels of intensity of other negative emotions (e.g., fear) may result in these physiological responses, no other emotion accomplishes this end with the regularity and efficiency of disgust. For example, being compelled to eat, or even simply being exposed to, disgusting food increases the likelihood of the physiological reactions of nausea and vomiting.

Of course, what is disgusting for a particular person is not determined solely by chemical and biological variables. The range of stimuli that become capable of eliciting disgust responses is influenced by cultural practices and idiosyncratic learning. Thus contamination may be ideational or chemical or both (Rozin & Fallon, 1987). In some cases, disgust protects people from harmful substances. In other cases, it protects people from the psychological consequences of violating cultural norms.

Certain features of the disgust reaction—facial behavior, food rejection—can be elicited in newborns, even in anencephalic newborns (Steiner, 1979). This suggests that the original and primary function of disgust is to protect the body from substances sensed as harmful. The potential harmfulness may be real or a learned misconception. A strong case has been made for learned food disgust that can be elicited by either real or imagined contamination (Rozin & Fallon, 1987).

Through conditioning and social learning, anything that is offensive, whether real or abstract, may become a stimulus for disgust. The offense can be to the senses or to one's psychological taste. Even one's own self can be the offender, and the disgust can be directed inward.

The Functions of Shame

The capacity for experiencing shame reflects the vulnerability of the individual to the sanctions and criticisms of parents, other adults, and peers. Persons who fail to fulfill their responsibility in the community may become the subjects of ridicule and contempt—strong stimuli for shame. Thus shame acts as a force for social conformity and social cohesion, and the anticipation of shame or shame avoidance motivates the individual to accept his or her share of responsibility for the welfare of the community (see Lewis, 1971; Tomkins, 1962).

No other emotion is as effective as shame in calling attention to failures and weaknesses in the functioning of the self. Shame results from conditions that heighten self-awareness, and shame is more likely to occur when the exposed self is found inadequate. The exposure one feels during the experience of shame highlights personal inadequacies in performance and feelings of incompetence. Because of this relation between the vulnerability of the self and proneness to shame, shame anticipation and shame avoidance motivate the acquisition of skills and competencies. In this way, shame plays a significant role in the development of self-adequacy (see Lewis, 1971; Lynd, 1961; Tangney, 1990; Tomkins, 1963).

The Functions of Fear

The unique function of fear is to motivate escape from dangerous situations. Fear anticipation motivates avoidance behavior. Neither escape nor avoidance implies that the behavior must involve flight. Indeed, fear sometimes disengages the motor system, resulting in freezing behavior. Furthermore, the threat may be psychological as well as physical. Threats to one's self-concept, one's integrity, or one's psychological well-being can elicit fear, and such threats are rarely eliminated by physically running away. Nevertheless, whether the threat is physical or mental or both, fear performs its basic function of motivating escape and alleviating fear-eliciting conditions.

Fear provides an excellent example of the power of emotion to organize and direct perceptual and cognitive processes. Fear tends to produce "tunnel vision" by focusing attention on the source of the threat and restricting cue utilization (see Easterbrook, 1959). Keen attention to the threatening agent or situation can be adaptive in guiding self-protective behavior. Such restrictions on attentional processes in unrealistic or unwarranted fear are maladaptive.

EMOTIONS AND MALADAPTIVE BEHAVIOR

As everyone knows, emotions are not always associated with adaptive behavior. Theory and evidence strongly support the notion that each emotion has an inherently adaptive function (Izard, 1989; Plutchik, 1980; Leventhal, 1980; Lazarus & Smith, 1988), but this does not mean that emotion guarantees an effective response to threat or challenge. The relation between emotion and adaptive behavior is a function of the mechanisms and processes that link emotion, cognition, and action, and those that effect emotion regulation. Chief among the regulatory mechanisms are neural inhibitory structures, which are significantly influenced by genetic and maturational processes, and cognitive development and social learning, which are greatly influenced by the environment.

If the individual's resources for emotion regulation are inadequate, in terms of either neural or cognitive–behavioral controls, the emotion can go awry and become maladaptive. However, even in extreme fear (as in other intense emotional states), maladaptive behavior is never simply a function or the fear experience. Maladaptive behavior usually reflects problems in emotion–cognition relations and in emotion–cognition–action patterns. If the motivational component of fear (or any emotion) has been linked to inappropriate cognition to form maladaptive affective–cognitive structures, then activation of the emotion will result in maladaptive behavior.

THE FUNCTIONS OF EMOTIONS IN THE DEVELOPMENT OF PERSONALITY

A major general function of the emotions and the emotions system is the organization of traits and dimensions of personality (Izard, 1991; Malatesta, 1990). That emotions affect the development of personality is a truism, but the matter of how this is accomplished is not so obvious.

I have argued that emotions are motivational and that they organize and motivate cognition and action. It follows that emotions would affect an individual's characteristic way of thinking and acting—his or her personality. This is especially true if we accept the assumption of some theories that some emotion at some level of intensity is continually present in consciousness (e.g., Izard, 1989). Furthermore, I have maintained that each emotion influences perception, cognition, and action in a particular way. This suggests that specific emotions help shape specific traits, and that particular patterns of emotions influence particular broad dimensions of personality. There are some empirical data to support the notion that emotions have rather specific effects in shaping personality; more conservatively, this evidence shows significant correlations among measures of emotion experiences and personality traits.

MECHANISMS AND PROCESSES IN EMOTION–PERSONALITY RELATIONS

Before discussing some empirical findings on relations among emotion experiences and personality traits, I present some propositions about mechanisms and processes by which emotions influence personality. Some of these may be thought of as structural characteristics of emotions and others as functional characteristics, but this distinction does not imply a hard dichotomy.

Two structural features of emotions that affect personality are genetically influenced individual differences in activation thresholds and the stability of emotionality. Common observation suggests that people differ widely in readiness or proneness to express different emotions. Such differences help account for the difficulty researchers have experienced in finding emotion-specific stimuli, particularly for experiments with adults. Self-report measures reveal wide individual differences in the frequency with which older children and adults experience the various emotions (Blumberg & Izard, 1986; Tangney, 1990).

A good example of population differences in emotion activation thresholds is in the research on children with Down's syndrome. Cicchetti and Sroufe (1976) have shown that these children are less likely to respond emotionally to a variety of positive and negative stimuli than are normal children. These differences hold even when the two groups are matched on indices of cognitive development. Because it is known that Down's syndrome is a specific genetic defect, the foregoing finding is consistent with the notion that genes influence emotion activation thresholds.

Evidence for individual stability of emotionality (individuals' maintaining their rank order within the group) is at the same time evidence for differences in emotion activation thresholds. If, for example, there is individual stability in indices of anger expression or positive emotionality, then there must be individual differences in proneness to experience or display anger or positive emotions. A number of investigators have shown that positive emotionality and negative emotionality have stability over time (Diener & Larsen, 1984; Epstein, 1980; Tellegen, 1985).

Others have found stability of indices of discrete emotions for periods of up to 3 years (Izard et al., in press). In the latter study, indices of 11 discrete emotions showed individual stability even during the first 6 months after childbirth, when important hormonal and social changes occur (O'Hara, 1987). These changes sometimes result in "postpartum blues," a phenomenon that resembles depression. In the Izard et al. (in press) study, indices of four depression-related emotion experiences did show changes or group instability during the first 6 months after childbirth. They were significantly elevated at 2.5 months after childbirth. They decreased to a normal level 4 months later and remained stable at this level over the next 2.5 years of the study. Even during the postpartum period, when indices of some emotion experiences showed group instability, these and all other indices continued to show individual stability. Thus during the period of "postpartum blues," when there were significant changes in group means, individuals tended to retain their rank within the group.

As already noted, in differential-emotions theory (Izard, 1991; Izard, et al., in press) the chief functional characteristic of emotions is their capacity to organize and motivate behavior. Yet emotions do not motivate random responses. Each discrete emotion motivates a particular type or range of cognitions and actions. Although the repertoire of responses associated with an emotion undergoes age-appropriate changes, it continues to serve the basic functions of the emotion. Therefore, if a given emotion is experienced frequently, a particular type of thought and action is more likely to occur frequently. Thus as a child develops characteristic patterns of emotion–cognition–action sequences, personality traits are formed.

Two other concepts help clarify the role of emotions in the development of personality—stable patterns of emotions and affective-cognitive structures. Not only is there stability in the frequency of experiencing a particular emotion, but some emotions co-occur with regularity. Such co-occurrence is probably a function of both innate and learned relationships among emotions (Tomkins, 1962; Izard, 1972). An example of a stable pattern of emotions is the sadness–anger pattern that characterizes depression (Blumberg & Izard, 1985, 1986). Frequently occurring stable patterns of emotions influence cognition and actions in particular ways, and as these responses and response tendencies become characteristic of the individual, they are tantamount to traits.

An affective–cognitive structure, as defined earlier, is a bond or association between an emotion or pattern of emotions and a thought or set of thoughts (schema or script). Such affective–cognitive structures or emotion scripts, or related sets of them, can motivate a related pattern of behaviors that are manifested as a characteristic or trait. As indicated earlier, emotion experiences typically influence normal personality functioning through affective–cognitive structures. The important exceptions are emotion experiences that are not labeled or cognitively articulated or emotion experiences that have become dissociated from the cognition once associated with it. Such unlabeled or dissociated emotion experiences are conceived of as the major source of unconscious motivation.

To summarize the role of emotions in personality development, individual differences in emotion activation thresholds lead to differences in the frequency of emotion experiences. Frequent experiences of a particular emotion tend to organize particular types of cognition and action, and recurring patterns of emotion-cognition–action sequences lead to the development of a characteristic way of responding—a personality trait. For example, people with low thresholds for positive emotions are characteristically happy, and their positive emotionality tends to be stable over time. For many people, positive mood lowers the threshold for social interaction, and because of this, positive emotionality in infancy and childhood increases the likelihood of the emergence of the personality dimension of extraversion. In a similar fashion, low thresholds for negative emotions set the stage for the development of the personality dimension of negative emotionality or neuroticism.

EMPIRICAL STUDIES OF EMOTION–PERSONALITY RELATIONS

A number of studies have examined the relations between indices of emotion experience and dimensions of personality, as assessed by tests based on the five-factor model (e.g., McCrae & Costa, 1987). This approach leads to measures of extraversion (E), neuroticism (N), openness to experience (O), agreeableness (A), and conscientiousness (C). Correlations of about .60 have been found consistently between positive emotionality and E, and between negative emotionality and N. Watson and Clark (1992) found that their specific emotion scales of fear, sadness, guilt, and hostility were also strongly related to N. Their indices of positive emotions (joviality, self-assurance, attentiveness) were moderately related to E and C.

Several researchers have related emotion experience measures to the three-factor Eysenck Personality Questionnaire (e.g., Larsen & Ketelaar, 1989). They also found that positive and negative emotionality correlated significantly with Eysenck's E and N, respectively.

A study by Emmons and Diener (1986) suggests that the activation of emotions associated with a personality trait is primed or facilitated by situations that are congruent with the trait.

For example, people who scored high on E were happier when allowed to choose to be with others than when they were required to be alone. This seems consistent with the argument that emotions motivate traits and trait-related behaviors. Thus, extraverts seek social situations as opportunities to experience their interest in and enjoyment of people.

The foregoing argument—that low threshold for interest and joy facilitates the development of extraversion and social behavior—does not explain the happy shy person. On the average, shyness correlates negatively with E (Izard et al., 1992), but the correlation is not strong enough to suggest anything close to a one-to-one relation. Indeed, some shy people are sociable (Jones, Cheeks, & Briggs, 1986), though probably not extraverted. In any case, the interrelations among the positive emotions, E, shyness, and sociability make it clear that an emotion or pattern of emotions can relate to (organize and motivate) more than one personality trait.

Although we must be aware of the complexity of the relations among emotions and traits, the evidence for these relations is growing. The Izard et al. (in press) study not only found significant relations between broad dimensions of emotionality and broad dimensions of personality; it also demonstrated a number of relations between specific emotions, as measured by the Differential Emotions Scale (Izard, 1972), and specific traits, as measured by the Personality Research Form (Jackson, 1984). For example, the emotion of interest correlated with the traits of achievement and endurance, and the emotion of enjoyment correlated with the trait of affiliation. Furthermore, this study found a predicted relation between the emotions of anger, disgust, and contempt (the "hostility triad") and the trait of aggression.

SUMMARY

This chapter is based on the assumption that the emotions system constitutes the primary motivational system for human behavior, and that each discrete emotion serves unique functions in coping and adaptation. The chief premise of the chapter is that each of the emotions organizes and motivates perception, cognition, and actions (behavior) in particular ways. Therefore, individual differences in emotion thresholds lead to individual differences in patterns of behavior that become organized as traits of personality.

The chapter presents evidence and argument for the unique organizing and motivational functions of discrete emotions. Finally, it discusses a sample of the growing body of research that shows relations between indices of emotion experiences and indices of traits and dimensions of personality.

Acknowledgments. This work was supported in part by National Science Foundation Grant No. BND8706146 and National Institute of Mental Health Grant No. MH4205005003.

REFERENCES

Averill, J. R. (1968). Grief: Its nature and significance. *Psychological Bulletin*, 70, 721–748.

Averill, J. R. (1983). Studies on anger and aggression: Implications for theories of emotion. *American Psychologist*, 38, 1145–1162.

Blumberg, S. H., & Izard, C. E. (1985). Affective and cognitive characteristics of depression in 10- and 11-year-old children. *Journal of Personality and Social Psychology*, 49(1), 194–202.

Blumberg, S. H., & Izard, C. E. (1986). Discriminating patterns of emotions in 10- and 11-year-old children's anxiety and depression. *Journal of Personality and Social Psychology*, 51(4), 852–857.

Bower, G. H. (1987). Commentary on mood and memory. *Behaviour Research and Therapy*, 25(6), 443–455.

Bower, G. H., & Gilligan, S. (1984). Cognitive consequences of emotional arousal. In C. E. Izard, J. Kagan, & R. B. Zajonc (Eds.), *Emotions, cognition, and behavior* (pp. 547–588). New York: Cambridge University Press.

Campos, J. J., & Barrett, K. C. (1984). Toward a new understanding of emotions and their development. In C. E. Izard, J. Kagan, & R. B. Zajonc (Eds.), *Emotions, cognition, and behavior* (pp. 229–263). New York: Cambridge University Press.

Cannon, W. B. (1929). *Bodily changes in pain, hunger, fear and rage: An account of recent researches into the function of emotional excitement*. New York: Appleton-Century-Crofts.

Chevalier-Skolnikoff, S. (1973). Facial expression of emotion in nonhuman primates. In P. Ekman (Ed.), *Darwin and facial expression* (pp. 11–89). New York: Academic Press.

Cicchetti, D. (1990). Perspectives on the interface between normal and atypical development. In D. Cicchetti (Ed.), *Development and psychopathology* (Vol. 2, pp. 329–333). New York: Cambridge University Press.

Cicchetti, D., & Sroufe, L. A. (1976). The relationship between affective and cognitive development in Down syndrome infants. *Child Development*, 47, 920–929.

Darwin, C. R. (1965). *The expression of the emotions in man and animals*. Chicago: University of Chicago Press. (Original work published 1872)

Diener, E., & Larsen, R. J. (1984). Temporal stability and cross-situational consistency of affective, cognitive, and behavioral responses. *Journal of Personality and Social Psychology, 47*, 871–883.

Duffy, E. (1941). An explanation of "emotional" phenomena without the use of the concept "emotion." *Journal of General Psychology, 25*, 283–293.

Easterbrook, J. A. (1959). The effect of emotion on cue utilization and the organization of behavior. *Psychological Bulletin, 66*(3), 183–201.

Eisenberg, N., & Strayer, J. (Eds.). (1987). *Empathy and its development.* New York: Cambridge University Press.

Ekman, P. (1972). Universals and cultural differences in facial expressions of emotion. In J. R. Cole (Ed.), *Nebraska Symposium on Motivation* (Vol. 19, pp. 207–283). Lincoln: University of Nebraska Press.

Ekman, P., Friesen, W. V., & Ellsworth, P. C. (1972). *Emotion in the human face: Guidelines for research and an integration of findings.* Elmsford, NY: Pergamon Press.

Emde, R. (1980). Levels of meaning in infant development. In W. A. Collins (Ed.), *Minnesota Symposium on Child Psychology* (Vol. 13, pp. 1–37). Hillsdale, NJ: Erlbaum.

Emmons, R. A., & Diener, E. (1986). An interactional approach to the study of personality and emotion. *Journal of Personality, 54*(2), 1221–1228.

Epstein, S. (1980). The stability of behavior: II. Implications for psychological research. *American Psychologist, 35*, 790–806.

Hamburg, D. A. (1963). Emotions in the perspective of human evolution. In P. H. Knapp (Ed.), *Expression of emotions in man* (pp. 300–317). New York: International Universities Press.

Harris, P. L. (1989). *Children and emotions: The development of psychological understanding.* Oxford: Blackwell.

Izard, C. E. (1971). *The face of emotion.* New York: Appleton-Century-Crofts.

Izard, C. E. (1972). *Patterns of emotions: A new analysis of anxiety and depression.* New York: Academic Press.

Izard, C. E. (1977). *Human emotions.* New York: Plenum Press.

Izard, C. E. (1989). The structure and functions of emotions: Implications for cognition, motivation, and personality. In I. S. Cohen (Ed.), *The G. Stanley Hall lecture series* (Vol. 9, pp. 35–73). Washington, DC: American Psychological Association.

Izard, C. E. (1990). Facial expressions and the regulation of emotions. *Journal of Personality and Social Psychology, 58*(3), 487–498.

Izard, C. E. (1991). *The psychology of emotions.* New York: Plenum Press.

Izard, C. E. (1992). Basic emotions, relations among emotions, and emotion-cognition relations. *Psychological Review, 99*, 561–565.

Izard, C. E., Haynes, O. M., Libero, D. Z., & Putnam, P. (in press). Stability of emotion experiences and their relations to traits of personality. *Journal of Personality and Social Psychology.*

Izard, C. E., Hembree, E. A., & Huebner, R. R. (1987). Infants' emotion expressions to acute pain: Developmental change and stability of individual differences. *Developmental Psychology, 23*(1), 105–113.

Izard, C. E., & Malatesta, C. Z. (1987). Perspectives on emotional development: I. Differential emotions theory of early emotional development. In J. D. Osofsky (Ed.), *Handbook of infant development* (2nd ed., pp. 494–554). New York: Wiley.

Izard, C. E., Wehmer, G. M., Livsey, W., & Jennings, J. R. (1965). Affect, awareness, and performance. In S. S. Tomkins & C. E. Izard (Ed.), *Affect, cognition, and personality* (pp. 2–41). New York: Springer.

Jackson, D. N. (1984). *Personality Research Form manual* (3rd ed.). London, Ontario: Research Psychologists Press.

Jones, W. H., Cheeks, J. M., & Briggs, S. R. (Eds.). (1986). *Shyness: Perspectives on research and treatment.* New York: Plenum Press.

Laird, J. D. (1974). Self-attribution of emotion: The effects of expressive behavior on the quality of emotional experience. *Journal of Personality and Social Psychology, 29*, 475–486.

Lang, P. J. (1984). Cognition in emotion: Cognition in action. In C. E. Izard, J. Kagan, & R. B. Zajonc (Eds.), *Emotions, cognition, and behavior* (pp. 192–226). New York: Cambridge University Press.

Larsen, R. J., & Ketelaar, T. (1989). Extraversion, neuroticism, and susceptibility to positive/negative mood induction procedures. *Personality and Individual Differences, 10*(2), 1221–1228.

Lazarus, R. S., Kanner, A. D., & Folkman, S. (1980). Emotions: A cognitive–phenomenological analysis. In R. Plutchik & H. Kellerman (Eds.), *Emotion: Theory, research, and experience. Vol. 1. Theories of emotion* (pp. 189–217). New York: Academic Press.

Lazarus, R. S., & Smith, C. A. (1988). Knowledge and appraisal in the emotion–cognition relationship. *Cognition and Emotion, 2*, 281–300.

Lelwica, M., & Haviland, J. M. (1983, April). *Response or imitation: Ten-week-old infants' reactions to three emotion expressions.* Paper presented at the biennial meeting of the Society for Research in Child Development, Detroit.

Leventhal, H. (1980). Toward a comprehensive theory of emotion. In L. Berkowitz (Ed.), *Advances in experimental social psychology* (Vol. 13, pp. 141–165). New York: Academic Press.

Lewis, H. (1971). *Shame and guilt in neurosis.* New York: International Universities Press.

Libero, D. Z., & Izard, C. E. (1992). *Mothers' emotion experiences and nonmaternal care influence infant–mother attachment.* Unpublished manuscript, University of Delaware, Newark.

Lindsley, D. B. (1951). Emotion. In S. S. Stevens (Ed.), *Handbook of experimental psychology* (pp. 473–516). New York: Wiley.

Lynd, H. M. (1961). *On shame and the search for identity.* New York: Science Editions.

Malatesta, C. Z. (1990). The role of emotions in the development and organization of personality. In R. A. Thompson (Ed.), *Nebraska Symposium on Motivation: Vol. 36. Socioemotional development* (pp. 1–56). Lincoln: University of Nebraska Press.

McCrae, R. R., & Costa, P. T. (1987). Validation of a five-factor model of personality across instruments and observers. *Journal of Personality and Social Psychology, 52*, 81–90.

Mellen, S. L. W. (1981). *The evolution of love.* San Francisco: W. H. Freeman.

Moore, B., Underwood, B., & Rosenhan, D. L. (1984). Emotion, self, and others. In C. E. Izard, J. Kagan, & R. B. Zajonc (Eds.), *Emotions, cognition, and behavior* (pp. 464–483). New York: Cambridge University Press.

O'Hara, M. W. (1987). Postpartum "blues," depression and

psychosis: A review. *Journal of Psychosomatic Obstetrics and Gynecology*, 7(3), 205–227.

Plutchik, R. (1962). *The emotions: Facts, theories, and a new model*. New York: Random House.

Plutchik, R. (1980). *Emotion: A psychoevolutionary synthesis*. New York: Harper & Row.

Roseman, I. J. (1984). Cognitive determinants of emotions: A structural theory. In P. Shaver (Ed.), *Review of personality and social psychology: Emotions, relationships, and health* (Vol. 5, pp. 11–36). Beverly Hills, CA: Sage.

Roseman, I. J., Weist, C., & Swartz, T. (in press). Phenomenology, behaviors and goals differentiate discrete emotions. *Journal of Personality and Social Psychology*.

Rozin, P., & Fallon, A. E. (1987). A perspective on disgust. *Psychological Review*, 94(1), 23–41.

Schlosberg, H. S. (1941). A scale for the judgement of facial expressions. *Journal of Experimental Psychology*, 29, 497–510.

Smith, C. A., & Ellsworth, P. C. (1985). Patterns of cognitive appraisal in emotion. *Journal of Personality and Social Psychology*, 48, 813–838.

Spencer, H. (1890). *The principles of psychology* (Vol. 1). New York: Appleton.

Steiner, J. E. (1979). Human facial expressions in response to taste and smell stimulation. *Advances in Child Development and Behavior*, 12, 257–295.

Tangney, J. P. (1990). Assessing individual differences in proneness to shame and guilt: Development of the self-conscious affect and attribution inventory. *Journal of Personality and Social Psychology*, 59, 102–111.

Tellegen, A. (1985). Structures of mood and personality and their relevance to assessing anxiety, with an emphasis on self-report. In A. H. Tuma & J. D. Maser (Eds.), *Anxiety and the anxiety disorders* (pp. 681–706). Hillsdale, NJ: Erlbaum.

Termine, N. T., & Izard, C. E. (1988). Infants' responses to their mothers' expressions of joy and sadness. *Developmental Psychology*, 24(2), 223–229.

Tomkins, S. S. (1962). *Affect, imagery, consciousness: Vol. 1. The positive affects*. New York: Springer.

Tomkins, S. S. (1963). *Affect, imagery, consciousness: Vol. 2. The negative affects*. New York: Springer.

Tomkins, S. S. (1991). *Affect, imagery, consciousness: Vol. 3. The negative affects: Anger and fear*. New York: Springer.

Watson, D., & Clark, L. A. (1992). On traits and temperament: General and specific factors of emotional experience and their relation to the five-factor model. *Journal of Personality*, 60, 441–476.

Watson, D., & Tellegen, A. (1985). Toward a consensual structure of mood. *Psychological Bulletin*, 98, 219–235.

Weiner, B. (1989). An attributional theory of achievement motivation and emotion. *Psychological Review*, 89(4), 548–573.

Woodworth, R. S. (1938). *Experimental psychology*. New York: Holt.

Wundt, W. (1897). *Outlines of psychology* (C. H. Judd, Trans.). New York: G. E. Stechert.

Index

Acetylcholine, affecting emotions, 91
ACTH
  affecting emotions, 95–96
  release in stress, 115
  releasing factor affecting emotions, 92
Action readiness
  in emotion, 353–354
  in moods, 355
Adenosine, affecting emotions, 91
Adrenal response to stress, 92, 115
Adrenocortical responses to emotion, in infants,
      172, 178–179, 230
Affect
  alterations without cognitive activity, 218–219
  anthropology of, 29–37
  assessment in psychotherapy, 503–504
  classification of, 68
  control theory, 47–50, 493–494
  and daily life, 307–308
  and decision making, 261–275
  disease related to, 366–368
  and drug abuse, 307
  network theory of, 397–398
  and personality development, 251–254, 301–
      309
  persuasive communications affecting, 469–
      470
  phenomenological theory of, 303
  psychoanalytic theory of, 302–303
  in psychomotor epilepsy, 78–79
  trait theory of, 303–305
Affective states, 381–399
  consequents of, 393–398
  emotion in, 382–384
    antecedents and functions of, 387–388
  emotion episodes in, 385–387
    antecedents and functions of, 388
  moods in, 381, 384–385
    antecedents and functions of, 388–390
  phenomena in, 381–382
  variety and structure of, 390–392

Aggression
  anger in, 537–545. *See also* Anger
  and sadness, 554
Agoraphobia, 513–514, 518, 531
Alcohol intake, inducing exhilaration, 612
Ambiguous visual figures, perception of, 138–139
Amines, biogenic, affecting emotions, 90
Amino acids, affecting emotions, 89–90
Amygdala
  lesions affecting affect and memory, 218–219
  role in emotions, 77, 110–113
Anger, 537–545
  autonomic activity in, 120–121
  in childhood
    parental reactions to, 540–541
    peers as socializers of, 541–542
  concepts in different languages, 34
  developmental course of, 538–540
  emergence in infants, 233
  emotional impact on children, 542–544
  in families, 19
  feelings of, 10–11
  functions of, 537–538, 635
  goal outcome patterns in, 291–297
  as moral emotion, 588
  and psychosocial development, 253
  and sadness, 554–556
  and shame, 248, 254
  social role of, 350–351
  vocal expression of, 188
Angiotensin, psychobehavioral effects of, 98
Animal emotions, 155–164
  biological basis of, 162–164
  definition of, 156–157
  in insects and other invertebrates, 158–160
  in rats and mice, 160–162
Animal food prohibitions, 582
Anthropological research, 22, 25, 29–37
  and emotions as social discourse, 35–37
  interpretations of emotional meanings in, 33–35
  sadness in, 550–556

Breaching of rules, emotions in, 489–490
Breathing, nasal, affecting temperature of brain, 213–214, 216, 218

C

Calcitonin gene-related peptide, psychobehavioral effects of, 98–99
Catecholamines affecting emotions, 90
Causal explanations of emotions, 12–13
Cavernous sinus role in hypothalamic cooling, 212–213
Cerebral evolution of emotion, 67–82
    forebrain and neural chassis in, 69
    mammalian origins in, 69
    operational terms in, 67–69
Change
    in attitudes, emotional appeals in, 461–470
    in emotional experiences and contexts, 17–27
        and acceptance of new standards, 25
    in emotional states, techniques used by children, 241
    in psychotherapy, 499–507
Chaotic systems theory. *See* Dynamic systems theory
Chewong society, 346
Childhood
    development of emotions in. *See* Infant emotions
    personality development in, 254–256
Cholecystokinin, psychobehavioral effects of, 96–97
Christian philosophy of emotions, in Middle Ages, 5–6
Cingulate gyrus, role in emotions, 77, 109
Cognitive–experiential self-theory, 321–324
    emotions in, 321
    experiential and rational systems in, 323
    needs and beliefs in, 321–323
    personal theories of reality in, 323–324
Cognitive processes
    in anxiety, 532
    development in infants, 233–234
    dissonance in, and arousal, 468–469
    in emotion, 11–12, 30, 500
    in emotional experiences, 228–229, 633–634
        disease related to, 372–373
    in emotional well-being, 412
    in mediation of emotions, 441
    moods affecting, 394
    organization of, positive affect in, 263–267
    persuasive communications affecting, 469–470
    in self-conscious emotions, 563, 566–568
    and self-theory, 315–316
    and social-cognitive theories

affect and personality in, 305–306
    self development in, 319–320
    in temperament, 357–358
Coherence principle in self-development, 318–319
Communication
    of emotion, vocal expression in, 185–195
    persuasive, 461–470
Companionate love, 601–603
Comparative neurobehavioral studies, reptilian complex in, 71–74
Compulsive behavior, lack of emotion in, 73
Conditioning
    affecting attitudes, 463–464
    to feared stimuli, 522–523
Conflicts
    in hierarchies, 62
    territorial, 62
Constructionism, social, 17–18, 341–351, 491–492
Contamination response to disgusting contacts, 582–583
    interpersonal contagion in, 586
Contempt, origins of, 588–589
Contentment, and psychosocial development, 253
Coping mechanisms
    in anxiety, 529
    in existential crises, 63–64
Corpus striatum lesions, effects of, 73
Corticotropin. *See* ACTH
Cortisol levels, in infant emotions, 172, 179
Crying, mechanisms in, 81–82
Cultural factors
    in development of disgust, 587–588
    in psychology of emotions, 417–428
        in ancient Sanskrit text, 419–424
        anthropological studies of, 22, 25, 29–37
        in contemporary Hindu concepts, 426–428
        symbolic approach in, 425–426
    in sadness, 550–556
    in social construction of emotions, 341–351
    in socialization of emotion, 435–444
    in temperament, 360–361

D

Daily life, affect factors in, 307–308
Death
    and coping with loss or separation, 63
    relation to disgust, 584
Decay, as disgust substance, 579–580
Decision making, positive affect in, 261–275
Decoding
    of acoustic cues, 189–192
    of expressive cues, 452